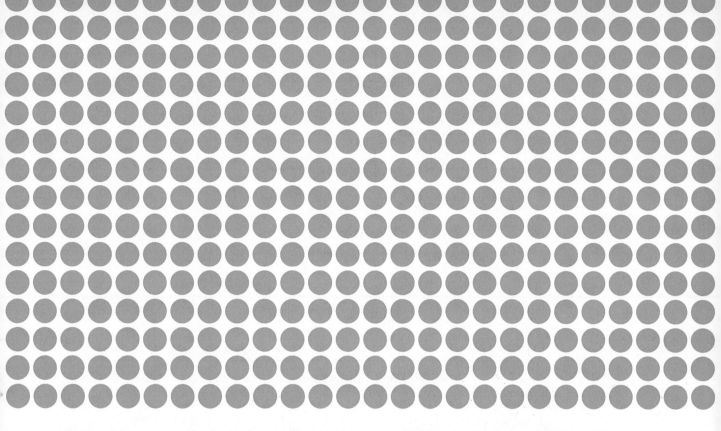

ORGANIZATIONAL BEHAVIOUR

UNDERSTANDING AND MANAGING LIFE AT WORK   SEVENTH EDITION

GARY JOHNS
CONCORDIA UNIVERSITY

ALAN M. SAKS
UNIVERSITY OF TORONTO

PEARSON

Prentice
Hall

Toronto

For Bill and Jean Johns, and for Monika Jörg.   Gary Johns

For Kelly, Justin, and Brooke, and Simon and Renee Saks.   Alan M. Saks

Library and Archives Canada Cataloguing in Publication

Johns, Gary, 1946–
    Organizational behaviour: understanding and managing life at work / Gary Johns,
    Alan M. Saks. — 7th ed.

Includes bibliographical references and index.
ISBN-13: 978-0-13-613436-7
ISBN-10: 0-13-613436-X

1. Organizational behaviour—Textbooks. 2. Management—Textbooks. I. Saks, Alan M.
(Alan Michael), 1960– II. Title.

HD58.7.J64 2007   302.3'5   C2006-906396-6

ISBN-13: 978-0-13-613436-7
ISBN-10: 0-13-613436-X

Editor-in-Chief: Gary Bennett
Sponsoring Editor: Lori Will
Acquisitions Editor: Karen Elliott
Executive Marketing Manager: Cas Shields
Developmental Editor: José Sevilla
Production Editors: Leanne Rancourt/Cheryl Jackson
Copy Editor: Leanne Rancourt
Proofreader: Ann McInnis
Production Coordinator: Andrea Falkenberg
Compositor: Nelson Gonzalez
Photo Research: Lisa Brant
Permissions Research: Christina Beamish
Art Director: Julia Hall
Interior and Cover Design: Miguel Acevedo
Cover Image: Veer/Digital Vision

2 3 4 5   11 10 09 08

Printed and bound in the United States.

BRIEF CONTENTS

CONTENTS

PART 3   Social Behaviour and Organizational Processes   223

CHAPTER 7   Groups and Teamwork   224

PREFACE

Welcome to the seventh edition of *Organizational Behaviour: Understanding and Managing Life at Work*! This edition marks the twenty-fifth anniversary of the text, which has been rigorously updated over the years to present students with the latest knowledge and research on both the science and practice of organizational behaviour. First published in 1983, *Organizational Behaviour* is the longest-running, continuously published, regularly revised organizational behaviour textbook authored in Canada.

In writing the seventh edition of this book, we have been guided by three goals. First, we wish to convey the genuine excitement inherent in the subject of organizational behaviour by sharing our enthusiasm about the subject with students who are reading and learning about it for the first time.

Second, we want the presentation of the material to have both academic and practical integrity, acknowledging the debt of the field to both behavioural science research and organizational practice. To put it another way, we want this book to be useful and enjoyable to read without oversimplifying key subjects on the premise that this somehow makes them easier to understand. This requires striking a balance between research and theory on the one hand, and practice and application on the other hand. The seventh edition of *Organizational Behaviour* includes the most recent research and theory in the field (e.g., employee engagement in Chapter 5; the GLOBE project in Chapters 4 and 9; the "Research Focus" feature) as well as many examples of the application and practice of organizational behaviour throughout the text and in the chapter-opening vignettes, the "Applied Focus" feature, and the "You Be the Manager" feature.

Third, we want students to not only learn about organizational behaviour, but also to understand the connections and linkages across topics and how to integrate theory, principles, and concepts across chapters rather than see them as separate or isolated topics. Special features in this edition designed to enhance this skill include an integrative case that runs through each section of the text, integrative discussion questions at the end of every chapter, and the "OB Flashback" feature that shows how material in a current chapter is linked and related to material in previous chapters. We sincerely hope these goals have resulted in a textbook that is interesting and enjoyable to read and that conveys the importance of organizational behaviour.

NEW TO THE SEVENTH EDITION

The seventh edition of *Organizational Behaviour* adds substantial new content, features, and pedagogy while remaining faithful to the general format and structure of the sixth edition.

While the major topics of the sixth edition remain in this edition, we have added new content to reflect recent research as well as new and emerging themes in organizational behaviour literature and practice in every chapter of the text. Examples of new topics and sections that can be found in the seventh edition include:

- Chapter 1: evidence-based management
- Chapter 2: behavioural modelling training; total rewards; peer recognition programs
- Chapter 3: social identity theory; perceptions of recruitment and selection
- Chapter 4: interactional fairness; the GLOBE project
- Chapter 5: employee engagement

- Chapter 6: stretch assignments
- Chapter 8: proximal and distal socialization outcomes; organizational identification
- Chapter 9: leader reward and punishment behaviour; the GLOBE project; ethical leadership
- Chapter 10: signalling aspects of office decor
- Chapter 12: facets of political skill; whistle-blowing
- Chapter 13: bullying; hindrance versus challenge stressors
- Chapter 14: transition from organic to mechanistic structures
- Chapter 16: the learning organization; the knowing–doing gap
- Appendix: moderating and mediating variables; threats to internal validity

We have updated many other areas throughout the text with the most current and recent research from practising management literature, academic literature, and the popular and business press. We have also replaced the content of many of the features and added new ones. In total, the seventh edition contains 11 new chapter-opening vignettes, 25 new "Focus" boxes, and 12 new "You Be the Manager" features. These features have been carefully chosen to represent current and exciting examples of organizational behaviour. Of those examples that we have retained from the sixth edition, many have been substantially updated.

In addition to new and updated content, the seventh edition includes many new exhibits showing information such as the most admired corporate cultures in Canada (Exhibit 8.6) and common activities included in diversity programs (Exhibit 3.8). New figures concerning the determinants of self-efficacy (Exhibit 2.5), the impact of emotional labour on pay (Exhibit 4.5), the "honeymoon-hangover" effect (Exhibit 4.8), the socialization process (Exhibit 8.1), inferences made from office decor (Exhibit 10.2), and the psychological conditions of employee engagement (Exhibit 5.3) have also been added.

Finally, in the end-of-chapter material, 12 new cases have been added as well as three new case incidents and three new exercises. You will also find many new discussion questions. In addition, we have added a new pedagogical feature called "On-the-Job Challenge Question" (see "Pedagogical Features" on page xxiii for more information).

ABOUT THE COVER

The cover of the seventh edition of *Organizational Behaviour: Understanding and Managing Life at Work,* along with the pictures throughout the text, features musicians from a performing jazz band. What does a jazz band have to do with organizational behaviour? Actually, a great deal. Jazz has been used as a metaphor for organizations and organizational behaviour for many years.

In 1998, the journal *Organizational Science* published a special issue on jazz improvisation as a metaphor for organizations (vol. 9, no. 5), a result of a symposium called "Jazz as a Metaphor for Organizing in the Twenty-First Century" that was held at the 1995 Academy of Management Conference in Vancouver, British Columbia. The idea was to think about the twenty-first-century organization in the context of the jazz metaphor for organizing. The jazz metaphor has also been adopted by some organizations. In its 1996 annual report, the LEGO Corporation featured its top-management team as a jazz ensemble with the CEO playing the saxophone—the CEO wanted to highlight the importance of improvisation at all levels of management.

Organizations and organizational behaviour are like jazz in many ways. Jazz involves improvisation, innovation, and flexibility, all of which are important attributes of individuals and groups in organizations as well as organizations themselves. Organizations and the people in them must be flexible and capable of innovation and improvisation to survive and adapt to change. Innovation and flexibility are especially important for contemporary organizations.

In his book *Leadership Jazz*, Max De Pree argues that leadership in organizations is like a jazz band: "Jazz-band leaders must choose the music, find the right musicians, and perform—in public. But the effect of the performance depends on so many things—the environment, the volunteers playing in the band, the need for everybody to perform as individuals and as a group, the absolute dependence of the leader on the members of the band, the need of the leader for the followers to play well. What a summary of an organization!"

Finally, as noted by Mary Jo Hatch, one of the chairs of the jazz symposium, the characteristics that are associated with the twenty-first-century organization are very similar to those of a jazz band: It is flexible, adaptable, and responsive to the environment, and it has loose boundaries and minimal hierarchy. Organizational behaviour is very much like a jazz band—individuals working together in the spirit of innovation, improvisation, and inspiration.

GENERAL CONTENT AND WRITING STYLE

Organizational Behaviour, Seventh Edition, is comprehensive—the material is authoritative and up to date, and reflects current research and practical concerns. Both traditional subjects (such as expectancy theory) and newer topics (like employee engagement, bullying, whistle-blowing, ethical leadership, virtual teams, mood and emotions, emotional intelligence, and organizational learning) are addressed. Balanced treatment is provided to micro topics (covered in the earlier chapters) and macro topics (covered in the later chapters).

Although *Organizational Behaviour* is comprehensive, we have avoided the temptation to include too many concepts, theories, and ideas. Rather than composing a long laundry list of marginally related concepts, each chapter is organized in interlocked topics. The topics are actively interrelated and are treated in enough detail to ensure understanding. Special attention has been devoted to the flow and sequencing of the topics.

The writing style is personal and conversational. Excessive use of jargon is avoided and important ideas are well defined and illustrated. Special attention has been paid to consistency of terminology throughout the book. We have tried to foster critical thinking about the concepts under discussion by using devices like asking the reader questions in the body of the text.

Believing that a well-tailored example can illuminate the most complex concept, we have used examples liberally throughout the text to clarify the points under consideration. The reader is not left wondering how a key idea applies to the world of organizations. The book is illustrated with exhibits, cartoons, and excerpts from the business press, such as *Report on Business*, *Canadian Business*, *Fortune*, and the *Globe and Mail*, to enhance the flow of the material and reinforce the relevance of the examples for students.

We have treated the subject matter generically, recognizing that organizational behaviour occurs in all organizations. The reader will find examples, cases, "Focus" selections, and "You Be the Manager" features drawn from a variety of settings, including large and small businesses, high-technology firms, manufacturing firms, hospitals, schools, and the military. In addition, care has been taken to demonstrate that the material covered is relevant to various levels and jobs within these organizations.

ORGANIZATION

Organizational Behaviour is organized in a simple but effective building-block manner. "Part One: An Introduction" defines organizational behaviour, discusses the nature of organizations, introduces the concept of management, and reviews contemporary management concerns. "Part Two: Individual Behaviour" covers the topics of personality, learning, perception, attribution, diversity, attitudes, job satisfaction, organizational commitment, and motivation. "Part Three: Social Behaviour and Organizational Processes" discusses groups, teamwork, socialization, culture, leadership, communication, decision making, power, politics, ethics, conflict, negotiation, and stress. "Part Four: The Total Organization" considers organizational structure, environment, strategy, technology, change, and innovation.

Some instructors may prefer to revise the order in which students read particular chapters, and they can accomplish this easily. However, Chapter 5, "Theories of Work Motivation," should be read before Chapter 6, "Motivation in Practice." Also, Chapter 14, "Organizational Structure," should be read before Chapter 15, "Environment, Strategy, and Technology." The book has been designed to be used in either a quarter or semester course.

MAJOR THEMES AND CONTENT

In preparing the seventh edition of *Organizational Behaviour*, we concentrated on developing several themes that are current in contemporary organizational life. This development included adding new content, expanding previous coverage, and addressing the themes throughout the text to enhance integration.

The **global aspects of organizational life** continue to receive strong treatment in this edition to enable students to become more comfortable and competent in dealing with people from other cultures. Major sections on this theme appear in Chapters 4, 5, 9, and 10, which deal respectively with values, motivation, leadership, and communication. Pedagogical support for the global theme includes "Global Focus" features (Chapters 2, 4, 7, 8, and 15), an "Applied Focus" (Chapter 7), a "You Be the Manager" feature (Chapter 10), and an experiential exercise (Chapter 10).

The changing nature of workplace demographics and a need to provide a welcoming work environment for all organizational members has led to explicit coverage of **workforce diversity**. The major treatment of this topic occurs in Chapter 3 in the context of interpersonal perception and attribution. Additional treatment occurs in the context of motivation (Chapter 5), teams (Chapter 7), and communication (Chapter 10). Pedagogical support for the diversity theme can be found in the "You Be the Manager" feature in Chapter 3. We also see it in some "Applied Focus" features (Chapter 3), a chapter-opening vignette (Chapter 3), and two exercises (Chapters 3 and 10).

Contemporary organizations are focusing more and more on **teamwork**. This has led to expanded coverage of teams (such as virtual teams), and the most recent research findings on team characteristics and group effectiveness can be found in Chapter 7. Coverage of group decision making is included in Chapter 11. Pedagogical backup for the teamwork theme includes a chapter-opening vignette, "You Be the Manager" feature, "Global Focus" feature, and a case study and case incident (all in Chapter 7). In addition, the case study in Chapter 10 and two experiential exercises (Chapters 7 and 11) cover aspects of teamwork.

Many organizations continue to undergo major *change* and *transformation*. Interrelated topics involving organizational change such as **reengineering, downsizing,** and **advanced technology** continue to receive detailed coverage and are the focus of another theme highlighted in this edition. Coverage of reengineering can be found in

Chapter 16, and related coverage on downsizing can be found in Chapter 14. Although principal coverage of advanced technology is discussed in Chapter 15, the role of technology in communication and decision making can also be found in Chapters 10 and 11, where computer-mediated communication, company television networks and intranets, and electronic brainstorming are covered. Other relevant topics include telecommuting (Chapter 6) as well as sections on virtual, modular, and boundaryless organizational structures (Chapter 14). Several features also portray the use of advanced technology, such as the "You Be the Manager" feature in Chapter 14, the "Research Focus" features in Chapters 12 and 15, and the "OB Flashback" in Chapter 15. Pedagogical backup for the change theme includes three chapter-opening vignettes (Chapters 13, 15, and 16), five "You Be the Manager" features (Chapters 1, 6, 8, 10, 15, and 16), two "Applied Focus" features (Chapters 14 and 16), an "OB Flashback" (Chapter 16), four case studies (Chapters 8, 14, 15, and 16), two case incidents (Chapters 2 and 16), and the integrative case.

Finally, the seventh edition of *Organizational Behaviour* reflects the continuing issue of **ethics** in organizational decision making. The major formal coverage of ethics is included in Chapter 12 with a discussion of power and politics. Pedagogical support for the ethics theme can be found in several chapter-opening vignettes (Chapters 11 and 12), a number of "Ethical Focus" features (Chapters 5, 9, 10, 12, and 13), and the "You Be the Manager" feature in Chapter 12. Case studies are particularly good vehicles for examining the complexity surrounding ethical issues, and the case incidents for Chapters 9 and 12 and the case for Chapter 12 concern explicit ethical dilemmas.

PEDAGOGICAL FEATURES

The seventh edition's pedagogical features are designed to complement, supplement, and reinforce the textual material. More specifically, they are designed to promote self-awareness, critical thinking, and an appreciation of how the subject matter applies in actual organizations. The seventh edition of *Organizational Behaviour* includes all of the features found in the previous edition, including three different kinds of cases (case studies, case incidents, and an integrative case), four types of Focus boxes (Applied Focus, Research Focus, Ethical Focus, and Global Focus), You Be the Manager features, and "OB Flashback" features. New to this edition is the "On-the-Job Challenge Question," which can be found at the end of each chapter, along with discussion questions for each chapter and integrative discussion questions.

- All chapters begin with an **Opening Vignette** chosen to stimulate interest in the chapter's subject matter. All of these vignettes concern real people in real organizations. Each vignette is carefully analyzed at several points in the chapter to illustrate the ideas under consideration. For example, Chapter 3 begins with a discussion of stereotypes and diversity programs at the Bank of Montreal, and Chapter 10 describes communication at UPS.

- Each chapter opens with several **Learning Objectives** to help focus the student's attention on the chapter's subject matter.

- In each chapter, students encounter a **"You Be the Manager"** feature that invites them to stop and reflect on the relevance of the material they are studying to a real problem in a real organization. Venues range from RAC call centres (Chapter 4) to Hudson's Bay Company (Chapter 6). Problems range from improving customer service (Chapter 4) to bullying at work (Chapter 13). At the end of each chapter, **"The Manager's Notebook"** offers some observations about the problem and reveals what the organization actually did.

- All chapters contain some combination of the following "Focus" features: "**Research Focus**," "**Applied Focus**," "**Global Focus**," or "**Ethical Focus**." These features illustrate or supplement the textual material with material from the practising management literature (e.g., *Harvard Business Review*), the research literature (e.g., the *Academy of Management Journal*), and the popular press (e.g., the *Globe and Mail*). They are chosen to exemplify real-world problems and practices as they relate to organizational behaviour. The "Research Focus" feature provides examples of organizational behaviour research, such as the effects of a computer-based orientation program on new hires' socialization (Chapter 8) and research on the effects of traumatic national events on stress and work behaviour (Chapter 13). The "Applied Focus" features provide practical examples of the application of the text material in organizations. For example, the "Applied Focus" box in Chapter 3 describes diversity at Procter & Gamble, and the one in Chapter 12 describes employee empowerment programs at Delta Hotels and Resorts. These two features help to reinforce the importance of both the research and practice of organizational behaviour. The "Ethical Focus" feature provides examples of ethics in organizational behaviour research, such as the effects of goal setting on ethical behaviour (Chapter 5) and the effects of workplace violence and stress (Chapter 13). This feature helps to reinforce the importance of ethics in management and organizational behaviour. The "Global Focus" feature provides examples of organizational behaviour around the globe, such as Walt Disney's operations in Japan and France (Chapter 4) and the culture of Mary Kay Cosmetics in China (Chapter 8). This feature helps to reinforce the importance of cross-cultural issues in management and organizational behaviour.

- Several chapters of the text have an "**OB Flashback**" feature at the end of the chapter. This feature is an example of our efforts to improve the integration of material throughout the text and to encourage integrative thinking, something that has been suggested by reviewers over the years. The "OB Flashback" appears at the end of eight chapters (Chapters 3, 6, 8, 9, 11, 15, and 16). Each one shows how the material in a current chapter has implications for understanding the material in an earlier chapter. For example, the "OB Flashback" in Chapter 8 (*The Effect of Culture on Learning*) shows students that culture (in particular, a continuous learning culture) has a strong influence on employee learning, which is covered in Chapter 2. The "OB Flashback" in Chapter 3 (*Self-Monitoring and Negative Gender Stereotypes*) describes how women who are high on self-monitoring (discussed in Chapter 2) are able to overcome negative gender stereotypes. Thus, this feature demonstrates how different topics in the text are related and how knowledge of one topic can shed light on our understanding of other topics.

- **Key terms** in each chapter are set in boldface type when they are discussed in the body of the text and are defined in the margin in a **Running Glossary**. To help students find the definitions they need, key terms are highlighted in the index, with page references for definitions, also in boldface.

- Each chapter concludes with a **Learning Objectives Checklist** (keyed to the chapter **Learning Objectives**) and **Discussion Questions**. In addition, each chapter includes two or three **Integrative Discussion Questions**. While the traditional discussion questions deal with issues within each chapter, the integrative discussion questions require the student to relate and integrate the material in a current chapter with concepts and theories from previous chapters. For example, one of the questions in Chapter 12 ("Power, Politics, and Ethics") requires students to use the material on organizational learning practices (Chapter 2) and contributors to organizational culture (Chapter 8) to understand how an organization can create an ethical workplace. This feature is designed to facilitate student integration of various concepts and theories throughout the text.

- New to this edition is the **On-the-Job Challenge Question** that appears after the integrative discussion questions in each chapter. These questions differ from the other discussion questions in several respects. First, they are based on real issues and problems facing organizations. Second, they are more complex and challenging in that they require students to use their knowledge of all the material in the chapter. Third, these questions are very practical and require students to apply the text material to an actual situation or event facing an organization. For example, the question in Chapter 8 asks students to consider how important it is for Ford to change its culture to restore the company to profitability, how likely it is that they will be able to do this, and how they should proceed. Thus, the answers to these questions are not simple or straightforward and require the student to apply the text material to a real issue or problem facing an organization. We hope that these questions provide students with an interesting and engaging opportunity to use their knowledge of organizational behaviour to address real problems facing organizations today.

- Each chapter includes an **Experiential Exercise**. These exercises span individual self-assessment, role-playing, and group activities. The seventh edition of *Organizational Behaviour* includes four new exercises. In addition, to enhance student understanding and encourage discussion and interaction, most of the exercises have been updated to include a group component in which groups of students work together on an exercise or discuss the results of a self-assessment and answer a series of questions. To ensure confidence in the feedback students receive, the self-assessments generally have a research base.

- A **Case Study** is found in each chapter. The cases are of medium length, allowing great flexibility in tailoring their use to an instructor's personal style. We have selected cases that require active analysis and decision making, not simply passive description. Cases span important topics in contemporary organizations, such as discrimination and workplace diversity (Chapter 3), introducing teams (Chapter 7), and changing corporate culture (Chapter 8). The seventh edition of *Organizational Behaviour* includes 11 new cases.

- **Case Incidents** are included in every chapter. Case incidents are shorter than the case studies and are designed to focus on a particular topic within a chapter. Because they are short (one or two paragraphs) and deal with realistic scenarios of organizational life, they enable an instructor to quickly generate class discussion on a key theme within each chapter. They can be used at the beginning of a class to introduce a topic and to stimulate student thinking and interest, during the class when a particular topic is being discussed, or at the end of a class when the focus turns to the application of the text material. The seventh edition of *Organizational Behaviour* includes four new case incidents.

- The **Integrative Case** is first presented at the end of Part One. Unlike the case studies, which focus only on the material in each chapter, the integrative case requires students to use the material throughout the text to understand the case material. Integrative case questions can be found at the end of each of the four parts of the text. The questions deal with the main issues and themes of the chapters within each part. This enables students to gain an increasing awareness and understanding of the case material upon completion of each part of the text. Answering the case questions requires the integration of material from the chapters within each part as well as preceding parts of the text. Therefore, upon completion of the text and the integrative case questions, the student will have acquired a comprehensive understanding of the case through the integration of issues pertaining to individual behaviour, social behaviour and organizational processes, and the total organization.

SUPPLEMENTS

Instructor's Resource CD-ROM. This resource provides all of the following supplements in one convenient package:

Instructor's Resource Manual. Written by the text authors to ensure close coordination with the book, this extensive manual includes chapter objectives, a chapter outline, answers to all of the text questions and cases, supplemental lecture material, video case teaching notes, and teaching notes for each chapter.

Pearson Education Canada Test Generator. This software enables instructors to view and edit the existing test bank questions, add new questions, and generate custom tests. It includes about 1700 questions, including a mix of factual and application questions. Multiple-choice, true/false, and short-answer formats are provided. Like the instructor's resource manual, the questions in the test generator have been written by the text authors.

PowerPoint® Slides. Each chapter of the text is outlined in a series of PowerPoint slides prepared by the text authors, which include key points, figures, and tables. The slides include detailed teaching notes accessed through PowerPoint's "notes" function.

CBC/Pearson Education Canada Video Library. This collection of video cases includes segments from CBC's *Venture* and *The National*, covering topics such as recruiting a new generation of workers, finding and keeping workers, workplace stress, work–life balance, alternative working schedules, whistle-blowing, team-based work arrangements, and how to communicate in a cross-cultural world. Written cases and questions to accompany the segments can be found on our password-protected Video Central website, accessible through a link on the Companion Website at **www.pearsoned.ca/johns**. Both the cases and answers to the questions are provided in the Instructor's Video Guide.

Companion Website. Found at **www.pearsoned.ca/johns**, this website acts as an online study guide for students, and to ensure close coordination with the book, it has been prepared by the authors of the text. It includes chapter summaries, self-tests, and research-style questions that direct students to access Research Navigator, which is a database of primary source materials, as well as weblinks and search tools.

Research Navigator™. Research Navigator™ has been packaged with this text. This research tool helps students complete research assignments efficiently and with confidence by providing three exclusive databases of high-quality scholarly and popular press articles accessed by easy-to-use search engines. Gain access to Research Navigator by using the access code found in the guide that has been packaged with your text.

ACKNOWLEDGMENTS

Books are not written in a vacuum. In writing *Organizational Behaviour*, Seventh Edition, we have profited from the advice and support of a number of individuals. This is our chance to say thank you.

First, we would like to thank our reviewers for this edition, who provided us with a wealth of insights about how to improve the text:

Garfield Du Couturier-Nichol, McGill University
David Girard, British Columbia Institute of Technology
Anne Hardacre, St. Lawrence College
Greg Irving, Wilfred Laurier University
Steve Lynch, University of Guelph

Second, we wish to thank our many colleagues who have provided us with helpful feedback, insights, and general support for the book: Blake Ashforth, Jennifer Berdahl, Stéphane Côté, Jamie Gruman, Geoffrey Leonardelli, Julie McCarthy, Samantha Montes, Phani Radhakrishnan, Simon Taggar, Soo Min Toh, John Trougakos, Mark Weber, V.V. Baba, and David Zweig.

Third, we want to thank Eric Patton, whose excellent research skills, both in-library and online, contributed greatly to the timeliness and relevance of the revision.

Fourth, we want to thank the team at Pearson Education Canada. We wish to extend our genuine appreciation to a group of extremely competent professionals who were wonderful to work with and who have greatly contributed to the quality of this text: Karen Elliott (Acquisitions Editor), Lori Will (Sponsoring Editor), José Sevilla (Media Developmental Editor), Pamela Voves (Senior Developmental Editor), and Leanne Rancourt (Production Editor and Copy Editor). Finally, we wish to thank the design and production team: Miguel Acevedo (Designer), Andrea Falkenberg (Production Coordinator), and Nelson Gonzalez (Formatter), for making this text look so wonderful. We did our best to make this book interesting, informative, and enjoyable to read; making it look as good as it does is icing on the cake. Thanks to everyone at Pearson who contributed to this book. They represent a great example of what this textbook is all about: *individuals working together to accomplish goals through group effort.*

Finally, each of us wishes to give thanks to those in our lives who have contributed to our work and the writing of this text:

I (Gary Johns) am grateful to my Concordia University Management Department colleagues for their interest, support, and ideas. Additionally, I would like to thank my students over the years. In one way or another, many of their questions, comments, challenges, and suggestions are reflected in the book. Also, thanks to all my colleagues who have taken time to suggest ideas for the book when we have met at professional conferences. Finally, thanks to Monika Jörg for her continuing enthusiasm, caring, humour, support, and advice.

I (Alan Saks) am grateful to my colleagues at the University of Toronto who have all been very supportive of this textbook. I would like to express my appreciation to my parents, Renee and Simon Saks, who have provided me with love and support throughout my education and career and continue to celebrate every step along the way. I also wish to thank my wife, Kelly, and my children, Justin and Brooke, who have had to endure my long hours of work for the past year. Although they did not write a single word in this book, in many ways their contribution is as significant as mine. Thanks for understanding, making me laugh, and for waiting so long for it to end!

Gary Johns   Alan M. Saks

Gary Johns (PhD, Wayne State University) is Professor of Management and the Concordia University Research Chair in Management in the John Molson School of Business, Concordia University, Montreal. He has research interests in absenteeism from work, presenteeism, personality, job design, self-serving behaviour, research methodology, and the impact of context on organizational behaviour. He has published in *Journal of Applied Psychology*, *Academy of Management Journal*, *Academy of Management Review*, *Organizational Behavior and Human Decision Processes*, *Personnel Psychology*, *Journal of Management*, *Research in Organizational Behavior*, *Research in Personnel and Human Resources Management*, *Journal of Organizational Behavior*, *Journal of Occupational and Organizational Psychology*, *International Review of Industrial and Organizational Psychology*, *Canadian Psychology*, *Human Resource Management Review*, *Human Relations*, *Canadian Journal of Administrative Sciences*, and *Psychology Today*. Co-author of *Organizational Behavior: Understanding and Managing Life at Work* (Seventh Edition, Pearson Prentice Hall). Recipient of Academy of Management Organizational Behavior Division's New Concept Award, Society for Industrial and Organizational Psychology's Edwin E. Ghiselli Research Design Award, the Concordia University Research Award, and the award for the best article published in *Human Relations* in 2007. Elected Fellow of SIOP, American Psychological Association, and Canadian Psychological Association. Former Chair of the Canadian Society for Industrial and Organizational Psychology. Currently on editorial boards of *Organizational Behavior and Human Decision Processes*, *Journal of Occupational Health Psychology*, *Human Relations*, *International Journal of Selection and Assessment*, and *Applied Psychology: An International Review*. Formerly on editorial boards of *Academy of Management Journal*, *Journal of Management*, *Personnel Psychology*, *Canadian Journal of Administrative Sciences*, and *Journal of Occupational and Organizational Psychology*. Consulting (Associate) Editor of *Journal of Organizational Behavior*, 1998–2006.

Alan M. Saks (PhD, University of Toronto) is a Professor of Organizational Behaviour and Human Resource Management at the University of Toronto, where he holds a joint appointment in the Department of Management—UTSC, the Centre for Industrial Relations and Human Resources, and the Joseph L. Rotman School of Management. He conducts research in a number of areas in human resources and organizational behaviour including recruitment, job search, training, employee engagement, and the socialization of new employees. His research has been published in refereed journals such as the *Journal of Applied Psychology*, *Personnel Psychology*, *Industrial and Organizational Psychology*, *Academy of Management Journal*, *Journal of Organizational Behavior*, *Journal of Vocational Behavior*, *Human Resource Management*, *Human Relations*, *International Journal of Selection and Assessment*, and *Human Resource Development Quarterly*, as well as in professional journals such as the *HR Professional Magazine*, *The Training Report*, *The Learning Journal*, *Canadian HR Reporter*, and the *HRM Research Quarterly*. In addition to this text, he is also the author of *Research, Measurement, and Evaluation of Human Resources*, and co-author of *Managing Performance through Training and Development*.

A Great Way to Learn and Instruct Online

The Pearson Education Canada Companion Website is easy to navigate and is organized to correspond to the chapters in this textbook. Whether you are a student in the classroom or a distance learner you will discover helpful resources for in-depth study and research that empower you in your quest for greater knowledge and maximize your potential for success in the course.

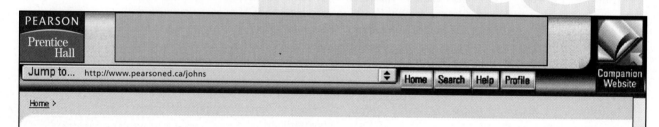

[**www.pearsoned.ca/johns**]

Enter

PEARSON
Prentice
Hall

Jump to...   http://www.pearsoned.ca/johns   Home   Search   Help   Profile

Companion
Website

Home >

Companion Website

Organizational Behaviour: Understanding and Managing Life at Work, Seventh Edition, by Johns and Saks

Student Resources

The modules in this section provide students with tools for learning course material. These modules include:

- Learning Objectives
- Chapter Summary
- Practice Quizzes
- Internet Exercises
- Research Navigator™
- Weblinks
- Glossary and Glossary Flashcards

In the quiz modules students can send answers to the grader and receive instant feedback on their progress through the Results Reporter. Coaching comments and references to the textbook may be available to ensure that students take advantage of all available resources to enhance their learning experience.

Instructor Resources

A link to this book on the Pearson Education Canada online catalogue (www.pearsoned.ca) provides instructors with additional teaching tools. Downloadable PowerPoint Presentations and an Instructor's Manual are just some of the materials that may be available. The catalogue is password protected. To get a password, simply contact your Pearson Education Canada Representative or call Faculty Sales and Services at 1-800-850-5813.

CHAPTER

1 Organizational Behaviour and Management

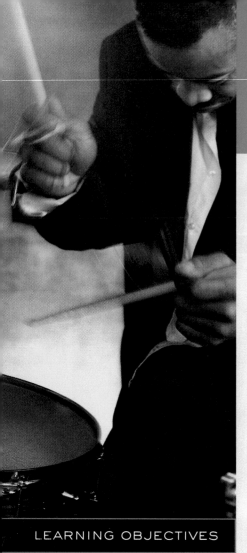

CHAPTER I

Organizational Behaviour and Management

Have you ever wondered what it would be like to be employed at the best workplace in Canada? You would be working at Vancity Credit Union in British Columbia, which was selected by *Canadian Business* magazine as the best workplace in Canada in 2006 and ranked as the best place to work in Canada by *Maclean's* magazine in 2005. In 2006, the company was also chosen as one of the *Financial Post*'s 10 best companies to work for as well as one of BC's top 20 employers.

Formed in 1945, Vancity is Canada's largest credit union, with $11.8 billion in assets, more than 330 000 members, and 46 branches throughout Greater Vancouver, the Fraser Valley, and Victoria. The credit union is considered one of Canada's most progressive companies for its support of and involvement in community-related and environmental causes. In fact, the effect of the company's initiatives on the community and the quality of life in the community is as important as making money, and in some cases even more important. It donates $1 million each year to a local BC-based non-profit organization chosen by its clients for an innovative community project.

What makes Vancity Canada's best workplace? There are a number of factors: its employee-centred culture that encourages making people proud and happy to work there, its commitment to employees, and its progressive workplace policies. Vancity is committed to treating its employees well. It provides a host of benefits and perks, including three weeks of vacation in the first year plus an option to trade unused benefits for more days off; low-interest loans, mortgages, and credit lines; and transit subsidies for Vancouver's light rail transit system. The head office has meditation and lactation rooms and an employee-run library and subsidized parking for those who carpool. The company also pays the full cost of a flexible benefits plan.

Although Vancity is small compared to the Big Five banks, it pays its employees on par with its larger rivals. Support staff is paid slightly better than industry average. Bonuses are calculated based on Vancity's profits and the performance of the employee's branch or department. Vancity

LEARNING OBJECTIVES

After reading Chapter 1, you should be able to:

1. Define *organizations* and describe their basic characteristics.

2. Explain the concept of *organizational behaviour* and describe the goals of the field.

3. Define *management* and describe what managers do to accomplish goals.

4. Contrast the *classical viewpoint* of management with that which the *human relations movement* advocated.

5. Describe the *contemporary contingency approach* to management.

6. Explain what managers do—their roles, activities, agendas for action, and thought processes.

7. Describe the societal and global trends that are shaping contemporary management concerns.

Vancity Credit Union has been ranked as the best place to work in Canada thanks to an employee-centred culture and progressive workplace practices.

also hosts a range of social events such as "recognition nights," family picnics, winter skating, an annual gala and themed costume parties, and has softball, dragon boat, and kayak teams.

Vancity also provides employees with opportunities for learning and career development. The company operates a web portal for career planning called Discoveru to help employees advance in their careers and has a tuition reimbursement program in which they reimburse employees up to $2500 a year in tuition as long as the employee receives a passing grade. Employees have access to internal training and development programs as well as outside courses to advance their careers. And even if training isn't directly related to an employee's current job, Vancity will still cover half the cost. There is a strong focus on helping employees achieve their personal goals.

Vancity Credit Union
www.vancity.com

Another key factor is the company's emphasis on internal communications. Twice a year Vancity's 15-person senior management team travels in pairs to the credit union's 60 divisions to sit down and talk with all 2000 employees. Anything goes and any question is fair game. For a manager to do well at Vancity, the most important thing is to address problems. These visits have become a critical way for senior managers to connect directly with employees. The company also has four employees dedicated to internal communications. They distribute memos in weekly e-newsletter briefs and post short stories about employee and community achievements in lunchrooms and elevators.

Vancity's focus on employees is also apparent in its executive compensation model, which is based on five equal performance measures. In addition to profitability, membership growth, the number and size of accounts, and member satisfaction, executive compensation is also based on employee surveys. Manager's bonuses are tied not just to business performance but to employee engagement, which is tracked by the surveys. According to CEO Dave Mowat, making sure employees are engaged is critical.

The annual surveys are also used to identify areas for improvement. For example, in 2004 the survey indicated that only 63 percent of employees felt they could voice their opinions. Executives asked the company's Employee Advisory Committee, a group with a representative from every branch and department, to gather stories about experiences in their workplaces and to offer ideas. What they discovered was that loyalty to teams at Vancity is so strong that individuals are often reluctant to offer opinions that counter the perceived consensus. The executive team then set a goal to improve employee voice and wrote a four-point commitment statement. They also began a program to recognize employees who speak up and a program called "Courageous Conversations" that teaches managers how to engage employees in open dialogue. Mowat wrote an all-employee letter to express his personal surprise about the problem and what management was going to do about it.

Vancity's trust in the role of employees is especially apparent in how it has used employees' ideas to update the company's vision. In 2003, the company undertook an 18-month process in which employees and members were asked what they felt makes Vancity special. The themes that emerged were then put into the Story of Vancity, a 48-page book that informs everything from executive decisions to Vancity's branding and advertising. It is also a template for how everyone—from members to front-line tellers right up to the CEO—talks about the organization.

According to Mowat, the company's initiatives resonate because Vancity's culture stresses that success starts with employees. "We don't do it to be nice and win awards," he says, "We're doing it because our ability to compete with companies 35 times as big as we are rests in the fact that when somebody walks through our door, an employee will walk up to them and treat them really well, treat them with respect. And that makes us money."

In the past few years, Vancity has seen record earnings and membership growth as well as the highest employee engagement scores in the organization's history. Is it any wonder that Canadians are clamouring to work at Vancity? The company has received as many as 12 000 applications a year—one of the highest per-employee ratios in Canada.[1]

What we have here is an example of worklife and management—just what this book is about. The example also highlights many important aspects of organizational behaviour such as channels of communication, organizational culture, employee engagement, motivation, and job attitudes. It raises some very interesting questions: Why are manager's bonuses tied to employee engagement? Why does the company offer employees so many benefits and perks and what effect does this have on their attitudes and motivation? Why does the senior management team hold meetings with employees every year? This book will help you uncover the answers to these kinds of questions.

There are a variety of different organizations in which individuals work together to accomplish goals through group effort. Though the motivation of a television news station might differ from other organizations, all organizations strive for goal accomplishment and survival.

In this chapter, we will define *organizations* and *organizational behaviour* and examine its relationship to management. We will explore historical and contemporary approaches to management and consider what managers do and how they think. The chapter concludes with some issues of concern to contemporary managers.

WHAT ARE ORGANIZATIONS?

This book is about what happens in organizations. **Organizations** are social inventions for accomplishing common goals through group effort. Vancity is obviously an organization, but so are the Calgary Flames, the CBC, the Tragically Hip, and a college sorority or fraternity.

Organizations. Social inventions for accomplishing common goals through group effort.

Social Inventions

When we say that organizations are social inventions, we mean that their essential characteristic is the coordinated presence of *people*, not necessarily things. Vancity owns a lot of things, such as equipment and offices. However, you are probably aware that through advanced information technology and contracting out work, some contemporary organizations make and sell products, such as computers or clothes, without owning much of anything. Also, many service organizations, such as consulting firms, have little physical capital. Still, these organizations have people—people who present both opportunities and challenges. *The field of organizational behaviour is about understanding people and managing them to work effectively.*

Goal Accomplishment

Individuals are assembled into organizations for a reason. The organizations mentioned above have the very basic goals of providing financial services, delivering news, and winning hockey games. Non-profit organizations have goals such as saving souls, promoting the arts, helping the needy, or educating people. Virtually all organizations have survival as a goal. Despite this, consider the list of organizations that have failed to survive: Canadian Airlines, Eaton's, Jetsgo, and a ton of American savings and loan companies. *The field of organizational behaviour is concerned with how organizations can survive and adapt to change.* Certain behaviours are necessary for survival and adaptation. People have to

- be motivated to join and remain in the organization;
- carry out their basic work reliably, in terms of productivity, quality, and service;
- be willing to continuously learn and upgrade their knowledge and skills; and
- be flexible and innovative.[2]

The field of organizational behaviour is concerned with all these basic activities. Innovation and flexibility, which provide for adaptation to change, are especially important for contemporary organizations. Management guru Tom Peters has gone so far as to advise firms to "Get Innovative or Get Dead."[3]

Tom Peters
www.tompeters.com

Group Effort

The final component of our definition of organizations is that they are based on group effort. At its most general level, this means that organizations depend on interaction and coordination among people to accomplish their goals. Much of the intellectual and physical work done in organizations is quite literally performed by groups, whether they are permanent work teams or short-term project teams. Also, informal grouping occurs in all organizations because friendships develop and individuals form informal alliances to accomplish work. The quality of this informal contact in terms of communication and morale can have a strong impact on goal achievement. For all these reasons, *the field of organizational behaviour is concerned with how to get people to practise effective teamwork.*

Now that we have reviewed the basic characteristics of organizations, let's look more directly at the meaning and scope of organizational behaviour.

WHAT IS ORGANIZATIONAL BEHAVIOUR?

Organizational behaviour.
The attitudes and behaviours of individuals and groups in organizations.

Organizational behaviour refers to the attitudes and behaviours of individuals and groups in organizations. The discipline of organizational behaviour systematically studies these attitudes and behaviours and provides insight about effectively managing and changing them. It also studies how organizations can be structured more effectively and how events in their external environments affect organizations. Those who study organizational behaviour are interested in attitudes—how satisfied people are with their jobs, how committed they feel to the goals of the organization, or how supportive they are of promoting women or minorities into management positions. Behaviours like cooperation, conflict, innovation, resignation, or ethical lapses are important areas of study in the field of organizational behaviour.

Using an organizational behaviour perspective, reconsider the Vancity vignette that opened the chapter. The immediate question is: *What are the factors that make an organization a great place to work and a success?* Although we will not answer this question directly, we can pose some subsidiary questions highlighting some of the topics that the field of organizational behaviour covers, which we will explore in later chapters.

- How do employees in organizations learn and what is the role of training and career planning? At Vancity, employees have access to internal training, a tuition reimbursement program, and outside courses to help them advance in their careers through Discoveru, a resource for career planning. Learning is important for employee behaviour and performance and is discussed in Chapter 2.
- How can organizations motivate employees and how important is compensation? At Vancity, employees receive many benefits and perks and also receive bonuses based on company profits and productivity. Managers' bonuses are tied to

employee engagement. Chapter 5 describes different theories of motivation and the role of money as a motivator, and different ways of linking pay to performance are described in Chapter 6.

- What is a strong organizational culture and what role does it play in an organization's effectiveness? Vancity has a very unique and strong culture that emphasizes social responsibility and concern and caring for employees. How cultures are built and maintained is covered in Chapter 8.

- What style of leadership is most effective? At Vancity, senior management sits down with all 2000 employees every year and employee input, voice, and involvement in company decisions is encouraged. Leadership is one of the most important ingredients for an organization's success. As you will learn in Chapter 9, the field of organizational behaviour has a longstanding interest in leadership.

- How should managers communicate to employees? Communication is the process of exchanging information, and effective organizational communication is essential for organizational competitiveness. At Vancity, the senior management team holds meetings with all of the company's employees every year and open dialogue between management and employees is encouraged. A group of employees dedicated to internal communications distribute memos in weekly e-newsletter briefs and post short stories about employee and community achievements in lunchrooms and elevators. Communication is the focus of Chapter 10.

These questions provide a good overview of some issues that those in the field of organizational behaviour study. Accurate answers to these questions would go a long way toward understanding why Vancity is a successful organization and how other organizations can make changes to become more effective. Analysis followed by action is what organizational behaviour is all about.

WHY STUDY ORGANIZATIONAL BEHAVIOUR?

Why should you attempt to read and understand the material in *Organizational Behaviour*?

Organizational Behaviour Is Interesting

At its core, organizational behaviour is interesting because it is about people and human nature. Why are employees at Vancity so proud of their organization and so highly engaged? These questions are interesting because they help us understand why employees become committed to an organization and what motivates them to work hard.

Organizational Behaviour includes interesting examples of success as well as failure. Later in the text, we will study a company that receives thousands of job applications a week (WestJet), a company with strong values for treating people and the environment with respect (Husky Injection Molding Systems), and a company that has implemented equality and diversity programs and is considered a model for how to tie diversity to business success (Bank of Montreal). All of these companies are extremely successful, and organizational behaviour helps explain why.

Organizational behaviour does not have to be exotic to be interesting. Anyone who has negotiated with a recalcitrant bureaucrat or had a really excellent boss has probably wondered what made them behave the way they did. Organizational behaviour provides the tools to find out why.

Organizational Behaviour Is Important

Looking through the lens of other disciplines, it would be possible to frame Vancity's success in terms of economics or finance. Notice, however, that underlying all these perspectives, it is *still* about organizational behaviour. What happens in organizations often has a profound impact on people. It is clear that the impact of organizational behaviour does not stop at the walls of the organization. The consumers of an organization's products and services are also affected, such as the customers who rely on Vancity for loans and mortgages. Thus, organizational behaviour is important to managers, employees, and consumers; and understanding it can make us more effective managers, employees, or consumers.

We sometimes fail to appreciate that there is tremendous variation in organizational behaviour. For example, skilled salespeople in insurance or real estate make many, many more sales than some of their peers. Similarly, for every Greenpeace or Sierra Club, there are dozens of failed organizations that were dedicated to saving the environment. The field of organizational behaviour is concerned with explaining these differences and using the explanations to improve organizational effectiveness and efficiency.

Greenpeace International
www.greenpeace.org

Organizational Behaviour Makes a Difference

Does organizational behaviour matter for an organization's competitiveness and performance? In his book, *Competitive Advantage Through People*, Jeffrey Pfeffer argues that organizations can no longer achieve a competitive advantage through the traditional sources of success, such as technology, regulated markets, access to financial resources, and economies of scale.[4] Today, the main factor that differentiates organizations is their workforce, and the most successful organizations are those that effectively manage their employees. In other words, sustained competitive advantage and organizational effectiveness are increasingly related to management and organizational behaviour. On the basis of a review of the popular and academic literature, Pfeffer identified 16 practices of companies that are effective through their management of people. Many of these practices, such as incentive pay, participation and empowerment, teams, job redesign, and training and skill development, are important topics in organizational behaviour and are discussed in this book. Pfeffer's research helps to point out that organizational behaviour is not just interesting and important but that it also makes a big difference for the effectiveness and competitiveness of organizations.

Jeffrey Pfeffer
www.pfdf.org/leaderbooks/pfeffer

There is increasing evidence that management practices and organizational behaviour not only influence employee attitudes and behaviour, but also have an effect on an organization's effectiveness. In fact, companies like RBC Financial Group are at the forefront of a new wave of management practices that recognize that satisfied, high-performing employees are good for profits. A major overhaul of this company's human resources and management practices resulted in an improvement in both employee and customer satisfaction.[5]

RBC Financial Group
www.rbc.com

This raises an interesting question: Are companies with good management who have implemented practices from organizational behaviour more successful? Are the best companies to work for also the most profitable? Some might argue that just because an organization is a great place to work does not necessarily mean that it is a great organization in terms of its competitiveness and performance. What do you think? To find out more, see the "Research Focus: *Are the Best Companies to Work for the Best Companies?*"

HOW MUCH DO YOU KNOW ABOUT ORGANIZATIONAL BEHAVIOUR?

Although this is probably your first formal course in organizational behaviour, you already have a number of opinions about the subject. To illustrate this, consider whether the following statements are true or false. Please jot down a one-sentence rationale for your answer. There are no tricks involved!

RESEARCH FOCUS

Are the Best Companies to Work for the Best Companies?

In recent years, surveys of the best companies to work for have become very popular. The Globe and Mail's *Report on Business Magazine* publishes its annual list of the "50 Best Employers in Canada"; *Maclean's* magazine has its annual list of "Canada's Top 100 Employers"; and *Canadian Business* has its annual list of the "Best Workplaces in Canada." In the United States, *Fortune* magazine publishes an annual list of the "100 Best Companies to Work for in America." While there is no doubt that being a great place to work is important, some have wondered whether the best places to work are also the best companies. For example, are the additional costs associated with being a great place to work (e.g., employee-friendly practices, outstanding pay and benefits) justified by higher firm performance? Do good employee relations and positive job attitudes contribute to the bottom line?

To find out, Ingrid Fulmer, Barry Gerhart, and Kimberly Scott conducted a study in which they compared 50 of the companies from *Fortune* magazine's 100 best list in 1998 to a matched set of firms that have never been on the 100 best list but are comparable in terms of industry, size, and operating performance. Comparisons between the two samples indicated that the 100 best companies outperformed the matched group of companies on financial performance and stock returns. Financial performance as measured by return on assets (ROA) and market-to-book value of equity was generally better among the 100 best than the matched group of organizations over a six-year period. Further, the six-year cumulative stock returns of the companies on the 100 best list outperformed a composite market index by 183 percentage points, or 95 percent!

The authors were also interested in finding out what it was about the 100 best companies that caused them to be more effective. They suggested that it has to do with more positive employee relations and job attitudes. To be sure, they compared the sample from the 100 best companies to another sample of organizations from Hewitt Associates and The Gallup Organization on a measure of employee attitudes. The results indicated that the companies on the 100 best list did have more positive employee relations and attitudes compared to the other companies. Further, to assess the stability of job attitudes, the authors examined the relationship between the employee attitude measure in 1998 and 1999. The results indicated that the relationship was positive and significant and that there was little change from one year to the next. In other words, employee attitudes at the 100 best firms were highly positive and stable over time, providing some support for the belief that positive employee relations are a source of sustainable competitive advantage.

According to the authors, these findings provide the strongest evidence to date of a direct positive link between employee relations and employee attitudes and financial performance. They suggest that companies can create attractive workplaces without hurting the bottom line, and in many cases the 100 best exhibit superior performance.

What about the best companies to work for in Canada? Do they have superior financial performance? In terms of shareholder return and sales growth, the answer is "Yes." Thirty-one of the 50 best companies to work for in Canada in 2003, whose shares trade publicly, outperformed the S&P/TSX Composite Index by 14.4 percent in annual total shareholder return, and by 5 percent in average annual sales growth over a period of five years. The share prices of the best employers of 2004 increased by an average of 10.2 percent a year over the past 10 years compared to 6.2 percent for the S&P/TSX Composite Index.

So what's the bottom line? Positive employee relations do not come at the expense of financial performance. Organizations can have both!

Sources: Based on Fulmer, I.S., Gerhart, B., & Scott, K.S. (2003). Are the 100 best better? An empirical investigation of the relationship between being a "great place to work" and firm performance. *Personnel Psychology, 56,* 965–993; Romero, E.J. (2004). Are the great places to work also great performers? *Academy of Management Executive, 18,* 150–152; Brearton, S., & Daly, J. (2003, January). The fifty best companies to work for in Canada. *Report on Business, 19(7),* 53–65, 60; Brearton, S. & Daly, J. (2004, January). The 50 best companies to work for in Canada. *Report on Business, 20(7),* 33.

1. Effective organizational leaders tend to possess identical personality traits.
2. Nearly all workers prefer stimulating, challenging jobs.
3. Managers have a very accurate idea about how much their peers and superiors are paid.
4. Workers have a very accurate idea about how often they are absent from work.
5. Pay is the best way to motivate most employees and improve job performance.

Now that you have your answers, do one more thing. Assume that the correct answer is opposite to the one you have given; that is, if your answer is "true" for a statement, assume that it is actually false, and vice versa. Now, give a one-sentence rationale why this opposite answer could also be correct.

Each of these statements concerns the behaviour of people in organizations. Furthermore, each statement has important implications for the functioning of organizations. If effective leaders possess identical personality traits, then organizations might sensibly hire leaders who have such traits. Similarly, if most employees prefer stimulating jobs, there are many jobs that could benefit from upgrading. In this book, we will investigate the extent to which statements such as these are true or false and why they are true or false.

The answers to this quiz may be surprising. Substantial research indicates that each of the statements in the quiz is essentially false. Of course, there are exceptions, but in general, researchers have found that the personalities of effective leaders vary a fair amount, many people prefer routine jobs, managers are not well informed about the pay of their peers and superiors, workers underestimate their own absenteeism, and pay is not always the most effective way to motivate workers and improve job performance. However, you should not jump to unwarranted conclusions based on the inaccuracy of these statements until we determine *why* they tend to be incorrect. There are good reasons for an organization to tie pay to job performance to motivate employees and to improve their performance. Also, we can predict who might prefer challenging jobs and who will be motivated by pay. We will discuss these issues in more detail in later chapters.

Experience indicates that people are amazingly good at giving sensible reasons as to why the same statement is either true or false. Thus, pay will always motivate workers because most people want to make more money and will work harder to get more pay. Conversely, workers will only work as hard as they have to regardless of how much money they are paid. The ease with which people can generate such contradictory responses suggests that "common sense" develops through unsystematic and incomplete experiences with organizational behaviour.

However, because common sense and opinions about organizational behaviour do affect management practice, practice should be based on informed opinion and systematic study. To learn more about how to study organizational behaviour, see the Appendix. Now, let's consider the goals of organizational behaviour.

GOALS OF ORGANIZATIONAL BEHAVIOUR

Like any discipline, the field of organizational behaviour has a number of commonly agreed-on goals. Chief among these are effectively predicting, explaining, and managing behaviour that occurs in organizations. For example, in Chapter 6 we will discuss the factors that predict which pay plans are most effective in motivating employees. Then we will explain the reasons for this effectiveness and describe how managers can implement effective pay plans.

Predicting Organizational Behaviour

Predicting the behaviour of others is an essential requirement for everyday life, both inside and outside of organizations. Our lives are made considerably easier by our ability to anticipate when our friends will get angry, when our professors will respond favourably to a completed assignment, and when salespeople and politicians are telling us the truth about a new product or the state of the nation. In organizations, there is considerable interest in predicting when people will make ethical decisions, create innovative products, or engage in sexual harassment.

The very regularity of behaviour in organizations permits the prediction of its future occurrence. However, untutored predictions of organizational behaviour are not always as accurate. Through systematic study, the field of organizational behaviour provides a scientific foundation that helps improve predictions of organizational events. Of course, being able to predict organizational behaviour does not guarantee that we can explain the reason for the behaviour and develop an effective strategy to manage it. This brings us to the second goal of the field.

Explaining Organizational Behaviour

Another goal of organizational behaviour is to explain events in organizations—why do they occur? Prediction and explanation are not synonymous. Ancient societies were capable of predicting the regular setting of the sun, but were unable to explain where it went or why it went there. In general, accurate prediction precedes explanation. Thus, the very regularity of the sun's disappearance gave some clues about why it was disappearing.

Organizational behaviour is especially interested in determining why people are more or less motivated, satisfied, or prone to resign. Explaining events is more complicated than predicting them. For one thing, a particular behaviour could have multiple causes. People may resign from their jobs because they are dissatisfied with their pay, because they are discriminated against, or because they have failed to respond appropriately to an organizational crisis. An organization that finds itself with a "turnover problem" is going to have to find out why this is happening before it can put an effective correction into place. This behaviour could have many different causes, each of which would require a specific solution. Furthermore, explanation is also complicated by the fact that the underlying causes of some event or behaviour can change over time. For example, the reasons people quit may vary greatly depending on the overall economy and whether there is high or low unemployment in the field in question. Throughout the book, we will consider material that should improve your grasp of organizational behaviour. The ability to understand behaviour is a necessary prerequisite for effectively managing it.

Managing Organizational Behaviour

Management is defined as the art of getting things accomplished in organizations. Managers acquire, allocate, and utilize physical and human resources to accomplish goals.[6] This definition does not include a prescription about how to get things accomplished. As we proceed through the text, you will learn that a variety of management styles might be effective depending on the situation at hand.

If behaviour can be predicted and explained, it can often be controlled or managed. That is, if we truly understand the reasons for high-quality service, ethical behaviour, or anything else, we can often take sensible action to manage it effectively. If prediction and explanation constitute analysis, then management constitutes action. Unfortunately, we see all too many cases in which managers act without analysis, looking for a quick fix to problems. The result is often disaster. The point is not to

Management. The art of getting things accomplished in organizations through others.

overanalyze a problem. Rather, it is to approach a problem with a systematic understanding of behavioural science. Such an approach is known as evidence-based management. To learn more, see "Applied Focus: *Evidence-Based Management in Organizational Behaviour.*"

EARLY PRESCRIPTIONS CONCERNING MANAGEMENT

For many years, experts interested in organizations were concerned with prescribing the "correct" way to manage an organization to achieve its goals. There were two basic phases to this prescription, which experts often call the classical view and the human relations view. A summary of these viewpoints will illustrate how the history of management thought and organizational behaviour has developed.

The Classical View and Bureaucracy

Most of the major advocates of the classical viewpoint were experienced managers or consultants who took the time to write down their thoughts on organizing. For the most part, this activity occurred in the early 1900s. The classical writers acquired their experience in military settings, mining operations, and factories that produced everything from cars to candy. Prominent names include Henri Fayol, General Motors executive James D. Mooney, and consultant Lyndall Urwick.[7] Although exceptions existed, the **classical viewpoint** tended to advocate a very high degree of specialization of labour and a very high degree of coordination. Each department was to tend to its own affairs, with centralized decision making from upper management providing coordination. To maintain control, the classical view suggested that managers have fairly few workers, except for lower-level jobs where machine pacing might substitute for close supervision.

> **Classical viewpoint.** An early prescription on management that advocated high specialization of labour, intensive coordination, and centralized decision making.

Frederick Taylor (1856–1915), the father of **Scientific Management**, was also a contributor to the classical school, although he was mainly concerned with job design and the structure of work on the shop floor.[8] Rather than informal "rules of thumb" for job design, Taylor's Scientific Management advocated the use of careful research to determine the optimum degree of specialization and standardization. Also, he supported the development of written instructions that clearly defined work procedures, and he encouraged supervisors to standardize workers' movements and breaks for maximum efficiency. Taylor even extended Scientific Management to the supervisor's job, advocating "functional foremanship," whereby supervisors would specialize in particular functions. For example, one might become a specialist in training workers, while another might fulfill the role of a disciplinarian.

> **Scientific Management.** Frederick Taylor's system for using research to determine the optimum degree of specialization and standardization of work tasks.

The practising managers and consultants had an academic ally in Max Weber (1864–1920), the distinguished German social theorist. Weber made the term "bureaucracy" famous by advocating it as a means of rationally managing complex organizations. During Weber's lifetime, managers were certainly in need of advice. In this time of industrial growth and development, most management was done by intuition, and nepotism and favouritism were rampant. According to Weber, a **bureaucracy** has the following qualities:

> **Bureaucracy.** Max Weber's ideal type of organization that included a strict chain of command, detailed rules, high specialization, centralized power, and selection and promotion based on technical competence.

- A strict chain of command in which each member reports to only a single superior.
- Criteria for selection and promotion based on impersonal technical skills rather than nepotism or favouritism.
- A set of detailed rules, regulations, and procedures ensuring that the job gets done regardless of who the specific worker is.
- The use of strict specialization to match duties with technical competence.
- The centralization of power at the top of the organization.[9]

APPLIED FOCUS

Evidence-Based Management in Organizational Behaviour

How do managers make decisions about what courses of action to take to address organizational concerns and solve problems? Can they adequately predict and explain organizational behaviour to determine the most appropriate and effective course of action?

The answer is "yes." In one real-life example, the executive director of a health care system with 20 rural clinics noted that performance differed tremendously among the clinics. The differences had nothing to do with patient mix or employee characteristics. To get to the bottom of the issue, the director interviewed clinic members and discovered that they were frustrated with the sheer number of metrics they had to report on (200+ indicators sent monthly, comparing each clinic to the other 19). The director recalled a principle from a course in psychology taken a long time ago: humans can only process a limited amount of information at any one time. With this in mind, a redesigned feedback system was put in place. The new system was created with input from clinic staff and uses three performance categories—care quality, cost, and employee satisfaction. Because of the new, employee-friendly feedback system, the health care system's performance improved across the board over the next year, with low-performing units showing the greatest improvement.

This example shows how a principle (human beings can process only a limited amount of information) is translated into practice (asking for feedback on a few critical performance indicators using terms people easily understand). In other words, the executive director was able to use sound research to predict, explain, and manage clinic members' behaviour and performance. This is what evidence-based management is all about.

Evidence-based management involves translating principles based on best scientific evidence into organizational practices. By using evidence-based management, managers can make decisions based on the best available scientific evidence from social science and organizational research, rather than personal preference and unsystematic experience. As the example demonstrates, evidence-based management derives principles from research evidence and translates them into practices that solve organizational problems. The use of evidence-based management is more likely to result in the attainment of organizational goals,

including those affecting employees, stockholders, and the public in general.

Evidence-based practice is nothing new. It has taken the medical establishment by storm in the last decade and is also used in policing and education. Decisions in medical care are based on the latest and best knowledge of what actually works. Unfortunately, this is not the case in management as many managers today continue to rely largely on personal experience, obsolete knowledge, hype, dogma, advice from consultants based on weak evidence, or mimicry of top performers. According to Jeffrey Pfeffer and Robert Sutton, "If doctors practiced medicine like many companies practice management, there would be more unnecessary sick or dead patients and many more doctors in jail or suffering other penalties for malpractice."

What evidence should managers use to solve problems and implement better decisions? First, managers should be aware of the knowledge derived from organizational research about cause-effect relationships (e.g., specific goals are more effective than do-your-best goals). Second, they should obtain local or organization-specific evidence about events in their own organization. This involves systematically gathering data in a particular setting to inform decision making and choose appropriate courses of action. So if employee absenteeism is on the rise, gather data to try and find out what is causing it. Managers need to obtain relevant evidence based on scientific principles as well as organization-specific facts to solve problems and make effective decisions that help to realize organizational goals.

According to Pfeffer and Sutton, managers (like doctors) can practise their craft more effectively if they are routinely guided by the best logic and evidence—and if they relentlessly seek new knowledge and insight—both from inside and outside their companies—to keep updating their assumptions, knowledge, and skills. The managers and companies that practise evidence-based management have a pronounced competitive advantage.

Sources: Based on Rousseau, D.M. (2006). Is there such a thing as "evidence-based management"? *Academy of Management Review, 31,* 256–269; Pfeffer, J., & Sutton, R.I. (2006). Evidence-based management. *Harvard Business Review,* 62–74.

Weber saw bureaucracy as an "ideal type" or theoretical model that would standardize behaviour in organizations and provide workers with security and a sense of purpose. Jobs would be performed as intended rather than following the whims of the specific role occupant. In exchange for this conformity, workers would have a fair chance of being promoted and rising in the power structure. Rules, regulations, and a clear-cut chain of command that further clarified required behaviour provided the workers with a sense of security.

Even during this period, some observers, such as the "business philosopher" Mary Parker Follett (1868–1933), noted that the classical view of management seemed to take for granted an essential conflict of interest between managers and employees.[10] This sentiment found expression in the human relations movement.

The Human Relations Movement and a Critique of Bureaucracy

Hawthorne studies. Research conducted at the Hawthorne plant of Western Electric in the 1920s and 1930s that illustrated how psychological and social processes affect productivity and work adjustment.

The human relations movement generally began with the famous **Hawthorne studies** of the 1920s and 1930s.[11] These studies, conducted at the Hawthorne plant of Western Electric near Chicago, began in the strict tradition of industrial engineering. They were concerned with the impact of fatigue, rest pauses, and lighting on productivity. However, during the course of the studies, the researchers (among others, Harvard University's Elton Mayo and Fritz Roethlisberger and Hawthorne's William J. Dickson) began to notice the effects of psychological and social processes on productivity and work adjustment. This impact suggested that there could be dysfunctional aspects to how work was organized. One obvious sign was resistance to management through strong informal group mechanisms like norms that limited productivity to less than what management wanted.

Human relations movement. A critique of classical management and bureaucracy that advocated management styles that were more participative and oriented toward employee needs.

After World War II, a number of theorists and researchers, who were mostly academics, took up the theme begun at Hawthorne. Prominent names included Chris Argyris, Alvin Gouldner, and Rensis Likert. The **human relations movement** called attention to certain dysfunctional aspects of classical management and bureaucracy and advocated more people-oriented styles of management that catered more to the social and psychological needs of employees. This critique of bureaucracy addressed several specific problems:

- Strict specialization is incompatible with human needs for growth and achievement.[12] This can lead to employee alienation from the organization and its clients.

- Strong centralization and reliance on formal authority often fail to take advantage of the creative ideas and knowledge of lower-level members, who are often closer to the customer.[13] As a result, the organization will fail to learn from its mistakes, which threatens innovation and adaptation. Resistance to change will occur as a matter of course.

- Strict, impersonal rules lead members to adopt the minimum acceptable level of performance that the rules specify.[14] If a rule states that employees must process at least eight claims a day, eight claims will become the norm, even though higher performance levels are possible.

- Strong specialization causes employees to lose sight of the overall goals of the organization.[15] Forms, procedures, and required signatures become ends in themselves, divorced from the true needs of customers, clients, and other departments in the organization. This is the "red-tape mentality" that we sometimes observe in bureaucracies.

Obviously, not all bureaucratic organizations have these problems. However, they were common enough that human relations advocates and others began to call for the adoption of more flexible systems of management and the design of more interesting jobs. They also advocated open communication, more employee participation in decision making, and less rigid, more decentralized forms of control.

CONTEMPORARY MANAGEMENT— THE CONTINGENCY APPROACH

How has the apparent tension between the classical approach and the human relations approach been resolved? First, contemporary scholars and managers recognize the merits of both approaches. The classical advocates pointed out the critical role of control and coordination in getting organizations to achieve their goals. The human relationists pointed out the dangers of certain forms of control and coordination and addressed the need for flexibility and adaptability. Second, as we will study in later chapters, contemporary scholars have learned that management approaches need to be tailored to fit the situation. For example, we would generally manage a payroll department more bureaucratically than a research and development department. Getting out a payroll every week is a routine task with no margin for error. Research requires creativity that is fostered by a more flexible work environment.

Reconsider the five questions we posed earlier about the factors that make an organization a great place to work and a success. Answering these questions is not an easy task, partly because human nature is so complex. This complexity means that an organizational behaviour text cannot be a "cookbook." In what follows, you will not find formulas to improve job satisfaction or service quality with one cup of leadership style and two cups of group dynamics. We have not discovered a simple set of laws of organizational behaviour that you can memorize and then retrieve when necessary to solve any organizational problem. It is this "quick fix" mentality that produces simplistic and costly management fads and fashions.[16]

There is a growing body of research and management experience to help sort out the complexities of what happens in organizations. However, the general answer to many of the questions we will pose in the following chapters is "It depends." Which leadership style is most effective? This depends on the characteristics of the leader, those of the people being led, and what the leader is trying to achieve. Will an increase in pay lead to an increase in performance? This depends on who is getting the increase and the exact reason for the increase. These dependencies are called contingencies. The **contingency approach** to management recognizes that there is no one best way to manage; rather, an appropriate style depends on the demands of the situation. Thus, the effectiveness of a leadership style is contingent on the abilities of the followers, and the consequence of a pay increase is partly contingent on the need for money. Contingencies illustrate the complexity of organizational behaviour and show why we should study it systematically. Throughout the text we will discuss organizational behaviour with the contingency approach in mind.

Contingency approach. An approach to management that recognizes that there is no one best way to manage, and that an appropriate management style depends on the demands of the situation.

WHAT DO MANAGERS DO?

Organizational behaviour is not just for managers or aspiring managers. As we noted earlier, a good understanding of the field can be useful for consumers or anyone else who has to interact with organizations or get things done through them. Nevertheless, many readers of this text have an interest in management as a potential career. Managers can have a strong impact on what happens in and to organizations. They both influence and are influenced by organizational behaviour, and the net result can have important consequences for organizational effectiveness.

There is no shortage of texts and popular press books oriented toward what managers *should* do. However, the field of organizational behaviour is also concerned with what really happens in organizations. Let's look at several research studies that explore what managers *do* do. This provides a context for appreciating the usefulness of understanding organizational behaviour.

Managerial Roles

Canadian management theorist Henry Mintzberg conducted an in-depth study of the behaviour of several managers.[17] The study earned him a Ph.D. from the Massachusetts Institute of Technology (MIT) in 1968. In the Appendix, we discuss how he conducted the study and some of its more basic findings. Here, however, we are concerned with Mintzberg's discovery of a rather complex set of roles played by the managers: figurehead, leader, liaison person, monitor, disseminator, spokesperson, entrepreneur, disturbance handler, resource allocator, and negotiator. These roles are summarized in Exhibit 1.1.

Interpersonal Roles. Interpersonal roles are expected behaviours that have to do with establishing and maintaining interpersonal relations. In the *figurehead role*, the manager serves as a symbol of his or her organization rather than an active decision maker. Examples of the figurehead role are making a speech to a trade group, entertaining clients, or signing legal documents. In the *leadership role*, the manager selects, mentors, rewards, and disciplines employees. In the *liaison role*, the manager maintains horizontal contacts inside and outside the organization. This might include discussing a project with a colleague in another department or touching base with an embassy delegate of a country where one hopes to do future business.

Informational Roles. These roles are concerned with the various ways the manager receives and transmits information. In the *monitor role,* the manager scans the internal and external environments of the firm to follow current performance and to keep himself informed of new ideas and trends. For example, the head of research and development might attend a professional engineering conference. In the *disseminator role*, managers send information on both facts and preferences to others. For example, the R&D head might summarize what she learned at the conference in an electronic mail message to employees. The *spokesperson role* concerns mainly sending messages into the organization's external environment—for example, drafting an annual report to stockholders or giving an interview to the press.

Decisional Roles. The final set of managerial roles Mintzberg discussed deals with decision making. In the *entrepreneur role,* the manager turns problems and opportunities into plans for improved changes. This might include suggesting a new product or service that will please customers. In the *disturbance handler role,* the manager deals with problems stemming from employee conflicts and addresses threats to resources and turf. In their *resource allocation roles*, managers decide how to deploy time, money, personnel, and other critical resources. Finally, in their *negotiator roles*, managers conduct major negotiations with other organizations or individuals.

EXHIBIT 1.1
Mintzberg's managerial roles.

Adapted from Mintzberg, H. (1973). *The nature of managerial work.* New York: Harper & Row.

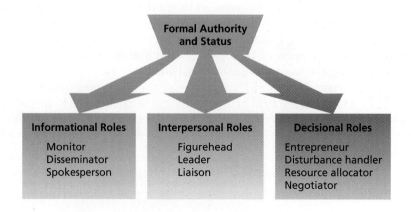

Of course, the relative importance of these roles will vary with management level and organizational technology.[18] First-level supervisors do more disturbance handling and less figureheading. Still, Mintzberg's major contribution to organizational behaviour is to highlight the *complexity* of the roles managers are required to play and the variety of skills they must have to be effective, including leadership, communication, and negotiation. His work also illustrates the complex balancing act managers face when they must play different roles for different audiences. A good grasp of organizational behaviour is at the heart of acquiring these skills and performing this balancing act.

Managerial Activities

Fred Luthans, Richard Hodgetts, and Stuart Rosenkrantz studied the behaviour of a large number of managers in a variety of different kinds of organizations.[19] They determined that the managers engage in four basic types of activities:

- *Routine communication.* This includes the formal sending and receiving of information (as in meetings) and handling paperwork.
- *Traditional management.* Planning, decision making, and controlling are the primary types of traditional management.
- *Networking.* Networking consists of interacting with people outside of the organization and informal socializing and politicking with insiders.
- *Human resource management.* This includes motivating and reinforcing, disciplining and punishing, managing conflict, staffing, and training and developing employees.

Exhibit 1.2 summarizes these managerial activities and shows how a sample of 248 managers divided their time and effort, as determined by research observers (discipline and punishment were done in private and were not open to observation). Perhaps the most striking observation about this figure is how all these managerial activities involve dealing with people.

One of Luthans and colleagues' most fascinating findings is how emphasis on these various activities correlated with managerial success. If we define success as moving up the ranks of the organization quickly, networking proved to be critical. The people who were promoted quickly tended to do more networking (politicking, socializing, and making contacts) and less human resource management than the averages in Exhibit 1.2. If we define success in terms of unit effectiveness and employee satisfaction and commitment, the more successful managers were those who devoted more time and effort to human resource management and less to networking than the averages in the exhibit. A good understanding of organizational behaviour should help you

EXHIBIT 1.2
Summary of managerial activities.

Note: Figures do not total 100% due to rounding. Source: Adapted from Luthans, F., Hodgetts, R.M., & Rosenkrantz, S.A. (1988). *Real managers.* Cambridge, MA: Ballinger.

manage this trade-off more effectively, reconciling the realities of organizational politics with the demands of accomplishing things through others.

Managerial Agendas

John Kotter studied the behaviour patterns of a number of successful general managers.[20] Although he found some differences among them, he also found a strong pattern of similarities that he grouped into the categories of agenda setting, networking, and agenda implementation.

Agenda Setting. Kotter's managers, given their positions, all gradually developed agendas of what they wanted to accomplish for the organization. Many began these agendas even before they assumed their positions. These agendas were almost always informal and unwritten, and they were much more concerned with "people issues" and were less numerical than most formal strategic plans. The managers based their agendas on wide-ranging informal discussions with a wide variety of people.

Networking. Kotter's managers established a wide formal and informal network of key people both inside and outside of their organizations. Insiders included peers, employees, and bosses, but they also extended to these people's employees and bosses. Outsiders included customers, suppliers, competitors, government officials, and the press. This network provided managers with information and established cooperative relationships relevant to their agendas. Formal hiring, firing, and reassigning shaped the network, but so did informal liaisons in which they created dependencies by doing favours for others.

Agenda Implementation. The managers used networks to implement the agendas. They would go *anywhere* in the network for help—up or down, in or out of the organization. In addition, they employed a wide range of influence tactics, from direct orders to subtle language and stories that conveyed their message indirectly.

The theme that runs through Kotter's findings is the high degree of informal interaction and concern with people issues that were necessary for the managers to achieve their agendas. To be sure, the managers used their formal organizational power, but they often found themselves dependent on people over whom they wielded no power. An understanding of organizational behaviour helps to recognize and manage these realities.

John Kotter's research of successful business managers showed that exemplary managers practise agenda setting, networking, and agenda implementation. Michael Dell, of Dell Computers, is an example of such a manager.

Managerial Minds

In contrast to how managers act, which is the focus of the previous section, Herbert Simon and Daniel Isenberg have both explored how managers think.[21] Although they offer a wealth of observations, we will concentrate here on a specific issue that each examined in independent research—managerial intuition.

Some people think that organizational behaviour and its implications for management are just common sense. However, careful observers of successful managers have often noted that intuition seems to guide many of their actions. Isenberg's research suggests that experienced managers use intuition in several ways:

● to sense that a problem exists;

● to perform well-learned mental tasks rapidly (e.g., sizing up a written contract);

● to synthesize isolated pieces of information and data; and

● to double-check more formal or mechanical analyses ("Do these projections look correct?").

Does the use of intuition mean that managerial thinking is random, irrational, or undisciplined? Both Simon and Isenberg say no. In fact, both strongly dispute the idea that intuition is the opposite of rationality or that intuitive means unanalytical. Rather, good intuition is problem identification and problem solving based on a long history of systematic education and experience that enables the manager to locate problems within a network of previously acquired information. The theories, research, and management practices that we cover in *Organizational Behaviour* will contribute to your own information network and give you better managerial intuition about decisions that involve how to make an organization a great place to work and a financial success.

International Managers

The research we discussed above describes how managers act and think in North America. Would managers in other global locations act and think the same way? Up to a point, the answer is probably yes. After all, we are dealing here with some very basic managerial behaviours and thought processes. However, the style in which managers do what they do and the emphasis given to various activities will vary greatly across cultures because of cross-cultural variations in values that affect both managers' and employees' expectations about interpersonal interaction. Thus, in Chapter 5 we will study cross-cultural differences in motivation. In Chapter 9 we study cultural differences in leadership, and in Chapter 10 we will explore how communication varies across cultures.

Geert Hofstede has done pioneering work on cross-cultural differences in values that we will study in Chapter 4. Hofstede provides some interesting observations about how these value differences promote contrasts in the general role that managers play across cultures.[22] He asserts that managers are cultural heroes and even a distinct social class in North America where individualism is treasured. In contrast, Germany tends to worship engineers and have fewer managerial types. In Japan, managers are required to pay obsessive attention to group solidarity rather than to star employees. In the Netherlands, managers are supposed to exhibit modesty and strive for consensus. In the family-run businesses of Taiwan and Singapore, "professional" management, North American style, is greatly downplayed. The contrasts that Hofstede raises are fascinating because the technical requirements for accomplishing goals are actually the same across cultures. It is only the *behavioural* requirements that differ. Thus, national culture is one of the most important contingency variables in organizational behaviour. The appropriateness of various leadership styles, motivation techniques, and communication methods depends on where one is in the world.

International managers must adapt to cross-cultural differences to successfully interact with potential clients and overseas affiliates.

SOME CONTEMPORARY MANAGEMENT CONCERNS

To conclude the chapter, we will briefly examine four issues with which organizations and managers are currently concerned. As with previous sections, our goal is to illustrate how the field of organizational behaviour can help you understand and manage these issues.

Diversity—Local and Global

The demographics of the North American population and workforce are changing, and as a result, both the labour force and customers are becoming increasingly culturally diverse. Contributing to this is the increased movement of women into paid employment, as well as immigration patterns. In Canada, visible minorities are the fastest growing segment of the population.[23] The annual report of Employment and Immigration Canada has projected that two-thirds of today's new entrants to the Canadian labour force will be women, visible minorities, aboriginal people, and persons with disabilities.[24] A recent report by Statistics Canada predicted that the number of visible minorities in Canada is expected to double by 2017 and form more than half the population in greater Toronto and Vancouver, and immigrants will account for 22 percent of the population.[25] Native-born Caucasian North Americans frequently find themselves working with people whose ethnic backgrounds are very different from their own.

Citizenship and Immigration Canada www.cic.gc.ca

Diversity of age is also having an impact in organizations. In less than a decade, the workforce will be dominated by people over the age of 40. By the year 2015, 48 percent of Canada's working-age population will be between the ages of 45 and 64, compared to 29 percent in 1991.[26] With the elimination of mandatory retirement at age 65, a growing number of Canadians over 65 will remain in the workforce. A recent survey found that older Canadians are redefining the concept of retirement and that 75 percent of the participants who had not yet retired expected to continue working post-retirement.[27] Perhaps you have observed people of various ages working in fast-food restaurants that were at one time staffed solely by young people. Both the re-entry of retired people into the workforce and the trend to remove vertical layers in organizations have contributed to much more intergenerational contact in the workplace than was common in the past. Organizations are beginning to adopt new programs in response to this demographic shift, such as flexible benefit plans, compressed work-days, and part-time jobs, to attract and retain older workers. For example, Orkin/PCO Services Corp. of Mississauga, a pest-control service, dealt with a shortage of pest-control specialists by introducing a more flexible part-time schedule with benefits to attract and retain employees who would otherwise have retired or left the industry.[28]

Diversity is also coming to the fore as many organizations realize that they have not treated certain segments of the population, such as women, homosexuals, and the disabled, fairly in many aspects of employment. Organizations have to be able to get the best from *everyone* to be truly competitive. Although legal pressures (such as the *Employment Equity Act*) have contributed to this awareness, general social pressure, especially from customers and clients, has also done so.

Employment Equity Act
http://lois.justice.gc.ca/en/
E-5.401/index.html

Finally, diversity issues are having an increasing impact as organizations "go global." Foreign sales by multinational corporations have exceeded $7 trillion and are growing 20 to 30 percent faster than their sales of exports.[29] Multinational expansion, strategic alliances, and joint ventures increasingly require employees and managers to come into contact with their counterparts from other cultures. Although many of these people have an interest in North American consumer goods and entertainment, it is naïve to assume that business values are rapidly converging on some North American model. As a result, North American organizations that operate in other countries need to understand how the workforce and customers in those countries are diverse and culturally different.

What does diversity have to do with organizational behaviour? The field has long been concerned with stereotypes, conflict, cooperation, and teamwork. These are just some of the factors that managers must manage effectively for organizations to benefit from the considerable opportunities that a diverse workforce affords.

Employee–Organization Relationships

Downsizing, restructuring, re-engineering, and outsourcing have had a profound effect on North American and European organizations in the past two decades. Companies such as General Motors, Ford, Levi Strauss, IBM, Air Canada, and Nortel each have laid off thousands of workers. These companies have eliminated high-paying manufac-turing jobs, the once-secure middle-management jobs, and high-tech jobs. As well, there has been a major structural change in work arrangements. Full-time, full-year perma-nent jobs are being replaced by part-time work and temporary or contract work. It is expected that these work arrangements will become the future standard forms of work, and they will forever change the nature of employee–organization relationships.[30]

Surveys suggest that the consequences of these events are decreased trust, morale, commitment, and shifting loyalties. Study after study shows an increasing decline in workers' attitudes toward their jobs and organizations, suggesting that employee loy-alty is a thing of the past. A survey by Towers Perrin management consultants found that one-third of employees are profoundly unhappy in their work and more than half of the employees sampled in both Canada and the United States have negative feelings about their jobs and are either actively or passively looking for other work. The key reasons for employees' unhappiness included boredom, overwork, concern about their future, and a lack of support and recognition from their bosses. The study also found that trust in senior management is declining, and only 17 percent of Canadian workers are highly engaged in their jobs and willing to put in extra effort.[31] In another study, the results indicated that employee morale and job satisfaction levels have fallen in the last decade. Employee satisfaction with bonuses, promotion policies, training pro-grams, and co-workers is on the decline.[32]

Absenteeism in Canadian organizations is also on the rise. According to Statistics Canada, there has been an alarming and unprecedented increase in absenteeism rates since the mid-1990s. In 2002, Canadians lost more than 92 million workdays due to illness, injury, and personal reasons. Full-time Canadian workers missed an average of nine work days, up from eight days in 2000. Furthermore, the increase in absenteeism has been found across all age groups and sectors, and translates into millions of dollars in lost productivity. It has been estimated that the total cost of reported absenteeism in Canada is $15 billion annually. Although there is no one definitive cause, increasing stress levels and poorly designed jobs are major contributors. In fact, all types of employees are experiencing more workplace stress today than a decade ago, and the incidence of work-related illness is also on the rise.[33] A recent study of Canadian employees estimated that the direct cost of absenteeism due to high work–life conflict—a major stressor in the workplace—is approximately $3–5 billion per year, and when both direct and indirect costs are included in the calculation, work–life conflict costs Canadians approximately $6–10 billion per year.[34] Exhibit 1.3 presents some of the major findings from this study.

The field of organizational behaviour offers many potential solutions to these kinds of problems. To take just a few examples, consider Radical Entertainment, a software company in Vancouver that has been ranked as one of Canada's best-managed private companies, where taking care of employees and creating a great place to work is a high priority. Employees have access to a fully equipped gym, flexible hours, enriched maternity leaves, and breakfast every morning. According to former company CEO Ian Wilkinson, "If creating a good place to work means that the people who work here will be inspired and that they will stay with us, then it's worth the cost."[35]

This book provides many other examples of organizations that have been able to build and maintain strong and positive employee–organization relationships. For now, consider this: How can an organization improve relations with employees after years of downsizing and declining morale? Read the You Be the Manager feature, *Saving Dofasco*, and answer the questions. At the end of the chapter, find out what Dofasco did in The Manager's Notebook. This is not a test, but rather an exercise to improve critical thinking, analytical skills, and management skills. Pause and reflect on these application features as you encounter them in each chapter.

Radical Entertainment
www.radical.ca

Dofasco Inc.
www.dofasco.ca

EXHIBIT 1.3
Work–Life Conflict in Canadian Organizations.

Higgins C. and Duxbury, L. (2003). *2001 National Work-Life Conflict Study* (Ottawa: Health Canada). Reproduced with permission of the authors.

These findings are based on a sample of 31 571 Canadian employees who work for 100 medium to large organizations in the public, private, and nonprofit sections of the economy. The authors of the report concluded that the majority of Canada's largest employers cannot be considered to be best-practice employers.

What Workers Experience	Percentage of Employees
Employees reporting high levels of role overload	58%
Work responsibilities interfere with the ability to fulfill responsibilities at home	28%
Negative spillover from work to family	44%
Employees reporting high levels of stress	33%
Employees reporting high levels of burnout	32%
Employees reporting highly depressed mood	36%
Employees reporting high levels of job satisfaction	46%
Employees reporting high levels of organizational commitment	53%
Employees who think of leaving their current organization once a week or more	28%
Employees indicating high levels of absenteeism	46%
Employees reporting high levels of life satisfaction	41%

A Focus on Quality, Speed, and Flexibility

Intense competition for customers, both locally and globally, has given rise to a strong emphasis on the quality of both products and services. Correctly identifying customer needs and satisfying them before, during, and after the sale (whether the consumer purchased a car or health care) are now seen as key competitive advantages. To obtain these advantages, many organizations have begun to pursue programs to achieve continuous improvement in the quality of their products or services.

Quality can be very generally defined as everything from speedy delivery to producing goods or services in an environmentally friendly manner. For example, AT&T used its quality program to radically reduce paper pollution in its operations. Other firms that make notable quality efforts include Cadillac, Xerox, FedEx, and Motorola.[36] In the auto industry, quality is considered to be a critical indicator of success. Thus, it is not surprising that in North America, automakers have been making changes to improve the quality of their vehicles. For example, Ford Motor Company has implemented quality-control initiatives that include more rigorous inspection processes, and executives conduct quality blitzes at the plant level and within engineering and purchasing operations.[37]

Ford Canada
www.ford.ca

Quality tactics include extensive training, frequent measurement of quality indicators, meticulous attention to work processes, and an emphasis on preventing (rather than correcting) service or production errors. Maine's L.L.Bean mail-order clothing and camping operation claims to have shipped 500 000 orders without an error over a period of several months. Automakers focus on solving problems that customers are most concerned about, such as wind noise, brake noise, fuel consumption, and ease of operating doors and hatches.[38]

Closely allied with quality is speed. Lenscrafters makes glasses "in about an hour," and Domino's became famous for speedy pizza delivery. Local car dealers now do on-the-spot oil changes, whereas customers previously had to make an appointment days in advance. Perhaps even more important than this external manifestation of speed is the behind-the-scenes speed that has reduced the cycle time for getting new products to the market. Firms such as Benetton and The Limited can move new fashions into stores in a couple of months instead of a couple of years, the former norm. American automakers are beginning to approach the Japanese standard for getting a new car design into the showroom in three years instead of five. Such speed can prove to be a real competitive advantage. Sega successfully challenged Nintendo in the video game market by being the first to launch a 16-bit system.

Finally, in addition to improving quality and speed, flexibility on the part of employees and organizations is also an important competitive advantage. Organizations today must operate in increasingly uncertain, turbulent, and chaotic environments that are being driven by the technological revolution and increasing globalization. For some organizations, the competition has become so fierce that it has been referred to as hypercompetition. Hypercompetitive environments are characterized by constant change and high levels of uncertainty. In order to survive in such an environment, organizations need to be flexible so that they can rapidly respond to changing conditions.

A good example of this is happening in the manufacturing sector, where organizations have begun to create jobs that are more mobile and flexible. At Lincoln Electric Co., the world's largest producer of arc welding equipment, workers receive continual cross-training and they are moved wherever they are needed depending on the type and volume of orders the company receives. For example, salaried workers have been moved to hourly clerical jobs and are paid a different wage for each job assignment. Such job flexibility allows the company to operate with a lean workforce that has for decades contributed to productivity growth and profitability. Apex Precision Technologies Inc. trains workers on all of its equipment so they can shift jobs depending on the orders the company receives each week. As these examples

Lincoln Electric Co.
www.lincolnelectric.com

👉 YOU BE THE
Manager

Saving Dofasco

The steel industry had always had to contend with cyclical ups and downs in demand. But in the 1980s and 1990s that pattern was being overrun by turmoil that evaporated a full third of the continent's steel-making capacity. American giant LTV Corp. filed for bankruptcy in 1986, eventually to be followed by Bethlehem Steel and National Steel. The first rumblings of trouble were felt at Dofasco in 1980 as a recession cut deeply into demand: the company shut down for a week, without layoffs. But in 1982, it laid off 2000 employees—an enormous breach of trust for an employer that had always offered a lifetime security blanket. A year after that, all 2000 were invited back. All but 160 returned, and the company rode out the decade. There was no reconsideration of the overall modus operandi.

Instead, Dofasco tried to buy security. In short order, it invested $425 million for a new hot strip mill, $450 million for plant upgrades, and $300 million for a continuous slab caster. Then, in 1988, it purchased Algoma Steel of Sault Ste. Marie, Ontario, for $560 million, propelling Dofasco past Stelco as the country's largest steelmaker. But demand fell, there were two different cultures and lots of distrust, and there was a long strike at Algoma. By 1991, the company had walked away from Algoma, written off $700 million, and embarked on a painful company-wide restructuring.

Dofasco was losing money and deeply in debt after Algoma. As a result, the company embarked on some downsizing programs and shut down some obsolete facilities. A workforce of close to 12 000 would bottom out at approximately 7000 (all but 400 departed "voluntarily," left via attrition, retired, or were offered severance packages). On the production side, management made a key decision. Under its Solutions in Steel scheme, Dofasco would concentrate less on unprocessed, rolled steel and more on value-added product developed specifically for the needs of its customers, the auto industry above all. According to then CEO John Mayberry, "We spent a year and a half figuring out who we were, what we were good at and where we wanted to go."

The challenge of handling the layoffs was abated by an over-funded pension plan. The company established

| When massive layoffs led to a crash in employee morale, Dofasco had to think fast. |

a centre to help the departing employees find new work, or return to school to get new training with tuition paid for. Those who remained worried and wondered what was next. According to former CEO Don Pether, "There were a lot of unhappy folks here, because they were being totally disrupted. They were staying but their best buddy might have been retired. So you go through all of that angst."

The drop in morale among staff was all the more worrisome because Mayberry and his team knew they needed to get employees engaged with a new long-term vision of the company. But how could they maintain the old, worker-centred philosophy of the founding Sherman family, while at the same time adapting to a shifting business environment?

The company brought in consultants, as is the norm. But it also tapped into the brainpower of a select group of its brightest young employees, who were asked to come up with a series of made-in-Hamilton initiatives.

What initiatives do you think are needed to restore employee–organization relations and save Dofasco? You be the manager.

QUESTIONS

1. What initiatives do you think are required to restore employee–organization relations and get employees engaged with a new long-term vision of the company?

2. Is it possible to change a company with such a long history and strong culture? What are the consequences of doing so?

To find out what Dofasco did and the results, see The Manager's Notebook at the end of the chapter.

Source: Excerpted from Brunt, S. (2004, June). *Heavy mettle. Report on Business*, 58–70. Reprinted with permission from the *Globe and Mail*.

demonstrate, organizations require multiskilled workers as well as new organizational structures, cultures, and leaders to build an organization with strategic flexibility to survive and compete in the twenty-first century.[39]

Another good example of the importance of speed and flexibility is the adoption of flexible manufacturing in the auto industry. Because the vehicle market has become so fragmented, companies must be able to react quickly to changes in consumer demand. As a result, instead of producing one variety of car or truck in a plant, many are now able to turn out several models off one or more platforms. A good example of this is Ford's new Oakville Assembly Complex, which is the company's first flexible plant in Canada and its seventh in North America (see Chapter 15).

What does the passion for quality, speed, and flexibility have to do with organizational behaviour? For one thing, all of these require a high degree of employee *involvement* and *commitment*. Often, this means that management must give employees the power to make on-the-spot decisions that were previously reserved for managers. In addition, quality, speed, and flexibility all require a high degree of *teamwork* between individuals and groups who might have some natural tendency to be uncooperative (such as the engineers and accountants involved in car design). The field of organizational behaviour is deeply concerned with such issues.

Employee Recruitment and Retention

One of the greatest challenges facing organizations today is how to attract and retain skilled employees. The ability of organizations to attract and retain talent has always been important; however, today it has become especially critical for many organizations that are struggling to find the employees they need to compete and survive. An increasing number of organizations are having trouble finding qualified people, a problem stemming in part from changing demographics that will result in a dramatic shortage of skilled workers over the next 10 years. The baby boomers will begin to retire in the next few years, which will create a large skills gap. It is predicted that there will be a 30 percent shortfall of workers between the ages of 25 and 44. This, combined with the increasing willingness of knowledge workers to relocate anywhere in the world and fewer Canadians entering the skilled trades, means that Canadian organizations will increasingly face severe shortages of labour. There are already shortages in scientific, technical, and high-tech industries, and in senior management, communications, and marketing positions. A recent poll found that more than 60 percent of Canadian employers say that labour shortages are limiting their productivity and efficiency. The shortage of labour is so serious in Alberta that businesses are closing early or shutting down altogether because they cannot find enough staff. In fact, most of Canada's top CEOs believe that retaining employees has become their number-one priority and attracting new employees is their fourth priority, just behind financial performance and profitability. Three-quarters of CEOs say they can't find enough competent employees.[40]

The problem is just as severe in the United States, where 80 percent of employers say they are having trouble attracting and retaining employees with critical skills, and some report having difficulty hiring employees with non-critical skills. Given that the key to an organization's success and very survival is its people, the ability to successfully recruit and retain employees has become a critical concern for managers and organizations.[41]

It is now well known that it takes more than money and competitive wages to recruit and retain skilled and talented employees. Pay is only one factor, and for many employees it is not the most important factor for joining or remaining in an organization. So what can managers and organizations do to recruit and retain skilled employees?

DuPont Canada
www.dupont.ca

Consider how DuPont Canada has been successful in retaining its employees. Every new employee receives extensive training in systemic thinking skills with an orientation toward problem solving to maintain operational effectiveness. Employees are told everything that is important about what they are doing. Their input on important issues is sought out by management, and they share in the responsibility for the health of the company. The rate of employee turnover at DuPont is low compared to its competitors and to the industry average. In fact, the average length of employment for an employee at DuPont is over 15 years.[42]

Coastal Pacific Xpress Inc.
www.cpx.ca

One industry where there is already a substantial labour shortage is the trucking industry, where the average turnover is 120 percent. However, for long-haul trucking company Coastal Pacific Xpress (CPX) of Surrey, BC, the turnover rate is only 20 percent. The owners attribute this to the way the company treats its employees. The company provides a supportive environment that treats employees with respect. It pays for fitness memberships, offers flex-time, recognizes staff birthdays, and encourages colleagues to thank their co-workers with candy and thank-you notes. The company also has a profit-sharing program that has paid out more than $400 000 to employees in recent years (see Chapter 6).[43]

Many of the solutions to improving recruitment and retention can be found in organizational behaviour. For example, providing opportunities for learning, improving employees' job satisfaction and organizational commitment, designing jobs that are challenging and meaningful, providing recognition and monetary rewards for performance, managing a diverse workforce, offering flexible work arrangements, and providing effective leadership are just some of the factors that can improve employee recruitment and retention. These are, of course, some of the practices of the best companies to work for in Canada, and their annual rate of turnover is lower than the national average and is half that of other companies.[44] Organizational behaviour has a great deal to offer companies that seek to improve recruitment and retention and to become an employer of choice. To learn more about the management practices of the best companies to work for in Canada, see Exhibit 1.4.

We hope this brief discussion of some of the issues that are of concern to organizations and managers has reinforced your awareness of using organizational behaviour to better understand and manage life at work. These concerns permeate today's workplace, and we will cover them in more detail throughout the book.

- Flexible work schedules (flex-time, telecommuting, job sharing, and compressed workweek)
- Stock options, profit sharing plans, and performance bonuses
- Extensive training and development programs
- Family assistance programs
- On-site fitness facilities, daycare, and wellness programs
- Career days and formal career plans
- Flexible or cafeteria-style benefit plans
- Monthly staff socials, family Christmas parties, and picnics
- Stress reduction programs
- Monthly all-employee meetings
- Formal workplace diversity programs to encourage women and minorities
- Employee recognition and reward programs

EXHIBIT 1.4
Management practices of the best companies to work for in Canada.

Sources: Brearton, S., & Daly, J. (2003, January). The 50 best companies to work for in Canada. *Report on Business Magazine, 19(2)*, 53–66; Hannon, G. (2002, January). The 50 best companies to work for. *Report on Business Magazine, 18(7)*, 41–52.

 THE MANAGER'S

Notebook

Saving Dofasco

Dofasco is a good example of an organization that experienced years of downsizing and declining employee morale. As a result, they had to improve relations with employees and make changes that would enable the company to survive in an industry that was changing and becoming more global. Here's what they did to improve employee–organization relationships and get employees involved in the new Dofasco.

1. Dofasco needed to get employees involved in creating a new vision and future for the company. To do so, they adopted a team approach in the workplace, tearing down barriers between departments, and drastically reducing layers of management. Even more significantly, Dofasco adjusted its fundamental premise as an employer: rather than a paternalistic, entitlement-oriented environment, it would encourage what Mayberry and Pether call an "earnings mentality," adding a system of variable compensation pay to the existing profit-sharing program. A rank-and-file employee's wage can be topped up by as much as 20 percent if the company outperforms its targets. Persuading the employees to buy in required both re-establishing the faith that had been shattered by the layoffs and educating them about Dofasco's place in the evolving global steel industry. To that end, the company invited every employee, in a series of small groups, to a retreat at Ontario's Talisman Mountain Resort, where they were encouraged to air their fears and grievances, offer suggestions, and learn more about the business. They were also asked to take part in a "pole and rope" course designed to inspire teamwork and trust. More than 90 percent of employees voluntarily participated.

2. Most of the people working at Dofasco today are survivors of all that upheaval, which finally came to a head in the early 1990s. Many of them are over 45 and began their working lives in a much larger, much different company, doing very different jobs. They talk admiringly about the team approach that Dofasco has adopted—no time clocks, shared responsibilities, flexibility, and self-sufficiency. For workers, the changes the company endured were painful; there are regrets about lost colleagues and about some lost aspects of the old Dofasco culture. But there is also a keen understanding about the larger steel industry, the company's place in it, and a tangible pride in the fact that while others have fallen hard, Dofasco has survived and prospered. And today, Dofasco is Canada's most successful steel producer and a global industry leader that is surviving and thriving in an industry that has been revolutionized by mini-mill technology and buffeted by low-cost offshore competition. The rate of attrition remains low as very few employees leave of their own volition. In 2004, Dofasco was named one of the 50 best employers in Canada, and in 2006 it was named one of the *Financial Post*'s 10 best companies to work for in Canada. Dofasco has succeeded because of what changed and also because of what remained exactly the same—like Dofasco's annual Christmas party where the company's executives greet employees and their families, shake hands, and smile. The symbolism of the gesture is obvious: the men and women in suits and the men and women lining up are all in it together.

LEARNING OBJECTIVES CHECKLIST

1. *Organizations* are social inventions for accomplishing common goals through group effort. The basic characteristic of organizations is that they involve the coordinated efforts of people working together to accomplish common goals.

2. *Organizational behaviour* refers to the attitudes and behaviours of individuals and groups in an organizational context. The field of organizational behaviour systematically studies these attitudes and behaviours and provides advice about how organizations can manage them effectively. The goals of the field include the prediction, explanation, and management of organizational behaviour.

3. *Management* is the art of getting things accomplished in organizations through others. It consists of acquiring, allocating, and utilizing physical and human resources to accomplish goals.

4. The *classical view* of management advocated a high degree of employee specialization and a high degree of coordination of labour from the top of the organization. Taylor's Scientific Management and Weber's views on bureaucracy are in line with the classical position. The *human relations movement* pointed out

the "people problems" that the classical management style sometimes provoked and advocated more interesting job design, more employee participation in decisions, and less centralized control.

5. The *contemporary contingency approach* to management suggests that the most effective management styles and organizational designs are dependent on the demands of the situation.

6. Research on what managers do shows that they fulfill interpersonal, informational, and decisional roles. Important activities include routine communication, traditional management, networking, and human resource management. Managers pursue agendas through networking and use intuition to guide decision making. The demands on managers vary across cultures. A good grasp of organizational behaviour is essential for effective management.

7. A number of societal and global trends are shaping contemporary management concerns, including local and global diversity; changes in employee–organization relationships; the need to improve quality, speed, and flexibility; and the need to recruit and retain employees.

DISCUSSION QUESTIONS

1. What are your goals in studying organizational behaviour? What practical advantages might this study have for you?

2. Consider absence from work as an example of organizational behaviour. What are some of the factors that might *predict* who is likely to be absent from work? How might you *explain* absence from work? What are some techniques that organizations use to *manage* absence?

3. Describe the assumptions about organizational behaviour that are reflected in television shows, such as situation comedies and police dramas. How accurate are these portrayals? Do they influence our thinking about what occurs in organizations?

4. To demonstrate that you grasp the idea of contingencies in organizational behaviour, consider how closely managers should supervise the work of their employees. What are some factors on which closeness of supervision might be contingent?

5. Management is the art of getting things accomplished in organizations through others. Given this definition, what are some factors that make management a difficult, or at least a challenging, occupation?

6. Use the contingency approach to describe a task or an organizational department where a more classical management style might be effective. Then do the same for a task or department where the human relations style would be effective.

7. Give an example of a managerial *figurehead* role, *negotiator* role, and *disseminator* role.

8. Why do studies of managerial behaviour reveal the importance of networking? What about human resource management? Explain the differences between these two behaviours and their importance for success.

9. What are some of the demands that increased workforce diversity and increased global operations make on managers? What are some of the opportunities that these trends offer to managers?

10. Describe how management practices and organizational behaviour can help organiza-tions deal with the contemporary manage-ment concerns discussed in the chapter. In other words, what are some of the things that organizations can do to (a) manage local and global diversity, (b) improve the nature of employee–organization relationships, (c) improve quality, speed, and flexibility, and (d) improve the recruitment and retention of employees?

11. What is evidence-based management and how can it help promote the goals of organi-zational behaviour? Give an example of how evidence-based management might be used to predict, explain, and manage organizational behaviour.

ON-THE-JOB CHALLENGE QUESTION

A number of surveys in recent years have indi-cated that Canadian workers are less engaged and loyal today than in the past. A study conducted by Towers Perrin HR Services found that Canadian workers are becoming less "engaged" in their work and more likely to quit because they have seen little payback for sacrifices they made when times were tougher. Only 17 percent of Canadian employees are "highly engaged" and willing to put in extra effort. According to a survey by Watson Wyatt Canada, Canadian employees are so disenchanted that 46 percent said they would consider jumping ship if a com-parable job were available. The survey also found a deepening disengagement among Canadian employees. Another survey by Watson Wyatt indicated that two out of every three Canadians keep their resumes up to date, and less than half are committed to staying with their present employer. However, a survey of Canadians con-ducted by The Izzo Group found that 71 percent of Canadians under 40 would still prefer to stay with one company for their entire career—if their needs were met by the company.

What do the results of these surveys tell us about employees and organizations? What can organizations do to improve employee engage-ment, loyalty, and commitment and lower the probability that employees will quit? How can the goals of organizational behaviour and evi-dence-based management help organizations solve the increasing discontent of employees?

Sources: Galt, V. (2005, January 26). This just in: Half your employees ready to jump ship. *Globe and Mail*, B1, B9; Galt, V. (2005, November 15). Fewer workers willing to put in 110%. *Globe and Mail*, B8; Izzo, J. (2006, March 3). Employee loyalty: Not dead, just different. *Globe and Mail*, C1, C2.

EXPERIENTIAL EXERCISE

Good Job, Bad Job

The purpose of this exercise is to help you get acquainted with some of your classmates by learning something about their experiences with work and orga-nizations. To do this, we will focus on an important and traditional topic in organizational behaviour— what makes people satisfied or dissatisfied with their jobs (a topic that we will cover in detail in Chapter 4).

1. Students should break into learning groups of four to six people. Each group should choose a recording secretary.

2. In each group, members should take turns intro-ducing themselves and then describing to the others either the best job or the worst job that they have ever had. Take particular care to explain why this particular job was either satisfying or dissatisfying. For example, did factors such as pay, co-workers, your boss, or the work itself affect your level of sat-isfaction? The recording secretary should make a list of the jobs group members held, noting which were "good" and which were "bad." (15 minutes)

3. Using the information from Step 2, each group should develop a profile of four or five characteristics that seem to contribute to dissatisfaction in a job and four or five characteristics that contribute to job satisfaction. In other words, are there some common experiences among the group members? (10 minutes)

4. Each group should write its "good job" and "bad job" characteristics on the board. (3 minutes)

5. The class should reconvene, and each group's recording secretary should report on the specific jobs the group considered good or bad. The instructor will discuss the profiles on the board, noting similarities and differences. Other issues worth probing are behavioural consequences of job attitudes (e.g., quitting) and differences of opinion within the groups (e.g., one person's bad job might have seemed attractive to someone else). (15 minutes)

6. Why do you think that a good job for some people might be a bad job for others and vice versa? What are the implications of this for management and organizational behaviour?

EXPERIENTIAL EXERCISE

OB on TV

The purpose of this exercise is to explore the portrayal of organizational behaviour on television. Most experts on the function of TV as a communication medium agree on two points. First, although TV may present an inaccurate or distorted view of many specific events, the overall content of TV programming does accurately reflect the general values and concerns of society. Second, experts generally agree that TV has the power to shape the attitudes and expectations of viewers. If this is so, we should pay some attention to the portrayal of work and organizational behaviour on TV.

Prepare this exercise before its assigned class:

1. Choose a prime-time TV show that interests you. (This means a show that airs between 8 p.m. and 10 p.m. in your viewing area. If your schedule prohibits this, choose another time.) The show in question could be a comedy, a drama, or a documentary, for example, *Law and Order*, *CSI*, or *The Office*. Your instructor may give you some more specific instructions about what to watch.

2. On a piece of paper, list the name of the program and its date and time of broadcast. Write the answers to the following questions during or immediately following the broadcast:

   a. What industry is the primary focus of the program? Use the following list to categorize your answer: agriculture; mining; construction; manufacturing; transportation; communication; wholesale trade; retail trade; finance; service; public administration. (Examples of service industries include hotel, health, law, education, newspaper, entertainment, and private investigation. Examples of public administration include justice, police work, and national security.)

   b. What industries or occupations are of secondary focus in the program?

   c. What exact job categories or occupational roles do the main characters in the program play? Use this list to categorize your answers: managerial; clerical; professional; sales; service; craftsperson; machine operator; labourer; lawbreaker; military personnel; customer/patient/client; housework.

   d. Write several paragraphs describing how organizational life is portrayed in the program. For example, is it fun or boring? Does it involve conflict or cooperation? Are people treated fairly? Do they seem motivated? Is work life stressful?

   e. What aspects of the TV portrayal of organizational behaviour do you think were realistic? Which were unrealistic?

3. Be prepared to discuss your findings in class. Your instructor will have some research information about how organizational life has actually been portrayed on TV over the years.

Source: Inspired by the research of Leah Vande Berg and Nick Trujillo, as reported in: Vande Berg, L., & Trujillo, N. (1989). *Organizational life on television*. Norwood, NJ: Ablex.

CASE INCIDENT

My Mother's Visit

Last year, George was preparing for his mother's first visit to Canada. George had immigrated to Canada from Haiti six years ago. His dream was for his mother to come to Canada to meet his family and share in his success. He had been working hard and saving money for years to pay for his mother's airfare. Finally, everything was coming together. His mother's flight was booked and a big celebration was planned to mark her arrival. George had arranged to leave work at lunch to pick his mother up at the airport and take her to his house where the guests would be waiting. He spent months planning the celebration and making the arrangements. However, when the big day arrived, his boss handed him an assignment and told him he was not to leave until it was completed. When George described his plans, his boss cut him off and reminded him that the organization depends on employees to do whatever it takes to get the job done: "No excuses George. You are not to leave until the job is done!" George had to arrange for a taxi to pick up his mother and her welcome celebration took place without him. George did not get home until late in the evening. The guests had left and his mother had gone to bed. George wondered why the assignment could not have waited until the next day, or why one of his co-workers couldn't have done it.

1. What does this incident tell you about management and organizational behaviour at George's organization?

2. How can organizational behaviour help to predict and explain the behaviour of George and his boss? What advice would you give to George and his boss in terms of managing organizational behaviour in the future?

3. What does this incident tell us about management and organizational behaviour in general?

CASE STUDY

My First Day on the Kill Floor

In the mid-1990s, McCain bought a majority stake in Maple Leaf Foods. As company president, Michael McCain had been pressured to stage a turnaround of Maple Leaf's moribund meat division. So McCain got down to work with his management team. They drafted a strategy to build a pork powerhouse, and gobbled up competitors like Burns Foods Ltd., which had previously purchased Gainers.

The centrepiece of the company's plan was a world-class processing plant in Brandon, Manitoba. The location would allow the company proximity to cheap grain to feed its pigs, space in which to raise them, and a ready transportation route to the burgeoning Japanese pork market. In terms of sheer size, the Brandon plant's capacity would be staggering: 90 000 hogs a week. It was to be a technological marvel in a landscape of aging, lethargic plants across the country. But Maple Leaf also envisioned cost cuts that would herald a new era of tension between the company and its workers.

At the same time the company was drawing up a blueprint for its state-of-the-art plant in Brandon, some 2300 workers were on strike or locked out at Maple Leaf facilities across the country. It was the beginning of an aggressive drive to reduce costs through massive wage rollbacks—similar to the decade-long battles that had already played out in the United States. Not only had the US industry undergone a staggering period of restructuring and consolidation, it had also tightened its grip on workers. In a campaign to slash costs, many American companies fought the unions very aggressively and drove down wages.

By the time the Maple Leaf facility opened its doors in Brandon in August, 1999, the company had negotiated a new deal with the United Food and Commercial Workers Union, slicing wages by 40 percent at the new plant, similar to what it had already done in other locations. Brandon's $150 million plant opened amid great pomp and pageantry, with both provincial and city officials extolling its benefits to the community. Everyone, it seemed, was happy; everyone but the workers.

With that, I arrived on the doorstep, application in hand. Two weeks later, I'm hired. For $9.45 an hour, I will work the factory floor alongside some 1300 jaw-breakers, pig chasers, and kidney poppers, in one of the most dangerous and gruesome jobs in the country. For eight hours a day I'll be in "by-products," slicing the cheeks out of hogs heads. How bad could it possibly be?

Monday: my first day on the job. It's just past 6:30 a.m., and the parking lot is already teeming, filled with dozens of young men in muscle shirts and women pinched into low riding jeans. They walk two by two, the sound of gravel skidding beneath their feet. In the distance, a truck is busy unloading today's hog kill. The constant drone of the engine muffles the sound of their collective squeal.

In the bowels of a building with walls that sweat gristle and blood, we're standing in a semi-circle on the kill floor, 25 fresh recruits, our mouths agape. Mike, a short, squat factory-floor veteran stuffed into a bloody lab coat, is leading our tour. Hundreds of hogs swing by on a conveyer line; flayed and shackled up by their hind legs, their heads dangling by a flap of skin, they smack together like bowling pins.

We stare at the blank faces of the men who thrust in and out of the hogs' bellies with knives, yanking out glistening tubes of red and grey entrails, bowels, hearts, and livers that will eventually be chopped, packaged, and shipped off to dinner tables. "We'd harvest the farts if we could," Mike offers with a certain morbid glee. "Yup, we use just about everything. Only three percent of the pig goes to waste around here."

My tongue suddenly feels like it's caked with the stench of sweat and scared animals. My head begins to swing like a seesaw. "Don't you dare puke," Mike snorts, grabbing at my helmet to take note of my name, displayed there in bold lettering. "Suck it up, Princess." I'm praying for a miracle—that I won't toss my cookies. Or worse, be tossed out tush over teakettle my first day on the job. "It's the smell," I responded weakly. And then with all the moxie I can muster: "I'll get used to it."

With that, Mike cocks his head and inhales deeply before he begins a spiel he's surely mouthed dozens of times before. "You know what that smell is?" he growls rhetorically. "That," he says, leaning in for emphasis, "is the smell of money."

Upstairs, high above the kill floor, the 25 of us are gathered in a room with posters trumpeting Maple Leaf Food products: loins, hams, ribs, and pork bellies. The floor beneath our feet is rumbling, set into motion by the thrum of the butchery below. Robert Panontin, a 30-something Maple Leaf labour relations specialist who's dressed in a company shirt and canvas pants, arrives and pounds the table with a raft of documents. He's setting the mood by scaring the heck out of us. The statistics aren't pretty. He knows most of us will leave long before we reach probation, like some 4000 other workers since the plant opened, many because their hands had become too crippled from working all day with a knife or because the work was too dark and surreal.

The problem extends far beyond the Brandon city limits. In fact, there is a revolving door of workers across the continent. Turnover rates of between 40 percent and 100 percent annually are common among US industry giants such as Tyson Foods Inc., one of the companies that masterminded the low-wage scale. Faced with a limited labour pool in North America for demanding, low-paying jobs, Maple Leaf has followed the lead of the US industry and has hired foreign workers from Mexico and Central America.

Panontin then goes on to exalt the perks that will bulk up our pay packet and keep us punching the company clock. For a perfect attendance record over four weeks an extra dollar an hour gets tacked onto our cheque and we're given a shot at a company draw for $1500. We can also rack up "pork bucks," allowing us to buy our roasts and ribs direct from the factory floor at just a fraction above cost.

Panontin then hunches forward in a listen-up posture. "I just want you to know we're watching you like a hawk," he warns, surveying the room to gauge whether his tone has invoked the intended effect. "You have signed an employee/employer contract with us. We've agreed to pay you a wage and you agree to come to work. We are looking for commitment."

With that, Panontin gathers his training materials and readies to leave. But he stops short of the door and swivels: "I just want you to know I have a really good friend in security at the mall. If I'm doing an investigation on you, I'll go down there to watch his security videos. God help you if I catch you goofing off at the mall on video."

It's a revolving door of corporate types and pep talks and motivational videos until we're handed over to Randie Mulligan, our health and safety supervisor. With charts and handouts, she offers tips on good grooming and work-floor hygiene: how to keep the "product" free of our microbes. "Your quality of life shouldn't change while you're working at Maple Leaf," she assures us in one breath, warning us in the next that two-thirds of us, it's assumed, will get hurt from everything from minor cuts to full-scale injuries in the next three months on the job.

Meanwhile, the nurses' station is busy taking care of today's injuries. We pass by on our way for lunch at Hamlets, the company's main cafeteria. A half-dozen workers are slumped in chairs, waiting for treatment. Inside the cafeteria, the din of the coffee cups is muted by the singsong of the chain-link belly belts that chime as the workers file in line for today's grub. The daily special? Pork chops, mashed potatoes, and gravy.

Soon we are herded back to the training room, where we'll be fitted in the costume of the factory floor. Rubber boots with steel toes; whites still stained with the memory of yesterday's slaughter; a belly belt to protect the organs; earplugs, a hair net, and helmet; and a mesh glove that extends to the elbow. I'm now dressed to kill, or at least butcher. I feel like a snow-white Darth Vader.

Jesus Zavala, who has worked his way up to trainer in less than two years on the job, is to be our mentor. He leads us deep into the basement of the building. A crypt, really, where there is no clock, no window, no vestige of the outside world. It's now 1:30, and with their bellies full from lunch, workers are busy single-mindedly hacking pork from shoulder bones. Men on the dressing floor are pulling livers and hearts, which they place on a pulley of spikes behind them. If the line fails to keep pace, the kill men have to slow down, backing up the process. The quota must be met or it will mean overtime—part of our collective agreement with the company. One hour, two hours . . . whatever it takes to get the job done.

Our first day on the line, and we learn we're in for an hour's overtime. There's a problem at the gam table, first stop for the freshly killed hogs as they topple from a tumbler to have their tendons slit and be skewered up by their hind legs. Several workers are off sick. Sherri, our floor supervisor, arrives to gather four strong volunteers for the gam table. For the rest of us, it's show time.

Zavala clamps on his hearing gear, slips on a pair of goggles and motions us through. We enter a room reverberating in a chorus of hum and hiss, clang and thud. I step over strings of slippery yellow gristle and pools of blood, past plumes of steam that rise from the floor to my workstation.

On the right, workers are hunched over a conveyer line of disembodied heads. Some are sawing off ears with pneumatic knives. Others are skewering heads onto spikes. The thrum of the line triggers the beasts' mouths in motion, as though they're in conversation. They round the corner, tumbling onto another conveyer belt. Piled three by three, they're headed straight at me.

With all of the skill and artistry of a sculptor, Zavala reaches forward, picking a head up by the esophagus, and begins chiselling. First he slices the cheeks from the outside of the head, then the inside. He plops the flesh onto a smaller conveyer belt below, and thrusts the hog's head down a chute, on its way to rendering. "Now, you try," he says, handing me a razor-sharp knife and smiling with encouragement.

I grasp at a snout, and haul 20 pounds of head toward me. It's heavier than I imagined and I stumble. The head rolls from my carving station, falling face up on my boot. Mouth ajar, eyes still open, cheeks twitching, it stares up at me as if stuck in some sort of somnolent scream.

I do better next time. Soon, dozens of hogs' heads later, I can feel the blood trickling down my cheek and seeping into my bra. But what makes me really woozy is the sensation of warm, sticky flesh on the other side of my plastic glove each time I lay hold of an esophagus.

By quitting time, my carving hand is starting to give out. My back aches. But it's my cheeks that hurt the most from sucking in my lips all day, hoping to keep the blood and guts from getting into my mouth.

We gather around the sink to clean the little pieces of fat and meat from our tools. By 6:30, I'm standing in a hot shower, trying to wash it all away. By 7:30, I'm able to eat for the first time that day. By 8:30, I'm in bed, dreading the thought of tomorrow.

Source: Excerpted from Bourette, S. (2003, December). Butchered. *Report on Business* 46–56. Susan Bourette won a National Magazine Award in investigative reporting for this story. She is a Toronto author and writer.

1. Refer to the case and describe how it sheds light on the meaning of organizations and organizational behaviour.

2. Use examples from the case to explain the goals of organizational behaviour. In other words, what are some important events that the company can predict, explain, and manage? What are they doing to manage employee behaviour and do you think they will be effective? Explain your answer.

3. Relate the management practices described in the case to the different prescriptions of management described in the chapter. Is the approach to management characteristic of the classical view and bureaucracy or the human relations movement? Give specific examples to support your answer. What are the implications of the company's approach to management for employees and the organization?

4. Compare and contrast the management practices described in the case to those of the best companies to work for in Canada (see Exhibit 1.4). Is there anything the company can do to change its style of management or is it constrained by the nature of the work?

5. Consider the case in terms of the contemporary management concerns described in the chapter. In other words, to what extent is diversity, employee–organization relationships, a focus on quality, speed, and flexibility, and employee recruitment and retention a concern? What is the organization doing about these issues? What should they be doing?

6. What does this case tell us about management and organizational behaviour?

INTEGRATIVE CASE

Ace Technology

The meeting ran an hour overtime, and Bill was glad it did. The senior managers finally reached a consensus on the strategy for Ace Technology. The consensus was a critical milestone for the company and set the stage for a number of important change strategies. The task ahead was to make these plans a reality.

A critical topic in the planning session was the antiquated compensation programs. The senior managers agreed that the compensation programs were too complicated and they conflicted with the key themes of the company's new strategy. The base pay program emphasized the hierarchy of the organization and was not customer focused. The incentive plans were tied to individual accountability rather than group effort. The recognition programs were too limited in both who was selected and who used them.

Change needed to happen quickly if Ace Technology was going to regain its market leadership. Bill knew that changing the compensation plans was going to be very challenging, but it was too important to be delayed.

As he entered his office, Bill thought, "What do I do now?"

Bill called his management team together to discuss linking human resources programs to the organization's new business strategy. He reviewed the changing conditions in the business environment and the rise of new competitive forces. Although there were many opinions, few team members disagreed about the need to change.

Bill reviewed the mission, vision, and values of the company. Although his staff members had heard this before, Bill outlined the company's strategy against the critical success factors. Bill's team began to see the pay program in context of the new strategy. The team members were able to examine what programs support or defend the new goals. Their discussion consumed most of the three-hour meeting.

Other Ace Technology executives met and conducted intense discussions with their own staff as well. Afterward, Bill and the other executives met to discuss what they had found. Bill summarized the comments he heard from each executive and offered a set of "action themes" that would be important for focusing their initiatives. The executives were making real progress on developing concrete action plans and employees were becoming genuinely excited about the new direction. But, the executives knew the excitement would not be sustained unless the plans could be reinforced.

At the next meeting of Ace Technology's senior management team, the firm's new strategic plan was finalized. The executives identified several common themes in the firm's strategy and established eight critical success factors, as follows:

- Be more responsive and valuable to our customers than our competitors.

- Manage costs so that pricing can be lower than our primary competitors but also so that the firm remains financially strong.

- Continue to seek ways to improve processes of the organization and transfer knowledge across all areas.

- Create a work environment where people feel valued for their contributions.

- Continue to advance the technology and capabilities of our products through research and development.

- Give the customer the products and services they need, when they need them.

- Provide such high-quality products and services that our customers have confidence in our organization.

- Continue to seek ways to be more attractive in the marketplace.

These critical success factors summarized many management initiatives that were in place for years. In light of the eight factors, the executives saw that Ace's success rested on shareholders, customers, and employees. Although these were not new concepts, the list strengthened the understanding of what the company needed to do.

Bill then led the executive team in a discussion about action needed. Once the group found key behaviours, Bill used the desired behaviours as the foundation for developing a reward strategy and determining what programs needed to be developed or changed. He also saw how these desired behaviours could serve to refocus other human resources and management initiatives.

The key behaviours the executive team finally developed are as follows:

- Focus on the customers and treat them as we want to be treated.

- Take the initiative to do what needs to be done, for our customers and for ourselves.

- Utilize resources in a responsible manner, and find ways to improve efficiency.

- Continue to increase knowledge and job capabilities.

- Be innovative and resourceful in how to approach work. Experiment with new methods, learn from these experiences, and share the knowledge with others.

- Work as a team with a high degree of mutual respect and collaboration.

- Fulfill the commitment to achieve desired results for the customer and the company.

The executive team realized these actions would need to be modified to fit its specific units. Andrea would need to integrate them differently in Operations than Frank would in Finance. Regardless of the interpretation, the actions provided the missing link between strategy and behaviour.

As Bill and the executives worked on the reward strategy, it became clear that the program did not need to be complicated—the value would be in its simplicity. The group also tried to use many of the programs already in place, making minor modifications. It wanted a flexible reward strategy that could change over time.

The Ace Technology Overall Reward Strategy

Because people are critical to Ace Technology's competitiveness, it is essential that we create a link between the strategy of the company and employee action, between company competitiveness and employee contributions, between the well being of the company and personal well being. As the company prospers, so will our employees. As we face challenging times in the marketplace, we will meet competitive demands effectively. Our reward systems will provide an integrated set of programs in which all members will participate. With such a program, we are demonstrating that Ace Technology is its people, and the people are the company.

Base Compensation

The base pay program will support Ace's ability to acquire and develop superior talent by emphasizing critical competencies. There will be core competencies that reflect the shared values of the company and competencies that focus on the unique requirements of each major functional area. These competencies will be the measuring stick for managing performance, directing careers, investing in training and development, and providing competitive compensation. The base pay levels will be parallel to the median of the market where we compete for talent and business. We will make special provisions for specific functions that are in high demand. Compensation growth will be based on demonstrated competencies that improve the firm's performance and competitiveness.

Variable Compensation

Variable pay programs will focus on specific performance requirements for the organization. The purpose of the variable pay program will be to create a clear and significant stake for each individual in the performance of his or her business unit and the company. Cash compensation will emphasize short-term performance requirements and the measures will link directly to the strategic goals of the company. The variable plans will primarily emphasize team performance. Individual incentives will be used if they are clearly aligned with Ace's strategy. In addition, the company will make use of stock options and restricted stock to provide selected people with a meaningful stake in the future of the company. In combination, these variable pay programs will encourage and reinforce desired performance.

Recognition Management

Recognizing and rewarding employee contributions are essential to this organization. The firm will provide and promote a series of formal recognition programs that will reward the contributions of employees. Managers can supplement these specific programs with practices that are of particular relevance to their business units. Business units will focus their recognition process on the contributions of individuals and teams. Recognition will not emphasize high-expense items, except in extraordinary cases. Instead, through a combination of special events, poster boards, newsletters, public meetings, and private discussions, individuals will be appreciated for their contributions. Senior management's role will be to recognize and reward those who do a particularly good job at recognizing others. Ace Technology will continue to make recognition something special.

Management Reaction

Several weeks after the reward strategy was developed, human resources managers presented an evaluation of the reward systems to Ace's executives. Managers' opinions differed on whether reward systems would impact behaviour. Many believed that change would cause disruption and were concerned about the impact. As the discussion unfolded, it became apparent to the group that to do nothing or make only incremental efforts would have a more negative impact than making a mistake. The firm's new strategy depended on a difference in how employees are rewarded. The executives decided implementation needed to move in stages and be supported by improvements in information availability. The new reward systems will need to support the firm's new strategy directly—by following the changes in some areas or by serving as a catalyst for change in other areas.

In short, Ace Technology determined the following action plan:

- The company-wide performance-sharing program (i.e., profit sharing) will be eliminated and the dollars will be channelled to support unit-based incentive plans. The reallocation will create a strong line of sight between actions and results with a focus on growth, productivity, cost reductions, delivery performance, and other key success factors.

- Unit-based incentive plans will be developed for all critical functional areas. The incentives will emphasize teams. The measures will use a balanced scorecard approach, emphasizing issues relevant to the unit. The new plan will enhance teamwork, drive a customer focus deep into the organization, and clearly define the commitment to performance.

- The current recognition program will be revamped, providing more opportunities for recognition. A set of tiers will be developed, providing a variety of involvement and reward opportunities. Further, the executive team will review these programs regularly and become active at cross-function events. The emphasis of the recognition program will be innovation, initiative, and outstanding customer service. The program will be transformed from a "nice thing to do" to one that is clearly aligned with desired behaviours.

- The base pay program will shift from being based solely on the market to a combination of competencies and market. The program will emphasize developing a series of career levels tied to the requirements of each major operating unit. Pay opportunities will be tied to career pay bands and increases will be a function of competencies. This will clearly emphasize increasing knowledge, taking responsibility and initiative for personal development, and fulfilling commitments. The base pay program will directly reflect what is important to the company and the employees.

The presentation and discussion demonstrated the group's commitment to link the company's rewards to the critical success factors. Further, the proposed reward programs would form a system of rewards where each element was integrated with the others. The attention was not only on the results, but on the process as well.

Source: From Wilson, T.B. (1998, Summer). Reward strategy—Time to rethink the methods and the messages. *ACA Journal*, pp. 63–69. Reprinted with permission.

QUESTIONS

1. What are some organizational behaviour topics and issues that relate to the circumstances at Ace Technology?

2. Discuss the relevance of each of the goals of organizational behaviour for Ace Technology. What

does the company want to predict, explain, and manage?

3. Consider Bill's role as a manager in terms of Mintzberg's managerial roles. What roles does he exhibit and how effective is he in performing these roles?

4. What are some of the implications of the events in the case for individuals, groups, and the organization?

5. Discuss the effect that the action plans might have on the relationship between Ace Technology and its employees and the ability of the company to recruit and retain employees.

PART ② Individual Behaviour

CHAPTER 2

Personality and Learning

TELUS

TELUS is the largest telecommunications company in Western Canada and the second largest in Canada with 25 000 employees. The company provides a wide range of telecommunications products and services, including data, voice, and TELUS mobility wireless services across Canada, utilizing next generation Internet protocol–based network technologies. TELUS is also known as an organization with a strong commitment to learning and employee development.

At TELUS, investing in employee capabilities is one of six strategic imperatives, and optimizing the learning environment is one of five strategic thrusts in human resources. In 2004, the company completed 139 000 e-learning courses and 30 000 classroom courses. Furthermore, about 2 percent of payroll budgets goes to training. According to Josh Blair, TELUS vice-president of learning and development, "TELUS strives to make it easy for team members to learn the skills they need to meet their career goals and to keep up with the latest technologies and industry developments."

If you were an employee at TELUS, you would have a customized career development plan and participate in a four-step process called Growing for High Performance, which helps team members grow their careers and develop to their highest potential. At TELUS, employees at all levels are expected to create a plan that sets out personal objectives for both performance and learning. The program is designed to align individual performance objectives with corporate strategy.

The first step involves learning about the corporate strategy, business expectations, and what the company expects of you personally. Employees have a range of opportunities for learning that include monthly or quarterly performance meetings with a team leader, a weekly

LEARNING OBJECTIVES

After reading Chapter 2, you should be able to:

1   Define *personality* and discuss its general role in influencing organizational behaviour.

2   Describe the dispositional, situational, and interactionist approaches to organizational behaviour.

3   Discuss the Five-Factor Model of personality.

4   Discuss the consequences of *locus of control, self-monitoring,* and *self-esteem.*

5   Discuss *positive* and *negative affectivity, proactive personality, general self-efficacy,* and *core self-evaluations.*

6   Define *learning* and describe what is learned in organizations.

7   Explain *operant learning* theory and differentiate between *positive* and *negative reinforcements.*

8   Explain when to use immediate versus delayed reinforcement and when to use continuous versus partial reinforcement.

9   Distinguish between *extinction* and *punishment* and explain how to use punishment effectively.

10 Explain social cognitive theory and discuss *modelling, self-efficacy,* and *self-regulation.*

11 Describe the various organizational learning practices.

TELUS has received international awards for its commitment to employee learning and development and for using learning to drive corporate performance.

online video, an online magazine, weekly e-letters from the CEO, company-wide e-mails and voicemail messages, and a portal providing information on business units, human resources, news developments, and share prices. Employees also learn about the TELUS values, which indicate how the company expects groups and individuals to approach their work and the corporate competencies that drive excellence.

TELUS
www.telus.ca

In the second step, employees assess themselves against the set expectations so that growth and developmental opportunities can be determined. This can be done using a TELUS self-assessment tool, a 360-degree survey tool, or through discussions with one's manager.

In the third step, employees create a customized career development plan and set personal performance objectives. This involves a contract between employees and their manager as to what learning they will do in the next year and what learning will be made available.

The fourth step is to pursue learning options such as e-courses, instructor-led courses, job shadowing, mentoring, and individual coaching. For example, if you are a new hire in the credit department, you would receive new-hire training in a blended delivery format. The six-day program enables you to participate in a group overview, a debrief, and discussion sessions, interspersed with interactive e-learning modules that provide the core theory content. Job aids, system exercises, and moderated on-the-job experience would make you a contributing member of the team as early as your third day. To graduate from the program, your score on the final exam must be at least 85.

TELUS also offers a wide range of innovative programs to help team members enhance key skills such as leadership, ethics, business acumen, customer service, strategic sales, project management, financial management, technology support, and on-the-job safety. The company has received numerous awards for its programs. For example, TELUS won a Program of the Year award in 2005 for two of its leadership and development programs. One is a blended learning program for training front-line staff in TELUS's credit department, and the other is a comprehensive leadership development program for all levels of the organization. Other innovative programs include TELUS's ethics training or e-Ethics. This is the company's most ambitious training program and is completed by all employees. The course incorporates guidelines and theory with review questions and case study scenarios as it strives to take the ethical standards from the conceptual to the specific and sets the corporate standard for ethical behaviour.

All these initiatives and many others are driven by TELUS's corporate commitment to learning, development, and performance. "The training and development function is now more than ever linked to improving the performance of individuals and the organization as a whole," explains Viki MacMillan, director of HR strategic partnerships and training excellence. "All of our programs are tied to TELUS's values competencies and future direction," she says.

In 2005, TELUS was the only Canadian company to receive an international award in recognition of its commitment to employee learning. Josh Blair was named the Learning Leader of the Year, and TELUS was recognized for its excellence in enterprise learning. According to Judy Shuttleworth, executive vice-president of human resources, "Under Josh's leadership, we have put strategies, programs, technologies and tools in place that enabled TELUS to become a true learning organization." In 2003 and 2004, TELUS was the only Canadian company to receive one of the American Society of Training and Development's BEST awards. In 2004, TELUS was ranked sixth overall out of 24 recipients from five countries for using learning to drive corporate performance. TELUS is a good example of how learning can be incorporated into the culture of an organization and how learning is a key component of corporate strategy.[1]

Learning is a critical requirement for effective organizational behaviour, and as you probably know, for organizations to remain competitive in today's rapidly changing environment, employee learning must be continuous and life-long. As you can tell from the opening vignette, this is something that TELUS has clearly mastered and, in fact, has turned the company into a recognized world leader. But how has TELUS created a "learning organization" in which learning has become a regular part of every employee's job? In this chapter we will focus on the learning process and see how learning in organizations takes place. While learning is necessary for the acquisition of knowledge, skills, and behaviours, studies in organizational behaviour have shown that behaviour is also a function of people's personalities. Therefore, we begin this chapter by considering personality and organizational behaviour.

WHAT IS PERSONALITY?

The notion of personality permeates thought and discussion in our culture. We are bombarded with information about "personalities" in the print and broadcast media. We are sometimes promised exciting introductions to people with "nice" personalities. We occasionally meet people who seem to have "no personality." But exactly what *is* personality?

Personality is the relatively stable set of psychological characteristics that influences the way an individual interacts with his or her environment and how he or she feels, thinks, and behaves. An individual's personality summarizes his or her personal style of dealing with the world. You have certainly noticed differences in personal style on the part of your parents, friends, professors, bosses, and employees. It is reflected in the distinctive way that they react to people, situations, and problems.

Where does personality come from? Personality consists of a number of dimensions and traits that are determined in a complex way by genetic predisposition and by one's long-term learning history. Although personality is relatively stable, it is certainly susceptible to change through adult learning experiences. And while we often use labels such as "high self-esteem" to describe people, we should always remember that people have a *variety* of personality characteristics. Excessive typing of people does not help us to appreciate their unique potential to contribute to an organization.

Personality. The relatively stable set of psychological characteristics that influences the way an individual interacts with his or her environment.

PERSONALITY AND ORGANIZATIONAL BEHAVIOUR

Personality has a rather long and rocky history in organizational behaviour. Initially, it was believed that personality was an important factor in many areas of organizational behaviour, including motivation, attitudes, performance, and leadership. In fact, after World War II, the use of personality tests for the selection of military personnel became widespread, and in the 1950s and 1960s it became popular in business organizations. This approach to organizational behaviour is known as the "dispositional approach" because it focuses on individual dispositions and personality. According to the dispositional approach, individuals possess stable traits or characteristics that influence their attitudes and behaviours. In other words, individuals are predisposed to behave in certain ways. However, decades of research produced mixed and inconsistent findings that failed to support the usefulness of personality as a predictor of organizational behaviour and job performance. As a result, there was a dramatic decrease in personality research and a decline in the use of personality tests for selection. Researchers began to shift their attention to factors in the work environment that might predict and explain organizational behaviour. This approach became known as the "situational approach." According to the situational approach, characteristics of the organizational setting, such as rewards and punishment, influence people's feelings, attitudes, and behaviour. For example, many studies have shown that job satisfaction and other work-related attitudes are largely determined by situational factors such as the characteristics of work tasks.[2]

Over the years, proponents of both approaches have argued about the importance of dispositions versus the situation in what is known as the "person–situation debate." While researchers argued over which approach was the right one, it is now believed that both approaches are important for predicting and understanding organizational behaviour. This led to a third approach to organizational behaviour, known as the "interactionist approach," or "interactionism." According to the interactionist approach, organizational behaviour is a function of both dispositions and the situation. In other words, to predict and understand organizational behaviour, one must know something about an individual's personality and the setting in which he or she works. This approach is now the most widely accepted perspective within organizational behaviour.[3]

To give you an example of the interactionist perspective, consider the role of personality in different situations. To keep it simple, we will describe situations as being either "weak" or "strong." In weak situations it is not always clear how a person should behave, while in strong situations there are clear expectations for appropriate behaviour. As a result, personality has the most impact in weak situations. This is because in these situations (e.g., a newly formed volunteer community organization) there are loosely defined roles, few rules, and weak reward and punishment contingencies. However, in strong situations, which have more defined roles, rules, and contingencies (e.g., routine military operations), personality tends to have less impact.[4] Thus, as you can see, the extent to which personality influences people's attitudes and behaviour depends on the situation. Later in the text you will learn that the extent to which stressors are perceived as stressful as well as the way that people react to stress is also influenced by one's personality. This is another example of the interactionist approach to organizational behaviour.

One of the most important implications of the interactionist perspective is that some personality characteristics are useful in certain organizational situations. Thus, there is no one best personality, and managers need to appreciate the advantages of employee diversity. A key concept here is *fit*: putting the right person in the right job, group, or organization and exposing different employees to different management styles.

In recent years, there has been a resurgence of interest in personality research in organizational behaviour. One of the main problems with the early research on personality was the use of inadequate measures of personality characteristics. However, advances in measurement and trends in organizations have prompted renewed interest. For example, increased emphasis on service jobs with customer contact, concern about ethics and integrity, and contemporary interest in teamwork and cooperation all point to the potential contribution of personality.[5]

Another reason for the renewed interest in personality has been the development of a framework of personality characteristics known as the Five-Factor Model, or the "Big Five," which provides a framework for classifying personality characteristics into five general dimensions. This framework makes it much easier to understand and study the role of personality in organizational behaviour.[6]

In what follows, we first discuss the five general personality dimensions of the Five-Factor Model. Then we cover three well-known personality characteristics with special relevance to organizational behaviour. We then discuss recent developments in personality research. Later in the text, we will explore the impact of personality characteristics on job satisfaction, motivation, leadership, ethics, organizational politics, and stress.

The Five-Factor Model of Personality

People are unique, people are complex, and there are literally hundreds of adjectives that we can use to reflect this unique complexity. Yet, over the years, psychologists have discovered that there are about five basic but general dimensions that describe personality. These "Big Five" dimensions are known as the Five-Factor Model (FFM) of personality and are summarized in Exhibit 2.1 along with some illustrative traits.[7] The dimensions are:

- *Extraversion*—this is the extent to which a person is outgoing versus shy. High extraverts enjoy social situations while those low on this dimension (introverts) avoid them.

- *Emotional stability/Neuroticism*—the degree to which a person has appropriate emotional control. People with high emotional stability (low neuroticism) are self-confident and have high self-esteem. Those with lower emotional stability (high neuroticism) tend toward self-doubt and depression.

● *Agreeableness*—the extent to which a person is friendly and approachable. More agreeable people are warm and considerate. Less agreeable people tend to be cold and aloof.

● *Conscientiousness*—the degree to which a person is responsible and achievement oriented. More conscientious people are dependable and positively motivated. Less conscientious people are unreliable.

● *Openness to experience*—the extent to which a person thinks flexibly and is receptive to new ideas. More open people tend toward creativity and innovation. Less open people favour the status quo.

These dimensions are relatively independent. That is, you could be higher or lower in any combination of dimensions. Also, they tend to hold up well cross-culturally. Thus, people in different cultures use these same dimensions when describing the personalities of friends and acquaintances. There is also evidence that the "Big Five" traits have a genetic basis.[8]

Research has linked these personality dimensions to organizational behaviour. First, there is evidence that each of the "Big Five" dimensions is related to job performance.[9] Generally, traits like those in the top half of Exhibit 2.1 lead to better job performance. One review found that high extraversion was important for managers and salespeople and that high conscientiousness facilitated performance for all occupations. In fact, conscientiousness has been found to be the strongest predictor of all the "Big Five" dimensions of overall job performance.[10] And in support of the interactionist approach, one study showed that high conscientiousness and extraversion contributed more to managerial performance for managers who had more autonomy in the way they handled their jobs.[11]

Second, research has also found that the "Big Five" are related to other work behaviours. For example, one study showed that conscientiousness is related to retention and attendance at work and is also an important antidote for counterproductive behaviours such as theft, absenteeism, and disciplinary problems.[12] Extraversion has also been found to be related to absenteeism, but in a positive direction. In other words, extraverts tend to be absent more often than introverts.[13]

The "Big Five" are also related to work motivation and job satisfaction. In a study that investigated the relationship between the "Big Five" and different indicators of work motivation, the "Big Five" were found to be significantly related to motivation. Among the five dimensions, neuroticism and conscientiousness were the strongest predictors of motivation, with the former being negatively related and the latter being positively related.[14] In another study, the "Big Five" were shown to be significantly related to job satisfaction. The strongest predictor was neuroticism (i.e., emotional stability) followed by conscientiousness, extraversion, and to a lesser extent, agreeableness. Openness to experience was not related to job satisfaction. Higher neuroticism was associated with lower job satisfaction, while higher extraversion, conscientiousness, and agreeableness were associated with higher job satisfaction. Similar results have been found for life satisfaction. In addition, individuals with higher conscientiousness,

EXHIBIT 2.1
The Five-Factor Model of Personality.

Extraversion	Emotional Stability	Agreeableness	Conscientiousness	Openness to Experience
Sociable, Talkative vs. Withdrawn, Shy	Stable, Confident vs. Depressed, Anxious	Tolerant, Cooperative vs. Cold, Rude	Dependable, Responsible vs. Careless, Impulsive	Curious, Original vs. Dull, Unimaginative

extraversion, agreeableness, and emotional stability perform better on a team in terms of their performance of important team-relevant behaviours such as cooperation, concern, and courtesy to team members.[15]

The "Big Five" are also related to job search and career success. For example, extraversion, conscientiousness, openness to experience, and agreeableness were found to relate positively to the intensity of a job seeker's job search, while neuroticism was negatively related. As well, conscientiousness was found to be positively related to the probability of obtaining employment.[16] In addition, high conscientiousness and extraversion and low neuroticism have been found to be associated with a higher income and occupational status. Perhaps most interesting is the fact that these personality traits were related to career success even when the influence of general mental ability has been taken into account. Furthermore, both childhood and adult measures of personality predicted career success during adulthood over a period of 50 years. These results suggest that the effects of personality on career success are relatively enduring.[17]

Finally, the "Big Five" are also related to vocational interests and preferences. In particular, extraversion is related to an enterprising and social vocational orientation, and openness to experience is related to an artistic and investigative vocational orientation.[18] As for specific occupations, entrepreneurs have been found to be higher on conscientiousness and openness to experience and lower on neuroticism and agreeableness in comparison to individuals in managerial positions.[19]

As noted earlier, the "Big Five" personality dimensions are basic and general. However, years of research have also identified a number of more specific personality characteristics that influence organizational behaviour, including locus of control, self-monitoring, and self-esteem.

Locus of Control

Locus of control. A set of beliefs about whether one's behaviour is controlled mainly by internal or external forces.

EXHIBIT 2.2
The internal/external locus of control continuum.

Consider the following comparison. Laurie and Stan are both management trainees in large banks. However, they have rather different expectations regarding their futures. Laurie has just enrolled in an evening Master of Business Administration (MBA) program in a nearby university. Although some of her MBA courses are not immediately applicable to her job, Laurie feels that she must be prepared for greater responsibility as she moves up in the bank hierarchy. Laurie is convinced that she will achieve promotions because she studies hard, works hard, and does her job properly. She feels that an individual makes her own way in the world, and that she can control her own destiny. She is certain that she can someday be the president of the bank if she really wants to be. Her personal motto is: "I can do it."

Stan, on the other hand, sees no use in pursuing additional education beyond his bachelor's degree. According to him, such activities just do not pay off. People who get promoted are just plain lucky or have special connections, and further academic preparation or hard work has nothing to do with it. Stan feels that it is impossible to predict his own future, but knows that the world is pretty unfair.

Laurie and Stan differ on a personality dimension called **locus of control**. This variable refers to individuals' beliefs about the *location* of the factors that control their behaviour. At one end of the continuum are high internals (like Laurie) who believe that the opportunity to control their own behaviour resides within themselves. At the other end of the continuum are high externals (like Stan) who believe that external forces determine their behaviour. Not surprisingly, compared with internals, externals see the world as an unpredictable, chancy place in which luck, fate, or powerful people control their destinies.[20] (See Exhibit 2.2.)

Internals tend to see stronger links between the effort they put into their jobs and the performance level that they achieve. In addition, they perceive to a greater degree than externals that the organization will notice high performance and reward it.[21] Since internals believe that their work behaviour will influence the rewards they achieve, they are more likely to be aware of and to take advantage of information that will enable them to perform effectively.[22]

Research shows that locus of control influences organizational behaviour in a variety of occupational settings. Evidently, because they perceive themselves as being able to control what happens to them, people who are high on internal control are more satisfied with their jobs, earn more money, and achieve higher organizational positions.[23] In addition, they seem to perceive less stress, to cope with stress better, and to engage in more careful career planning.[24]

Self-Monitoring

We are sure that you have known people who tend to "wear their hearts on their sleeves." These are people who act the way they feel and say what they think in spite of their social surroundings. We are also sure that you have known people who are a lot more sensitive to their social surroundings, a lot more likely to fit what they say and do to the nature of those surroundings, regardless of how they think or feel. What we have here is a contrast in **self-monitoring**, which is the extent to which people observe and regulate how they appear and behave in social settings and relationships.[25] The people who "wear their hearts on their sleeves" are low self-monitors. They are not so concerned with scoping out and fitting in with those around them. Their opposites are high self-monitors, who take great care to observe and control the images that they project. In this sense, high self-monitors behave somewhat like actors. In particular, high self-monitors tend to show concern for socially appropriate behaviour, to tune in to social and interpersonal cues, and to regulate their behaviour and self-presentation according to these cues.

How does self-monitoring affect organizational behaviour?[26] For one thing, high self-monitors tend to gravitate toward jobs that require, by their nature, a degree of role-playing and the exercise of their self-presentation skills. Sales, law, public relations, and politics are examples. In such jobs, the ability to adapt to one's clients and contacts is critical; so are communication skills and persuasive abilities, characteristics that high self-monitors frequently exhibit. High self-monitors perform particularly well in occupations that call for flexibility and adaptiveness in dealings with diverse constituencies. As well, a number of studies show that managers are inclined to be higher self-monitors than nonmanagers in the same organization. Self-monitoring is also significantly related to a number of work-related outcomes. High self-monitors tend to be more involved in their jobs, to perform at a higher level, and are more likely to emerge as leaders. However, high self-monitors are also likely to experience more role stress and show less commitment to their organization.[27]

Promotion in the management ranks is often a function of subjective performance appraisals, and the ability to read and conform to the boss's expectations can be critical for advancement. Thus, the ability to regulate and adapt one's behaviour in social situations and to manage the impressions others form of them might be a career advantage for high self-monitors. In fact, in a study that tracked the careers of a sample of Master's of Business Administration graduates, high self-monitors were more likely to change employers and locations and to receive more promotions than low self-monitors.[28]

Are high self-monitors always at an organizational advantage? Not likely. They are unlikely to feel comfortable in ambiguous social settings in which it is hard to determine exactly what behaviours are socially appropriate. Dealing with unfamiliar cultures (national or corporate) might provoke stress. Also, some roles require people to go against the grain or really stand up for what they truly believe in. Thus, high self-monitoring types would seem to be weak innovators and would have difficulty resisting social pressure.

Self-monitoring. The extent to which people observe and regulate how they appear and behave in social settings and relationships.

Self-Esteem

Self-esteem. The degree to which a person has a positive self-evaluation.

How well do you like yourself? This is the essence of the personality characteristic called self-esteem. More formally, **self-esteem** is the degree to which a person has a positive self-evaluation. People with high self-esteem have favourable self-images. People with low self-esteem have unfavourable self-images. They also tend to be uncertain about the correctness of their opinions, attitudes, and behaviours. In general, people tend to be highly motivated to protect themselves from threats to their self-esteem.

Behavioural plasticity theory. People with low self-esteem tend to be more susceptible to external and social influences than those who have high self-esteem.

One of the most interesting differences between people with high and low self-esteem has to do with the *plasticity* of their thoughts, attitudes, and behaviour, or what is known as "behavioural plasticity." According to **behavioural plasticity theory**, people with low self-esteem tend to be more susceptible to external and social influences than those who have high self-esteem—that is, they are more pliable. Thus, events and people in the organizational environment have more impact on the beliefs and actions of employees with low self-esteem. This occurs because, being unsure of their own views and behaviour, they are more likely to look to others for information and confirmation. In addition, people who have low self-esteem seek social approval from others, approval that they might gain from adopting others' views, and they do not react well to ambiguous and stressful situations. This is another example of interactionism in that the effect of the work environment on people's beliefs and actions is partly a function of their self-esteem.[29]

Employees with low self-esteem also tend to react badly to negative feedback—it lowers their subsequent performance.[30] This means that managers should be especially cautious when using negative reinforcement and punishment, as discussed later in this chapter, with employees with low self-esteem. If external causes are thought to be responsible for a performance problem, this should be made very clear. Also, managers should direct criticism at the performance difficulty and not at the person. As we will explain shortly, modelling the correct behaviour should be especially effective with employees with low self-esteem, who are quite willing to imitate credible models and also respond well to mentoring. Finally, organizations should try to avoid assigning those with low self-esteem to jobs (such as life insurance sales) that inherently provide a lot of negative feedback.

Organizations will generally benefit from a workforce with high self-esteem. Such people tend to make more fulfilling career decisions, they exhibit higher job satisfaction and job performance, and they are generally more resilient to the strains of everyday worklife.[31] What can organizations do to bolster self-esteem? Opportunity for participation in decision making, autonomy, and interesting work have been fairly consistently found to be positively related to self-esteem.[32] Also, organizations should avoid creating a culture with excessive and petty work rules that signal to employees that they are incompetent or untrustworthy.[33]

Recent Developments in Personality and Organizational Behaviour

In recent years, there has been a number of exciting developments in personality research in organizational behaviour. In this section, we briefly review five personality variables that have been found to be important for organizational behaviour: positive and negative affectivity, proactive personality, general self-efficacy, and core self-evaluations.

Positive and Negative Affectivity. Have you ever known somebody who is always happy, cheerful, and in a good mood? Or perhaps you know someone who is always unhappy and in a bad mood. Chances are you have noticed these differences in people. Some people are happy most of the time, while others are almost always unhappy. These differences reflect two affective dispositions known as positive affectivity (PA) and negative affectivity (NA). Research has found that they are enduring personality characteristics and that there might be a genetic and biological basis to them.

People who are high on **positive affectivity** experience positive emotions and moods and view the world in a positive light, including themselves and other people. They tend to be cheerful, enthusiastic, lively, sociable, and energetic. People who are high on **negative affectivity** experience negative emotions and moods and view the world in a negative light. They have an overall negative view of themselves and the world around them and they tend to be distressed, depressed, and unhappy.[34]

Unlike the other personality traits discussed in this chapter, positive and negative affectivity are emotional dispositions that predict people's general emotional tendencies. Thus, they can influence people's emotions and mood states at work and influence job attitudes and work behaviour. Research on affective dispositions has found that people who are high on PA report higher job satisfaction while those high on NA report lower job satisfaction. There is also some evidence that PA is positively related to job performance, and NA is negatively related. Employees who have higher PA have also been found to be more creative at work. People who have high NA tend to experience more stressful conditions at work and report higher levels of workplace stress and strain. Finally, there is some evidence that positive affect is a key factor that links happiness to success in life and at work.[35]

Proactive Personality. How effective are you at taking initiative and changing your circumstances? Taking initiative to improve one's current circumstances or creating new ones is known as **proactive behaviour.** It involves challenging the status quo rather than passively adapting to present conditions. Some people are actually better at this than others because they have a stable disposition toward proactive behaviour, known as a "proactive personality." Individuals who have a **proactive personality** are relatively unconstrained by situational forces and act to change and influence their environment. Proactive personality is a stable personal disposition that reflects a tendency to take personal initiative across a range of activities and situations and to effect positive change in one's environment.[36]

Proactive individuals search for and identify opportunities, show initiative, take action, and persevere until they bring about meaningful change. People who do not have a proactive personality are more likely to be passive and to react and adapt to their environment. As a result, they tend to endure and to be shaped by the environment instead of trying to change it.[37] Proactive personality has been found to be related to a number of work outcomes, including job performance, tolerance for stress in demanding jobs, leadership effectiveness, participation in organizational initiatives, work team performance, and entrepreneurship. One study found that proactive personality is associated with higher performance evaluations because individuals with a proactive personality develop strong supportive networks and perform initiative–taking behaviours such as implementing solutions to organization or departmental problems or spearheading new programs. There is also evidence that persons with a proactive personality are more successful in searching for employment and career success. They are more likely to find a job, to receive higher salaries and more frequent promotions, and to have more satisfying careers.[38]

General Self-Efficacy. General self-efficacy (GSE) is a general trait that refers to an individual's belief in his or her ability to perform successfully in a variety of challenging situations.[39] GSE is considered to be a *motivational* trait rather than an *affective* trait because it reflects an individual's belief that he or she can succeed at a variety of tasks rather than how an individual feels about him or herself. An individual's GSE is believed to develop over the life span as repeated successes and failures are experienced across a variety of tasks and situations. Thus, if you have experienced many successes in your life, you probably have high GSE, whereas somebody who has experienced

Positive affectivity. Propensity to view the world, including oneself and other people, in a positive light.

Negative affectivity. Propensity to view the world, including oneself and other people, in a negative light.

Proactive behaviour. Taking initiative to improve current circumstances or creating new ones.

Proactive personality. A stable personal disposition that reflects a tendency to take personal initiative across a range of activities and situations and to effect positive change in one's environment.

General self-efficacy. A general trait that refers to an individual's belief in his or her ability to perform successfully in a variety of challenging situations.

many failures probably has low GSE. Individuals who are high on GSE are better able to adapt to novel, uncertain, and adverse situations. In addition, employees with higher GSE have higher job satisfaction and job performance.[40]

Core Self-Evaluations. Unlike the other personality characteristics described in this chapter, which are specific in themselves, **core self-evaluations** refers to a broad personality concept that consists of more specific traits. The idea behind the theory of core self-evaluations is that individuals hold evaluations about themselves and their self-worth or worthiness, competence, and capability.[41] In a review of the personality literature, Timothy Judge, Edwin Locke, and Cathy Durham identified four traits that make up a person's core self-evaluation. The four traits have already been described in this chapter and include self-esteem, general self-efficacy, locus of control, and neuroticism (emotional stability). Research on core self-evaluations has found that these traits are among the best dispositional predictors of job satisfaction and job performance. People with more positive self-evaluations have higher job satisfaction and job performance. Furthermore, research has shown that core self-evaluations measured in childhood and in early adulthood are related to job satisfaction in middle adulthood. This suggests that core self-evaluations are related to job satisfaction over time. Core self-evaluations have also been found to be positively related to life satisfaction. One of the reasons for the relationship between core self-evaluations and job satisfaction is because individuals with a positive self-regard are more likely to perceive their jobs as interesting, significant, and autonomous than individuals with a negative self-regard. Persons with a positive self-regard experience their job as more intrinsically satisfying, and they are also more likely to have more complex jobs.[42]

To summarize, you now know that a number of general and more specific personality characteristics have important implications for employees' workplace attitudes and behaviour. However, what if you wanted to work in another country? Would your personality be an important factor in your ability to adjust and your job performance? To find out, see "Global Focus: *Personality and Expatriate Effectiveness*."

WHAT IS LEARNING?

So far in this chapter we have described how people's personalities can influence their work attitudes and behaviours. However, recall our earlier discussion that people's experiences and the work environment also have a strong effect on attitudes and behaviour. As you will learn in this section, the environment can change people's behaviour and even shape personalities. To understand how this can happen, let's examine the concept of learning.

Learning occurs when practice or experience leads to a relatively permanent change in behaviour potential. The words *practice* or *experience* rule out viewing behavioural changes caused by factors like drug intake or biological maturation as learning. One does not learn to be relaxed after taking a tranquilizer, and a boy does not suddenly learn to be a bass singer at the age of 14. The practice or experience that prompts learning stems from an environment that gives feedback concerning the consequences of behaviour.

But what do employees learn in organizations? Learning in organizations can be understood in terms of taxonomies that indicate what employees learn, how they learn, and different types of learning experiences. The "what" aspect of learning can be described as learning content, of which there are four primary categories: practical skills, intrapersonal skills, interpersonal skills, and cultural awareness.[43]

Practical skills include job-specific skills, knowledge, and technical competence. For example, if you were a salesperson at TELUS, you would attend a workshop to learn how to sell strategically. Employees frequently learn new skills and technologies to continually improve performance and to keep organizations competitive. Constant

Core self-evaluations. A broad personality concept that consists of more specific traits that reflect the evaluations people hold about themselves and their self-worth.

Learning. A relatively permanent change in behaviour potential that occurs due to practice or experience.

GLOBAL FOCUS

Personality and Expatriate Effectiveness

Managing international assignments is both challenging and complex for organizations. While in the past many expatriates had previous overseas experience, the number of first-time expatriates is increasing. Furthermore, the expatriate workforce is becoming more varied and global as multinational corporations rely more heavily on third-country nationals and less expensive intraregion transfers. Thus, the major international assignment challenge for organizations is expatriate selection.

However, when it comes to selecting candidates for expatriate assignments, many companies base assignee selection decisions on technical expertise and employee (or familial) willingness to go. Unfortunately, the result of this strategy is often failed expatriate adjustment and early return as well as inadequate job performance. With an estimated US$150 000 or more per person for adjustment failure in addition to an estimated US$80 000 for training, relocation, and compensation, organizations can ill afford to continue making expatriate selection decisions based on technical expertise and willingness to go.

But what factors might be important for predicting expatriate adjustment and effectiveness? To find out, Margaret Shaffer, Hal Gregersen, David Harrison, J. Stewart Black, and Lori Ferzandi studied individual differences as potential predictors of several dimensions of expatriate adjustment. The individual differences included broad, stable personality traits (the "Big Five") as well as some specific cross-cultural competencies that represent knowledge and skills that are important for successful international assignments and can be acquired through training (i.e., cultural flexibility, task orientation, people orientation, and ethnocentrism). Expatriate effectiveness included three kinds of adjustment (work adjustment, interaction adjustment, and cultural adjustment), intentions to quit the assignment, and job performance.

To study these relationships, the researchers collected data from a sample of expatriates and their spouses and colleagues from many nations living and working in Hong Kong, as well as Korean and Japanese expatriates on international assignments in numerous countries around the world. Because expatriates face highly uncertain and ambiguous situations, it represents a good example of a "weak situation" in which the norms for behaviour are unclear and individuals do not share a common understanding of what is expected

of them. As a result, personality and individual traits are especially likely to influence the behaviour of expatriates and expatriate effectiveness.

As expected, the study results support the importance of personality and individual differences for expatriate effectiveness. Among the "Big Five" personality dimensions, emotional stability was positively related to an expatriate's work adjustment and negatively related to intentions to quit. Agreeableness was positively related to interaction adjustment; openness to experience was positively related to work adjustment and job performance; and extraversion was positively related to cultural adjustment. However, conscientiousness was not related to any indicator of expatriate effectiveness. Among the cross-cultural competencies, cultural flexibility was a positive predictor of work and cultural adjustment and performance; task orientation was a positive predictor of work adjustment and was negatively related to intentions to quit; people orientation was a positive predictor of work and cultural adjustment and performance; and ethnocentrism was a negative predictor of interaction adjustment and performance, and a positive predictor of intentions to quit.

Overall, the results of this study demonstrate that both broad, stable personality traits (the "Big Five") as well as specific individual differences (cross-cultural competencies) are important predictors of international assignment effectiveness. Each of the "Big Five" personality traits (except for conscientiousness) was a significant predictor of at least one form of expatriate effectiveness. In addition, each of the cross-cultural competencies was related to several indicators of effectiveness, with ethnocentrism being related to all forms of expatriate effectiveness. According to the study authors, the results indicate that the assessment of individual differences can provide value to organizations looking for adaptable, committed, and socially and technically competent individuals for international assignments. Expatriates who are emotionally stable, outgoing and agreeable, and high on openness to experience seem to function better than others. As well, the selection of individuals with specific cross-cultural competencies should also be a priority.

Source: Based on Shaffer, M.A., Gregersen, H., Harrison, D.A., Black, J.S., & Ferzandi, L.A. (2006). You can take it with you: Individual differences and expatriate effectiveness. *Journal of Applied Psychology, 91,* 109–125.

improvement has become a major goal in many organizations today, and training can give an organization a competitive advantage.[44]

Intrapersonal skills are skills such as problem solving, critical thinking, learning about alternative work processes, and risk taking. At TELUS, all employees take the company's ethics training program and learn how to respond to ethical dilemmas.

Interpersonal skills include interactive skills such as communicating, teamwork, and conflict resolution. As noted earlier, TELUS has a comprehensive leadership program for all levels of the organization. Later in this book, we will discuss the ways in which teams are becoming the major building blocks of organizations as well as the importance of effective communication for organizational success.

Finally, *cultural awareness* involves learning the social norms of organizations, understanding company goals, business operations, and company expectations and priorities. All employees need to learn the cultural norms and expectations of their organizations to function as effective organizational members. At TELUS, the first step of the Growing for High Performance program involves learning about the corporate strategy, business expectations, and the TELUS values that indicate how the company expects groups and individuals to approach their work and the corporate competencies that drive excellence.

Now that we have considered the content of learning in organizations, let's now turn to two theories that describe how people learn in organizations.

Operant Learning Theory

In the 1930s, psychologist B.F. Skinner investigated the behaviour of rats confined in a box containing a lever that delivered food pellets when pulled. Initially, the rats ignored the lever, but at some point they would accidentally pull it and a pellet would appear. Over time, the rats gradually acquired the lever-pulling response as a means of obtaining food. In other words, they *learned* to pull the lever. The kind of learning Skinner studied is called **operant learning** because the subject learns to operate on the environment to achieve certain consequences. The rats learned to operate the lever to achieve food. Notice that operantly learned behaviour is controlled by the consequences that follow it. These consequences usually depend on the behaviour, and this connection is what is learned. For example, salespeople learn effective sales techniques to achieve commissions and avoid criticism from their managers. The consequences of commissions and criticism depend on which sales behaviours salespeople exhibit.

Operant learning can be used to increase the probability of desired behaviours and to reduce or eliminate the probability of undesirable behaviours. Let's now consider how this is done.

Operant learning. The subject learns to operate on the environment to achieve certain consequences.

INCREASING THE PROBABILITY OF BEHAVIOUR

One of the most important consequences that influence behaviour is reinforcement. **Reinforcement** is the process by which stimuli strengthen behaviours. Thus, a *reinforcer* is a stimulus that follows some behaviour and increases or maintains the probability of that behaviour. The sales commissions and criticism mentioned earlier are reinforcers for salespeople. In each case, reinforcement serves to strengthen behaviours, such as proper sales techniques, that fulfill organizational goals. In general, organizations are interested in maintaining or increasing the probability of behaviours such as correct performance, prompt attendance, and accurate decision making. As we shall see, positive reinforcers work by their application to a situation, while negative reinforcers work by their removal from a situation.

Reinforcement. The process by which stimuli strengthen behaviours.

Positive Reinforcement

Positive reinforcement increases or maintains the probability of some behaviour by the *application* or *addition* of a stimulus to the situation in question. Such a stimulus is a positive reinforcer. In the basic Skinnerian learning situation described earlier, we can assume that reinforcement occurred because the probability of the lever operation increased over time. We can further assume that the food pellets were positive reinforcers because they were introduced after the lever was pulled.

Consider the experienced securities analyst who tends to read a particular set of financial newspapers regularly. If we had been able to observe the development of this reading habit, we might have found that it occurred as the result of a series of successful business decisions. That is, the analyst learns to scan those papers because his or her reading is positively reinforced by subsequent successful decisions. In this example, something is added to the situation (favourable decisions) that increases the probability of certain behaviour (selective reading). Also, the appearance of the reinforcer is dependent or contingent on the occurrence of that behaviour.

In general, positive reinforcers tend to be pleasant things, such as food, praise, money, or business success. However, the intrinsic character of stimuli does not determine whether they are positive reinforcers, and pleasant stimuli are not positive reinforcers when considered in the abstract. Whether or not something is a positive reinforcer depends only on whether it increases or maintains the occurrence of some behaviour by its application. Thus, it is improbable that the holiday turkey that employers give to all the employees of a manufacturing plant positively reinforces anything. The only behaviour that the receipt of the turkey is contingent on is being employed by the company during the third week of December. It is unlikely that the turkey increases the probability that employees will remain for another year or work harder.

Negative Reinforcement

Negative reinforcement increases or maintains the probability of some behaviour by the *removal* of a stimulus from the situation in question. Also, negative reinforcement occurs when a response *prevents* some event or stimulus from occurring. In each case, the removed or prevented stimulus is a *negative reinforcer*. Negative reinforcers are usually aversive or unpleasant stimuli, and it stands to reason that we will learn to repeat behaviours that remove or prevent these stimuli.

Let's repeat this point, because it frequently confuses students of organizational behaviour: Negative reinforcers *increase* the probability of behaviour. Suppose we rig a cage with an electrified floor so that it provides a mild shock to its inhabitant. In addition, we install a lever that will turn off the electricity. On the first few trials, a rat put in the cage will become very upset when shocked. Sooner or later, however, it will accidentally operate the lever and turn off the current. Gradually, the rat will learn to operate the lever as soon as it feels the shock. The shock serves as a negative reinforcer for the lever pulling, increasing the probability of the behaviour by its removal.

Managers who continually nag their employees unless they work hard are attempting to use negative reinforcement. The only way employees can stop the aversive nagging is to work hard and be diligent. The nagging maintains the probability of productive responses by its removal. In this situation, employees often get pretty good at anticipating the onset of nagging by the look on their boss's face. This look serves as a signal that they can avoid the nagging altogether if they work harder.

Negative reinforcers generally tend to be unpleasant things, such as shock, nagging, or threat of fines. Again, however, negative reinforcers are defined only by what they do and how they work, not by their unpleasantness. Above, we indicated that nagging could serve as a negative reinforcer to increase the probability of productive responses. However, nagging could also serve as a positive reinforcer to increase the probability

Positive reinforcement.
The application or addition of a stimulus that increases or maintains the probability of some behaviour.

Negative reinforcement.
The removal of a stimulus that, in turn, increases or maintains the probability of some behaviour.

of unproductive responses if an employee has a need for attention and nagging is the only attention the manager provides. In the first case, nagging is a negative reinforcer—it is terminated following productive responses. In the second case, nagging is a positive reinforcer—it is applied following unproductive responses. In both cases, the responses increase in probability.

Organizational Errors Involving Reinforcement

Experience indicates that managers sometimes make errors in trying to use reinforcement. The most common errors are confusing rewards with reinforcers, neglecting diversity in preferences for reinforcers, and neglecting important sources of reinforcement.

Confusing Rewards with Reinforcers. Organizations and individual managers frequently "reward" workers with things such as pay, promotions, fringe benefits, paid vacations, overtime work, and the opportunity to perform challenging tasks. Such rewards can fail to serve as reinforcers, however, because organizations do not make them contingent on specific behaviours that are of interest to the organization, such as attendance, innovation, or productivity. For example, many organizations assign overtime work on the basis of seniority, rather than performance or good attendance, even when the union contract does not require it. Although the opportunity to earn extra money might have strong potential as a reinforcer, it is seldom made contingent on some desired behaviour.

Neglecting Diversity in Preferences for Reinforcers. Organizations often fail to appreciate individual differences in preferences for reinforcers. In this case, even if managers administer rewards after a desired behaviour, they might fail to have a reinforcing effect. Intuitively, it seems questionable to reinforce a workaholic's extra effort with time off from work, yet such a strategy is fairly common. A more appropriate reinforcer might be the assignment of some challenging task, such as work on a very demanding key project. Some labour contracts include clauses that dictate that supervisors assign overtime to the workers who have the greatest seniority. Not surprisingly, high-seniority workers are often the best paid and the least in need of the extra pay available through overtime. Even if it is administered so that the best-performing high-seniority workers get the overtime, such a strategy might not prove reinforcing—the usual time off might be preferred over extra money.

Managers should carefully explore the possible range of stimuli under their control (such as task assignment and time off from work) for their applicability as reinforcers for particular employees. Furthermore, organizations should attempt to administer their formal rewards (such as pay and promotions) to capitalize on their reinforcing effects for various individuals. One way for organizations to do this is by creating a total rewards program. To learn more, see "Applied Focus: *Total Rewards at TransAlta Corporation and Sysco Food Services of Ontario, Inc.*"

Neglecting Important Sources of Reinforcement. There are many reinforcers of organizational behaviour that are not especially obvious. While concentrating on potential reinforcers of a formal nature, such as pay or promotions, organizations and their managers often neglect those which are administered by co-workers or intrinsic to the jobs being performed. Many managers cannot understand why a worker would persist in potentially dangerous horseplay despite threats of a pay penalty or dismissal. Frequently, such activity is positively reinforced by the attention provided by the joker's co-workers. In fact, on a particularly boring job, such threats might act as positive reinforcers for horseplay by relieving the boredom, especially if the threats are never carried out.

TransAlta Corporation
www.transalta.com

Sysco Food Services of
Ontario, Inc.
www.sysco.com

APPLIED FOCUS

Total Rewards at TransAlta Corporation and Sysco Food Services of Ontario, Inc.

Total rewards is a catch-all phrase used to describe everything an organization offers employees. Different organizations have varying views as to what should be included, but generally speaking, total rewards can include pay, variable compensation, core benefits (such as health, dental, and vision coverage), recognition, pensions, voluntary benefits, and training and development. The idea is to pull all of these rewards together in a total rewards package that can be marketed to existing and potential employees. A total rewards program can also involve an open dialogue with employees to find out what they value in rewards. Companies that involve employees in the development of their programs use employee surveys, focus groups, or committees. Organizations can then tailor what they offer to best suit employees' needs.

The results of a survey conducted by *Canadian HR Reporter* revealed that many organizations have adopted a formalized total rewards strategy to compensation and benefits. Further, most of the organizations that do not have a formalized total rewards program said they are considering implementing one. The driving force for organizations that have a total rewards program is to ensure employees are aware of the full range of benefits and their value, and that salary isn't the only form of remuneration available.

TransAlta Corporation is a power-generation firm with 2500 employees based in Calgary, Alberta. A key part of its total rewards program is firmly tying performance and rewards together. As part of the company's

total rewards strategy, it implemented a new performance management program and linked it to a wide range of rewards, including base pay, medium-term incentive compensation (for meeting a three-year target), long-term incentives such as stock options, and a performance share plan. The basic philosophy is that superior performance will be met with superior pay. On the non-financial side, the company has identified career opportunities and training and development as areas to focus on. TransAlta has also launched a recognition program it calls "Above and Beyond." Rewards vary from something as simple as a letter of commendation from the CEO to thousands of dollars in cash.

At Sysco Food Services of Ontario, Inc., a food distributor in Kingston, Ontario, rewards for employees include pay, benefits, a defined contribution pension plan, employee stock purchase plan, and tuition reimbursement. The company recently implemented a quarterly recognition program, on top of its service awards, to reward its 146 staff for productivity, attendance, and safety. Peers can also nominate each other for recognition. Winners are given gift certificates that can be redeemed at selected retail stores around the city. Altogether, the company spends about $25 000 a year on the quarterly recognition program.

Sources: Based on Humber, T. (2004, February 23). TransAlta Corporation keeps pay, performance the focus of total rewards. *Canadian HR Reporter, 17(4)*, G12; Humber, T. (2005, February 14). Total rewards: One concept, many monikers. *Canadian HR Reporter, 18(3)*, R3; Anonymous (2005, February 14). The total rewards concept defined. *Canadian HR Reporter, 18(3)*, R2.

One very important source of reinforcement that managers often ignore is information that accompanies the successful performance of tasks. **Performance feedback** involves providing quantitative or qualitative information on past performance for the purpose of changing or maintaining performance in specific ways. This reinforcement is available for jobs that provide feedback concerning the adequacy of performance. For example, in some jobs, feedback contingent on performance is readily available. Doctors can observe the success of their treatment by observing the progress of their patients' health, and mechanics can take the cars they repair for a test drive. In other jobs, organizations must design some special feedback mechanism into the job. Performance feedback is most effective when it is (a) conveyed in a positive manner, (b) delivered immediately after observing performance, (c) represented visually, such as in graph or chart form, and (d) specific to the behaviour that is being targeted for feedback.[45]

Performance feedback. Providing quantitative or qualitative information on past performance for the purpose of changing or maintaining performance in specific ways.

Social recognition.
Informal acknowledge-
ment, attention, praise,
approval, or genuine
appreciation for work well
done from one individual
or group to another.

Another important source of reinforcement is social recognition. **Social recognition** involves informal acknowledgement, attention, praise, approval, or genuine appreciation for work well done from one individual or group to another. Research has shown that when social recognition is made contingent on employee behaviour it can be an effective means for performance improvement.[46] Thus, managers should understand that positive feedback and a "pat on the back" for a job well done is a positive reinforcer that is easy to administer and is likely to reinforce desirable behaviour.

Reinforcement Strategies

What is the best way to administer reinforcers? Should we apply a reinforcer immediately after the behaviour of interest occurs, or should we wait for some period of time? Should we reinforce every correct behaviour, or should we reinforce only a portion of correct responses?

To obtain the *fast acquisition* of some response, continuous and immediate reinforcement should be used—that is, the reinforcer should be applied every time the behaviour of interest occurs, and it should be applied without delay after each occurrence. Many conditions exist in which the fast acquisition of responses is desirable. These include correcting the behaviour of "problem" employees, training employees for emergency operations, and dealing with unsafe work behaviours. Consider the otherwise excellent performer who tends to be late for work. Under pressure to demote or fire this good worker, the boss might sensibly attempt to positively reinforce instances of prompt attendance with compliments and encouragement. To modify the employee's behaviour as quickly as possible, the supervisor might station herself near the office door each morning to supply these reinforcers regularly and immediately.

You might wonder when one would not want to use a continuous, immediate reinforcement strategy to mould organizational behaviour. Put simply, behaviour that individuals learn under such conditions tends not to persist when reinforcement is made less frequently or stopped. Intuitively, this should not be surprising. For example, under normal conditions, operating the power switch on your stereo system is continuously and immediately reinforced by music. If the system develops a short circuit and fails to produce music, your switch-operating behaviour will cease very quickly. In the example in the preceding paragraph, the need for fast learning justified the use of continuous, immediate reinforcement. Under more typical circumstances, we would hope that prompt attendance could occur without such close attention.

Behaviour tends to be *persistent* when it is learned under conditions of partial and delayed reinforcement. That is, it will tend to persist under reduced or terminated reinforcement when not every instance of the behaviour is reinforced during learning or when some time period elapses between its enactment and reinforcement. In most cases, the supervisor who wishes to reinforce prompt attendance knows that he will not be able to stand by the shop door every morning to compliment his crew's timely entry. Given this constraint, the supervisor should compliment prompt attendance occasionally, perhaps later in the day. This should increase the persistence of promptness and reduce the employees' reliance on the boss's monitoring.

To repeat, continuous, immediate reinforcement facilitates fast learning, and delayed, partial reinforcement facilitates persistent learning (see Exhibit 2.3). Notice that it is impossible to maximize both speed and persistence with a single reinforcement strategy. Also, many responses in our everyday lives cannot be continuously and immediately reinforced, so in many cases it pays to sacrifice some speed in learning to prepare the learner for this fact of life. All this suggests that managers have to tailor reinforcement strategies to the needs of the situation. Often, managers must alter the strategies over time to achieve effective learning and maintenance of behaviour. For example, the manager training a new employee should probably use a reinforcement strategy that is fairly continuous and immediate (whatever the reinforcer). Looking over the employee's shoulder to obtain the fast acquisition of behaviour is appropriate.

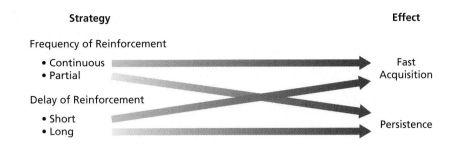

EXHIBIT 2.3
Summary of
reinforcement strategies
and their effects.

Gradually, however, the supervisor should probably reduce the frequency of reinforcement and perhaps build some delay into its presentation to reduce the employee's dependency on his or her attention.

REDUCING THE PROBABILITY OF BEHAVIOUR

Thus far in our discussion of learning, we have been interested in *increasing* the probability of various work behaviours, such as attendance or good performance. Both positive and negative reinforcement can accomplish this goal. However, in many cases, we encounter learned behaviours that we wish to *stop* from occurring. Such behaviours are detrimental to the operation of the organization and could be detrimental to the health or safety of an individual employee.

There are two strategies that can reduce the probability of learned behaviour: extinction and punishment.

Extinction

Extinction simply involves terminating the reinforcement that is maintaining some unwanted behaviour. If the behaviour is not reinforced, it will gradually dissipate or be extinguished.

Consider the case of a bright, young marketing expert who was headed for the "fast track" in his organization. Although his boss, the vice-president of marketing, was considering him for promotion, the young expert had developed a very disruptive habit—the tendency to play comedian during department meetings. The vice-president observed that this wisecracking was reinforced by the appreciative laughs of two other department members. He proceeded to enlist their aid to extinguish the joking. After the vice-president explained the problem to them, they agreed to ignore the disruptive one-liners and puns. At the same time, the vice-president took special pains to positively reinforce constructive comments by the young marketer. Very quickly, joking was extinguished, and the young man's future with the company improved.[47]

This example illustrates that extinction works best when coupled with the reinforcement of some desired substitute behaviour. Remember that behaviours that have been learned under delayed or partial reinforcement schedules are more difficult to extinguish than those learned under continuous, immediate reinforcement. Ironically, it would be harder to extinguish the joke-telling behaviour of a partially successful committee member than of one who was always successful at getting a laugh.

Punishment

Punishment involves following an unwanted behaviour with some unpleasant, aversive stimulus. In theory, this should reduce the probability of the response when the actor learns that the behaviour leads to unwanted consequences. Notice the difference between punishment and negative reinforcement. In negative reinforcement a nasty stimulus is *removed* following some behaviour, increasing the probability of that behav-

Extinction. The gradual dissipation of behaviour following the termination of reinforcement.

Punishment. The application of an aversive stimulus following some behaviour designed to decrease the probability of that behaviour.

iour. With punishment, a nasty stimulus is *applied* after some behaviour, *decreasing* the probability of that behaviour. If a boss criticizes her secretary after seeing the secretary use the office phone for personal calls, we expect to see less of this activity in the future. Exhibit 2.4 compares punishment with reinforcement and extinction.

Using Punishment Effectively

In theory, punishment should be useful in eliminating unwanted behaviour. After all, it seems unreasonable to repeat actions that cause us trouble. Unfortunately, punishment has some unique characteristics that often limit its effectiveness in stopping unwanted activity. First of all, while punishment provides a clear signal as to which activities are inappropriate, it does not by itself demonstrate which activities should *replace* the punished response. Reconsider the executive who chastises her secretary for making personal calls at the office. If the secretary makes personal calls only when she has caught up on her work, she might legitimately wonder what she is supposed to be doing during her occasional free time. If the boss fails to provide substitute activities, the message contained in the punishment might be lost.

Both positive and negative reinforcers specify which behaviours are appropriate. Punishment indicates only what is not appropriate. Since no reinforced substitute behaviour is provided, punishment only temporarily suppresses the unwanted response. When surveillance is removed, the response will tend to recur. Constant monitoring is very time consuming, and individuals become amazingly adept at learning when they can get away with the forbidden activity. The secretary will soon learn when

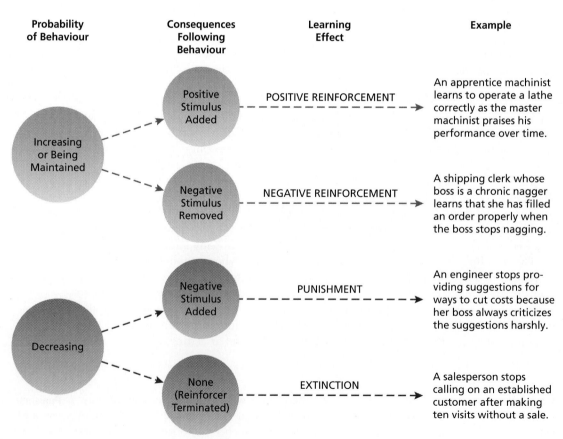

Probability of Behaviour	Consequences Following Behaviour	Learning Effect	Example
Increasing or Being Maintained	Positive Stimulus Added	POSITIVE REINFORCEMENT	An apprentice machinist learns to operate a lathe correctly as the master machinist praises his performance over time.
	Negative Stimulus Removed	NEGATIVE REINFORCEMENT	A shipping clerk whose boss is a chronic nagger learns that she has filled an order properly when the boss stops nagging.
Decreasing	Negative Stimulus Added	PUNISHMENT	An engineer stops providing suggestions for ways to cut costs because her boss always criticizes the suggestions harshly.
	None (Reinforcer Terminated)	EXTINCTION	A salesperson stops calling on an established customer after making ten visits without a sale.

EXHIBIT 2.4
Summary of learning effects.

she can make personal calls without detection. The moral here is clear: *Provide an acceptable alternative for the punished response.*

A second difficulty with punishment is that it has a tendency to provoke a strong emotional reaction on the part of the punished individual.[48] This is especially likely when the punishment is delivered in anger or perceived to be unfair. Managers who try overly hard to be patient with employees and then finally blow up risk overemotional reactions. So do those who tolerate unwanted behaviour on the part of their employees and then impulsively decide to make an example of one individual by punishing him or her. Managers should be sure that their own emotions are under control before punishing, and they should generally avoid punishment in front of observers.[49] Because of the emotional problems involved in the use of punishment, some organizations have downplayed its use in discipline systems. They give employees who have committed infractions *paid* time off to think about their problems.

In addition to providing correct alternative responses and limiting the emotions involved in punishment, there are several other principles that can increase the effectiveness of punishment.

- *Make sure the chosen punishment is truly aversive.* Organizations frequently "punish" chronically absent employees by making them take several days off work. Managers sometimes "punish" ineffective performers by requiring them to work overtime, which allows them to earn extra pay. In both cases, the presumed punishment might actually act as a positive reinforcer for the unwanted behaviour.

- *Punish immediately.* Managers frequently overlook early instances of rule violations or ineffective performance, hoping that things will "work out."[50] This only allows these behaviours to gain strength through repetition. If immediate punishment is difficult to apply, the manager should delay action until a more appropriate time and then reinstate the circumstances surrounding the problem behaviour. For example, the bank manager who observes her teller exhibiting inappropriate behaviour might ask this person to remain after work. She should then carry out punishment at the teller's window rather than in her office, perhaps demonstrating correct procedures and role-playing a customer to allow the employee to practise them.

- *Do not reward unwanted behaviours before or after punishment.* Many supervisors join in horseplay with their employees until they feel it is time to get some work done. Then, unexpectedly, they do an about-face and punish those who are still "goofing around." Sometimes, managers feel guilty about punishing their employees for some rule infraction and then quickly attempt to make up with displays of good-natured sympathy or affection. For example, the boss who criticizes her secretary for personal calls might show up an hour later with a gift of flowers. Such actions present employees with extremely confusing signals about how they should behave, since the manager could be inadvertently reinforcing the very response that he or she wants to terminate.

- *Do not inadvertently punish desirable behaviour.* This happens commonly in organizations. The manager who does not use all his capital budget for a given fiscal year might have the department's budget for the next year reduced, punishing the prudence of his employees. Government employees who "blow the whistle" on wasteful or inefficient practices might find themselves demoted.[51] University professors who are considered excellent teachers might be assigned to onerous, time-consuming duty on a curriculum committee, cutting into their class preparation time.

In summary, punishment can be an effective means of stopping undesirable behaviour. However, managers must apply it very carefully and deliberately to achieve this effectiveness. In general, reinforcing correct behaviours and extinguishing unwanted responses are safer strategies for managers than the frequent use of punishment.

SOCIAL COGNITIVE THEORY

It has perhaps occurred to you that learning and behaviour sometimes takes place in organizations without the conscious control of positive and negative reinforcers by managers. People often learn and behave through their own volition and self-influence. Thus, human behaviour is not simply due to environmental influences. Rather, people have the cognitive capacity to regulate and control their own thoughts, feelings, motivation, and actions. So, unlike operant learning theory, social cognitive theory emphasizes the role of *cognitive processes* in regulating people's behaviour. For example, people learn by observing the behaviour of others. Individuals can also regulate their behaviour by thinking about the consequences of their actions (forethought), setting performance goals, monitoring their performance and comparing it to their goals, and rewarding themselves for goal accomplishment. People also develop beliefs about their abilities through their interaction with the environment that influences their thoughts and behaviour.[52]

According to social cognitive theory, human behaviour can best be explained through a system of *triadic reciprocal causation* in which personal factors and environmental factors work together and interact to influence people's behaviour. In addition, people's behaviour also influences personal factors and the environment. Thus, operant learning theory and social cognitive theory complement each other in explaining learning and organizational behaviour.[53]

According to Albert Bandura, social cognitive theory involves three components: modelling, self-efficacy, and self-regulation.[54]

Albert Bandura and Theory
http://www.ship.edu/
~cgboeree/bandura.html

Modelling

Besides directly experiencing consequences, humans also learn by observing the behaviour of others. For instance, after experiencing just a couple of executive committee meetings, a newly promoted vice-president might look like an "old pro," bringing appropriate materials to the meeting, asking questions in an approved style, and so on. How can we account for such learning?

Modelling. The process of imitating the behaviour of others.

Modelling is the process of imitating the behaviour of others. With modelling, learning occurs by observing or imagining the behaviour of others, rather than through direct personal experience.[55] Generally, modelling involves examining the behaviour of others, seeing what consequences they experience, and thinking about what might happen if we act the same way. If we expect favourable consequences, we might imitate the behaviour. Thus, the new vice-president doubtless modelled his behaviour on that of the more experienced peers on the executive committee. But has reinforcement occurred here? It is *self-reinforcement* that occurs in the modelling process. For one thing, it is reinforcing to acquire an understanding of others who are viewed positively. In addition, we are able to imagine the reinforcers that the model experiences coming our way when we imitate his or her behaviour. Surely, this is why we imitate the behaviour of sports heroes and entertainers, a fact that advertisers capitalize on when they choose them to endorse products. In any event, modelling is an important aspect of social cognitive theory.

What kinds of models are likely to provoke the greatest degree of imitation? In general, attractive, credible, competent, high-status people stand a good chance of being imitated. In addition, it is important that the model's behaviour provoke consequences that are seen as positive and successful by the observer. Finally, it helps if the model's behaviour is vivid and memorable—bores do not make good models.[56] In business schools, it is not unusual to find students who have developed philosophies or approaches that are modelled on credible, successful, high-profile business leaders. Popular examples include Microsoft's Bill Gates and former General Electric CEO Jack Welch, both of whom have been the object of extensive coverage in the business and popular press.

The extent of modelling as a means of learning in organizations suggests that managers should pay more attention to the process. For one thing, managers who operate on a principle of "do as I say, not as I do" will find that what they do is more likely to be imitated, including undesirable behaviours such as expense account abuse. Also, in the absence of credible management models, workers might imitate dysfunctional peer behaviour if peers meet the criteria for strong models. For example, one study found that the antisocial behaviour of a work group was a significant predictor of an individual's antisocial workplace behaviour. Thus, individual's antisocial workplace behaviour can be shaped, in part, through the process of observation and modelling.[57] On a more positive note, well-designed performance appraisal and reward systems permit organizations to publicize the kind of organizational behaviour that should be imitated.

Self-Efficacy

While modelling may have helped the vice-president learn how to behave in an executive committee meeting, you may have wondered what made him so confident. Was he not full of self-doubt and worried that he would fail? Such beliefs are known as self-efficacy. **Self-efficacy** refers to beliefs people have about their ability to successfully perform a specific task. At this point, it is important to note the difference between task-specific self-efficacy and some of the general personality traits discussed earlier in the chapter. In particular, unlike self-esteem and general self-efficacy, which are general personality traits, self-efficacy is a task-specific cognitive appraisal of one's ability to perform a specific task. Thus, it is not a generalized personality trait. Furthermore, people can have different self-efficacy beliefs for different tasks. For example, the vice-president might have strong self-efficacy for conducting an executive committee meeting, but low self-efficacy for doing well in a course on organizational behaviour![58]

> **Self-efficacy.** Beliefs people have about their ability to successfully perform a specific task.

Because self-efficacy is a cognitive belief rather than a stable personality trait, it can be changed and modified in response to different sources of information. As shown in Exhibit 2.5, self-efficacy is influenced by one's experiences and success performing the task in question (performance mastery), observation of others performing the task, verbal persuasion and social influence, and one's physiological or emotional state. Thus, the self-efficacy of the vice-president could have been strengthened by observing the behaviour of others during meetings, encouragement from peers that he would do a great job, and perhaps by his own sense of comfort and relaxation rather than anxiety and stress while attending meetings. Finally, his mastery displayed during the meeting is also likely to further strengthen his self-efficacy beliefs.

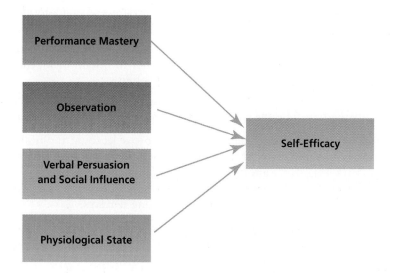

EXHIBIT 2.5
Determinants of Self-Efficacy.

Self-efficacy is a critical component of behaviour that can influence the activities people choose to perform, the amount of effort and persistence devoted to a task, affective and stress reactions, and job performance.[59] In the case of the vice-president, his strong sense of self-efficacy obviously contributed to his ability to perform like an "old pro" at the meeting.

Self-Regulation

In much of this chapter, we have been concerned with how organizations and individual managers can use learning principles to manage the behaviour of organizational members. However, according to social cognitive theory, employees can use learning principles to manage their *own* behaviour, making external control less necessary. This process is called **self-regulation**.[60]

Self-regulation. The use of learning principles to regulate one's own behaviour.

How can self-regulation occur? You will recall that modelling involved factors such as observation, imagination, imitation, and self-reinforcement. Individuals can use these and similar techniques in an intentional way to control their own behaviour. The basic process involves observing one's own behaviour, comparing the behaviour with a standard, and rewarding oneself if the behaviour meets the standard. A key part of the process is people's pursuit of self-set goals that guide their behaviour. When there exists a discrepancy between one's goals and performance, individuals are motivated to modify their behaviour in the pursuit of goal attainment (a process known as *discrepancy reduction*). When individuals attain their goals, they are likely to set even higher and more challenging goals, a process known as *discrepancy production*. In this way, people continually engage in a process of setting goals in the pursuit of ever higher levels of performance. Thus, discrepancy reduction and discrepancy production lie at the heart of the self-regulatory process.[61]

To illustrate some specific self-regulation techniques, consider the executive who finds that she is taking too much work home to do in the evenings and over weekends. While her peers seem to have most evenings and weekends free, her own family is ready to disown her due to lack of attention! What can she do?[62]

- *Collect self-observation data.* This involves collecting objective data about one's own behaviour. For example, the executive might keep a log of phone calls and other interruptions for a few days if she suspects that these contribute to her inefficiency.

- *Observe models.* The executive might examine the time-management skills of her peers to find someone successful to imitate.

- *Set goals.* The executive might set specific short-term goals to reduce telephone interruptions and unscheduled personal visits, enlisting the aid of her secretary and using self-observation data to monitor her progress. Longer-term goals might involve four free nights a week and no more than four hours of work on weekends.

- *Rehearse.* The executive might anticipate that she will have to educate her co-workers about her reduced availability. So as not to offend them, she might practise explaining the reason for her revised accessibility.

- *Reinforce oneself.* The executive might promise herself a weekend at the beach with her family the first time she gets her take-home workload down to her target level.

Research has found that self-regulation can improve learning and result in a change in behaviour. For example, one study showed how a self-regulation program was used to improve work attendance among unionized maintenance employees. Those who had used over half their sick leave were invited by the human resources department to participate in an eight-week program with the following features:

- Discussion of general reasons for use of sick leave. High on the list were transportation problems, family difficulties, and problems with supervisors and co-workers.

- Self-assessment of personal reasons for absence and development of personal coping strategies.
- Goal setting to engage in behaviours that should improve attendance (short-term goals) and to improve attendance by a specific amount (long-term goal).
- Self-observation using charts and diaries. Employees recorded their own attendance, reasons for missing work, and steps they took to get to work.
- Identification of specific reinforcers and punishers to be self-administered for reaching or not reaching goals.

Compared with a group of employees who did not attend the program, the employees who were exposed to the program achieved a significant improvement in attendance, and they also felt more confident (i.e., higher self-efficacy) that they would be able to come to work when confronted with various obstacles to attendance.[63] In another study, training in self-regulation was found to significantly improve the sales performance of a sample of insurance salespeople.[64] Self-regulation programs have been successful in positively changing a variety of work behaviours and are an effective method of training and learning.[65]

ORGANIZATIONAL LEARNING PRACTICES

We began our discussion of learning by describing learning content, and then we focused on how people learn. In this final section, we review a number of organizational learning practices, including an application of operant learning called organizational behaviour modification, employee recognition programs, training programs, and career development.

Organizational Behaviour Modification

Most reinforcement occurs naturally, rather than as the result of a conscious attempt to manage behaviour. **Organizational behaviour modification** (O.B. Mod) involves the systematic use of learning principles to influence organizational behaviour. For example, consider how one company used organizational behaviour modification through the reinforcement of safe working behaviour in a food-manufacturing plant. At first glance, accidents appeared to be chance events or wholly under the control of factors such as equipment failures. However, the researchers felt that accidents could be reduced if specific safe working practices could be identified and reinforced. These practices were identified with the help of past accident reports and advice from supervisors. Systematic observation of working behaviour indicated that employees followed safe practices only about 74 percent of the time. A brief slide show was prepared to illustrate safe versus unsafe job behaviours. Then, two reinforcers of safe practices were introduced into the workplace. The first consisted of a feedback chart that was conspicuously posted in the workplace to indicate the percentage of safe behaviours observers noted. This chart included the percentages achieved in observational sessions before the slide show, as well as those achieved every three days after the slide show. A second source of reinforcement was supervisors, who were encouraged to praise instances of safe performance that they observed. These interventions were successful in raising the percentage of safe working practices to around 97 percent almost immediately. When the reinforcers were terminated, the percentage of safe practices quickly returned to the level before the reinforcement was introduced. (See Exhibit 2.6.)[66]

In general, research supports the effectiveness of organizational behaviour modification programs. In addition to improvements in safety, O.B. Mod has also been found to have a positive effect on improving work attendance and task performance. The effects on task performance, however, tend to be stronger in manufacturing than in service organizations. As well, money, feedback, and social recognition have all been

Organizational behaviour modification. The systematic use of learning principles to influence organizational behaviour.

EXHIBIT 2.6
Percentage of safe working practices achieved with and without reinforcement.

Source: Adapted from Komaki, J., et al. (1978, August). A behavioral approach to occupational safety: Pinpointing and reinforcing safe performance in a food manufacturing plant. *Journal of Applied Psychology, 63(4)*, 439. Copyright © 1978 by American Psychological Association. Adapted by permission.

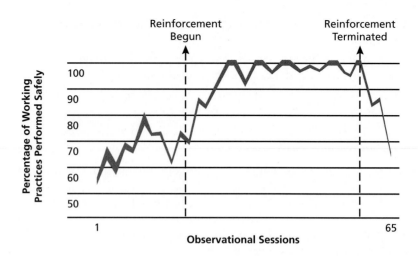

found to be effective forms of positive reinforcement. Although money has been found to have stronger effects on performance than social recognition and performance feedback, the use of all three together has the strongest effect on task performance. Research has also found that the effect of money on performance is greater when it is provided systematically through O.B. Mod compared to a routine pay-for-performance program.[67]

Employee Recognition Programs

Another example of an organizational learning practice that uses positive reinforcement is employee recognition programs. **Employee recognition programs** are formal organizational programs that publicly recognize and reward employees for specific behaviours. To be effective, a formal employee recognition program must specify (a) how a person will be recognized, (b) the type of behaviour being encouraged, (c) the manner of the public acknowledgement, and (d) a token or icon of the event for the recipient. A key part of an employee recognition program is public acknowledgment. Thus, a financial reward for good performance would not qualify as an employee recognition program if it was not accompanied by some form of public praise and recognition.[68]

Employee recognition programs have been found to be related to a number of individual and organizational outcomes, including job satisfaction, performance and productivity, and lower turnover.[69] One study compared a public recognition program for improving work attendance with several other interventions. Employees with perfect attendance for an entire month had their names posted with a gold star for that month. At the end of each quarter, employees with no more than two absences received a personal card notifying and congratulating them. In addition, at the end of the year there was a plant-wide meeting to recognize good attendance and small, engraved mementos were awarded to employees who had perfect attendance during the entire year. The results indicated that employees had favourable perceptions of the program and the program resulted in a decrease in absenteeism.[70]

Many companies in Canada have some form of employee recognition program and employees in the best companies to work for in Canada believe that they receive adequate recognition beyond compensation for their contributions and accomplishments. At Canadian Tire, for example, the head office has a Wall of Winners, which displays photographs of exceptional customer service. At Fidelity Investments Canada Ltd., up to five employees are honoured each quarter for outstanding performance. They receive $500, a letter of recognition, and a lunch. Once a year the "best of the best" receives $1000. Toronto-based pharmaceutical company Janssen-Ortho recognizes top

Employee recognition programs. Formal organizational programs that publicly recognize and reward employees for specific behaviours.

Canadian Tire
www.canadiantire.ca

Fidelity Investments Canada
www.fidelity.ca

performers with peer-chosen bronze, silver, and gold Medallion Awards.[71] A recent survey of 26 000 employees in 31 organizations in the United States found that companies that invest the most in recognition programs have more than triple the profits of those that invest the least.[72]

An increasing number of organizations have begun to implement a new kind of recognition program called *peer recognition*. Before continuing, consider the You Be the Manager feature.

Training Programs

Training is one of the most common types of formal learning in organizations. As described at the beginning of the chapter, TELUS invests about 2 percent of payroll budgets on training and offers a wide variety of training programs to its employees. **Training** refers to planned organizational activities that are designed to facilitate knowledge and skill acquisition to change behaviour and improve performance.[73] Employees learn a variety of skills by attending formal training programs. In addition to teaching employees technical skills required to perform their jobs, training programs also teach employees nontechnical skills such as how to work in teams, how to provide excellent customer service, and ways to understand and appreciate cultural diversity.

Effective training programs include many of the principles of learning described earlier in the chapter, such as positive reinforcement, feedback, learning by observation, strengthening employees' self-efficacy, and self-regulation. One of the most widely used and effective methods of training is *behaviour modelling training* (BMT), which is based on the modelling component of social cognitive theory and involves the following steps:[74]

- Describing to trainees a set of well-defined behaviours (skills) to be learned.
- Providing a model or models displaying the effective use of those behaviours.
- Providing opportunities for trainees to practise using those behaviours.
- Providing feedback and social reinforcement to trainees following practice.
- Taking steps to maximize the transfer of those behaviours to the job.

Training. Planned organizational activities that are designed to facilitate knowledge and skill acquisition to change behaviour and improve performance.

Delta Hotels and Resorts Ltd.
www.deltahotels.com

Island Savings Credit Union
www.iscu.com

Ceridian Canada Ltd.
www.ceridian.ca

YOU BE THE
Manager

Peer Recognition Programs

Peer recognition programs are showing up in organizations all across Canada as a growing number of employers see the value in encouraging employees to support each other. It is a trend that goes along with a less hierarchical workplace where teamwork is valued over competition, and employees are more likely to get ahead by patting each other on the back rather than by stabbing each other in the back. More companies are seeing the importance of recognizing their employees as a boost to morale, loyalty, retention, and recruiting. About 35 percent of major US companies now have peer recognition programs, up from 25 percent five years ago.

In Canada, Delta Hotels is one company with a peer recognition program. According to Bill Pallett, senior vice-president of people and quality, "It's an inclusive process, whereby employees recognize their own. We're getting away from politicized employee of the month, management's favourite person." Delta is a subsidiary of Fairmont Hotels & Resorts Inc., which has several peer recognition programs. Employees nominate peers for recognition rewards in several categories that correspond to corporate objectives, such as customer service, community service, and maintaining the National Quality Institute's standards for a healthy workplace.

Duncan, BC–based Island Savings Credit Union has several peer recognition programs, including one that allows employees to hand out "WOW" points that can be redeemed for gift certificates and other rewards, including services volunteered by senior managers such as babysitting for employees working on Saturdays, a round of golf, or a trip on a yacht.

Employees at Markham, Ontario–based Ceridian Canada Ltd. have good reason to be excited about the top rewards offered in its program. Ceridian recognizes 28 "star" employees each quarter and gives each a $100 gift certificate. At year end, 15 are selected to go on an overseas trip with spouses and senior executives. The destinations in previous years have included London, Paris, and Costa Rica, and the next trip will visit several African countries. "With prizes like these, the quest for recognition is 'quite competitive,'" says Jim Thomson, director of human resources operations.

> ### Peer recognition programs are popping up all across Canada

He says that Ceridian's employees appreciate having an opportunity to praise each other. "We don't have to push this program at all," he says. "The employees like working with one another and, when one of their co-workers does something above and beyond, they know they have a way of rewarding that."

What do you think about peer recognition programs? Are they an effective way to reward employees? You be the manager.

QUESTIONS

1. Based on operant learning theory, what is necessary to make peer recognition programs effective?

2. How should peer recognition programs be designed to be most effective?

To find out how to make peer recognition programs effective, see The Manager's Notebook.

Source: Based on Marron, K. (2006, February 15). High praise from colleagues counts. *Globe and Mail*, C1, C6. Reprinted with permission from Kevin Marron, freelance journalist, author, business writer.

Many organizations have used behavioural modelling training to develop supervisory, communications, sales, and customer service skills. A recent review of behavioural modelling training research concluded that it has a positive effect on learning, skills, and job behaviour. The effects on behaviour were greatest when trainees were instructed to set goals and when rewards and sanctions were used in the trainees' work environment.[75] Training has also been found to increase trainees' self-efficacy in addition to having a positive effect on learning and job behaviour.[76]

Career Development

While training can help employees learn to perform their current jobs more effectively, career development helps employees prepare for future roles and responsibilities. This is clearly the case at TELUS, where all employees have a customized career development plan to grow their careers and develop to their highest potential. **Career development** is an ongoing process in which individuals progress through a series of stages that consist of a unique set of issues, themes, and tasks. This usually involves a career planning and career management component. Career planning involves the assessment of an individual's interests, skills, and abilities in order to develop goals and career plans. Career management involves taking the necessary steps that are required to achieve an individual's goals and career plans. This often involves special assignments and activities that are designed to assist employees in their career development.[77]

Career development.
An ongoing process in which individuals progress through a series of stages that consist of a unique set of issues, themes, and tasks.

THE MANAGER'S

Notebook

Peer Recognition Programs

1. Peer recognition programs use rewards as a way to recognize employees who have demonstrated outstanding performance. According to operant learning theory, to be most effective the rewards must be contingent on specific behaviours that are of interest to the organization, such as attendance, innovation, or productivity. This is especially important since employees are responsible for choosing co-workers for recognition, and such choices should not simply be based on who is most liked or who has the most friends in the company. The program also has to consider individual preferences for reinforcers. Rewards will not have a reinforcing effect if they are not desired by the employee. Therefore, it is important that a variety of rewards be available to suit individual preferences. Clearly, there are many rewards other than pay and promotions that can be effective reinforcers. A good example is Island Savings Credit Union's use of points that can be redeemed for gift certificates and other rewards.

2. Peer recognition programs should be designed in the same manner as formal employee recognition programs. To be effective, they should specify (a) how a person will be recognized, (b) the type of behaviour being encouraged, (c) the manner of the public acknowledgement, and (d) a token or icon of the event for the recipient. Because one's peers are responsible for deciding who will be recognized, careful attention should be given to how this is done to ensure that the process is fair and that the expected behaviour has been demonstrated. It also needs to be clear about what types of behaviours will be rewarded. Recognizing the wrong people and being inconsistent in how rewards are granted can create problems and undermine the program. Therefore, the program must have clear guidelines about what kind of behaviour will be recognized and how this will be done. At Ceridian, there are stringent criteria for nominations, and selections are made by committees composed of a mix of employees and managers. The company also holds employee focus groups to solicit feedback on its program and has acted on recommendations such as having more front-line staff and fewer senior executives on the selection committees.

Dun & Bradstreet Canada
www.dnb.ca

Given the increasing emphasis and importance of continuous and life-long learning, many organizations now have career development programs. For example, Dun & Bradstreet Canada, a business information services company, has a career development program for all of its employees. Employees have a file called a Leadership Action Plan that lists their strengths and career aspirations as well as a plan on how they will achieve their goals. The file is reviewed by a supervisor four times a year. In addition, an intranet site is available to help employees perform career assessments and access information about job opportunities within the company. The company believes that its career development program will provide it with a learning, knowledge, and skills advantage.[78] When TD Bank Financial Group surveyed its employees, it found that skills development and career development were the most important factors for them. As a result, the company decided to invest more in employee career management and created a website to help employees with all aspects of managing their careers. The Career Advisor site is a comprehensive tool that enables employees to determine how best to develop themselves and overcome career challenges. Employees have access to a combination of interactive diagnostic instruments, personal reports, advice, tools, and action planning exercises.[79]

TD Bank Financial Group
www.td.com

LEARNING OBJECTIVES CHECKLIST

1. *Personality* is the relatively stable set of psychological characteristics that influences the way we interact with our environment. It has more impact on behaviour in weak situations than in strong situations.

2. According to the dispositional approach, stable individual characteristics influence people's attitudes and behaviours. The situational approach argues that characteristics in the work environment influence people's attitudes and behaviour. The interactionist approach posits that organizational behaviour is a function of both dispositions and the situation.

3. The Five-Factor Model consists of five basic dimensions of personality: extraversion, emotional stability/neuroticism, agreeableness, conscientiousness, and openness to experience. Research has found that the "Big Five" are related to motivation, job satisfaction, job performance, and career outcomes.

4. People who have an *internal locus of control* are more satisfied with their jobs, earn more money, and achieve higher organizational positions. High *self-monitors* have good communication skills and persuasive abilities and are more likely to change employers and locations and to receive more promotions than individuals who are low self-monitors. People

with high *self-esteem* tend to make more fulfilling career decisions, to exhibit higher job satisfaction and job performance, and to be generally more resilient to the strains of everyday worklife.

5. People who are high on *positive affectivity* experience positive emotions and moods and tend to view the world in a positive light, including oneself and other people. People who are high on *negative affectivity* experience negative emotions and moods and tend to view the world in a negative light. *Proactive personality* is a stable personal disposition that reflects a tendency to take personal initiative across a range of activities and situations and to effect positive change in one's environment. *General self-efficacy* (GSE) is a general trait that refers to an individual's belief in his or her ability to perform successfully in a variety of challenging situations. *Core self-evaluations* refers to a broad personality concept that consists of more specific traits.

6. *Learning* occurs when practice or experience leads to a relatively permanent change in behaviour potential. The content of learning in organizations consists of practical, intrapersonal, and interpersonal skills and cultural awareness.

7. *Operant learning* occurs as a function of the consequences of behaviour. If some behaviour is occurring regularly or increasing in probability, you can assume that it is being reinforced. If the reinforcer is added to the situation following the behaviour, it is a *positive reinforcer*. If the reinforcer is removed from the situation following the behaviour, it is a *negative reinforcer*.

8. Behaviour is learned quickly when it is reinforced immediately and continuously. Behaviour tends to be persistent under reduced or terminated reinforcement when it is learned under conditions of delayed or partial reinforcement.

9. If some behaviour decreases in probability, you can assume that it is being either extinguished or punished. If the behaviour is followed by no observable consequence, it is being extinguished; that is, some reinforcer that was maintaining the behaviour has been terminated. If the behaviour is followed by the application of some unpleasant consequence, it is being punished.

10. According to social cognitive theory, people have the cognitive capacity to regulate and control their own thoughts, feelings, motivation, and actions. The main components of social cognitive theory are modelling, self-efficacy, and self-regulation. *Modelling* is the process of imitating others. Models are most likely to be imitated when they are high in status, attractive, competent, credible, successful, and vivid. *Self-efficacy* is the belief that one can successfully perform a specific task and is influenced by performance mastery, observation of others performing the task, verbal persuasion and social influence, and physiological arousal. *Self-regulation* occurs when people use learning principles to manage their own behaviour, thus reducing the need for external control. Aspects of self-regulation include collecting self-observation data, observing models, goal setting, rehearsing, and using self-reinforcement.

11. Organizational learning practices include organizational behaviour modification, employee recognition programs, training programs, and career development. *Organizational behaviour modification* is the systematic use of learning principles to influence organizational behaviour. Companies have successfully used it to improve employees' attendance, task performance, and workplace safety. *Employee recognition programs* are formal organizational programs that publicly recognize and reward employees for specific behaviours. *Training programs* involve planned organizational activities that are designed to facilitate knowledge and skill acquisition to change behaviour and improve performance. *Career development* is an ongoing process in which individuals progress through a series of stages that consist of a unique set of issues, themes, and tasks.

DISCUSSION QUESTIONS

1. Consider the relevance of the dispositional, situational, and interactionist approaches to your own behaviour. Describe examples of your behaviour in a school or work situation that demonstrates each perspective of organizational behaviour.

2. Suppose that you are the manager of two employees, one of whom has an internal locus of control and another who has an external locus of control. Describe the leadership tactics that you would use with each employee. Contrast the management styles that you would employ for employees with high versus low self-esteem.

3. Consider some examples of behaviour that you repeat fairly regularly (such as studying or going to work every morning). What are the positive and negative reinforcers that maintain this behaviour?

4. We pointed out that managers frequently resort to punishing ineffective behaviour. What are some of the practical demands of the typical manager's job that lead to this state of affairs?

5. Discuss a situation that you have observed in which the use of punishment was ineffective in terminating some unwanted behaviour. Why was punishment ineffective in this case?

6. Describe a situation in which you think an employer could use organizational behaviour modification and an employee recognition program to improve or correct employee behaviour. Can you anticipate any dangers in using these approaches?

7. A supervisor in a textile factory observes that one of her employees is violating a safety rule that could result in severe injury. What combination of reinforcement, punishment, extinction, and social cognitive theory could she use to correct this behaviour?

8. Describe a job in which you think an employee recognition program might be an effective means for changing and improving employee behaviour. Explain how you would design the program and how principles from operant learning theory and social cognitive theory could be used.

9. Refer to the Global Focus feature, "Personality and Expatriate Effectiveness," and consider the relationship between the "Big Five" personality characteristics and expatriate effectiveness. Why do you think that conscientiousness was the only trait not related to expatriate effectiveness, given that it has been found to be the best predictor of job performance among the "Big Five"? Why is openness to experience and agreeableness more important to expatriate effectiveness?

10. Compare and contrast operant learning theory and social cognitive theory. Describe how you would change an individual's behaviour according to each theory. What do you think is the best approach?

INTEGRATIVE DISCUSSION QUESTIONS

1. Refer to the material in Chapter 1 on Mintzberg's managerial roles and consider how personality might be a factor in how effectively a manager performs each role. Discuss the relationship among the "Big Five" personality dimensions, locus of control, self-monitoring, self-esteem, proactive personality, and general self-efficacy with each of the managerial roles.

2. Discuss how each of the organizational learning practices discussed in the chapter can be used by organizations to deal effectively with the contemporary management concerns discussed in Chapter 1 (i.e., diversity—local and global, employee–organization relationships, quality, speed, and flexibility, and employee recruitment and retention).

ON-THE-JOB CHALLENGE QUESTION

In 2005, BioWare Corp., an Edmonton-based video game developer, had a good year so it pulled out all the stops for its holiday party. The company's 480 employees and guests attended a dinner and dance at an upscale hotel and enjoyed a paid taxi ride home. Once over, employees had the following two weeks off with pay—in addition to their regular vacation entitlements. The party is only one of many celebrations—from employee barbecues to ski trips, movie nights to champagne toasts on the launch of new games— all of which are meant to acknowledge employee efforts throughout the year. The result, according to the company's human resources manager, is high morale. In fact, 57 percent of human resources managers at 99 Canadian companies surveyed by Hewitt Associates said the reason their companies have holiday parties is to acknowledge the efforts of their employees. Another 26 percent said it's considered important for staff morale. The remainder said the party is a holiday tradition.

What do you think about holiday parties and BioWare Corp.'s many other celebrations? Are they a good way to reward the efforts of employees? What are the advantages and disadvantages of them? What advice do you have to organizations thinking about having a holiday party?

Source: Immen, W. (2005, December 7). Holiday party: a booster or buster to morale? *Globe and Mail*, C1, C7. Reprinted with permission from the *Globe and Mail*.

EXPERIENTIAL EXERCISE

Proactive Personality Scale

Do you have a proactive personality? To find out, answer the 17 questions below as frankly and honestly as possible using the following response scale:

1–Disagree very much   5–Agree slightly

2–Disagree moderately   6–Agree moderately

3–Disagree slightly   7–Agree very much

4–Neither agree or disagree

_____ 1. I am constantly on the lookout for new ways to improve my life.

_____ 2. I feel driven to make a difference in my community, and maybe the world.

_____ 3. I tend to let others take the initiative to start new projects.

_____ 4. Wherever I have been, I have been a powerful force for constructive change.

_____ 5. I enjoy facing and overcoming obstacles to my ideas.

_____ 6. Nothing is more exciting than seeing my ideas turn into reality.

_____ 7. If I see something I don't like, I fix it.

_____ 8. No matter what the odds, if I believe in something I will make it happen.

_____ 9. I love being a champion for my ideas, even against others' opposition.

_____ 10. I excel at identifying opportunities.

_____ 11. I am always looking for better ways to do things.

_____ 12. If I believe in an idea, no obstacle will prevent me from making it happen.

_____ 13. I love to challenge the status quo.

_____ 14. When I have a problem, I tackle it head-on.

_____ 15. I am great at turning problems into opportunities.

_____ 16. I can spot a good opportunity long before others can.

_____ 17. If I see someone in trouble, I help out in any way I can.

Scoring and Interpretation

You have just completed the Proactive Personality Scale developed by Thomas Bateman and J. Michael Crant. To score your scale, first subtract your response to question 3 from 8. For example, if you gave a response of 7 to question 3, give yourself a 1 (8 minus 7). Then add up your scores to all 17 items. Your total should be somewhere between 17 and 119. The higher you scored, the more *proactive* your personality is—you feel that you can change things in your environment.

The average score of 134 first-year MBA students with full-time work experience was 90.7. Thus, these people tended to see themselves as very proactive. In this research, people with a proactive personality tended to report more extracurricular and service activities and major personal achievements that involve constructive environmental change.

To facilitate class discussion and your understanding of proactive personality, form a small group with several other members of the class and consider the following questions:

1. Each group member should present their proactive personality score. Next, consider the extent to which each member has been involved in extracurricular and service activities as well as personal accomplishments that involved environmental change. Have students with higher proactive personality scores been more involved in extracurricular and service activities? What about personal accomplishments and constructive change? (Alternatively, each member of the class might write their proactive personality score and extracurricular and service activities and personal accomplishments on a piece of paper and hand it in to the instructor. The instructor can then write the responses on the board for class discussion).

2. When is a proactive personality most likely to be beneficial? When is it least likely to be beneficial?

3. Do you think organizations should hire people based on whether or not they have a proactive personality? What are the implications of this?

4. How can knowledge of your proactive personality score help you at school and at work? What can you do to become more proactive?

Source: Bateman, T.S., & Crant, J.M. (1993). The proactive component of organizational behavior: A measure and correlates. *Journal of Organizational Behavior, 14,* 103–118.

CASE INCIDENT

Courier Cats

To stay competitive, many organizations have to regularly upgrade their computer technology. This was certainly the case for Courier Cats, a small but profitable courier firm. To improve the delivery and tracking of parcels, the company decided to invest in a new software program. It was expected that the new software would not only allow the company to expand its business, but would also improve the quality of service. Because the new software was much more complex and sophisticated than what the company had been using, employees attended a one-day training program to learn how to use the new system. However, six months after the system was implemented, most employees were still using the old system. Some employees refused to use the new software, while others did not think they would ever be able to learn how to use it.

1. Why do you think that the employees did not use the new software?

2. What are some of the implications that stem from operant learning theory and social cognitive theory for increasing the probability that the employees will use the new software? What do you recommend for improving the use of the new software?

CASE STUDY

Club Chaos

Club Chaos is an exclusive, upscale, non-profit private organization that provides members with an array of facilities. The club includes a golf club (complete with a pro shop and instructors), indoor/outdoor tennis courts (with professional instructors), a curling rink, swimming pool, private meeting rooms, and extensive dining facilities (banquets, catered meetings, fine dining, sports lounge, a patio BBQ, a poolside BBQ/snack bar, an in-house bakeshop, and catering outside the club for members). Club Chaos employs over 200 people and has an extensive organizational structure. (See Exhibit 2.7 for an organizational chart.)

The club's general manager is Antonio, a man with little formal education. Antonio can usually be found out on the golf course or playing tennis (usually in the company of his wife). He has recently created the position of clubhouse manager and promoted his friend Rocco, the former head of the maintenance department, to fill it. Rocco is also a self-taught individual, with limited formal education or business experience. Rocco ran a two-person home renovation company for a few years, the club's maintenance department for three, and now finds himself in charge of the majority of club operations. Rocco can often be seen in the lounge drinking with the club members for extended periods, and it is widely rumoured that Rocco is to be the "broom" in a "clean sweep" of the organization.

Cathy was the head of catering and was known for her efficiency in heading up the Food and Beverage operation and her savvy in dealing with customers.

EXHIBIT 2.7
Club Chaos catering department (F&B) flow chart.

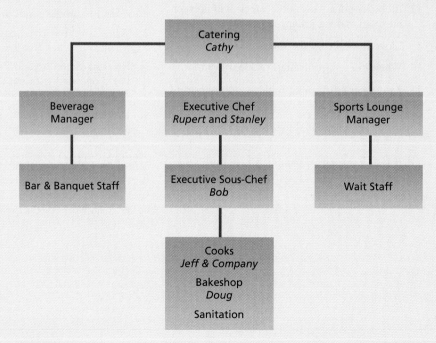

Soon after Rocco's promotion, Cathy was told in a meeting with him that she was to dismiss her assistant Jan (who is also Cathy's sister-in-law). The position of catering assistant was to be terminated, as the budget was being trimmed to boost revenue so that a new clubhouse could be built for the members. Cathy soon resigned as well, and the department fell into disarray. Rocco was playing an active role in the catering office, but new people occupied and left the position of catering manager at the rate of one every three months. Contracts came in late, last minute changes were frequent, and many details were left out of the function planning sheets. On one occasion, a contract for a wedding party of 160 people was overlooked until the morning of the event.

During this time, Rocco was also putting extreme pressure on the executive chef, Rupert. Demands were made to increase the kitchen's revenue, and the inconsistent quality of the food was a frequent criticism. On the other hand, Rupert was instructed to keep food and labour costs low and service levels high. Antonio and Rocco suspected that theft was the cause of high food costs lately. Rumours were circulating throughout the close-knit culinary group that Club Chaos was actively seeking a new executive chef, and phone calls by potential applicants were unwittingly forwarded directly to Rupert's office. Rupert soon resigned from his position, and Stanley was hired to replace him. Although Stanley had very odd behavioural quirks—he could be seen running through the kitchen on his hands and knees barking like a dog and playfully biting his employees—he did create control systems that revealed what had been suspected. Large amounts of inventory were missing from the kitchen on a daily basis.

Rocco posted threatening notices in all staff common areas and the chef took charge of the scheduling from the executive sous-chef, Bob, explaining that he wanted to phase out suspected thieves from the schedule and have them replaced. After three months, only 6 original employees of 26 remained, most having been forced to quit and one employee having been dismissed by the chef for a violent outburst. No formal training for new employees, performance evaluations, or raises took place. Rocco explained to staff that there was no money in the budget for such activities. With the high rate of turnover, the rate of missing inventory slowed marginally at first, but soon picked up speed

again, while the quality of the food the kitchen produced was still inconsistent—at best.

One day, executive sous-chef Bob was putting empty milk crates in the loading dock when he spotted something suspicious. Upon investigation, he found a heavily wrapped package that contained six pounds of ribs with all the trimmings. He left the evidence in place and consulted Stanley on the matter. Bob was ordered to keep an eye on the area, effectively setting a trap. Later that afternoon, Bob spotted two of the few remaining long-term, productive employees quietly leaving the facility through the loading dock. Bob not only found Jeff with the ribs, but the pastry chef, Doug, was pulling out a bag of assorted canned goods and a cake from under a pile of empty boxes.

This case is based on original work by Judson Bray, from *Organizational Behaviour: Canadian Cases and Exercises*, 5th ed., by Randy Hoffman and Fred Ruemper (Concord, ON: Captus Press Inc., 2004), pp. 54–57. Reprinted with permission of Captus Press Inc. www.captus.com.

1. What are the problems facing Club Chaos and what are some possible reasons for these problems?

2. In learning theory terms, what behaviours are being reinforced and punished? What behaviours are not being reinforced?

3. Consider the role of the situation and personality in the case. What factors explain employee behaviours? Does it make sense to change the people or the situation?

4. What kind of system was Rocco implementing when he posted threatening notices, and what effect did this have on employees' behaviour?

5. How might operant learning theory principles be used to increase desirable behaviours and eliminate undesirable behaviours? Be specific in terms of the relevant behaviours you would try to increase and decrease.

6. Discuss the potential of organizational learning practices for improving the situation at Club Chaos. What organizational learning practices would you recommend and how should they be implemented?

CHAPTER 3

Perception, Attribution, and Judgment of Others

BANK OF MONTREAL (BMO)

In 1991, Bank of Montreal (BMO) executives discovered an alarming statistic. Although women made up 75 percent of the company's workforce, only 9 percent of the company's executives and 13 percent of its senior managers were women. Overall, 91 percent of the company's women employees were in nonmanagement positions. Then CEO Tony Comper described the bank's performance in achieving equality for women as "dismal."

In order to address this problem, the executives created a Task Force on the Advancement of Women to identify and break down the barriers to women's advancement and to develop an action plan. Members of the task force interviewed almost 300 employees and conducted the company's largest employee survey ever, with more than 9000 responses.

Based on the results, the task force identified three major barriers to women's advancement. First, it was found that many employees in the company had false assumptions about women. In fact, a key finding was that women were not advancing because of stereotypical attitudes, myths, and "conventional wisdom." For example, women at the bank were perceived as either too young or too old to compete with men for promotions. They were seen as less committed to their careers because they have babies and leave the bank while their children are young. It was believed that more women needed to be better educated to compete in significant numbers with men and that women don't have the "the right stuff" to compete for more senior jobs. Second, the task force discovered that the bank had failed to provide women with the encouragement, opportunities, and the information they needed to advance in their careers. Third, the bank had been unsupportive of employees' personal and family commitments, something that most severely affected women with children.

To remove these barriers, a number of actions were taken. To dispel the myths and faulty stereotypes about the bank's women employees, a document that contained the bank's workforce statistics was distributed to employees. The statistics showed that the age distribution of men and

LEARNING OBJECTIVES

After reading Chapter 3, you should be able to:

1. Define *perception* and discuss some of the general factors that influence perception.

2. Explain *social identity theory* and *Bruner's model* of the perceptual process.

3. Describe the main biases in person perception.

4. Describe how people form *attributions* about the causes of behaviour.

5. Discuss various biases in attribution.

6. Discuss the concepts of *workforce diversity* and valuing diversity.

7. Discuss how racial, ethnic, gender, and age *stereotypes* affect organizational behaviour and what organizations can do to manage diversity.

8. Define *trust* perceptions and *perceived organizational support* and discuss the factors that influence them.

9. Discuss person perception and perceptual biases in human resources.

BMO has received many awards for its Workplace Equality Programs and is a model for how to tie workplace diversity to business success.

women in the bank was nearly equivalent. In response to the myth that women quit the company after having children, the statistics showed that women at all levels except senior management had longer overall service records than men. Regarding the myth that women are not educated enough to take top positions in the bank, the statistics showed that at nonmanagement and junior-management levels, more women had degrees than men. And in response to the myth that women don't have "the right stuff," the statistics indicated that a larger percentage of women than men at all levels received top performance ratings. Thus, contrary to the myths and stereotypes, the bank's female employees were just as qualified for advancement as men in every respect.

Bank of Montreal
www.bmo.com

In addition to removing the stereotypes of the bank's women employees, the action plan also included enhanced training, better posting of job vacancies, redesigned career development opportunities, job information counsellors to help employees determine their suitability for particular positions, and more flexible work arrangements. A monitoring system was also set up to ensure that the bank would examine the rate of women's advancement on a regular basis. Within two years, there were substantial gains in the percentages of women at all management levels, and by 1997, 23 percent of executives were women.

The women's equality initiatives led to an overhaul of the entire diversity system at the bank. Within 13 months of the women's task force, the bank created task forces on the hiring and advancement of aboriginal people, people with disabilities, and members of visible minorities. Once again, it was found that a major barrier involved misperceptions and myths. For example, the task force found that there existed a perception that persons with disabilities were less productive, took more sick leave, and were not qualified. The task force dealt with these misperceptions with information and action plans. For example, managers received training to increase their understanding of applicants with disabilities.

Action plans to improve the hiring and advancement of aboriginal people, people with disabilities, and members of visible minorities included targeted recruitment materials, career guidance, a mentoring program, employee networks, diversity courses and action teams, advisory councils that involve employees in promoting equality, student-employment programs and internships, and partnerships with community groups.

In addition, the bank's managers are required to set goals and action plans for the hiring, development, and promotion of women, aboriginal people, persons with disabilities, and visible minority members as part of the annual business plan process, and they are held accountable for achieving these goals in their annual performance review. Managers who promote equality receive monetary and emotional recognition.

Today, an executive committee oversees equity and diversity issues in the bank. As a result of their efforts, 37 percent of the bank's executives are now women, the number of workers who have a disability or are members of visible minorities has doubled, and the number of aboriginal workers has tripled. Not surprisingly, BMO has received many awards for its Workplace Equality Programs and is now considered a model for how to tie diversity to business success.[1]

Why has the Bank of Montreal made workplace equality and diversity a top business priority? What effect do equality and diversity programs have on employee attitudes and behaviour? And why do organizations often harbour false assumptions and myths about women and visible minority employees? These are the kinds of questions that we will attempt to answer in this chapter. First, we will define perception and examine how various aspects of the perceiver, the object or person being perceived, and the situation influence perception. Following this, we will present a theory and model of the perceptual process, and we will consider some of the perceptual tendencies that we employ in forming impressions of people and attributing causes to their behaviour. We will then examine the role of perception in achieving a diverse workforce and how to manage diversity, perceptions of trust and perceived organizational support, and person perception in human resources. In general, you will learn that perception and attribution influence who gets into organizations, how they are treated as members, and how they interpret this treatment.

WHAT IS PERCEPTION?

Perception. The process of interpreting the messages of our senses to provide order and meaning to the environment.

Perception is the process of interpreting the messages of our senses to provide order and meaning to the environment. Perception helps sort out and organize the complex and varied input received by our senses of sight, smell, touch, taste, and hearing. The key word in this definition is *interpreting*. People frequently base their actions on the

"I'm only firing you to impress the people that I'm not firing."

interpretation of reality that their perceptual system provides, rather than on reality itself. If you perceive your pay to be very low, you might seek employment in another firm. The reality—that you are the best-paid person in your department—will not matter if you are unaware of the fact. However, to go a step further, you might be aware that you are the best-paid person and *still* perceive your pay as low in comparison with that of the CEO of BMO or your ostentatious next-door neighbour.

Some of the most important perceptions that influence organizational behaviour are the perceptions that organizational members have of each other. Because of this, we will concentrate on person perception in this chapter.

COMPONENTS OF PERCEPTION

Perception has three components—a perceiver, a target that is being perceived, and some situational context in which the perception is occurring. Each of these components influences the perceiver's impression or interpretation of the target (Exhibit 3.1).

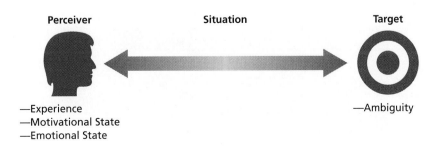

Perceiver	Situation	Target
—Experience		—Ambiguity
—Motivational State		
—Emotional State		

EXHIBIT 3.1
Factors that influence perception.

The Perceiver

The perceiver's experience, needs, and emotions can affect his or her perceptions of a target.

Fortune 500
www.money.cnn.com/
magazines/fortune/
fortune500/

One of the most important characteristics of the perceiver that influences his or her impressions of a target is experience. Past experiences lead the perceiver to develop expectations, and these expectations affect current perceptions. An interesting example of the influence of experience on perception is shown in Exhibit 3.2. It illustrates the perceptions of 268 managerial personnel in a Fortune 500 company concerning the influence of race and gender on promotion opportunities. As you can see, Caucasian men were much less likely to perceive race or gender barriers to promotion than were Caucasian women, non-Caucasian men, and non-Caucasian women.[2] Remember, these people were ostensibly viewing the same "objective" promotion system.

Frequently, our needs unconsciously influence our perceptions by causing us to perceive what we wish to perceive. Research has demonstrated that perceivers who have been deprived of food will tend to "see" more edible things in ambiguous pictures than will well-fed observers. Similarly, lonely university students might misperceive the most innocent actions of members of the opposite sex as indicating interest in them.

Emotions, such as anger, happiness, or fear, can influence our perceptions. We have all had the experience of misperceiving the innocent comment of a friend or acquaintance when we were angry. For example, a worker who is upset about not getting a promotion might perceive the consolation provided by a co-worker as gloating condescension. On the other hand, consider the worker who does get a promotion. She is so happy that she fails to notice how upset her co-worker is because he was not the one promoted.

Perceptual defence. The tendency for the perceptual system to defend the perceiver against unpleasant emotions.

In some cases, our perceptual system serves to defend us against unpleasant emotions. This phenomenon is known as **perceptual defence**. We have all experienced cases in which we "see what we want to see" or "hear what we want to hear." In many of these instances, our perceptual system is working to ensure that we do not see or hear things that are threatening.

The Target

Perception involves interpretation and the addition of meaning to the target, and ambiguous targets are especially susceptible to interpretation and addition. Perceivers have a need to resolve such ambiguities. You might be tempted to believe that providing more information about the target will improve perceptual accuracy. Unfortunately, this is not always the case. Writing clearer memos might not always get the message across. Similarly, assigning minority workers to a prejudiced manager will not always improve his or her perceptions of their true abilities. As we shall see shortly, the perceiver does not or cannot always use all the information provided by the target. In these cases, a reduction in ambiguity might not be accompanied by greater accuracy.

EXHIBIT 3.2
Ratings of the perceived importance of race and gender for promotion opportunity in executive jobs.

Note: Table values are the percentages saying that race or gender was important or very important. N = number of cases. Source: Cox, T., Jr. (1993). *Cultural diversity in organizations: Theory, research, & practice.* San Francisco: Berrett-Koehler, p. 119.

	Caucasian Men (N = 123)	Caucasian Women (N = 76)	Non-Caucasian Men (N = 52)	Non-Caucasian Women (N = 17)
Race	26	62	75	76
Gender	31	87	71	82

The Situation

Every instance of perception occurs in some situational context, and this context can affect what one perceives. The most important effect that the situation can have is to add information about the target. Imagine a casual critical comment about your performance from your boss the week before she is to decide whether or not you will be promoted. You will likely perceive this comment very differently from how you would if you were not up for promotion. Also, a worker might perceive a racial joke overheard on the job very differently before and after racial strife has occurred in the plant. In both of these examples, the perceiver and the target are the same, but the perception of the target changes with the situation.

SOCIAL IDENTITY THEORY

In the previous section, we described how characteristics of the perceiver, target, and the situation influence the perceiver's interpretation of the target. In this section, we discuss a theory called social identity theory to help us understand how this happens. Let's begin with a simple question: "Who are you?" Chances are when you answer this question you say things like, "student," "Canadian," "accountant," and so on. In other words, you respond in terms of various social categories to which you believe you belong. This is what social identity theory is all about.

According to social identity theory, people form perceptions of themselves based on their characteristics and memberships in social categories. As a result, our sense of self is composed of a personal identity and a social identity. Our *personal identity* is based on our unique personal characteristics, such as our interests, abilities, and traits. *Social identity* is based on our perception that we belong to various social groups, such as our gender, nationality, religion, occupation, and so on. Personal and social identities help us answer the question, "Who am I?"

But why and how do we do this? As individuals, we categorize ourselves and others to make sense of and understand the social environment. The choice of specific categories depends on what is most salient and appropriate to the situation. For example, we might define people in a meeting according to their job title. Once a category is chosen, we tend to see members of that category as embodying the most typical attributes of that category, or what are called "prototypes." Similarly, once we locate ourselves in a social category we tend to perceive ourselves as embodying the prototypical characteristics of the category. In this way, we develop a sense of who and what we are as well as our values, beliefs, and ways of thinking, acting, and feeling.[3]

In addition to forming self-perceptions based on our social memberships, we also form perceptions of others based on their memberships in social categories. This is because social identities are relational and comparative. In other words, we define members of a category relative to members of other categories. For example, the category of professor is meaningful in relation to the category of student. As the comparison category changes, so will certain aspects of the focal social identity. So when the authors of this text are in the classroom, they are perceived as professors by their students and as having whatever attributes the students attribute to professors. However, one of the authors of this text lives next door to a university student who perceives him not as a professor, but as a "baby boomer." Notice how her social categorization differs from those of the students in the classroom. As a result, her perception of the author will also differ because the attributes and characteristics associated with the age category of a "baby boomer" differ from those of a "professor."

Social identity theory helps us understand how the components of the perceptual system operate in the formation of perceptions. We perceive people in terms of the attributes and characteristics that we associate with their social category relative to other categories. Thus, your perception of others is a function of how you categorize yourself (e.g., student) and your target (e.g., professor). If the situation changes, so might the categorization and the relation between the perceiver and the target. For example, in a hospital, medical students might be perceived as doctors by nurses and patients, but in the classroom they are likely to be perceived as medical students by their professors.[4]

Because people tend to perceive members of their own social categories in more positive and favourable ways than those who are different and belong to other categories, social identity theory is useful for understanding stereotyping and discrimination, topics we discuss later in this chapter. Now let's turn to a more detailed understanding of the perceptual process.

A MODEL OF THE PERCEPTUAL PROCESS

Jerome Bruner and Theory
www.gwu.edu/~tip/
bruner.html

In the previous section, we described how we form perceptions of ourselves and others based on social categories. But exactly how does the perceiver go about putting together the information contained in the target and the situation to form a picture of the target? Respected psychologist Jerome Bruner has developed a model of the perceptual process that can provide a useful framework for this discussion.[5] According to Bruner, when the perceiver encounters an unfamiliar target, the perceiver is very open to the informational cues contained in the target and the situation surrounding it. In this unfamiliar state, the perceiver really needs information on which to base perceptions of the target and will actively seek out cues to resolve this ambiguity. Gradually, the perceiver encounters some familiar cues (note the role of the perceiver's experience here) that enable her to make a crude categorization of the target, which follows from social identity theory. At this point, the cue search becomes less open and more selective. The perceiver begins to search out cues that confirm the categorization of the target. As this categorization becomes stronger, the perceiver actively ignores or even distorts cues that violate initial perceptions (see the left side of Exhibit 3.3). This does not mean that an early categorization cannot be changed. It does mean, however, that it will take a good many contradictory cues before one recategorizes the target, and that these cues will have to overcome the expectations that have been developed.

Let's clarify your understanding of Bruner's perceptual model with an example, shown on the right side of Exhibit 3.3. Imagine that a woman who works as an engineer for a large aircraft company is trying to size up a newly hired co-worker. Since he is an unfamiliar target, she will probably be especially open to any cues that might provide information about him. In the course of her cue search, she discovers that he has

EXHIBIT 3.3
Bruner's model of the perceptual process and an example.

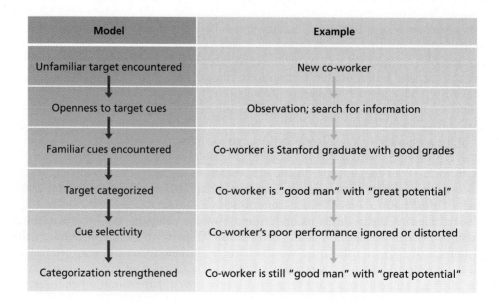

Model	Example
Unfamiliar target encountered	New co-worker
Openness to target cues	Observation; search for information
Familiar cues encountered	Co-worker is Stanford graduate with good grades
Target categorized	Co-worker is "good man" with "great potential"
Cue selectivity	Co-worker's poor performance ignored or distorted
Categorization strengthened	Co-worker is still "good man" with "great potential"

a Master's degree in aeronautical engineering from Stanford University, and that he graduated with top grades. These are familiar cues because she knows that Stanford is a top school in the field, and she has worked with many excellent Stanford graduates. She then proceeds to categorize her new co-worker as a "good man" with "great potential." With these perceptions, she takes a special interest in observing his performance, which is good for several months. This increases the strength of her initial categorization. Gradually, however, the engineer's performance deteriorates for some reason, and his work becomes less and less satisfactory. This is clear to everyone except the other engineer, who continues to see him as adequate and excuses his most obvious errors as stemming from external factors beyond his control.

Bruner's model demonstrates three important characteristics of the perceptual process. First, perception is *selective*. Perceivers do not use all the available cues, and those they do use are thus given special emphasis. This means that our perception is efficient, and this efficiency can both aid and hinder our perceptual accuracy. Second, Bruner's model illustrates that our perceptual system works to paint a constant picture of the target. Perceptual *constancy* refers to the tendency for the target to be perceived in the same way over time or across situations. We have all had the experience of "getting off on the wrong foot" with a teacher or a boss and finding it difficult to change his or her constant perception of us. Third, the perceptual system also creates a consistent picture of the target. Perceptual *consistency* refers to the tendency to select, ignore, and distort cues in such a manner that they fit together to form a homogeneous picture of the target. We strive for consistency in our perception of people. We do not tend to see the same person as both good and bad or dependable and untrustworthy. Often, we distort cues that are discrepant with our general image of a person to make the cues consistent with this image.

To test your understanding of Bruner's model, refer back to the example in Exhibit 3.3 and explain the role of selectivity, constancy, and consistency. In the next section, we consider some specific perceptual biases that contribute to selectivity, constancy, and consistency in our perception of people.

BASIC BIASES IN PERSON PERCEPTION

For accuracy's sake, it would be convenient if we could encounter others under laboratory conditions, in a vacuum or a test tube, as it were. Because the real world lacks such ideal conditions, the impressions that we form of others are susceptible to a number of perceptual biases.

Primacy and Recency Effects

Given the examples of person perception that we have discussed thus far, you might gather that we form our impressions of others fairly quickly. One reason for this fast impression formation is our tendency to rely on the cues that we encounter early in a relationship. This reliance on early cues or first impressions is known as the **primacy effect**. Primacy often has a lasting impact. Thus, the worker who can favourably impress his or her boss in the first few days on the job is in an advantageous position due to primacy. Similarly, the labour negotiator who comes across as "tough" on the first day of contract talks might find this image difficult to shake as the talks continue. Primacy is a form of selectivity, and its lasting effects illustrate the operation of constancy. Sometimes, a **recency effect** occurs in which people give undue weight to the cues they encountered most recently. In other words, last impressions count most. Landing a big contract today might be perceived as excusing a whole year's bad sales performance.

Primacy effect. The tendency for a perceiver to rely on early cues or first impressions.

Recency effect. The tendency for a perceiver to rely on recent cues or last impressions.

Reliance on Central Traits

Central traits. Personal characteristics of a target person that are of particular interest to a perceiver.

Even though perceivers tend to rely on early information when developing their perceptions, these early cues do not receive equal weight. People tend to organize their perceptions around **central traits**, personal characteristics of the target that are of special interest to them. In developing her perceptions of her new co-worker, the experienced engineer seemed to organize her impressions around the trait of intellectual capacity. The centrality of traits depends on the perceiver's interests and the situation. Thus, not all engineers would organize their perceptions of the new worker around his intellectual abilities, and the established engineer might not use this trait as a central factor in forming impressions of the people she meets at a party.

Central traits often have a very powerful influence on our perceptions of others. Physical appearance is a common central trait in work settings that is related to a variety of job-related outcomes. Research shows an overwhelming tendency for those who are "attractive" to also be perceived as "good," especially when it comes to judgments about their social competence, qualifications, and potential job success.[6] In general, research shows that conventionally attractive people are more likely to fare better than unattractive people in terms of a variety of job-related outcomes, including employment potential, getting hired, being chosen as a business partner, given good performance evaluations, or being promoted.[7] Physical height, which is one of the most obvious aspects of appearance, has also been found to be related to job performance, promotions, and career success.[8] Taller and more attractive people are also more likely to be paid more, as discussed in "Research Focus: *Physical Attractiveness and Height Pay Off.*"

Implicit Personality Theories

Implicit personality theories. Personal theories that people have about which personality characteristics go together.

Each of us has a "theory" about which personality characteristics go together. These are called **implicit personality theories**. Perhaps you expect hardworking people to also be honest. Perhaps you feel that people of average intelligence tend to be most friendly. To the extent that such implicit theories are inaccurate, they provide a basis for misunderstanding.[9] The employee who assumes that her very formal boss is also insensitive might be reluctant to discuss a work-related problem with him that could be solved fairly easily.

Projection

Projection. The tendency for perceivers to attribute their own thoughts and feelings to others.

In the absence of information to the contrary, and sometimes in spite of it, people often assume that others are like themselves. This tendency to attribute one's own thoughts and feelings to others is called **projection**. In some cases, projection is an efficient and sensible perceptual strategy. After all, people with similar backgrounds or interests often *do* think and feel similarly. Thus, it is not unreasonable for a capitalistic businessperson to assume that other businesspeople favour the free enterprise system and disapprove of government intervention in this system. However, projection can also lead to perceptual difficulties. The chairperson who feels that an issue has been resolved and perceives committee members to feel the same way might be very surprised when a vote is taken. The honest warehouse manager who perceives others as honest might find stock disappearing. In the case of threatening or undesirable characteristics, projection can serve as a form of perceptual defence. The dishonest worker might say, "Sure I steal from the company, but so does everyone else." Such perceptions can be used to justify the perceiver's thievery.

Stereotyping

One way to form a consistent impression of other people is simply to assume that they have certain characteristics by virtue of some category that they fall into as suggested

Physical Attractiveness and Height Pay Off

Consistent with evidence that physical attractiveness is related to obtaining employment and promotion, more attractive employees have also been found to enjoy more economic success in their careers. A recent study looked at the careers of 2500 law students from a prestigious law school in the United States. An independent panel of raters rated the students' appearance on a scale from one to five. Five years after graduation, those of above-average attractiveness were earning eight to nine percent more than those of below-average attractiveness. After 15 years, those of above-average appearance were earning 12 to 13 percent more.

The research on attractiveness and salaries also suggests that attractiveness is more consistently related to economic success for men than for women. Roszell, Kennedy, and Grabb (1989) examined the relationship of attractiveness to income attainment for over 1000 Canadians. Attractive persons earned higher annual salaries than less attractive persons. With each increase in rated attractiveness on a five-point scale, the 1981 annual income of the respondent increased by $1988. After controlling for respondent gender, the gender composition of the job, and 1979 salaries, this figure dropped to $1046, but was still statistically significant. This relationship was found for men, older employees, and those engaged in male-dominated occupations, but not for women, younger employees, and those in female-dominated occupations.

In another study, Frieze, Olson, and Russell (1991) asked a group of people with corporate management experience to rate the physical attractiveness of 700 MBA graduates on a five-point scale. The starting salaries of male graduates receiving the highest attractiveness rating were approximately $5000 a year more than those receiving the lowest attractiveness rating. After five years, those receiving the highest rating earned $10 000 more than those receiving the lowest

rating. Attractiveness had no impact on starting salaries of women but was related to later salaries, although not as strongly as for men. For each increment in attractiveness on the five-point scale, women earned $2000 more in salary five years later.

Several studies have also found physical height to be positively related to income. In one study, Good, Olson, and Frieze (1986) used height, weight, and body mass (weight relative to height) as indicators of physical attractiveness. They surveyed over 2000 MBA graduates of the University of Pittsburgh who graduated between 1973 and 1982. For men, weight but not height was found to predict starting salary, and both height and weight predicted the current (1983) salary. For each one-inch increase in height, the salary of the man was $600 higher. Overweight men earned $4000 less in salary than those of men with a normal weight. However, neither of these variables predicted the starting and current salary of the women in the sample.

More recently, Timothy Judge and Daniel Cable found that height was positively related to income for both men and women, an effect that appears to be stable over the course of one's career. Their results indicate that each one-inch increase in height results in a predicted increase in annual earnings of about $800. Further, an individual who is 72 inches tall would be expected to earn $5525 more per year than someone who is 65 inches tall, or almost $166 000 more across a 30-year career.

Source: Excerpted from Stone, E.F., Stone D.L., &. Dipboye, R.L. (1992). Stigmas in organizations: Race, handicaps, and physical unattractiveness. In K. Kelley (Ed.), *Issues, theory, and research in industrial/organizational psychology*. New York: Elsevier, 419–420; McFarland, J. (1996, January 23). The ugly truth: Looks count. *Globe and Mail*, B12; Judge, T.A., & Cable, D.M. (2004). The effect of physical height on workplace success and income: Preliminary test of a theoretical model. *Journal of Applied Psychology, 89*, 428–441.

by social identity theory. This perceptual tendency is known as **stereotyping**, or the tendency to generalize about people in a social category and ignore variations among them. Categories on which people might base a stereotype include race, age, gender, ethnic background, social class, occupation, and so on.[10] There are three specific aspects to stereotyping.[11]

Stereotyping. The tendency to generalize about people in a certain social category and ignore variations among them.

- We distinguish some category of people (college professors).
- We assume that the individuals in this category have certain traits (absent-minded, disorganized, ivory-tower mentality).

● We perceive that everyone in this category possesses these traits ("All my professors this year will be absent-minded, disorganized, and have an ivory-tower mentality").

People can evoke stereotypes with incredibly little information. In a "first impressions" study, the mere designation of a woman as preferring to be addressed as "Ms." led to her being perceived as more masculine, more achievement oriented, and less likeable than those who preferred the traditional titles "Miss" or "Mrs."[12]

Not all stereotypes are unfavourable. You probably hold favourable stereotypes of the social categories of which you are a member, such as student. However, these stereotypes are often less well developed and less rigid than others you hold. Stereotypes help us develop impressions of ambiguous targets, and we are usually pretty familiar with the people in our own groups. In addition, this contact helps us appreciate individual differences among group members, and such differences work against the development of stereotypes.

Language can be easily twisted to turn neutral or even favourable information into a basis for unfavourable stereotypes. For example, if British people do tend to be reserved, it is fairly easy to interpret this reserve as snobbishness. Similarly, if women who achieve executive positions have had to be assertive, it is easy to interpret this assertiveness as pushiness.

Knowing a person's occupation or field of study, we often make assumptions about his or her behaviour and personality. Accountants might be stereotyped as compulsive, precise, and one-dimensional, while engineers might be perceived as cold and calculating. Reflect on your own stereotypes of psychology or business students.

On average, not all stereotypes are inaccurate. You probably hold fairly correct stereotypes about the educational level of the typical university professor and the on-the-job demeanour of the typical telephone operator. These accurate stereotypes ease the task of developing perceptions of others. However, it is probably safe to say that most stereotypes are inaccurate, especially when we use them to develop perceptions of specific individuals. This follows from the fact that stereotypes are most likely to develop when we do not have good information about a particular group.

This raises an interesting question: If many stereotypes are inaccurate, why do they persist?[13] After all, reliance on inaccurate information to develop our perceptions would seem to be punishing in the long run. In reality, a couple of factors work to *reinforce* inaccurate stereotypes. For one thing, even incorrect stereotypes help us process information about others quickly and efficiently. Sometimes, it is easier for the perceiver to rely on an inaccurate stereotype than it is to discover the true nature of the target. The male manager who is required to recommend one of his 20 employees for a promotion might find it easier to automatically rule out promoting a woman than to carefully evaluate all his employees, regardless of gender. Second, inaccurate stereotypes are often reinforced by selective perception and the selective application of language that was discussed above. The Hispanic worker who stereotypes all non-Hispanic managers as unfair might be on the lookout for behaviours to confirm these stereotypes and fail to notice examples of fair and friendly treatment. If such treatment *is* noticed, it might be perceived as patronizing rather than helpful.

ATTRIBUTION: PERCEIVING CAUSES AND MOTIVES

Attribution. The process by which causes or motives are assigned to explain people's behaviour.

Thus far, we have considered social identity theory, Bruner's model of perception, and discussed some specific perceptual tendencies that operate as we form impressions of others. We will now consider a further aspect of impression formation—how we perceive people's motives. **Attribution** is the process by which we assign causes or motives to explain people's behaviour. The attribution process is important because many rewards and punishments in organizations are based on judgments about what really caused a target person to behave in a certain way.

In making attributions about behaviour, an important goal is to determine whether the behaviour is caused by dispositional or situational factors. **Dispositional attributions** suggest that some personality or intellectual characteristic unique to the person is responsible for the behaviour, and that the behaviour thus reflects the "true person." If we explain a behaviour as a function of intelligence, greed, friendliness, or laziness, we are making dispositional attributions. In general, the business press attributed the turnaround of the Chrysler Corporation to Lee Iacocca's leadership skills and market savvy, not to government loan guarantees or an improving economy.

Situational attributions suggest that the external situation or environment in which the target person exists was responsible for the behaviour, and that the person might have had little control over the behaviour. If we explain behaviour as a function of bad weather, good luck, proper tools, or poor advice, we are making situational attributions.

Obviously, it would be nice to be able to read minds to understand people's motives. Since we cannot do this, we are forced to rely on external cues and make inferences from these cues. Research indicates that as we gain experience with the behaviour of a target person, three implicit questions guide our decisions as to whether we should attribute the behaviour to dispositional or situational causes.[14]

- Does the person engage in the behaviour regularly and consistently? (Consistency cues)
- Do most people engage in the behaviour, or is it unique to this person? (Consensus cues)
- Does the person engage in the behaviour in many situations, or is it distinctive to one situation? (Distinctiveness cues)

Let's examine consistency, consensus, and distinctiveness cues in more detail.

Consistency Cues

Consistency cues reflect how consistently a person engages in some behaviour over time. For example, unless we see clear evidence of external constraints that force a behaviour to occur, we tend to perceive behaviour that a person performs regularly as indicative of his or her true motives. In other words, high consistency leads to dispositional attributions. Thus, one might assume that the professor who has generous office hours and is always there for consultation really cares about his students. Similarly, we are likely to make dispositional attributions about workers who are consistently good or poor performers, perhaps perceiving the former as "dedicated" and the latter as "lazy." When behaviour occurs inconsistently, we begin to consider situational attributions. For example, if a person's performance cycles between mediocre and excellent, we might look to variations in workload to explain the cycles.

Consensus Cues

Consensus cues reflect how a person's behaviour compares to that of others. In general, acts that deviate from social expectations provide us with more information about the actor's motives than conforming behaviours do. Thus, unusual, low-consensus behaviour leads to more dispositional attributions than typical, high-consensus behaviour. The person who acts differently from the majority is seen as revealing more of his or her true motives. The informational effects of low-consensus behaviour are magnified when the actor is expected to suffer negative consequences because of the deviance. Consider the job applicant who makes favourable statements about the role of big business in society while being interviewed for a job at General Motors. Such statements are so predictable in this situation that the interviewer can place little confidence in what they really indicate about the candidate's true feelings and motives. On

Dispositional attributions. Explanations for behaviour based on an actor's personality or intellect.

Situational attributions. Explanations for behaviour based on an actor's external situation or environment.

Consistency cues. Attribution cues that reflect how consistently a person engages in some behaviour over time.

Consensus cues. Attribution cues that reflect how a person's behaviour compares with that of others.

General Motors
www.gm.com

the other hand, imagine an applicant who makes critical comments about big business in the same situation. Such comments are hardly expected and could clearly lead to rejection. In this case, the interviewer would be more confident about the applicant's true disposition regarding big business.

A corollary to this suggests that we place more emphasis on people's private actions than their public actions when assessing their motives.[15] When our actions are not open to public scrutiny, we are more likely to act out our genuine motives and feelings. Thus, we place more emphasis on a co-worker's private statements about his boss than we do on his public relations with the boss.

Distinctiveness Cues

Distinctiveness cues.
Attribution cues that reflect the extent to which a person engages in some behaviour across a variety of situations.

Distinctiveness cues reflect the extent to which a person engages in some behaviour across a variety of situations. When a behaviour occurs across a variety of situations, it lacks distinctiveness, and the observer is prone to provide a dispositional attribution about its cause. We reason that the behaviour reflects a person's true motives if it "stands up" in a variety of environments. Thus, the professor who has generous office hours, stays after class to talk to students, and attends student functions is seen as truly student oriented. The worker whose performance was good in his first job as well as several subsequent jobs is perceived as having real ability. When a behaviour is highly distinctive, in that it occurs in only one situation, we are likely to assume that some aspect of the situation caused the behaviour. If the only student-oriented behaviour that we observe is generous office hours, we assume that they are dictated by department policy. If a worker performed well on only one job, back in 1985, we suspect that his uncle owns the company!

Attribution in Action

Frequently, observers of real life behaviour have information at hand about consistency, consensus, and distinctiveness. Let's take an example that shows how the observer puts such information together in forming attributions. At the same time, the example will serve to review the previous discussion. Imagine that Smith, Jones, and Kelley are employees who work in separate firms. Each is absent from work today, and a manager must develop an attribution about the cause to decide which action is warranted.

- *Smith*—Smith is absent a lot, his co-workers are seldom absent, and he was absent a lot in his previous job.
- *Jones*—Jones is absent a lot, her co-workers are also absent a lot, but she was almost never absent in her previous job.
- *Kelley*—Kelley is seldom absent, his co-workers are seldom absent, and he was seldom absent in his previous job.

Just what kind of attributions are managers likely to make regarding the absences of Smith, Jones, and Kelley? Smith's absence is highly consistent, it is a low-consensus behaviour, and it is not distinctive, since he was absent in his previous job. As shown in Exhibit 3.4, this combination of cues is very likely to prompt a dispositional attribution, perhaps that Smith is lazy or irresponsible. Jones is also absent consistently, but it is high-consensus behaviour in that her peers also exhibit absence. In addition, the behaviour is highly distinctive—she is absent only on this job. As indicated, this combination of cues will usually result in a situational attribution, perhaps that working conditions are terrible, or that the boss is nasty. Finally, Kelley's absence is inconsistent. In addition, it is similar to that of co-workers and not distinctive, in that he was inconsistently absent on his previous job as well. As shown, this combination of cues suggests that some temporary, short-term situational factor causes his absence. It is possible that a sick child occasionally requires him to stay home.

	Consistency	Consensus	Distinctiveness	Likely Attribution
Smith	High	Low	Low	Disposition
Jones	High	High	High	Situation
Kelley	Low	High	Low	Temporary Situation

EXHIBIT 3.4
Cue combinations and resulting attributions.

Biases in Attribution

As the preceding section indicates, observers often operate in a rational, logical manner in forming attributions about behaviour. The various cue combinations and the resulting attributions have a sensible appearance. This does not mean that such attributions are always correct, but that they do represent good bets about why some behaviour occurred. Having made this observation, it would be naive to assume that attributions are always free from bias or error. Earlier, we discussed a number of very basic perceptual biases, and it stands to reason that the complex task of attribution would also be open to bias. Let's consider three biases in attribution: the fundamental attribution error, actor–observer effect, and self-serving bias.[16]

Fundamental Attribution Error. Suppose you make a mistake in attributing a cause to someone else's behaviour. Would you be likely to err on the side of a dispositional cause or a situational cause? Substantial evidence indicates that when we make judgments about the behaviour of people other than ourselves, we tend to overemphasize dispositional explanations at the expense of situational explanations. This is called the **fundamental attribution error.**[17]

Why does the fundamental attribution error occur? For one thing, we often discount the strong effects that social roles can have on behaviour. We might see bankers as truly conservative people because we ignore the fact that their occupational role and their employer dictate that they act conservatively. Second, many people whom we observe are seen in rather constrained, constant situations (at work, or at school) that reduce our appreciation of how their behaviour can vary in other situations. Thus, we fail to realize that the observed behaviour is distinctive to a particular situation. That conservative banker might actually be a weekend skydiver!

The fundamental attribution error can lead to problems for managers of poorly performing employees. It suggests that dispositional explanations for the poor performance will sometimes be made even when situational factors are the true cause. Laziness or low aptitude might be cited, while poor training or a bad sales territory is ignored. However, this is less likely when the manager has had actual experience in performing the employee's job and is thus aware of situational roadblocks to good performance.[18]

Fundamental attribution error. The tendency to overemphasize dispositional explanations for behaviour at the expense of situational explanations.

Actor–Observer Effect. It is not surprising that actors and observers often view the causes for the actor's behaviour very differently. This difference in attributional perspectives is called the **actor–observer effect.**[19] Specifically, while the observer might be busy committing the fundamental attribution error, the actor might be emphasizing the role of the situation in explaining his or her own behaviour. Thus, as actors, we are often particularly sensitive to those environmental events that led us to be late or absent. As observers of the same behaviour in others, we are more likely to invoke dispositional causes.

We see some of the most striking examples of this effect in cases of illegal behaviour, such as price fixing and the bribery of government officials. The perpetrators and those close to them often cite stiff competition or management pressure as causes of their ethical lapses. Observers see the perpetrators as immoral or unintelligent.[20]

Actor–observer effect. The propensity for actors and observers to view the causes of the actor's behaviour differently.

Why are actors prone to attribute much of their own behaviour to situational causes? First, they might be more aware than observers of the constraints and advantages that the environment offered. At the same time, they are aware of their private thoughts, feelings, and intentions regarding the behaviour, all of which might be unknown to the observer. Thus, I might know that I sincerely wanted to get to the meeting on time, that I left home extra early, and that the accident that delayed me was truly unusual. My boss might be unaware of all of this information and figure that I am just unreliable.

Self-serving bias. The tendency to take credit for successful outcomes and to deny responsibility for failures.

Self-Serving Bias. It has probably already occurred to you that certain forms of attributions have the capacity to make us feel good or bad about ourselves. In fact, people have a tendency to take credit and responsibility for successful outcomes of their behaviour and to deny credit and responsibility for failures.[21] This tendency is called **self-serving bias**, and it is interesting because it suggests that people will explain the very same behaviour differently on the basis of events that happened *after* the behaviour occurred. If the vice-president of marketing champions a product that turns out to be a sales success, she might attribute this to her retailing savvy. If the very same marketing process leads to failure, she might attribute this to the poor performance of the marketing research firm that she used. Notice that the self-serving bias can overcome the tendency for actors to attribute their behaviour to situational factors. In this example, the vice-president invokes a dispositional explanation ("I'm an intelligent, competent person") when the behaviour is successful.

Self-serving bias can reflect intentional self-promotion or excuse making. However, again, it is possible that it reflects unique information on the part of the actor. Especially when behaviour has negative consequences, the actor might scan the environment and find situational causes for the failure.[22] To be sure, when a student does very well on an exam he is very likely to make a dispositional attribution. However, upon receiving a failing grade, the same student is much more likely to find situational causes to explain his grade!

PERSON PERCEPTION AND WORKFORCE DIVERSITY

The realities of workforce diversity have become an important factor for many organizations in recent years. **Workforce diversity** refers to differences among employees or potential recruits in characteristics such as gender, race, age, religion, cultural background, physical ability, or sexual orientation. The interest in diversity stems from at least two broad facts. First, the workforce is becoming more diverse. Second, there is growing recognition that many organizations have not successfully managed workforce diversity.

Workforce diversity. Differences among recruits and employees in characteristics such as gender, race, age, religion, cultural background, physical ability, or sexual orientation.

The Changing Workplace

As we mentioned in Chapter 1, the composition of the labour force is changing.[23] Thirty years ago, it was mainly Caucasian and male. Now, changing immigration patterns, the aging of baby boomers, and the increasing movement of women into paid employment make for a lot more variety. Immigrants to Canada from all parts of the world are making the Canadian population and labour force increasingly multicultural and multiethnic. According to Statistics Canada, the number of visible minorities in Canada is expected to double by 2017 and will form more than half the population in greater Toronto and Vancouver. If current trends continue, then one in every five persons in Canada will be non-white when Canada celebrates its 150th birthday in 2017.[24] And in less than a decade, 48 percent of Canada's working-age population will be between the ages of 45 and 64.[25]

Not only is the labour pool changing, but many organizations are seeking to recruit more representatively from this pool so that they employ people who reflect their customer base—an effort to better mirror their markets. This is especially true in the growing service sector, where contact between organizational members and customers is very direct. As discussed in the chapter opening vignette, the Bank of Montreal has been very active in developing programs to hire, develop, and promote visible minorities, women, aboriginal people, and disabled persons, as have many other companies, including the YMCA in Toronto, Shell Canada Ltd., Federal Express Canada Ltd., the Royal Bank of Canada (RBC), and the RCMP, among others.[26]

The changing employment pool is not the only factor that has prompted interest in diversity issues. Globalization, mergers, and strategic alliances mean that many employees are required to interact with people from substantially different national or corporate cultures. Compounding all this is an increased emphasis on teamwork as a means of job design and quality enhancement.

Valuing Diversity

In the past, organizations were thought to be doing the right thing if they merely tolerated diversity—that is, if they engaged in fair hiring and employment practices with respect to women and minorities. Firms were considered to be doing especially well if they assisted these people to "fit in" with the mainstream corporate culture by "fixing" what was different about them.[27] For example, women managers were sometimes given assertiveness training to enable them to be as hard-nosed and aggressive as their male counterparts!

Recently, some have argued that organizations should *value* diversity, not just tolerate it or try to blend everyone into a narrow mainstream. To be sure, a critical motive is the basic fairness of valuing diversity. However, there is increasing awareness that diversity and its proper management can yield strategic and competitive advantages. These advantages include the potential for improved problem solving and creativity when diverse perspectives are brought to bear on an organizational problem, such as product or service quality. They also include improved recruiting and marketing when the firm's human resources profile matches that of the labour pool and customer base (see Exhibit 3.5). The results of a recent study indicate that more organizations are adopting diversity as part of their corporate strategy to improve their competitiveness in global markets. Another study found that organizations with more gender-diverse management teams have superior financial performance.[28]

Procter & Gamble
www.pg.ca

At IBM, diversity is embedded in the overall strategy, business goals, and policies toward employees, and the company is now regarded as a leader in workplace diversity. At IBM Canada, 26 percent of those in senior leadership positions are women, and one-third of employees are women.[29] The Bank of Montreal also believes that building a diverse workforce that reflects the communities and individuals it serves and giving all employees equal opportunities to reach their career goals is its greatest competitive advantage. Procter & Gamble also values diversity and even celebrates it. To find out how, see "Applied Focus: *Celebrating Diversity at Procter & Gamble.*"

Employees at Procter & Gamble headquarters in Toronto take part in an international celebration of the company's diversity.

EXHIBIT 3.5
Competitive advantages
to valuing and managing
a diverse workforce.

Source: Cox, T.H., & Blake, S. (1991,
August). Managing cultural diversity:
Implications for organizational com-
petitiveness. *Academy of Management
Executive, 47*, 45–56.

1. Cost Argument	As organizations become more diverse, the cost of a poor job in integrating workers will increase. Those who handle this well will thus create cost advantages over those who don't.
2. Resource-Acquisition Argument	Companies develop reputations on favourability as prospective employers for women and ethnic minorities. Those with the best reputations for managing diversity will win the competition for the best personnel. As the labour pool shrinks and changes composition, this edge will become increasingly important.
3. Marketing Argument	For multinational organizations, the insight and cultural sensitivity that members with roots in other countries bring to the marketing effort should improve these efforts in important ways. The same rationale applies to marketing to subpopulations within domestic operations.
4. Creativity Argument	Diversity of perspectives and less emphasis on conformity to norms of the past (which characterize the modern approach to management of diversity) should improve the level of creativity.
5. Problem-Solving Argument	Heterogeneity in decision and problem solving groups potentially produces better decisions through a wider range of perspectives and more thorough critical analysis of issues.
6. System Flexibility Argument	An implication of the multicultural model for managing diversity is that the system will become less determinant, less standardized, and therefore more fluid. The increased fluidity should create greater flexibility to react to environmental changes (i.e., reactions should be faster and at less cost).

Stereotypes and Workforce Diversity

If there is a single concept that serves as a barrier to valuing diversity, it is the stereo-type. Let's examine several workplace stereotypes and their consequences. Common workplace stereotypes are based on gender, age, race, and ethnicity.

Racial and Ethnic Stereotypes. Racial and ethnic stereotypes are pervasive, persistent, frequently negative, and often self-contradictory. Most of us hold at least some stereotypical views of other races or cultures. Over the years, such stereotypes exhibit remarkable stability unless some major event, such as a war, intervenes to change them. Then, former allies can acquire negative attributes in short order.

Personal experience is unnecessary for such stereotype formation. In one study, people were asked to describe the traits of a number of ethnic groups, including several fictional ones. Although they had never met a Danerian, a Pirenian, or a Wallonian, this did not inhibit them from assigning traits, and those they assigned were usually unfavourable![30] Such stereotypes often contain contradictory elements. A common reaction is to describe a particular group as being too lazy, while at the same time criticizing it for taking one's job opportunities away.

There is a remarkable shortage of serious research into racial and ethnic matters in organizations.[31] Nevertheless, what follows is a sample of some typical findings. Just getting in the door can be a problem:

The Urban Institute
www.urban.org

> *The Urban Institute sent out teams of black and white job applicants with equal credentials. The men applied for the same entry-level jobs in Chicago and Washington, D.C., within hours of each other. They were the same age and physical size, had identical education and work experience, and shared similar personalities. Yet in almost 20% of the 476 audits, whites advanced farther in the hiring process, researchers found.*[32]

APPLIED FOCUS

Celebrating Diversity at Procter & Gamble

Procter & Gamble employees in Toronto and elsewhere around the world celebrate their diversity with jerk pork samosas, Romanian meatballs, and, playfully, Fruit To Go from the gay, bisexual, lesbian, and transgendered employees booth. But it is more than just a feel-good event for the 800 employees who work out of the Toronto headquarters of P&G Canada—employees who represent more than 40 different countries and speak at least 30 different languages. There is a bottom-line purpose as well for the world's largest consumer goods company. For one, employees are more productive in an environment that respects and accepts their differences. Also, by "leveraging that diversity," Procter & Gamble believes it can sell more soap and toothpaste.

The company today is a far cry from the staid, predominantly male, white organization that Tim Penner, president of P&G Canada, joined 27 years ago. "And we're richer for it," said Penner, adding that diversifying the workforce is now a core strategic mission. P&G's continued success in marketing its household-name products—Crest, Mr. Clean, Tide, Pampers—to even more households rides on expanding its reach as the cultural makeup of Canada changes and new consumer markets open up around the world.

"Have fun, learn a lot, enjoy your day and . . . increase your cultural competency," Penner told employees, who were among more than 20 000 company P&G employees joining the "international celebration" in several countries around the world.

At P&G, said Penner, "it's not as superficial as saying someone who is black can market better to black people, or that French people can market better

to French people, that women can market better to women." Instead, it enriches everyone in the organization to have exposure to more cultures and, ultimately, gives all P&G employees a better understanding of their customers. He said the best and most creative decisions are made by teams drawn from a diverse cross-section of employees.

There are eight official "affinity groups" at P&G Canada, one of which is the gay, bisexual, lesbian, and transgendered employee group. The others are the Asian Professional Network, the Black Professional Network, the Latino Network, The French Canadian Network, the Women's Leadership Council, the Christian Network, and the Jewish Network.

These networks exist primarily to make the employees feel more comfortable about participating fully in corporate life, but they also exist as resource groups for colleagues who might want advice on targeting a specific market sector. The fact that colleagues will actively seek out others from different backgrounds signals an acceptance that is not always found in other workplaces. But quite apart from the marketing aspect, there is a real benefit to having more diverse employees involved in making decisions as the company moves forward. The most diverse teams have better ideas and get the best business results as measured by the bottom line. For P&G, diversity is a competitive advantage.

Sources: Excerpted from Galt, V. (2005, April 7). P&G leverages its cultural diversity. *Globe and Mail*, B1, B18. Reprinted with permission from the *Globe and Mail*; Noik-Bent, S. (2004, November 24). By being visible: How to manage multiculti maze. *Globe and Mail*, C1, C2.

Even after getting in the door, career tracking based on racial or ethnic stereotypes is common. For instance, one study found that a stereotype that "African Americans can't handle pressure" was partially responsible for a lack of acceptance of African Americans in managerial roles.[33] Many companies have promoted African American executives to positions having to do with affirmative action, diversity, or urban affairs in spite of their extensive credentials in other substantive areas of business. Similarly, the stereotype of Asian Americans as technical wizards has interfered with their opportunity to ascend to high general management positions.[34]

Attributions can play an important role in determining how job performance is interpreted. For example, one study found that good performance on the part of African American managers was seen to be due to help from others (a situational attribution), while good performance by Caucasian managers was seen to be due to their effort and abilities (a dispositional attribution).[35]

Racial and ethnic stereotypes are also important in the context of the increasing globalization of business. In one study, researchers asked American business students to describe Japanese and American managers along a number of dimensions. The students viewed Japanese managers as having more productive employees and being better overall managers. However, the students preferred to work for an American manager.[36] One can wonder how such students will respond to international assignments. Of course, all groups have stereotypes of each other. Japanese stereotypes of Americans probably contribute to Americans not being promoted above a certain level in Japanese firms.

Finally, recent evidence suggests that organizations are simply reflections of the environments in which they are a part. Thus, if prejudice, negative stereotyping, ethnocentrism, and discrimination exist within the environment that an organization inhabits, it is very likely that these problems will surface within the organization itself. [37]

Gender Stereotypes. One of the most problematic stereotypes for organizations is the gender stereotype. Considering their numbers in the workforce, women are severely underrepresented in managerial and administrative jobs. Although women now occupy a significant and growing proportion of entry- and mid-level management positions, this is not the case for top-level positions. According to a study of 500 of Canada's top companies by Catalyst Canada, women hold only 14.4 percent of corporate officer positions including presidents, executive vice-presidents, and chief operating officers. As a result, it's predicted that women's overall representation in corporate Canada will not reach 25 percent until 2025.[38]

There is evidence that gender stereotypes are partially responsible for discouraging women from business careers and blocking their ascent to managerial positions. This underrepresentation of women managers and administrators happens because stereotypes of women do not correspond especially well with stereotypes of businesspeople or managers. As indicated in the chapter opening vignette, a major barrier to women's advancement to managerial positions in the Bank of Montreal was myths about the company's female employees. These myths have their basis in gender stereotypes.

What is the nature of gender stereotypes? A series of studies have had managers describe men in general, women in general, and typical "successful middle managers." These studies have determined that successful middle managers are perceived as having traits and attitudes that are similar to those generally ascribed to men. That is, successful managers are seen as more similar to men in qualities such as leadership ability, competitiveness, self-confidence, ambitiousness, and objectivity.[39] Thus, stereotypes of successful middle managers do not correspond to stereotypes of women. The trend over time in the results of these studies contains some bad news and some good news. The bad news is that *male* managers today hold the same dysfunctional stereotypes about women and management that they held in the early 1970s when researchers conducted the first of these studies. At that time, women managers held the same stereotypes as the men. The good news is that the recent research shows a shift by the women—they now see successful middle managers as possessing attitudes and characteristics that describe *both* men and women in general. However, although good managers are described today as possessing less masculine characteristics than in past decades, the most recent research indicates that both men and women of varying age, education, and work experience still describe a good manager as possessing predominantly masculine characteristics.[40]

Granting that gender stereotypes exist, do they lead to biased human resources decisions? The answer would appear to be yes. In a typical study, researchers asked male bank supervisors to make hypothetical decisions about workers who were described equivalently except for gender.[41] Women were discriminated against for promotion to a branch manager's position. They were also discriminated against when they requested to attend a professional development conference. In addition, female supervisors were less likely than their male counterparts to receive support for their request that a problem employee be fired. In one case, bias worked to *favour* women. The bank supervisors were more likely to approve a request for a leave of absence to care for one's children when it came from a female. This finding is similar to others that show that gender stereotypes tend to favour women when they are being considered for "women's" jobs (such as secretary) or for "women's" tasks (such as supervising other women), but not traditional male jobs.[42] One recent study found that when women are successful in traditional male jobs, they are less liked, and being disliked had a negative effect on their evaluations and recommendations for rewards, including salary and special job opportunities.[43]

In general, research suggests that the above findings are fairly typical. Women suffer from a stereotype that is detrimental to their hiring, development, promotion, and salaries. Female managers are also more likely than male managers to have to make off-the-job sacrifices and compromises in family life to maintain their careers.[44] However, there is growing evidence that the detrimental effects of such stereotypes are reduced or removed when decision makers have good information about the qualifications and performance of particular women and an accurate picture of the job that they are applying for or seeking promotion into.[45] In particular, several studies reveal convincingly that women do not generally suffer from gender stereotypes in *performance evaluations* that their supervisors provide.[46] This is not altogether surprising. As we noted earlier, stereotypes help us process information in ambiguous situations. To the extent that we have good information on which to base our perceptions of people, reliance on stereotypes is less necessary. Day-to-day performance is often fairly easy to observe, and gender stereotypes do not intrude on evaluations.

On the other hand, hiring and promotion decisions might confront managers with ambiguous targets or situations and prompt them to resort to gender stereotypes in forming impressions. In fact, one recent study found that when participants read descriptions of mixed-sex pairs' team performance and were asked to evaluate the male and female members, females were rated as less competent, less influential in achieving a successful team outcome, and less likely to have taken on a leadership role unless there was specific information about the female member's excellent performance, her contribution to the success of the team was irrefutable, or there was definitive information about the excellence of her past performance.[47] Thus, participants resorted to negative stereotype-based attributions in evaluating women's performance when there was ambiguity about the source of the team's success.

In another study, women were perceived as less competent and characterized as less achievement oriented than men when there was ambiguity about how successful they had been when performing a traditional male job. However, when success was made explicit, women were not perceived as less competent than men.[48] Finally, when women make up a very *small* proportion of an employee group (15–20 percent), they tend to suffer a "tokenism" effect that exaggerates the effect of stereotypes.[49] Under such circumstances, research shows that women's performance appraisals suffer.[50] Evidently, people view token women as less capable of doing a "man's" job.

Fortunately, as shown in Exhibit 3.6, an increasing number of Canadian organizations like BMO have been removing barriers to women's advancement in organizations. For example, at Dominion of Canada General Insurance Company, 7 of the 12 senior executives at the Toronto-based property and casualty insurer are women.[51] Shell Canada Ltd. of Calgary now has more women than men on its list of potential senior managers.[52] And women have made the most significant progress moving into senior management and executive positions in the financial services industry. On the other hand, industries that tend to be stereotypically male, such as paper and forest products, steel production, motor vehicles and parts, oil and gas, and general manufacturing and construction, continue to have the lowest representation of women in senior positions.[53]

The Dominion of Canada General Insurance Company
www.thedominion.ca

Shell Canada Ltd.
www.shell.ca

At Dominion of Canada General Insurance Company, 7 of the 12 senior executives are women.

EXHIBIT 3.6

Canada's 10 Most Powerful Women Corporate Executives

Sources: Canada's most powerful women: Top 100.™ Women's Executive Network.™

Name	Title	Company
Deborah Alexander	Executive VP, General Counsel and Secretary	Scotiabank
Diane Bean	Executive VP, Corporate Affairs and Human Resources	Manulife Financial
Elisabetta Bigsby	Group Head, Implementation Office and Human Resources	RBC Financial Group
Alberta Cefis	Executive VP, Retail Lending Services and President and CEO, Scotia Mortgage Corporation	Scotiabank
Sylvia Chrominska	Executive VP, Human Resources and Public, Corporate and Government Affairs	Scotiabank
Lisa Colnett	Senior VP, Human Resources	Celestica
Sherry Cooper	Executive VP and Global Economic Strategist; Chief Economist	BMO Financial Group; BMO Nesbitt Burns
Isabelle Courville	President, Enterprise Group	Bell Canada
Elizabeth Del Bianco	Senior VP, Chief Legal Officer and Corporate Secretary	Celestica
Bonnie DuPont	Group VP, Corporate Resources	Enbridge

Organizations that remove perceptual barriers to the advancement of women have much to gain. A study of Fortune 500 companies found that companies with the highest representation of women in senior management positions have a 35 percent higher return on equity and a 34 percent greater return to shareholders than firms with the fewest women in senior positions.[54]

Age Stereotypes. Another kind of stereotype that presents problems for organizations is the age stereotype. Knowing that a person falls into a certain age range, we have a tendency to make certain assumptions about the person's physical, psychological, and intellectual capabilities. Exhibit 3.7 presents generation stereotypes in terms of work characteristics.

What is the nature of work-related age stereotypes? Older workers are seen as having less *capacity for performance*. They tend to be viewed as less productive, creative, logical, and capable of performing under pressure than younger workers. In addition, older workers are seen as having less *potential for development*. Compared with younger workers, they are considered more rigid and dogmatic and less adaptable to new corporate cultures. Not all stereotypes of older workers are negative, however. They tend to be perceived as more honest, dependable, and trustworthy (in short, more *stable*). In general, these stereotypes are held by both younger and older individuals.[55] It is worth noting that these stereotypes are essentially inaccurate. For example, age seldom limits the capacity for development until post-employment years.[56] Further, research has found that age and performance are unrelated, and some recent studies indicate a shift toward a more positive perception about older workers.[57]

However, the relevant question remains: Do age stereotypes affect human resources decisions? It would appear that such stereotypes can affect decisions regarding hiring, promotion, and skills development. In one study, researchers had university students make hypothetical recommendations regarding younger and older male workers. An older man was less likely to be hired for a finance job that required rapid, high-risk decisions. An older man was considered less promotable for a marketing position that required creative solutions to difficult problems. Finally, an older worker was less likely to be permitted to attend a conference on advanced production systems.[58] These decisions reflect the stereotypes of the older worker depicted above, and they are doubtless indicative of the tendency for older employees to be laid off during corporate restructuring.

Unfortunately, the reality for older workers is consistent with the research. According to the Ontario Human Rights Commission, discrimination on the basis of age is experienced by people as young as 40 to 45, who are often passed over for merit pay and promotions or pressured to take early retirement. In a blatant example of such discrimination, a job fair held in Toronto several years ago stated that the target audience was 18 to 54 year olds. Many older workers were offended, and a complaint was made to the Ontario Human Rights Commission.[59] Again, however, we should recognize that age stereotypes may have less impact on human resources decisions when managers have good information about the capacities of the particular employee in question.

Ontario Human Rights Commission
www.ohrc.on.ca

A literature review on generational diversity by psychologist Constance Patterson indicates differences in work ethics and values among traditionalists, baby boomers, Gen-Xers, and millennials.

Traditionalists (1925 to 1945)	Baby Boomers (1946 to 1960)	Generation X (1961 to 1980)	Millennials (1981 to present)
• Practical	• Optimistic	• Skeptical	• Hopeful
• Patient, loyal, and hardworking	• Teamwork and cooperation	• Self-reliant	• Meaningful work
• Respectful of authority	• Ambitious	• Risk-taking	• Diversity and change valued
• Rule followers	• Workaholic	• Balances work and personal life	• Technology savvy

EXHIBIT 3.7
Generation Stereotypes

Source: Dittmann, M. (2005, June). Generational differences at work. *Monitor on Psychology*, 54–55.

A public awareness campaign to combat age stereotypes and discrimination sponsored by Canada's Association for the Fifty-Plus and the Ontario Human Rights Commission featured this poster with the tag line: "Nobody has a shelf life."

Canada's Association for the 50 Plus
www.carp.ca

To combat age stereotypes and discrimination, Canada's Association for the 50 Plus (CARP) has worked with the Ontario Human Rights Commission on a public awareness campaign that included a poster featuring photographs of older people with the tag line, "Nobody has a shelf life. Stop age discrimination now."[60] The association has also begun to award the best employers for older workers in an attempt to overcome negative assumptions that older workers are costly, unproductive, harder to work with, and too set in their ways. Companies are scored based on how they treat older workers in areas such as recruitment, retention, skill development, compensation and benefits, retirement planning, and education. Previous winners have included the Royal Bank, Merck Frosst, Home Depot Canada, and Avis Rent A Car.[61]

Managing Diversity

Given the prevalence of the stereotypes noted above, valuing diversity is not something that occurs automatically. Rather, diversity needs to be *managed* to have a positive impact on work behaviour and an organization. Before continuing, read the You Be the Manager feature to find out what the Ottawa Police Service is doing to manage diversity.

Ottawa Police Service
www.ottawapolice.ca

So what can organizations do to achieve and manage a diverse workforce? Some common examples are listed below.[62] For a more extensive list see Exhibit 3.8.

- Select enough minority members to get them beyond token status. When this happens, the majority starts to look at individual accomplishments rather than group membership because they can see variation in the behaviours of the minority.
- Encourage teamwork that brings minority and majority members together.
- Ensure that those making career decisions about employees have accurate information about them rather than having to rely on hearsay and second-hand opinion.
- Train people to be aware of stereotypes.

Ford Australia
www.ford.com.au

A good example of a company that has a diverse workforce is Ford Australia, which has been recognized as a leader of diversity management. Ford Australia believes

☞ YOU BE THE
Manager

Wanted: Diversity at Ottawa Police Service

The Ottawa Police Service has a big problem on its hands. It is facing the total turnover of its senior ranks. The majority of them will be retiring within the next five to ten years. And if that's not enough, most of those who will replace them have less than five years of experience. Set against this reality is the changing face of the city. One in five residents is born outside of Canada, and while this immigrant population isn't as sizable as it is in some other municipalities, it is still growing at twice the rate of the general population. With such a population shift, police chief Vince Bevan has stated that, "we would not be a legitimate police organization unless we had the capacity to communicate with and understand the diverse population that calls Ottawa home . . . If we can't communicate with the victims, who is going to investigate crimes committed against them? And if we can't penetrate organized crime because we can't speak the language and don't understand the culture, who's going to halt its spread?"

Recruitment is also part of the problem. According to sergeant Syd Gravel, when police services talk of recruiting, what they usually mean is processing applications. "If the chief comes to me and says, 'We've got to hire 30 people,' I go and pull out 200 files from the filing cabinet from people who were naturally attracted to policing. And I go through the files and bring them down to 30 excellent candidates, and we would hire 30 people." The problem is that the names in that filing cabinet resemble less and less the names one encounters on Ottawa's streets.

Immigrant communities, however, have traditionally shown little interest in policing. Many immigrants come from nations where the police oppress rather than serve the public. Others arrive in Canada only to find themselves or their youth too often targeted by police using racial profiling. For these communities, a policing career for their children just doesn't come up as an option to consider.

In addition to the difficulties in recruiting from immigrant communities, the retention of women and visible minorities is also a problem. The results from focus groups that included officers and civilian staff who were women, visible minorities, gay, lesbian, bisexual, or transgender indicated that while white male officers didn't believe the organization had a retention problem, the female officers voiced discontent and a desire to leave the service. Civilian employees in the focus groups

> **Recruiting and retaining visible minority and female employees is a big problem for the Ottawa Police Service**

felt the same way, and while visible minority officers found the recruitment process to be fair and welcoming, once on board they felt that their peers viewed them as "employment equity" hires. When a consultant looked at the retention rates of the 1200-strong force, he discovered that white men stayed roughly 29 years, women stayed 15 years, and visible minorities 8 years. Thus, retention is a problem for some groups.

What should the Ottawa Police Service do to create a more diverse workforce? You be the manager.

QUESTIONS

1. **What should the Ottawa Police Service do to begin the process of creating a more diverse workforce?**

2. **What are some specific strategies that the Ottawa Police Service might employ to recruit and retain employees from diverse backgrounds?**

To find out what the Ottawa Police Service is doing, consult The Manager's Notebook at the end of the chapter.

Source: Excerpted from Vu, U. (2005, April 25). Ottawa cops pursuing diversity. *Canadian HR Reporter, 18(8)*, 1, 5; Crawford, T. (2006, April 1). A better mix. *Toronto Star*, L1, L2.

EXHIBIT 3.8
Common activities included in diversity programs.

Source: Jayne, M.E.A., & Dipboye, R.L. (2004, Winter). Leveraging diversity to improve business performance: Research findings and recommendations for organizations. *Human Resource Management, 43(4)*, 409–424.

Strategic Initiative	Sample Interventions
Recruiting	• Employee referral programs • Diverse recruiting teams • Internship programs and sponsored scholarships • Job posting and advertising initiatives targeting specific groups • Minority conference and job fair attendance • Recruiting efforts targeting universities and community colleges with diverse student bodies
Retention	• Corporate-sponsored employee resource or affinity groups • Employee benefits (e.g., adoption, domestic partner, eldercare, flexible health, and dependent spending accounts) • Work-life programs and incentives (e.g., on-site childcare, flexible work schedules, on-site lactation facilities)
Development	• Leadership development training programs • Mentoring programs
External Partnership	• Minority supplier programs • Community service outreach
Communication	• Award programs providing public recognition of managers and employees for diversity achievement • Newsletters, internal websites on diversity • Senior leadership addresses, town hall meetings, business updates
Training	• Awareness training on the organization's diversity initiative • Issue-based/prevention training (e.g., sexual harassment, men and women as colleagues) • Team-building and group-process training
Staffing and Infrastructure	• Dedicated diversity staff • Executive and local diversity councils

that having a diverse workforce is important for understanding the needs of their customers and that diversity has many benefits that provide a competitive advantage in the marketplace. The company uses the following strategies for managing diversity:[63]

- Recruits a diverse workforce that resembles and understands the company's customers. Ford Australia currently has over 68 nationalities represented in its plants.

- The company has extensive training programs to ensure that its diversity mission is understood, supported, and acted on at every work site.

- Builds respect in the workforce through celebration and acknowledgment. Harmony Day is a celebration that actively promotes workforce diversity in a fun and celebratory way. It is an example of how Ford Australia constantly reinforces the positive benefits of diversity. The celebrations include international food, music, decorations, and dancing.

- Strategies to optimize the benefits of women in the workforce. Ford Australia offers flexible work arrangements such as job sharing, telecommuting, childcare facilities, and work–life balance programs. The company has been recognized as an employer of choice for women.

- Uses surveys and other measurement tools to communicate the diversity message and track the effectiveness of its diversity programs. The company continuously seeks feedback from the workforce to ensure that its diversity programs and practices are working effectively; employees participate in focus groups to identify what diversity initiatives are working; the workforce is given a Pulse Survey that assesses Ford Australia's commitment to and performance in achieving a diverse workforce; and all managers at Ford Australia are assessed for their ability to manage, support, and improve diversity initiatives as part of their performance review. The assessments are a way for the company to hold managers accountable for diversity.

At IBM, diversity is considered to be a fundamental value and business imperative. The company has implemented many programs to ensure that the workplace is free of discrimination and harassment and full of opportunity for all people. In addition to race, gender, and physical disabilities, diversity at IBM also includes human differences such as culture, lifestyle, age, religion, economic status, sexual orientation, gender identity and expression, martial status, thought, and geography.[64]

Diversity at FedEx Canada focuses on communicating respect and fostering awareness of the importance of diversity to the business. Managers are held accountable in their performance appraisal for creating a diverse workplace. A guaranteed fair treatment process policy enables employees to bring any instance of perceived or real discrimination to management for redress. The importance of diversity is communicated in a variety of ways, including lectures on various topics to Diversity Month celebrations that take place at FedEx offices across the country.[65]

FedEx Canada
www.fedex.ca

BC Hydro has an Aboriginal Cross-Cultural Awareness Program that focuses on building relationships. BC Hydro's transmission lines cross more than 500 aboriginal reserves, so employees need to be aware of aboriginal rights and customs and the laws that protect aboriginal lands. Employees learn how diversity can affect their work in a particular community. Aboriginals serve as subject-matter experts for the training program, which includes face-to-face meetings. Training takes place in a traditional setting within a particular community and has included dancing and singing.[66]

BC Hydro
www.bchydro.com

Although diversity training programs are one of the most common approaches for managing diversity, there is little hard research on the success of these programs. However, there is some anecdotal evidence that these programs can actually cause disruption and bad feelings when all they do is get people to open up and generate stereotypes and then send them back to work.[67] Awareness training should be accompanied by skills training that is relevant to the particular needs of the organization. This might include training in resolving intercultural conflict, team building, handling a charge of sexual harassment, or learning a second language.

Basic awareness and skills training are not the only components of managing diversity. Organizations must use a number of other tactics. In future chapters, we will consider the following:

- Comprehensive attitude change programs that focus on diversity (Chapter 4).
- Recognizing diversity in employee needs and motives (Chapter 5).
- Using alternative working schedules to offer employees flexibility (Chapter 6).
- Using employee surveys to foster better communication (Chapters 10 and 16).

In summary, many organizations today have implemented programs to manage diversity. In fact, it is estimated that organizations spend $8 billion annually on diversity training. For many organizations, diversity is believed to be a business imperative that can improve competitiveness and firm performance. Although some have questioned the benefits of diversity programs, it is generally believed that diversity can result in positive outcomes when organizations take certain actions in the management of diversity. According to Michele Jayne and Robert Dipboye, diversity programs will be most successful when the following actions are taken as part of a diversity initiative:[68]

- *Build senior management commitment and accountability.* Diversity programs involve change for the organization, and to be successful they require the visible, active, and ongoing involvement and commitment of senior management.

- *Conduct a thorough needs assessment.* To be effective, diversity programs need to be tailored to an organization's business, culture, and people. A thorough needs assessment of employees, jobs, and the organization will help to ensure that the right issues are identified and appropriate interventions are implemented.

- *Develop a well-defined strategy tied to business results.* The foundation for a successful diversity program is tying the diversity strategy to the business strategy and results. The diversity strategy should guide decision making and help employees understand and accept the business case for change and how diversity supports the business strategy.

- *Emphasize team building and group process training.* Team building and group process training can help ensure that the different skills and perspectives of a diverse group are used to improve task performance. These efforts encourage group members to share information and develop a deeper understanding of the resources available to the team.

- *Establish metrics and evaluate the effectiveness of diversity initiatives.* Diversity metrics should be established to track progress and evaluate the effectiveness of a diversity program.

PERCEPTIONS OF TRUST

Do you trust your boss? This is a question that more and more people are asking themselves today. In the last several years, the importance of trust in organizations has become especially evident in the face of the Enron and WorldCom scandals. Not surprisingly, employee trust toward management is reported to be on the decline.[69] One survey found that 47 percent of those who responded agreed that a lack of trust is a problem in their organization. In another survey, 40 percent indicated that they do not believe what management says.[70] A decline in trust can be a serious problem because trust perceptions influence organizational processes and outcomes, such as sales levels, net profits, and employee turnover.[71]

While most of us have some basic understanding of what trust means, most definitions of **trust** refer to it as a willingness to be vulnerable and to take risks with respect to the actions of another party.[72] More specifically, "trust is a psychological state comprising the intention to accept vulnerability based upon positive expectations of the intentions or behaviour of another."[73] Trust perceptions toward management are based on three distinct perceptions: ability, benevolence, and integrity.[74] *Ability* refers to employee perceptions regarding managements' competence and skills. *Benevolence* refers to the extent that employees perceive management as caring and concerned for their interests and willing to do good for them. *Integrity* refers to employee perceptions that management adheres to and behaves according to a set of values and principles that the employee finds acceptable. The combination of these three factors influences perceptions of trust.

Keeping in mind that trust refers to a willingness to be vulnerable to the actions of others, how trusting would you be if you perceived your boss to be incompetent, unconcerned about your welfare, or driven by a set of values that you find unaccept-

Trust. A psychological state in which one has a willingness to be vulnerable and to take risks with respect to the actions of another party.

able? Not surprisingly, higher perceptions of management ability, benevolence, and integrity are associated with greater perceptions of trust. Furthermore, perceptions of trust in management are positively related to job satisfaction, organizational commitment, job performance and organizational citizenship behaviour, and negatively related to turnover intentions.[75] How is it that trust results in positive attitudes and behaviours? A recent study conducted in a small manufacturing firm that produces tools found that perceptions of trust in the plant manager and the top management team were positively related to employees' ability to focus. Thus, trust in management allows employees to focus their attention on value-producing activities.[76]

PERCEIVED ORGANIZATIONAL SUPPORT

Whether or not you trust your boss probably has a lot to do with how much they support you, or rather, your perceptions of their support. **Perceived organizational support** (POS) refers to employees' general belief that their organization values their contribution and cares about their well-being. When employees have positive perceptions of organizational support, they believe that their organization will provide assistance when it is needed for them to perform their job effectively and to deal with stressful situations.[77]

According to *organizational support theory*, employees who have strong perceptions of organizational support feel an obligation to care about the organization's welfare and to help the organization achieve its objectives. They feel a greater sense of purpose and meaning and a strong sense of belonging to the organization. As a result, employees incorporate their membership and role within the organization into their social identity. In addition, when POS is strong, employees feel obligated to reciprocate the organization's care and support. As a result, POS has a number of positive consequences. Research has found that employees who have greater POS have higher job performance and are more satisfied with their jobs, more committed to the organization, and less likely to be absent from work and to quit. They are also more likely to have a positive mood at work and to be more involved in their job, and they are less likely to experience strain symptoms such as fatigue, burnout, anxiety, and headaches.[78]

As shown in Exhibit 3.9, there are a number of factors that contribute to employees' POS. First, because supervisors function as representatives of their organizations through their actions and decisions, they represent the organization to employees. As a result, favourable treatment and support from supervisors, or *perceived supervisor support*, contributes strongly to POS. Interestingly, supervisors with more positive perceptions of POS are themselves perceived by employees as being more supportive. Thus, supervisors who experience greater POS provide more support to others.[79] In addition, fair organizational procedures as well as favourable rewards and job conditions are also strongly related to POS.

What can organizations do to develop employee perceptions of organizational support? One study found that supportive human resources practices that demonstrate an investment in employees and recognition of employee contributions are most likely to lead to the development of greater POS. Such practices signal to employees that the organization values and cares about them. Some examples of supportive human resources practices include participation in decision making, opportunities for growth and development, and a fair reward and recognition system.[80] Of course, equality and diversity programs such as those at the Bank of Montreal are also good examples of how an organization invests in its employees and develops a high level of POS.

> **Perceived organizational support.** Employees' general belief that their organization values their contribution and cares about their well-being.

EXHIBIT 3.9
Predictors and consequences of perceived organizational support.

Source: Based on Rhoades, L., & Eisenberger, R. (2002). Perceived organizational support: A review of the literature. *Journal of Applied Psychology, 87*, 698–714.

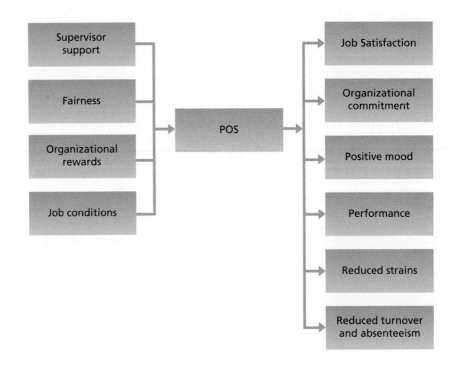

PERSON PERCEPTION IN HUMAN RESOURCES

Perceptions play an important role in human resources and can influence who gets hired and how one is evaluated once they are hired. Job applicants also form perceptions during the recruitment and selection process, and their perceptions influence their attraction to an organization and whether or not they decide to accept a job offer. In this section, we consider the role of perceptions in three important areas of human resources: the employment interview, applicant perceptions of recruitment and selection, and the performance appraisal.

Perceptions in the Employment Interview

You have probably had the pleasure (or displeasure!) of sitting through one or more job interviews in your life. After all, the interview is one of the most common organizational selection devices, applied with equal opportunity to applicants for everything from the janitorial staff to the executive suite. With our futures on the line, we would like to think that the interview is a fair and accurate selection device, but is it? Research shows that the interview is a valid selection device, although it is far from perfectly accurate, especially when the interviewer conducts it in an unstructured, free-form format. However, the validity of the interview improves when interviewers conduct a more structured interview.[81]

What factors threaten the validity of the interview? To consider the most obvious problem first, applicants are usually motivated to present an especially favourable impression of themselves. As our discussion of the perception of people implies, it is difficult enough to gain a clear picture of another individual without having to cope with active deception! A couple of the perceptual tendencies that we already discussed in this chapter can also operate in the interview. For one thing, there is evidence that interviewers compare applicants to a stereotype of the ideal applicant.[82] In and of itself, this is not a bad thing. However, this ideal stereotype must be accurate, and this requires a clear understanding of the nature of the job in question and the kind of person who can do well in this job. This is a tall order, especially for the interviewer

The interview is a difficult setting in which to form accurate impressions about a candidate. Interview validity increases when interviews are more structured.

who is hiring applicants for a wide variety of jobs. Second, interviewers have a tendency to exhibit primacy reactions.[83] Minimally, this means that information the interviewer acquired early in the interview will have an undue impact on the final decision. However, it also means that information the interviewer obtained *before* the interview (for instance, by scanning the application form or resumé) can have an exaggerated influence on the interview outcome.

A couple of perceptual tendencies that we have not discussed are also at work in interviews. First, interviewers have a tendency to give less importance to positive information about the applicant.[84] This tendency means that negative information has undue impact on the decision.[85] It might occur because interviewers get more feedback about unsuccessful hiring than successful hiring ("Why did you send me that idiot?"). It might also happen because positive information is not perceived as telling the interviewer much, since the candidate is motivated to put up a good front. In addition, **contrast effects** sometimes occur in the interview.[86] This means that the applicants who have been interviewed earlier affect the interviewer's perception of a current applicant, leading to an exaggeration of differences between applicants. For example, if the interviewer has seen two excellent candidates and then encounters an average candidate, she might rate this person lower than if he had been preceded by two average applicants (see Exhibit 3.10). This is an example of the impact of the situation on perception.

It is clear that the interview constitutes a fairly difficult setting in which to form accurate impressions about others. It is of short duration, a lot of information is generated, and the applicant is motivated to present a favourable image. Thus, interviewers often adopt "perceptual crutches" that hinder accurate perception.

Earlier, we noted that the validity of the interview improves when it is structured. But what exactly is a structured interview? According to Derek Chapman of the University of Calgary and David Zweig of the University of Toronto, interview structure involves four dimensions: *evaluation standardization* (the extent to which the interviewer uses standardized and numeric scoring procedures); *question sophistication* (the extent to which the interviewer uses job-related behavioural questions and situational questions); *question consistency* (the extent to which the interviewer asks the same questions in the same order of every candidate); and *rapport building* (the extent to which the interviewer does *not* ask personal questions that are unrelated to the job). They also found that interviews were more likely to be structured when the interviewer had formal interview training and focused on selection rather than recruitment during the interview.[87] Structured interviews probably reduce information overload and ensure that applicants can be more easily compared, since they have all responded to an identical sequence of questions.[88]

Contrast effects.
Previously interviewed job applicants affect an interviewer's perception of a current applicant, leading to an exaggeration of differences between applicants.

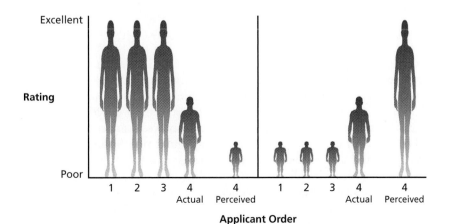

EXHIBIT 3.10
Two examples of contrast effects.

Perceptions of Recruitment and Selection

When you meet company recruiters and complete selection tests, chances are you form perceptions of recruiters and the organization. In fact, research on recruitment and selection indicates that how job applicants are treated during the recruitment and selection process influences their perceptions toward the organization and their likelihood of accepting a job offer. According to *signalling theory*, job applicants interpret their recruitment experiences as cues or signals about what it is like to work in an organization. For example, questions that are invasive and discriminatory might send a signal that the organization discriminates and does not value diversity; poor treatment during the hiring process might signal a lack of professionalism and respect of employees. These perceptions are important because they influence a job applicant's likelihood of remaining in the selection process and accepting a job offer.[89]

Applicants also form perceptions toward organizations based on the selection tests they are required to complete. This research has its basis in *organizational justice theory*, which is described in more detail in Chapter 4. Essentially, job applicants tend to form more positive perceptions of the selection process when selection procedures are perceived to be fair. Furthermore, applicants who have more positive perceptions of selection fairness are more likely to view the organization favourably and to have stronger intentions to accept a job offer and recommend the organization to others. Among various selection procedures, employment interviews and work samples are perceived more favourably than cognitive ability tests, which are perceived more favourably than personality tests and honesty tests.[90] Thus, how job applicants are treated during the recruitment and selection process has important implications for their perceptions, attitudes, intentions, and behaviour.

Perceptions and the Performance Appraisal

Once a person is hired, however imperfectly, further perceptual tasks confront organization members. Specifically, the organization will want some index of the person's job performance for decisions regarding pay raises, promotions, transfers, and training needs.

Objective and Subjective Measures. It is possible to find objective measures of performance for certain aspects of some jobs. These are measures that do not involve a substantial degree of human judgment. The number of publications that a professor has in top journals is a good example. In general, though, as we move up the organizational hierarchy, it becomes more difficult to find objective indicators of performance. Thus, it is often hard to find quantifiable evidence of a manager's success or failure. When objective indicators of performance do exist, they are often contaminated by situational factors. For example, it might be very difficult to compare the dollar sales of a snowmobile salesperson whose territory covers British Columbia with one whose territory is Nova Scotia. Also, while dollar sales might be a good indicator of current sales performance, it says little about a person's capacity for promotion to district sales manager.

Because of the difficulties that objective performance indicators present, organizations must often rely on subjective measures of effectiveness, usually provided by managers. However, the manager is confronted by a number of perceptual roadblocks. He or she might not be in a position to observe many instances of effective and ineffective performance. This is especially likely when the employee's job activities cannot be monitored directly. For example, a police sergeant cannot ride around in six squad cars at the same time, and a telephone company supervisor cannot visit customers' homes or climb telephone poles with all of his or her installers. Such situations mean that the target (the employee's performance) is frequently ambiguous, and we have seen that the perceptual system resolves ambiguities in an efficient but often inaccurate manner.

Even when performance is observable, employees often alter their behaviour so that they look good when their manager is around.

Rater Errors. Subjective performance appraisal is susceptible to some of the perceptual biases we discussed earlier—primacy, recency, and stereotypes. In addition, a number of other perceptual tendencies occur in performance evaluation. They are often called rater errors. One interrelated set of these tendencies includes leniency, harshness, and central tendency (Exhibit 3.11). **Leniency** refers to the tendency to perceive the performance of one's ratees as especially good, while **harshness** is the tendency to see their performance as especially ineffective. Lenient raters tend to give "good" ratings, and harsh raters tend to give "bad" ratings. Professors with reputations as easy graders or tough graders exemplify these types of raters. **Central tendency** involves assigning most ratees to a middle-range performance category—the extremes of the rating categories are not used. The professor who assigns 80 percent of her students C's is committing this error.

Each of these three rating tendencies is probably partially a function of the rater's personal experiences. For example, the manager who has had an especially good group of employees might respond with special harshness when management transfers him to supervise a group of slightly less able workers. It is worth noting that not all instances of leniency, harshness, and central tendency necessarily represent perceptual errors. In some cases, raters intentionally commit these errors, even though they have accurate perceptions of workers' performance. For example, a manager might use leniency or central tendency in performance reviews so that his employees do not react negatively to his evaluation.

Another perceptual error that is frequently committed by performance raters is called the **halo effect**.[91] The halo effect occurs when the observer allows the rating of an individual on one trait or characteristic to colour the ratings on other traits or characteristics. For example, in a teacher evaluation system, a student might perceive his instructor as a nice person, and this might favourably influence his perception of the instructor's knowledge of the material and speed in returning exams and papers. Similarly, a manager might rate an employee as frequently late for work, and this might in turn lead her to devalue the employee's productivity and quality of work. As these examples illustrate, halo can work either for or against the ratee. In both cases, the rater fails to perceive differences *within* ratees. The halo effect tends to be organized around central traits that the rater considers important. The student feels that being nice is an especially important quality, while the manager places special emphasis on promptness. Ratings on these characteristics then affect the rater's perceptions of other characteristics.

Leniency. The tendency to perceive the job performance of ratees as especially good.

Harshness. The tendency to perceive the job performance of ratees as especially ineffective.

Central tendency. The tendency to assign most ratees to middle-range job performance categories.

Halo effect. The rating of an individual on one trait or characteristic tends to colour ratings on other traits or characteristics.

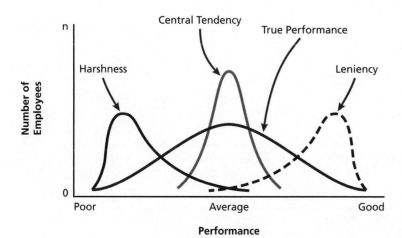

EXHIBIT 3.11
Leniency, harshness, and central tendency rater errors.

Similar-to-me effect. A rater gives more favourable evaluations to people who are similar to the rater in terms of background or attitudes.

The **similar-to-me effect** is an additional rater error that may, in part, reflect perceptual bias. The rater tends to give more favourable evaluations to people who are similar to the rater in terms of background or attitudes. For example, the manager with an MBA degree who comes from an upper-middle-class family might perceive a similar employee as a good performer even though the person is only average. Similarly, a rater might overestimate the performance of an individual who holds similar religious and political views. Such reactions probably stem from a tendency to view our own performance, attitudes, and background as "good." We then tend to generalize this evaluation to others who are, to some degree, similar to us. Raters with diverse employees should be especially wary of this error.

Given all these problems, it should be clear that it is difficult to obtain good subjective evaluations of employee performance. Because of this, human resources specialists have explored various techniques for reducing perceptual errors and biases. There has been a tendency to attempt to reduce rater errors by using rating scales with more specific behavioural labels. The assumption here is that giving specific examples of effective and ineffective performance will facilitate the rater's perceptual processes and recall.

Exhibit 3.12 shows a behaviourally anchored rating scale that gives very specific behavioural examples (from top to bottom) of good, average, and poor customer service. It was developed for the J.C. Penney Company. With such an aid, the rater may

J.C. Penney Co.
www.jcpenney.com

EXHIBIT 3.12
Behaviourally anchored scale for rating customer service.

Source: Campbell, J.P., Dunnette, M.D., Lawler, E.E., III, & Weick, K.E., Jr. (1970). *Managerial behavior, performance, and effectiveness.* New York: McGraw-Hill.

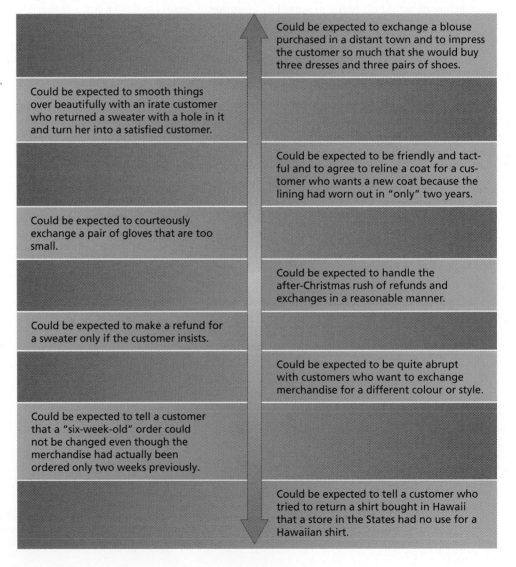

Could be expected to exchange a blouse purchased in a distant town and to impress the customer so much that she would buy three dresses and three pairs of shoes.

Could be expected to smooth things over beautifully with an irate customer who returned a sweater with a hole in it and turn her into a satisfied customer.

Could be expected to be friendly and tactful and to agree to reline a coat for a customer who wants a new coat because the lining had worn out in "only" two years.

Could be expected to courteously exchange a pair of gloves that are too small.

Could be expected to handle the after-Christmas rush of refunds and exchanges in a reasonable manner.

Could be expected to make a refund for a sweater only if the customer insists.

Could be expected to be quite abrupt with customers who want to exchange merchandise for a different colour or style.

Could be expected to tell a customer that a "six-week-old" order could not be changed even though the merchandise had actually been ordered only two weeks previously.

Could be expected to tell a customer who tried to return a shirt bought in Hawaii that a store in the States had no use for a Hawaiian shirt.

be less susceptible to perceptual errors when completing the rating task, although the evidence for this is mixed.[92] Furthermore, there is also some evidence that a performance appraisal system that accurately measures employees' performance and ties it to rewards can increase employees' perceptions of trust toward management.[93]

☞ THE MANAGER'S

Notebook

Wanted: Diversity at Ottawa Police Service

1. In order to reach out to the diverse groups in Ottawa, the Ottawa Police Service needed to first find out how it is perceived as an employer. So they launched a process of consultation with community groups to find out what strategies they should put in place to help recruit a police service that reflects the community. The service's corporate planning section also put together focus groups of officers and civilian staff representing different groups. The recommendations of the community groups and the police staff were very similar. Telephone surveys of sworn officers and civilian employees on changes that management needed to make were also conducted. More than 90 recommendations emerged that were eventually distilled into 17 that formed the blueprint for the services outreach recruitment program. A project team then took the recommendations to the Police Services Board and made a case for making the first recommendation—to be a diverse and bias-free organization—one of the 10 organizational values. The board approved, which means that henceforth, the chief is required by the *Police Services Act* to go to the board every three years and report on how the service is living up to that value.

2. In order to recruit and retain a more diverse workforce, the Ottawa Police Service developed programs to recruit from immigrant communities that have traditionally shown little interest in policing. For example, a volunteer recruiter initiative brings on board people from various communities to help the police recruit. After training, they go out with a pair of police employees, one uniformed and one civilian, to job fairs and career days to speak about policing as a career. Another program has the Ottawa police teaming up with the Ontario Provincial Police to go into an English-as-second-language class to teach young newcomers *Criminal Code* terminology and to talk about policing as a career. To help young candidates with entry requirements, the police service is setting up information sessions to prepare people for the aptitude tests, which are set out by the province. Holding information sessions to explain to young immigrants what the tests are about, or matching up mentors with young candidates to answer their questions one on one, begins to put them on an equal footing to start the application process, says staff sergeant Syd Gravel. And if that's not enough, police and Somali youth play in a competitive basketball league in the hopes that Somali kids will see policing as a future occupation. To make the case that diversity means reaching out to all, not to some, the police service framed all the work in terms of being an employer of choice for all. According to police chief Vince Bevan, "We wanted to make sure that we had a workplace where they would thrive, where they would be successful, and where they would be good ambassadors back to the community about what it was like to work for the Ottawa Police Service."

Source: Excerpted from Vu, U. (2005, April 25). Ottawa cops pursuing diversity. *Canadian HR Reporter, 18(8)*, 1, 5; Crawford, T. (2006, April 1). A better mix. *Toronto Star,* L1, L2.

LEARNING OBJECTIVES CHECKLIST

1. *Perception* involves interpreting the input from our senses to provide meaning to our environment. Any instance of perception involves a perceiver, a target, and a situational context. The experience, needs, and emotions of the perceiver affect perception, as does the ambiguity of the target.

2. According to *social identity theory*, people form perceptions of themselves and others based on their characteristics and memberships in social categories. *Bruner's model* of the perceptual process suggests that we are very receptive to cues provided by the target and the situation when we encounter an unfamiliar target. However, as we discover familiar cues, we quickly categorize the target and process other cues in a selective manner to maintain a consistent and constant picture of the target.

3. The main biases in person perception include *primacy, recency, implicit personality theory, reliance on central traits, projection,* and *stereotyping.* Gender, age, race, and ethnic stereotypes are especially problematic for organizations.

4. *Attribution* is the process of assigning causes or motives to people's behaviour. The observer is often interested in determining whether the behaviour is due to dispositional (internal) or situational (external) causes. Behaviour is likely to be attributed to the disposition of the actor when the behaviour (1) is performed consistently, (2) differs from that exhibited by other people, and (3) occurs in a variety of situations or environments. An opposite set of cues will prompt a situational attribution.

5. The tendency of observers to overemphasize dispositional attributions is known as the *fundamental attribution error.* In contrast, actors are more likely to explain their own behaviour in situational terms, and this actor–observer difference in attributions is known as the *actor–observer effect.* Our tendency to take credit for success and to deny responsibility for failure is known as the *self-serving bias.*

6. The changing nature of the workplace and increasing diversity has highlighted the importance of valuing and managing employee diversity, which can yield strategic and competitive advantages for the organization.

7. Racial, ethnic, gender, and age *stereotypes* can result in discriminatory human resources decisions and are a major barrier to valuing diversity. Organizations can use a number of tactics, including training, to manage diversity.

8. Perceptions of *trust* involve a willingness to be vulnerable and to take risks with respect to the actions of another party. Trust perceptions toward management are based on perceptions of ability, benevolence, and integrity. *Perceived organizational support (POS)* refers to perceptions about how much an organization values an individual's contribution and cares about one's well-being. POS perceptions are influenced by perceived supervisor support, fairness, rewards, and job conditions.

9. Judging the suitability of job applicants in an interview and appraising job performance are especially difficult perceptual tasks, in part because the target is motivated to convey a good impression. In addition, interviewers and performance raters exhibit a number of perceptual tendencies that are reflected in inaccurate judgments, including *contrast effects, leniency, harshness, central tendency, halo,* and *similar-to-me effects.* Structured interviews can improve the accuracy of perceptions in the employment interview, and behaviourally anchored rating scales can improve performance appraisals. According to signalling theory, job applicants form perceptions about organizations on the basis of their recruitment and selection experiences and their perceptions influence the likelihood that they will accept a job offer. Job applicants form more positive perceptions of the selection process when the selection procedures are perceived as being fair.

OB FLASHBACK

Self-Monitoring and Negative Gender Stereotypes

In Chapter 2, you learned about a personality variable called self-monitoring, which is the extent to which people observe and regulate how they appear and behave in social settings and relationships. Low self-monitors are not concerned about how they appear to others and fitting in with those around them. Their opposites are high self-monitors, who take great care to observe and control the images they project. High self-monitors tend to show concern for socially appropriate behaviour, to tune in to social and interpersonal cues, and to regulate their behaviour and self-presentation according to these cues. Self-monitoring has a positive effect on a number of important work outcomes such as promotions, interview success, performance, and job satisfaction.

High self-monitors have an advantage in social situations where strong norms exist and adherence to them is rewarded. This is because high self-monitors have a tendency to closely observe social cues and use them as guides for how to present themselves. Because they are concerned about how others perceive them, high self-monitors are more likely to change their behaviour to suit different situations and others' expectations. If they believe that others are likely to view them negatively, high self-monitors will be inclined to behave in a way that counteracts the negative perception. This has implications for work situations where negative stereotypes disadvantage women. In particular, can self-monitoring help women overcome negative gender stereotypes?

To find out, Francis Flynn and Daniel Ames of Columbia University conducted a study in which graduate students worked in mixed-sex groups (which are often subjected to negative gender stereotypes). The researchers reasoned that because of negative gender stereotypes, women face a dilemma when performing traditional male tasks. To be perceived favourably when performing a traditional male task, women might adopt stereotypical masculine behaviours (e.g., assertiveness) to counter negative female stereotypes. However, such behaviours violate the traditional female role and could result in a backlash from others. Flynn and Ames reasoned that self-monitoring might help women decide when it is appropriate to violate the female stereotype and demonstrate traditional masculine behaviours. They might also be able to minimize any potential backlash when social cues suggest that others perceive them as being overly assertive. Thus, women who are high self-monitors might be able to overcome the negative gender stereotype ascribed to them and also minimize any backlash associated with exhibiting stereotypical male behaviours.

Participants were required to complete a semester-long group project as part of the first-year curriculum in a master's of business administration (MBA) program. At the beginning of the term, students were assigned to a four- or five-member team. Each team included at least one woman. The teams had to conduct a rigorous analysis of a corporation of their choosing in terms of the firm's revenues and costs, projections of the firm's future growth and profitability, as well as an analysis of the firm's industry, competitive strategy, and corporate structure. At the end of the semester, each team submitted a single report of its analysis and recommendations.

Participants then completed several surveys in which they provided ratings of their self-monitoring and rated each team member on his or her social influence and contribution to the project. Consistent with negative gender stereotypes, women were rated as having less influence than men over group decisions and outcomes and were perceived as less valuable contributors than men. However, women who were high self-monitors were rated as being more influential and as having contributed more to the group than women who were low self-monitors. Self-monitoring did not have the same beneficial effects for men.

In a second study, the authors had MBA students participate in a mixed-sex dyadic negotiation exercise. The negotiation task involved the acquisition of a food exporter and the objective was to maximize one's payoff. The results indicated that, once again, self-monitoring had a positive effect on the performance of women but not men. Self-monitoring was especially beneficial for women on distributive bargaining issues in which a unit of gain for one party entails a unit of loss for the other. One of the reasons for this finding is that the women who were high self-monitors were more responsive to their partners' assertive behaviour than women who were low self-monitors. In other words, high self-monitoring women were able to adapt to an assertive negotiating partner by behaving more assertively themselves, something that low self-monitoring women were not able to do.

In summary, the results of this study suggest that women who are high self-monitors are able to overcome negative gender stereotypes in situations where traditional masculine characteristics are perceived as being necessary for effective task performance. As a result, high self-monitoring women were perceived as having more influence and making a greater contribution to the group compared to women who were low self-monitors.

Thus, the effect of self-monitoring appears to be different for men and women and more beneficial for women because they experience different gender stereotypes.

Source: Based on Flynn, F.J., & Ames, D.R. (2006). What's good for the goose may not be as good for the gander: The benefits of self-monitoring for men and women in task groups and dyadic conflicts. *Journal of Applied Psychology, 91*, 272–281.

DISCUSSION QUESTIONS

1. Discuss how differences in the experiences of students and professors might affect their perceptions of students' written work and class comments.

2. Using implicit personality theory, explain how physical attractiveness influences job-related outcomes in employment interviews and performance appraisals.

3. Discuss the occupational stereotypes that you hold about computer programmers, the clergy, truck drivers, bartenders, and bankers. How do you think these stereotypes have developed? Has an occupational stereotype ever caused you to commit a socially embarrassing error when meeting someone for the first time?

4. Use Bruner's perceptual model (Exhibit 3.3) and social identity theory to explain why performance appraisals and interviewers' judgments are frequently inaccurate.

5. Discuss how perceptions of organizational support can influence employees' attitudes and behaviour. What can organizations do to develop positive perceptions of organizational support?

6. Suppose an employee does a particularly poor job on an assigned project. Discuss the attribution process that this person's manager will use to form judgments about this poor performance. Be sure to discuss how the manager will use consistency, consensus, and distinctiveness cues.

7. A study of small business failures found that owners generally cited factors such as economic depression or strong competition as causes. However, creditors of these failed businesses were much more likely to cite ineffective management. What attribution bias is indicated by these findings? Why do you think the difference in attribution occurs?

8. Discuss the factors that make it difficult for employment interviewers to form accurate perceptions of interviewees. Explain why a gender or racial stereotype might be more likely to affect a hiring decision than a performance appraisal decision. How can interviews and performance appraisals be designed to improve the accuracy of perceptions?

9. What are the implications of social identity theory for diversity in organizations? Describe some of the things that an organization can do to remove the barriers to workplace diversity. List some of the advantages gained by organizations that effectively manage a diverse workforce.

INTEGRATIVE DISCUSSION QUESTIONS

1. Describe how the principles of operant learning theory and social cognitive theory can be used to manage workplace diversity and reduce the effects of workplace stereotypes. How can the organizational learning practices described in Chapter 2 be used for managing diversity?

2. Consider how the four basic types of managerial activities described in Chapter 1 (i.e., routine communication, traditional management, networking, and human resource management) can influence employees' perceptions of trust and perceived organizational support (POS). How should managers perform each of these activities to improve employees' perceptions of trust and POS?

ON-THE-JOB CHALLENGE QUESTION

Telecom giant LM Ericsson AB is the world's biggest supplier of mobile phone equipment and networks. Currently, the company employs 21 300 people in Sweden and about 50 500 in 140 other countries around the world. The company is now offering buyouts to up to 1000 of its employees in Sweden. It is a voluntary package, but it is only being offered to employees between the ages of 35 and 50. The company also announced plans to hire 900 new employees over the next three years, but only those who are under the age of 30. According to the company's global head of human resources, "The purpose of this program is to correct an age structure that is unbalanced . . . We would like to make sure we employ more young people in order not to miss a generation in 10 years' time."

What do you think of Ericsson's voluntary buyout package and new hiring plans? Do perceptions have anything to do with their hiring plans? Is this something that Canadian organizations should consider? What are the implications?

Source: Acharya-Tom Yew, Madhavi. (2006, April 26). Is age 35 not judted as over the hill? *Toronto Star*, E1, E8. Reprinted with permission from Torstar Syndication Services.

EXPERIENTIAL EXERCISE

Beliefs about Older Workers

The items on the next page are an attempt to assess the attitudes people have about older workers. The statements cover many different opposing points of view; you may find yourself agreeing strongly with some of the statements, disagreeing just as strongly with others, and perhaps feeling uncertain about others.

Scoring and Interpretation

The scale you have just completed measures your attitudes toward older workers. To score your beliefs about older workers, subtract your responses to each of the following items from 6: 1, 2, 5, 6, 7, 8, 11, 13, 16, 17, 22, and 25. For example, if you put 2 for item 1, give yourself a 4 (6 minus 2). Then simply add up your resulting responses to all 27 items. Your score should fall somewhere between 27 and 135. Low scores indicate an overall negative belief about older workers, while high scores indicate positive beliefs. Thus, the higher your score, the more favourable your attitudes are toward older workers.

Research on older workers has generally found that a negative stereotype of older workers exists in organizations. The danger of this is that it can lead to negative attitudes and discriminatory behaviour toward older workers.

A recent study of 179 employees from three organizations obtained scores that ranged from 54 to 118. The average score was 90, which indicated somewhat positive beliefs about older workers. As reported in other studies, older workers had more positive beliefs about older workers than younger workers. However, younger workers who had more interactions with older workers were found to have more positive beliefs about older workers.

To facilitate class discussion and your understanding of age stereotypes, form a small group with several other members of the class and consider the following questions. (Note that the instructor can also do this as a class exercise. Students should write their score, age, and interactions with older workers on a piece of paper and hand it in to the instructor, who can then determine the relationship between age,

Read each statement carefully. Using the numbers from 1 to 5 on the rating scale, mark your personal opinion about each statement in the blank space next to each statement. Remember, give your personal opinion according to how much you agree or disagree with each item. In all cases, older refers to those who are 50 years of age or older.

—1—	—2—	—3—	—4—	—5—
Strongly agree	Agree	Neither agree nor disagre	Disagree	Strongly disagree

____ 1. Older employees have *fewer accidents* on the job.

____ 2. Most companies are *unfair* to older employees.

____ 3. Older employees are *harder to train* for jobs.

____ 4. Older employees are *absent more often* than younger employees.

____ 5. Younger employees have more *serious accidents* than older workers.

____ 6. If two workers had similar skills, I'd *pick the older worker to work with me*.

____ 7. *Occupational diseases* are more likely to occur among younger employees.

____ 8. Older employees usually turn out work of *higher quality*.

____ 9. Older employees are *grouchier* on the job.

____ 10. Younger workers are *more cooperative* on the job.

____ 11. Older workers are more *dependable*.

____ 12. Most older workers cannot keep up with the *speed of modern industry*.

____ 13. Older employees are *most loyal* to the company.

____ 14. Older workers *resist change* and are *too set in their ways*.

____ 15. Younger workers are more interested than older workers in *challenging jobs*.

____ 16. Older workers can *learn new skills* as easily as other employees.

____ 17. Older employees are *better* employees.

____ 18. Older employees *do not want* jobs with *increased responsibilities*.

____ 19. Older workers are not interested in *learning new skills*.

____ 20. Older employees should 'step aside' (take a less demanding job) to give younger employees advancement opportunities.

____ 21. The majority of older employees would *quit work* if they could *afford it*.

____ 22. Older workers are usually *outgoing and friendly* at work.

____ 23. Older workers prefer *less challenging jobs* than those they held *when* they were *younger*.

____ 24. It is a *better investment* to *train younger workers* rather than older workers.

____ 25. Older employees in our department *work just as hard* as anyone else.

____ 26. Given a choice, I would *not work with an older worker* on a daily basis.

____ 27. A person's *performance declines significantly* with age.

interactions with older workers, and beliefs about older workers.)

1. Students should first compare their scores to each other and to the average score indicated above (90). Do group members have positive or negative beliefs about older workers? Do some group members have more positive or negative beliefs than others in the group?

2. Each member of the group should indicate their age. Determine the average age of the group and categorize those members above the average as being "older" and those below the average as being "younger." Then calculate the average score of the two age groups. Is there a difference in beliefs about older workers between older and younger group members?

3. Each group member should indicate how often they interact with older workers (daily, several times a week, once a week, or monthly). Based on group members' responses, create two categories that correspond to high and low interactions with older workers. Calculate the average score of these two groups. Is there a difference in beliefs about older workers between those who have more and those you have less interaction with older workers?

4. Why do some students have positive or negative beliefs about older workers? What are the implications of these beliefs at work and outside of work?

5. What can you do to develop more positive beliefs about older workers?

Source: Hassell, B.L., & Perrewe, P.L. (1995). An examination of beliefs about older workers: Do stereotypes still exist? *Journal of Organizational Behavior, 16,* 457–468.

CASE INCIDENT

Evaluating Gregory

After six months in her new position as manager, Nina was faced with the task of having to conduct performance reviews of her staff. She was worried because she had never done performance reviews and was not sure how to do them. However, to ease her way into it, she decided to start with Gregory. Gregory was a recent hire in her department, and Nina felt that he was the most attractive-looking guy she had hired since she became manager. She felt it would be easy to evaluate his performance.

1. Using Bruner's model of the perceptual process, discuss how Nina's perception of Gregory might influence her evaluation of his performance. What are some of the perceptual biases that might come into play?

2. What can Nina do to prevent perceptual errors and bias in her performance evaluations?

CASE STUDY

Accounting for Failure

It had been a long two years, but Nancy Koharski had at last gained some peace of mind. She was struck with the irony of how the same company that acted as a consultant to help other firms increase productivity and employee morale could be so blind to its own problems.

Company Background

Berry, Hepworth & Associates (BH&A) is a large regional accounting firm headquartered in Calgary. Over 125 professionals work at the Calgary office, and additional branch offices are located in Edmonton, Red Deer, and Regina. BH&A is the dominant audit firm in the region and has earned a solid reputation in bank auditing and management information systems. The company was founded in the 1940s and has experienced tremendous growth in recent years.

BH&A is divided into four departments: Commercial Audit, Healthcare, Financial Institutions Audit Group (FIAG), and the Management Information Systems Group. The latter is composed mainly of computer programmers, but includes two psychologists who consult with clients on organizational behaviour issues. Among the audit staff it is informally recognized that Commercial Audit is the best department in terms of clientele and working conditions, but opportunities are limited owing to a large number of staff. The bank audits performed by FIAG are widely seen as boring and therefore undesirable, and the FIAG staff are quietly referred to as "nerds" and "brown-nosers." However, it is acknowledged that FIAG does offer a good career path, as banks constitute a significant portion of BH&A's business. In fact, because they are so terribly overworked, FIAG actively recruits (in effect, forces) BH&A people into the department.

All new staff persons are first assigned to Commercial Audit; the "choice" to specialize is made after a year or so of experience. There is no direct supervisor responsible for any particular person's training and development. Instead, the manager or "in-charge" on a particular assignment is responsible for helping the new "junior" on the job. While the in-charge is required to provide a verbal review after each assignment, focusing on areas for improvement, these are seldom provided. Every six months, a formal professional appraisal is held. In preparation, review forms are completed anonymously by everyone in the firm. Each junior can review in-charges and managers, who in turn evaluate the juniors.

Scheduling for jobs is, according to company policy, unbiased: juniors are to be assigned to upcoming jobs purely on a rotational basis. No in-charge can request that a particular junior be placed or withheld from a job.

The Working Environment

BH&A is a very conservative firm. Most of the partners come from small towns or rural environments. Among the entire professional staff at Calgary, there is only one divorcee, fewer than 10 smokers, and one "possible" homosexual. The older members of the firm believe that while the firm has grown, it has not sacrificed the positive qualities it enjoyed as a smaller firm, including company loyalty and pride.

Chartered accounting at BH&A is structured to be competitive. More staff are hired each year than is necessary. It is commonly understood that one must outperform one's peers to survive. The six-month review is especially dreaded because BH&A tends to fire the two lowest-ranked juniors—despite assurances that the firm will retain newcomers at least until they have met the two-year requirement for the Chartered Accountant licence. Juniors are apprehensive about the anonymous comments because they figure prominently in the review process, and yet juniors are unable to defend themselves against unknown sources. Numerous juniors reported being afraid to open a small envelope that appeared unexpectedly during review time (the envelopes in fact contained the employee's income tax statement). Much gallows humour can be heard around review time, and juniors tend to develop a real sense of comradeship.

The high performance expectations of BH&A appear to have given a rise to a "martyr complex," a curious blend of masochism and machoism. Ulcers and other stress-related illnesses are seen as evidence of hard work and status symbols. Numerous complaints are made about long working hours, but in reality these are boasts about how hard one is working. Overtime statistics are kept informally and compared among co-workers as if they were baseball statistics. FIAGs are particularly notorious for this sort of behaviour. Calling in sick is not acceptable as it is seen as a sign of weakness and lack of dedication. One manager was in a car accident and taken to the hospital with a concussion. He returned to work that afternoon wearing the hospital bandage around his head.

It is understood that people must prove their loyalty by working very hard for years on end. The ultimate payoff is elevation to partnership. Currently, there are only 35 partners dividing the profits of one of the top accounting firms in the region. The monetary reward should be great indeed for those who survive.

Golden Boys and Audit Drones

The college recruiter who first interviewed Nancy Koharski spoke at length about the informal, family atmosphere at BH&A, and how Nancy would find greater personal attention and a more relaxed working environment than at a traditional accounting firm. BH&A, he had gone on to say, was proud of its success in attracting women to the firm. He noted that the first female professional had been hired in 1977, and related several humorous stories about the "early pioneers." One story concerned a female auditor who was not strong enough to carry the old-fashioned adding machines to clients. Rather than admit it, she kept "forgetting" to bring the machine. Nancy was impressed by the interview and eventually accepted an offer from BH&A.

Nancy was determined to make partner, and to that end she threw herself into her new job with a vengeance. She took considerable pride in her hard work and initial accomplishments during her first few months. This pride, however, was tempered with a gnawing feeling that her efforts were not being noticed and that she was being passed over for more important assignments and being given more than her fair share of "grunt work." She noticed that, somehow, certain male juniors were always assigned to the prize jobs and clients and worked repeatedly for the same managers. These "golden boys," as her colleagues sarcastically nicknamed them, also seemed to learn the office gossip and other information well before the women in the office. They seemed to enjoy excellent personal relationships with the managers, playing together on company-sponsored sports teams and joking about incidents that happened while they roomed together while out of town.

In contrast, Nancy's female friends at the office referred to themselves and most other women at BH&A as "audit drones." Each staff member was required to complete time sheets that billed time to clients at quarter-hour intervals. It was regarded as a major humiliation to write "unassigned," especially after having been at the firm for a while. It soon became apparent to Nancy that the audit drones were often left to fend for themselves over long periods, trying to scrounge up work. They were usually the last to be assigned to jobs, which tended to be the dreaded bank audits. When unassigned, they had little choice but to go door to door asking for any kind of menial work, while the golden boys worked overtime on plum assignments. One of Nancy's female friends put the situation this way: "I'm not given the chance to develop. But what can I do? If I complain, I could be replaced by somebody fresh out of school who could do what I'm doing inside a week. And for less money." Another friend remarked that "the most a woman can hope for here is to avoid being fired."

Nancy also began to hear stories that were considerably more disturbing than the ones the interviewer had first told her. One story described the difficult transition period at BH&A when women first joined the company at the professional level. Apparently, some men openly blamed the women for upsetting what had been a comfortable work environment. A second story concerned the lone woman assigned to the Red Deer office. She was told by co-workers that the manager "hated to waste time developing women who would eventually end up leaving the firm." She was assigned to Commercial Audit, but it became so obvious that she was not being scheduled for commercial jobs that her male co-workers commented on it to her. She spoke with the managing partner of the office and, after apparently receiving no help, felt compelled to join the FIAGs as the only way to work in the office. Another story concerned a pregnant manager who was said to have been relieved of her clients as soon as she began to "show," and was not allowed to work on engagements outside the office. Following her pregnancy, she was apparently told she had lost her "special relationship" with clients. Further, her requests for occasional time off for childcare were denied.

Most disturbing of all were the statements of a number of male colleagues. Female staff members were told repeatedly and directly that "Women don't belong in accounting" as it was "no place for a woman." Since women would "obviously" marry and want children, it was inevitable that they would eventually leave the firm. These men pointed to the high turnover rate for female staff members as proof of the validity of their beliefs. They explained that because the work was so demanding and time consuming, it would be "impossible" for women to combine family life with an accounting career.

Nancy was startled to learn that these attitudes were espoused, not only by older men at the firm, but by a number of younger men as well. The more sympathetic men admitted that it was "unfair that they didn't have to make the same choice . . ." but they had wives at home or in less demanding jobs who could manage the family in their absence.

This belief in the unsuitability of women was never openly questioned by male staff members. If a woman countered with something like: "The job is only impossible for working mothers if the company chooses to make it impossible," she was apt to be met with blank stares. Working mothers were told that BH&A could not offer them special treatment, shorter hours, or less travel time because the men who had accepted these hardships would rebel. The more arguments and stories that Nancy heard with a similar ring, the more she began to resent the company and the golden boys.

The Dragon Lady

Several of the older women at BH&A struck Nancy as being rather cold and demanding. Indeed, the most loathed of these women was nicknamed "dragon lady." While they were always very professional in their dress and manner, they did not go out of their way to offer support or encouragement to the younger female staff members. Three of these women tended to fawn over two influential male partners. It was rumoured that one of these women had supported the policy of selected firings as a "way to shut them up and make them work harder."

The Confrontation

Two women who had been at the firm for several years complained to the partners about the apparent bias in the scheduling of work assignments. They were told that they were "imagining things" because the company policy was designed to prohibit such abuses. When pressed to explain why women were always the "extra junior" on bank jobs, the partners responded that this was because there were higher-level women in FIAG with whom they could room while out of town, but none at Commercial Audit. The cost of an extra hotel room for a lone woman was not feasible, given the tight budgets. The women were also told that, while the men at the firm were liberal and had no problems working with women, many of the older clients would not accept dealing with a female authority figure. To avoid this problem, women were not assigned where it was felt they would not be accepted. Finally, it was explained that if any one woman had been neglected, it was a "regrettable oversight" in trying to assign so many employees. The meeting was concluded with a promise to review the situation. Nothing more was heard.

The Decision

One by one, Nancy's more senior female friends quit the firm after they had "served time," that is, fulfilled the two-year licensing requirement. If they were mentioned in the company at all after they left, it was along the lines of "They obviously weren't Berry, Hepworth material," or "They couldn't hack life in Calgary."

After two years and six days with BH&A, Nancy, too, announced that she was leaving. One colleague, the "dragon lady," urged her to voice her complaints about the treatment of women at the firm to the human resources partner during her exit interview. Nancy decided to do so, and received what she concluded was a fitting send-off: throughout the entire interview, the partner sat clipping his nails and declined to respond to a single issue she raised.

Source: Case prepared by Kathleen Solonika and Blake Ashforth. From Kelly, J., Prince, J.B., & Ashforth, B. (1991). *Organizational Behavior: Readings, Cases, and Exercises* (2nd ed.), Scarborough: Prentice-Hall Canada.

1. Discuss several examples of conflicting or contradictory perceptions at BH&A. What effect do these perceptions have on organizational members' attitudes and behaviour? What effect do they have on the organization?

2. Use social identity theory and Bruner's model of the perceptual process to explain the various perceptions of the employees and partners at BH&A.

3. The chapter discusses how selection interviewers can make perceptual errors. What does the case say about perceptual errors on the part of job applicants? Use signalling theory to explain Nancy's perceptions of BH&A.

4. Use the concepts of stereotyping and the halo effect to explain the contrast between the golden boys and the audit drones.

5. Are there any aspects to the organization of work at BH&A that could lead to perceptual problems in performance appraisals? What should be done about this?

6. Compare and contrast this case with the BMO vignette that opened the chapter.

7. Suppose that you were appointed to a newly created position at BH&A, manager of diversity. What would you do to better manage diversity at the firm?

CHAPTER 4

Values, Attitudes, and Work Behaviour

HUSKY INJECTION MOLDING SYSTEMS LTD.

Ontario-based Husky Injection Molding Systems Ltd. manufactures injection molding equipment—high-tech beasts resembling immense waffle irons that pump out everything from yogurt containers to car bumpers. More than 90 percent of its machinery is exported to 80 countries, with some 3600 Husky machines now operating globally. Husky employs approximately 3000 people in 40 locations around the world.

Since producing their first mold for a coffee cup in 1958, Husky has become a world leader in producing machinery used to create PET (polyethylene terephthalate) molds. Over the last two decades, its sales have soared from US$72 million in 1985 to over $1 billion. Husky alone is credited, in large measure, for Canada's shift from a trade deficit to a surplus position in plastics machinery.

How has Husky achieved such a stellar record of financial success? The answer is a strong value system that it lives consistently and brings to life in its buildings, its employees, and its products. At Husky, treating people and the environment with respect is paramount, and when it comes to labour–management relations, Husky is clearly no ordinary company.

According to Husky founder Robert Schad, Husky is a company with a conscience and one that is built on values. Those values are apparent as soon as you arrive at Husky's 21.5-hectare headquarters and manufacturing plant in Bolton, Ontario, just north of Toronto, where everything is spotlessly clean and well lit. Manufacturing areas are bright and air-conditioned, and the walls, even in washrooms, are adorned with framed nature paintings, photos, or prints. Books on wildlife greet visitors in the waiting rooms. In the cafeterias, staff dine on organic, vegetarian meals, served hot and subsidized by the company. Herbal teas are free. Candy, doughnuts, and vending machines are nonexistent. The entire building is smoke free, and signs about nutrition are everywhere. In addition to the fitness centre, a nurse, naturopath, chiropractor, and massage therapist are on site most days, and employees receive a $500 annual benefit for vitamins. Husky nurtures the mind as well as the body, paying 100 percent of tuition and book costs for employees who attend university or college.

LEARNING OBJECTIVES

After reading Chapter 4, you should be able to:

1 Define *values* and discuss the implications of cross-cultural variation in values for organizational behaviour.

2 Define *attitudes* and explain how people develop and change attitudes.

3 Explain the concept of *job satisfaction* and discuss some of its key contributors, including discrepancy, fairness, disposition, mood, and emotion in promoting job satisfaction.

4 Outline the various consequences of job satisfaction and explain the relationship between job satisfaction and absenteeism, turnover, performance, organizational citizenship behaviour, and customer satisfaction.

5 Differentiate *affective, continuance,* and *normative commitment* and explain how organizations can foster *organizational commitment*.

Husky Injection Molding
Systems Ltd.
www.husky.ca

World Wildlife Fund
www.worldwildlife.org

The firm's governing ethos is strict egalitarianism. Executives use the same parking lot, dining room, and washrooms as everyone else. No titles denoting position are posted. Offices for executives are small and spartan. Casual dress is *de rigueur*. Employees with children can bring them to Husky's 15 500-square-foot, $5 million childcare centre, considered to be a model of contemporary daycare.

In keeping with Husky's concern for environmental responsibility, it recycles 95 percent of its industrial, office, and food waste, uses electric rather than gas-powered fork lifts, and is moving to ammonia-cooled air-conditioning systems. In addition, 5 percent of after-tax company profits go to charities and environmental causes, such as the World Wildlife Fund and the Canadian College of Naturopathic Medicine. Robert Schad is also a strong proponent of the Kyoto environmental accord, and threatened to quit the powerful Canadian Manufacturers and Exporters industry association over the group's anti-Kyoto position. Husky also introduced a program that allows employees to earn company shares by helping the environment and community through activities such as walking to work, photocopying on both sides of the paper, and coaching a sports team. Corporate Knights, an organization specializing in corporate ethics and social performance, recognized Husky in 2002 as Canada's most environmentally responsible company.

These benefits have allowed Husky to attract the best people and to keep them productive, happy, and proud of where they work. As well, Husky's emphasis on health and humanity pays concrete dividends. According to Schad, although Husky spends $2 to $3 million on social and environmental programs every year, they save $6 million a year on recycling, low absenteeism, and low turnover. There are also lower Workers' Compensation Board claims and more accident-free days. At the same time, such a work environment is not for everyone and obligations run both ways. "Values, intelligence and spark fit our culture. If you don't measure up, you don't stay," commented Schad.

Husky has exported its healthy habits and concern for the environment to the United States and Asia. At the opening of a $80 million manufacturing plant, Schad told the audience, "We don't want to build molds and machines, we want to build a company that's a role model for lasting business success based on our values." The governor of the state of Vermont described it this way: "This is the most remarkable plant in the state of Vermont, and it may be the most remarkable plant in the United States . . . It's a corporate example of how to do business." In 2004, Husky opened a new technical centre in Shanghai, China—a facility deemed one of the most energy-efficient industrial buildings in Asia because of its natural ventilation system, natural lighting, and naturalized landscaping. Overall, the Shanghai centre uses 40 percent of the average amount of energy required for a building of its size.

In late 2004, Robert Schad announced that he was stepping down as president and CEO of the firm he had built for over 50 years. When the new CEO, John Galt, was named in December 2005, the 76-year-old Schad emphasized that Galt had a strong belief in Husky's values through his 20 years of experience with the company. In reflecting on his career at Husky and the legacy he was leaving, Schad commented, "I hope my greatest legacy is that values are a foundation of successful and lasting businesses. This issue will become more and more important in selecting the people who run companies. I haven't quite proven this point yet, because Husky is not profitable enough. It's important that profitability go with the values, but it doesn't come first: Values come first, and because of the values you run a profitable and successful company."[1]

Would you be happy working at Husky? This would probably depend on your values and attitudes, important topics that we will cover in this chapter. Our discussion of values will be particularly oriented toward cross-cultural variations in values and their implications for organizational behaviour. Our discussion of attitudes will cover attitude formation and change. Two critical attitudes are job satisfaction and organizational commitment. We will consider the causes and consequences of both.

WHAT ARE VALUES?

We might define **values** as "a broad tendency to prefer certain states of affairs over others."[2] The *preference* aspect of this definition means that values have to do with what we consider good and bad. Values are motivational, since they signal the attractive aspects of our environment that we seek and the unattractive aspects that we try to avoid or change. The words *broad tendency* mean that values are very general, and that they do not predict behaviour in specific situations very well. Knowing that a person generally embraces the values that support capitalism does not tell us much about how he or she will respond to a homeless person on the street this afternoon.

Values. A broad tendency to prefer certain states of affairs over others.

It is useful to classify values into several categories: intellectual, economic, aesthetic, social, political, and religious.[3] Not everyone holds the same values. Managers might value high productivity (an economic value), while union officials might be more concerned with enlightened supervision and full employment (social values). Husky supports stronger social and health values than the typical organization. We learn values through the reinforcement processes we discussed in Chapter 2. Most are socially reinforced by parents, teachers, and representatives of religions.

To solidify your understanding of values and their impact on organizational behaviour, let's examine some occupational differences in values and see how work values differ across cultures.

Occupational Differences in Values

Members of different occupational groups espouse different values. A research program showed that university professors, city police officers, oil company salespeople, and entrepreneurs had values that distinguished them as groups from the general population.[4] For example, the professors valued "equal opportunity for all" more highly than the average person does. On the other hand, the salespeople and entrepreneurs ranked social values (peace, equality, freedom) lower than the average person does. Value differences such as these might be partially responsible for the occupational stereotypes that we discussed in Chapter 3. Further, these differences can cause conflict between organizations and within organizations when members of different occupations are required to interact with each other. For instance, doctors frequently report that their social values are at odds with the economic values of hospital administrators. In general, a good "fit" between the values of supervisors and employees promotes employee satisfaction and commitment.[5] There is also evidence that a good "fit" between an individual's values and the values of his or her organization (person–organization fit) also enhances job attitudes and behaviours.[6]

Do differences in occupational values develop after a person enters an occupation, or do such differences cause people to gravitate to certain occupations? Given the fact that values are relatively stable, and that many values are acquired early in life, it would appear that people choose occupations that correspond to their values.[7]

Values across Cultures

It is by now a cliché to observe that business has become global in its scope—Korean cars dot North American roads; your Dell helpdesk service provider resides in India; entire lines of "Italian" cookware are made in China. All this activity obscures just how difficult it can be to forge business links across cultures. For example, research shows that anywhere from 16 to 40 percent of managers who receive foreign assignments terminate them early because they perform poorly or do not adjust to the culture.[8] Similarly, a lengthy history of failed business negotiations is attributable to a lack of understanding of cross-cultural differences. At the root of many of these problems is a lack of appreciation of basic differences in work-related values across cultures. On the other hand, consider the opportunities for organizations that are globally adept (and for graduating students who are cross-culturally sensitive!).

Work Centrality. Work itself is valued differently across cultures. One large-scale survey of over 8000 individuals in several nations found marked cross-national differences in the extent to which people perceived work as a central life interest.[9] Japan topped the list, with very high work centrality. Belgians and Americans exhibited average work centrality, and the British scored low. One question in the survey asked respondents whether they would continue working if they won a large amount of money in a lottery. Those with more central interest in work were more likely to report that they would continue working despite the new-found wealth.

Customer-friendly service is a high work priority in Japan. Tokyo Disneyland is considered the safest, cleanest, and most orderly Disney park in the world.

The survey also found that people for whom work was a central life interest tended to work more hours. A reflection of this can be seen in Exhibit 4.1, which shows great variation in vacation time across cultures. This illustrates how cross-cultural differences in work centrality can lead to adjustment problems for foreign employees and managers. Imagine the unprepared British executive who is posted to Japan only to find that Japanese managers commonly work late and then socialize with co-workers or customers long into the night. In Japan, this is all part of the job, often to the chagrin of the lonely spouse. On the other hand, consider the Japanese executive posted to Britain who finds out that an evening at the pub is *not* viewed as an extension of the day at the office and not a place to continue talking business.

Hofstede's Study. Dutch social scientist Geert Hofstede questioned over 116 000 IBM employees located in 40 countries about their work-related values.[10] (There were 20 different language versions of the questionnaire.) Virtually everyone in the corporation participated. When Hofstede analyzed the results, he discovered four basic dimensions along which work-related values differed across cultures: power distance, uncertainty

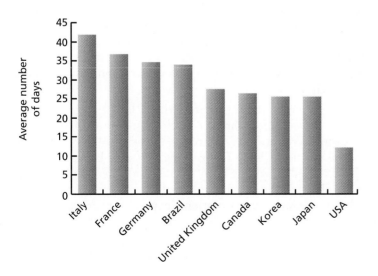

EXHIBIT 4.1
Vacation time across cultures.

Source: World Tourism Organization (WTO) as cited in Travel Industry Association of America (2002). *World Tourism Overview.* Retrieved July 18, 2003, from http://www.tia.org/ivis/worldtourism.asp#vacation.

avoidance, masculinity/femininity, and individualism/collectivism. Subsequent work with Canadian Michael Bond that catered more to Eastern cultures resulted in a fifth dimension, the long-term/short-term orientation.[11] More recently, the dimensions were verified and supplemented by the GLOBE project, headed by Professor Robert House.[12] You will learn more about this research that studied over 17 000 managers in 62 societies when we cover leadership in Chapter 9.

Power distance. The extent to which an unequal distribution of power is accepted by society members.

- *Power distance.* **Power distance** refers to the extent to which society members accept an unequal distribution of power, including those who hold more power and those who hold less. In small power distance cultures, inequality is minimized, superiors are accessible, and power differences are downplayed. In large power distance societies, inequality is accepted as natural, superiors are inaccessible, and power differences are highlighted. Small power distance societies include Denmark, New Zealand, Israel, and Austria. Large power distance societies include the Philippines, Venezuela, and Mexico. Out of 40 societies, Canada and the United States rank 14 and 15, respectively, falling on the low power distance side of the average, which would be 20.

Uncertainty avoidance. The extent to which people are uncomfortable with uncertain and ambiguous situations.

- *Uncertainty avoidance.* **Uncertainty avoidance** refers to the extent to which people are uncomfortable with uncertain and ambiguous situations. Strong uncertainty avoidance cultures stress rules and regulations, hard work, conformity, and security. Cultures with weak uncertainty avoidance are less concerned with rules, conformity, and security, and hard work is not seen as a virtue. However, risk taking is valued. Strong uncertainty avoidance cultures include Japan, Greece, and Portugal. Weak uncertainty avoidance cultures include Singapore, Denmark, and Sweden. On uncertainty avoidance, the United States and Canada are well below average (i.e., exhibiting weak uncertainty avoidance), ranking 9 and 10, respectively, out of 40.

- *Masculinity/femininity.* More masculine cultures clearly differentiate gender roles, support the dominance of men, and stress economic performance. More feminine cultures accept fluid gender roles, stress sexual equality, and stress quality of life. In Hofstede's research, Japan is the most masculine society, followed by Austria, Mexico, and Venezuela. The Scandinavian countries are the most feminine. Canada ranks about mid-pack, and the United States is fairly masculine, falling about halfway between Canada and Japan. The GLOBE research identified two aspects to this dimension—how assertive people are and how much they value gender equality.

Individualistic vs. collective. Individualistic societies stress independence, individual initiative, and privacy. Collective cultures favour interdependence and loyalty to family or clan.

- *Individualism/collectivism.* More **individualistic** societies tend to stress independence, individual initiative, and privacy. More **collective** cultures favour interdependence and loyalty to one's family or clan. The United States, Australia, Great Britain, and Canada are among the most individualistic societies. Venezuela, Columbia, and Pakistan are among the most collective, with Japan falling about mid-pack. The GLOBE research uncovered two aspects to this dimension—how much the collective distribution of resources is stressed and how much one's group or organization elicits loyalty.

- *Long-term/short-term orientation.* Cultures with a long-term orientation tend to stress persistence, perseverance, thrift, and close attention to status differences. Cultures with a short-term orientation stress personal steadiness and stability, face-saving, and social niceties. China, Hong Kong, Taiwan, Japan, and South Korea tend to be characterized by a long-term orientation. The United States, Canada, Great Britain, Zimbabwe, and Nigeria are more short-term oriented. Hofstede and Bond argue that the long-term orientation, in part, explains prolific East Asian entrepreneurship.

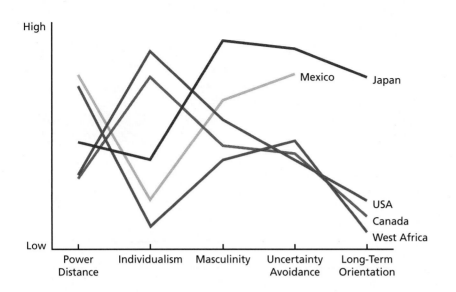

EXHIBIT 4.2
Cross-cultural value
comparisons.

Source: Graph by authors. Data from
Hofstede, G. (1991). *Cultures and
organizations: Software of the mind.*
London: McGraw-Hill. (Time orientation
data for Mexico unavailable.)

Exhibit 4.2 compares the United States, Canada, Mexico, Japan, and West Africa on Hofstede's value dimensions. Note that the profiles for Canada and the United States are very similar, but they differ considerably from that of Mexico.

Hofstede has produced a number of interesting "cultural maps" that show how countries and regions cluster together on pairs of cultural dimensions. The map in Exhibit 4.3 shows the relationship between power distance and degree of individualism. As you can see, these two values tend to be related. Cultures that are more individualistic tend to downplay power differences, while those that are more collectivistic tend to accentuate power differences.

Implications of Cultural Variation

Exporting OB Theories. An important message from the cross-cultural study of values is that organizational behaviour theories, research, and practices from North America might not translate well to other societies, even the one located just south of Texas.[13] The basic questions (How should I lead? How should we make this decision?) remain the same. It is just the *answers* that differ. For example, North American managers tend to encourage participation in work decisions by employees. This corresponds to the fairly low degree of power distance valued here. Trying to translate this leadership style to cultures that value high power distance might prove unwise. In these cultures, people might be more comfortable deferring to the boss's decision. Thus, it is unlikely that Husky could translate their low power distance and egalitarian style to all overseas locations. Similarly, in individualistic North America, calling attention to one's accomplishments is expected and often rewarded in organizations. In more collective Asian or South American cultures, individual success might be devalued, and it might make sense to reward groups rather than individuals. Finally, in extremely masculine cultures, integrating women into management positions might require special sensitivity.

A good fit between company practices and the host culture is important. In general, the American culture is more similar to the French culture than the Japanese culture. However, the Walt Disney Company found that its specific human resources practices fit well with Japanese culture, but not French culture (see "Global Focus: *Disney in Japan vs. Disney in France*").

Disneyland Paris
www.disneylandparis.com

Importing OB Theories. Not all theories and practices that concern organizational behaviour are designed in North America or even in the West. The most obvious examples are "Japanese management" techniques, such as quality circles, total quality

EXHIBIT 4.3
Power distance and individualism values for various countries and regions.

Source: Adapted from Hofstede, G. (1984). The cultural relativity of the quality of life concept. *Academy of Management Review, 9,* p. 391. Reprinted with permission. This material is protected by copyright and is being used with permission from *Access Copyright.* Any alteration of its content or further copying in any form whatsoever is strictly prohibited.

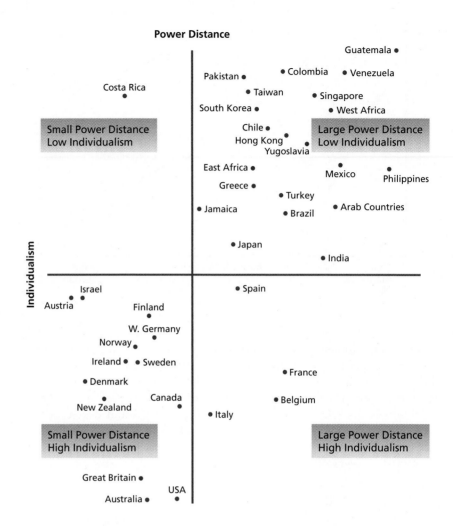

management, and just-in-time production. Although there are success stories of importing these techniques from Japan to North America, there are also examples of difficulties and failure. Many of the problems stem from basic value differences between Japan and North America. For example, the quest for continuous improvement and the heavy reliance on employee suggestions for improvement has had a mixed reaction.[14] In Japan, cultural values have traditionally dictated a fairly high degree of employment security. Thus, working at a fast pace and providing suggestions for improvement will not put one out of a job. North American workers are uncertain about this.

Many of the Japanese-inspired means of organizing work are team oriented. Since Japan has fairly collective cultural values, submerging one's own interests in those of the team is natural. Although employers have successfully used teams in North America, as you will see in Chapter 7, our more individualistic culture dictates that careful selection of team members is necessary.

Understanding cultural value differences can enable organizations to successfully import management practices by tailoring the practice to the home culture's concerns.

Appreciating Global Customers. An appreciation of cross-cultural differences in values is essential to understanding the needs and tastes of customers or clients around the world. Once relegated to the status of a marketing problem, it is now clear that such understanding fundamentally has to do with organizational behaviour. Errors

GLOBAL FOCUS

Disney in Japan vs. Disney in France

Disney prides itself on friendly service and safe, clean, and orderly surroundings. And Disney feels that its employees, or "cast," must have what it calls a "wholesome American look" to be able to properly execute their smiling "roles" in the "happiest place on Earth." New employees are taught about these things at Disney University.

Providing this kind of service and atmosphere at Tokyo Disneyland was not difficult, because Disney's type of service orientation meshes easily with Japanese cultural norms. In fact, customer-friendly service is so important in Japanese corporate culture that new hires at Japanese companies have to take a 6- to 12-month training program just to learn customer service techniques. Among other things, they learn to adopt a special high-pitched voice as a mark of respect when talking to customers. The match between Disney's corporate norms and Japanese cultural norms is so good that of all the Disney theme parks worldwide, Tokyo Disneyland is the safest, cleanest, and most orderly.

At Disneyland Paris, on the other hand, Disney had trouble achieving its standards for customer service and park surroundings. Because French workplaces tend not to have dress codes, employees felt that Disney's dress code—which includes allowable lengths for dress, hair, and fingernails—limited their right to personal expression. Disneyland Paris also had

problems getting its employees to smile the way they were taught at Disney University.

Inspections at Disneyland Paris have revealed all sorts of problems that make for a less than customer-friendly experience: messy grounds that lack the numerous sidewalk sweepers that are so prominent at other Disney parks, messy bathrooms with many broken stall doors, and unsmiling personnel. In one case, a food server got into an argument with a guest over the bill.

Unlike the custom in Japan and the United States, in France the customer isn't necessarily right. For example, waiters feel perfectly comfortable telling diners in their restaurant when they disapprove of their choice of dishes. Indeed, they take pride in doing so.

The mismatch between Disney's corporate norms and French cultural norms has resulted in a lot of negative press coverage. And in January 1995, Disneyland Paris was charged with having violated French labour laws for its attempt to impose the US dress code on its workers. Clearly, Disney's one-size-fits-all mentality needed to be adjusted to the differing cultural norms of France.

Source: Brannen, M.Y. (2004). When Mickey loses face: Recontextualization, semantic fit, and the semiotics of foreignness. *Academy of Management Review*, *29*, 593–616.

occur with regularity. For instance, the initial French response to the Disneyland Paris theme park was less enthusiastic than Disney management expected, probably due in part to Disney's failure to truly appreciate French tastes in food, lifestyle, and entertainment. South Korea's Samsung recalled a calendar featuring models displaying its products that was destined for overseas customers. Some North Americans were offended by Miss July's see-through blouse.

Samsung Electronics
www.samsungelectronics.com

Appreciating the values of global customers is also important when the customers enter your own culture. Many firms have profited from an understanding of the increasing ethnic diversity in the United States, Canada, and Australia.

Developing Global Employees. Success in translating management practices to other cultures, importing practices developed elsewhere, and appreciating global customers are not things that happen by accident. Rather, companies need to select, train, and develop employees to have a much better appreciation of differences in cultural values and the implications of these differences for behaviour in organizations.

To get their designers to better appreciate the values of the North American market, Japanese and Korean car makers, including Nissan, Toyota, Hyundai, and Kia,

General Motors
www.gm.com

have design studios in California. The top ranks of Detroit's automakers, once the protected realm of mid-westerners, are now liberally filled with Europeans or those with European or Asian experience. For example, Robert Lutz, vice-chairman of global product development at General Motors, did previous stints at BMW and Ford Europe. This has led to the development of cars that are more suitable for global markets. Korea's Samsung sends its most promising young employees overseas for a year, simply to immerse themselves in the values of another culture (as one executive put it, "to goof off at the mall"). The company feels that this will pay long-term dividends in terms of international competition.[15]

As you proceed through the text, you will encounter further discussion about the impact of cultural values on organizational behaviour. Now, let's examine attitudes and see how they are related to values.

WHAT ARE ATTITUDES?

Attitude. A fairly stable evaluative tendency to respond consistently to some specific object, situation, person, or category of people.

An **attitude** is a fairly stable evaluative tendency to respond consistently to some specific object, situation, person, or category of people. First, notice that attitudes involve *evaluations* directed toward *specific* targets. If I inquire about your attitude toward your boss, you will probably tell me something about how well you *like* him or her. This illustrates the evaluative aspect of attitudes. Attitudes are also much more specific than values, which dictate only broad preferences. For example, you could value working quite highly but still dislike your specific job.

The definition states that attitudes are *relatively stable*. Under normal circumstances, if you truly dislike German food or your boss today, you will probably dislike them tomorrow. Of course, some attitudes are less strongly held than others and are thus more open to change. If your negative attitude toward German cuisine stems from only a couple of experiences, I might be able to improve it greatly by exposing you to a home-cooked German meal. This provides you with some new information.

Our definition indicates that attitudes are *tendencies to respond* to the target of the attitude. Thus, attitudes often influence our behaviour toward some object, situation, person, or group:

Attitude ⟶ Behaviour

This is hardly surprising. If you truly dislike German food, I would not expect to see you eating it. By the same token, if you like your boss, it would not be surprising to hear you speaking well of him:

Dislike German Food ⟶ Don't Eat German Food

Like Boss ⟶ Praise Boss

Of course, not everyone who likes the boss goes around praising him in public, for fear of being seen as too political. Similarly, people who dislike the boss do not always engage in public criticism, for fear of retaliation. These examples indicate that attitudes are not always consistent with behaviour, and that attitudes provide useful information over and above the actions that we can observe.

Where do attitudes come from? Put simply, attitudes are a function of what we think and what we feel. That is, attitudes are the product of a related belief and value. If you believe that your boss is consultative, and you value consultation, we can conclude that you might have a favourable attitude toward the boss. We can represent this relationship in the form of a simple syllogism.[16] For example:

If the boss is consultative, (Belief)

And consultation is good, (Value)

Then the boss is good. (Attitude)

Given this point of view, we can now expand the attitude model presented earlier to include the thinking and feeling aspects of attitudes represented by beliefs and values:

$$\text{BELIEF} + \text{VALUE} \Rightarrow \text{Attitude} \longrightarrow \text{Behaviour}$$

Thus, we can imagine the following sequence of ideas in the case of a person experiencing work-family conflict:

"My job is interfering with my family life." (Belief)

"I dislike anything that hurts my family." (Value)

"I dislike my job." (Attitude)

"I'll search for another job." (Behaviour)

This simple example shows how attitudes (in this case, job satisfaction) develop from basic beliefs and values, and how they affect organizational behaviour (in this case, turnover from the organization).

Organizations often attempt to change employee attitudes. Most attempts at attitude change are initiated by a communicator who tries to use persuasion of some form to modify the beliefs or values of an audience that supports a currently held attitude.[17] For example, management might hold a seminar to persuade managers to value workforce diversity, or it might develop a training program to change attitudes toward workplace safety. Persuasion that is designed to modify or emphasize values is usually emotionally oriented. A safety message that concentrates on a dead worker's weeping, destitute family exemplifies this approach. Persuasion that is slanted toward modifying certain beliefs is usually rationally oriented. A safety message that tries to convince workers that hard hats and safety glasses are not uncomfortable to wear reveals this angle. You have probably seen both these approaches used in AIDS and anti-smoking campaigns.

The specific attitudes we are now going to cover, job satisfaction and organizational commitment, have a strong impact on people's positive contributions to their work.[18]

WHAT IS JOB SATISFACTION?

Job satisfaction refers to a collection of attitudes that people have about their jobs. We can differentiate two aspects of satisfaction. The first of these is facet satisfaction, the tendency for an employee to be more or less satisfied with various facets of the job. The notion of facet satisfaction is obvious when we hear someone say, "I love my work but hate my boss," or, "This place pays lousy, but the people I work with are great." Both these statements represent different attitudes toward separate facets of the speaker's job. Research suggests that the most relevant attitudes toward jobs are contained in a rather small group of facets: the work itself, compensation, career opportunities, recognition, benefits, working conditions, supervision, co-workers, and organizational policy.[19]

In addition to facet satisfaction, we can also conceive of overall satisfaction, an overall or summary indicator of a person's attitude toward his or her job that cuts across the various facets.[20] The statement, "On the whole, I really like my job, although a couple of aspects could stand some improvement," is indicative of the nature of overall satisfaction. Overall satisfaction is an average or total of the attitudes individuals hold toward various facets of the job. Thus, two employees might express the same level of overall satisfaction for different reasons.

The most popular measure of job satisfaction is the *Job Descriptive Index* (JDI).[21] This questionnaire is designed around five facets of satisfaction. Employees are asked to respond "yes," "no," or "?" (cannot decide) in describing whether a particular word

Job satisfaction. A collection of attitudes that workers have about their jobs.

EXHIBIT 4.4

Sample items from the Job Descriptive Index with "satisfied" responses.

Source: The Job Descriptive Index, revised 1985, is copyrighted by Bowling Green State University. The complete forms, scoring key, instructions, and norms can be obtained from the Department of Psychology, Bowling Green State University, Bowling Green, Ohio, 43404. Reprinted with permission.

Work

- N Routine
- Y Creative
- N Tiresome
- Y Gives sense of accomplishment

People

- Y Stimulating
- Y Ambitious
- N Talk too much
- N Hard to meet

Promotions

- Y Good opportunity for advancement
- Y Promotion on ability
- N Dead-end job
- N Unfair promotion policy

Supervision

- Y Asks my advice
- Y Praises good work
- N Doesn't supervise enough
- Y Tells me where I stand

Pay

- Y Income adequate for normal expenses
- N Bad
- N Less than I deserve
- Y Highly paid

or phrase is descriptive of particular facets of their jobs. Exhibit 4.4 shows some sample JDI items under each facet, scored in the "satisfied" direction. A scoring system is available to provide an index of satisfaction for each facet. In addition, an overall measure of satisfaction can be calculated by adding the separate facet indexes.

Another carefully constructed measure of satisfaction, using a somewhat different set of facets, is the *Minnesota Satisfaction Questionnaire* (MSQ).[22] On this measure, respondents indicate how happy they are with various aspects of their job on a scale ranging from "very satisfied" to "very dissatisfied." Sample items from the short form of the MSQ include the following:

- The competence of my supervisor in making decisions
- The way my job provides for steady employment
- The chance to do things for other people
- My pay and the amount of work I do

Scoring the responses to these items provides an index of overall satisfaction as well as satisfaction on the facets on which the MSQ is based.

Firms such as Sears, Marriott, 3M, and Microsoft make extensive use of employee attitude surveys. We will cover the details of such surveys in Chapter 10 when we explore communication and in Chapter 16 when we cover organizational change and development. For now, consider "Applied Focus: *High Tech Needs High Satisfaction.*"

WHAT DETERMINES JOB SATISFACTION?

When employees on a variety of jobs complete the JDI or the MSQ, we often find differences in the average scores across jobs. Of course, we could almost expect such differences. The various jobs might differ objectively in the facets that contribute to satisfaction. Thus, you would not be astonished to learn that a corporate vice-president was more satisfied with her job than a janitor in the same company. Of greater interest is the fact that we frequently find decided differences in job satisfaction expressed by individuals performing the same job in a given organization. For example, two nurses who work side by side might indicate radically different satisfaction in response to the MSQ item "The chance to do things for other people." How does this happen?

APPLIED FOCUS

High Tech Needs High Satisfaction

In the high tech and creative domains, much of organizational success depends on attracting and retaining the very best talent and creating an atmosphere free from distractions and inconveniences so that the creative juices can flow. The stress of project deadlines is commonplace. Because of these factors, firms such as Pixar Animation Studios and Microsoft go to extraordinary lengths to foster employee job satisfaction.

Pixar, acquired in 2006 by Disney, is responsible for the animated blockbusters *Toy Story*, *Finding Nemo*, and most recently *Cars*. The 16-acre Pixar campus in Emeryville, California, boasts an Olympic-size pool, sports courts and fields, a health club, and communal scooters. Some animators are given a budget to construct highly personalized "offices" within the large studio workspace; one resembles a mini suburban house, and another mimics a Tahitian grass hut with a hammock! "Pixar University" supports study related to the film in progress, such as scuba diving lessons for *Finding Nemo* and a performance driving course for *Cars*.

Responding to sagging attitude survey figures and stiff competition for top talent from Google and other Internet companies, Microsoft has acted decisively to bolster employee satisfaction. Pay increases and enhanced stock rewards form part of the package. Amenities that combat life's hassles and distractions are meant to counter Google's three free meals a day, free commuter transport, on-site car service, and free laundry. At Microsoft, these include on-site cleaning and laundry, grocery delivery from Safeway, and take-home dinners from Wolfgang Puck.

Sources: Mandel, D. (2006, May 29). A Cars is born. *AutoWeek*, 12–17; Bass, D. (2006, May 20). Microsoft pumps up pay, perks to head off worker exodus. *Ottawa Citizen*, D3.

Pixar Animation Studios
www.pixar.com

Discrepancy

You will recall that attitudes, such as job satisfaction, are the product of associated beliefs and values. These two factors cause differences in job satisfaction even when jobs are identical. First, people might differ in their beliefs about the job in question. That is, they might differ in their *perceptions* concerning the actual nature of the job. For example, one of the nurses might perceive that most of her working time is devoted to direct patient care, while the other might perceive that most of her time is spent on administrative functions. To the extent that they both value patient care, the former nurse should be more satisfied with this aspect of the job than the latter nurse. Second, even if individuals perceive their jobs as equivalent, they might differ in what they *want* from the jobs. Such desires are preferences that are dictated, in part, by the workers' value systems. Thus, if the two nurses perceive their opportunities to engage in direct patient care as high, the one who values this activity more will be more satisfied with the patient care aspect of work. The **discrepancy theory** of job satisfaction asserts that satisfaction is a function of the discrepancy between the job outcomes people want and the outcomes that they perceive they obtain.[23] For instance, there is strong evidence that satisfaction with one's pay is high when there is a small gap between the pay received and the perception of how much pay *should* be received.[24]

Discrepancy theory. A theory that job satisfaction stems from the discrepancy between the job outcomes wanted and the outcomes that are perceived to be obtained.

Fairness

In addition to the discrepancy between the outcomes people receive and those they desire, the other factor that determines job satisfaction is fairness. Issues of fairness affect both what people want from their jobs and how they react to the inevitable discrepancies of organizational life. As you will see, there are three basic kinds of fairness. Distributive fairness has to do with the outcomes we receive, procedural fairness concerns the process that led to those outcomes, and interactional fairness concerns how these matters were communicated to us.[25]

Distributive fairness. Fairness that occurs when people receive what they think they deserve from their jobs.

Equity theory. A theory that job satisfaction stems from a comparison of the inputs one invests in a job and the outcomes one receives in comparison with the inputs and outcomes of another person or group.

Inputs. Anything that people give up, offer, or trade to their organization in exchange for outcomes.

Outcomes. Factors that an organization distributes to employees in exchange for their inputs.

Distributive Fairness. **Distributive fairness** (often called distributive justice) occurs when people receive what they think they deserve from their jobs; that is, it involves the ultimate *distribution* of work rewards and resources. Above, we indicated that what people want from their jobs is a partial function of their value systems. In fact, however, there are practical limitations to this notion. You might value money and the luxurious lifestyle that it can buy very highly, but this does not suggest that you expect to receive a salary of $200 000 a year. In the case of many job facets, individuals want "what's fair." And how do we develop our conception of what is fair? **Equity theory** states that the inputs that people perceive themselves as investing in a job and the outcomes that the job provides are compared against the inputs and outcomes of some other relevant person or group.[26] Equity will be perceived when the following distribution ratios exist:

$$\frac{\text{My outcomes}}{\text{My inputs}} = \frac{\text{Other's outcomes}}{\text{Other's inputs}}$$

In these ratios, **inputs** consist of anything that individuals consider relevant to their exchange with the organization, anything that they give up, offer, or trade to their organization. These might include factors such as education, training, seniority, hard work, and high-quality work. **Outcomes** are those factors that the organization distributes to employees in return for their inputs. The most relevant outcomes are represented by the job facets we discussed earlier—pay, career opportunities, supervision, the nature of the work, and so on. The "other" in the ratio above might be a co-worker performing the same job, a number of co-workers, or even one's conception of all the individuals in one's occupation.[27] For example, the CEO of the Ford Motor Company probably compares his outcome/input ratio with those that he assumes exist for the CEOs of General Motors and DaimlerChrysler. You probably compare your outcome/input ratio in your organizational behaviour class with that of one or more fellow students.

Equity theory has important implications for job satisfaction. First, inequity itself is a dissatisfying state, especially when we are on the "short end of the stick." For example, suppose you see the hours spent studying as your main input to your organizational behaviour class and the final grade as an important outcome. Imagine that a friend in the class is your comparison person. Under these conditions, the following situations appear equitable and should not provoke dissatisfaction on your part:

You	Friend		You	Friend
C grade	A grade	or	A grade	C grade
50 hours	100 hours		60 hours	30 hours

In each of these cases, a "fair" relationship seems to exist between study time and grades distributed. Now consider the following relationships:

You	Friend		You	Friend
C grade	A grade	or	A grade	C grade
100 hours	50 hours		30 hours	60 hours

In each of these situations, an unfair connection appears to exist between study time and grades received, and you should perceive inequity. However, the situation on the left, in which you put in more work for a lower grade, should be most likely to prompt dissatisfaction. This is a "short end of the stick" situation. For example, the employee who frequently remains on the job after regular hours (input) and receives no special praise or extra pay (outcome) might perceive inequity and feel dissatisfied. Equity considerations also have an indirect effect on job satisfaction by influencing what people want from their jobs. If you study for 100 hours while the rest of the class averages 50 hours, you will expect a higher grade than the class average.

Recently, Bell Canada settled a 14-year, $100 million pay equity dispute with thousands of former and current telephone operators, most of them women. At the core of the dispute was the fact that the women were paid less and had less opportunity than those employed in "men's" jobs that required equivalent work inputs.[28]

Bell Canada
www.bell.ca

In summary, the equitable distribution of work outcomes contributes to job satisfaction by providing for feelings of distributive fairness. However, let's remember our earlier discussion of cross-cultural differences in values. The equity concept suggests that outcomes should be tied to individual contributions or inputs. This corresponds well with the individualistic North American culture. In more collective cultures, *equality* of outcomes might produce more feelings of distributive fairness. In more feminine cultures, allocating outcomes according to *need* (rather than performance) might provide for distributive fairness.

Procedural Fairness. **Procedural fairness** (often called procedural justice) occurs when individuals see the process used to determine outcomes as reasonable; that is, rather than involving the actual distribution of resources or rewards, it is concerned with how these outcomes are decided and allocated. An example will illustrate the difference between distributive and procedural fairness. Out of the blue, Greg's boss tells him that she has completed his performance evaluation and that he will receive a healthy pay raise starting next month. Greg has been working very hard, and he is pleased with the pay raise (distributive fairness). However, he is vaguely unhappy about the fact that all this occurred without his participation. Where he used to work, the employee and the boss would complete independent performance evaluation forms and then sit down and discuss any differences. This provided good feedback for the employee. Greg wonders how his peers who got less generous raises are reacting to the boss's style.

Procedural fairness.
Fairness that occurs when the process used to determine work outcomes is seen as reasonable.

Procedural fairness is particularly relevant to outcomes such as performance evaluations, pay raises, promotions, layoffs, and work assignments. In allocating such outcomes, the following factors contribute to perceptions of procedural fairness.[29] The allocator

- follows consistent procedures over time and across people;
- uses accurate information and appears unbiased;
- allows two-way communication during the allocation process; and
- welcomes appeals of the procedure or allocation.

As you might imagine, procedural fairness seems especially likely to provoke dissatisfaction when people also see distributive fairness as being low.[30] One view notes that dissatisfaction will be "maximized when people believe that they *would* have obtained better outcomes if the decision maker had used other procedures that *should* have been implemented."[31] (Students who receive lower grades than their friends will recognize the wisdom of this observation!) Thus, Greg, mentioned above, will probably not react too badly to the lack of consultation, while his peers who did not receive large raises might strongly resent the process that the boss used.

Interactional Fairness. **Interactional fairness** (often called interactional justice) occurs when people feel that they have received respectful and informative communication about some outcome.[32] In other words, it extends beyond the actual procedures used to the interpersonal treatment received when learning about the outcome. Respectful communication is sincere and polite and treats the individual with dignity; informative communication is candid, timely, and thorough. Interactional fairness is important because it is possible for absolutely fair outcomes or procedures to be perceived as unfair when they are inadequately or uncaringly explained.

Interactional fairness.
Fairness that occurs when people feel they have received respectful nd informative communication about an outcome.

Sometimes, lower-level managers have little control over procedures that are used to allocate resources. However, they almost always have the opportunity to explain these procedures in a thorough, truthful, and caring manner. Frequently, people who experience procedural unfairness are dissatisfied with the "system." On the other hand, people who experience interactional unfairness are more likely dissatisfied with the boss.

Both procedural and interactional fairness can to some extent offset the negative effects of distributive unfairness. In one interesting study, nurses who received a pay cut due to hospital policy changes exhibited less insomnia when their supervisors were trained in the principles of interactional fairness compared to nurses with untrained supervisors.[33]

Disposition

Could your personality contribute to your feelings of job satisfaction? This is the essential question guiding research on the relationship between disposition and job satisfaction. Underlying the previous discussion is the obvious implication that job satisfaction can increase when the work environment changes to increase fairness and decrease the discrepancy between what an individual wants and what the job offers. Underlying the dispositional view of job satisfaction is the idea that some people are *predisposed* by virtue of their personalities to be more or less satisfied despite changes in discrepancy or fairness. This follows from the discussion in Chapter 2 on the dispositional approach and personality.

Some of the research that suggests that disposition contributes to job satisfaction is fascinating. Although each of these studies has some problems, as a group they point to a missing dispositional link.[34] For example:

- Identical twins raised apart from early childhood tend to have similar levels of job satisfaction.

- Job satisfaction tends to be fairly stable over time, even when changes in employer occur.

- Disposition measured early in adolescence is correlated with one's job satisfaction as a mature adult.

Taken together, these findings suggest that some personality characteristics originating in genetics or early learning contribute to adult job satisfaction.

Recent research on disposition and job satisfaction has centred around the "Big Five" personality traits (Chapter 2). People who are extraverted and conscientious tend to be more satisfied with their jobs, while those high in neuroticism are less satisfied.[35] Also, people who are high in self-esteem and internal locus of control are more satisfied.[36] Thus, in general, people who are more optimistic and proactive report higher job satisfaction. Mood and emotion may contribute to this connection, so we will now examine these topics.

Mood and Emotion

The picture we have painted so far of the determinants of job satisfaction has been mostly one of calculation and rationality: people calculate discrepancies, compare job inputs to outcomes, and so on. But what about the intense feelings that are sometimes seen in work settings—the joy of a closed business deal or the despair that leads to workplace homicides? Or what about that vague feeling of a lack of accomplishment that blunts the pleasure of a dream job? We are speaking here about the role of affect as a determinant of job satisfaction. Affect is simply a broad label for feelings. These feelings include **emotions**, which are intense, often short-lived, and caused by a particular event such as a bad performance appraisal. Common emotions include joy, pride, anger, fear, and sadness. Affect also refers to **moods**, which are less intense, longer-lived, and more diffuse feelings.

How do emotions and moods affect job satisfaction? Affective events theory, proposed by Howard Weiss and Russell Cropanzano, addresses this question.[37] Basically,

Emotions. Intense, often short-lived feelings caused by a particular event.

Moods. Less intense, longer-lived, and more diffuse feelings.

the theory reminds us that jobs actually consist of a series of events and happenings that have the potential to provoke emotions or to influence moods, depending on how we appraise these events and happenings. Thus, seeing a co-worker being berated by a manager might provoke emotional disgust and lower one's job satisfaction, especially if it is a frequent occurrence. This illustrates that perceived unfairness, as discussed earlier, can affect job satisfaction via emotion. Also, a person's disposition can interact with job events to influence satisfaction. For instance, those who are neurotic and pessimistic may react to a minor series of job setbacks with a negative mood that depresses their job satisfaction.

An interesting way in which mood and emotion can influence job satisfaction is through **emotional contagion**. This is the tendency for moods and emotions to spread between people or throughout a group. Thus, people's moods and emotions tend to converge with interaction. Generally, teams experiencing more positive affect tend to be more cooperative, helpful, and successful, all of which are conditions that contribute to job satisfaction.[38] Emotional contagion can also occur in dealing with customers, such that pleasant service encounters contribute to the service provider's satisfaction as well as to that of the customer.

> **Emotional contagion.** Tendency for moods and emotions to spread between people or throughout a group.

Another interesting way in which mood and emotion can influence job satisfaction is through the need for **emotional regulation**. This is the requirement for people to conform to certain "display rules" in their job behaviour, in spite of their true mood or emotions. Often, this is referred to informally as "emotional labour." In one version, employees are expected to be perky and upbeat, whether they feel that way or not, thus exaggerating positive emotions. In the other version, employees are supposed to remain calm and civil even when hassled or insulted, thus suppressing negative emotions. One study found that call centre employees averaged 10 incidents of customer aggression a day.[39] All jobs have their implicit display rules, such as not acting angry in front of the boss. However, service roles such as waiter, bank teller, and flight attendant are especially laden with display rules, some of which may be made explicit in training and via cues from managers.

> **Emotional regulation.** Requirement for people to conform to certain "display rules" in their job behaviour in spite of their true mood or emotions.

What are the consequences of the requirement for emotional regulation? There is growing evidence that the frequent need to suppress negative emotions takes a toll on job satisfaction and increases stress.[40] Flight attendants can only humour so many drunk or angry air passengers before the experience wears thin! On the other hand, the jury is still out on the requirement to express positive emotions. Some research suggests that this display rule boosts job satisfaction.[41] If so, positive contagion from happy customers may be responsible. Of course, disposition may again enter the picture, as extraverts may be energized by requirements for positive display.

Do organizations pay a premium for emotional labour? The answer is sometimes. Theresa Glomb, John Kammeyer-Mueller, and Maria Rotundo studied the emotional labour and cognitive demands (thinking, decision making) required in various occupations (see Exhibit 4.5).[42] They found that those in occupations with high cognitive demands (the upper portion of the exhibit) tend to be paid more when the jobs are also high in emotional labour. Thus, lawyers tend to earn more than zoologists. On the other hand, occupations with low cognitive demands entail a wage penalty when emotional labour is higher. Thus, the "people jobs" in the lower right quadrant of the exhibit tend to be less well paid than the jobs in the lower left quadrant. As we will see shortly, pay is an important determinant of job satisfaction.

Consideration of mood and emotion helps explain a curious but commonplace phenomenon: how people with similar beliefs and values doing the same job for the same compensation can still exhibit very different satisfaction levels. This difference is probably a result of emotional events and subtle differences in mood that add up over time. We will revisit emotion when we study emotional intelligence (Chapter 5), decision making (Chapter 11), stress (Chapter 13), and organizational change (Chapter 16).

EXHIBIT 4.5
Occupations plotted by
emotional labour and
cognitive demands.

Source: Adapted from Glomb, T.M.,
Kammeyer-Mueller, J.D., & Rotundo, M.
(2004). Emotional labor demands and
compensating wage differentials.
Journal of Applied Psychology, 89,
700–714.

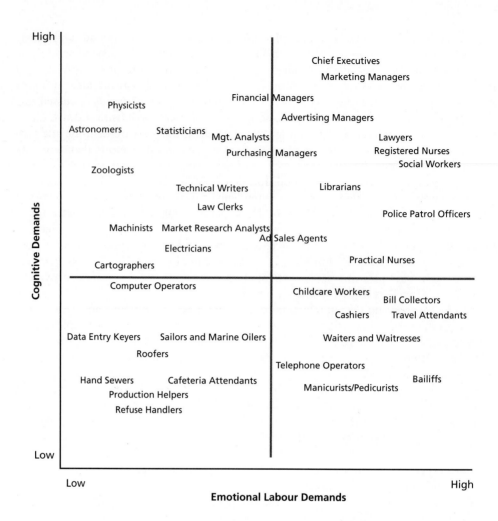

Exhibit 4.6 summarizes what research has to say about the determinants of job satisfaction. To recapitulate, satisfaction is a function of certain dispositional factors, the discrepancy between the job outcomes a person wants and the outcomes received, and mood and emotion. More specifically, people experience greater satisfaction when they meet or exceed the job outcomes they want, perceive the job outcomes they receive as equitable compared with those others receive, and believe that fair procedures deter-

EXHIBIT 4.6
How discrepancy,
fairness, disposition,
mood, and emotion
affect job satisfaction.

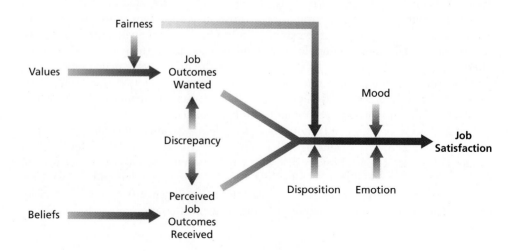

mine job outcomes. The outcomes that people want from a job are a function of their personal value systems, moderated by equity considerations. The outcomes that people perceive themselves as receiving from the job represent their beliefs about the nature of that job.

Key Contributors to Job Satisfaction

From what we have said thus far, you might expect that job satisfaction is a highly personal experience. While this is essentially true, we can make some general statements about the facets that seem to contribute the most to feelings of job satisfaction for most North American workers. These include mentally challenging work, adequate compensation, career opportunities, and friendly or helpful colleagues.[43]

Mentally Challenging Work. This is work that tests employees' skills and abilities and allows them to set their own working pace. Employees usually perceive such work as personally involving and important. It also provides the worker with clear feedback regarding performance. Of course, some types of work can be too challenging, and this can result in feelings of failure and reduced satisfaction. In addition, some employees seem to prefer repetitive, unchallenging work that makes few demands on them.

Adequate Compensation. It should not surprise you that pay and satisfaction are positively related. Employee job satisfaction at Husky is probably partly due to industry-high salaries as well as bonuses received as part of the company's profit-sharing plan. However, not everyone is equally desirous of money, and some people are certainly willing to accept less responsibility or fewer working hours for lower pay. In most companies, one finds a group of employees who are especially anxious to earn extra money through overtime and another group that actively avoids overtime work.

Career Opportunities. The availability of career opportunities contributes to job satisfaction. Opportunity for promotion is an important contributor to job satisfaction because promotions contain a number of valued signals about a person's self-worth. Some of these signals may be material (such as an accompanying raise), while others are of a social nature (recognition within the organization and increased prestige in the community). Of course, there are cultural and individual differences in what people see as constituting a fair promotion system. Some employees might prefer a strict seniority system, while others might wish for a system based strictly on job performance. Many of today's flatter organizations no longer offer the promotion opportunities of the past. Well-run firms have offset this by designing lateral moves that provide for challenging work. Also, as discussed in Chapter 2, career development helps prepare employees to assume challenging assignments.

People. It should not surprise you that friendly, considerate, good-natured superiors and co-workers contribute to job satisfaction, especially via positive moods and emotions. There is, however, another aspect to interpersonal relationships on the job that contributes to job satisfaction. Specifically, we tend to be satisfied in the presence of people who help us attain job outcomes that we value. Such outcomes might include doing our work better or more easily, obtaining a raise or promotion, or even staying alive. For example, a company of soldiers in battle might be less concerned with how friendly their commanding officer is than with how competently he is able to act to keep them from being overrun by the enemy. Similarly, an aggressive young executive might like a considerate boss but prefer even more a boss who can clarify her work objectives and reward her for attaining them. The friendliness aspect of interpersonal relationships seems most important in lower-level jobs with clear duties and various dead-end jobs. If pay is tied to performance, or as jobs become more complex or promotion opportunities increase, the ability of others to help us do our work well contributes more to job satisfaction.

For some types of jobs, the challenge of achieving employee satisfaction can be particularly difficult. Consider the example in the You Be the Manager feature.

RAC Motoring Services
www.rac.co.uk

☞ YOU BE THE
Manager

RAC's Call Centres

In today's service-oriented economy with its focus on high-tech communication, call centres have become one of the most popular means of delivering customer service. Unfortunately, call centres have come to be viewed by many as the sweatshops of the twenty-first century, where employees are overworked, underpaid, and highly stressed. They are also often characterized by close supervision, as call statistics are meticulously examined and calls are regularly listened in on, with or without the knowledge of the employee.

While employee well-being has been identified as a problem, call centres can also have an important impact on organizational outcomes. Call centres have been shown to have very high turnover and absenteeism rates, which result in extra costs for employers. Furthermore, call centre employees are often the primary contact between customers and the company. As such, it has been suggested that the job satisfaction of call centre employees can influence customer satisfaction, which can impact company revenues in future years. Given the popularity of call centres, the stress experienced by their workers, and the potential impact on the bottom line, how can employers increase the job satisfaction of their call centre employees? This was the question faced by RAC Motoring Services, the UK's second-largest automotive membership organization.

In 1996, RAC, which is similar to AAA (American Automobile Association) in the United States or CAA (Canadian Automobile Association) in Canada, lost three-quarters of a million customers to competitors or through non-renewals. Given the nature of their services (car buying guides, travel planning, roadside assistance), managers at RAC recognized that keeping customers happy was the best way to compete in this tough market. As such, they decided to focus on their call centre operations to improve service quality for existing and potential customers. In the company's review of its two call centres in England, serious problems were uncovered, including a lack of one-stop shopping for customers, inflexible working practices, an inability to attract and retain staff, low employee morale, and poor training and development.

> ### RAC combats traditional call centre problems.

In response to this review, a customer service director was appointed to initiate a number of important changes in how the call centres operate. Imagine you have just been appointed to this new position and consider the following two questions:

QUESTIONS

1. **What are some of the reasons underlying the fact that so many practices commonly used in call centres lead to poor employee satisfaction?**

2. **Given the nature of the work, what are some concrete steps or programs that you could put in place to improve job satisfaction for RAC's call centre employees?**

To find out what RAC did, see The Manager's Notebook at the end of the chapter.

Sources: Barnes, P.C. (2001, July). People problems in call centres, *Management Services, 7*, 30–31; Holman, D. (2002). Employee well being in call centres. *Human Resource Management Journal, 12*, 35–50; Hutchinson, S., Purcell, J., & Kinnie, N. (2000). Evolving high commitment management and the experience of the RAC call centre. *Human Resource Management Journal, 10*, 63–78.

CONSEQUENCES OF JOB SATISFACTION

Dell, Sears, and L'Oréal Canada are firms that have maintained a competitive advantage by paying particular attention to employee satisfaction. Why is this so? Let's look at some consequences of job satisfaction.

Absence from Work

At Husky Injection Molding Systems, the rate of absenteeism is much lower than at other organizations. This is no small feat, as absenteeism is an expensive behaviour in North America. One estimate pegs the annual American cost at up to $46 billion and the Canadian cost at up to $10 billion and on the rise.[44] Such costs are attributable to "sick pay," lost productivity, and chronic overstaffing to compensate for absentees. Many more days are lost to absenteeism than to strikes and other industrial disputes. Is some of this absenteeism the product of job dissatisfaction? Research shows that less-satisfied employees are indeed more likely to be absent, and that satisfaction with the content of the work is the best predictor of absenteeism.[45] However, the absence–satisfaction connection is not very strong. Several factors probably constrain the ability of many people to convert their like or dislike of work into corresponding attendance patterns:

- Some absence is simply unavoidable because of illness, weather conditions, or daycare problems. Thus, some very happy employees will occasionally be absent owing to circumstances beyond their control.

- Opportunities for off-the-job satisfaction on a missed day may vary. Thus, you might love your job but love skiing or sailing even more. In this case, you might skip work while a dissatisfied person who has nothing better to do shows up.

- Some organizations have attendance control policies that can influence absence more than satisfaction does. In a company that doesn't pay workers for missed days (typical of many hourly paid situations), absence may be more related to economic needs than to dissatisfaction. The unhappy worker who absolutely needs money will probably show up for work. By the same token, dissatisfied and satisfied workers might be equally responsive to threats of dismissal if they are absent.

- On many jobs, it might be unclear to employees how much absenteeism is reasonable or sensible. With a lack of company guidelines, workers might look to the behaviour of their peers for a norm to guide their behaviour. This norm and its corresponding "absence culture" (see Chapter 7) might have a stronger effect than the individual employee's satisfaction with his or her job.[46]

The connection between job satisfaction and good attendance probably stems in part from the tendency for job satisfaction to facilitate mental health and satisfaction with life in general.[47] Content people will attend work with enthusiasm.

Turnover

Turnover refers to resignation from an organization, and it can be incredibly expensive. For example, it costs several thousand dollars to replace a nurse or a bank teller who resigns. As we move up the organizational hierarchy, or into technologically complex jobs, such costs escalate dramatically. For example, it costs millions of dollars to hire and train a single military fighter pilot. Estimates of turnover costs usually include the price of hiring, training, and developing to proficiency a replacement employee. Such figures probably underestimate the true costs of turnover, however, because they do not include intangible costs, such as work group disruption or the loss of employees who informally acquire special skills and knowledge over time on a job. All this would not be so bad if turnover were concentrated among poorer performers. Unfortunately, this is not always the case. In one study, 23 percent of scientists and engineers who left an organization were among the top 10 percent of performers.[48]

What is the relationship between job satisfaction and turnover? Research indicates a moderately strong connection, with less-satisfied workers being more likely to quit.[49] Thus, it is not surprising that Husky has a low turnover rate. However, the relationship between the attitude (job satisfaction) and the behaviour in question (turnover) is far from perfect. Exhibit 4.7 presents a model of turnover that can help explain this.[50] In the model, circles represent attitudes, ovals represent elements of the turnover process, and squares denote situational factors. The model shows that job satisfaction as well as commitment to the organization and various "shocks" (both discussed below) can contribute to intentions to leave. Research shows that such intentions are very good predictors of turnover.[51] As shown, such intentions sometimes prompt turnover directly, even impulsively. On the other hand, reduced satisfaction or commitment can also stimulate a more deliberate evaluation of the utility of quitting and a careful job search and evaluation of job alternatives. The following are some reasons why satisfied people sometimes quit their jobs or dissatisfied people stay:

- Certain "shocks," such as a marital breakup, the birth of a child, or an unsolicited job offer in an attractive location, might stimulate turnover despite satisfaction with the current job.

- An employee's dissatisfaction with his or her specific job might be offset by a strong commitment to the overall values and mission of the organization.

- An employee might be so embedded in the community (due to involvement with churches, schools, or sports) that he or she is willing to endure a dissatisfying job rather than move.

- A weak job market might result in limited employment alternatives. Dissatisfaction is most likely to result in turnover when jobs are plentiful.[52]

Despite these exceptions, a decrease in job satisfaction often precedes turnover, and those who quit experience a boost in satisfaction on their new job. However, some of this boost might be due to a "honeymoon effect" in which the bad facets of the old job

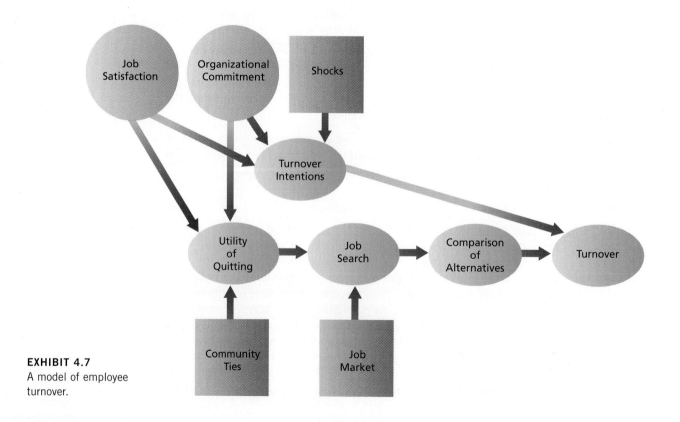

EXHIBIT 4.7
A model of employee turnover.

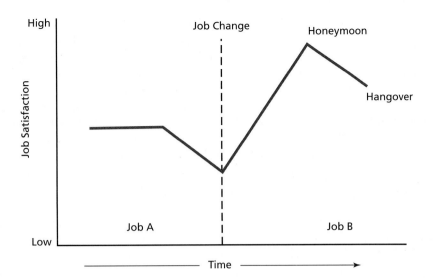

EXHIBIT 4.8
The honeymoon-hangover effect.

Source: Based on Boswell, W.R., Boudreau, J.W., & Tichy, J. (2005). The relationship between employee job change and job satisfaction: The honeymoon-hangover effect. *Journal of Applied Psychology, 90,* 882–892.

are gone, the good facets of the new job are apparent, and the bad facets of the new job are not yet known. Over time, as these bad facets are recognized, a "hangover effect" can occur in which overall satisfaction with the new job decreases.[53] This pattern is shown in Exhibit 4.8, which traces job satisfaction at five points in time as a person moves between jobs A and B.

Performance

It seems sensible that job satisfaction contributes to less absenteeism and turnover, but does it also lead to improved job performance? After all, employees might be so "satisfied" that no work is accomplished! In fact, research has confirmed what folk wisdom and business magazines have advocated for many years—job satisfaction is associated with enhanced performance.[54] However, the connection between satisfaction and performance is complicated, because many factors influence motivation and performance besides job satisfaction (as we'll see in Chapter 5). Thus, research has led to some qualifications to the idea that "a happy worker is a productive worker."

All satisfaction facets are not equal in terms of stimulating performance. The most important facet has to do with the content of the work itself.[55] Thus, interesting, challenging jobs are most likely to stimulate high performance (we will see how to design such jobs in Chapter 6). One consequence of this is the fact that the connection between job satisfaction and performance is stronger for complex high-tech jobs in science, engineering, and computers and less strong for more routine labour jobs. In part, this is because people doing complex jobs have more control over their level of performance.

Another issue in the connection between job satisfaction and performance has to do with which of these is the cause and which the effect. Although job satisfaction contributes to performance, performance probably also contributes to job satisfaction.[56] How does this happen? When good performance is *followed by rewards*, employees are more likely to be satisfied. Thus, the standout computer analyst who is given a bonus should register an increase in job satisfaction. This reversed causality is beneficial because the other benefits of high satisfaction accrue. However, many organizations do not reward good performance sufficiently, thus setting a limit on the connection between satisfaction and performance.

In addition to boosting formal job performance, satisfaction can also contribute to employees' informal, everyday behaviour and actions that help their organizations and their co-workers. Let's turn now to a discussion of this.

Organizational Citizenship Behaviour

Organizational citizenship behaviour (OCB) is voluntary, informal behaviour that contributes to organizational effectiveness.[57] In many cases, the formal performance evaluation system does not detect and reward it. Job satisfaction contributes greatly to the occurrence of OCB.[58]

An example of OCB should clarify the concept. You are struggling to master a particularly difficult piece of software. A colleague at the next desk, busy on her own rush job, comes over and offers assistance. Irritated with the software, you are not even very grateful at first, but within 10 minutes you have solved the problem with her help. Notice the defining characteristics of this example of OCB:

- The behaviour is voluntary. It is not included in her job description.
- The behaviour is spontaneous. Someone did not order or suggest it.
- The behaviour contributes to organizational effectiveness. It extends beyond simply doing you a personal favour.
- The behaviour is unlikely to be explicitly picked up and rewarded by the performance evaluation system, especially since it is not part of the job description.

What are the various forms that OCB might take? As the software example indicates, one prominent form is *helping* behaviour, offering assistance to others. Another might be *conscientiousness* to the details of work, including getting in on the snowiest day of the year and not wasting organizational resources. A third form of OCB involves being a *good sport* when the inevitable frustrations of organizational life crop up—not everyone can have the best office or the best parking spot. A final form of OCB is *courtesy and cooperation*.[59] Examples might include warning the photocopy unit about a big job that is on the way or delaying one's own work to assist a colleague on a rush job.

Just how does job satisfaction contribute to OCB? Fairness seems to be the key.[60] Although distributive fairness (especially in terms of pay) is important, procedural and interactional fairness from a supportive manager seem especially critical.[61] If the manager strays from the prescriptions for procedural fairness we gave earlier, OCB can suffer. If one feels unfairly treated, it might be difficult to lower formal performance for fear of dire consequences. It might be much easier to withdraw the less visible,

Organizational citizenship behaviour. Voluntary, informal behaviour that contributes to organizational effectiveness.

When one worker voluntarily helps out another, it is an example of organizational citizenship, which positively affects organizational effectiveness.

informal activities that make up OCB. On the other hand, fair treatment and its resulting satisfaction might be reciprocated with OCB, a truly personalized input.

It is interesting that OCB is also influenced by employees' mood at work. People in a pleasant, relaxed, optimistic mood are more likely to provide special assistance to others.[62] Some of this research is based on studies with salespeople, so OCB might make customer service more competitive. Let's look at this issue.

Customer Satisfaction and Profit

So far, we have established that job satisfaction can reduce employee absenteeism and turnover and increase employee performance and citizenship behaviour. But is it possible that employee satisfaction could actually affect *customer* satisfaction? That is, do happy employees translate into happy customers? And do happy employees actually contribute to the bottom line of the organization by increasing organizational profits? After all, we have warned that the translation of positive attitudes into positive employee behaviours is less than perfect and such attitudes therefore might not affect the bottom line.

A growing body of evidence has established that employee job satisfaction is indeed translated into customer or client satisfaction and organizational profitability.[63] Thus, organizations with higher average levels of employee satisfaction are more effective. The same applies to units within larger organizations. Hence, local bank branches or insurance claims offices with more satisfied employees should tend to have more satisfied clients and generate more profits for the larger firm. Thus, it makes good sense to use employee satisfaction as one criterion in judging the effectiveness of local unit managers.

How does employee satisfaction translate into customer satisfaction? Reduced absenteeism and turnover contribute to the seamless delivery of service, as do the OCBs that stimulate good teamwork. Also, the mood mechanism, mentioned earlier, should not be discounted, as good mood among employees can be contagious for customers.

The Ford Motor Company (see Chapter 16) and Sears have been particularly attentive to the links among employee satisfaction, customer satisfaction, and profit. In an 800-store study, Sears found a clear positive relationship between employee satisfaction and store profitability. In addition, improvements in employee satisfaction were mirrored in customer satisfaction, resulting in an estimated $200 million in added annual revenue.[64]

Sears Canada
www.sears.ca

Let's turn now to another important work attitude—organizational commitment.

WHAT IS ORGANIZATIONAL COMMITMENT?

Organizational commitment is an attitude that reflects the strength of the linkage between an employee and an organization. This linkage has implications for whether someone tends to remain in an organization. Researchers John Meyer and Natalie Allen have identified three very different types of organizational commitment:[65]

Organizational commitment. An attitude that reflects the strength of the linkage between an employee and an organization.

- **Affective commitment** is commitment based on a person's identification and involvement with an organization. People with high affective commitment stay with an organization because they *want* to. Employees at Husky have high affective commitment. They participate in rotating council meetings where they make suggestions for improvements and they are proud of where they work.

Affective commitment. Commitment based on identification and involvement with an organization.

- **Continuance commitment** is commitment based on the costs that would be incurred in leaving an organization. People with high continuance commitment stay with an organization because they *have* to.

Continuance commitment. Commitment based on the costs that would be incurred in leaving an organization.

Normative commitment. Commitment based on ideology or a feeling of obligation to an organization.

- **Normative commitment** is commitment based on ideology or a feeling of obligation to an organization. People with high normative commitment stay with an organization because they think that they *should* do so.

Employees can be committed not only to their organization, but also to various constituencies within and outside the organization. Thus, each type of commitment could also apply to one's work team, union, or profession.[66]

Key Contributors to Organizational Commitment

The causes of the three forms of commitment tend to differ. By far the best predictor of affective commitment is interesting, satisfying work of the type found in enriched jobs (see Chapter 6).[67] One mistake that organizations sometimes make is starting employees out in unchallenging jobs so they do not make any serious errors. This can have a negative impact on affective commitment. Role clarity and having one's expectations met after being hired also contribute to affective commitment.[68]

Continuance commitment occurs when people feel that leaving the organization will result in personal sacrifice, or they perceive that good alternative employment is lacking. Building up "side bets" in pension funds, obtaining rapid promotion, or being well integrated into the community where the firm is located can lock employees into organizations even though they would rather go elsewhere. Not surprisingly, continuance commitment increases with the time a person is employed by an organization.

Normative commitment ("I *should* stay here") can be fostered by benefits that build a sense of obligation to the organization. These might include tuition reimbursements or special training that enhances one's skills. Strong identification with an organization's product or service ("I should stay here because the Sierra Club is doing important work") can also foster normative commitment. Finally, certain socialization practices (see Chapter 8) that emphasize loyalty to the organization can stimulate normative commitment. For example, sports coaches often haze players who miss practice to stress the importance of loyalty to the team.

Consequences of Organizational Commitment

There is good evidence that all forms of commitment reduce turnover intentions and actual turnover.[69] Organizations plagued with turnover problems among key employees should look carefully at tactics that foster commitment. This is especially called for when turnover gets so bad that it threatens customer service. Many service organizations (e.g., restaurants and hotels), however, have traditionally accepted high turnover rates.

Organizations should take care, though, in their targeting of the kind of commitment to boost. Affective commitment is positively related to performance because it focuses attention on goals and thus enhances motivation (see Chapter 5).[70] However, continuance commitment is *negatively* related to performance, something you might have observed in dealing with burned-out bureaucrats.[71] An especially bad combination for both the employee and the organization is high continuance commitment coupled with low affective commitment—people locked into organizations that they detest. This happens very frequently during recessions.

Is there a downside to organizational commitment? Very high levels of commitment can cause conflicts between family life and worklife. Also, very high levels of commitment have often been implicated in unethical and illegal behaviour, including a General Electric price-fixing conspiracy. Finally, high levels of commitment to a particular *form or style* of organization can cause a lack of innovation and lead to resistance when a change in the culture is necessary.[72]

General Electric
www.ge.com

Changes in the Workplace and Employee Commitment

Organizations are experiencing unprecedented change as a result of shifts in workforce demographics, technological innovations, and global competition.[73] In an era of lay-offs, downsizing, outsourcing, restructuring, and reengineering, there is evidence that employees are losing commitment to their organizations.[74] People often view their careers as a series of jobs with a variety of potential employers, or they even see themselves as freelancers rather than having a series of jobs in one organization. Because of the consequences of employee commitment for individuals and organizations, it is important to understand how these changes might affect employee commitment.

John Meyer, Natalie Allen, and Laryssa Topolnytsky have studied commitment in a changing world of work, and they note that the impact of changes in the workplace on employee commitment can be seen in three main areas:[75]

- *Changes in the nature of employees' commitment to the organization.* Depending on the nature of workplace changes and how they are managed, employees' levels of affective, continuance, and normative commitment can increase or decrease. Thus, the commitment profiles of employees following a change will be different from what they were prior to the change, and maintaining high levels of affective commitment will be particularly challenging. Changes that are made in the organization's best interest but that are detrimental to employees' well-being are most likely to damage affective commitment.

- *Changes in the focus of employees' commitment.* As mentioned earlier, the focus of the three types of commitment can include entities other than the organization. Thus, employees generally have multiple commitments. In particular, employee commitment can be directed to others within the organization, such as subunits or divisions, teams, the "new" organization, as well as entities outside the organization, such as one's occupation, career, and union. Therefore, changes in the workplace might alter the focus of employees' commitments both within and outside of the organization. For example, as organizations increase in size following mergers and acquisitions, employees are likely to shift their commitment to smaller organizational units, such as their particular division, branch, or team. As well, changes that threaten employees' future in the organization might result in a shift in commitment to entities outside the organization, such as one's profession, occupation, or personal career.

- *The multiplicity of employer–employee relationships within organizations.* As organizations attempt to cope and adapt to rapid change, they need to be flexible enough to shrink and expand their workforce. At the same time, they need a workforce that is flexible enough to get any job done. This creates a potential conflict as employees who do not have a guarantee of job security may be unwilling to be as flexible as the organization would like or to have a strong affective commitment toward the organization. A potential solution to this problem is for organizations to have different relationships with employees and employee groups. For example, an organization might have a group of core employees who perform the key operations required for organizational success. It would be important for this group of employees to have a high level of affective organizational commitment. Other employee groups would consist of those with contractual arrangements or individuals hired on a temporary basis who do not perform the core tasks and whose commitment to the organization is not as important. The idea of a multiplicity of employee–organization relationships enables organizations to have a flexible workforce and at the same time foster a high level of affective commitment among a core group of employees.

In summary, changes in the workplace are having an impact on the nature of employee commitment and employee–employer relationships. It is therefore important that organizations understand how changes in the workplace can change the profile and focus of employees' commitment and the impact this can have on employee behaviour and organizational success.

  THE MANAGER'S

Notebook

RAC's Call Centres

1. Call centres represent a difficult work setting for several reasons. While the actual work can vary from one call centre to the next, tasks in call centres are generally highly scripted and closely monitored. Furthermore, tasks are repetitive and workers have little control over the pace of the work. Although some have made comparisons between call centres and assembly lines, it is important to note that call centre work often involves contact with customers who may have complaints or be hostile during the interaction; as such, although monotonous and repetitive, call centre work can also be very emotional and stressful. Furthermore, given the high turnover rates, the frequent use of temporary employees, and the solitary nature of the work, long-lasting friendships and pleasant social interactions with co-workers can be difficult to achieve. Finally, pay is generally low and opportunities for advancement are extremely limited. In sum, job satisfaction in call centres is at risk because of the lack of mentally challenging work, the lack of social interaction with colleagues, and the low pay and close supervision that can be seen as threats to distributive and procedural fairness.

2. RAC used a bundle of human resources initiatives to enhance employee satisfaction and improve performance. First, greater emphasis was placed on people, and concerted attempts were made to relieve the pressure and routine of call centre work. The organizational structure was flattened from seven levels to four, and a new team environment was created. One of the team manager's functions was to put some "fun" into the workplace through activities and prizes. Team bonding was also encouraged through social events. Second, efforts were made to make the call centre jobs more mentally challenging. The old functional separation between sales and service was eliminated, and new multi-skilled customer adviser positions were created. A suggestion scheme called "Bright Ideas," which rewards good ideas with a chance for prizes, was created to encourage staff to think up ways of improving service. Third, perceptions of distributive and procedural fairness were enhanced through a new, more generous, pay system. Finally, RAC focused on the attitudes of its workers through recruiting and training. The goal was to have a more reliable, committed, and skilled workforce. What were the results? Performance indicators at RAC's Bristol call centre improved immediately in terms of calls per hour and customer satisfaction. Turnover, which had averaged between 27 and 35 percent over the three years prior to the changes, fell to 8 percent in 1997 and 2 percent in 1998, while absenteeism decreased by 5 percent from 1997 to 1998. Job satisfaction also rose after the changes were implemented, and reported levels of satisfaction remained high four years after the changes.

LEARNING OBJECTIVES CHECKLIST

1. *Values* are broad preferences for particular states of affairs. Values tend to differ across occupational groups and across cultures. Critical cross-cultural dimensions of values include power distance, uncertainty avoidance, masculinity/femininity, individualism/collectivism, and time orientation. Differences in values across cultures set constraints on the export and import of organizational behaviour theories and management practices. They also have implications for satisfying global customers and developing globally aware employees.

2. *Attitudes* are a function of what we think about the world (our beliefs) and how we feel about the world (our values). Attitudes are important because they influence how we behave, although we have discussed several factors that reduce the correspondence between our attitudes and behaviours.

3. *Job satisfaction* is an especially important attitude for organizations. Satisfaction is a function of the discrepancy between what individuals want from their jobs and what they perceive that they obtain, taking into account fairness. Dispositional factors, moods, and emotions also influence job satisfaction. Factors such as challenging work, adequate compensation, career opportunities, and friendly, helpful co-workers contribute to job satisfaction.

4. Job satisfaction is important because it promotes several positive outcomes for organizations. Satisfied employees tend to be less absent and less likely to leave their jobs. While links between satisfaction and performance are not always strong, satisfaction with the work itself has been linked to better performance. Satisfaction linked to perceptions of fairness can also lead to citizenship behaviours on the part of employees. Satisfied workers may also enhance customer satisfaction.

5. *Organizational commitment* is an attitude that reflects the strength of the linkage between an employee and an organization. *Affective commitment* is based on a person's identification with an organization. *Continuance commitment* is based on the costs of leaving an organization. *Normative commitment* is based on ideology or feelings of obligation. Changes in the workplace can change the nature and focus of employee commitment as well as employer–employee relationships. To foster commitment, organizations need to be sensitive to the expectations of employees and consider the impact of policy decisions beyond economic issues.

DISCUSSION QUESTIONS

1. What are some of the conditions under which a person's attitudes might not predict his or her work behaviour?

2. What is the difference between procedural and interactional fairness? Give an example of each.

3. Explain how these people might have to regulate their emotions when doing their jobs: hair salon owner; bill collector; police officer; teacher. How will this regulation of emotion affect job satisfaction?

4. Using the model of the turnover process in Exhibit 4.7, explain why a very dissatisfied employee might not quit his or her job.

5. Explain why employees who are very satisfied with their jobs might not be better performers than those who are less satisfied.

6. Use equity theory to explain why a dentist who earns $100 000 a year might be more dissatisfied with her job than a factory worker who earns $40 000.

7. Mexico has a fairly high power distance culture, while the United States and Canada have lower power distance cultures. Discuss how effective management techniques might vary between Mexico and its neighbours to the north.

8. Describe some job aspects that might contribute to job satisfaction for a person in a more collective culture. Do the same for a person in a more individualistic culture.

9. Give an example of an employee who is experiencing distributive fairness but not procedural fairness. Give an example of an employee who is experiencing procedural fairness but not distributive fairness.

INTEGRATIVE DISCUSSION QUESTIONS

1. What role do perceptions play in the determination of job satisfaction? Refer to the components of perception in Chapter 3 and describe how perception plays a role in the determination of job satisfaction according to discrepancy theory, equity theory, and dispositions. How can perceptions be changed to increase job satisfaction?

2. Does personality influence values and job attitudes? Discuss how the "Big Five" personality dimensions, locus of control, self-monitoring, self-esteem, and positive and negative affectivity might influence occupational choice, job satisfaction, and organizational commitment (affective, continuance, and normative). If personality influences job satisfaction and organizational commitment, how can organizations foster high levels of these attitudes?

ON-THE-JOB CHALLENGE QUESTION

In 2006, Mr. Arthur Winston died at age 100 after having worked for 76 years for the Los Angeles Metropolitan Transportation Authority cleaning trains and buses. Although this is remarkable enough, it is even more remarkable that he missed only one day of work in his last 72 years, the day of his wife's funeral in 1988. At the time of his retirement on the eve of becoming 100, he headed a crew of 11 workers. Although he had aspired to become a mechanic when younger, the racial biases of the 1930s and 1940s prevented this career advancement. In 1996, Mr. Winston received a congressional citation from the US President as "Employee of the Century." Mr. Winston's incredible record was the object of extensive media coverage, both at home and abroad.

Use the material in the chapter to speculate on various reasons for Mr. Winston's awesome attendance record. What accounts for the great media interest in Mr. Winston?

Sources: (2006, April 14). MTA employee who retired at 100 has died in his sleep. CBS2.com; Marquez, M. (2006, March 22). Los Angeles man retires at 100. ABC News, US.

EXPERIENTIAL EXERCISE

Attitudes toward Absenteeism from Work

In this exercise we will examine your attitudes toward absenteeism from work. Although you learned in the chapter that absence can stem from job dissatisfaction, the scenarios below show that a number of other factors can also come into play.

1. Working alone, please indicate the extent to which you think that the employee's absence in each of the following scenarios is legitimate or illegitimate by using one of the six answer categories that appear below. A legitimate absence might be considered acceptable, while an illegitimate absence might be considered unacceptable. This is a measure of your personal attitudes; there are no right or wrong answers. Add up your scores and divide by 7 to obtain an average. Lower scores represent less favourable attitudes toward absenteeism.

2. Working in groups of 3–5 people, discuss the ratings that each of you gave to each scenario. What are the major reasons that contributed to each of your ratings? Compare your average scores.

3. As a group, decide which scenario is *most* legitimate, and explain why. Then decide which scenario is *least* legitimate, and explain why. Compare with the norms provided below.

4. As managers, how would you react to the least legitimate situation? What would you do?

6	5	4	3	2	1
Extremely legitimate	Moderately legitimate	Slightly legitimate	Slightly illegitimate	Moderately illegitimate	Extremely illegitimate

1. Susan is a highly productive employee, but she is absent more often than her co-workers. She has decided to be absent from work to engage in some recreational activities because she believes that her absence would not affect her overall productivity. ___

2. John is an active member of his community social club. Occasionally, the club organizes community activities with the aim of improving the quality of community life. A few days before a planned community activity, much of the work has not been done and the club members are concerned that the activities will be unsuccessful. John has therefore decided to be absent from work to help the club organize its forthcoming activities. ___

3. Peter is a member of a project team that was charged with the responsibility of converting the company's information systems. The work entailed long hours, but the team was able to finish the project on time. Now that the project is completed, the long working hours have taken a toll and Peter feels quite stressed so he has decided to stay away from work to recuperate. ___

4. Jane works in a low-paying job for which she is overqualified. She has been searching for a more suitable job through advertisements in the newspapers. She has been called for a job interview and has decided to call in sick to attend the interview. ___

5. Frank has a few months before his retirement and has lost the enthusiasm he used to have for his work. He believes he has contributed to making the company the success it is today. He recently joined a retired persons association where he feels his services are needed more. The association is organizing a safety awareness program for senior citizens, so he has decided to stay away from work to help. ___

6. Joan's co-workers normally use up all their sick leave. She is moving into a new house, and since she has not used up all her permitted sick leave, she has decided to call in sick so that she can finish packing for the move. ___

7. Anne does not feel challenged by her job and believes that she is not making any meaningful contribution to her organization. Her mother is going to the doctor for a routine medical checkup and because Anne believes the company will not miss her, she decided to stay away from work to accompany her mother. ___

Source: Scenarios developed by Helena M. Addae. Used with permission.

Scoring and Interpretation

As noted, lower scores represent less favourable attitudes toward absenteeism. Helena Addae, who developed the scenarios, administered them to over 1500 employees in nine countries. The average rating across the 7 scenarios was 3.09. Respectively, the average ratings for each scenario were: S1=2.39; S2=2.88; S3=3.96; S4=3.52; S5=3.12; S6=3.03; S7=2.70. Higher numbers indicate more legitimacy.

CASE INCIDENT

How Much Do You Get Paid?

Joan had been working as a reporter for a large television network for seven years. She was an experienced and hardworking reporter who had won many awards over the years for her outstanding work. The work was exciting and challenging, and at $75 000 a year plus benefits she felt well-paid and satisfied. Then she found out that two recent graduates from one of the best schools of journalism in the United States had just been hired by her network at a starting salary of $80 000.

Further, two other reporters who worked with Joan and had similar track records had just received job offers from American networks and were being offered $150 000 plus $10 000 for every award won for their reporting.

1. According to equity theory, how will these incidents influence Joan's job satisfaction and behaviour?

2. What should Joan do in response to her situation? What should her organization do?

CASE STUDY

The Well-Paid Receptionist

Harvey Finley did a quick double take when he caught a glimpse of the figure representing Ms. Brannen's salary on the year-end printout. A hurried call to payroll confirmed it. Yes, his receptionist had been paid $127 614.21 for her services last year. As he sat in stunned silence, he had the sudden realization that since his firm was doing so well this year, she would earn at least 10 to 15 percent more money during the current fiscal year. This was a shock, indeed.

Background

Harvey began his career as a service technician for a major manufacturer of copy machines. He received rather extensive technical training, but his duties were limited to performing routine, on-site maintenance and service for customers. After a year's experience as a service technician, he asked for and received a promotion to sales representative. In this capacity, he established many favourable contacts in the business community of Troupville and the surrounding towns. He began to think seriously about capitalizing on his success by opening his own business.

Then, seven years ago, he decided to take the plunge and start his own firm. He was tired of selling for someone else. When he mentioned his plan to his friends, they all expressed serious doubts; Troupville, a city of approximately 35 000 people located in the deep South, had just begun to recover from a severe recession. The painful memories of the layoffs, bankruptcies, and plummeting real estate values were too recent and vivid to be forgotten.

Undeterred by the skeptics, Harvey was optimistic that Troupville's slow recovery would soon become a boom. Even though his firm would certainly have to be started on a shoestring, Harvey thought his sales experience and technical competence would enable him to survive what was sure to be a difficult beginning. He was nervous but excited when he signed the lease on the first little building. A lifelong dream was either about to be realized or dashed forever. Troupville Business Systems was born.

While he had managed to borrow, rent, lease, or subcontract for almost everything that was absolutely necessary, he did need one employee immediately. Of course, he hoped the business would expand rapidly and that he would soon have a complete and competent staff. But until he could be sure that some revenue would be generated, he thought he could get by with one person who would be a combination receptionist/secretary and general assistant.

The typical salary for such a position in the area was about $30 000 per year; for Harvey, this was a major expense. Nevertheless, he placed what he thought was a well-worded ad in the "Help Wanted" section of the local newspaper. There were five applicants, four of whom just did not seem quite right for the position he envisioned. The fifth applicant, Ms. Cathy Brannen, was absolutely captivating.

Ms. Brannen was 27 years old with one child. Her resumé showed that she had graduated from a two-year office administration program at a state university. She had worked for only two employers following graduation, one for five years and the most recent for two years. Since returning to her hometown of Troupville two months ago, following her divorce, she had not been able to find suitable employment.

From the moment she sat down for the interview, Harvey and Ms. Brannen seemed to be on exactly the same wavelength. She was very articulate, obviously quite bright, and most importantly, very enthusiastic about assisting with the start-up of the new venture. She seemed to be exactly the sort of person Harvey had envisioned when he first began to think seriously about taking the plunge. He resisted the temptation to offer her the job on the spot, but ended the hour-long interview by telling her that he would check her references and contact her again very soon.

Telephone calls to her two former employers convinced Harvey that he had actually underestimated Ms. Brannen's suitability for the position. Each one said without equivocation that she was the best employee he had ever had in any position. Both former employers concluded the conversation by saying they would rehire her in a minute if she were still available. The only bit of disturbing information gleaned from these two calls was the fact that her annual salary had risen to $32 900 in her last job. Although Harvey thought that the cost of living was probably a bit higher in Houston, where she had last worked, he was not sure she would react favourably to the $30 000 offer he was planning to make. However, he was determined that, somehow, Cathy Brannen would be his first employee.

Ms. Brannen seemed quite pleased when Harvey telephoned her at home that same evening. She said she would be delighted to meet him at the office the next morning to discuss the position more fully.

Cathy Brannen was obviously very enthusiastic about the job as outlined in the meeting. She asked all the right questions, responded quickly and articulately to every query posed to her, and seemed ready to accept the position even before the offer was extended. When Harvey finally got around to mentioning the salary, there was a slight change in Cathy's eager expression. She stiffened. Since Harvey realized that salary might be a problem, he decided to offer Cathy an incentive of sorts in addition to the $30 000 annual salary. He told her that he realized his salary offer was lower than the amount she had earned on her last job. And he told her he understood that a definite disadvantage of working for a new firm was the complete absence of financial security. Although he was extremely reluctant to guarantee a larger salary because of his own uncertainty regarding the future, he offered her a sales override in the amount of two percent of sales. He explained that she would largely determine the success or failure of the firm. She needed to represent the firm in the finest possible manner to potential customers who telephoned and to those who walked in the front door. For this reason, the sales override seemed to be an appropriate addition to her straight salary. It would provide her with incentive to take an active interest in the firm.

Cathy accepted the offer immediately. Even though she was expecting a salary offer of $32 500, she hoped the sales override might make up the difference. "Who knows," she thought, "two percent of sales may amount to big money someday." It did not, however, seem very likely at the time.

Troupville Business Systems began as a very small distributor of copy machines. The original business plan was just to sell copy machines and provide routine, on-site service. More extensive on-site service and repairs requiring that a machine be removed from a customer's premises were to be provided by a regional distributor located in a major city approximately 100 miles from Troupville.

Troupville Business Systems did well from the start. Several important changes were made in the services the firm offered during the first year. Harvey soon found that there was a greater demand for the leasing of copy machines, particularly the large expensive models that he originally planned to sell. He also soon discovered that his customers wanted to be able to contract directly with his firm for all their service needs. Merely guaranteeing that he could get the machines serviced was not sufficient in the eyes of potential customers. In attempting to accommodate the market, he developed a complete service facility and began to offer leasing options on all models. These changes in the business all occurred during the first year. Growth during that year was steady, but not spectacular. While sales continued to grow steadily the second year, it was early in the third year that Harvey made what turned out to be his best decision. He entered the computer business.

Harvey had purchased a personal computer soon after Troupville Business Systems was founded. The machine and its capabilities fascinated him, although he knew virtually nothing about computers. He was soon a member of a local users club, was subscribing to all the magazines, and was taking evening computer courses at the local university—in short, he became a computer buff. Harvey recognized the business potential of the rapidly growing personal computer market, but he did not believe that his original business was sufficiently stable to introduce a new product line just yet.

During his third year of operations, he decided the time was right to enter the computer business. He added to his product line a number of personal computers popular with small businesses in the area. This key decision caused a virtual explosion in the growth of his firm. Several key positions were added, including that of a comptroller. By the fourth year of operations, computers produced by several other manufacturers had been added to Harvey's product line, and he had developed the capability of providing complete service for all products carried. His computer enterprise was not limited to business customers, because he quickly developed a significant walk-in retail trade. Rapid growth continued unabated.

During the first seven years of the company's existence, Cathy Brannen had proven truly indispensable. Her performance exceeded Harvey's highest expectations. Although her official position remained that of secretary/receptionist, she took it on herself to learn about each new product or service. During the early years, Harvey often thought that she did a better job than he did whenever a potential customer called in his absence. Even after he acquired a qualified sales staff, Harvey had no concerns when Cathy had to field questions from a potential customer because a regular salesperson was not available. The customer never realized that the professional young lady capably handling all inquiries was "only" the receptionist.

Cathy began performing fewer sales functions because of the increased number of professional salespersons, but her secretarial duties had expanded tremendously. She was still Harvey's secretary, and she continued to answer virtually every telephone call coming into the business. Since her office was in an open area, she still was the first to greet many visitors.

Cathy took a word-processing course at a local business school shortly after joining the firm. As she began working with Harvey's first personal computer, she, too, developed into a computer aficionado and became the best computer operator in the firm.

The Current Situation

Harvey was shaken by the realization that Cathy Brannen had been paid over $127 000 last year. As he wondered what, if anything, should be done about her earnings, he began to reflect on the previous seven years.

Success had come almost overnight. It seemed as though Troupville Business Systems could do nothing wrong. The workforce had grown at a rate of approximately 15 percent per year since the third year of operations. Seventeen people were now employed by the firm. While Harvey did acknowledge that some of this success was due to being in the right place at the right time, he also had reason to be proud of the choices he had made. Time had proven that all his major decisions had been correct. He also could not overestimate Cathy's contribution to the success of the firm. Yes, certainly, one of the most important days in the life of the firm was the day when Cathy responded to his ad in the newspaper.

Success had brought with it the ever-increasing demands on his time. He had never worked so hard, but the rewards were certainly forthcoming. First, there was the new Jaguar, then the new home on Country Club Drive, the vacation home on the coast, the European trips . . . Yes, success was wonderful.

During these years Cathy, too, had prospered. Harvey had not thought much about it, but he did remember making a joking comment the first day she drove her new Mercedes to work. He also remembered commenting on her mink coat at the company banquet last December. Cathy had been dazzling.

Now that Harvey realized what he was paying Cathy, he was greatly disturbed. She was making almost twice as much money as anyone else in the firm with the exception of himself. The best salesman had earned an amount in the low nineties last year. His top managers were paid salaries ranging from the high sixties to the mid-seventies. The average salary in the area for executive secretaries was now probably between $30 000 and $35 000 per year. A good receptionist could be hired for under $28 000, and yet Cathy had been paid $127 614.21 last year. The sales override had certainly enabled Cathy to share in the firm's success. Yes, indeed.

As Harvey thought more and more about the situation, he kept returning to the same conclusion. He felt something had to be done about her compensation. It was just too far out of line with other salaries in the firm. Although Harvey was drawing over $200 000 per year in salary and had built an equity in the business of more than $1 million, these facts did not seem relevant as he pondered what to do. It seemed likely that a number of other employees did know about Cathy's compensation level. Harvey wondered why no one ever mentioned it. Even the comptroller never mentioned Cathy's compensation. This did seem quite odd to Harvey, as the comptroller, Frank Bain, knew that Harvey did not even attempt to keep up with the financial details. He relied on Frank to bring important matters to his attention.

With no idea of how to approach this problem, Harvey decided to begin by making a list of alternatives. He got out a piece of paper and, as he stared at the blank lines, overheard Cathy's cheerful exchange with a customer in the next room.

---

1. Use the ideas of distributive fairness and equity theory to explain why Harvey Finley thinks he pays Cathy Brannen too much.

2. Use the ideas of distributive fairness and equity theory to explain why Cathy Brannen might feel that her pay is fair.

3. What are the likely consequences for job satisfaction, organizational commitment, and behaviour if Ms. Brannen's pay level is known to other organizational members? Use equity theory to support your answer.

4. Suppose that you had been in Mr. Finley's position at the time that he hired Ms. Brannen. What would you have done differently to avoid the current situation while still attracting her to join the fledgling firm?

5. How might emotions be relevant to the events in the case?

6. What ethical or moral issues does this case raise?

7. What should Mr. Finley do now? Be sure to consider procedural and interactional fairness in framing your answer.

CHAPTER 5

Theories of Work Motivation

WestJet Airlines

Based on the principles and success of discount airlines in the United States like Dallas-based discount carrier Southwest Airlines Company, four Calgary entrepreneurs saw an opportunity to provide low-fare air travel across Western Canada. So on February 29, 1996, with 220 employees and three aircraft, Calgary-based WestJet Airlines began operations, charging only $118 for a return fare to Vancouver while the major airlines were charging up to $600.

Unlike major airlines, WestJet keeps costs down by using various cost-saving measures such as operating only with confirmation numbers rather than tickets; having no central booking and no meals in flight; and using only Boeing 737 aircraft, which are the cheapest aircraft to maintain. And while a full-service airline like Air Canada operates with more than 140 people per aircraft, WestJet operates with about 59 people per aircraft.

In its first 10 months of operation, the debt-free airline brought in $37.2 million in revenues while operating only three aircraft between Calgary, Vancouver, Kelowna, Winnipeg, and Edmonton. By 1998, revenues had grown to $125.8 million, more western cities were added, the number of employees had doubled, and earnings grew from $870 000 to $6.5 million. WestJet was making money while its big competitors continued to record huge losses. In fact, it has consistently ranked as one of the most profitable airlines in North America. And since its initial public offering of 2.5 million common shares in 1999, its share price has increased more than 240 percent.

In addition to its discount fares and low-cost operation, WestJet is also well known for how it motivates its employees. In order to motivate its workforce, the company aligns employees' interests with the interests of the company through a number of policies and programs that make everyone at WestJet an owner. For example, WestJet has a generous profit sharing plan that is designed to encourage everyone to maximize profits. Employees share in profits that are equivalent to the company's profit margin, up to 20 percent. So if the airline's profit margin is 10 percent, then 10 percent of the net income is spread among employees (prorated

LEARNING OBJECTIVES

After reading Chapter 5, you should be able to:

1 Define *motivation*, discuss its basic properties, and distinguish it from *performance*.

2 Compare and contrast *intrinsic* and *extrinsic motivation*.

3 Explain and discuss the different factors that predict *performance* and define *general cognitive ability* and *emotional intelligence*.

4 Define employee *engagement* and describe what contributes to it.

5 Explain and discuss *need theories* of motivation.

6 Explain and discuss *expectancy theory*.

7 Explain and discuss *equity theory*.

8 Explain and discuss *goal setting theory* and *goal orientation*.

9 Discuss the cross-cultural limitations of theories of motivation.

10 Summarize the relationship among the various theories of motivation, performance, and job satisfaction.

WestJet uses a number of motivational practices that align the interests of employees with those of the organization, including profit sharing and employee stock ownership plans.

WestJet Airlines
www.westjet.com

to salary). "Profit Sharing Day" is held twice a year at which time cheques are handed out to employees. The company has handed out more than $8 million on such days, with an average cheque amount of $9000.

WestJet also has an employee stock ownership plan. Employees are encouraged to buy shares in the company, and for every $1 a worker invests, the company matches it. Employees can also choose to receive up to 20 percent of their salary in shares, which the company then matches 100 percent. Over 80 percent of the airline's employees are shareholders, and many of the original employees who invested in the company before it went public now have generous portfolios. In fact, some of WestJet's flight attendants have more than $400 000 in stock, and some of its pilots are millionaires.

In addition to profit sharing and employee stock ownership plans, WestJet also provides employees with a great deal of freedom and autonomy in how they perform their jobs. In fact, a pillar of the company's culture is that employees in direct contact with customers not only have a stake in the success of the company through profit sharing, but are also openly encouraged to contribute ideas about how the airline runs. In addition, employees are given the freedom to make judgment calls when dealing directly with customers without having to check in with a supervisor. For example, call centre representatives have the authority to waive fees and override fares in certain circumstances. Flight attendants are expected to serve customers in a caring, positive, and cheerful manner, but the rest is up to them. WestJet's cabin crews are famous for their in-flight antics, such as singalongs, bowling with oranges, contests, playing games with passengers, and editorial commentary from the flight deck. WestJet employees make decisions about what they are doing and how they do it. They take ownership of their jobs.

WestJet has become the most successful low-cost carrier in Canadian history. Today, it flies to 34 cities in Canada and the United States, including the Hawaiian Islands, and boasts the most modern fleet of airplanes in North America. Despite the troubles of the volatile and uncertain airline industry, the company is viewed as a solid long-term investment. In 2006, the company surged and recorded record first- and second-quarter profits. Over the next three years, WestJet could become larger than Canadian Airlines was when it was absorbed by Air Canada.

WestJet is also one of Canada's top 100 employers and one of the most respected companies in Canada. In 2005 and 2006, it was ranked as having the most admired Canadian corporate culture. Perhaps it's not surprising that the company receives an average of 1700 unsolicited resumés every week![1]

Would you be motivated if you worked for WestJet Airlines? What kind of person would respond well to WestJet's motivational techniques? What underlying philosophy of motivation is WestJet using? These are some of the questions that this chapter will explore.

First, we will define motivation and distinguish it from performance and employee engagement. After this, we will describe several popular theories of work motivation and contrast them. Then we will explore whether these theories translate across cultures. Finally, we will present a model that links motivation, performance, and job satisfaction.

WHY STUDY MOTIVATION?

Why should you study motivation? Motivation is one of the most traditional topics in organizational behaviour, and it has interested managers, researchers, teachers, and sports coaches for years. However, a good case can be made that motivation has become even more important in contemporary organizations. Much of this is a result of the need for increased productivity to be globally competitive. It is also a result of the rapid changes that contemporary organizations are undergoing. Stable systems of rules, regulations, and procedures that once guided behaviour are being replaced by requirements for flexibility and attention to customers that necessitate higher levels of initiative. This initiative depends on motivation.

What would a good motivation theory look like? In fact, as we shall see, there is no single all-purpose motivation theory. Rather, we will consider several theories that serve somewhat different purposes. In combination, though, a good set of theories should recognize human diversity and consider that the same conditions will not motivate everyone. Also, a good set of theories should be able to explain how it is that some people seem to be self-motivated, while others seem to require external motivation. Finally, a good set of theories should recognize the social aspect of human beings—people's motivation is often affected by how they see others being treated. Before getting to our theories, let's define motivation more precisely.

WHAT IS MOTIVATION?

The term *motivation* is not easy to define. However, from an organization's perspective, when we speak of a person as being motivated, we usually mean that the person works "hard," "keeps at" his or her work, and directs his or her behaviour toward appropriate outcomes.

Basic Characteristics of Motivation

Motivation. The extent to which persistent effort is directed toward a goal.

We can formally define **motivation** as the extent to which persistent effort is directed toward a goal.[2]

Effort. The first aspect of motivation is the strength of the person's work-related behaviour, or the amount of *effort* the person exhibits on the job. Clearly, this involves different kinds of activities on different kinds of jobs. A loading dock worker might exhibit greater effort by carrying heavier crates, while a researcher might reveal greater effort by searching out an article in some obscure foreign technical journal. Both are exerting effort in a manner appropriate to their jobs.

Persistence. The second characteristic of motivation is the *persistence* that individuals exhibit in applying effort to their work tasks. The organization would not be likely to think of the loading dock worker who stacks the heaviest crates for two hours and then goofs off for six hours as especially highly motivated. Similarly, the researcher who makes an important discovery early in her career and then rests on her laurels for five years would not be considered especially highly motivated. In each case, workers have not been persistent in the application of their effort.

Direction. Effort and persistence refer mainly to the quantity of work an individual produces. Of equal importance is the quality of a person's work. Thus, the third characteristic of motivation is the *direction* of the person's work-related behaviour. In other words, do workers channel persistent effort in a direction that benefits the organization? Employers expect motivated stockbrokers to advise their clients of good investment opportunities and motivated software designers to design software, not play computer games. These correct decisions increase the probability that persistent effort is actually translated into accepted organizational outcomes. Thus, motivation means working smart as well as working hard.

Goals. Ultimately, all motivated behaviour has some goal or objective toward which it is directed. We have presented the preceding discussion from an organizational perspective—that is, we assume that motivated people act to enhance organizational objectives. In this case, employee goals might include high productivity, good attendance, or creative decisions. Of course, employees can also be motivated by goals that are contrary to the objectives of the organization, including absenteeism, sabotage, and embezzlement. In these cases, they are channelling their persistent efforts in directions that are dysfunctional for the organization.

Extrinsic and Intrinsic Motivation

Some hold the view that people are motivated by factors in the external environment (such as supervision or pay), while others believe that people can, in some sense, be self-motivated without the application of these external factors. You might have experienced this distinction. As a worker, you might recall tasks that you enthusiastically performed simply for the sake of doing them and others that you performed only to keep your job or placate your boss.

Experts in organizational behaviour distinguish between intrinsic and extrinsic motivation. At the outset, we should emphasize that there is only weak consensus concerning the exact definitions of these concepts and even weaker agreement about whether we should label specific motivators as intrinsic or extrinsic.[3] However, the following definitions and examples seem to capture the distinction fairly well.

Intrinsic motivation stems from the direct relationship between the worker and the task and is usually self-applied. Feelings of achievement, accomplishment, challenge, and competence derived from performing one's job are examples of intrinsic motivators, as is sheer interest in the job itself. Being able to make decisions about what they are doing and how they do it, and the freedom to make judgment calls when dealing directly with customers are good examples of intrinsic motivation for WestJet employees. Off the job, avid participation in sports and hobbies is often intrinsically motivated.

Extrinsic motivation stems from the work environment external to the task and is usually applied by someone other than the person being motivated. Pay, fringe benefits, company policies, and various forms of supervision are examples of extrinsic motivators. At WestJet, profit sharing and the employee stock ownership plan are examples of extrinsic motivators.

Obviously, employers cannot package all conceivable motivators as neatly as these definitions suggest. For example, a promotion or a compliment might be applied by the boss, but might also be a clear signal of achievement and competence. Thus, some motivators have both extrinsic and intrinsic qualities.

Despite the fact that the distinction between intrinsic and extrinsic motivation is fuzzy, many theories of motivation implicitly make the distinction. However, the relationship between intrinsic and extrinsic motivators has been the subject of a great deal of debate.[4] Some research studies have reached the conclusion that the availability of extrinsic motivators can reduce the intrinsic motivation stemming from the task itself.[5] The notion is that when extrinsic rewards depend on performance, then the motivating potential of intrinsic rewards decreases. Proponents of this view have suggested that making extrinsic rewards contingent on performance makes individuals feel less competent and less in control of their own behaviour. That is, they come to believe that their performance is controlled by the environment and that they perform well only because of the money.[6] As a result, their intrinsic motivation suffers.

However, a review of research in this area reached the conclusion that the negative effect of extrinsic rewards on intrinsic motivation occurs only under very limited conditions, and they are easily avoidable.[7] As well, in organizational settings in which individuals see extrinsic rewards as symbols of success and as signals of what to do to achieve future rewards, they increase their task performance.[8] Thus, it is safe to assume that both kinds of rewards are important and compatible in enhancing work motivation.

Motivation and Performance

At this point, you might well be saying, "Wait a minute, I know many people who are 'highly motivated' but just don't seem to perform well. They work long and hard, but they just don't measure up." This is certainly a sensible observation, and it points to the important distinction between motivation and performance. **Performance** can be defined as the extent to which an organizational member contributes to achieving the objectives of the organization.

Some of the factors that contribute to individual performance in organizations are shown in Exhibit 5.1.[9] While motivation clearly contributes to performance, the relationship is not one-to-one because a number of other factors also influence performance. For example, recall from Chapter 2 that personality traits such as the "Big Five" and core self-evaluations also predict job performance. You might also be wondering about the role of intelligence—doesn't it influence performance? The answer, of course, is yes—intelligence, or what is also known as mental ability, does predict performance.

Intrinsic motivation. Motivation that stems from the direct relationship between the worker and the task; it is usually self-applied.

Extrinsic motivation. Motivation that stems from the work environment external to the task; it is usually applied by others.

Performance. The extent to which an organizational member contributes to achieving the objectives of the organization.

EXHIBIT 5.1
Factors contributing to individual job performance.

General cognitive ability. A person's basic information processing capacities and cognitive resources.

Emotional intelligence. The ability to understand and manage one's own and other's feelings and emotions.

Two forms of intelligence that are particularly important are general cognitive ability and emotional intelligence. Let's consider each before we discuss motivation.

General Cognitive Ability. The term *cognitive ability* is often used to refer to what most people call intelligence or mental ability. Although there are many different types of specific cognitive abilities, in organizational behaviour we are often concerned with what is known as *general cognitive ability*. **General cognitive ability** is a term used to refer to a person's basic information processing capacities and cognitive resources. It reflects an individual's overall capacity and efficiency for processing information, and it includes a number of cognitive abilities such as verbal, numerical, spatial, and reasoning abilities that are required to perform mental tasks. Cognitive ability is usually measured by a number of specific aptitude tests that measure these abilities.[10]

Research has found that general cognitive ability predicts learning and training success as well as job performance in all kinds of jobs and occupations, including those that involve both manual and mental tasks. This should not come as a surprise because many cognitive skills are required to perform most kinds of jobs. General cognitive ability is an even better predictor of performance for more complex and higher-level jobs that require the use of more cognitive skills and involve more information processing.[11] Thus, both general cognitive ability and motivation are necessary for performance.

Research has also found that general cognitive ability and motivation are required for career success. In a study on the early career success of MBA graduates, students with higher general cognitive ability in combination with higher motivation were more successful in their job search at graduation, obtained higher salaries and more rapid pay increases, and received more promotions. The results of this study indicate the importance of both general cognitive ability and motivation for career success and performance.[12]

Emotional Intelligence. Although the importance of general cognitive ability for job performance has been known for many years, researchers have recently begun to study emotional intelligence. **Emotional intelligence** (EI) has to do with an individual's ability to understand and manage his or her own and others' feelings and emotions. It involves the ability to perceive and express emotion, assimilate emotion in thought, understand and reason about emotions, and manage emotions in oneself and others. People with emotional intelligence are able to identify and recognize the meanings of emotions and to manage and regulate their emotions as a basis for problem solving, reasoning, thinking, and action.[13]

Peter Salovey and John Mayer, who are credited with first coining the term *emotional intelligence*, have developed an EI model that consists of four interrelated sets of skills or branches. The four skills represent sequential steps that form a hierarchy. The perception of emotion is at the bottom of the hierarchy, followed by (in ascending order) the integration and assimilation of emotions, the knowledge and understanding of emotions, and the management and regulation of emotions. Salovey and Mayer's EI model is shown in Exhibit 5.2 and described below:[14]

1. *The perception of emotions:* This involves the ability to perceive emotions and to accurately identify one's own emotions and the emotions of others. An example of this is the ability to accurately identify emotions in people's faces and nonverbal behaviour. People differ in the extent to which they can accurately identify emotions in others, particularly from facial expressions.[15] This step is the most basic level of EI and is necessary to be able to perform the other steps in the model.

2. *The integration and assimilation of emotions:* This refers to the ability to use and assimilate emotions and emotional experiences to guide and facilitate one's thinking and reasoning. This means that one is able to use emotions in functional

ways, such as making decisions and other cognitive processes (e.g., creativity, integrative thinking, inductive reasoning). This stage also involves being able to shift one's emotions and generate new emotions that can help one to see things in different ways and from different perspectives. This is an important skill because, as described in Chapter 11, emotions and moods affect what and how people think when making decisions.[16]

3. *Knowledge and understanding of emotions:* This stage involves being able to understand emotional information, the determinants and consequences of emotions, and how emotions evolve and change over time. At this stage, people understand how different situations and events generate emotions as well as how they and others are influenced by various emotions.[17] Individuals who are good at this know not to ask somebody who is in a bad mood for a favour, but rather to wait until the person is in a better mood or to just ask somebody else!

4. *Management of emotions:* This involves the ability to manage one's own and others' feelings and emotions as well as emotional relationships. This is the highest level of EI because it requires one to have mastered the previous stages. At this stage, an individual is able to regulate, adjust, and change his or her own emotions as well as others' emotions to suit the situation. Examples of this include being able to stay calm when feeling angry or upset; being able to excite and enthuse others; or being able to lower another person's anger. To be effective at managing emotions, one must be able to perceive emotions, integrate and assimilate emotions, and be knowledgeable of and understand emotions.

Research on EI has found that it predicts performance in a number of areas, including job performance and academic performance.[18] One study found that college students' EI measured at the start of the academic year predicted their grade point averages at the end of the year. There is also some evidence that EI is most strongly related to job performance in jobs that require high levels of emotional intelligence, such as police officers and customer service representatives.[19] However, some studies have suggested that there is no relation or an inconsistent relation between emotional intelligence and job performance, leading some to question the importance of emotional intelligence for job performance. To learn more about the relationship between emotional intelligence and job performance, see "Research Focus: *Does Emotional Intelligence Predict Job Performance?*"

In summary, it is certainly possible for performance to be low even when a person is highly motivated. In addition to personality and levels of general cognitive ability and emotional intelligence, poor performance could also be due to a poor understanding of the task or luck and chance factors that can damage the performance of the most highly motivated individuals. Of course, an opposite effect is also conceivable. An individual with rather marginal motivation might have high general cognitive ability or emotional intelligence, or might understand the task so well that some compensation occurs—what little effort the individual makes is expended very efficiently in terms of goal accomplishment. Also, a person with weak motivation might perform well because of some luck or chance factor that boosts performance. Thus, it is no wonder that workers sometimes complain that they receive lower performance ratings than colleagues who "don't work as hard."

In this chapter, we will concentrate on the motivational components of performance, rather than on the other determinants in Exhibit 5.1. However, the moral here should be clear: We cannot consider motivation in isolation; high motivation will not result in high performance if employees have low general cognitive ability and emotional intelligence, do not understand their jobs, or encounter unavoidable obstacles over which they have no control. Motivational interventions, such as linking pay to performance, simply *will not work* if employees are deficient in important skills and abilities.[20]

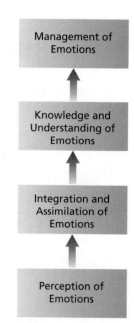

EXHIBIT 5.2
Salovey and Mayer's model of emotional intelligence.

Source: Based on Mayer, J.D., Caruso, D.R., & Salovey, P. (2000). Emotional intelligence meets traditional standards for an intelligence. *Intelligence, 27,* 267–298; Salovey, P., & Mayer, J.D. (1990). Emotional intelligence. *Imagination, Cognition and Personality, 9,* 185–211.

RESEARCH FOCUS

Does Emotional Intelligence Predict Job Performance?

In recent years, there has been a great deal of interest on the part of researchers and organizations in emotional intelligence. Although a number of studies have found that emotional intelligence predicts job performance, some studies have reported no relationship or inconsistent relations. This has led some to question whether or not emotional intelligence really predicts job performance and has created some controversy about the usefulness of emotional intelligence for organizational research and managerial practice.

To learn more about the relationship between emotional intelligence and job performance, Stéphane Côté and Christopher Miners of the University of Toronto conducted a study in which they developed and tested a compensatory model of the relationship between emotional intelligence and job performance.

They suggested that compensatory effects might explain why emotional intelligence predicts job performance in some studies but not in others. That is, emotional intelligence might compensate for the lack of other abilities and therefore be more important for job performance for some people than others. In particular, they suggested that emotional intelligence might compensate for low levels of cognitive intelligence.

According to Côté and Miners, emotional intelligence represents the specialization of general intelligence in the area of emotions in ways that reflect experience and learning about emotions. Cognitive intelligence represents the specialization of general intelligence in the domain of cognition in ways that reflect experience and learning about cognitive processes, such as memory.

The basic premise behind their compensatory model is that when job performance is not attained through cognitive intelligence, it might be attained through emotional intelligence. In other words, emotional intelligence is most likely to enhance the job performance of individuals with low levels of cognitive intelligence.

To test the model, they conducted a study with a 175 full-time employees of a large public university. Participants were asked to complete tests of emotional intelligence and cognitive intelligence. The supervisor of each participant was then contacted and asked to complete a measure of the participant's job performance.

The results indicated that both cognitive intelligence and emotional intelligence were positively related to job performance. However, more importantly, the results provided support for their compensatory model. The relationship between emotional intelligence and job performance was positive for participants with low cognitive intelligence, but not related to job performance for those with higher cognitive intelligence.

This study helps to reconcile the differences found across studies of the relationship between emotional intelligence and job performance and indicates that emotional intelligence and cognitive intelligence are compensatory in the prediction of job performance. In other words, emotional intelligence is important for the job performance of employees with lower levels of cognitive intelligence and of less importance for the job performance of employees with high levels of cognitive intelligence.

Source: Based on Côté, S. & Miners, C.T.H. (2006). Emotional intelligence, cognitive intelligence, and job performance. *Administrative Science Quarterly, 51*, 1–28.

WHAT IS EMPLOYEE ENGAGEMENT?

Before discussing the theories of motivation, we will introduce you to a topic that has received a great deal of attention in recent years—*employee engagement*. Much has been written about the decline in employee engagement. Several recent surveys indicate that there is a deepening disengagement among Canadian employees; only 17 percent of Canadians are highly engaged at work, 66 percent are moderately engaged, and 17 percent are disengaged.[21] But what is employee engagement and how does it differ from motivation?

Although employee engagement might seem to be similar to motivation, especially intrinsic motivation, it is not the same. While employee engagement does involve some degree of effort, it has more to do with *how* individuals perform their jobs rather than how motivated they are to do them.

According to William Kahn, who has conducted a major study of employee engagement, **engagement** involves the extent to which an individual immerses his or her true self into his or her work roles. When people are engaged, they employ and express themselves physically, cognitively, and emotionally during role performances. When a person is disengaged, they remove or decouple their true selves from their role. They withdraw and defend themselves physically, cognitively, or emotionally during role performances. Thus, when people are engaged, they display their true selves—what they think and feel, their creativity, their beliefs and values, and their personal connections to others—whereas disengaged individuals hide and conceal their true selves.[22]

Two important components of employee engagement are attention and absorption. *Attention* refers to the amount of time one spends thinking about a role, and *absorption* refers to being engrossed in a role and the intensity of one's focus on his or her role. Thus, when an individual is engaged they exhibit a high degree of attention and absorption. By contrast, people who are disengaged tend to be uninvolved, detached, and distracted from their work. In more simple terms, employee engagement means being psychologically present at work and in the performance of one's work roles.[23]

What factors contribute to people's engagement at work? Based on his observations and interviews with summer camp counsellors and members of an architectural firm, Kahn found that three psychological conditions contribute to engagement: psychological meaningfulness, safety, and availability (see Exhibit 5.3).

- People experience *psychological meaningfulness* when there are incentives for them to engage, they receive a return on their investment, and they feel worthwhile, useful, valuable, and not taken for granted.

- People experience *psychological safety* when they can employ and express themselves without fear of negative consequences to their self-image, status, or career.

- People experience *psychological availability* when they feel they have the physical, emotional, and cognitive resources required to engage themselves in a situation.[24]

Although engagement is still a new and emerging topic in organizational behaviour, there is some evidence that the three psychological conditions are related to engagement and that engagement leads to important outcomes for individuals and organizations.[25] One study found that business units with more engaged employees had more

Engagement. The extent to which an individual immerses his or her true self into his or her work roles. When people are engaged, they employ and express themselves physically, cognitively, and emotionally during role performances.

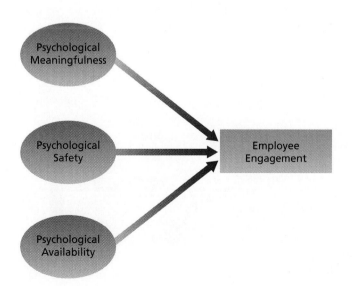

EXHIBIT 5.3
Psychological Conditions of Engagement

Source: Based on Kahn, W.A. (1990). Psychological conditions of personal engagement and disengagement at work. *Academy of Management Journal, 33,* 692–724.

positive business outcomes such as profitability, productivity, customer satisfaction, and lower turnover.[26]

Now that you know how employee engagement differs from motivation, let's take a look at the different theories of motivation.

NEED THEORIES OF WORK MOTIVATION

Need theories. Motivation theories that specify the kinds of needs people have and the conditions under which they will be motivated to satisfy these needs in a way that contributes to performance.

The first three theories of motivation that we will consider are **need theories**. These theories attempt to specify the kinds of needs people have and the conditions under which they will be motivated to satisfy these needs in a way that contributes to performance. Needs are physiological and psychological wants or desires that individuals can satisfy by acquiring certain incentives or achieving particular goals. It is the behaviour stimulated by this acquisition process that reveals the motivational character of needs:

$$\text{NEEDS} \longrightarrow \text{BEHAVIOUR} \longrightarrow \text{INCENTIVES AND GOALS}$$

Notice that need theories are concerned with *what* motivates workers (needs and their associated incentives or goals). They can be contrasted with *process theories,* which are concerned with exactly *how* various factors motivate people. Need and process theories are complementary rather than contradictory. Thus, a need theory might contend that money can be an important motivator (what), and a process theory might explain the actual mechanics by which money motivates (how).[27] In this section, we will examine three prominent need theories of motivation.

Maslow's Hierarchy of Needs

Abraham Maslow was a psychologist who, over a number of years, developed and refined a general theory of human motivation.[28] According to Maslow, humans have five sets of needs that are arranged in a hierarchy, beginning with the most basic and compelling needs (see the left side of Exhibit 5.4). These needs include:

1. *Physiological needs.* These include the needs that must be satisfied for the person to survive, such as food, water, oxygen, and shelter. Organizational factors that might satisfy these needs include the minimum pay necessary for survival and working conditions that promote existence.

2. *Safety needs.* These include needs for security, stability, freedom from anxiety, and a structured and ordered environment. Organizational conditions that might meet these needs include safe working conditions, fair and sensible rules and regulations, job security, a comfortable work environment, pension and insurance plans, and pay above the minimum needed for survival.

EXHIBIT 5.4
Relationship between Maslow's and Alderfer's need theories.

3. *Belongingness needs.* These include needs for social interaction, affection, love, companionship, and friendship. Organizational factors that might meet these needs include the opportunity to interact with others on the job, friendly and supportive supervision, opportunity for teamwork, and opportunity to develop new social relationships.

4. *Esteem needs.* These include needs for feelings of adequacy, competence, independence, strength, and confidence, and the appreciation and recognition of these characteristics by others. Organizational factors that might satisfy these needs include the opportunity to master tasks leading to feelings of achievement and responsibility. Also, awards, promotions, prestigious job titles, professional recognition, and the like might satisfy these needs when they are felt to be truly deserved.

5. *Self-actualization needs.* These needs are the most difficult to define. They involve the desire to develop one's true potential as an individual to the fullest extent and to express one's skills, talents, and emotions in a manner that is most personally fulfilling. Maslow suggests that self-actualizing people have clear perceptions of reality, accept themselves and others, and are independent, creative, and appreciative of the world around them. Organizational conditions that might provide self-actualization include absorbing jobs with the potential for creativity and growth as well as a relaxation of structure to permit self-development and personal progression.

Given the fact that individuals may harbour these needs, in what sense do they form the basis of a theory of motivation? That is, what exactly is the motivational premise of **Maslow's hierarchy of needs?** Put simply, the lowest-level unsatisfied need category has the greatest motivating potential. Thus, none of the needs is a "best" motivator; motivation depends on the person's position in the need hierarchy. According to Maslow, individuals are motivated to satisfy their physiological needs before they reveal an interest in safety needs, and safety must be satisfied before social needs become motivational, and so on. When a need is unsatisfied, it exerts a powerful effect on the individual's thinking and behaviour, and this is the sense in which needs are motivational. However, when needs at a particular level of the hierarchy are satisfied, the individual turns his or her attention to the next higher level. Notice the clear implication here that a *satisfied need is no longer an effective motivator.* Once one has adequate physiological resources and feels safe and secure, one does not seek more of the factors that met these needs but looks elsewhere for gratification. According to Maslow, the single exception to this rule involves self-actualization needs. He felt that these were "growth" needs that become stronger as they are gratified.

> **Maslow's hierarchy of needs.** A five-level hierarchical need theory of motivation that specifies that the lowest-level unsatisfied need has the greatest motivating potential.

Alderfer's ERG Theory

Clayton Alderfer developed another need-based theory, called **ERG theory.**[29] It streamlines Maslow's need classifications and makes some different assumptions about the relationship between needs and motivation. The name ERG stems from Alderfer's compression of Maslow's five-category need system into three categories—existence, relatedness, and growth needs:

> **ERG theory.** A three-level hierarchical need theory of motivation (existence, relatedness, growth) that allows for movement up and down the hierarchy.

1. *Existence needs.* These are needs that are satisfied by some material substance or condition. As such, they correspond closely to Maslow's physiological needs and to those safety needs that are satisfied by material conditions rather than interpersonal relations. These include the need for food, shelter, pay, and safe working conditions.

2. *Relatedness needs.* These are needs that are satisfied by open communication and the exchange of thoughts and feelings with other organizational members. They correspond fairly closely to Maslow's belongingness needs and to those esteem needs that involve feedback from others. However, Alderfer stresses that related-

ness needs are satisfied by open, accurate, honest interaction rather than by uncritical pleasantness.

3. *Growth needs*. These are needs that are fulfilled by strong personal involvement in the work setting. They involve the full utilization of one's skills and abilities and the creative development of new skills and abilities. Growth needs correspond to Maslow's need for self-actualization and the aspects of his esteem needs that concern achievement and responsibility.

As you can see in Exhibit 5.4, Alderfer's need classification system does not represent a radical departure from that of Maslow. In addition, Alderfer agrees with Maslow that as lower-level needs are satisfied, the desire to have higher-level needs satisfied will increase. Thus, as existence needs are fulfilled, relatedness needs gain motivational power. Alderfer explains this by arguing that as more "concrete" needs are satisfied, energy can be directed toward satisfying less concrete needs. Finally, Alderfer agrees with Maslow that the least concrete needs—growth needs—become *more* compelling and *more* desired as they are fulfilled.

It is, of course, the differences between ERG theory and the need hierarchy that represent Alderfer's contribution to the understanding of motivation. First, unlike the need hierarchy, ERG theory does not assume that a lower-level need *must* be gratified before a less concrete need becomes operative. Thus, ERG theory does not propose a rigid hierarchy of needs, and some individuals, owing to background and experience, might seek relatedness or growth even though their existence needs are ungratified. Hence, ERG theory seems to account for a wide variety of individual differences in motive structure. Second, ERG theory assumes that if the higher-level needs are ungratified, individuals will increase their desire for the gratification of lower-level needs. Notice that this represents a *radical* departure from Maslow. According to Maslow, if esteem needs are strong but ungratified, a person will not revert to an interest in belongingness needs because these have necessarily already been gratified. (Remember, he argues that satisfied needs are not motivational.) According to Alderfer, however, the frustration of higher-order needs will lead workers to regress to a more concrete need category. For example, the software designer who is unable to establish rewarding social relationships with superiors or co-workers might increase his interest in fulfilling existence needs, perhaps by seeking a pay increase. Thus, according to Alderfer, an apparently satisfied need can act as a motivator by substituting for an unsatisfied need.

Given the preceding description of ERG theory, we can identify its two major motivational premises as follows:

1. The more lower-level needs are gratified, the more higher-level need satisfaction is desired;

2. The less higher-level needs are gratified, the more lower-level need satisfaction is desired.

McClelland's Theory of Needs

Psychologist David McClelland has spent several decades studying the human need structure and its implications for motivation. According to **McClelland's theory of needs**, needs reflect relatively stable personality characteristics that one acquires through early life experiences and exposure to selected aspects of one's society. Unlike Maslow and Alderfer, McClelland has not been interested in specifying a hierarchical relationship among needs. Rather, he has been more concerned with the specific behavioural consequences of needs. In other words, under what conditions are certain needs likely to result in particular patterns of motivation? The three needs that McClelland studied most have special relevance for organizational behaviour—needs for achievement, affiliation, and power.[30]

McClelland's theory of needs. A nonhierarchical need theory of motivation that outlines the conditions under which certain needs result in particular patterns of motivation.

Individuals who are high in **need for achievement** (*n* Ach) have a strong desire to perform challenging tasks well. More specifically, they exhibit the following characteristics:

- *A preference for situations in which personal responsibility can be taken for outcomes.* Those high in *n* Ach do not prefer situations in which outcomes are determined by chance because success in such situations does not provide an experience of achievement.

- *A tendency to set moderately difficult goals that provide for calculated risks.* Success with easy goals will provide little sense of achievement, while extremely difficult goals might never be reached. The calculation of successful risks is stimulating to the high–*n* Ach person.

- *A desire for performance feedback.* Such feedback permits individuals with high *n* Ach to modify their goal attainment strategies to ensure success and signals them when success has been reached.[31]

People who are high in *n* Ach are concerned with bettering their own performance or that of others. They are often concerned with innovation and long-term goal involvement. However, these things are not done to please others or to damage the interests of others. Rather, they are done because they are *intrinsically* satisfying. Thus, *n* Ach would appear to be an example of a growth or self-actualization need.

People who are high in **need for affiliation** (*n* Aff) have a strong desire to establish and maintain friendly, compatible interpersonal relationships. In other words, they like to like others, and they want others to like them! More specifically, they have an ability to learn social networking quickly and a tendency to communicate frequently with others, either face to face, by telephone, or by letter. Also, they prefer to avoid conflict and competition with others, and they sometimes exhibit strong conformity to the wishes of their friends. The *n* Aff motive is obviously an example of a belongingness or relatedness need.

People who are high in **need for power** (*n* Pow) strongly desire to have influence over others. In other words, they wish to make a significant impact or impression on them. People who are high in *n* Pow seek out social settings in which they can be influential. When in small groups, they act in a "high-profile," attention-getting manner. There is some tendency for those who are high in *n* Pow to advocate risky positions. Also, some people who are high in *n* Pow show a strong concern for personal prestige. The need for power is a complex need because power can be used in a variety of ways, some of which serve the power seeker and some of which serve other people or the organization. However, *n* Pow seems to correspond most closely to Maslow's self-esteem need.

McClelland predicts that people will be motivated to seek out and perform well in jobs that match their needs. Thus, people with high *n* Ach should be strongly motivated by sales jobs or entrepreneurial positions, such as running a small business. Such jobs offer the feedback, personal responsibility, and opportunity to set goals, as noted above. People who are high in *n* Aff will be motivated by jobs such as social work or customer relations because these jobs have as a primary task establishing good relations with others. Finally, high *n* Pow will result in high motivation in jobs that enable one to have a strong impact on others—jobs such as journalism and management. In fact, McClelland has found that the most effective managers have a low need for affiliation, a high need for power, and the ability to direct power toward organizational goals.[32] (We will study this further in Chapter 12.)

Research Support for Need Theories

Maslow's need hierarchy suggests two main hypotheses. First, specific needs should cluster into the five main need categories that Maslow proposes. Second, as the needs

Need for achievement. A strong desire to perform challenging tasks well.

Need for affiliation. A strong desire to establish and maintain friendly, compatible interpersonal relationships.

Need for power. A strong desire to influence others, making a significant impact or impression.

in a given category are satisfied, they should become less important, while the needs in the adjacent higher-need category should become more important. This second hypothesis captures the progressive, hierarchical aspect of the theory. In general, research support for both these hypotheses is weak or negative. This is probably a function of the rigidity of the theory, which suggests that most people experience the same needs in the same hierarchical order. However, there is fair support for a simpler two-level need hierarchy comprising the needs toward the top and the bottom of Maslow's hierarchy.[33]

This latter finding provides some indirect encouragement for the compressed need hierarchy found in Alderfer's ERG theory. Several tests indicate fairly good support for many of the predictions generated by the theory, including expected changes in need strength. Particularly interesting is the confirmation that the frustration of relatedness needs increases the strength of existence needs.[34] The simplicity and flexibility of ERG theory seem to capture the human need structure better than the greater complexity and rigidity of Maslow's theory.

McClelland's need theory has generated a wealth of predictions about many aspects of human motivation. Recently, researchers have tested more and more of these predictions in organizational settings, and the results are generally supportive of the idea that particular needs are motivational when the work setting permits the satisfaction of these needs.[35]

Managerial Implications of Need Theories

The need theories have some important things to say about managerial attempts to motivate employees.

Appreciate Diversity. The lack of support for the fairly rigid need hierarchy suggests that managers must be adept at evaluating the needs of individual employees and offering incentives or goals that correspond to their own needs. Unfounded stereotypes about the needs of the "typical" employee and naïve assumptions about the universality of need satisfaction are bound to reduce the effectiveness of chosen motivational strategies. The best salesperson might not make the best sales manager! The needs of a young recent college graduate probably differ from those of an older employee preparing for retirement. Thus, it is important to survey employees to find out what their needs are and then offer programs that meet their needs.

Appreciate Intrinsic Motivation. The need theories also serve the valuable function of alerting managers to the existence of higher-order needs (whatever specific label we apply to them). The recognition of these needs in many employees is important for two key reasons. One of the basic conditions for organizational survival is the expression of some creative and innovative behaviour on the part of members. Such behaviour seems most likely to occur during the pursuit of higher-order need fulfillment, and ignorance of this factor can cause the demotivation of the people who have the most to offer the organization. Second, observation and research evidence support Alderfer's idea that the frustration of higher-order needs prompts demands for greater satisfaction of lower-order needs. This can lead to a vicious motivational circle—that is, because the factors that gratify lower-level needs are fairly easy to administer (e.g., pay and fringe benefits), management has grown to rely on them to motivate employees. In turn, some employees, deprived of higher-order need gratification, come to expect more and more of these extrinsic factors in exchange for their services. Thus, a circle of deprivation, regression, and temporary gratification continues at great cost to the organization.[36]

How can organizations benefit from the intrinsic motivation that is inherent in strong higher-order needs? First, such needs will fail to develop for most employees unless lower-level needs are reasonably well gratified.[37] Thus, very poor pay, job insecurity, and unsafe working conditions will preoccupy most workers at the expense of higher-order outcomes. Second, if basic needs are met, jobs can be "enriched" to be more stimulating and challenging and to provide feelings of responsibility and achievement (we will have more to say about this in Chapter 6). Finally, organizations could pay more attention to designing career paths that enable interested workers to progress through a series of jobs that continue to challenge their higher-order needs. Individual managers could also assign tasks to employees with this goal in mind.

PROCESS THEORIES OF WORK MOTIVATION

In contrast to need theories of motivation, which concentrate on *what* motivates people, **process theories** concentrate on *how* motivation occurs. In this section, we will examine three important process theories—expectancy theory, equity theory, and goal setting theory.

Process theories. Motivation theories that specify the details of how motivation occurs.

Expectancy Theory

The basic idea underlying **expectancy theory** is the belief that motivation is determined by the outcomes that people expect to occur as a result of their actions on the job. Psychologist Victor Vroom is usually credited with developing the first complete version of expectancy theory and applying it to the work setting.[38] The basic components of Vroom's theory are shown in Exhibit 5.5 and are described in more detail below:

- **Outcomes** are the consequences that may follow certain work behaviours. First-level outcomes are of particular interest to the organization; for example, high productivity versus average productivity, illustrated in Exhibit 5.5, or good attendance versus poor attendance. Expectancy theory is concerned with specifying how an employee might attempt to choose one first-level outcome instead of another. Second-level outcomes are consequences that follow the attainment of a particular first-level outcome. Contrasted with first-level outcomes, second-level outcomes are most personally relevant to the individual worker and might involve amount of pay, sense of accomplishment, acceptance by peers, fatigue, and so on.

- **Instrumentality** is the probability that a particular first-level outcome (such as high productivity) will be followed by a particular second-level outcome (such as pay). For example, a bank teller might figure that the odds are 50/50 (instrumentality = .5) that a good performance rating will result in a pay raise.

- **Valence** is the expected value of outcomes, the extent to which they are attractive or unattractive to the individual. Thus, good pay, peer acceptance, the chance of being fired, or any other second-level outcome might be more or less attractive to particular workers. According to Vroom, the valence of first-level outcomes is the sum of products of the associated second-level outcomes and their instrumentalities—that is,

$$\text{the valence of a particular first-level outcome} = \Sigma \; instrumentalities \times second\text{-}level \; valences$$

In other words, the valence of a first-level outcome depends on the extent to which it leads to favourable second-level outcomes.

- **Expectancy** is the probability that the worker can actually achieve a particular first-level outcome. For example, a machinist might be absolutely certain (expectancy = 1.0) that she can perform at an average level (producing 15 units a day), but less certain (expectancy = .6) that she can perform at a high level (producing 20 units a day).

- **Force** is the end product of the other components of the theory. It represents the relative degree of effort that will be directed toward various first-level outcomes.

Expectancy theory. A process theory that states that motivation is determined by the outcomes that people expect to occur as a result of their actions on the job.

Outcomes. Consequences that follow work behaviour.

Instrumentality. The probability that a particular first-level outcome will be followed by a particular second-level outcome.

Valence. The expected value of work outcomes; the extent to which they are attractive or unattractive.

Expectancy. The probability that a particular first-level outcome can be achieved.

Force. The effort directed toward a first-level outcome.

EXHIBIT 5.5
A hypothetical expectancy model (E = Expectancy, I = Instrumentality, V = Valence).

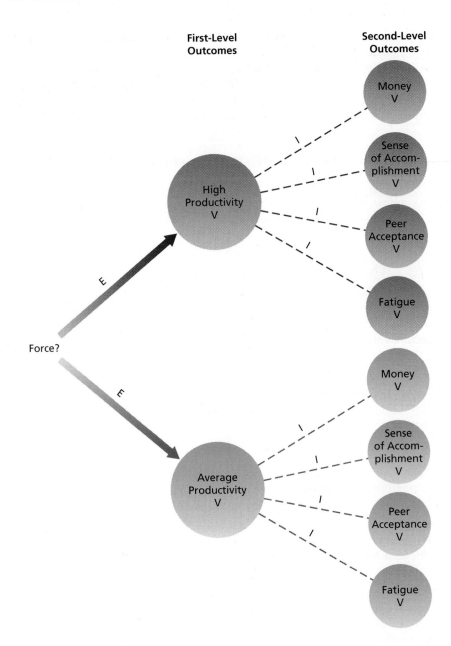

According to Vroom, the force directed toward a first-level outcome is a product of the valence of that outcome and the expectancy that it can be achieved. Thus,

force = first-level valence × expectancy

We can expect an individual's effort to be directed toward the first-level outcome that has the largest force product. Notice that no matter how valent a particular first-level outcome might be, a person will not be motivated to achieve it if the expectancy of accomplishment approaches zero.

Believe it or not, the mechanics of expectancy theory can be distilled into a couple of simple sentences! In fact, these sentences nicely capture the premises of the theory:

- People will be motivated to perform in those work activities that they find attractive and that they feel they can accomplish.

- The attractiveness of various work activities depends on the extent to which they lead to favourable personal consequences.

It is extremely important to understand that expectancy theory is based on the perceptions of the individual worker. Thus, expectancies, valences, instrumentalities, and relevant second-level outcomes depend on the perceptual system of the person whose motivation we are analyzing. For example, two employees performing the same job might attach different valences to money, differ in their perceptions of the instrumentality of performance for obtaining high pay, and differ in their expectations of being able to perform at a high level. Therefore, they would likely exhibit different patterns of motivation.

Although expectancy theory does not concern itself directly with the distinction between extrinsic and intrinsic motivators, it can handle any form of second-level outcome that has relevance for the person in question. Thus, some people might find second-level outcomes of an intrinsic nature, such as feeling good about performing a task well, positively valent. Others might find extrinsic outcomes, such as high pay, positively valent.

To firm up your understanding of expectancy theory, consider Tony Angelas, a middle manager in a firm that operates a chain of retail stores (Exhibit 5.6). Second-level outcomes that are relevant to him include the opportunity to obtain a raise and the chance to receive a promotion. The promotion is more highly valent to Tony than the raise (7 versus 5 on a scale of 10) because the promotion means more money *and* increased prestige. Tony figures that if he can perform at a very high level in the next few months, the odds are 6 in 10 that he will receive a raise. Thus, the instrumentality of high performance for obtaining a raise is .6. Promotions are harder to come by, and Tony figures the odds at .3 if he performs well. The instrumentality of average performance for achieving these favourable second-level outcomes is a good bit lower (.2 for

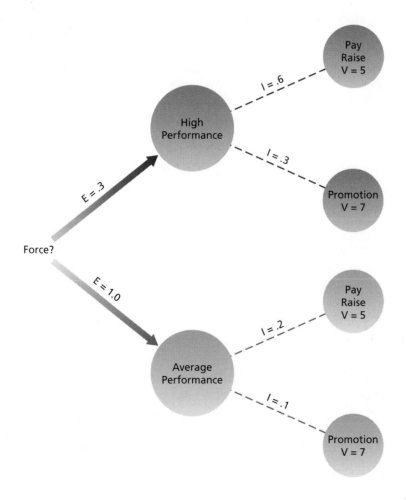

EXHIBIT 5.6
Expectancy model for Tony Angelas
(E = Expectancy,
I = Instrumentality,
V = Valence).

the raise and only .1 for the promotion). Recall that the valence of a first-level outcome is the sum of the products of second-level outcomes and their instrumentalities. Thus, the valence of high performance for Tony is $(5 \times .6) + (7 \times .3) = 5.1$. Similarly, the valence of average performance is $(5 \times .2) + (7 \times .1) = 1.7$. We can conclude that high performance is more valent for Tony than average performance.

Does this mean that Tony will necessarily try to perform at a high level in the next few months? To determine this, we must take into account his expectancy that he can actually achieve the competing first-level outcomes. As shown in Exhibit 5.6, Tony is absolutely certain that he can perform at an average level (expectancy = 1.0) but much less certain (.3) that he can sustain high performance. Force is a product of these expectancies and the valence of their respective first-level outcomes. Thus, the force associated with high performance is $.3 \times 5.1 = 1.53$, while that associated with average performance is $1.0 \times 1.7 = 1.70$. As a result, although high performance is attractive to Tony, he will probably perform at an average level.

With all this complicated figuring, you might be thinking "Look, would Tony really do all this calculation to decide his motivational strategy? Do people actually think this way?" The answer to these questions is probably no. Rather, the argument is that people *implicitly* take expectancy, valence, and instrumentality into account as they go about their daily business of being motivated. If you reflect for a moment on your behaviour at work or school, you will realize that you have certain expectancies about what you can accomplish, the chances that these accomplishments will lead to certain other outcomes, and the value of these outcomes for you.

Research Support for Expectancy Theory

Tests have provided moderately favourable support for expectancy theory.[39] In particular, there is especially good evidence that the valence of first-level outcomes depends on the extent to which they lead to favourable second-level consequences. We must recognize, however, that the sheer complexity of expectancy theory makes it difficult to test. We have already suggested that people are not used to *thinking* in expectancy terminology. Thus, some research studies show that individuals have a difficult time discriminating between instrumentalities and second-level valences. Despite this and other technical problems, experts in motivation generally accept expectancy theory.

Managerial Implications of Expectancy Theory

The motivational practices suggested by expectancy theory involve "juggling the numbers" that individuals attach to expectancies, instrumentalities, and valences.

Boost Expectancies. One of the most basic things managers can do is ensure that their employees *expect* to be able to achieve first-level outcomes that are of interest to the organization. No matter how positively valent high productivity or good attendance might be, the force equation suggests that workers will not pursue these goals if expectancy is low. Low expectancies can take many forms, but a few examples will suffice to make the point.

- Employees might feel that poor equipment, poor tools, or lazy co-workers impede their work progress.
- Employees might not understand what the organization considers to be good performance or see how they can achieve it.
- If performance is evaluated by a subjective supervisory rating, employees might see the process as capricious and arbitrary, not understanding how to obtain a good rating.

Although the specific solutions to these problems vary, expectancies can usually be enhanced by providing proper equipment and training, demonstrating correct work procedures, carefully explaining how performance is evaluated, and listening to employee performance problems. The point of all this is to clarify the path to beneficial first-level outcomes.

Clarify Reward Contingencies. Managers should also attempt to ensure that the paths between first- and second-level outcomes are clear. Employees should be convinced that first-level outcomes desired by the organization are clearly *instrumental* in obtaining positive second-level outcomes and avoiding negative outcomes. If a manager has a policy of recommending good performers for promotion, she should spell out this policy. Similarly, if managers desire regular attendance, they should clarify the consequences of good and poor attendance. To ensure that instrumentalities are strongly established, they should be clearly stated and then acted on by the manager. Managers should also attempt to provide stimulating, challenging tasks for workers who appear to be interested in such work. On such tasks, the instrumentality of good performance for feelings of achievement, accomplishment, and competence is almost necessarily high. The ready availability of intrinsic motivation reduces the need for the manager to constantly monitor and clarify instrumentalities.[40]

Appreciate Diverse Needs. Obviously, it might be difficult for managers to change the valences that employees attach to second-level outcomes. Individual preferences for high pay, promotion, interesting work, and so on are the product of a long history of development and are unlikely to change rapidly. However, managers would do well to analyze the diverse preferences of particular employees and attempt to design individualized "motivational packages" to meet their needs. Of course, all concerned must perceive such packages to be fair. Let's examine another process theory that is concerned specifically with the motivational consequences of fairness.

Equity Theory

In Chapter 4, we discussed the role of **equity theory** in explaining job satisfaction. To review, the theory asserts that workers compare the inputs that they invest in their jobs and the outcomes that they receive against the inputs and outcomes of some other relevant person or group. When these ratios are equal, the worker should feel that a fair and equitable exchange exists with the employing organization. Such fair exchange contributes to job satisfaction. When the ratios are unequal, workers perceive inequity, and they should experience job dissatisfaction, at least if the exchange puts the worker at a disadvantage vis-à-vis others.

But in what sense is equity theory a theory of motivation? Put simply, *individuals are motivated to maintain an equitable exchange relationship.* Inequity is unpleasant and tension producing, and people will devote considerable energy to reducing inequity and achieving equity. What tactics can do this? Psychologist J. Stacey Adams has suggested the following possibilities:[41]

- Perceptually distort one's own inputs or outcomes.
- Perceptually distort the inputs or outcomes of the comparison person or group.
- Choose another comparison person or group.
- Alter one's inputs or alter one's outcomes.
- Leave the exchange relationship.

Notice that the first three tactics for reducing inequity are essentially psychological, while the last two involve overt behaviour.

To clarify the motivational implications of equity theory, consider Terry, a middle manager in a consumer products company. He has five years' work experience and an

Equity theory. A process theory that states that motivation stems from a comparison of the inputs one invests in a job and the outcomes one receives in comparison with the inputs and outcomes of another person or group.

MBA degree and considers himself a good performer. His salary is $75 000 a year. Terry finds out that Maxine, a co-worker with whom he identifies closely, makes the same salary he does. However, she has only a Bachelor's degree and one year of experience, and he sees her performance as average rather than good. Thus, from Terry's perspective, the following outcome/input ratios exist:

$$\frac{\text{TERRY } \$75\ 000}{\text{Good performance, MBA, 5 years}} \neq \frac{\text{MAXINE } \$75\ 000}{\text{Average performance, Bachelor's, 1 year}}$$

In Terry's view, he is underpaid and should be experiencing inequity. What might he do to resolve this inequity? Psychologically, he might distort the outcomes that he is receiving, rationalizing that he is due for a certain promotion that will bring his pay into line with his inputs. Behaviourally, he might try to increase his outcomes (by seeking an immediate raise) or reduce his inputs. Input reduction could include a decrease in work effort or perhaps excessive absenteeism. Finally, Terry might resign from the organization to take what he perceives to be a more equitable job somewhere else.

Let's reverse the coin and assume that Maxine views the exchange relationship identically to Terry—same inputs, same outcomes. Notice that she too should be experiencing inequity, this time from relative overpayment. It does not take a genius to understand that Maxine would be unlikely to seek equity by marching into the boss's office and demanding a pay cut. However, she might well attempt to increase her inputs by working harder or enrolling in an MBA program. Alternatively, she might distort her view of Terry's performance to make it seem closer to her own. As this example implies, equity theory is somewhat vague about just when individuals will employ various inequity reduction strategies.

Gender and Equity. As an addendum to the previous example, it is extremely interesting to learn that both women and men have some tendency to choose same-sex comparison persons—that is, when judging the fairness of the outcomes that they receive, men tend to compare themselves with other men, and women tend to compare themselves with other women. This might provide a partial explanation for why women are paid less than men, even for the same job. If women restrict their equity comparisons to (lesser paid) women, they are less likely to be motivated to correct what we observers see as wage inequities.[42]

Research Support for Equity Theory. Most research on equity theory has been restricted to economic outcomes and has concentrated on the alteration of inputs and outcomes as a means of reducing inequity. In general, this research is very supportive of the theory when inequity occurs because of *underpayment*.[43] For example, when workers are underpaid on an hourly basis, they tend to lower their inputs by producing less work. This brings inputs in line with (low) outcomes. Also, when workers are underpaid on a piece-rate basis (e.g., paid $1 for each market research interview conducted), they tend to produce a high volume of low-quality work. This enables them to raise their outcomes to achieve equity. Finally, there is also evidence that underpayment inequity leads to resignation. Presumably, some underpaid workers thus seek equity in another organizational setting.

The theory's predictions regarding *overpayment* inequity have received less support.[44] The theory suggests that such inequity can be reduced behaviourally by increasing inputs or by reducing one's outcomes. The weak support for these strategies suggests either that people tolerate overpayment more than underpayment, or that they use perceptual distortion to reduce overpayment inequity.

Managerial Implications of Equity Theory. The most straightforward implication of equity theory is that perceived underpayment will have a variety of negative motivational consequences for the organization, including low productivity, low quality, theft, or turnover. On the other hand, attempting to solve organizational problems through overpayment (disguised bribery) might not have the intended motivational effect. The trick here is to strike an equitable balance.

But how can such a balance be struck? Managers must understand that feelings about equity stem from a *perceptual* social comparison process in which the worker "controls the equation"—that is, employees decide what are considered relevant inputs, outcomes, and comparison persons, and management must be sensitive to these decisions. For example, offering the outcome of more interesting work might not redress inequity if better pay is considered a more relevant outcome. Similarly, basing pay only on performance might not be perceived as equitable if employees consider seniority an important job input.

Understanding the role of comparison people is especially crucial.[45] Even if the best engineer in the design department earns $2000 more than anyone else in the department, she might still have feelings of inequity if she compares her salary with that of more prosperous colleagues in *other* companies. Awareness of the comparison people chosen by workers might suggest strategies for reducing felt inequity. Perhaps the company will have to pay even more to retain its star engineer. Equity is achieved at WestJet Airlines by treating all employees as owners and by including all employees in the company's profit sharing program and employee stock ownership plan.

Goal Setting Theory

One of the basic characteristics of all organizations is that they have goals. A goal is the object or aim of an action.[46] At the beginning of this chapter, individual performance was defined as the extent to which a member contributes to the attainment of these goals or objectives. Thus, if employees are to achieve acceptable performance, some method of translating organizational goals into individual goals must be implemented.

Unfortunately, there is ample reason to believe that personal performance goals are vague or nonexistent for many organizational members. Employees frequently report that their role in the organization is unclear, or that they do not really know what their boss expects of them. Even in cases in which performance goals would seem to be obvious because of the nature of the task (e.g., filling packing crates to the maximum to avoid excessive freight charges), employees might be ignorant of their current performance. This suggests that the implicit performance goals simply are not making an impression.

The notion of **goal setting** as a motivator has been around for a long time. However, theoretical developments and some very practical research have demonstrated when and how goal setting can be effective.[47]

Goal setting. A motivational technique that uses specific, challenging, and acceptable goals and provides feedback to enhance performance.

What Kinds of Goals Are Motivational?

A large body of evidence suggests that goals are most motivational when they are *specific, challenging,* and when organizational members are *committed* to them. In addition, *feedback* about progress toward goal attainment should be provided.[48] The positive effects of goals are due to four mechanisms: they *direct* attention toward goal-relevant activities; they lead to greater *effort*; they increase and prolong *persistence*; and they lead to the discovery and use of task-relevant *strategies* for goal attainment.[49] Exhibit 5.7 shows the kinds of goals that are motivational and the mechanisms that explain the effects of goals on performance.

Goal Specificity. Specific goals are goals that specify an exact level of achievement for people to accomplish in a particular time frame. For example, "I will enroll in five courses next semester and achieve a *B* or better in each course" is a specific goal. Similarly, "I will increase my net sales by 20 percent in the coming business quarter" is a specific goal. On the other hand, "I will do my best" is not a specific goal, since level of achievement and time frame are both vague.

EXHIBIT 5.7
The mechanisms of goal setting.

Source: Locke, E.A., & Latham, G.P. (2002). Building a practically useful theory of goal setting and task motivation. *American Psychologist, 57,* 705–717.

Goal Challenge. Obviously, specific goals that are especially easy to achieve will not motivate effective performance. However, goal challenge is a much more personal matter than goal specificity, since it depends on the experience and basic skills of the organizational member. One thing is certain, however—when goals become so difficult that they are perceived as *impossible* to achieve, they will lose their potential to motivate. Thus, goal challenge is best when it is pegged to the competence of individual workers and increased as the particular task is mastered. One practical way to do this is to base initial goals on past performance. For example, an academic counsellor might encourage a *D* student to set a goal of achieving Cs in the coming semester and encourage a *C* student to set a goal of achieving Bs. Similarly, a sales manager might ask a new salesperson to try to increase his sales by 5 percent in the next quarter and ask an experienced salesperson to try to increase her sales by 10 percent.

Goal Commitment. Individuals must be committed to specific, challenging goals if the goals are to have effective motivational properties. The effect of goals on performance is strongest when individuals have high goal commitment. In a sense, goals really are not goals and cannot improve performance unless an individual accepts them and is committed to working toward them. This is especially important when goals are challenging and difficult to achieve. In a following section, we will discuss some factors that affect goal commitment.

Goal Feedback. Specific and challenging goals have the most beneficial effect when they are accompanied by ongoing feedback that enables the person to compare current performance with the goal. This is why a schedule of tasks to be completed often motivates goal accomplishment. Progress against the schedule provides feedback. To be most effective, feedback should be accurate, specific, credible, and timely.

Enhancing Goal Commitment

It has probably not escaped you that the requirements for goal challenge and goal commitment seem potentially incompatible. After all, you might be quite amenable to accepting an easy goal but balk at accepting a tough one. Therefore, it is important to consider some of the factors that might affect commitment to challenging, specific goals, including participation, rewards, and management support.

Participation. It seems reasonable that organizational members should be more committed to goals that are set with their participation than to those simply handed down by their superior. Sensible as this sounds, the research evidence on the effects of participation is very mixed—sometimes participation in goal setting increases performance, and sometimes it does not.[50] If goal commitment is a potential *problem,* participation might prove beneficial.[51] When a climate of distrust between superiors and employees exists, or when participation provides information that assists in the establishment of fair, realistic goals, then it should facilitate performance. On the other hand, when employees trust their boss, and when the boss has a good understanding of the capability of the employees, participation might be quite unnecessary for goal commitment.[52] Interestingly, research shows that participation can improve performance by increasing the *difficulty* of the goals that employees adopt.[53] This might occur because participation induces competition or a feeling of team spirit among members of the work unit, which leads them to exceed the goal expectations of the supervisor.

Rewards. Will the promise of extrinsic rewards (such as money) for goal accomplishment increase goal commitment? Probably, but there is plenty of evidence that goal setting has led to performance increases *without* the introduction of monetary incentives for goal accomplishment. One reason for this might be that many ambitious goals involve no more than doing the job as it was designed to be done in the first place. For example, encouraging employees to pack crates or load trucks to within 5 percent of their maximum capacity does not really involve a greater expenditure of effort or more work. It simply requires more attention to detail. Goal setting should, however, be compatible with any system to tie pay to performance that already exists for the job in question.

Supportiveness. There is considerable agreement about one factor that will *reduce* commitment to specific, challenging performance goals. When supervisors behave in a coercive manner to encourage goal accomplishment, they can badly damage employee goal commitment. For goal setting to work properly, supervisors must demonstrate a desire to assist employees in goal accomplishment and behave supportively if failure occurs, even adjusting the goal downward if it proves to be unrealistically high. Threat and punishment in response to failure will be extremely counterproductive.[54]

Goal Orientation

A recent development in goal setting theory has been research on different types of goals, or what is known as *goal orientation*. Two goal orientations that are particularly important are a learning goal orientation and a performance goal orientation. **Learning goals** are process-oriented goals that focus on learning. They enhance understanding of a task and the use of task strategies. **Performance goals** are outcome-oriented goals that focus attention on the achievement of specific performance outcomes.[55]

Individuals appear to differ in their goal preference and goal orientation. In fact, goal orientation has been found to be a stable individual difference. Some individuals have a preference for learning goals while others have a preference for performance goals. Individuals with a learning goal orientation are most concerned about learning something new and developing their competence in an activity by acquiring new skills and mastering new situations; they focus on acquiring new knowledge and skills and developing their competence. Individuals with a performance goal orientation are most concerned about demonstrating their competence in performing a task by seeking favourable judgments and avoiding negative judgments; they focus on the outcome of their performance.[56]

Goal orientation is important because it can influence performance as well as cognitive, affective, and motivational processes. In the last several years, research has found that a learning goal orientation is especially important for performance and leads to higher performance compared to a performance goal orientation. One study on the salespeople of a medical supplies distributor found that a learning goal orientation was positively related to sales performance, but a performance goal orientation was not. A learning goal orientation has also been found to be positively related to effort, self-efficacy, and goal setting level.[57]

Learning goals. Process-oriented goals that focus on learning and enhance understanding of a task and the use of task strategies.

Performance goals. Outcome-oriented goals that focus attention on the achievement of specific performance outcomes.

Research Support for and Managerial Implications of Goal Setting Theory

Research Support. Several decades of research has demonstrated that specific, difficult goals lead to improved performance and productivity on a wide variety of tasks and occupations, including servicing drink machines, entering data, selling, teaching, and typing text. Studies reveal that the positive results of goal setting are not short lived—they persist over a long enough time to have practical value.[58] For example, in a now classic study conducted at Weyerhaeuser Company, a large forest products firm headquartered in Tacoma, Washington, truck drivers were assigned a specific, challenging performance goal of loading their trucks to 94 percent of legal weight capacity. Before setting this goal, management had simply asked the drivers to do their best to maximize their weight. Over the first several weeks, load capacity gradually increased to over 90 percent and remained at this high level for seven years! In the first nine months alone, the company accountants conservatively estimated the savings at $250 000. These results were achieved without driver participation in setting the goal and without monetary incentives for goal accomplishment. Drivers evidently found the 94-percent goal motivating in and of itself; they frequently recorded their weights in informal competition with other drivers.[59]

In recent years, however, research has found that the effects of goal setting on performance depend on a number of factors. For example, when individuals lack the knowledge or skill to perform a complex task effectively, a specific and challenging performance goal can decrease rather than increase performance relative to a do-your-best goal. On the other hand, when a task is straightforward, a specific, high performance goal results in higher performance than a do-your-best goal. In addition, a specific, high learning goal is more effective than a specific, high performance goal or a do-your-best goal when individuals are learning to perform a complex task. This is because effective performance of complex tasks requires the acquisition of knowledge and skills, and a specific learning goal focuses one's attention on learning.[60] Some research has also suggested that goal setting might have some unintended consequences. To learn more, see "Ethical Focus: *Goal Setting and Unethical Behaviour.*"

Weyerhaeuser Company
www.weyerhaeuser.com

Drivers at Weyerhaeuser Company were assigned a specific, challenging performance goal of loading their trucks to 94 percent of legal weight capacity.

ETHICAL FOCUS

Goal Setting and Unethical Behaviour

Many studies have demonstrated that individuals exert more effort and display greater persistence in the pursuit of specific and difficult goals compared to "do your best" goals. In fact, hundreds of studies have found that specific and challenging goals have a positive effect on task performance. The evidence is so strong that goal setting theory is now considered to be one of the most important theories in organizational behaviour, with over a thousand articles and reviews published on the topic in the last 30 years.

However, the use of goal setting in some organizations has resulted in some unintended consequences, such as "cooked books" and false sales reports. This has led some to speculate that goal setting might have some negative consequences on people's behaviour. For example, is it possible that goal setting motivates unethical behaviour?

To find out, Maurice Schweitzer, Lisa Ordonez, and Bambi Douma conducted a study in which participants had to create words using seven letters listed at the top of a page. Participants also had to check all of their work at the end of the study and indicate if they had met their goal. This enabled the authors to find out if people are likely to misrepresent and overstate their performance—an example of unethical behaviour—when they fall short of meeting their goals.

There were three goal setting conditions: Do-your-best goals, mere goals, and reward goals. In the do-your-best condition, participants were told to "do your best to create as many words as you can." In the mere goal condition, participants were given the goal of creating nine or more words for each round. In the reward goal condition, participants were given the goal of creating nine words for each round and told that they would earn $2 for each round in which the goal was met.

Following a practice round, participants completed seven experimental rounds. For each round, they were given seven letters and one minute to create words. Participants in the reward goal condition were each given an envelope that contained 14 one-dollar bills. They were told to keep $2 for each of the seven experimental rounds in which they met the goal and to return unearned money at the end of the study.

At the end of the seven rounds, participants were asked to check their work. They were given dictionaries and an answer sheet on which they had to indicate whether or not they created nine or more valid words in each round. Participants then deposited their workbooks and answer sheets in separate sealed boxes. Reward goal participants also had envelopes in which to deposit any unearned money along with their answer sheets.

To measure unethical behaviour, the authors compared the actual performance of each participant to each participant's claims about their performance to determine if participants overstated their performance. As expected, participants in the mere goal and reward goal conditions were more likely to overstate their performance than those in the do-your-best condition. The results also indicated that participants were most likely to overstate their performance when they were close to rather than far from reaching their goals. In fact, the relationship between goal setting and unethical behaviour was particularly strong when people fell just short of reaching their goals.

Thus, while goal setting can be used constructively to motivate desirable behaviour, the results of this study suggest that goal setting can lead to unethical behaviour. Therefore, managers need to be vigilant for unethical behaviour when they use goal setting to motivate employees.

Source: Based on Schweitzer, M.E., Ordonez, L., & Douma, B. (2004). Goal setting as a motivator of unethical behaviour. *Academy of Management Journal, 47*, 422–432.

Finally, although we have focused on individual goal setting, the effect of group goal setting on group performance is similar to the effect of individual goal setting. Group goals result in superior group performance, especially when groups set specific goals and when the group members participate in setting the goals.[61]

Managerial Implications. The managerial implications of goal setting theory seem straightforward: Set specific and challenging goals and provide ongoing feedback so that individuals can compare their performance with the goal. While goals can be motivational in certain circumstances, they obviously have some limitations. For example, as indicated earlier, the performance impact of specific, challenging goals is stronger for simpler jobs than for more complex jobs such as scientific and engineering work. Thus, when a task is novel or complex and individuals need to acquire new knowledge and skills for good performance, setting a specific learning goal will be more effective than setting a high performance goal. Setting a high performance goal will be most effective when individuals already have the ability to perform a task effectively.[62]

Microsoft is one of many organizations today that incorporate goals and the goal setting process in the performance management system. General Electric's goal setting program is credited with making the organization more effective along a number of financial and productivity dimensions.[63] In the next chapter, we will discuss a more elaborate application of goal setting theory, called *management by objectives*.

Now that you are familiar with motivation theories, try to use them to evaluate an actual motivation program. Please consult "You Be the Manager: *Purolator's Early and Safe Return to Work Program*."

Purolator
www.purolator.com

DO MOTIVATION THEORIES TRANSLATE ACROSS CULTURES?

Are the motivation theories that we have described in this chapter culture bound? That is, do they apply only to North America, where they were developed? The answer to this question is important for North American organizations that must understand motivational patterns in their international operations. It is also important to foreign managers, who are often exposed to North American theory and practice as part of their training and development.

It is safe to assume that most theories that revolve around human needs will come up against cultural limitations to their generality. For example, both Maslow and Alderfer suggest that people pass through a social stage (belongingness, relatedness) on their way to a higher-level personal growth or self-actualization stage. However, as we discussed in Chapter 4, it is well established that there are differences in the extent to which societies value a more collective or a more individualistic approach to life.[64] In individualistic societies (e.g., Canada, the United States, Great Britain, Australia), people tend to value individual initiative, privacy, and taking care of oneself. In more collective societies (e.g., Mexico, Singapore, Pakistan), more closely knit social bonds are observed, in which members of one's in-group (family, clan, organization) are expected to take care of each other in exchange for strong loyalty to the in-group.[65] This suggests that there might be no superiority to self-actualization as a motive in

Cultures differ in how they define achievement. In collective societies where group solidarity is dominant, achievement may be more group oriented than in individualistic societies.

more collective cultures. In some cases, for example, appealing to employee loyalty might prove more motivational than the opportunity for self-expression because it relates to strong belongingness needs that stem from cultural values. Also, cultures differ in the extent to which they value achievement as it is defined in North America, and conceptions of achievement might be more group oriented in collective cultures than in individualistic North America. Similarly, the whole concept of intrinsic motivation might be more relevant to wealthy societies than to the developing societies.

☞ YOU BE THE

Manager

Purolator's Early and Safe Return to Work Program

When Doug Kube describes Purolator's workers' compensation premiums as a "pretty big number," it sounds like an understatement. With 2130 claims filed in 2005, the company's bill for workers' compensation premiums came in around $13 million for the year. At Purolator, which employs 11 600 people across Canada, including 3000 couriers, 300 line haul truck drivers, and 500 call centre operators, 90 percent of the workers' compensation claims can be traced back to employees in two occupations: couriers and sorters.

Because their jobs require constant hauling, lifting, pushing, and pulling, soft tissue, orthopaedic and joint injuries make up the bulk of the claims. Psychological disability is also common, accounting for about one in five claims. Kube, director of human resources, says the numbers are on par with the industry average. But recognizing that the costs were too high, particularly on the workers' compensation side, Purolator put in place a program to improve claims management and disability accommodation.

Purolator developed a commitment to "early and safe return to work," fleshed out the models and processes to support that commitment, and hired a total of six occupational nurses and workers' compensation specialists to step into the roles of return-to-work coordinators. Their primary job is to coach managers and HR people on accommodating injured workers, and to liaise with physicians, unions, and workers' compensation boards.

One of the guiding principles in Purolator's return-to-work program is that it's not good enough just to put people back in an easy or light-duty job. "Our belief is we shouldn't be taking couriers and putting them into an office. We should find jobs that are similar in the depot, that take advantage of the skills and knowledge they have," says Kube. That means that a courier might be put back into the job he had before he became a courier, or a worker on the dock who was loading trailers before he was injured might return to a job scanning freight or something similar.

Employee absence because of work-related injuries was becoming a problem at Purolator.

However, making this happen and getting the numbers down also requires a change in people's behaviour. How can Purolator motivate managers to change their behaviour to help employees return to work and lower the number of days lost? You be the manager.

QUESTIONS

1. What should Purolator do to motivate managers to help employees return to work and lower the number of days lost to injuries?

2. How effective do you think a motivational program might be for lowering the days lost to injury?

To find out what Purolator did and the results, see The Manager's Notebook at the end of the chapter.

Source: Excerpt from Vu, U. (2006, March 13). How Purolator dealt with skyrocketing costs. *Canadian HR Reporter*, 9, 10.

Turning to equity theory, we noted earlier that people should be appropriately motivated when outcomes received "match" job inputs. Thus, higher producers are likely to expect superior outcomes compared with lower producers. This is only one way to allocate rewards, however, and it is one that is most likely to be endorsed in individualistic cultures. In collective cultures, there is a tendency to favour reward allocation based on equality rather than equity.[66] In other words, everyone should receive the same outcomes despite individual differences in productivity, and group solidarity is a dominant motive. Trying to motivate employees with a "fair" reward system might backfire if your definition of fairness is equity and theirs is equality.

Because of its flexibility, expectancy theory is very effective when applied cross-culturally. The theory allows for the possibility that there may be cross-cultural differences in the expectancy that effort will result in high performance. It also allows for the fact that work outcomes (such as social acceptance versus individual recognition) may have different valences across cultures.[67]

Finally, setting specific and challenging goals should also be motivational when applied cross-culturally and, in fact, goal setting has been found to predict, influence, and explain behaviour in numerous countries around the world.[68] However, for goal setting to be effective, careful attention will be required to adjust the goal setting process in different cultures. For example, individual goals are not likely to be accepted or motivational in collectivist cultures, where group rather than individual goals should be used. Power distance is also likely to be important in the goal setting process. In cultures where power distance is large, it would be expected that goals be assigned by superiors. However, in some small power distance cultures in which power differences are downplayed, participative goal setting would be more appropriate. One limitation to the positive effect of goal setting might occur in those (mainly Far Eastern) cultures in which saving face is important. That is, a specific and challenging goal may not be very motivating if it suggests that failure could occur and if it results in a negative reaction. This would seem to be especially bad if it were in the context of the less-than-preferred individual goal setting. Failure in the achievement of a very specific goal could lead to loss of face. As well, in the so-called "being-oriented" cultures where people work only as much as needed to live and avoid continuous work, there tends to be some resistance to goal setting.[69]

International management expert Nancy Adler has exemplified how cultural blinders often lead to motivational errors.[70] A primary theme running through this discussion is that appreciating cultural diversity is critical in maximizing motivation.

PUTTING IT ALL TOGETHER: INTEGRATING THEORIES OF WORK MOTIVATION

In this chapter, we have presented several theories of work motivation and attempted to distinguish between motivation and performance. In Chapter 4, we discussed the relationship between job performance and job satisfaction. At this point, it seems appropriate to review just how all these concepts fit together. Exhibit 5.8 presents a model that integrates these relationships.

Each of the theories helps us to understand the motivational process. First, in order for individuals to obtain rewards, they must achieve designated levels of performance. We know from earlier in this chapter that performance is a function of motivation as well as other factors such as personality, general cognitive ability, emotional intelligence, understanding of the task, and chance. In terms of motivation, we are concerned with the amount, persistence, and direction of effort. Therefore, Boxes 1 through 5 in Exhibit 5.8 explain these relationships.

Perceptions of expectancy and instrumentality (expectancy theory) relate to all three components of motivation (*Box 1*). In other words, individuals direct their effort toward a particular first-level outcome (expectancy) and increase the amount and

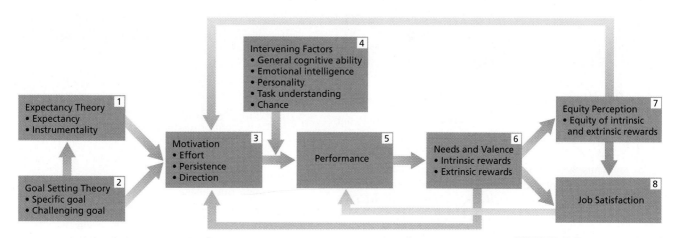

EXHIBIT 5.8
Integrative model of motivation theories.

persistence of effort to the extent that they believe it will result in second-level outcomes (instrumentality). Goal setting theory (*Box 2*) indicates that specific and challenging goals will have a positive effect on amount, persistence, and direction of effort. Goal specificity should also strengthen both expectancy and instrumentality connections. The individual will have a clear picture of a first-level outcome to which her effort should be directed and greater certainty about the consequences of achieving this outcome.

Boxes 3 through 5 illustrate that motivation (*Box 3*) will be translated into good performance (*Box 5*) if the worker has the levels of general cognitive ability and emotional intelligence relevant to the job, and if the worker understands the task (*Box 4*). Chance can also help to translate motivation into good performance. If these conditions are not met, high motivation will not result in good performance.

Second, a particular level of performance (*Box 5*) will be followed by certain outcomes. To the extent that performance is followed by outcomes that fulfill individual needs (need theory) and are positively valent second-level outcomes (expectancy theory), they can be considered rewards for good performance (*Box 6*). In general, the connection between performance and the occurrence of intrinsic rewards should be strong and reliable because such rewards are self-administered. For example, the nurse who assists several very sick patients back to health is almost certain to feel a sense of competence and achievement because such feelings stem directly from the job. On the other hand, the connection between performance and extrinsic rewards might be much less reliable because the occurrence of such rewards depends on the actions of management. Thus, the head nurse may or may not recommend attendance at a nursing conference (an extrinsic fringe benefit) for the good performance.

Third, to the extent that the rewards fulfill individual needs (need theory), then they will be motivational as depicted by the path from rewards (*Box 6*) to motivation (*Box 3*). In addition, the rewards that individuals receive are also the outcomes of the equity theory equation and will be used by individuals to form perceptions of equity (*Box 7*). Perceptions of equity also influence motivation (*Box 3*) and job satisfaction (*Box 8*). You will recall that this relationship between job outcomes, equity, and job satisfaction was discussed in Chapter 4. According to equity theory, individuals in a state of equity have high job satisfaction. Individuals who are in a state of inequity experience job dissatisfaction. Also recall from Chapter 4 that good performance leads to job satisfaction if that performance is rewarded, and job satisfaction in turn leads to good performance.

In summary, each theory of motivation helps us to understand a different part of the motivational process. Understanding how the different theories of motivation can be integrated brings us to the topic of the next chapter—practical methods of motivation that apply the theories we have been studying in this chapter.

Notebook

Purolator's Early and Safe Return to Work Program

1. Given that the focus of Purolator's program is to get employees back to work early and to lower the number of days lost to injury, it is possible to set clear targets. Thus, goal setting is particularly relevant in this situation and played a key part in the program. In rolling out the program, Purolator measured the lost time and severity of injuries at each of its 120 facilities across the country. Then they set targets (goals) for the company as a whole, for each division, each of the three depots, and each of the terminals. Another theory that is relevant is expectancy theory. Recall that according to expectancy theory, people will be motivated to perform those work activities that they find attractive and that they feel they can accomplish. The attractiveness of various work activities depends on the extent to which they lead to favourable personal consequences. So the question for Purolator was how they could get managers to be attracted to lowering the days lost to injuries? What they did was strengthen the *instrumentality* linkage—the probability that a first-level outcome (targets for lost days) will be followed by a particular second-level outcome. The second-level outcome was the manager's pay.

One of the most important things that Purolator did was to link performance to managers' compensation. About 10 percent of the managers' bonuses depends on meeting the targets for lost time and severity.

2. Managers were resistant to the program and saw accommodation as a potential drag on their productivity goals. But instead of softening productivity goals, Purolator held the line believing that employees who were sitting at home doing nothing could contribute to productivity goals. After showing managers a breakdown of the costs and demonstrating that for every dollar a claim costs the company in workers' compensation, another four dollars are spent on indirect costs, managers got the message. Now they work with HR on getting employees back to work and accommodated. The feedback from employees has been very positive. They feel that the company cares about them and they are more willing to come back and be engaged and work for the company. As for the number of days lost to injuries? In 2002 it was 9700, and in 2005 it was 6039. "That's 3000 days that people are working instead of sitting at home," says Doug Kube.

LEARNING OBJECTIVES CHECKLIST

1. *Motivation* is the extent to which persistent effort is directed toward a goal. *Performance* is the extent to which an organizational member contributes to achieving the objectives of the organization.

2. *Intrinsic motivation* stems from the direct relationship between the worker and the task and is usually self-applied. *Extrinsic motivation* stems from the environment surrounding the task and is applied by others.

3. Performance is influenced by motivation as well as personality, general cognitive ability, emotional intelligence, task understanding, and chance factors. *General cognitive ability* refers to a person's basic information pro-

cessing capacities and cognitive resources. *Emotional intelligence* refers to the ability to manage one's own and other's feelings and emotions. Motivation will be translated into good performance if an individual has the general cognitive ability and emotional intelligence relevant to the job, and if he or she understands the task.

4. *Engagement* involves the extent to which an individual immerses his or her true self into his or her work roles. When people are engaged, they employ and express themselves physically, cognitively, and emotionally during role performances. The main contributors to engagement are psychological meaningfulness, safety, and availability.

5. *Need theories* propose that motivation will occur when employee behaviour can be directed toward goals or incentives that satisfy personal wants or desires. The three need theories discussed are *Maslow's need hierarchy*, *Alderfer's ERG theory*, and *McClelland's theory of needs* for achievement, affiliation, and power. Maslow and Alderfer have concentrated on the hierarchical arrangement of needs and the distinction between intrinsic and extrinsic motivation. McClelland has focused on the conditions under which particular need patterns stimulate high motivation.

6. *Process theories* attempt to explain how motivation occurs rather than what specific factors are motivational. *Expectancy theory* argues that people will be motivated to engage in work activities that they find attractive and that they feel they can accomplish. The attractiveness of these activities depends on the extent to which they lead to favourable personal consequences.

7. *Equity theory* states that workers compare the inputs that they apply to their jobs and the outcomes that they get from their jobs with the inputs and outcomes of others. When these outcome/input ratios are unequal, inequity exists, and workers will be motivated to restore equity.

8. *Goal setting theory* states that goals are motivational when they are specific and challenging and when workers are committed to them. In some cases, companies can facilitate goal commitment through employee participation in goal setting and by financial incentives for goal attainment, but freedom from coercion and punishment seems to be the key factor in achieving goal commitment. Goals also can vary in terms of whether they are learning or performance goals. *Learning goals* are process-oriented goals that focus on learning. *Performance goals* are outcome-oriented goals that focus attention on the achievement of specific performance outcomes.

9. There are some cross-cultural limitations of the theories of motivation. For example, most theories that revolve around human needs will come up against cultural limitations to their generality as a result of differences in values across cultures. As for equity theory, trying to motivate employees with a "fair" reward system might backfire if the definition of fairness is other than equity (e.g., equality). Because of its flexibility, expectancy theory is very effective when applied cross-culturally and allows for the possibility that there may be cross-cultural differences in the expectancy that effort will result in high performance. It also allows for the fact that work outcomes (such as social acceptance versus individual recognition) may have different valences across cultures. Setting specific and challenging goals should also be motivational when applied cross-culturally. However, for goal setting to be effective, careful attention will be required to adjust the goal setting process in different cultures.

10. Performance is a function of motivation as well as other factors such as personality, general cognitive ability, emotional intelligence, understanding of the task, and chance. Perceptions of expectancy and instrumentality influence motivation as do specific and challenging goals. Motivation will be translated into good performance if the worker has the levels of general cognitive ability and emotional intelligence relevant to the job, and if the worker understands the task. Chance can also help to translate motivation into good performance. To the extent that performance leads to rewards that fulfill individual needs and are positively valent, they will be motivational. When the rewards are perceived as equitable, they will have a positive effect on motivation and job satisfaction. Furthermore, good performance leads to job satisfaction if that performance is rewarded, and job satisfaction in turn leads to good performance.

DISCUSSION QUESTIONS

1. Many millionaires continue to work long, hard hours, sometimes even beyond the usual age of retirement. Use the ideas developed in the chapter to speculate about the reasons for this motivational pattern. Is the acquisition of wealth still a motivator for these individuals?

2. Discuss a time when you were highly motivated to perform well (at work, at school, in a sports contest) but performed poorly in spite of your high motivation. How do you know that your motivation was really high? What factors interfered with good performance? What did you learn from this experience?

3. Use Maslow's hierarchy of needs and Alderfer's ERG theory to explain why assembly line workers and executive vice-presidents might be susceptible to different forms of motivation.

4. Colleen is high in need for achievement, Eugene is high in need for power, and Max is high in need for affiliation. They are thinking about starting a business partnership. To maximize the motivation of each, what business should they go into, and who should assume which roles or jobs?

5. Reconsider the case of Tony Angelas, which was used to illustrate expectancy theory. Imagine that you are Tony's boss and you think that he can be motivated to perform at a high level. Suppose you cannot modify second-level outcomes or their valences, but you can affect expectancies and instrumentalities. What would you do to motivate Tony? Prove that you have succeeded by recalculating the force equations to demonstrate that Tony will now perform at a high level.

6. Debate the following statements: Of all the motivational theories we discussed in this chapter, goal setting is the simplest to implement. Goal setting is no more than doing what a good manager should be doing anyway.

7. What are the implications of goal orientation for motivating a group of employees? When would it be best to set a learning goal versus a performance goal? Describe a situation in which it would be best to set a learning goal and a situation in which it would be best to set a performance goal.

8. Critique the following assertion: People are basically the same. Thus, the motivation theories discussed in the chapter apply equally around the globe.

9. Discuss how goal setting might motivate unethical behaviour. Think of some actual work situations where this might happen and what managers can do to prevent it.

10. What is the relationship between cognitive ability and emotional intelligence with job performance? When would emotional intelligence be most important for a person's job performance? When is cognitive ability especially important for job performance?

11. What is employee engagement and how is it different from motivation? Describe a work situation in which you were highly engaged and a situation in which you were disengaged. What factors contributed to your levels of engagement and disengagement? What should managers do to engage employees?

INTEGRATIVE DISCUSSION QUESTIONS

1. Refer to the cross-cultural dimensions of values described in Chapter 4 (i.e., work centrality, power distance, uncertainty avoidance, masculinity/femininity, individualism/collectivism, and long-term/short-term orientation) and discuss the implications of each value for exporting the work motivation theories discussed in this chapter across cultures. Based on your analysis, how useful are the theories described in this chapter for understanding and managing motivation across cultures? What are the implications?

2. Consider the basic characteristics of motivation in relation to operant learning theory and social cognitive theory. What are the implications of operant learning theory and social cognitive theory for motivation, and how do they compare to the theories of work motivation described in this chapter?

ON-THE-JOB CHALLENGE QUESTION

Many companies in Canada today are facing a serious problem—finding and keeping employees. Canada has one of the most serious labour shortages in the industrial world. The problem is especially serious for small businesses that cannot compete with the wages and benefits offered by large companies. As a result, small businesses are beginning to compete for staff with creative perks. Some are offering flexible schedules, health programs, and paid volunteer time. Some fast food chains reward good workers with mountain bikes and iPod music players. A new Calgary restaurant is giving away a Mexican vacation and a $500 signing bonus to all full-time staff who provide three months of service; part-timers also get the cash after the three months, but not the vacation. Susan Nelson, owner of Inn on the Lake, a 40-room hotel in Fall River, Nova Scotia,

has a program in which staff can earn points to be redeemed for cash. For example, an employee earns 30 points for a favourable mention from a guest or 60 points for coming up with a proven cost-cutting tip for the business. Employees receive one dollar for every 10 points, and each year Nelson budgets $5000 to give away as part of the incentive program.

Comment on the "creative perks" being used by companies to motivate their employees. How effective do you think these perks are? What do the need and process theories of motivation say about the motivational effects of these programs? What else can small businesses do to motivate their employees?

Source: Based on Bouw, B. (2006, March 17). No help at the inn. *Globe and Mail*, B1, B12.

EXPERIENTIAL EXERCISE

Emotional Intelligence

The following scale is a self-report measure of emotional intelligence. Answer each of the statements as accurately and honestly as possible using the following response scale:

1–Strongly disagree   4–Agree

2–Disagree   5–Strongly agree

3–Neither agree or disagree

____ 1. I know when to speak about personal problems to others.

____ 2. When I am faced with obstacles, I remember times I faced similar obstacles and overcame them.

____ 3. I expect that I will do well on most things I try.

____ 4. Other people find it easy to confide in me.

____ 5. I find it hard to understand the nonverbal messages of other people.

____ 6. Some of the major events of my life have led to me to re-evaluate what is important and not important.

____ 7. When my mood changes, I see new possibilities.

____ 8. Emotions are one of the things that make my life worth living.

____ 9. I am aware of my emotions as I experience them.

____ 10. I expect good things to happen.

____ 11. I like to share my emotions with others.

____ 12. When I experience a positive emotion, I know how to make it last.

____ 13. I arrange events others enjoy.

____ 14. I seek out activities that make me happy.

____ 15. I am aware of the nonverbal messages I send to others.

____ 16. I present myself in a way that makes a good impression on others.

____ 17. When I am in a positive mood, solving problems is easy for me.

____ 18. By looking at their facial expressions, I recognize the emotions people are experiencing.

____ 19. I know why my emotions change.

____ 20. When I am in a positive mood, I am able to come up with new ideas.

____ 21. I have control over my emotions.

____ 22. I easily recognize my emotions as I experience them.

____ 23. I motivate myself by imagining a good outcome on tasks I take on.

____ 24. I compliment others when they have done something well.

____ 25. I am aware of the nonverbal messages other people send.

____ 26. When another person tells me about an important event in his or her life, I almost feel as though I have experienced this event myself.

____ 27. When I feel a change in emotions, I tend to come up with new ideas.

____ 28. When I am faced with a challenge, I give up because I believe I will fail.

____ 29. I know what other people are feeling just by looking at them.

____ 30. I help other people feel better when they are down.

____ 31. I use good moods to help myself keep trying in the face of obstacles.

____ 32. I can tell how people are feeling by listening to the tone of their voice.

____ 33. It is difficult for me to understand why people feel the way they do.

Scoring and Interpretation

To obtain your score, first subtract your response to questions 5, 28, and 33 from 6. For example, if you gave a response of 1 to question 5, give yourself a 5 (6 minus 1). Then add up your scores to all 33 items. Your total should be somewhere between 33 and 165. The higher your score, the higher your emotional intelligence. Because this is a self-report measure of EI, it is susceptible to bias. As a result, your score might differ somewhat on a more objective measure of EI.

In a study that compared the EI scores of psychotherapists, prisoners, and substance-abuse clients, the EI was highest for the psychotherapists (134.92), followed by the substance-abuse clients (122.23), and then the prisoners (120.08). As well, the women in the sample had higher EI scores (130.94) than the men (124.78). In addition, the EI of college students who completed this scale was significantly related to grade point averages at the end of their first year. In other words, higher EI was associated with a higher grade point average. Higher scores on this EI scale have also been found to be related to openness to experience, but not to any of the other dimensions of the Five-Factor Model of personality.

To facilitate class discussion and your understanding of emotional intelligence, form a small group with several other members of the class and consider the following questions:

1. Each group member should present their EI score. Next, consider your grade point averages. Do the students with a higher EI score have a higher GPA? (Alternatively, each member of the class might write their EI score and GPA on a piece of paper and hand it in to the instructor. The instructor can then write the responses on the board for class discussion).

2. When is EI most likely to be related to grades and job performance? Explain why somebody with a low EI score might have a high grade point average or high job performance?

3. Compare and contrast the type of jobs that those scoring high and low on EI have had and prefer. Do group members with a higher EI score prefer jobs that are different from those with lower EI scores? What kind of jobs are people with high EI scores likely to be good at and prefer?

4. How can knowledge of your EI help you in your interactions with others and in your job? What can you do to improve your EI?

Source: Reprinted from *Personality and Individual Differences*, vol 25, no 2 by Schutte, N.S., Malouff, J.M., Hall, L.E., Haggerty, D.J., Cooper, J.T., Golden, C.J., & Dornheim, L. (1998). Development and validation of a measure of emotional intelligence, 167–177, © 1998, with permission from Elsevier.

CASE INCIDENT

Mayfield Department Stores

As competition in the retail market began to heat up, it became necessary to find ways to motivate the sales staff of Mayfield Department Stores to increase sales. Therefore, a motivational program was developed with the help of a consulting firm. Each month, employees in the department with the highest sales would have a chance to win a trip to Florida. At the end of the year, the names of all employees in those departments that had the highest sales for at least one month would have their name entered into a draw, and then three names would be chosen to win a one-week trip to Florida paid for by Mayfield.

1. According to need theories of motivation and goal setting theory, will this program be motivational?

2. Discuss the motivational potential of this program according to expectancy theory and equity theory. Will the program motivate the sales staff and improve sales?

3. How would you change the program to make it more effective for motivating employees?

CASE STUDY

The Boiler Room

These days, everyone complains about the way tele-marketers interfere with their lives. People complain about how they always seem to phone when it is least convenient, and that they are pushy and aggressive on the phone. The telemarketing that most people complain about is those phone calls that begin with a few seconds of silence when you answer the phone, followed by the polite voice of a person who tries to get you to take on a new credit card, or buy insurance for your mortgage, or purchase some product or service from a national organization.

These calls originate from large call centres located in parts of the country with an ample supply of cheap labour and with a government willing to install the telecommunications infrastructure necessary to support the industry. Increasingly, these call centres are being located offshore, where labour is even cheaper. The calls are dialled centrally by a computer, and when the phone is answered the call is switched to a telemarketer who goes into the pitch. There have been efforts to curtail this telephone sales activity by legislating rights to privacy. The reality is that telemarketing has been around as long as the telephone.

I'm from the old school and there are plenty like me around. I don't sell products or services over the phone. My customers are salespeople who buy lists of prospects from me and then sell those people products or services that they don't have.

Here's how it works. I call up someone and tell them I'm conducting market research on consumer goods and services. I assure them I'm not selling anything and that this survey will only take a few minutes of their time. Let's say I'm working with someone who is selling vacuum cleaners. I ask the person a variety of questions, but all I really want to know is whether they have a built-in vacuum cleaner and whether they have a credit card. The name, address, and phone number of someone who does not have a built-in vacuum cleaner and does have a credit card is worth money to a vacuum cleaner salesperson. These people will follow up with a strong pitch to get an appointment to demonstrate their expensive product in the home. Usually they offer an incentive, because if they can get in the door a sale is very likely. The sales commission can run to hundreds of dollars for a single evening of work.

This is all done on a local basis. I work with sales-people from my area who buy my lists of prospects. Sometimes we work out of the same location, such as a back room in the warehouse district. We don't need a storefront location. The reason they will pay me for the list of prospects is that it takes time to find people who meet the qualifications of a sales prospect. The vacuum cleaner salespeople are better off spending their time in customers' homes trying to close deals on vacuum cleaners, rather than spending time on the phone trying to find prospects. They only want to talk to customers who are "qualified" to buy a vacuum cleaner.

Obviously, I can do things to improve the likelihood of a sale by finding out other information, such as whether they have recently bought a vacuum cleaner, whether they have a high enough limit on their credit card for a costly purchase, whether they have carpet throughout their home, and so on. These enhancements to the information on a list of prospects make it a hotter property, and in my business my reputation is made by the quality of the prospects I find.

I run my operation in direct conjunction with a team of salespeople who are pushing a particular product, such as vacuum cleaners, and I am part of the team. Nonetheless, I am still independent, and have found ways to get the most income out of my prospect lists. When I am gathering information about prospective customers, I usually ask them about all of their household appliances and, as a result, have valuable information for other sales operations; I can sell my list to several other clients.

However, there is no way I can do all of the phoning myself and still earn what I consider a decent income. It can take a dozen or more calls to find one person who will talk to me. So I hire people to do the phoning for me at minimum wage. I hire them to come in for a few hours each evening, usually from 5:00 p.m. to 9:00 p.m., to make calls. I write a script for them to follow that I feel will give the best results. My telemarketers just sit at a table with a phone, photocopied pages from a phone book, the script, and an information sheet to be filled out on each prospect. This workplace is called a boiler room.

For my employees, it is not very desirable work. What they do is phone people who don't want to hear from them, try to convince people to answer questions about their household and their finances, and try to prevent these people from hanging up before they get enough information to know if they are "qualified" to buy the product. Generally, the location of boiler rooms is not convenient for after-hours work, and the work environment is not particularly comfortable.

Usually, my operation is "off the books," and I pay in cash. This allows me to recruit people who would not otherwise be willing to take the work. I get a lot of single mothers on welfare, students with student loans, people on disability pensions, people in bankruptcy, and moonlighting workers of all sorts. My requirement for workers can fluctuate wildly, and my workforce is very transient. We can be very busy for a month, and then shut down for a few weeks while the salespeople catch up on the prospects we have provided.

Typically, there is a brief training period where we work with new employees to help them catch on to the process. We give them tips about the patter to use, how to answer common questions, and how to modify the tone of their voice to assure the people that it's okay to answer the question. Later, they will learn tricks of the trade about how to deviate from the script to improve responses. For example, we offer only a vague identification of who we are. We never give a name that is in the phone book, and we regularly change the business name. If the customer thinks we are from a well-known polling organization or Statistics Canada, well so be it. Our relationship with them will end in a couple of minutes, and no real harm has been done. We play things pretty close to the edge: but if we don't do it, others would.

So here I am with a dozen or so irregular employees. People often don't show up for work. They call in at the last minute to say they can't make it because their kid is sick or their childcare arrangement fell through, or they do show up, but they're drunk. And sometimes they show up and just sit there like a lump, expecting to be paid for doing as little as possible.

My main motivational strategy is to fire anyone who doesn't meet the quota. I monitor the phone calls to see how they're doing and to validate their report sheets. They learn it doesn't pay to fake their results. Usually, I pay them cash at the end of each week, and if they want to be paid, they had better do their job. This works, to a certain extent. I get rid of the slackers who do very little, but it doesn't seem to do much to motivate my best employees. If I spend a shift on the phones, I can easily get twice as many "qualified" prospects as my best employee. I know they can do better, but I can't seem to get them to do more than the minimum required to keep their job. I need some better motivational strategies in the boiler room.

This case is based on original work by Laura Tannis, from *Organizational Behaviour: Canadian Cases and Exercises*, 5th ed., by Randy Hoffman and Fred Ruemper (Concord, ON: Captus Press Inc., 2004), pp.163–165. Reprinted with permission of Captus Press Inc. www.captus.com. Questions prepared by Alan Saks.

1. What factors do you think contribute to the performance of the employees in the boiler room? Refer to Exhibit 5.1 to explain your answer.

2. Consider the needs of the employees in the boiler room. What is most likely to motivate them? How important are intrinsic and extrinsic motivators?

3. Discuss the motivational strategies being used in the boiler room. Why have these strategies failed to motivate the employees? How do the theories of motivation help us to understand why the employees are not motivated to perform better?

4. Consider the engagement of the employees in the boiler room. How engaged or disengaged are they? What can be done to improve their engagement?

5. Using the theories of motivation, what advice would you give the owner on how to motivate the employees in the boiler room? Be sure to refer to the need theories and the process theories of motivation.

6. What would you do to motivate employees to come to work, get more prospects, and not quit?

CHAPTER 6

Motivation in Practice

BC BIOMEDICAL LABORATORIES LTD.

BC Biomedical is British Columbia's largest community laboratory and an integral part of the British Columbia health care system. It is the primary diagnostic lab that doctors in greater Vancouver send their patients to for a wide array of medical tests. The company is owned and operated by 42 pathologists and employs more than 650 employees who serve more than 1.6 million patients each year. The workforce is diverse and includes a high percentage of women, employees over the age of 50 and close to retirement, as well as employees under 40 who have young families.

If you work for BC Biomedical your job might involve conducting laboratory testing services such as blood work, drug screening, pre-employment screening, occupational health testing, scientific research, or clinical trials at one of the company's 45 patient centres throughout the Lower Mainland.

But how motivated would you be if you worked for BC Biomedical? Chances are you would be very motivated. In addition to providing top pay and benefits, the company also has a profit sharing plan based on company results. In the past, employees have received an increase of about 5 percent. The company also has a health program that provides employees with a $250 disbursement each year in addition to their regular benefits. Employees can spend the funds on any health-related service.

Employees at BC Biomedical are also empowered and accountable for what they do. This is partly due to the company's flat organizational structure. There are no more than two people in the hierarchy between the CEO and any employee in the organization, and many employees receive no day-to-day supervision. Access to and communication with the CEO is relatively easy, and employees can and do frequently drop by to talk to the CEO about their work and personal concerns. They can also pick up the phone and call the CEO anytime. In addition to improving the flow of communication, this also results in a consensus-building style of leadership and provides employees with a great deal of autonomy.

Another important factor is the company's flexible work schedules, which include part-time and full-time positions, flexible work hours, four-day work weeks, and job sharing. Two employees who share a job each receive full benefits and they work out their own schedules and holidays.

What is the impact of these programs on BC Biomedical and its employees? For starters, BC Biomedical was ranked number one on

LEARNING OBJECTIVES

After reading Chapter 6, you should be able to:

1. Discuss how to tie pay to performance on production jobs and the difficulties of *wage incentive plans*.

2. Explain how to tie pay to performance on white-collar jobs and the difficulties of *merit pay plans*.

3. Understand how to use pay to motivate teamwork.

4. Describe the details of the *Job Characteristics Model*.

5. Discuss the motivational properties of *job enrichment*.

6. Understand the connection between goal setting and *Management by Objectives*.

7. Explain how *alternative work schedules* respect employee diversity.

8. Describe the factors that organizations should consider when choosing motivational practices.

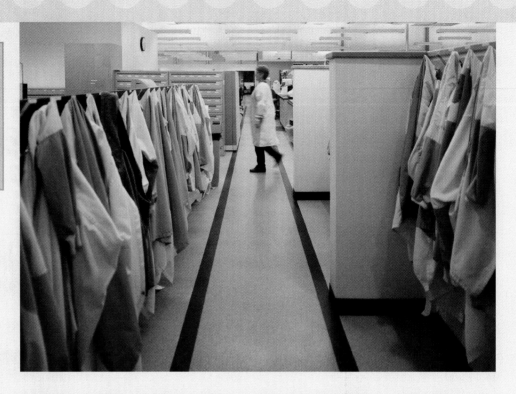

BC Biomedical has been ranked as the best employer in Canada and has received top marks for employee motivation thanks to its profit sharing plan and alternative working schedules.

BC Biomedical
Laboratories Ltd.
www.bcbio.com

Report on Business Magazine's 50 Best Employers in Canada in 2003, 2004, and 2005 receiving top marks in almost all areas, including motivation among employees. The company also boasts a high level of employee loyalty and commitment, quality service for the company's customers/patients, and high technical quality in tests and analyses. It also means an extremely low employee turnover rate that barely surpasses 2 percent![1]

Notice the motivational strategies that BC Biomedical employs: top pay and benefits, a profit sharing plan, flexible work schedules, a health program, and freedom and autonomy in how employees perform their job. In this chapter, we will discuss four motivational techniques: money, job enrichment, Management by Objectives, and alternative working schedules. In each case, we will consider the practical problems that are involved in implementing these techniques. The chapter will conclude with a discussion of the factors that an organization needs to consider when choosing a motivational strategy.

MONEY AS A MOTIVATOR

The money that employees receive in exchange for organizational membership is in reality a package made up of pay and various fringe benefits that have dollar values, such as insurance plans, sick leave, and vacation time. Here, we will be concerned with the motivational characteristics of pay itself.

So just how effective is pay as a motivator? How important is pay for you? Chances are you don't think pay is as important as it really is. In fact, employees and managers seriously underestimate the importance of pay as a motivator.[2] Yet the motivation theories described in Chapter 5 suggest that pay is indeed a very important motivator.

According to Maslow and Alderfer, pay should prove especially motivational to people who have strong lower-level needs. For these people, pay can be exchanged for food, shelter, and other necessities of life. However, suppose you receive a healthy pay raise. Doubtless, this raise will enable you to purchase food and shelter, but it might also give you prestige among friends and family, signal your competence as a worker, and demonstrate that your boss cares about you. Thus, using need hierarchy terminology, pay can also function to satisfy social, self-esteem, and self-actualization needs. If pay has this capacity to fulfill a variety of needs, then it should have especially good potential as a motivator. How can this potential be realized? Expectancy theory provides the clearest answer to this question. According to expectancy theory, if pay can satisfy a variety of needs, it should be highly valent, and it should be a good motivator to the extent that *it is clearly tied to performance.*

Research on pay and financial incentives is consistent with the predictions of need theory and expectancy theory. Financial incentives and pay-for-performance plans have been found to increase performance and lower turnover. Research not only supports

"Because of my ridiculously low pay per course,
I will only be able to give partial answers, vague suggestions,
and half-truths. Okay--let's get started . . . ."

the motivational effects of pay, but it also suggests that pay may well be the most important and effective motivator of performance. In general, the ability to earn money for outstanding performance is a competitive advantage for attracting, motivating, and retaining employees.[3] Let's now find out how to link pay to performance on production jobs.

Linking Pay to Performance on Production Jobs

Piece-rate. A pay system in which individual workers are paid a certain sum of money for each unit of production completed.

The prototype of all schemes to link pay to performance on production jobs is piece-rate. In its pure form, **piece-rate** is set up so that individual workers are paid a certain sum of money for each unit of production they complete. For example, sewing machine operators might be paid two dollars for each dress stitched, or punch press operators might be paid a few cents for each piece of metal fabricated. More common than pure piece-rate is a system whereby workers are paid a basic hourly wage and paid a piece-rate differential on top of this hourly wage. For example, a forge operator might be paid 8 dollars an hour plus 30 cents for each unit he produces. In some cases, of course, it is very difficult to measure the productivity of an individual worker because of the nature of the production process. Under these circumstances, group incentives are sometimes employed. For example, workers in a steel mill might be paid an hourly wage and a monthly bonus for each ton of steel produced over some minimum quota. These various schemes to link pay to performance on production jobs are called **wage incentive plans.**

Wage incentive plans. Various systems that link pay to performance on production jobs.

Compared with straight hourly pay, the introduction of wage incentives usually leads to substantial increases in productivity.[4] One review reports a median productivity improvement of 30 percent following the installation of piece-rate pay, an increase not matched by goal setting or job enrichment.[5] Also, a study of 400 manufacturing companies found that those with wage incentive plans achieved 43 to 64 percent greater productivity than those without such plans.[6]

Lincoln Electric Company
www.lincolnelectric.com

One of the best examples of the successful use of a wage incentive plan is the Lincoln Electric Company. Lincoln Electric is the world's largest producer of arc welding equipment, and it also makes electric motors. The company offers what some say are the best-paid factory jobs in the world. The company uses an intricate piece-rate pay plan that rewards workers for what they produce. The firm has turned a handsome profit every quarter for over 50 years and has not laid anyone off for over

Wage incentive programs that link pay to performance on production jobs have been shown to improve employee productivity.

40 years. Employee turnover is extremely low, and Lincoln workers are estimated to be roughly twice as productive as other manufacturing workers.[7] Other companies that use wage incentive plans include Steelcase, the Michigan manufacturer of office furniture, and Nucor, a steel producer. However, not as many organizations use wage incentives as we might expect. What accounts for this relatively low utilization of a motivational system that has proven results?[8]

Potential Problems with Wage Incentives

Despite their theoretical and practical attractiveness, wage incentives have some potential problems when they are not managed with care.

Lowered Quality. It is sometimes argued that wage incentives can increase productivity at the expense of quality. While this may be true in some cases, it does not require particular ingenuity to devise a system to monitor and maintain quality in manufacturing. However, the quality issue can be a problem when employers use incentives to motivate faster "people processing," such as conducting consumer interviews on the street or in stores. Here, quality control is more difficult.

Differential Opportunity. A threat to the establishment of wage incentives exists when workers have different opportunities to produce at a high level. If the supply of raw materials or the quality of production equipment varies from workplace to workplace, some workers will be at an unfair disadvantage under an incentive system. In expectancy theory terminology, workers will differ in the expectancy that they can produce at a high level.

Reduced Cooperation. Wage incentives that reward individual productivity might decrease cooperation among workers. For example, to maintain a high wage rate, machinists might hoard raw materials or refuse to engage in peripheral tasks, such as keeping the shop clean or unloading supplies. Consider what happened when Solar Press, an Illinois printing and packaging company, installed a team wage incentive.

> It wasn't long before both managers and employees began to spot problems. Because of the pressure to produce, teams did not perform regular maintenance on the equipment, so machines broke down more often than before. When people found better or faster ways to do things, some hoarded them from fellow employees for fear of reducing the amount of their own payments. Others grumbled that work assignments were not fairly distributed, that some jobs demanded more work than others. They did, but the system did not take this into account.[9]

Incompatible Job Design. In some cases, the way jobs are designed can make it very difficult to implement wage incentives. On an assembly line, it is almost impossible to identify and reward individual contributions to productivity. As pointed out above, wage incentive systems can be designed to reward team productivity in such a circumstance. However, as the size of the team *increases,* the relationship between any individual's productivity and his or her pay *decreases.* For example, the impact of your productivity in a team of two is much greater than the impact of your productivity in a team of ten. As team size increases, the linkage between your performance and your pay is erased, removing the intended incentive effect.

Restriction of Productivity. A chief psychological impediment to the use of wage incentives is the tendency for workers to restrict productivity. This restriction is illustrated graphically in Exhibit 6.1. Under normal circumstances, without wage incentives, we can often expect productivity to be distributed in a "bell-shaped" manner—a few workers are especially low producers, a few are especially high producers, and most produce in the middle range. When wage incentives are introduced, however, workers sometimes come to an informal agreement about what constitutes a fair day's work and artificially limit their output accordingly. In many cases, this **restriction of productivity** can decrease the expected benefits of the incentive system, as in Exhibit 6.1.

Restriction of productivity. The artificial limitation of work output that can occur under wage incentive plans.

Why does restriction often occur under wage incentive systems? Sometimes it happens because workers feel that increased productivity due to the incentive will lead to reductions in the workforce. More frequently, however, employees fear that if they produce at an especially high level, an employer will reduce the rate of payment to cut labour costs. In the early days of industrialization, when unions were nonexistent or weak, this often happened. Engineers studied workers under normal circumstances, and management would set a payment rate for each unit of productivity. When management introduced the incentive system, workers employed legitimate shortcuts that they had learned on the job to produce at a higher rate than expected. In response to this, management simply changed the rate to require more output for a given amount of pay! Stories of such rate-cutting are often passed down from one generation of workers to another in support of restricting output under incentive systems. As you might expect, restriction seems less likely when a climate of trust and a history of good relations exist between employees and management.

Linking Pay to Performance on White-Collar Jobs

Compared to production jobs, white-collar jobs (including clerical, professional, and managerial) frequently offer fewer objective performance criteria to which pay can be tied. To be sure, company presidents are often paid annual bonuses that are tied to the profitability of the firm, and salespeople are frequently paid commissions on sales. However, trustworthy objective indicators of individual performance for the majority of white-collar jobs are often difficult to find. Thus, performance in many such jobs is evaluated by the subjective judgment of the performer's manager.

Merit pay plans. Systems that attempt to link pay to performance on white-collar jobs.

Attempts to link pay to performance on white-collar jobs are often called **merit pay plans.** Just as straight piece-rate is the prototype for most wage incentive plans, there is also a prototype for most merit pay plans: Periodically (usually yearly), managers are required to evaluate the performance of employees on some form of rating scale or by means of a written description of performance. Using these evaluations, the managers then recommend that some amount of merit pay be awarded to individuals over and above their basic salaries. This pay is usually incorporated into the subsequent year's salary cheques. Since the indicators of good performance on some white-collar jobs (especially managerial jobs) can be unclear or highly subjective, merit pay can provide an especially tangible signal that the organization considers an employee's performance "on track." Individuals who see a strong link between rewards and performance tend to perform better.[10] In addition, white-collar workers (especially managers) particularly support the notion that performance should be an important determinant of pay.[11]

EXHIBIT 6.1
Hypothetical productivity distributions, with and without wage incentives, when incentives promote restriction.

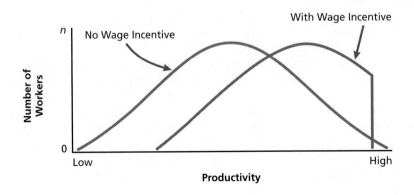

Merit pay plans are employed with a much greater frequency than wage incentive plans and and have become one of the most common forms of motivation in Canadian organizations.[12] In an increasingly tight labour market, merit pay is being used by organizations to attract and retain employees and as an alternative to wage increases.[13]

However, despite the fact that merit pay can stimulate effective performance, that substantial support exists for the idea of merit pay, and that most organizations claim to provide merit pay, it appears that many of these systems now in use are *ineffective*. In fact, a recent survey found that 83 percent of organizations with a pay-for-performance system said it was only somewhat successful or not working at all.[14] Many individuals who work under such plans do not perceive a link between their job performance and their pay. There is also evidence that pay is, in fact, *not* related to performance under some merit plans.[15] Adding more evidence of ineffectiveness are studies that track pay increases over time. For example, one study of managers showed that pay increases in a given year were often uncorrelated with pay increases in adjacent years.[16] From what we know about the consistency of human performance, such a result seems unlikely if organizations are truly tying pay to performance. In most organizations, seniority, the number of employees, and job level account for more variation in pay than performance does. Perhaps it is not surprising then that there has been an increasing number of disputes over unpaid or underpaid bonuses that are winding up in the courts.[17]

Potential Problems with Merit Pay Plans

As with wage incentive plans, merit pay plans have several potential problems if employers do not manage them carefully. Before continuing, read the You Be the Manager feature, *"Employees Oppose Merit Pay Plan at Hudson's Bay Company."*

Hudson's Bay Company
www.hbc.com

Low Discrimination. One reason that many merit pay plans fail to achieve their intended effect is that managers might be unable or unwilling to discriminate between good performers and poor performers. In Chapter 3, we pointed out that subjective evaluations of performance can be difficult to make and are often distorted by a number of perceptual errors. In the absence of performance rating systems designed to control these problems, managers might feel that the only fair response is to rate most employees as equal performers. Good rating systems are rarely employed. Surveys show consistent dissatisfaction with both giving and receiving performance evaluations.[18] Even when managers feel capable of clearly discriminating between good and poor performers, they might be reluctant to do so. If the performance evaluation system does not assist the manager in giving feedback about his or her decisions to employees, the equalization strategy might be employed to prevent conflicts with them or among them. If there are true performance differences among employees, equalization overrewards poorer performers and underrewards better performers.[19]

Small Increases. A second threat to the effectiveness of merit pay plans exists when merit increases are simply too small to be effective motivators. In this case, even if rewards are carefully tied to performance and managers do a good job of discriminating between more and less effective performers, the intended motivational effects of pay increases might not be realized. Ironically, some firms all but abandon merit when inflation soars or when they encounter economic difficulties. Just when high motivation is needed, the motivational impact of merit pay is removed. Sometimes a reasonable amount of merit pay is provided, but its motivational impact is reduced because it is spread out over a year or because the organization fails to communicate how much of a raise is for merit and how much is for cost of living. To overcome this visibility problem, some firms have replaced conventional merit pay with a **lump sum bonus** that is paid out all at one time and not built into base pay. Such bonuses have become a common method to motivate and retain employees at all levels of an organization.

Lump sum bonus. Merit pay that is awarded in a single payment and not built into base pay.

☞ YOU BE THE
Manager

Employees Oppose Merit Pay Plan at Hudson's Bay Company

In August of 2002, Hudson's Bay Company (HBC) reported a 65-percent drop in quarterly profits. At the same time, the company planned to introduce "an enhanced pay-for-performance program" to improve service and make more sales.

The merit pay system was designed to reward employees who worked hard while raising productivity at the stores. According to HBC's senior vice-president of human resources, "It was designed to increase sales by giving better service to our customers." He also said that it was not designed to cut labour costs or cut wages. "It will not result in any wage reductions for associates."

However, employees did not agree. More than 800 sales and clerical workers went on strike at five Ontario stores of The Bay department store chain. National CAW union representative Bill Gibson said that "The Bay is trying to turn back the labour relations clock some 25 years," citing attempts to replace traditional progressive wage scales with a merit pay system based on favouritism and profit margins.

A spokesperson for the CAW said this was one of the first times union members have struck at a Canadian department store. The retail workers union struck at Eaton's in the early 1980s, which resulted in a long and bitter strike that lasted for months.

The strike at HBC came at a difficult time for the company. It reported a sharp drop in profits in the quarter ending July 31, a performance it blamed on poor weather in the crucial spring fashion season and poor margins when the unsold spring fashions were sold off at a discount in July. Analysts also pointed to tough competition from Wal-Mart Canada, which has taken a hefty slice of business away from HBC's Zellers division.

What do you think HBC should do about the new merit pay plan? You be the manager.

> **Employees at five Ontario stores went on strike after HBC announced plans to introduce a merit pay system.**

QUESTIONS

1. Why do you think HBC employees opposed the merit pay plan?

2. What do you think HBC should do? Is the merit pay plan a good approach for motivating employees and improving service and sales?

To find out why employees revolted and what HBC did, see The Manager's Notebook at the end of the chapter.

Source: Bertin, O. (2002, August 30). Workers strike five Bay stores. *Globe and Mail*, B5. Reprinted with the permission of the *Globe and Mail*.

Ford Motor Company
www.ford.com

They get people's attention! Ford Motor Company recently reinstated employee bonuses for salaried employees in Canada and the United States after withholding them since 2002 as a cost-cutting measure.[20]

When merit pay makes up a substantial portion of the compensation package, management has to take extreme care to ensure that it ties the merit pay to performance criteria that truly benefit the organization. Otherwise, employees could be motivated to earn their yearly bonus at the expense of long-term organizational goals.

Pay Secrecy. A final threat to the effectiveness of merit pay plans is the extreme secrecy that surrounds salaries in most organizations. It has long been a principle of human resource management that salaries are confidential information, and management frequently implores employees who receive merit increases not to discuss these increases with their co-workers. Notice the implication of such secrecy for merit pay plans: Even if merit pay is administered fairly, is contingent on performance, and is generous, employees might remain ignorant of these facts because they have no way of comparing their own merit treatment with that of others. As a consequence, such secrecy might severely damage the motivational impact of a well-designed merit plan. Rather incredibly, many organizations fail to inform employees about the average raise received by those doing similar work.

Given this extreme secrecy, you might expect that employees would profess profound ignorance about the salaries of other organizational members. In fact, this is not true—in the absence of better information, employees are inclined to "invent" salaries for other members. Unfortunately, this invention seems to reduce both satisfaction and motivation. Specifically, several studies have shown that managers have a tendency to overestimate the pay of their employees and their peers and to underestimate the pay of their superiors (see Exhibit 6.2).[21] In general, these tendencies will reduce satisfaction with pay, damage perceptions of the linkage between performance and rewards, and reduce the valence of promotion to a higher level of management.

An interesting experiment examined the effects of pay disclosure on the performance and satisfaction of pharmaceutical salespeople who operated under a merit pay system.

At the time of a regularly scheduled district sales meeting, each of the 14 managers in the experimental group presented to his/her employees the new open salary administration program. The sales staff were given the individual low, overall average, and individual high merit raise amounts for the previous year. The raises ranged from no raise to $75 a month, with a company average of $43. Raises were classified according to district, region, and company increases in pay. Likewise, salary levels (low, average, and high) were given for sales staff on the basis of their years with the company (1 to 5; 5 to 10; 10 to 20; and more than 20 years). Specific individual names and base salaries were not disclosed to the sales staff. However, this information could be obtained from the supervisor. Each person's performance evaluation was also made available by the district manager for review by his/her other sales staff.[22]

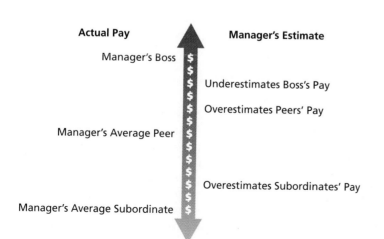

EXHIBIT 6.2
A manager's estimates of pay earned by boss, peers, and subordinates.

After the pay disclosure was implemented, the sales staff in the experimental group revealed significant increases in performance and satisfaction with pay. However, since performance consisted of supervisory ratings, it is possible that supervisors felt pressured to give better ratings under the open pay system, in which their actions were open to scrutiny. This, of course, raises an important point. If performance evaluation systems are inadequate and poorly implemented, a more open pay policy will simply expose the inadequacy of the merit system and lead managers to evaluate performance in a manner that reduces conflict. Unfortunately, this might be why most organizations maintain relative secrecy concerning pay. One exception was the now defunct NeXT Computers, founded by Steve Jobs, which had a completely open salary system. Although many public and civil service jobs have open pay systems, most make little pretence of paying for performance.

Using Pay to Motivate Teamwork

Some of the dysfunctional aspects of wage incentives and merit pay stem from their highly individual orientations. People sometimes end up pursuing their own agendas (and pay) at the expense of the goals of their work group, department, or organization. As a result, some firms have either replaced or supplemented individual incentive pay with plans designed to foster more cooperation and teamwork.[23] Notice that each of the plans we discuss below has a somewhat different motivational focus. Organizations have to choose pay plans that support their strategic needs.

Profit sharing. The return of some company profit to employees in the form of a cash bonus or a retirement supplement.

Air Canada Jazz
www.flyjazz.ca

Profit Sharing. **Profit sharing** is one of the most commonly used group-oriented incentive systems. In years in which the firm makes a profit, some of this is returned to employees in the form of a bonus, sometimes in cash and sometimes in a deferred retirement fund. This is, of course, one of the motivational strategies at BC Biomedical. Such money is surely welcome, and it might reinforce some identification with the organization. Air Canada Jazz recently announced that it will be offering a profit-sharing program in which employees will be able to receive as much as $2000 depending on the airline's performance.[24]

However, it is unlikely that profit sharing, as normally practised, is highly motivational. Its greatest problem is that too many factors beyond the control of the workforce (such as the general economy) can affect profits no matter how well people perform their jobs. Also, in a large firm, it is difficult to see the impact of one's own actions on profits. For example, for two years after Chrysler Corporation's first profit-sharing payment, the company made no payments. And with a workforce of 63 000, one's impact on profits would be completely obscured.

Profit sharing seems to work best in smaller firms that regularly turn a handsome profit, like BC Biomedical. WestJet is another good example. The company is small and has been profitable for 25 consecutive quarters. For another example of a small company with a profit sharing plan, see "Applied Focus: *Respect and Profit Sharing at Coastal Pacific Xpress.*"

Coastal Pacific Xpress
www.cpx.com

Employee stock ownership plans (ESOPs). Incentive plans that allow employees to own a set amount of a company's shares and provide employees with a stake in the company's future earnings and success.

Employee Stock Ownership Plans (ESOPs). In recent years, **employee stock ownership plans (ESOPs)** have also become a popular group-oriented incentive. These plans allow employees to own a set amount of the company's shares. Employees are often allowed to purchase shares at a fixed price and some organizations, like WestJet, match employee contributions. ESOPs provide employees with a stake in a company's future earnings and success. They also serve a number of other purposes, including attracting and retaining talent; motivating employee performance; focusing employee attention on organizational performance; creating a culture of ownership; educating employees about the business; and conserving cash by substituting options for cash.[25]

In Canada, many of the best companies to work for offer stock options to a majority of their employees. For example, at the Royal Bank of Canada, 85 percent of

APPLIED FOCUS

Respect and Profit Sharing at Coastal Pacific Xpress

Coastal Pacific Xpress (CPX) is one of BC's biggest trucking companies. The Surrey-based company began with one truck and trailer and now has 160 trucks and 250 trailers, making it one of the fastest-growing temperature-controlled truckload carriers in British Columbia. The company operates throughout North America and serves major markets in Canada and the United States. It focuses on temperature-controlled and just-in-time overnight deliveries. Over the past five years the company has grown by 500 percent.

This might not seem like such a big deal if it wasn't for the fact that there is an alarming shortage of long-haul truck drivers in Canada and the United States. According to Statistics Canada, 18 percent of Canadian truck drivers are 55 or older (compared with 13 percent of the general workforce), making it one of the oldest workforces in the country. According to the Canadian Trucking Human Resources Council, the industry currently employs more than 500 000 people and needs to attract 30 000 to 45 000 new drivers annually. However, in recent years it has hired only between 5700 and 18 100.

Part of the problem is the relatively low pay, long hours, and extended periods on the road that keep young job seekers away from an occupation that is perceived as unattractive. But this doesn't seem to be a problem at CPX, whose guiding principle is employees come first, customers come second, and profits third.

What does it mean to put employees first? The owners say they set out to build a company that treats truck drivers with respect. According to co-owner Jim Mickey, "Our intention has always been to create a shared success, shared reward-type environment, one where the president isn't necessarily more valuable than a truck driver."

In August of 2005 they put their money where their mouths are. They handed out bonus cheques totalling more than $400 000 to more than 400 employees. The owners intend to give out bonuses every year that the company makes a profit. "My goal is to do $1 million next year. I would love to have a BBQ and pass out double what we did this year," says Mickey.

The company's approach seems to be working. In an industry with an average turnover of 120 percent, CPX is doing far better with only 20 percent turnover in 2006, down from 22 percent in 2005—one of the lowest in the industry. Further, its employees' drive to cut waste and keep costs down generates profit margins at CPX that exceed the industry average.

And what about the intention to hand out bonuses every year the company makes a profit? In August of 2006, the company paid out more than $400 000 in profits to 475 employees and drivers in recognition of their role in helping the company generate revenue of $100 million for the fiscal year that ended May 31, 2006—a 41 percent ($71 million) increase over 2005!

Sources: Klie, S. (2005, September 26). 'Employees first' at CPX. *Canadian HR Reporter*, 1, 3; Galt, V. (2006, February 24). Better shifts, better training, better pay. *Globe and Mail*, C1; Hood, S.B. (2006, April 10–23). Truck stop: A shortage of long-haul drivers threatens to impede commerce. *Canadian Business*, 79(8), 24; Anonymous. (2006, August 10). Breaking the rules: Hundreds of CPX o-o's see big raises from profit sharing program. *Today's Trucking Online*, www.todaystrucking.com/news.cfm?intDocID=16557&CFID=

employees are enrolled in a share ownership plan that matches 50 cents for every dollar an employee invests up to 6 percent of their salary. At PCL Constructors in Edmonton, only employees are permitted to own company stocks.[26] Husky Injection Molding Systems Ltd. has a share-purchasing plan in which approximately 25 percent of the company's shares are held by employees. Employees at Husky can earn company shares by doing things that help the environment and community. At Hudson's Bay Company, employees receive $1 worth of company shares for every $6 they invest, an immediate return of 17 percent.[27]

Employee stock options are believed to increase employees' loyalty and motivation because they align employees' goals and interests with those of the organization and create a sense of legal and psychological ownership. There is some evidence that ESOPs can improve employee retention and profitability.[28] However, like profit sharing, these programs work best in small organizations that regularly turn a profit. In larger organizations it is more difficult for employees to see the connection between their efforts and company profits because many factors can influence the value of a company's stock besides employee effort and performance. In addition, ESOPs lose their motivational potential in a weak economy when a company's share price goes down.

Gainsharing. **Gainsharing** plans are group incentive plans that are based on improved productivity or performance over which the workforce has some control.[29] Such plans often include reductions in the cost of labour, material, or supplies. When measured costs decrease, the company pays a monthly bonus according to a predetermined formula that shares this "gain" between employees and the firm. For example, a plan installed by Canadian pulp and paper producer Fraser Papers rewards employees for low scrap and low steam usage during production. The plan sidesteps the cost of steam generation and the international price for paper, things over which the workforce lacks control.[30]

Gainsharing plans have usually been installed using committees that include extensive workforce participation. This builds trust and commitment to the formulas that are used to convert gains into bonuses. Also, most plans include all members of the work unit, including production people, managers, and support staff.

The most common gainsharing plan is the Scanlon Plan, developed by union leader Joe Scanlon in the 1930s.[31] The plan stresses participatory management and joint problem solving between employees and managers, but it also stresses using the pay system to reward employees for this cooperative behaviour. Thus, pay is used to align company and employee goals. The Scanlon Plan has been used successfully by many small, family-owned manufacturing firms. Also, in recent years, many large corporations (such as General Electric, Motorola, Carrier, and Dana) have installed Scanlon-like plans in some manufacturing plants.[32] The turnaround of the motorcycle producer Harley-Davidson is, in part, attributed to the institution of gainsharing.

In a recent study in a unionized auto parts manufacturing plant, a Scanlon gainsharing program was negotiated as part of a joint union–management effort to respond to economic downturns and competitive challenges in the auto industry. Management and the union were extensively involved in the development and implementation of the plan, which consisted of a formal employee suggestion program and a formula for determining the amount of total cost savings that was to be divided equally among plant employees. The plan had a positive effect on the number of suggestions provided by employees and the cumulative number of suggestions implemented was associated with lower production costs.[33] In general, productivity improvements following the introduction of Scanlon-type plans support the motivational impact of this group wage incentive.[34] However, perception that the plan is fair is critical.[35]

Skill-Based Pay. The idea behind **skill-based pay** (also called pay for knowledge) is to motivate employees to learn a wide variety of work tasks, irrespective of the job that they might be doing at any given time. The more skills that are acquired, the higher the person's pay.[36] Companies use skill-based pay to encourage employee flexibility in task assignments and to give them a broader picture of the work process. It is especially useful on self-managed teams (Chapter 7), in which employees divide up the work as they see fit. It is also useful in flexible manufacturing (Chapter 15), in which rapid changes in job demands can occur. Quebec's Bell Helicopter Textron plant uses skill-based pay for its aircraft assemblers to enhance their flexibility.

Training costs can be high with a skill-based pay system. Also, when the system is in place, it has to be used. Sometimes, managers want to keep employees on a task they are good at rather than letting them acquire new skills. However, skill-based programs can have positive consequences. A recent study on the effects of a skill-based pay system in a large organization that manufactures vehicle safety systems reported an increase in productivity, lower labour costs per part, and a reduction in scrap following implementation of a skill-based pay program.[37]

Gainsharing. A group pay incentive plan based on productivity or performance improvements over which the workforce has some control.

Fraser Papers
www.fraserpapers.com

Harley-Davidson
www.harley-davidson.com

Skill-based pay. A system in which people are paid according to the number of job skills they have acquired.

Bell Helicopter Textron
www.bellhelicopter.textron.com

At Quebec's Bell Helicopter Textron plant, skill-based pay encourages flexibility in the aircraft assemblers' work assignments and provides them with an overall picture of the work process.

Exhibit 6.3 compares the various pay plans that organizations use to motivate teamwork. An interesting issue that arises when examining these pay plans is whether or not they are more effective than non-financial incentives. To learn about a study that compared the effects of financial and non-financial incentives, see "Research Focus: *Effects of Financial and Non-Financial Incentives on Business-Unit Outcomes.*"

EXHIBIT 6.3
Characteristics of team-oriented incentive plans.

Source: Perry, N.J. (1988, December 19). Here come richer, riskier pay plans. *Fortune*, 50–58, p. 52.

PLAN TYPE	HOW IT WORKS	WHAT IT REQUIRES TO BE EFFECTIVE	ADVANTAGES	DISADVANTAGES
Profit sharing and employee stock ownership	Employees receive a varying annual bonus based on corporate profits and/or can purchase a certain amount of the company's shares. Payments can be made in cash or deferred into a retirement fund.	• Participating employees collectively must be able to influence profits. • Owners must value employees' contributions enough to be willing to share profits and ownership.	• The incentive formula is simple and easy to communicate. • The plan is guaranteed to be affordable: It pays only when the firm is sufficiently profitable. • It unites the financial interests of owners and employees.	• Annual payments may lead employers to ignore long-term performance. • Factors beyond the employee's control can influence profits. • The plan forces private companies to open their books.
Gainsharing	When a unit beats predetermined performance targets, all members get bonuses. Objectives often include better productivity, quality, and customer service.	• Objectives must be measurable. • Management must encourage employee involvement. • Employees must have a high degree of trust in management.	• The plan enhances coordination and teamwork. • Employees learn more about the business and focus on objectives. • Employees work harder and smarter.	• Plans that focus only on productivity may lead employees to ignore other important objectives, such as quality. • The company may have to pay bonuses even when unprofitable.
Skill-based pay	An employee's salary or wage rises with the number of tasks he or she can do, regardless of the job performed.	• Skills must be identified and assigned a pay grade. • The company must have well-developed employee assessment and training procedures.	• By increasing flexibility, the plan lets the company operate with a leaner staff. • The plan gives workers a broader perspective, making them more adept at problem solving.	• Most employees will learn all applicable skills, raising labour costs. • Training costs are high.

RESEARCH FOCUS

Effects of Financial and Non-Financial Incentives on Business-Unit Outcomes

Most of the research that has been conducted on financial incentives has focused on the motivation and performance of individuals. This research has shown that both financial and non-financial incentives have a positive effect on individual performance. Much less attention has been given to the effects of incentives on business-unit outcomes, even though outcomes such as profitability, customer service, and employee retention are crucial to an organization's competitive advantage.

To test the effects of financial and non-financial incentives on business-unit outcomes, Suzanne Peterson and Fred Luthans conducted a study in 21 fast-food franchises owned by one company. Each store had an average of two managers and 25 employees. The 21 stores were randomly assigned to one of three conditions: 1. Financial incentive, 2. Non-financial incentive, and 3. Control—No incentives.

In the financial incentive condition, managers were trained to identify critical employee behaviours and to clearly communicate them to employees along with the specifics of the pay distribution plan. Employees were told that a lump-sum monetary bonus would be received by everyone in the store when members of the store collectively engaged in specific critical performance behaviours. Thus, the money would only be distributed on the basis of pay for contingent group performance behaviour. Managers then observed employees on a set number of randomly spaced times and marked down the critical performance behaviours they observed on tally sheets they were given for this purpose. At the end of each month, the bonuses were given based on the number of critical behaviours exhibited by the employees in the entire store.

In the non-financial condition, managers were trained to deliver performance feedback and social recognition to the store employees as a group. They developed charts of the frequency of the group's critical performance behaviours that were placed in a prominent place where all members of the unit could readily see the results. Managers were also trained to administer positive recognition to individuals, groups, and the entire store for performing the critical behaviours. The managers also gave a memo to each employee on a weekly basis that summarized in a positive way how the unit was progressing on the critical behaviours.

The three groups were then compared on three key business-unit outcomes: profit performance of each unit, drive-through time (minutes it takes for customers to approach the restaurant, order their food, pay, and leave the restaurant), and employee turnover. Comparisons were made after three, six, and nine months.

After three, six, and nine months, the financial incentive and non-financial incentive conditions outperformed the control condition on all three outcomes with higher profits, lower drive-through times, and lower employee turnover. Further, the financial incentive condition outperformed the non-financial incentive condition on all three outcomes after three months. However, after six and nine months, the financial incentive condition outperformed the non-financial condition only on employee turnover.

The results of this study indicate that group-based financial and non-financial incentives increased business-unit profit performance, improved customer service, and lowered employee turnover. Further, the financial and non-financial incentives were equally effective for profit performance and customer service over time; financial incentives, however, had a greater effect in reducing employee turnover. The results show that group-based financial incentives can have a positive effect on the collective efforts of employees and business-unit outcomes. Perhaps not surprisingly, top management of the firm indicated that they would be using both financial and non-financial incentives in all their restaurants.

Source: Peterson, S., & Luthans, F. (2006). The impact of financial and nonfinancial incentives on business-unit outcomes over time. *Journal of Applied Psychology, 91*, 156–165.

JOB DESIGN AS A MOTIVATOR

If the use of money as a motivator is primarily an attempt to capitalize on extrinsic motivation, current approaches to using job design as a motivator represent an attempt to capitalize on intrinsic motivation. In essence, the goal of job design is to identify the characteristics that make some tasks more motivating than others and to capture these characteristics in the design of jobs.

Traditional Views of Job Design

From the beginning of the Industrial Revolution until the 1960s, the prevailing philosophy regarding the design of most nonmanagerial jobs was job simplification. The historical roots of job simplification are found in social, economic, and technological forces that existed even before the Industrial Revolution. This preindustrial period was characterized by increasing urbanization and the growth of a free market economy, which prompted a demand for manufactured goods. Thus, a division of labour within society occurred, and specialized industrial concerns using newly developed machinery emerged to meet this demand. With complex machinery and an uneducated, untrained workforce, these organizations recognized that *specialization* was the key to efficient productivity. If the production of an object could be broken down into very basic, simple steps, even an uneducated and minimally trained worker could contribute his or her share by mastering one of these steps.

The zenith of job simplification occurred in the early 1900s when industrial engineer Frederick Winslow Taylor presented the industrial community with his principles of Scientific Management.[38] From Chapter 1, you will recall that Taylor advocated extreme division of labour and specialization, even extending to the specialization of supervisors in roles such as trainer, disciplinarian, and so on. Also, he advocated careful standardization and regulation of work activities and rest pauses. Intuitively, jobs designed according to the principles of scientific management do not seem intrinsically motivating. The motivational strategies that management used during this period consisted of close supervision and the use of piece-rate pay. It would be a historical disservice to conclude that job simplification was unwelcomed by workers, who were mostly nonunionized, uneducated, and fighting to fulfill their basic needs. Such simplification helped them to achieve a reasonable standard of living. However, with a better-educated workforce whose basic needs are fairly well met, behavioural scientists have begun to question the impact of job simplification on performance, customer satisfaction, and the quality of working life.

Job Scope and Motivation

Job scope can be defined as the breadth and depth of a job.[39] Breadth refers to the number of different activities performed on the job, while depth refers to the degree of discretion or control the worker has over how these tasks are performed. "Broad" jobs require workers to *do* a number of different tasks, while "deep" jobs emphasize freedom in *planning* how to do the work.

As shown in Exhibit 6.4, jobs that have great breadth and depth are called high-scope jobs. A professor's job is a good example of a high-scope job. It is broad because it involves the performance of a number of different tasks, such as teaching, grading, doing research, writing, and participating in committees. It is also deep because there is considerable discretion in how academics perform these tasks. In general, professors have a fair amount of freedom to choose a particular teaching style, grading format, and research area. Similarly, management jobs are high-scope jobs. Managers perform a wide variety of activities (supervision, training, performance evaluation, report writing) and have some discretion over how they accomplish these activities.

The classic example of a low-scope job is the traditional assembly line job. This job is both "shallow" and "narrow" in the sense that a single task (such as bolting on car wheels) is performed repetitively and ritually, with no discretion as to method. Traditional views of job design were attempts to construct low-scope jobs in which workers specialized in a single task.

Occasionally, we encounter jobs that have high breadth but little depth, or vice versa. For motivational purposes, we can also consider these jobs to be relatively low

EXHIBIT 6.4
Job scope as a function of job depth and job breadth.

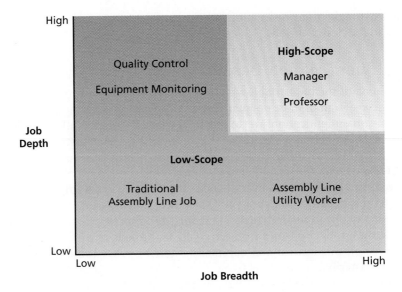

The motivational theories we discussed in the previous chapter suggest that high-scope jobs (*both* broad and deep) should provide more intrinsic motivation than low-scope jobs. Maslow's need hierarchy and ERG theory both seem to indicate that people can fulfill higher-order needs by the opportunity to perform high-scope jobs. Expectancy theory suggests that high-scope jobs can provide intrinsic motivation if the outcomes derived from such jobs are attractive.

in scope. For example, a utility worker on an assembly line fills in for absent workers on various parts of the line. While this job involves the performance of a number of tasks, it involves little discretion as to when or how the worker performs the tasks. On the other hand, some jobs involve a fair amount of discretion over a single, narrowly defined task. For example, quality control inspectors perform a single, repetitive task, but they might be required to exercise a fair degree of judgment in performing this task. Similarly, workers who monitor the performance of equipment (such as in a nuclear power plant) might perform a single task but again be required to exercise considerable discretion when a problem arises.

In his classic film *Modern Times*, Charlie Chaplin performed a typical low-scope job working on an assembly line.

One way to increase the scope of a job is to assign employees *stretch assignments*, something that many organizations have begun to do. Stretch assignments offer employees challenging opportunities to broaden their skills by working on a variety of tasks with new responsibilities. Oakville, Ontario-based Javelin Technologies Inc., which develops design and engineering software for the manufacturing industry, uses stretch assignments as a way to keep employees interested and challenged in their positions.[40] In the next section, we discuss a model of how to design high-scope jobs.

Javelin Technologies Inc.
www.javelin-tech.com

The Job Characteristics Model

The concept of job scope provides an easy-to-understand introduction to why some jobs seem more intrinsically motivating than others. However, we can find a more rigorous delineation of the motivational properties of jobs in the Job Characteristics Model that J. Richard Hackman and Greg Oldham developed (Exhibit 6.5).[41] As you can observe, the Job Characteristics Model proposes that there are several "core" job characteristics that have a certain psychological impact on workers. In turn, the psychological states induced by the nature of the job lead to certain outcomes that are relevant to the worker and the organization. Finally, several other factors (moderators) influence the extent to which these relationships hold true.

Core Job Characteristics. The Job Characteristics Model shows that there are five core job characteristics that have particularly strong potential to affect worker motivation: skill variety, task identity, task significance, autonomy, and job feedback. These characteristics are described in detail in Exhibit 6.6. In general, higher levels of these characteristics should lead to the favourable outcomes shown in Exhibit 6.5. Notice that **skill variety**, the opportunity to do a variety of job activities using various skills and talents, corresponds fairly closely to the notion of job breadth we discussed earlier. **Autonomy**, the freedom to schedule one's own work activities and decide work procedures, corresponds to job depth. However, Hackman and Oldham recognized that one could have a high degree of control over a variety of skills that were perceived as meaningless or fragmented. Thus, the concepts of task significance and task identity were introduced. **Task significance** is the impact that a job has on others. **Task identity** is the extent to which a job involves doing a complete piece of work, from beginning to end. In addition, they recognized that **feedback**, information about one's performance effectiveness, is also essential for high intrinsic motivation. People are not motivated for long if they do not know how well they are doing.

Hackman and Oldham developed a questionnaire called the Job Diagnostic Survey (JDS) to measure the core characteristics of jobs. The JDS requires job holders to report the amount of the various core characteristics contained in their jobs. From these reports, we can construct profiles to compare the motivational properties of various jobs. For example, Exhibit 6.7 shows JDS profiles for lower-level managers in a utility company (collected by one of the authors of this text) and those for keypunchers in another firm (reported by Hackman and Oldham). While the managers perform a full range of managerial duties, the keypunchers perform a highly regulated job—anonymous work from various departments is assigned to them by a supervisor, and their output is verified for accuracy by others. Not surprisingly, the JDS profiles reveal that the managerial jobs are consistently higher on the core characteristics than are the keypunching jobs.

According to Hackman and Oldham, an overall measure of the motivating potential of a job can be calculated by the following formula:

Skill variety. The opportunity to do a variety of job activities using various skills and talents.

Autonomy. The freedom to schedule one's own work activities and decide work procedures.

Task significance. The impact that a job has on other people.

Task identity. The extent to which a job involves doing a complete piece of work, from beginning to end.

Feedback. Information about the effectiveness of one's work performance.

$$\text{Motivating potential score} = \frac{\text{Skill variety} + \text{Task identity} + \text{Task significance}}{3} \times \text{Autonomy} \times \text{Job feedback}$$

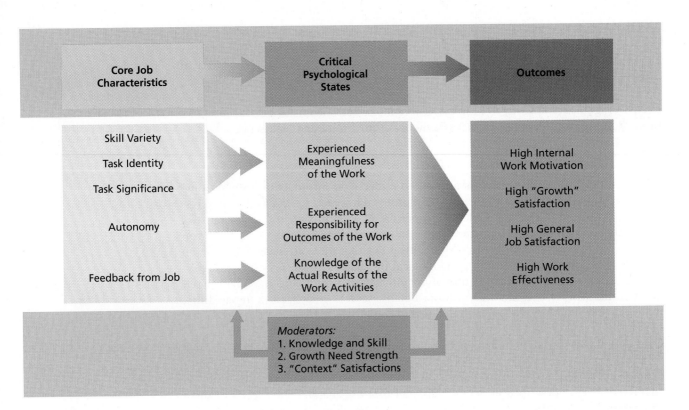

EXHIBIT 6.5

The Job Characteristics Model.

Source: Hackman, J.R., & Oldham, G.R. (1980). *Work redesign.* Reading, MA: Addison-Wesley. Copyright © 1980 by Addison-Wesley Publishing Company. Figure 4.6. Reprinted with permission of the publisher.

Since the JDS measures the job characteristics on seven-point scales, a motivating potential score could theoretically range from 1 to 343. For example, the motivating potential score for the keypunchers' jobs shown in Exhibit 6.7 is 20, while that for the managers' jobs is 159. Thus, the managers are more likely than the keypunchers to be motivated by the job itself. The average motivating potential score for 6930 employees on 876 jobs has been calculated at 128.[42]

Critical Psychological States. Why are jobs that are higher on the core characteristics more intrinsically motivating? What is their psychological impact? Hackman and Oldham argue that work will be intrinsically motivating when it is perceived as *meaningful*, when the worker feels *responsible* for the outcomes of the work, and when the worker has *knowledge* about his or her work progress. As shown in Exhibit 6.5, the Job Characteristics Model proposes that the core job characteristics affect meaningfulness, responsibility, and knowledge of results in a systematic manner. When an individual uses a variety of skills to do a "whole" job that is perceived as significant to others, he or she perceives the work as meaningful. When a person has autonomy to organize and perform the job as he or she sees fit, the person feels personally responsible for the outcome of the work. Finally, when the job provides feedback about performance, the worker will have knowledge of the results of this opportunity to exercise responsibility.

Outcomes. The presence of the critical psychological states leads to a number of outcomes that are relevant to both the individual and the organization. Chief among these is high intrinsic motivation. When the worker is truly in control of a challenging job that provides good feedback about performance, the key prerequisites for intrinsic motivation are present. The relationship between the work and the worker is emphasized, and the worker is able to draw motivation from the job itself. This will result in high-quality productivity. By the same token, workers will report satisfaction with higher-order needs (growth needs) and general satisfaction with the job itself. This should lead to reduced absenteeism and turnover.

1. **Skill variety:** The degree to which a job requires a variety of different activities in carrying out the work, involving the use of a number of different skills and talents of the person.
   High variety: The owner-operator of a garage who does electrical repair, rebuilds engines, does body work, and interacts with customers.
   Low variety: A body shop worker who sprays paint eight hours a day.

2. **Task identity:** The degree to which a job requires completion of a "whole" and identifiable piece of work, that is, doing a job from beginning to end with a visible outcome.
   High identity: A cabinet maker who designs a piece of furniture, selects the wood, builds the object, and finishes it to perfection.
   Low identity: A worker in a furniture factory who operates a lathe solely to make table legs.

3. **Task significance:** The degree to which a job has substantial impact on the lives of other people, whether those people are in the immediate organization or in the world at large.
   High significance: Nursing the sick in a hospital intensive care unit.
   Low significance: Sweeping hospital floors.

4. **Autonomy:** The degree to which the job provides substantial freedom, independence, and discretion to the individual in scheduling the work and determining the procedures to be used in carrying it out.
   High autonomy: A telephone installer who schedules his or her own work for the day, makes visits without supervision, and decides on the most effective techniques for a particular installation.
   Low autonomy: A telephone operator who must handle calls as they come according to a routine, highly specified procedure.

5. **Job feedback:** The degree to which carrying out the work activities required by the job provides the individual with direct and clear information about the effectiveness of his or her performance.
   High feedback: An electronics factory worker who assembles a radio and then tests it to determine if it operates properly.
   Low feedback: An electronics factory worker who assembles a radio and then routes it to a quality control inspector who tests it for proper operation and makes needed adjustments.

EXHIBIT 6.6
Core job characteristics and examples.

Source: Definitions from Hackman, J.R., & Oldham, G.R. (1980). The properties of motivating jobs. *Work redesign.* Reading, MA: Addison-Wesley. Copyright © 1980 by Addison-Wesley Publishing Company, Reading, Massachusetts. Reprinted with permission of the publisher. Examples by authors.

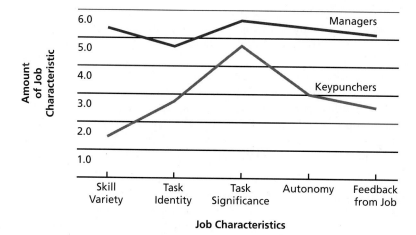

EXHIBIT 6.7
Levels of core job characteristics for managers and keypunchers.

Source: Hackman, J.R., & Oldham, G.R. (1980). *Work redesign.* Reading, MA: Addison-Wesley. Copyright © 1980 by Addison-Wesley Publishing Company. Figure 6.2. Reprinted with permission of the publisher. (Managers' data collected by Gary Johns.)

Moderators. Hackman and Oldham recognize that jobs that are high in motivating potential do not *always* lead to favourable outcomes. Thus, as shown in Exhibit 6.5, they propose certain moderator or contingency variables (Chapter 1) that intervene between job characteristics and outcomes. One of these is the job-relevant knowledge and skill of the worker. Put simply, workers with weak knowledge and skills should not respond favourably to jobs that are high in motivating potential, since such jobs will prove too demanding. Another proposed moderator is **growth need strength**, which refers to the extent to which people desire to achieve higher-order need satisfaction by performing their jobs. Hackman and Oldham argue that those with high growth needs should be most responsive to challenging work. Finally, they argue that workers who are dissatisfied with the context factors surrounding the job (such as pay, supervision, and company policy) will be less responsive to challenging work than those who are reasonably satisfied with context factors.

Research Evidence. In tests of the Job Characteristics Model, researchers usually require workers to describe their jobs by means of the JDS and then measure their reactions to these jobs. Although there is some discrepancy regarding the relative importance of the various core characteristics, these tests have generally been very supportive of the basic prediction of the model—workers tend to respond more favourably to jobs that are higher in motivating potential.[43] The results of one study indicated that job characteristics predicted absenteeism up to six years after the job characteristics were assessed. Among the five job characteristics, skill variety, task identity, and autonomy were negatively and consistently related to absenteeism.[44] Where the model seems to falter is in its predictions about growth needs and context satisfaction. Evidence that these factors influence reactions to job design is weak or contradictory.[45]

Job Enrichment

Job enrichment is the design of jobs to enhance intrinsic motivation, the quality of working life, and job involvement. **Job involvement** refers to a cognitive state of psychological identification with one's job and the importance of work to one's total self-image. Employees who have challenging and enriched jobs tend to have higher levels of job involvement. In fact, all of the core job characteristics have been found to be positively related to job involvement. Employees who are more involved in their job have higher job satisfaction and organizational commitment and are less likely to consider leaving their organization.[46]

BC Biomedical is a good example of the benefits of job enrichment. As indicated in the chapter opening vignette, BC Biomedical employees have a high degree of latitude in how they perform their jobs, without interference from supervisors, and they make decisions about what they do and how they do it. This helps to explain the high degree of job involvement and positive job attitudes among BC Biomedical employees, as well as the company's low turnover rate.

In general, job enrichment involves increasing the motivating potential of jobs via the arrangement of their core characteristics. There are no hard and fast rules for the enrichment of jobs. Specific enrichment procedures depend on a careful diagnosis of the work to be accomplished, the available technology, and the organizational context in which enrichment is to take place. However, *many job enrichment schemes combine tasks, establish client relationships, reduce supervision, form teams, or make feedback more direct.*[47]

- *Combining tasks.* This involves assigning tasks that might be performed by different workers to a single individual. For example, in a furniture factory a lathe operator, an assembler, a sander, and a stainer might become four "chair makers"; each worker would then do all four tasks. Such a strategy should increase the variety of skills employed and might contribute to task identity as each worker approaches doing a unified job from start to finish.

Growth need strength. The extent to which people desire to achieve higher-order need satisfaction by performing their jobs.

Job enrichment. The design of jobs to enhance intrinsic motivation, quality of working life, and job involvement.

Job involvement. A cognitive state of psychological identification with one's job and the importance of work to one's total self-image.

- *Establishing external client relationships.* This involves putting employees in touch with people outside the organization who depend on their products or services. An example of this might be to give line workers letters from customers who have problems with service or a product.[48] Such a strategy might involve the use of new (interpersonal) skills, increase the identity and significance of the job, and increase feedback about one's performance.

- *Establishing internal client relationships.* This involves putting employees in touch with people who depend on their products or services within the organization. For example, billers and expediters in a manufacturing firm might be assigned permanently to certain salespeople, rather than working on any salesperson's order as it comes in. The advantages are similar to those mentioned for establishing external client relationships.

- *Reducing supervision or reliance on others.* The goal here is to increase autonomy and control over one's own work. For example, management might permit clerical employees to check their own work for errors instead of having someone else do it. Similarly, firms might allow workers to order needed supplies or contract for outside services up to some dollar amount without obtaining permission. As indicated earlier, the lack of interference from supervisors at BC Biomedical is an example of this job enrichment technique.

- *Forming work teams.* Management can use this format as an alternative to a sequence of "small" jobs that individual workers perform when a product or service is too large or complex for one person to complete alone. For example, social workers who have particular skills might operate as a true team to assist a particular client, rather than passing the client from person to person. Similarly, stable teams can form to construct an entire product, such as a car or boat, in lieu of an assembly line approach. Such approaches should lead to the formal and informal development of a variety of skills and increase the identity of the job.

- *Making feedback more direct.* This technique is usually used in conjunction with other job design aspects that permit workers to be identified with their "own" product or service. For example, an electronics firm might have assemblers "sign" their output on a tag that includes an address and toll-free phone number. If a customer encounters problems, he or she contacts the assembler directly. In Sweden, workers who build trucks by team assembly are responsible for service and warranty work on "their" trucks that are sold locally.

Potential Problems with Job Enrichment

Despite the theoretical attractiveness of job enrichment as a motivational strategy, and despite the fact that many organizations have experimented with such programs, enrichment can encounter a number of challenging problems.

Poor Diagnosis. Problems with job enrichment can occur when it is instituted without a careful diagnosis of the needs of the organization and the particular jobs in question. Some enrichment attempts might be half-hearted tactical exercises that really do not increase the motivating potential of the job adequately. An especially likely error here is increasing job breadth by giving employees more tasks to perform at the same level while leaving the other crucial core characteristics unchanged—a practice known as **job enlargement**. Thus, workers are simply given *more* boring, fragmented, routine tasks to do, such as bolting intake manifolds and water pumps onto engines. On the other side of the coin, in their zeal to use enrichment as a cure-all, organizations might attempt to enrich jobs that are already perceived as too rich by their incumbents (some refer to this as *job engorgement!*).[49] This has happened in some "downsized" firms in which the remaining employees have been assigned too many extra responsibilities. Rather than increasing motivation, this can lead to role overload and work stress.

Job enlargement. Increasing job breadth by giving employees more tasks at the same level to perform but leaving other core characteristics unchanged.

Lack of Desire or Skill. Put simply, some workers do not *desire* enriched jobs. Almost by definition, enrichment places greater demands on workers, and some might not relish this extra responsibility. Even when people have no basic objections to enrichment in theory, they might lack the skills and competence necessary to perform enriched jobs effectively. Thus, for some poorly educated or trained workforces, enrichment might entail substantial training costs. In addition, it might be difficult to train some workers in certain skills required by enriched jobs, such as social skills. For example, part of the job enrichment scheme at a Philips television manufacturing plant in the Netherlands required TV assemblers to initiate contacts with high-status staff members in other departments when they encountered problems. This is an example of the establishment of an internal client relationship, and many workers found this job requirement threatening.[50]

Demand for Rewards. Occasionally, workers who experience job enrichment ask that greater extrinsic rewards, such as pay, accompany their redesigned jobs. Most frequently, this desire is probably prompted by the fact that such jobs require the development of new skills and entail greater responsibility. For example, one enrichment exercise for clerical jobs in a US government agency encountered this reaction.[51] Sometimes, such requests are motivated by the wish to share in the financial benefits of a successful enrichment exercise. In one documented case, workers with radically enriched jobs in a General Foods dog food plant in Topeka sought a financial bonus based on the system's success.[52] Equity in action!

Union Resistance. Traditionally, North American unions have not been enthusiastic about job enrichment. In part, this is due to a historical focus on negotiating with management about easily quantified extrinsic motivators, such as money, rather than the soft stuff of job design. Also, unions have tended to equate the narrow division of labour with preserving jobs for their members. Faced with global competition, the need for flexibility, and the need for employee initiative to foster quality, companies and unions have begun to dismantle restrictive contract provisions regarding job design. Fewer job classifications mean more opportunities for flexibility by combining tasks and using team approaches.

Supervisory Resistance. Even when enrichment schemes are carefully implemented to truly enhance the motivating potential of deserving jobs, they might fail because of their unanticipated impact on other jobs or other parts of the organizational system. A key problem here concerns the supervisors of the workers whose jobs have been enriched. By definition, enrichment increases the autonomy of employees. Unfortunately, such a change might "disenrich" the boss's job, a consequence that will hardly facilitate the smooth implementation of the job redesign. Some organizations have responded to this problem by effectively doing away with direct supervision of workers performing enriched jobs. Others use the supervisor as a trainer and developer of individuals in enriched jobs. Enrichment can increase the need for this supervisory function.

MANAGEMENT BY OBJECTIVES

In Chapter 5, we discussed goal setting theory, which states that a specific, challenging goal can be established to solve a particular performance problem. In this basic form, goal setting is rather lacking in the potential to assist in employee development over time. Usually, management makes no particular provisions for counselling employees in goal accomplishment or for changing goals in some systematic manner as the need arises. It might also occur to you that certain jobs require the simultaneous accomplishment of *several* goals, and that managers and employees might differ in the importance that they attach to these goals or disagree about how to evaluate goal accomplishment. This is particularly likely in the more complex jobs that exist at higher levels in the organization, such as management jobs and staff jobs (e.g., the human resources department or the research and development department).

Management by Objectives (MBO) is an elaborate, systematic, ongoing management program designed to facilitate goal establishment, goal accomplishment, and employee development.[53] The concept was developed by management theorist Peter Drucker. The objectives in MBO are simply another label for goals. In a well-designed MBO program, objectives for the organization as a whole are developed by top management and diffused down through the organization through the MBO process. In this manner, organizational objectives are translated into specific behavioural objectives for individual members. Our primary focus here is with the nature of the interaction between managers and individual workers in an MBO program. Although there are many variations on the MBO theme, most manager–employee interactions share the following similarities:

1. The manager meets with individual workers to develop and agree on employee objectives for the coming months. These objectives usually involve both current job performance and personal development that may prepare the worker to perform other tasks or seek promotion. The objectives are made as specific as possible and quantified, if feasible, to assist in subsequent evaluation of accomplishment. Time frames for accomplishment are specified, and the objectives may be given priority according to their agreed importance. The methods to achieve the objectives might or might not be topics of discussion. Objectives, time frames, and priorities are put in writing.

2. There are periodic meetings to monitor employee progress in achieving objectives. During these meetings, people can modify objectives if new needs or problems are encountered.

3. An appraisal meeting is held to evaluate the extent to which the agreed upon objectives have been achieved. Special emphasis is placed on diagnosing the reasons for success or failure so that the meeting serves as a learning experience for both parties.

4. The MBO cycle is repeated.

Over the years, a wide variety of organizations have implemented MBO programs. At Hewlett-Packard, MBO and metrics to measure progress was the cornerstone of the company's management philosophy for nearly six decades.[54] At Toronto-based pharmaceutical firm Janssen-Ortho Inc., each employee's goals are tied to a list of corporate objectives. Employees can earn a yearly bonus of up to 20 percent if they and the company meet their goals.[55]

Research Evidence. Overall, the research evidence shows that MBO programs result in clear productivity gains.[56] However, a number of factors are associated with the failure of MBO programs. For one thing, MBO is an elaborate, difficult, time-consuming process, and its implementation must have the full commitment of top management. One careful review showed a 56-percent average gain in productivity for programs with high top management commitment, and a 6-percent gain for those with low commitment.[57] If such commitment is absent, managers at lower levels simply go through the motions of practising MBO. At the very least, this reaction will lead to the haphazard specification of objectives and thus subvert the very core of MBO—goal setting. A frequent symptom of this degeneration is the complaint that MBO is "just a bunch of paperwork."[58] Indeed, at this stage, it is!

Even with the best of intentions, setting specific, quantifiable objectives can be a difficult process. This might lead to an overemphasis on measurable objectives at the

Management by Objectives (MBO). An elaborate, systematic, ongoing program designed to facilitate goal establishment, goal accomplishment, and employee development.

Janssen-Ortho Inc.
www.janssen-ortho.com

expense of more qualitative objectives. For example, it might be much easier to agree on production goals than on goals that involve employee development, although both might be equally important. Also, excessive short-term orientation can be a problem with MBO. Finally, even if reasonable objectives are established, MBO can still be subverted if the performance review becomes an exercise in browbeating or punishing employees for failure to achieve objectives.[59]

ALTERNATIVE WORKING SCHEDULES AS MOTIVATORS FOR A DIVERSE WORKFORCE

Royal Bank of Canada
www.royalbank.com

Most Canadians work a five-day week of approximately 40 hours—the "nine-to-five grind." However, many organizations have begun to experiment with modifying these traditional working schedules. The purpose of these modifications is not to motivate people to work harder and thus produce direct performance benefits. Rather, the purpose is to meet diverse workforce needs and promote job satisfaction. In turn, this should facilitate recruiting the best personnel and reduce costly absenteeism and turnover. For example, realizing that the traditional banking approach of rigid schedules and inattention to employee's personal preferences was driving staff away and compromising customer service, the Royal Bank of Canada made some major changes to its human resources policies. As a result, the bank now offers its employees flexible work hours, compressed workweeks, job sharing, telecommuting, and other innovative work arrangements. These changes appear to be paying off. Employees are happier, more customers are giving the bank their business, and the bank has been ranked as the most respected company in Canada.[60]

As indicated at the beginning of the chapter, an important component of the motivational system at BC Biomedical is the company's flexible work arrangements, which include flexible work hours, four-day work weeks, and job sharing. Let's now look more closely at these alternative working schedules.

Flex-Time

Flex-time. An alternative work schedule in which arrival and departure times are flexible.

One alternative to traditional working schedules is **flex-time**, which was first introduced on a large scale in Europe. In its most simple and common form, management requires employees to report for work on each working day and work a given number of hours. However, the times at which they arrive and leave are flexible, as long as they are present during certain core times. For example, companies might permit employees to begin their day anytime after 7 a.m. and work until 6 p.m., as long as they put in eight hours and are present during the core times of 9:15 until noon and 2:00 until 4:15 (Exhibit 6.8). Other systems permit employees to tally hours on a weekly or monthly basis, although they are still usually required to be present during the core time of each working day.[61]

Flex-time is obviously well suited to meeting the needs of a diverse workforce since it allows employees to tailor arrival and departure times to their own transportation and childcare situations. It should reduce absenteeism, since employees can handle personal matters during conventional business hours.[62] Also, flexible working hours signal a degree of prestige and trust that is usually reserved for executives and professionals.

When jobs are highly interdependent, such as on an assembly line, flex-time becomes an unlikely strategy. To cite an even more extreme example, we simply cannot have members of a hospital operating room team showing up for work whenever it suits them! In addition, flex-time might lead to problems in achieving adequate supervisory coverage. For these reasons, not surprisingly, flex-time is most frequently implemented in office environments. For instance, in a bank, the core hours might be when the bank is open to the public.

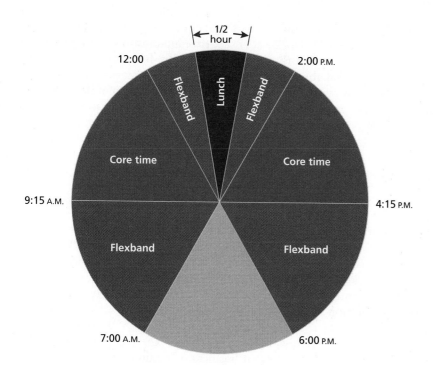

EXHIBIT 6.8
An example of a flex-time
schedule.

Source: Adapted from Ronen, S.
(1981). *Flexible working hours: An
innovation in the quality of work life.*
New York: McGraw-Hill, p. 42.
Reprinted by permission.

Although flex-time has generally been limited to white-collar personnel, it has been applied in a variety of organizations, including insurance companies (ING Insurance), financial institutions (RBC), and government offices (many Canadian and American civil service positions). According to one survey, 66 percent of organizations offered flexible work schedules.[63]

Source: David Harbaugh

Research Evidence. We can draw a number of conclusions from the research on flex-time.[64] First, employees who work under flex-time almost always prefer the system to fixed hours. In addition, work attitudes generally become more positive, and employers report minimal abuse of the arrangement. When measured, absenteeism and tardiness have often shown decreases following the introduction of flex-time, and first-line supervisors and managers are usually positively inclined toward the system. Interestingly, slight productivity gains are often reported under flex-time, probably due to better use of scarce resources or equipment rather than to increased motivation. A review of research on flex-time concluded that it has a positive effect on productivity, job satisfaction, satisfaction with work schedule, and lowers employee absenteeism.[65]

Compressed Workweek

Compressed workweek. An alternative work schedule in which employees work fewer than the normal five days a week but still put in a normal number of hours per week.

A second alternative to traditional working schedules is the **compressed workweek**. This system compresses the hours worked each week into fewer days. The most common compressed workweek is the 4–40 system, in which employees work four 10-hour days each week rather than the traditional five 8-hour days. Thus, the organization or department might operate Monday through Thursday or Tuesday through Friday, although rotation schemes that keep the organization open five days a week are also employed.[66]

Like flex-time, the shorter workweek might be expected to reduce absenteeism because employees can pursue personal business or family matters in what had been working time. In addition, the 4–40 schedule reduces commuting costs and time by 20 percent and provides an extra day a week for leisure or family pursuits. Although the longer workday could pose a problem for single parents, a working couple with staggered off-days could actually provide their own childcare on two of five "working" days.

Technical roadblocks to the implementation of the 4–40 workweek include the possibility of reduced customer service and the negative effects of fatigue that can accompany longer working days. The latter problem is likely to be especially acute when the work is strenuous.

Research Evidence. Although research on the effects of the four-day week is less extensive than that for flex-time, a couple of conclusions do stand out.[67] First, people who have experienced the four-day system seem to *like* it. Sometimes this liking is accompanied by increased job satisfaction, but the effect might be short-lived.[68] In many cases, the impact of the compressed workweek might be better for family life than for work-life. Second, workers have often reported an increase in fatigue following the introduction of the compressed week. This might be responsible for the uneven impact of the system on absenteeism, sometimes decreasing it and sometimes not. Potential gains in attendance might be nullified as workers take an occasional day off to recuperate from fatigue.[69] Finally, the more sophisticated research studies do not report lasting changes in productivity due to the shortened workweek.[70] According to a review of research on the compressed workweek, there is a positive effect on job satisfaction and satisfaction with work schedule, but no effect on absenteeism or productivity.[71]

Job Sharing

Job sharing. An alternative work schedule in which two part-time employees divide the work of a full-time job.

Job sharing occurs when two part-time employees divide the work (and perhaps the benefits) of a full-time job.[72] The two can share all aspects of the job equally, or some kind of complementary arrangement can occur in which one party does some tasks and the co-holder does other tasks.

Job sharing is obviously attractive to people who want to spend more time with small children or sick elders than a conventional five-day-a-week routine permits. By the same token, it can enable organizations to attract or retain highly capable employees who might otherwise decide against full-time employment.

Job sharing is also an effective strategy for avoiding layoffs. For example, NORDX/CDT, a Montreal-based firm that makes cables used in fibre-optic networks, introduced a job sharing program sponsored by the federal government to cut costs while keeping workers employed. The program reduces the workweek by one to three days for some employees over a short-term period; 272 employees work one day less per week. Employees receive employment-insurance benefits for the days they are not working. Other companies, such as Air Canada, have also participated in the government program, enabling them to reduce the number of employees laid off. The government program has saved thousands of jobs in recent years, including many in the technology sector.[73]

NORDX/CDT
www.nordx.com

Research Evidence. There is virtually no hard research on job sharing. However, anecdotal reports suggest that the job sharers must make a concerted effort to communicate well with each other as well as with superiors, co-workers, and clients. Such communication is greatly facilitated by contemporary computer technology and voice mail. However, coordination problems are bound to occur if there is not adequate communication. Also, problems with performance appraisal can occur when two individuals share one job.

Telecommuting

In recent years, an increasing number of organizations have begun to offer employees telecommuting, or what is sometimes called "telework." By **telecommuting**, employees are able to work at home but stay in touch with their offices through the use of communications technology, such as a computer network, voice mail, and electronic messages.[74] Like the other types of alternative working arrangements, telecommuting provides workers with greater flexibility in their work schedules.

Telecommuting. A system by which employees are able to work at home but stay in touch with their offices through the use of communications technology, such as a computer network, voice mail, and electronic messages.

Many companies first began implementing telecommuting in response to employee requests for more flexible work arrangements.[75] With the growth in communication technologies, however, other factors have also influenced the spread of telecommuting. For example, telecommuting is changing the way that organizations recruit and hire people. When telecommuting is an option, companies can hire the best person for a

job, regardless of where they live in the world, through *distant staffing*.[76] Distant staffing enables employees to work for a company without ever having to come into the office or even be in the same country!

Telecommuting has grown considerably over the last few years and demand is expected to continue to grow in the coming years. Today, it is estimated that approximately 11 million North Americans are telecommuting, and 51 percent of North American companies offer some form of telecommuting, including one in four Fortune 1000 companies. In Canada, it has been estimated that more than 1.5 million Canadians are telecommuting.[77]

An interesting trend in telecommuting that has started to appear in the United States and Canada are telework centres that provide workers all of the amenities of a home office in a location close to their home. Related to this is the emergence of *distributed work programs*, which involve a combination of remote work arrangements that allow employees to work at their business office, a satellite office, and a home office. At Bell Canada, all employees are eligible to participate in the company's distributed work program. Employees can choose to work from home all of the time or they can also work a few days a week at one of Bell's satellite offices.[78]

Research Evidence. Although research on telecommuting is limited, it is believed to have a number of advantages for employees and organizations. Organizations benefit from lower costs as a result of a reduction in turnover and the need for less office space and equipment, and they can attract employees who see it as a desirable benefit.[79] The results of one survey found that telecommuting had a positive effect on productivity, flexibility, and work–life balance.[80] AT&T has calculated that its telework program resulted in savings of $100 million (US) from increased productivity, $18 million because of lower turnover, and $25 million in reduced real estate costs.[81]

Some negative aspects of telecommuting, however, can result because of the potential damage to informal communication. These included decreased visibility when promotions are considered, problems in handling rush projects, and workload spillover for non-telecommuters.[82] Other potential problems include distractions in the home environment, feelings of isolation, and overwork.

Despite the potential benefits and the growing popularity of telecommuting, many companies are hesitant to implement telecommuting programs because of concerns about trust and control. Many managers are uncomfortable with the prospect of not being able to keep an eye on their employees while they work.[83] Therefore, it is important that there is a strong perception of trust between employees and management as well as careful planning and clear guidelines before an organization implements a telecommuting program.

MOTIVATION PRACTICES IN PERSPECTIVE

As the earlier sections illustrate, organizations have a lot of options when it comes to motivating their employees. Confused about what they should do? The concepts of *fit* and *balance* can help resolve this confusion. First, the motivational systems chosen should have a good fit with the strategic goals of the organization. Ultimately, attraction, retention, speed, quality, and volume of output involve some tradeoffs, and an organization will not be able to achieve all of these outcomes with one motivational strategy. Second, balance among the components of a motivational system is critical. Job design and work schedules must allow employees to achieve the goals that are set, and the reward system needs to be directed toward this achievement.

As we indicated in Chapter 1, there are no simple formulas to improve employee attitudes and performance or a set of laws of organizational behaviour that can be used to solve organizational problems. Like all of organizational behaviour, when it comes to employee motivation, there is no "cookbook" to follow. Thus, while many of the

Bell Canada
www.bell.ca

AT&T
www.att.com

best companies to work for in Canada use the motivational practices described in this chapter, this does not mean that these practices will always be effective or that other organizations should follow suit. Clearly, the motivational practices used by the best companies are effective because they *fit* into and are part of a larger organizational culture and system of management practices. For example, the motivational practices of BC Biomedical described at the beginning of the chapter are part of an organizational culture that fosters a family atmosphere and fit with the company's employee-centred management practices.

The choice of motivational practices requires a thorough diagnosis of the organization as well as a consideration of employee needs. Keep in mind the relevance of the theories of motivation discussed in Chapter 5. Employees will be motivated by things that will fulfill their needs (need theory) and that they find highly valent (expectancy theory). It is therefore important to understand employees and their needs, the nature of jobs, organizational characteristics, and the primary motivational outcome that an organization wants to achieve.

For example, some employees, such as those with high self-efficacy and a high need for achievement, tend to prefer pay that is contingent on individual performance.[84] Employees who perform relatively simple tasks often do not wish to have their jobs enriched. Thus, linking pay to performance would be a more effective motivational practice than job enrichment. Similarly, young employees in the early stages of their career tend to prefer challenging and enriched job opportunities, while those with young families prefer alternative working schedules.

The nature of the job will also influence the choice of a motivational practice. For example, jobs that require knowledge and skill upgrading lend themselves to a skill-based pay system, and jobs in which it is possible to identify the outputs of individuals are better suited to piece-rate plans.

In terms of organizational characteristics, alternative working schedules are effective for organizations where diversity is a top priority, while organizations that are most concerned with the alignment of employee and organization goals would be more likely to benefit from profit sharing, employee stock ownership programs, and management by objectives.

It is also important to consider the motivational outcome of most importance to an organization. That is, what is it that the organization wants employees to be motivated to do? Are they concerned with attracting new employees, diversity, employee output, quality, learning, or perhaps employee retention? In this regard, pay-for-performance systems are most effective for increasing employee performance and productivity and employee retention. Skill-based pay systems are effective when an organization wants to motivate employees to continuously learn and acquire new knowledge and skills. Job enrichment is particularly effective for increasing intrinsic motivation and job involvement, while alternative working schedules tend to be effective for applicant attraction, employee retention, and workforce diversity.

In summary, while there are many motivational practices that organizations can employ to motivate their workforce, it is important to keep in mind that the most effective approach will depend on a combination of factors, including employee characteristics and needs, the nature of the job, characteristics of the organization (e.g., strategy, culture, management practices), and the outcome that an organization wants to achieve. Ultimately, motivational systems that make use of a variety of motivators—such as performance-based pay and job enrichment—used in conjunction with one another are likely to be most effective.[85]

THE MANAGER'S

Notebook

Employees Oppose Merit Pay Plan at Hudson's Bay Company

1. More than 800 sales and clerical staff at five Ontario stores revolted against the plan to introduce the merit pay system. Although the company claimed that the purpose of a pay-for-performance program was to improve service and increase sales, the striking employees said that the plan would open them up to the abuses of favouritism and bias by management. CAW national representative Bill Gibson said, "workers are entitled to know what their wages will be" without worrying that "their supervisor doesn't like them or because a change in corporate accounting practice changes the profit statement."

Employee reactions can be understood in terms of three aspects of organizational behaviour. First, it appears that employees did not believe that pay would in fact be linked to performance. Recall that this is one of the reasons why merit pay plans are often ineffective. This is due in part to poor performance appraisals that do not accurately measure employees' performance. Second, the fact that employees believe that favouritism and bias will determine their pay suggests a lack of trust in management. Recall from Chapter 3 that trust has to do with perceptions of management ability, benevolence, and integrity. Thus, employees might not trust management because they do not believe that management has the competence to evaluate their performance; they do not believe that management is concerned about their interests and is willing to do good for them; and they do not believe that management adheres to a set of values and principles that they find acceptable. Finally, employees obviously do not believe that a merit pay plan will be fair. Based on the discussion of fairness in Chapter 4, it would seem that employees have low perceptions of procedural and distributive justice. That is, they do not believe that fair procedures will be used to determine their merit pay, and they do not believe that the amount of pay they receive under a merit pay plan will be fair.

2. The strike lasted two weeks and did not end until management backed down and resurrected the flat-wage system. Whether or not the system would have motivated employees and improved service and sales if it had not been opposed is difficult to say. However, it is clear that implementing a system without employee input and involvement is doomed to failure. Perhaps if employees had participated in the development of the new pay system they would have accepted it. It might also have helped if a new performance appraisal system was designed to reduce perceptual errors and biases in the evaluation of employees' performance and to increase the fairness and accuracy of performance ratings. Recall from Chapter 3 that behaviourally anchored rating scales are designed for this purpose. Replacing a performance appraisal system with a new system that is fair, accurate, and linked to rewards has been found to be more acceptable to employees and to increase perceptions of trust toward management. It would also help if procedures were implemented to ensure perceptions of procedural fairness as described in Chapter 4. This, along with a new performance appraisal system, would have helped to create more positive perceptions of distributive and procedural fairness. Finally, it is also important to recognize that introducing a merit pay system based on individual performance might not fit an organization's culture. In some cases, it might be better to design a group-based merit pay program rather than an individual-based system. Employees at HBC might have been more accepting of the merit pay plan if it had been based on department performance rather than individual performance. Combining a group merit system along with some friendly competition between departments might be more acceptable, motivational, and more likely to improve service and sales.

LEARNING OBJECTIVES CHECKLIST

1. Money should be most effective as a motivator when it is made contingent on performance. Schemes to link pay to performance on production jobs are called *wage incentive plans*. Piece-rate, in which workers are paid a certain amount of money for each item produced, is the prototype of all wage incentive plans. In general, wage incentives increase productivity, but their introduction can be accompanied by a number of problems, one of which is the restriction of production.

2. Attempts to link pay to performance on white-collar jobs are called *merit pay plans*. Evidence suggests that many merit pay plans are less effective than they could be because merit pay is inadequate, performance ratings are mistrusted, or extreme secrecy about pay levels prevails.

3. Compensation plans to enhance teamwork include *profit sharing, employee stock ownership, gainsharing*, and *skill-based pay*. Each of these plans has a different motivational focus, so organizations must choose a plan that supports their strategic needs.

4. Recent views advocate increasing the scope (breadth and depth) of jobs to capitalize on their inherent motivational properties, as opposed to the job simplification of the past. The *Job Characteristics Model*, developed by Hackman and Oldham, suggests that jobs have five core characteristics that affect their motivating potential: *skill variety, task identity, task significance, autonomy*, and *feedback*. When jobs are high in these characteristics, favourable motivational and attitudinal consequences should result.

5. *Job enrichment* involves designing jobs to enhance intrinsic motivation, *job involvement*, and the quality of working life. Some specific enrichment techniques include combining tasks, establishing client relationships, reducing supervision and reliance on others, forming work teams, and making feedback more direct.

6. *Management by Objectives* (MBO) is an elaborate goal-setting and evaluation process that organizations typically use for management jobs. Objectives for the organization as a whole are developed by top management and diffused down through the organization and translated into specific behavioural objectives for individual members.

7. Some organizations have adopted *alternative working schedules*, such as *flex-time, compressed workweeks, job sharing*, or *telecommuting*, with expectations of motivational benefits. These schemes should have little effect on productivity, and they have the potential to reduce absenteeism and turnover and to enhance the quality of working life for a diverse workforce.

8. Organizations need to conduct a diagnostic evaluation to determine the motivational practice that will be most effective. This requires a consideration of employee characteristics and needs, the nature of the job, organizational characteristics, and the outcome that is of most concern to the organization.

OB FLASHBACK

Making Pay-for-Performance More Effective with Goal Setting

In a recent article in the *Wall Street Journal,* it was reported that 83 percent of companies with some type of pay-for-performance program say that it is only somewhat successful or not working at all. According to Hewitt Associates, the consulting firm that conducted the survey, many of the companies that report poor results from performance-based pay programs might not be adequately articulating goals to employees. Those companies that have achieved some success with performance-based pay programs are reported to be setting clear goals and motivating employees to achieve them.

This raises an interesting question: Can pay-for-performance plans be more effective if they are used with goal setting? In Chapter 5, you learned about goal setting theory and that goals are most motivational when they are specific and challenging and when individuals are committed to them and receive feedback about their progress towards goal attainment.

According to Edwin Locke, one of the originators of goal setting theory, you can make pay-for-performance programs more effective by linking them to goals. He describes four methods of doing this.

The first method involves assigning employees difficult or *stretch* goals and then providing a substantial bonus if they are reached and no bonus if they are not reached. This method provides a strong incentive for goal attainment and leaves no ambiguity as to what is required to receive the bonus. However, a weakness of this method is that employees might focus on the short term and take shortcuts or even cheat to receive the bonus (see the Ethical Focus feature in Chapter 5 on goal setting and unethical behaviour). Another weakness with this method is that high performance that falls short of the goal results in no bonus at all, which can be very demoralizing.

The second method involves assigning multiple goal levels and with a different bonus level attached to each. This way the higher the goal level attained the higher the bonus. This method ensures that employees will get a bonus even if they fall short of the highest level, so they will be less likely to take shortcuts or cheat. A weakness, however, is that some employees might be content with the lowest level and not be motivated to pursue the highest level. In addition, once the highest level is reached there is no motivation to do better.

The third method is a linear or continuous bonus system. This is in contrast to the previous method, which involved increments. In the previous method, an individual might fall just below a goal level and so his or her bonus will actually be based on a lower level (if an employee achieves 24 percent sales and the sales goals are 5, 10, 15, 20, and 25 percent, he or she will get rewarded only for achieving the 20 percent goal and will have just missed the 25 percent goal). With a continuous bonus system, an employee might get a 2 percent bonus for every 1 percent increase in sales. As a result, employees get rewarded for exactly what they achieve. Further, unlike the previous two methods, there is no upper limit so there is an incentive to attain higher goals. However, because there is a minimum level, some employees might not be motivated to pursue higher level goals.

The fourth method involves setting specific and challenging goals, but the decision about bonus rewards is made after the fact to take into account the full context in which the goal was pursued, such as how the company did as a whole, how difficult the goal really was in light of various factors such as resources, obstacles, and market conditions, as well as the methods the employee used to attain the goals. The bonus decision might then be made by a management team that is knowledgeable about these factors. This is a more flexible and comprehensive method than the other three because it takes into account factors that might have made it very easy or difficult to attain a goal. However, it requires management to be knowledgeable about the context and to be objective to avoid favouritism and bias.

Which method is best? This depends on many factors. According to Locke, organizations should choose the type of bonus system that is right for the company with full awareness of the pros and cons of each method. Whatever method is chosen, goals should be set for important and desired outcomes. They should be clear and challenging and, if necessary, they should be set for the actions that lead to the desired outcomes and not just the outcomes themselves. Make sure the number of goals assigned is reasonable and do not change the goals too readily.

Source: Based on Locke, E.A. (2004). Linking goals to monetary incentives. *Academy of Management Executive, 18,* 130–133.

DISCUSSION QUESTIONS

1. Describe some jobs for which you think it would be difficult to link pay to performance. What is it about these jobs that provokes this difficulty?

2. Why do you think employees and managers seriously underestimate the importance of pay as a motivator? What are the implications of this for organizations' use of pay to motivate employees? What are the consequences?

3. Imagine two insurance companies that have merit pay plans for salaried, white-collar personnel. In one organization, the plan truly rewards good performers, while in the other it does not. Both companies decide to make salaries completely public. What will be the consequences of such a change for each company? (Be specific, using concepts such as expectancy, instrumentality, job satisfaction, and turnover.)

4. You are, of course, familiar with the annual lists of the world's 10 worst-dressed people or the 10 worst movies. Here's a new one: A job enrichment consultant has developed a list of the 10 worst jobs, which includes a highway toll collector, pool typist, bank guard, and elevator operator. Use the five core job characteristics to describe each of these jobs. Could you enrich any of these jobs? How? Which should be completely automated? Can you add some jobs to the list?

5. What are the essential distinctions between gainsharing, profit sharing, and employee stock ownership? How effective is each pay plan and what are the advantages and disadvantages?

6. Some observers have argued that the jobs of the prime minister of Canada and the president of the United States are "too big" for one person to perform adequately. This probably means that the jobs are perceived as having too much scope or being too enriched. Use the Job Characteristics Model to explore the accuracy of this observation.

7. Imagine an office setting in which a change to a four-day workweek, flex-time, or telecommuting would appear to be equally feasible to introduce. What would be the pros and cons of each system? How would factors such as the nature of the business, the age of the workforce, and the average commuting distance affect the choice of systems?

8. How is the concept of workforce diversity related to the motivational techniques discussed in the chapter?

9. Although an increasing number of organizations are offering their employees the opportunity to telecommute, many employees who have tried it don't like it and prefer to be in the workplace. Why do you think some employees do not want to telecommute and some have even returned to the workplace after trying it? What can organizations do to ensure that employees' telecommuting experiences are successful?

10. Why does BC Biomedical use some motivational practices and not others? Review the chapter opening vignette and explain the extent to which the motivational practices used by BC Biomedical "fit" the organization and the extent to which they would work in other organizations. Describe situations in which you think BC Biomedical's motivational practices will be effective and situations in which you think they will be less effective.

INTEGRATIVE DISCUSSION QUESTIONS

1. Merit pay plans often require that managers conduct performance evaluations of their employees to determine the amount of merit pay to be awarded. Discuss some of the perceptual problems and biases described in Chapter 3 that could create problems for a merit pay plan. What can be done to improve performance evaluations and the success of merit pay plans?

2. Using each of the motivation theories described in Chapter 5, explain how job design and job enrichment can be motivational. According to each theory, when is job design and job enrichment most likely to be effective for motivating workers?

3. In Chapter 2, employee recognition programs were discussed as an organizational learning practice. Using the material presented in this chapter, describe the potential for employee recognition programs as a motivational practice. What aspects of employee recognition programs might be especially important for a motivational program?

ON-THE-JOB CHALLENGE QUESTION

A new and popular trend in human resources is to offer employees longer vacations, more personal leave entitlements, extra days off, and more flexible work arrangements. Toronto-based Carlson Wagonlit Travel Canada changed its vacation policy in response to an employee survey. Employees now get four weeks of paid vacation after five years of service. The previous policy required ten years of service to qualify for four weeks of paid vacation. Toronto-based investment management firm Frank Russell Canada Ltd. grants all employees four weeks of paid vacation after one year of service. The company also entitles long-service employees to eight-week paid sabbaticals every 10 years.

Comment on the motivational effects of these policies, paying particular attention to the characteristics and needs of employees, the nature of the job, organizational characteristics, and the desired outcome. In other words, will these policies motivate employees, and if so, when, how, and why? What do you think of this new trend?

Source: Galt, V. (2004, December 28). Gift of time pays off for savvy employers. *Globe and Mail*, B3.

EXPERIENTIAL EXERCISE

Choose Your Job

People differ in the kinds of jobs they prefer. The questions on the next page give you a chance to consider just what it is about a job that is most important to *you*. For each question, indicate the extent to which you would prefer Job A or Job B if you had to make a choice between them. In answering, assume that everything else about the two jobs is the same except the characteristics being compared. There are no "correct" answers. Just give your personal choice.

—1—	—2—	—3—	—4—	—5—
Strongly Prefer A	Slightly Prefer A	Neutral	Slightly Prefer B	Strongly Prefer B

JOB A

JOB B

_____ 1. A job where the pay is very good. | A job where there is considerable opportunity to be creative and innovative.

_____ 2. A job where you are often required to make important decisions. | A job with many pleasant people to work with.

_____ 3. A job in which greater responsibility is given to those who do the best work. | A job in which greater responsibility is given to loyal employees who have the most seniority.

_____ 4. A job in an organization which is in financial trouble—and might have to close down within the year. | A job in which you are not allowed to have any say whatever in how your work is scheduled, or in the procedures to be used in carrying it out.

_____ 5. A very routine job. | A job where your co-workers are not very friendly.

_____ 6. A job with a supervisor who is often very critical of you and your work in front of other people. | A job which prevents you from using a number of skills that you worked hard to develop.

_____ 7. A job with a supervisor who respects you and treats you fairly. | A job which provides constant opportunities for you to learn new and interesting things.

_____ 8. A job where there is a real chance you could be laid off. | A job with very little chance to do challenging work.

_____ 9. A job in which there is a real chance for you to develop new skills and advance in the organization. | A job which provides lots of vacation time and an excellent fringe benefit package.

_____ 10. A job with little freedom and independence to do your work in the way you think best. | A job where the working conditions are poor.

_____ 11. A job with very satisfying teamwork. | A job which allows you to use your skills and abilities to the fullest extent.

_____ 12. A job which offers little or no challenge. | A job which requires you to be completely isolated from co-workers.

Scoring and Interpretation

These questions make up the growth need strength measure from J. Richard Hackman and Greg Oldham's Job Diagnostic Survey. To determine your own growth need strength, first subtract your responses on items 2, 3, 4, 6, 8, and 9 from 6. Then, add up the resulting scores on all 12 items and divide the total by 12. This is your growth need strength score. It should fall somewhere between 1 and 5.

People with high growth needs have a strong desire to obtain growth satisfaction from their jobs. The average growth score for thousands of individuals employed in a wide variety of jobs is 4.23. Here are some other growth need norms based on occupation, education, and age:

4.46 White-collar
4.00 Blue-collar
4.92 Middle managers
4.62 First-line managers
4.76 Professional and technical
4.18 Clerical
4.25 Ages 20–29

4.92 Sales
4.13 Machine trades
4.16 Construction
4.02 High school graduates
4.72 University graduates
4.01 Under age 20

Source: Hackman, J.R., & Oldham, G.R. (1974). _The Job Diagnostic Survey: An instrument for the diagnosis of jobs and the evaluation of job redesign projects._ Yale University Department of Administrative Sciences Technical Report No. 4.

To facilitate class discussion and your understanding of growth need strength and job design, form a small group with several other members of the class and consider the following questions.

1. Each group member should present their growth need strength (GNS) score. Next, consider the types of jobs you have had in the past and their job scope. Make a list of your previous jobs and their job scope (for each job, rate it as high or low on job breadth and job depth; see Exhibit 6.4). For each job, indicate your motivation and satisfaction (low, average, high). Next, relate your GNS score to the scope of your jobs and your level of motivation and satisfaction. Are group members with higher GNS more motivated and satisfied in jobs with higher job scope?

2. To what extent has your GNS been a factor in your motivation, satisfaction, and performance in your previous and current job? To what extent has it been a factor in your decision to quit a job? Explain your answer.

3. How can knowledge of your GNS assist you in your decision to accept a job? How can it assist you in knowing how much you will like a job and how you will perform?

4. What are the implications of GNS for job design? How can knowledge of employees' GNS help organizations design jobs that will motivate their employees?

CASE INCIDENT

The Junior Accountant

After graduating from business school, Sabrita received a job offer from a large accounting firm to work as a junior accountant. She was ranked in the top 10 of her class and could not have been happier. During the first six months, however, Sabrita began to reconsider her decision to join a large firm. This is how she described her job: Every day her supervisor brought several files for her to audit. He told her exactly in what order to do them and how to plan her day and work. At the end of the day, the supervisor would return to pick up the completed files. The supervisor collected the files from several other junior accountants, and then put them all together and completed the audit himself. The supervisor would then meet the client to review and discuss the audit. Sabrita did not ever meet the clients, and her

supervisor never talked about his meeting with them or the final report. Sabrita felt very discouraged and wanted to quit. She was even beginning to reconsider her choice of accounting as a career.

1. Describe the job characteristics and critical psychological states of Sabrita's job. According to the Job Characteristics Model, how motivated is Sabrita and what is she likely to do?

2. How would you redesign Sabrita's job to increase its motivating potential? Be sure to describe changes you would make in the core job characteristics as well as job enrichment schemes that you might use to redesign her job.

3. What do you think Sabrita's supervisor should do?

CASE STUDY

Hewlett-Packard's Team-Based Pay System

In an effort to support a transition to self-managed teams and encourage a focus on teamwork rather than individual performance, Hewlett-Packard (HP) initiated a team pay-for-performance (TPP) plan at one of its sites. Previously, responsibility for implementing HP's merit based pay philosophy for managing the development of employees was given to individual managers who would divide work group objectives into individual assignments and then monitor individual contributions. Under the new self-managing-teams structure, a layer of supervision had been removed, and managers had wider spans of control and less manager/subordinate interaction.

Teams themselves divided up the work and were guided by a set of business objectives. Consequently, managers were not as well-positioned to make merit increase decisions or to manage the development of

individual employees. Therefore, management put together a TPP plan to ensure employees focused on team performance and to encourage them to manage their own development and acquire the broader set of skills that would be required by team responsibilities.

Team pay-for-performance was established to motivate achievement of specific team goals, such as team-process improvement, production, and quality goals. The team-based pay for achieving certain goals was added incrementally to base pay. There was no "take-away" for failing to meet team goals.

Three levels of team performance were possible within the pay structure. Ninety percent of the teams were expected to achieve Level I performance and thus receive a payout. Fifty percent were expected to reach Level II performance, and 10 to 15 percent Level III performance, the highest level. For achieving Level III performance, for example, members of a particular work team would receive between $150–$200 additional pay at the end of the following month. Teams also had production coaches to assist them.

The new pay package also included a skill-based pay system called pay-for-contribution (PFC). Instead of the typical merit system, employees would advance from a starting rate by demonstrating competence to perform additional sets of tasks within the team. The system was intended to motivate employees to learn new skills on an ongoing basis. Possession of a new skill set was measured and certified by "subject matter experts." The goal was to create a continuously learning workforce capable of adapting to new situations.

During the first six months, team members liked the TPP program and significantly outperformed the performance goals set at the beginning of the experiment, with a majority of the teams reaching Level II and III. However, because the TPP program paid out more than expected, management concluded that they had set the performance standards too low and decided to adjust them. This effort was met with great resistance from team members, who complained bitterly. They had built a lifestyle around the higher monthly pay they had come to expect, and now saw the program as taking something away. Managers also concluded that workers' attention was now focused on their pay instead of their work.

Another drawback of pay-for-performance that managers saw had to do with factors outside of the team's control that affected team performance. For example, delays in shipment of parts or a mechanical breakdown in the assembly line prevented teams from building the units they needed to meet their goals for that month. This caused serious dissatisfaction with the pay system. Team members felt as though they had very little control over their performance.

Furthermore, high-performing teams often refused to admit anyone to their team who they thought might be below their level of competence. This resulted in self-reinforcing positive and negative spirals in team performance. Some teams had many top performers, while others stagnated with low performers who needed further training. Furthermore, barriers to employee mobility between teams reduced the capacity of the organization to transfer learning from one team to another, a major barrier in a dynamic environment.

Regarding the skill-based PFC system, management reported that the majority of employees disliked this system. They did not like the additional pressure of taking tests to increase their pay, some in how to read and write and do math. Because they were afraid it wouldn't leave them enough time to study and test for new work skills, employees would often refuse new job assignments. Moreover, many of the newly acquired skills were not used on the job. Furthermore, at the beginning of the program, employees had to demonstrate proficiency on skills required in their current job to maintain their skill classification. If they failed, the system called for them to drop to a lower classification and pay level. Managers found it difficult to do this, however. These constituted takeaways from expected levels of pay that had been established in the minds of employees.

Local site managers concluded that a team structure together with training would have provided the same benefits as the team structure combined with team- and skill-based pay, but without the additional effort, money, and communications demanded by the team-based pay system. Managers also concluded that the pay system did not motivate employees to work harder or learn, though it did stimulate them to better understand relevant performance metrics, the manufacturing system as a whole, and the company's broader goals. This improved understanding may have been used by employees to define their own interests rather than the broader interests of the organization as a whole when TPP stopped paying off.

One of the largest of the divisions dropped the pay program after about a year. Managers were tired of having to constantly reengineer the pay system to overcome its numerous problems. Surveys indicated that employees preferred to switch back to HP's standard pay structure. When management of that division announced they would drop the pay program, employees threw a party to show their gratitude.

The rest of the divisions eventually dropped the program as well, due to a major manufacturing reorganization. The divisions found that team-based pay made it extremely difficult to maintain consistency in the pay system across the whole site.

Source: Excerpt from Beer, M., & Cannon, M.D. (2004). Promise and peril in implementing pay-for-performance. *Human Resource Management, 43*, 3–20. Reprinted with permission of John Wiley & Sons, Inc.

1. Why did the company initiate a team-based pay system and what implications did this have for team members and managers? Was it a good idea?

2. What effect did the team pay-for-performance plan have on team members? Why wasn't it more effective?

3. What effect did the skill-based pay system have on team members? Why wasn't it more effective?

4. Comment on management's role in implementing and maintaining the team-based pay system. Did they help or hinder the success of the programs? What should they have done differently?

5. If you had to redesign the team-based pay system, what would you do to make it more effective?

6. What does this case tell us about team-based pay systems and pay-for-performance plans?

INTEGRATIVE CASE

Ace Technology

At the end of Chapter 1 you were introduced to the Ace Technology Integrative Case. It focused on issues pertaining to managerial roles and organizational behaviour in general. You were also asked to consider the implications of the events at Ace Technology for individuals, groups, and the organization. Now that you have completed Part 2 of the text and the chapters on Individual Behaviour, you can return to the Ace Technology Integrative Case and focus on issues related to learning, job attitudes, motivation, pay systems, and incentive plans by answering the following questions.

QUESTIONS

1. What behaviours are employees at Ace Technology expected to learn?

2. Describe the reward and reinforcement strategies being used to change employees' behaviour at Ace Technology. Do you think that employees will change their behaviour? Why or why not?

3. Describe the revamped employee recognition program and evaluate it using the material discussed in Chapter 2 about employee recognition programs. How effective do you think the revamped program will be? How would you revamp the recognition program to make it more effective?

4. Discuss the implications of the new strategy and compensation program for employee job satisfaction in terms of equity theory and distributive and procedural fairness. How will the new system impact distributive and procedural fairness?

5. What are the differences between Ace Technology's "antiquated" and new compensation programs? Consider the implications and effectiveness of the new compensation program according to Maslow's and Alderfer's need theories, expectancy theory, and goal setting theory. What are the advantages and disadvantages of the new program according to each theory?

6. How is money being used to motivate employees at Ace Technology? What other programs might be useful for improving employee motivation?

7. Describe the incentive plans being considered by Ace Technology. What are the potential problems with these incentive plans, and how effective do you think they will be for motivating employees and implementing the new strategy?

PART ❸ Social Behaviour and Organizational Processes

CHAPTER 7

Groups and Teamwork

RALSTON FOODS

Headquartered in St. Louis, Missouri, Ralcorp has more than 3000 employees and is the largest store-brand manufacturer in the United States. It includes four separate food categories: Ralston ready-to-eat and hot cereals; Bremner crackers and cookies; Nutcracker/Flavor House Brands jar and can snack nuts and candy; and Carriage House mayonnaise, salad dressings, jams, jellies, and peanut butter.

The Ralston Foods' Sparks, Nevada, plant, located on the outskirts of Reno, is a small segment of Ralcorp's $1.2-billion organization. The plant opened as a pet-food producer in 1972, but was shut down as a pet-food operation in 1990. At that time, Daniel Kibbe was brought in to retrofit the facility into a cereal plant. Kibbe viewed this major change as a way to create a new culture at the Sparks plant: a culture focused on groups and teams.

Many millions of dollars were spent redesigning and retrofitting the plant over an 18-month period, from mid-1990 to 1991. In July 1991, Kibbe and his management team met with 58 laid-off employees and explained the new participative culture to them. At first they were pretty skeptical. Their response was, "We've heard that before; you'll never let us do those things." But Kibbe stayed the course. Initially, they started delegating a lot of little things that were empowering in nature such as allowing the workers to renegotiate the vending service contract at the plant that had previously been a source of dissatisfaction. That kind of empowerment spread throughout the plant as they moved into the start-up process. Group members were involved in all aspects of the start-up process—hiring, equipment checkout, developing work rules, skill-based pay, schedules, and training.

The Sparks culture is based on the recognition that traditional systems have failed to tap the true potential of group members. The system is based on an environment of credibility, trust, and openness. The work group orientation drives the organization. There are operating work groups, support work groups, and a leadership work group composed of the entire management staff, including operating and staff managers, group leaders, and the plant manager. In most cases, work groups, which range in size from 8 to 50 members, are broken down into smaller teams ranging from 3 to 10 members. The six operating work groups function in

LEARNING OBJECTIVES

After reading Chapter 7, you should be able to:

1. Define *groups* and distinguish between *formal* and *informal groups*.

2. Discuss group development.

3. Explain how group size and member diversity influence what occurs in groups.

4. Review how *norms*, *roles*, and *status* affect social interaction.

5. Discuss the causes and consequences of *group cohesiveness*.

6. Explain the dynamics of *social loafing*.

7. Discuss how to design and support *self-managed teams*.

8. Explain the logic behind *cross-functional teams* and describe how they can operate effectively.

9. Understand *virtual teams* and what makes them effective.

Ralston Foods has been able to use self-directed work groups to its advantage in its Sparks, Nevada cereal plant.

all areas of the plant, including three in operations, which comprises the mill, processing, and packing areas, plus three more in the maintenance, storeroom, and warehouse areas. Two of these groups are totally self-directed; four are semiautonomous.

In addition to work groups, there are cross-functional committees that meet regularly. Most committee members are volunteers, and group members represent their work group. Some are only formed for short-term needs, such as business response, specific continuous improvement projects, and culture day (an off-site day in which all group members participate in team-building activities and training). There are also ongoing committees responsible for the following areas or issues: continuous improvement, food safety, community activities, employee activities, hiring task force, policy, safety, and PEO (Plant Emergency Organization).

Ralston Foods
www.ralstonfoods.com

The two self-directed work groups in the plant are the warehouse and mill groups. Neither of these groups has had a group leader for five or six years. The self-directed groups consistently have a better, more dependable performance than those with group leaders. They also tend to be tougher on disciplinary problems than work groups with leaders. The work groups with leaders have gotten good at referring to the group leader for decisions they are reluctant to make—such as dealing with a poor performer. Self-directed groups do meet with a group manager once a week, but other than that, the groups have to deal with all the issues themselves. They just elevate themselves to the level needed.

Productivity numbers at the plant—measured in terms of total cost per unit—have steadily improved. From their first full year through 1998, the plant improved productivity by over 55 percent. Total costs also improved significantly, being cut by over

5 percent per year for the first six years. The year 2000 was the first year in which not all financial goals were met. Today, the plant has a much more difficult product mix, yet they have kept costs flat for the past several years. The Sparks plant has also led the company/division in safety, quality, sanitation, yields, and other significant performance categories on a frequent basis. Through a mix of trust, performance measurement and rewards, training and development, and leadership, Kibbe has succeeded in transforming the culture at Ralston's Sparks plant and has demonstrated the power of teamwork.[1]

This vignette shows how critical groups or teams are in determining organizational success. In this chapter, we will define the term *group* and discuss the nature of formal groups and informal groups in organizations. After this, we will present the details of group development. Then, we will consider how groups differ from one another structurally and explore the consequences of these differences. We will also cover the problem of social loafing. Finally, we will examine teams and how to design effective work teams.

WHAT IS A GROUP?

Group. Two or more people interacting interdependently to achieve a common goal.

We use the word *group* rather casually in everyday discourse—special-interest group, ethnic group, and others. However, for behavioural scientists, a **group** consists of two or more people interacting interdependently to achieve a common goal.

Interaction is the most basic aspect of a group—it suggests who is in the group and who is not. The interaction of group members need not be face to face, and it need not be verbal. For example, employees who "telecommute" can be part of their work group at the office even though they live miles away and communicate with a modem. Interdependence simply means that group members rely to some degree on each other to accomplish goals. All groups have one or more goals that their members seek to achieve. These goals can range from having fun to marketing a new product to achieving world peace.

Group memberships are very important for two reasons. First, groups exert a tremendous influence on us. They are the social mechanisms by which we acquire many beliefs, values, attitudes, and behaviours. Group membership is also important because groups provide a context in which *we* are able to exert influence on *others*.

Formal work groups. Groups that are established by organizations to facilitate the achievement of organizational goals.

Formal work groups are groups that organizations establish to facilitate the achievement of organizational goals. They are intentionally designed to channel individual effort in an appropriate direction. The most common formal group consists of a manager and the employees who report to that manager. In a manufacturing company, one such group might consist of a production manager and the six shift supervisors who report to him or her. In turn, the shift supervisors head work groups composed of themselves and their respective subordinates. Thus, the hierarchy of most organizations is a series of formal interlocked work groups. As the Ralston Foods case shows, all this direct supervision is not always necessary. Nevertheless, Ralston's self-managed teams are still formal work groups.

Other types of formal work groups include task forces and committees. *Task forces* are temporary groups that meet to achieve particular goals or to solve particular problems, such as suggesting productivity improvements. *Committees* are usually permanent groups that handle recurrent assignments outside the usual work group structures. For example, a firm might have a standing committee on work–family balance. Although their terminology varies a bit, Ralston Foods makes extensive use of committees and task forces.

In addition to formal groups sanctioned by management to achieve organizational goals, informal grouping occurs in all organizations. **Informal groups** are groups that emerge naturally in response to the common interests of organizational members. They are seldom sanctioned by the organization, and their membership often cuts across formal groups. Informal groups can either help or hurt an organization, depending on their norms for behaviour. We will consider this in detail later.

> **Informal groups.** Groups that emerge naturally in response to the common interests of organizational members.

GROUP DEVELOPMENT

Even relatively simple groups are actually complex social devices that require a fair amount of negotiation and trial and error before individual members begin to function as a true group. While employees often know each other before new teams are formed, simple familiarity does not replace the necessity for team development.

Typical Stages of Group Development

Leaders and trainers have observed that many groups develop through a series of stages over time.[2] Each stage presents the members with a series of challenges they must master to achieve the next stage. These stages (forming, storming, norming, performing, and adjourning) are presented in Exhibit 7.1.

Forming. At this early stage, group members try to orient themselves by "testing the waters." What are we doing here? What are the others like? What is our purpose? The situation is often ambiguous, and members are aware of their dependency on each other.

Storming. At this second stage, conflict often emerges. Confrontation and criticism occur as members determine whether they will go along with the way the group is developing. Sorting out roles and responsibilities is often at issue here. Problems are more likely to happen earlier, rather than later, in group development.

EXHIBIT 7.1
Stages of group development.

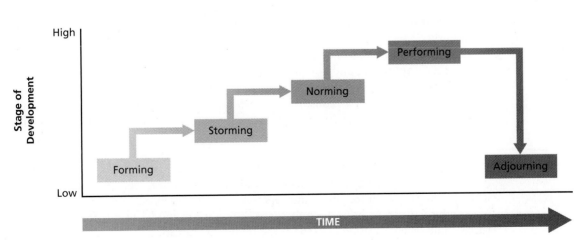

Norming. At this stage, members resolve the issues that provoked the storming, and they develop social consensus. Compromise is often necessary. Interdependence is recognized, norms are agreed to, and the group becomes more cohesive (we will study these processes later). Information and opinions flow freely.

Performing. With its social structure sorted out, the group devotes its energies toward task accomplishment. Achievement, creativity, and mutual assistance are prominent themes of this stage.

Adjourning. Some groups, such as task forces and design project teams, have a definite life span and disperse after achieving their goals. Also, some groups disperse when corporate layoffs and downsizing occur. At this adjourning stage, rites and rituals that affirm the group's previous successful development are common (such as ceremonies and parties). Members often exhibit emotional support for each other.[3]

The stages model is a good tool for monitoring and troubleshooting how groups are developing. However, not all groups go through these stages of development. The process applies mainly to new groups that have never met before. Well-acquainted task forces and committees can short-circuit these stages when they have a new problem to work out.[4] Also, some organizational settings are so structured that storming and norming are unnecessary for even strangers to coalesce into a team. For example, most commercial airline cockpit crews perform effectively even though they can be made up of virtual strangers who meet just before takeoff.[5]

Punctuated Equilibrium

When groups have a specific deadline by which to complete some problem-solving task, we can often observe a very different development sequence from that described above. Connie Gersick, whose research uncovered this sequence, describes it as a **punctuated equilibrium model** of group development.[6] *Equilibrium* means stability, and the research revealed apparent stretches of group stability punctuated by a critical first meeting, a midpoint change in group activity, and a rush to task completion. Along with many real-world work groups, Gersick studied student groups doing class projects, so see if this sequence of events sounds familiar to you.

> **Punctuated equilibrium model.** A model of group development that describes how groups with deadlines are affected by their first meetings and crucial midpoint transitions.

Phase 1. Phase 1 begins with the first meeting and continues until the midpoint in the group's existence. The very first meeting is critical in setting the agenda for what will happen in the remainder of this phase. Assumptions, approaches, and precedents that members develop in the first meeting end up dominating the first half of the group's life. Although it gathers information and holds meetings, the group makes little visible progress toward the goal.

Midpoint Transition. The midpoint transition occurs at almost exactly the halfway point in time toward the group's deadline. For instance, if the group has a two-month deadline, the transition will occur at about one month. The transition marks a change in the group's approach, and how the group manages it is critical for the group to show progress. The need to move forward is apparent, and the group may seek outside advice. This transition may consolidate previously acquired information or even mark a completely new approach, but it crystallizes the group's activities for Phase 2 just like the first meeting did for Phase 1.

Phase 2. For better or for worse, decisions and approaches adopted at the midpoint get played out in Phase 2. It concludes with a final meeting that reveals a burst of activity and a concern for how outsiders will evaluate the product.

Exhibit 7.2 shows how the punctuated equilibrium model works for groups that successfully or unsuccessfully manage the midpoint transition.

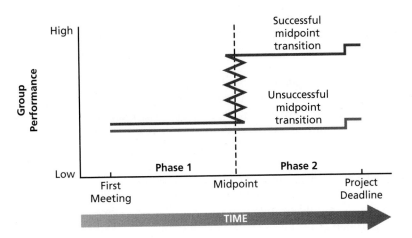

EXHIBIT 7.2
The punctuated equilibrium model of group development for two groups.

What advice does the punctuated equilibrium model offer for managing product development teams, advertising groups, or class project groups?[7]

- Prepare carefully for the first meeting. What is decided here will strongly determine what happens in the rest of Phase 1. If you are the coach or advisor of the group, stress *motivation and excitement* about the project.

- As long as people are working, do not look for radical progress during Phase 1.

- Manage the midpoint transition carefully. Evaluate the strengths and weaknesses of the ideas that people generated in Phase 1. Clarify any questions with whoever is commissioning your work. Recognize that a fundamental change in approach must occur here for progress to occur. Essential issues are not likely to "work themselves out" during Phase 2. At this point, a group coach should focus on the *strategy* to be used in Phase 2.

- Be sure that adequate resources are available to actually execute the Phase 2 plan.

- Resist deadline changes. These could damage the midpoint transition.

As noted, the concept of punctuated equilibrium applies to groups with deadlines. Such groups might also exhibit some of the stages of development noted earlier, with a new cycle of storming and norming following the midpoint transition.

GROUP STRUCTURE AND ITS CONSEQUENCES

Group structure refers to the characteristics of the stable social organization of a group—the way a group is "put together." The most basic structural characteristics along which groups vary are size and member diversity. Other structural characteristics are the expectations that members have about each other's behaviour (norms), agreements about "who does what" in the group (roles), the rewards and prestige allocated to various group members (status), and how attractive the group is to its members (cohesiveness).

Group Size

Of one thing we can be certain—the smallest possible group consists of two people, such as a manager and a particular employee. It is possible to engage in much theoretical nitpicking about just what constitutes an upper limit on group size. However, given the definition of group that we presented earlier, it would seem that congressional or parliamentary size (300 to 400 members) is somewhere close to this limit. In practice, most work groups, including task forces and committees, usually have between 3 and 20 members.

Size and Satisfaction. The more the merrier? In theory, yes. In fact, however, members of larger groups rather consistently report less satisfaction with group membership than those who find themselves in smaller groups.[8] What accounts for this apparent contradiction?

For one thing, as opportunities for friendship increase, the chance to work on and develop these opportunities might decrease owing to the sheer time and energy required. In addition, in incorporating more members with different viewpoints, larger groups might prompt conflict and dissension, which work against member satisfaction. As group size increases, the time available for verbal participation by each member decreases. Also, many people are inhibited about participating in larger groups.[9] Finally, in larger groups, individual members identify less easily with the success and accomplishments of the group. For example, a particular member of a four-person cancer research team should be able to identify his or her personal contributions to a research breakthrough more easily than a member of a 20-person team can.

Size and Performance. Satisfaction aside, do large groups perform tasks better than small groups? This question has great relevance to practical organizational decisions: How many people should a bank assign to evaluate loan applications? How many carpenters should a construction company assign to build a garage? If a school system decides to implement team teaching, how big should the teams be? The answers to these and similar questions depend on the exact task that the group needs to accomplish and on how we define good performance.[10]

Some tasks are **additive tasks.** This means that we can predict potential performance by adding the performances of individual group members together. Building a house is an additive task, and we can estimate potential speed of construction by adding the efforts of individual carpenters. Thus, for additive tasks, the potential performance of the group increases with group size.

Some tasks are **disjunctive tasks.** This means that the potential performance of the group depends on the performance of its *best member*. For example, suppose that a research team is looking for a single error in a complicated computer program. In this case, the performance of the team might hinge on its containing at least one bright, attentive, logical-minded individual. Obviously, the potential performance of groups doing disjunctive tasks also increases with group size because the probability that the group includes a superior performer is greater.

We use the term "potential performance" consistently in the preceding two paragraphs for the following reason: As groups performing tasks get bigger, they tend to suffer from process losses.[11] **Process losses** are performance difficulties that stem from the problems of motivating and coordinating larger groups. Even with good intentions, problems of communication and decision making increase with size—imagine 50 carpenters trying to build a house. Thus, actual performance = potential performance − process losses.

These points are summarized in Exhibit 7.3. As you can see in part (a), both potential performance and process losses increase with group size for additive and disjunctive tasks. The net effect is shown in part (b), which demonstrates that actual performance increases with size up to a point and then falls off. Part (c) shows that the *average* performance of group members decreases as size gets bigger. Thus, up to a point, larger groups might perform better as groups, but their individual members tend to be less efficient.

We should note one other kind of task. **Conjunctive tasks** are those in which the performance of the group is limited by its *poorest performer*. For example, an assembly-line operation is limited by its weakest link. Also, if team teaching is the technique used to train employees how to perform a complicated, sequential job, one poor teacher in the sequence will severely damage the effectiveness of the team. Both the potential and actual performance of conjunctive tasks would decrease as group size increases because the probability of including a weak link in the group goes up.

Additive tasks. Tasks in which group performance is dependent on the sum of the performance of individual group members.

Disjunctive tasks. Tasks in which group performance is dependent on the performance of the best group member.

Process losses. Group performance difficulties stemming from the problems of motivating and coordinating larger groups.

Conjunctive tasks. Tasks in which group performance is limited by the performance of the poorest group member.

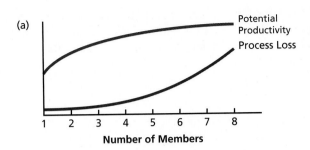

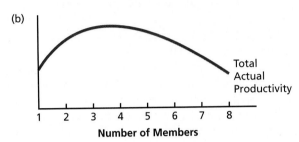

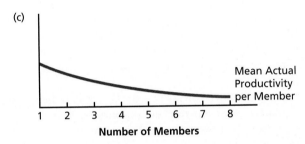

EXHIBIT 7.3
Relationships among group size, productivity, and process losses.

Source: From Steiner, I.D. (1972). *Group process and productivity.* New York: Academic Press, p. 96. Copyright © 1972, by Harcourt Brace Jovanovich, Inc., reprinted by permission of the publisher and the author.

In summary, for additive and disjunctive tasks, larger groups might perform better up to a point, but at increasing costs to the efficiency of individual members. By any standard, performance on purely conjunctive tasks should decrease as group size increases.

Diversity of Group Membership

Imagine an eight-member product development task force composed exclusively of 30-something white males of basically Western European heritage. Then imagine another task force with 50 percent men and 50 percent women, from eight different ethnic or racial backgrounds, and an age range from 25 to 55. The first group is obviously homogeneous in its membership, while the latter is heterogeneous or diverse. Which task force do you think would develop more quickly as a group? Which would be most creative?

Group diversity has a strong impact on interaction patterns—more diverse groups have a more difficult time communicating effectively and becoming cohesive (we will study cohesiveness in more detail shortly).[12] This means that diverse groups might tend to take longer to do their forming, storming, and norming.[13] Once they do develop, more and less diverse groups are equally cohesive and productive.[14] However, diverse groups sometimes perform better when the task requires cognitive, creativity-demanding tasks and problem solving rather than more routine work because members consider a broader array of ideas.[15] In general, any negative effects of "surface diversity" in age, gender, or race seem to wear off over time. However, "deep diversity" in attitudes toward work or how to accomplish a goal can badly damage cohesiveness.[16]

All this speaks well for the concepts of valuing and managing diversity, which we discussed in Chapter 3. When management values and manages diversity, it offsets some of the initial process loss costs of diversity and capitalizes on its benefits for group performance.

Group Norms

Norms. Collective expectations that members of social units have regarding the behaviour of each other.

Social **norms** are collective expectations that members of social units have regarding the behaviour of each other. As such, they are codes of conduct that specify what individuals ought and ought not to do and standards against which we evaluate the appropriateness of behaviour.

Much normative influence is unconscious, and we are often aware of such influence only in special circumstances, such as when we see children struggling to master adult norms or international visitors sparring with the norms of our culture. We also become conscious of norms when we encounter ones that seem to conflict with each other ("Get ahead," but "Don't step on others") or when we enter new social situations. For instance, the first day on a new job, workers frequently search for cues about what is considered proper office etiquette: Should I call the boss "mister"? Can I personalize my work space?

Norm Development. *Why* do norms develop? The most important function that norms serve is to provide regularity and predictability to behaviour. This consistency provides important psychological security and permits us to carry out our daily business with minimal disruption.

What do norms develop *about*? Norms develop to regulate behaviours that are considered at least marginally important to their supporters. For example, managers are more likely to adopt norms regarding the performance and attendance of employees than norms concerning how employees personalize and decorate their offices. In general, less deviation is accepted from norms that concern more important behaviours.

How do norms develop? As we discussed in Chapter 4, individuals develop attitudes as a function of a related belief and value. In many cases, their attitudes affect their behaviour. When the members of a group *share* related beliefs and values, we can expect them to share consequent attitudes. These shared attitudes then form the basis for norms.[17] Notice that it really does not make sense to talk about "my personal norm." Norms are *collectively* held expectations, depending on two or more people for their existence.

Why do individuals tend to comply with norms? Much compliance occurs simply because the norm corresponds to privately held attitudes. In addition, even when norms support trivial social niceties (such as when to shake hands or when to look serious), they often save time and prevent social confusion. Most interesting, however, is the case in which individuals comply with norms that *go against* their privately held attitudes and opinions. For example, couples without religious convictions frequently get married in religious services, and people who hate neckties often wear them to work. In short, groups have an extraordinary range of rewards and punishments available to induce conformity to norms. In the next chapter, we will examine this process in detail.

Some Typical Norms. There are some classes of norms that seem to crop up in most organizations and affect the behaviour of members. They include the following:

- *Dress norms.* Social norms frequently dictate the kind of clothing people wear to work.[18] Military and quasi-military organizations tend to invoke formal norms that support polished buttons and razor-sharp creases. Even in organizations that have adopted casual dress policies, employees often express considerable concern about what they wear at work. Such is the power of social norms.

- *Reward allocation norms.* There are at least four norms that might dictate how rewards, such as pay, promotions, and informal favours, could be allocated in organizations:

  a. Equity—reward according to inputs, such as effort, performance, or seniority.

  b. Equality—reward everyone equally.

  c. Reciprocity—reward people the way they reward you.

  d. Social responsibility—reward those who truly need the reward.[19]

  Officially, of course, most Western organizations tend to stress allocation according to some combination of equity and equality norms—give employees what they deserve, and no favouritism.

- *Performance norms.* The performance of organizational members might be as much a function of social expectations as it is of inherent ability, personal motivation, or technology.[20] Work groups provide their members with potent cues about what an appropriate level of performance is. New group members are alert for these cues: Is it all right to take a break now? Under what circumstances can I be absent from work without being punished? (See "Research Focus: *Absence Cultures—Norms in Action.*") The official organizational norms that managers send to employees usually favour high performance. However, work groups often establish their own informal performance norms, such as those that restrict productivity under a piece-rate pay system. The self-directed warehouse and mill groups at Ralston Foods, which are tougher disciplinarians than groups with conventional leaders, are clear exceptions.

Roles

Roles are positions in a group that have a set of expected behaviours attached to them. Thus, roles represent "packages" of norms that apply to particular group members. As we implied in the previous section, many norms apply to all group members to be sure that they engage in *similar* behaviours (such as restricting productivity or dressing a certain way). However, the development of roles is indicative of the fact that group members might also be required to act *differently* from one another. For example, in a committee meeting, not every member is required to function as a secretary or a chairperson, and these become specific roles that are fulfilled by particular people.

In organizations, we find two basic kinds of roles. *Designated* or *assigned roles* are formally prescribed by an organization as a means of dividing labour and responsibility to facilitate task achievement. In general, assigned roles indicate "who does what" and "who can tell others what to do." In a software firm, labels that we might apply to formal roles include president, software engineer, analyst, programmer, and sales manager. In addition to assigned roles, we invariably see the development of *emergent roles*. These are roles that develop naturally to meet the social-emotional needs of group members or to assist in formal job accomplishment. The class clown and the office gossip fulfill emergent social-emotional roles, while an "old pro" might emerge to assist new group members learn their jobs. Other emergent roles might be assumed by informal leaders or by scapegoats who are the targets of group hostility.

Role Ambiguity. **Role ambiguity** exists when the goals of one's job or the methods of performing it are unclear. Ambiguity might be characterized by confusion about how performance is evaluated, how good performance can be achieved, or what the limits of one's authority and responsibility are.

Exhibit 7.4 shows a model of the process that is involved in assuming an organizational role. As you can see, certain organizational factors lead role senders (such as managers) to develop role expectations and "send" roles to focal people (such as

Roles. Positions in a group that have a set of expected behaviours attached to them.

Role ambiguity. Lack of clarity of job goals or methods.

RESEARCH FOCUS

Absence Cultures—Norms in Action

On first thought, you might assume that absenteeism from work is a very individualized behaviour, a product of random sickness or of personal job dissatisfaction. Although these factors contribute to absenteeism, there is growing evidence that group norms also have a strong impact on how much work people miss.

We can see cross-national differences in absenteeism. Traditionally, absence has been rather high in Scandinavia, lower in the United States and Canada, and lower yet in Japan and Switzerland. Clearly, these differences are not due to sickness, but rather to differences in cultural values about the legitimacy of taking time off work. These differences get reflected in work group norms.

Within the same country and company, we can still see group differences in absenteeism. A company that Gary Johns studied had four plants that made the same products and had identical human resources policies. Despite this, one plant had a 12 percent absence rate while another had an absence rate of 5 percent. Within one plant, some departments had virtually no absence while others approached a rate of 25 percent!

Moving to the small group level, Johns also studied small customer service groups in a utility company.

Despite the fact that all employees were doing the same work in the same firm, there were again striking cross-group differences in absenteeism, ranging from 1 to 13 percent.

These normative differences in absenteeism across groups are called *absence cultures*. How do they develop? People tend to adjust their own absence behaviour to what they see as typical of their group. Then, other factors come into play. In the utility company study, the groups that monitored each others' behaviour more closely had lower absence. A Canadian study found that air-traffic controllers traded off calling in sick so that their colleagues could replace them at double overtime. A UK study found that industrial workers actually posted "absence schedules" so that they could take time off without things getting out of hand! All these are examples of norms in action.

The norms underlying absence cultures can dictate presence as well as absence. Recent studies show that "presenteeism," coming to work when feeling unwell, is prevalent in many human services occupations.

Source: Some of the research bearing on absence cultures is described in Johns, G. (2003). How methodological diversity has improved our understanding of absenteeism from work. *Human Resource Management Review, 13*, 157–184.

employees). The focal person "receives" the role and then tries to engage in behaviour to fulfill the role. This model reveals a variety of elements that can lead to ambiguity.

- *Organizational factors.* Some roles seem inherently ambiguous because of their function in the organization. For example, middle management roles might fail to provide the "big picture" that upper management roles do. Also middle management roles do not require the attention to supervision necessary in lower management roles.

- *The role sender.* Role senders might have unclear expectations of a focal person. Even when the sender has specific role expectations, they might be ineffectively sent to the focal person. A weak orientation session, vague performance reviews, or inconsistent feedback and discipline may send ambiguous role messages to employees.

- *The focal person.* Even role expectations that are clearly developed and sent might not be fully digested by the focal person. This is especially true when he or she is new to the role. Ambiguity tends to decrease as length of time in the job role increases.[21]

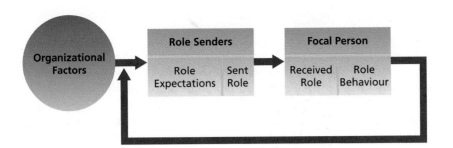

EXHIBIT 7.4
A model of the role
assumption process.

Source: Adapted from Katz, D., et al.
(1966, 1978). *The social psychology of
organizations.* New York: Wiley, p. 196.
Copyright © 1966, 1978, by John Wiley
& Sons, Inc. Reprinted by permission
of John Wiley & Sons, Inc.

What are the practical consequences of role ambiguity? The most frequent outcomes appear to be job stress, dissatisfaction, reduced organizational commitment, lowered performance, and intentions to quit.[22] Managers can do much to reduce unnecessary role ambiguity by providing clear performance expectations and performance feedback, especially for new employees and for those in more intrinsically ambiguous jobs.

Role Conflict. **Role conflict** exists when an individual is faced with incompatible role expectations. Conflict can be distinguished from ambiguity in that role expectations might be crystal clear but incompatible in the sense that they are mutually exclusive, cannot be fulfilled simultaneously, or do not suit the role occupant.

- **Intrasender role conflict** occurs when a single role sender provides incompatible role expectations to the role occupant. For example, a manager might tell an employee to take it easy and not work so hard, while delivering yet another batch of reports that requires immediate attention. This form of role conflict seems especially likely to also provoke ambiguity.

- If two or more role senders differ in their expectations for a role occupant, **intersender role conflict** can develop. Employees who straddle the boundary between the organization and its clients or customers are especially likely to encounter this form of conflict. Intersender conflict can also stem exclusively from within the organization. The classic example here is the first-level manager, who serves as the interface between "management" and "the workers." From above, the manager might be pressured to get the work out and keep the troops in line. From below, he or she might be encouraged to behave in a considerate and friendly manner.

- Organizational members necessarily play several roles at one time, especially if we include roles external to the organization. Often, the expectations inherent in these several roles are incompatible, and **interrole conflict** results.[23] One person, for example, might fulfill the roles of a functional expert in marketing, head of the market research group, subordinate to the vice-president of marketing, and member of a product development task force. This is obviously a busy person, and competing demands for her time are a frequent symptom of interrole conflict.

- Even when role demands are clear and otherwise congruent, they might be incompatible with the personality or skills of the role occupant—thus, **person–role conflict** results.[24] Many examples of "whistle-blowing" are signals of person–role conflict. The organization has demanded some role behaviour that the occupant considers unethical.

As with role ambiguity, the most consistent consequences of role conflict are job dissatisfaction, stress reactions, lowered organizational commitment, and turnover intentions.[25] Managers can help prevent employee role conflict by avoiding self-contradictory messages, conferring with other role senders, being sensitive to multiple role demands, and fitting the right person to the right role.

Role conflict. A condition of being faced with incompatible role expectations.

Intrasender role conflict. A single role sender provides incompatible role expectations to a role occupant.

Intersender role conflict. Two or more role senders provide a role occupant with incompatible expectations.

Interrole conflict. Several roles held by a role occupant involve incompatible expectations.

Person–role conflict. Role demands call for behaviour that is incompatible with the personality or skills of a role occupant.

Status

Status. The rank, social position, or prestige accorded to group members.

Status is the rank, social position, or prestige accorded to group members. Put another way, it represents the group's *evaluation* of a member. Just *what* is evaluated depends on the status system in question. However, when a status system works smoothly, the group will exhibit clear norms about who should be accorded higher or lower status.

Formal Status Systems. All organizations have both formal and informal status systems. Since formal systems are most obvious to observers, let's begin there. The formal status system represents management's attempt to publicly identify those people who have higher status than others. It is so obvious because this identification is implemented by the application of *status symbols* that are tangible indicators of status. Status symbols might include titles, particular working relationships, pay packages, work schedules, and the physical working environment. Just what are the criteria for achieving formal organizational status? One criterion is often seniority in one's work group. Employees who have been with the group longer might acquire the privilege of choosing day shift work or a more favourable office location. Even more important than seniority, however, is one's assigned role in the organization—one's job. Because they perform different jobs, secretaries, labourers, managers, and executives acquire different statuses. Organizations often go to great pains to tie status symbols to assigned roles.

Why do organizations go to all this trouble to differentiate status? For one thing, status and the symbols connected to it serve as powerful magnets to induce members to aspire to higher organizational positions (recall Maslow's need for self-esteem). Second, status differentiation reinforces the authority hierarchy in work groups and in the organization as a whole, since people *pay attention* to high-status individuals.

Informal Status Systems. In addition to formal status systems, one can detect informal status systems in organizations. Such systems are not well advertised, and they might lack the conspicuous symbols and systematic support that people usually accord the formal system. Nevertheless, they can operate just as effectively. Sometimes, job performance is a basis for the acquisition of informal status. The "power hitters" on a baseball team or the "cool heads" in a hospital emergency unit might be highly evaluated by co-workers for their ability to assist in task accomplishment. Some managers who perform well early in their careers are identified as "fast trackers" and given special job assignments that correspond to their elevated status. Just as frequently, though, informal status is linked to factors other than job performance, such as gender or race. For example, the man who takes a day off work to care for a sick child may be praised as a model father. The woman who does the same may be questioned about her work commitment.

Consequences of Status Differences. Status differences have a paradoxical effect on communication patterns. Most people like to communicate with others at their own status or higher, rather than with people who are below them.[26] The result should be a tendency for communication to move up the status hierarchy. However, if status differences are large, people can be inhibited from communicating upward. These opposing effects mean that much communication gets stalled.

Status also affects the amount of various group members' communication and their influence in group affairs. As you might guess, higher-status members do more talking and have more influence.[27] Some of the most convincing evidence comes from studies of jury deliberations, in which jurors with higher social status (such as managers and professionals) participate more and have more effect on the verdict.[28] Unfortunately, there is no guarantee that the highest-status person is the most knowledgeable about the problem at hand!

Reducing Status Barriers. Although status differences can be powerful motivators, their tendency to inhibit the free flow of communication has led many organizations to downplay status differentiation by doing away with questionable status symbols. The goal is to foster a culture of teamwork and cooperation across the ranks. The high-tech culture of Silicon Valley has always been pretty egalitarian and lacking in conspicuous status symbols, but even old-line industries are getting on the bandwagon. For example at GM's Saturn plant, the big boss wears the same gear as the line workers, and the executive team at Levi Strauss & Co. wears examples of its own informal clothing line.[29]

GM Saturn
www.saturn.com

Levi Strauss & Co.
www.levistrauss.com

Some organizations employ phoney or misguided attempts to bridge the status barrier. Some examples of "casual Friday" policies (wearing casual clothes on Fridays) only underline status differences the rest of the week if no other cultural changes are made.

Many observers note that e-mail has levelled status barriers.[30] High-speed transmission, direct access, and the opportunity to avoid live confrontation often encourage lower-status parties to communicate directly with organizational VIPs. This has even been seen in the rank-conscious military.

GROUP COHESIVENESS

Group cohesiveness is a critical property of groups. Cohesive groups are those that are especially attractive to their members. Because of this attractiveness, members are especially desirous of staying in the group and tend to describe the group in favourable terms.[31]

Group cohesiveness. The degree to which a group is especially attractive to its members.

The arch-stereotype of a cohesive group is the major league baseball team that begins September looking like a good bet to win its division and make it to the World Series. On the field we see well-oiled, precision teamwork. In the clubhouse, all is sweetness and joviality, and interviewed players tell the world how fine it is to be playing with "a great bunch of guys."

Cohesiveness is a relative, rather than absolute, property of groups. While some groups are more cohesive than others, there is no objective line between cohesive and noncohesive groups. Thus, we will use the adjective *cohesive* to refer to groups that are more attractive than average for their members.

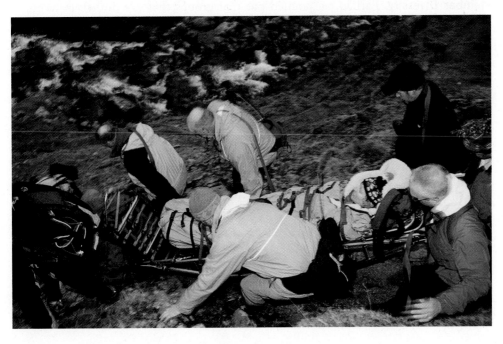

Cohesive groups lead to effective goal accomplishment.

Factors Influencing Cohesiveness

What makes some groups more cohesive than others? Important factors include threat, competition, success, member diversity, group size, and toughness of initiation.

Threat and Competition. External threat to the survival of the group increases cohesiveness in a wide variety of situations.[32] As an example, consider the wrangling, uncoordinated corporate board of directors that quickly forms a united front in the face of a takeover bid. Honest competition with another group can also promote cohesiveness.[33] This is the case with the World Series contenders.

Why do groups often become more cohesive in response to threat or competition? They probably feel a need to improve communication and coordination so that they can better cope with the situation at hand. Members now perceive the group as more attractive because it is seen as capable of doing what has to be done to ward off threat or to win. There are, of course, limits to this. Under *extreme* threat or very *unbalanced* competition, increased cohesiveness will serve little purpose. For example, the partners in a firm faced with certain financial disaster would be unlikely to exhibit cohesiveness because it would do nothing to combat the severe threat.

Success. It should come as no surprise that a group becomes more attractive to its members when it has successfully accomplished some important goal, such as defending itself against threat or winning a prize.[34] By the same token, cohesiveness will decrease after failure, although there may be "misery loves company" exceptions. The situation for competition is shown graphically in Exhibit 7.5. Fit-Rite Jeans owns two small clothing stores (A and B) in a large city. To boost sales, it holds a contest between the two stores, offering $150 worth of merchandise to each employee of the store that achieves the highest sales during the next business quarter. Before the competition begins, the staff of each store is equally cohesive. As we suggested above, when competition begins, both groups become more cohesive. The members become more cooperative with each other, and in each store there is much talk about "us" versus "them." At the end of the quarter, store A wins the prize and becomes yet more cohesive. The group is especially attractive to its members because it has succeeded in the attainment of a desired goal. On the other hand, cohesiveness plummets in the losing store B—the group has become less attractive to its members.

Member Diversity. Earlier, we pointed out that groups that are diverse in terms of gender, age, and race can have a harder time becoming cohesive than more homogeneous groups. However, if the group is in agreement about how to accomplish some

EXHIBIT 7.5
Competition, success, and cohesiveness.

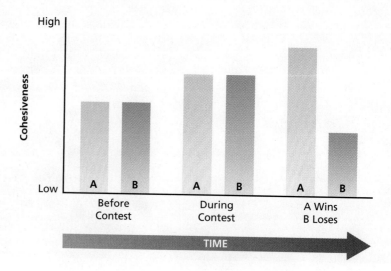

particular task, its success in performing the task will often outweigh surface dissimilarity in determining cohesiveness.[35] For example, one study found no relationship between cohesiveness and similarity of age or education for industrial work groups.[36] Another found that the cohesiveness of groups composed of African American and Caucasian southern soldiers was dependent on successful task accomplishment rather than racial composition.[37]

Size. Other things being equal, bigger groups should have a more difficult time becoming and staying cohesive. In general, such groups should have a more difficult time agreeing on goals and more problems communicating and coordinating efforts to achieve those goals. Earlier, we pointed out that large groups frequently divide into subgroups. Clearly, such subgrouping is contrary to the cohesiveness of the larger group.

Toughness of Initiation. Despite its rigorous admissions policies, the Harvard Business School does not lack applicants. Similarly, exclusive yacht and golf clubs might have waiting lists for membership extending several years into the future. All this suggests that groups that are tough to get into should be more attractive than those that are easy to join.[38] This is well known in the armed forces, where rigorous physical training and stressful "survival schools" precede entry into elite units, such as the Special Forces or the Rangers.

Consequences of Cohesiveness

From the previous section, it should be clear that managers or group members might be able to influence the level of cohesiveness of work groups by using competition or threat, varying group size or composition, or manipulating membership requirements. The question remains, however, as to whether *more* or *less* cohesiveness is a desirable group property. This, of course, depends on the consequences of group cohesiveness and who is doing the judging.

More Participation in Group Activities. Because members wish to remain in the group, voluntary turnover from cohesive groups should be low. Also, members like being with each other; therefore, absence should be lower than that exhibited by less cohesive groups. In addition, participation should be reflected in a high degree of communication within the group as members strive to cooperate with and assist each other. This communication might well be of a more friendly and supportive nature, depending on the key goals of the group.[39]

More Conformity. Because they are so attractive and coordinated, cohesive groups are well equipped to supply information, rewards, and punishment to individual members. These factors take on special significance when they are administered by those who hold a special interest for us. Thus, highly cohesive groups are in a superb position to induce conformity to group norms.

Members of cohesive groups are especially motivated to engage in activities that will *keep* the group cohesive. Chief among these activities is applying pressure to deviants to get them to comply with group norms. Cohesive groups react to deviants by increasing the amount of communication directed at these individuals.[40] Such communication contains information to help the deviant "see the light," as well as veiled threats about what might happen if he or she does not. Over time, if such communication is ineffective in inducing conformity, it tends to decrease. This is a signal that the group has isolated the deviant member to maintain cohesiveness among the majority.

More Success. Above, we pointed out that successful goal accomplishment contributes to group cohesiveness. However, it is also true that cohesiveness contributes to group success—in general, cohesive groups are good at achieving their goals. Research has found that group cohesiveness is related to performance.[41] Thus, there is a reciprocal relationship between success and cohesiveness.

Why are cohesive groups effective at goal accomplishment? Probably because of the other consequences of cohesiveness we discussed above. A high degree of participation and communication, coupled with active conformity to group norms and commitment, should ensure a high degree of agreement about the goals the group is pursuing and the methods it is using to achieve those goals. Thus, coordinated effort pays dividends to the group.

Since cohesiveness contributes to goal accomplishment, should managers attempt to increase the cohesiveness of work groups by juggling the factors that influence cohesiveness? To answer this question, we must emphasize that cohesive groups are especially effective at accomplishing *their own* goals. If these goals happen to correspond with those of the organization, increased cohesiveness should have substantial benefits for group performance. If not, organizational effectiveness might be threatened. In fact, one study found that group cohesiveness was related to the productivity of paper-machine work crews that accepted the goals of the organization. Cohesiveness did not improve productivity in work crews that did not accept the goals of the organization.[42] One large-scale study of industrial work groups reached the following conclusions:

- In highly cohesive groups, the productivity of individual group members tends to be fairly similar to that of other members. In less cohesive groups there is more variation in productivity.

- Highly cohesive groups tend to be *more* or *less* productive than less cohesive groups, depending on a number of variables.[43]

These two facts are shown graphically in Exhibit 7.6. The lower variability of productivity in more cohesive groups stems from the power of such groups to induce conformity. To the extent that work groups have productivity norms, more cohesive groups should be better able to enforce them. Furthermore, if cohesive groups accept organizational norms regarding productivity, they should be highly productive. If cohesive groups reject such norms, they are especially effective in limiting productivity.

One other factor that influences the impact of cohesiveness on productivity is the extent to which the task really requires interdependence and cooperation among group

EXHIBIT 7.6
Hypothetical productivity curves for groups varying in cohesiveness.

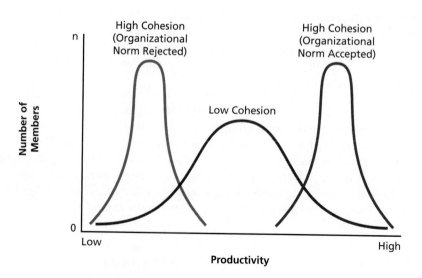

members (e.g., a football team versus a golf team). Cohesiveness is more likely to pay off when the task requires more interdependence.[44]

In summary, cohesive groups tend to be successful in accomplishing what they wish to accomplish. In a good labour relations climate, group cohesiveness on interdependent tasks should contribute to high productivity. If the climate is marked by tension and disagreement, cohesive groups might pursue goals that result in low productivity.

SOCIAL LOAFING

Have you ever participated in a group project at work or school in which you did not contribute as much as you could have because other people were there to take up the slack? Or have you ever reduced your effort in a group project because you felt that others were not pulling their weight? If so, you have been guilty of social loafing. **Social loafing** is the tendency that people have to withhold physical or intellectual effort when they are performing a group task.[45] The implication is that they would work harder if they were alone rather than part of the group. Earlier we said that process losses in groups could be due to coordination problems or to motivation problems. Social loafing is a motivation problem.

People working in groups often feel trapped in a social dilemma, in that something that might benefit them individually—slacking off in the group—will result in poor group performance if everybody behaves the same way. Social loafers resolve the dilemma in a way that hurts organizational goal accomplishment. Notice that the tendency for social loafing is probably more pronounced in individualistic North America than in more collective and group-oriented cultures.

As the questions above suggest, social loafing has two different forms. In the *free rider effect*, people lower their effort to get a free ride at the expense of their fellow group members. In the *sucker effect*, people lower their effort because of the feeling that others are free riding, that is, they are trying to restore equity in the group. You can probably imagine a scenario in which the free riders start slacking off and then the suckers follow suit. Group performance suffers badly.

What are some ways to counteract social loafing?[46]

- *Make individual performance more visible.* Where appropriate, the simplest way to do this is to keep the group small in size. Then, individual contributions are less likely to be hidden. Posting performance levels and making presentations of one's accomplishments can also facilitate visibility.

- *Make sure that the work is interesting.* If the work is involving, intrinsic motivation should counteract social loafing.

- *Increase feelings of indispensability.* Group members might slack off because they feel that their inputs are unnecessary for group success. This can be counteracted by using training and the status system to provide group members with unique inputs (e.g., having one person master computer graphics programs).

- *Increase performance feedback.* Some social loafing happens because groups or individual members simply are not aware of their performance. Increased feedback, as appropriate, from the boss, peers, and customers (internal or external) should encourage self-correction. Group members might require assertiveness training to provide each other with authentic feedback.

- *Reward group performance.* Members are more likely to monitor and maximize their own performance (and attend to that of their colleagues) when the group receives rewards for effectiveness.

Social loafing. The tendency to withhold physical or intellectual effort when performing a group task.

WHAT IS A TEAM?

We began this chapter with a simple question: "What is a group?" Now you may be asking yourself, "What is a team?" Some writers have suggested that a team is something more than a group. They suggest that a group becomes a team when there exists a strong sense of shared commitment and when a synergy develops such that the group's efforts are greater than the sum of its parts.[47] While such differences might be evident in some instances, our definition of a group is sufficient to describe most teams that can be found in organizations. The term "team" is generally used to describe "groups" in organizational settings. Therefore, for our purposes in this chapter, we use the terms interchangeably.

In recent years, many organizations have, like Ralston, begun to use team-based work arrangements. Other well-known examples include GM's Saturn Plant, Rubbermaid, Xerox, Federal Express, and General Electric. Indeed, teams have become a major building block of organizations and are now quite common in North America.[48] The reasons for this vary, but in many cases it is an attempt to improve efficiency, quality, customer satisfaction, innovation, or the speed of production. Research has shown improvements in organizational performance in terms of both efficiency and quality as a result of team-based work arrangements.[49]

DESIGNING EFFECTIVE WORK TEAMS

The double-edged nature of group cohesiveness suggests that a delicate balance of factors dictates whether a work group is effective or ineffective. In turn, this raises the idea that organizations should pay considerable attention to how work groups are designed and managed. At first, the notion of designing a work group might seem strange. After all, don't work groups just "happen" in response to the demands of the organization's goals or technology? While these factors surely set some limits on how groups are organized and managed, organizations are finding that there is still plenty of scope for creativity in work group design.

A good model for thinking about the design of effective work groups is to consider a successful sports team, whether professional or amateur. In most cases, such teams are small groups made up of highly skilled individuals who are able to meld these skills into a cohesive effort. The task they are performing is intrinsically motivating and provides very direct feedback. If there are status differences on the team, the basis for these differences is contribution to the team, not some extraneous factor. The team shows an obsessive concern with obtaining the right personnel, relying on tryouts or player drafts, and the team is "coached," not supervised. With this informal model in mind, let's examine the concept of group effectiveness more closely.

J. Richard Hackman of Harvard University (co-developer of the Job Characteristics Model, Chapter 6) has written extensively about work group effectiveness.[50] According to Hackman, a work group is effective when (1) its physical or intellectual output is acceptable to management and to the other parts of the organization that use this output, (2) group members' needs are satisfied rather than frustrated by the group, and (3) the group experience enables members to *continue* to work together.

What leads to group effectiveness? In colloquial language, "sweat, smarts, and style." More formally, Hackman notes that group effectiveness occurs when high effort is directed toward the group's task, when great knowledge and skill are directed toward the task, and when the group adopts sensible strategies for accomplishing its goals. And just how does an organization achieve this? As with Ralston Foods, there is growing awareness in many organizations that the answer is self-managed work teams.

Self-Managed Work Teams

Although the exact details vary tremendously, **self-managed work teams** generally provide their members with the opportunity to do challenging work under reduced supervision. Other labels that we often apply to such groups are autonomous, semiautonomous, and self-directed. The general idea, which is more important than the label, is that the groups regulate much of their own members' behaviour. Much interest in such teams was spurred by the success of teams in Japanese industry.

Critical to the success of self-managed teams are the nature of the task, the composition of the group, and the various support mechanisms in place.[51] Notice that many of the suggestions that follow should improve coordination and discourage social loafing.

Self-managed work teams. Work groups that have the opportunity to do challenging work under reduced supervision.

Tasks for Self-Managed Teams. Experts agree that tasks assigned to self-managed work teams should be complex and challenging, requiring high interdependence among team members for accomplishment. In general, these tasks should have the qualities of enriched jobs, which we described in Chapter 6. Thus, teams should see the task as significant, they should perform the task from beginning to end, and they should use a variety of skills. The point here is that self-managed teams have to have something useful to self-manage, and it is fairly complex tasks that capitalize on the diverse knowledge and skills of a group. Taking a bunch of olive stuffers on a food-processing assembly line, putting them in distinctive jumpsuits, calling them the Olive Squad, and telling them to self-manage will be unlikely to yield dividends in terms of effort expended or brainpower employed. The basic task will still be boring, a prime recipe for social loafing!

Outside the complexity requirement, the actual range of tasks for which organizations have used self-managed teams is wide, spanning both blue- and white-collar jobs. In the white-collar domain, complex service and design jobs seem especially conducive to self-management. Organizations such as 3M and Federal Express make extensive use of teams. At Federal Express, for example, self-managed back-office clerical teams are credited with improving billing accuracy and reducing lost packages for a savings of millions of dollars.[52]

Federal Express
www.fedex.com

In the blue-collar domain, Kodak, General Mills, GM's Saturn plant, and Chaparral Steel of Midlothian, Texas, make extensive use of self-managed work groups. In general, these groups are responsible for dividing labour among various subtasks as they see fit and making a variety of decisions about matters that impinge on the group. When a work site is formed from scratch and lacks an existing culture, the range of these activities can be very broad. Consider the self-managed teams formed in a new UK confectionery plant.

Production employees worked in groups of 8 to 12 people, all of whom were expected to carry out each of eight types of jobs involved in the production process. Group members were collectively responsible for allocating jobs among themselves, reaching production targets and meeting quality and hygiene standards, solving local production problems, recording production data for information systems, organizing breaks, ordering and collecting raw materials and delivering finished goods to stores, calling for engineering support, and training new recruits. They also participated in selecting new employees. Within each group, individuals had considerable control over the amount of variety they experienced by rotating their tasks, and each production group was responsible for one product line. Group members interacted informally throughout the working day but made the most important decisions—for example, regarding job allocation—at formal weekly group meetings where performance was also discussed.[53]

Motorola
www.motorola.com

If a theme runs through this discussion of tasks for self-managed teams, it is the breakdown of traditional, conventional, specialized *roles* in the group. Group members adopt roles that will make the group effective, not ones that are simply related to a narrow specialty. For another example of using self-managed teams, consider the You Be the Manager feature on teams at Motorola.

Composition of Self-Managed Teams. How should organizations assemble self-managed teams to ensure effectiveness? "Stable, small, and smart" might be a fast answer.[54]

- *Stability.* Self-managed teams require considerable interaction and high cohesiveness among their members. This, in turn, requires understanding and trust. To achieve this, group membership must be fairly stable. Rotating members into and out of the group will cause it to fail to develop a true group identity.[55]

- *Size.* In keeping with the demands of the task, self-managed teams should be as small as is feasible. The goal here is to keep coordination problems and social loafing to a minimum. These negative factors can be a problem for all groups, but they can be especially difficult for self-managed groups. This is because reduced supervision means that there is no boss to coordinate the group's activities and search out social loafers who do not do their share of the work.

- *Expertise.* It goes without saying that group members should have a high level of expertise about the task at hand. Everybody does not have to know everything, but the group as a *whole* should be very knowledgeable about the task. Again, reduced supervision discourages "running to the boss" when problems arise, but the group must have the resources to successfully solve these problems. One set of skills that all members should probably possess to some degree is *social skills.* Understanding how to talk things out, communicate effectively, and resolve conflict is especially important for self-managed groups.

- *Diversity.* Put simply, a team should have members who are similar enough to work well together and diverse enough to bring a variety of perspectives and skills to the task at hand. A product planning group consisting exclusively of new, male MBAs might work well together but lack the different perspectives that are necessary for creativity.

One way of maintaining appropriate group composition might be to let the group choose its own members, as occurred at the confectionery plant we described above. In the GM Saturn start-up, a panel of union and management members evaluated applications for all blue- and white-collar jobs, paying particular attention to social skills.[56] A potential problem with having a group choose its own members is that the group might use some irrelevant criterion (such as race or gender) to unfairly exclude others. Thus, human resources department oversight is necessary, as are very clear selection criteria (in terms of behaviours, skills, and credentials). The selection stage is critical, since some studies (including the one conducted in the confectionery plant) have shown elevated turnover in self-managed teams.[57] "Fit" is important and well worth expending the extra effort to find the right people.

The theme running through this discussion of team composition favours *high cohesiveness* and the development of group *norms* that stress group effectiveness.

Supporting Self-Managed Teams. A number of support factors can assist self-managed teams in becoming and staying effective. Reports of problems with teams can usually be traced back to inadequate support.

- *Training.* In almost every conceivable instance, members of self-managed teams will require extensive training. At Saturn, for example, new workers receive five full

YOU BE THE
Manager

Teams at Motorola

Motorola is a world leader in cell phone manufacturing and wireless communications with additional activities in satellite and microwave communications equipment. A few years ago, Motorola discovered that a part-testing failure had disrupted the schedule and increased the cost of a previously successful manufacturing program. To correct the problem and attempt to reduce part defects, management decided to double the number of assemblers on the project. The logic was that many hands make light work, and that several heads and eyes are better than just a few. Did the increased size of the unit lead to the desired outcomes? In a word, no! In fact, things got worse. The new, additional people created tension and increased conflicts within the team, which resulted in more delays and a significant increase in costs.

Why did things get worse? Probably because the proposed solution did not get to the heart of the problem. At the time, Motorola used a traditional unit structure in which each production line group consisted of a project leader, a production leader, a group leader, and assemblers who built the products as directed. Under this arrangement, all of the responsibility for quality, production, and improvements were placed solely on the shoulders of the production manager. Assemblers could suggest an improvement, but this would be filtered through the group leader, who would decide if it was worth mentioning to the production manager. By the time problems were identified and consultation took place with production control and engineers, a week would usually pass before any corrective action could take place. It would take, on average, another week of testing and monitoring to verify if the proposed solutions actually worked.

Obviously, it is difficult to see how adding more assemblers could solve problems of quality and speed under this arrangement. The project leader turned to the section manager for advice on how to improve this wors-

Motorola implements self-managed teams to solve production problems.

ening situation. The section manager believed the way to solve the problems was by getting the people close to the action more involved. Could self-managed teams be the answer?

QUESTIONS

1. Comment on why increasing group size did not have the desired effect in reducing defects at Motorola.

2. How could a move to self-managed teams solve Motorola's parts defect problem?

To find out what Motorola did, see The Manager's Notebook at the end of the chapter.

Source: Adapted from B. Carroll. The self management payoff: Making ten years of improvements in one. *National Productivity Review, 19*, 61–67. © 2000 John Wiley & Sons. Reprinted with permission of John Wiley & Sons, Inc.

days of training. The kind of training depends on the exact job design and on the needs of the workforce. However some common areas include:

- *Technical training.* This might include math, computer use, or any tasks that a supervisor formerly handled. Cross-training in the specialties of other team-mates is common.

- *Social skills*. Assertiveness, problem solving, and routine dispute resolution are skills that help the team operate smoothly.

- *Language skills*. This can be important for ethnically diverse teams. Good communication is critical on self-managed teams.

- *Business training*. Some firms provide basic elements of finance, accounting, and production so that employees can better grasp how their team's work fits into the larger picture.

- *Rewards*. The general rule here is to try to tie rewards to team accomplishment rather than to individual accomplishment while still providing team members with some individual performance feedback. Microsoft's European product support group went from individual rewards to team-based rewards when it found that the former discouraged engineers from taking on difficult cases.[58] Gain sharing, profit sharing, and skill-based pay (Chapter 6) all seem to be compatible reward systems for a team environment. Skill-based pay, used at Ralston Foods, is especially attractive because it rewards the acquisition of multiple skills that can support the team. To provide individual performance feedback, some firms have experimented with peer (e.g., team member) performance appraisals. Many have also done away with status symbols that are unrelated to group effectiveness (such as reserved parking and dining areas).

- *Management*. Self-management will not receive the best support when managers feel threatened and see it as reducing their own power or promotion opportunities. Some schooled in the traditional role of manager may simply not adapt. Those who do can serve important functions by mediating relations *between* teams and by dealing with union concerns, since unions are often worried about the cross-functional job sharing in self-management. One study found that the most effective managers in a self-management environment encouraged groups to observe, evaluate, and reinforce their own task behaviour.[59] This suggests that coaching teams to be independent enhances their effectiveness.[60]

Michael Campion and his colleagues have studied team characteristics and group effectiveness in teams of professional and nonprofessional workers.[61] Their results provide strong support for many of the relationships shown in Exhibit 7.7. For example, they found that task characteristics were related to most measures of group effectiveness, including productivity, team member satisfaction, and manager and employee judgments of group effectiveness. Group composition characteristics were related to only a few of the effectiveness measures. In particular, teams perceived as too large for their tasks were rated as less effective than teams perceived as an appropriate

EXHIBIT 7.7

Factors influencing work group effectiveness.

Source: Based in part on Hackman, J.R. (1987). The design of work teams. In J.W. Lorsch (Ed.), *Handbook of organizational behavior*. Englewood Cliffs, NJ: Prentice-Hall.

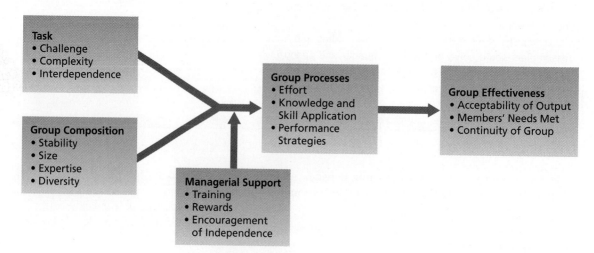

size or too small. Managerial support was related to many of the measures of effectiveness and was found to be one of the best predictors of group performance in another recent study.[62] Campion and colleagues found that group processes were the best predictors of group effectiveness, which is consistent with Exhibit 7.7. Overall, research has shown improvements in team productivity, quality, customer satisfaction, and safety following the implementation of self-managed work teams.[63]

Finally, in keeping with some of the issues introduced in earlier chapters, you might be wondering what role values play in the use and effectiveness of self-managed work teams in different cultures. To find out, check out "Global Focus: *Diversity on Multicultural Self-Managed Work Teams*."

Cross-Functional Teams

Let's look at another kind of team that contemporary organizations are using with increasing frequency. **Cross-functional teams** bring people with different functional specialties together to better invent, design, or deliver a product or service.

A cross-functional team might be self-managed and permanent if it is doing a recurrent task that is not too complex. For example, UPS has multiskilled sales teams that sell and deliver products and services. If the task is complex and unique (such as designing a car), cross-functional teams require formal leadership, and their lives will generally be limited to the life of the specific project. In both cases, the "cross-functional" label means such diverse specialties are necessary so that cross-training is not feasible. People have to be experts in their own area but able to cooperate with others.

Cross-functional teams, which have been used in service industries such as banking and hospitals, are probably best known for their successes in product development.[64] Thus, Rubbermaid uses teams to invent and design a remarkable variety of innovative household products. Similarly, Thermos used a team to invent a very successful ecologically friendly electric barbecue grill. It sped to the market in record time.

The general goals of using cross-functional teams include some combination of innovation, speed, and quality that come from early coordination among the various specialties. We can see their value by looking at the traditional way auto manufacturers designed cars in North America.[65] First, stylists determined what the car would look like and then passed their design on to engineering, which developed mechanical specifications and blueprints. In turn, manufacturing considered how to construct what the stylists and engineers designed. Somewhere down the line, marketing and accounting got their say. This process invariably leads to problems. One link in the chain might have a difficult time understanding what the previous link meant. Worse, one department might resist the ideas of another simply because they "were not invented here." The result of all this is slow, expensive development and early quality problems. In contrast, the cross-functional approach gets all the specialties working together from day one. A complex project, such as a car design, might have over 30 cross-functional teams working at the same time. Particular beneficiaries have been the Dodge Viper sports car and Ford's Mustang. Even venerable Rolls-Royce is using such teams.

The speed factor can be dramatic. Manufacturers have reduced the development of a new car model by several years. Boeing used a cross-functional team to reduce certain design analyses from two weeks to only a few minutes.

Principles for Effectiveness. Research has discovered a number of factors that contribute to the effectiveness of cross-functional teams.[66]

- *Composition.* All relevant specialties are obviously necessary, and effective teams are sure not to overlook anyone. Auto companies put labour representatives on car design teams to warn of assembly problems. On the Mustang and Thermos projects, the companies included outside suppliers.

Cross-functional teams.
Work groups that bring people with different functional specialties together to better invent, design, or deliver a product or service.

Rubbermaid
www.rubbermaid.com

Thermos
www.thermos.com

Ford Mustang
www.fordvehicles.com/cars/mustang

GLOBAL FOCUS

Diversity on Multicultural Self-Managed Work Teams

Over the last several decades, companies have turned to self-managed work teams (SMWTs) to accomplish important tasks and solve organizational problems. For managers and researchers alike, the issue of how to assemble a strong team has been of great interest. The advent of the global economy has added a new question concerning successful team composition: How can managers build an effective team made up of individuals from different cultures? Furthermore, since various cultures can be represented in a single country, this question not only concerns multinational teams, but within-nation teams made up of individuals with different cultural values.

Researchers Bradley Kirkman and Debra Shapiro undertook a study to assess how cultural diversity affects SMWT performance. Instead of simply using nationality as a measure of culture, Kirkman and Shapiro measured cultural values directly to capture within-country differences. They believed that diversity in cultural values would be more important for team performance than how high a team scored on a particular value. They also believed that diversity on various cultural values would affect performance differently in different countries, depending on their dominant cultural orientation. To test these beliefs, Kirkman and Shapiro studied 15 SMWTs in an American chemical firm and 19 SMWTs in an electronic component manufacturer in the Philippines, and assessed how cultural value diversity affected team performance. The cultural values considered included *collectivism* (the

extent to which people promote their group's welfare over their own personal welfare), *power distance* (the extent to which people value equality over status differentiation), *doing orientation* (the extent to which people prefer work activities to nonwork activities), and *determinism* (the extent to which individuals believe that one's fate is determined by forces beyond his or her control).

What did they find? Cultural diversity measured directly had a greater impact on team performance than simple demographic (e.g., age, gender) diversity. They also found that diversity in cultural values within teams affected performance more than whether a team had an overall high or low score on a particular value. Finally, they found a different pattern of results concerning diversity and performance for the American teams versus the teams from the Philippines. For example, diversity on collectivism, power distance, and determinism had negligible or positive effects on performance on the Philippine teams, but negative effects on the US teams. Overall, the lessons for managers are that (a) cultural diversity on SMWTs is not automatically good or bad, (b) managers need to carefully consider cultural diversity issues when assembling a team, and (c) managers need to understand that diversity effects can vary across countries.

Source: Based on Kirkman, B.L., & Shapiro, D.L. (2005). The impact of cultural value diversity on multicultural team performance. *Advances in International Management (Managing Multinational Teams: Global Perspectives), 18,* 33–67.

Superordinate goals.
Attractive outcomes that can only be achieved by collaboration.

- *Superordinate goals.* **Superordinate goals** are attractive outcomes that can only be achieved by collaboration. They override detailed functional objectives that might be in conflict (e.g., finance versus design). On the Mustang project, the superordinate goal was to keep the legendary name alive in the face of corporate cost cutting.

- *Physical proximity.* Team members have to be located (sometimes relocated) close to each other to facilitate informal contact. Mustang used a former furniture warehouse in Allen Park, Michigan, to house its teams.

- *Autonomy.* Cross-functional teams need some autonomy from the larger organization, and functional specialists need some authority to commit their function to project decisions. This prevents meddling or "micromanaging" by upper level or functional managers.

- *Rules and procedures.* Although petty rules and procedures are to be avoided, some basic decision procedures must be laid down to prevent anarchy. On the Mustang project, it was agreed that a single manufacturing person would have a veto over radical body changes.

- *Leadership*. Because of the potential for conflict, cross-functional team leaders need especially strong people skills in addition to task expertise. The "tough engineer" who headed the Mustang project succeeded in developing his people skills for that task.

We will consider other material relevant to cross-functional teams when we cover conflict management and organizational design. Now, let's consider virtual teams.

Virtual Teams

With the increasing trends toward globalization and the rapid development of high-tech communication tools, a new type of team has emerged that will surely be critical to organizations' success for years to come: virtual teams. **Virtual teams** are work groups that use technology to communicate and collaborate across space, time, and organizational boundaries.[67] Along with their reliance on computer and electronic technology, the primary feature of these teams is the lack of face-to-face contact between team members due to geographic dispersion. This geographic separation often entails linkages across countries and cultures. Furthermore, virtual teams are often cross-functional in nature. Technologies used by virtual teams can be either asynchronous ones (e-mail, faxes, voice mail), which allow team members to reflect before responding, or synchronous ones (chat, groupware), through which team members communicate dynamically in real time. Although in the past they were only a dream, virtual teams are now spreading across the business landscape and are used by numerous companies such as Chevron, Sabre Inc., IBM, and Texas Instruments.

Virtual teams. Work groups that use technology to communicate and collaborate across time, space, and organizational boundaries.

Advantages of Virtual Teams. Why are these teams becoming so popular? Because managers are quickly learning that linking minds through technology has some definite advantages:

- *Around-the-clock work*. Globally, using a virtual team can create a 24-hour team that never sleeps. In these "follow the sun" teams, a team member can begin a process in London and pass it on to another team member in New York for more input. From New York, the work can be forwarded to a colleague in San Francisco who, after more work, can send it along to Hong Kong for completion.[68] In today's non-stop economy, the benefits of such continuous workflows are huge. For an example, see "Applied Focus: *The "Night Shift" in India Gives CAE's Montreal Engineers a Break*."

- *Reduced travel time and cost*. Virtual teaming reduces travel costs associated with face-to-face meetings. In the past, important meetings, key negotiation sessions, and critical junctures in projects required team members to board planes and travel long distances. In the virtual environment, expensive and time-consuming travel can be mostly eliminated. As such, virtual teams can lead to significant savings of time and money. In addition to these savings, security concerns over air travel also make virtual teams an attractive alternative.

- *Larger talent pool*. Virtual teams allow companies to expand their potential labour markets and to go after the best people, even if these people have no interest in relocating. The nature of virtual teams can also give employees added flexibility, allowing for a better work–life balance, which is an effective recruiting feature.[69]

Challenges of Virtual Teams. While the advantages highlighted above are appealing, many commentators have pointed out that virtual teams can also involve some disadvantages.[70] The lesson seems to be that managers must recognize that these teams

APPLIED FOCUS

The "Night Shift" in India Gives CAE's Montreal Engineers a Break

Before CAE Inc.'s aerospace engineers in Montreal shut down their computers and head home, they hit the send button to transfer files to India, all in the name of efficiency. In an effort to help boost productivity and speed delivery times for flight simulators, CAE hired 50 engineers in Bangalore 18 months ago. That trial in exchanging electronic files by e-mail has proven to be such a success that CAE is now in a hiring mode to soon double the number of staff in the Indian office to 100 employees. Overnight, as CAE engineers in Montreal sleep, their colleagues half a world away pore over intricate software programs in a process that has virtually created round-the-clock work flows.

"When the people in Montreal come into the office in the morning, the work has been completed," CAE chief executive officer Robert Brown said in an interview. "It's complementary from a time-zone point of view and certainly builds on efficiency." Mr. Brown emphasizes that the 1200 engineers at CAE's Montreal headquarters remain the company's core strength. But he adds that the Bangalore workers are valuable. He said they help troubleshoot, doing labour-intensive chores by revising and testing software that simulates the "visual reality" of piloting an array of aircraft.

CAE officials declined to comment on the wage scales in Canada and India. But some industry observers say there are large labour cost savings from farming out numerous duties to India, in addition to the productivity gains in the Montreal–Bangalore cooperative system.

Indian staff help build databases for visual systems. They also contribute to developing simulation software and testing software originating from Montreal. CAE's Montreal engineers understandably don't relish an overnight shift, so it's much more practical to have the Indian staff on "day duty" in Bangalore while Canadians get ready for bed, said Ted Larkin, an analyst with Orion Securities Inc. "The turnaround time is faster. This is a supplementary thing, a support effort," Mr. Larkin said.

The Montreal–Bangalore connection, along with various other manufacturing improvements, means that an Airbus A320 full-flight simulator now takes 14 months to build, compared with 20 months previously. Having the global high-tech link allows CAE to effectively benefit from two shifts, and on occasions when extended hours on both sides of the world are needed to complete a project, it's 24/7 treatment.

Source: Excerpted from Jang, B. (2006, May 23). The night shifter in India give CAE's Montreal engineers a break. *Globe and Mail*, B1, B2. Reprinted with permission from the *Globe and Mail*.

---

present unique challenges and should not simply be treated as regular teams that just happen to use technology.

- *Miscommunication.* The loss of face-to-face communication presents certain risks for virtual teams. Humans use many nonverbal cues to communicate meaning and feeling in a message. Using technology, the richness of face-to-face communication is lost and miscommunication can result (see Chapter 10). These risks can be particularly high on global virtual teams, as attempts at humour or the use of unfamiliar terms can be misconstrued. Some organizations like Chevron encourage global team members to avoid humour or metaphors when communicating online.[71]

Chevron Corporation
www.chevron.com

- *Trust.* Several commentators have noted that trust is difficult to develop between virtual team members. People typically establish trust through physical contact and socialization, which are simply not available to virtual team members.

- *Isolation.* People have needs for companionship. In self-contained offices, co-workers can meet for lunch, share stories, talk about their kids, and socialize outside of work. Unfortunately, these more casual interactions are not usually possible for virtual teams, a lack which can lead to team members having feelings of isolation and detachment.

- *High costs.* Savings in other areas such as travel must be weighed against the costs of cutting-edge technology. Initial set-up costs can be substantial. Budgets must also be devoted to maintenance since, in the virtual environment, the firm's technology must run flawlessly, 24 hours a day, 7 days a week.

- *Management issues.* For managers, virtual teams can create new challenges in terms of dealing with subordinates who are no longer in view. How can you assess individual performance, monitor diligence, and ensure fairness in treatment when your team is dispersed around the globe?

Bradley Kirkman and colleagues studied 65 virtual teams at Sabre Inc., a leader in web-based travel reservations, and found that many of these challenges could be managed, and in some cases, turned into opportunities.[72] They found that trust, although developed differently than in face-to-face teams, was still possible through team member responsiveness, consistency, and reliability. Training and once-a-year team-building exercises in which members actually meet also build trust and clarify communication standards at Sabre. Furthermore, Kirkman and colleagues found that virtual communication reduced instances of stereotyping, discrimination, personality conflicts, and the formation of cliques, which often create problems in conventional work environments. Finally, in terms of performance assessments, the view at Sabre is that technology actually leads to more objective, transparent, and unbiased information being available to both employees and managers.

Sabre Inc.
www.sabretravelnetwork.com

Lessons Concerning Virtual Teams. Overall, a number of lessons are beginning to emerge about what managers must do or keep watch for when developing virtual teams.[73]

- *Recruitment.* Choose team members carefully in terms of attitude and personality so that they are excited about these types of teams and can handle the independence and isolation that often define them. Find people with good interpersonal skills, not just technical expertise.

- *Training.* Invest in training for both technical and interpersonal skills. At Sabre, cooperation and interpersonal skills were rated much higher in importance than technical skills by virtual team members.

- *Personalization.* Encourage team members to get to know each other, either through informal communication using technology or by arranging face-to-face meetings whenever possible. Reduce feelings of isolation by setting aside time for chit-chat, acknowledging birthdays, and so on.

- *Goals and ground rules.* On the management side, virtual team leaders should define goals clearly, set rules for communication standards and responses, and provide feedback to keep team members informed of progress and the big picture.

The key appears to be in recognizing the ways in which these teams are different than those based in a single office environment, but not falling into the trap of focusing solely on technology. Many of the general recommendations that apply to any work team also apply to virtual teams. These teams are still made up of individuals who have the same feelings and needs as workers in more traditional environments. Virtual teams must be real teams, if not by location, then in mind and spirit.

A WORD OF CAUTION: TEAMS AS A PANACEA

Teams can be a powerful resource for organizations, and this chapter has identified some of the important lessons leading to team success. However, switching from a traditional structure to a team-based configuration is not a cure-all for an organization's problems, even though some managers fall prey to the "romance of teams."[74] It is likely that the research to date on teams has focused almost exclusively on viable, ongoing teams, with little attention being paid to failed or unsuccessful teams. Also, the emergence of many teams has been a result not of employee demand but of managers' desire for greater organizational returns. As such, some suggest that the team approach puts unwanted pressure and responsibilities on workers. Some observers have noted that many organizations have rushed to deploy teams with little planning, often resulting in confusion and contradictory signals to employees. Good planning and continuing support are necessary for the effective use of teams.[75]

 THE MANAGER'S

Notebook

Teams at Motorola

1. In the traditional work group structure at Motorola, the role of assembler consisted of building products. Given that the goal was to increase speed and improve quality, simply increasing the size of the group proved ineffective. As noted, the increase in size led to conflicts and problems among the group members, which in turn resulted in process losses. Coordinating and motivating this larger group became much more difficult. Furthermore, as the goal was speed and quality, the extra workers frustrated assemblers who tried to have their suggestions heard. The additional workers also put added stress on the group leader, who was responsible for filtering more suggestions, supervising and monitoring more employees, and dealing with more conflict. The production leader was faced with more problems from below and had little help in implementing the improvements that were ultimately his or her responsibility. Had the goal been to increase production, an increase in workers might have been appropriate, with the proper support; however, given that the focus was on speed and quality, adding workers was an ill-fated strategy leading to process losses.

2. By creating self-managed teams, organizations can challenge employees, empower them to go the extra mile, increase flexibility, and ultimately improve organizational performance. At Motorola, management decided that quality problems should be handled by those closest to the situation—the assembly workers. A five-year plan was implemented, and workers were trained to expand their skills and tackle problems at the source. Over time, layers of supervision and support staff were removed, and after three-and-a-half years the team was self-managed. Common titles eliminated functional barriers, team members rotated in attending the project leader's regular meetings, and the team met every morning to openly and honestly discuss problems and to work on solutions that could be implemented quickly. The team readily accepted its new responsibilities and the workers became excited, motivated, and energized. For Motorola, the benefits exceeded all expectations: The production cycle time fell from 22 weeks to 5, defects per million went from 750 to 22, and space needs were cut from 8000 square feet to 3500 while production increased. Time needed to install a new assembly component went from 4 days to 4 hours. In the new team structure, the section manager faded into the background and became more of an advisor, facilitator, and enabler. The roles of all the team members changed, and it became clear that the workers themselves were the best-equipped individuals to identify and solve problems.

LEARNING OBJECTIVES CHECKLIST

1. A *group* consists of two or more people interacting interdependently to achieve a common goal. *Formal work groups* are groups that organizations establish to facilitate the achievement of organizational goals. *Informal groups* are groups that emerge naturally in response to the common interests of organizational members.

2. Some groups go through a series of developmental stages: forming, storming, norming, performing, and adjourning. However, the *punctuated equilibrium model* stresses a first meeting, a period of little apparent progress, a critical midpoint transition, and a phase of goal-directed activity.

3. As groups get bigger, they provide less opportunity for member satisfaction. When tasks are *additive* (performance depends on the addition of individual effort) or *disjunctive* (performance depends on that of the best member), larger groups should perform better than smaller groups if the group can avoid *process losses* due to poor communication and motivation. When tasks are *conjunctive* (performance is limited by the weakest member), performance decreases as the group gets bigger, because the chance of adding a weak member increases. Diverse groups will generally develop at a slower pace and be less cohesive than homogeneous groups. While the effects of surface-level demographic diversity can wear off over time, deep diversity differences regarding attitudes are more difficult to overcome.

4. *Norms* are expectations that group members have about each other's behaviour. They provide consistency to behaviour and develop as a function of shared attitudes. In organizations, both formal and informal norms often develop to control dress, reward allocation, and performance. *Roles* are positions in a group that have a set of expected behaviours associated with them. *Role ambiguity* refers to a lack of clarity of job goals or methods. *Role conflict* exists when an individual is faced with incompatible role expectations, and it can take four forms: *intrasender, intersender, interrole,* and *person–role*. Both ambiguity and conflict have been shown to provoke job dissatisfaction, stress, and lowered commitment. *Status* is the rank or prestige that a group accords its members. Formal status systems use status symbols to reinforce the authority hierarchy and reward progression. Informal status systems also operate in organizations. Although status differences are motivational, they also lead to communication barriers.

5. *Cohesive groups* are especially attractive to their members. Threat, competition, success, and small size contribute to cohesiveness, as does a tough initiation into the group. The consequences of cohesiveness include increased participation in group affairs, improved communication, and increased conformity. Cohesive groups are especially effective in accomplishing their own goals, which may or may not be those of the organization.

6. *Social loafing* occurs when people withhold effort when performing a group task. This is less likely when individual performance is visible, the task is interesting, there is good performance feedback, and the organization rewards group achievement.

7. Members of *self-managed work teams* do challenging work under reduced supervision. For greatest effectiveness, such teams should be stable, small, well-trained, and moderately diverse in membership. Group-oriented rewards are most appropriate.

8. *Cross-functional teams* bring people with different functional specialties together to better invent, design, or deliver a product or service. They should have diverse membership, a *superordinate goal,* some basic decision rules, and reasonable autonomy. Members should work in the same physical location, and leaders require people skills as well as task skills.

9. *Virtual teams* use technology to communicate and collaborate across time, space, and organizational boundaries. These teams offer many advantages such as reduced travel costs, greater potential talent, and continuous workflows, but pose dangers in terms of miscommunication, trust, and feelings of isolation.

DISCUSSION QUESTIONS

1. Describe the kind of skills that you would look for in members of self-managed teams. Explain your choices. Do the same for virtual teams.

2. Debate: Effective teamwork is more difficult for individualistic Americans, Canadians, and Australians than for more collectivist Japanese.

3. When would an organization create self-managed teams? When would it use cross-functional teams? When would it employ virtual teams?

4. Suppose that a group of United Nations representatives from various countries forms to draft a resolution regarding world hunger. Is this an additive, disjunctive, or conjunctive task? What kinds of process losses would such a group be likely to suffer? Can you offer a prediction about the size of this group and its performance?

5. Explain how a cross-functional team could contribute to product or service quality. Explain how a cross-functional team could contribute to speeding up product design.

6. Mark Allen, a representative for an international engineering company, is a very religious person and an elder in his church. Mark's direct superior has instructed him to use "any legal means" to sell a large construction project to a foreign government. The vice-president of international operations had informed Mark that he could offer a generous "kickback" to government officials to clinch the deal, although such practices are illegal. Discuss the three kinds of role conflict that Mark is experiencing.

7. Some organizations have made concerted efforts to do away with many of the status symbols associated with differences in organizational rank. All employees park in the same lot, eat in the same dining room, and have similar offices and privileges. Discuss the pros and cons of such a strategy. How might such a change affect organizational communications?

8. You are an executive in a consumer products corporation. The president assigns you to form a task force to develop new marketing strategies for the organization. You are permitted to choose its members. What things would you do to make this group as cohesive as possible? What are the dangers of group cohesiveness for the group itself and for the organization of which the group is a part?

INTEGRATIVE DISCUSSION QUESTIONS

1. What role do perceptions play in group development? Refer to the perceptual process and biases in Chapter 3 and discuss the implications for each stage of group development. What are the implications for improving the development of groups?

2. How can groups be motivated? Consider the implications of each of the work motivation theories described in Chapter 5. What do the theories tell us about how to motivate groups?

ON-THE-JOB CHALLENGE QUESTION

ISE Communications was one of the pioneers in using self-managed work teams. The teams were put in place to improve manufacturing flexibility and customer service, both factors being crucial in the highly competitive circuit board industry. Its conversion from an assembly-line style of circuit board manufacturing to teams who identified with "their own" products and customers was deemed a great success by industry observers. One interesting result was that the teams were extremely obsessed with monitoring the promptness and attendance of their members, more so

than managers had been before the conversion to teams. They even posted attendance charts and created punishments for slack team members.

Use your understanding of both group dynamics and teams to explain why the employees became so concerned about attendance when they were organized into teams. What had changed?

Source: Barker, J.R. (1993). Tightening the iron cage: Concertive control in self-managing teams. *Administrative Science Quarterly, 38,* 408–437.

EXPERIENTIAL EXERCISE

NASA

The purpose of this exercise is to compare individual and group problem solving and to explore the group dynamics that occur in a problem-solving session. It can also be used in conjunction with Chapter 11. The instructor will begin by forming groups of four to seven members.

The situation described in this problem is based on actual cases in which men and women lived or died, depending on the survival decisions they made. Your "life" or "death" will depend on how well your group can share its present knowledge of a relatively unfamiliar problem, so that the group can make decisions that will lead to your survival.

The Problem

You are a member of a space crew originally scheduled to rendezvous with a mother ship on the lighted surface of the moon. Due to mechanical difficulties, however, your ship was forced to land at a spot some 200 miles from the rendezvous point. During landing, much of the equipment aboard was damaged, and, because survival depends on reaching the mother ship, the most critical items available must be chosen for the 200-mile trip. On the next page are listed the fifteen items left intact and undamaged after the landing. Your task is to rank them in terms of their importance to your crew in reaching the rendezvous point. In the first column (step 1) place the number 1 by the first most important, and so on, through number 15, the least important. You have fifteen minutes to complete this phase of the exercise.

After the individual rankings are complete, participants should be formed into groups having from four to seven members. Each group should then rank the fifteen items as a team. This group ranking should be a general consensus after a discussion of the issues, not

just the average of each individual ranking. While it is unlikely that everyone will agree exactly on the group ranking, an effort should be made to reach at least a decision that everyone can live with. It is important to treat differences of opinion as a means of gathering more information and clarifying issues and as an incentive to force the group to seek better alternatives. The group ranking should be listed in the second column (step 2).

The third phase of the exercise consists of the instructor providing the expert's rankings, which should be entered in the third column (step 3). Each participant should compute the difference between the individual ranking (step 1) and the expert's ranking (step 3), and between the group ranking (step 2) and the expert's ranking (step 3). Then add the two "difference" columns—the smaller the score, the closer the ranking is to the view of the experts.

From *Organization and People,* 3rd edition, by Ritchie. © 1984. Reprinted with permission of South-Western, a division of Thomson Learning: www.thomsonrights.com. Fax 800 730-2215.

Discussion

The instructor will summarize the results on the board for each group, including (a) the average individual accuracy score, (b) the group accuracy score, (c) the gain or loss between the average individual score and the group score, and (d) the lowest individual score (i.e., the best score) in each group.

The following questions will help guide the discussion:

1. As a group task, is the NASA exercise an additive, disjunctive, or conjunctive task?

2. What would be the impact of group size on performance in this task?

3. Did any norms develop in your group that guided how information was exchanged or how the decision was reached?

4. Did any special roles emerge in your group? These could include a leader, a secretary, an "expert," a critic, or a humorist. How did these roles contribute to or hinder group performance?

5. Consider the factors that contribute to effective self-managed teams. How do they pertain to a group's performance on this exercise?

6. How would group diversity help or hinder performance on the exercise?

NASA tally sheet

Items	Step 1 Your individual ranking	Step 2 The team's ranking	Step 3 Survival expert's ranking	Step 4 Difference between Step 1 & 3	Step 5 Difference between Step 2 & 3
Box of matches					
Food concentrate					
50 feet of nylon rope					
Parachute silk					
Portable heating unit					
Two .45 calibre pistols					
One case dehydrated milk					
Two 100-lb. tanks of oxygen					
Stellar map (of the moon's constellation)					
Life raft					
Magnetic compass					
5 gallons of water					
Signal flares					
First aid kit containing injection needles					
Solar-powered FM receiver-transmitter					
Total					

(The lower the score the better) | Your score | Team score |

CASE INCIDENT

The Group Assignment

Janet, a student, never liked working on group assignments; however, this time she thought it would be different because she knew most of the people in her group. But it was not long before things started going badly. After the first meeting, the group could not agree when to meet again. When they finally did agree to meet, nobody had done anything, and the assignment was due in two weeks. The group then agreed to meet again the next day to figure out what to do. However, two of the group members did not show up. The following week Janet tried in vain to arrange for another meeting, but the other group members said they were too busy, and that it would be best to divide the assignment up and have each member work on a section. The night before the assignment was due the group members met to give Janet their work. Finally, Janet thought, we are making progress. However, when she got home and read what the other members had written she was shocked at how bad it was. Janet spent the rest of the night and early morning doing the whole assignment herself. Once the course ended, Janet never spoke to any of the group members again.

1. Refer to the typical stages of group development and explain the development of Janet's group.

2. To what extent was group cohesiveness a problem in Janet's work group? What might have made the group more cohesive?

CASE STUDY

Levi Strauss & Co.'s Flirtation with Teams

Levi Strauss & Co. is the largest maker of brand-name clothing in the world. It has had a long history of being profitable, good to its workers, and charitable to its factory towns. Compared with other companies in the apparel industry, Levi Strauss had been known for generous wages and good working conditions. According to chairman Robert Haas, Levi's treatment of its workers and concern for their welfare is far greater than in other companies in the industry.

When other American apparel firms moved their manufacturing offshore, Levi Strauss & Co. maintained a large American manufacturing base and was often ranked as one of the best companies to work for. In fact, in 1997 the company received an award from the United Nations for improving global workplace standards.

Up until 1992, Levi's employees worked on their own operating machines in which they performed a single, specific, and repetitive task, such as sewing zippers or belt loops on jeans. Pay was based on a piece-rate system, in which workers were paid a set amount for each piece of work completed. A worker's productivity and pay was highly dependent on levels of skill, speed, and stamina.

By 1992, however, Levi Strauss & Company began to feel the pressure of overseas, low-cost competitors, and realized it needed to increase productivity and reduce costs to remain competitive and keep their North American plants open. The company decided that the best solution was teamwork. In a memo sent to workers, Levi's operations vice-president wrote, "This change will lead to a self-managed work environment that will reduce stress and help employees become more productive." Teamwork was felt to be a humane, safe, and profitable solution that would be consistent with the company's philosophy.

Under the new philosophy, gone was the old system of performing a single task all the time and the piece-rate system that went with it. Now groups of 10 to 50 workers shared the tasks and would be paid for the total number of trousers that the group completed. The team system was expected to lower the monotony of piecework by enabling workers to do different tasks and to therefore lower repetitive-stress injuries.

Although employees were given brief seminars and training on team building and problem solving, it was not long before problems began to arise. Top performers complained about their less skilled and slower teammates who caused a decline in their wages. Meanwhile, the wages of lower-skilled workers increased. Threats, insults, and group infighting became a regular part of daily work as faster workers tried to rid their group of slower workers. To make matters worse, top performers responded to their lower wages by reducing their productivity. Not surprisingly, employee morale began to deteriorate.

Another problem was that whenever a group member was absent or slow, the rest of the team had to make up for it. This exacerbated the infighting among team members and resulted in excessive peer pressure. In one instance, an enraged worker had to be restrained from throwing a chair at a team member who constantly harassed her about working too slowly, and in another incident, a worker threatened to kill a member of her team. An off-duty sheriff's deputy had to be placed at the plant's front entrance.

Because the groups had limited supervision, they had to resolve group problems on their own, and they also divided up the work of absent members themselves. In some plants, team members would chase each other out of the bathroom and nurse's station. Slower teammates were often criticized, needled, and resented by their group. Some could not take the resentment and simply quit. In one group, a member was voted off her team because she planned to have hand surgery.

And although workers were now part of a team system, management was not given guidance on how to implement the system. As a result, each manager had his or her own idea of how the team system should work, including team size, structure, pay formulas, and shop-floor layouts. One former production manager described the situation as worse than chaos and more like hell!

To make matters worse, the team system did not improve the situation for Levi's. Labour and overhead costs increased by up to 25 percent during the first years of the team system.

Efficiency, based on the quantity of pants produced per hour worked, dropped to 77 percent of pre-team levels. Although productivity began to improve, it is now only at 93 percent of the piecework level. Even in some of the company's best plants, production has fallen and remained at lower levels since the introduction of teams. And although one of the reasons for adopting the team system was to lower the high costs of injuries that resulted from workers pushing themselves to achieve piece-rate goals, these costs continued to rise in many plants even after the team approach was implemented.

Profit margins also began to decline as competitors began offering private-label jeans at two-thirds the price of Levi's, and Levi's market share of men's denim jeans in the United States fell from 48 percent in 1990 to 26 percent in 1997. As costs continued to increase, plant managers were warned that they would face an uncertain future unless they cut costs by 28 percent by the end of year.

Teams did, however, result in some improvements. For example, the average turnaround time of receiving an order and shipping it was reduced from nine to seven weeks. As well, because the teams were responsible for producing completed pairs of pants, there was less work-in-process at the end of each day compared with the piece-rate system, where each worker did only one part of the job. And according to Robert Haas, teams allowed workers to manage themselves and to find better and safer ways of working.

Nonetheless, the team system did not help Levi's achieve its objectives. In February 1997, then-CEO and current board chair Robert Haas announced that the company would cut its salaried workforce by 20 percent in the next 12 months. The following November, the company closed 11 factories in the United States and laid off 6395 workers. In an unusual response to being laid off, one worker described it as a "relief" from the burden and stress that had become part of her job.

Commenting on the team approach, a now-retired former manufacturing manager said, "We created a lot of anxiety and pain and suffering in our people, and for what?" According to a production manager who has taken early retirement, "It's just not the same company anymore. The perceived value of the individual and the concern for people just is not there." A veteran worker who had gone back to the old system of doing a single task and was now paid in part for what she produced said, "I hate teams. Levi's is not the place it used to be."

In February 1999, as sales of Levi's jeans continued to fall, the company let go another 5900 workers, or 30 percent of its workforce of 19 900 in the United States and Canada, and announced that it would close 11 of its remaining 22 plants in North America. According to company officials, plant closings might have been sooner and job losses greater if they had not adopted the team system. In 2003, due to substantial drops in net sales over the last three years, the company implemented more measures to recoup some of its losses, including closing 37 of its factories worldwide and instead using independent contract manufacturers. The company closed its remaining North American manufacturing facilities; its San Antonio operations closed at the end of 2003 and its three Canadian operations closed in March 2004. The closures affected some 2000 employees. The Canadian plants were considered among the most efficient in the company. As such, Levi Strauss & Co. now manufactures 100 percent of its jeans for the North American market outside of North America, compared with 15 percent in 1991, and none 20 years ago.

Sources: Gilbert, C. (1998, September). Did modules fail Levi's or did Levi's fail modules? *Apparel Industry Magazine*, 88–92; King, R.T., Jr. (1998, May 20). Levi's factory workers are assigned to teams and morale takes a hit. *Wall Street Journal*, A1, A6; Levi Strauss & Co. (2003, September 15). *Hoover's Company Capsules* (L), p. 40278. Retrieved September 30, 2003, from ProQuest database; McFarland, J. (1999, February 23). Levi Strauss slashes 5,900 jobs. *Globe and Mail*, B5; Paddon, D. (2003, September 26). Levi Strauss closing plants. *Montreal Gazette*, B2; Steinhart, D. (1999, February 23). Levi to shut plants in Cornwall, *U.S. Financial Post*, C1, C9.

1. Discuss the stages of group development and the implications of them for the development of the teams at Levi Strauss.

2. Discuss some of the norms that emerged in the teams. What was their function and how did they influence the behaviour of group members?

3. Discuss the role dynamics that emerged in the groups. Is there any evidence of role ambiguity or role conflict?

4. How cohesive were the groups at Levi Strauss? What factors contribute to the level of cohesiveness?

5. Analyze and evaluate the effectiveness of the teams using the concepts summarized in Exhibit 7.7.

6. The teams were supposed to be self-managing teams. Critique this idea in terms of the principles for effectiveness for such teams given in the text.

7. Do you think it was a good idea for Levi Strauss & Co. to implement a team system? Was it the best solution to deal with increased global competition? Why wasn't the team approach at Levi Strauss & Co. more effective, and with your knowledge of groups, what might you have done differently if you had to implement a team system at Levi Strauss?

8. What does the Levi Strauss experience tell us about the use of teams and their effectiveness?

CHAPTER 8

Social Influence, Socialization, and Culture

FAIRMONT HOTELS & RESORTS AND THE RITZ-CARLTON HOTEL COMPANY

Fairmont Hotels & Resorts and The Ritz-Carlton Hotel Company are two successful hotel chains with strong cultures and extensive orientation programs for new hires.

Fairmont Hotels & Resorts is the largest luxury hotel company in North America, with 26 000 employees. Their individual properties include bustling downtown hotels, luxury resorts, and historic landmarks. The key to Fairmont's success is its excellent customer service, which is all about making sure guests leave with lasting memories.

Individual Fairmont hotels are given some leeway in how to introduce the property and the work environment to new employees, but each orientation session covers certain basics.

Before their first day of orientation, new employees get a formal invitation to the hotel. On their first day, they get to experience the hotel as a guest would. At many Fairmont hotels, when new employees arrive, they are treated to valet parking. Then they are greeted by senior hotel management and served coffee and breakfast in one of the guest dining rooms. They have an informal discussion about various aspects of the hotel, and later they are served a meal or receive vouchers for an overnight stay. Finally, they are shown a welcome video from the executive.

On the second day, new employees engage in role-playing to prepare them for interactions with guests. The orientation trainers follow the company's customer service policies when interacting with the new employees: The new employees are treated like special guests, so they know first-hand how it feels to stay at the hotel.

Individual hotels come up with different ways to make employee training fun and to help new employees feel connected to the history and culture of their particular property. Some hotels engage new employees in friendly competition through scavenger hunts. Others provide tours connected to celebrities; for example, the room at the Queen Elizabeth Hotel in Montreal where John Lennon and Yoko Ono held their "Bed-in for

LEARNING OBJECTIVES

After reading Chapter 8, you should be able to:

1. Understand the difference between *information dependence* and *effect dependence*.

2. Differentiate *compliance, identification,* and *internalization* as motives for social conformity.

3. Describe the *socialization* process and the stages of organizational socialization.

4. Describe the implications of *unrealistic expectations* and the *psychological contract* for socialization.

5. Describe the main *methods of socialization* and how newcomers can be proactive in their socialization.

6. Define *organizational culture* and discuss the contributors to a culture.

7. Discuss the assets and liabilities of *strong organizational cultures*.

8. Describe how to diagnose an organizational culture.

Fairmont Hotels &
Resorts
www.fairmont.com

The Ritz-Carlton
www.ritzcarlton.com

Employees at Fairmont Hotels & Resorts learn about the company's history and culture through an extensive socialization program.

Peace." The Fairmont Banff Springs in Alberta provides a different kind of tour—of rooms that are said to be haunted by ghosts.

Of course employees need to learn about the corporate strategy, but when they learn about the stories and history of the hotel as well, they feel more connected to their workplace. And once they are working in the hotel, they can share this kind of background information with guests, making for a more interesting and unique hotel visit.

When new employees have been working at a Fairmont Hotels & Resorts property for two or three months, they participate in a third orientation: they are paired with a mentor they have chosen from among the more established staff. They also have an interview with a supervisor to identify career goals, talk about their experiences so far (including any problems), and receive feedback.

The Ritz-Carlton company, while smaller (with 59 hotels in 20 countries), is also very successful largely because of its customer service. The Ritz-Carlton recognizes that employees do not necessarily know how to provide great customer service when they first start, so teaching them this skill is priority.

The orientation program for new employees emphasizes company culture and company philosophy. As the company's Leadership Center vice-president puts it, "The most important thing for us is the depth of our culture. We are ladies and gentlemen serving ladies and gentlemen. And the entire company culture is based around this: If we are treated with respect and dignity and there is pride and joy in the workplace, the automatic human reaction is that we will turn around and make magic for the customers."

The company's philosophy is "You get the problem, you own it." Employees are taught to take personal responsibility for any problems they encounter and to deal with them promptly. The company's culture and philosophy combined result in great customer service, which is all about ensuring guests have a relaxing and stress-free stay.

Employees are reminded of the company culture, its credo, motto, and customer service ethic daily during the so-called daily line-ups—15-minute mandatory meetings that are held three times a day for each shift. During the line-up, company standards are reinforced and a speaker covers a daily script and speaks briefly about the importance of one of the 20 Basics. The line-ups also provide an opportunity to discuss any problems from the day before. These meetings help to emphasize the company's culture by reinforcing it each and every day.

Like Fairmont Hotels & Resorts, The Ritz-Carlton teaches by example. During the two-day orientation program, employees receive the same level of service as they would if they were a guest. New employees get a handwritten card welcoming them and are then asked to name their favourite snack, which is waiting for them when they take a break. During their orientation, new employees at The Ritz-Carlton use the same meeting rooms used by the guests and eat in the guest restaurant. New employees can take advantage of so-called interpreters, who will help them out during orientation. And at the end of the orientation, they are paired with a departmental trainer who mentors them for at least three weeks, longer if necessary.

During follow-up, employees are asked whether the job is living up to their expectations. The first follow-up happens at three weeks, and a second one happens at one year. At this time, the no-longer-new employees attend a ceremony during which they receive a pin to mark one year of service.

At both these hotels, customer service is not left to chance. It is central to these businesses' success and is, therefore, the focus of high-quality training and follow-up.[1]

This description of the orientation of new employees and the culture at Fairmont Hotels & Resorts and The Ritz-Carlton Hotel Company raises a number of interesting questions. Why do these companies spend so much time and effort on the orientation of new employees? Do employees actually accept the ideas and values that they encounter during their orientation? What is the effect of this type of orientation on employees' attitudes and behaviour? What does it mean to have a strong culture and how are cultures built and maintained? These are the kinds of questions that we will probe in this chapter.

First, we will examine the general issue of social influence in organizations—how members have an impact on each other's behaviour and attitudes. Social norms hold an organization together, and conformity to such norms is a product of social influence. Thus, the next section discusses conformity. Following this, we consider the elaborate process of organizational socialization, the learning of the organization's norms and roles. Socialization both contributes to and results from the organizational culture, the final topic that we will explore.

SOCIAL INFLUENCE IN ORGANIZATIONS

In the previous chapter, we pointed out that groups exert influence over the attitudes and behaviour of their individual members. As a result of social influence, people often feel or act differently from how they would as independent operators. What accounts for such influence? In short, in many social settings, and especially in groups, people are highly *dependent* on others. This dependence sets the stage for influence to occur.

Information Dependence and Effect Dependence

We are frequently dependent on others for information about the adequacy and appropriateness of our behaviour, thoughts, and feelings. How satisfying is this job of mine? How nice is our boss? How much work should I take home to do over the weekend? Should we protest the bad design at the meeting? Objective, concrete answers to such questions might be hard to come by. Thus, we must often rely on information that others provide.[2] In turn, this **information dependence** gives others the opportunity to influence our thoughts, feelings, and actions via the signals they send to us.[3]

Information dependence. Reliance on others for information about how to think, feel, and act.

Individuals are often motivated to compare their own thoughts, feelings, and actions with those of others as a means of acquiring information about their adequacy. The effects of social information can be very strong, often exerting as much or more influence over others as objective reality.[4]

As if group members were not busy enough tuning into information provided by the group, they must also be sensitive to the rewards and punishments the group has at its disposal. Thus, individuals are dependent on the *effects* of their behaviour as determined by the rewards and punishments provided by others. **Effect dependence** actually involves two complementary processes. First, the group frequently has a vested interest in how individual members think and act because such matters can affect the goal attainment of the group. Second, the member frequently desires the approval of the group. In combination, these circumstances promote effect dependence.

Effect dependence. Reliance on others due to their capacity to provide rewards and punishment.

In organizations, plenty of effects are available to keep individual members "under the influence." Managers typically have a fair array of rewards and punishments available, including promotions, raises, and the assignment of more or less favourable tasks. At the informal level, the variety of such effects available to co-workers is staggering. They might reward cooperative behaviour with praise, friendship, and a helping hand on the job. Lack of cooperation might result in nagging, harassment, name calling, or social isolation.

SOCIAL INFLUENCE IN ACTION

One of the most obvious consequences of information and effect dependence is the tendency for group members to conform to the social norms that have been established by the group. In the last chapter, we discussed the development and function of such norms, but we have postponed until now the discussion of why norms are supported. Put simply, much of the information and many of the effects on which group members are dependent are oriented toward enforcing group norms.

Motives for Social Conformity

The fact that Roman Catholic priests conform to the norms of the church hierarchy seems rather different from the case in which convicts conform to norms that prison officials establish. Clearly, the motives for conformity differ in these two cases. What is needed, then, is some system to classify different motives for conformity.[5]

Compliance. Conformity to a social norm prompted by the desire to acquire rewards or avoid punishment.

Compliance. Compliance is the simplest, most direct motive for conformity to group norms. It occurs because a member wishes to acquire rewards from the group and avoid punishment. As such, it primarily involves effect dependence. Although the complying individual adjusts his or her behaviour to the norm, he or she does not really subscribe to the beliefs, values, and attitudes that underlie the norm. Most convicts conform to formal prison norms out of compliance. Similarly, very young children behave themselves only because of external forces.

Identification. Some individuals conform because they find other supporters of the norm attractive. In this case, the individual identifies with these supporters and sees him or herself as similar to them. Although there are elements of effect dependence here, information dependence is especially important—if someone is basically similar to you, then you will be motivated to rely on them for information about how to think and act. **Identification** as a motive for conformity is often revealed by an imitation process in which established members serve as models for the behaviour of others. For example, a newly promoted executive might attempt to dress and talk like her successful, admired boss. Similarly, as children get older, they might be motivated to behave themselves because such behaviour corresponds to that of an admired parent with whom they are beginning to identify.

Identification. Conformity to a social norm prompted by perceptions that those who promote the norm are attractive or similar to oneself.

Internalization. Some conformity to norms occurs because individuals have truly and wholly accepted the beliefs, values, and attitudes that underlie the norm. As such, **internalization** of the norm has happened, and conformity occurs because it is seen as *right,* not because it achieves rewards, avoids punishment, or pleases others. That is, conformity is due to internal, rather than external, forces. In general, we expect that most religious leaders conform to the norms of their religion for this reason. Similarly, the career army officer might come to support the strict discipline of the military because it seems right and proper, not simply because colleagues support such discipline. In certain organizational settings, some of these motives for conformity are more likely than others.

Internalization. Conformity to a social norm prompted by true acceptance of the beliefs, values, and attitudes that underlie the norm.

The Subtle Power of Compliance

In many of the examples given in the previous section, especially those dealing with effect dependence, it is obvious that the doubting group member is motivated to conform only in the *compliance* mode—that is, he or she really does not support the belief, value, and attitude structure underlying the norm but conforms simply to avoid trouble or obtain rewards. Of course, this happens all the time. Individuals without religious beliefs or values might agree to be married in a church service to please others. Similarly, a store cashier might verify a credit card purchase by a familiar customer even though he feels that the whole process is a waste of time. These examples of compliance seem trivial enough, but a little compliance can go a long way.

A compliant individual is necessarily *doing* something that is contrary to the way he or she *thinks* or *feels*. Such a situation is highly dissonant and arouses a certain tension in the individual. One way to reduce this dissonance is to cease conformity. This is especially likely if the required behaviour is at great variance with one's values or moral standards. However, this might require the person to adopt an isolated or scapegoat role, which are equally unpleasant prospects. The other method of reducing dissonance is to gradually accept the beliefs, values, and attitudes that support the norm in question. This is more likely when the required behaviour is not so discrepant with one's current value system.

Consider Mark, an idealistic graduate of a college social work program who acquires a job with a social services agency. Mark loves helping people but hates the bureaucratic red tape and reams of paperwork that is necessary to accomplish this goal. However, to acquire the approval of his boss and co-workers and to avoid trouble, he follows the rules to the letter of the law. This is pure compliance. Over time, however, Mark begins to *identify* with his boss and more experienced co-workers because they are in the enviable position of controlling those very rewards and punishments that are so important to him. Obviously, if he is to *be* one of them, he must begin to think and feel like them. Finally, Mark is promoted to a supervisory position, partly because he is so cooperative. Breaking in a new social worker, Mark is heard to say, "Our rules and forms are very important. You don't understand now, but you will." The metamorphosis is complete—Mark has *internalized* the beliefs and values that support the bureaucratic norms of his agency.

Although this story is slightly dramatized, the point that it makes is accurate—simple compliance can set the stage for more complete identification and involvement with organizational norms and roles. The process through which this occurs in organizations is known as *organizational socialization*, the focus of the next section.

ORGANIZATIONAL SOCIALIZATION

The story of Mark, the social worker, in the previous section describes how one individual was socialized into a particular organization. In the chapter opening vignette, we described how new hires are socialized at Fairmont Hotels & Resorts and The Ritz-Carlton. **Socialization** is the process by which people learn the norms and roles that are necessary to function in a group or organization. It is a learning process in which new members must acquire knowledge, change their attitudes, and perform new behaviours. Socialization is also the primary means by which organizations communicate the organization's culture and values to new members. In human resources, this process is often referred to today as "onboarding."

Exhibit 8.1 depicts the socialization process. In particular, it shows how different socialization methods influence a number of immediate or proximal socialization outcomes such as learning, task mastery, social integration, role conflict, role ambiguity, and person–job and person–organization fit. These proximal outcomes then lead to more distal or longer-term outcomes such as job satisfaction, organizational commitment, organizational identification, organizational citizenship behaviour, job performance, stress, and turnover.

Learning during socialization has often been described in terms of content areas or domains of learning such as the task, role, group, and organization domain. Newcomers need to acquire the knowledge and skills necessary to perform their job duties and tasks; they need to learn the appropriate behaviours and expectations of their role; they need to learn the norms and values of their work group; and they need to learn about the organization, such as its history, traditions, language, politics, mission, and culture. As newcomers learn about each of these areas they should begin to

Socialization. The process by which people learn the norms and roles that are necessary to function in a group or organization.

EXHIBIT 8.1
The socialization process.

Socialization Methods	Proximal Socialization Outcomes	Distal Socialization Outcomes
Realistic job previews	Learning	Job satisfaction
Employee orientation programs	Task mastery	Organizational commitment
Socialization tactics	Social integration	Organizational identification
Mentoring	Role conflict	Organizational citizenship behaviour
Proactive tactics	Role ambiguity	Job performance
	Person–job fit	Stress
	Person–organization fit	Turnover

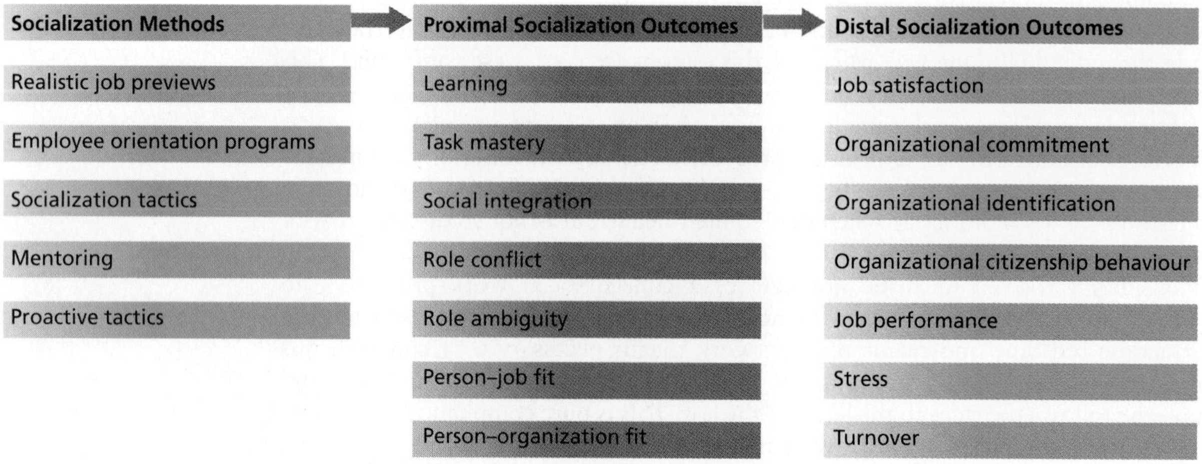

master their tasks and integrate with others in their work group and the organization. This should also help to reduce their role ambiguity and role conflict. In Chapter 7 we described how different factors can lead to role ambiguity and role conflict. One of the goals of socialization is to provide new hires with information and knowledge about their role to avoid problems of role conflict and role ambiguity.

Another important proximal outcome of organizational socialization is for newcomers to achieve a good fit. There are generally two kinds of fit that are important for socialization. First, newcomers must acquire the knowledge and skills necessary to perform their work tasks and roles. This is known as person–job fit, or P–J fit. **Person–job fit** refers to the match between an employee's knowledge, skills, and abilities and the requirements of a job. Second, newcomers must also learn the values and beliefs that are important to the group and organization. This is known as **person–organization fit**, or P–O fit, and refers to the match between an employee's personal values and the values of an organization.[6] Research has found that both P–J and P–O fit are strongly related to job attitudes and behaviours.[7]

In summary, socialization is important because it has a direct effect on proximal socialization outcomes (e.g., better P–J and P–O fit, lower role ambiguity), which lead to more positive distal outcomes (e.g., job satisfaction, organizational commitment). As we shall see, some of this process might occur before organization membership formally begins, while some occurs once the new member enters the organization. Furthermore, socialization is an ongoing process by virtue of continuous interaction with others in the workplace. However, there is good reason to believe that socialization is most potent during certain periods of membership transition, such as when one is promoted or assigned to a new work group, and especially when one joins a new organization.[8]

Person–job fit. The match between an employee's knowledge, skills, and abilities and the requirements of a job.

Person–organization fit. The match between an employee's personal values and the values of an organization.

Stages of Socialization

Since organizational socialization is an ongoing process, it is useful to divide this process into three stages.[9] One of these stages occurs before entry, another immediately follows entry, and the last occurs after one has been a member for some period of time. In a sense, the first two stages represent hurdles for achieving passage into the third stage (see Exhibit 8.2).

Anticipatory Socialization. A considerable amount of socialization occurs even before a person becomes a member of a particular organization. This process is called anticipatory socialization. Some anticipatory socialization includes a formal process of skill and attitude acquisition, such as that which might occur by attending college or university. Other anticipatory socialization might be informal, such as that acquired through a series of summer jobs or even by watching the portrayal of organizational life in television shows and movies. Some organizations begin to socialize job candidates

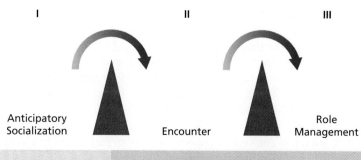

EXHIBIT 8.2
Stages of organizational socialization.

Source: Based on Feldman, D.C. (1976). A contingency theory of socialization. *Administrative Science Quarterly, 21,* 433–452; Feldman, D.C. (1981). The multiple socialization of organization members. *Academy of Management Review, 6,* 309–318.

even before they are hired at recruitment events where organizational representatives discuss the organization with potential hires. As we shall see shortly, organizations vary in the extent to which they encourage anticipatory socialization in advance of entry. As well, not all anticipatory socialization is accurate and useful for the new member.

Encounter. In the encounter stage, the new recruit, armed with some expectations about organizational life, encounters the day-to-day reality of this life. Formal aspects of this stage might include orientation programs, such as those at Fairmont Hotels & Resorts and The Ritz-Carlton, and rotation through various parts of the organization. Informal aspects include getting to know and understand the style and personality of one's boss and co-workers. At this stage, the organization and its experienced members are looking for an acceptable degree of conformity to organizational norms and the gradual acquisition of appropriate role behaviour. At Fairmont Hotels & Resorts, such behaviours include making guests feel special, valued, and appreciated, and at The Ritz-Carlton it means providing first-class service in accordance with the company's Gold Standard. Recruits, on the other hand, are interested in having their personal needs and expectations fulfilled. If successful, the recruit will have complied with critical organizational norms and should begin to identify with experienced organizational members.

Role Management. Having survived the encounter stage and acquired basic role behaviours, the new member's attention shifts to fine tuning and actively managing his or her role in the organization. Following some conformity to group norms, the new recruit might now be in a position to modify the role to better serve the organization. This might require forming connections outside the immediate work group. The organizational member must also confront balancing the now-familiar organizational role with nonwork roles and family demands. Each of these experiences provides additional socialization to the role occupant, who might begin to internalize the norms and values that are prominent in the organization.

Now that we have seen a basic sketch of how socialization proceeds, let's look in greater detail at some of the key issues in the process.

Unrealistic Expectations and the Psychological Contract

People seldom join organizations without expectations about what membership will be like and what they expect to receive in return for their efforts. In fact, it is just such expectations that lead them to choose one career, job, or organization over another. Management majors have some expectations about what they will be doing when they become management trainees at IBM. Similarly, even 18-year-old army recruits have notions about what military life will be like. Unfortunately, these expectations are often unrealistic and obligations between new members and organizations are often breached.

Unrealistic Expectations. Research indicates that people entering organizations hold many expectations that are inaccurate and often unrealistically high. As a result, once they enter an organization they experience a reality shock and their expectations are not met.[10] In one study of telephone operators, for example, researchers obtained people's expectations about the nature of the job *before* they started work. They also looked at these employees' perceptions of the actual job shortly *after* they started work. The results indicated that many perceptions were less favourable than expectations. A similar result occurred for students entering an MBA program.[11] Such changes, which are fairly common, support the notion that socialization has an important impact on new organizational members.

Why do new members often have unrealistic expectations about the organizations they join?[12] To some extent, occupational stereotypes, such as those we discussed in Chapter 3, could be responsible. The media often communicate such stereotypes. For example, a person entering nurses' training might have gained some expectations about hospital life from watching the television show *Grey's Anatomy*. Those of us who teach might also be guilty of communicating stereotypes. After four years of study, the new management trainee at IBM might be dismayed to find that the emphasis is on *trainee* rather than *management*! Finally, unrealistic expectations may also stem from overzealous recruiters who paint rosy pictures to attract job candidates to the organization. Taken together, these factors demonstrate the need for socialization.

Psychological Contract. When people join organizations, they have beliefs and expectations about what they will receive from the organization in return for what they give the organization. Such beliefs form what is known as the psychological contract. A **psychological contract** refers to beliefs held by employees regarding the reciprocal obligations and promises between them and their organization.[13] For example, an employee might expect to receive bonuses and promotions in return for hard work and loyalty.

> **Psychological contract.** Beliefs held by employees regarding the reciprocal obligations and promises between them and their organization.

Unfortunately, psychological contract breach appears to be a common occurrence. Perceptions of psychological contract breach occur when an employee perceives that his or her organization has failed to fulfill one or more promised obligations of the psychological contract. One study found that 55 percent of recent MBA graduates reported that some aspect of their psychological contract had been broken by their employer.[14] This often results in feelings of anger and betrayal and can have a negative effect on employees' work attitudes and behaviour. A recent study of customer service employees found that psychological contract breach was related to lower organizational trust, which was in turn related to less cooperative employment relations and higher levels of absenteeism.[15]

Why does psychological contract breach occur? As is the case with unrealistic expectations, recruiters are often tempted to promise more than their organization can provide to attract the best job applicants. In addition, newcomers often lack sufficient information to form accurate perceptions concerning their psychological contract. As a result, there will be some incongruence or differences in understandings between an employee and the organization about promised obligations. In addition, organizational changes, such as downsizing and restructuring, can cause organizations to knowingly break promises made to an employee that they are either unable or unwilling to keep.[16]

It is therefore important that newcomers develop accurate perceptions in the formation of a psychological contract. Many of the terms of the psychological contract are established during anticipatory socialization. Therefore, organizations need to ensure that truthful and accurate information about promises and obligations is communicated to new members before and after they join an organization. Incongruence and psychological contract breach are less likely in organizations where socialization is intense.[17] Recall that at The Ritz-Carlton the company meets with employees on day 21 to make sure they have delivered on the promises they made to new hires. This further demonstrates the importance of and need for organizational socialization.

METHODS OF ORGANIZATIONAL SOCIALIZATION

Organizations differ in the extent to which they socialize their new hires. This is in part owing to the fact that some organizations make use of other organizations to help socialize their members. For example, hospitals do not develop experienced cardiologists from scratch. Rather, they depend on medical schools to socialize potential doctors in the basic role requirements of being a physician. Similarly, business firms rely on business schools to send them recruits who think and act in a business-like manner.

In this way, a fair degree of anticipatory socialization may exist before a person joins an organization. On the other hand, organizations such as police forces, the military, and religious institutions are less likely to rely on external socialization. Police academies, boot camps, and seminaries are set up as extensions of these organizations to aid in socialization.

Organizations that handle their own socialization are especially interested in maintaining the continuity and stability of job behaviours over a period of time. Conversely, those that rely on external agencies to perform anticipatory socialization are oriented toward maintaining the potential for creative, innovative behaviour on the part of members—there is less "inbreeding." Of course, reliance on external agents might present problems. The engineer who is socialized in university courses to respect design elegance might find it difficult to accept cost restrictions when he or she is employed by an engineering firm. For this reason, organizations that rely heavily on external socialization always supplement it with formal training and orientation or informal on-the-job training.

Thus, organizations differ in terms of *who* does the socializing, *how* it is done, and *how much* is done. Most organizations, however, make use of a number of methods of socialization including realistic job previews, employee orientation programs, socialization tactics, and mentoring.

Realistic Job Previews

We noted earlier that new organizational members often harbour unrealistic, inflated expectations about what their jobs will be like. When the job actually begins and it fails to live up to these expectations, individuals experience "reality shock," and job dissatisfaction results. As a consequence, costly turnover is most likely to occur among newer employees who are unable to survive the discrepancy between expectations and reality. For the organization, this sequence of events represents a failure of socialization.

Realistic job previews.
The provision of a balanced, realistic picture of the positive and negative aspects of a job to applicants.

Obviously, organizations cannot control all sources of unrealistic job expectations, such as those provided by television shows and glorified occupational stereotypes. However, they *can* control those generated during the recruitment process by providing job applicants with realistic job previews. **Realistic job previews** provide a balanced, realistic picture of the positive and negative aspects of the job to applicants.[18] Thus, they provide "corrective action" to expectations at the anticipatory socialization stage. Exhibit 8.3 compares the realistic job preview process with the traditional preview process that often sets expectations too high by ignoring the negative aspects of the job.

How do organizations design and conduct realistic job previews? Generally, they obtain the views of experienced employees and human resources officers about the positive and negative aspects of the job. Then, they incorporate these views into booklets or videotape presentations for applicants.[19] For example, a video presentation might involve interviews with job incumbents discussing the pros and cons of their jobs. Some companies have managers and employees communicate realistic information to job candidates. For example, Scotiabank has managers from various business lines explain the day-to-day job realities to prospective job candidates. Steel maker Dofasco Inc. of Hamilton, Ontario, has a team of employees, which includes members from the senior ranks to the most recently hired, join student ambassadors at campus recruitment events where they are available for one-on-one conversations with job candidates.[20] Realistic previews have been designed for jobs as diverse as telephone operators, life insurance salespeople, US Marine Corps recruits, and supermarket workers.

Ontario Provincial Police
www.opp.ca

Sometimes realistic previews use simulations to permit applicants to actually sample the work. For example, in an effort to recruit more women, the Ontario Provincial Police (OPP) staged a five-day recruiting camp for 100 women who were selected from close to 3000 applicants interested in a career in policing. During the five-day recruiting camp, the women experienced typical OPP policing activities, including shooting a handgun, completing 6 a.m. fitness drills, and responding to mock

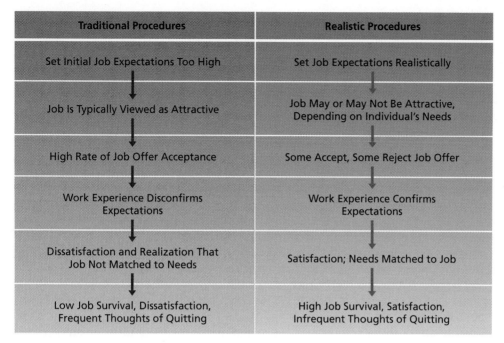

Traditional Procedures	Realistic Procedures
Set Initial Job Expectations Too High	Set Job Expectations Realistically
Job Is Typically Viewed as Attractive	Job May or May Not Be Attractive, Depending on Individual's Needs
High Rate of Job Offer Acceptance	Some Accept, Some Reject Job Offer
Work Experience Disconfirms Expectations	Work Experience Confirms Expectations
Dissatisfaction and Realization That Job Not Matched to Needs	Satisfaction; Needs Matched to Job
Low Job Survival, Dissatisfaction, Frequent Thoughts of Quitting	High Job Survival, Satisfaction, Infrequent Thoughts of Quitting

EXHIBIT 8.3
Traditional and realistic job previews compared.

crimes. Eighty-three of the women decided to complete the first stage of testing and, if successful, they will go through a lengthy application and selection process with very realistic expectations.[21]

Evidence shows that realistic job previews are effective in reducing inflated expectations and turnover and improving job performance.[22] What is less clear is exactly why turnover reduction occurs. Reduced expectations and increased job satisfaction are part of the answer. It also appears that realistic previews cause those not cut out for the job to withdraw from the application process, a process known as self-selection.[23] As a result, applicants who perceive a good P–J and P–O fit are more likely to

The Ontario Provincial Police staged a five-day recruiting camp in which female recruits participated in realistic work simulations.

remain in the hiring process and to accept a job offer. Although the turnover reductions generated by realistic previews are small, they can result in substantial financial savings for organizations.[24] Providing realistic job previews can also help prevent perceptions of psychological contract breach.[25]

Employee Orientation Programs

Once newcomers enter an organization, socialization during the encounter stage usually begins with an orientation program. Orientation programs are designed to introduce new employees to their job, the people they will be working with, and the organization. The main content of most orientation programs consists of health and safety issues, terms and conditions of employment, and information about the organization, such as its history and traditions. Another purpose of new employee orientation programs is to begin conveying and forming the psychological contract and to teach newcomers how to cope with stressful work situations.[26]

Most orientation programs take place during the first week of entry and last one day to one week. Some organizations, such as Fairmont Hotels & Resorts and The Ritz-Carlton, realize the importance of orientation and invest a considerable amount of time and resources in it. Another good example of this is Starbucks, where new employees receive 24 hours of training in their first 80 hours of employment. CEO Howard Schultz greets new hires via video and they learn about the company's history and its obsession with quality and customer service. According to Schultz, "For people joining the company we try to define what Starbucks stands for, what we're trying to achieve, and why that's relevant to them." Not surprisingly, the turnover rate at Starbucks is considerably less than the average rate in the specialty-coffee industry.[27]

Orientation programs are an important method of socialization because they can have an immediate effect on learning and a lasting effect on the job attitudes and behaviours of new hires. One study found that newly hired employees who attended an orientation program were more socialized in terms of their knowledge and understanding of the organization's goals and values, history, and involvement with people, and also reported higher organizational commitment compared to employees who did not attend the orientation program.[28] A study conducted at Corning Inc. concluded that employees who completed a full orientation program were 69 percent more likely to remain with the company after three years. Other companies have also seen substantial decreases in their rate of turnover as a result of new employee orientation programs.[29]

With the increasing use of computers for employee training, some organizations have begun to use computer-based orientation programs. To learn more, see "Research Focus: *The Effects of a Computer-Based Orientation Program on the Socialization of New Hires.*"

Socialization Tactics

Although realistic job previews and orientation programs play an important role in the socialization of new employees, the socialization process does not end at the conclusion of an orientation program. So what happens to new hires once the orientation program has ended? Consider how the new hires at Fairmont Hotels & Resorts are socialized. They are first greeted by senior management and receive a message from the corporate executive team. They go through their socialization together as a group at their respective hotel. They know that their orientation will occur during the first two days and a third orientation day will take place on the job 60 to 90 days later when they will be paired with a mentor and meet with their supervisor. As you can see, there is a deliberate, conscious, and structured manner in which the new hires at Fairmont Hotels & Resorts are socialized.

Starbucks
www.starbucks.com

Corning Inc.
www.corning.com

RESEARCH FOCUS

The Effects of a Computer-Based Orientation Program on the Socialization of New Hires

One of the main ways that new employees learn about their new job and become socialized is by attending orientation programs. Most organizations provide some form of orientation to help new employees adjust and become socialized. New-employee orientation programs usually take place when an employee first begins employment with an organization. They are designed to help newcomers adjust and facilitate the process of socialization by introducing them to people in the organization, their roles within the organization, and the organization itself.

A major development in the training field has been the growth of computer-based training programs. Many companies have converted their traditional training programs into computer-based programs. Some have begun to make the move from traditional group-based orientation programs to computer-based orientation programs. Multimedia programs in which text, graphics, animation, audio, and video are used through the computer to facilitate learning are particularly popular.

However, is a computer-based orientation program as effective for the socialization of new hires as a more traditional program? To find out, Michael J. Wesson and Celile Itir Gogus conducted a study in which 261 newcomers from a large technology-based consulting firm attended either a traditional orientation program or a computer-based orientation program.

The traditional orientation program was a one-week program created to familiarize new hires with the organization and its practices and procedures as well as to give a sense of community and belonging. Newcomers were flown to a central location in the United States where they spent the week in an orientation program, secluded with a group of new hires, orientation instructors, and guest speakers from various parts of the organization. The orientation program consisted of presentations, videos, reading assignments, team-building activities, and question-and-answer sessions.

The computer-based program was a self-guided orientation program that covered all of the same material as the traditional program through the use of a full-fledged, multimedia orientation that included written, audio, and video-based sessions. The program was designed to take two to three days to complete.

The new hires were asked to complete surveys after two and four months on the job to assess their socialization and job attitudes; their supervisors also completed a survey after four months. The results indicated that newcomers who attended the computer-based orientation program had lower scores on social-related outcomes including organizational goals and values, politics, and people, but not for more information-based outcomes such as knowledge of the organization's history and language or performance proficiency. In addition, newcomers in the computer-based orientation program reported lower levels of job satisfaction and organizational commitment, and their supervisors rated them lower on organizational goal-value socialization and role understanding.

These results indicate that the computer-based orientation program hindered the socialization of newcomers on socially oriented content areas of socialization, but not on information-based content areas. The study demonstrates the importance of employee orientation programs for the socialization of new hires and that to be most effective, orientation programs should provide newcomers with opportunities for social interaction.

Source: Wesson, M.J. & Gogus, C.I. (2005). Shaking hands with a computer: An examination of two methods of organizational newcomer orientation. *Journal of Applied Psychology, 90,* 1018–1026.

John Van Maanen and Edgar Schein developed a theory of socialization that helps us understand and explain the socialization process that is used at companies like Fairmont Hotels & Resorts and The Ritz-Carlton. They suggested that there are six **socialization tactics** that organizations can use to structure the early work experiences of newcomers and individuals who are in transition from one role to another. Each of the six tactics consists of a bipolar continuum and are described below.[30] Exhibit 8.4 depicts the six socialization tactics.

Socialization tactics. The manner in which organizations structure the early work experiences of newcomers and individuals who are in transition from one role to another.

EXHIBIT 8.4

Socialization tactics.

Source: Jones, G.R. Socialization tactics, self-efficacy, and newcomers' adjustments to organizations. *Academy of Management Journal, 29*, 262–279. This material is protected by copyright and is being used with permission from *Access Copyright*. Any alteration of its content or further copying in any form whatsoever is strictly prohibited.

Tactics concerned mainly with:	INSTITUTIONALIZED	INDIVIDUALIZED
CONTEXT	Collective Formal	Individual Informal
CONTENT	Sequential Fixed	Random Variable
SOCIAL ASPECTS	Serial Investiture	Disjunctive Divestiture

Collective versus Individual Tactics. Organizations can use a *collective* or an *individual* socialization tactic. When using the collective tactic, a number of new members are socialized as a group, going through the same experiences and facing the same challenges, as is the case at Fairmont Hotels & Resorts and The Ritz-Carlton. Army boot camps, fraternity pledge classes, and training classes for salespeople and airline attendants are also common examples. In contrast, the individual tactic consists of socialization experiences that are tailor-made for each new member. Simple on-the-job training and apprenticeship to develop skilled craftspeople constitute individual socialization.

Formal versus Informal Tactics. Socialization tactics can also be *formal* or *informal*. Formal tactics involve segregating newcomers from regular organizational members and providing them with formal learning experiences during the period of socialization. Informal tactics, however, do not distinguish a newcomer from more experienced members and rely more on informal and on-the-job learning. The first two days of orientation at Fairmont Hotels & Resorts is a good example of formal tactics.

Sequential versus Random Tactics. *Sequential* versus *random* tactics have to do with whether there is a clear sequence of steps or stages during the socialization process. With a sequential tactic, there is a fixed sequence of steps leading to the assumption of the role, compared with the random tactic, in which there is an ambiguous or changing sequence. The socialization process at Fairmont Hotels & Resorts and The Ritz-Carlton is a good example of sequential socialization. For example, notice how at The Ritz-Carlton the process begins with a two-day orientation program followed by three weeks on the job with a departmental trainer, a follow-up on day 21, and another follow-up on day 365.

Fixed versus Variable Tactics. Socialization tactics can also be distinguished in terms of the existence of a time frame during which the socialization period lasts. If the socialization tactic is *fixed*, there is a time table for the assumption of the role. If the tactic is *variable*, then there is no time frame to indicate when the socialization process ends and the newcomer assumes his or her new role. At Fairmont Hotels & Resorts and The Ritz-Carlton, socialization is fixed. A good example of this is the pin ceremony on day 365 at The Ritz-Carlton that signals the end of socialization and the newcomers' assumption of their new role.

Serial versus Disjunctive Tactics. Socialization tactics also vary in terms of whether or not experienced members of the organization participate in the socialization of new members. The *serial* tactic refers to a process in which newcomers are socialized by experienced members of the organization, as is the case at Fairmont Hotels & Resorts and The Ritz-Carlton. The *disjunctive* tactic refers to a socialization process where role models and experienced organization members do not groom new members or "show them the ropes."

Investiture versus Divestiture Tactics. Finally, socialization tactics can be either *investiture* or *divestiture*. Divestiture tactics refer to what is also known as debasement and hazing. This is seen when organizations put new members through a series of experiences that are designed to humble them and strip away some of their initial self-confidence. Debasement is a way of testing the commitment of new members and correcting for faulty anticipatory socialization. Having been humbled and stripped of preconceptions, members are then ready to learn the norms of the organization. An extreme example is the rough treatment and shaved heads of US Marine Corps recruits. Sometimes organizations prefer not to use debasement or hazing as part of the socialization of newcomers. Rather, they employ the investiture socialization tactic, which affirms the incoming identity and attributes of new hires rather than denies and strips them away. Organizations that carefully select new members for certain attributes and characteristics would be more likely to use this tactic. This is certainly the case at The Ritz-Carlton where service professionals selected to work at the hotel are in the top 1 percent of the industry.

Institutionalized versus Individualized Socialization. The six socialization tactics can be grouped into two separate patterns of socialization. *Institutionalized socialization* consists of collective, formal, sequential, fixed, serial, and investiture tactics. *Individualized socialization* consists of individual, informal, random, variable, disjunctive, and divestiture tactics. The main difference between these two dimensions is that institutionalized socialization reflects a more formalized and structured program of socialization that reduces uncertainty and encourages new hires to accept organizational norms and maintain the status quo. On the other hand, individualized socialization reflects a relative absence of structure that creates ambiguity and encourages new hires to question the status quo and develop their own approach to their role. In addition, the tactics have also been distinguished in terms of the *context* in which information is presented to new hires, the *content* provided to new hires, and the *social* aspects of socialization.[31] As shown in Exhibit 8.4, the collective-individual and formal-informal tactics represent the context of socialization; the sequential-random and fixed-variable represent the content of socialization; and the serial-disjunctive and investiture-divestiture represent the social aspects of socialization.

Institutionalized socialization tactics are especially effective in inducing uniform behaviour because there are so many others present who are undergoing the same experience. In addition, the individuals being socialized might pressure each other to

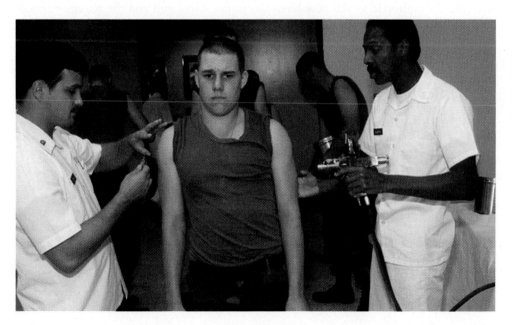

Some socialization tactics, such as debasement and hazing, are designed to strip new members of their old beliefs, values, and attitudes and get them to internalize new ones.

toe the line and "do things right." Thus, in institutionalized socialization, one's peers prove to be especially potent sources of information.

When socialization is individualized, new members are more likely to take on the particular characteristics and style of those who are socializing them. Thus, two newly hired real estate agents who receive on-the-job training from their bosses might soon think and act more like their bosses than like each other. As you can see, uniformity is less likely under individualized socialization.

On the basis of this description, it should be apparent to you that the socialization process at Fairmont Hotels & Resorts and The Ritz-Carlton is formalized and structured and hence more institutionalized than individualized. Why do you think that this approach is used to socialize new hires? Just consider the desired outcome of both company's socialization program—great customer service in accordance with the company's values and culture. Institutionalized socialization tactics are effective in promoting organizational loyalty, esprit de corps, and uniformity of behaviour among those being socialized. This last characteristic is often very important. No matter where they are in the world, soldiers know whom to salute and how to do it. Similarly, air passengers need not expect any surprises from cabin attendants, thanks to the attendants' institutionalized socialization. And employees at Fairmont Hotels & Resorts and The Ritz-Carlton know how to welcome, greet, and treat customers in a consistent manner around the world.

Institutionalized socialization is always followed up by some individualized socialization as the member joins his or her regular work unit. For example, rookie police officers are routinely partnered with more experienced officers. At this point, they will begin to develop some individuality in the style with which they perform their jobs. This is the case for the new hires at Fairmont Hotels & Resorts who are paired with a mentor once they have been on the job for several months and at The Ritz-Carlton where new hires work for three weeks with a departmental trainer who can remain a mentor to the new hire indefinitely.

Research Evidence. Research on socialization tactics supports the basic predictions regarding the effects of institutionalized and individualized socialization on newcomers' roles, attitudes, and behaviour. Institutionalized socialization tactics have been found to be related to proximal outcomes, such as lower role ambiguity and conflict and more positive perceptions of P–J and P–O fit, as well as more distal outcomes, such as more positive job satisfaction and organizational commitment and lower stress and turnover. In addition, the institutionalized socialization tactics result in a more custodial role orientation in which new hires accept the status quo and the requirements of their tasks and roles. On the other hand, the individualized socialization tactics tend to result in a more innovative role orientation in which new recruits might change or modify the way they perform their tasks and roles. It is also worth noting that among the different socialization tactics, the social tactics (serial-disjunctive and investiture-divestiture) have been found to be the most strongly related to socialization outcomes. This is consistent with research that has found that organizations that are more successful at socializing newcomers help them to establish a broad network of relationships with co-workers.[32]

Mentoring

It should be apparent from our discussion of socialization tactics that supervisors and peers play an important role in the socialization process. While effective relationships between supervisors and their employees obviously influence the socialization and career success of individuals within an organization, one particularly important relationship is that between a newcomer or apprentice and a mentor.

A **mentor** is an experienced or more senior person in the organization who gives a junior person special attention, such as giving advice and creating opportunities to

Mentor. An experienced or more senior person in the organization who gives a junior person special attention, such as giving advice and creating opportunities to assist him or her during the early stages of his or her career.

assist him or her during the early stages of his or her career. Recall that newcomers at Fairmont Hotels & Resorts are paired with a mentor once they have been on the job for several months, and at The Ritz-Carlton new hires work with a departmental trainer who can also become a mentor. While someone other than the junior person's boss can serve as a mentor, often the supervisor is in a unique position to provide mentoring. For mentors to be effective, they must perform two types of mentor functions: career and psychosocial functions.

Career Functions of Mentoring. A mentor provides many career-enhancing benefits to an apprentice.[33] These benefits are made possible by the senior person's experience, status, knowledge of how the organization works, and influence with powerful people in the organization. The career functions of mentoring include:

- *Sponsorship.* The mentor might nominate the apprentice for advantageous transfers and promotions.
- *Exposure and visibility.* The mentor might provide opportunities to work with key people and see other parts of the organization.
- *Coaching and feedback.* The mentor might suggest work strategies and identify strengths and weaknesses in the apprentice's performance.
- *Developmental assignments.* Challenging work assignments a mentor can provide will help develop key skills and knowledge that are crucial to career progress.

Psychosocial Functions of Mentoring. Besides helping directly with career progress, mentors can provide certain psychosocial functions that are helpful in developing the apprentice's self-confidence, sense of identity, and ability to cope with emotional traumas that can damage a person's effectiveness. These include:

- *Role modelling.* This provides a set of attitudes, values, and behaviours for the junior person to imitate.
- *Acceptance and confirmation.* The mentor can also provide encouragement and support and help the apprentice gain self-confidence.
- *Counselling.* This provides an opportunity to discuss personal concerns and anxieties concerning career prospects, work–family conflicts, and so on.

Research Evidence. Many research efforts have documented the importance of having a mentor when starting one's career and how it can influence career success.[34] A recent review of this research found that mentored individuals had higher objective career outcomes, such as compensation and the number of promotions, as well as higher subjective outcomes, including greater satisfaction with one's job and career and greater career commitment, and they were more likely to believe that they will advance in their career. However, mentoring tends to be more strongly related to the subjective than the objective career outcomes. Furthermore, when comparing the effects of the two mentoring functions, the psychosocial function was found to be more strongly related to satisfaction with the mentoring relationship while the career function was more strongly related to compensation and advancement. Both functions were found to be just as important in generating positive attitudes toward one's job and career.[35] Positive relationships have also been found for mentoring and socialization. One study on mentoring provided by experienced peers found that both the career and psychosocial functions of mentoring were related to the successful socialization of newcomers, and socialization was negatively related to work stress. As well, both mentoring functions were related to the amount of help in coping with stress that mentored employees received from their mentors.[36]

Many research efforts have documented the importance of having a mentor when starting one's career and how it can influence career success.

Formal Mentoring Programs. Mentoring relationships have often been of an informal nature, such that the individuals involved chose to enter into a mentoring relationship with each other without the direct involvement of their organization. However, can organizations formally assign mentors to apprentices and achieve the career outcomes normally associated with more spontaneous, informal mentor–apprentice relationships? The answer appears to be yes as formal mentoring programs have become increasingly popular in recent years.[37] For example, Telvent Canada Ltd., a Calgary-based company that develops information management systems, started a formal mentoring program a number of years ago. Although it was originally offered to new hires to help get them up to speed, it is now available to all of the company's employees. Bell Canada launched a company-wide online mentor program several years ago called Mentor Match that is open to all of its employees. The program is available on the company's intranet, and employees must apply to be either a mentor or protégé.[38]

Telvent Canada Inc.
www.telvent.com

Bell Canada
www.bell.ca

Research on formal mentoring programs has found that they are just as beneficial as informal relationships and are certainly more beneficial than not having mentors at all. In addition, formal mentoring programs have been found to be most effective when the mentor and protégé have input into the matching process and when they receive training prior to the mentoring relationship, especially training that is perceived to be of a high quality.[39]

While all mentors, by definition, provide some subset of the career functions, mentors do not always provide the psychosocial functions. A network of close peers can go a long way in providing functions that one's mentor is not able to. People starting their careers should be aware of the importance of these career and psychosocial functions and should attempt to establish a social network that will fulfill them. A mentor relationship is usually a key element in this broader set of relationships. To some extent, a supportive and well-connected social network can substitute for not having an effective mentor.[40]

Women and Mentors. One factor that inhibits women's career development compared with their male counterparts is the difficulty women have historically faced in establishing an apprentice–mentor relationship with a senior person in the organization.[41] The lack of mentors and role models is a major barrier for the career advancement of many women.[42] The problem goes well beyond the traditional gender stereotyping we discussed in Chapter 3. It stems from the fact that senior people, who are in the best position to be mentors, are frequently men. A young woman attempting to establish a productive relationship with a senior male associate faces complexities that the male apprentice does not. Part of the problem is the lack of experience many male mentor candidates have in dealing with a woman in roles other than daughter, wife, or lover. Often, a woman's concerns are going to be different from those her male mentor experienced at that stage in his career. As a result, the strategies that he models might have limited relevance to the female apprentice. Perhaps the greatest difficulty is associated with fears that their relationship will be perceived as involving sexual intimacy. Concerns about appearances and what others will say can make both people uncomfortable and get in the way of a productive relationship.

Because of these concerns, the prospective female apprentice faces more constraints than her male counterpart. Research has confirmed that cross-gender mentor–apprentice dyads are less likely to get involved in informal after-work social activities. These activities can help apprentices establish relationships with other influential people in a relaxed setting. Research also confirms that apprentices in a cross-gender dyad are less likely to see their mentor as a role model and, therefore, are less likely to realize the developmental benefits of an effective model.[43]

How critical is mentoring to a woman's career? The research evidence suggests that mentoring is even more critical to women's career success than it is to men's. Women who make it to executive positions invariably had a mentor along the way. This is true for half to two-thirds of male executives.[44] Recent studies also indicate that a majority (61 percent) of women have had a mentor, and almost all (99 percent) say that their mentor has had an impact on the advancement of their careers.[45]

Thus, for women with these career aspirations, finding a mentor appears to be a difficult but crucial task. The good news is that an increasing number of organizations are developing mentoring and networking programs. For example, Deloitte has a program called Developing Leaders in which experienced partners mentor and coach male and female partners who demonstrate leadership potential. Mentors are carefully chosen and their skills and experience are matched to the new partner's goals and aspirations. In addition, women at Deloitte have developed networking and mentoring opportunities for themselves through a program called Women's Business Development Groups. The group organizes networking events and meets with other women's business groups, and an annual Spring Breakfast is held in which prominent women are invited to speak.[46] These kinds of networking opportunities are extremely important because research has found that exclusion from informal networks is one of the major roadblocks to the advancement of women.[47]

Deloitte
www.deloitte.com

The Bank of Montreal also has a mentoring program as part of its equality and diversity efforts. When the bank asked employees how they could assist women in advancing in their careers, the most important factor suggested by senior women in management was a mentoring program. A formal mentoring program was implemented, and one of the results has been an increasing amount of informal mentoring throughout the bank. In addition, mentored employees have become much more proactive about managing their own careers, something that we discuss later in this chapter.[48]

Bank of Montreal
www.bmo.com

For women who are unable to find an effective mentor, establishing an informed and supportive social network is a way to obtain some of the career and psychosocial functions we discussed above.

Race, Ethnicity, and Mentoring. Limited racial and ethnic diversity at higher levels of organizations constrain the mentoring opportunities available to younger minority group employees. Research shows that mentors tend to select apprentices who are similar to them in terms of race and nationality as well as gender.[49] While there are exceptions, research confirms that minority apprentices in cross-ethnic group mentoring relationships tend to report less assistance compared with those with same-race mentors.[50]

IBM
www.ibm.com

Cross-race mentoring relationships seem to focus on instrumental or career functions of mentoring (e.g., sponsorship, coaching, and feedback) and provide less psychosocial support functions (e.g., role modelling, counselling) than is generally seen in same-race dyads.[51] Although the increasing diversity of organizations makes this tendency less problematic, it suggests that minority group members should put extra efforts into developing a supportive network of peers who can provide emotional support and role modelling as well as the career functions. It also means that organizations must do more to provide mentoring opportunities for minority employees, just as some have done for women. One organization that is doing this is IBM, where an Asian Task Force identifies and develops talented Asian employees across North America who might benefit from mentoring.[52]

Proactive Socialization: What Newcomers Can Do to Socialize Themselves

On the basis of what you have read so far in this chapter, you might have the impression that individuals are at the mercy of organizations to socialize them and help them progress in their careers. This, however, is not the case. You may recall from Chapter 2 that individuals also learn by interacting and observing the behaviour of others and through self-regulation. You also learned how people with a proactive personality have a tendency to behave proactively and to effect positive change in their environment. Thus, it should not surprise you that newcomers can be proactive in their socialization and in the management of their careers through the use of proactive behaviours. In fact, observation has been found to be one of the most common ways that newcomers learn on the job, and newcomer self-regulation behaviour has been found to be related to lower anxiety and stress and to a more successful socialization.[53]

Proactive socialization.
The process through which newcomers play an active role in their own socialization through the use of a number of proactive socialization tactics.

Proactive socialization refers to the process in which newcomers play an active role in their socialization through the use of a number of proactive tactics. Exhibit 8.5 describes the major types of proactive socialization tactics. One of the most important proactive tactics that newcomers can employ during socialization is to request feedback about their performance and to seek information about their work tasks and roles as well as about their group and organization. Recall that organizational socialization is about learning the attitudes, knowledge, and behaviours that are necessary to function as an effective member of a group and organization. One way for new employees to learn is to seek information from others in the organization.[54]

Newcomers can acquire information by requesting it, by asking questions, and by observing the behaviour of others. In addition, there are different sources that can be used to acquire information, such as supervisors, co-workers, mentors, and written documents. However, research has found that newcomers rely primarily on observation, followed by interpersonal sources (i.e., supervisors and co-workers). Furthermore, they tend to seek out task-related information the most, especially during the early period of socialization, followed by role, group, and organization information. Research has also found that feedback and information seeking is related to greater knowledge of different content areas as well as to higher job satisfaction, organizational commitment, job performance, and lower levels of stress, intentions to quit, and turnover. Furthermore, supervisors are the information source most strongly related to positive socialization outcomes.[55]

In addition to feedback and information seeking, there are a number of other proactive tactics that newcomers can use, such as socializing, networking, and building relationships with co-workers and members of the organization, negotiating job changes to improve P–J fit, career enhancing strategies to improve one's career opportunities, involvement in different work-related activities to acquire new knowledge and skills, and finding a mentor.[56] As indicated earlier, having a mentor is extremely important for one's socialization and career development. Thus, new hires should be proactive in finding a mentor if their organization does not have a formal mentoring program.

General socializing. Participating in social office events and attending social gatherings (e.g., parties, outings, clubs, lunches).

Boss relationship building. Initiating social interactions to get to know and form a relationship with one's boss.

Networking. Socializing with and getting to know members of the organization from various departments and functions.

Feedback-seeking. Requesting information about how one is performing one's tasks and role.

Information-seeking. Requesting information about one's job, role, group and organization.

Observation. Observing and modelling the behaviour of appropriate others.

Behavioural self-management. Managing one's socialization through self-observation, self-goal setting, self-reward, and rehearsal.

Relationship building. Initiating social interactions and building relationships with others in one's area or department.

Job change negotiation. Attempts to change one's job duties or the manner and means by which one performs one's job in order to increase the fit between oneself and the job.

Involvement in work-related activities. Participating in "extra-curricular" work-related activities that are work-related but not part of one's job.

Career-enhancing strategies. Engaging in behaviours to improve one's career opportunities, such as working on varied tasks and job assignments and seeking additional job responsibilities.

Informal mentor relationships. Forming relationships with experienced organization members who act as informal mentors.

EXHIBIT 8.5 Proactive socialization tactics.

Sources: Ashford, S.J., & Black, J.S. (1996). Proactivity during organizational entry: The role of desire for control. *Journal of Applied Psychology, 81*, 199–214; Feij, J.A., Whitely, W.T., Peiro, J.M., & Taris, T.W. (1995). The development of career-enhancing strategies and content innovation: A longitudinal study of new workers. *Journal of Vocational Behavior, 46*, 231–256; Griffin, A.E.C., Colella, A., & Goparaju, S. (2000). Newcomer and organizational socialization tactics: An interactionist perspective. *Human Resource Management Review, 10*, 453–474.

One of the primary goals of organizational socialization is to ensure that new employees learn and understand the key beliefs, values, and assumptions of an organization's culture and for individuals to define themselves in terms of the organization and what it is perceived to represent. This is known as **organizational identification,** and as shown in Exhibit 8.1, it is also an outcome of socialization. Organizational identification reflects an individual's learning and acceptance of an organization's culture, and it has been found to be positively related to work attitudes, intentions, and behaviours.[57] In the next section, we will describe the meaning and role of organizational culture.

Organizational identification. The extent to which an individual defines him or herself in terms of the organization and what it is perceived to represent.

ORGANIZATIONAL CULTURE

The last several pages have been concerned with socialization into an organization. To a large degree, the course of that socialization both depends on and shapes the culture of the organization. As indicated in the chapter opening vignette, learning about the company's culture is the most important outcome of the socialization process at The Ritz-Carlton. Let's examine culture, a concept that has gained the attention of both researchers and practising managers.

What Is Organizational Culture?

At the outset, we can say that organizational culture is not the easiest concept to define. Informally, culture might be thought of as an organization's style, atmosphere, or personality. This style, atmosphere, or personality is most obvious when we contrast what it must be like to work in various organizations such as Suncor Energy Inc., the Royal Bank of Canada, WestJet, or The Ritz-Carlton. Even from their mention in the popular press, we can imagine that these organizations provide very different work environments. Thus, culture provides uniqueness and social identity to organizations.

More formally, **organizational culture** consists of the shared beliefs, values, and assumptions that exist in an organization.[58] In turn, these shared beliefs, values, and assumptions determine the norms that develop and the patterns of behaviour that emerge from these norms. The term *shared* does not necessarily mean that members are in close agreement on these matters, although they might well be. Rather, it means that they have had uniform exposure to them and have some minimum common understanding of them. This is, of course, the result of the socialization process at Fairmont Hotels & Resorts and The Ritz-Carlton where they engage in the culture each and every day. Several other characteristics of culture are important.

Organizational culture. The shared beliefs, values, and assumptions that exist in an organization.

- Culture represents a true "way of life" for organizational members, who often take its influence for granted. Frequently, an organization's culture becomes obvious only when it is contrasted with that of other organizations or when it undergoes changes.

- Because culture involves basic assumptions, values, and beliefs, it tends to be fairly stable over time. In addition, once a culture is well established, it can persist despite turnover among organizational personnel, providing social continuity.

- The content of a culture can involve matters that are internal to the organization or external. Internally, a culture might support innovation, risk taking, or secrecy of information. Externally, a culture might support "putting the customer first" or behaving unethically toward competitors.

- Culture can have a strong impact on both organizational performance and member satisfaction.

Culture is truly a social variable, reflecting yet another aspect of the kind of social influence that we have been discussing in this chapter. Thus, culture is not simply an automatic consequence of an organization's technology, products, or size. For example, there is some tendency for organizations to become more bureaucratic as they get larger. However, the culture of a particular large organization might support an informal, nonbureaucratic atmosphere.

Subcultures. Smaller cultures that develop within a larger organizational culture that are based on differences in training, occupation, or departmental goals.

Can an organization have several cultures? The answer is yes. Often, unique **subcultures** develop that reflect departmental differences or differences in occupation or training.[59] A researcher who studied Silicon Valley computer companies found that technical and professional employees were divided into "hardware types" and "software types." In turn, hardware types subdivided into engineers and technicians, and software types subdivided into software engineers and computer scientists. Each group had its own values, beliefs, and assumptions about how to design computer systems.[60] Effective organizations will develop an overarching culture that manages such divisions. For instance, a widely shared norm might exist that in effect says, "We fight like hell until a final design is chosen, and then we all pull together."

The "Strong Culture" Concept

Strong culture. An organizational culture with intense and pervasive beliefs, values, and assumptions.

Some cultures have more impact on the behaviour of organizational members than others. In a **strong culture**, the beliefs, values, and assumptions that make up the culture are both intense and pervasive across the organization.[61] In other words, they are strongly supported by the majority of members, even cutting across any subcultures that might exist. Thus, the strong culture provides great consensus concerning "what the organization is about" or what it stands for. In weak cultures, on the other hand, beliefs, values, and assumptions are less strongly ingrained or less widely shared across the organization. Weak cultures are thus fragmented and have less impact on organizational members. All organizations have a culture, although it might be hard to detect the details of weak cultures.

To firm up your understanding of strong cultures, let's consider thumbnail sketches of some organizations that are generally agreed to have strong cultures.

- *Hilti (Canada) Corp.* For ten years, the construction-equipment manufacturer in Mississauga, Ontario, developed a can-do attitude using Gung Ho! as its mantra and a culture that emphasizes the importance of worthwhile work, being in control of achieving your goals, and celebrating others' successes. The company takes its culture so seriously that last year Gung Ho! was transformed into a new program called Culture Journey to ensure that all employees know what Hilti stands for and expects. Most of the company's employees have gone through the mandatory two-day Culture Journey, which reintroduces them to the company's culture. In addition, all new recruits now get two days of "culture training" before they begin four weeks of product and sales training, and that's after four weeks of pre-training! In 2006, Hilti was selected by *Maclean's* magazine as one of the best workplaces in Canada.[62]

Hilti Canada
www.hilti.ca

- *Flight Centre.* Flight Centre is an Australia-based company that has 170 stores and over 900 employees in North America. The company is known for its youthful and energetic staff and for an egalitarian culture that is also fun and caring. In fact, the company's annual reports state that "Fun is an essential part of our company." Monthly parties and thank-you trips are part of a culture that some employees jokingly refer to as a "cult."[63]

- *Suncor Energy Inc.* Suncor Energy Inc. is an integrated energy company headquartered in Calgary, Alberta. The company was recently selected by *Maclean's* magazine as one of Canada's top 100 employers and in 2005 was ranked fifth on a list of Canada's most admired corporate cultures. CEO Rick George describes Suncor's culture as being open and non-bureaucratic, with a clear strategy that employees relate to, enabling them to learn from mistakes.[64]

Suncor Energy Inc.
www.suncor.com

Fun is an essential part of the culture of Flight Centre, where employees attend monthly parties called "buzz nights."

WestJet
www.westjet.com

- *WestJet Airlines.* Since its inception in 1996, the Calgary-based company has turned a consistent profit in the turbulent airline industry by focusing on low-cost, short-distance flights. WestJet is known for its relaxed, fun, and youthful culture and for fostering a family atmosphere and a desire to maximize profits that has inspired extremely high employee motivation and commitment. WestJet was ranked as having the most admired Canadian corporate culture in Canada in 2005 and 2006. Interestingly, the airline and its culture are modelled after the successful Dallas-based airline, Southwest Airlines.[65] To find out about some of the other companies with the most admired corporate cultures in Canada, see Exhibit 8.6.

Three points are worth emphasizing about strong cultures. First, an organization need not be big to have a strong culture. If its members agree strongly about certain beliefs, values, and assumptions, a small business, school, or social service agency can have a strong culture. Second, strong cultures do not necessarily result in blind conformity. For example, a strong culture at 3M supports and rewards *non*conformity in the form of innovation and creativity. Finally, Hilti, Flight Centre, Suncor, and WestJet are obviously successful organizations. Thus, there is a strong belief that strong cultures are associated with greater success and effectiveness.

Assets of Strong Cultures

Organizations with strong cultures have several potential advantages over those lacking such a culture.

Coordination. In effective organizations, the right hand (e.g., finance) knows what the left hand (e.g., production) is doing. The overarching values and assumptions of strong cultures can facilitate such communication. In turn, different parts of the organization can learn from each other and can coordinate their efforts. This is especially important in decentralized, team-oriented organizations.

Saturn
www.saturn.com

Comparing the General Motors Saturn organization to established GM divisions provides a good contrast in cultural strength and coordination. Saturn, which has a strong culture oriented toward customer service, received praise from the automotive press for its communication with customers and dealers when inevitable early-model quality problems cropped up. When quality problems arose with the new Chevy Camaro and Pontiac Firebird, GM received praise for not shipping defective cars, but it was criticized for not communicating well with customers and dealers.[66] Ironically, GM developed Saturn in part to serve as a cultural model for the established GM divisions that have long had rather fragmented cultures.

Conflict Resolution. You might be tempted to think that a strong culture would produce strong conflicts within an organization—that is, you might expect the intensity associated with strongly held assumptions and values to lead to friction among orga-

Rank	Organization
#1	WestJet Airlines
#2	Royal Bank of Canada
#3	Canadian Tire Corporation
#4	Tim Hortons Inc.
#5	Dell Inc. (Canada)
#6	Microsoft Canada Co.
#7	Four Seasons Hotels Inc.
#8	Research in Motion Limited
#9	Starbucks Coffee Canada Inc.
#10 (Tie)	Yellow Pages Group Co.
#10 (Tie)	Manulife Financial Corporation

nizational members. There might be some truth to this. Nevertheless, sharing core values can be a powerful mechanism that helps to ultimately resolve conflicts—a light in a storm, as it were. For example, in a firm with a core value of fanatical customer service, it is still possible for managers to differ about how to handle a particular customer problem. However, the core value will often suggest an appropriate dispute resolution mechanism—"Let's have the person who is closest to the customer make the final decision."

Financial Success. Does a strong culture pay off in terms of dollars and cents—that is, do the assets we discussed above get translated into bottom-line financial success? The answer seems to be yes, as long as the liabilities discussed below can be avoided.

One study of insurance companies found that firms whose managers responded more consistently to a culture survey (thus indicating agreement about the firm's culture) had greater asset and premium growth than those with disagreement.[67] Another study had members of six international accounting firms complete a value survey, the results of which you see in Exhibit 8.7. Because all firms were in the same business, there is some similarity to their value profiles (e.g., attention to detail is valued over innovation). However, close inspection shows that the six firms actually differ a good deal in their value profiles. Firms E and F tended to emphasize the work task values of detail and stability and to deemphasize a team orientation and respect for people. Comparatively, firms A, B, and C tended to emphasize these interpersonal relationship values. The author determined that firms E and F had much higher employee turnover rates compared with firms A, B, and C, a fact that was estimated to cost firms E and F between $6 and $9 million a year.[68]

There is growing consensus that strong cultures contribute to financial success and other indicators of organizational effectiveness *when the culture supports the mission, strategy, and goals of the organization.*[69] This is certainly the case for The Ritz-Carlton, where the company's culture is considered to be integral to the hotel's success. Another good example is WestJet Airlines. A key aspect of WestJet's corporate culture is a universal desire to maximize profits. The company has not only become one of the most profitable airlines in North America, but it is also the most successful low-cost carrier in Canadian history. According to company CEO Clive Beddoe, WestJet's corporate culture is the primary reason for its extraordinary performance. "The entire environment is conducive to bringing out the best in people," he says. "It's the culture that creates the passion to succeed."[70]

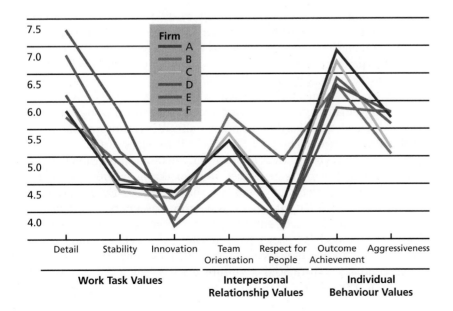

EXHIBIT 8.7

Scores on organizational culture values across six accounting firms.

Source: Sheridan, J.E. (1992). Organizational culture and employee retention. *Academy Management Journal, 35*, 1036–1056. Reprinted with permission. This material is protected by copyright and is being used with permission from *Access Copyright.* Any alteration of its content or further copying in any form whatsoever is strictly prohibited.

Perhaps it's no wonder, then, that executives across Canada ranked WestJet as having the most admired corporate culture in Canada. Most of the executive respondents also believe that there is a direct correlation between culture and an organization's health and financial performance, and that corporate culture has a tangible impact on their long-term success and an organization's ability to recruit, manage, and retain the best people. In fact, the 10 Canadian organizations listed in Exhibit 8.6 had a three-year average revenue growth of almost three times that of the S&P/TSX 60, and a three-year asset growth almost four times that of the S&P/TSX 60.[71]

Liabilities of Strong Cultures

On the other side of the coin, strong cultures can be a liability under some circumstances.

Resistance to Change. The mission, strategy, or specific goals of an organization can change in response to external pressures, and a strong culture that was appropriate for past success might not support the new order. That is, the strong consensus about common values and appropriate behaviour that makes for a strong culture can prove to be very resistant to change. This means that a strong culture can damage a firm's ability to innovate.

An excellent example is the case of IBM. A strong culture dedicated to selling and providing excellent service for mainframe computers contributed to the firm's remarkable success. However, this strong culture also bred strong complacency that damaged the company's ability to compete effectively with smaller, more innovative firms. IBM's strong mainframe culture limited its competitiveness in desktop computing, software development, and systems compatibility.

Oracle Corporation
www.oracle.com

Another good example is the sales culture of software giant Oracle Corporation, which has been described as hyperaggressive and tough as nails—the toughest ever seen in the industry. Oracle salespeople have been accused of using brute-force tactics, heavy-handed sales pitches, and even routinely running roughshod over customers. Although the culture was once the envy of the industry and the major reason Oracle became the world's second-largest software company, the industry has changed and now the culture has been described as its own worst enemy. CEO Larry Ellison set out to change the company's aggressive sales culture, and one of the first things he did was eliminate a long-established incentive system that encouraged furious sales pushes, over-promising, and steep discounts.[72]

Security Pacific
www.securitypacific.com

Hewlett-Packard
www.hp.com

Culture Clash. Strong cultures can mix as badly as oil and water when a merger or acquisition pushes two of them together under the same corporate banner.[73] Both General Electric and Xerox, large organizations with strong cultures of their own, had less-than-perfect experiences when they acquired small high-tech Silicon Valley companies with unique cultures. The merger of BankAmerica and Security Pacific resulted in a particularly strong culture clash. In each of these cases, the typical scenario concerns a freewheeling smaller unit confronting a more bureaucratic larger unit.

The merger of Hewlett-Packard and Compaq also raised concerns about a culture clash given the different work habits, attitudes, and strategies of the two companies. For example, Hewlett-Packard is known for careful, methodical decision making while Compaq has a reputation for moving fast and correcting mistakes later. Hewlett-Packard is engineering oriented and Compaq is sales oriented. The merger involved a vicious battle inside Hewlett-Packard that was described as a corporate civil war. Now that the companies have merged, employees who were once rivals have to work together and learn new systems. They have to resolve culture clashes and overcome the fact that more often than not, high-tech mergers fail. This, however, is nothing new to Compaq. The company experienced a culture clash when it merged with Digital Equipment Corp. in 1998. Many of the promised benefits did not materialize, product decisions were not made quickly or were changed, and confused customers took their business elsewhere.[74]

Pathology. Some strong cultures can threaten organizational effectiveness simply because the cultures are, in some sense, pathological.[75] Such cultures may be based on beliefs, values, and assumptions that support infighting, secrecy, and paranoia, pursuits that hardly leave time for doing business. The collapse of Enron has been blamed in part on a culture that valued lies and deception rather than honesty and truths, and the collapse of WorldCom has been attributed to a culture of secrecy and blind obedience in which executives were encouraged to hide information from directors and auditors and told to simply follow orders. The use of unethical and fraudulent accounting practices was part and parcel of both cultures (see Chapter 12).[76]

Another example of a pathological culture is NASA's culture of risk taking. Although the cause of the fatal crash of the Columbia space shuttle in February 2003 was a chunk of foam about the size of a briefcase, the root cause was NASA's culture that downplayed space-flight risks and suppressed dissent. A report by the Columbia Accident Investigation Board concluded that "NASA's organizational culture had as much to do with this accident as foam did." The report indicated that the culture of NASA has sacrificed safety in the pursuit of budget efficiency and tight schedules. One of the Board's recommendations was that the "self-deceptive" and "overconfident" culture be changed.[77]

NASA
www.nasa.gov

Contributors to the Culture

How are cultures built and maintained? In this section, we consider two key factors that contribute to the foundation and continuation of organizational cultures. Before continuing, please consult the You Be the Manager feature, *"A Shift in Culture for Yellow Pages Group."*

Yellow Pages Group
www.yellowpages.ca

The Founder's Role. It is certainly possible for cultures to emerge over time without the guidance of a key individual. However, it is remarkable how many cultures, especially strong cultures, reflect the values of an organization's founder.[78] The imprint of Walt Disney on the Disney Company, Sam Walton on Wal-Mart, Ray Kroc on McDonald's, Thomas Watson on IBM, Frank Stronach on Magna International, Mary Kay Ash on Mary Kay Cosmetics, and Bill Gates on Microsoft is obvious. As we shall see shortly, such imprint is often kept alive through a series of stories about the founder passed on to successive generations of new employees. This provides continuing reinforcement of the firm's core values.

CEO Frank Stronach of Magna International is a classic example of a founder whose values have shaped the organization's culture.

In a similar vein, most experts agree that top management strongly shapes the organization's culture. The culture will usually begin to emulate what top management "pays attention to." For example, the culture of IBM today is much different than it was under the leadership of Thomas Watson who created a culture that reflected his own personality. Louis Gerstner, Jr., who took over as CEO in 1993 until his retirement in 2002, made diversity a top priority. As a result, the culture of IBM became a more people-friendly one in which individuals are valued for their unique traits, skills, and contributions—a sharp contrast to the culture of conformity under the leadership of Thomas Watson. Today, IBM is regarded as a leader in workplace diversity.[79]

Sometimes the culture begun by the founder can cause conflict when top management wishes to see an organization change directions. At Apple Computer, Steven Jobs nurtured a culture based on new technology and new products—innovation was everything. When top management perceived this strategy to be damaging profits, it introduced a series of controls and changes that led to Jobs' resignation as board chair.[80] At Oracle, many people who are familiar with the company believed that to change the culture they must also change the CEO.

Apple Computer
www.apple.com

☞ YOU BE THE
Manager

A Shift in Culture for Yellow Pages Group

With over 2000 employees, Montreal-based Yellow Pages Group (YPG) is Canada's largest telephone directories publisher and has been an industry leader since it published its first directory in 1908. YPG is the official publisher for Bell's directories in Canada and for TELUS directories. YPG now publishes more than 330 directories with a total circulation of 28 million copies reaching over 90 percent of Canadians. It also owns some of Canada's leading Internet directories, such as YellowPages.ca, and seven local online guides, generating an average of five million unique visitors each month.

Today, YPG's market performance is impressive, with 12-month increases of 113 percent in revenues, 580 percent in profits, and 310 percent in earnings per share. However, achieving this success has required a considerable change in the company's culture. In the 1980s, the introduction of the colour red into advertisements in the profitable yet lethargic telephone business was considered "innovative." Today, the business has changed drastically in response to new competitive pressures like the Internet that require content-rich product offerings, brand leadership, and innovative thinking. It also requires a customer-focused and result-oriented corporate culture, according to YPG president and CEO, Marc P. Tellier.

However, YPG's culture was less than dynamic. According to Tellier, there was a "sense of entitlement" in the business and little accountability for results. The culture needed to change. "We like to characterize this business as a 100-year-old start-up," says Tellier. The cultural shift started with internal marketing of three new YPG guiding principles after Kohlberg Kravis Roberts & Co. and Ontario Teachers' Merchant Bank acquired control of YPG from BCE Inc. in 2002. First, says Tellier, there had to be open, honest, and timely communication. "We put a lot of emphasis on the three words because if it's not open, it's not honest," he says. "And importantly, if it's not timely, what's the point?" Second, the organization would promote the "sense of

Rejuvenating a 100-year-old "start-up"

excellence." Third, there would only be fact-based decision making. "There are no sacred cows," says Tellier, "Everything should be questioned."

But what should the new culture be like? What values are required to respond to new competitive pressures? And what will it take to change employee behaviours and accept the new culture? You be the manager.

QUESTIONS

1. What kind of culture should the company build and what values should be emphasized?

2. What should the company do to build the culture and change employee behaviours?

To find out about YPG's new culture and how it was changed, see The Manager's Notebook at the end of the chapter.

Source: Excerpt from 2005 Canadian corporate culture study. Waterstone Human Capital Ltd. Toronto, Ontario.

Another potential source of conflict can arise when an organization expands into a country where the national culture conflicts with the organization's culture. For a good example of this, see "Global Focus: *Mary Kay Cosmetics Goes to China.*"

Mary Kay Cosmetics
www.marykay.com

Socialization. The precise nature of the socialization process is a key to the culture that emerges in an organization because socialization is one of the primary means by which individuals can learn the culture's beliefs, values, and assumptions. Weak or fragmented cultures often feature haphazard selection and a nearly random series of job assignments that fail to present the new hire with a coherent set of experiences. On the other hand, Richard Pascale of Stanford University notes that organizations with strong cultures go to great pains to expose employees to a careful step-by-step socialization process (Exhibit 8.8).[81]

GLOBAL FOCUS

Mary Kay Cosmetics Goes to China

Mary Kay Cosmetics provides a good example of how a company that is founded on a particular set of social values can successfully penetrate a market whose national culture is very different.

Mary Kay Cosmetics has been a fixture in North America since 1963 and first entered the Chinese market in 1995. While there were some problems at first, the company is now doing well there. Since the difficult five-month period in 1998 when the Chinese government banned the kind of direct sales that the company relies on, company earnings have almost doubled.

Apart from the direct-sales embargo, the company's first stumbling blocks upon entering the Chinese market were cultural: In North America, Mary Kay's corporate values are "God first, family second, and career third." The company had to make some changes to these values to be accepted in China. The country is officially atheist, so most Chinese are not very comfortable with the concept of God. Mary Kay China therefore changed "God first" to "Principle first," but it stood by the remainder of its tenets, providing a challenge for some of its employees—since many Chinese consider their career more important than their family.

Other parts of Mary Kay's corporate culture and values, however, mesh more easily with Chinese culture. The company's golden rule, treat others as you want to be treated, is a big part of traditional Chinese culture, as is the social activism the company encourages. As a demonstration of their commitment to social causes, Mary Kay China employees collected $500 000 to help victims of the 2004 tsunami in the Indian Ocean. The golden rule also makes Mary Kay a loyal employer: During the Chinese government's ban on direct sales, not a single employee was laid off.

The philosophy, according to Paul Mak, president of Mary Kay China, is "Don't sell to people; care for people, and that will help you to sell. If you don't have the company culture, you won't have business."

The approach of Mary Kay Cosmetics is also based on a pro-feminist philosophy of personal empowerment—with the underlying goal of enriching each woman's life. Mary Kay China has 370 full-time employees, including the 120 people who work in the Mary Kay China factory and the 50 people who supply the products to the consultants and motivate them. The average age of an employee is 30. Adjusting to the Mary Kay corporate culture has clearly been easier for young people, who have, perhaps, been less influenced by socialist doctrine.

As in North America, the actual selling of Mary Kay products is done by independent contractors, who are called "beauty consultants." Mary Kay China now has about 250 000 beauty consultants, approximately 100 000 of whom are very active. Just as in North America, these consultants are motivated by incentives: Thousands have earned Mary Kay pink cell phones, and the top "prize" is currently a Mary Kay pink Buick. But soon top sellers will be able to earn that North American icon, the coveted Mary Kay pink Cadillac. Mary Kay has truly arrived in China!

Source: Booe, M. (2005, April). Sales force at Mary Kay China embraces the American way. *Workforce Management, 84(4)*, 24–25.

EXHIBIT 8.8
Socialization steps in strong cultures.

Source: From Pascale, R. The paradox of "corporate culture": Reconciling ourselves to socialization. Copyright © 1985, by The Regents of the University of California. Reprinted from the *California Management Review*, Vol. 27, No. 2. By permission of The Regents.

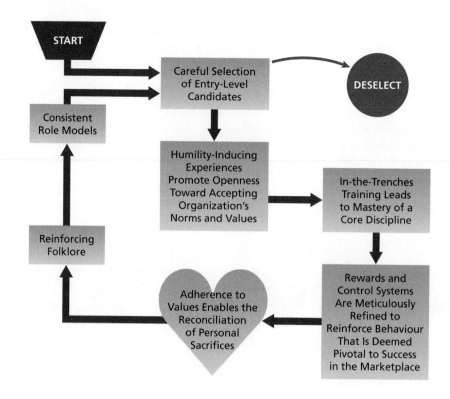

- *Step 1—Selecting Employees.* New employees are carefully selected to obtain those who will be able to adapt to the existing culture, and realistic job previews are provided to allow candidates to deselect themselves (i.e., self-selection). As an example, Pascale cites Procter & Gamble's series of individual interviews, group interviews, and tests for brand management positions.

- *Step 2—Debasement and Hazing.* Debasement and hazing provoke humility in new hires so that they are open to the norms of the organization.

- *Step 3—Training "in the Trenches."* Training begins "in the trenches" so that employees begin to master one of the core areas of the organization. For example, even experienced MBAs will start at the bottom of the professional ladder to ensure that they understand how *this* organization works. At Lincoln Electric, an extremely successful producer of industrial products, new MBAs literally spend eight weeks on the welding line so that they truly come to understand and appreciate Lincoln's unique shop floor culture.

- *Step 4—Reward and Promotion.* The reward and promotion system is carefully used to reinforce those employees who perform well in areas that support the goals of the organization.

- *Step 5—Exposure to Core Culture.* Again and again, the culture's core beliefs, values, and assumptions are asserted to provide guidance for member behaviour. This is done to emphasize that the personal sacrifices required by the socialization process have a true purpose.

- *Step 6—Organizational Folklore.* Members are exposed to folklore about the organization, stories that reinforce the nature of the culture. We examine this in more detail below.

- *Step 7—Role Models.* Identifying people as "fast-trackers" provides new members with role models whose actions and views are consistent with the culture. These role models serve as tangible examples for new members to imitate.

Pascale is careful to note that it is the *consistency* among these steps and their mutually reinforcing properties that make for a strong culture. Given that they are socializing theme park employees rather than rocket scientists, it is remarkable how many of these tactics the Disney company uses. Selection is rigorous, and grooming standards serve as mild debasement. Everyone begins at the bottom of the hierarchy. Pay is low, but promotion is tied to performance. Folklore stresses core values ("Walt's in the park."). And better performers serve as role models at Disney University or in paired training. At Four Seasons Hotels and Resorts, where the company wants new employees to buy into the team philosophy and a "service mindset," all new hires—from hotel managers to dishwashers—go through four interviews during the selection process and once hired they enter a three-month socialization program.[82]

Four Seasons Hotels & Resorts
www.fourseasons.com

Diagnosing a Culture

Earlier, we noted that culture represents a "way of life" for organizational members. Even when the culture is strong, this way of life might be difficult for uninitiated outsiders to read and understand. One way to grasp a culture is to examine the symbols, rituals, and stories that characterize the organization's way of life. For insiders, these symbols, rituals, and stories are mechanisms that teach and reinforce the culture.

Symbols. At the innovative Chaparral Steel Company in Texas, employees have to walk through the human resources department to get to their lockers. Although this facilitates communication, it also serves as a powerful symbol of the importance that the company places on its human resources. For years, IBM's "respect for the individual" held strong symbolic value that was somewhat shaken with its first-ever layoffs. Such symbolism is a strong indicator of corporate culture.[83]

Chaparral Steel
www.chaparralsteel.com

Some executives are particularly skilled at using symbols consciously to reinforce cultural values. Retired chairman and CEO Carl Reichardt of Wells Fargo was known as a fanatic cost cutter. According to one story, Reichardt received managers requesting capital budget increases while sitting in a tatty chair. As managers made their cases, Reichardt picked at the chair's exposed stuffing, sending a strong symbolic message of fiscal austerity. This was in case they had missed the message conveyed by having to pay for their own coffee and their own office Christmas decorations![84]

Wells Fargo
www.wellsfargo.com

Rituals. Observers have noted how rites, rituals, and ceremonies can convey the essence of a culture.[85] For example, at Tandem, a California computer company, Friday afternoon "popcorn parties" are a regular ritual. (For years, these parties were called "beer busts." We will leave it up to you to decide whether this change of names is symbolic of a major cultural shift!) The parties reinforce a "work hard, play hard" atmosphere and reaffirm the idea that weekly conflicts can be forgotten. The Disney picnics, beach parties, and employee nights are indicative of a peer-oriented, youth-oriented culture. At Flight Centre, the monthly parties called "buzz nights," at which employees are recognized for their accomplishments, are indicative of a youthful, energetic, and fun culture. At Mary Kay Cosmetics, elaborate "seminars" with the flavour of a Hollywood premiere combined with a revival meeting are used to make the sales force feel good about themselves and the company. Pink Cadillacs and other extravagant sales awards reinforce the cultural imperative that any Mary Kay woman can be successful. Rituals need not be so exotic to send a cultural message. In some companies, the annual performance review is an act of feedback and development. In others, it might be viewed as an exercise in punishment and debasement.

Stories. As we noted earlier, the folklore of organizations—stories about past organizational events—is a common aspect of culture. These stories, told repeatedly to successive generations of new employees, are evidently meant to communicate "how things work," whether they are true, false, or a bit of both. Anyone who has spent much time in a particular organization is familiar with such stories, and they often appear to reflect the uniqueness of organizational cultures. However, research indicates that a few common themes underlie many organizational stories.

- Is the big boss human?
- Can the little person rise to the top?
- Will I get fired?
- Will the organization help me when I have to move?
- How will the boss react to mistakes?
- How will the organization deal with obstacles?[86]

McDonald's
www.mcdonalds.com

Issues of equality, security, and control underlie the stories that pursue these themes. Also, such stories often have a "good" version, in which things turn out well, and a "bad" version, in which things go sour. For example, there is a story that Ray Kroc, McDonald's founder, cancelled a franchise after finding a single fly in the restaurant.[87] This is an example of a sour ending to a "how will the boss react to mistakes?" story. Whether the story is true or not, its retelling is indicative of one of the core values of the McDonald's culture—a fanatical dedication to clean premises.

☞ THE MANAGER'S
Notebook

A Shift in Culture for Yellow Pages Group

The Yellow Pages Group is an excellent example of how an organization can change its values and culture and the actions involved in the process. In 2005 and 2006, the company was ranked as having one of the 10 most admired corporate cultures in Canada.

1. Management's objectives included building a performance-driven culture that focused on results with more employee accountability and respect in the workplace. Six values, or "ground rules," were promoted to encourage behavioural changes: customer focus, compete to win, teamwork, passion, respect, and open communication.

2. One of the first things the company did was to demonstrate that the organization's own people were important contributors. Internal talent was promoted to highly visible positions, while others were recruited from the outside for some key roles. According to Tellier, efforts were made to ensure they had the "right people in the right seat on the right bus." In addition, small things like printing the ground rules on the back of employees' security access cards had a big impact. And because the company did not have a common message or language in the marketplace, they developed the YPG Value Equation, which became a kind of internal script that highlights the organization's strengths and superior market position. "You have to create a framework in terms of how you get there and how you live it day-in and day-out with a set of values that people can relate to," says Tellier. Management also played an important role. In its efforts to question internal processes, the company ended up redesigning all reporting methods to encourage greater individual accountability. Senior management also demonstrated teamwork, such as spending one day a week making calls with the advertising force. Most importantly, "we were conscious about not making cultural change an objective in and of itself. While corporate culture is what we're trying to drive," says Tellier, "culture is a by-product of other behaviours. Our focus was on accomplishments that we were incredibly proud of, such as our heritage, brand, and products. We then made people accountable for their actions and started expecting more of ourselves."

LEARNING OBJECTIVES CHECKLIST

1. There are two basic forms of social dependence. *Information dependence* means that we rely on others for information about how we should think, feel, and act. *Effect dependence* means that we rely on rewards and punishments provided by others. Both contribute to conformity to norms.

2. There are several motives for conformity to social norms. One is *compliance,* in which conformity occurs mainly to achieve rewards and avoid punishment. It is mostly indicative of effect dependence. Another motive for conformity is *identification* with other group members. Here, the person sees himself or herself as similar to other organizational members and relies on them for information. Finally, conformity may be motivated by the *internalization* of norms, and the person is no longer conforming simply because of social dependence.

3. *Socialization* is the process by which people learn the norms and roles that are necessary to function in a group or organization. It is a process that affects proximal socialization outcomes (i.e., learning about one's tasks, roles, group, and organization; role conflict; role ambiguity; task mastery; social integration; and person–job and person–organization fit) as well as distal socialization outcomes (job satisfaction, organizational commitment, organizational identification, organizational citizenship behaviour, stress, job performance, and turnover). Organizational members learn norm and role requirements through three stages of socialization: anticipatory, encounter, and role management.

4. People entering organizations tend to have expectations that are inaccurate and unrealistically high that can cause them to experience a reality shock when they enter an organization. The *psychological contract* refers to beliefs held by employees regarding the reciprocal obligations and promises between them and their organization. Psychological contract breach is common and can have a negative effect on employees' work attitudes and behaviours. Socialization programs can help new hires form realistic expectations and accurate perceptions of the psychological contract.

5. *Realistic job previews* can help new members cope with initial unrealistic expectations. *Employee orientation programs* introduce new employees to their job, the people they will be working with, and the organization. *Socialization tactics* refer to the manner in which organizations structure the early work experiences of newcomers and individuals who are in transition from one role to another. Institutionalized socialization reflects a formalized and structured program of socialization, while individualized socialization reflects a relative absence of structure. *Mentors* can assist new members during socialization and influence their career success by performing career and psychosocial functions. New members can play an active role in their socialization through the use of *proactive socialization tactics,* such as feedback and information seeking. An important outcome of organizational socialization is *organizational identification,* which refers to the extent to which an individual defines him or herself in terms of the organization and what it is perceived to represent.

6. *Organizational culture* consists of the shared beliefs, values, and assumptions that exist in an organization. *Subcultures* can develop that reflect departmental or occupational differences. In *strong cultures,* beliefs, values, and assumptions are intense, pervasive, and supported by consensus. An organization's founder and its socialization practices can strongly shape a culture.

7. The assets of a strong culture include good coordination, appropriate conflict resolution, and financial success. Liabilities of a strong culture include inherent pathology, resistance to change, and culture clash when mergers or acquisitions occur.

8. Symbols, rituals, and stories are often useful for diagnosing a culture.

OB FLASHBACK

The Effect of Culture on Learning

In Chapter 2, a number of organizational learning practices were described, including organizational behaviour modification, employee recognition programs, training, and career development. These practices are often used by organizations so that employees learn new skills and change their behaviour. However, research has shown that they are not always effective. For example, research on training has found that employees do not always apply what they learn in training back on the job.

The degree to which employees apply the knowledge, skills, and behaviours acquired in training on the job is known as the *transfer of training*. Over the years, training researchers have noted the relatively low rates of transfer of training, and some have suggested that there exists a transfer problem in organizations. Why do you think that training programs sometimes fail to transfer?

J. Bruce Tracey, Scott Tannenbaum, and Michael Kavanagh suggested that for training to transfer, the culture of an organization must support learning. In particular, they suggested that a critical factor in the transfer of training is the extent to which an organization has a continuous-learning culture. A continuous-learning culture is a culture in which the members of an organization share perceptions and expectations that learning is an important part of everyday worklife. These perceptions and expectations constitute important organizational values and beliefs, and they are influenced by a number of factors such as challenging jobs; supportive social, reward, and development systems; and an innovative and competitive work setting. In a continuous-learning culture, knowledge and skill acquisition is the responsibility of every employee and supported by social interaction and work relationships. Learning is a taken-for-granted part of every job in the organization. Thus, a continuous-learning culture is one component of an organization's overall culture that promotes the acquisition, application, and sharing of knowledge, skills, and behaviours through a variety of means and sources.

To investigate the effects of a continuous-learning culture on employee learning and behaviour, the authors conducted a study in 52 stores of a large supermarket chain. The sample included 104 store managers who attended a three-day training program on basic supervisory behaviour and skills that included interpersonal skills like customer and employee relations and various administrative procedures. Following the training, the trainees as well as members of their work group, including their supervisors and four or five of their managerial co-workers, completed a questionnaire to measure the degree to which there exists a continuous-learning culture. At approximately six to eight weeks after training, trainees' supervisors completed a questionnaire to measure their use and application of the trained supervisory skills and behaviours on the job.

The results indicated that the manager trainees' use and application of the supervisory training skills and behaviours on the job was strongly influenced by the degree to which they work in a continuous-learning culture. In particular, trainees who worked in a continuous-learning culture were more likely to use and apply the trained supervisory skills and behaviours on the job. Thus, a continuous-learning culture was a major factor in the transfer of training.

This research is a good example of the importance of an organization's culture for learning. It is also a good demonstration of the influence of the situation on employee learning and behaviour. In particular, the results indicate that the work environment plays a critical role in employee learning and the application of newly acquired knowledge, skills, and behaviour on the job. Thus, to be most effective, organizational learning practices must be supported by a learning culture.

Source: Adapted from Tracey, J.B., Tannenbaum, S.I., & Kavanagh, M.J. (1995). Applying trained skills on the job: The importance of the work environment. *Journal of Applied Psychology, 80*, 239–252. Copyright by the American Psychological Association. Adapted with permission.

DISCUSSION QUESTIONS

1. Compare and contrast information dependence with effect dependence. Under which conditions should people be especially information dependent? Under which conditions should people be especially effect dependent?

2. Describe an instance of social conformity that you have observed in an organizational setting. Did compliance, identification, or internalization motivate this incident? Were the results beneficial for the organization? Were they beneficial to the individual involved?

3. Consider how you were socialized into the college or university where you are taking your organizational behaviour course. Did you have some unrealistic expectations? Where did your expectations come from? What outside experiences prepared you for college or university? Did you experience institutionalized or individualized socialization? What proactive socialization tactics did you employ to facilitate your socialization?

4. What are the pros and cons of providing realistic job previews for a job that is objectively pretty bad?

5. Imagine that you are starting a new business in the retail trade. You are strongly oriented toward providing excellent customer service. What could you do to nurture a strong organizational culture that would support such a mission?

6. Discuss the advantages and disadvantages of developing a strong organizational culture and some socialization practices that you would recommend for building a strong organizational culture.

7. Describe how you would design a new employee orientation program. Be sure to indicate the content of your program and what knowledge and information employees will acquire from attending the program. What are some of the outcomes that you would expect from your orientation program?

INTEGRATIVE DISCUSSION QUESTIONS

1. What are the implications of social cognitive theory for social influence and socialization? Discuss the practical implications of each component of social cognitive theory (i.e., modelling, self-efficacy, and self-regulation) for the socialization of new organization members. Describe how you would design an orientation program for new employees based on social cognitive theory. Consider the implications of social cognitive theory for mentoring. What does social cognitive theory say about why mentoring is important and how to make it effective?

2. Refer to the work-related values that differ across cultures in Chapter 4 (i.e., work centrality, power distance, uncertainty avoidance, masculinity/femininity, individualism/collectivism, long-term/short-term orientation) and consider how the culture of an organization in Canada might lead to conflicts in a country with different work-related values than Canada. Give some examples of the kind of organizational culture that might conflict with the various work-related values in other countries. What are the implications of this for Canadian companies that wish to expand abroad?

ON-THE-JOB CHALLENGE QUESTION

In an effort to transform its US operation, which continues to lose money and threatens to bring down the entire corporation, Ford Motor Company has embarked on an ambitious people management restructuring plan. Its "Way Forward" plan will attempt to transform the company's workforce from a culture of bureaucrats monitoring clock watchers to a collaborative team focused on making customers happy. This will involve a dramatic shift to a less bureaucratic and more responsive and flexible management style. It plans to restore North America to profitability by 2008. According to former Ford chairman and CEO Bill Ford, "We are going to be a big company that thinks like a small company." In September of 2006, Bill Ford stepped down as president and chief executive officer of Ford Motor Company, handing over the reins to Alan Mulally. Mulally was formally the executive vice-president of Boeing Company, where he is credited with the turnaround of the company's commercial airplane division.

How important is it for Ford to change its culture? What do they need to do to change it and restore the company to profitability? Was it a good idea for Bill Ford to step down as CEO? What effect might the appointment of Alan Mulally as CEO have on the transformation of the company's culture? What advice would you give Mulally about trying to change the culture? How likely is it that Ford will achieve its goal to transform the company's workforce and culture?

Sources: Based on original work by Laura Tannis, from *Organizational Behaviour: Canadian Cases and Exercises*, 5th ed., by Randy Hoffman and Fred Ruemper (Concord, ON: Captus Press Inc., 2004), pp.163–165. Reprinted with permission of Captus Press Inc. www.captus.com.

EXPERIENTIAL EXERCISE

The Organizational Culture–Values Survey

The purpose of the Organizational Culture–Values Survey is for you to learn about those values that are most important to you and to develop a values profile of yourself. You can also compare your values with those of a current or previous organization where you were employed. By comparing the rankings of each list you can determine the degree of person–organization fit between your values and those of the organization.

First, rank the values in the order of most importance to you. Place the number 1 next to the value you feel is most important and the number 16 next to the one you think is least important. Then number the second and fifteenth and so on. Second, do the same thing for your current organization if you are employed or the most recent organization where you were last employed.

Scoring and Interpretation

Compare your values profile to the values orientation of your organization. For each value, calculate the difference between the two rankings in the space indicated, and then calculate a total difference score. A small difference indicates a better person–organization fit between your values and those of your organization. Large differences indicate a lack of person–organization fit or a mismatch. Research indicates that a good person–organization fit between an employee's values and those of the organization is positively related to job attitudes and work behaviour.

To facilitate class discussion and your understanding of values and organizational culture, form a small group with several other members of the class and consider the following issues.

Your Values	Organizational Values	Difference
_____ Ambition	____ Ambition	_____
_____ Broadmindedness	____ Broadmindedness	_____
_____ Competence	____ Competence	_____
_____ Cheerfulness	____ Cheerfulness	_____
_____ Cleanliness	____ Cleanliness	_____
_____ Courage	____ Courage	_____
_____ Helpfulness	____ Helpfulness	_____
_____ Honesty	____ Honesty	_____
_____ Imagination	____ Imagination	_____
_____ Independence	____ Independence	_____
_____ Intelligence	____ Intelligence	_____
_____ Obedience	____ Obedience	_____
_____ Politeness	____ Politeness	_____
_____ Responsibility	____ Responsibility	_____
_____ Self-control	____ Self-control	_____
_____ Tolerance	____ Tolerance	_____

Source: Based on original work by Laura Tannis, from *Organizational Behaviour: Canadian Cases and Exercises*, 5th ed., by Randy Hoffman and Fred Ruemper (Concord, ON: Captus Press Inc., 2004), pp.163–165. Reprinted with permission of Captus Press Inc. www.captus.com.

1. Each group member should present their total difference score and explain how different their values are from the values of their organization and the effect this had on their job attitudes and behaviour. Do students with smaller difference scores report more positive job attitudes and are they less likely to quit?

2. How can an understanding of the values that are most important to you assist in your decision to join an organization? Make a list of what group members have done in the past to determine if their values are a good match for an organization they considered working for. What should you do next time you decide to apply for and accept a job offer?

3. What are the implications for organizations that hire employees whose values differ from those of the organization, and what should they do about it?

4. How can organizational socialization be used to ensure that new hires have values that are consistent with the organization's culture?

CASE INCIDENT

The Reality Shock

Soon after starting his new job, Jason began to wonder about the challenging work he was supposed to be doing, the great co-workers he was told about, and the ability to attend training and development programs. None of these things seemed to be happening as he had expected. To make matters worse, he had spent most of the first month working on his own and reading about the organization's mission, history, policies, and so on. Jason is beginning to wonder if this is the right job and organization for him. He is feeling very dissatisfied and is seriously thinking about quitting.

1. Explain how Jason's anticipatory socialization might be contributing to his disappointment and job attitudes. How might this situation have been prevented?

2. Given Jason's current situation, is there anything the organization can do to prevent him from quitting? Is there anything they should do so other new hires don't have the same experience as Jason?

3. Explain how unrealistic expectations and the psychological contract can help us understand Jason's situation.

CASE STUDY

Changing the Culture at Home Depot

When Robert Nardelli arrived at Home Depot in December 2000, the deck seemed stacked against the new CEO. He had no retailing experience and, in fact, had spent an entire career in industrial, not consumer, businesses. His previous job was running General Electric's power systems division, whose multimillion-dollar generating plants for industry and governments were a far cry from $10 light switches for do-it-yourselfers. Nardelli was also taking over what seemed to be a wildly successful company with a 20-year record of growth that had outpaced even Wal-Mart—but with latent financial and operational problems that threatened its continued growth, and even its future, if they weren't quickly addressed.

Over the past five years, Home Depot's performance has indeed been put on a stable footing. Although its share price is well below the peak it achieved shortly before Nardelli arrived, and the rate of revenue increase has cooled from the breakneck pace of the late 1990s, the company continues to enjoy robust and profitable growth. Revenue climbed to around $80 billion in 2005, and earnings per share have more than doubled since 2000. Just as important, a platform has been built to generate future growth.

Home Depot is one of the business success stories of the past quarter century. Founded in 1978 in Atlanta, the company grew to more than 1100 big-box stores by the end of 2000; it reached the $40 million revenue mark faster than any retailer in history. The company's success stemmed from several distinctive characteristics, including the warehouse feel of its orange stores, complete with low lighting, cluttered aisles, and sparse signage; a "stack it high, watch it fly" philosophy that reflected a primary focus on sales growth; and extraordinary store manager autonomy, aimed at spurring innovation and allowing managers to act quickly when they sensed a change in local market conditions.

Home Depot's culture, set primarily by the charismatic Bernard Marcus (known universally among employees as Bernie), was itself a major factor in the company's success. It was marked by an entrepreneurial high-spiritedness and a willingness to take risks; a passionate commitment to customers, colleagues, the company, and the community; and an aversion to anything that felt bureaucratic or hierarchical.

Long-time Home Depot executives recall the disdain with which store managers used to view directives from headquarters. Because everyone believed that managers should spend their time on the sales floor with customers, company paperwork often ended up buried under piles on someone's desk, tossed in a wastebasket, or even marked with a company-supplied "B.S." stamp and sent back to the head office. Such behaviour was seen as a sign of the company's unflinching focus on the customer. "The idea was to challenge senior managers to think about whether what they were sending out to the stores was worth store managers' time," says Tom Taylor, who started at Home Depot in 1983 as a parking lot attendant and today is executive vice-president for merchandising and marketing.

There was a downside to this state of affairs, though. Along with arguably low-value corporate paperwork, an important store safety directive might disappear among the unread memos. And while their sense of entitled autonomy might have freed store managers to respond to local market conditions, it paradoxically made the company as a whole less flexible. A regional buyer might agree to give a supplier of, say, garden furniture, prime display space in dozens of stores in exchange for a price discount of 10 percent—only to have individual store managers ignore the agreement because they thought it was a bad idea. And as the chain mushroomed in size, the lack of strong career development programs was leading Home Depot to run short of the talented store managers on whom its business model depended.

All in all, the cultural characteristics that had served the retailer well when it had 200 stores started to undermine it when Lowe's began to move into Home Depot's big metropolitan markets from its small-town base in the mid-1990s. Individual autonomy and a focus on sales at any cost eroded profitability, particularly as stores weren't able to benefit from economies of scale that an organization the size of Home Depot should have enjoyed.

Nardelli's arrival at Home Depot came as a shock. No one had expected that Marcus (then chairman) and Arthur Blank (then CEO) would be leaving anytime soon. Most employees simply couldn't picture the company without these father figures. And if there was going to be change at the top of this close-knit organization, in which promotions had nearly always come from within, no one wanted, as Nardelli himself acknowledges, an outsider who would "GE-ize their company and culture."

To top it off, Nardelli's exacting and tough-minded approach, which he learned at General Electric, set him on a collision course with the freewheeling yet famously close-knit culture fostered by his predecessors, Home Depot's legendary co-founders, Marcus and Blank. It was this culture that Nardelli had to reshape if he hoped to bring some big-company muscle to the entrepreneurial organization (which, with revenue of $46 billion in 2000, was sometimes referred to as a "$40 billion start-up") and put the retailer's growth on a secure foundation.

Nardelli laid out a three-part strategy: enhance the core by improving the profitability of current and future stores in existing markets; extend the business by offering related services such as tool rental and home installation of Home Depot products; and expand the market, both geographically and by serving new kinds of customers, such as big construction contractors.

To meet his strategy goals, Nardelli had to build an organization that understood the opportunity in, and the importance of, taking advantage of its growing scale. Some functions, such as purchasing (or merchandising), needed to be centralized to leverage the buying power that a giant company could wield. Previously autonomous functional, regional, and store operations needed to collaborate—merchandising needed to work more closely with store operations, for instance, to avoid conflicts like the one over the placement of garden furniture. This would be aided by making detailed performance data transparent to all the relevant parties simultaneously so that people could base decisions on shared information. The merits of the current store environment needed to be re-evaluated; its lack of signage and haphazard layout made increasingly less sense for time-pressed shoppers. And a new emphasis needed to be placed on employee training, not only to bolster the managerial ranks but also to transform orange-aproned sales associates from cheerful greeters into knowledgeable advisers who could help customers solve their home improvement problems. As Nardelli likes to say, "What so effectively got Home Depot from zero to $50 billion in sales wasn't going to get it to the next $50 billion." The new strategy would require a careful renovation of Home Depot's strong culture.

Shortly after arriving, Nardelli hired an old colleague from GE, Dennis Donovan, as his head of human resources. By placing a trusted associate in a position known for its conspicuous lack of influence in most executive suites—and by making him one of Home Depot's highest-paid executives—Nardelli signalled that changing the culture would be central to getting the company where it needed to go.

Source: Excerpt from Charan, R. (2006). Home Depot's blueprint for culture change. *Harvard Business Review, 84(4)*, 60–70.

1. Why does Home Depot need to change its culture? What are the consequences it faces if it does not change the culture?

2. Describe Home Depot's culture and the role it has played in the company's success. How should the culture change? What norms and patterns of behaviour need to be developed? How should the new culture differ from the old culture?

3. Do you agree with the board's decision to hire an outsider as the new CEO, especially someone who has worked in a company with a very different culture? What are the advantages and disadvantages of this?

4. What are some of the risks and obstacles that Nardelli faces in trying to change the culture of Home Depot? What should he do to manage them?

5. How should Nardelli change the culture of Home Depot? What does he have to do, and how should he proceed?

CHAPTER 9

Leadership

Rajesh Subramaniam is by all measures an example of an effective leader. He is the youngest senior executive ever to be named by FedEx, and his rise through the ranks is considered meteoric. After 15 years of working for the company in the United States and Hong Kong, Subramaniam was named head of Canadian operations in 2003. As president of FedEx Canada, he is responsible for overseeing the strategic direction and the management of sales, marketing, air and ground operations, customer service, and customs brokerage for FedEx Canada.

However, getting to the top was not so easy. Subramaniam had a tough time getting hired by any company after finishing his MBA degree at the University of Texas at Austin. He was on a student visa and needed employer sponsorship to stay in the United States—but it was 1991, the height of a recession. He was turned down in many job interviews, but FedEx decided to take a chance on him, hiring him as a junior marketing analyst. After shining in Memphis, he was sent to head up marketing in FedEx's Hong Kong office. After seven years there, he landed the top job in Canada, where he is credited with improving employee morale and profits.

When Subramaniam was appointed in 2003 to head Canadian operations, morale was bad and profits were flat. Today, according to in-house surveys, morale is soaring and profit is up 19 percent. An informal survey of employees elicits effusive praise for Subramaniam. What is Subramaniam's philosophy for success? "If you take good care of your people, they will go the extra mile to deliver the best service, and then profit takes care of itself," he explains. He vowed to personally meet each of FedEx's 5000 Canadian employees, and after 18 months into the job he had shaken hands with about 90 percent of them.

As part of CBC *Venture's* "The Big Switcheroo," Subramaniam traded in his suit and corner office for a FedEx uniform. For a week he worked at front-line jobs—as a courier delivering parcels, a runner in the hub locating parcels, a mechanic, and taking orders over the phone. "I didn't crash the truck," laughs Subramaniam. "Seriously, it was a terrific experience. It made crystal clear to me how important providing a good customer experience is to our success. There is a moment of magic when an employee hands off a package to a customer." Subramaniam found working different jobs so invaluable that he had his senior management team also do service on the front lines for a day. Not only was the stint

1. Define and discuss the role of both formal and emergent *leadership*.

2. Explain and critically evaluate the *trait* approach to leadership.

3. Explain the *task* function and *social-emotional* function of emergent leadership and the concepts of *consideration, initiating structure, reward,* and *punishment leader behaviour* and their consequences.

4. Describe and evaluate *Fiedler's Contingency Theory*.

5. Describe and evaluate *House's Path-Goal Theory*.

6. Explain how and when to use *participative leadership*.

7. Describe and evaluate *Leader–Member Exchange Theory*.

8. Discuss the merits of *transformational* and *transactional leadership*.

9. Describe and evaluate *strategic leadership*.

10. Explain the role that culture plays in leadership effectiveness and describe *global leadership*.

11. Define and discuss *ethical leadership*.

12. Describe gender differences in leadership styles.

Rajesh Subramaniam is the youngest senior executive ever to be named by FedEx, and his rise through the ranks has been meteoric.

FedEx Canada
www.fedex.ca

eye-opening for Subramaniam, it endeared him to FedEx employees and garnered their respect.

Everyone at FedEx—from the receptionist to his senior executive team—calls him Raj, not Mr. Subramaniam. "That's my dad; plus, they can't pronounce it anyway," he jokes. And it is easy to see why. "He's a people person. He makes you feel like what you do is important," says receptionist Germina Dias.

According to another employee, before Subramaniam arrived employees didn't feel appreciated. That changed when Subramaniam instituted policies such as an across-the-board Christmas bonus and allowing couriers to be off the road by 1 p.m. in the event of bad winter weather. "That shows how caring he is. He doesn't put profits ahead of staff safety. He's a down-to-earth guy who listens to us," says Leon Gayle, a FedEx courier. Gayle was so impressed with the new boss that he sent him a "Bravo Zulu," an in-house award typically sent from managers to employees to recognize outstanding work. Though Subramaniam has a host of awards in his office, he prizes the Bravo Zulu from Gayle the most. "It blew me away. It was so unusual and so touching. It was a signal that I was moving in the right direction."

In March of 2006, the International Association of Business Communicators (IABC) named Subramaniam as the recipient of the 2006 Excellence in Communication Leadership (EXCEL) Award. The EXCEL Award is the organization's highest award given to non-members and recognizes individuals who exhibit strong leadership in fostering excellence in communication and who contribute to the development and support of organizational communication.

Throughout his career at FedEx, Subramaniam's leadership has been key to developing and executing successful strategies for revenue growth, profitability, brand awareness, and corporate reputation. According to Warren Bickford, chair of IABC, "Rajesh recognizes the communication challenges unique to the structure of the FedEx operation with 85 percent of employees, primarily on-road couriers, without regular intranet or e-mail access. He ensured that systems were in place so that these front-line employees were kept informed and engaged in their organization. Rajesh makes communication a key component of his business decision making and understands the value and importance of strategic communication in achieving business success."

In June 2006, Rajesh Subramaniam was appointed to the position of senior vice-president of international marketing for FedEx Services. He will be responsible for developing and implementing strategic international marketing plans and directing the development of new service opportunities around the globe.[1]

Rajesh Subramaniam's story is a case study in successful leadership. But what exactly is leadership, and what makes a leader successful? Would Rajesh Subramaniam be successful in other leadership situations? These are the kinds of issues that this chapter tackles.

First, we will define leadership and find out if we can identify special leadership traits. After this, we will explore how leaders emerge in groups. Next, we will examine the consequences of various leadership behaviours and examine theories contending that effective leadership depends on the nature of the work situation. Following this are discussions of participation, leader–member exchange theory, transformational leadership, strategic leadership, culture and global leadership, and ethical leadership. We conclude the chapter with a discussion of gender differences in leadership style.

WHAT IS LEADERSHIP?

Several years ago, an article in *Report on Business Magazine* highlighted the perceived importance of leadership in business and public affairs. The cover story, "The toughest SOBs in business," profiles Canada's toughest bosses and suggests that effective leaders have a rare combination of vision, skills, expertise, and toughness. More recently, the magazine's cover story featured the 25 most powerful executives in Canada, noting that to make the list you need influence, the ability to get your way with governments, the public, partners, and peers. It is therefore not surprising that corporations in North America spend billions of dollars each year to make their leaders more effective.[2]

Leadership occurs when particular individuals exert influence on the goal achievement of others in an organizational context. Thus, *Report on Business Magazine* argues for the merits of "toughness," "influence," and "power" and points out that one trait shared by effective leaders is the ability to drive relentlessly toward a goal, even if it means being intimidating or infuriating. Effective leadership exerts influence in a way that achieves organizational goals by enhancing the productivity, innovation, satisfaction, and commitment of the workforce.

In theory, *any* organizational member can exert influence on other members, thus engaging in leadership. In practice, though, some members are in a better position to be leaders than others. Individuals with titles such as *manager, executive, supervisor,* and *department head* occupy formal or assigned leadership roles. As part of these roles they are *expected* to influence others, and they are given specific authority to direct employees. Of course, the presence of a formal leadership role is no guarantee that there is leadership. Some managers and supervisors fail to exert any influence on

Leadership. The influence that particular individuals exert on the goal achievement of others in an organizational context.

others. These people will usually be judged to be ineffective leaders. Thus, leadership involves going beyond formal role requirements to influence others.

Individuals might also emerge to occupy informal leadership roles. Since informal leaders do not have formal authority, they must rely on being well liked or being perceived as highly skilled to exert influence. In this chapter we will concentrate on formal leadership, although we will consider informal leadership as well.

ARE LEADERS BORN? THE SEARCH FOR LEADERSHIP TRAITS

Throughout history, social observers have been fascinated by obvious examples of successful interpersonal influence, whether the consequences of this influence were good, bad, or mixed. Individuals such as Henry Ford, Martin Luther King, Jr., Barbara Jordan, Ralph Nader, and Jack Welch have been analyzed and reanalyzed to discover what made them leaders and what set them apart from less successful leaders. The implicit assumption here is that those who become leaders and do a good job of it possess a special set of traits that distinguish them from the masses of followers. While philosophers and the popular media have advocated such a position for centuries, trait theories of leadership did not receive serious scientific attention until the 1900s.

Research on Leadership Traits

During World War I the US military recognized that it had a leadership problem. Never before had the country mounted such a massive war effort, and able officers were in short supply. Thus, the search for leadership traits that might be useful in identifying potential officers began. Following the war, and continuing through World War II, this interest expanded to include searching for leadership traits in populations as diverse as school children and business executives. Some studies tried to differentiate traits of leaders and followers, while others were a search for traits that predicted leader effectiveness or distinguished lower-level leaders from higher-level leaders.[3]

Traits. Individual characteristics such as physical attributes, intellectual ability, and personality.

Just what is a trait, anyway? **Traits** are personal characteristics of the individual, including physical characteristics, intellectual ability, and personality. Research has shown that many, many traits are not associated with whether people become leaders or how effective they are. However, research also shows that some traits are associated with leadership. Exhibit 9.1 provides a list of these traits.[4] As you might expect, leaders (or more successful leaders) tend to be higher than average on these dimensions, although the connections are not very strong. Notice that the list portrays a high energy person who really wants to have an impact on others but at the same time is smart and stable enough not to abuse his or her power. Interestingly, this is a very accurate summary description of Suncor Energy Inc. CEO Rick George, who is credited with saving the once struggling company and was named Canada's CEO of the year in 1999.

In recent years, there has been a renewed interest in the study of leadership traits, and a number of studies have shown that certain traits are more closely linked to leadership emergence and effectiveness. For example, one study found that three of the "Big Five" dimensions of personality (agreeableness, extraversion, and openness to experience) are related to leadership behaviours. A review of research on intelligence and leadership found that although there is a significant relationship between intelligence and leadership, it is considerably lower than previously thought.[5] In addition, research that compared top performers with average performers in senior leadership positions found that the most effective leaders have high levels of emotional intelligence. The emotional intelligence of leaders has also been found to be positively related to the job satisfaction and organizational citizenship behaviour of employees.[6] Many

Intelligence
Energy
Self-confidence
Dominance
Motivation to lead
Emotional stability
Honesty and integrity
Need for achievement

EXHIBIT 9.1
Traits associated with leadership effectiveness.

prominent firms use personality tests and assessment centres to measure leadership traits when making hiring and promotion decisions. However, there are some aspects to the trait approach that limit its ultimate usefulness.

Limitations of the Trait Approach

Even though some traits appear to be related to leadership, there are several reasons why the trait approach is not the best means of understanding and improving leadership.

In many cases, it is difficult to determine whether traits make the leader or whether the opportunity for leadership produces the traits. For example, do dominant individuals tend to become leaders, or do employees become more dominant *after* they successfully occupy leadership roles? This distinction is important. If the former is true, we might wish to seek out dominant people and appoint them to leadership roles. If the latter is true, this strategy will not work.

Even if we know that dominance, intelligence, or tallness is associated with effective leadership, we have few clues about what dominant or intelligent or tall people *do* to influence others successfully. As a result, we have little information about how to train and develop leaders and no way to diagnose failures of leadership.

Rick George, CEO of Suncor Energy Inc., exhibits many of the traits associated with leadership effectiveness and was named Canada's CEO of the year in 1999.

The most crucial problem of the trait approach to leadership is its failure to take into account the *situation* in which leadership occurs. Intuitively, it seems reasonable that top executives and first-level supervisors might require different traits to be successful. Similarly, physical prowess might be useful in directing a logging crew but irrelevant to managing a team of scientists.

In summary, although there are some traits that are associated with leadership success, traits alone are not sufficient for successful leadership. Traits are only a precondition for certain actions that a leader must take to be successful. In other words, possessing the appropriate traits for leadership makes it possible—and even more likely—that certain actions will be taken and will be successful.[7] Let's now consider what "actions" are important for leadership.

LESSONS FROM EMERGENT LEADERSHIP

The trait approach is mainly concerned with what leaders *bring* to a group setting. The limitations of this approach gradually promoted an interest in what leaders *do* in group settings. Of particular interest were the behaviours of certain group members that caused them to *become* leaders. As we shall see, this study of emergent leadership gives us some good clues about what formally assigned or appointed leaders must do to be effective.

Imagine that a grass-roots organization has assembled to support the election of a local politician. In response to a newspaper ad, 30 individuals show up, all of whom admire Jonathan Greed, the aspiring candidate. The self-appointed chairperson begins the meeting and asks for volunteers for various subcommittees. The publicity subcommittee sounds interesting, so you volunteer and find yourself with six other volunteers, none of whom knows the others. Your assigned goal is to develop an effective public relations campaign for Greed. From experience, you are aware that someone will emerge to become the leader of this group. Who will it be?

Without even seeing your group interact, we can make a pretty good guess as to who will become the leader. Quite simply, it will be the person who *talks* the most, as long as he or she is perceived as having relevant expertise.[8] Remember, leadership is a form of influence, and one important way to influence the group is by speaking a lot. What would the "big talker" talk about? Probably about planning strategy, getting organized, dividing labour, and so on—things to get the task at hand accomplished. We often call such a leader a **task leader**, because he or she is most concerned with accomplishing the task at hand.

Suppose the group members are also asked who they *liked* the most in the group. Usually, there will be a fair amount of agreement, and the nominated person might be called the **social-emotional leader**. Social-emotional influence is more subtle than task influence, and it involves reducing tension, patching up disagreements, settling arguments, and maintaining morale.

In many cases, the task and social-emotional leadership roles are performed by the same group member.[9] In some instances, though, two separate leaders emerge to fill these roles. When this happens, these two leaders usually get along well with each other and respect each other's complementary skills.[10]

The emergence of two leadership roles has been noted again and again in a wide variety of groups. This suggests that task leadership and social-emotional leadership are two important functions that must occur in groups. On the one hand, the group must be structured and organized to accomplish its tasks. On the other hand, the group must stick together and function well as a social unit, or even the best structure and organization will be useless. Thus, in general, leaders must be concerned with both the social-emotional and task functions. Furthermore, organizations almost never appoint *two* formal leaders to a work group. Thus, the formal appointed leader must often be concerned with juggling the demands of two distinct roles.

There is an important qualifier to the preceding paragraph. It should be obvious that task and social-emotional functions are both especially important in the case of newly developing groups. However, for mature, ongoing groups, one leadership role might be more important than the other. For example, if group members have learned to get along well with each other, the social-emotional role might decrease in importance. Also, the two leadership roles may have different significance in different situations. Suppose a team of geologists is doing a routine series of mineral prospecting studies in a humid, bug-infested jungle. In this case, its leader might be most concerned with monitoring morale and reducing tensions provoked by the uncomfortable conditions. If the team becomes lost, task leadership should become more important—a logical plan for finding the way must be developed.

THE BEHAVIOUR OF ASSIGNED LEADERS

We turn now to the behaviour of assigned or appointed leaders, as opposed to emergent leaders. What are the crucial behaviours such leaders engage in, and how do these behaviours influence employee performance and satisfaction? In other words, is there a particular *leadership style* that is more effective than other possible styles?

Task leader. A leader who is concerned with accomplishing a task by organizing others, planning strategy, and dividing labour.

Social-emotional leader. A leader who is concerned with reducing tension, patching up disagreements, settling arguments, and maintaining morale.

Consideration and Initiating Structure

The most involved, systematic study of leadership to date was begun at Ohio State University in the 1940s. The Ohio State researchers began by having employees describe their superiors along a number of behavioural dimensions. Statistical analyses of these descriptions revealed that they boiled down to two basic kinds of behaviour—consideration and initiating structure.

Consideration is the extent to which a leader is approachable and shows personal concern and respect for employees. The considerate leader is seen as friendly, egalitarian, expresses appreciation and support, and is protective of group welfare. This is a pretty accurate description of Rajesh Subramaniam. Co-operators president and CEO Kathy Bardswick is also a good example of leader consideration behaviour. After she became CEO in 2001, she participated in 90 town hall meetings across the country to learn about employee concerns and answer their questions. Upon learning that employees were stressed and feeling the heat of public outrage at the high cost of auto insurance, she introduced a number of initiatives to assist employees, including a wellness program, recognition programs, and flexible work hours. In 2004, for the first time, the Co-operators were named one of the 50 Best Employers in Canada.[11] Obviously, consideration is related to the social-emotional function discovered in studies of emergent leadership.

Initiating structure is the degree to which a leader concentrates on group goal attainment. The structuring leader clearly defines and organizes his or her role and the roles of followers, stresses standard procedures, schedules the work to be done, and assigns employees to particular tasks. Clearly, initiating structure is related to the task function revealed in studies of emergent leadership.

It is important to note that consideration and initiating structure are not incompatible; a leader could be high, low, or average on one or both dimensions.

The Consequences of Consideration and Structure

The association between leader consideration, leader initiating structure, and employee responses has been the subject of hundreds of research studies. In general, this research shows that consideration and initiating structure both contribute positively to employees' motivation, job satisfaction, and leader effectiveness. However, consideration tends to be more strongly related to follower satisfaction (leader satisfaction and job satisfaction), motivation, and leader effectiveness, while initiating structure is slightly more strongly related to leader job performance and group performance.[12] In addition, there is some evidence that the relative importance of consideration and initiating structure varies according to the nature of the leadership situation. To be sure, consider the following:

- When employees are under a high degree of pressure due to deadlines, unclear tasks, or external threat, initiating structure increases satisfaction and performance. (Soldiers stranded behind enemy lines should perform better under directive leadership.)

- When the task itself is intrinsically satisfying, the need for high consideration and high structure is generally reduced. (The teacher who really enjoys teaching should be able to function with less social-emotional support and less direction from the principal.)

- When the goals and methods of performing the job are very clear and certain, consideration should promote employee satisfaction, while structure might promote dissatisfaction. (The job of refuse collection is clear in goals and methods. Here, employees should appreciate social support but view excessive structure as redundant and unnecessary.)

Co-operators president and CEO Kathy Bardswick is a good example of leader consideration behaviour.

Consideration. The extent to which a leader is approachable and shows personal concern and respect for employees.

Initiating structure. The degree to which a leader concentrates on group goal attainment.

- When employees lack knowledge as to how to perform a job, or the job itself has vague goals or methods, consideration becomes less important while initiating structure takes on additional importance. (The new astronaut recruit should appreciate direction in learning a complex, unfamiliar job.)[13]

As you can see, the effects of consideration and initiating structure often depend on characteristics of the task, the employee, and the setting in which work is performed.

Leader Reward and Punishment Behaviours

Leader reward behaviour.
The leader's use of compliments, tangible benefits, and deserved special treatment.

Leader punishment behaviour. The leader's use of reprimands or unfavourable task assignments and the active withholding of rewards.

Assigned leaders can do other things besides initiate structure and be considerate. Two additional leader behaviours that have been the focus of research are leader reward behaviour and leader punishment behaviour. **Leader reward behaviour** provides employees with compliments, tangible benefits, and deserved special treatment. When such rewards are made *contingent on performance*, employees should perform at a high level and experience job satisfaction. Under such leadership, employees have a clear picture of what is expected of them, and they understand that positive outcomes will occur if they achieve these expectations. **Leader punishment behaviour** involves the use of reprimands or unfavourable task assignments and the active withholding of raises, promotions, and other rewards. You will recall from Chapter 2 that punishment is extremely difficult to use effectively, and when it is perceived as random and not contingent on employee behaviour, employees react negatively with great dissatisfaction.

How effective is leader reward and punishment behaviour? A recent study examined research on leader reward and punishment behaviour and found these behaviours to be very effective. Contingent leader reward behaviour was found to be positively related to employees' perceptions (e.g., trust in supervisor), attitudes (e.g., job satisfaction and organizational commitment), and behaviour (e.g., effort, performance, organizational citizenship behaviour). And while contingent leader punishment behaviour was positively related to employee perceptions, attitudes, and behaviour, *noncontingent* punishment behaviour was negatively related. The authors noted that the relationships were much stronger when rewards and punishment were made contingent on employee behaviour, leading them to conclude that the manner in which leaders administer rewards and punishment is a critical determinant of their effectiveness. In other words, as described in Chapter 2, the key to effective reward and punishment is that it be administered contingent on employee behaviour and performance. The study also suggested that the reason leader reward and punishment behaviour is related to employee attitudes and behaviours is because it leads to more positive perceptions of justice and lower role ambiguity.[14]

SITUATIONAL THEORIES OF LEADERSHIP

We have referred to the potential impact of the situation on leadership effectiveness several times. Specifically, *situation* refers to the *setting* in which influence attempts occur. The basic premise of situational theories of leadership is that the effectiveness of a leadership style is contingent on the setting. The setting includes the characteristics of the employees, the nature of the task they are performing, and characteristics of the organization.

WestJet Airlines
www.westjet.com

A good example of the importance of the setting for the effectiveness of a leader comes from WestJet Airlines. A number of years ago, the airline hired Steve Smith to take over as CEO. At the time, Smith was running Air Canada's regional airline in Ontario. WestJet liked his amiable, energetic personality. However, once on the job it became apparent that Smith's top-down leadership style and lack of openness with employees did not fit with WestJet's more open, bottom-up, collaborative style of leadership. WestJet's employee association resented his approach and Smith eventually resigned. This is a good example of how the effectiveness of a leader's style is contingent on the setting.[15]

Situational theories of leadership explain how leadership style must be tailored to the demands of the task and the qualities of employees.

The two situational leadership theories described below are among the best known and most studied. They consider situational variables that seem especially likely to influence leadership effectiveness.

Fiedler's Contingency Theory

Fred Fiedler of the University of Washington has spent over three decades developing and refining a situational theory of leadership called **Contingency Theory**.[16] This name stems from the notion that the association between *leadership orientation* and *group effectiveness* is contingent on (depends on) the extent to which the *situation is favourable* for the exertion of influence. In other words, some situations are more favourable for leadership than others, and these situations require different orientations on the part of the leader.

Contingency Theory. Fred Fiedler's theory that states that the association between leadership orientation and group effectiveness is contingent on how favourable the situation is for exerting influence.

Leadership Orientation. Fiedler has measured leadership orientation by having leaders describe their **Least Preferred Co-Worker (LPC)**. This person may be a current or past co-worker. In either case, it is someone with whom the leader has had a difficult time getting the job done. To obtain an LPC score, the troublesome co-worker is described on eighteen scales of the following nature:

Least Preferred Co-Worker. A current or past co-worker with whom a leader has had a difficult time accomplishing a task.

$$\text{PLEASANT} :\_:\_:\_:\_:\_:\_:\_:\_: \text{UNPLEASANT}$$
$$\qquad\qquad 8\ \ 7\ \ 6\ \ 5\ \ 4\ \ 3\ \ 2\ \ 1$$

$$\text{FRIENDLY} :\_:\_:\_:\_:\_:\_:\_:\_: \text{UNFRIENDLY}$$
$$\qquad\qquad 8\ \ 7\ \ 6\ \ 5\ \ 4\ \ 3\ \ 2\ \ 1$$

The leader who describes the LPC relatively favourably (a high LPC score) can be considered *relationship* oriented—that is, despite the fact that the LPC is or was difficult to work with, the leader can still find positive qualities in him or her. On the other hand, the leader who describes the LPC unfavourably (a low LPC score) can be considered *task* oriented. This person allows the low-task competence of the LPC to colour his or her views of the personal qualities of the LPC ("If he's no good at the job, then he's not good, period.").

Fiedler has argued that the LPC score reveals a personality trait that reflects the leader's motivational structure. High LPC leaders are motivated to maintain interpersonal relations, while low LPC leaders are motivated to accomplish the task. Despite the apparent similarity, the LPC score is *not* a measure of consideration or initiating structure. These are observed *behaviours,* while the LPC score is evidently an *attitude* of the leader toward work relationships.

Situational Favourableness. Situational favourableness is the "contingency" part of Contingency Theory—that is, it specifies when a particular LPC orientation should contribute most to group effectiveness. According to Fiedler, a favourable leadership situation exists when the leader has a high degree of control and when the results of this control are very predictable. Factors that affect situational favourableness, in order of importance, are the following:

- *Leader–member relations.* When the relationship between the leader and the group members is good, the leader is in a favourable situation to exert influence. A poor relationship should damage the leader's influence and even lead to insubordination or sabotage.

- *Task structure.* When the task at hand is highly structured, the leader should be able to exert considerable influence on the group. Clear goals, clear procedures to achieve these goals, and straightforward performance measures enable the leader to set performance standards and hold employees responsible.

- *Position power.* Position power is the formal authority granted to the leader by the organization to tell others what to do. The more position power the leader holds, the more favourable is the leadership situation.

In summary, the situation is most favourable for leadership when leader–member relations are good, the task is structured, and the leader has strong position power— for example, a well-liked army sergeant who is in charge of servicing jeeps in the base motor pool. The situation is least favourable when leader–member relations are poor, the task is unstructured, and the leader has weak position power—for instance, the disliked chairperson of a voluntary homeowner's association who is trying to get agreement on a list of community improvement projects.

The Contingency Model. Under what conditions is one leadership orientation more effective than another? As shown in Exhibit 9.2, we can arrange the possible combinations of situational factors into eight octants that form a continuum of favourability. The model indicates that a task orientation (low LPC) is most effective when the leadership situation is very favourable (octants I, II, and III) *or* when it is very unfavourable (octant VIII). On the other hand, a relationship orientation (high LPC) is most effective in conditions of medium favourability (octants IV, V, VI, and VII). Why is this so? In essence, Fiedler argues that leaders can "get away" with a task orientation when the situation is favourable—employees are "ready" to be influenced. Conversely, when the situation is very unfavourable for leadership, task orientation is necessary to get any-

EXHIBIT 9.2
Predictions of leader effectiveness from Fiedler's Contingency Theory of leadership.

Favourableness	High ⬅							Low
Leader-Member Relations	Good				Poor			
Task Structure	Structured		Unstructured		Structured		Unstructured	
Position Power	Strong	Weak	Strong	Weak	Strong	Weak	Strong	Weak
	I	II	III	IV	V	VI	VII	VIII
Most Effective Leader Orientation	Task				Relationship			Task

thing accomplished. In conditions of medium favourability, the boss is faced with some combination of an unclear task or a poor relationship with employees. Here, a relationship orientation will help to make the best of a situation that is stress provoking but not impossibly bad.

Evidence and Criticism. The conclusions about leadership effectiveness in Exhibit 9.2 are derived from many studies that Fiedler summarizes.[17] However, Contingency Theory has been the subject of as much debate as any theory in organizational behaviour.[18] Fiedler's explanation for the superior performance of high LPC leaders in the middle octants is not especially convincing, and the exact meaning of the LPC score is one of the great mysteries of organizational behaviour. It does not seem to be correlated with other personality measures or predictive of specific leader behaviour. It now appears that a major source of the many inconsistent findings regarding Contingency Theory is the small sample sizes that researchers used in many of the studies. Advances in correcting for this problem statistically have led recent reviewers to conclude that there is reasonable support for the theory.[19] However, Fiedler's prescription for task leadership in octant II (good relations, structured task, weak position power) seems contradicted by the evidence, suggesting that his theory needs some adjustment.

House's Path-Goal Theory

Robert House, building on the work of Martin Evans, has proposed a situational theory of leadership called Path-Goal Theory.[20] Unlike Fiedler's Contingency Theory, which relies on the somewhat ambiguous LPC trait, **Path-Goal Theory** is concerned with the situations under which various leader *behaviours* are most effective.

Path-Goal Theory. Robert House's theory concerned with the situations under which various leader behaviours (directive, supportive, participative, achievement oriented) are most effective.

The Theory. Why did House choose the name Path-Goal for his theory? According to House, the most important activities of leaders are those that clarify the paths to various goals of interest to employees. Such goals might include a promotion, a sense of accomplishment, or a pleasant work climate. In turn, the opportunity to achieve such goals should promote job satisfaction, leader acceptance, and high effort. Thus, *the effective leader forms a connection between employee goals and organizational goals.*

House argues that to provide *job satisfaction* and *leader acceptance,* leader behaviour must be perceived as immediately satisfying or as leading to future satisfaction. Leader behaviour that employees see as unnecessary or unhelpful will be resented. House contends that to promote employee *effort,* leaders must make rewards dependent on performance and ensure that employees have a clear picture of how they can achieve these rewards. To do this, the leader might have to provide support through direction, guidance, and coaching. For example, the bank teller who wishes to be promoted to supervisor should exhibit superior effort when his boss promises a recommendation contingent on good work and explains carefully how the teller can do better on his current job.

Leader Behaviour. Path-Goal Theory is concerned with four specific kinds of leader behaviour. These include:

- *Directive behaviour.* Directive leaders schedule work, maintain performance standards, and let employees know what is expected of them. This behaviour is essentially identical to initiating structure.
- *Supportive behaviour.* Supportive leaders are friendly, approachable, and concerned with pleasant interpersonal relationships. This behaviour is essentially identical to consideration.
- *Participative behaviour.* Participative leaders consult with employees about work-related matters and consider their opinions.

- *Achievement-oriented behaviour.* Achievement-oriented leaders encourage employees to exert high effort and strive for a high level of goal accomplishment. They express confidence that employees can reach these goals.

According to Path-Goal Theory, the effectiveness of each set of behaviours depends on the situation that the leader encounters.

Situational Factors. Path-Goal Theory has concerned itself with two primary classes of situational factors—employee characteristics and environmental factors. Exhibit 9.3 illustrates the role of these situational factors in the theory. Put simply, the impact of leader behaviour on employee satisfaction, effort, and acceptance of the leader depends on the nature of the employees and the work environment. Let's consider these two situational factors in turn, along with some of the theory's predictions.

According to the theory, different types of employees need or prefer different forms of leadership. For example:

- Employees who are high need achievers (Chapter 5) should work well under achievement-oriented leadership.
- Employees who prefer being told what to do should respond best to a directive leadership style.
- When employees feel that they have rather low task abilities, they should appreciate directive leadership and coaching behaviour. When they feel quite capable of performing the task, they will view such behaviours as unnecessary and irritating.

As you can observe from these examples, leaders might have to tailor their behaviour to the needs, abilities, and personalities of individual employees.

Also, according to the theory, the effectiveness of leadership behaviour depends on the particular work environment. For example:

- When tasks are clear and routine, employees should perceive directive leadership as a redundant and unnecessary imposition. This should reduce satisfaction and acceptance of the leader. Similarly, participative leadership would not seem to be useful when tasks are clear, since there is little in which to participate. Obviously, such tasks are most common at lower organizational levels.
- When tasks are challenging but ambiguous, employees should appreciate both directive and participative leadership. Such styles should clarify the path to good performance and demonstrate that the leader is concerned with helping employees to do a good job. Obviously, such tasks are most common at higher organizational levels.
- Frustrating, dissatisfying jobs should increase employee appreciation of supportive behaviour. To some degree, such support should compensate for a disliked job, although it should probably do little to increase effort.

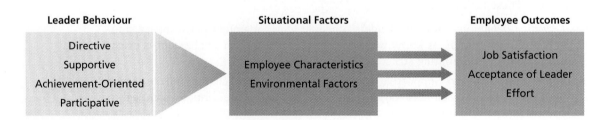

EXHIBIT 9.3
The Path-Goal Theory of leadership.

Source: From *Journal of Contemporary Business, 3(4)*, 89. Reprinted by permission.

As you can see from these examples of environmental factors, effective leadership should *take advantage of* the motivating and satisfying aspects of jobs while *offsetting or compensating for* those job aspects that demotivate or dissatisfy.

Evidence and Criticism. In general, there is some research support for most of the situational propositions discussed above. In particular, there is substantial evidence that supportive or considerate leader behaviour is most beneficial in supervising routine, frustrating, or dissatisfying jobs and some evidence that directive or structuring leader behaviour is most effective on ambiguous, less-structured jobs.[21] The theory appears to work better in predicting employees' job satisfaction and acceptance of the leader than in predicting job performance.[22]

PARTICIPATIVE LEADERSHIP: INVOLVING EMPLOYEES IN DECISIONS

In the discussion of Path-Goal Theory, we raised the issue of participative leadership. Because this is such an important topic, we will devote further attention to participation.

What Is Participation?

At a very general level, **participative leadership** means involving employees in making work-related decisions. The term *involving* is intentionally broad. Participation is not a fixed or absolute property, but a relative concept. This is illustrated in Exhibit 9.4. Here, we see that leaders can vary in the extent to which they involve employees in decision making. Minimally, participation involves obtaining employee opinions before making a decision. Maximally, it allows employees to make their own decisions within agreed-on limits. As the "area of freedom" on the part of employees increases, the leader is behaving in a more participative manner. There is, however, an upper limit to the area of employee freedom available under participation. Participative leadership should not be confused with the *abdication* of leadership, which is almost always ineffective.

Participation can involve individual employees or the entire group of employees that reports to the leader. For example, participation on an individual basis might work best when setting performance goals for particular employees, planning employee development, or dealing with problem employees. On the other hand, the leader might

Participative leadership. Involving employees in making work-related decisions.

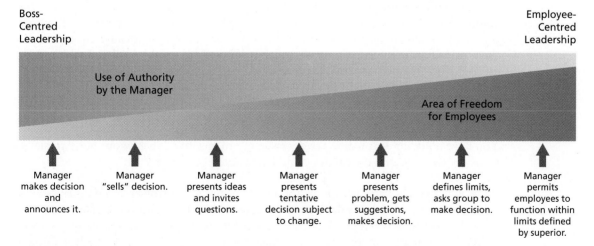

EXHIBIT 9.4
Employee participation in decision making can vary.

involve the entire work group in decision making when determining vacation schedules, arranging for telephone coverage during lunch hour, or deciding how to allocate scarce resources, such as travel money or secretarial help. As these examples suggest, the choice of an individual or group participation strategy should be tailored to specific situations.

Potential Advantages of Participative Leadership

Just why might participation be a useful leadership technique? What are its potential advantages?

Motivation. Participation can increase the motivation of employees.[23] In some cases, participation permits them to contribute to the establishment of work goals and to decide how they can accomplish these goals. It might also occur to you that participation can increase intrinsic motivation by enriching employees' jobs. In Chapter 6, you learned that enriched jobs include high task variety and increased employee autonomy. Participation adds some variety to the job and promotes autonomy by increasing the "area of freedom" (see Exhibit 9.4).

Quality. Participation can enhance quality in at least two ways. First, an old saying argues that "two heads are better than one." While this is not always true, there do seem to be many cases in which "two heads" (participation) lead to higher-quality decisions than the leader could make alone.[24] In particular, this is most likely when employees have special knowledge to contribute to the decision. In many research and engineering departments, it is common for the professional employees to have technical knowledge that is superior to that of their boss. This occurs either because the boss is not a professional or because the boss's knowledge has become outdated. Under these conditions, participation in technical matters should enhance the quality of decisions.

Participation can also enhance quality because high levels of participation often empower employees to take direct action to solve problems without checking every detail with the boss. Empowerment gives employees the authority, opportunity, and motivation to take initiative and solve problems.

Acceptance. Even when participation does not promote motivation or increase the quality of decisions, it can increase the employees' acceptance of decisions. This is especially likely when issues of *fairness* are involved.[25] For example, consider the problems of scheduling vacations or telephone coverage during lunch hours. Here, the leader could probably make high-quality decisions without involving employees. However, the decisions might be totally unacceptable to the employees because they perceive them as unfair. Involving employees in decision making could result in solutions of equal quality that do not provoke dissatisfaction. Public commitment and ego involvement probably contribute to the acceptance of such decisions.

Potential Problems of Participative Leadership

You have no doubt learned that every issue in organizational behaviour has two sides. Consider the potential difficulties of participation.

Time and Energy. Participation is not a state of mind. It involves specific behaviours on the part of the leader (soliciting ideas, calling meetings), and these behaviours use time and energy. When a quick decision is needed, participation is not an appropriate leadership strategy. The hospital emergency room is not the place to implement participation on a continuous basis!

Loss of Power. Some leaders feel that a participative style will reduce their power and influence. Sometimes, they respond by asking employees to make trivial decisions of the "what colour shall we paint the lounge" type. Clearly, the consequences of such decisions (for motivation, quality, and acceptance) are near-zero. A lack of trust in employees and a fear that they will make mistakes is often the hallmark of an insecure manager. On the other hand, the contemporary call for flatter hierarchies and increased teamwork make such sharing of power inevitable.

Lack of Receptivity or Knowledge. Employees might not be receptive to participation. When the leader is distrusted, or when a poor labour climate exists, they might resent "having to do management's work." Even when receptive, employees might lack the knowledge to contribute effectively to decisions. Usually, this occurs because they are unaware of *external constraints* on their decisions.

A Situational Model of Participation

How can leaders capitalize on the potential advantages of participation while avoiding its pitfalls? Victor Vroom and Arthur Jago have developed a model that attempts to specify in a practical manner when leaders should use participation and to what extent they should use it (the model was originally developed by Vroom and Philip Yetton).[26]

Vroom and Jago begin with the recognition that there are various degrees of participation that a leader can exhibit. For issues involving the entire work group, the following range of behaviours is plausible (*A* stands for autocratic, *C* for consultative, and *G* for group; I indicates an individual, and II indicates that a group is involved):

AI. You solve the problem or make the decision yourself, using information available to you at the time.

AII. You obtain the necessary information from your employees, then decide the solution to the problem yourself. You may or may not tell your employees what the problem is in getting the information from them. The role played by your employees in making the decision is clearly one of providing the necessary information to you, rather than generating or evaluating alternative solutions.

CI. You share the problem with the relevant employees individually, getting their ideas and suggestions without bringing them together as a group. Then you make the decision, which may or may not reflect your employees' influence.

CII. You share the problem with your employees as a group, obtaining their collective ideas and suggestions. Then you make the decision, which may or may not reflect your employees' influence.

GII. You share the problem with your employees as a group. Together you generate and evaluate alternatives and attempt to reach agreement (consensus) on a solution. Your role is much like that of chairperson. You do not try to influence the group to adopt "your" solution, and you are willing to accept and implement any solution that has the support of the entire group.[27]

Which of these strategies is most effective? According to Vroom and Jago, this depends on the situation or problem at hand. In general, the leader's goal should be to make high-quality decisions to which employees will be adequately committed without undue delay. To do this, he or she must consider the questions in Exhibit 9.5. The quality requirement (QR) for a problem might be low if it is very unlikely that a technically bad decision could be made or all feasible alternatives are equal in quality. Otherwise, QR is probably high. The commitment requirement (CR) is likely to be high if employees are very concerned about which alternative is chosen or if they will have to actually implement the decision. The problem is structured (ST) when the leader understands the current situation, the desired situation, and how to get from one to the other. Unfamiliarity, uncertainty, or novelty in any of these matters reduces problem structure. The other questions in Exhibit 9.5 are fairly self-explanatory. Notice, however, that all are oriented toward preserving either decision quality or commitment to the decision.

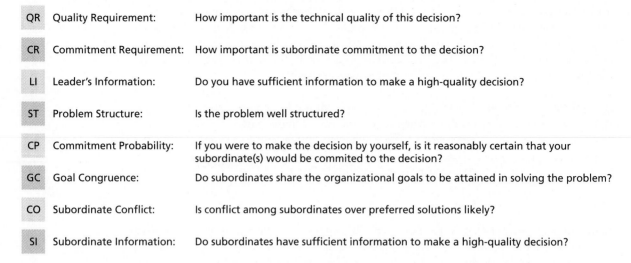

QR	Quality Requirement:	How important is the technical quality of this decision?
CR	Commitment Requirement:	How important is subordinate commitment to the decision?
LI	Leader's Information:	Do you have sufficient information to make a high-quality decision?
ST	Problem Structure:	Is the problem well structured?
CP	Commitment Probability:	If you were to make the decision by yourself, is it reasonably certain that your subordinate(s) would be commited to the decision?
GC	Goal Congruence:	Do subordinates share the organizational goals to be attained in solving the problem?
CO	Subordinate Conflict:	Is conflict among subordinates over preferred solutions likely?
SI	Subordinate Information:	Do subordinates have sufficient information to make a high-quality decision?

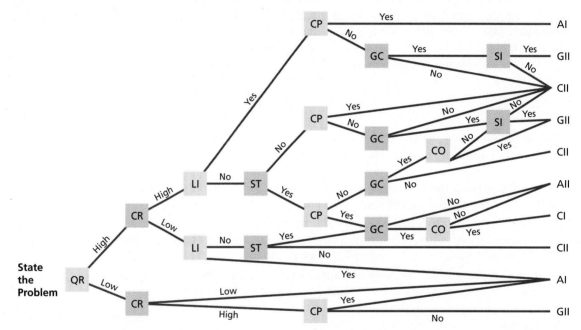

EXHIBIT 9.5

The Vroom and Jago decision tree for participative leadership.

Source: Reprinted from Vroom, V.H., & Jago, A.G. (1988). *The new leadership: Managing participation in organizations.* Englewood Cliffs, NJ: Prentice-Hall. Copyright © 1987 by Vroom, V.H., & Jago, A.G.

By tracing a problem through the decision tree, the leader encounters the prescribed degree of participation for that problem. In every case, the tree shows the fastest approach possible (i.e., the most autocratic) that still maintains decision quality and commitment. In many cases, if the leader is willing to sacrifice some speed, a more participative approach could stimulate employee development (as long as quality or commitment is not threatened).

The original decision model developed by Vroom and Yetton, on which the Vroom and Jago model is based, has substantial research support.[28] Following the model's prescriptions is more likely to lead to successful managerial decisions than unsuccessful decisions. The model has been used frequently in management development seminars.

Does Participation Work?

Now we come to the bottom line—does participative leadership result in beneficial outcomes? There is substantial evidence that employees who have the opportunity to participate in work-related decisions report more job satisfaction than those who do not. Thus, most workers seem to *prefer* a participative work environment. However, the positive effects of participation on productivity are open to some debate. For participation to be translated into higher productivity, it would appear that certain facilitating conditions must exist. Specifically, participation should work best when employees feel favourably toward it, when they are intelligent and knowledgeable about the issue at hand, and when the task is complex enough to make participation useful.[29] In general, these conditions are incorporated into the Vroom and Jago model. Like any other leadership strategy, the usefulness of participation depends on the constraints of the situation.

LEADER–MEMBER EXCHANGE (LMX) THEORY

An important component of leadership is the nature of the relationship that develops between leaders and employees. One theory of leadership that explains leader–employee relationships is **Leader–Member Exchange** or **LMX Theory**. Unlike other theories of leadership that focus on leader traits and behaviours, the focus of LMX theory is on the dyadic relationship between a leader and an employee. In other words, it is a relationship-based approach to leadership.

Leader–Member Exchange (LMX) Theory. A theory of leadership that focuses on the quality of the relationship that develops between a leader and an employee.

The basic idea is that over time and through the course of their interactions, different types of relationships develop between leaders and employees. As a result, each relationship that a leader develops with an employee will be different and unique. In terms of LMX theory, these relationships will differ in terms of the *quality* of the relationship. Effective leadership processes result when leaders and employees develop and maintain high-quality social exchange relationships.[30]

Research on LMX theory has shown that the relationships between leaders and employees do in fact differ in terms of the quality of the relationship. High-quality relationships, or high LMX, involve a high degree of mutual influence and obligation as well as trust, loyalty, and respect between a leader and an employee. High LMX leaders provide employees with challenging tasks and opportunities, greater latitude and discretion, task-related resources, and recognition. In high-quality relationships, employees perform tasks beyond their job descriptions. At the other extreme are low-quality relationships, or low LMX. Low LMX is characterized by low trust, respect, obligation, and mutual support. In low-quality relationships, the leader provides less attention and latitude to employees, and employees do only what their job descriptions and formal role requirements demand.[31]

Research has found that the quality of LMX is related to a number of employee outcomes, including higher overall satisfaction, satisfaction with supervision, organizational commitment, role clarity, and job performance, and lower role conflict and turnover intentions. In general, research on LMX theory has found that higher-quality LMX relationships result in a number of positive outcomes for leaders, employees, work units, and organizations.[32]

TRANSFORMATIONAL AND TRANSACTIONAL LEADERSHIP

Thus far in the chapter, we have been studying various aspects of what we can call *transactional leadership*. Transactional leadership is leadership that is based on a fairly straightforward exchange between the leader and the followers—employees perform well, and the leader rewards them; the leader uses a participatory style, and the employees come up with good ideas. For the most part, transactional leadership behaviour involves contingent reward behaviour as discussed earlier in the chapter and management by exception. Similar to path-goal theory, the leader clarifies expectations and establishes the rewards for meeting them. **Management by exception** is the degree to which the leader takes corrective action on the basis of results of leader–follower transactions. Thus, they monitor follower behaviour, anticipate problems, and take corrective actions before the behaviour creates serious problems.[33] Although it might be difficult to do well, such leadership is routine, in the sense that it is directed mainly toward bringing employee behaviour in line with organizational goals.

However, you might have some more dramatic examples of leadership in mind, examples in which leaders have had a more profound effect on followers by giving them a new vision that instilled true commitment to a project, a department, or an organization. Such leadership is called **transformational leadership** because the leader decisively changes the beliefs and attitudes of followers to correspond to this new vision and motivates them to achieve performance beyond expectations.[34]

Popular examples of transformational leadership are easy to find—consider Herb Kelleher's founding of Southwest Airlines, Disney CEO Michael Eisner's role in improving Disney's performance, Steven Jobs's vision in bringing the Apple Macintosh to fruition, or former Hewlett-Packard CEO Carly Fiorina's orchestration of the merger with Compaq Computer and her transformation of Hewlett-Packard's structure and culture. Each of these leaders went beyond a mere institutional figurehead role and even beyond a transactional leadership role to truly transform employees' thinking about the nature of their businesses. However, these prominent examples should not obscure the fact that transformational leadership can occur in less visible settings. For example, a new coach might revitalize a sorry peewee soccer team or an energetic new director might turn around a moribund community association using the same types of skills.

But what *are* the skills of these exceptional transformational leaders who encourage considerable effort and dedication on the part of followers? Bernard Bass of the State University of New York at Binghamton has conducted extensive research on transformational leaders.[35] Bass notes that transformational leaders are usually good at the transactional aspects of clarifying paths to goals and rewarding good performance. But he also notes other qualities that set transformational leaders apart from their transactional colleagues. In particular, there are four key dimensions of transformational leader behaviour: intellectual stimulation, individualized consideration, inspirational motivation, and charisma.[36]

Intellectual Stimulation

Intellectual stimulation contributes, in part, to the "new vision" aspect of transformational leadership. People are stimulated to think about problems, issues, and strategies in new ways. The leader challenges assumptions, takes risks, and solicits followers' ideas. Often, creativity and novelty are at work here. For example, Steve Jobs was convinced that the Apple Macintosh had to be extremely user friendly. As you might imagine, many of the technical types who wanted to sign on to the Mac project needed to be convinced of the importance of this quality, and Jobs was just the person to do it, raising their consciousness about what it felt like to be a new computer user.

Individualized Consideration

Individualized consideration involves treating employees as distinct individuals, indicating concern for their needs and personal development, and serving as a mentor or coach when appropriate. The emphasis is a one-on-one attempt to meet the concerns and needs of the individual in question in the context of the overall goal or mission. Bass implies that individualized consideration is particularly striking when military

Management by exception. The leader takes corrective action on the basis of results of leader–follower transactions.

Transformational leadership. Providing followers with a new vision that instills true commitment.

Apple Computer Inc.
www.apple.com

leaders exhibit it because the military culture generally stresses impersonality and "equal" treatment. General "Stormin'" Norman Schwarzkopf, commander of American troops during the Gulf War, was noted for this.

Inspirational Motivation

Inspirational motivation involves the communication of visions that are appealing and inspiring to followers. Leaders with inspirational motivation have a strong vision for the future based on values and ideals. They stimulate enthusiasm, challenge followers with high standards, communicate optimism about future goal attainment, and provide meaning for the task at hand. They inspire followers using symbolic actions and persuasion.[37]

Charisma

Charisma (also known as *idealized influence*) is the fourth and by far the most important aspect of transformational leadership. In fact, many authors simply talk about charismatic leadership, although a good case can be made that a person could have charisma without being a leader. **Charisma** is a term stemming from a Greek word meaning *favoured* or *gifted*.

> **Charisma.** The ability to command strong loyalty and devotion from followers and thus have the potential for strong influence among them.

Charismatic individuals have been portrayed throughout history as having personal qualities that give them the potential to have extraordinary influence over others. They tend to command strong loyalty and devotion, and this, in turn, inspires enthusiastic dedication and effort directed toward the leader's chosen mission. In terms of the concepts we developed in Chapter 8, followers come to trust and *identify* with charismatic leaders and to *internalize* the values and goals they hold. Charisma provides the *emotional* aspect of transformational leadership.

It appears that the emergence of charisma is a complex function of traits, behaviours, and being in the right place at the right time.[38] Prominent traits include self-confidence, dominance, and a strong conviction in one's beliefs. Charismatics often act to create an impression of personal success and accomplishment. They hold high expectations for follower performance while at the same time expressing confidence in followers' capabilities. This enhances the self-esteem of the followers. The goals set by charismatic leaders often have a moral or ideological flavour to them. In addition, charismatic leaders often emerge to articulate the feelings of followers in times of stress or discord. If these feelings go against an existing power structure, the leader might be perceived as especially courageous.

Charisma has been studied most intensively among political leaders and the leaders of social movements. Winston Churchill, Martin Luther King, Jr., Nelson Mandela, Pierre Elliott Trudeau, and Gandhi appear charismatic. Among American presidents, one study concludes that Jefferson, Jackson, Lincoln, Kennedy, and Reagan were charismatic, while Coolidge, Harding, and Buchanan were not.[39] Among business leaders, Frank Stronach, Richard Branson, and Jack Welch are often cited as charismatic.

Although charisma is considered to be an important aspect of transformational leadership, it has also been treated as a distinct theory of leadership in its own right and often studied independent of the other dimensions of transformational leadership. Charismatic leadership has been found to be strongly related to follower satisfaction and leadership effectiveness.[40] Several studies have investigated the charisma of CEOs and its relationship to organizational performance. The results of these studies, however, are mixed. Although CEOs who are perceived to be more charismatic tend to be perceived as more effective, only one study has found charismatic leadership to be directly related to firm performance, and two studies found a relationship, but only when the environment was perceived to be uncertain.[41] Thus, it is still unclear as to whether or not CEO charisma leads to better firm performance.

Richard Branson of Virgin Group is a charismatic leader who commands strong loyalty and devotion from his employees.

Virgin Group
www.virgin.com

In passing, we must also mention that charisma has a dark side, a side that is revealed when charismatics abuse their strong influence over others for purely personal reasons.[42] Such people often exploit the needs of followers to pursue a reckless goal or mission. Adolf Hitler and cult leader David Koresh personify extreme examples of charismatic abuse. We will explore the abuse of power further in Chapter 12.

Research Evidence. In the last two decades, there have been more published studies on transformational leadership than all other popular theories of leadership. A recent review of all these studies found transformational leadership to be strongly related to follower motivation and satisfaction (satisfaction with leader and job satisfaction), leader performance, leader effectiveness, and group and organization performance. Interestingly, contingent reward leadership behaviour was also strongly related to all of these outcomes, and management by exception was moderately related to follower motivation, satisfaction with the leader, leader job performance, and leader effectiveness. Comparisons between transformational leadership and contingent reward behaviours indicated that transformational leadership was more strongly related to follower satisfaction with the leader and leader effectiveness, while contingent reward was more strongly related to follower job satisfaction and leader job performance.[43]

Why are transformational leaders so effective? According to recent studies, transformational behaviours are instrumental in developing high-quality LMX relationships and for enhancing employees' perceptions of the five core job characteristics of the job characteristics model (see Chapter 6).[44] Overall, research supports the contention that the best leaders are both transformational and transactional.

An interesting debate about transformational leadership is whether or not transformational leaders are born or if they can be trained. To find out more, see "Research Focus: *Are Transformational Leaders Born or Made?*"

STRATEGIC LEADERSHIP

In today's rapidly changing and uncertain environment, leaders must be much more strategic than in the past when the environment was more certain and stable. Recall from the chapter opening vignette that as president of FedEx Canada, Rajesh Subramaniam was responsible for overseeing the strategic direction of the company. In his new position as senior vice-president of international marketing, he is responsible for developing and implementing strategic international marketing plans. But what does it mean to be a strategic leader, and how can organizations develop strategic leadership? Before continuing, consult the You Be the Manager feature on page 318.

RESEARCH FOCUS

Are Transformational Leaders Born or Made?

Although research has found that transformational leadership is related to leadership effectiveness across different types of organizations, leadership levels, and even cultures, it remains unclear as to whether or not this is a trait or behavioural theory of leadership and whether transformational leaders are born or made. It is possible that some aspects of transformational leadership, such as charisma, are actually traits or are influenced by traits.

To answer this question, Timothy Judge and Joyce Bono of the University of Iowa conducted a study on the "Big Five" dimensions of personality (see Chapter 2) and transformational leadership behaviour that included leaders from over 200 organizations. Leaders were asked to complete a survey to measure their personality on each of the "Big Five" dimensions. They were also asked to give a survey to several of their employees to measure their transformational leadership behaviour and to measure employees' attitudes and motivation. A survey was also given to each leader's supervisor to measure the leader's effectiveness.

The results indicated that extraversion, agreeableness, and openness to experience were positively related to transformational leadership behaviour. Neuroticism and conscientiousness were not related to transformational leadership. In a subsequent review of research on personality and transformational leadership, the authors found that extraversion was the strongest and most consistent predictor of transformational leadership and neuroticism was negatively related. Further, the charisma dimension of transformational leadership was the most strongly related to personality. These results provide some support for a dispositional basis of transformational leadership, especially with respect to charisma.

However, because personality traits have their basis in genetics as well as one's life-long learning experiences, this study does not provide conclusive evidence that transformational leaders are born. For this, we have to consider a study by Richard Arvey and colleagues that looked at the role of genetics, personality, and cognitive factors in leadership. They studied 646 identical and fraternal male twins who completed a survey about their occupancy in leadership roles in work settings.

The results indicated that one's occupancy in a leadership role could be explained by personality and cognitive factors as well as genetic factors. Thus, on the basis of this study, the authors concluded that

genetics influence personality, cognitive factors, and leadership. Overall, the results indicated that 30 percent of the variance in leadership role occupancy was explained by genetic factors, providing some evidence that leaders are born.

However, genetic factors did not completely explain leadership. Thus, leadership and, more specifically, transformational leadership must also be a function of non-genetic factors. Does this mean that transformational leaders can be made?

As it turns out, there is some evidence that transformational leadership behaviour can be learned. In one of the first studies to test the effects of transformational leadership training, Julian Barling, Tom Weber, and Kevin Kelloway studied branch managers in a large bank in Canada who received training in transformational leadership. Compared to a group of managers who did not receive the training, the employees of the trained managers perceived their managers to be higher on intellectual stimulation, charisma, and individualized consideration and reported higher organizational commitment. In addition, the branches in which the managers were trained reported better financial performance. In another study, military leaders who were trained in transformational leadership had a positive effect on followers' development and performance. Finally, in a study on charismatic leadership training, managers received training on the inspirational communication component of charismatic leadership. Following the training program the managers' showed significant improvements in their skills to charismatically communicate a vision. The results of these three studies indicate that leaders can, in fact, be trained to be transformational leaders.

So, are transformational leaders born or made? The answer appears to be both!

Sources: Arvey, R.D., Rotundo, M., Johnson, W., Zang, Z., & McGue, M. (2006). The determinants of role occupancy: Genetic and personality factors. *The Leadership Quarterly, 17,* 1–20; Frese, M., Beimel, S., & Schoenborn, S. (2003). Action training for charismatic leadership: Two evaluations of studies of a commercial training module on inspirational communication of a vision. *Personnel Psychology, 56,* 671–697; Judge, T.A. & Bono, J.E. (2000). Five-factor model of personality and transformational leadership. *Journal of Applied Psychology, 85,* 751–765; Bono, J.E. & Judge, T.A. (2004). Personality and transformational and transactional leadership: A meta-analysis. *Journal of Applied Psychology, 89,* 901–910; Barling, J., Weber, T., & Kelloway, E.K. (1996). Effects of transformational leadership training on attitudinal and financial outcomes: A field experiment. *Journal of Applied Psychology, 81,* 827–832; Dvir, T., Eden, D., Avolio, B.J., & Shamir, B. (2002). Impact of transformational leadership on follower development and performance: A field experiment. *Academy of Management, 45,* 735–744.

☞ YOU BE THE

Manager

Developing Strategic Leaders at RBC Financial Group

RBC Financial Group is one of the oldest and most admired companies in Canada. It has financed much of the commercial growth within Canada over the years while more recently becoming a player in the global-financial-services arena. In 2001, it became Canada's most valuable (in terms of market capitalization) and most profitable company.

But not long ago, RBC's future strategic course seemed in doubt. By the mid- to late-1990s, it was clear that the group's prospects for growth within Canada were becoming saturated. RBC attempted to pursue growth by merging with rival Bank of Montreal; the two banks developed a proposal to create what would have been a North American financial services powerhouse. That proposal, however, was rejected by Canada's Competition Bureau, which contended that the merger would create a monopoly environment.

RBC's leadership then saw only two scenarios: The bank could do nothing and watch its hard-earned market share deteriorate, or it could leverage its strengths in Canada to grow outside the country. RBC's board and its top team agreed unanimously to pursue that latter scenario. The bank's leaders refined the strategy by articulating that most of RBC's growth in the first decade of the new millennium would take place in the United States; the company would grow in this way to become a major North American presence.

Within just a few years, RBC's acquisitions in the United States included Centura Banks and Liberty Insurance in the South, Prism Mortgage and Dain Rauscher Wessels in the Midwest, Tucker Anthony in the Northeast, and Sutro in the West. To more accurately reflect the new composition of businesses within the RBC family, the company added the Group Management Committee (GMC) to its top management team. The GMC would be composed of the leaders of the group's five divisions (called platforms), RBC's major functional leaders, and the CEO.

On the surface, the strategy seemed to be unfolding flawlessly. But Gordon Nixon, RBC's CEO, was concerned. Company surveys and focus groups indicated

> **When big changes happened at RBC, new leadership was needed to guide the company into the future.**

that RBC's employees were feeling confused about the company's vision, strategy, and core values. Before the acquisitions, when RBC was a big fish in a small pond, employees had always been clear about the bank's strategy and had understood its core values implicitly.

What should RBC do about the confusion over the company's vision, strategy, and core values? Is leadership development an option? You be the manager.

QUESTIONS

1. What should RBC do and to what extent should they involve the company's leaders?

2. How should RBC develop high-potential leaders for the future?

To find out what RBC did, see The Manager's Notebook at the end of the chapter.

Source: Excerpt from Ready, D.A. (2002). How storytelling builds next-generation leaders. *MIT Sloan Management Review, 43(4),* 63–69.

RBC Financial Group
www.rbc.com

Strategic leadership refers to a leader's "ability to anticipate, envision, maintain flexibility, think strategically, and work with others to initiate changes that will create a viable future for the organization."[45] Strategic leaders can provide an organization with a sustainable competitive advantage by helping their organizations compete in turbulent and unpredictable environments and by exploiting growth opportunities.[46]

According to Duane Ireland and Michael Hitt, there are six components to effective strategic leadership:[47]

- *Determining the firm's purpose or vision.* Strategic leaders must have a clear vision of their organization and its purpose, and provide guidelines for where the firm is going and how it will get there.

- *Exploiting and maintaining core competencies.* Core competencies refer to the resources and capabilities that provide an organization with a competitive advantage. Strategic leaders must be able to develop and exploit their organization's core competencies in new and competitive ways.

- *Developing human capital.* Human capital refers to the knowledge and skills of an organization's workforce. Strategic leaders invest in the education and development of their organization's workforce and view the workforce as a critical resource.

- *Sustaining an effective organizational culture.* As described in Chapter 8, organizational culture refers to the shared beliefs, values, and assumptions that exist in an organization. An organization's culture can be a source of competitive advantage. Therefore, strategic leaders must be able to shape an organization's culture so that it is effective and can provide the organization with a competitive advantage.

- *Emphasizing ethical practices.* Strategic leaders will establish ethical principles that guide the practices and behaviour of the organization and its members and will develop a culture in which ethical principles and practices are the norm and the foundation for decisions.

- *Establishing balanced organizational controls.* Organizational controls are formal procedures that guide work and organizational activities toward the achievement of performance objectives. Strategic leaders must establish strategic and financial controls to facilitate flexible, creative, and innovative behaviours.

In addition to these six elements, the authors also recommend that strategic leaders focus on growth opportunities, create, manage, and mobilize knowledge and intellectual capital, be open and honest in their interactions with all the organization's stakeholders, and focus on the future.

As the economy becomes increasingly global and competitive, leaders must learn to become more strategic in their approach to leadership and understand how it can be a competitive advantage. According to Duane Ireland and Michael Hitt, "Strategic leadership may prove to be one of the most critical issues facing organizations. Without effective strategic leadership, the probability that a firm can achieve superior or even satisfactory performance when confronting the challenges of the global economy will be greatly reduced."[48]

CULTURE AND GLOBAL LEADERSHIP

Are various leadership styles equally effective across cultures? This is a question that researchers have been asking for decades. Fortunately, we have learned a great deal about this over the last 10 years thanks to the most extensive and ambitious study ever undertaken on global leadership. The Global Leadership and Organizational Behaviour (GLOBE) research project involved 170 researchers who worked together for 10 years collecting and analyzing data on cultural values and practices and leadership attributes from over 17 000 managers in 62 societal cultures. The results provide a rich and detailed account of cultural attributes and global leadership dimensions around the world.[49]

Strategic leadership.
Leadership that involves the ability to anticipate, envision, maintain flexibility, think strategically, and work with others to initiate changes that will create a viable future for the organization.

The project team first identified nine cultural dimensions that distinguish one society from another and have important managerial implications. Some of these dimensions are similar to Hofstede's, which were described in Chapter 4, but many of them were developed by GLOBE. Exhibit 9.6 lists and defines the nine cultural dimensions. Using these nine dimensions, GLOBE identified 10 culture clusters from the 62 culture samples. The culture clusters differ with respect to how they score on the nine culture dimensions.

Second, GLOBE wanted to know if the same attributes that lead to successful leadership in one country lead to success in other countries. What they found was that citizens in each nation have implicit assumptions regarding requisite leadership qualities, something known as implicit leadership theory. According to **implicit leadership theory**, individuals hold a set of beliefs about the kinds of attributes, personality characteristics, skills, and behaviours that contribute to or impede outstanding leadership. These belief systems are assumed to affect the extent to which an individual accepts and responds to others as leaders. GLOBE found that these belief systems are shared among individuals in common cultures, something they call *culturally endorsed implicit leadership theory (CLT)*. Further, they identified 21 primary and 6 global leadership dimensions that are contributors to or inhibitors of outstanding leadership. The six global leadership dimensions are as follows:[50]

- *Charismatic/Value-Based*. A broadly defined leadership dimension that reflects the ability to inspire, to motivate, and to expect high performance outcomes from others on the basis of firmly held core beliefs.

Implicit leadership theory. Individuals hold a set of beliefs about the kinds of attributes, personality characteristics, skills, and behaviours that contribute to or impede outstanding leadership.

EXHIBIT 9.6

Cultural Dimensions from the GLOBE Project

Source: Javidan, M., Dorfman, P.W., de Luque, M.S., & House, R.J. In the eye of the beholder: Cross-cultural lessons in leadership from Project GLOBE. *Academy of Management Perspectives, 20*, 67–90.

The GLOBE conceptualized and developed measures of nine cultural dimensions. These are aspects of a country's culture that distinguish one society from another and have important managerial implications. The nine cultural dimensions are as follows:

Performance Orientation: The degree to which a collective encourages and rewards (and should encourage and reward) its members for improvement and excellence in their performance.

Assertiveness: The degree to which individuals are (and should be) assertive, confrontational, and aggressive in their interactions with others.

Future Orientation: The extent to which individuals prepare (and should prepare) for the future, for example, by delaying gratification, planning ahead, and investing in the future.

Humane Orientation: The degree to which a collective encourages and rewards (and should encourage and reward) individuals for their fairness, altruism, generosity, caring, and kindness to others.

Institutional Collectivism: The degree to which the institutional practices of organizations and society encourage and reward (and should encourage and reward) collective distribution of resources and collective action.

In-Group Collectivism: The degree to which individuals express (and should express) pride, loyalty, and cohesiveness in their families or organizations.

Gender Egalitarianism: The degree to which a collective minimizes (and should minimize) gender inequality.

Power Distance: The degree to which members of a collective expect (and should expect) power to be distributed evenly.

Uncertainty Avoidance: The extent to which a society, organization, or group relies (and should rely) on social norms, rules, and procedures to lessen the unpredictability of future events.

- *Team-Oriented*. Emphasizes effective team building and implementation of a common purpose or goal among team members.
- *Participative*. The degree to which managers involve others in making and implementing decisions.
- *Humane-Oriented*. Reflects supportive and considerate leadership, but also includes compassion and generosity.
- *Autonomous*. Refers to independent and individualistic leadership.
- *Self-Protective*. Focuses on ensuring the safety and security of the individual.

Third, GLOBE created leadership profiles for each national culture and cluster of cultures based on their scores on the six global leadership dimensions. They then compared the ten culture clusters on the leadership profiles and found that cultures and clusters differ significantly on all six of the global leadership dimensions. For example, compared to other culture clusters, Canada and the United States score high on the charismatic/value-based, participative, and humane-oriented dimensions, low on the self-protective dimension, and medium on the team-oriented and the autonomous dimensions.

Finally, to determine what is considered important for leadership effectiveness across cultures, GLOBE examined a large number of leader attributes. They found that while the cultures do differ on many aspects of leadership effectiveness, they also have many similarities. In fact, they found many attributes such as being honest, decisive, motivational, and dynamic to be universally desirable and are believed to facilitate outstanding leadership in all GLOBE countries. They also found leadership attributes such as loners, irritable, egocentric, and ruthless to be deemed ineffective in all GLOBE countries. And as you might expect, they also found that some attributes are *culturally contingent*. In other words, some attributes are effective in some cultures but are either ineffective or even dysfunctional in others. Exhibit 9.7 provides some examples of universally desirable, universally undesirable, and culturally contingent leadership attributes.[51]

The results of the GLOBE project are important because they show that while there are similarities across cultures in terms of what are considered to be desirable and undesirable leadership attributes, there are also important differences. This means that managers need to understand the similarities and differences in what makes someone an effective leader across cultures if they are to be effective global leaders.

The following is a partial list of leadership attributes that are universal facilitators, universal inhibitors, or culturally contingent.

Universal Facilitators of Leadership Effectiveness

- Demonstrating trustworthiness, a sense of justice, and honesty
- Having foresight and planning ahead
- Encouraging, motivating, and building confidence; being positive and dynamic
- Being communicative, informed, a coordinator, and team integrator (team builder)

Universal Impediments to Leadership Effectiveness

- Being a loner and asocial
- Being irritable and uncooperative
- Imposing your views on others

Culturally Contingent Endorsement of Leader Attributes

- Being individualistic
- Being constantly conscious of status
- Taking risks

EXHIBIT 9.7
Cultural Views of Leadership Effectiveness from the GLOBE Project.

Source: Javidan, M., Dorfman, P.W., de Luque, M.S., & House, R.J. In the eye of the beholder: Cross-cultural lessons in leadership from Project GLOBE. *Academy of Management Perspectives, 20*, 67–90.

Global Leadership

For multinational organizations, global leadership is a critical success factor. But what is global leadership? **Global leadership** involves having leadership capabilities to function effectively in different cultures and being able to cross language, social, economic, and political borders.[52] The essence of global leadership is the ability to influence people who are not like the leader and come from different cultural backgrounds. This means that to succeed, global leaders need to have a global mindset, tolerate high levels of ambiguity, and exhibit cultural adaptability and flexibility.[53]

A good example of a global leader is SNC-Lavalin Group's CEO Jacques Lamarre. SNC-Lavalin is Canada's premier engineering firm and has been described as a planetary powerhouse because it has projects in more than 100 countries. In Lamarre's 10 years as CEO, sales have grown fourfold to more than $4 billion. Much of the credit for the company's success and status as a global giant goes to Lamarre's cultural skills and adaptability, which enable him to understand his clients all over the globe.[54]

According to Hal Gregersen, Allen Morrison, and Stewart Black, global leaders have the following four characteristics:[55]

- *Unbridled inquisitiveness.* Global leaders must be able to function effectively in different cultures in which they are required to cross language, social, economic, and political borders. A key characteristic of global leaders is that they relish the opportunity to see and experience new things.

- *Personal character.* Personal character consists of two components: an emotional connection to people from different cultures and uncompromising integrity. The ability to connect with others involves a sincere interest and concern for them, and a willingness to listen to and understand others' viewpoints. Global leaders also demonstrate an uncompromising integrity by maintaining high ethical standards and loyalty to their organization's values. This demonstration of integrity results in a high level of trust throughout the organization.

- *Duality.* For global leaders, duality means that they must be able to manage uncertainty and balance global and local tensions. Global leaders are able to balance the tensions and dualities of global integration and local demands.

- *Savvy.* Because of the greater challenges and opportunities of global business, global leaders need to have business and organizational savvy. Global business savvy means that global leaders understand the conditions they face in different countries and are able to recognize new market opportunities for their organization's goods and services. Organizational savvy means that global leaders are well informed of their organization's capabilities and international ventures.

Earlier in this chapter, we discussed research on leadership traits. By now you might be wondering if global leaders are born or made. The answer appears to be both; that is, "global leaders are born and then made." Individuals with the potential to become global leaders have experience working or living in different cultures, they speak more than one language, and have an aptitude for global business.

However, becoming an effective global leader requires extensive training that consists of travel to foreign countries, teamwork with members of diverse backgrounds, and formal training programs that provide instruction on topics such as international and global strategy, business and ethics, cross-cultural communication, and multicultural team leadership. The most powerful strategy for developing global leaders is work experience, transfers, and international assignments. Transfers and international assignments enable leaders to develop many of the characteristics that global leaders require to be successful. Long-term international assignments are considered to be especially effective.[56] Rajesh Subramaniam's assignments in the United States and Hong Kong before coming to Canada are a good example of this. Many companies such as GE, Citigroup, Shell, Siemens, and Nokia use international assignments to develop global leaders.[57]

Global leadership. A set of leadership capabilities required to function effectively in different cultures and the ability to cross language, social, economic, and political borders.

SNC-Lavalin Group
www.snc-lavalin.com

Jacques Lamarre, CEO of SNC-Lavalin Group, is an example of a quintessential global business leader.

In summary, developing global leaders is becoming increasingly important for organizations around the world. To be successful in the global economy, it is critical for an organization to identify and develop leaders who have the capability to become global leaders. For many organizations, however, this will not be easy, as most report that they do not have enough global leaders now or for the future, and they do not have a system in place for developing them.[58]

However, there is some evidence that certain countries produce more global leaders than others. Karl Moore and Henry Mintzberg of McGill University found that those countries that are considered to be the most global in terms of their involvement in world trade and investment, such as Canada, the Netherlands, Switzerland, Belgium, Ireland, Sweden, Denmark, Singapore, Australia, and Finland, tend to have more than their share of good global leaders given their size. Why is this? They are all middle-economy countries that are dependent on foreign trade. As a result, they must be able to understand and empathize with persons in other cultures. For Canadians, this comes naturally. According to Moore and Mintzberg, it is a strength of Canadians that they learn from the cradle to take into account other perspectives, a key requirement of global managers working for global companies. Living in a multicultural environment like Canada is excellent preparation for being a global manager. As a result, Canadian companies like Bombardier are way ahead of most organizations in big countries like the United States when it comes to global leadership.[59]

Bombardier
www.bombardier.com

ETHICAL LEADERSHIP

You might recall that both strategic and global leadership emphasize the importance of ethical practices and high ethical standards. However, most of the material presented in this chapter deals with what might be called the "technical" effectiveness and competence of leaders. This should not be surprising, as most organizations and their shareholders want competent leaders who can make the company profitable. However, the high profile ethical scandals in recent years involving leaders such as Kenneth Lay of Enron and Bernard Ebbers of WorldCom have raised concerns about ethics and leadership. The public trust of organizations has become an issue, and important questions about the role of leadership in shaping ethical conduct in organizations are being asked. It has also brought to the forefront an important dimension of leadership that has largely been ignored: ethics and the effect of ethical and unethical leadership behaviour on an organization and its members.[60]

Effective leadership requires more than the single-minded pursuit of organizational goals. It also has a moral and ethical dimension to it, and as a result, an effective leader must also be ethical in how he or she exerts influence. For example, consider Rajesh Subramaniam's decision to allow couriers to be off the road by 1 p.m. in the event of bad winter weather. Other leaders might be more concerned about profits and less concerned about employee safety. Subramaniam's concern for employee safety is an example of ethical leadership. Some leaders, such as oil company BP PLC CEO Sir John Browne and Suncor Energy Inc. CEO Rick George, display ethical leadership by supporting environmentally friendly programs and policies.[61]

So what exactly is ethical leadership? **Ethical leadership** involves the demonstration of normatively appropriate conduct (e.g., openness and honesty) through personal actions and interpersonal relationships, and the promotion of such conduct to followers through two-way communication, reinforcement, and decision making. Thus, ethical leaders model what is deemed to be normatively appropriate behaviour, such as honesty, trustworthiness, fairness, and care. They make ethics salient in the workplace and draw attention to it by engaging in explicit ethics-related communications and by setting ethical standards. They reward ethical conduct and discipline those who don't follow ethical standards (notice the use of contingent leader reward and punishment behaviour). Ethical leaders also consider the ethical consequences of their decisions and make principled and fair decisions that can be observed and emulated by others.[62]

Ethical leadership. The demonstration of normatively appropriate conduct through personal actions and interpersonal relationships, and the promotion of such conduct to followers through two-way communication, reinforcement, and decision making.

Some leaders, like oil company BP PLC CEO Sir John Browne, display ethical leadership by supporting environmentally friendly programs and policies.

Ethical leadership is a critical factor in the development of an ethical culture. As described in Chapter 8, the norms and patterns of behaviour in an organization are a result of the culture of the organization, which is largely influenced by the organization's leaders. Employees determine what is ethically right or wrong on the basis of the culture of their organization and the accepted norms. At Enron, for example, executives engaged in and supported unethical practices, which became acceptable organizational norms. Thus, the ethical conduct of employees within an organization is largely a result of the ethical practices and behaviour of its leaders.[63]

What should leaders do to develop an ethical culture and workplace? According to Terry Thomas, John Schermerhorn, and John Dienhart, leaders must have a strong commitment to ethics and be willing to do even the small things every day that help to raise awareness of and reinforce the importance of ethics, including:[64]

- *Communicate a clear and consistent positive ethics message from the top.* Commitment to ethics must be stated often and clearly; ethics messages must be supported by positive examples of senior executives making tough choices that are driven by company values.

- *Create and embrace opportunities for everyone in the organization to communicate positive ethics, values, and practices.* Everyone must experience a "voice" in the ethics culture, being encouraged to express concerns and preferences; they must have easy and secure access to mechanisms for doing so, including advice lines and tip lines for reporting violations; all questions and concerns must be followed to closure; all systematic sources of recurring problems must be traced and rectified.

- *Ensure consequences for ethical and unethical conduct.* Ethical performance should be recognized and rewarded, visibly and regularly; unethical behaviour should be met with sanctions up to and including termination, with no exclusions for senior executives.

The Boeing Company
www.boeing.com

Boeing's CEO Jim McNerney is a good example of an ethical leader who has taken these kinds of initiatives in an effort to build an ethical culture. For example, he has linked pay and bonuses to how well executives embrace "Boeing values," such as promoting integrity and avoiding abusive behaviour. He has also established financial incentives for managers not based solely on a rising stock price, but on improved performance.[65]

Ethical leadership is a new and emerging area of leadership research, and as a result, very little research has been conducted. However, in one of the few studies that have been conducted, ethical leadership was positively associated with employee perceptions of honesty, fairness, and effectiveness. Employees of ethical leaders were more satisfied with their supervisor, more willing to devote extra effort to one's job, and more willing to report problems to management. In another recent study, the extent to which ethics was an important part of an organization's culture was influenced by the ethics and moral development of the leader. In other words, the ethical behaviour of leaders had a significant influence on the ethical culture of the organization.[66]

Clearly, leaders have an important role to play as models of ethical behaviour for employees to identify with and emulate. The culture of an organization and employee behaviour is strongly influenced by the ethics of its leaders. As the Enron, WorldCom, and Arthur Andersen scandals demonstrate, a lack of ethical leadership can have substantial consequences for employees and organizations and even destroy a company. It is now generally understood that ethical leadership is a critical component of leadership effectiveness and long-term business success.

For a good example of the effects of unethical leadership, see "Ethical Focus: *The Ethics of the Privacy Czar.*"

GENDER AND LEADERSHIP STYLE

Do men and women adopt different leadership styles? Recently, a number of popular books have argued that women leaders tend to be more intuitive, less hierarchically oriented, and more collaborative than their male counterparts. Is this true? Notice that two opposing logics could be at work here. On the one hand, different socialization experiences could lead men and women to learn different ways of exerting influence on others. On the other hand, men and women should be equally capable of gravitating toward the style that is most appropriate in a given setting. This would result in no general difference in style.

However, a number of reviews have found that there are some differences in leadership style between men and women in organizational settings. For example, researchers Alice Eagly and Blair Johnson concluded that women have a tendency to be more participative or democratic than men.[67] Interestingly, an article in *Fortune* magazine on the 50 most powerful women in American business noted that women leaders are making the business world much less macho. Why is this so? One theory holds that women have better social skills that enable them to successfully manage the give-and-take that participation requires. Another theory holds that women avoid more autocratic styles because they violate gender stereotypes and lead to negative reactions. This might explain why a study on gender and leadership found that women are perceived by themselves and their co-workers as performing significantly better as managers than men.[68] Exhibit 9.8 on page 327 highlights some of the qualities of successful women executives.

In a review of the leadership styles of men and women based on 45 studies, women leaders were found to be more transformational than men leaders, and they also engaged in more of the contingent reward behaviours associated with transactional leadership. Men leaders engaged in more of the other components of transactional leadership, such as management by exception as well as **laissez-faire leadership**, which is the avoidance or absence of leadership. What is most interesting about these findings is that those aspects of leadership style in which women exceed men are all positively related to leadership effectiveness, while those leadership aspects in which men exceed women have weak, negative, or null relations to leadership effectiveness. The authors concluded that these findings attest to the ability of women to be highly effective leaders in contemporary organizations.[69]

Laissez-faire leadership. A style of leadership that involves the avoidance or absence of leadership.

ETHICAL FOCUS

The Ethics of the Privacy Czar

In June of 2003, former federal privacy commissioner George Radwanski resigned from his position before a parliamentary committee could recommend he be fired for his lavish and unjustifiable spending. An investigation into Canada's Privacy Commission by Auditor General Sheila Fraser found that the scope of the abuses, cronyism, extravagance, and misuse of hundreds of thousands of taxpayers' dollars by the Commission was beyond her "wildest dreams" and so extreme that the RCMP had been called in to investigate.

The Auditor General's report revealed abuses on a scale that shocked MPs, bureaucrats, and ministers in what has been described as a management free-for-all. The report indicates a "major breakdown" in financial controls that "allowed the abuse of the public treasury for the benefit of the former commissioner and a few senior executives." The abuses included three senior executives' falsification of financial statements to Parliament to hide the fact that the commission overspent its budget by $234 000; the overpayment of executives by more than $250 000; unclaimed taxable benefits by senior executives; the reclassification of executives' jobs without justification to pay them higher salaries; unreasonable and extravagant spending on travel and hospitality that exceeded the allowable maximum spending limits; favoured executives receiving rapid promotions and raises as high as 20 percent; all executives receiving the maximum bonus; contracts and jobs being handed out to friends of Radwanski and his officials; and the payment of two $15 000 advances to Radwanski without justification.

The Auditor General said she was "outraged" at the climate of "fear and arbitrariness" that led to a "complete breakdown in controls in all aspects of management." According to Fraser, Radwanski and his senior managers "turned a blind eye" to abuses of the laws and policies that govern the public service. She said that she was most "saddened" by the treatment of employees who worked in what she described as a "poisoned work environment" of abuse, intimidation, and humiliation. Employees broke down when telling stories of verbal abuse, intimidation, inappropriate comments, and humiliation in front of their colleagues. They described Radwanski's leadership as a "reign of terror" in which they feared reprisals if they reported abuses. Workers who displeased Radwanski were banished to another floor, had their work taken away or contracted out, were excluded from meetings, or were not allowed to put their names on reports. Employees who were favoured and were part of Radwanski's "inner circle" were treated very well and received promotions and raises. The report found that favouritism was rife at the Commission, and job competitions and postings were orchestrated and manipulated so they could be steered to whom they wanted.

In March of 2006, more than two years after Radwanski resigned, the RCMP formally laid charges of breach of trust and fraud over $5000. Radwanski's former chief of staff, Arthur Lamarche, has also been charged with the same two offences. Criminal lawyer Edward Greenspan, who is representing Radwanski, said he will "vigorously defend" the charges, adding that his client considers the upcoming court case an opportunity for vindication. Radwanski claims he is the victim of a political vendetta and that he has been unfairly scapegoated. He has blamed poor bookkeeping at the Commission for the irregular transactions. The fraud charges carry a maximum sentence of 10 years in prison, while the maximum sentence for breach of trust is 5 years.

Sources: Gordon, S. (2006, March 16). Ex-privacy czar facing charges. *Toronto Star*, A1, A19; Curry, B. (2006, March 16). Mounties lay fraud charges against former privacy czar. *Globe and Mail*, A1, A6; Clark, C. (2003, October 1). Radwanski accused of falsifying documents. *Globe and Mail*, A4; Clark, C. (2003, October 1). Radwanski audit details junkets and cronyism. *Globe and Mail*, A1, A4; Lawton, V. (2003, October 1). Watchdog ruled with a "reign of terror" report says. *Toronto Star*, A1, A9; Lawton, V. (2003, October 1). Radwanski blames staff for mistakes. *Toronto Star*, A9; May, K. (2003, October 1). Auditor finds "reign of terror." *National Post*, A1.

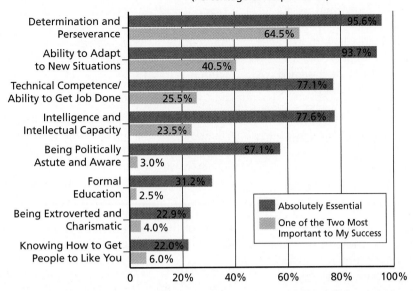

Qualities of Successful Women Executives
(Percentage of Respondents)

- Determination and Perseverance: 95.6% / 64.5%
- Ability to Adapt to New Situations: 93.7% / 40.5%
- Technical Competence/ Ability to Get Job Done: 77.1% / 25.5%
- Intelligence and Intellectual Capacity: 77.6% / 23.5%
- Being Politically Astute and Aware: 57.1% / 3.0%
- Formal Education: 31.2% / 2.5%
- Being Extroverted and Charismatic: 22.9% / 4.0%
- Knowing How to Get People to Like You: 22.0% / 6.0%

Legend:
- Absolutely Essential
- One of the Two Most Important to My Success

(Scale: 0 / 20% / 40% / 60% / 80% / 100%)

EXHIBIT 9.8
Qualities of successful women executives.

Source: *Women in Management,* Richard Ivey School of Business, The University of Western Ontario.

THE MANAGER'S

Notebook

Developing Strategic Leaders at RBC Financial Group

The need to develop next-generation leaders who can translate strategy into results and core values into day-to-day behaviours has become a major challenge for organizations, and this is a good example of what one company is doing to develop strategic leadership.

1. Elisabetta Bigsby, RBC's senior executive vice president for human resources and transformation, shared CEO Gordon Nixon's concerns. She recommended that the company initiate a process that would bring RBC's top team together with its next-generation leaders. The goal would be to build a bridge between RBC's new strategic direction and the leadership capabilities that would be required to implement that strategy. The CEO agreed to the proposal, adding that he wanted to engage in a widespread series of discussions with RBC's high-potential leaders that would focus on understanding core values as well as strategy. Involving leaders in the development of future leaders was crucial.

2. A series of discussions with members of the Group Management Committee (GMC) and the CEO were held to obtain their views on the company's leadership-development challenges. As a result of these efforts, the GMC developed a collective and well-articulated point of view on what leadership effectiveness meant for RBC and came to believe that it was

critical to design and implement an RBC-specific leadership program. GMC members were persuaded to become leader coaches for what became known as the RBC Leadership Dialogues. With the help of an adviser, the GMC members framed stories from their experiences that would help RBC's next-generation leaders. The program began in April 2001 with Jim Rager, RBC's vice chairman and head of the personal and commercial banking platform, telling his story to an audience of 25 of RBC's senior managers who had been identified as likely to move up to senior-executive leadership positions. Rager's story wove back and forth between strategy and values, showing how he had struggled to balance choices that reflected RBC's strategy with those that were in keeping with RBC's values of integrity, trust, and fairness. Although his story itself only took 30 minutes to tell, he and another leader coach engaged with the participants in a dialogue that lasted for two days. The participants had all gone through a 360-degree feedback process on their leadership effectiveness beforehand, so they had an idea of the challenges they needed to address. Toward the end of the session, each group member prepared a developmental action plan that he or she would follow with the supervision of his or her boss and a leadership coach.

Source: Excerpt from Ready, D.A. (2002). How storytelling builds next-generation leaders. *MIT Sloan Management Review, 43(4),* 63–69.

LEARNING OBJECTIVES CHECKLIST

1. *Leadership* occurs when an individual exerts influence on others' goal achievement in an organizational context. Individuals with titles such as manager, executive, supervisor, and department head occupy formal or assigned leadership roles. As part of these roles they are expected to influence others, and they are given specific authority to direct employees. Individuals might also emerge to occupy informal leadership roles. Since informal leaders do not have formal authority, they must rely on being well liked or being perceived as highly skilled to exert influence.

2. Early studies of leadership were concerned with identifying physical, psychological, and intellectual *traits* that might predict leader effectiveness. While some traits appear to be related to leadership capacity, there are no traits that guarantee leadership across various situations.

3. Studies of emergent leadership have identified two important leadership functions—the *task function* and the *social-emotional function*. The former involves helping the group achieve its goals through planning and organizing, while the latter involves resolving disputes and maintaining a pleasant group environment. Explorations of the behaviour of assigned leaders have concentrated on *initiating structure* and *consideration*, which are similar to task behaviour and social-emotional behaviour, as well as *leader reward* and *punishment behaviours*. Both consideration and initiating structure contribute positively to employees' motivation, job satisfaction, and leader effectiveness. Consideration tends to be more strongly related to follower satisfaction, motivation, and leader effectiveness, while initiating structure is slightly more strongly related to leader job performance and group performance. Leader contingent reward and punishment behaviour is positively related to employees' perceptions, attitudes, and behaviour.

4. *Fiedler's Contingency Theory* is a situational theory of leadership that suggests that different leadership orientations are necessary depending on the favourableness of the situation for the leader. Favourableness depends on the structure of the task, the position power of the leader, and the relationship between the leader and the group. Fiedler argues that *task-oriented* leaders perform best in situations that are either very favourable or very unfavourable. *Relationship-oriented* leaders are said to perform best in situations of medium favourability.

5. *House's Path-Goal Theory* is a situational theory of leadership that suggests that leaders will be most effective when they are able to clarify the paths to various subordinate goals that are also of interest to the organization. According to House, the effectiveness of directive, supportive, participative, and achievement-oriented behaviour depends on the nature of the subordinates and the characteristics of the work environment.

6. *Participative* leader behaviour involves employees in work decisions. Participation can increase employee motivation and lead to higher-quality and more acceptable decisions. The *Vroom and Jago model* specifies how much participation is best for various kinds of decisions. Participation works best when employees are desirous of participation, when they are intelligent and knowledgeable, and when the task is reasonably complex.

7. *Leader–Member Exchange Theory* is concerned with the quality of the relationship that develops between a leader and an employee. High-quality relationships, or high LMX, involve a high degree of mutual influence and obligation as well as trust, loyalty, and respect between a leader and an employee. Higher-quality LMX relationships result in positive outcomes for leaders, employees, work units, and organizations.

8. *Transformational* leaders modify the beliefs and attitudes of followers to correspond to a new vision. They provide *intellectual stimulation, individualized consideration, and inspirational motivation*. They also have *charisma*, the ability to command extraordinary loyalty, dedication, and effort from followers. *Transactional* leadership is leadership that is based on a straightforward exchange between the leader and the followers and involves *contingent reward behaviour* and *management by exception*.

9. *Strategic leadership* involves the ability to anticipate, envision, maintain flexibility, think strategically, and work with others to initiate changes that will create a viable future for the organization.

10. The GLOBE project found that there are many leadership attributes that are universally desirable or universally undesirable in all cultures, as well as some attributes that are *culturally contingent*, that is, they will be effective in some cultures but ineffective or dysfunctional in others. *Global leaders* can function effectively in different cultures and are characterized by their inquisitiveness, personal character, global business and organizational savvy, and their ability to manage the dualities of global integration and local demands.

11. *Ethical leadership* involves the demonstration of normatively appropriate conduct through personal actions and interpersonal relationships, and the promotion of such conduct to followers through two-way communication, reinforcement, and decision making.

12. There are some differences in leadership style between men and women in organizational settings. Women leaders tend to be more transformational than men leaders, and they also engage in more contingent reward behaviours. Men leaders engage in more management by exception and laissez-faire leadership.

OB FLASHBACK

Leadership and Emotions

In Chapter 4, we discussed how emotions and moods affect job satisfaction. We defined emotions as intense, often short-lived, feelings caused by a particular event and moods as less intense, longer-lived, and more diffuse feelings. In Chapter 5, we discussed the importance of emotional intelligence for job performance. We defined emotional intelligence (EI) as an individual's ability to understand and manage his or her own and others' feelings and emotions. Emotional intelligence involves the ability to perceive and express emotion, assimilate emotion in thought, understand and reason about emotions, and manage emotions in oneself and others. Given that leadership involves exerting influence on the goal achievement of others, it would seem that emotions are probably very important.

According to Jennifer George, leadership is an emotion-laden process from both the leader's and follower's perspective. Thus, emotions and moods should play an important role in leadership, and emotional intelligence is very likely a key contributor to leadership effectiveness. How does emotional intelligence contribute to leadership effectiveness? According to George, emotional intelligence can help leaders carry out five key elements of leadership effectiveness.

First, leaders with emotional intelligence should be better at developing a collective sense of goals and objectives and how to go about achieving them. Leaders with emotional intelligence are better able to come up with a compelling vision and to communicate it throughout the organization. Second, leaders with emotional intelligence should be better at instilling in others

knowledge and appreciation of the importance of work activities and behaviour, and making them aware of problems and major issues facing an organization. This requires a leader to understand and influence follower's emotions. Third, leaders with higher EI should be better at generating and maintaining excitement, enthusiasm, confidence, and optimism in an organization as well as cooperation and trust. This is because they are able to appraise how their followers feel and know how to influence their feelings. Fourth, leaders who are knowledgeable about emotions and able to manage emotions should be better at encouraging flexibility in decision making and change, since emotions play an important role in these processes. Leaders must be able to assess how others feel and respond to and even alter feelings to overcome resistance to change. Finally, leaders with higher EI will be better at establishing and maintaining a meaningful identity for an organization. This involves the development and expression of an organization's culture, which requires a leader to invoke feelings and emotions that support the norms and values of the organization.

What do leaders think about the role of emotions in leadership? Karl Moore of McGill University recently interviewed eight CEOs in Canada and discovered that there are some common themes that have helped them shape their careers. One of the common themes is emotions. According to Moore, business schools focus on the analytic side of leadership. However, the CEOs indicate that their emotions and those of the people around them are just as important if not more so to running an organization. According to Paul Tellier, former CEO of Canadian National Railway Company and Bombardier Inc., "Business is very cerebral, but there is a lot of room for feelings and emotions."

Moore also discovered that the executives bring to work a passion for their companies, their products, and most fundamentally their people, and they all genuinely love their jobs. "We enjoy what we do," said Pierre Beaudoin, president of Bombardier Inc.'s aerospace division. "If you are in a job like mine and you don't enjoy it, you've got to think of something else because it's your life . . . I'm going to do this until I don't like doing this. If it is not fun any more, I will do something else." Nearly every CEO echoed that notion: Love your job or leave it.

The executives also recognized the importance of emotions in the people they lead. Robert Dutton, CEO of Rona Inc., said he once fired a manager for trying to run his operation on fear. When asked about the importance of emotions at work, he said, "When people realize that you understand their feelings, that's key to a personal touch with them. And you develop a specific relationship with them." Richard Evans, president and CEO of Alcan Inc., said this about emotions: "Emotions colour a lot of activities. You can have

clear, hard facts that point in one direction but if there's not an emotional acceptance that the values on which those facts are based are right values, or that the person presenting those facts is trustworthy . . . you're going to reject that at the gut level. Trust and confidence in someone are very important."

And what about the emotional intelligence of the CEOs? Research conducted by Daniel Goleman indicates that the most effective leaders have a high degree of emotional intelligence. He also found that emotional intelligence plays an increasingly important role at the highest levels of an organization. When he compared star performers to average ones in senior leadership positions, almost 90 percent of the difference in their profiles was due to emotional intelligence factors rather than cognitive abilities. Thus, emotional intelligence is a distinguishing factor for outstanding leaders, especially those at the highest levels of an organization.

Sources: George, J.M. (2000). Emotions and leadership: The role of emotional intelligence. *Human Relations, 53,* 1027–1055; Goleman, D. (1998, Nov–Dec). What makes a leader? *Harvard Business Review, 76,* 92–102; Moore, K. (2006, September 4). It seems that CEOs, too, must have the Right Stuff. *Globe and Mail*, B9; Moore, K. (2006, July 31). A hardware guy learns value of kid gloves. *Globe and Mail*, B10.

DISCUSSION QUESTIONS

1. Are leaders born or made? Consider each perspective (leaders born versus made) and the implications of each for organizations. What does each perspective suggest that organizations must do to ensure that they have effective leaders?

2. Discuss a case of emergent leadership that you have observed. Why did the person in question emerge as a leader? Did he or she fulfill the task role, the social-emotional role, or both?

3. Contrast the relative merits of consideration and initiating structure as well as leader reward and punishment behaviour in the following leadership situations: running the daily operations of a bank branch; commanding an army unit under enemy fire; supervising a group of college students who are performing a hot, dirty, boring summer job. Use House's Path-Goal Theory to support your arguments.

4. Fred Fiedler argues that leader LPC orientation is difficult to change, and that situations should be "engineered" to fit the leader's LPC orientation. Suppose that a relationship-

oriented (high LPC) person finds herself assigned to a situation with poor leader–member relations, an unstructured task, and weak position power. What could she do to make the situation more favourable for her relationship-oriented leadership?

5. Describe a situation that would be ideal for having employees participate in a work-related decision. Discuss the employees, the problem, and the setting. Describe a situation in which participative decision making would be an especially unwise leadership strategy. Why is this so?

6. What are transformational leaders skilled at doing that gives them extraordinary influence over others? Why do you think women are more likely to be transformational leaders than men? Describe a leadership situation in which a transformational leader would probably *not* be the right person for the job.

7. What are the main findings from the GLOBE project and what are the implications for leadership across cultures? If a leader from Canada takes on an assignment in another

culture, will he or she be successful? What is most likely to improve the chances of success?

8. Identify a leader who you think is a global leader and describe the characteristics and behaviours that make that person a global leader. Do you think that global leaders are born or made? What advice would you give an organization that needs more global leaders?

9. Leadership traits are considered to be important for leadership because they can lead to certain actions that are required for effective leadership. Review each of the traits in Exhibit 9.1 and discuss how they might be related to different leadership styles and behaviours (e.g., consideration, initiating structure, directive, supportive, participative, achievement oriented, transformational, LMX, strategic, global).

10. What does it mean to be an ethical leader and how can ethical or unethical leadership impact an organization?

INTEGRATIVE DISCUSSION QUESTIONS

1. Consider the relationship between leadership and organizational culture. Using the approaches to leadership discussed in this chapter (e.g., leadership traits, behaviours, situational theories, participative leadership, LMX theory, and transformational leadership), describe how a leader can influence the culture of an organization. Based on your analysis, do you think that leaders have a strong influence on an organization's culture?

2. What effect does leadership have on employee motivation? Using each of the theories of motivation described in Chapter 5, discuss the implications for leadership. In other words, according to each theory, what should a leader do to motivate employees?

3. Refer to the material in Chapter 3 on perceptions and gender stereotypes and compare and contrast what is known about gender stereotypes and women in management. Why do you think women are more likely to be transformational leaders than men? What does this tell us about perceptions, stereotypes, and reality?

4. Refer to the material in Chapter 2 on learning and discuss the implications of learning theories for ethical leadership. Similarly, refer to the material in Chapter 8 on culture and explain what a leader might do to create an ethical organizational culture.

ON-THE-JOB CHALLENGE QUESTION

In March of 2006, Richard Evans became the new president and CEO of Alcan Inc. Evans is a 37-year veteran of the aluminum business. In the late seventies and early eighties he was employed as works manager for a Kaiser Aluminum facility in the politically unstable West African country of Ghana. Not only did he turn around the strike-plagued operations in difficult conditions, he was there at a time when the plant survived three coups and two monetary crises. It's fair to say that in his new job as president and chief executive officer of Montreal-based Alcan—the world's second-largest production of primary aluminum after Alcoa Inc.—he won't face quite the same set of crisis-management situations. But he does have his work cut out for him in the wake of two company-transforming moves: the blockbuster acquisition of French rival Pechiney SA in 2003 and the later spinoff of Alcan's rolled products division. Asked about his vision for the company in a recent interview, Evans said that in the short term, the top job at Alcan is following through on the $6-billion (US) Pechiney purchase with consistently solid bottom-line results and enhanced profit margins. "We need to deliver on the promises we made about Pechiney. That's a first priority. If we don't do that, we ourselves are a takeover target," he said.

What do you think Richard Evans needs to do to be an effective leader for Alcan? Using the theories and approaches to leadership discussed in the chapter, what kind of a leader should he be and what must he do to be effective?

Source: Excerpt from Marotte, B. (2006, May 8). New CEO Evans inherits a company on the move. Globe and Mail, B1, B4.

EXPERIENTIAL EXERCISE

Leadership Jazz

The purpose of this exercise is to learn about the effect of leadership on individual and group creativity. It can also be used in conjunction with Chapter 16 (i.e., creativity). For this exercise, students will work in small groups (no larger than five people). The instructor will assign a leader to each group and will also decide what kind of leader he or she will be. Each group will be required to create musical instruments using only the resources they have with them, which they will use to play a tune/song in front of the class. The class will evaluate each group's performance.

Procedure

Students should form small groups with no more than five people. The instructor will then assign a leader in each group and instruct that person on what kind of leader to be (e.g., transactional, transformational, considerate, task-oriented, participative, etc.). This will enable comparisons across groups. Alternatively, the instructor can let the leaders choose their own leadership style. The leader of each group is responsible for his or her group's performance in creating musical instruments and for their performance of a tune/song. Once the groups have been formed and the leaders assigned, the exercise should proceed as follows:

Step 1: Each group will have 10–15 minutes to create musical instruments using any materials they have with them. They must not leave the room or their workspace to search for materials. Groups should try to create as many musical instruments as they can as well as a variety of instruments that can be used in a band or orchestra. Thus, the goal is both quantitative (number of instruments) and qualitative (variety of instruments).

Step 2: Each group will have 10–15 minutes to decide on several tunes/songs to play and to rehearse them in preparation for their performance in front of the class. The group should decide on what tune to play for the class and to focus on the quality of their performance. Each group should have a backup tune/song in case another group plays the same one they have chosen. This will help to ensure that each group plays a different tune/song. Keep in mind that the quality of the performance is important.

Step 3: Each group will perform a tune/song (two to three minutes maximum) in front of the class that no other group has performed (each group should be prepared to perform more than one song in case their first choice is played by another group).

Step 4: The class will rate the performance of each group using the following criteria:

- quantity of instruments used
- variety of instruments used
- recognizability of tune/song
- uniqueness of tune/song
- quality of performance

After all the groups have performed their tune/song, the class votes for the best group for each of the criteria listed above and the overall best group.

Discussion

The discussion should focus on how the group members responded to the leader and the effect of the leader on the group's creativity and performance. To facilitate class discussion, consider the following questions:

1. How did group members respond to their leader and what effect did the leader have on individual group member's behaviour, creativity, and performance?

2. What effect did the leader have on the creativity and performance of each group? Group members should comment on what their leader did that was helpful and encouraged creativity, and what their leader did that was not helpful and did not encourage creativity. What else could the leader have done to improve the group's creativity and performance? How important is leadership for individual and group creativity? What can leaders do to encourage creativity?

3. What style of leadership was most effective? At this point, the leader's can disclose their leadership style. What type of leader was associated with the group that received the highest score on the performance criteria? What type of leader was associated with the group that received the lowest score on the performance criteria? What type of leadership was most effective for overall group creativity and performance?

4. Consider the role of situational theories of leadership. Does the task of creating and playing musical instruments require a certain style of leadership? Did some members of each group respond better to their leader than others?

5. If you were to do this task over again, what type of leader would you prefer and why? What type of leader would be most effective? Discuss the theories of leadership to support your answers.

Source: Lengnick-Hall, M.L., & Lengnick-Hall, C.A. (1999). Leadership jazz: An exercise in creativity. *Journal of Management Education, 23,* 65–70.

CASE INCIDENT

Fran-Tech

A mid-level manager at Fran-Tech, a Seattle software company, received a CD-ROM set containing the source code for a competitor's software product. The competitor is the market leader in the software niche in which both companies compete; it is crushing Fran-Tech in the marketplace. An anonymous note accompanying the package stated that the package was sent by a disgruntled employee of the competitor and urged the recipient to use the data "as you see fit." The manager receiving the data was considered to be a "star" performer by her boss and her peers.

1. What do you think the manager is likely to do in this situation? What should she do and why?

2. Explain the relevance of ethical leadership in this situation. What will an ethical leader do and why? What will an unethical leader do?

3. Consider how the manager's response to this situation can impact the ethical behaviour of her employees in the organization. What are some of the potential implications of her actions for employees and the organization?

Source: Thomas, T., Schermerhorn, J.R., Jr., & Dienhart, J.W. (2004). Strategic leadership of ethical behavior in business. *Academy of Management Executive*, 18, 56–66.

CASE STUDY

Computer Services Team at AVIONICS

John Johnson, a top executive at AVIONICS who is partially responsible for information systems, is contemplating a government contract directive that calls for an integration of the computer information systems into a "service centre" concept. He is also aware that management has issued a directive to cut costs, and that he has not been inspired by the service centre manager's performance for some time. He wondered if the service contract idea is an opportunity to address all three issues at once.

John is known for his ability to empower people. He is dedicated to continual process improvement techniques, and he has put together a number of process improvement teams, focusing on concurrent engineering and total quality management (TQM). He prides himself on his ability to help teams improve quality and process. People respect John's abilities, and he has moved up rapidly in the organization. His excellent interpersonal skills have made him well-liked and influential at AVIONICS.

In John's readings of total quality management and process improvement, he has been impressed with the concept of a "leaderless team" or "autonomous work group." He wonders if the service centre concept could be an opportunity to experiment with the idea. After some thought, he decides to lay off the computer information systems supervisor and create a leaderless team. He changed the name from "computer information systems" to "computer service centre," and let team members know that their purpose was to integrate their systems to provide quality service to the customers.

As John expected, the laid-off supervisor, Glen Smith, was not happy and immediately filed a grievance, requesting reinstatement. He was allowed to stay as a member of the team until a decision could be made about his status. Even with the grievance, John felt satisfied that he had solved some of his problems. Glen wouldn't be a problem now that he was just a member.

John decided to start the team off right with a two-day, intensive training session. At the training session, he told the team members he was empowering them to change their own destiny. "You have the opportunity to control your own work," John enthusiastically told them. "No one is a leader—you are *all* responsible. That means if you have a problem, don't come running to me—you are in charge!"

Using large sheets of newsprint, the group listed their goals and expectations. They decided they wanted to achieve a collective identity. John instructed them on breakthrough analysis and told them about leaderless teams. Team members were impressed by John's knowledge of the subject. William Ashby, a Macintosh specialist, listened with interest. He really liked what John was saying about total quality management. He had read a few books on the subject and, listening to John, he felt inspired about really doing it.

The First Meeting

Shortly after the off-site training session, team members gathered for their first meeting. Eight people sat at a large rectangular table. William, the Macintosh specialist, looked around the room. He had more or less worked with several of these people in the past; at least they had shared the same large office space. There was Alyne, the VAX systems administrator, and her assistant, Frank. William recognized Russ, the IBM PC specialist and his counterpart. Glen, their former supervisor, was there, trying to blend in. Three other people he didn't know very well were also present: Rachel, the database support specialist, Harold, from business operations, and the assistant business manager, Carol.

A few people chatted with each other. Carol appeared engrossed in a memo. Glen sat with his arms folded, leaning back in his chair. William wondered who was going to get the meeting started. People were looking uncomfortable, waiting and wondering what would happen next. "Maybe I should say something," William thought to himself. He cleared his throat.

"Well, here we all are," he said. William hesitated, to see if anyone else wanted to take the lead. Everyone except Carol, who still seemed engrossed in her memo, stared at him. "I guess we should get started," William announced, hoping someone would offer a suggestion. He waited again. Again, everyone stared at him.

"Well, I for one was really excited about what John had to say at our off-site training." William looked around the room; a few people's heads nodded. "So I guess we should get started," William repeated, feeling a bit foolish.

Glen, the former supervisor, sat watching the group. "Oh, brother!" he thought. "This is going to be a problem, a real problem." He watched William struggle to lead the group.

William continued: "John suggested that we elect a leader from among ourselves to act as a volunteer leader of sorts. Does anyone have any suggestions?"

"Yeah, let's hurry this up," said Russ, the IBM PC specialist. "I've got 10 people who need to be hard-wired breathing down my neck." Russ continued, "I nominate you, William. You seem interested, and I really don't care who our leader is."

Some of the people looked at Russ with embarrassment. They had lots of work to do, too, but wouldn't have put it so bluntly. "He sure is a pain," thought Alyne. She turned to William and smiled. "Yes, I think William would be good. Would you be interested, William?" she asked.

"Well, I guess I would. I've never played on a formal team before, and I don't know what to do, but I'm willing to give it a shot." William felt the blood rising up to his ears. "I guess, unless there are any objections, I'll volunteer to be leader." Since no one said anything, William became the leader.

The group spent the next 20 minutes trying to figure out what it was supposed to be doing. They weren't sure what a TQM team was, or what it meant to integrate their various jobs to "create a service team." Most of the people sat and listened while William, Alyne, and Rachel talked. Russ stated again that he really needed to get back to work. The group decided to continue the discussion during the next meeting, a week away.

The Volunteer Leader Prepares

William told his wife that night about his election as leader of the group. "I'm not sure what to do. Maybe I'll check out the bookstore, and see if I can find some books on the subject." William drove to the bookstore and searched through the business section. He found several books on TQM that looked promising, plus one called *How to Make Prize Winning Teams*, which he thought was a real find. That night, William began reading the book. He was inspired by what he read, and he thought it was "doable" for his team.

The next week, the team gathered once more around the rectangular table. Russ, the IBM specialist, was absent because of "pressing business," but everyone else was present. William started things off by telling them about the books. He suggested that everyone should get a copy and read it.

"I think we need to begin figuring out how to improve our work," William told them. He proceeded to tell them about how they should look at each of their areas, and look for ways to improve it. William looked down at the notes he had taken from the book. He wanted to make sure he told them all exactly how it should be done; he didn't want to get it wrong.

Alyne interrupted him. She didn't like the way William seemed to be telling them what to do. "I think before we go charging down that street, we need to decide how we are going to decide things. I, for one, don't want people telling me what to do about my area." A few people nodded. "I think everyone should have a vote in these changes."

"Yes, I agree," said Frank, her assistant. "Majority rules; no one should have more say-so than anyone else."

"Fine," said William, but he couldn't help feeling that something had just gone wrong. The team agreed to vote on all matters. People started fidgeting in their seats, so William suggested that they end the meeting. "Everyone should try to buy the books and read them before our next meeting," he said.

During the next few months, William tried in vain to get the group to read the books. He thought if they would read them, they'd understand what he'd been talking about.

He felt pretty disheartened as he spoke to his wife that night. "Everyone wants to just go along," he told her. "We've got all these individuals on the team, and they only seem to care about their own turf. I thought we were starting to make progress last week when a few people started talking about the common complaint their customers had about reaching them, but then it became a discussion about why their customers didn't understand. I've learned you can't dictate to them. I have to win them over, but I don't know how. I'm going for a drive to think this out."

As William drove toward the beach, he thought about his job. He wasn't having much fun. Every meeting was the same thing. Members had to vote on every little thing that was brought up. If someone in the group didn't want to do it, that person just didn't vote. Or the person would go along with everyone else and vote but not follow through. He saw no evidence that anyone wanted to make it work. He wished he could go to his supervisor, John, but John had maintained a strict hands-off approach with the team since the in-service training. He felt that John had cut them loose, to sink or swim. They were definitely sinking.

"Maybe there is too much diversity on this team," he thought. "I need training on how to bring a diverse group together." He decided to see if he could get some training to help him out of the hole he'd crawled into.

William Voted Out

When William approached the human resources department about the training, he was told that his group did not have the budget for that kind of training. William angrily left the office, feeling very discouraged.

Over the next two months, it became painfully obvious that the group wasn't working. Some team members argued constantly, and some avoided conflict at all cost. Carol, the assistant business manager, requested a stress leave. She felt she couldn't take the problems and responsibility any longer. No one could agree on the team's goals, or how they were going to integrate their "service team." They felt frustrated with John, their manager, and thought he was unpredictable. John had a reputation for being a supportive and creative manager, yet with this team he was distant. They wondered why he didn't act like the manager others said he was.

Finally, at one meeting six months after the team began, Alyne, the VAX specialist, spoke up, "Look, William, this isn't working. We need a new leader." Everyone else agreed and, after some discussion, they voted in Glen, their former supervisor, as their "volunteer" leader. Glen, who had recently won his grievance against the layoff, was ready for the assignment.

William felt hurt. "That's it, I give up," he thought. "From now on, I'm looking out for my own group. I've been neglecting the Mac users, but no more."

About the time that Glen became "volunteer" leader, John was transferred to another assignment, and Barbara, the director of business management, became the group's manager. She told team members they needed to get better at serving their customers.

Glen, who had more leadership skills than William, recognized that the team was at a crisis point. He decided to try to build trust among the team members by working on continuous process improvement (CPI). He thought they might be able to pull it off if they just had enough time.

After four months, Barbara, the team manager, pulled the plug and ordered the team to go back to the structure it had nearly a year ago. A few people, and particularly Glen, were disappointed. "I was just beginning to feel like we were going to make it. The other team members were right—the company doesn't support teams. They just give a lot of lip service, but there is no management commitment."

The team went back to its old structure. John, their former manager, looked back at what happened. "They are still having problems serving their customers. I ran a bizarre experiment by cutting them loose. I took away all their support systems, and told them they were all equal people. It was a big mistake."

Source: *Understanding diversity: Cases, readings and exercises*, by Harvey/Allard, pp. 242–244. © 1995 Addison Wesley Longman, Inc. Reprinted by permission of Pearson Education, Inc., Upper Saddle River, NJ.

1. Discuss the leadership situation in the computer services team in terms of emergent leadership and the behaviour of assigned leaders. Why did William become the leader of the team and what behaviours did he exhibit? Why wasn't he a more effective leader?

2. Discuss John's and William's leadership behaviour in terms of consideration, initiating structure, reward, and punishment. What behaviours did they exhibit and which behaviours do you think they should have exhibited? Explain your answer.

3. Use House's Path-Goal Theory to analyze the leadership situation facing the computer services team. What leadership behaviour does the theory suggest? What leadership behaviour did John and William exhibit and what effect did it have on members of the team?

4. Use Fiedler's Contingency Theory to analyze the leadership situation. What leadership style does the theory suggest? What leadership style did John and William exhibit and what does the theory say about their effectiveness as leaders?

5. Discuss the merits of LMX theory and transactional and transformational leadership for the computer services team. What do these theories tell us about how John and William could have been more effective leaders?

6. What do the events in the case tell us about the effects of leadership on individuals, teams, and organizations? Was the computer services team a big mistake or could things have turned out differently? Explain your answer.

CHAPTER 10

Communication

UNITED PARCEL SERVICE

United Parcel Service (UPS) is the world's largest package delivery company and a leading global provider of specialized transportation and logistics services. One of the company's missions is to maintain a financially sound company, with broad employee ownership, that offers a long-term competitive return to shareowners. This ownership culture is demonstrated through ownership guidelines for managers and supervisors as well as several employee stock programs. The ownership culture is vigorously promoted throughout UPS by a variety of communication channels. Employee ownership is core to the UPS culture, and it translates into a strong work ethic, with employees engaged in growing the business and committed to the company's success.

UPS's "Winning Team" strategic imperative is a human resources effort to attract, develop, and retain a skilled, motivated, and diverse global workforce. The Winning Team initiative strives to develop not only an effective workforce, but also one whose interests and values align with UPS, which subsequently results in highly engaged employees. It also is intended to preserve and build upon UPS's culture and legacy of integrity, ownership, performance, respect, innovation, personal growth, and service excellence. UPS's success in meeting business goals and in fulfilling the strategic imperative requires a broad communicative effort to its over 400 000 employees throughout the United States, Canada, Asia, Europe, Africa, and Latin America. Employees must know what UPS is doing, why the company is engaging in various activities, and what their individual roles are in making the business successful. They also must understand the principles that are guiding the strategic imperatives, which are found in the UPS Charter. That charter, which includes the company's strategy, mission, purpose, and values, sets forth the principles that guide decisions made and solutions developed every day at UPS.

In creating a thorough understanding of the Winning Team initiative and developing supporting relationships throughout UPS, a number of media and deliverables are used. There are frequent communication meetings throughout the operating districts among staff, operations, managers, and first-line employees. In addition, UPSers.com, the employee portal, provides the most up-to-date information about UPS, technology, industry news, employee services, and business initiatives. This communication channel, which employees can access from work or home, is needed, because with more than 70 000 drivers, UPS is truly a mobile workforce.

Excellent communication between management and employees has helped make UPS the largest package delivery company in the world.

UPSers.com includes links to the medical, dental, vision, and prescription carriers, as well as other benefit providers for US employees. It also includes links to the administrator for the UPS Savings Advantage (401(k) plan) and the Discounted Employee Stock Purchase Plan. There is also a site where employees can view executive speech summaries and biographies to better understand who the UPS leaders are and what they are saying to the public about the business.

United Parcel Service
www.ups.com

Historically, UPS employees receive feedback in three-minute daily group meetings. Today, in addition to the three-minute Prework Communications Meeting, a progressive employee relations initiative is in place. Known as "One Vision," this hour-long one-to-one conversation between the supervisors and first-line employees focuses on UPS's competition, technology, health and safety, opinion survey feedback, UPS supply-chain solutions, stock purchasing, and recognition. It also encompasses "Project LEAD," a program that rewards employees who obtain sales leads for the company. In short, this conversation states what UPS has done, where UPS is presently, and the future of UPS. It is seen as a forum for the supervisor and first-line employees to communicate openly with each other and talk about the challenges the company faces, business initiatives, and how all can work together for success.[1]

UPS exemplifies the importance of good communication for organizational success. It also illustrates how employees and managers can communicate with each other and the importance of good electronic and face-to-face communication.

In this chapter, we will explore these and other aspects of communication in organizations. First, we will define communication and present a model of the communication process. We will investigate manager–employee communication, the "grapevine," the verbal and nonverbal language of work, gender differences, cross-cultural communication, and computer-mediated communication. Finally, we will discuss personal and organizational means of improving communication.

WHAT IS COMMUNICATION?

Communication. The process by which information is exchanged between a sender and a receiver.

Communication is the process by which information is exchanged between a sender and a receiver. The kind of communication we are concerned with in this chapter is *interpersonal* communication—the exchange of information between people. The simplest prototype for interpersonal communication is a one-on-one exchange between two individuals. Exhibit 10.1 presents a model of the interpersonal communication process and an example of a communication episode between a purchasing manager and her assistant. As you can see, the sender must *encode* his or her thoughts into some form that can be *transmitted* to the receiver. In this case, the manager has chosen to encode her thoughts in writing and transmit them via e-mail. Alternatively, the manager could have encoded her thoughts in speech and transmitted them via voice mail or face to face. The assistant, as a receiver, must *perceive* the message and accurately decode it to achieve accurate understanding. In this case, the assistant uses an online parts catalogue to decode the meaning of an "A-40." To provide *feedback*, the assistant might send the manager a copy of the order for the flange bolts. Such feedback involves yet another communication episode that tells the original sender that her assistant received and understood the message.

This simple communication model is valuable because it points out the complexity of the communication process and demonstrates a number of points at which errors can occur. Such errors lead to a lack of correspondence between the sender's initial thoughts and the receiver's understanding of the intended message. A slip of the finger

EXHIBIT 10.1
A model of the communication process and an example.

Source: From *Management*, 2nd Edition, by Glueck. © 1980. Reprinted with permission of South-Western, a division of Thomson Learning: www.thomsonrights.com. Fax 800-730-2215. Example by authors.

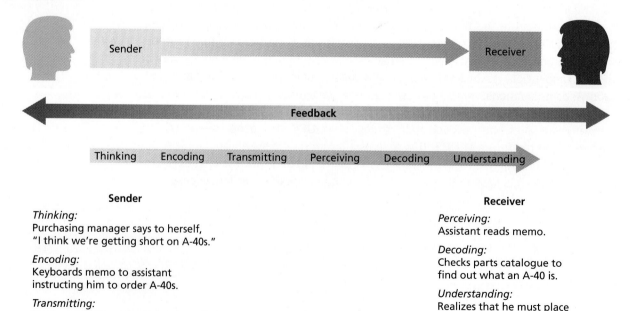

Sender	Receiver
Thinking: Purchasing manager says to herself, "I think we're getting short on A-40s."	*Perceiving:* Assistant reads memo.
Encoding: Keyboards memo to assistant instructing him to order A-40s.	*Decoding:* Checks parts catalogue to find out what an A-40 is.
Transmitting: Sends memo through electronic mail.	*Understanding:* Realizes that he must place an order for flange bolts.

on the keyboard can lead to improper encoding. A poor e-mail system can lead to ineffective transmission. An outdated parts catalogue can result in inaccurate decoding. As you might imagine, encoding and decoding may be prone to even more error when the message is inherently ambiguous or emotional. This is because the two parties may have very different perceptions of the "facts" at hand.

Effective communication occurs when the right people receive the right information in a timely manner. Violating any of these three conditions results in a communication episode that is ineffective.

Effective communication. The right people receive the right information in a timely manner.

BASICS OF ORGANIZATIONAL COMMUNICATION

Let's consider a few basic issues about organizational communication.

Communication by Strict Chain of Command

The lines on an organizational chart represent lines of authority and reporting relationships. For example, a vice-president has authority over the plant manager, who has authority over the production supervisors. Conversely, production workers report to their supervisors, who report to the plant manager, and so on. In theory, organizational communication could stick to this strict **chain of command**. Under this system, three necessary forms of communication can be accomplished.

Chain of command. Lines of authority and formal reporting relationships.

Downward communication flows from the top of the organization toward the bottom. For example, a vice-president of production might instruct a plant manager to gear up for manufacturing a new product. In turn, the plant manager would provide specifics to supervisors, who would instruct the production workers accordingly.

Downward communication. Information that flows from the top of the organization toward the bottom.

Upward communication flows from the bottom of the organization toward the top. For instance, a chemical engineer might conceive a new plastic formula with unique properties. She might then pass this on to the research and development manager, who would then inform the relevant vice-president.

Upward communication. Information that flows from the bottom of the organization toward the top.

Horizontal communication occurs between departments or functional units, usually as a means of coordinating effort. Within a strict chain of command, such communication would flow up to and then down from a *common manager*. For example, suppose a salesperson gets an idea for a new product from a customer. To get this idea to the research staff, it would have to be transmitted up to and down from the vice-presidents of marketing and research, the common managers for these departments.

Horizontal communication. Information that flows between departments or functional units, usually as a means of coordinating effort.

Clearly, a lot of organizational communication does follow the formal lines of authority shown on organizational charts. This is especially true for the examples of upward and downward communication given above—directives and instructions usually pass downward through the chain of command, and ideas and suggestions pass upward. However, the reality of organizational communication shows that the formal chain of command is an incomplete and sometimes ineffective path of communication.

Deficiencies in the Chain of Command

Managers recognize that sticking strictly to the chain of command is often ineffective.

Informal Communication. The chain of command obviously fails to consider *informal* communication between members. In previous chapters, we discussed how informal interaction helps people accomplish their jobs more effectively. Of course, not all informal communication benefits the organization. An informal grapevine might spread unsavoury, inaccurate rumours across the organization.

Filtering. Getting the right information to the right people is often inhibited by filtering. **Filtering** is the tendency for a message to be watered down or stopped altogether at some point during transmission, and it is something of a double-edged sword.

Filtering. The tendency for a message to be watered down or stopped during transmission.

On the one hand, employees are *supposed* to filter information. For example, CEOs are not expected to communicate every detail of the management of the company right down to the shop floor. On the other side of the coin, overzealous filtering will preclude the right people from getting the right information, and the organization will suffer accordingly. Upward filtering often occurs because employees are afraid that their boss will use the information against them. Downward filtering is often due to time pressures or simple lack of attention to detail, but more sinister motives may be at work. As the old saying goes, "information is power," and some managers filter downward communications to maintain an edge on their subordinates. For example, a manager who feels that an up-and-coming employee could be promoted over her might filter crucial information to make the subordinate look bad at a staff meeting.

Obviously, the potential for filtering increases with the number of links in the communication chain. For this reason, organizations establish channels in addition to those revealed in the formal chain of command. For instance, many managers establish an **open door policy** in which any organizational member below them can communicate directly without going through the chain.[2] Such a policy should decrease the upward filtering of sensitive information if subordinates trust the system. To prevent downward filtering, many organizations attempt to communicate directly with potential receivers, bypassing the chain of command. For example, the CEO of a company might use closed circuit TV to accurately inform employees about intended layoffs.

Slowness. Even when the chain of command transmits information faithfully, it can be painfully slow. The chain of command can be even slower for horizontal communication between departments, and it is not a good mechanism for reacting quickly to customer problems. Cross-functional teams and employee empowerment, concepts we introduced earlier in the text, have been used to improve communication in these areas by short-circuiting the chain of command.

In summary, informal communication and the recognition of filtering and time constraints guarantee that organizations will develop channels of communication beyond the strict chain of command.

MANAGER–EMPLOYEE COMMUNICATION

Manager–employee communication consists of the one-to-one exchange of information between a boss and an employee. As such, it represents a key element in upward and downward communication in organizations. Ideally, such exchange should enable the boss to instruct the employee in proper task performance, clarify reward contingencies, and provide social-emotional support. In addition, it should permit the employees to ask questions about their work role and make suggestions. Perceptions that managers are good communicators tend to be correlated positively with organizational performance.[3] At UPS, the daily group meetings and the longer "One Vision" meetings are designed to foster good communication between managers and employees.

How Good Is Manager–Employee Communication?

The extent to which managers and employees agree about work-related matters and are sensitive to each other's point of view is one index of good communication. Research indicates that managers and employees often differ in their perceptions of the following issues:

- How employees should and do allocate time
- How long it takes to learn a job
- The importance employees attach to pay

Open door policy. The opportunity for employees to communicate directly with a manager without going through the chain of command.

- The amount of authority the employee has
- The employee's skills and abilities
- The employee's performance and obstacles to good performance
- The manager's leadership style[4]

Perceptual differences like these suggest a lack of openness in communication, which might contribute to much role conflict and ambiguity, especially on the part of employees. In addition, a lack of openness in communication reduces employee job satisfaction.[5]

Barriers to Effective Manager–Employee Communication

What causes communication problems between managers and employees? In addition to basic differences in personality (Chapter 2) and perception (Chapter 3), the following factors have been implicated.

Conflicting Role Demands. In the previous chapter, we noted that the leadership role requires managers to attend to both task and social-emotional functions. Many managers have difficulties balancing these two role demands. For example, consider the following memo from a sales manager to one of the company's younger sales representatives:

> *I would like to congratulate you on being named Sales Rep of the Month for March. You can be very proud of this achievement. I now look forward to your increased contribution to our sales efforts, and I hope you can begin to bring some new accounts into the company. After all, new accounts are the key to our success.*

In congratulating the young sales rep and in suggesting that he increase his performance in the future, the manager tries to take care of social-emotional business and task business in one memo. Unfortunately, the sales rep might be greatly offended by this communication episode, feeling that it slights his achievement and implies that he has not been pulling his weight in the company. In this case, two separate communiqués, one dealing with congratulations and the other with the performance directive, would probably be more effective.

The Mum Effect. Another factor inhibiting effective manager–employee communication is the **mum effect**. This distinctive term refers to the tendency to avoid communicating unfavourable news to others.[6] Often, people would rather "keep mum" than convey bad news that might provoke negative reactions on the part of the receiver. The sender need not be *responsible* for the bad news for the mum effect to occur. For instance, a structural engineer might be reluctant to tell her boss that there are cracks in the foundation of a building, even though a subcontractor was responsible for the faulty work. It should be obvious, though, that the mum effect is even more likely when the sender *is* responsible for the bad news. For example, the nurse who mistakenly administers an incorrect drug dose might be very reluctant to inform the head nurse of her error. Employees with strong aspirations for upward mobility are especially likely to encounter communication difficulties with their bosses.[7] This might be due, in part, to the mum effect—employees who desire to impress their bosses to achieve a promotion have strong motives to withhold bad news.[8]

The mum effect does not apply only to employees. The boss might be reluctant to transmit bad news downward. In research conducted by one of your authors, it was found that employees who had good performance ratings were more likely to be informed of those ratings than employees who had bad ratings. Managers evidently avoided communicating bad news for which they were partly responsible, since they

Mum effect. The tendency to avoid communicating unfavourable news to others.

themselves had done the performance ratings. Given this, it is not surprising that managers and their employees often differ in their perceptions of employee performance.[9]

THE GRAPEVINE

Just inside the gates of the steel mill where one of your authors used to work there was a large sign that read "*X* days without a major accident." The sign was revised each day to impress on the workforce the importance of safe working practices. A zero posted on the sign caught one's attention immediately, since this meant that a serious accident or fatality had just occurred. Seeing a zero on entering the mill, workers seldom took more than five minutes to find someone who knew the details. While the victim's name might be unknown, the location and nature of the accident were always accurate, even though the mill was very large and the accident had often occurred on the previous shift. How did this information get around so quickly? It travelled through the "grapevine."

Characteristics of the Grapevine

Grapevine. An organization's informal communication network.

The **grapevine** is the informal communication network that exists in any organization. As such, the grapevine often cuts across formal lines of communication that are recognized by management. Observation suggests several distinguishing features of grapevine systems:

- We generally think of the grapevine as communicating information by word of mouth. However, written notes, e-mails, and fax messages can contribute to the transmission of information. For example, a fax operator in the New York office might tell the Zurich office that the chairman's wife just had a baby.
- Organizations often have several grapevine systems, some of which may be loosely coordinated. For instance, a secretary who is part of the "office grapevine" might communicate information to a mail carrier, who passes it on to the "warehouse grapevine."
- The grapevine can transmit information relevant to the performance of the organization as well as personal gossip.[10] Many times, it is difficult to distinguish between the two: "You won't *believe* who just got fired!"

How accurate is the grapevine? One expert concludes that at least 75 percent of the noncontroversial organizationally related information carried by the grapevine is correct.[11] Personal information and emotionally charged information are most likely to be distorted.

Grapevine information does not run through organizations in a neat chain in which person A tells only person B who tells only person C. Neither does it sweep across the organization like a tidal wave, with each sender telling six or seven others, who each, in turn, transmit the information to six or seven *other* members. Rather, only a proportion of those who receive grapevine news pass it on, with the net effect that more "know" than "tell."[12]

Who Participates in the Grapevine?

Just who is likely to tell—that is, who is likely to be a transmitter of grapevine information? Personality characteristics may play a role. For instance, extraverts might be more likely to pass on information than introverts. Similarly, those who lack self-esteem might pass on information that gives them a personal advantage.

The nature of the information might also influence who chooses to pass it on. In a hospital, the news that a doctor has obtained a substantial cancer research grant might follow a very different path from news involving his affair with a nurse!

Finally, it is obvious that the *physical* location of organizational members is related to their opportunity to both receive and transmit news via the "vine." Occupants of work stations that receive a lot of traffic are good candidates to be grapevine transmitters. A warm control room in a cold plant or an air-conditioned computer room in a sweltering factory might provide their occupants with a steady stream of potential receivers for juicy information. On the other side of the coin, jobs that require movement throughout the organization also give their holders much opportunity to serve as grapevine transmitters. Mail carriers and IT troubleshooters are good examples.

Pros and Cons of the Grapevine

Is the grapevine desirable from the organization's point of view? For one thing, it can keep employees informed about important organizational matters, such as job security. In some organizations, management is so notoriously lax at this that the grapevine is a regular substitute for formal communication. The grapevine can also provide a test of employee reactions to proposed changes without making formal commitments. Managers have been known to "leak" ideas (such as a change to a four-day workweek) to the grapevine to probe their potential acceptance. Anita Roddick, the founder of The Body Shop, was known for planting ideas with the office gossips to tap into the organization's informal networks.[13] Finally, participation in the grapevine can add a little interest and diversion to the work setting.

The grapevine can become a real problem for the organization when it becomes a constant pipeline for rumours. A **rumour** is an unverified belief that is in general circulation.[14] The key word here is *unverified*—although it is possible for a rumour to be true, it is not likely to *remain* true as it runs through the grapevine. Because people cannot verify the information as accurate, rumours are susceptible to severe distortion as they are passed from person to person.

> **Rumour.** An unverified belief that is in general circulation.

Rumours seem to spread fastest and farthest when the information is especially ambiguous, when the content of the rumour is important to those involved, when the rumour seems credible, and when the recipient is anxious.[15]

Increasingly difficult global competition, staff reductions, and restructuring have placed a premium on rumour control. At the same time, organizations should avoid the tendency to be mum about giving bad news. For a concrete example of the pros and cons of the grapevine, see "Ethical Focus: *Blogs: Effective Communication Tool or Cyberspace Menace?*"

THE VERBAL LANGUAGE OF WORK

A friend of one of your authors just moved into a new neighbourhood. In casual conversation with a neighbour, he mentioned that he was "writing a book on OB." She replied with some enthusiasm, "Oh, that's great. My husband's in obstetrics too!" The author's friend, of course, is a management professor who was writing a book on organizational behaviour. The neighbour's husband was a physician who specialized in delivering babies.

Every student knows what it means to do a little "cramming in the caf" before an exam. Although this phrase might sound vaguely obscene to the uninitiated listener, it reveals how circumstances shape our language and how we often take this shaping for granted. In many jobs, occupations, and organizations we see the development of a specialized language, or **jargon**, that members use to communicate with each other. Thus, OB means *organizational behaviour* to management professors and *obstetrics* to physicians.

> **Jargon.** Specialized language used by job holders or members of particular occupations or organizations.

Rosabeth Moss Kanter, in studying a large corporation, discovered its attempt to foster COMVOC, or "common vocabulary," among its managers.[16] Here, the goal was to facilitate communication among employees who were often geographically separated, unknown to each other, and "meeting" impersonally through telex or memo.

ETHICAL FOCUS

Blogs: Effective Communication Tool or Cyberspace Menace?

Web logs, popularly known as blogs, are online journals in which an individual can share his or her personal thoughts and views on almost any topic. Blogs are becoming one of the most popular forms of communication in cyberspace and allow their authors to publish opinions on movies, politics, fashion, and so on and give their readers a peek into their daily lives. Increasingly, employees are using blogs to communicate information and views concerning their employers. This can represent both an opportunity and a threat for companies. On the one hand, some companies have embraced blogs as a way of assessing the internal climate of the workforce and gaining access to the employee grapevine. Microsoft has over 2000 in-house bloggers and views them in a positive light, as many blogs actually promote company products. Other companies arrange blogs themselves or set up internal blogs as an extension of their intranet. The ultimate employee blog is the chief executive's, who can use the Internet to connect with employees and disseminate information. Companies who manage their company-related blogs well can reap the benefits of improved communication.

Blogs, however, also have a dark side. They can be a breeding ground for personal attacks against managers, unfounded rumours and gossip, and also disseminate confidential company information. To make matters worse, the more vicious bloggers usually use their computer expertise to remain anonymous. "A blogger can go out and make any statement about anybody, and you can't control it," says Steven Down, general manager of bike lock maker Kryptonite, a company that was under attack from bloggers over flaws in their products, many of the claims proving to be untrue. To defend against potential brand damage caused by smear campaigns, employers can engage and respond to the bloggers directly, which could open them to further ridicule, or pursue legal action, which may be difficult if the blogger's identity cannot be easily determined.

The risks can also be high for the bloggers themselves. While blogging during working hours can lead to disciplinary action, and disclosing confidential company information or slandering managers is grounds for dismissal and legal action, some bloggers have found out the hard way that their tongue-in-cheek musings about work can be a fast track to the unemployment line. Companies such as Google, Delta Airlines, and the Wells Fargo bank have fired employees for their blogging activities. Mark Jen, formally of Google, and Joe Gordon, formally of the UK bookstore chain Waterstone's, were both fired due to blog posts that management viewed as damaging to the company. The bloggers indicated that their web logs were similar to chatting about work with family and friends, and both offered to stop blogging about work if the company desired it; but they were fired anyway.

Experts recommend that companies create policies on blogging for their employees, outlining what is and is not acceptable in blogs. For instance, IBM has developed guidelines concerning blogging. Overall, it seems clear that web logs are here to stay, and that what goes on in the workplace will always be a favourite topic for bloggers. Whether or not blogs represent a positive tool for employee communication, however, remains to be seen.

Sources: Brody, R.G., & Wheelin, B.J. (2005). Blogging: The new computer "virus" for employers. *HR. Human Resource Planning, 28,* 12; Lyons, D. (2005, November 14). Attack of the Blogs. *Forbes,* 128–138 (Down quote); Murphy, C. (2006, March 21). Blogging. *Personnel Today,* 26–27; Weinman, J.J. (2005). What the dooce! Blogging about work. *Journal of Internet Law, 9,* 3–6.

COMVOC provided a common basis for interaction among virtual strangers. In addition, managers developed their own informal supplements to COMVOC. Upward mobility, an especially important topic in the corporation, was reflected in multiple labels for the same concept:

Fast trackers	One performers
High fliers	Boy (girl) wonders
Superstars	Water walkers

While jargon is an efficient means of communicating with peers and provides a touch of status to those who have mastered it, it can also serve as a *barrier* to communicating with others. For example, local jargon might serve as a barrier to clear communication between departments such as sales and engineering. New organizational members often find the use of jargon especially intimidating and confusing.

A second serious problem with the use of jargon is the communication barrier that it presents to those *outside* of the organization or profession. Consider the language of the corporate takeover, with its greenmail, poison pills, and white knights! Kanter, the researcher who studied COMVOC in a large corporation, found that wives of male executives could generate a total of 103 unfamiliar terms and phrases that their husbands used in relation to work! Such a situation might contribute to a poor understanding of what the spouse does at work and how work can make such heavy demands on family life.

THE NONVERBAL LANGUAGE OF WORK

Have you ever come away from a conversation having heard one thing yet believing the opposite of what was said? Professors frequently hear students say that they understand a concept but somehow know that they do not. Students often hear professors say, "Come up to my office any time," but somehow know that they do not mean it. How can we account for these messages that we receive in spite of the words we hear? The answer is often nonverbal communication.

Nonverbal communication refers to the transmission of messages by some medium other than speech or writing. As indicated above, nonverbal messages can be very powerful, in that they often convey "the real stuff," while words serve as a smoke screen. Raised eyebrows, an emphatic shrug, or an abrupt departure convey a lot of information with great economy. The minutes of dramatic meetings (or even verbatim transcripts) can make for extremely boring reading because they are stripped of nonverbal cues. These examples involve the transmission of information by body language. Below, we consider body language and the manipulation of objects as major forms of nonverbal communication.

Nonverbal communication. The transmission of messages by some medium other than speech or writing.

Body Language

Body language is nonverbal communication that occurs by means of the sender's bodily motions and facial expressions or the sender's physical location in relation to the receiver.[17] Although we can communicate a variety of information via body language, two important messages are the extent to which the sender likes and is interested in the receiver and the sender's views concerning the relative status of the sender and the receiver.

In general, senders communicate liking and interest in the receiver when they

Body language. Nonverbal communication by means of a sender's bodily motions, facial expressions, or physical location.

- position themselves physically close to the receiver;
- touch the receiver during the interaction;
- maintain eye contact with the receiver;
- lean forward during the interaction; and
- direct the torso toward the receiver.[18]

As you can see, each of these behaviours demonstrates that the sender has genuine consideration for the receiver's point of view.

Senders who feel themselves to be of higher status than the receiver act more *relaxed* than those who perceive themselves to be of lower status. Relaxation is demonstrated by

- the casual, asymmetrical placement of arms and legs;

- a reclining, nonerect seating position; and
- a lack of fidgeting and nervous activity.[19]

In other words, the greater the difference in relaxation between two parties, the more they communicate a status differential to each other.

People often attempt to use nonverbal behaviour to communicate with others, just like they use verbal behaviour. This use could include showing our true feelings, "editing" our feelings, or trying to actively deceive others. It is difficult to regulate nonverbal behaviour when we are feeling very strong emotions. However, people are otherwise pretty good at nonverbal "posing," such as looking relaxed when they are not. On the other hand, observers also show some capacity to detect such posing.[20]

One area in which research shows that body language has an impact is on the outcome of employment interview decisions. Employment interviewers are usually faced with applicants who are motivated to make a good verbal impression. Thus, in accordance with the idea that "the body doesn't lie," interviewers might consciously or unconsciously turn their attention to nonverbal cues on the assumption that they are less likely to be censored than verbal cues. Nonverbal behaviours, such as smiling, gesturing, and maintaining eye contact, have a favourable impact on interviewers when they are not overdone.[21] However, it is unlikely that such body language can overcome bad credentials or poor verbal performance.[22] Rather, increased body language might give the edge to applicants who are otherwise equally well-qualified. Remember, in an employment interview, it is not just what you say, but also what you do!

Props, Artifacts, and Costumes

In addition to the use of body language, nonverbal communication can also occur through the use of various objects such as props, artifacts, and costumes.

Office Decor and Arrangement. Consider the manner in which people decorate and arrange their offices. Does this tell visitors anything about the occupant? Does it communicate any useful information? The answer is yes. One study found that students would feel more welcome and comfortable in professors' offices when the office was (1) tidy, (2) decorated with posters and plants, and (3) the desk was against the wall instead of between the student and the professor.[23] A neat office evidently signalled

The decor and arrangement of furniture in a person's office conveys nonverbal information to visitors.

that the professor was well organized and had time to talk to them. Perhaps personal decoration signalled, "I'm human." When the desk was against the wall, there was no tangible barrier between the parties. Inferences of this type appear to have some validity. A recent study found that strangers were able to accurately infer certain "Big Five" personality traits (Chapter 2) of the occupants of business offices. In particular, they could assess how conscientious and how open to experience the person was simply by seeing his or her office. Neatness was a typical cue for conscientiousness and distinctive decor for openness.[24]

Researcher Kimberly Elsbach found that middle managers working in the California information technology sector (mostly at Intel and Hewlett-Packard) used office decor to "profile" the identity and status of office occupants.[25] Exhibit 10.2 shows some of the inferences they made about their fellow employees, both flattering and unflattering.

Does Clothing Communicate? "Wardrobe engineer" John T. Molloy is convinced that the clothing organizational members wear sends clear signals about their competence, seriousness, and promotability—that is, receivers unconsciously attach certain stereotyped meanings to various clothing and then treat the wearer accordingly. For example, Molloy insists that a black raincoat is the kiss of death for an aspiring male executive. He claims that black raincoats signal "lower-middle class," while beige raincoats lead to "executive" treatment both inside and outside the firm. For the same reason, Molloy strongly vetoes sweaters for women executives. Molloy stresses, however, that proper clothing will not make up for a lack of ambition, intelligence, and savvy. Rather, he argues that the wrong clothing will prevent others from detecting these qualities. To this end, he prescribes detailed "business uniforms," the men's built around a conservative suit and the women's around a skirted suit and blouse.[26] The rise in the number of image consultants who help aspiring executives "dress for success" testifies to the popularity of such thinking.

Research reveals that clothing does indeed communicate.[27] Even at the ages of 10 to 12 years, children associate various brand names of jeans with different personality characteristics of the wearer! Such effects persist into adulthood. Research simulations have shown that more masculinely dressed and groomed women are more likely to be

EXHIBIT 10.2
Inferences from office decor.

Source: Elsbach, K.D. (2004) Interpreting Workplace Identities: The Role of Office Décor. *Journal of Organizational Behavior*, 25 © John Wiley & Sons Limited. Reproduced with permission.

Office Decor	Distinctiveness Categorizations	Status Categorizations
Family photos	Family oriented, balanced, not work focused	Not a 'player'
Hobby photos, calendar, poster, artifacts	Ambitious, outgoing, well-rounded	Unprofessional
Funny, unusual artifacts and conversation pieces	Fun person, joker, off-beat, approachable, lazy, needs attention	Not serious, unprofessional
Formal decor, artifacts	Professional, successful, vain, distant, snobbish	High status, authority figure
Informal, messy office	Easy-going, busy, true engineer, disorganized, unskilled	Unprofessional
Awards, diplomas	Show-off, hard-working, successful, pretentious, vain	Accomplished, intimidating
Professional products	Functional expert, 'company person,' geek	Accomplished
Ideological artifacts	Patriotic, says 'I have a social conscience,' extreme, radical	Insecure, unprofessional
Salient, flashy artifacts	Needs to get attention, flashy	Insecure
High conformity artifacts	Predictable, reliable, conservative, not innovative	Insecure

selected for executive jobs. However, one study shows that there might be a point at which women's dress becomes "too masculine" and thus damages their prospects.[28] Women's clothing styles have been of special research interest because there is less consensus about just how female executives should dress.

If clothing does indeed communicate, it might do so partly because of the impact it has on the wearer's own self-image. Proper clothing might enhance self-esteem and self-confidence to a noticeable degree. One study contrived to have some student job applicants appear for an interview in street clothes, while others had time to dress in more appropriate formal interview gear. Those who wore more formal clothes felt that they had made a better impression on the interviewer. They also asked for a starting salary that was $4000 higher than the job seekers who wore street clothes![29]

GENDER DIFFERENCES IN COMMUNICATION

Do men and women communicate differently? According to Deborah Tannen, not only are there gender differences in communication styles, but these differences influence the way that men and women are perceived and treated in the workplace. Gender differences in communication have their origin in childhood. Girls see conversations as a way to develop relationships and networks of connection and intimacy. Boys view conversations as a way for them to achieve status within groups and to maintain independence. These childhood differences persist in the workplace, where they influence who gets recognized and who is valued.[30]

The typical example of how these differences are played out is in a business meeting in which a woman comes up with a great idea and by the end of the meeting one of her male peers receives the credit for it. Similarly, a woman might have a great idea for a new product but nobody pays any attention to it until a man suggests it.[31] In these instances, what often happens is that a man picks up the idea of a female co-worker and spends more time talking about it. As a result, he gets the credit.[32]

Gender differences in communication revolve around what Tannen refers to as the "One Up, One Down" position. Men tend to be more sensitive to power dynamics and will use communication as a way to position themselves in a one-up situation. Women are more concerned with rapport building, and they communicate in ways that avoid putting others down. As a result, women often find themselves in a one-down position, which can have a negative effect on the rewards they receive and their careers.[33]

On the basis of her research, Tannen has found that there are a number of key differences in male and female communication styles and rituals that often place women in a one-down position:

- *Getting credit.* Men are more likely than women to blow their horn about something good they have done.

- *Confidence and boasting.* Men tend to be more boastful about themselves and their capabilities and to minimize their doubts, compared with women, who downplay their certainty. As a result, men tend to be perceived as more confident.

- *Asking questions.* Most people know that men do not like to ask for directions when they are lost. This is because they realize that asking questions can put them in a one-down position and reflect negatively on them. Therefore, men are less likely than women to ask questions.

- *Apologies.* Women will often say "I'm sorry" as a way of expressing concern, such as when a friend has had a bad day. For women, apologies are part of a ritual that is used to establish rapport. Men, however, avoid such ritual apologies because for them it is a sign of weakness.

- *Feedback.* Men and women differ in the way they use feedback. Women will often buffer criticism by beginning with praise as a way to save face for the person receiving the criticism and avoid putting them in a one-down position. Men, however, tend to be much more blunt and straightforward. These differences can lead to misunderstandings, as when a man interprets a woman's praise, rather than the criticism, as the main message.

- *Compliments*. If a friend of yours has just completed a class presentation and asks for your thoughts about it, what would you say? Women are more likely to provide a compliment such as "Great presentation" or "Good job." Men, however, are more likely to interpret the question literally and provide a critique, not realizing that all that is expected is a compliment.

- *Ritual opposition*. Men often use ritual opposition or fighting as a form of communication and to exchange ideas. This often takes the form of attacking others' points of view, challenging them in public, and being combative and argumentative. For women, this type of ritual opposition is seen as a personal attack and something to be avoided.

- *Managing up and down*. Men and women differ in the way they communicate with those above and below them in the chain of command. Many women believe that to be recognized and rewarded, what matters most is doing a good job. Unfortunately, this is not always the case. What also matters is whom you communicate with and what you discuss. Men spend much more time communicating with their superiors and talking about their achievements. Not surprisingly, this type of communication influences who gets recognized and promoted. When in positions of power, women tend to downplay their superiority, leading others to believe that they are not capable of projecting their authority.

- *Indirectness*. What would be your response if your supervisor asked you a relatively simple question such as, "How would you feel about helping the human resources department hire a new person for our department?" Would you then think about how you "feel" about helping or would you interpret this as a request to actually do it? In North America, persons in positions of authority are expected to give direct orders when asking subordinates to do something. Women in positions of authority, however, tend to be indirect when giving orders. For instance, in the above example, what is really being said is, "Help the human resource department hire a person for our department." Such indirectness can lead to misunderstandings and be perceived as a lack of appropriate demeanour and confidence.[34]

As the examples indicate, the differences in communication styles between men and women almost always reflect negatively on women and place them in a one-down position. Does this mean that women should change the way they communicate? Not necessarily. It depends on the person they are communicating with and the situation. For example, the communication styles that women are accustomed to are most appropriate when communicating with other women, and the same goes for men. Problems and misunderstandings arise when those communicating do not understand the rituals and styles of each other. The key, according to Deborah Tannen, is to recognize that people have different linguistic styles and to be flexible so that you can adjust your style when necessary. For example, men should learn to admit when they make a mistake and women could learn to be more direct when asking subordinates to do something. Being able to use different communication styles allows people to adjust their style to any given situation.[35] This is also important for effective cross-cultural communication, which is our next topic.

CROSS-CULTURAL COMMUNICATION

Consider a commonplace exchange in the world of international business:

A Japanese businessman wants to tell his Norwegian client that he is uninterested in a particular sale. To be polite, the Japanese says, "That will be very difficult." The Norwegian interprets the statement to mean that there are still unresolved problems, not that the deal is off. He responds by asking how his company can help solve the problems. The Japanese, believing he has sent the message that there will be no sale, is mystified by the response.[36]

Obviously, ineffective communication has occurred between our international businesspeople, since the Norwegian has not received the right information about the (non)sale. From the Norwegian's point of view, the Japanese has not encoded his message in a clear manner. The Japanese, on the other hand, might criticize the weak decoding skills of his Scandinavian client. Thus, we see that problems in communication across cultures go right to the heart of the communication model that we studied at the beginning of the chapter.

In Chapter 4, we learned that various societies differ in their underlying value systems. In turn, these differences lead to divergent attitudes about a whole host of matters ranging from what it means to be on time for a meeting to how to say "no" to a business deal (as illustrated above). In Chapter 4, we also noted that a surprising number of managers do not work out well in international assignments. Many of these failures stem from problems in cross-cultural communication. Let's examine some important dimensions of such communication.

Language Differences

Communication is generally better between individuals or groups who share similar cultural values. This is even more true when they share a common language. Thus, despite acknowledged differences in terminology ("lift" versus "elevator," "petrol" versus "gasoline"), language should not be a communication barrier for the North American executive who is posted to a British subsidiary. Despite this generality, the role of language in communication involves some subtle ironies. For example, a common language can sometimes cause visitors to misunderstand or be surprised by legitimate cultural differences because they get lulled into complacency. Boarding a Qantas Airlines flight in Australia, one of your authors was attempting to pick up a magazine from a rack in the 747 when he was admonished by a flight attendant with the sharp words "First class, mate." Grinning sheepishly, he headed back to his tourist class seat without the magazine. Wise to the ways of Australia, he was not offended by this display of brash informality. However, a less familiar North American, assuming that "they speak English, they're just like us," might have been less forgiving, attributing the flight attendant's behaviour to a rude personality rather than national style. By the same token, the flight attendant would be surprised to learn that someone might be offended by his words.

As the Qantas example indicates, speaking the same language is no guarantee of perfect communication. In fact, the Norwegian and Japanese businesspeople described above might have negotiated in a common language, such as English. Even then, the Norwegian did not get the message. Speaking generally, however, learning a second language should facilitate cross-cultural communication. This is especially true when the second-language facility provides extra insight into the communication style of the other culture. Thus, the Norwegian would profit from understanding that the Japanese have sixteen subtle ways to say no, even if he could not understand the language perfectly.[37]

Nonverbal Communication across Cultures

From our earlier discussion of nonverbal communication, you might be tempted to assume that it would hold up better than verbal communication across cultures. While there are some similarities across cultures in nonverbal communication, there are also many differences. Here are a few examples.

- *Facial expressions.* People are very good at decoding basic, simple emotions in facial expressions, even across cultures. Americans, Japanese, and members of primitive New Guinea tribes can accurately detect anger, surprise, fear, and sadness in the same set of facial photographs.[38] Thus, paying particular attention to the face in cross-cultural encounters will often yield communication dividends. However, this does not always work because some cultures (such as that of Japan) frown on the display of negative facial expressions, no doubt prompting the "inscrutable" label.

- *Gestures.* Except for literal mimicry ("I need food," "Sign here"), gestures do not translate well across cultures. This is because they involve symbolism that is not shared. Most amusing are those cases in which the same gesture has different meanings across cultures:

    In the United States, a raised thumb is used as a signal of approval or approbation, the "thumbs up" signal, but in Greece, it is employed as an insult, often being associated with the expression "katsa pano" or "sit on this." Another example is the ring sign, performed by bringing the tips of the thumb and finger together so that they form a circle. For most English-speaking people it means O.K. and is, in fact, known as the "O.K. gesture." But in some sections of France, the ring means zero or worthless. In English-speaking countries, disagreement is signalled by shaking the head, but in Greece and southern Italy the head-toss is employed to signify "no."[39]

- *Gaze.* There are considerable cross-cultural differences in the extent to which it is considered suitable to look others directly in the eye. Latin Americans and Arabs favour an extended gaze, while Europeans do not. In many parts of East Asia, avoiding eye contact is a means of showing respect. In North America, it often connotes disrespect.

- *Touch.* In some cultures, people tend to stand close to one another when meeting and often touch each other as an adjunct to conversation. This is common in Arab, Latin American, and Southern European countries. On the other hand, Northern Europeans and North Americans prefer to "keep their distance."[40]

In an interesting experiment on nonverbal cross-cultural communication, English people received training in social skills that were appropriate to the Arab world. These included standing or sitting close to others and looking into their eyes, coupled with extensive touching, smiling, and handshaking. Experimenters then introduced Arabs to a trained subject and to a control subject who had only been exposed to general information about the Middle East. When asked whom they liked better, the Arabs preferred the people who had received training in their own nonverbal communication style.[41] We can well imagine a business meeting between English and Saudi bankers, both true to their cultures. The Saudis, gazing and touching, finish the meeting wondering why the English are so inattentive and aloof. The English, avoiding eye contact and shrinking from touch, wonder why the Saudis are so aggressive and threatening!

Etiquette and Politeness across Cultures

Cultures differ considerably in how etiquette and politeness are expressed.[42] Very often, this involves saying things that one does not literally mean. The problem is that the exact form that this takes varies across cultures, and careful decoding is necessary to avoid confusion and embarrassment. Literal decoding will almost always lead to trouble. Consider the North American manager who says to an employee, "Would you like to calculate those figures for me?" This is really a mild order, not an opportunity to say no to the boss's "invitation." However, put yourself in the place of a foreign employee who has learned that Americans generally speak directly and expect directness in return. Should she say no to the boss?

In some cultures, politeness is expressed with modesty that seems excessive to North Americans. Consider, for example, the Chinese visitor's response to a Canadian who told him that his wife was very attractive. The Chinese modestly responded, "No, no, my wife is ugly." Needless to say, what was said was not what was meant.

In social situations, the Japanese are particularly interested in maintaining feelings of interdependence and harmony. To do this, they use a large number of set phrases or "lubricant expressions" to express sympathy and understanding, soften rejection, say no indirectly, or facilitate apology.[43] When the Japanese told the Norwegian "that will be very difficult," rather than "no," he was using such an expression. To Northern Europeans and North Americans, who do not understand the purpose of these ritual expressions, they seem at best to be small talk and at worst to be insincere.

Social Conventions across Cultures

Over and above the issue of politeness and etiquette, there are a number of social conventions that vary across cultures and can lead to communication problems.[44] We have already alluded to the issue of directness. Especially in business dealings, North Americans tend to favour "getting down to brass tacks" and being specific about the issue at hand. Thus, the uninitiated businessperson might be quite surprised at the rather long period of informal chat that will begin business meetings in the Arab world or the indirectness and vagueness of many Japanese negotiators.

Greetings and how people say hello also vary across cultures, and these differences can lead to misunderstandings (Exhibit 10.3). For example, in North America people often greet one another by asking "How are you?" and yet seem uninterested in the response. While this is an acceptable way of saying hello to North Americans, visitors from other cultures find this to be hypocritical. In other cultures, people greet each other by asking, "Where are you going?" Such a question is considered intrusive to North Americans who do not realize that this too is just a way of greeting somebody.[45]

What individuals consider a proper degree of loudness for speech also varies across cultures, and people from "quieter" societies (such as the United Kingdom) might unfairly view those from "louder" societies (such as the Middle East) as pushy or intimidating.

What people consider proper punctuality also varies greatly around the world. In North America and Japan, punctuality at meetings and social engagements is expected and esteemed. In the Arab world and Latin America, being late for a meeting is not

EXHIBIT 10.3
Greetings from around the world: Cultural differences in saying "hello."

Source: Data from Axtell, R.E. (1991). *Gestures: The do's and taboos of body language around the world.* New York: Wiley.

Greetings from Around the World:
Cultural Differences in Saying "Hello"

Culture	Description
Japan	The bow—bending forward and down at the waist.
India	*Namaste*—placing hands at the chest in a praying position and bowing slightly.
Thailand	*Wai*—same as namaste (India).
Middle East	*Salaam*—used primarily among the older generation. Right hand moves upward, touching first the heart, then the forehead, an then moving up into the air.
Maori tribespeople (New Zealand) and Inuit	Rubbing noses.
East African tribes	Spitting at each other's feet.
Tibetan tribesmen	Sticking out their tongues at each other.
Bolivia	Handshake accompanied by a hearty clap on the back.
Russia	Friends begin with a handshake and move to a "bear hug."
Latin America	*Abrazo*—embracing with both arms.

viewed negatively. In fact, one study found that being on time for an appointment connoted success in the United States and being *late* connoted success in Brazil.[46] Notice how an American businessperson might decode a Brazilian's lateness as disrespect, while the Brazilian was just trying to make a proper impression.

Exhibit 10.4 shows the results of a study of differences in the pace of life across cultures. It illustrates the accuracy of clocks, the time to walk 100 feet, and the time to get served in a post office. As you can see, Japan is the most time conscious, while Indonesia is quite leisurely. Such differences are especially likely to provoke communication problems when we attribute them to a *person* and ignore the overall influence of the culture.

Finally, nepotism, favouring one's relatives in spite of their qualifications, is generally frowned on in more individualistic societies, such as North America and Northern Europe. However, in more collective cultures, such as those found in Africa and Latin America, people are expected to help their relatives. Hence, an American manager might view his Nigerian colleague's hiring his own son as irresponsible. The Nigerian might see it as irresponsible *not* to hire his own flesh and blood.

Cultural Context

In the previous sections, we provided many examples of communication differences across cultures. Is there some organizing principle underlying these differences, something that helps to summarize them? The concept of *cultural context* provides a partial answer. **Cultural context** is the cultural information that surrounds a communication episode. It is safe to say that context is always important in accurately decoding a message. Still, as Exhibit 10.5 shows, cultures tend to differ in the importance to which context influences the meaning to be put on communications.[47]

Some cultures, including many East Asian, Latin American, African, and Arab cultures, are high-context cultures. This means that the message contained in communication is strongly influenced by the context in which the message is sent. In high-context cultures, literal interpretations are often incorrect. Examples include those mentioned earlier—the Japanese really meant that the business deal was dead, and the Chinese did not really mean that his wife was unattractive.

Cultural context. The cultural information that surrounds a communication episode.

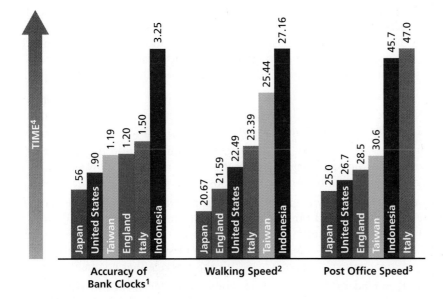

EXHIBIT 10.4
Pace of life in six countries.

Source: Levine, R., & Wolff, E. (1985, March). Social time: The heartbeat of culture. *Psychology Today*, 26–35. Reprinted with permission from *Psychology Today Magazine*, copyright © 1985 Sussex Publishers, Inc.

¹ Deviations are reported in minutes
²,³ Speeds are in seconds
⁴ Smaller numbers indicate more accurate clocks, faster walking speeds, and faster office speeds, respectively

EXHIBIT 10.5
High- versus low-context cultures.

Source: Klopf, D.W. (1995). *Intercultural encounters: The fundamentals of intercultural communication*, p. 33. Englewood, Colorado: Morton Publishing Company.

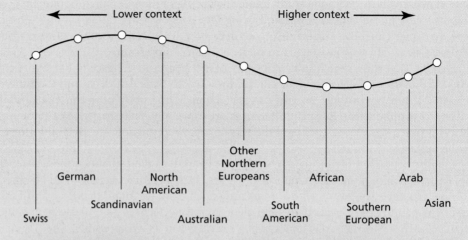

Low-context cultures include North America, Australia, Northern Europe (excluding France), and Scandinavia. Here, messages can be interpreted more literally because more meaning resides in the message than in the context in which the communication occurs. The "straight talk" that Americans favour is such an example. However, such straight talk is not any straighter in meaning than that heard in high-context cultures if one also learns to attend to the context when decoding messages.

Differences in the importance of context across cultures have some interesting implications for organizational communication, especially when we consider what might occur during business negotiations. Consider the following:[48]

- People from high-context cultures want to know about you and the company that you represent in great detail. This personal and organizational information provides a context for understanding your messages to them.

- Getting to the point quickly is not a style of communication that people in high-context cultures favour. Longer presentations and meetings allow people to get to know one another and to consider a proposal in a series of stages.

- When communicating with people from a high-context culture, give careful consideration to the age and rank of the communicator. Age and seniority tend to be valued in high-context cultures, and the status of the communicator is an important contextual factor that gives credibility to a message. Younger fast-trackers will do fine in low-context cultures where "it's the message that counts."

- Because they tend to devalue cultural context, people from low-context cultures tend to favour very detailed business contracts. For them, the meaning is in the message itself. High-context cultures place less emphasis on lengthy contracts because the context in which the deal is sealed is critical.

Some more general advice for good cross-cultural communication will be presented shortly, but for now, consider the You Be the Manager feature about cross-cultural communication when a company expands to a new country, as was the case when Four Seasons took over one of Paris's most renowned hotels.

Four Seasons Hotels and Resorts
www.fourseasons.com

COMPUTER-MEDIATED COMMUNICATION

Does communicating electronically differ from face-to-face communication? This is clearly an important topic given the pervasive use of routine e-mail, "chat" type decision support software, teleconferencing, videoconferencing, and other electronic communication media. A good way to begin thinking about this issue is to consider **information richness**, the potential information-carrying capacity of a communication medium.[49] As you can see in Exhibit 10.6, we can rank various media in terms of their information richness. A face-to-face transmission of information is very high in richness because the sender is personally present, audio and visual channels are used, body language and verbal language are occurring, and feedback to the sender is immediate and ongoing. At UPS, management recognizes that face-to-face meetings are a good way to communicate with their employees, in keeping with the firm's "One Vision" initiative. A telephone conversation is also fairly rich, but it is limited to the audio channel, and it does not permit the observation of body language. At the other extreme, communicating via numeric computer output lacks richness because it is impersonal and uses only numeric language. Feedback on such communication might also be very slow.

Information richness. The potential information-carrying capacity of a communication medium.

Exhibit 10.7 (page 357) shows two important dimensions of information richness: the degree to which information is synchronous between senders and receivers, and the extent to which both parties can receive nonverbal and paraverbal cues. Highly synchronous communication, such as face-to-face speech, is two-way, in real time. On the low side of synchronization, memos, letters, and even e-mails are essentially a series of one-way messages, although e-mail has the clear potential for speedy response. Face-to-face interaction and videoconferencing are high in nonverbal (e.g., body language) and paraverbal (e.g., tone of voice) cues, while these are essentially absent in the text-based media. In general, the media in the upper right sector of Exhibit 10.7 (highly synchronous, high in nonverbal and paraverbal cues) exemplify the most information richness and those in the lower left sector exhibit the least richness.

As shown in Exhibit 10.7, e-mail, chat systems, teleconferencing, and videoconferencing are commonly classified as **computer-mediated communication (CMC)** in that they rely on computer technology to facilitate information exchange. All of these media permit discussion and decision making without employees having to be in the

Computer-mediated communication (CMC). Communication that relies on computer technology to facilitate information exchange.

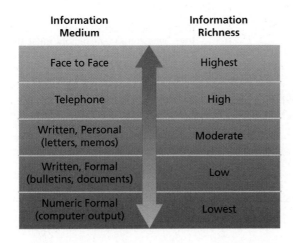

Information Medium	Information Richness
Face to Face	Highest
Telephone	High
Written, Personal (letters, memos)	Moderate
Written, Formal (bulletins, documents)	Low
Numeric Formal (computer output)	Lowest

EXHIBIT 10.6
Communication media and information richness.

Source: Daft, R.L., & Lengel, R.H. (1984). Information richness: A new approach to managerial behavior and organization design. *Research in Organizational Behavior, 6,* 191–233, p. 196. Reprinted by permission of JAI Press, Inc.

☞ YOU BE THE Manager

Four Seasons Goes to Paris

In 2006, Four Seasons Hotels and Resorts managed 70 properties in 30 countries and was widely regarded as the world's leading operator of luxury hotels. For nine years in a row, the Canadian company had made *Fortune's* list of the top 100 best companies to work for in North America, and had also seen impressive financial results during that same period.

Four Seasons is known for its strong organizational culture, which is based on the Golden Rule of "treating others as you wish they would treat you." The culture is supported by a philosophy focusing on modesty, individual accountability, a strong allegiance to the firm, global service standards, and intelligent, anticipatory, and enthusiastic customer service. When Four Seasons decided to expand internationally, many wondered if it's corporate culture—undoubtedly a major factor in its North American success—would be easy to transfer to employees in other countries. This question was particularly important when Four Seasons signed a deal to manage the famous George V hotel in Paris in 1996.

The French have a distinct national culture and a particular philosophy of customer service. They believe it is degrading to be "in the service" of someone else, but honourable to "give service" if it is deserved. This view is quite the opposite of what Four Seasons' North American employees believe. The French have also had management–employee relationships that traditionally tended to be adversarial, not cooperative, and they are not known for taking initiative without checking with a higher up first. At the Four Seasons, however, the culture focuses on individual initiative with accountability, and strong cooperation between managers and employees.

A further problem for the Four Seasons was France's strong labour laws. The company was forced to keep all existing employees who wished to stay with the hotel. The George V is one of six grand, historic, and luxurious hotels in Paris classified as "Palaces," but in the 1980s and 1990s service had lapsed to the point where many wondered if it was worthy of the "Palace" name. Having to keep some of the employees who worked during these down years meant that communicating and implementing a new, customer-focused culture would be difficult, to say the least. The Four Seasons also had to contend with France's past experiences with other North American firms who showed little cultural sensitivity when they came to Europe and earned the resentment and ridicule of the French. Disney is one of the best

The George V balances Four Seasons corporate culture with French national culture.

examples of corporate culture clash in France (see the Global Focus feature in Chapter 4).

To contend with all of these daunting hurdles, Four Seasons played up its Canadian identity to emphasize its open-mindedness to different cultures. Further, Didier Le Calvez, a native of France who had spent the last 25 years working outside of the country, was appointed as general manager of the George V. Le Calvez and his team knew that "Four Seasonizing" the hotel would be no easy task.

QUESTIONS

1. Given Four Seasons' operations in 30 different countries, what important factors must the firm's managers be aware of to properly communicate with staff at their hotels? Should all policies and procedures be communicated and implemented universally?

2. Considering France's national culture, and the fact that the George V had been acquired and is now being operated by foreign interests, what specific tactics could Le Calvez use to communicate Four Seasons' culture and approach to employees and to the French public?

To find out what Four Seasons did, see The Manager's Notebook at the end of the chapter.

Source: Adapted (with updates) from Hallowell, R., Bowen, D.E., & Knoop, C.I. (2002, November). Four Seasons goes to Paris. *Academy of Management Executive*, 7–24.

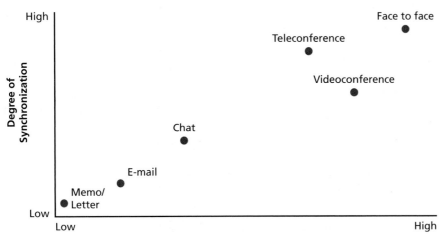

EXHIBIT 10.7
Communication media arranged according to synchronization and cue availability.

Source: Baltes, B.B., Dickson, M.W., Sherman, M.P., Bauer, C.C., & LaGanke, J.S. (2002). Computer-mediated communication and group decision making: A meta-analysis. *Organizational Behavior and Human Decision Processes, 87*, 156–179.

same location, potentially saving time, money, and travel hassles. But does such potential efficiency result in effective communication, as we defined it earlier?

Most research to date has focused on "chat"-type group-decision support systems that rely on text-based computer conferencing to generate ideas and make decisions. Such systems have been shown to enhance the sheer number of ideas regarding some problem generated under "brainstorming" conditions (Chapter 11).[50] Several factors contribute to this. In electronic groups, computer memory means that people can "talk" at the same time. Also, some systems permit the anonymous generation of ideas. This means that those who are shy may be less inhibited in offering suggestions. Also, anonymity can

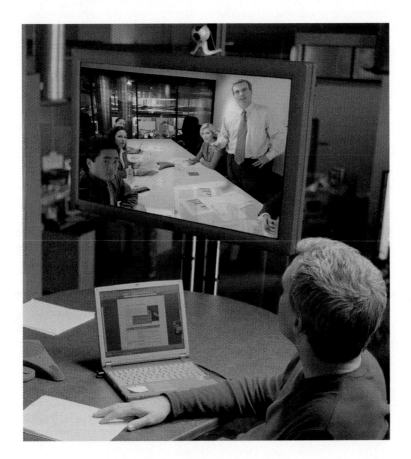

Computer-mediated communication includes videoconferencing.

erase perceived or actual status differences. In one study of executives, men were five times more likely than women to offer an initial idea in a face-to-face meeting. In an electronic meeting, men and women were equally likely to offer the first idea.[51]

By almost any criterion other than generating ideas, computer-mediated groups perform more poorly than face-to-face groups, at least when they meet for only a single session. A careful review concluded that computer-mediated decision groups generally take more time, make less effective decisions, and have less satisfied members than face-to-face groups.[52] However, recent research suggests that time is an issue, and that computer-mediated groups gradually develop increased trust and cooperation over repeated meeting sessions.[53] What accounts for the slow development of trust using computer-mediated communication (a point we noted in Chapter 7 with reference to virtual teams)? Some observers have noted that the detachment of electronic communication can give rise to rude, impulsive messages and to the expression of extreme views, sometimes called "flaming." Others have noted that electronic media elicit informal modes of expression that are prone to misinterpretation. The consequent use of emotional icons ("emoticons") such as the smiley face

: -)

can only go so far as trust builders.[54] In addition, the lack of nonverbal cues may make it difficult to recognize subtle trends toward consensus. Finally, although computer mediation can reduce status differences and promote equality, people can still detect some differences in text-based messages. For instance, people exhibit some degree of accuracy in deducing whether a message was sent by a man or a woman![55]

As suggested by Exhibit 10.7, e-mail may be even more prone to miscommunication than chat formats. Jason Kruger and colleagues conducted five experiments that showed that people strongly overestimated their skill in both communicating and interpreting sarcasm, humour, and emotions via e-mail. They concluded that people tend to be egocentric and exaggerate the extent to which others share their own perspective.[56]

To summarize, a good rule to follow is that less routine communication requires richer communication media.[57] Memos, reports, and e-mails are fine for recurrent, non-controversial, impersonal communication in which information is merely being disseminated. Important decisions, news, intended changes, controversial messages, and emotional issues generally call for richer (i.e., face-to-face or video) media. At UPS, the web portal UPSers.com is used for the routine dissemination of information and face-to-face meetings are used for less routine matters. For an example of the need for a rich communication medium, see "Research Focus: *Explaining Controversial Policies*."

PERSONAL APPROACHES TO IMPROVING COMMUNICATION

What can you do to improve your own ability to communicate better with your boss, your subordinates, your peers, as well as customers, clients, or suppliers? Good question. More and more people are learning that developing their communication skills is just as sensible as developing their accounting skills, their computer skills, or anything else that will give them an edge in the job market.

Improvements in communication skills are very reinforcing. When you communicate well, people generally respond to you in a positive way, even if they are not totally happy with your message. Poor communication can provoke a negative response that is self-perpetuating, in that it leads to even *poorer* communication. This happens when the other party becomes resistant, defensive, deceptive, or hostile.

Basic Principles of Effective Communication

Let's consider some basic principles of effective face-to-face communication.[58] These principles are basic, in that they apply to upward, downward, horizontal, and outside

RESEARCH FOCUS

Explaining Controversial Policies

Organizations sometimes have to enact controversial policies that have the potential to spark much employee resistance. Examples might involve restructuring, layoffs, pay rollbacks, smoking bans, or affirmative action programs. Often, there are good business or social reasons for the introduction of such policies. However, in line with the mum effect, many organizations simply announce such policies with little or no explanation, evidently fearing to dwell on negative news or provoke lawsuits. Research shows that this is a bad idea, and there are communication approaches that can greatly improve the perceived fairness of controversial policies. Notions of procedural and interactional fairness (Chapter 4) underlie such effective communication.

Two factors are critical to the perceived fairness of controversial policies: the adequacy of the explanation and the style with which it is delivered. Adequate explanations are specific and detailed, highlighting the reasons for the policy, how the decision was made, and the benefits that will accrue from it. Equally important,

the delivery of the message should be truthful, sincere, respectful, and sensitive. When appropriate, the communicator should express sincere remorse for having to implement the policy (e.g., a pay rollback) and acknowledge any suffering that the policy might cause. Needless to say, all of this requires the use of a rich communication medium, such as a personal appearance by the CEO or other high organizational representative. A research review by John Shaw and colleagues concluded that an adequate explanation for a policy decision reduced employees' tendencies to retaliate by 43 percent. It also concluded that an inadequate explanation is seen as less fair than no explanation at all.

Sources: Bobocel, D.R., & Zdaniuk, A. (2005). How can explanations be used to foster organizational justice? In J. Greenberg & J.A. Colquitt (Eds.), *Handbook of organizational justice.* Mahwah, NJ: Lawrence Erlbaum; Greenberg, J., & Lind, E.A. (2000). The pursuit of organizational justice: From conceptualization to implication to application. In C.L. Cooper & E.A. Locke (Eds.), *Industrial and organizational psychology: Linking theory with practice.* Oxford: Blackwell; Shaw, J.C., Wild, E., & Colquitt, J.A. (2003). To justify or excuse? A meta-analytic review of the effects of explanations. *Journal of Applied Psychology, 88,* 444–458.

communication. They generally apply to cross-cultural encounters, too, as long as they are applied in conjunction with the advice in the following section, "When in Rome. . . ."

Take the Time. Good communication takes time. Managers in particular have to devote extra effort to developing good rapport with employees. Not taking adequate time often leads to the selection of the wrong communication medium. One of your authors has seen a "don't do this" memo sent to 130 employees because two of them committed some offence. Of course, the memo irritated 128 people and the two offenders really did not grasp the problem. The boss should have taken the time to meet face-to-face with the two people in question. At UPS, the short, daily three-minute prework meetings are supplemented by the much longer one-hour conversations.

Be Accepting of the Other Person. Try to be accepting of the other person as an individual who has the right to have feelings and perceptions that may differ from your own. You can accept the person even if you are unhappy with something that he or she has done. Having empathy with others (trying to put yourself in their place and see things from their perspective) will increase your acceptance of them. Acting superior or arrogant works against acceptance.

Do Not Confuse the Person with the Problem. Although you should be accepting of others, it is generally useful to be problem oriented rather than person oriented. For example, suppose an employee does something that you think might have offended a client. It is probably better to focus on this view of the problem than to impute motives to the employee ("Don't you care about the client's needs?"). The focus should be on what the person did, not who the person is. Along these same lines, try to be more descriptive rather than evaluative. Again, focus on what exactly the employee did to the client, not how bad the consequences are.

Say What You Feel. More specifically, be sure that your words, thoughts, feelings, and actions exhibit congruence—that they all contain the same message. A common problem is soft-pedalling bad news, such as saying that someone's job is probably secure when you feel that it probably is not. However, congruence can also be a problem with positive messages. Some managers find it notoriously difficult to praise excellent work or even to reinforce routine good performance. Congruence can be thought of as honesty or authenticity, but you should not confuse it with brutal frankness or cruelty. Also, remember that in some high-context cultures, "saying what you feel" is done very indirectly. Still, the words and feelings are congruent in their own context.

Listen Actively. Effective communication requires good listening. People who are preoccupied with themselves or who simply hear what they expect to hear are not good listeners. Good listening improves the accuracy of your reception, but it also shows acceptance of the speaker and encourages self-reflection on his or her part. Developing good listening skills can be harder than acquiring good speaking skills. Good listening is not a passive process. Rather, good communicators employ active listening to get the most out of an interaction. Techniques of **active listening** include the following:

- *Watch your body language.* Sit up, lean forward, and maintain eye contact with the speaker. This shows that you are paying attention and are interested in what the speaker is saying (this is another aspect of congruence).
- *Paraphrase what the speaker means.* Reflecting back what the speaker has said shows interest and ensures that you have received the correct message.
- *Show empathy.* When appropriate, show that you understand the feelings that the speaker is trying to convey. A phrase such as "Yes, that client has irritated me, too" might fill the bill.
- *Ask questions.* Have people repeat, clarify, or elaborate what they are saying. Avoid asking leading questions that are designed to pursue some agenda that *you* have.
- *Wait out pauses.* Do not feel pressured to talk when the speaker goes silent. This discourages him or her from elaborating.

The San Francisco Police Department has trained several hundred officers in active listening as part of its peer support program to deal with work stress.[59]

Give Timely and Specific Feedback. When you initiate communication to provide others with feedback about their behaviour, do it soon and be explicit. Speed maximizes the reinforcement potential of the message, and explicitness maximizes its usefulness to the recipient. Say *what* was good about the person's presentation to the client, and say it soon.

When in Rome . . .

Frankly, you are off to a pretty good start in cross-cultural communication if you can do a careful job of applying the basic communication principles we discussed above. However, people's basic skills sometimes actually *deteriorate* when they get nervous about a cross-cultural encounter. Let's cover a few more principles for those situations.

Assume Differences Until You Know Otherwise. The material we presented earlier on cross-cultural communication and that in Chapter 3 on workforce diversity should sensitize you to the general tendency for cross-cultural differences to exist. In a cross-

---

Congruence. A condition in which a person's words, thoughts, feelings, and actions all contain the same message.

Active listening. A technique for improving the accuracy of information reception by paying close attention to the sender.

San Francisco Police Department
www.sfgov.org/police

cultural situation, caution dictates assuming that such differences exist until we are proven wrong. Remember, we have a tendency to project our own feelings and beliefs onto ambiguous targets (Chapter 3), leading us to ignore differences. Be particularly alert when dealing with good English speakers from cultures that emphasize harmony and avoidance of conflict (e.g., Japan). Their good English will tempt you to think that they think like you do, and their good manners will inhibit them from telling you otherwise.

Recognize Differences within Cultures. Appreciating differences between cultures can sometimes blind us to the differences among people within a culture. This, of course, is what stereotypes do (Chapter 3). Remember, your German employees will have as many different personalities, skills, and problems as your North American employees. Remember, too, that there are occupational and social class differences in other countries just like there are at home, although they can be harder to decipher (this is why one of the authors once shook hands with the chef at a French business school, mistaking him for the dean!).

Watch Your Language (and Theirs). Unless the person with whom you are communicating is very fluent in English, speak particularly clearly, slowly, and simply. Avoid clichés, jargon, and slang. Consider how mystifying phrases such as "I'm all ears," "let's get rolling," and "so long" must be.[60] By the same token, do not assume that those who can speak your language well are smarter, more skilled, or more honest than those who cannot.

ORGANIZATIONAL APPROACHES TO IMPROVING COMMUNICATION

In this section, we discuss some organizational techniques that can improve communication. We consider other techniques in Chapter 13 (concerning conflict reduction) and Chapter 16 (with regard to organizational development).

360-Degree Feedback

Traditionally, employee performance appraisal has been viewed as an exercise in downward communication in which the boss tells the employee how he or she is doing. More recently, performance appraisal has become a two-way communication process in which employees are also able to have upward impact concerning their appraisal. Most recently, some firms have expanded the communication channels in performance appraisal to include not only superior and self-ratings, but also ratings by subordinates, peers, and clients or customers. This is called *multisource* or **360-degree feedback**. Firms that have tried it include Honeywell, Sprint, Amoco, and Burger King. At Nebraska's Midlands Community Hospital, patients are incorporated into the process when nurses receive feedback.[61]

360-degree feedback. Performance appraisal that uses the input of supervisors, employees, peers, and clients or customers of the appraised individual.

The 360-degree system usually focuses on required behavioural competencies rather than bottom-line performance. It is usually used for employee development rather than salary determination. It is possible that the various sources of feedback could contradict each other, and ratees may need some assistance in putting all this input together. However, in a well-designed 360-degree system, the various information sources ideally provide unique data about a person's performance. When supervisors receive performance ratings from multiple employees, it is called *upward feedback*. A study on upward feedback over a five-year period found that managers who were initially rated as poor or moderate showed significant improvements in feedback ratings, especially when the managers met with their employees to discuss their upward feedback.[62]

Employee Surveys and Survey Feedback

Surveys of the attitudes and opinions of current employees can provide a useful means of upward communication. Since surveys are usually conducted with questionnaires that provide for anonymous responses, employees should feel free to voice their genuine views. A good **employee survey** contains questions that reliably tap employee concerns and also provide information that is useful for practical purposes. Survey specialists must summarize (encode) results in a manner that is easily decoded by management. Surveys are especially useful when they are administered periodically. In this case, managers can detect changes in employee feelings that might deserve attention.

When survey results are fed back to employees, along with management responses and any plans for changes, this feedback should enhance downward communication. Survey feedback shows employees that management has heard and considered their comments. Plans for changes in response to survey concerns indicate a commitment to two-way communication.[63] In Chapter 16 you will learn more about employee surveys.

Employee survey. An anonymous questionnaire that enables employees to state their candid opinions and attitudes about an organization and its practices.

Suggestion Systems and Query Systems

Suggestion systems are designed to enhance upward communication by soliciting ideas for improved work operations from employees. They represent a formal attempt to encourage useful ideas and prevent their filtering through the chain of command. The simplest example of a suggestion system involves the use of a suggestion box into which employees put written ideas for improvements (usually anonymously). This simple system is usually not very effective, since there is no tangible incentive for making a submission and no clear mechanism to show that management considered a submission.

Suggestion systems. Programs designed to enhance upward communication by soliciting ideas for improved work operations from employees.

Much better are programs that *reward* employees for suggestions that are actually adopted and provide feedback as to how management evaluated each suggestion. For simple suggestions a flat fee is usually paid (perhaps $500). For complex suggestions of a technical nature that might result in substantial savings to the firm, a percentage of the anticipated savings is often awarded (perhaps several thousand dollars). An example of such a suggestion might be how to perform machinery maintenance without costly long-term shutdowns. When strong publicity follows the adopted suggestions (such as explaining them in the organization's employee newsletter), downward communication is also enhanced, since employees receive information about the kind of innovations desired. At RBC Financial Group, employees can receive up to $25 000 for a suggestion, and around 550 a month are submitted.[64]

RBC Financial Group
www.rbc.com

Related to suggestion systems are *query systems* that provide a formal means of answering questions that employees may have about the organization. These systems foster two-way communication and are most effective when questions and answers are widely disseminated. Many organizations have a column of questions and answers in their employee newsletters, the content ranging from questions about benefits to the firm's stock performance.

Telephone Hotlines, TV Networks, and Intranets

Many organizations have adopted *telephone hotlines* to further communication. Some are actually query systems, in that employees can call in for answers to their questions. More common are hotlines that use a news format to present company information. News may be presented live at prearranged times or recorded for 24-hour availability. Such hotlines prove especially valuable at times of crisis, such as during storms or strikes.[65] Companies also use their intranets as a means of communicating important announcements. Intranets represent an important information source on various topics of interest to employees and can also allow employees to communicate information to the organization, such as changes of address or benefits enrolment.[66]

One excellent technique for fostering communication is a company-operated television network. Prominent firms with their own TV networks include IBM, Federal Express, J.C. Penney, Ford, and DaimlerChrysler. Because TV networks constitute a rich communication medium, they are especially good for rumour control, training, and new product introduction. DaimlerChrysler uses its system to train mechanics right at their own dealerships.

DaimlerChrysler
www.daimlerchrysler.com

Management Training

Proper training can improve the communication skills of managers. Notice the specific use of the word *skills* here. Vague lectures about the importance of good communication simply do not tell managers *how* to communicate better. However, isolating specific communication skills and giving the boss an opportunity to practise these skills should have positive effects. The manager who has confidence in how to handle delicate matters should be better able to handle the balance between social-emotional and task demands.

 THE MANAGER'S

Notebook

Four Seasons Goes to Paris

1. While Four Seasons encourages strict adherence to its core values, it allows the management and employees of each hotel to be true to their national culture. As such, Four Seasons takes a "when in Rome . . ." approach to the hotel business. Not every country has the same social conventions, or the same idea of what is considered polite and proper etiquette. Four Seasons goes out of its way to ensure that its hotels communicate fundamental values to staff and guests, but in a way that allows employees to have discretion at the local level. To underline this point, Four Seasons trimmed its written operating standards from 800 to 270 to allow greater discretion at the local level when dealing with different social conventions across cultures. As such, an Italian employee in Italy or an Egyptian employee in Egypt would be free to behave in a manner and provide service in a way that is congruent with their national identities. Four Seasons' cultural sensitivity extends to human resource practices, such as performance evaluations, that are not common in Europe and the Middle East. Managers are free to modify human resource forms and procedures to respect local customs and traditions.

2. Four Seasons' managers noted that, in France, words were not enough to communicate values and that French employees take a wait-and-see approach before jumping on board. As such, how the values were presented to employees and enacted by managers were key parts of the communication process. In addition to the presentation style, some concrete communication tactics were also used. A 35-person task force was assembled to help people understand how the company does things, to listen for problems, and to control the rumour mill. In an attempt to diffuse the traditional labour tensions in France, Le Calvez took the representatives of the various unions to lunch so that important conversations could take place face to face in an inclusive manner. The company also carefully explained the use of procedures, such as employee evaluations, and framed them as opportunities for open and constructive dialogue. Furthermore, to promote communication and problem solving, Four Seasons implemented a "direct line" process in which, once a month, the general manager would meet with employees, supervisors, and managers in groups of 30. Finally, Le Calvez and his team carefully cultivated culturally sensitive external communications with the press. So what was the outcome? Responses from employee surveys have been extremely positive, clearly showing that employees have bought into the culture. Furthermore, the hotel received several industry awards since Four Seasons took control. Overall, through intelligent communication tactics and cultural sensitivity, Four Seasons was able to maintain the standards of excellence at the George V and to make believers of employees and the public alike.

Effective training programs often present videotaped models correctly handling a typical communication problem. Managers then role-play the problem and are reinforced by the trainers when they exhibit effective skills. At General Electric, for example, typical communication problems that this kind of training addresses have included discussing undesirable work habits, reviewing work performance, discussing salary changes, and dealing with employee-initiated discussions.[67] North Carolina's Center for Creative Leadership incorporates 360-degree feedback data from peers, superiors, and subordinates into its training.

It might seem that training of this nature is essentially focused on downward communication. However, the disclosure of one's attitudes and feelings promotes reciprocity on the part of the receiver.[68] Thus, the manager who can communicate effectively downward can expect increased upward communication in return.

LEARNING OBJECTIVES CHECKLIST

1. *Communication* is the process by which information is exchanged between a sender and a receiver. Effective communication involves getting the right information to the right people in a timely manner. Although much routine communication can occur via the chain of command, the chain tends to be slow and prone to filtering. It also ignores informal communication.

2. *Manager–employee communication* is frequently ineffective. The manager might have difficulty balancing task and social-emotional demands, and both parties might be reluctant to inform each other of bad news (the mum effect).

3. The *grapevine* is an organization's informal communication network. Only a portion of people who receive grapevine information pass it on. Key physical locations or jobs that require movement around the organization encourage certain members to pass on information. The grapevine can be useful to the organization, and it often transmits information accurately. However, it becomes problematic when rumours (unverified beliefs) circulate.

4. Verbal language that is tailored to the needs of a particular occupation or organization is known as *jargon*. While jargon aids communication between experienced co-workers, it can often prove confusing for new organizational members and people outside the organization. *Nonverbal communication* is the transmission of messages by a medium other than speech or writing. One major form is *body language*, which involves body movement or the placement of the body in relation to the receiver. Much body language is subtle and automatic, communicating factors such as liking, interest, and status differences. Other forms of nonverbal communication involve office decoration, office arrangement, and the clothing worn at work.

5. Differences in communication styles between men and women have their origin in childhood but persist in the workplace, where they can influence the way men and women are perceived and treated.

6. Communication across cultures can be difficult owing to obvious language differences, but also to less obvious differences in nonverbal style, social conventions, and matters of etiquette. In low-context cultures, individuals can interpret messages more literally than in high-context cultures, where issues surrounding a message are more critical to understanding it. When communicating cross-culturally, assume cultural differences until you know otherwise, recognize differences within cultures, and use simple language.

7. *Computer-mediated communication* is communication that relies on computer technology to facilitate information exchange. Examples include e-mail, chat systems, teleconferencing, and videoconferencing. Computer-mediated communication is useful for disseminating routine messages and soliciting ideas, but richer (e.g., face-to-face) communication media are superior for non-routine decision tasks and messages.

8. Personal approaches to improving communication include taking time, being accepting of others, concentrating on the problem, saying what you feel, listening actively, and giving timely and specific feedback. Organizational approaches to improving communication include 360-degree feedback, employee surveys, suggestion and query systems, hotlines, TV networks and intranets, and management training.

DISCUSSION QUESTIONS

1. Using Exhibit 10.1 as a guide, describe a communication episode that you have observed in an organization. Who were the sender and receiver? Was the episode effective? Why or why not?

2. Debate: Since more and more global business is being conducted in English, North Americans will not have cross-cultural communication problems in the future.

3. Why is computer-mediated communication attractive? What are its problems?

4. "It is very difficult to establish good manager–employee communication." Why?

5. Discuss the pros and cons of the existence of the grapevine in organizations. Suppose an organization wanted to "kill" the grapevine. How easy do you think this would be?

6. Discuss a case in which you heard one message communicated verbally and "saw" another transmitted nonverbally. What was the content of each message? Which one did you believe?

7. Under what conditions might body language or clothing have a strong communicative effect? When might the effect be weaker?

8. Debate: As more women move into management positions in organizations, the gender differences in communication between men and women will eventually disappear and so will communication problems.

INTEGRATIVE DISCUSSION QUESTIONS

1. What role do perceptions play in gender differences in communication? Refer to the perceptual system in Chapter 3 and use its components to explain how differences in communication styles between men and women can result in misunderstandings and inaccurate perceptions. What effect might these misunderstandings and inaccurate perceptions have on gender stereotypes?

2. How does a manager's leadership style affect manager–employee communication? Refer to the theories of leadership described in Chapter 9 (e.g., leadership traits, behaviours, situational theories, participative leadership, and LMX theory) and explain their implications for effective manager–employee communication.

ON-THE-JOB CHALLENGE QUESTION

Wal-Mart, the world's largest corporate employer, invests tremendous energy in hiring and retaining good employees. Retention is a particular issue in the retail industry, where loyalty to employers is generally low and expensive employee turnover is common. Coleman H. Peterson is the former chief human resource officer of Wal-Mart. When visiting stores and distribution centres, he would regularly walk around and strike up conversations with associates. When it came to asking about supervision, his favourite question was to ask employees the name of their store or centre manager.

What did Peterson's practice of walking around and talking with Wal-Mart associates have to do with retaining employees? Why do you think he asked if they knew the manager's name? What if they did? What if they didn't?

Source: Peterson, C.H. (2005). Employee retention: The secrets behind Wal-Mart's successful hiring policies. *Human Resource Management, 44,* 85–88.

EXPERIENTIAL EXERCISE

Cross-Cultural Communication Quiz

This quiz will give you an idea of how much you already know about cross-cultural communication. In some cases, there is more than one correct response to each question.

_____ 1. On average, how long do native-born Americans maintain eye contact?
   a. 1 second
   b. 15 seconds
   c. 30 seconds

_____ 2. True or false: One of the few universal ways to motivate workers, regardless of cultural background, is through the prospect of a promotion.

_____ 3. Learning to speak a few words of the language of immigrant clients, customers, and workers is:
   a. Generally a good idea, as the effort communicates respect for the other person
   b. Generally not a good idea because they might feel patronized
   c. Generally not a good idea because they might be offended if a mistake is made in vocabulary or pronunciation

_____ 4. True or false: North American culture has no unique characteristics; it is composed only of individual features brought from other countries.

_____ 5. When communicating across language barriers, using the written word:
   a. Should be avoided; it can insult the immigrant or international visitor's intelligence
   b. Can be helpful; it is usually easier to read English than to hear it
   c. Can be confusing; it is usually easier to hear English than to read it

_____ 6. True or false: Behaving formally around immigrant colleagues, clients, and workers— that is, using last names, observing strict rules of etiquette—is generally not a good idea as it gives the impression of coldness and superiority.

_____ 7. In times of crisis, the immigrant's ability to speak English:
   a. Diminishes because of stress
   b. Stays the same
   c. Improves because of the necessity of coping with the crisis
   d. Completely disappears

_____ 8. The number of languages spoken in the United States today is:
   a. 0–10
   b. 10–50
   c. 50–100
   d. 100+

_____ 9. True or false: Immigrant families in the United States largely make decisions as individuals and have generally abandoned the practice of making decisions as a group.

_____ 10. When you have difficulty understanding someone with a foreign accent:
   a. It probably means that he or she cannot understand you either.
   b. It probably means that he or she is recently arrived in your country.
   c. It is helpful if you listen to all that he or she has to say before interrupting, as the meaning might become clear in the context of the conversation.
   d. It is helpful for you to try to guess what the speaker is saying and to speak for him or her so as to minimize the risk of embarrassment.

_____ 11. When an Asian client begins to give you vague answers before closing a deal, saying things like "It will take time to decide," or "We'll see," the best thing to do is:
   a. Back off a bit, he or she may be trying to say "no" without offending you.
   b. Supply more information and data about your service or product, especially in writing.
   c. Push for a "close." His or her vagueness is probably a manipulative tactic.
   d. State clearly and strongly that you are dissatisfied with his or her reaction so as to avoid any misunderstanding.

_____ 12. Apparent rudeness and abruptness in immigrants is often due to:
   a. Lack of facility with the English language
   b. A difference in cultural style
   c. Differing tone of voice

_____ 13. True or false: Many immigrant and ethnic cultures place greater importance on how something is said (body language and tone of voice) than on the words themselves.

_____ 14. The avoidance of public embarrassment (loss of face) is of central concern to which of the following cultures?
   a. Hispanic
   b. Mainstream American
   c. Asian
   d. Middle Eastern

_____ 15. True or false: One of the few universals in etiquette is that everyone likes to be complimented in front of others.

_____ 16. In a customer service situation, when communicating to a decision maker through a child who is functioning as interpreter, it is best to:
   a. Look at the child as you speak so that he or she will be certain to understand you.

b. Look at the decision maker.

c. Look back and forth between the two.

____ 17. Which of the following statements is (are) true?

    a. Most Asian workers like it when the boss rolls up his or her sleeves to work beside employees.

    b. Taking independent initiative on tasks is valued in most workplaces throughout the world.

    c. Many immigrant workers are reluctant to complain to the boss as they feel it is a sign of disrespect.

    d. Asians are quick to praise superiors to their face in an attempt to show respect.

____ 18. True or false: The "V" sign for victory is a universal gesture of goodwill and triumph.

____ 19. Which of the following statements is (are) true?

    a. It is inappropriate to touch Asians on the hand.

    b. Middle-Eastern men stand very close as a means of dominating the conversation.

    c. Mexican men will hold another man's lapel during a conversation as a sign of good communication.

____ 20. Building relationships slowly when doing business with Hispanics is:

    a. A bad idea; if you do not move things along, they will go elsewhere.

    b. A bad idea; they will expect native-born professionals to move quickly, so will be disoriented if you do not.

    c. A good idea; it may take longer, but the trust you build will be well worth the effort.

Scoring and Interpretation

Below are the correct answers to each of the 20 questions in the quiz. To score your quiz, simply add up the number of correct answers. If your score is above 15, you are quite knowledgeable about cross-cultural communication. If your score is below 15, you need to improve your knowledge of cross-cultural communication.

1. a 2. False 3. A 4. False 5. b 6. False 7. a 8. d 9. False 10. c 11. a 12. a, b, and c 13. True 14. a, c, and d 15. False 16. b 17. c 18. False 19. c 20. c

Source: Thiederman, S.B. (1991). *Profiting in America's multicultural workplace: How to do business across cultural lines*, 245–247. Reprinted with permission of Lexington Books, an imprint of the Rowman & Littlefield Publishing Group.

CASE INCIDENT

The "Philanderer"

Phil is the manager of a small division of an international construction company. At one point, Phil was trying to get in touch with a client to advise him that he would be late getting to the site, but he was unable to get through on his client's cell phone. Alternatively, Phil called his own secretary, Carol, and asked her to call the client's office so that they would relay a message to the client, advising him that Phil would be a bit late. Carol called the client's office and left Phil's message.

When Phil got to the construction site, the client was not there. One of the construction workers indicated that the client had been there earlier, had waited awhile, looked at his watch and left. Phil then drove to the client's office and found that the client had not received the message that he would be late. Suspecting that Carol had neglected to relay the message, Phil apologized to his client, but said nothing to Carol.

Four months later, Carol and Phil sat down together for her annual performance review and Phil indicated that he was terribly disappointed in Carol since she had not been very good at relaying messages, as he requested. He pointed out the incident where his client had not been at the construction site since he had not received the message that Phil would be late. Livid, Carol insisted that she had relayed the message and asked Phil why he didn't tell her about this problem at the time it occurred. Phil shrugged his shoulders and looked away.

Source: Prepared by Nicole Bérubé. Used with permission.

1. Why did Phil wait until the performance review to raise the miscommunication problem with Carol?

2. If you were Phil, what would you do now?

CASE STUDY

eProcure: The Project

Sonya Richardson, tired and frustrated, sat at her desk and stared at the design documents spread in front of her. She had just finished a design team meeting with her manager, Molly Berkson, and her fellow team member, Claire Bishop. Sonya and Claire had just presented Molly with the software designs they had been working on for the past three weeks. During the meeting, they realized that the modules that Claire and Sonya had designed weren't integrated.

Sonya was extremely frustrated with what had just happened. She had spent day and night for the past three weeks working on her designs and put together all the necessary documentation for the designs to be passed to the technical development team. She had also been preparing for the final design presentation, which was only a week away. She and Claire were scheduled to present the final software designs to the co-founders of eProcure and to the Excel Consulting managing partner in charge of the project. This presentation was her opportunity to prove herself to the leadership and now she felt she had messed everything up. Sonya realized that she and Claire would have to work closely together for the next week and make their best attempt at fixing the designs, redoing all of the design documentation and putting together a final presentation. If only they had figured this out sooner.

Company Information

Sonya, Claire, and Molly all worked for Excel Consulting, a leading global provider of management and technology services and solutions. With more than 35 000 employees, a global reach including over 55 offices in 20 countries, and serving mainly Fortune 100 and Fortune 500 companies, Excel was one of the largest and most reputable consulting firms.

Excel's primary focuses were delivering innovative solutions to clients and providing exceptional client service. Excel delivered its services and solutions to clients by organizing its professionals into focused industry groups. This industry focus allowed the firm's professionals to develop a thorough understanding of the client's industry, business issues, and applicable technologies to deliver tailored solutions to each client. Each professional is further aligned to a specific service function, such as strategy, process, human performance, or technology. This alignment allows an individual to develop specialized skills and knowledge in an area of expertise. The organizational structure encourages a collaborative and team-based atmosphere. Most client teams included professionals from a similar industry focus, but from several different service function specialties.

Most Excel employees, however, display a variety of educational, cultural and geographical backgrounds, but most share similar skills and attributes, including leadership, intelligence, innovation, integrity and dedi-cation. Many professionals began their careers with Excel directly after completing an undergraduate degree; however, Excel hired experienced professionals as well. The career path at Excel generally made the following progression: analyst, consultant, manager, associate partner, and partner. A new hire, directly after graduating with a university undergraduate degree, would begin as an analyst and then, typically after two years, would be promoted to consultant. After consultant, it would typically take another three years before promotion to a manager position within the firm.

Along with its focus on client service, Excel also emphasized employee satisfaction. It conducted regular satisfaction surveys and had many corporate policies in place to help ensure work–life balance. These policies included flexible working hours and the assignment of professionals in the city of their home office to limit their travel. Partners and managers had the flexibility and discretion to implement these policies on their individual projects. In practice, most projects were unable to effectively implement these policies due to constrained timelines and budgets. Balancing client service and employee satisfaction was a challenge at the firm, and one that it shared with most consulting companies.

Client and Project Information

eProcure, an Internet start-up company based in Baltimore, Maryland, was founded by two former executives from a large, diversified, multinational firm who realized the critical need for a holistic sourcing/procurement solution. They founded eProcure in June 1999 to deliver a technology-based strategic sourcing solution for procuring goods and services. The Strategic eProcure (SeP) software that eProcure was building focused on providing purchasing professionals with the tools they needed to source and negotiate contracts with their suppliers online. The software incorporated the enabling technologies of online auctions, private bids, and communication tools.

The vision of the eProcure solution was to allow purchasing professionals to electronically research, evaluate, plan, and negotiate the lowest total cost for both direct and indirect goods and services. These goods and services could include both tactical and strategic buys within an organization. The SeP, web-based software solution was intended to enable buyers to analyze both internal purchasing and external industry data to determine and execute effective eNegotiation strategies. Those strategies could then be shared across the enterprise for repeat savings of money and time.

eProcure formed a strategic alliance with Excel Consulting in July 1999. Excel would contribute intellectual property in return for a percentage of equity ownership in eProcure. Excel had many years of experience in strategic sourcing through its numerous clients in a variety of industries. Currently, strategic sourcing was a manual process. Excel would help clients research and analyze their internal and external data and conduct negotiations with suppliers in order to procure goods and services in the most cost-efficient manner. These were long-term projects for Excel, typically ranging from three months to two years. Procurement and supply chain effectiveness was a very popular line of business for Excel as many large organizations had begun to shift their focus to operational cost savings. This partnership was seen as beneficial to both eProcure and Excel. eProcure needed Excel's experience and client base, and Excel was interested in getting more exposure to the booming start-up industry.

In August 1999, a project team was formed in Baltimore, which included the eight eProcure employees and 20 Excel consultants from all over North America. The team's mandate was to work together to design and develop the SeP software solution. All members were distributed amongst several smaller teams, including process design, technical design, and technical development/infrastructure. Each of these teams included an Excel manager and several Excel consultants and/or analysts. The eProcure employees would rotate among the different teams and help when and where they were needed. The entire project was overseen by George Fry, an Excel partner, along with William Sheppard and Steve Miller, the eProcure co-founders.

Sonya Richardson

Sonya was an analyst with Excel in the business process functional area at the Toronto office. She began working with Excel in May 1998, right after graduating from the University of Western Ontario with an honours business degree from the Richard Ivey School of Business.

Sonya had received a personal phone call from Molly, a supply chain manager from the Atlanta office, asking her to join the design team of the eProcure project. Sonya had just completed a strategic sourcing project for a financial institution in Toronto, and her manager from this project had recommended her to Molly as a valuable resource for the eProcure project. Sonya was interested in the supply chain line of business and was excited about working on her first out-of-town project. Sonya was also up for early promotion to consultant in December 1999; therefore, she wanted to ensure that she took a role that would give her the opportunities and exposure to prove herself worthy of an early advancement. After listening to the role description, Sonya was pleased with the prospects and immediately accepted the role.

The design team was managed by Molly, and consisted of Claire Bishop, Maria Hodge, and Sonya. Claire and Maria were both analysts from the Atlanta office. Claire began working with Excel at the same time as Sonya and therefore she was also being considered for early promotion in December. Maria was a new analyst who had only been at the firm for two months.

During their first meeting with Molly, both Sonya and Claire were informed that they were responsible for the conceptual and detail designs of the SeP project. Since a technical tool had never been developed for strategic sourcing, there were no previous projects or experiences they could rely on. As such, Sonya and Claire needed to research and analyze the manual process, and creatively design a technical solution for it. Molly had decided that the software would consist of four main modules: internal analysis, supplier analysis, strategy, and eNegotiation. Sonya was responsible for designing the first two modules since she had hands-on experience with these parts of the process, and Claire was responsible for the other two modules. Since Maria was new to the firm, she was there to support both Sonya and Claire by conducting research and putting final design documents together. They were told that they had three weeks to work on the designs. Upon completion, they would make a presentation to George Fry, William Sheppard, and Steve Miller. Molly asked for weekly status reports to be completed by all team members. She would use these status reports to update the project timeline and to inform other Excel team members of her team's progress.

Molly Berkson

Molly was a senior manager with Excel in the supply chain line of business at the Atlanta office. Molly had begun working with Excel in April 1993, after she graduated with an MBA from the University of Kansas.

Molly had been asked by George Fry to join the team in early August. She had worked in numerous strategic sourcing engagements throughout the firm and was considered an expert in the area. Due to her expertise, Molly had been assigned to lead the design efforts of the SeP software product. Her specific responsibilities involved managing all design efforts for the project, including managing a team of three professionals and ensuring project deadlines and deliverables were met. In addition, since Molly was one of only a few people with strategic sourcing knowledge, she was responsible for assisting all of the teams by answering any questions and helping people to understand specific strategic sourcing concepts.

Although Molly was excited about the prospects of working for an Internet start-up company, she wasn't very excited about leading the design team. As a senior manager, she was beginning to look for opportunities to increase her exposure to senior executives both inside and outside the firm. She hoped to be promoted to associate partner in a year or two. Leading the design team would be similar to many of her past management roles, and therefore Molly was concerned that this role might hold her back from other opportunities. Since she had worked with George in the past, and he had asked her personally to join the team, Molly found it difficult to refuse the role.

The Design

Sonya and Claire began working on the designs immediately after their first meeting with Molly. Three weeks was a short period of time to complete all the research and designs and documentation. With the added pressure of making a final presentation to the co-founders and the Excel partner, Sonya was even more eager to get a head start. She intended to work extremely hard over the next few weeks in order to come up with the most impressive designs. Sonya knew this project was her chance to prove herself and make a positive impression on Molly and, more importantly, on George.

Sonya had worked on a strategic sourcing project in the past and was familiar with the Excel methodology. She had also developed relationships with other supply chain managers in the Toronto office, so she was able to call them for reference materials and help with any questions. Sonya felt uncomfortable approaching Molly with too many questions for a variety of reasons: Molly always seemed busy or preoccupied; Molly was never very friendly or warm toward her; and Sonya didn't want to leave the impression that she needed a lot of help and couldn't handle the task herself. Sonya spent a lot of time researching the first few steps of the project and researched day and night trying to come up with good ideas for the designs. She had developed a good relationship with Maria, the junior analyst on her team. Maria was very helpful in conducting any research and putting together the documentation that was necessary.

Sonya thought it was important that she work together with Claire on the designs in order to integrate them, but she found Claire to be very secretive about her designs and any progress she had made with them. Sonya knew that Claire would have to spend more time upfront understanding the process because she didn't have any previous experience with strategic sourcing. Sonya had offered Claire help if she had any questions about the process, but Claire only asked Molly any questions that she had. Although Sonya had tried to make several attempts to talk to and work with Claire on the designs, she had been unsuccessful.

Sonya felt that there was obvious tension on the team, but unfortunately, Claire had made no effort to get to know either Sonya or Maria. Sonya and Maria went for lunch together every day and whenever they asked Claire, she always responded that she was busy and went for lunch with Molly or with an eProcure employee instead. Maria found Claire difficult to deal with as well. In particular, Maria complained to Sonya that Claire treated her like a secretary, ordering her around to do research and to complete documents, instead of treating her as a colleague. Although Maria recognized that she was new to the firm, all three of them on the team were at the same analyst level.

Sonya had noticed that Claire and Molly had recently become very good friends. They often went to the gym together after work and met for coffee in the morning. This made Sonya feel very uncomfortable because she knew that both she and Claire were up for early promotion within a few months. Sonya had never been the type of person to get ahead purely because of relationships with people. Although she always got along with everyone on her team, she was usually quieter and really focused on producing quality work. She believed that hard work and initiative would get her ahead, and she hoped that Molly would appreciate this too.

Recent Events

Three weeks had passed and Molly had scheduled a team meeting to go over the designs before the final presentation at the end of the week. Both Claire and Sonya had sent their documentation to Molly a few days before the meeting. Molly had been unable to look at anything before the meeting, however, because she had been busy helping other teams on the project. Sonya and Claire were supposed to practise presenting their designs to Molly and Maria during the meeting.

Sonya presented her designs first, since she had designed the first two modules. Molly was impressed with all the work she had done and congratulated Sonya for her efforts. Claire presented next, but within 15 minutes of the presentation, Molly told her to stop and asked, "Why are the designs not integrated?"

Sonya wasn't sure how to respond. She didn't want to complain about Claire, but at the same time she didn't want it to seem like she had never thought about integrating the designs. As she was trying to think of a reasonable response to Molly's question, Claire immediately responded:

> I realized the importance of integration early on and talked about it to Sonya within the first few days. I have been trying to find time with Sonya to sit down to discuss how to integrate the designs as smoothly as possible; however Sonya has been very busy working on her own designs and documentation. Therefore, I have been working on my designs by getting ideas from the eProcure employees and other Excel personnel and have been concentrating on putting together as many creative ideas as possible for the product. My designs are very flexible and I can easily work with Sonya to make sure they are integrated by the end of the week.

Sonya couldn't believe that Claire had completely lied, but she felt that she couldn't say anything about it to Molly, especially during a team meeting. Therefore, Sonya just responded that she had thought the same and had also been very busy working on her designs. She also assured Molly that integration would not be a problem.

Molly told them that she wished they had approached her earlier with any questions or concerns; however, she now just wanted to be sure that they could integrate the designs within the next few days. It was Monday and the final presentation was exactly a week away. Molly wanted to see all of the final integrated designs by the end of Thursday. She informed the team to cancel their flights home as they would be staying in Baltimore for the weekend to finish. Molly then asked Claire to finish her presentation. After the presentation, she brainstormed various ideas for Claire and Sonya and provided them with her feedback on the designs. She was generally happy, but Claire's section needed a lot more work. The eNegotiation module was probably one of the toughest to design, and therefore Molly asked that the entire team spend a few hours together to brainstorm ideas for the design in order to help Claire.

The meeting lasted about six hours in total and Molly asked the team to get back to work and reconvene the next afternoon. She wanted to stay involved and make sure that she managed the rest of the week very closely. She was upset that the team had been unable to take the initiative to manage the design process on its own and she wondered why they had not been proactive in asking her questions and getting feedback during the process. She knew that she had been very busy lately helping other teams on the project, but she always thought of herself as accessible. The final presentation to the leadership would be a reflection on her as well; therefore, Molly wanted to ensure that her team was able to integrate the designs and complete all of the necessary documentation before Thursday.

Next Steps

Sonya left the meeting feeling very frustrated. She had spent so many weeks working on her designs and now she had to spend the rest of the week working on the integration of the designs. This weekend was her best friend's birthday and she had planned the party weeks in advance. Now Sonya would have to call her and explain that she wasn't going to be there. Work was definitely different than she had expected.

There were numerous issues that were bothering Sonya. First, she was upset that the team was in this situation in the first place. She had tried to speak to Claire earlier, but that obviously didn't work. She wondered what else she could have done. She realized that she probably should have spoken to Molly earlier, but she was afraid of the perception Molly may have developed of her if she had. Molly may have thought that

she wasn't able to handle the responsibility and Sonya didn't want to jeopardize any chance of an early promotion. Sonya also wondered what Molly could have done to have prevented this from happening.

In addition, Sonya was upset with the relationship she had with Claire. It was difficult when team members didn't get along and now that they had to work very closely together for the rest of the week, she was worried about the impact their personal relationship would have on the final designs. She wondered how much of her relationship with Claire had to do with personal differences and to what extent it was based on both of them being up for early promotion at the same time. She knew that there was a sense of competition between them as soon as they had met. They were both trying to impress Molly and the leadership so they could be promoted earlier. Could Excel and the eProcure leadership team have managed this better?

Sonya was definitely learning a lot from her first job out of Ivey. She realized that she needed to put these thoughts behind her right now and focus on the designs since she had a meeting with Molly the next afternoon. The first thing Sonya needed to do was talk to Claire. She wondered if she should say anything to Claire about her comments in the meeting or just forget about them and focus on working on the designs. Sonya decided to make the first move and talk to Claire immediately.

Source: Prepared by Monica Kumar under the supervision of Professor Lyn Purdy. Copyright © 2002, Ivey Management Services.

1. Use the section of the chapter "Basic Principles of Effective Communication" to critique the respective communication skills of Molly, Sonya, and Claire.

2. How did the respective career motives of Molly, Sonya, and Claire affect the communication on the project?

3. Describe any examples of the mum effect.

4. As the team leader, how should Molly have proceeded when the team was formed to avoid the problems seen in the case?

5. What should Sonya say to Claire now?

CHAPTER 11

Decision Making

THE LOSS OF THE SPACE SHUTTLE COLUMBIA

On February 1, 2003, the space shuttle *Columbia* exploded during re-entry over Texas, killing all seven astronauts aboard. The most likely cause of the accident, as determined by the Columbia Accident Investigation Board, was that a piece of hardened foam the size of a suitcase struck the left side of the shuttle at the speed of 500 mph during takeoff, causing damage that allowed heat to enter the shuttle as it tried to re-enter the Earth's atmosphere. As the hearings into the *Columbia* tragedy progressed, the focus shifted from the technical aspects of the voyage to the decision-making procedures at NASA, and many concluded that NASA had not learned the painful lessons from the space shuttle *Challenger* explosion in 1986.

Top NASA officials indicated that they had noted the foam incident during the takeoff, but decided that it had caused no damage that could put the shuttle at risk. As the hearings continued, however, it became clear that this view was not shared by all. A series of e-mails between NASA engineers that were made public clearly revealed that many feared the worst as a result of the foam incident, and that some viewed the assessment that "all was fine" as very premature. Some of the e-mails proved eerily clairvoyant as they predicted almost the exact sequence of events during the eventual tragedy. When pressed by the investigation board, top NASA officials admitted that no managers involved with the failed mission had been aware of these e-mails, and suggested that they represented typical "what-if" speculation and healthy debate among mid-level employees.

Others suggested that the failure to recognize danger was a systematic problem at NASA. Professor Diane Vaughan, a witness at the *Columbia* hearings whose scholarly review of the 1986 *Challenger* crash pointed to a culture of denial at NASA, suggested that, for all of NASA's talk about free thinking and healthy debate, decisions at the space agency are very data and procedure driven. While the engineers who predicted the eventual crash in their e-mails used a common-sense approach of what would happen when a hard projectile hits a craft at very high speed, they had no solid data to support their views. As such, their fears were not communicated to the proper individuals. According to Professor Vaughan, "One of the characteristics in shifting from *Apollo* culture to shuttle-era culture is that 'intuition and hunch' do not carry any weight. They do in everyday decision making. But when it comes to formal decisions, hard data-numbers are required."

LEARNING OBJECTIVES

After reading Chapter 11, you should be able to:

1. Define *decision making* and differentiate well-structured and ill-structured problems.

2. Compare and contrast perfectly *rational decision making* with decision making under *bounded rationality*.

3. Discuss the impact of *framing* and *cognitive biases* on the decision process.

4. Explain the process of *escalation of commitment* to an apparently failing course of action.

5. Consider how emotions and mood affect decision making.

6. Summarize the pros and cons of using groups to make decisions, with attention to the *groupthink* phenomenon and risk assessment.

7. Discuss techniques for improving organizational decision making.

The *Columbia* space shuttle tragedy revealed flawed decision making.

Other witnesses pointed to NASA's faulty assessment of risk and the lack of follow-up on reported problems. It was revealed during the hearings that falling foam was a common occurrence during shuttle takeoffs and that foam had struck the space shuttle *Atlantis* on a previous mission in the fall of 2002. Unlike *Columbia*, however, *Atlantis* had completed its mission without incident.

NASA
www.nasa.gov

Investigation witness Robert Thompson, who ran the shuttle program until 1981, said he could not imagine allowing the shuttle to fly knowing that a hunk of foam could strike the wing at nearly 500 mph (800 kph), and could not understand how this risk was downplayed. Thompson likened NASA's attitude about falling debris to that of a person who narrowly escapes several gunshots and then assumes future gunshots pose no danger. Several other witnesses alluded to an organizational culture where managers were lulled into a false sense of security when problems did not lead to tragedy. It was also revealed that NASA did not have a proper safety database of reported problems and that the analytical tools used to conclude that the foam had caused no damage were technologically crude.

Finally, it was suggested that decisions in Washington to cut funding had a trickle-down effect by which NASA's workforce decreased in both size and expertise, and the agency came to rely more and more on contractors from private industry, especially for the shuttle program. NASA's problems with contractors was nothing new, as witnessed by the technical flaws of NASA's Hubble Space Telescope in the 1990s, which required $600 million in repairs. It was also noted that NASA transferred control of the shuttle program from the Johnson Space Center in Houston to the NASA deputy associate administrator for space flights in Washington in 2002, which moved decisions away from the people who had real responsibility and technical expertise.

In July 2005, over two years after the *Columbia* tragedy, NASA launched the space shuttle *Discovery* to take supplies to the International Space Station. In the two years since *Columbia*, NASA named a new chief administrator and spent billions on safety improvements to both prevent and monitor falling debris. Despite all the planning and precautions, problems still arose. First, the launch was delayed due to a faulty fuel sensor. After engineers conducted several tests, the launch was deemed safe. Incredibly, a chunk of foam became dislodged and struck *Discovery* on lift-off in a scenario eerily similar to what had occurred two years previously. When fabric was shown to be protruding from the shuttle, there was discussion of docking *Discovery* at the space station and sending a rescue shuttle to retrieve the crew. However, after a great deal of testing by engineers on earth and a space-walk repair job with duct tape and scissors that was similar to the intuitive quick-thinking style of the *Apollo* missions, it was decided that *Discovery* was in no danger. With the world holding its collective breath, *Discovery* made a textbook landing in early August 2005.

While *Discovery* was still in orbit, NASA's new head Michael Griffin announced that the fleet would be grounded and all future launches suspended until the debris problem is finally resolved. When *Discovery* was launched next in July 2006, NASA's safety chief and chief engineer recommended scrapping the mission because of their belief that the foam problem was still not fixed. After numerous delays, the mission took place without incident and the message appears to be that falling debris is simply a risk that will always exist.[1]

In the case of the *Columbia* disaster, how could so many smart people misjudge such risks and make a series of such apparently bad decisions? We will find out in this chapter. First, we will define decision making and present a model of a rational decision-making process. As we work through this model, we will be especially concerned with the practical limitations of rationality. After this, we will investigate the use of groups to make decisions. Finally, the chapter closes with a description of some techniques to improve decision making.

WHAT IS DECISION MAKING?

Consider the following questions that might arise in a variety of organizational settings:

- How much inventory should our store carry?
- Where should we locate the proposed community mental health centre?
- Should I remain at this job or accept another?
- How many classes of Philosophy 200 should our department offer next semester?
- Should our diplomats attend the summit conference?

Decision making. The process of developing a commitment to some course of action.

Common sense tells us that someone is going to have to do some decision making to answer such questions. **Decision making** is the process of developing a commitment to some course of action.[2] Three things are noteworthy about this definition. First, decision making involves making a *choice* among several action alternatives—the store can carry more or less inventory, and the mental health centre can be located at the north or south end of town. Second, decision making is a *process* that involves more than simply the final choice among alternatives—if you decide to accept the offer of a new job, we want to know *how* this decision was reached. Finally, the "commitment" mentioned in the definition usually involves some commitment of *resources,* such as time, money, or personnel—if the store carries a large inventory, it will tie up cash; if the chairperson of Philosophy offers too many introductory classes, he might have no one available to teach a graduate seminar. NASA shuttle launches require a substantial resource commitment.

In addition to conceiving of decision making as the commitment of resources, we can also describe it as a process of problem solving.[3] A **problem** exists when a gap is perceived between some existing state and some desired state. For example, the chairperson of the Philosophy department might observe that there is a projected increase in university enrolment for the upcoming year and that his course schedule is not completed (existing state). In addition, he might wish to adequately service the new students with Philosophy 200 classes and at the same time satisfy his dean with a timely, sensible schedule (desired state). In this case, the decision-making process involves the perception of the existing state, the conception of the desired state, and the steps that the chairperson takes to move from one state to the other.

Problem. A perceived gap between an existing state and a desired state.

Well-Structured Problems

For a **well-structured problem,** the existing state is clear, the desired state is clear, and how to get from one state to the other is fairly obvious. Intuitively, these problems are simple, and their solutions arouse little controversy. This is because such problems are repetitive and familiar.

Well-structured problem. A problem for which the existing state is clear, the desired state is clear, and how to get from one state to the other is fairly obvious.

- Assistant bank manager—which of these 10 car loan applications should I approve?
- Welfare officer—how much assistance should this client receive?
- Truck driver—how much weight should I carry?

Because decision making takes time and is prone to error, organizations (and individuals) attempt to program the decision making for well-structured problems. A **program** is simply a standardized way of solving a problem. As such, programs short-circuit the decision-making process by enabling the decision maker to go directly from problem identification to solution.

Program. A standardized way of solving a problem.

Programs usually go under labels such as *rules, routines, standard operating procedures,* or *rules of thumb.* Sometimes, they come from experience and exist only "in the head." Other programs are more formal. You are probably aware that routine loan applications are "scored" by banks according to a fixed formula that takes into account income, debt, previous credit, and so on. Some programs exist in the form of straightforward rules—"Truck drivers will always carry between 85 and 95 percent of legal weight."

Many of the problems encountered in organizations are well structured, and programmed decision making provides a useful means of solving these problems. However, programs are only as good as the decision-making process that led to the adoption of the program in the first place. In computer terminology, "garbage in" will result in "garbage out." Another difficulty with decision programs is their tendency to persist even when problem conditions change.

These difficulties of programmed decision making are seen in the ineffective hiring procedures that some firms use. To solve the recurrent problem of choosing employees for lower-level jobs, almost all companies use application forms. These forms are part of a decision program. However, some firms have persisted in asking for information (such as age or marital status) that violates equal employment and human rights legislation or is not job related. Costly lawsuits have resulted. Furthermore, there is seldom evidence that this information is a valid predictor of job performance (garbage in—garbage out).

III-Structured Problems

Ill-structured problem. A problem for which the existing and desired states are unclear, and the method of getting to the desired state is unknown.

The extreme example of an **ill-structured problem** is one in which the existing and desired states are unclear, and the method of getting to the desired state (even if clarified) is unknown. For example, a vice-president of marketing might have a vague feeling that the sales of a particular product are too low. However, she might lack precise information about the product's market share (existing state) and the market share of its most successful competitor (ideal state). In addition, she might be unaware of exactly how to increase the sales of this particular product.

Ill-structured problems are generally unique, that is, they are unusual and have not been encountered before. In addition, they tend to be complex and involve a high degree of uncertainty. As a result, they frequently arouse controversy and conflict among the people who are interested in the decision. For example, consider the following:

- Should we vaccinate the population against a new flu strain when the vaccination might have some bad side effects?
- Should we implement a risky attempt to rescue political hostages?
- In which part of the country should we build a new plant?

It should be obvious that ill-structured problems such as these cannot be solved with programmed decisions. Rather, the decision makers must resort to nonprogrammed decision making. This simply means that they are likely to try to gather more information and be more self-consciously analytical in their approach. Ill-structured problems can entail high risk and stimulate strong political considerations. This was apparent in the chaos and political blame game that followed Hurricane Katrina's devastation of New Orleans in 2005. We will concentrate on such ill-structured problems in this chapter.

THE COMPLEAT DECISION MAKER—A RATIONAL DECISION-MAKING MODEL

Exhibit 11.1 presents a model of the decision process that a rational decision maker might use. When a problem is identified, a search for information is begun. This information clarifies the nature of the problem and suggests alternative solutions. These are carefully evaluated, and the best is chosen for implementation. The implemented solution is then monitored over time to ensure its immediate and continued effectiveness. If difficulties occur at any point in the process, repetition or recycling may be effected.

It might occur to you that we have not yet determined exactly what a "rational" decision maker is. Before we discuss the specific steps of the model in detail, let's contrast two forms of rationality.

Perfect versus Bounded Rationality

Perfect rationality. A decision strategy that is completely informed, perfectly logical, and oriented toward economic gain.

The prototype for **perfect rationality** is the familiar Economic Person (formerly Economic Man), whom we meet in the first chapter of most introductory textbooks in economics. Economic Person is the perfect, cool, calculating decision maker. More specifically, he or she

- can gather information about problems and solutions without cost and is thus completely informed;
- is perfectly logical—if solution A is preferred over solution B, and B is preferred over C, then A is necessarily preferable to C; and
- has only one criterion for decision making—economic gain.

While Economic Person is useful for theoretical purposes, the perfectly rational characteristics embodied in Economic Person do not exist in real decision makers.

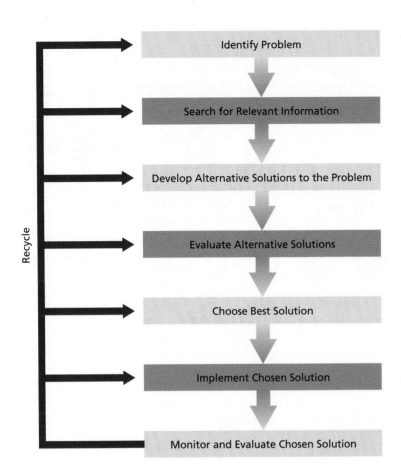

EXHIBIT 11.1
The rational decision-making process.

Nobel Prize winner Herbert Simon recognized this and suggested that managers use **bounded rationality** rather than perfect rationality.[4] That is, while they try to act rationally, they are limited in their capacity to acquire and process information. In addition, time constraints and political considerations (such as the need to please others in the organization) act as bounds to rationality.

Framing and cognitive biases both illustrate the operation of bounded rationality, as does the impact of emotions and mood on decisions. **Framing** refers to the (sometimes subtle) aspects of the presentation of information about a problem that are assumed by decision makers.[5] A frame could include assumptions about the boundaries of a problem, the possible outcomes of a decision, or the reference points used to decide if a decision is successful.[6] As we shall see, how problems and decision alternatives are framed can have a powerful impact on resulting decisions.

Cognitive biases are tendencies to acquire and process information in a particular way that is prone to error. These biases constitute assumptions and shortcuts that can improve decision-making efficiency, but they frequently lead to serious errors in judgment. We will see how they work in the following pages.

After we work through the rational decision-making model, we will consider how emotions and mood affect decisions.

Problem Identification and Framing

You will recall that a problem exists when a gap occurs between existing and desired conditions. Such gaps might be signalled by dissatisfied customers or vigilant employees. Similarly, the press might contain articles about legislation or ads for competing products that signal difficulties for the organization. The perfectly rational

Bounded rationality. A decision strategy that relies on limited information and that reflects time constraints and political considerations.

Framing. Aspects of the presentation of information about a problem that are assumed by decision makers.

Cognitive biases. Tendencies to acquire and process information in an error-prone way.

Source: *Current Contents*, July 17, 1989.

decision maker, infinitely sensitive and completely informed, should be a great problem identifier. Bounded rationality, however, can lead to the following difficulties in problem identification:[7]

- *Perceptual defence.* In Chapter 3, we pointed out that the perceptual system may act to defend the perceiver against unpleasant perceptions. For example, the down-playing of recurring problems during shuttle launches by NASA managers could have been due to their perceptual systems' incapacity to dwell on disaster scenarios. For more on how inaccurate perceptions affect decision making see "OB Flashback: *How Can Managers Make Good Decisions Despite Inaccurate Perceptions?*" at the end of the chapter.

- *Problem defined in terms of functional specialty.* Selective perception can cause decision makers to view a problem as being in the domain of their own specialty even when some other perspective might be warranted. For example, employees with a marketing background might fixate on a marketing solution to poor sales even though the problem resides in bad design.

- *Problem defined in terms of solution.* This form of jumping to conclusions effectively short-circuits the rational decision-making process. When Coca-Cola changed its time-honoured formula to produce a "new" Coke, it appears that its market share problem was prematurely defined in terms of a particular solution— we need to change our existing product. More recently, BMW's attempt to enhance the technology quotient of its cars led to the adoption of the electronic iDrive interface. Many auto writers found the system cumbersome and wondered whether this was the way to showcase technology.

- *Problem diagnosed in terms of symptoms.* "What we have here is a morale problem." While this might be true, a concentration on surface symptoms will provide the decision maker with few clues about an adequate solution. The real problem here involves the cause of the morale problem. Low morale due to poor pay suggests different solutions than does low morale due to boring work.

Coca-Cola
www.coca-cola.com

BMW
www.bmw.com

When a problem is identified, it is necessarily framed in some way. Consider how different it is to frame a $10 000 expenditure as a cost (something to be avoided) versus an investment (something to be pursued). Or, consider how different it is to frame a new product introduction as a military campaign against competitors versus a crusade to help customers. Or, consider how a firm might view a new piece of technology as a threat to its business or an opportunity to be exploited. In each case, the facts of the matter might be the same, but the different decision frames might lead to very different decisions.

Rational decision makers should try to be very self-conscious about how they have framed problems ("We have assumed that this is a product innovation problem."). Also, they should try out alternative frames ("Let's imagine that we don't need a new product here."). Finally, decision makers should avoid overarching, universal frames (corporate culture gone wild). While it is a good idea to "put customers first," we do not want to frame every problem as a customer service problem.[8]

Information Search

As you can see in Exhibit 11.1, once a problem is identified, a search for information is instigated. This information search may clarify the nature or extent of the problem and begin to suggest alternative solutions. Again, our perfectly rational Economic Person is in good shape at this second stage of the decision-making process. He or she has free and instantaneous access to all information necessary to clarify the problem and develop alternative solutions. Bounded rationality, however, presents a different picture. The information search might be slow and costly.

Too Little Information. Sometimes, decision makers do not acquire enough information to make a good decision. Several cognitive biases contribute to this. For one thing, people tend to be mentally lazy and use whatever information is most readily available to them. Often, this resides in the memory, and we tend to remember *vivid, recent* events.[9] Although such events might prove irrelevant in the context of the current problem, we curtail our information search and rely on familiar experience. The manager who remembers that "the last time we went to an outside supplier for parts, we got burned" may be ignoring the wisdom of contracting out a current order.

Another cognitive bias that contributes to an incomplete information search is the well-documented tendency for people to be overconfident in their decision making.[10] This difficulty is exacerbated by **confirmation bias**, the tendency to seek out information that conforms to one's own definition of or solution to a problem. Both these biases can lead people to shirk the acquisition of additional information. Indeed, critics of the US invasion of Iraq cited both overconfidence and confirmation bias. Similarly, in the fatal 1986 *Challenger* space launch, only a limited range of data about the impact of temperature on mechanical failure was examined. In 2005, however, NASA had much more information at its disposal when evaluating the problems with *Discovery*.

Confirmation bias. The tendency to seek out information that conforms to one's own definition of or solution to a problem.

Too Much Information. While the bounds of rationality often force us to make decisions with incomplete or imperfect information, *too much* information can also damage the quality of decisions. **Information overload** is the reception of more information than is necessary to make effective decisions. As you might guess, information overload can lead to errors, omissions, delays, and cutting corners.[11] In addition, decision makers facing overload often attempt to use all the information at hand, then get confused and permit low-quality information or irrelevant information to influence their decisions.[12] Perhaps you have experienced this when writing a term paper—trying to incorporate too many references and too many viewpoints into a short paper can lead to a confusing, low-quality end product. More is not necessarily better.

Information overload. The reception of more information than is necessary to make effective decisions.

Information overload can lead to errors, omissions, delays, and stress.

However, decision makers seem to *think* that more is better. In one study, even though information overload resulted in lower-quality decisions, overloaded decision makers were more *satisfied* than those who did not experience overload.[13] Why is this so? For one thing, even if decisions do not improve with additional information, confidence in the decisions may increase ("I did the best I could"). Second, decision makers may fear being "kept in the dark" and associate the possession of information with power. One research review concludes that managers

- gather much information that has little decision relevance;

- use information that they collected and gathered after a decision to justify that decision;

- request information that they do not use;

- request more information, regardless of what is already available; and

- complain that there is not enough information to make a decision even though they ignore available information.[14]

In conclusion, although good information improves decisions, organizational members often obtain more or less information than is necessary for adequate decisions.

Alternative Development, Evaluation, and Choice

Perfectly informed or not, the decision maker can now list alternative solutions to the problem, examine the solutions, and choose the best one. For the perfectly rational, totally informed, ideal decision maker, this is easy. He or she conceives of all alternatives, knows the ultimate value of each alternative, and knows the probability that each alternative will work. In this case, the decision maker can exhibit **maximization**—that is, he or she can choose the alternative with the greatest expected value. Consider a simple example:

Maximization. The choice of the decision alternative with the greatest expected value.

	Ultimate Value	Probability	Expected Value
Alternative 1	$100 000 Profit	.4	$40 000 Profit
Alternative 2	$ 60 000 Profit	.8	$48 000 Profit

Here, the expected value of each alternative is calculated by multiplying its ultimate value by its probability. In this case, the perfectly rational decision maker would choose to implement the second alternative.

Unfortunately, things do not go so smoothly for the decision maker working under bounded rationality. He may not know all alternative solutions, and he might be ignorant of the ultimate values and probabilities of success of those solutions that he knows. Again, cognitive biases come into play. In particular, people are especially weak intuitive statisticians, and they frequently violate standard statistical principles. For example:[15]

- People avoid incorporating known existing data about the likelihood of events ("base rates") into their decisions. For instance, firms continue to launch novelty food products (e.g., foods squeezed from tubes or foods developed by celebrities) even though they have a very high failure rate in the market.

- Large samples warrant more confidence than small samples. Despite this, data from a couple of (vivid) focus groups might be given more weight than data from a large (but anonymous) national survey.

- Decision makers often overestimate the odds of complex chains of events occurring—the scenario sounds sensible despite being less likely with every added link in the chain. "This product will be successful because the price of oil will fall *and* our competitors won't master the technology *and* free trade laws will be enacted."

- People are poor at revising estimates of probabilities and values as they acquire additional information. A good example is the **anchoring effect**, which illustrates that decision makers do not adjust their estimates enough from some initial estimate that serves as an anchor. For example, in one study, real estate agents allowed the *asking price* of a house to unduly influence their *professional evaluation* of the house.[16]

Anchoring effect. The inadequate adjustment of subsequent estimates from an initial estimate that serves as an anchor.

It is possible to reduce some of these basic cognitive biases by making people more accountable for their decisions. This might include requiring reasoned reports, formal presentations of how the decision was reached, and so on. However, it is critical that this accountability be in place *before* a decision is reached. After-the-fact accountability often increases the probability of biases, as people try to protect their identity as good decision makers.[17]

The perfectly rational decision maker can evaluate alternative solutions against a single criterion—economic gain. The decision maker who is bounded by reality might have to factor in other criteria as well, such as the political acceptability of the solution to other organizational members—will the boss like it? Since these additional criteria have their own values and probabilities, the decision-making task increases in complexity. Decision expert Paul Nutt found that the search for alternatives is often very limited in strategic decision making and that firms invest very little money in exploring alternatives. He cites Quaker's dubious purchase of Snapple as an example.[18]

Quaker
www.quakeroats.com

The bottom line here is that the decision maker working under bounded rationality frequently "satisfices" rather than maximizes.[19] **Satisficing** means that the decision maker establishes an adequate level of acceptability for a solution and then screens solutions until he or she finds one that exceeds this level. When this occurs, evaluation of alternatives ceases, and the solution is chosen for implementation. For instance, the human resources manager who feels that absenteeism has become too high might choose a somewhat arbitrary acceptable level (e.g., the rate one year earlier), then accept the first solution that seems likely to achieve this level. Few organizations seek to *maximize* attendance.

Satisficing. Establishing an adequate level of acceptability for a solution to a problem and then screening solutions until one that exceeds this level is found.

Risky Business

Choosing between decision alternatives often involves an element of risk, and the research evidence on how people handle such risks is fascinating. Consider this scenario that decision researcher Max Bazerman developed. Which alternative solution would you choose?

> *Robert Davis, head of the legal staff of a Fortune 500 company, has delayed making one of the most critical recommendations in the organization's history. The company is faced with a class action suit from a hostile group of consumers. While the organization believes that it is innocent, it realizes that a court may not have the same perspective. The organization is expected to lose $50 million if the suit is lost in court. Davis predicts a 50 percent chance of losing the case. The organization has the option of settling out of court by paying $25 million to the "injured" parties. Davis's senior staff has been collecting information and organizing the case for over six months. It is time for action. What should Davis recommend?*

Alternative A   Settle out of court and accept a sure *loss* of $25 000 000,

or

Alternative B   Go to court expecting a 50 percent probability of a $50 000 000 loss.[20]

Notice that these two solutions are functionally equivalent in terms of dollars and cents (50 percent of $50 million = $25 million). Nonetheless, you probably tended to choose alternative B—about 80 percent of students do. Notice also that alternative B is the riskier of the two alternatives in that it exposes the firm to a *potential* for greater loss.

Now, consider two further descriptions of the alternatives. Which solution would you choose?

Alternative C   Settle out of court and *save* $25 000 000 that could be lost in court,

or

Alternative D   Go to court expecting a 50 percent probability of *saving* $50 000 000.

Again, these two solutions are functionally equivalent in monetary terms (and equivalent to options A and B). Yet, you probably chose solution C—80 percent of students do. Notice that this is the *less* risky alternative, in that the firm is not exposed to a potential $50 million loss.

This is a graphic example of the power of framing. Alternatives A and B frame the problem as a choice between losses, while C and D frame it as a choice between gains or savings. Research by Daniel Kahneman and Amos Tversky shows that when people view a problem as a choice between losses, they tend to make risky decisions, rolling the dice in the face of a sure loss. When people frame the alternatives as a choice between gains they tend to make conservative decisions, protecting the sure win.[21]

It is very important to be aware of what reference point you are using when you frame decision alternatives. It is not necessarily wrong to frame a problem as a choice between losses, but this can contribute to a foolish level of risk taking. In the *Columbia* example, experts testified that had the foam incident been deemed a serious problem, NASA would have been faced with a costly, risky, and perhaps impossible rescue attempt. As such, had the shuttle been deemed at serious risk, decision makers would have been faced with two very negative alternatives: Risk the loss of the shuttle, or attempt a costly, dangerous, and very uncertain rescue attempt. The difficult alternatives could have influenced decision makers to go with experience and assume that the foam caused no serious damage.

We should emphasize that learning history can modify these general preferences for or against risk.[22] For example, suppose that a firm has become very successful by virtue of a series of risky decisions and is now faced with sitting on a handsome market share or investing in a product that could boost its share even higher. This win-win scenario would normally provoke conservatism, but the firm's historical success may tempt managers to choose the risky course of action and invest in the new product.

Solution Implementation

When a decision is made to choose a particular solution to a problem, the solution must be implemented. The perfectly rational decision maker will have factored any possible implementation problems into his or her choice of solutions. Of course, the bounded decision maker will attempt to do the same when estimating probabilities of success. However, in organizations, decision makers are often dependent on others to implement their decisions, and it might be difficult to anticipate their ability or motivation to do so.

A good example of implementation problems occurs when products such as cars are designed, engineered, and produced in a lengthy series of stages. For example, engineering might have to implement decisions made by designers, and production planning might have to implement decisions made by engineering. As we noted in Chapter 7, this sequential process frequently leads to confusion, conflict, and delay, unless cross-functional teams are used during the decision-making process. When they work well, such teams are sensitive to implementation problems.

Solution Evaluation

When the time comes to evaluate the implemented solution, the decision maker is effectively examining the possibility that a new problem has occurred: Does the (new) existing state match the desired state? Has the decision been effective? For all the reasons we stated previously, the perfectly rational decision maker should be able to evaluate the effectiveness of the decision with calm, objective detachment. Again, however, the bounded decision maker might encounter problems at this stage of the process.

Justification. As we said earlier, people tend to be overconfident about the adequacy of their decisions. Thus, substantial dissonance can be aroused when a decision turns out to be faulty. One way to prevent such dissonance is to avoid careful tests of the adequacy of the decision. As a result, many organizations are notoriously lax when it comes to evaluating the effectiveness of expensive training programs or advertising campaigns. If the bad news cannot be avoided, the erring decision maker might devote his or her energy to trying to justify the faulty decision.

The justification of faulty decisions is best seen in the irrational treatment of sunk costs. **Sunk costs** are permanent losses of resources incurred as the result of a decision.[23] The key word here is "permanent." Since these resources have been lost (sunk) due to a past decision, they should not enter into future decisions. Despite this, psychologist Barry Staw has studied how people often "throw good resources after bad," acting as if they can recoup sunk costs. This process is **escalation of commitment** to an apparently failing course of action, in which the escalation involves devoting more and more resources to actions implied by the decision.[24] For example, suppose an executive authorizes the purchase of several new machines to improve plant productivity. The machines turn out to be very unreliable, and they are frequently out of commission for repairs. Perfect rationality suggests admitting to a mistake here. However, the executive might authorize an order for more machines from the same manufacturer to "prove" that he was right all along, hoping to recoup sunk costs with improved productivity from an even greater number of machines. Dissonance reduction is not the only reason that escalation of commitment to a faulty decision may occur. In addition,

Sunk costs. Permanent losses of resources incurred as the result of a decision.

Escalation of commitment. The tendency to invest additional resources in an apparently failing course of action.

a social norm that favours *consistent* behaviour by managers might be at work.[25] Changing one's mind and reversing previous decisions might be perceived as a sign of weakness, a fate to be avoided at all costs.

Escalation of commitment sometimes happens even when the current decision maker is not responsible for previous sunk costs. For example, politicians might continue an expensive, unnecessary public works project that was begun by a previous political administration. Here, dissonance reduction and the appearance of consistency are irrelevant, suggesting some other causes of escalation. For one thing, decision makers might be motivated to not appear wasteful.[26] ("Even though the airport construction is way over budget and flight traffic doesn't justify a new airport, let's finish the thing. Otherwise, the taxpayers will think we've squandered their money.") Also, escalation of commitment might be due to the way in which decision makers frame the problem once some resources have been sunk. Rather than seeing the savings involved in reversing the decision, the problem might be framed as a decision between a sure loss of x dollars (which have been sunk) and an uncertain loss of $x + y$ dollars (maybe the additional investment will succeed). As we noted earlier, when problems are framed this way, people tend to avoid the certain loss and go with the riskier choice, which in this case is escalation.[27] In addition to these situational causes, personality, moods, and emotions can affect escalation. For instance, people high on neuroticism and negative affectivity (Chapter 2) are *less* likely to escalate since they try to avoid stressful predicaments.[28]

Escalation can occur in both competitive and noncompetitive situations. A noncompetitive example can be seen in the overvaluation of stocks by Wall Street analysts in advance of a market crash. Competitive, auction-like situations seem especially likely to prompt escalation because they often involve time pressure, rivalry, interested audiences, and the desire to be the first mover. These factors contribute to emotional arousal (see below) and stimulate escalation. An example was the bidding war between CBS and NBC for the TV show *Frasier*.[29]

Are there any ways to prevent the tendency to escalate commitment to a failing course of action? Logic and research suggest the following:[30]

- Encourage continuous experimentation with reframing the problem to avoid the decision trap of feeling that more resources *have* to be invested. Shift the frame to saving rather than spending.

- Set specific goals for the project in advance that must be met if more resources are to be invested. This prevents escalation when early results are "unclear."

- Place more emphasis in evaluating managers on *how* they made decisions and less on decision outcomes. This kind of accountability is the sensible way to teach managers not to fear failure.

- Separate initial and subsequent decision making so that individuals who make the initial decision to embark on a course of action are assisted or replaced by others who decide if a course of action should be continued. Banks often do this when trying to decide what to do about problem loans.

It may be tempting to think that using groups to make decisions will reduce the tendency toward escalation. However, groups are *more* prone than individuals to escalate commitment.[31] Certainly, many of the most prominent escalation fiascos have been group decisions.

Hindsight. The careful evaluation of decisions is also inhibited by faulty hindsight. **Hindsight** refers to the tendency to review the decision-making process that was used to find out what was done right (in the case of success) or wrong (in the case of failure). While hindsight can prove useful, it often reflects a cognitive bias.

The classic example of hindsight involves the armchair quarterback who "knew" that a chancy intercepted pass in the first quarter was unnecessary because the team

Hindsight. The tendency to review the decision-making process to find what was done right or wrong.

won the game anyway! The armchair critic is exhibiting the knew-it-all-along effect. This is the tendency to assume, after the fact, that we knew all along what the outcome of a decision would be. In effect, our faulty memory adjusts the probabilities that we estimated before making the decision to correspond to what actually happened.[32] This can prove quite dangerous. The money manager who consciously makes a very risky investment that turns out to be successful might revise her memory to assume that the decision was a sure thing. The next time, the now-confident investor might not be so lucky!

Another form of faulty hindsight is the tendency to take personal responsibility for successful decision outcomes while denying responsibility for unsuccessful outcomes.[33] Thus, when things work out well, it is because *we* made a careful, logical decision. When things go poorly, some unexpected *external* factor messed up our sensible decision!

How Emotion and Mood Affect Decision Making

Thus far, we have discussed decision making from a mainly cognitive perspective, focusing on the rational decision-making model and illustrating the limits to rationality. However, our coverage of decision justification and hindsight suggests a considerable emotional component to many organizational decisions—people don't like to be wrong, and they often become emotionally attached to the failing course of action that signals escalation of commitment.

At the outset, it should be emphasized that emotionless decision making would be poor decision making, and the rational model is not meant to suggest otherwise. Some of the most graphic evidence for this comes from unfortunate cases in which people suffer brain injuries that blunt their emotions while leaving their intellectual functions intact. Such individuals often proceed to make a series of poor life decisions because they are unable to properly evaluate the impact of these decisions on themselves and others; they have no feeling.[34] One can imagine the negative consequences if NASA's manned spacecraft were designed by emotionless rather than caring engineers. In fact, during the 2005 *Discovery* mission, it was suggested that some of the caution-focused decisions, such as the delay in landing and decision to set down in California, were made by mission control personnel still suffering emotional effects of the *Columbia*

Decision makers in a good mood can overestimate the likelihood of good events and use shortcut decision strategies.

tragedy. Strong emotions frequently figure in the decision-making process that corrects ethical errors (Chapter 12), and so-called whistle-blowers often report that they were motivated by emotion to protest decision errors. Strong (positive) emotion has also been implicated in creative decision making and the proper use of intuition to solve problems. Such intuition (Chapter 1) can lead to the successful short-circuiting of the steps in the rational model when speed is of the essence.

Despite these examples of how emotion can help decision making, there are many cases in which strong emotions are a hindrance. The folk saying "blinded by emotion" has some truth to it, as people experiencing strong emotions are often self-focused and distracted from the actual demands of the problem at hand. Most of our information about the impact of emotions on decisions is anecdotal, because people are often reluctant to participate in field research about emotional issues and because it is not ethical to invoke strong emotions in lab research. One clever field study did document how excessive pride led highly paid CEOs to pay too much for firms they were acquiring.[35] Other business-press evidence implicates angry CEOs losing their heads in competitive bidding for acquisitions (escalation of commitment). A common theme over the years has been how excessive emotional conflict between business partners or family business members provokes questionable business decisions.

In addition to escalation situations, emotions can also be a factor in risk assessment. Consider the example in the You Be the Manager feature on the 2005 World Aquatic Championships.

In contrast to the case for strong emotions, there is much research on the impact of mood on decision making. You will recall from Chapter 4 that moods are relatively mild, unfocused states of positive or negative feeling. The research on mood and decision making reveals some very interesting paradoxes. For one thing, mood is a pretty low-key state, and you might be inclined to think it would not have much impact on decisions. In fact, there is plenty of evidence that mood affects *what* and *how* people think when making decisions. Also, you might imagine that the impact of mood would be restricted to mundane, structured decision problems. In fact, mood has its greatest impact on uncertain, ambiguous decisions of the type that are especially crucial for organizations. Here is what the research reveals:[36]

- People in a positive mood tend to remember positive information. Those in a negative mood remember negative information.

- People in a positive mood tend to evaluate objects, people, and events more positively. Those in a negative mood provide more negative evaluations.

- People in a good mood tend to overestimate the likelihood that good events will occur and underestimate the occurrence of bad events. People in a bad mood do the opposite.

- People in a good mood adopt simplified, shortcut decision-making strategies, more likely violating the rational model. People in a negative mood are prone to approach decisions in a more deliberate, systematic, detailed way.

- Positive mood promotes more creative, intuitive decision making.

As you can see, it makes perfect sense to hope for your job interview to be conducted by a person in a good mood or to try to create a good mood on the part of your clients! Notice that the impact of mood on decision making is not necessarily dysfunctional. If the excesses of optimism can be controlled, those in a good mood can make creative decisions. If the excesses of pessimism can be controlled, those in a negative mood can actually process information more carefully and effectively. In a very interesting simulation of foreign currency trading, it was found that traders in a good mood performed more poorly (by losing money) than those in bad or neutral moods. Those in a bad mood performed better, but were rather conservative. Traders in a neutral mood did best, tolerating risk but not being overconfident.[37] Thus, the investment practitioners' advice to remain calm during turbulent markets has some validity.

FINA
www.fina.org

☞ YOU BE THE
Manager

Sink or Swim? The 2005 World Aquatic Championships.

In 2001, Montreal was awarded the 2005 World Aquatic Championships, the most important aquatic event outside of the Olympics. All levels of government pledged millions of dollars toward the event ($16 million from the Canadian government, $14.1 million from the Quebec provincial government, and $11 million from the city of Montreal) while the official organizing committee was charged with raising the additional $18 million required through corporate sponsorships.

In December 2004, however, it became clear that the organizing committee was not fulfilling its mandate. Not only were few Montrealers aware of the event, but the total amount of sponsorships secured amounted to a mere $400 000. With a looming shortfall of over $17 million and the event less than eight months away, FINA, the world governing body for swimming competitions, threatened to pull the games out of Montreal. In early January 2005, the head of FINA travelled to Montreal to ask the three levels of government to pledge additional funding. The provincial minister in charge of sports suggested that FINA provide funding, apparently offending the visiting official. On January 19th, FINA officially stripped Montreal of the event.

The shockwaves were felt immediately. The event, which was to attract over 2000 athletes, had already resulted in over 50 000 hotel reservations that would now be cancelled. The projected $80 million in revenue to the local economy would also be lost. Politicians demanded to know what had happened to the millions already spent on the event. Sports officials suggested that the pullout would severely hurt Montreal's reputation, as well as Quebec and Canada's, on the international sports scene. Finally, on February 2nd, in the midst of all the controversy, the head of the organizing committee committed suicide.

The mayor of Montreal, Gérald Tremblay, however, was not ready to give up just yet. During the last week of January, he flew to Paris to meet with FINA officials and asked them to reverse their decision. Upon his return, he kept up the pressure by stating that the city of Montreal would cover any deficits. FINA was facing pressure as well. It had already invested several months and millions of dollars on Montreal and was now scrambling to find a replacement city for a huge event to be held in less than seven months. FINA announced that it would decide on the event location on February 15th. On February 10th, Mayor Tremblay flew to Frankfurt to address FINA in a last ditch effort to bring the games back to Montreal. While many believed the chances of

The repercussions of poor decision making hit hard when Montreal was stripped of the 2005 World Aquatic Championships.

success were slim, the entire city was now watching to see how the drama would end. In November, almost nobody in the city knew about the event; in February, it was now a different story.

QUESTIONS

1. In terms of evaluation and risk, how could FINA's decision to strip Montreal of the event be explained? Could the mayor's offer to cover any deficits be effective?

2. What role could emotions have played in FINA's decision to pull the games and the mayor's attempts to save them? Is the mayor demonstrating escalation of commitment to a failing course of action?

To find out what FINA and the mayor did, check The Manager's Notebook at the end of the chapter.

Sources: All sources from *The Gazette* (Montreal): Carroll, A. (2005, February 11). 'Mr. Tremblay did a fantastic lobbying job,' FINA boss says, A3; Gyulai, L. (2006, January 31). $4.77-million aquatics loss was worth it, mayor says, A8; Guylai, L. (2005, December 13). City still crunching aquatics numbers, A6; Guylai, L., & Branswell, B. (2005, January 24). Tremblay still trying to revive aquatics meet, A7; Ravensbergen, J. (2005, February 8). All washed up? We should know Thursday, A6; Ravensbergen, J, Riga, A., & Stubbs, D. (2005, January 20). FINA pulls plug on Montreal aquatics: Mayor offers to dump deficit on taxpayers, A1; Riga, A. (2005, February 4). Tremblay still intent on hosting aquatics: Mayor not deterred by CEO's suicide, A1; Stubbs, D. (2005, June 1). Legault dives into worlds, C1.

A fine example of how mood and emotion can lead to faulty decision making can be seen in the "dot.com meltdown" that began in the late 1990s (see our case at the end of the chapter). In this era, hundreds of firms were formed to exploit the potential wealth of e-commerce. An economic boom, ready capital, advancing technology, and the model of a few overnight "Internet millionaires" created a positive mood that led to overly intuitive decisions, false creativity, and exaggerated optimism. Mood is contagious, and many start-up firms, fearing to be left behind, were founded with vague goals and vaguer business plans. Many consisted of little more than a website, and "hits" were confused with cash flow. The ensuing crash left the firms founded on careful business decision-making principles to enjoy the spoils of the technology revolution.

Rational Decision Making—A Summary

The rational decision-making model in Exhibit 11.1 provides a good guide for how many decisions *should* be made, but offers only a partially accurate view of how they *are* made. For complex, unfamiliar decisions, such as choosing an occupation, the rational model provides a pretty good picture of how people actually make decisions.[38] Also, organizational decision makers often follow the rational model when they agree about the goals they are pursuing.[39] On the other hand, there is plenty of case study evidence of short-circuiting the rational model in organizational decisions, in part because of the biases we discussed above.[40] Thus, it should not be surprising that a study of 356 decisions in medium to large organizations in the United States and Canada found that half the decisions made in organizations fail. These failures were found to be primarily due to the use of poor tactics on the part of managers who impose solutions, limit the search for alternatives, and use power to implement their plans.[41] However, true experts in a field will often short-circuit the rational model, using their intuitive knowledge base stored in memory to skip steps logically.[42] Exhibit 11.2 summarizes the operation of perfect and bounded rationality at each stage of the decision process. Exhibit 11.3 summarizes the various cognitive biases that we have covered.

EXHIBIT 11.2
Perfectly rational decision making contrasted with bounded rationality.

Stage	Perfect Rationality	Bounded Rationality
Problem Identification	Easy, accurate perception of gaps that constitute problems	Perceptual defence; jump to solutions; attention to symptoms rather than problems; mood affects memory
Information Search	Free; fast; right amount obtained	Slow; costly; reliance on flawed memory; obtain too little or too much
Development of Alternative Solutions	Can conceive of all	Not all known
Evaluation of Alternative Solutions	Ultimate value of each known; probability of each known; only criterion is economic gain	Potential ignorance of or miscalculation of values and probabilities; criteria include political factors; affected by mood
Solution Choice	Maximizes	Satisfices
Solution Implementation	Considered in evaluation of alternatives	May be difficult owing to reliance on others
Solution Evaluation	Objective, according to previous steps	May involve justification, escalation to recover sunk costs, faulty hindsight

- Decision makers tend to be overconfident about the decisions that they make.
- Decision makers tend to seek out information that confirms their own problem definitions and solutions. (Confirmation bias)
- Decision makers tend to remember and incorporate vivid, recent events into their decisions.
- Decision makers fail to incorporate known existing data about the likelihood of events into their decisions.
- Decision makers ignore sample sizes when evaluating samples of information.
- Decision makers overestimate the odds of complex chains of events occurring.
- Decision makers do not adjust estimates enough from some initial estimate that serves as an anchor as they acquire more information. (Anchoring effect)
- Decision makers have difficulty ignoring sunk costs when making subsequent decisions.
- Decision makers overestimate their ability to have predicted events after-the-fact, take responsibility for successful decision outcomes, and deny responsibility for unsuccessful outcomes. (Hindsight)

EXHIBIT 11.3
Summary of cognitive biases in decision making.

GROUP DECISION MAKING

Many, many organizational decisions are made by groups rather than individuals, especially when problems are ill structured. In this section, we consider the advantages and problems of group decision making.

Why Use Groups?

There are a number of reasons for employing groups to make organizational decisions.

Decision Quality. Experts often argue that groups or teams can make higher-quality decisions than individuals. This argument is based on the following three assumptions:

- Groups are *more vigilant* than individuals are—more people are scanning the environment.
- Groups can *generate more ideas* than individuals can.
- Groups can *evaluate ideas better* than individuals can.

At the problem identification and information search stages, vigilance is especially advantageous. A problem that some group members miss might be identified by others. For example, a member of the board of directors might notice a short article in an obscure business publication that has great relevance for the firm. In searching for information to clarify the problem suggested in the article, other members of the board might possess unique information that proves useful.

When it comes to developing alternative solutions, more people should literally have more ideas, if only because someone remembers something that others have forgotten. In addition, members with different backgrounds and experiences may bring different perspectives to the problem. This is why undergraduate students, graduate students, faculty, and administrators are often included on university task forces to improve the library or course evaluation system.

When it comes to evaluating solutions and choosing the best one, groups have the advantage of checks and balances—that is, an extreme position or incorrect notion held by one member should be offset by the pooled judgments of the rest of the group.

These characteristics suggest that groups *should* make higher-quality decisions than individuals can. Shortly, we will find out whether they actually do.

Decision Acceptance and Commitment. As we pointed out in our discussion of participative leadership in Chapter 9, groups are often used to make decisions on the premise that a decision made in this way will be more acceptable to those involved. Again, there are several assumptions underlying this premise:

- People wish to be involved in decisions that will affect them.
- People will better understand a decision in which they participated.
- People will be more committed to a decision in which they invested personal time and energy.

The acceptability of group decisions is especially useful in dealing with a problem described earlier—getting the decision implemented. If decision makers truly understand the decision and feel committed to it, they should be willing to follow through and see that it is carried out.

Diffusion of Responsibility. High quality and acceptance are sensible reasons for using groups to make decisions. A somewhat less admirable reason to employ groups is to allow for **diffusion of responsibility** across the members in case the decision turns out poorly. In this case, each member of the group will share part of the burden of the negative consequences, and no one person will be singled out for punishment. Of course, when this happens, individual group members often "abandon ship" and exhibit biased hindsight—"I knew all along that the bid was too high to be accepted, but they made me go along with them."

> **Diffusion of responsibility.** The ability of group members to share the burden of the negative consequences of a poor decision.

Do Groups Actually Make Higher-Quality Decisions Than Individuals?

The discussion in the first part of the previous section suggested that groups *should* make higher-quality decisions than individuals. But *do* they? Is the frequent use of groups to make decisions warranted by evidence? The answer is yes. One review concludes that "groups usually produce more and better solutions to problems than do individuals working alone."[43] Another concludes that group performance is superior to that of the average individual in the group.[44] More specifically, groups should perform better than individuals when

- the group members differ in relevant skills and abilities, as long as they do not differ so much that conflict occurs;
- some division of labour can occur;
- memory for facts is an important issue; and
- individual judgments can be combined by weighting them to reflect the expertise of the various members.[45]

To consolidate your understanding of these conditions, consider a situation that should favour group decision making: A small construction company wishes to bid on a contract to build an apartment complex. The president, the controller, a construction boss, and an engineer work together to formulate the bid. Since they have diverse backgrounds and skills, they divide the task initially. The president reviews recent bids on similar projects in the community; the controller gets estimates on materials costs; the engineer and boss review the blueprints. During this process, each racks his or her brain to recall lessons learned from making previous bids. Finally, they put their information together, and each member voices an opinion about what the bid should be. The president decides to average these opinions to arrive at the actual bid, since each person is equally expert in his or her own area.

Disadvantages of Group Decision Making

Although groups have the ability to develop high-quality, acceptable decisions, there are a number of potential disadvantages to group decision making.

Time. Groups seldom work quickly or efficiently compared with individuals. This is because of the process losses (Chapter 7) involved in discussion, debate, and coordination. The time problem increases with group size. When the speed of arriving at a solution to a problem is a prime factor, organizations should avoid using groups.

Conflict. Many times, participants in group decisions have their own personal axes to grind or their own resources to protect. When this occurs, decision quality may take a back seat to political wrangling and infighting. In the example about the construction company we presented earlier, the construction boss might see it to his advantage to overestimate the size of the crew required to build the apartments. On the other hand, the controller might make it her personal crusade to pare labour costs. A simple compromise between these two extreme points of view might not result in the highest-quality or most creative decision.

Domination. The advantages of group decision making will seldom be realized if meetings are dominated by a single individual or a small coalition. Even if a dominant person has good information, this style is not likely to lead to group acceptance and commitment. If the dominant person is particularly misinformed, the group decision is very likely to be ineffective.

Groupthink. In retrospect, have you ever been involved in a group decision that you knew was a "loser" but that you felt unable to protest? Perhaps you thought you were the only one who had doubts about the chosen course of action. Perhaps you tried to speak up, but others criticized you for not being on the team. Maybe you found yourself searching for information to confirm that the decision was correct and ignoring evidence that the decision was bad. What was happening? Were you suffering from some strange form of possession? Mind control?

In Chapter 8, we discussed the process of conformity. As you might expect, conformity can have a strong influence on the decisions that groups make. The most extreme influence is seen when **groupthink** occurs. This happens when group pressures lead to reduced mental efficiency, poor testing of reality, and lax moral judgment.[46] In effect, unanimous acceptance of decisions is stressed over quality of decisions.

Psychologist Irving Janis, who developed the groupthink concept, felt that high group cohesiveness was at its root. It now appears that other factors are more important.[47] These include strong identification with the group, concern for their approval, and the isolation of the group from other sources of information. However, the promotion of a particular decision by the group leader appears to be the strongest cause.[48] Janis provides a detailed list of groupthink symptoms:

Groupthink. The capacity for group pressure to damage the mental efficiency, reality testing, and moral judgment of decision-making groups.

- *Illusion of invulnerability.* Members are overconfident and willing to assume great risks. They ignore obvious danger signals.
- *Rationalization.* Problems and counterarguments that members cannot ignore are "rationalized away." That is, seemingly logical but improbable excuses are given.
- *Illusion of morality.* The decisions the group adopts are not only perceived as sensible, they are also perceived as *morally* correct.
- *Stereotypes of outsiders.* The group constructs unfavourable stereotypes of those outside the group who are the targets of their decisions.
- *Pressure for conformity.* Members pressure each other to fall in line and conform with the group's views.

- *Self-censorship.* Members convince themselves to avoid voicing opinions contrary to the group.
- *Illusion of unanimity.* Members perceive that unanimous support exists for their chosen course of action.
- *Mindguards.* Some group members may adopt the role of "protecting" the group from information that goes against its decisions.[49]

For an example of some of these symptoms, see "Research Focus: 'Pluralistic Ignorance' on Corporate Boards."

Obviously, victims of groupthink are operating in an atmosphere of unreality that should lead to low-quality decisions. Groupthink has been implicated in the decision process that led to NASA's fatal launch of *Challenger* in 1986.[50] We can also see it in the decision-making process in the NASA Hubble example, where an aberration in the telescope's primary mirror was the source of the astronomical repair costs.[51] To begin with, a dominant leader in charge of the internal mirror tests appears to have isolated the mirror project team from outside sources of information. Symptoms of groupthink followed: At least three sets of danger signals that the mirror was flawed were ignored or explained away (illusion of invulnerability and rationalization); an outside firm, Kodak, was dismissed as too incompetent to test the mirror (stereotype of outsiders); the consultant who suggested that Kodak test the mirror received bitter criticism but still felt he did not protest enough in the end (mindguarding and self-censorship); the defence of the isolated working methods was viewed as more "theological" than technical (illusion of morality).

What can prevent groupthink? Leaders must be careful to avoid exerting undue pressure for a particular decision outcome and concentrate on good decision processes. Also, leaders should establish norms that encourage and even reward responsible dissent, and outside experts should be brought in from time to time to challenge the group's views.[52] Some of the decision-making techniques we discuss later in the chapter should help prevent the tendency as well.

RESEARCH FOCUS

"Pluralistic Ignorance" on Corporate Boards

Corporate boards of directors are appointed to oversee the strategy and performance of organizations. Many such boards are made up of highly qualified and experienced executives. Nonetheless, there are countless examples of boards seemingly ignoring prominent signals that the companies they govern are in serious trouble. What accounts for this apparent contradiction between board member expertise and failed oversight? Could group dynamics have something to do with it?

Researchers James Westphal and Michael Bednar studied the contribution of "pluralistic ignorance" to the failure of corporate boards to call for strategic change in the face of poor firm performance. Pluralistic ignorance occurs when most group members feel concern about certain policies or practices, but at the same time feel that the other group members *support* the policies and practices. It is thought that this ignorance stems from the self-censorship and illusion of una-

nimity aspects of groupthink—people are reticent to voice what they think are minority opinions.

Using questionnaires completed by outside directors of low-performing firms, Westphal and Bednar found that they underestimated the degree of concern felt by other board members. The stronger this tendency, the less likely board members were to voice their concerns and the more likely their firms were to persist in ineffective strategies. In direct contradiction to the idea that cohesiveness contributes to groupthink, boards with stronger friendship ties and those that were more homogeneous in terms of business background and gender were less likely to exhibit pluralistic ignorance.

Source: Westphal, J.D., & Bednar, M.K. (2005). Pluralistic ignorance in corporate boards and firms' strategic persistence in response to low firm performance. *Administrative Science Quarterly, 50,* 262–298.

How Do Groups Handle Risk?

Almost by definition, problems that are suitable for group decision making involve some degree of risk and uncertainty. This raises a very important question: Do groups make decisions that are more or less risky than those of individuals? Or will the degree of risk assumed by the group simply equal the average risk preferred by its individual members? The answer here is obviously important. Consider the following scenario:

> *An accident has just occurred at a nuclear power plant. Several corrections exist, ranging from expensive and safe to low-cost but risky. On the way to an emergency meeting, each nuclear engineer formulates an opinion about what should be done. But what will the group decide?*

Conventional wisdom provides few clear predictions about what the group of engineers will decide to do. On the one hand, it is sometimes argued that groups will make riskier decisions than individuals because there is security in numbers—that is, diffusion of responsibility for a bad decision encourages the group to take greater chances. On the other hand, it is often argued that groups are cautious, with the members checking and balancing each other so much that a conservative outcome is sure to occur. Just contrast the committee-laden civil service with the swashbuckling style of independent operators such as Ted Turner and Donald Trump!

Given this contradiction of common sense, the history of research into group decision making and risk is both interesting and instructive. A Massachusetts Institute of Technology student, J.A.F. Stoner, reported in a master's thesis that he had discovered clear evidence of a **risky shift** in decision making.[53] Participants in the research reviewed hypothetical cases involving risk, such as those involving career choices or investment decisions. As individuals, they recommended a course of action. Then they were formed into groups, and the groups discussed each case and came to a joint decision. In general, the groups tended to advise riskier courses of action than the average risk initially advocated by their members. This is the risky shift. As studies were conducted by others to explore the reasons for its causes, things got more complicated. For some groups and some decisions, **conservative shifts** were observed. In other words, groups came to decisions that were *less* risky than those of the individual members before interaction.

It is now clear that both risky and conservative shifts are possible, and they occur in a wide variety of real settings, including investment and purchasing decisions. But what determines which kind of shift occurs? A key factor appears to be the initial positions of the group members before they discuss the problem. This is illustrated in Exhibit 11.4. As you can see, when group members are somewhat conservative before interaction (the Xs), they tend to exhibit a conservative shift when they discuss the problem. When group members are somewhat risky initially (the ●s), they exhibit a risky shift after discussion. In other words, *group discussion seems to polarize or exaggerate the initial position of the group.*[54] Returning to the nuclear accident, if the engineers initially prefer a somewhat conservative solution, they should adopt an even more conservative strategy during the meeting.

Why do risky and conservative shifts occur when groups make decisions? Evidence indicates two main factors:[55]

- Group discussion generates ideas and arguments that individual members have not considered before. This information naturally favours the members' initial tendency toward risk or toward conservatism. Since discussion provides "more" and "better" reasons for the initial tendency, the tendency ends up being exaggerated.

- Group members try to present themselves as basically similar to other members but "even better." Thus, they try to one-up others in discussion by adopting a slightly more extreme version of the group's initial stance.

Risky shift. The tendency for groups to make riskier decisions than the average risk initially advocated by their individual members.

Conservative shift. The tendency for groups to make less risky decisions than the average risk initially advocated by their individual members.

EXHIBIT 11.4
The dynamics of risky and conservative shifts for two groups.

Position of Group Members Before Discussion:

Position of Group Members After Discussion:

A somewhat worrisome research finding is that groups that communicate electronically via computer-mediated methods (Chapter 10) are inclined to polarize even more than face-to-face groups.[56] Such electronic communication is very common during complex NASA missions.

In summary, managers should be aware of the tendency for group interaction to polarize initial risk levels. If this polarization results from the sensible exchange of information, it might actually improve the group's decision. However, if it results from one-upmanship, it might lead to low-quality decisions.

IMPROVING DECISION MAKING IN ORGANIZATIONS

Can the decision-making process and its outcomes be improved? One study found that managers can improve the success of their decisions by using various tactics, such as making the need for action clear at the outset, setting objectives, carrying out an unrestricted search for solutions, and getting key people to participate.[57] It stands to reason that organizational decision making can improve if decision makers receive encouragement to follow more closely the rational decision-making model shown in Exhibit 11.1. This should help to preclude the various biases and errors that we have alluded to throughout the chapter. Each of the following techniques has this goal.

Training Discussion Leaders

When organizations use group decision making, an appointed leader often convenes the group and guides the discussion. The actions of this leader can "make or break" the decision. On the one hand, if the leader behaves autocratically, trying to "sell" a preconceived decision, the advantages of using a group are obliterated, and decision acceptance can suffer. If the leader fails to exert *any* influence, however, the group might develop a low-quality solution that does not meet the needs of the organization. The use of role-playing training to develop these leadership skills has increased the quality and acceptance of group decisions. The following are examples of the skills that people learn in discussion leader training:[58]

- State the problem in a nondefensive, objective manner. Do not suggest solutions or preferences.

- Supply essential facts and clarify any constraints on solutions (e.g., "We can't spend more than $25 000.").

- Draw out all group members. Prevent domination by one person, and protect members from being attacked or severely criticized.
- Wait out pauses. Do not make suggestions or ask leading questions.
- Ask stimulating questions that move the discussion forward.
- Summarize and clarify at several points to mark progress.

Stimulating and Managing Controversy

Full-blown conflict among organizational members is hardly conducive to good decision making. Individuals will withhold information, and personal or group goals will take precedence over developing a decision that solves organizational problems. On the other hand, a complete lack of controversy can be equally damaging, since alternative points of view that may be very relevant to the issue at hand will never surface. Such a lack of controversy is partially responsible for the groupthink effect, and it also contributes to many cases of escalation of commitment to flawed courses of action. For example, opportunities to express concern over the fate of the *Columbia* shuttle were not seized upon during face-to-face meetings, but were kept in electronic form between a small circle of colleagues.

Research shows a variety of ways to stimulate controversy in decision-making groups: incorporating members with diverse ideas and backgrounds, forming subgroups to "tear the problem apart," and establishing norms that favour the open sharing of information.[59] However, these tactics must be managed carefully to ensure that open conflict does not result. The discussion skills covered in the previous section can help here.

One interesting method of controversy stimulation is the appointment of a **devil's advocate** to challenge existing plans and strategies. The advocate's role is to challenge the weaknesses of the plan or strategy and state why it should not be adopted. For example, a bank might be considering offering an innovative kind of account. Details to be decided include interest rate, required minimum balance, and so on. A committee might be assigned to develop a position paper. Before a decision is made, someone would be assigned to read the paper and "tear it apart," noting potential weaknesses. Thus, a decision is made in full recognition of the pros and cons of the plan.

The controversy promoted by the devil's advocate improves decision quality.[60] However, to be effective, the advocate must present his or her views in an objective, unemotional manner.

Devil's advocate. A person appointed to identify and challenge the weaknesses of a proposed plan or strategy.

Traditional and Electronic Brainstorming

Brainstorming is the "brain child" of a Madison Avenue advertising executive.[61] Its major purpose is to increase the number of creative solution alternatives to problems. Thus, **brainstorming** focuses on the *generation* of ideas rather than the *evaluation* of ideas. If a group generates a large number of ideas, the chance of obtaining a truly creative solution is increased.

Brainstorming was originally conceived as a group technique. It was assumed that in generating ideas, group members could feed off each other's suggestions and be stimulated to offer more creative solutions. To ensure this, the group is encouraged to operate in a free-wheeling, off-the-wall manner. No ideas should be considered too extreme or unusual to be voiced. In addition, no criticism of ideas should be offered, since this can inhibit useful lines of thinking. For instance, an advertising agency might convene a group to generate names for a new toothpaste or soft drink. Similarly, a government agency might convene a group to generate possible solutions for welfare fraud.

Traditional brainstorming has not fulfilled its full creative promise. Research has shown conclusively that individuals working alone tend to generate more ideas than

Brainstorming. An attempt to increase the number of creative solution alternatives to problems by focusing on idea generation rather than evaluation.

when in groups.[62] In other words, four people working independently (and encouraged to be creative and nonevaluative) will usually generate more ideas than the same people working as a team. Why is this? Likely explanations include inhibition, domination of the group by an ineffective member, or the sheer physical limitations of people trying to talk simultaneously. However, as "Applied Focus: *Brainstorming at IDEO*" illustrates, brainstorming can provide advantages that extend beyond the mere number of ideas generated.

IDEO
www.ideo.com

An alternative to traditional brainstorming is electronic brainstorming. **Electronic brainstorming** uses computer-mediated communication to accomplish the same goal as traditional brainstorming: the generation of novel ideas without evaluation. As we noted, face-to-face interaction actually reduces individual brainstorming performance. But what happens if people brainstorm as an electronic group?

Electronic brainstorming.
The use of computer-mediated technology to improve traditional brainstorming practices.

Once over the size of two members, electronic brainstorming groups perform better than face-to-face groups in terms of both quantity and quality of ideas.[63] Also, as electronic groups get larger, they tend to produce more ideas, but the ideas-per-person measure remains stable. In contrast, as face-to-face groups get bigger, fewer and fewer ideas per person are generated (remember social loafing from Chapter 7). What

---

APPLIED FOCUS

Brainstorming at IDEO

IDEO is the largest industrial design firm in the United States and one of the most innovative companies in the world. Founded in 1978 by David Kelley and headquartered in Palo Alto, California, the 350-person firm has offices in San Francisco, Chicago, Boston, London, and Munich, and does business all over the world for clients such as Hewlett-Packard, AT&T Wireless Services, Nestlé, Samsung, NASA, and the BBC.

In the 1980s and 1990s, IDEO was at the forefront of the tech boom, designing products such as Apple's first mouse, the Palm V handheld computer, and Polaroid's izone cameras. In the early 21st century, IDEO has shifted its focus from designing cutting edge products to helping companies design optimal interaction processes with customers in such areas as banking, shopping, and its current largest practice, health care. To offer its clients innovative products and processes, IDEO has assembled an eclectic workforce consisting of engineers, psychologists, sociologists, graphic designers, and anthropologists, among others. "They're creative and strategic, eclectic and passionate. They're cool but without attitude," is how one client put it.

A key element in IDEO's success is its use of brainstorming. IDEO mixes clients with designers, social scientists, and engineers in a room where all ideas are put on the table for discussion and scrutiny. "Rules" for brainstorming, prominently displayed on meeting room walls, include (1) one discussion at a time, (2) stay on topic, (3) build on others' ideas, (4) defer judgment, and (5) encourage wild ideas.

Researchers Robert Sutton and Andrew Hargadon were interested in why IDEO makes such extensive use of group brainstorming, in light of the research showing that the procedure does not result in more ideas being generated than occur when people "brainstorm" alone. What they found was that the procedure results in a number of other important creative and business advantages. In terms of the organizational culture, they found that it helped organizational memory and supported a culture of wisdom—that is, ideas from one session can be used on subsequent unrelated projects, and participants learn to appreciate the good ideas of others. At the individual level, the sessions motivate and stimulate the engineers and allow them to show off their good ideas to their colleagues. Finally, IDEO uses the brainstorming sessions to impress their clients, who really get to see how the design process unfolds. Thus, brainstorming shapes the organizational culture, helps retain good talent, and contributes to client confidence.

Sources: Morrison, S. (2005, February 18). Sharp focus gives design group the edge. *Financial Times*, 8; Nussbaum, B. (2004, May 17). The power of design. *Business Week*, 86–94 (client quote); Stone, B. (2003, October 27). Reinventing everyday life. *Newsweek*, 90–92; Sutton, R.I., & Hargadon, A. (1996). Brainstorming groups in context: Effectiveness in a product design firm. *Administrative Science Quarterly, 41*, 685–718.

accounts for the success of electronic brainstorming? Reduced inhibition about participating and the ability for people to enter ideas simultaneously without waiting for others seem to be the main reasons. Notice that these factors become especially critical as the group gets bigger. Some organizations have done electronic brainstorming with up to 30-member groups.

Nominal Group Technique

The fact that nominal (in name only) brainstorming groups generate more ideas than interacting brainstorming groups gave rise to the **nominal group technique** (NGT) of decision making. Unlike brainstorming, NGT is concerned with both the generation of ideas and the evaluation of these ideas:

> *Imagine a meeting room in which 7 to 10 individuals are sitting around a table in full view of each other; however, at the beginning of the meeting they do not speak to each other. Instead, each individual is writing ideas on a pad of paper in front of him or her. At the end of 5 to 10 minutes, a structured sharing of ideas takes place. Each individual, in round-robin fashion, presents one idea from his or her private list. A recorder writes that idea on a flip chart in full view of other members. There is still no discussion at this point of the meeting— only the recording of privately narrated ideas. Round-robin listing continues until all members indicate they have no further ideas to share. Discussion follows during the next phase of the meeting; however, it is structured so that each idea receives attention before independent voting. This is accomplished by asking for clarification, or stating support or nonsupport of each idea listed on the flip chart. Independent voting then takes place. Each member privately, in writing, selects priorities by rank-ordering (or rating). The group decision is the mathematically pooled outcome of the individual votes.*[64]

As you can see, NGT carefully separates the generation of ideas from their evaluation. Ideas are generated nominally (without interaction) to prevent inhibition and conformity. Evaluation permits interaction and discussion, but it occurs in a fairly structured manner to be sure that each idea gets adequate attention. NGT's chief disadvantage would seem to be the time and resources required to assemble the group for face-to-face interaction. The Delphi technique was developed, in part, to overcome this problem.

The Delphi Technique

The **Delphi technique** of decision making was developed at the Rand Corporation to forecast changes in technology. Its name derives from the future-telling ability of the famous Greek Delphic Oracle.[65] Unlike NGT, the Delphi process relies solely on a nominal group—participants do not engage in face-to-face interaction. Thus, it is possible to poll a large number of experts without assembling them in the same place at the same time. We should emphasize that these experts do not actually make a final decision; rather, they provide information for organizational decision makers.

The heart of Delphi is a series of questionnaires sent to respondents. Minimally, there are two waves of questionnaires, but more is not unusual. The first questionnaire is usually general in nature and permits free responses to the problem. For example, suppose the CEO of a large corporation wishes to evaluate and improve the firm's customer service. A random sample of employees who have worked closely with customers would receive an initial questionnaire asking them to list the strengths and weaknesses of the existing approach to customers. The staff would collate the responses and develop a second questionnaire that might share these responses and ask for suggested improvements. A final questionnaire might then be sent asking respondents to rate or rank each improvement. The staff would then merge the ratings or rankings mathematically and present them to the president for consideration.

Nominal group technique. A structured group decision-making technique in which ideas are generated without group interaction and then systematically evaluated by the group.

Delphi technique. A method of pooling a large number of expert judgments by using a series of increasingly refined questionnaires.

A chief disadvantage of Delphi is the rather lengthy time frame involved in the questionnaire phases, although fax and e-mail can speed up sending and receiving. In addition, its effectiveness depends on the writing skills of the respondents and their interest in the problem, since they must work on their own rather than as part of an actual group. Despite these problems, Delphi is an efficient method of pooling a large number of expert judgments while avoiding the problems of conformity and domination that can occur in interacting groups.

 THE MANAGER'S

Notebook

Sink or Swim? The 2005 World Aquatic Championships.

1. From December 2004 to February 2005, the situation had changed drastically for decision makers at FINA. From December to mid-January, due to the perceived incompetence of the organizing committee, the lack of support from the corporate community, and the refusal of the federal and provincial governments to provide more funding, it would have appeared to FINA that they were facing a sure loss if they kept the championships in Montreal. As such, they decided to pull the games. By early February, however, the loss seemed certain if they did not give the event back to Montreal. Time and money had already been invested in Montreal, and FINA realized that almost no other cities could host the event. Cities that were initially considered to be candidates such as Sydney, Australia, and Long Beach, California, indicated emphatically that they were not interested in the event. When Mayor Tremblay announced that the city would cover any losses incurred by the championships, the sure loss of Montreal looked more like a likely gain. On February 11, 2005, FINA awarded the games back to the city of Montreal. The event took place in July 2005 with 160 000 tickets sold and was a great success for both FINA and the city of Montreal.

2. Emotions played an important role in many decisions surrounding the World Aquatic Championships. First, it was suggested that the decision by FINA to strip Montreal of the event was influenced in part by the negative feelings experienced by the head of FINA when he lobbied the government for more funding in early January 2005. More importantly, Mayor Tremblay made his passion for Montreal the driving force in his push to regain the games for the city. While some observers viewed the loss of the games in a positive light and suggested that Montreal's winter climate made the city ill-suited for such an event, and almost everyone applauded the federal and provincial governments for not investing more taxpayer money into the championships, the mayor stressed that Montreal's international reputation was on the line. When FINA announced that Montreal was being given back the games, it made it clear that Mayor Tremblay's passion and emotion were important factors in the reversal. Once regained, Mayor Tremblay personally took over as president of the organizing committee. Did the mayor demonstrate escalation of commitment to a failing course of action? In the end, it appeared that he was justified in his efforts. While the city did incur a $4.7 million charge to cover the eventual deficit for the championships, this was seen as a small price for an event that was an economic and marketing success for the larger community.

LEARNING OBJECTIVES CHECKLIST

1. *Decision making* is the process of developing a commitment to some course of action. Alternatively, it is a problem-solving process. A *problem* exists when a gap is perceived between some existing state and some desired state. Some problems are well structured. This means that existing and desired states are clear, as is the means of getting from one state to the other. Well-structured problems are often solved with programs, which simply standardize solutions. Programmed decision making is effective as long as the program is developed rationally and as long as conditions do not change. Ill-structured problems contain some combination of an unclear existing state, an unclear desired state, or unclear methods of getting from one state to the other. They tend to be unique and nonrecurrent, and they require nonprogrammed decision making in which the rational model comes into play.

2. *Rational decision making* includes (1) problem identification, (2) information search, (3) development of alternative solutions, (4) evaluation of alternatives, (5) choice of the best alternative, (6) implementation, and (7) ongoing evaluation of the implemented alternative. The imaginary, perfectly rational decision maker has free and easy access to all relevant information, can process it accurately, and has a single ultimate goal— economic maximization. Real decision makers must suffer from *bounded rationality*. They do not have free and easy access to information, and the human mind has limited information processing capacity and is susceptible to a variety of cognitive biases. In addition, time constraints and political considerations can outweigh anticipated economic gain. As a result, bounded decision makers usually *satisfice* (choose a solution that is "good enough") rather than maximize.

3. *Framing* refers to the aspects of the presentation of information about a problem that are assumed by decision makers. A frame could include assumptions about the boundaries of a problem, the possible outcomes of a decision, or the reference points used to decide if a decision is successful. Problems that are framed as an investment versus a cost, or as a potential gain versus a potential loss, can affect decision-making processes. *Cognitive biases* are tendencies to acquire and process information in a particular way that is prone to error. These biases constitute assumptions and shortcuts that can improve decision-making efficiency, but they frequently lead to serious errors in judgment. Examples include overemphasizing recent information, overconfidence based on past success, perceptual defence, and faulty hindsight.

4. *Escalation of commitment* is the tendency to invest additional resources in an apparently failing course of action. This tendency emerges from people's desires to justify past decisions and attempts to recoup sunk costs incurred as the result of a past decision.

5. Although emotions can enhance the decision-making process in relation to correcting ethical errors or when dealing with creative problems, they can also distract and unsettle decision makers and lead to poor choices. Research has shown that mood can also have an important impact on the decision-making process, especially for uncertain or ambiguous problems. Mood can affect information recall, evaluation, creativity, time reference, and projected outcomes.

6. Groups can often make higher-quality decisions than individuals because of their vigilance and their potential capacity to generate and evaluate more ideas. Also, group members might accept more readily a decision that they have been involved in making. Given the proper problem, groups will frequently make higher-quality decisions than individuals. However, using groups takes a lot of time and might provoke conflict. In addition, groups might fall prey to *groupthink*, in which social pressures to conform to a particular decision outweigh rationality. Groups might also make decisions that are more risky or conservative than those of individuals.

7. Attempts to improve organizational decision making have involved training discussion leaders, stimulating controversy, *brainstorming*, the *nominal group technique,* and the *Delphi technique.*

OB FLASHBACK

How Can Managers Make Good Decisions Despite Inaccurate Perceptions?

In Chapter 3 we defined perception as the process of interpreting the messages of our senses to provide order and meaning to the environment. Logically, accurate perceptions would seem to be crucial for successful decision making. Johns Mezias and William Starbuck reviewed considerable evidence showing that managers' perceptions are typically quite inaccurate, even among those from very successful organizations. For instance, managers tend to misperceive the degree of stability of their business's environment, inaccurately report firm and industry sales, and misjudge their business unit's quality performance. Given such inaccurate perceptions, how can organizations manage to adapt and prosper? At least three factors may explain how good decisions can be made despite individual manager's perceptual errors. First, Mezias and Starbuck conclude that focusing on general long-term goals may reduce the impact of specific inaccurate perceptions. For example, correctly deciding how to improve quality may not require an exact grasp of current quality levels. Second, important organizational decisions are seldom made by individual managers, and consensus may average out errors to provide accurate decision data. Third, Chip Heath, Richard Larrick, and Joshua Klayman describe how organizations put in place routines and procedures that make "cognitive repairs" to faulty individual perceptions. Examples include formal decision checklists, regular staff meetings, and the provision of buffer time. Microsoft builds buffer time into its project schedules to compensate for people's tendency to underestimate how long tasks take to complete.

Sources: Mezias, J.M., & Starbuck, W.H. (2003). Studying the accuracy of managers' perceptions: A research odyssey. *British Journal of Management, 14*, 3–17; Heath, C., Larrick, R.P., & Klayman, J. (1998). Cognitive repairs: How organizational practices can compensate for individual shortcomings. *Research in Organizational Behavior, 20*, 1–37.

DISCUSSION QUESTIONS

1. The director of an urban hospital feels that there is a turnover problem among the hospital's nurses. About 25 percent of the staff resign each year, leading to high replacement costs and disruption of services. Use the decision model in Exhibit 11.1 to explore how the director might proceed to solve this problem. Discuss probable bounds to the rationality of the director's decision.

2. Describe a decision-making episode (in school, work, or your personal life) in which you experienced information overload. How did you respond to this overload? Did it affect the quality of your decision?

3. Many universities must register thousands of students for courses each semester. Is this a well-structured problem or an ill-structured problem? Does it require programmed decisions or nonprogrammed decisions? Elaborate.

4. An auditing team fails to detect a case of embezzlement that has gone on for several months at a bank. How might the team members use hindsight to justify their faulty decisions?

5. A very cohesive planning group for a major oil company is about to develop a long-range strategic plan. The head of the unit is aware of the groupthink problem and wishes to prevent it. What steps should she take?

6. Discuss the implications of diffusion of responsibility, risky shift, and conservative shift for the members of a parole board. Also, consider the role of emotion and mood.

7. Discuss how the concepts of groupthink and escalation of commitment might be related to some cases of unethical decision making (and its cover-up) in business.

8. What are the similarities and differences of the nominal group technique and the Delphi technique? What are the comparative advantages and disadvantages?

INTEGRATIVE DISCUSSION QUESTIONS

1. Consider the role of communication in decision making. Explain how barriers to effective manager–employee communication can affect decision making in organizations. How can personal and organizational approaches for improving communication improve decision making?

2. Does group structure influence group decision making? Explain how each of the following structural characteristics might influence group decision quality, acceptance and commitment, and diffusion of responsibility: group size, diversity, norms, roles, status, and cohesiveness.

ON-THE-JOB CHALLENGE QUESTION

Although automotive journalists love BMW's award-winning cars, they have complained for years about BMW's complicated iDrive electronic interface. The menu-driven interface, which uses a knob on the centre console and a display screen, controls several hundred functions related to climate control, sound system, and navigation. A recent issue of *Car and Driver* magazine used the words "maddening," "exasperating," and "curse" in referring to iDrive. Most automotive journalists seem to dislike the feature, even though BMW feels that it reinforces their image as a technology leader and represents the wave of the future in automotive electronics.

All car companies are sensitive to complaints by automotive journalists, and BMW is obviously aware of the repeated criticism. What factors might account for their decision not to do away with or significantly simplify iDrive?

Source: Among many such complaints, see Swann, T. (2006, November). Four upscale sedans to ward off old-guy blues. *Car and Driver*, 88–97.

EXPERIENTIAL EXERCISE

The New Truck Dilemma

Preparation for Role-Playing

The instructor will:

1. Read the general instructions to the class as a whole.

2. Place data regarding name, length of service, and make and age of truck on the chalkboard for ready reference by all.

3. Divide the class into groups of six. Any remaining members should be asked to join one of the groups and serve as observers.

4. Assign roles to each group by handing out slips with the names Chris Marshall, Terry, Sal, Jan, Sam, and Charlie. Ask each person to read his or her own role only. Instructions should not be consulted once role-playing has begun.

5. Ask the Chris Marshalls to stand up when they have completed reading their instructions.

6. When all Chris Marshalls are standing, ask that each crew member display conspicuously the slip of paper with his or her role name so that Chris can tell who is who.

The Role-Playing Process

1. The instructor will start the role-playing with a statement such as the following: "Chris Marshall has asked the crew to wait in the office. Apparently Chris wants to discuss something with the crew. When Chris sits down that will mean he or she has returned. What you say to each other is entirely up to you. Are you ready? All Chris Marshalls please sit down."

2. Role-playing proceeds for 25 to 30 minutes. Most groups reach agreement during this interval.

Collection of Results

1. Each supervisor in turn reports his or her crew's solution. The instructor summarizes these on the chalkboard by listing the initials of each repair person and indicating with arrows which truck goes to whom.

2. A tabulation should be made of the number of people getting a different truck, the crew members considering the solution unfair, and the supervisor's evaluation of the solution.

Discussion of Results

1. A comparison of solutions will reveal differences in the number of people getting a different truck, who gets the new one, the number dissatisfied, etc. Discuss why the same facts yield different outcomes.

2. The quality of the solution can be measured by the trucks retained. Highest quality would require the poorest truck to be discarded. Evaluate the quality of the solutions achieved.

3. Acceptance is indicated by the low number of dissatisfied repair people. Evaluate solutions achieved on this dimension.

4. List problems that are similar to the new truck problem. See how widely the group will generalize.

General Instructions

This is a role-playing exercise. *Do not read the roles given below until assigned to do so by your instructor*!

Assume that you are a repair person for a large utility company. Each day you drive to various locations in the city to do repair work. Each repair person drives a small truck, and you take pride in keeping it looking good. You have a possessive feeling about your truck and like to keep it in good running order. Naturally, you would like to have a new truck, too, because a new truck gives you a feeling of pride.

Here are some facts about the trucks and the crew that reports to Chris Marshall, the supervisor of repairs:

> Terry—17 years with the company, has a 2-year-old Ford
>
> Sal—11 years with the company, has a 5-year-old Dodge
>
> Jan—10 years with the company, has a 4-year-old Ford
>
> Sam—5 years with the company, has a 3-year-old Ford
>
> Charlie—3 years with the company, has a 5-year-old Chevrolet

Most of you do all your driving in the city, but Jan and Sam cover the jobs in the suburbs.

You will be one of the people mentioned above and will be given some further individual instructions. In acting your part in role-playing, accept the facts as well as assume the attitude supplied in your specific role. From this point on, let your feelings develop in accordance with the events that transpire in the role-playing process. When facts or events arise that are not covered by the roles, make up things that are consistent with the way it might be in a real-life situation.

When the role-playing begins, assume that Chris Marshall called the crew into the repair office.

Role for Chris Marshall, Supervisor. You are the supervisor of a repair crew, each of whom drives a small service truck to and from various jobs. Every so often you get a new truck to exchange for an old one, and you have the problem of deciding which one of your crew gets the new truck. Often there are hard feelings because each person seems to feel entitled to the new truck, so you have a tough time being fair. As a matter of fact, it usually turns out that whatever you decide, most of the crew consider it wrong. You now have to face the issue again because a new truck has just been allocated to you for assignment. The new truck is a Chevrolet.

To handle this problem, you have decided to put the decision up to the crew themselves. You will tell them about the new truck and will put the problem in terms of what would be the fairest way to assign the truck. *Do not take a position yourself because you want to do what the crew thinks is most fair.* However, be sure that the group reaches a decision.

Role for Terry. When a new Chevrolet truck becomes available, you think you should get it because you have most seniority and do not like your present truck. Your own car is a Chevrolet, and you prefer a Chevrolet truck such as you drove before you got the Ford.

Role for Sal. You feel you deserve a new truck. Your present truck is old, and since the more senior crew member has a fairly new truck, you should get the next one. You have taken excellent care of your present Dodge and have kept it looking like new. People deserve to be rewarded if they treat a company truck like their own.

Role for Jan. You have to do more driving than most of the other crew because you work in the suburbs. You have a fairly old truck and feel you should have a new one because you do so much driving.

Role for Sam. The heater in your present truck is inadequate. Since Charlie backed into the door of your truck, it has never been repaired to fit right. The door lets in too much cold air, and you attribute your frequent colds to this. You want a warm truck since you have a good deal of driving to do. As long as it has good tires, brakes, and is comfortable, you do not care about its make.

Role for Charlie. You have the poorest truck in the crew. It is five years old, and before you got it, it had been in a bad wreck. It has never been good, and you have put up with it for three years. It is about time you got a good truck to drive, and you feel the next one should be yours. You have a good accident record. The only accident you had was when you sprung the door of Sam's truck when he opened it as you backed out of the garage. You hope the new truck is a Ford, since you prefer to drive one.

Source: Adapted from Maier, N.R.F., & Verser, G.C. (1982). *Psychology in industrial organizations* (5th ed.). Copyright 1982 by Houghton Mifflin Company. Adapted with permission.

CASE INCIDENT

The Restaurant Review

After immigrating from New Orleans to his adopted city of Vancouver, Christophe Touché had worked as head chef at a neighborhood pub for five years while saving money and planning to open his own restaurant. At the pub, he perfected several Cajun specialities that would form the core of the menu of his new restaurant, Cajun Sensation. After being open for two months, Christophe was delighted to receive a phone call from the local newspaper food critic who had dined anonymously at the restaurant the previous evening and was calling to verify some of the ingredients and techniques he used in his cooking. Two days later, delight turned to dismay as Christophe read the restaurant review. Although the critic praised the inventiveness of some dishes, others were described as "heavy handed." The staff were described as "charming but amateurish." And the wine list was described as "well chosen, but overpriced." The review concluded, "In sum, this very new restaurant has both problems and promise." It was local custom to post restaurant reviews prominently at the restaurant entrance to capture walk-by trade. At a staff meeting, opinions varied about what to do. One member suggested posting the review, as it noted that the new establishment had been open only two months. Another suggested posting only favourable excerpts from the review. A third offered to write an angry letter to the paper's editor. Christophe wasn't sure what to do.

1. What are some of the factors that might lead Christophe to make a poor decision about the review?

2. What would you do in this situation, and why?

CASE STUDY

Dot-com Meltdown

I strode confidently into the cookie-cutter office building in the Washington suburbs, ready to conquer the New Economy and pocket my share of that promised IPO.

When I told my colleagues and friends that I was chucking a good job and a decent wage for a below-market salary at an Internet start-up, no one said, "Kevin, you're nuts." On the contrary. They gazed at me with envy and muttered something about how they hoped I would remember them when my stock options landed me my first million bucks.

I arrived early that first day in January 2000, intent on impressing my new bosses with my punctuality and proper business attire. What an Old Economy way of thinking! There was no receptionist to take my name and buzz me in. Instead, I said hello to the Mr. Potato Head grinning from a desk in the lobby, grabbed a coffee from the kitchen and went looking for my new mates on my maiden voyage to dot-com land.

I found the vice-president of marketing, who greeted me enthusiastically. We made our way past a row of empty offices and entered a large open room crammed with desks, computers and about 15 people. The unusual seating arrangement was designed to encourage teamwork and smash the traditional pecking order that dictates who gets the corner suite with the mahogany credenza and who gets the windowless cubicle. Excitement and optimism were in the air.

"This," the marketing VP beamed, "is gonna work."

My title was director of business development. I was the company's seventeenth hire. My job duties were a bit vague, but I wasn't daunted. I was quite certain I'd find out soon enough. The important things were set. We had several million dollars in venture capital, and the possibility of millions more. We had "content"—an innovative information package for consumers in search of certain services—that our backers thought would bring millions of "eyeballs" and those critical advertising dollars to our website. (I have omitted further identifying details out of kindness and humility.)

The fact that we had no revenue and no product to sell (the service was free) was beside the point. We weren't necessarily in it for the long haul. We would ramp up and go public just as soon as we could.

I was ready. I was willing to work the dot-com way, subsisting on caffeine and adrenaline and logging those 18-hour days that I had read so much about.

To my surprise, long hours and hard work were not an essential part of the culture. Most days, the place didn't really get hopping until after 10 a.m. Although we disdained hierarchies and fancy offices, we were overstocked with vice-presidents, directors, and managers. And then there was the Friday afternoon happy hour. That seemed a little much, I thought at first, but hey—why argue about beer in the work place?

This was gonna work.

February

As I got to know my fellow dot-commies, I became a student of their attire. Some went corporate, dressing in expensive outfits. Others followed the lead of our 32-year-old CEO, who favoured casual chic. Some days, he opted for the worn look, even wearing a sweater with a hole in the armpit and pants with a split seam. Some employees went barefoot around the office. It was laid back. It was cool. It was so New Economy.

Like many of our dot-com brethren, our top people were long on youth and light on experience. Several managers were under 25. Another was a relative of the

CEO. Of course, none of this meant that we weren't going to make it. But it contributed to my discomfort about whether we had the crew we needed to create a successful business from scratch. I began to wonder if I had done enough homework before accepting the job.

Skepticism began to creep into my conversations with colleagues. It wasn't welcomed. My bosses frequently would remind us: "We have the best content on the web." One day I started to ask, "Yes, but how are we going to make money. . . ." The room grew quiet. I felt as if it were somehow disloyal to voice doubts. Soon, it became apparent that managers who challenged the wisdom of company initiatives were labelled as "negative." In dot-com land, where revenue is theoretical and image is everything, it was, like, totally uncool to be anything but a cheerleader.

The CEO gushed over toadies who nodded and smiled in meetings. His favourite expressions were "Awesome!" and, of course, "This is gonna work." If you could produce an Excel spreadsheet, you were golden. It didn't matter what the figures meant; if you could express yourself in numbers and neat columns, then you were destined for greatness in our company. For the first time in my career, I resolved to keep my concerns to myself—at least for a while.

Fortunately, a new set of venture capitalists took a look at the company and liked our business plan enough to invest. Just days before the Nasdaq crash in April, we closed a $10 million round of financing, bringing our bank account up to nearly $12 million. It didn't take long to spend.

April

We started by making a big splash at the Internet World Convention in Los Angeles. For dot-coms, it's considered a must-be-seen-at trade show. While most in the industry were sweating over where the Nasdaq was headed, we were hosting lavish nightly cocktail parties, sponsoring breakfasts, and flying the staff cross-country to traipse around the L.A. Convention Center's floors and eat catered lunches and dinners. The marketing VP was busy positioning our CEO as an "Internet visionary." It didn't matter that our chief hadn't worked in the industry before. "Well, I know he's not really a visionary now," she said, "but he will be." She wasn't being ironic; she was a believer. She repeated the "gonna work" mantra until the day she was laid off.

She snared our CEO a coveted spot on an Internet World panel discussion with other "visionaries." Fresh from that triumph, he returned to the office ready to spend. We went on a hiring spree, bringing in people by the dozen. Everyone was prepared to learn on the company dime. By June, we had about 100 people on the payroll and took over another floor in our office building. We signed a landmark portal deal that, we were told, would ensure our position as an industry leader. The price tag was $15 million—or $3 million more than the total amount of venture capital we had

raised. In return, the portal would give us links to our site and keyword-based advertising. In retrospect, it seems clear that we had spent too much for too little. But that reality could not penetrate the CEO's happy-happy armour. This was gonna work.

July–August

So, what were those 100 people doing? We weren't always sure. There was a lot of gazing at computer screens by people who weren't producing content. In the most egregious case, one bright and enthusiastic hire asked her new boss what she should do. His response? "Surf the net." Four months later, she was still surfing.

She made no secret or protest of this daily exercise. While many of her co-workers came to work in sweat pants, blue jeans, and T-shirts, this woman would arrive each day looking like an IBM corporate clone. Her clothes were freshly dry cleaned, her makeup flawless, her hair just so. What was she learning? Who knew? Formal reports and work products weren't part of the assignment. Her job was to keep surfing while her boss presumably was thinking of something for her to do.

By midsummer, the widespread lack of productivity was starting to show and our board of directors was getting antsy. It wanted to see revenue, and our senior management bristled at the board's nerve. Ignoring what the rest of the world already knew about the futility of banner ads on the web, the management team decided to put a significant focus on selling banners. We would spare no expense in hiring a team. After interviewing a parade of candidates eager to hit the lottery and snag the incredible six-figure base salary (plus commissions), we hired a sales executive from radio. She knew almost nothing about the Internet. But, we were told, she was a team player and had a positive outlook.

Three months and many costly business trips later, our ad sales manager had little to show for her efforts. This was due, in part, to the implausible sales team she assembled. Our New York City sales rep, for example, lived in Ocean City, Maryland, and had apparently never heard of Silicon Alley.

In the office, we began to wonder: Just when was this gonna work?

October

After a nerve-racking summer that saw many dot-com stocks begin to tank, fall arrived along with whispers of layoffs. Several senior staffers left the company, and I became addicted to dot-com "deadpool" sites, nervously scanning the growing lists of failed companies, wondering how much time we had. Round One of our layoffs came on Halloween. Imagine showing up for an office costume party and being handed your pink slip while dressed as a scarecrow. It happened at our firm.

Just six months after his triumphant coming-out party in LA, the CEO began to preside over a series of layoffs that reduced the company to a skeletal staff. Mine was a fitting end: I was laid off in a conference call on December 7th. I received an e-mail at home and was told to call a number at 5:30 p.m. It turned out to be a long-distance call. So adding insult to my lost dream of IPO riches, I had to pay to learn about my own layoff—they didn't even spring for a toll-free line to fire us.

In the end, it had taken only seven months to burn through most of our venture capital. The portal never got its $15 million, the company never went public, and I turned 30 without retiring. Not everyone faced the axe, however. The CEO and his inner circle survived, along with his confidence. He really believed that a company with no products to sell could still work.

Source: Naff, K.C. (2001, March 17). Diary of a dot-com casualty: No one told me I was nuts to take this job. *The Gazette* (Montreal), B1. Copyright Southam Publications Inc.

1. Do you think that the author of the case, Kevin Naff, used a rational decision model in choosing to work at the dot-com start-up? Did emotion affect his decision process?

2. Perceptual defence can work against proper problem identification. Can you find evidence of perceptual defence in the case?

3. Naff describes some rather extravagant spending at the start-up company. How would the flamboyant "visionary" CEO frame this spending to justify it? How would a conservative outside consultant frame the spending?

4. Is there evidence of groupthink in the case? If so, which symptoms are evident?

5. Is there escalation of commitment in the case? On whose part?

6. How do you think mood and emotion affected the events in the company?

7. Are there ethical issues in the case?

CHAPTER 12

Power, Politics, and Ethics

ENRON, WORLDCOM, AND ARTHUR ANDERSEN

When energy-trading giant Enron filed for bankruptcy in December 2001, it was the seventh-largest corporation in the United States. A firm that had been the darling of the investment community, and had been called America's most innovative company by *Fortune*, was gone with no apparent warning. What caused Enron's downfall? The house of cards collapsed when it was revealed that the firm had used shady accounting practices to hide over a billion dollars of debt and losses in outside firms that it had created. Transferring poor financial results to these partnership firms made it appear that Enron was in excellent financial health and allowed its stock price to soar. As such, executives got rich and investors were defrauded. In the end, rank-and-file employees, the vast majority of whom knew nothing about these partnership firms, suffered the most through the loss of their jobs, and, in many cases, the loss of their life savings.

On the heels of the Enron fiasco, the corporate world was floored by the news in June 2002 that WorldCom, the second-largest long distance telecommunications company in the United States, had used fraudulent accounting practices in misstating over $9 billion of expenses. WorldCom, with close to $110 billion in assets, became the largest bankruptcy in US history when it filed for Chapter 11 in July 2002. Millions of investors lost money, banks and suppliers were rocked, and 17 000 employees lost their jobs.

The fall of Enron and WorldCom also ensnared Arthur Andersen, the fifth-largest accounting firm in the United States until it was destroyed by the Enron mess. As Enron's external auditors, many questioned how Andersen could have approved these financial practices for years. Although the accounting firm stated it had been duped by Enron, it was revealed that it shredded thousands of documents relating to Enron between September and December 2001. Andersen was indicted on obstruction of justice charges in March 2002 and was found guilty that June. Andersen was also WorldCom's external auditor during their years of fraud. By the time the WorldCom indiscretions came to light, however, the accounting firm was already ruined.

As investigations into the unethical and illegal activities unfolded, it became clear that power, politics, and corporate cultures fuelled by greed

1400 Smith Street

Enron illustrates how the abuse of power and politics contributes to unethical corporate behaviour.

were an important part of the story. Enron had been a traditional energy company in the 1980s with regular assets such as oil pipelines. In the 1990s, Jeff Skilling was chosen by CEO Kenneth Lay to steer the company in a new direction. As Lay faded into the background, Skilling transformed Enron's business and culture, and the company sold off hard assets and entered the complicated business of energy trading. Enron went from a traditional energy company to the biggest e-commerce company in the United States. For several years, the wheeling and dealing paid off, and Enron executives became rich beyond their wildest dreams. Underlying the apparent success, however, was a corporate culture based on cutthroat competition, paranoia, and the relentless pursuit of profit. Skilling created an in-your-face culture in which positive results and growth were all that mattered. Those who preached fundamentals or suggested more traditional business approaches were labelled dinosaurs and were marginalized. Skilling also used political tactics and power to out-manoeuvre potential internal rivals. By December 2000, Skilling had surrounded himself with a team of yes-people, had wiped out all internal opponents, and collected his ultimate prize: promotion to the position of CEO, replacing Ken Lay, who stayed on as board chair. In Skilling's Enron, his right-hand man was CFO Andrew Fastow, another young shark who rose quickly and was not afraid to use bully tactics. Fastow set up and partially owned many of the partnership firms in which Enron hid its losses. It has been reported that Fastow made over $30 million from these partnerships and enriched family and friends along the way. By the second half of 2002, it became clear that Enron's fortune and success were mere illusions. Barely six months into his term as CEO, Skilling resigned, citing personal reasons. In November 2002, Fastow was charged in criminal court with fraud, money laundering, and conspiracy. More indictments followed in May 2003, including one for Fastow's wife. Fastow was convicted

Enron
www.enron.com

MCI (formerly WorldCom)
www.mci.com

and sentenced to 10 years in prison. Jeff Skilling and Ken Lay were indicted on fraud and insider trading charges and were convicted in 2006. Skilling faces life in prison and fines of up to $80 million. Lay died of a massive heart attack only weeks after his conviction. Among the most shocking revelations was that Enron executives cashed out $1.1 billion of stock from 1999 to 2001 before any trouble was disclosed to the public, and that Ken Lay continued to encourage employees to buy stock even after executive whistle-blower Sherron Watkins had warned him of the fraudulent practices.

The story of WorldCom also features a powerful, maverick CEO and an accounting whiz kid out of control. Canadian-born Bernard Ebbers, WorldCom's CEO until he was forced out in April 2002, had built the company through a dizzying number of acquisitions and big deals, the biggest of which was the acquisition of MCI in 1997. His right-hand man was CFO Scott Sullivan, who navigated all of the financial deals. Two reports released in June 2003 underline a culture of greed at WorldCom in which positive results were the only concern, and a corporate environment in which no one would ever question the powerful Ebbers or Sullivan. In August 2002, Sullivan was arrested on federal fraud charges and pleaded guilty in March 2004. Ebbers was charged in federal court on fraud and conspiracy charges, was found guilty in March 2005, and received a 25-year prison sentence. WorldCom received a $750 million fine for its false accounting reports. In 2004, it emerged from bankruptcy under the MCI name and was acquired by Verizon in 2006.

In the case of Andersen, many point to the $1 million per week for auditing and the $27 million in consulting revenue that the accounting firm received from Enron as the reason they did not stop the questionable practices. Information has also surfaced about the culture of greed within the accounting firm in which income apparently overruled the obligation to be impartial and vigilant.

In all, three once-respected firms have been destroyed, public confidence in corporations and entities designed to stop fraud has been shaken, and millions of people have been adversely affected by these scandals in very concrete ways. Not the most promising start for business in the 21st century.[1]

This vignette illustrates the main themes of this chapter—power, politics, and ethics. First, we will define power and discuss the bases of individual power. Then we will examine how people get and use power and who seeks it. After this, we will explore how organizational subunits, such as particular departments, obtain power, define organizational politics, and explore the relationship of politics to power. Finally, we will look at ethics in organizations and sexual harassment.

At one time, power and politics were not considered polite topics for coverage in organizational behaviour textbooks. At best, they were seen as irrational and, at worst, as evil. Now, though, organizational scholars recognize what managers have known all along—that power and politics are *natural* expressions of life in organizations. They often develop as a rational response to a complex set of needs and goals, and their expression can be beneficial. However, they can also put a strain on ethical standards, as was the case at Enron and WorldCom.

WHAT IS POWER?

Power is the capacity to influence others who are in a state of dependence. First, notice that power is the *capacity* to influence the behaviour of others. Power is not always perceived or exercised.[2] For example, most professors hold a great degree of potential power over students in terms of grades, assignment load, and the ability to embarrass students in class. Under normal circumstances, professors use only a small amount of this power.

Second, the fact that the target of power is dependent on the powerholder does not imply that a poor relationship exists between the two. For instance, your best friend has power to influence your behaviour and attitudes because you are dependent on him or her for friendly reactions and social support. Presumably, you can exert reciprocal influence for similar reasons.

Third, power can flow in any direction in an organization. Often, members at higher organizational levels have more power than those at lower levels. However, in specific cases, reversals can occur. For example, the janitor who finds the president in a compromising position with a secretary might find himself in a powerful position if the president wishes to maintain his reputation in the organization!

Finally, power is a broad concept that applies to both individuals and groups. On the one hand, an individual production manager might exert considerable influence over the supervisors who report to her. On the other, the marketing department at XYZ Foods might be the most powerful department in the company, able to get its way more often than other departments. But from where do the production manager and the marketing department obtain their power? We explore this issue in the following sections. First, we consider individual bases of power. Then we examine how organizational subunits, such as the marketing department, obtain power.

Power. The capacity to influence others who are in a state of dependence.

THE BASES OF INDIVIDUAL POWER

If you wanted to marshal some power to influence others in your organization, where would you get it? As psychologists John French and Bertram Raven explained, power can be found in the *position* that you occupy in the organization or the *resources* that you are able to command.[3] The first base of power—legitimate power—is dependent on one's position or job. The other bases (reward, coercive, referent, and expert power) involve the control of important resources. If other organizational members do not respect your position or value the resources that you command, they will not be dependent on you, and you will lack the power to influence them.

Legitimate Power

Legitimate power derives from a person's position or job in the organization. It constitutes the organization's judgment about who is formally permitted to influence whom, and it is often called authority. As we move up the organization's hierarchy, we find that members possess more and more legitimate power. In theory, organizational equals (e.g., all vice-presidents) have equal legitimate power. Of course, some people are more likely than others to *invoke* their legitimate power—"Look, *I'm* the boss around here."

Organizations differ greatly in the extent to which they emphasize and reinforce legitimate power. At one extreme is the military, which has many levels of command, differentiating uniforms, and rituals (e.g., salutes), all designed to emphasize legitimate power. On the other hand, the academic hierarchy of universities tends to downplay differences in the legitimate power of lecturers, professors, chairpeople, and deans.

When legitimate power works, it often does so because people have been socialized to accept its influence. Experiences with parents, teachers, and law enforcement officials cause members to enter organizations with a degree of readiness to submit to (and

Legitimate power. Power derived from a person's position or job in an organization.

exercise) legitimate power. In fact, studies consistently show that employees cite legitimate power as a major reason for following their boss's directives, even across various cultures.[4] This is one reason why juries failed to believe that Skilling and Lay were "out of the loop" in the Enron fiasco.

Reward Power

Reward power. Power derived from the ability to provide positive outcomes and prevent negative outcomes.

Reward power means that the powerholder can exert influence by providing positive outcomes and preventing negative outcomes. In general, it corresponds to the concept of positive reinforcement discussed in Chapter 2. Reward power often backs up legitimate power. That is, managers are given the chance to recommend raises, do performance evaluations, and assign preferred tasks to employees. Of course, *any* organizational member can attempt to exert influence over others with praise, compliments, and flattery, which also constitute rewards.

At Enron, those who bought into Jeff Skilling's vision for the company were well rewarded. Many became rich beyond their wildest dreams. Lavish parties, exclusive clubs, and special privileges for managers and their families were available for those who went along with the change of direction. Around Houston, the company's home base, Porsches became known as Enron's company car.

Coercive Power

Coercive power. Power derived from the use of punishment and threat.

Coercive power is available when the powerholder can exert influence using punishment and threat. Like reward power, it is often a support for legitimate power. Managers might be permitted to dock pay, assign unfavourable tasks, or block promotions. Despite a strong civil service system, even US government agencies provide their executives with plenty of coercive power. At Enron, while employees who followed Jeff Skilling's cultural shift were rewarded, the consequences for those who did not were very unpleasant. Executives who clashed with Skilling were shipped off to other departments, sometimes overseas, and all managers faced regular performance reviews that could be particularly brutal. In fact, after every review, the bottom 15 percent would be fired immediately.

Of course, coercive power is not perfectly correlated with legitimate power. Lower-level organizational members can also apply their share of coercion. For example, consider work-to-rule campaigns that slow productivity by adhering religiously to organizational procedures. Cohesive work groups are especially skilful at enforcing such campaigns.

In Chapter 2, we pointed out that the use of punishment to control behaviour is very problematic because of emotional side effects. Thus, it is not surprising that when managers use coercive power, it is generally ineffective and can provoke considerable employee resistance.[5]

Referent Power

Referent power. Power derived from being well liked by others.

Referent power exists when the powerholder is *well liked* by others. It is not surprising that people we like readily influence us. We are prone to consider their points of view, ignore their failures, seek their approval, and use them as role models. In fact, it is often highly dissonant to hold a point of view that is discrepant from that held by someone we like.[6]

Referent power is especially potent for two reasons. First, it stems from *identification* with the powerholder. Thus, it represents a truer or deeper base of power than reward or coercion, which may stimulate mere compliance to achieve rewards or avoid punishment. In this sense, charismatic leaders (Chapter 9) have referent power. Second, *anyone* in the organization may be well liked, irrespective of his or her other bases of power. Thus, referent power is available to everyone from the janitor to the president.

Friendly interpersonal relations often permit influence to extend across the organization, outside the usual channels of legitimate authority, reward, and coercion. For example, a production manager who becomes friendly with the design engineer through participation in a task force might later use this contact to ask for a favour in solving a production problem.

Expert Power

A person has **expert power** when he or she has special information or expertise that the organization values. In any circumstance, we tend to be influenced by experts or by those who perform their jobs well. However, the more crucial and unusual this expertise, the greater is the expert power available. Thus, expert power corresponds to difficulty of replacement. Consider the business school that has one highly published professor who is an internationally known scholar and past federal cabinet minister. Such a person would obviously be difficult to replace and should have much greater expert power than an unpublished lecturer.

One of the most fascinating aspects of expert power occurs when lower-level organizational members accrue it. Many secretaries have acquired expert power through long experience in dealing with clients, keeping records, or sparring with the bureaucracy. Frequently, they have been around longer than those they serve. In this case, it is not unusual for bosses to create special titles and develop new job classifications to reward their expertise and prevent their resignation.

Expert power is especially common among lower-level members in scientific and technical areas. Consider the solid-state physicist who has just completed her Ph.D. dissertation on a topic of particular interest to her new employer. Although new to the firm, she might have considerable expert power. Put simply, she *knows* more than her boss, whose scientific knowledge in this area is now outdated.

Expert power is a valuable asset for managers. Of all the bases of power, expertise is most consistently associated with employee effectiveness.[7] Also, research shows that employees perceive women managers as more likely than male managers to be high in expert power.[8] Women often lack easy access to more organizationally based forms of power, and expertise is free for self-development. Thus, being "better" than their male counterparts is one strategy that women managers have used to gain influence.

Exhibit 12.1 summarizes likely employee responses to various bases of managerial power. As you can see, coercion is likely to produce resistance and lack of cooperation. Legitimate power and reward power are likely to produce compliance with the boss's wishes. Referent and expert power are most likely to generate true commitment and enthusiasm for the manager's agenda.

Expert power. Power derived from having special information or expertise that is valued by an organization.

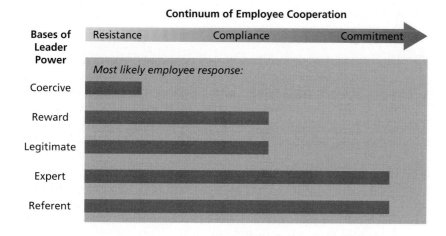

EXHIBIT 12.1
Employee responses to bases of power.

Source: Steers, R.M., & Black, J.S. (1994). *Organizational behavior* (5th ed). New York: HarperCollins.

HOW DO PEOPLE OBTAIN POWER?

Now that we have discussed the individual bases of power, we can turn to the issue of how people *get* power—that is, how do organizational members obtain promotions to positions of legitimate power, demonstrate their expertise, and get others to like them? And how do they acquire the ability to provide others with rewards and punishment? Rosabeth Moss Kanter, an organizational sociologist, has provided some succinct answers: Do the right things, and cultivate the right people.[9]

Doing the Right Things

According to Kanter, some activities are "righter" than others for obtaining power. She argues that activities lead to power when they are extraordinary, highly visible, and especially relevant to the solution of organizational problems.

Extraordinary Activities. Excellent performance of a routine job might not be enough to obtain power. What one needs is excellent performance in *unusual* or *nonroutine* activities. In the large company that Kanter studied, these activities included occupying new positions, managing substantial changes, and taking great risks. For example, consider the manager who establishes and directs a new customer service program. This is a risky, major change that involves the occupancy of a new position. If successful, the manager should acquire substantial power.

Visible Activities. Extraordinary activities will fail to generate power if no one knows about them. People who have an interest in power are especially good at identifying visible activities and publicizing them. The successful marketing executive whose philosophy is profiled in *Fortune* will reap the benefits of power. Similarly, the innovative surgeon whose techniques are reported in the *New England Journal of Medicine* will enhance her influence in the hospital.

Relevant Activities. Extraordinary, visible work may fail to generate power if no one cares. If nobody sees the work as relevant to the solution of important organizational problems, it will not add to one's influence. The English professor who wins two Pulitzer Prizes will probably not accrue much power if his small college is financially strapped and hurting for students. He would not be seen as contributing to the solution of pressing organizational problems. In another college, these extraordinary, visible activities might generate considerable influence.

Cultivating the Right People

An old saying advises, "It's not what you know, it's *who* you know." In reference to power in organizations, there is probably more than a grain of truth to the latter part of this statement. Kanter explains that developing informal relationships with the right people can prove a useful means of acquiring power.

Outsiders. Establishing good relationships with key people outside one's organization can lead to increased power within the organization. Sometimes this power is merely a reflection of the status of the outsider, but all the same, it may add to one's internal influence. The assistant director of a hospital who is friendly with the president of the American Medical Association might find herself holding power by association. Cultivating outsiders may also contribute to more tangible sources of power. Organizational members who are on the boards of directors of other companies might acquire critical information about business conditions that they can use in their own firms. Enron cultivated strong political ties in Washington through large contributions to political parties. Although they were abandoned by political friends once the problems were revealed, many suggest that their contacts allowed them to operate with little oversight and to gain many favours over the years.

Subordinates. At first blush, it might seem unlikely that power can be enhanced by cultivating relationships with subordinates. However, as Kanter notes, an individual can gain influence if she is closely identified with certain up-and-coming subordinates—"I taught her everything she knows." In academics, some professors are better known for the brilliant Ph.D. students they have supervised than for their own published work. Of course, there is also the possibility that an outstanding subordinate will one day become one's boss! Having cultivated the relationship earlier, one might then be rewarded with special influence.

Cultivating subordinate interests can also provide power when a manager can demonstrate that he or she is backed by a cohesive team. The research director who can oppose a policy change by honestly insisting that "My people won't stand for this" knows that there is strength in numbers.

At Enron, a team of key subordinates helped Jeff Skilling advance his vision for the firm and build his internal empire. As a result, these subordinates were given a very long leash and a great deal of power for themselves. In the end, these powerful subordinates were allowed to operate with little oversight, which eventually led to the ethical lapses.

Peers. Cultivating good relationships with peers is mainly a means of ensuring that nothing gets in the way of one's *future* acquisition of power. As one moves up through the ranks, favours can be asked of former associates, and fears of being "stabbed in the back" for a past misdeed are precluded. Organizations often reward good "team players" with promotions on the assumption that they have demonstrated good interpersonal skills. On the other side of the coin, people often avoid contact with peers whose reputation is seen as questionable.

Superiors. Liaisons with key superiors probably represent the best way of obtaining power through cultivating others. As we discussed in Chapter 8, such superiors are often called *mentors* or *sponsors* because of the special interest they show in a promising subordinate. Mentors can provide power in several ways. Obviously, it is useful to be identified as a protégé of someone higher in the organization. More concretely, mentors can provide special information and useful introductions to other "right people."

EMPOWERMENT—PUTTING POWER WHERE IT IS NEEDED

Early organizational scholars treated power as something of a fixed quantity: An organization had so much, the people on the top had a lot, and lower-level employees had a little. Our earlier analysis of the more informal sources of power (such as being liked and being an expert) hints at the weakness of this idea. Thus, contemporary views of power treat it less as a fixed-sum phenomenon. This is best seen in the concept of **empowerment,** which means giving people the authority, opportunity, and motivation to take initiative to solve organizational problems.[10]

In practice, having the authority to solve an organizational problem means having legitimate power. This might be included in a job description, or a boss might delegate it to a subordinate.

Having opportunity usually means freedom from bureaucratic barriers and other system problems that block initiative. In a service encounter, if you have ever heard "Sorry, the computer won't let me do that" or "that's not my job," you have been the victim of limited opportunity. Opportunity also includes any relevant training and information about the impact of one's actions on other parts of the organization.

The motivation part of the empowerment equation suggests hiring people who will be intrinsically motivated by power and opportunity and aligning extrinsic rewards

Empowerment. Giving people the authority, opportunity, and motivation to take initiative and solve organizational problems.

"… *Don't think of this as your cubicle, think of it as an empowerment zone* …"

with successful performance. Also, leaders who express confidence in subordinates' abilities (especially transformational leaders, Chapter 9) can contribute to empowerment. A good example occurred when a nay-saying union shop steward, doubting General Electric's commitment to changing its corporate culture, explained a recurrent problem with a supplier's component. His manager, sensing he was correct, chartered a plane, and the subordinate left that same night to visit the supplier and solve the problem.[11] It goes without saying that managers have to be tolerant of occasional mistakes from empowered employees.

In Chapter 2, we discussed self-efficacy in the context of social cognitive theory. People who are empowered have a strong sense of self-efficacy, the feeling that they are capable of doing their jobs well and "making things happen." Empowering lower-level employees can be critical in service organizations, where providing customers with a good initial encounter or correcting any problems that develop can be essential for repeat business. The Nordstrom chain of stores is one firm that is known for empowering sales personnel to make on-the-spot adjustments or search out merchandise at other stores. Customers have even had enthusiastic store personnel change flat tires. This dedication to customer service enables Nordstrom to spend only a fraction of the industry average on advertising.

There is growing evidence that empowerment fosters job satisfaction and high performance.[12] However, empowerment does not mean providing employees with a maximum amount of unfettered power. Rather, used properly, empowerment puts power where it is *needed* to make the organization effective. This depends on organizational strategy and customer expectations. The average Taco Bell customer does not expect highly empowered counter personnel who offer to make adjustments to the posted menu—a friendly, fast, efficient encounter will do. On the other hand, the unempowered waiter in a fancy restaurant who is fearful of accommodating reasonable adjustments and substitutions can really irritate customers. Speaking generally, service encounters predicated on high volume and low cost need careful engineering. Those predicated on customized, personalized service need more empowered personnel.[13] For a good example of this, see "Applied Focus: *Delta Hotels Focuses on Empowerment.*"

General Electric
www.ge.com

Nordstrom
www.nordstrom.com

Delta Hotels and Resorts
www.deltahotels.com

APPLIED FOCUS

Delta Hotels Focuses on Empowerment

Delta Hotels is one of Canada's largest hotel companies, with 39 locations and over 7000 employees. When the company decided to make quality the core of its strategy in the mid-1990s, management felt they needed to get employees involved in a concrete way. In an industry traditionally characterized by high turnover and a diverse workforce, often with little formal hospitality training, the challenge was daunting. But Delta's management team understood that frontline employees are better placed to understand and respond to the needs of hotel guests than vice-presidents sitting in boardrooms at the head office in Toronto.

As such, Delta Hotels established a formal empowerment program called Power to Please. "We educate our frontline troops that empowerment is key," comments William Pallett, Delta's senior vice-president of people, resources, and quality. "Employees have to feel they're contributing." Staff at Delta Hotels have the authority to handle special guest requests without seeking manager approval, deal with customer complaints on the spot, and have input on how they fulfill their tasks. For example, staff can handle requests for extra towels or more coffee directly, housekeepers have input on the type of cleaning products the hotel uses, and a front desk staffer can take it upon him or herself to send up a platter from room service following a guest complaint. For Pallett, the important thing is "people gaining a little more control over their work area and having a say and being included in the decision-making. People feel they have an impact on the outcome of the business."

From their first day with the company, Delta employees are repeatedly reminded that what they think counts and that the success of the company is in their hands. The hotel holds departmental and town hall meetings, has problem-solving teams, and encourages one-on-one discussions between managers and staff to ensure that staffers' voices are heard and that they get the feedback they need. The Power to Please program is supported by extensive training and innovative compensation practices. Training on employee empowerment also extends to managers. A successful manager at Delta, according to Pallett, is one who empowers his or her employees; managers who take a command-and-control approach don't last at Delta.

The results for Delta Hotels have been impressive. In 2000, they were the first-ever hotel to receive the prestigious National Quality Institute's (NQI) Canada Award for Excellence, an award they won again in 2004. The company was recognized as one of "The 50 Best Employers in Canada" by *Report on Business* in 2001, 2002, 2003, and 2005. For Pallett, empowering employees is good for their well-being and good for the company's bottom line: "Being concerned and proactive, empowering your workforce and ensuring you have a healthy workplace is good for business. Employee satisfaction drives guest satisfaction. With high customer loyalty and satisfaction, you should be doing pretty well on the revenue side."

Sources: Lowe, E. (2005, October). Response-ability and the Power to Please: Delta Hotels. *Social Innovations*, 7–8, Retrieved July 12, 2006, from the Vanier Institute of the Family website: http://www.vifamily.ca/library/social/delta.html (Pallett quotes); Anonymous (2004). Happy employees put Delta in the honors. *Human Resource Management International Digest, 12,* 32–34; Pallett, W.J., Taylor, W.W., & Jayawardena, C. (2003). People and quality: The case of Delta Hotels. *International Journal of Contemporary Hospitality Management, 15,* 349–351; Social Development Canada (2001). *Organizational profiles: Delta Hotels.* Retrieved July 10, 2006, from http://www.sdc.gc.ca/asp/gateway.asp?hr=/en/lp/spila/wlb/ell/06delta_hotels.shtml&hs=wnc

You might wonder whether organizational members could have *too much* power. Exhibit 12.2 nicely illustrates the answer. People are empowered, and should exhibit effective performance, when they have sufficient power to carry out their jobs. Above, we mainly contrasted empowerment with situations in which people had inadequate power for effective performance. However, as the exhibit shows, excessive power can lead to abuse and ineffective performance. One is reminded of the recurrent and inappropriate use of government aircraft by political bigwigs as an example. As we will see in the following sections, the fact that people can have too much power does not always inhibit them from seeking it anyway!

INFLUENCE TACTICS—PUTTING POWER TO WORK

Influence tactics. Tactics that are used to convert power into actual influence over others.

As we discussed earlier, power is the potential to influence others. But exactly how does power result in influence? Research has shown that various **influence tactics** convert power into actual influence. These are specific behaviours that powerholders use to affect others.[14] These tactics include the following:

- Assertiveness—ordering, nagging, setting deadlines, and verbal confrontation;
- Ingratiation—using flattery and acting friendly, polite, or humble;
- Rationality—using logic, reason, planning, and compromise;
- Exchange—doing favours or offering to trade favours;
- Upward appeal—making formal or informal appeals to organizational superiors for intervention; and
- Coalition formation—seeking united support from other organizational members.

What determines which influence tactics you might use? For one thing, your bases of power.[15] Other things being equal, someone with coercive power might gravitate toward assertiveness, someone with referent power might gravitate toward ingratiation, and someone with expert power might try rationality. Of course, rationality or its appearance is a highly prized quality in organizations, and its use is viewed positively by others. Thus, surveys show that people report trying to use rationality very frequently.

As you can guess, the use of influence tactics is also dependent on just whom you are trying to influence—subordinates, peers, or superiors. Subordinates are more likely to be the recipients of assertiveness than peers or superiors. Despite the general popularity of rationality, it is most likely to be directed toward superiors. Exchange, ingratiation, and upward appeal are favoured tactics for influencing both peers and subordinates.[16]

EXHIBIT 12.2
Relationship between power and performance.

Source: Adapted from Whetten, D.A., & Cameron, K.S. (1995). *Developing management skills*. New York: HarperCollins.

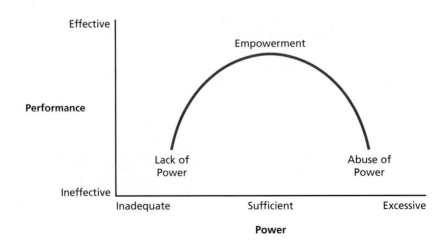

Which influence tactics are most effective? Some of the most interesting research has concerned upward influence attempts directed toward superiors. It shows that, at least for men, using rationality as an influence tactic was associated with receiving better performance evaluations, earning more money, and experiencing less work stress. A particularly ineffective influence style is a "shotgun" style that is high on all tactics with particular emphasis on assertiveness and exchange. In this series of studies, women who used ingratiation as an influence tactic received the highest performance evaluations (from male managers).[17]

WHO WANTS POWER?

Who wants power? At first glance, the answer would seem to be everybody. After all, it is both convenient and rewarding to be able to exert influence over others. Power whisks celebrities to the front of movie lines, gets rock stars the best restaurant tables, and enables executives to shape organizations in their own image. Actually, there are considerable individual differences in the extent to which individuals pursue and enjoy power. On television talk shows, we occasionally see celebrities recount considerable embarrassment over the unwarranted power that public recognition brings.

Earlier we indicated that some people consider power a manifestation of evil. This is due, in no small part, to the historic image of power seekers that some psychologists and political scientists have portrayed. This is that power seekers are neurotics who are covering up feelings of inferiority, striving to compensate for childhood deprivation, or substituting power for lack of affection.[18]

There can be little doubt that these characteristics do apply to some power seekers. Underlying this negative image of power seeking is the idea that some power seekers feel weak and resort primarily to coercive power to cover up, compensate for, or substitute for this weakness. Power is sought for its own sake and is used irresponsibly to hurt others. Adolf Hitler comes to mind as an extreme example.

But can one use power responsibly to influence others? Psychologist David McClelland says yes. In Chapter 5, we discussed McClelland's research on need for power (n Pow). You will recall that n Pow is the need to have strong influence over others. This need is a reliable personality characteristic—some people have more n Pow than others.[19] Also, just as many women have high n Pow as men.[20] People who are high in n Pow in its "pure" form conform to the negative stereotype depicted above—they are rude, sexually exploitative, abuse alcohol, and show a great concern with status symbols. However, when n Pow is responsible and controlled, these negative properties are not observed. Specifically, McClelland argues that the most effective managers

- have high n Pow;
- use their power to achieve organizational goals;
- adopt a participative or "coaching" leadership style; and
- are relatively unconcerned with how much others like them.

McClelland calls such managers *institutional managers* because they use their power for the good of the institution rather than for self-aggrandizement. They refrain from coercive leadership but do not play favourites, since they are not worried about being well liked. His research reveals that institutional managers are more effective than *personal power managers*, who use their power for personal gain, and *affiliative managers*, who are more concerned with being liked than with exercising power. Exhibit 12.3 shows that institutional managers are generally superior in giving subordinates a sense of responsibility, clarifying organizational priorities, and instilling team spirit.[21] We can conclude that the need for power can be a useful asset, as long as it is not a neurotic expression of perceived weakness.

EXHIBIT 12.3
Responses of
subordinates of
managers with different
motive profiles.

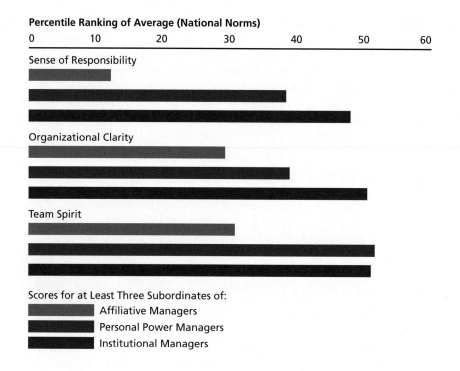

Percentile Ranking of Average (National Norms)

Scores for at Least Three Subordinates of:
Affiliative Managers
Personal Power Managers
Institutional Managers

Finally, what happens when people want power but cannot get it because they are locked in a low-level job or faced with excessive rules and regulations? People react to such powerlessness by trying to gain control, but if they cannot succeed, they feel helpless and become alienated from their work.[22] This is something that empowerment is designed to prevent.

CONTROLLING STRATEGIC CONTINGENCIES— HOW SUBUNITS OBTAIN POWER

Thus far, we have been concerned with the bases of *individual* power and how individual organizational members obtain influence. In this section, we shift our concern to **subunit power**. Most straightforwardly, the term subunit applies to organizational departments. In some cases, subunits could also refer to particular jobs, such as those held by software engineers or environmental lawyers.

How do organizational subunits acquire power—that is, how do they achieve influence that enables them to grow in size, get a bigger share of the budget, obtain better facilities, and have greater impact on decisions? In short, they control **strategic contingencies**, which are critical factors affecting organizational effectiveness. This means that the work *other* subunits perform is contingent on the activities and performance of a key subunit. Again, we see the critical role of *dependence* in power relationships. If some subunits are dependent on others for smooth operations (or their very existence), they are susceptible to influence. We turn now to the conditions under which subunits can control strategic contingencies.

Subunit power. The degree of power held by various organizational subunits, such as departments.

Strategic contingencies. Critical factors affecting organizational effectiveness that are controlled by a key subunit.

Scarcity

Differences in subunit power are likely to be magnified when resources become scarce.[23] When there is plenty of budget money or office space or support staff for all subunits, they will seldom waste their energies jockeying for power. If cutbacks occur, however, differences in power will become apparent. For example, well-funded quality-of-worklife programs or organizational development efforts might disappear when economic setbacks occur because the subunits that control them are not essential to the firm's existence.

Subunits tend to acquire power when they are able to *secure* scarce resources that are important to the organization as a whole. One study of a large state university found that the power of academic departments was associated with their ability to obtain funds through consulting contracts and research grants. This mastery over economic resources was more crucial to their power than was the number of undergraduates taught by the department.[24]

Uncertainty

Organizations detest the unknown. Unanticipated events wreak havoc with financial commitments, long-range plans, and tomorrow's operations. The basic sources of uncertainty exist mainly in the organization's environment—government policies might change, sources of supply and demand might dry up, or the economy might take an unanticipated turn. It stands to reason that the subunits that are most capable of coping with uncertainty will tend to acquire power.[25] In a sense, these subunits are able to protect the others from serious problems. By the same token, uncertainty promotes confusion, which permits *changes* in power priorities as the organizational environment changes. Those functions that can provide the organization with greater control over what it finds problematic and can create more certainty will acquire more power.[26]

Changes in the sources of uncertainty frequently lead to shifts in subunit power. Thus, centralized mainframe-oriented IT departments lost power with the advent of PC-based distributed computing, and HR departments gained power when government legislation regarding employment opportunity was first passed. Units dealing with business ethics or environmental concerns gain or lose power in response to the latest scandal or the newest piece of legislation involving clean air or water.

Centrality

Other things being equal, subunits whose activities are most central to the work flow of the organization should acquire more power than those whose activities are more peripheral.[27] A subunit's activities can be central in at least three senses. First, they may influence the work of most other subunits. The finance or accounting department is a good example here—its authority to approve expenses and make payments affects every other department in the firm.

Centrality also exists when a subunit has an especially crucial impact on the quantity or quality of the organization's key product or service. This is one reason for the former low power of human resources departments—their activities were then seen as fairly remote from the primary goals of the organization.

Finally, a subunit's activities are more central when their impact is more immediate. As an example, consider a large city government that includes a fire department, a police department, and a public works department. The impact of a lapse in fire or police services will be felt more immediately than a lapse in street repairs. This gives the former departments more potential for power acquisition.

Substitutability

A subunit will have relatively little power if others inside or outside the organization can perform its activities. If the subunit's staff is nonsubstitutable, however, it can acquire substantial power.[28] One crucial factor here is the labour market for the specialty performed by the subunit. A change in the labour market can result in a change in the subunit's influence. For example, the market for scientists and engineers is notoriously cyclical. When jobs are plentiful, these professionals command high salaries and high influence in organizations. When jobs are scarce, this power wanes. In the 1990s there was a shortage of engineers and scientists, with a consequent increase in their bargaining power. Precisely in line with the strategic contingencies idea, this shortage provided real opportunities for properly trained women and members of minorities to move into positions of power from which they were excluded when there were plenty of white male engineers and scientists to go around.[29]

If the labour market is constant, subunits whose staff is highly trained in technical areas tend to be less substitutable than those which involve minimal technical expertise. For example, in a telecommunications company, managers can fill in for striking telephone operators, but not for highly trained IT personnel.

Finally, if work can be contracted out, the power of the subunit that usually performs these activities is reduced. Typical examples include temporary office help, off-premises data entry, and contracted maintenance, laboratory, and security services. The subunits that control these activities often lack power because the threat of "going outside" can counter their influence attempts.

For an example of changing power priorities, see "Research Focus: *Technology-Mediated Learning Shifts Subunit Power*."

ORGANIZATIONAL POLITICS—USING AND ABUSING POWER

In the previous pages, we have avoided using the terms *politics* or *political* in describing the acquisition and use of power. This is because not all uses of power constitute politics.

RESEARCH FOCUS

Technology-Mediated Learning Shifts Subunit Power

Researchers Maryam Alavi and Brent Gallupe studied the use of technology-mediated learning (TML) in business and management education programs at Duke University, Ohio University, Wake Forest University, UCLA, and the University of Phoenix Online Campus. The various programs either use distance learning or offer intensive "laptop environments." In the words of the researchers, here is how TML changes the balance of power:

TML initiatives lead to change. Most institutions did not anticipate the degree of change involved. On the administrative side, TML projects change administrative responsibilities and power relationships. For example, the technology support group that might have little power before the TML initiative now may have substantial influence not only in the way the technology infrastructure is set up and maintained, but also in the delivery of programs and courses. Meanwhile, on the teaching side, the TML initiative may dramatically change the role of the instructor from the primary source of knowledge to a facilitator for student knowledge acquisition. This can be challenging to students and teachers alike. It must be recognized that this is a major cultural change for teachers who have themselves been taught using a particular method, only to find that this method no longer applies. Some will be able to adapt and some may experience great difficulties. On the students' side, TML initiatives give students much more power. Using the technology and services available to them, they now can access knowledge more quickly and easily than ever before. No longer do they rely solely on instructors as the "knowledge providers." They can bring to class, or to the course Web site, information that the instructor and other students have never seen before.

Source: Excerpted from Alavi, M., & Gallupe, R.B. (2003, June). Using information technology in learning: Case studies in business and management education programs. *Academy of Management Learning and Education*, p. 152.

The Basics of Organizational Politics

Organizational politics is the pursuit of self-interest within an organization, whether or not this self-interest corresponds to organizational goals.[30] Frequently, politics involves using means of influence that the organization does not sanction or pursuing ends or goals that are not sanctioned by the organization.[31]

We should make several preliminary points about organizational politics. First, political activity is self-conscious and intentional. This separates politics from ignorance or lack of experience with approved means and ends. Second, implicit in all but the mildest examples of politics is the idea of resistance, the idea that political influence would be countered if detected by those with different agendas. Third, we can conceive of politics as either individual activity or subunit activity. Either a person or a whole department could act politically. Finally, it is possible for political activity to have beneficial outcomes for the organization, even though these outcomes are achieved by questionable tactics.

We can explore organizational politics using the means/ends matrix in Exhibit 12.4. It is the association between influence means and influence ends that determines whether activities are political and whether these activities benefit the organization.

- *I. Sanctioned means/sanctioned ends.* Here, power is used routinely to pursue agreed-on goals. Familiar, accepted means of influence are employed to achieve sanctioned outcomes. For example, a manager agrees to recommend a raise for an employee if she increases her net sales by 30 percent in the next six months. There is nothing political about this.

- *II. Sanctioned means/nonsanctioned ends.* In this case, acceptable means of influence are abused to pursue goals that the organization does not approve. For instance, a head nurse agrees to assign a subordinate nurse to a more favourable job if the nurse agrees not to report the superior for stealing medical supplies. While job assignment is often a sanctioned means of influence, covering up theft is not a sanctioned end. This is dysfunctional political behaviour.

- *III. Nonsanctioned means/sanctioned ends.* Here, ends that are useful for the organization are pursued through questionable means. For example, although officials of the Salt Lake City Olympic Committee were pursuing a sanctioned end—the 2002 Winter Olympics—the use of bribery and vote-buying as a means of influence was not sanctioned by the Committee.

- *IV. Nonsanctioned means/nonsanctioned ends.* This quadrant may exemplify the most flagrant abuse of power, since disapproved tactics are used to pursue disapproved outcomes. For example, to increase his personal power, the head of an already overstaffed legal department wishes to increase its size. He intends to hire several of his friends in the process. To do this, he falsifies workload documents and promises special service to the accounting department in exchange for the support of its manager.

Organizational politics.
The pursuit of self-interest in an organization, whether or not this self-interest corresponds to organizational goals.

Influence Ends

Influence Means	Organizationally Sanctioned	Not Sanctioned by Organization
Organizationally Sanctioned	Nonpolitical Job Behaviour **I**	**II** Organizationally Dysfunctional Political Behaviour
Not Sanctioned by Organization	Political Behaviour Potentially Functional to the Organization **III**	**IV** Organizationally Dysfunctional Political Behaviour

EXHIBIT 12.4
The dimensions of organizational politics.

Source: From Mayes, B.T., & Allen, R.T. (1977). Toward a definition of organizational politics, *Academy of Management Review, 2,* 672–678, p. 675. Reprinted by permission.

We have all seen cases in which politics have been played out publicly to "teach someone a lesson." More frequently, though, politicians conceal their activities with a "cover story" or "smoke screen" to make them appear legitimate.[32] Such a tactic will increase the odds of success and avoid punishment from superiors. A common strategy is to cover nonsanctioned means and ends with a cloak of rationality.

Do political activities occur under particular conditions or in particular locations in organizations? Research suggests the following:[33]

- Managers report that most political manoeuvring occurs among middle and upper management levels rather than at lower levels.

- Some subunits are more prone to politicking than others. Clear goals and routine tasks (e.g., production) might provoke less political activity than vague goals and complex tasks (e.g., research and development).

- Some issues are more likely than others to stimulate political activity. Budget allocation, reorganization, and personnel changes are likely to be the subjects of politicking. Setting performance standards and purchasing equipment are not.

- In general, scarce resources, uncertainty, and important issues provoke political behaviour.

Highly political climates result in lowered job satisfaction, lowered feelings of organizational support, and increased turnover intentions.[34] When it comes to performance, evidence indicates that politics take a toll on older workers but not younger workers, perhaps due to stress factors.[35]

At Enron, the upper management echelons were steeped in organizational politics. Jeff Skilling's strongest rival at the firm was Rebecca Mark, another hotshot brought in by Ken Lay who became known as one of America's most powerful women in business. Skilling used political tactics to outmanoeuvre and undercut Mark at every turn. In the end, he received the ultimate reward when he was named as Lay's replacement.

The Facets of Political Skill

It is one thing to engage in organizational politics, but it is another thing to do it skilfully, because pursuing self-interest can encounter resistance. Gerald Ferris and colleagues define **political skill** as "the ability to understand others at work and to use that knowledge to influence others to act in ways that enhance one's personal or organizational objectives."[36] Notice that this definition includes two aspects—comprehending others and translating this comprehension into influence. Research by Ferris and colleagues indicates that there are four facets to political skill:

- *Social astuteness*. Good politicians are careful observers who are tuned in to others' needs and motives. They can "read" people and thus possess emotional intelligence, as discussed in Chapter 5. They are active self-monitors (Chapter 2) who know how to present themselves to others.

- *Interpersonal influence*. The politically skilled have a convincing and persuasive interpersonal style but employ it flexibly to meet the needs of the situation. They put others at ease.

- *Apparent sincerity*. Influence attempts will be seen as manipulative unless they are accompanied by sincerity. A good politician comes across as genuine and exhibits high integrity.

- *Networking ability*. **Networking** involves establishing good relations with key organizational members or outsiders to accomplish one's goals. Networks provide a channel for favours to be asked for and given. An effective network enhances one's organizational reputation, thus aiding influence attempts.

Political Skill. The ability to understand others at work and to use that knowledge to influence others to act in ways that enhance one's personal or organizational objectives.

Networking. Establishing good relations with key organizational members and outsiders to accomplish one's goals.

Political skill, as measured by these four facets, is positively related to rated job performance. Also, more skilled politicians are less inclined to feel stressed in response to role conflict, evidently due to better coping.[37] If you would like to assess your own political skill, complete the Experiential Exercise *Political Skill Inventory* at the end of the chapter.

Because networking is such a critical aspect of power acquisition and political success, let's examine it in more detail. In essence, networking involves developing informal social contacts to enlist the cooperation of others when their support is necessary. Upper-level managers often establish very large political networks both inside and outside the organization (Exhibit 12.5). Lower-level organizational members might have a more restricted network, but the principle remains the same. One study of general managers found that they used face-to-face encounters and informal small talk to bolster their political networks. They also did favours for others and stressed the obligations of others to them. Personnel were hired, fired, and transferred to bolster a workable network, and the managers forged connections among network members to create a climate conducive to goal accomplishment.[38]

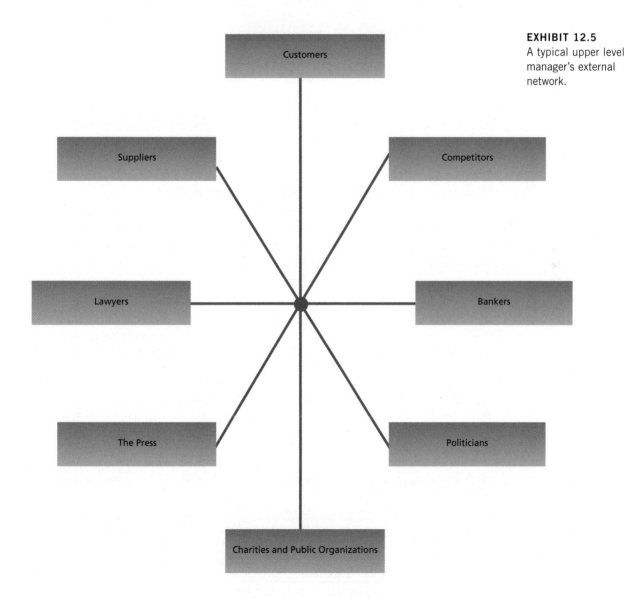

EXHIBIT 12.5
A typical upper level manager's external network.

Networking is an effective way to develop informal social contacts.

Monica Forret and Thomas Dougherty determined that there are several aspects to networking:[39]

- Maintaining contacts—giving out business cards; sending gifts and thank you notes
- Socializing—playing golf; participating in company sports leagues; having drinks after work
- Engaging in professional activities—giving a workshop; accepting a speaking engagement; teaching; publishing; appearing in the media
- Participating in community activities—being active in civic groups, clubs, and church events
- Increasing internal visibility—accepting high-profile work projects; sitting on important committees and task forces

The authors found that those high in self-esteem and extraversion (Chapter 2) were more likely to engage in networking behaviours. They also found that engaging in professional activities and increasing internal visibility were most associated with career success (i.e., compensation, promotions, perceived success). However, this applied only to men, despite the fact that men and women engaged in networking equally, except for socializing, where men perhaps had the edge. Forret and Dougherty make the important point that networking has increased in importance as people become more self-reliant and less reliant on organizations to plot their career futures.

Being central in a large network provides power because you have access to considerable resources, such as knowledge. This is especially true if the network is diverse (the people you know don't know each other) and consists of those who themselves hold power.[40]

High-powered executives are not the only people who are concerned about networking. Many telecommuters (Chapter 6) who work at home worry about being "cut out of the loop" of office influence because they are not physically present for informal office interaction. In turn, they fret that this will damage their promotion opportunities. Successful telecommuters report that they go to extra trouble to keep their bosses and co-workers informed about what they are doing at home and keeping their names visible in the communication network. At one prominent telecommunications firm, they showed their bosses videotapes of their home offices.[41]

Machiavellianism—The Harder Side of Politics

Have you ever known people who had the following characteristics?

- Act very much in their own self-interest, even at the expense of others.
- Cool and calculating, especially when others get emotional.
- High self-esteem and self-confidence.
- Form alliances with powerful people to achieve their goals.

These are some of the characteristics of individuals who are high on a personality dimension known as Machiavellianism. **Machiavellianism** is a set of cynical beliefs about human nature, morality, and the permissibility of using various tactics to achieve one's ends. The term derives from the 16th century writings of the Italian civil servant Niccolo Machiavelli, who was concerned with how people achieve social influence and the ability to manipulate others. Machiavellianism is a stable personality trait (Chapter 2).

Compared with "low Machs," "high Machs" are more likely to advocate the use of lying and deceit to achieve desired goals and to argue that morality can be compromised to fit the situation in question. In addition, high Machs assume that many people are excessively gullible and do not know what is best for themselves. Thus, in interpersonal situations, the high Mach acts in an exceedingly practical manner, assuming that the ends justify the means. Not surprisingly, high Machs tend to be convincing liars and good at "psyching out" competitors by creating diversions. Furthermore, they are quite willing to form coalitions with others to outmanoeuvre or defeat people who get in their way.[42] In summary, high Machs are likely to be enthusiastic organizational politicians.

Do high Machs feel guilty about the social tactics they utilize? The answer would appear to be no. Since they are cool and calculating rather than emotional, high Machs seem to be able to insulate themselves from the negative social consequences of their tactics. You might wonder how successful high Machs are at manipulating others and why others would tolerate such manipulation. After all, the characteristics we detail above are hardly likely to win a popularity contest, and you might assume that targets of a high Mach's tactics would vigorously resist manipulation by such a person. Again, the high Mach's rationality seems to provide an answer. Put simply, it appears that high Machs are able to accurately identify situations in which their favoured tactics will work. Such situations have the following characteristics:

- The high Mach can deal face to face with those he or she is trying to influence.
- The interaction occurs under fairly emotional circumstances.
- The situation is fairly unstructured, with few guidelines for appropriate forms of interaction.[43]

In combination, these characteristics reveal a situation in which the high Mach can use his or her tactics because emotion distracts others. High Machs, by remaining calm and rational, can create a social structure that facilitates their personal goals at the expense of others. Thus, high Machs are especially skilled at getting their way when power vacuums or novel situations confront a group, department, or organization. For example, imagine a small family business whose president dies suddenly without any plans for succession. In this power vacuum, a high Mach vice-president would have an excellent chance of manipulating the choice of a new president. The situation is novel, emotion provoking, and unstructured, since no guidelines for succession exist. In addition, the decision-making body would be small enough for face-to-face influence and coalition formation.

Machiavellianism. A set of cynical beliefs about human nature, morality, and the permissibility of using various tactics to achieve one's ends.

Defensiveness—Reactive Politics

So far, our discussion of politics has focused mainly on the proactive pursuit of self-interest. Another form of political behaviour, however, is more reactive, in that it concerns the defence or protection of self-interest. The goal here is to reduce threats to one's own power by avoiding actions that do not suit one's own political agenda or avoiding blame for events that might threaten one's political capital. Blake Ashforth and Ray Lee describe some tactics for doing both.[44]

Astute organizational politicians are aware that sometimes the best action to take is no action at all. A number of defensive behaviours can accomplish this mission:

- *Stalling.* Moving slowly when someone asks for your cooperation is the most obvious way of avoiding taking action without actually saying no. With time, the demand for cooperation may disappear. The civil service bureaucracy is infamous for stalling on demands from acting governments.

- *Overconforming.* Sticking to the strict letter of your job description or to organizational regulations is a common way to avoid action. Of course, the overconformer may be happy to circumvent his job description or organizational regulations when it suits his political agenda.

- *Buck passing.* Having someone else take action is an effective way to avoid doing it yourself. Buck passing is especially dysfunctional politics when the politician is best equipped to do the job but worries that it might not turn out successfully ("Let's let the design department get stuck with this turkey.").

Another set of defensive behaviours is oriented around the motto "If you can't avoid action, avoid blame for its consequences." These behaviours include:

- *Buffing.* Buffing is the tactic of carefully documenting information showing that an appropriate course of action was followed. Getting "sign offs," authorizations, and so on are examples. Buffing can be sensible behaviour, but it takes on political overtones when doing the documenting becomes more important than making a good decision. It is clearly dysfunctional politics if it takes the form of fabricating documentation.

- *Scapegoating.* Blaming others when things go wrong is classic political behaviour. Scapegoating works best when you have some power behind you. One study found that when organizations performed poorly, more-powerful CEOs stayed in office and the scapegoated managers below them were replaced. Less powerful CEOs were dismissed.[45]

The point of discussing these defensive political tactics is not to teach you how to do them. Rather, it is to ensure that you recognize them as political behaviour. Many of the tactics are quite mundane. However, viewing them in context again illustrates the sometimes subtle ways that individuals pursue political self-interest in organizations. Politics, like power, is natural in all organizations. Whether or not politics is functional for the organization depends on the ends that are pursued and the influence means that are used.

ETHICS IN ORGANIZATIONS

Smith Barney
www.smithbarney.com

In 2002, the investment firm Salomon Smith Barney (now Smith Barney, a division of Citigroup) was fined $5 million for misleading investors with biased stock research advice. At the core of the transgression was high-flying stock analyst Jack Grubman, whose enthusiastic "buy" recommendations for WorldCom and Winstar (both soon to be bankrupt) reflected the conflict of interest often observed in investment banks.[46] Such banks, which can earn hefty fees from such business, are reluctant to have their analysts issue negative reports about the prospects for their clients' stock. What are the ethics of this?

For our purposes, **ethics** can be defined as systematic thinking about the moral consequences of decisions. Moral consequences can be framed in terms of the potential for harm to any stakeholders in the decision. **Stakeholders** are simply people inside or outside the organization who have the potential to be affected by the decision. This could range from the decision makers themselves to "innocent bystanders."[47] Ethics is a major branch of philosophy, and we will not attempt to describe the various schools of ethical thought. Instead, we will focus on the kinds of ethical issues that organizational decision makers face and some of the factors that stimulate unethical decisions. As an example, see "Ethical Focus: *Canadian Employees and Workplace Fraud.*"

Over the years, researchers have conducted a number of surveys to determine managers' views about the ethics of decision making in business.[48] Some striking similarities across studies provide an interesting picture of the popular psychology of business ethics. First, far from being shy about the subject, a large majority agree that unethical practices occur in business. Furthermore, a substantial proportion (between 40 and 90 percent, according to the particular study) report that they have been pressured to

Ethics. Systematic thinking about the moral consequences of decisions.

Stakeholders. People inside or outside of an organization who have the potential to be affected by organizational decisions.

ETHICAL FOCUS

Canadian Employees and Workplace Fraud

Recent press coverage of so-called white-collar crimes has increased our awareness of fraud in the workplace. The Enron scandal is just one example, but others abound and some Canadians feel that this problem is spiralling out of control. Ernst and Young hired the polling firm Ipsos-Reid to provide a "reality check" to find out just how prevalent this kind of crime really is in Canada.

The poll indicates that 20 percent of working Canadians have witnessed fraudulent behaviour in their workplace during the past year, the most common being "taking office items or shoplifting" (41 percent). Other common fraudulent behaviours are "stealing or taking product or money" (20 percent), "inflating expense accounts" (16 percent), "claiming extra hours worked" (13 percent), "pocketing money from cash sales" (11 percent), "taking kickbacks from suppliers" (11 percent), and "creating phoney supplier invoices" (4 percent).

The poll asked working Canadians to rank the severity of various kinds of office fraud on a scale of zero to ten. The top crime was considered to be "altering the books to make profits or costs look better," but only 1 percent of respondents said they had actually encountered this type of fraud in their workplace.

In descending order, the other most serious frauds are considered to be "pocketing money from cash sales," "altering, creating or forging checks issued by your employer," "inflating expense accounts," "creating phoney supplier invoices," "taking office items or shoplifting from your employer of items more than

minor things like paper and pencils," and "taking kickbacks from suppliers."

When presented with a scenario of a co-worker who they knew was stealing goods (items worth more than a pad of paper or a couple of pencils) or money from the company, more than three-quarters (78 percent) of the people polled said that they would probably report the co-worker. Curiously, of the people polled who are actually aware of fraud in their workplace, only just over one-third (35 percent) reported it, while the remaining two-thirds did not.

The study also asked people what they thought of various fraud-prevention and -reduction methods. The preferred options are "better role models and leadership from managers and supervisors," "better communication to employees about what is allowed and what is not allowed," "tougher sanctions when employees are caught in a fraudulent act," and "better investigation of suspected problems." Methods that were deemed less effective include "more audits specifically to search for fraudulent acts," "improved screening of new employees," "more confidential counselling for employees with personal problems," "making someone specifically accountable for reducing fraud in the workplace," "a workplace version of a neighbourhood watch program where employees can report incidents anonymously," and "improved supervision and controls over employee's activities."

Source: Ipsos-Reid, (2002, August 8). One-fifth (20%) of Canadian workers are personally aware of fraud in their workplace. Retrieved June 25, 2003, from http://www.ipsos-reid.com/pdf/media/mr020808-1.pdf.

compromise their own ethical standards when making organizational decisions. Finally, in line with the concept of self-serving attributions, managers invariably tend to see themselves as having higher ethical standards than their peers and sometimes their superiors.[49] The unpleasant picture emerging here is one in which unethical behaviour tempts managers, who sometimes succumb but feel that they still do better than others on moral grounds.

In case you think that students are purer than organizational decision makers, think again. Research is fairly consistent in showing that business students have looser ethical standards than practising managers, at least when responding to written descriptions of ethical issues.[50] Among business students, undergraduates have been found to be more ethical than MBA students.[51] In addition, women have been found to have higher ethical standards than men when evaluating ethical business practices, especially among student samples.[52]

The Nature of Ethical Dilemmas

What are the kinds of ethical dilemmas that most frequently face organizational decision makers? Exhibit 12.6 shows the results of a Conference Board study of corporate codes of business ethics. The figures indicate the extent to which various issues are covered for the firms' own employees, its suppliers, and its joint venture partners. As can be seen, contractual and legally mandated issues find the most consensus (e.g., bribery, conflict of interest, proprietary information). The important but more subjective matters at the bottom of the list are less likely to be addressed.

Ethical issues are often occupationally specific. As an example, let's consider the ethical dilemmas that the various subspecialties of marketing face.[53] Among market researchers, telling research participants the true sponsor of the research has been an ongoing topic of debate. Among purchasing managers, where to draw the line in

EXHIBIT 12.6

Issues covered in corporate codes of ethics.

Source: *Global corporate ethics practices: A developing consensus* (Report Number: R-1243-99-RR), Ronald E. Berenbeim, The Conference Board, Inc. www.conference-board.org.

	Employees	Suppliers/ Vendors	Joint Venture Partners
Bribery/improper payments	92%	45%	27%
Conflict of interest	92	37	26
Security of proprietary information	92	30	25
Receiving gifts	90	46	25
Discrimination/equal opportunity	86	25	22
Giving gifts	84	48	26
Environment	78	27	24
Sexual harassment	78	22	17
Antitrust	76	27	23
Workplace safety	71	20	18
Political activities	71	11	13
Community relations	62	8	13
Confidentiality of personal information	52	11	11
Human rights	50	14	17
Employee privacy	48	8	10
Whistle-blowing	46	10	10
Substance abuse	42	12	12
Nepotism	28	5	8
Child labour	15	8	7

accepting favours (e.g., sports tickets) from vendors poses ethical problems. Among product managers, issues of planned obsolescence, unnecessary packaging, and differential pricing (e.g., charging more in the inner city) raise ethical concerns. When it comes to salespeople, how far to go in enticing customers and how to be fair in expense account use have been prominent ethical themes. Finally, in advertising, the range of ethical issues can (and does) fill books. Consider, for example, the decision to use sexual allure to sell a product.

In contrast to these occupationally specific ethical dilemmas, what are the common themes that run through ethical issues that managers face? An in-depth interview study of an occupationally diverse group of managers discovered seven themes that defined their moral standards for decision making.[54] Here are those themes and some typical examples of associated ethical behaviour:

- *Honest communication.* Evaluate subordinates candidly; advertise and label honestly; do not slant proposals to senior management.
- *Fair treatment.* Pay equitably; respect the sealed bid process; do not give preference to suppliers with political connections; do not use lower-level people as scapegoats.
- *Special consideration.* The "fair treatment" standard can be modified for special cases, such as helping out a long-time employee, giving preference to hiring the disabled, or giving business to a loyal but troubled supplier.
- *Fair competition.* Avoid bribes and kickbacks to obtain business; do not fix prices with competitors.
- *Responsibility to organization.* Act for the good of the organization as a whole, not for self-interest; avoid waste and inefficiency.
- *Corporate social responsibility.* Do not pollute; think about the community impact of plant closures; show concern for employee health and safety.
- *Respect for law.* Legally avoid taxes, do not evade them; do not bribe government inspectors; follow the letter and spirit of labour laws.

Causes of Unethical Behaviour

What are the causes of unethical behaviour? The answer to this question is important so that you can anticipate the circumstances that warrant special vigilance.

Knowing the causes of unethical behaviour can aid in its prevention. Because the topic is sensitive, you should appreciate that this is not the easiest area to research. The major evidence comes from surveys of executive opinion, case studies of prominent ethical failures, business game simulations, and responses to written scenarios involving ethical dilemmas.

Gain. Although the point might seem mundane, it is critical to recognize the role of temptation in unethical activity. The anticipation of healthy reinforcement for following an unethical course of action, especially if no punishment is expected, should promote unethical decisions.[55] Consider Dennis Levine, the Drexel Burnham Lambert investment banker, who was convicted of insider trading in one of Wall Street's biggest scandals.

> *It was just so easy. In seven years I built $39,750 into $11.5 million, and all it took was a 20-second phone call to my offshore bank a couple of times a month—maybe 200 calls total. My account was growing at 125% a year, compounded. Believe me, I felt a rush when I would check the price of one of my stocks on the office Quotron and learn I'd just made several hundred thousand dollars. I was confident that the elaborate veils of secrecy I had created—plus overseas bank-privacy laws—would protect me.*[56]

Role Conflict. Many ethical dilemmas that occur in organizations are actually forms of role conflict (Chapter 7) that get resolved in an unethical way. For example, consider the ethical theme of corporate social responsibility we listed above. Here, an executive's role as custodian of the environment (do not pollute) might be at odds with his or her role as a community employer (do not close the plant that pollutes).

A very common form of role conflict that provokes unethical behaviour occurs when our "bureaucratic" role as an organizational employee is at odds with our role as the member of a profession.[57] For example, engineers who in their professional role opposed the fatal launch of the space shuttle *Challenger* due to cold weather were pressured to put on their bureaucratic "manager's hats" and agree to the launch. Both the insurance and brokerage businesses have been rocked by similar ethics problems. Agents and brokers report being pressured as employees to push products that are not in the best interests of their clients. Frequently, reward systems (i.e., the commission structure) heighten the conflict, which then becomes a conflict of interest between self and client.

Competition. Stiff competition for scarce resources can stimulate unethical behaviour. This has been observed in both business game simulations and industry studies of illegal acts, in which trade offences, such as price fixing and monopoly violations, have been shown to increase with industry decline.[58] For example, observers cite a crowded and mature market as one factor prompting price fixing violations in the folding-carton packaging industry.[59] We should note one exception to the "competition stresses ethics" thesis. In cases in which essentially *no* competition exists, there is also a strong temptation to make unethical decisions. This is because the opportunity to make large gains is not offset by market checks and balances. Prominent examples have occurred in the defence industry, in which monopoly contracts to produce military hardware have been accompanied by some remarkable examples of overcharging taxpayers.

Personality. Are there certain types of personalities that are more prone to unethical decisions? Perhaps. Business game simulations have shown that people with strong economic values (Chapter 4) are more likely to behave unethically than those with weaker economic values.[60] Also, there are marked individual differences in the degree of sophistication that people use in thinking about moral issues.[61] Other things being equal, it is sensible to expect that people who are more self-conscious about moral matters will be more likely to avoid unethical decisions. Finally, people with a high need for personal power (especially Machiavellians) might be prone to make unethical decisions, using this power to further self-interest rather than for the good of the organization as a whole.

Remember that we have a tendency to exaggerate the role of dispositional factors, such as personality, in explaining the behaviour of others (Chapter 3). Thus, when we see unethical behaviour, we should look at situational factors, such as competition and the organization's culture, as well as the personality of the actor.

Organizational and Industry Culture. Bart Victor and John Cullen found that there were considerable differences in ethical values across the organizations they studied.[62] These differences involved factors such as consideration for employees, respect for the law, and respect for organizational rules. In addition, there were differences across groups within these organizations. This suggests that aspects of an organization's culture (and its subcultures) can influence ethics. This corresponds to the repeated finding in executive surveys that peer and superior conduct are viewed as strongly influencing ethical behaviour, for good or for bad. The presence of role models helps to shape the culture (Chapter 8). If these models are actually rewarded for unethical behaviour, rather than punished, the development of an unethical culture is likely. In fact, firms convicted of illegal acts often tend to be repeat offenders.[63] Remember, no one thing creates a "culture of corruption" in organizations. Rather, it is often a combination of factors such as evaluating managers solely "by the numbers," denying responsibility, denying injury to others, and teaching (low power) newcomers corrupt practices that lead to unethical corporate cultures.[64]

It has become clear that the illegal activities at Enron, WorldCom, and Andersen cannot simply be attributed to a few bad apples. Report after report has underlined the cultures of greed at these firms, which encouraged cutthroat politics, intimidation, and an almost exclusive focus on positive financial results. Since managers at these firms were excessively rewarded for such behaviours over the years, is it any wonder that things spun out of control?

Observers of the folding-carton price-fixing scandal we mentioned above noted how top managers frequently seemed out of touch with the difficulty of selling boxes in a mature, crowded market. They put in place goal setting and reward systems (e.g., commission forming 60 percent of income), systems that are much more appropriate for products on a growth cycle, that almost guaranteed unethical decisions.[65] In fact, research shows that upper-level managers generally tend to be naïve about the extent of ethical lapses in those below them. This can easily contribute to a success-at-any-cost culture.[66]

Finally, a consideration of culture suggests the conditions under which corporate codes of ethics might actually have an impact on decision making. If such codes are specific, tied to the actual business being done, and correspond to the reward system, they should bolster an ethical culture. If vague codes that do not correspond to other cultural elements exist, the negative symbolism might actually damage the ethical culture.

Before continuing, have a look at the You Be the Manager feature.

Whistle-blowing

In spite of the catalogue of causes of unethical behaviour discussed above, individuals occasionally step forward and "blow the whistle" on unethical actions. For instance, former tobacco executive Dr. Jeffrey Wigand (portrayed in the movie *The Insider*) leaked evidence to *60 Minutes* that consumers had been misled about the addictiveness of nicotine for many years. Similarly, Spc. Joseph Darby leaked photos showing abuse of prisoners at Iraq's Abu Ghraib prison.

Whistle-blowing occurs when a current or former organizational member discloses illegitimate practices to some person or organization that might be able to take action to correct these practices.[67] Thus, the whistle might be blown either inside or outside of the offending organization, depending on the circumstances. The courage of insiders to call attention to organizational misdoing is especially important in large contemporary organizations, because their very complexity often allows for such misdoing to be disguised from outsiders. Also, given pervasive conflicts of interest, there is no guarantee that external watchdogs (Arthur Andersen in the case of Enron) will do the job.[68] Most organizations seem to rely on vague open door policies (Chapter 10) rather than having specific channels and procedures for whistle-blowers to follow (see Exhibit 12.6). This is not the best way to encourage principled dissent.

Not everyone at Enron and WorldCom stood idly by while fraud unfolded around them. At Enron, Sherron Watkins, a vice-president with a master's degree in accounting, courageously spoke out against the fraudulent accounting practices and notified Ken Lay. Watkins' testimony at the hearings into the scandal also provided crucial information as to the breadth and depth of the problems at Enron. At WorldCom, Cynthia Cooper, an internal auditor, discovered the fraudulent bookkeeping entries. Cooper discussed her findings with the company's controller and with Scott Sullivan, but was told not to worry about it and to stop her review. Instead, she immediately went over her boss's head and called the board chair's audit committee.

Whistle-blowing.
Disclosure of illegitimate practices by a current or former organizational member to some person or organization that might be able to take action to correct these practices.

👉 YOU BE THE
Manager

Plagiarism at Raytheon

What would you do if you found out that the CEO of a big company had passed off someone else's work as his own?

This was the question faced by Carl Durrenberger, an engineer and market developer at Hewlett-Packard in San Diego. When he was cleaning out his desk in preparation for a move, he found a copy of *The Unwritten Laws of Engineering*, written by California engineering professor W.J. King and published by the American Society of Mechanical Engineers in 1944. It had been a present from his boss several years ago, and he stopped to read a couple of the rules, amused at the outdated language.

Imagine Durrenberger's surprise, though, when he read some of the rules again just a few days later, this time in a news article originally published in *USA Today* about the highly successful CEO of the Raytheon Company, a defence contractor based near Boston with annual sales of US$22 billion. The article referred to another publication, *Swanson's Unwritten Rules of Management,* by Raytheon's CEO, William Swanson. According to Swanson, his book was a compilation of management tips he had come up with and written down over the years. A few years ago, because the maxims had become very popular with corporate executives, Raytheon published the rules in a booklet to give away.

Durrenberger grabbed his copy of King's book and noted the following similarities between Swanson's rules and King's book, published some 50 years earlier:

Swanson: "Cultivate the habit of boiling matters down to the simplest terms: the proverbial 'elevator speech' is the best way."
King: "Cultivate the habit of 'boiling matters down' to their simplest terms."
Swanson: "Don't get excited in engineering emergencies: Keep your feet on the ground."
King: "Do not get excited in engineering emergencies—keep your feet on the ground."
Swanson: "Cultivate the habit of making quick, clean-cut decisions."
King: "Cultivate the habit of making brisk, clean-cut decisions."

Durrenberger initially gave Swanson the benefit of the doubt, thinking that perhaps the writer of the *USA Today* article had forgotten to credit King. He e-mailed the writer to point out the omission. He then did a bit of

> ### A question of plagiarism lands Raytheon's CEO in an embarrassing situation.

research on the Internet and discovered that the problem lay with Swanson: He had been passing the rules off as his own for years.

When Durrenberger hadn't heard back from *USA Today* after a day, he decided to publish his e-mail to the newspaper on his blog. He titled the entry "Bill Swanson of Raytheon is a Plagiarist." A *New York Times* reporter read it, and soon the story became nationwide news.

At first, Swanson and Raytheon claimed that the lack of attribution of King's book was an oversight on the part of Swanson's staff. But when it appeared that this explanation would not satisfy the public, Swanson finally accepted personal responsibility for the omission. During Raytheon's annual meeting, he apologized to the company's board, its shareholders, its employees, and "to those whose material I wish I had treated with greater care."

QUESTIONS

1. What is the nature of Swanson's breach of ethics? Suggest some possible causes that could explain Swanson's plagiarism.

2. Prior to the scandal, Swanson was regarded as a very successful CEO and had received a large raise in March 2006 (only a month before the disclosures of

plagiarism) based on Raytheon's strong financial performance. Who are the stakeholders affected by Swanson's actions? Do you believe that Swanson should be fired for his indiscretion? How does it compare to student plagiarism?

To find out how Raytheon's board reacted, see The Manager's Notebook at the end of the chapter.

Sources: Darce, K. (2006, May 13). How, why a blogger calls CEO a plagiarist. *San Diego Union-Tribune*, H1; Marquez, J. (2006, May 22). Sanctions on Raytheon CEO deemed fitting. *Workforce Management*, *85*, 8 (Trevino and Sonnenfeld quotes—Manager's Notebook); Cullen, L.T. (2006, May 15). Rule No. 1: Don't copy. *Time*, *167*, 41 (Wicks quote—Manager's Notebook); Weisman, R. (2006, March 16). Raytheon chief's pay jumps 25.5 percent to over $7M. *Boston Globe*, A1.

Two weeks later, WorldCom disclosed its misstatements. In the end, both women were singled out for their courage to speak up under conditions of intense pressure to remain silent. For their actions, Sherron Watkins and Cynthia Cooper, along with whistle-blower Coleen Rowley of the FBI, were named *Time*'s Persons of the Year for 2002.[69]

A lot of what we know about whistle-blowing comes from the study of sexual harassment. Let's turn to that topic.

Sexual Harassment—When Power and Ethics Collide

As indicated in Exhibit 12.6, 78 percent of the codes of ethics examined by the Conference Board mentioned sexual harassment. In recent years, a number of high-profile sexual harassment cases have made news headlines and brought increased attention to this problem. For example, a cover story in *Maclean's* reported that sexual harassment and assault in the Canadian Forces is common.[70] In addition to the numerous cases of sexual harassment reported in the American and Canadian military, many organizations, including Mitsubishi, Astra, Sears, and Del Laboratories, have found themselves involved in costly litigation cases.[71] The failure of these organizations to effectively respond to charges of sexual harassment has cost them millions of dollars in settlements as well as lower productivity, increased absenteeism, and turnover. Sexual harassment in the US army is reported to cost $250 million a year in lost productivity, absenteeism, and the replacement and transfer of employees.[72] As well, the effects on employees can include decreased morale and job satisfaction, as well as negative effects on psychological and physical well-being.[73]

The following is a fairly comprehensive definition of sexual harassment:

The EEOC [Equal Employment Opportunity Commission] regulatory guidelines state that unwelcome sexual advances, requests for sexual favours, and other verbal or physical conduct of a sexual nature constitute sexual harassment when submission to requests for sexual favours is made explicitly or implicitly a term or condition of employment; submission to or rejection of such requests is used as a basis for employment decisions; or such conduct unreasonably interferes with work performance or creates an intimidating, hostile, or offensive work environment. On the basis of these guidelines, current legal frameworks generally support two causes of action that claimants may state: coercion of sexual cooperation by threat of job-related consequences (quid pro quo harassment) and unwanted and offensive sex-related verbal or physical conduct, even absent any job-related threat (hostile work environment).[74]

Sexual harassment is a form of unethical behaviour that stems, in part, from the abuse of power and the perpetuation of a gender power imbalance. Managers who use their position, reward, or coercive power to request sexual favours, demonstrate verbal or physical conduct of a sexual nature as a condition of employment, or as a basis for employment decisions toward those in less powerful positions, are abusing their power and acting in an unethical manner. While the most severe forms of sexual harassment are committed by supervisors, the most frequent perpetrators are actually co-workers.

Although co-workers do not necessarily have the same formal power bases as supervisors, power differences often exist among co-workers and can also play a role in co-worker sexual harassment. Whether the harasser is a supervisor or a co-worker, he or she is likely to be more powerful than the person being harassed,[75] and the most vulnerable victims are those who cannot afford to lose their jobs.[76]

Sexual harassment is also prevalent in hostile work environments that perpetuate the societal power imbalance between men and women. For example, the higher incidences of sexual harassment reported in the military are believed to be partly a function of the rigid hierarchy and power differentials in the organizational structure.[77] Incidents of harassment and organizational inaction to complaints of harassment are also more likely in male-dominated industries and organizations in which men attempt to maintain their dominance relative to women.[78]

Unfortunately, many organizations are slow to react to complaints of sexual harassment, and many do nothing about it until the complainant has reported it to the EEOC. For example, until recently, the Canadian Forces denied that a problem exists and has been accused of mishandling sexual assault cases.[79] This phenomenon has been referred to as the "deaf ear syndrome," which refers to the "inaction or complacency of organizations in the face of charges of sexual harassment."[80] A review of organizational inaction in response to sexual harassment allegations found three main reasons to explain why organizations fail to respond: inadequate organizational policies and procedures for managing harassment complaints; defensive managerial reactions and rationalizations for failing to act in the face of complaints; and organizational features that contribute to inertial tendencies (e.g., international companies in the United States have problems managing sexual harassment).[81]

Organizations can effectively deal with allegations of sexual harassment and increase their responsiveness by taking a number of important measures. Ellen Peirce, Carol Smolinski, and Benson Rosen offer the following recommendations:

- *Examine the characteristics of deaf ear organizations.* Managers should examine their own organizations to determine if they have any of the characteristics that would make them susceptible to the deaf ear syndrome.

- *Foster management support and education.* Sexual harassment training programs are necessary to educate managers on how to respond to complaints in a sensitive and respectful manner.

- *Stay vigilant.* Managers must monitor the work environment and remove displays of a sexual nature and factors that can contribute to a hostile work environment.

- *Take immediate action.* Failure to act is likely to result in negative consequences for the organization and the victims of sexual harassment. Organizations considered to be the best places for women to work are known for their swift action and severe handling of harassers.

- *Create a state-of-the-art policy.* Sexual harassment policies and procedures need to clearly define what constitutes harassment and the sanctions that will be brought to bear on those found guilty of it.

- *Establish clear reporting procedures.* User-friendly policies need to be designed so that there are clear procedures for filing complaints and mechanisms in place for the impartial investigation of complaints. The privacy of those involved must also be protected.[82]

In general, organizations that are responsive to complaints of sexual harassment have top management support and commitment, provide comprehensive education and training programs, continuously monitor the work environment, respond to complaints in a thorough and timely manner, and have clear policies and reporting procedures.[83] An example of such an organization is E.I. du Pont de Nemours, which has developed a sexual harassment awareness program called A Matter of Respect, which

E.I. du Pont de Nemours
www.dupont.com

includes interactive training programs, peer-level facilitators who are trained to meet with victims or potential victims, and a 24-hour hotline. As the company has become more international, so has its training on sexual harassment, which is now provided in Japan, China, Mexico, and Puerto Rico.[84]

Employing Ethical Guidelines

A few simple guidelines, regularly used, should help in the ethical screening of decisions. The point is not to paralyze your decision making but to get you to think seriously about the moral implications of your decisions before they are made.[85]

- Identify the stakeholders that will be affected by any decision.

 THE MANAGER'S

Notebook

Plagiarism at Raytheon

1. Swanson's ethical breach can be framed in several ways. First, plagiarism represents dishonest communication. Second, plagiarism is a form of unfair treatment of an original author who is not getting credit for his or her own ideas. Third, Swanson's actions can be viewed as a breach of his responsibility toward Raytheon, which suffered negative publicity due to the story. Finally, plagiarism can be viewed as a lack of respect for copyright laws. How could such an ethical lapse be explained? While Swanson's mistake could possibly be an innocent oversight, there are several possible ethics-related explanations that could provide insight. First, while Swanson's maxims did not necessarily result in personal financial gain, they certainly earned him considerable fame. His book of "rules" was available for free download on the Raytheon website, and it is estimated that over 300 000 are in circulation. In addition to the distribution and initial positive news coverage of his "rules," Swanson was also a sought-after speaker. Second, personality could be an explanation for this type of breach by a CEO. Need for power, personal values, and moral reasoning can all influence a CEO's decisions and actions in such situations. Finally, there are also cultural factors that could explain how a CEO could be led to plagiarize. Many larger-than-life businesspeople, such as Jack Welch, Donald Trump, and Lee Iacocca, are known by the general public more for their business writings than their particular accomplishments. In this era of the CEO-superstar, the allure of publishing for the masses must be extremely appealing.

2. On the one hand, Swanson's indiscretion seems to be something of a victimless crime. No money changed hands, no individual was harmed in any way, and the original author is long deceased. Still, the slip seems particularly troubling because it came from the head of one of the country's most powerful corporations, one that is responsible for manufacturing high-security defence products for the military. In this era of heightened military security, questions about Swanson's integrity and honesty could damage the credibility of the company. "If I were a board member or a shareholder, it would raise questions in my mind about how honest, transparent and responsible a CEO is being in other dealings," says Andy Wicks, co-director of the University of Virginia's Olsson Center for Applied Ethics. As such, the primary stakeholder in this ethical breach appears to be Swanson's firm, Raytheon. How did Raytheon react? At the May 2006 annual shareholders' meeting, Raytheon's board announced that Swanson's raise was cancelled and that his eligible stock grants were being reduced by 20 percent. The salary cut represented a reduction of approximately $1 million. While the company hopes to put the incident behind it, ethics experts are still debating if the sanctions were harsh enough. According to Linda Trevino, director of the Shoemaker Program in Business Ethics at Pennsylvania State University, the board's response was entirely appropriate: "What he did was a mistake, and that was wrong, but he didn't profit from it and it wasn't intentional." Others, however, believe he got off easy. "If any of Raytheon's military customers did this when they were in school, they would have been thrown out," says Jeff Sonnenfeld, senior associate dean at the Yale School of Management.

- Identify the costs and benefits of various decision alternatives to these stakeholders.

- Consider the relevant moral expectations that surround a particular decision. These might stem from professional norms, laws, organizational ethics codes, and principles such as honest communication and fair treatment.

- Be familiar with the common ethical dilemmas that decision makers face in your specific organizational role or profession.

- Discuss ethical matters with decision stakeholders and others. Do not think ethics without talking about ethics.

- Convert your ethical judgments into appropriate action.

What this advice does is enable you to recognize ethical issues, make ethical judgments, and then convert these judgments into behaviour.[86]

Training and education in ethics have become very popular in North American organizations. Evidence indicates that formal education in ethics does have a positive impact on ethical attitudes.[87]

LEARNING OBJECTIVES CHECKLIST

1. *Power* is the capacity to influence others who are in a state of dependence. People have power by virtue of their position in the organization (legitimate power) or by virtue of the resources that they command (reward, coercion, friendship, or expertise).

2. People can obtain power by doing the right things and cultivating the right people. Activities that lead to power acquisition need to be extraordinary, visible, and relevant to the needs of the organization. People to cultivate include outsiders, subordinates, peers, and superiors.

3. *Empowerment* means giving people the authority, opportunity, and motivation to solve organizational problems. Power is thus located where it is needed to give employees the feeling that they are capable of doing their jobs well.

4. *Influence tactics* are interpersonal strategies that convert power into influence. They include assertiveness, ingratiation, rationality, exchange, upward appeal, and coalition formation. Rationality (logic, reason, planning, compromise) is generally the most efficient tactic.

5. Effective managers often have a high need for power. While individuals with high *n* Pow can, in some circumstances, behave in an abusive or dominating fashion, they can also use their power responsibly. Managers with high *n* Pow are effective when they use this power to achieve organizational goals.

6. Organizational subunits obtain power by controlling *strategic contingencies*. This means that they are able to affect events that are critical to other subunits. Thus, departments that can obtain resources for the organization will acquire power. Similarly, subunits gain power when they are able to reduce uncertainty, when their function is central to the workflow, and when other subunits or outside contractors cannot perform their tasks.

7. *Organizational politics* occur when influence means that are not sanctioned by the organization are used or when nonsanctioned ends are pursued. The pursuit of nonsanctioned ends is always dysfunctional, but the organization may benefit when nonsanctioned means are used to achieve approved goals. Several political tactics were discussed: *Networking* is establishing good relations with key people to accomplish goals. It contributes to political skill along with political astuteness, interpersonal influence, and apparent sincerity. *Machiavellianism* is a set of cynical beliefs about human nature, morality, and the permissibility of using various means to achieve one's ends. Situational morality, lying, and "psyching out" others are common tactics. *Defensiveness* means avoiding taking actions that do not suit one's political agenda and avoiding blame for negative events.

8. *Ethics* is systematic thinking about the moral consequences of decisions. Of particular interest is the impact on stakeholders, people who have the potential to be affected by a decision. Ethical dilemmas that managers face involve honest communication, fair treatment, special consideration, fair competition, responsibility to the organization, social responsibility, and respect for law. Causes of unethical behaviour include the potential for gain, role conflict, the extremes of business competition (great or none), organizational and industry culture, and certain personality characteristics.

9. *Sexual harassment* is a form of unethical behaviour that stems from the abuse of power and the perpetuation of a gender imbalance in the workplace. Steps that can be taken to deal with harassment include training and education, rapid response, clear and formal policies, vigilance, and detection of the "deaf ear" syndrome.

DISCUSSION QUESTIONS

1. Contrast the bases of power available to an army sergeant with those available to the president of a voluntary community association. How would these differences in power bases affect their influence tactics?

2. Are the bases of individual power easily substitutable for each other? Are they equally effective? For example, can coercive power substitute for expert power?

3. Suppose that you are an entrepreneur who has started a new chain of consumer electronics stores. Your competitive edge is to offer excellent customer service. What would you do to empower your employees to help achieve this goal?

4. Imagine that you are on a committee at work or in a group working on a project at school that includes a "high Mach" member. What could you do to neutralize the high Mach's attempts to manipulate the group?

5. Discuss the conditions under which the following subunits of an organization might gain or lose power: legal department; research and development unit; public relations department. Use the concepts of scarcity, uncertainty, centrality, and substitutability in your answers.

6. Differentiate between power and politics. Give an example of the use of power that is not political.

7. Is it unethical to occasionally surf the Internet at work? Is it unethical to download pornography? Defend your answers.

8. Is sexual harassment more likely to be a problem in some occupations and types of organizations? Describe those occupations and organizational cultures where sexual harassment is most likely to be a problem. What can be done to prevent sexual harassment in these occupations and organizations?

INTEGRATIVE DISCUSSION QUESTIONS

1. Consider the role of politics and ethics in decision making. How can organizational politics be a source of effective or ineffective decision making in organizations? In what way can the causes of unethical behaviour influence decision making?

2. How can an organization create an ethical workplace where ethical behaviour is the norm? Refer to the organizational learning practices in Chapter 2, attitude change in Chapter 4, ethical leadership in Chapter 9, and the contributors to organizational culture in Chapter 8 to answer this question.

ON-THE-JOB CHALLENGE QUESTION

In the fall of 2006, Patricia Dunn was removed as the chair of the board of Hewlett-Packard, one of the world's premier technology companies. Dunn, whose position earned $300 000 US a year, had been frustrated and angered by leaks to the media of sensitive boardroom discussions that might affect HP's stock price. To deal with the problem, she authorized a private investigation firm to seek out the identity of those responsible for the leaks. HP directors, employees, and journalists were the target of the investigation. Among other things, investigators posed as these people ("pretexting") to obtain their confidential telephone records and set up an e-mail sting to fool a reporter. Dunn claimed she was assured that all actions taken were legal and proper, but the invasion of privacy

did not sit well with a congressional committee investigating the matter. Two directors and a high-level legal advisor also resigned in the turmoil surrounding the events.

How were power and politics implicated in the events at HP? What are the ethics of using private investigators to probe leaks to the press? Was Dunn a victim in this affair?

Sources: Associated Press. (2006, September 28). Patricia Dunn: Others knew about HP probe. MSNBC.com; Robertson, J. (2006, September 26). Patricia Dunn resigns as HP chairwoman, Mark Hurd takes over as chairman. Canada.com, Canadian Press; Robertson, J. (2006; September 12). HP chairwoman Dunn to step down. globeandmail.com, Associated Press.

EXPERIENTIAL EXERCISE

Political Skill Inventory

Early in the chapter we discussed political skills. This exercise will allow you to assess your political skill set.

Instructions: Using the following 7-point scale, please place the number on the blank before each item that best describes how much you agree with each statement about yourself.

1 = strongly disagree
2 = disagree
3 = slightly disagree
4 = neutral
5 = slightly agree
6 = agree
7 = strongly agree

1. _____ I spend a lot of time and effort at work networking with others.

2. _____ I am able to make most people feel comfortable and at ease around me.

3. _____ I am able to communicate easily and effectively with others.

4. _____ It is easy for me to develop good rapport with most people.

5. _____ I understand people very well.

6. _____ I am good at building relationships with influential people at work.

7. _____ I am particularly good at sensing the motivations and hidden agendas of others.

8. _____ When communicating with others, I try to be genuine in what I say and do.

9. _____ I have developed a large network of colleagues and associates at work whom I can call on for support when I really need to get things done.

10. _____ At work, I know a lot of important people and am well connected.

11. _____ I spend a lot of time at work developing connections with others.

12. _____ I am good at getting people to like me.

13. _____ It is important that people believe I am sincere in what I say and do.

14. _____ I try to show a genuine interest in other people.

15. _____ I am good at using my connections and network to make things happen at work.

16. _____ I have good intuition or savvy about how to present myself to others.

17. _____ I always seem to instinctively know the right things to say or do to influence others.

18. _____ I pay close attention to people's facial expressions.

Scoring and Interpretation

To compute your overall political skill, add up your scores and divide the total by 18. Scores below 2.3 indicate low political skill and scores over 4.6 signal high political skill. You can also compute your scores for the various dimensions of political skill. To determine your social astuteness, sum answers 5, 7, 16, 17, and 18 and divide by 5. To determine your interpersonal influence, sum answers 2, 3, 4, and 12 and divide by 4. To assess your networking ability, sum answers 1, 6, 9, 10, 11, and 15 and divide by 6. Finally, to compute your apparent sincerity, sum answers 8, 13, and 14 and divide by 3. It is also useful to see how others rate your political skill. Have someone who knows you

well use the scale to rate you and compare his or her rating with yours.

Source: Ferris, G.R., Treadway, D.C., Kolodinsky, R.W., Hochwarter, W.A., Kacmar, C.J., Douglas, C., & Frink, D.D. (2005). Development and validation of the Political Skill Inventory. *Journal of Management*, 31, 126–152.

CASE INCIDENT

Doubling Up

The business school at Canadian Anonymous University prided itself on its international programs, which spanned Eastern Europe, North Africa, and South America. Many of the faculty enjoyed teaching in these programs, as it offered them a chance for free travel and the opportunity to sometimes avoid the harsh extremes of the Canadian climate. In addition, the teaching was well paid, offering a more reliable source of additional income than consulting. The university's auditor recently determined that several faculty members had been teaching in the international programs at the same time that they were scheduled to be teaching undergraduate classes at CAU. This was possibly due to the loose connection between the international programs office and the academic depart-

ments. After some investigation, it was determined that these faculty members had been subcontracting their CAU teaching to graduate students (at rather low rates) to enable themselves to teach internationally. One faculty member defended the practice as "gaining global exposure." Another claimed that developing countries "deserved experienced professors." A third claimed to be underpaid without the international teaching.

1. What kind of organizational politics are at work here?

2. What influence tactics might the profs have used to get the grad students to fill in for them?

3. Discuss the ethics of the professors "doubling up" on their teaching.

CASE STUDY

WestJet Spies on Air Canada

Stephen Smith is the type of boss who keeps his door open. As president of Zip, a short-lived Air Canada subsidiary, he was known as easygoing and approachable, regularly walking around the Calgary office to check in with people. He also happens to be the former CEO of WestJet Airlines, Air Canada's archrival. All of which may be why he was the one to receive a phone call last December from a man identifying himself only as a WestJet employee. "I'm all for tough competition," said the voice on the phone, "but I have to draw the line at dishonest conduct."

Then the caller dropped a bomb: WestJet was dipping into private Air Canada files online and passing the information around the executive suite. The tipster reported that he had seen a multicoloured page filled with Air Canada's flight load data—industry jargon for the number of passengers flying on a specific flight—on a senior executive's computer. Smith suddenly feared WestJet brass might have access to a private site used by Air Canada employees to book their own travel, from which the snoopers could gauge which routes make money and which don't—invaluable information in a business built on tight margins. If he was right, *this* could explain why WestJet seemed to be making all the right strategic decisions of late, such as flipping its Montreal–Vancouver flight from evening to morning.

Smith wasn't alone in his office when the call came. A colleague, Michael Rodyniuk, was also there,

according to an affidavit Smith filed later. Unbeknownst to the WestJet snitch, Smith's phone displayed his name and number. As Smith was jotting notes from the conversation, he pulled out an extra sheet of paper and says he indicated to Rodyniuk to write down the information.

That phone call, which couldn't have lasted more than five minutes, eventually triggered a massive civil lawsuit over corporate espionage, one that provides a rare glimpse of the dirty tricks rivals resort to in the name of competition. Although none of the parties would go on the record for this story, affidavits, transcripts and background interviews reveal just how ruthless the airline business has become in this country, where Air Canada is battling a posse of up-and-comers, most notably the feisty WestJet, as it emerges from bankruptcy protection. Even in its early stages the case has uncovered fresh incriminating material, but it will be months, possibly years, before the various players get their days in court. It may never get that far—many observers expect an out-of-court settlement. Still, the critical battle is playing out in the court of public opinion, where the two airlines' public personas so far seem reversed: Air Canada, long thought to be a corporate bully, appears to be the victim, while WestJet, for years the darling of investors and the flying public, has been cast as the bad guy.

In its statement of claim, which accuses WestJet of "high-handed and malicious" conduct, Air Canada says the company surreptitiously tapped into its employee website and set up a "screen scraper," a program designed to automatically lift data off one site and dump it into another. WestJet boosted its own profits using that information, says Air Canada, claiming a whopping $220 million in damages. In reply, WestJet dismissed the suit as an attempt to embarrass a rival and in a countersuit accuses the national carrier of stealing *its* confidential information. It says Air Canada sent investigators to pilfer one of its executive's garbage—and has pictures to prove it.

What pushes this story into the realm of the absurd is that neither airline denies the accusations—what's disputed is whether doing so was wrong. WestJet admits a senior executive, Mark Hill, entered Air Canada's website; Clive Beddoe, the company's CEO, even apologized to shareholders for Hill's actions while discussing WestJet's tumbling profits this summer. For its part, Air Canada readily admits it took the garbage—in fact, it uses the reconstituted pages as evidence for its case. But almost in mirror fashion, they both scoff at the recriminations. WestJet says its so-called crime coughed up data that was neither confidential nor important. Air Canada's investigators deny they trespassed on private property. If there weren't jobs and investors' money at stake, and possibly even the fragile health of the national airline industry, these suits and countersuits could be likened to a spat between siblings that's getting out of control.

And now Jetsgo Corporation, the young Montreal-based discounter, has entered the fray. Among the documents Air Canada had pasted back together, it discovered a summary of Jetsgo load factors. Last week, Jetsgo CEO Michel Leblanc asked Air Canada for a copy of that document. All of which poses an intriguing question: Just how widespread was WestJet's espionage?

While the audacity of the tactics may be shocking, there is nothing new in companies spying on each other, says Norman Inkster, who led the RCMP from 1987 to 1994 and now runs a private investigation firm. But in the old days it usually meant breaking into rivals' offices. Today, it's about hacking into websites and electronic files—tactics that Inkster says can be difficult to detect and hugely damaging. If Smith hadn't been tipped off, chances are Air Canada would never have discovered WestJet's scheme.

As much as five months before the mole's disturbing call, Rodyniuk, the executive who Smith says was in his office that day, had mentioned that a WestJet co-founder, Mark Hill, seemed to have oddly accurate data on Air Canada's flight loads. Rodyniuk, Zip's director of marketing and sales, had known Hill for more than a decade. The two regularly bantered back and forth by e-mail. Occasionally Hill, known as a genius for industry numbers, would taunt Rodyniuk about Air Canada's woes. "Winnipeg–London at 27 percent isn't doing much for your bottom line," he wrote on January 15, 2004. "I'd be willing to bet my next profit-share cheque that YWG-YXU [the airports'

call letters] has the lowest load factor of any domestic route operated by AC today. C'mon. Fess up."

Hill's name also came up in Smith's conversation with the informant, who said Hill was the source of the sensitive data. Smith immediately made two calls: one to Air Canada's CEO Robert Milton, and the other to security. An investigation was launched.

First stop: the employee website. A standard airline perk allows employees to travel almost for free on flights with open seats. Workers receive a personal code so they can check which flights are available. Air Canada's manager of online services, Gerald Gunn, found that someone—or something—had used a single access code to enter the site an astounding 243 630 times between May 15, 2003, and March 19, 2004, for an average of 786 hits a day. In one extraordinary day, the site was tapped 4973 times.

It didn't take long to determine the code used over and over belonged to Jeffrey Lafond, a former Canadian Airlines employee who had accepted a buyout as Canadian was being taken over by Air Canada. Part of his package included two Air Canada tickets a year for five years.

Last winter, as Air Canada secretly tried to piece together what WestJet knew and how, Rodyniuk continued his e-mail relationship with Hill. In February, he broached a new subject: He wondered if WestJet might have a job for him.

Here the storyline gets contentious. Air Canada claims Rodyniuk and Hill met for dinner on March 18. The following morning, Air Canada's employee website was entered using Lafond's code for the last time. On March 24, Rodyniuk quit his job at Zip. The next day, he showed up at WestJet as director of revenue. Air Canada believes Rodyniuk tipped Hill off to its investigation.

In his affidavit, Rodyniuk disputes Smith's account of the tipster phone call. He says he only learned about the call when Smith asked for help checking out a former Canadian Airlines employee. Rodyniuk admits he wrote down the name and number on the slip of paper, but that information didn't come from Smith's phone display; it came from directory assistance.

Meanwhile, as Gunn was combing through Air Canada's website looking for signs of infiltration, the company's law firm, Lerners, decided to engage in some espionage of its own. It hired a private detective agency, IPSA International, to do some sleuthing of a grittier nature than WestJet's high-tech screen scraping. Hill often worked from his home in Victoria's exclusive Oak Bay suburb. IPSA's job was to get Hill's trash: It might reveal how WestJet was using the data it took from Air Canada's site. Tipped off by a neighbour who'd seen a suspicious white truck, Hill caught the IPSA workers last April. "Do you work for Air Canada?" he shouted at them, snapping photos of the men and their truck as they loaded his trash and recycling bins into their pickup. The pictures were printed in newspapers, and the incident gave Hill and WestJet something to be indignant about. The garbage was on private property, says Hill, whose countersuit accuses the private dicks and Air Canada of trespassing.

Hill's recycling material included shredded papers. After sorting the trash, the IPSA men sent the strips to a company in Houston that specializes in reconstituting shredded papers. They turned out to be reports comparing Air Canada's and WestJet's flight loads, according to Air Canada affidavits.

The day after Hill snapped the photos, and two weeks after Rodyniuk jumped to WestJet, Air Canada filed a lawsuit against WestJet, Mark Hill, and Jeffrey Lafond. And that's when things got interesting.

Some of the best drama in the case—and some of Air Canada's best evidence—came in pre-trial cross-examinations, which took place in a vast glass-walled conference room at the company's law firm. Earl Cherniak, Air Canada's lawyer, is like a sharpshooter—quiet, precise, and dangerous. In late June, he questioned Lafond. The session was well attended: at least eight lawyers, a couple of airline executives, and Hill, who was to be examined immediately after. Lafond admitted providing his employee and personal ID numbers for Air Canada's website to Hill, but said he didn't think the load factor information was relevant. The transcript of the 2 ½ hour cross-examination reads like a school principal grilling a cheating student. Had Lafond asked Hill how the information would be used? Did he know it would be used 243 000 times? Did he know it was used on an automated basis? No, no, and no, Lafond answered.

"Mr. Hill never told you that?"

"No."

"So you had no idea, when you were giving Mr. Hill this access that he would use it in that way?"

"That's correct."

"Yes. But if you had known that, you wouldn't have given it to him, would you?"

"Again, I don't think the load factor information is very relevant," said Lafond. (He nonetheless asked Hill for—and got, on the same day he handed over the codes—an indemnity saying WestJet would take care of him for "any reason.")

At the beginning of Lafond's grilling, Hill kept busy doing a crossword puzzle. By the time it was his turn in the hot seat, however, Hill was no longer nonchalant. At one point during questioning, he was shaking, says one person who was in the room. Hill told Cherniak that when he first got Lafond's access code he spent 90 minutes each evening going into the Air Canada website and analyzing its data. Later, he asked a WestJet computer expert to create a program that would retrieve the data automatically. But, said Hill over and over, the load factor information was available from other sources. Airlines hire people to stand at airport gates and count passengers as they board or exit flights, he pointed out. And, over and over, Cherniak

told Hill that he was volunteering information for which he hadn't been asked. (Hill resigned from WestJet this summer, saying it was in his and WestJet's best interests they part company.)

In its defence, WestJet doesn't deny accessing Air Canada's website, but it points the finger at Hill as the one who did the dirty work. Besides, says WestJet, its rival's troubles aren't the result of Hill's actions, and the flight load information Hill obtained was of little value.

Much of the case will ultimately revolve around this point. As one lawyer put it, if you are hit by a car running a red light, the case against the driver will be much tougher if you were left brain-damaged than if you're lightly bruised. The next step in this case may well determine whether Air Canada was bruised or bashed by its rival's actions. In July, WestJet was ordered to turn over its executives' hard drives for an independent review, which should help answer some outstanding questions. Who at WestJet knew? Who used the data? And how useful was it? Claude Proulx, an airline analyst, noted in a July report that WestJet's load factors "deteriorated significantly" after it stopped scraping Air Canada's data. Meanwhile, Air Canada's traffic figures have improved substantially.

In the end, both airlines may be harshly judged. With few controls on its employee website, Air Canada left itself wide open to snoops. WestJet's Hill took advantage of his competition's lax security. But most importantly, both—whether as a tactic to divert attention from falling profits or a ploy to appear less of a bully—have blown things way out of proportion.

Source: Macklem, K. (2004, September 20). Spies in the skies. *Maclean's*, 20–22, 24.

1. Did WestJet employees engage in unethical behaviour in this series of events? Did Air Canada employees? Defend your answers.

2. Who are the relevant stakeholders in this situation?

3. Does Air Canada's apparently weak security in this matter reduce any blame to be accorded to WestJet?

4. Do arguments that the load data was useless or that it was available from other sources reduce the seriousness of the online snooping?

5. Who gained and lost power in this case?

6. On May 29, 2006, a settlement was announced. WestJet agreed to pay Air Canada $5 million in costs and to donate $10 million to children's charities in the name of the two airlines. It also apologized and described its conduct as unethical. Is this a fair outcome? Does it change your views about your answers to the previous questions?

CHAPTER 13

Conflict and Stress

> ## THE WALT DISNEY CORPORATION: TROUBLE IN THE MAGIC KINGDOM.

The position of chief executive officer of the Walt Disney Corporation is one of the most prestigious jobs in corporate America. More than running a multi-billion dollar company, it entails leading a beloved national institution that is about the magic of childhood. For over 20 years, from 1984 to 2005, Michael Eisner was the man at the helm. His tenure at Disney was marked by tremendous success, but his last years were marred by conflict and controversy, which eventually led to his departure.

When Eisner was recruited from Paramount in 1984 to take over at Disney, the company was floundering, the target of corporate raiders. During his first 10 years with the company, Eisner led a remarkable turnaround. He revitalized the company's theme parks, steered the company toward producing successful live-action motion pictures, and rejuvenated Disney's famous animation studio with such movies as *The Little Mermaid, Beauty and the Beast*, and *The Lion King*. He also capitalized on classic Disney movies through video and DVD, and oversaw successful productions of Disney-based Broadway plays. During his 21 years at Disney, the company's stock price rose by 15 percent (compared to 14 percent at General Electric and 11 percent at Sony) and Eisner delivered 27 percent annual growth in earnings per share (11 percent at GE and 1 percent at Sony). While these results can only be described as outstanding, Eisner exited Disney with little applause in 2005.

During his time at Disney, Eisner became known as a micromanager, a ruthless negotiator, and someone prone to conflict. When failures began to mount in the mid to late 1990s, Eisner's style, and his large compensation, became a problem. Several big budget movies that Eisner supported flopped, analysts estimated that he overpaid Fox by a billion dollars for its Family Channel, observers scoffed at his insistence on locating Euro Disney in France, and his purchase of the ABC network was widely panned. While the company was still in much better shape compared to the years before his arrival, these failures and a series of highly publicized conflicts eventually led to Eisner's demise at Disney.

One of the common complaints about Eisner was that he did not like having strong corporate talent in the company who would likely challenge him. In 1994, Eisner forced out studio chief Jeffrey Katzenberg, architect of Disney's wildly successful animated films in the late 1980s and early 1990s. Katzenberg, whom Eisner called a "little midget," sued

Disney for refusing to pay the royalties owed to him. Eisner refused to make a deal, and Katzenberg won a $280 million settlement. In 1995, Eisner hired his long-time friend Michael Ovitz as president. Ovitz only lasted 14 months before Eisner forced him out, but not without receiving a $140 million payout. Angry shareholders sued Disney's board of directors for approving the huge compensation package and acting in bad faith in the hiring and firing. Eisner also strengthened a central strategic planning department that became hated internally for regularly vetoing ideas from Disney's divisions.

Walt Disney Corporation
www.disney.com

Another high profile controversy surrounding Eisner concerned his failure to renew an agreement with Pixar Animation Studios. During the 1990s and 2000s, Pixar had provided Disney with its biggest hit movies, such as *Toy Story* and *Finding Nemo*, while most Disney animated features failed. When the distribution deal between Disney and Pixar came up for renegotiation, Eisner played hardball with Pixar's chairman, Steve Jobs, of Apple fame. When Jobs announced that there would be no deal with Disney and that Pixar would be looking at different studios, most believed that Eisner's hard negotiations and difficult personal style had killed any chance of a deal. Eisner also had a tumultuous relationship with Harvey Weinstein of Miramax, which is wholly owned by Disney. While Miramax produced 221 Oscar nominations, including 15 for best picture, Weinstein and Eisner waged a bitter battle over the types of films that Disney would agree to release. When Eisner blocked the release of Miramax's controversial *Fahrenheit 9/11*, Weinstein bought back the $6 million movie and sold it to another studio. It went on to make over $200 million worldwide. Eisner was branded a coward, censor, and bad businessman, and Weinstein indicated that he wanted out of his partnership with Disney due to his poor relationship with Eisner.

In 2004, Disney's shareholders, led by former board members Roy Disney and Stanley Gold, severely rebuked Eisner. Although Roy Disney, Walt's nephew, and Stanley Gold had both been instrumental in bringing Eisner to Disney in 1984, they both resigned in 2003 citing their inability to work with Eisner. Roy Disney suggested that Eisner was too concerned about profits and branding and did not adhere to his Uncle Walt's standard of quality and creating "magic" for children and families. Roy Disney and Gold rallied shareholders to withhold support from Eisner, and they responded: In March 2004, Eisner suffered a 43 percent vote of no confidence from investors. The board of directors immediately stripped him of his chairman's title, although he retained his position of CEO. Eisner announced that he would step down as CEO in September 2006 at the end of his contract. Critics such as Roy Disney and Gold were outraged that Eisner would stay on so long and threatened legal action when Eisner's handpicked successor, Robert Iger, was chosen to replace him. Eisner finally stepped down in October 2005 and Iger took over.

Since being tapped as successor, Iger has proven to be a different type of leader than Eisner. He quickly mended fences with Roy Disney and named him "director emeritus." He also disbanded the strategic planning department and vowed to get the heads of Disney's divisions more involved in decision making. Perhaps most importantly, Iger re-engaged Pixar in talks. Rather than taking a hard line, Iger used a personal approach with Steve Jobs and Pixar's creative head, John Lasseter, and focused on the companies' common belief in creating quality entertainment and lifelong memories for kids. The approach worked, and in a move that took almost everyone by surprise, Iger and Jobs announced in May 2006 that Pixar would become a wholly owned part of Disney.

In the final analysis, many of Michael Eisner's decisions in the final few years were successful. His choice of Robert Iger as successor, a decision that Eisner calls his best ever, has proven to be excellent. At 63, he is still eager to keep going. When asked in late 2004 to comment on the difficult few years that had led to his announced departure, Eisner remarked: "I felt, in my 20s at ABC and in my 30s at Paramount, enormous pressure every day making movies or dealing with producers . . . . That's been part of my life. Frankly, it has not added pressure—it's just added a lot of people who know about the pressure. The actual pressure seems to stimulate me and creates a competitive sense of wanting to succeed even more."[1]

In this chapter, we will define *interpersonal conflict*, discuss its causes, and examine various ways of handling conflict. We place particular emphasis on negotiation. Then we will explore *work stress*, noting its causes and the consequences that it can have for both individuals and organizations. Various strategies for reducing or coping with stress will be considered.

WHAT IS CONFLICT?

Interpersonal conflict is a process that occurs when one person, group, or organizational subunit frustrates the goal attainment of another. Thus, the curator of a museum might be in conflict with the director over the purchase of a particular work of art. Likewise, the entire curatorial staff might be in conflict with the financial staff over cutbacks in acquisition funds.

In its classic form, conflict often involves antagonistic attitudes and behaviours. As for attitudes, the conflicting parties might develop a dislike for each other, see each other as unreasonable, and develop negative stereotypes of their opposites ("Those scientists should get out of the laboratory once in a while"). Antagonistic behaviours might include name calling, sabotage, or even physical aggression. In some organizations, the conflict process is managed in a collaborative way that keeps antagonism at a minimum. In others, conflict is hidden or suppressed and not nearly so obvious (e.g., some gender conflict).[2]

Interpersonal conflict. The process that occurs when one person, group, or organizational subunit frustrates the goal attainment of another.

CAUSES OF ORGANIZATIONAL CONFLICT

It is possible to isolate a number of factors that contribute to organizational conflict.[3]

Group Identification and Intergroup Bias

An especially fascinating line of research has shown how identification with a particular group or class of people can set the stage for organizational conflict. In this work, researchers have typically assigned people to groups randomly or on the basis of some trivial characteristic, such as eye colour. Even without interaction or cohesion, people have a tendency to develop a more positive view of their own "in-group" and a less positive view of the "out-group" of which they are not a member.[4] The ease with which this unwarranted intergroup bias develops is disturbing.

Why does intergroup bias occur? Self-esteem is probably a critical factor. Identifying with the successes of one's own group and disassociating oneself from out-group failures boosts self-esteem and provides comforting feelings of social solidarity. Research by one of your authors, for example, found that people felt that their work group's attendance record was superior to that of their occupation in general (and, by extension, other work groups).[5] Attributing positive behaviour to your own work group should contribute to your self-esteem.

In organizations, there are a number of groups or classes with which people might identify. These might be based on personal characteristics (e.g., race or gender), job function (e.g., sales or production), or job level (e.g., manager or nonmanager). Furthermore, far from being random or trivial, differences between groups might be accentuated by real differences in power, opportunity, clients serviced, and so on. For instance, the merger between Air Canada and Canadian Airlines made firm identities very salient for employees, and these identities persisted even after the companies merged into a single entity. The best prognosis is that people who identify with some groups will tend to be leery of out-group members. The likelihood of conflict increases as the factors we cover below enter into the relationship between groups.

Air Canada
www.aircanada.com

The increased emphasis on teams in organizations generally places a high premium on getting employees to identify strongly with their team. The prevalence of intergroup bias suggests that organizations will have to pay special attention to managing relationships *between* these teams.

Interdependence

When individuals or subunits are mutually dependent on each other to accomplish *their own* goals, the potential for conflict exists. For example, the sales staff is dependent on the production department for the timely delivery of high-quality products.

This is the only way sales can maintain the good will of its customers. On the other hand, production depends on the sales staff to provide routine orders with adequate lead times. Custom-tailored emergency orders will wreak havoc with production schedules and make the production department look bad. In contrast, the sales staff and the office maintenance staff are not highly interdependent. Salespeople are on the road a lot and should not make great demands on maintenance. Conversely, a dirty office probably will not lose a sale.

Interdependence can set the stage for conflict for two reasons. First, it necessitates interaction between the parties so that they can coordinate their interests. Conflict will not develop if the parties can "go it alone." Second, as we noted in the previous chapter, interdependence implies that each party has some *power* over the other. It is relatively easy for one side or the other to abuse its power and create antagonism.

Interdependence does not *always* lead to conflict. In fact, it often provides a good basis for collaboration through mutual assistance. Whether interdependence prompts conflict depends on the presence of other conditions, which we will now consider.

Differences in Power, Status, and Culture

Conflict can erupt when parties differ significantly in power, status, or culture.

Power. If dependence is not mutual, but one way, the potential for conflict increases. If party A needs the collaboration of party B to accomplish its goals, but B does not need A's assistance, antagonism may develop. B has power over A, and A has nothing with which to bargain. A good example is the quality control system in many factories. Production workers might be highly dependent on inspectors to approve their work, but this dependence is not reciprocated. The inspectors might have a separate boss, their own office, and their own circle of friends (other inspectors). In this case, production workers might begin to treat inspectors with hostility, one of the symptoms of conflict.

Status. Status differences provide little impetus for conflict when people of lower status are dependent on those of higher status. This is the way organizations often work, and most members are socialized to expect it. However, because of the design of the work, there are occasions when employees with technically lower status find themselves giving orders to, or controlling the tasks of, higher-status people. The restaurant business provides a good example. In many restaurants, lower-status servers give orders and initiate queries to higher-status chefs. The latter might come to resent this reversal of usual lines of influence.[6] In some organizations, junior staff are more adept with information technology than senior staff. Some executives are defensive about this reversal of roles.

Culture. When two or more very different cultures develop in an organization, the clash in beliefs and values can result in overt conflict. Hospital administrators who develop a strong culture centred on efficiency and cost-effectiveness might find themselves in conflict with physicians who share a strong culture based on providing excellent patient care at any cost. A telling case of cultural conflict occurred when Apple Computer expanded and hired professionals away from several companies with their own strong cultures.

Hewlett-Packard
www.hp.com

Intel Corporation
www.intel.com

During the first couple of years Apple recruited heavily from Hewlett-Packard, National Semiconductor, and Intel, and the habits and differences in style among these companies were reflected in Cupertino. There was a general friction between the rough and tough ways of the semiconductor men (there were few women) and the people who made computers, calculators, and instruments at Hewlett-Packard. . . . Some of the Hewlett-Packard men began to see them-

selves as civilizing influences and were horrified at the uncouth rough-and-tumble practices of the brutes from the semiconductor industry. . . . Many of the men from National Semiconductor and other stern backgrounds harboured a similar contempt for the Hewlett-Packard recruits. They came to look on them as prissy fusspots.[7]

At Disney, conflict stemmed in part from tension between an "old school" set of values espoused by Roy Disney versus the more corporate values espoused by Michael Eisner.

Ambiguity

Ambiguous goals, jurisdictions, or performance criteria can lead to conflict. Under such ambiguity, the formal and informal rules that govern interaction break down. In addition, it might be difficult to accurately assign praise for good outcomes or blame for bad outcomes when it is hard to see who was responsible for what. For example, if sales drop following the introduction of a "new and improved" product, the design group might blame the marketing department for a poor advertising campaign. In response, the marketers might claim that the "improved" product is actually inferior to the old product.

Ambiguous performance criteria are a frequent cause of conflict between managers and employees. The basic scientist who is charged by a chemical company to "discover new knowledge" might react negatively when her boss informs her that her work is inadequate. This rather open-ended assignment is susceptible to a variety of interpretations. The conflict seen at Disney is not uncommon in the film and entertainment industry, in part because a great deal of ambiguity surrounds just what is needed to produce a hit movie or show.

Scarce Resources

In the previous chapter, we pointed out that differences in power are magnified when resources become scarce. This does not occur without a battle, however, and conflict often surfaces in the process of power jockeying. Limited budget money, secretarial support, or lab space can contribute to conflict. Scarcity has a way of turning latent or disguised conflict into overt conflict. Two scientists who do not get along very well may be able to put up a peaceful front until a reduction in lab space provokes each to protect his domain.

TYPES OF CONFLICT

Is all conflict the same? The answer is no. It is useful to distinguish among relationship, task, and process conflict.[8] **Relationship conflict** concerns interpersonal tensions among individuals that have to do with their relationship per se, not the task at hand. So-called "personality clashes" are examples of relationship conflicts. **Task conflict** concerns disagreements about the nature of the work to be done. Differences of opinion about goals or technical matters are examples of task conflict. Finally, **process conflict** involves disagreements about how work should be organized and accomplished. Disagreements about responsibility, authority, resource allocation, and who should do what all constitute process conflict.

In the context of work groups and teams, task, relationship, and process conflict tend to be detrimental to member satisfaction and team performance. In essence, such conflict prevents the development of cohesiveness (Chapter 7). Occasionally, some degree of task conflict might actually be beneficial for team performance, especially when the task is nonroutine and requires a variety of perspectives to be considered, and when it does not degenerate into relationship conflict.[9] Thus, not all conflict is detrimental, and we shall return to some potential benefits of conflict later in the chapter.

Relationship conflict.
Interpersonal tensions among individuals that have to do with their relationship per se, not the task at hand.

Task conflict.
Disagreements about the nature of the work to be done.

Process conflict.
Disagreements about how work should be organized and accomplished.

CONFLICT DYNAMICS

A number of events occur when one or more of the causes of conflict we noted above take effect. We will assume here that the conflict in question occurs between groups, such as organizational departments. However, much of this is also relevant to conflict within teams or between individuals. Specifically, when conflict begins, we often see the following events transpire:

- "Winning" the conflict becomes more important than developing a good solution to the problem at hand.

- The parties begin to conceal information from each other or to pass distorted information.

- Each side becomes more cohesive. Deviants who speak of conciliation are punished, and strict conformity is expected.

- Contact with the opposite party is discouraged except under formalized, restricted conditions.

- While the opposite party is negatively stereotyped, the image of one's own position is boosted.

- On each side, more aggressive people who are skilled at engaging in conflict may emerge as leaders.[10]

You can certainly see the difficulty here. What begins as a problem of identity, interdependence, ambiguity, or scarcity quickly escalates to the point that the conflict process *itself* becomes an additional problem. The elements of this process then work against the achievement of a peaceful solution. The conflict continues to cycle "on its own steam."

MODES OF MANAGING CONFLICT

How do you tend to react to conflict situations? Are you aggressive? Do you tend to hide your head in the sand? As conflict expert Kenneth Thomas notes, there are several basic reactions that can be thought of as styles, strategies, or intentions for dealing with conflict. As shown in Exhibit 13.1, these approaches to managing conflict are a function of both how *assertive* you are in trying to satisfy your own or your group's concerns and how *cooperative* you are in trying to satisfy those of the other party or group.[11] It should be emphasized that none of the five styles for dealing with conflict in Exhibit 13.1 is inherently superior. As we will see, each style might have its place given the situation in which the conflict episode occurs.

Avoiding

Avoiding. A conflict management style characterized by low assertiveness of one's own interests and low cooperation with the other party.

The **avoiding** style is characterized by low assertiveness of one's own interests and low cooperation with the other party. This is the "hiding the head in the sand" response. Although avoidance can provide some short-term stress reduction from the rigours of conflict, it does not really change the situation. Thus, its effectiveness is often limited.

Of course, avoidance does have its place. If the issue is trivial, information is lacking, people need to cool down, or the opponent is very powerful and very hostile, avoidance might be a sensible response.

Accommodating

Accommodating. A conflict management style in which one cooperates with the other party, while not asserting one's own interests.

Cooperating with the other party's wishes while not asserting one's own interests is the hallmark of **accommodating**. If people see accommodation as a sign of weakness, it does not bode well for future interactions. However, it can be an effective reaction when you are wrong, the issue is more important to the other party, or you want to build good will.

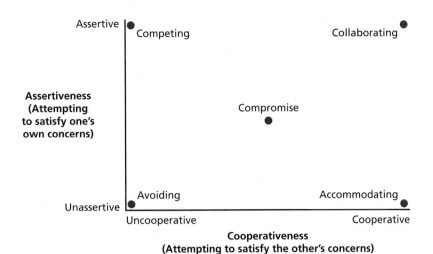

EXHIBIT 13.1
Approaches to managing organizational conflict.

Source: Taken from Thomas, K.W. (1992). Conflict and negotiation processes in organizations. In M.D. Dunnette & L.M. Hough (Eds.), *Handbook of industrial and organizational psychology.* (2nd ed., vol. 3). Palo Alto, CA: Consulting Psychologists Press.

Competing

A **competing** style tends to maximize assertiveness for your own position and minimize cooperative responses. In doing so, you tend to frame the conflict in strict win-lose terms. Full priority is given to your own goals, facts, or procedures. Bill Gates, the billionaire czar of Microsoft, tends to pursue the competing style:

> *Gates is famously confrontational. If he strongly disagrees with what you're saying, he is in the habit of blurting out, "That's the stupidest . . . . thing I've ever heard!" People tell stories of Gates spraying saliva into the face of some hapless employee as he yells, "This stuff isn't hard! I could do this stuff in a weekend!" What you're supposed to do in a situation like this, as in encounters with grizzly bears, is stand your ground: if you flee, the bear will think you're game and will pursue you, and you can't outrun a bear.*[12]

Others with this style include Hollywood producer Harvey Weinstein, lifestyle mogul Martha Stewart, and Apple's Steve Jobs.[13] The competing style holds promise when you have a lot of power, you are sure of your facts, the situation is truly win-lose, or you will not have to interact with the other party in the future.

Competing. A conflict management style that maximizes assertiveness and minimizes cooperation.

Microsoft
www.microsoft.com

Compromise

Compromise combines intermediate levels of assertiveness and cooperation. Thus, it is itself a compromise between pure competition and pure accommodation. In a sense, you attempt to satisfice (Chapter 11) rather than maximize your outcomes and hope that the same occurs for the other party. In the law, a plea bargain is an example of a compromise between the defending lawyer and the prosecutor.

Compromise places a premium on determining rules of exchange between the two parties. As such, it always contains the seeds for procedural conflict in addition to whatever else is being negotiated. Also, compromise does not always result in the most creative response to conflict. Compromise is not so useful for resolving conflicts that stem from power asymmetry, because the weaker party may have little to offer the stronger party. However, it is a sensible reaction to conflict stemming from scarce resources. Also, it is a good fall-back position if other strategies fail. In an interview, Michael Eisner reflected that he might have compromised more often for the good of Disney, even though he thought he was right.

Compromise. A conflict management style that combines intermediate levels of assertiveness and cooperation.

Collaborating

Collaborating. A conflict management style that maximizes both assertiveness and cooperation.

In the **collaborating** mode, both assertiveness and cooperation are maximized in the hope that an integrative agreement occurs that fully satisfies the interests of both parties. Emphasis is put on a win-win resolution in which there is no assumption that someone must lose something. Rather, it is assumed that the solution to the conflict can leave both parties in a better condition. Ideally, collaboration occurs as a problem-solving exercise (Chapter 11). It probably works best when the conflict is not intense and when each party has information that is useful to the other. Although, effective collaboration can take time and practice to develop, it frequently enhances productivity and achievement.[14]

Some of the most remarkable examples of collaboration in contemporary organizations are those between companies and their suppliers. Traditionally, adversarial competition in which buyers try to squeeze the very lowest price out of suppliers, who are frequently played off against each other, has dominated these relationships. This obviously does not provide much incentive for the perpetually insecure suppliers to invest in improvements dedicated toward a particular buyer. Gradually, things have changed, and now it is common for organizations to supply extensive engineering support and technical advice to their suppliers.

Collaboration also helps to manage conflict inside organizations. Our discussion of cross-functional teams in Chapter 7 is a good example. Also, research shows that collaboration between organizational departments is particularly important for providing good customer service.[15]

MANAGING CONFLICT WITH NEGOTIATION

Negotiation. A decision-making process among interdependent parties who do not share identical preferences.

The stereotype we have of negotiation is that it is a formal process of bargaining between labour and management or buyer and seller. However, job applicants negotiate for starting salaries, employees negotiate for better job assignments, and people with sick kids negotiate to leave work early. To encompass all these situations, we might define **negotiation** as "a decision-making process among interdependent parties who do not share identical preferences."[16] Negotiation constitutes conflict management, in that it is an attempt either to prevent conflict or to resolve existing conflict.

Collaboration can provide unions and management with win-win solutions.

Negotiation is an attempt to reach a satisfactory exchange among or between the parties. Sometimes, negotiation is very explicit, as in the case of the labour negotiation or the buyer–seller interaction. However, negotiation can also proceed in a very implicit or tacit way.[17] For instance, in trying to get a more interesting job assignment or to take off from work early, the terms of the exchange are not likely to be spelled out very clearly. Still, this is negotiation.

It has become common to distinguish between distributive and integrative negotiation tactics.[18] **Distributive negotiation** assumes a zero-sum, win-lose situation in which a fixed pie is divided up between the parties. If you re-examine Exhibit 13.1, you can imagine that distributive negotiation occurs on the axis between competition and accommodation. In theory, the parties will more or less tend toward some compromise. On the other hand, **integrative negotiation** assumes that mutual problem solving can result in a win-win situation in which the pie is actually enlarged before distribution. Integrative negotiation occurs on the axis between avoiding and collaborating, ideally tending toward the latter.

Distributive and integrative negotiations can take place simultaneously. We will discuss them separately for pedagogical purposes.

Distributive Negotiation Tactics

Distributive negotiation is essentially single-issue negotiation. Many potential conflict situations fit this scenario. For example, suppose you find a used car that you really like. Now, things boil down to price. You want to buy the car for the minimum reasonable price, while the seller wants to get the maximum reasonable price.

The essence of the problem is shown in Exhibit 13.2. Party is a consulting firm who would like to win a contract to do an attitude survey in Other's firm. Party would like to make $90 000 for the job (Party's target) but would settle for $70 000, a figure that provides for minimal acceptable profit (Party's resistance point). Other thinks that the survey could be done for as little as $60 000 (Other's target) but would be willing to spend up to $80 000 for a good job (Other's resistance point). Theoretically, an offer

Distributive negotiation.
Win-lose negotiation in which a fixed amount of assets is divided between parties.

Integrative negotiation.
Win-win negotiation that assumes that mutual problem solving can enlarge the assets to be divided between parties.

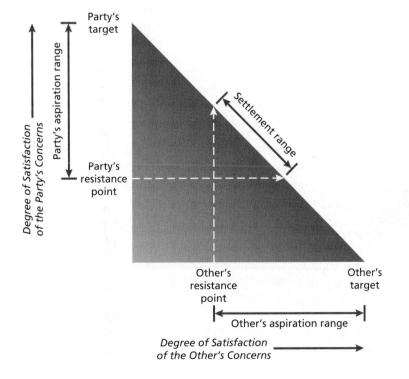

EXHIBIT 13.2
A model of distributive negotiation.

in the Settlement range between \$70 000 and \$80 000 should clinch the deal, if the negotiators can get into this range. Notice that every dollar that Party earns is a dollar's worth of cost for Other. How will they reach a settlement?[19]

Threats and Promises. *Threat* consists of implying that you will punish the other party if he or she does not concede to your position. For example, the Other firm might imply that it will terminate its other business with the consulting company if it does not lower its price on the attitude survey job. *Promises* are pledges that concessions will lead to rewards in the future. For example, Other might promise future consulting contracts if Party agrees to do the survey at a lower price. Of course, the difference between a threat and a promise can be subtle, as when the promise implies a threat if no concession is made.

Threat has some merit as a bargaining tactic if one party has power over the other that corresponds to the nature of the threat, especially if no future negotiations are expected or if the threat can be posed in a civil and subtle way.[20] If power is more balanced and the threat is crude, a counterthreat could scuttle the negotiations, despite the fact that both parties could be satisfied in the Settlement range. Promises have merit when your side lacks power and anticipates future negotiations with the other side. Both threat and promises work best when they send interpretable signals to the other side about your true position, what really matters to you. Careful timing is critical.

Firmness versus Concessions. How about intransigence—sticking to your target position, offering few concessions, and waiting for the other party to give in? Research shows that such a tactic is likely to be reciprocated by the other party, thus increasing the chances of a deadlock.[21] On the other hand, a series of small concessions early in the negotiation will often be matched. Good negotiators often use face-saving techniques to explain concessions. For example, the consulting firm might claim that it could reduce the cost of the survey by making it web-based rather than using paper questionnaires.

Persuasion. Verbal persuasion or debate is common in negotiations. Often, it takes a two-pronged attack. One prong asserts the technical merits of the party's position. For example, the consulting firm might justify its target price by saying "We have the most qualified staff. We do the most reliable surveys." The other prong asserts the fairness of the target position. Here, the negotiator might make a speech about the expenses the company would incur in doing the survey.

Verbal persuasion is an attempt to change the attitudes of the other party toward your target position. Persuaders are most effective when they are perceived as expert, likable, and unbiased. The obvious problem in distributive negotiations is bias—each party knows the other is self-interested. One way to deal with this is to introduce some unbiased parties. For example, the consulting firm might produce testimony from satisfied survey clients. Also, disputants often bring third parties into negotiations on the assumption that they will process argumentation in an unbiased manner.

Salary negotiation is a traditional example of distributive bargaining. A review of studies on gender differences in negotiation outcomes found that although men negotiated significantly better outcomes than women, the overall difference between men and women was small. However, even small differences in salary and wage negotiations could be perpetuated through subsequent salary increases based on percentage of pay. Furthermore, differences in negotiation outcomes could also be a factor in creating a "glass-ceiling" effect to the extent that women are less effective in negotiating opportunities and positions of power and status. Thus, training programs that enable women to negotiate better starting salaries comparable with men can have short- and long-term benefits.[22]

Integrative Negotiation Tactics

As we noted earlier, integrative negotiation rejects a fixed-pie assumption and strives for collaborative problem solving that advances the interests of both parties. At the outset, it is useful but sobering to realize that people have a decided bias for fixed-pie thinking. A good example is seen in the North American manufacturing sector, where such thinking by both unions and management badly damaged the global competitiveness of manufacturing firms.[23]

Why the bias for fixed-pie thinking? First, integrative negotiation requires a degree of creativity. Most people are not especially creative, and the stress of typical negotiation does not provide the best climate for creativity in any event. This means that many of the role models that negotiators have (e.g., following labour negotiations on TV) are more likely to use distributive than integrative tactics. To complicate matters, if you are negotiating for constituents, they are also more likely to be exposed to distributive tactics and likely to pressure you to use them. Nevertheless, attempts at integrative negotiation can be well worth the effort.[24]

Copious Information Exchange. Most of the information exchanged in distributive bargaining is concerned with attacking the other party's position and trying to persuade them of the correctness of yours. Otherwise, mum's the word. A freer flow of information is critical to finding an integrative settlement. The problem, of course, is that we all tend to be a bit paranoid about information being used against us in bargaining situations. This means that trust must be built slowly. One way to proceed is to give away some noncritical information to the other party to get the ball rolling. As we noted earlier, much negotiation behaviour tends to be reciprocated. Also, ask the other party a lot of questions, and *listen* to their responses. This is at odds with the tell-and-sell approach used in most distributive negotiations. If all goes well, both parties will begin to reveal their true interests, not just their current positions.

Framing Differences as Opportunities. Parties in a negotiation often differ in their preferences for everything from the timing of a deal to the degree of risk that each party wants to assume. Traditionally, such differences are framed as barriers to negotiations. However, such differences can often serve as a basis for integrative agreements because, again, they contain information that can telegraph each party's real interests. For instance, imagine that two co-workers are negotiating for the finishing date of a project that they have to complete by a certain deadline. Due to competing demands, one wants to finish it early, and the other wants to just make the deadline. In the course of the discussion, they realize that they can divide the labour such that one begins the project while the other finishes it, satisfying both parties fully (notice that this is not a compromise).

Cutting Costs. If you can somehow cut the costs that the other party associates with an agreement, the chance of an integrative settlement increases. For example, suppose that you are negotiating with your boss for a new, more interesting job assignment, but she does not like the idea because she relies on your excellent skills on your current assignment. By asking good questions (see above), you find out that she is ultimately worried about the job being done properly, not about your leaving it. You take the opportunity to inform her that you have groomed a subordinate to do your current job. This reduces the costs of her letting you assume the new assignment.

Integrative solutions are especially attractive when they reduce costs for *all* parties in a dispute. For example, firms in the computer and acoustics industries have joined together to support basic research on technology of interest to all firms. This reduces costly competition to perfect a technology that all parties need anyway.

Increasing Resources. Increasing available resources is a very literal way of getting around the fixed-pie syndrome. This is not as unlikely as it sounds when you realize that two parties, working together, might have access to twice as many resources as one party. One of your authors once saw two academic departments squabbling to get the approval to recruit one new faculty member for whom there was a budget line. Seeing this as a fixed pie leads to one department winning all or to the impossible compromise of half a recruit for each department. The chairs of the two departments used their *combined* political clout to get the dean to promise that they could also have exclusive access to one budget line the following year. The chairs then flipped a coin to see who would recruit immediately and who would wait a year. This minor compromise on time was less critical than the firm guarantee of a budget line.

Superordinate goals.
Attractive outcomes that can be achieved only by collaboration.

Introducing Superordinate Goals. As discussed in Chapter 7, **superordinate goals** are attractive outcomes that can be achieved only by collaboration.[25] Neither party can attain the goal on its own. Superordinate goals probably represent the best example of creativity in integrative negotiation because they change the entire landscape of the negotiation episode. Many observers have noted how the terrorist attacks on September 11, 2001, created a superordinate goal that prompted collaboration among nations that otherwise might have been mired in conflict over more trivial matters. At Disney, Eisner's successor, Robert Iger, invoked the superordinate goal of creating life-long memories for kids in his negotiations with Pixar.

Third Party Involvement

Sometimes, third parties come into play to intervene between negotiating parties. Often, this happens when the parties reach an impasse. For example, a manager might have to step into a conflict between two employees or even between two departments. In other cases, third party involvement exists right from the start of the negotiation. For example, real estate agents serve as an interface between home sellers and buyers.

Mediation. The process of mediation occurs when a neutral third party helps to facilitate a negotiated agreement. Formal mediation has a long history in labour disputes, international relations, and marital counselling. However, by definition, almost any manager might occasionally be required to play an informal mediating role.

What do mediators do?[26] First, almost anything that aids the *process* or *atmosphere* of negotiation can be helpful. Of course, this depends on the exact situation at hand. If there is tension, the mediator might serve as a lightning rod for anger or try to introduce humour. The mediator might try to help the parties clarify their underlying interests, both to themselves and to each other. Occasionally, imposing a deadline or helping the parties deal with their own constituents might be useful. Introducing a problem-solving orientation to move toward more integrative bargaining might also be appropriate.

The mediator might also intervene in the *content* of the negotiation, highlighting points of agreement, pointing out new options, or encouraging concessions.

Research shows that mediation has a fairly successful track record in dispute resolution. However, mediators cannot turn water into wine, and the process seems to work best when the conflict is not too intense and the parties are resolved to use negotiation to resolve their conflict. If the mediator is not seen as neutral or if there is dissension in the ranks of each negotiating party, mediation does not work so well.[27]

Arbitration. The process of arbitration occurs when a third party is given the authority to dictate the terms of settlement of a conflict (although there is nonbinding arbitration, which we will not consider here). Although disputing parties sometimes agree to arbitration, it can also be mandated formally by law or informally by upper management or parents. The key point is that negotiation has broken down, and the arbitrator has to make a final distributive allocation—this is not the way to integrative solutions.

In *conventional arbitration*, the arbitrator can choose any outcome, such as splitting the difference between the two parties. In *final offer arbitration*, each party makes a final offer, and the arbitrator chooses one of them. This latter invention was devised to motivate the two parties to make sensible offers that have a chance of being upheld. Also, fear of the all-or-nothing aspect of final arbitration seems to motivate more negotiated agreement.[28]

One of the most commonly arbitrated disputes between employers and employees is dismissal for excessive absenteeism. One study found that the arbitrators sided with the company in over half of such cases, especially when the company could show evidence of a fair and consistently applied absentee policy.[29]

IS ALL CONFLICT BAD?

In everyday life, there has traditionally been an emphasis on the negative, dysfunctional aspects of conflict. This is not difficult to understand. Discord between parents and children, severe labour strife, and international disputes are unpleasant experiences. To some degree, this emphasis on the negative aspects of conflict is also characteristic of thinking in organizational behaviour. However, there has been growing awareness of some potential *benefits* of organizational conflict. In fact, we suggested this in our previous distinction among task, process, and relationship conflict.

The argument that conflict can be functional rests mainly on the idea that it promotes necessary organizational change:

$$\text{CONFLICT} \longrightarrow \text{CHANGE} \longrightarrow \text{ADAPTATION} \longrightarrow \text{SURVIVAL}^{30}$$

In other words, for organizations to survive, they must adapt to their environments. This requires changes in strategy that may be stimulated through conflict. For example, consider the museum that relies heavily on government funding and consistently mounts exhibits that are appreciated only by "true connoisseurs" of art. Under a severe funding cutback, the museum can survive only if it begins to mount more popular exhibits. Such a change might occur only after much conflict within the board of directors.

Just how does conflict promote change? For one thing, it might bring into consideration new ideas that would not be offered without conflict. In trying to "one up" the opponent, one of the parties might develop a unique idea that the other cannot fail to appreciate. In a related way, conflict might promote change because each party begins to monitor the other's performance more carefully. This search for weaknesses means that it is more difficult to hide errors and problems from the rest of the organization. Such errors and problems (e.g., a failure to make deliveries on time) might be a signal that changes are necessary. Finally, conflict may promote useful change by signalling that a redistribution of power is necessary. Consider the human resources department that must battle with managers to get diversity programs implemented. This conflict might be a clue that some change is due in power priorities.

All this suggests that there are times when managers might use a strategy of **conflict stimulation** to cause change. But how does a manager know when some conflict might be a good thing? One signal is the existence of a "friendly rut," in which peaceful relationships take precedence over organizational goals. Another signal is seen when parties that should be interacting closely have chosen to withdraw from each other to avoid overt conflict. A third signal occurs when conflict is suppressed or downplayed by denying differences, ignoring controversy, and exaggerating points of agreement.[31]

The causes of conflict, discussed earlier, such as scarcity and ambiguity, could be manipulated by managers to achieve change.[32] For example, when he was appointed vice-chairman of product development at General Motors, Robert Lutz sent out a memo (promptly leaked to the automotive press) entitled "Strongly-Held Beliefs." In it, the product czar said that GM undervalued exciting design, and he panned corporate sacred cows such as the extensive use of consumer focus groups and product plan-

Conflict stimulation. A strategy of increasing conflict to motivate change.

ning committees. Lutz stimulated conflict by signalling a shift of resources from marketing to design.[33]

Conflict in organizations, warranted or not, often causes considerable stress. Let's now turn to this topic.

A MODEL OF STRESS IN ORGANIZATIONS

During the last decade, stress has become a serious concern for individuals and organizations. In fact, the headline of a news article referred to excessive stress as "the plague," and a popular business magazine named a special issue "The Limit," in recognition of workers being pushed to the limit like never before at all levels in the workplace.[34] The levels of stress in the workplace today are at an all-time high, and the implications of this are alarming. A recent US National Institute for Occupational Safety and Health survey found that 40 percent of workers found their jobs extremely or very stressful, and the Bureau of Labor Statistics determined that stress is a leading cause of worker disability.[35] In fact, the direct and indirect costs of stress-related and mental disorders in the United States is estimated to be about $100 billion.[36] The annual cost of time lost due to stress in Canada is $12 billion.[37]

These dramatic figures should not obscure the fact that stress can be part of the everyday routine of organizations. The model of a stress episode in Exhibit 13.3 can guide our introduction to this topic.[38]

Stressors

Stressors. Environmental events or conditions that have the potential to induce stress.

Stressors are environmental events or conditions that have the potential to induce stress. There are some conditions that would prove stressful for just about everyone. These include things such as extreme heat, extreme cold, isolation, or hostile people. More interesting is the fact that the individual personality often determines the extent to which a potential stressor becomes a real stressor and actually induces stress.

Stress

Stress. A psychological reaction to the demands inherent in a stressor that has the potential to make a person feel tense or anxious.

Stress is a psychological reaction to the demands inherent in a stressor that has the potential to make a person feel tense or anxious because the person does not feel capable of coping with these demands.[39] Stress is not intrinsically bad. All people require a certain level of stimulation from their environment, and moderate levels of stress can serve this function. In fact, one would wonder about the perceptual accuracy of a person who *never* experienced tension. On the other hand, stress does become a problem when it leads to especially high levels of anxiety and tension.

Stress Reactions

Stress reactions. The behavioural, psychological, and physiological consequences of stress.

Stress reactions are the behavioural, psychological, and physiological consequences of stress. Some of these reactions are essentially passive responses, over which the indi-

EXHIBIT 13.3
Model of a stress episode.

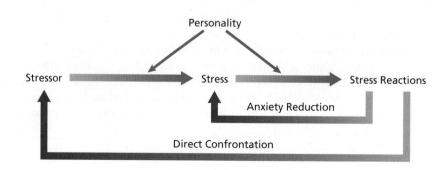

vidual has little direct control, such as elevated blood pressure or a reduced immune function. Other reactions are active attempts to *cope* with some previous aspect of the stress episode. Exhibit 13.3 indicates that stress reactions that involve coping attempts might be directed toward dealing directly with the stressor or simply reducing the anxiety generated by stress. In general, the former strategy has more potential for effectiveness than the latter because the chances of the stress episode being *terminated* are increased.[40]

Often, reactions that are useful for the individual in dealing with a stress episode may be very costly to the organization. The individual who is conveniently absent from work on the day of a difficult inventory check might prevent personal stress but leave the organization short handed (provoking stress in others). Thus, organizations should be concerned about the stress that individual employees experience.

Throughout the book, we have been careful to note cross-cultural differences in OB. However, the stress model presented here appears to generalize across cultures. That is, similar factors provoke stress and lead to similar stress reactions around the globe.[41]

Personality and Stress

Personality (Chapter 2) can have an important influence on the stress experience. As shown in Exhibit 13.3, it can affect both the extent to which potential stressors are perceived as stressful and the types of stress reactions that occur. Let's look at three key personality traits.

Locus of Control. You will recall from Chapter 2 that **locus of control** concerns people's beliefs about the factors that control their behaviour. Internals believe that they control their own behaviour, while externals believe that their behaviour is controlled by luck, fate, or powerful people. Compared with internals, externals are more likely to feel anxious in the face of potential stressors.[42] Most people like to feel in control of what happens to them, and externals feel less in control. Internals are more likely to confront stressors directly because they assume that this response will make a difference. Externals, on the other hand, are anxious but do not feel that they are masters of their own fate. Thus, they are more prone to simple anxiety-reduction strategies that only work in the short run.

Locus of control. A set of beliefs about whether one's behaviour is controlled mainly by internal or external forces.

Type A Behaviour Pattern. Interest in the Type A behaviour pattern began when physicians noticed that many sufferers of coronary heart disease, especially those who developed the disease relatively young, exhibited a distinctive pattern of behaviours and emotions.[43] Individuals who exhibit the **Type A behaviour pattern** tend to be aggressive and ambitious. Their hostility is easily aroused, and they feel a great sense of time urgency. They are impatient, competitive, and preoccupied with their work. The Type A individual can be contrasted with the Type B, who does not exhibit these extreme characteristics. Compared with Type B individuals, Type A people report heavier workloads, longer work hours, and more conflicting work demands.[44] We will see later that such factors turn out to be potent stressors. Thus, either Type A people encounter more stressful situations than Type Bs do, or they perceive themselves as doing so. In turn, Type A individuals are likely to exhibit adverse physiological reactions in response to stress. These include elevated blood pressure, elevated heart rate, and modified blood chemistry. Frustrating, difficult, or competitive events are especially likely to prompt these adverse reactions. Type A individuals seem to have a strong need to control their work environment. This is doubtless a full-time task that stimulates their feelings of time urgency and leads them to overextend themselves physically.[45]

Type A behaviour pattern. A personality pattern that includes aggressiveness, ambitiousness, competitiveness, hostility, impatience, and a sense of time urgency.

Research has made it increasingly clear that the major component of Type A behaviour that contributes to adverse physiological reactions is hostility and repressed anger. This may also be accompanied by exaggerated cynicism and distrust of others. When these factors are prominent in a Type A individual's personality, stress is most likely to take its toll.[46]

Negative affectivity. Propensity to view the world, including oneself and other people, in a negative light.

Negative Affectivity. Negative affectivity is the propensity to view the world, including oneself and other people, in a negative light. It is a stable personality trait that is a major component of the "Big Five" personality dimension neuroticism (Chapter 2). People high in negative affectivity tend to be pessimistic and downbeat. As a consequence, they tend to report more stressors in the work environment and to feel more subjective stress. They are particularly likely to feel stressed in response to the demands of a heavy workload.[47]

Several factors might be responsible for the susceptibility to stress of those who are high in negative affectivity. These include (a) a predisposition to *perceive* stressors in the workplace, (b) hypersensitivity to existing stressors, (c) a tendency to gravitate to stressful jobs, (d) a tendency to *provoke* stress through their negativity, or (e) the use of passive, indirect coping styles that avoid the real sources of stress.[48]

STRESSORS IN ORGANIZATIONAL LIFE

A recent study found that among a sample of employed Canadians, the most common source of stress is *workplace* stressors.[49] In this section, we will examine potential stressors in detail. Some stressors can affect almost everyone in any organization, while others are likely to affect people who perform particular roles.

Executive and Managerial Stressors

Executives and managers make key organizational decisions and direct the work of others. In these capacities, they experience some special forms of stress.

Role overload. The requirement for too many tasks to be performed in too short a time period.

Role Overload. Role overload occurs when one must perform too many tasks in too short a time period, and it is a common stressor for managers, especially in today's downsized organizations.[50] The open-ended nature of the managerial job is partly responsible for this heavy and protracted workload.[51] Management is an ongoing *process*, and there are few signposts to signify that a task is complete and that rest and relaxation are permitted. Especially when coupled with frequent moves or excessive travel, a heavy workload often provokes conflict between the manager's role as an

"You've been working awfully hard lately. If you need a little fresh air and sunshine, you can go to www.fresh-air-and-sunshine.com"

organizational member and his or her role as a spouse or parent. Thus, role overload may provoke stress, at the same time preventing the manager from enjoying the pleasures of life that can reduce stress.

Heavy Responsibility. Not only is the workload of the executive heavy, but it can have extremely important consequences for the organization and its members. A vice-president of labour relations might be in charge of a negotiation strategy that could result in either labour peace or a protracted and bitter strike. To complicate matters, the personal consequences of an incorrect decision can be staggering. For example, the courts have fined and even jailed executives who have engaged in illegal activities on behalf of their organizations. Finally, executives are responsible for people as well as things, and this influence over the future of others has the potential to induce stress. The executive who must terminate the operation of an unprofitable division, putting many out of work, or the manager who must lay off an employee, putting one out of work, might experience guilt and tension.[52]

Returning to the opening vignette on Disney, the film industry often entails heavy executive responsibility because so much rests on the success of a single movie.

Operative-Level Stressors

Operatives are individuals who occupy nonprofessional and nonmanagerial positions in organizations. In a manufacturing organization, operatives perform the work on the shop floor and range from skilled craftspeople to unskilled labourers. As is the case with other organizational roles, the occupants of operative positions are sometimes exposed to a special set of stressors.

Poor Physical Working Conditions. Operative-level employees are more likely than managers and professionals to be exposed to physically unpleasant and even dangerous working conditions. Although social sensibility and union activity have improved working conditions over the years, many employees must still face excessive heat, cold, noise, pollution, and the chance of accidents.

Poor Job Design. Although bad job design can provoke stress at any organizational level (executive role overload is an example), lower-level blue- and white-collar jobs are particular culprits. It might seem paradoxical that jobs that are too simple or not challenging enough can act as stressors. However, monotony and boredom can prove extremely frustrating to people who feel capable of handling more complex tasks. Thus, research has found that job scope can be a stressor at levels that are either too low or too high.[53]

According to Robert Karasek's **job demands–job control model**, jobs that make high demands on employees while giving them little control over workplace decisions are especially prone to produce stress and negative stress reactions.[54] High demands might include a hectic work pace, excessive workload, limited time to accomplish tasks, or responsibility for extreme economic loss. Lack of control means limited decision latitude and autonomy. Jobs that often involve high demand and little control include telephone operators, nurse's aides, assembly line workers, garment stitchers, and bus drivers. As Exhibit 13.4 demonstrates, these jobs fall into a zone of increased risk for heart disease (the area to the right of the dashed curve). Research has shown that both high job demands and low job control are stressors in their own right, and that their effects sometimes multiply to induce even more stress.[55]

Job demands–job control model. A model that asserts that jobs promote high stress when they make high demands while offering little control over work decisions.

EXHIBIT 13.4

Heart disease risk for various occupations.

Source: B. Nelson, "Bosses face less risk than bossed," *New York Times*, 1 April 1983. Section E, p. 16. Copyright © 1983 by The New York Times Co. Reprinted with permission.

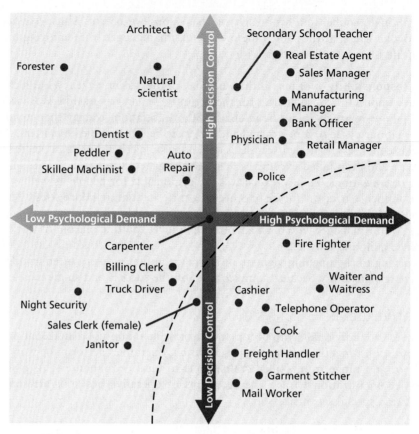

Note: High-risk occupations are to the right of the dotted line.

Boundary Role Stressors, Burnout, and Emotional Labour

Boundary roles. Positions in which organizational members are required to interact with members of other organizations or with the public.

Boundary roles are positions in which organizational members are required to interact with members of other organizations or with the public. For example, a vice-president of public relations is responsible for representing his or her company to the public. At the operative level, receptionists, salespeople, and installers often interact with customers or suppliers.

Occupants of boundary role positions are especially likely to experience stress as they straddle the imaginary boundary between the organization and its environment. This is yet another form of role conflict in which one's role as an organizational member might be incompatible with the demands made by the public or other organizations. A classic case of boundary role stress involves salespeople. In extreme cases, buyers desire fast delivery of a large quantity of custom-tailored products. The salesperson might be tempted to "offer the moon" but is at the same time aware that such an order could place a severe strain on his or her organization's production facilities. Thus, the salesperson is faced with the dilemma of doing his or her primary job (selling), while protecting another function (production) from unreasonable demands that could result in a broken delivery contract.

A particular form of stress experienced by some boundary role occupants is burnout. **Burnout,** as Christina Maslach and Susan Jackson define it, is a combination "of emotional exhaustion, depersonalization, and reduced personal accomplishment that can occur among individuals who work with people in some capacity."[56] Frequently, these other people are organizational clients who require very special attention or who are experiencing severe problems. Thus, teachers, nurses, paramedics, social workers, and police are especially likely candidates for burnout.

Burnout. Emotional exhaustion, depersonalization, and reduced personal accomplishment among those who work with people.

Burnout follows a process that begins with emotional exhaustion (Exhibit 13.5). The person feels fatigued in the morning, drained by the work, and frustrated by the day's events. One way to deal with this extreme exhaustion is to distance oneself from one's clients, the "cause" of the exhaustion. In an extreme form, this might involve treating them like objects and lacking concern for what happens to them. The clients might also be seen as blaming the employee for their problems. Finally, the burned-out individual develops feelings of low personal accomplishment—"I can't deal with these people, I'm not helping them, I don't understand them." In fact, because of the exhaustion and depersonalization, there might be more than a grain of truth to those feelings. Although the exact details of this progression are open to some question, these three sets of symptoms paint a reliable picture of burnout.[57]

Burnout seems to be most common among people who entered their jobs with especially high ideals. Their expectations of being able to "change the world" are badly frustrated when they encounter the reality shock of troubled clients (who are often perceived as unappreciative) and the inability of the organization to help them. Teachers get fed up with being disciplinarians, nurses get upset when patients die, and police officers get depressed when they must constantly deal with the "losers" of society.[58] For an illustration, see "Ethical Focus: *Workplace Violence Prompts Stress among Health and Social Service Providers.*"

What are the consequences of burnout? Some individuals bravely pursue a new occupation, often experiencing guilt about not having been able to cope in the old one. Others stay in the same occupation but seek a new job. For instance, the burned-out nurse might go into nursing education to avoid contact with sick patients. Some people pursue administrative careers in their profession, attempting to "climb above" the source of their difficulties. These people often set cynical examples for idealistic subordinates. Finally, some people stay in their jobs and become part of the legion of "deadwood," collecting their paycheques but doing little to contribute to the mission of the organization. Many "good bureaucrats" choose this route.[59]

It is perhaps not surprising to you that so much boundary role stress stems from the frequent need for such employees to engage in "emotional labour." You will recall from Chapter 4 that emotional labour involves regulating oneself to suppress negative emotions or to exaggerate positive ones. Thus, police officers are not supposed to express anger at unsafe motorists or drunks, and nurses are not supposed to express exasperation with uncooperative patients. Such suppression takes a toll on cognitive and emotional resources over time.

Some General Stressors

To conclude our discussion of stressors that people encounter in organizational life, we will consider some that are probably experienced equally by occupants of all roles.

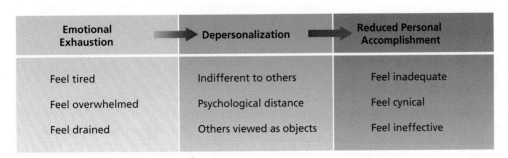

Emotional Exhaustion	Depersonalization	Reduced Personal Accomplishment
Feel tired	Indifferent to others	Feel inadequate
Feel overwhelmed	Psychological distance	Feel cynical
Feel drained	Others viewed as objects	Feel ineffective

EXHIBIT 13.5
The stages of burnout and their symptoms.

Source: Chart based on Organizational practices for preventing burnout, from *Handbook of Stress Coping Strategies* by Amarjit Singh Sethi and Randall S. Schuler, p. 92. Copyright © 1984 by Ballinger Publishing Company. Reprinted by permission of HarperCollins Publishers, Inc.

ETHICAL FOCUS

Workplace Violence Prompts Stress among Health and Social Service Providers

Health care and social assistance workers are much more likely to file compensation claims over violence in the workplace than employees in other Canadian sectors, a CBC News investigation suggests. In some provinces, the rate of violence-related claims is 12 times higher than for all other industries, according to databases from provincial workplace safety insurance boards that the CBC gained access to after three years of negotiation. Some of the databases are more detailed than others, and incidents are recorded in different ways, so numbers can't be compared across the board. However, the databases show the following:

- Nova Scotia health care and social assistance workers reported 3.59 violent incidents per 1000 workers between 1994 and 2004, among the highest rates in the country for workers in those sectors.
- Ontario health care and social assistance workers reported 5333 violent incidents between the years 1997 and 2004, out of 12 383 reported by all workers. That's an average of 1.21 incidents per 1000 workers, compared to 0.17 incidents per 1000 workers in other industries.
- Quebec's health and social assistance sector recorded 1.43 incidents per 1000 workers between 1994 and 2004.
- Annually, Ontario health care and social assistance workers lost 24.5 days per 1000 workers due to violence, compared to four lost days per 1000 workers in all other incidents.

Not even police officers are exposed to more violence at work than nurses, the numbers for at least two provinces indicate. In Nova Scotia, 358 registered nurses filed claims stemming from violence between 1994 and 2004, compared to 96 police officers who did so in the same time period. During the same decade in British Columbia, 769 practical nurses or nurses' aides filed claims based on violent incidents, compared to 335 police officers. Health care workers say the trend to de-institutionalize people with mental illnesses, bringing them into emergency rooms, is one reason for the increase in violence. And with an aging population, more people with dementia are in long-term care facilities. In addition, some nurses report they're so busy working in an overburdened system that they don't have time to defuse little crises before they escalate into full-fledged attacks.

A union representing 14 000 health care and social service workers in BC says they are being punched, grabbed, pushed, and threatened verbally by their patients and clients. In rare cases, some are even killed. "If you were working in a grocery store, you wouldn't tolerate someone ramming a grocery cart into you because the stock wasn't on the shelf," said Cindy Stewart, who speaks for the Health Sciences Association of British Columbia. "You wouldn't tolerate one of your customers punching you, or slapping you, grabbing you, or spitting on you, or verbally abusing you. That wouldn't be tolerated in those kinds of work environments—and yet it is a daily occurrence in the health sector."

One of the casualties was David Bland, a tall and soft-spoken employee at a mental health facility in Richmond, BC. Bland was fatally stabbed on January 19, 2005. A patient he had helped in the past is awaiting trial for his murder. "The last time I saw Dave was 5 or 10 minutes before he was killed," said Scott Elthinston, a colleague and friend. "We exchanged goodbyes." Bland was stabbed as he walked toward his car in the parking lot outside his office. Four colleagues found him on the ground. He managed to give the name of his attacker before he died. "My first thought was, 'Gee, the guy is so close to retirement,'" said Elthinston. "It could have been any one of us. I walked to my car a few minutes before Dave."

Anthony Pizzano researches health and safety for the Canadian Union of Public Employees. He says without tougher regulations, even more of his members will get injured. "What will happen is that we will have a reactive situation, whereas health and safety legislation in general is supposed to be preventive," he said. Few provinces other than BC and Saskatchewan have laws requiring employers and employees to deal with violence through measures such as safety audits. Among other things, audits could establish protocols for identifying dangerous patients.

Source: Excerpted from CBC News (2006). *Health, social service workers top targets of violence.* Retrieved April 24, 2006, from http://www.cbc.ca/story/canada/national/2006/04/24/workplace-violence060424.html.

Interpersonal Conflict. From our earlier discussion of interpersonal conflict, you might correctly guess that it can be a potent stressor, especially for those with strong avoidance tendencies. The entire range of conflict, from personality clashes to intergroup strife, is especially likely to cause stress when it leads to real or perceived attacks on our self-esteem or integrity. Although conflict can lead to stress in many settings outside of work, we often have the option of terminating the relationship, of "choosing our friends," as it were. This option is often not available at work.

A particular manifestation of interpersonal conflict which has received increased attention in recent years is workplace bullying. **Bullying** can be defined as repeated negative behaviour directed toward one or more individuals of lower power or status that creates a hostile work environment.[60]

A number of factors distinguish bullying as a stress-inducing form of conflict.[61] Although bullying can involve physical aggression, it is most commonly a more subtle form of psychological aggression and intimidation. This can take many forms, such as incessant teasing, demeaning criticism, social isolation, or sabotaging others' tools and equipment. An essential feature of bullying is its persistence, and a single harsh incident would not constitute such behaviour. Rather, it is the *repeated* teasing, criticism, or undermining that signals bullying. Another key feature of the bullying process is some degree of power or status imbalance between the bully and the victim. Thus, managers have often been identified as bullies by subordinates. However, power imbalance can be subtle, and in some settings even work peers might lack power due to their gender, race, physical stature, low job security, or educational credentials. Also, there is power in numbers such that subordinates might team up to harass their boss. This is an example of a phenomenon closely associated to bullying called *mobbing*. Mobbing occurs when a number of individuals, usually direct co-workers, "gang up" on a particular employee.[62] Mobbing can be especially intimidating and stressful because it restricts the availability of social support that might be present when there is only a single bully.

The essential point is that victims of bullying and mobbing experience stress because they feel powerless to deal with the perpetrator(s). Most observers note that a combination of factors work together to stimulate this dysfunctional behaviour.

Norway, Sweden, France, and the province of Quebec have enacted laws that pertain to bullying in the workplace.[63] Various organizations have also done their part. Ramsey County, Minnesota, the US Department of Veterans Affairs, and IBM all have active anti-bullying programs. IBM fired several factory workers who mobbed their new supervisor to drive home its seriousness about its policy.[64]

IBM
www.ibm.com

US Department of Veterans Affairs
www.va.gov

Before continuing, consider the You Be the Manager feature about bullying at Veterans Affairs.

Work-Family Conflict. A recent study on the costs of work-family conflict found that it is costing Canadian companies $6 to $10 billion a year in absenteeism, and the Canadian health care system $425 million as a result of increased visits to the doctor to treat problems associated with the conflict.[65]

Two facts of life in contemporary society have increased the stress stemming from the interrole conflict between being a member of one's family and the member of an organization. First, the increase in the number of homes in which both parents work and the increase in the number of single parent families has led to a number of stressors centred around childcare. Finding adequate daycare and disputes between partners about sharing childcare responsibilities can prove to be serious stressors.

Second, increased life spans have meant that many people in the prime of their careers find themselves providing support for elderly parents, some of whom may be seriously ill. This inherently stressful eldercare situation is often compounded by feelings of guilt about the need to tend to matters at work.

Women are particularly victimized by stress due to work-family conflict, although it is reported to be a rapidly growing problem for men as well.[66] Much anecdotal

☞ YOU BE THE
Manager

Bullying at Veterans Affairs

Jobs in the social service sector regularly entail emotional labour, with workers confronted on a daily basis with high demands from clients concerning social, emotional, and medical problems. While such client-service provider interactions can be emotionally draining, such a work environment can also be a breeding ground for workplace aggression and bullying.

With this in mind, the United States Department of Veterans Affairs (VA), in collaboration with other federal agencies and university researchers, launched the Workplace Stress and Aggression Project. The VA provides patient care and federal benefits to veterans and their dependents through central offices, benefits offices, and medical facilities. In the post–September 11 era, the VA has seen an increase in activity with the conflicts in Afghanistan and Iraq. The goal of the Workplace Stress and Aggression Project was to assess the prevalence of workplace aggression and bullying within the VA, to understand their impact on employee satisfaction, VA performance, and veteran satisfaction, and to develop intervention strategies to reduce aggression and bullying.

The research team used a multimethod approach featuring archival data, questionnaires to staff, interviews, and discussion groups. Twenty-six VA facilities participated in the project. Eleven of the sites, representing over 7200 employees, participated in a more comprehensive version of the project. Results of the initial surveys clearly indicated that workplace aggression and bullying were issues within the VA. Overall, 36 percent of employees surveyed reported being bullied at work. For the purposes of the survey, bullying was defined as persistent patterns of aggression that workers experienced at least once a week. Of the 36 percent, 29 percent indicated they experienced aggression in the workplace one to five times a week, while 7 percent reported experiencing six or more aggression episodes a week. Another 58 percent of employees reported that they experienced workplace aggression, albeit not on a weekly basis, while only 6 percent of employees indicated that they suffered no workplace aggression. Aggression could be physical or verbal, active (e.g., in a confrontation) or passive (e.g., through exclusion), or direct (e.g., personally targeted) or indirect (e.g., defacing property or spreading rumours). Most incidents were of the verbal, passive, and indirect variety.

> **High levels of bullying at various Veterans Affairs facilities worried executives, who decided to take action.**

Employees indicated that 44 percent of the aggression they experienced emanated from co-workers, 35 percent came from supervisors, and 12 percent came from veterans. In terms of impact on personal well-being, they suffered more stress and lower job satisfaction when a supervisor was the source of the aggression compared to aggression from co-workers or clients. The research team also found that bullying was linked to lower employee and organizational performance and increases in stress, absenteeism, lateness, turnover, and worker compensation claims.

With this data in hand, the project team's focus turned to understanding why aggression occurred and what could be done to reduce it.

QUESTIONS

1. What do you think some of the primary causes of workplace aggression and bullying within the VA might be? Do you think the causes would be different across the various VA facilities?

2. Suggest an intervention strategy to reduce the incidence of aggression and bullying in the VA workplace. Who should be involved?

To find out how the VA responded, see The Manager's Notebook at the end of the chapter.

Sources: Scaringi, J., et al. (Undated). *The VA workplace stress and aggression project—final report*; Neuman, J.H., & Keashly, L. (2005, August). Reducing aggression and bul-lying: An intervention project in the U.S. Department of Veterans Affairs. In J. Raver (Chair), *Workplace bullying: International perspectives on moving from research to practice*. Symposium presented at the annual meeting of the Academy of Management, Honolulu, HI; Neuman, J.H. (2004). Injustice, stress, and aggression in organizations. In R.W. Griffin & A.M. O'Leary-Kelly (Eds.), *The dark side of organizational behavior*. San Francisco, CA: Jossey-Bass.

evidence suggests that women who take time off work to deal with pressing family matters are more likely than men to be labelled disloyal or undedicated to their work. Also, many managers seem to be insensitive to the demands that these basic demographic shifts are making on their employees, again compounding the potential for stress.[67]

Job Insecurity and Change. Secure employment is an important goal for almost everyone, and stress may be encountered when it is threatened. During the last decade, organizations have undergone substantial changes that have left many workers unemployed and threatened the security of those who have been fortunate enough to remain in their jobs. The trend toward mergers and acquisitions, along with reengineering, restructuring, and downsizing, has led to increasingly high levels of stress among employees who have either lost their jobs or must live with the threat of more layoffs, the loss of friends and co-workers, and an increased workload.[68] The fear of job loss has become a way of life for employees at all organizational levels.[69]

At the operative level, unionization has provided a degree of employment security for some, but the vagaries of the economy and the threat of technology and other organizational changes hang heavy over many workers. Among professionals, the very specialization that enables them to obtain satisfactory jobs becomes a millstone whenever social or economic forces change. For example, aerospace scientists and engineers have long been prey to the boom-and-bust nature of their industry. When layoffs occur, these people are often perceived as overqualified or too specialized to easily obtain jobs in related industries. Finally, the executive suite does not escape job insecurity. Recent pressures for corporate performance have made cost cutting a top priority for many companies. One of the surest ways to cut costs in the short run is to reduce executive positions and thus reduce the total management payroll. Many corporations have greatly thinned their executive ranks in recent years.

Role Ambiguity. We have already noted how role conflict—having to deal with incompatible role expectations—can provoke stress. There is also substantial evidence that role ambiguity can provoke stress.[70] From Chapter 7, you will recall that role ambiguity exists when the goals of one's job or the methods of performing the job are unclear. Such a lack of direction can prove stressful, especially for people who are low in their tolerance for such ambiguity. For example, the president of a firm might be instructed by the board of directors to increase profits and cut costs. While this goal seems clear enough, the means by which it can be achieved might be unclear. This ambiguity can be devastating, especially when the organization is doing poorly and no strategy seems to improve things.

Sexual Harassment. In Chapter 12, we discussed sexual harassment in terms of the abuse of power and a form of unethical behaviour. Sexual harassment is a major workplace stressor with serious consequences for employees and organizations that are similar to or more negative than other types of job stressors.[71] Sexual harassment in the workplace is now considered to be widespread in both the public and private sectors, and most harassment victims are subjected to ongoing harassment and stress.[72] The negative effects of sexual harassment include decreased morale, job satisfaction, organizational commitment, and job performance, and an increase in absenteeism, turnover, and job loss. Sexual harassment has also been found to have serious effects on the psychological and physical well-being of harassment victims.[73] Victims of sexual harassment experience depression, frustration, nervousness, fatigue, nausea, hypertension, and symptoms of posttraumatic stress disorder.[74] Organizations in which sexual harassment is most likely to be a problem are those that have a climate that is tolerant of sexual harassment and where women are working in traditional male-dominated jobs and in a male-dominated workplace.[75]

Exhibit 13.6 summarizes the sources of stress at various points in the organization.

REACTIONS TO ORGANIZATIONAL STRESS

In this section, we examine the reactions that people who experience organizational stress might exhibit. These reactions can be divided into behavioural, psychological, and physiological responses.

Behavioural Reactions to Stress

Behavioural reactions to stress are overt activities that the stressed individual uses in an attempt to cope with the stress. They include problem solving, modified performance, withdrawal, and the use of addictive substances.

Problem Solving. In general, problem solving is directed toward terminating the stressor or reducing its potency, not toward simply making the person feel better in the short run. Problem solving is reality oriented, and while it is not always effective in combating the stressor, it reveals flexibility and realistic use of feedback. Most examples of a problem-solving response to stress are undramatic because problem solving is generally the routine, sensible, obvious approach that an objective observer might suggest. Consider the following examples of problem solving.

- *Delegation.* A busy executive reduces her stress-provoking workload by delegating some of her many tasks to a capable assistant.

- *Time management.* A manager who finds the day too short writes a daily schedule, requires his subordinates to make formal appointments to see him, and instructs his secretary to screen phone calls more selectively.

EXHIBIT 13.6
Sources of stress at various points in the organization.

Executives and Managers
- Heavy, Continuing Workload
- Heavy Responsibility

Boundary Roles
- Role Conflict
- Emotional Labour

All Employees
- Job Insecurity and Change
- Role Ambiguity
- Interpersonal Conflict
- Work-Family Conflict
- Sexual Harassment
- Bullying

Operative Employees
- Poor Physical Conditions
- Poor Job Design

- *Talking it out.* An engineer who is experiencing stress because of poor communication with her nonengineer superior resolves to sit down with the boss and hammer out an agreement concerning the priorities on a project.

- *Asking for help.* A salesperson who is anxious about his company's ability to fill a difficult order asks the production manager to provide a realistic estimate of the probable delivery date.

- *Searching for alternatives.* A machine operator who finds her monotonous job stress provoking applies for a transfer to a more interesting position for which the pay is identical.

Performance. Stress or stressors frequently cause reduced job performance.[76] However, this needs to be qualified slightly. Some stressors are "hindrance" stressors in that they directly damage goal attainment. These include things like role ambiguity and interpersonal conflict. Such stressors damage performance. On the other hand, some stressors are challenging. These include factors such as heavy workload and responsibility. Such stressors can damage performance, but they sometimes stimulate it via added motivation.[77]

Withdrawal. Withdrawal from the stressor is one of the most basic reactions to stress. In organizations, this withdrawal takes the form of absence and turnover. Compared with problem-solving reactions to stress, absenteeism fails to attack the stressor directly. Rather, the absent individual is simply attempting some short-term reduction of the anxiety prompted by the stressor. When the person returns to the job, the stress is still there. From this point of view, absence is a dysfunctional reaction to stress for both the individual and the organization. The same can be said about turnover when a person resigns from a stressful job on the spur of the moment merely to escape stress. However, a good case can be made for a well-planned resignation in which the intent is to assume another job that should be less stressful. This is actually a problem-solving reaction that should benefit both the individual and the organization in the long run. Absence, turnover, and turnover intentions have often been linked with stress and its causes.[78] For a dramatic example, see "Research Focus: *Traumatic National Events, Stress, and Work Behaviour.*"

Use of Addictive Substances. Smoking, drinking, and drug use represent the least satisfactory behavioural responses to stress for both the individual and the organization. These activities fail to terminate stress episodes, and they leave employees less physically and mentally prepared to perform their jobs. We have all heard of hard-drinking newspaper reporters and advertising executives, and it is tempting to infer that the stress of their boundary role positions is responsible for their drinking. Indeed, cigarette use and alcohol abuse are associated with the presence of work-related stress.[79]

Psychological Reactions to Stress

Psychological reactions to stress primarily involve emotions and thought processes rather than overt behaviour, although these reactions are frequently revealed in the individual's speech and actions. The most common psychological reaction to stress is the use of defence mechanisms.[80]

Defence mechanisms are psychological attempts to reduce the anxiety associated with stress. Notice that, by definition, defence mechanisms concentrate on *anxiety reduction* rather than on actually confronting or dealing with the stressor. Some common defence mechanisms include the following:

Defence mechanisms. Psychological attempts to reduce the anxiety associated with stress.

- *Rationalization* is attributing socially acceptable reasons or motives to one's actions so that they will appear reasonable and sensible, at least to oneself. For example, a

RESEARCH FOCUS

Traumatic National Events, Stress, and Work Behaviour

This chapter is mainly concerned with how factors at work promote stress. However, it is important to understand how off-the-job events influence stress and how such stress affects work behaviour. Everyday examples include the demands of childcare and eldercare. However, more dramatic examples can be found in examining how tragic national events can cause stress and influence work behaviour.

Talma Kushnir, Yitzhak Fried, and Ruth Malkinson studied how Israeli employees reacted to the November 5, 1995, assassination of Prime Minister Yitzhak Rabin by a fellow citizen. They reasoned that this would be a stressful event for many Israelis, and that this would influence their work behaviour. Indeed, employees who reported increased acute stress symptoms following the tragic event were more likely to also exhibit higher absenteeism from work. Women were more likely than men to translate stress into absenteeism, and optimists were less likely than pessimists to do so, in line with the idea that personality affects stress reactions.

Kristin Byron and Suzanne Peterson studied how US employees reacted to the deadly September 11, 2001, terrorist attacks on the World Trade Center and the Pentagon. Individuals who were more exposed to the events (e.g., knew victims, were physically close to the scene, watched much TV coverage) reported more acute stress. Furthermore, those who reported more stress were more likely to be absent from work in the ensuing weeks. The "optimism effect" noted by Kushnir and colleagues was not observed. However, employees who reported more organizational social support following the tragedy (e.g., patriotic displays, permitted discussion of events, fundraisers) were less likely to report feeling stress.

In both cases, absenteeism evidently served as a coping mechanism for stressed employees.

Sources: Byron, K., & Peterson, S. (2002). The impact of a large-scale traumatic event on individual and organizational outcomes: Exploring employee and company reactions to September 11, 2001. *Journal of Organizational Behavior, 23,* 895–910; Kushnir, T., Fried, Y., & Malkinson, R. (2001). Work absence as a function of a national traumatic event: The case of Prime Minister Rabin's assassination. *Work & Stress, 15,* 265–273.

male nurse who becomes very angry and abusive when learning that he will not be promoted to supervisor might justify his anger by claiming that the head nurse discriminates against men.

- *Projection* is attributing one's own undesirable ideas and motives to others so that they seem less negative. For example, a sales executive who is undergoing conflict about offering a bribe to an official of a foreign government might reason that the official is corrupt.

- *Displacement* is directing feelings of anger at a "safe" target rather than expressing them where they may be punished. For example, a construction worker who is severely criticized by the boss for sloppy workmanship might take out his frustrations in an evening hockey league.

- *Reaction formation* is expressing oneself in a manner that is directly opposite to the way one truly feels, rather than risking negative reactions to one's true position. For example, a low-status member of a committee might vote with the majority on a crucial issue rather than stating his true position and opening himself to attack.

- *Compensation* is applying one's skills in a particular area to make up for failure in another area. For example, a professor who is unable to get his or her research published might resolve to become a superb teacher.

Is the use of defence mechanisms a good or bad reaction to stress? Used occasionally to temporarily reduce anxiety, they appear to be a useful reaction. For example, the construction worker who displaces aggression in an evening hockey league rather than attacking a frustrating boss might calm down, return to work the next day, and "talk it out" with the boss. Thus, the occasional use of defence mechanisms as short-term anxiety reducers probably benefits both the individual and the organization. In fact, people with "weak defences" can be incapacitated by anxiety and resort to dysfunctional withdrawal or addiction.

When the use of defence mechanisms becomes a chronic reaction to stress, however, the picture changes radically. The problem stems from the very character of defence mechanisms—they simply do not change the objective character of the stressor, and the basic conflict or frustration remains in operation. After some short-term relief from anxiety, the basic problem remains unresolved. In fact, the stress might *increase* with the knowledge that the defence has been essentially ineffective.

Physiological Reactions to Stress

Can work-related stress kill you? This is clearly an important question for organizations, and it is even more important for individuals who experience excessive stress at work. Many studies of physiological reactions to stress have concentrated on the cardiovascular system, specifically on the various risk factors that might prompt heart attacks. For example, work stress is associated with electrocardiogram irregularities and elevated levels of blood pressure, cholesterol, and pulse.[81] Although dentists probably cause *you* stress, you might be surprised to learn that *they* also suffer from a fairly high rate of physiological problems that might be due to stress. One study found that the difficulties of building a dental practice, the image of the dentist as an inflictor of pain, and a lack of appreciation from patients were related to various cardiovascular risks.[82] Stress has also been associated with the onset of diseases such as respiratory and bacterial infections due to its ill effects on the immune system.[83] The accumulation of stress into burnout has been particularly implicated in cardiovascular problems.[84]

REDUCING OR COPING WITH STRESS

This chapter would be incomplete without a discussion of personal and organizational strategies that can reduce or cope with stress.

Job Redesign

Organizations can redesign jobs to reduce their stressful characteristics. In theory, it is possible to redesign jobs anywhere in the organization to this end. Thus, an overloaded executive might be given an assistant to reduce the number of tasks he or she must perform. In practice, most formal job redesign efforts have involved enriching operative-level jobs to make them more stimulating and challenging.

Especially for service jobs, there is growing evidence that providing more autonomy in how service is delivered can alleviate stress and burnout.[85] Call centre workers, fast-food employees, some salespeople, and some hospitality workers are highly "scripted" by employers with the idea that uniformity will be appreciated by customers. This is debatable, but it is not debatable that this lack of personal control goes against the research-supported prescriptions of job enrichment (Chapter 6), empowerment (Chapter 12), and the job demands–job control model of stress (this chapter). Boundary role service jobs require a high degree of emotional regulation in any event, and some degree of autonomy allows employees to cope with emotional labour by adjusting their responses to the needs of the moment in line with their own personalities. Guidelines about desired service outcomes can replace rigid scripts, especially for routine (non-emergency) encounters.

A special word should be said about the stressful job designs that often emerge from heavy-handed downsizings, restructurings, and mergers. Common symptoms of such jobs are extreme role overload, increased responsibility without corresponding authority to act, and the assignment of tasks for which no training is provided.

Executives overseeing such change efforts should obtain professional assistance to ensure proper job designs.

Social Support

Everyday experience suggests to us that the support of others can help us deal with stress. We have all seen children who are facing a tense experience run to an adult for support and comfort, and we have all seen on television the victims of natural disasters finding solace in others. Although the dynamics of job stress might be more subtle, there is every reason to believe that social support should work the same way for people who experience job stress.

Speaking generally, social support simply refers to having close ties with other people. In turn, these close ties could affect stress by bolstering self-esteem, providing useful information, offering comfort and humour, or even providing material resources (such as a loan). Research evidence shows that the benefits of social support are double barrelled. First, people with stronger social networks exhibit better psychological and physical well-being. Second, when people encounter stressful events, those with good social networks are likely to cope more positively. Thus, the social network acts as a buffer against stress.[86]

Off the job, individuals might find social support in a spouse, family, or friends. On the job, social support might be available from one's superior or co-workers. Research evidence suggests that the buffering aspects of social support are most potent when they are directly connected to the source of stress. This means that co-workers and superiors might be the best sources of support for dealing with work-related stress. In particular, most managers need better training to recognize employee stress symptoms, clarify role requirements, and so on. Unfortunately, some organizational cultures, especially those that are very competitive, do not encourage members to seek support in a direct fashion. In this event, relationships that people develop in professional associations can sometimes serve as an informed source of social support.

As described in Chapter 10, the San Francisco Police Department has an active peer support program that trains officers to detect stress and provide support to other officers. In one year, over 6000 peer-support contacts were reported.[87]

Police officers must deal with a unique type of on-the-job stress: workplace violence. There has been an upswing in psychological counselling for officers experiencing stress reactions.

"Family Friendly" Human Resource Policies

To reduce stress associated with dual careers, childcare, and eldercare, many organizations are beginning to institute "family friendly" human resource policies.[88] These policies generally include some combination of formalized social support, material support, and increased flexibility to adapt to employee needs. In fact, yummymummycareers.com is dedicated to hooking up working mothers with family friendly employers.

In the domain of social support, some firms distribute newsletters, such as *Work & Family Life,* that deal with work-family issues. Others have developed company support groups for employees dealing with eldercare problems. Some companies have contracted specialized consultants to provide seminars on eldercare issues.

A welcome form of material support consists of corporate daycare centres. Flexibility (which provides more *control* over family issues) is also important, and includes flex-time, telecommuting, and job sharing (Chapter 6), as well as family leave policies that allow time off for caring for infants, sick children, and aged dependents. Although many firms boast of having such flexible policies, a common problem is encouraging managers to *use* them in an era of downsizing and lean staffing.

Firms that are noted for their family-friendly human resource policies include Corning, IBM, American Express, and Zehrs Markets, a division of Toronto-based Loblaws.

Zehrs
www.zehrsmarkets.com

Stress Management Programs

Some organizations have experimented with programs designed to help employees "manage" work-related stress. Such programs are also available from independent off-work sources. Some of these programs help physically and mentally healthy employees prevent problems due to stress. Others are therapeutic in nature, aimed at individuals who are already experiencing stress problems. Although the exact content of the programs varies, most involve one or more of the following techniques: meditation; training in muscle-relaxation exercises; biofeedback training to control physiological processes; training in time management; and training to think more positively and realistically about sources of job stress.[89] Although each of these techniques has been useful in reducing anxiety and tension in other contexts, they have only recently been applied in the work setting. Tentative evidence suggests that these applications are useful in reducing physiological arousal, sleep disturbances, and self-reported tension and anxiety.[90]

Companies are striving to be much more "family friendly" than in the past. Some organizations offer daycare for children of employees.

Work–Life Balance Programs

Many people have argued that a balanced lifestyle that includes a variety of leisure activities combined with a healthy diet and physical exercise can reduce stress and counteract some of the adverse physiological effects of stress. For some organizations, work–life balance programs and quality-of-life benefits have become a strategic retention tool. Employees are increasingly demanding work–life balance benefits, and employers are realizing that by providing them they can increase commitment and reduce turnover.

Eddie Bauer Inc.
www.eddiebauer.com

Eddie Bauer Inc. offers work–life programs to their employees to help them lead more productive and balanced lives. Workers are encouraged to participate in mental and physical fitness through a variety of programs. Employee assistance programs are also available to help employees manage personal problems, mental and emotional difficulties, alcohol and chemical dependency, as well as legal and financial assistance.[91] At Husky Injection Molding Systems, the cafeteria only serves healthy food and at the company's head office in Bolton, Ontario, a naturopath, a chiropractor, a medical doctor, a nurse, and a massage therapist are on staff, and employees are encouraged to use the company's large fitness centre.[92] Starbucks also has a work–life program that includes on-site fitness services.[93]

Starbucks
www.starbucks.com

Studies show that fitness training is associated with improved mood, a better self-concept, reduced absenteeism, and reports of better performance. Work–life programs are also believed to result in lower health care costs. Some of these improvements probably stem from stress reduction.[94]

☞ THE MANAGER'S

Notebook

Bullying at Veterans Affairs

1. Many of the well-known sources of conflict in the workplace can lead to aggression and bullying. Power and status differences between individuals, rivalries between groups, uncertainty and competition, and a noxious organizational culture can all facilitate bullying and aggression. The VA project team found many of these conditions at the various sites. However, they generally found a distinctive pattern of causes of bullying at each facility. Through interviews and other methods, the research team attempted to paint a picture of each of the sites under study. At some sites, a lack of cooperation, respect, and fairness were drivers of aggression and bullying. At other sites, diversity management was the primary issue. Sites that had recently made significant new hires often had clashes between newcomers and old-timers. Sites with poor leadership and a lack of goal alignment were also problems. The results were often communication breakdowns, misinformation, and the growth of rumours. Overall, the project team identified issues in the work climate, although they varied in content from site to site, as the key factor in workplace aggression and bullying.

2. Unlike many organizational development prescriptions advocating the establishment of best practices to resolve problems, the VA project team realized that interventions to quell workplace aggression and bullying would need to be customized at each site to deal with each specific work climate. However, the *general* process they developed to do this was common to all. In the 11 sites that participated in the more comprehensive version of the project, the research team created action teams of organizational members to guide the project and develop needed interventions. The exercise of bringing people together to learn and discuss issues surrounding bullying and aggression in itself transformed the work climate in a positive way. Interventions often focused on some form of what are known as High Involvement Work Systems involving information sharing and empowerment. In a follow-up two years after the original data gathering exercise, the research team found that, compared to the 15 sites that did not participate in the intervention, the 11 focal sites reported fewer incidents of aggressive behaviour and fewer injury-stress–related behaviours. Work attitudes and performance indicators also improved at the 11 intervention sites compared to the 15 other sites.

LEARNING OBJECTIVES CHECKLIST

1. *Interpersonal conflict* is a process that occurs when one person, group, or organizational unit frustrates the goal attainment of another. Such conflict can revolve around facts, procedures, or the goals themselves. Causes of conflict include intergroup bias, high interdependence, ambiguous jurisdictions, and scarce resources. Differences in power, status, and culture are also a factor.

2. *Types of conflict* include *relationship, task,* and *process* conflict. Conflict dynamics include the need to win the dispute, withholding information, increased cohesiveness, negative stereotyping of the other party, reduced contact, and emergence of aggressive leaders.

3. Modes of managing conflict include *avoiding, accommodating, competing, compromise,* and *collaborating.*

4. *Negotiation* is a decision-making process among parties that do not have the same preferences. *Distributive negotiation* attempts to divide up a fixed amount of outcomes. Frequent tactics include threats, promises, firmness, concession making, and persuasion. *Integrative negotiation* attempts to enlarge the amount of outcomes available via collaboration or problem solving. Tactics include exchanging copious information, framing differences as opportunities, cutting costs, increasing resources, and introducing *superordinate goals.*

5. When managers perceive that employees are in a rut or avoiding disagreements at the cost of not dealing with important issues, they may want to *stimulate conflict* to reinvigorate the workplace. Although conflict is often considered a negative occurrence, conflict can also be necessary for and beneficial to organizational change initiatives. In the context of change, conflict can generate new ideas, lead to more careful monitoring of the actions of others, and lead to a redistribution of power within the organization.

6. *Stressors* are environmental conditions that have the potential to induce stress. *Stress* is a psychological reaction that can prompt tension or anxiety because an individual feels incapable of coping with the demands made by a stressor. *Stress reactions* are the behavioural, psychological, and physiological consequences of stress.

7. Personality characteristics can cause some individuals to perceive more stressors than others, experience more stress, and react more negatively to this stress. In particular, people with external *locus of control*, high *negative affectivity*, and *Type A behaviour pattern* are prone to such reactions.

8. At the *managerial* or *executive level*, common stressors include role overload and high responsibility. At the *operative level*, poor physical working conditions and underutilization of potential owing to poor job design are common stressors. *Boundary role occupants* often experience stress in the form of conflict between demands from inside the employing organization and demands from outside. Emotional labour may also provoke stress. *Burnout* may occur when interaction with clients produces emotional exhaustion, depersonalization, and low accomplishment. Job insecurity and change, role ambiguity, sexual harassment, interpersonal conflict, and work-family conflicts have the potential to induce stress in all organizational members.

9. *Behavioural reactions* to stress include problem solving, modified performance, withdrawal, and the use of addictive substances. *Problem solving* is the most effective reaction because it confronts the stressor directly and thus has the potential to terminate the stress episode. The most common psychological reaction to stress is the use of *defence mechanisms* to temporarily reduce anxiety. The majority of studies on physiological reactions to stress implicate cardiovascular risk factors. Strategies that can reduce organizational stress include job redesign, social support, family-friendly human resource policies, stress management programs, and work-life balance programs.

DISCUSSION QUESTIONS

1. The manager of a fast-food restaurant sees that conflict among the staff is damaging service. How might she implement a superordinate goal to reduce this conflict?

2. A company hires two finance majors right out of college. Being in a new and unfamiliar environment, they begin their relationship cooperatively. However, over time, they develop a case of deep interpersonal conflict. What factors could account for this?

3. What are some of the factors that make it a real challenge for conflicting parties to develop a collaborative relationship and engage in integrative negotiation?

4. Two social workers just out of college join the same county welfare agency. Both find their case loads very heavy and their roles very ambiguous. One exhibits negative stress reactions, including absence and elevated alcohol use. The other seems to cope very well. Use the stress episode model to explain why this might occur.

5. Imagine that a person who greatly dislikes bureaucracy assumes her first job as an investigator in a very bureaucratic government tax office. Describe the stressors that she might encounter in this situation. Give an example of a problem-solving reaction to this stress. Give an example of a defensive reaction to it.

6. What factors might explain why bullying persists? How do workplace bullies get away with it?

7. Compare and contrast the stressors that might be experienced by an assembly line worker and the president of a company.

8. Discuss the advantages and disadvantages of hiring employees with Type A personality characteristics.

INTEGRATIVE DISCUSSION QUESTIONS

1. Does personality influence the way individuals manage conflict? Consider the relationship among each of the following personality characteristics and the five approaches to managing conflict described in this chapter: the "Big Five" dimensions of personality, locus of control, self-monitoring, self-esteem, need for power, and Machiavellianism.

2. Can leadership be a source of stress in organizations? Refer to the leadership theories described in Chapter 9 (e.g., leadership traits, behaviours, situational theories, participative leadership, strategic leadership, and LMX theory) and explain how leadership can be a source of stress. According to each theory, what can leaders do to reduce stress and help employees cope with it?

ON-THE-JOB CHALLENGE QUESTION

When Air Canada and Canadian Airlines merged in 2000, one of the most difficult challenges was handling the integration of employees who had once been bitter rivals. In the months leading up to the merger, Canadian Airline employees began sporting "Better dead than red!" buttons in reference to their rival's corporate colour, while the head of Air Canada's pilots' union outraged Canadian Airlines pilots when he suggested that the successful Air Canada would be contaminated by a virus from the "sick" Canadian Airlines if the two airlines merged. Once the companies merged, a particular sore point became the question of seniority. Although Air Canada was the "winner" in the merger and the failing Canadian was the "loser," Canadian employees tended to have more overall seniority than their Air Canada peers. Conflict ensued, with Canadian employees expecting to be at the top of the seniority roster and Air Canada employees claiming that the Canadian people should feel lucky to have jobs at all. Years after the merger, this issue is still not fully resolved, and tension still runs high between the employees of the two former rivals.

What are the roots of the conflict between Air Canada employees and their colleagues who were previously part of Canadian Airlines? How could this conflict be better managed? On the seniority issue, what negotiation tactics would be recommended in this situation? What role could third parties play in the negotiation process?

Sources: Brent, P. (1999, December 6). Air Canada's challenge: Soothe bitter feelings of intense combatants. *National* Post, C4; Naumetz, T. (1999, September 30). Air Canada pilot fears "virus" from merger: Employees voice concerns for job security. *Ottawa Citizen*, C1; Nicol, J., & Clark, A. (2000, May 22). Unfriendly skies. *Maclean's*, 34–37; Viera, P. (2003, June 27). Labour board upholds seniority ruling covering airline pilots. *National Post*, FP5.

EXPERIENTIAL EXERCISE

Coping with Stress

To what extent does each of the following fit as a description of you? (Circle one number in each line across.)

	Very true	Quite true	Some-what true	Not very true	Not at all true
1. I "roll with the punches" when problems come up.	1	2	3	4	5
2. I spend almost all my time thinking about my work.	5	4	3	2	1
3. I treat other people as individuals and care about their feelings and opinions.	1	2	3	4	5
4. I recognize and accept my own limitations and assets.	1	2	3	4	5
5. There are quite a few people I could describe as "good friends."	1	2	3	4	5
6 I enjoy using my skills and abilities both on and off the job.	1	2	3	4	5
7. I get bored easily.	5	4	3	2	1
8. I enjoy meeting and talking with people who have different ways of thinking about the world.	1	2	3	4	5
9. Often in my job I "bite off more than I can chew."	5	4	3	2	1
10. I'm usually very active on weekends with projects or recreation.	1	2	3	4	5
11. I prefer working with people who are very much like myself.	5	4	3	2	1
12. I work primarily because I have to survive, and not necessarily because I enjoy what I do.	5	4	3	2	1
13. I believe I have a realistic picture of my personal strengths and weakness.	1	2	3	4	5
14. Often I get into arguments with people who don't think my way.	5	4	3	2	1
15. Often I have trouble getting much done on my job.	5	4	3	2	1
16. I'm interested in a lot of different topics.	1	2	3	4	5
17. I get upset when things don't go my way.	5	4	3	2	1
18. Often I'm not sure how I stand on a controversial topic.	5	4	3	2	1
19. I'm usually able to find a way around anything that blocks me from an important goal.	1	2	3	4	5
20. I often disagree with my boss or others at work.	5	4	3	2	1

Scoring and Interpretation

Dr. Alan A. McLean, who developed this checklist, feels that people who cope with stress effectively have five characteristics. First, they know themselves well and accept their own strengths and weaknesses. Second, they have a variety of interests off the job, and they are not total "workaholics." Third, they exhibit a variety of reactions to stress, rather than always getting a headache or always becoming depressed. Fourth, they are accepting of others who have values or styles different from their own. Finally, good copers are active and productive both on and off the job.

Add together the numbers you circled for the four questions contained in each of the five coping scales.

Coping scale	Add together your responses to these questions	Your score (write in)
Knows self	4, 9, 13, 18	_____
Many interests	2, 5, 7, 16	_____
Variety of reactions	1, 11, 17, 19	_____
Accepts other's values	3, 8, 14, 20	_____
Active and productive	6, 10, 12, 15	_____

Then, add the five scores together for your overall total score.

Scores on each of the five areas can vary between 5 and 20. Scores of 12 or above perhaps suggest that it might be useful to direct more attention to the area. The overall total score can range between 20 and 100. Scores of 60 or more may suggest some general difficulty in coping on the dimensions covered.

Source: McLean, A.A. (1979). *Work stress*. Reading, MA: Addison-Wesley, pp. 126–127. Copyright © 1976 by Management Decision Systems, Inc. Reprinted by permission.

CASE INCIDENT

Karoshi

Karoshi is Japanese for "death by overwork." This well-documented ailment, in which people develop illnesses from high stress and the pressures of overtime work—with many literally keeling over and dying at their desks, was officially recognized as a fatal illness by the Japanese in 1989. Officially, the first person who died of karoshi was a 48-year-old man who typically worked 15-hour days at an Osaka company and had worked 100 hours of overtime every month for a year. Eventually, this overload proved fatal. He died after putting in three consecutive 15-hour days.

Following are two examples of karoshi, whose toll runs to nearly 10 000 deaths each year in Japan.

Shinji Masami, 37, a design engineer at Hino Motors, a large subsidiary of Toyota that produces trucks, had to design parts that fit together well in final assembly. The job was intense and had pressing deadlines. From 1980 through 1986, Masami worked an average of 2600 hours, about 25 percent more than the average Japanese. Days before his death he complained of severe headaches and abdominal pains, yet he forced himself to go to work until his last day. He died of brain hemorrhage while at work in the office.

Jun Ishii, 47, a manager of Mitsui's Soviet division, collapsed and died at a business hotel after having spent his last five days escorting Russian visitors to local machine manufacturers. During the 10 months preceding his death, Ishii had made many business trips, totalling 103 days, to the Soviet Union, with little time for rest in between.

Source: Excerpted from Babbar, S., & Aspelin, D.J. (1998, February). The overtime rebellion: Symptom of a bigger problem? *Academy of Management Executive*, 68–76.

1. Do you think that incidents of karoshi like those described in the case incident can become a problem in North America? Does karoshi depend on whether the overtime work is voluntary or involuntary, and is personality a factor?

2. What can organizations in North America do to prevent karoshi?

CASE STUDY

The Last Straw

Jerry Lambert has been employed by the University of Upper Ontario for 26 years. He first came to the university in the mid 1970s as a master's student in information technology, and became a teaching assistant to Professor Jane Burnett. Eager to learn and thrilled with the teaching aspects of this job, Jerry convinced Professor Burnett to let him do some in-class work. The professor finally agreed, and was impressed with Jerry's natural teaching ability and dedication. At the end of the school year, the professor went on sabbatical and suggested to her department that Jerry take over her class for the time that she would be away. Because of the shortage of information technology professors at the time, and in light of Professor Burnett's glowing recommendation, Jerry was hired as an instructor.

In the meantime, Jerry had taken a summer job as a junior programmer in the university's computing services department. By the end of the summer, he had been offered a full-time job with this department. Since Jerry was thinking of marrying, he promptly decided to take the job, as well as the part-time teaching position. He also decided not to pursue his Ph.D. degree for the time being. Jerry soon earned a reputation as an excellent communicator, valiant worker, and dedicated instructor. Since information systems were relatively new at the time, most instructors and workers in this area were young. Jerry was young, had a friendly, outgoing personality, and was a quick learner. He fit in well and quickly built up a group of friends and associates within his department and elsewhere.

Over the years, Jerry obtained a number of promotions and more part-time teaching contracts. The teaching contracts were given on a one-semester basis. Therefore, Jerry had no guarantee of having any of them renewed. However, he had always had one or two classes per semester, so the situation seemed relatively stable. In the early 1980s, Jerry decided that he should pursue his Ph.D. degree and returned to school part-time. At the same time, he started to do some consulting work on his own. This very full schedule stimulated him, but left very little time for his personal life. Within a short time, he and his wife were divorced.

Jerry continued with his work, obtaining two more promotions. He was unable to continue his studies, however, because of lack of time. Finally, he became manager of training services for the university's information systems department. Jerry was very happy with this position, which gave him the opportunity to combine his interests. Three years after he had obtained this position, Jerry felt comfortable. He had a nice job, a cottage in the country, and had just bought a house in an affluent section of town. Although there was a large mortgage on the house, Jerry felt comfortable with it since his income allowed him to meet the payments. Jerry had recently remarried, and his wife was expecting a baby.

Three months ago, the university president announced that there would be massive cutbacks in management and support staff at the university. Within a month, Jerry heard rumours that his section was being targeted for downsizing. Jerry tried repeatedly to get confirmation or disconfirmation of these rumours from his boss, Patricia Jones. However, Patricia remained vague and evasive. At one point, Mario, a fellow manager, told Jerry in confidence that Patricia had asked other managers' opinion about Jerry's department and that some of these managers had said that they felt that Jerry's job and department were "nonessential." "I am not supposed to tell you this," Mario said, "but if I was in your shoes I'd like to know if my job was in danger." Jerry thanked him and kept the information confidential; however, he couldn't help feeling that his other colleagues, Mario excepted, were "stabbing him in the back." "They are all looking out for themselves without any thought as to what makes sense," he fumed. "What a bunch of self-centred turkeys!"

To make matters worse, a month later, Jerry stepped into the parking lot to find that his car had been stolen. Later on, he discovered that his insurance did not cover the full cost of replacing the car. His wife took this news badly and started feeling ill. Her doctor ordered complete bed rest for the next three months, until the

baby is due. She has told Jerry that she is tired of hearing about his speculations concerning doom and gloom at work. To avoid irritating his wife, Jerry has been keeping his work-related problems to himself. Last week, Jerry was told that some of his teaching contracts might not be renewed because the university planned to save money by assigning a larger teaching load to full-time professors. Concerned with the unstable situation of both his full-time job and his contract work at the university, Jerry pursued additional teaching assignments with the local community college. He is now teaching five nights a week and feeling exhausted since the workload amounts to having two full-time jobs. To make matters worse, constant worry is keeping him awake at night. In addition, he has been suffering from recurring colds and has been having frequent headaches.

This morning, his secretary walked into his office in tears, saying that Jerry's boss, Patricia, had just told her that she was being laid off. This was a shock for Jerry, who had not been forewarned about this by Patricia. Obviously, having his secretary laid off while being kept completely in the dark did not bode well for Jerry's department. Although he tried to sympathize with his secretary's plight, Jerry could not help but feel terribly angry at the way the situation was being handled. He tried to reach his boss but was told that Patricia was in a meeting. By the end of the day, Jerry still hadn't heard from Patricia. Feeling a knot in his stomach that would not go away, Jerry rushed from his office to his evening class, carrying a pile of assignments to return to his students. On the way out the door, a colleague bumped into him, sending the assignments flying. Upset, Jerry lashed out at his colleague, calling him an idiot.

Source: Case prepared by Nicole Bérubé. Used with permission.

1. Jerry is clearly experiencing stress. What stress reactions does he exhibit? What are the stressors that prompted this reaction?

2. Is Jerry experiencing burnout? If so, what factors might be responsible? Feel free to speculate, given the nature of his job and family situation.

3. Is interpersonal conflict an issue in the case? What are its causes?

4. Evaluate Patricia's management style. How should Jerry deal with her?

5. How could the University of Upper Ontario do a better job of dealing with the issues raised in the case?

INTEGRATIVE CASE

Ace Technology

At the end of Part Two of the text, on Individual Behaviour, you answered a number of questions about the Ace Technology Integrative Case that dealt with issues related to learning, job attitudes, motivation, pay systems, and incentive plans. Now that you have completed Part Three of the text and the chapters on Social Behaviour and Organizational Processes, you can return to the Ace Technology Integrative Case and enhance your understanding of some of the main issues associated with social behaviour and organizational processes by answering the following questions.

QUESTIONS

1. Discuss the culture at Ace Technology. Would you consider it a strong culture? Why or why not, and what are the implications of this for the new strategy? What effect will the new reward system have on the culture?

2. Consider Bill's leadership style and behaviour in the case. Use Fiedler's Contingency Theory and House's Path-Goal Theory to analyze the leadership situation confronting Bill. What leadership style does each theory suggest?

3. Run the new strategy and compensation plan through the Vroom and Jago decision tree (Exhibit 9.5). What level of participation is indicated?

4. Discuss the merits of transformational or charismatic leadership and LMX theory at Ace Technology. What do these theories suggest about the effectiveness of Bill's leadership?

5. Discuss communication at Ace Technology. How was the new strategy and compensation program communicated, and how effective is communication at Ace Technology?

6. Consider the decision-making process at Ace Technology. How was the decision made on the new strategy and compensation program, and how effective was it?

PART ④ The Total Organization

Organizational Structure

W.L. GORE & ASSOCIATES, INC.

Unless you are an avid hiker or camper, you may not be familiar with W.L. Gore & Associates, Inc. The firm, based in Newark, Delaware, is best known for the Gore-Tex brand fabric, a breathable, waterproof fabric laminate found in premium outdoor clothing and space suits. However, Gore also produces other high-tech products, including electrical cable, vascular grafts and other medical products, and a wide variety of environmental filters and other industrial products. Founded in 1958 by ex-DuPont R&D chemist Bill Gore in the basement of his home, the firm has 40 plants worldwide. Its annual revenue in 2005 was $1.84 billion, and it has posted good profits for over 30 years straight.

Gore's close to 7000 "associates" (not employees) operate under what the company describes as unmanagement. There are no titles, no bosses, and no budgets. By extension, there is no hierarchy or formal chain of command, no predetermined channels of communication, and no fixed organizational structure. People are not hired for a job, but rather, for a commitment. How does any work get done?

The company has a unique flat structure that it calls a lattice system in which an associate assumes responsibility for developing a new product. Then, he or she has to recruit volunteers from other parts of the company to form a team. This team could eventually become a plant, which would be divided into smaller teams that choose their own leaders. Gore intentionally limits plant size to no more than around 200 associates to foster good communication. Each plant is self-sufficient with its own manufacturing, finance, and research and development contained within the facility.

Instead of bosses, the company has sponsors. New hires are assigned to sponsors who help them understand their commitments and what is required to be successful in those commitments. Another important responsibility of a sponsor is to be a "positive advocate" for new associates. This involves gathering information and feedback about a new associate's personal development and presenting it to a compensation committee. The information is then used to rank all associates within a functional area to determine their compensation.

How did Gore come up with such a unique structure? The structure is a result of the core values that founder Bill Gore instituted to develop a

creative and energizing work environment. The key to Gore's success has been continual innovation, which is due, in large part, to the organization's cultural values of fairness, continuous learning, commitment, and consultation.

The lattice structure supports and reinforces the culture in a number of important ways. For example, because there are no formal channels of communication, associates must communicate and consult with each other. In addition, because associates do not have narrowly defined job titles that lock them into specific tasks, they are more likely to take on new and challenging assignments. Thus, the structure helps to foster communication and consultation among associates and in the development of new ideas and commitments.

What is it like to work in a lattice organizational structure compared with a more traditional hierarchical structure? According to a human resources leader at Gore, "Issuing orders, writing rules, and releasing memos is much easier than trying to obtain buy-in from a group, selling another associate on a new idea, or encouraging and motivating an individual or a team."

The challenges of the lattice system seem to have made a difference. W.L. Gore & Associates, Inc. have continued to grow and prosper, thanks to their unique structure that fosters a creative work environment and continual innovation. But how do Gore employees feel about working in a "lattice" organizational structure? It appears that the lattice system also fosters positive attitudes. In 2006, Gore earned a spot on *Fortune* magazine's 100 Best Companies to Work for in America for the ninth consecutive year![1]

W.L. Gore & Associates, Inc.
www.gore.com

Why is W.L. Gore & Associates, Inc. organized and structured the way it is? And how does its unique organizational structure affect Gore employees and the overall effectiveness of the organization? These are the kinds of questions that we shall attempt to answer in this chapter and the next.

First, we will define organizational structure and discuss the methods for dividing labour and forming departments. Then we will consider some methods for coordinating labour as well as traditional structural characteristics and the relationship between size and structure. Finally, we will review some signals of structural problems.

WHAT IS ORGANIZATIONAL STRUCTURE?

In previous chapters, we were concerned primarily with the bits and pieces that make up organizations. First, we analyzed organizational behaviour from the standpoint of the individual member—how his or her learning, personality, perception, attitudes, and motivation affect behaviour. Then we shifted our analysis to groups and to some of the processes that occur in organizations, including communication, leadership, and decision making. In this chapter we adopt yet another level of analysis by looking at the organization as a whole. Our primary interest is the causes and consequences of organizational structure.

Shortly, we will discuss organizational structure in detail. For now, it is enough to know that it broadly refers to how an organization's individuals and groups are *put together* or *organized* to accomplish work. This is an important issue. An organization could have well-motivated individual members and properly led groups, but still fail to fulfill its potential because of the way their efforts are divided and coordinated.

In Chapter 1, we defined organizations as social inventions for accomplishing common goals through group effort. In this chapter and the next, we shall see that organizational structure intervenes between goals and organizational accomplishments and thus influences organizational effectiveness. Among other things, structure affects how effectively and efficiently group effort is coordinated.

To achieve its goals, an organization has to do two very basic things: *divide* labour among its members and then *coordinate* what has been divided. For example, consider how a university divides its labour: some members teach, some run the graduate programs, some take care of accounts, and some handle registration. It is simply unlikely that anyone could do *all* these things well. Furthermore, within each of these subunits, labour would be further divided. For example, the registrar's office would include a director, secretaries, clerks, and so on. With all this division, some coordination is obviously necessary.

Organizational structure.
The manner in which an organization divides its labour into specific tasks and achieves coordination among these tasks.

We can conclude that **organizational structure** is the manner in which an organization divides its labour into specific tasks and achieves coordination among these tasks.[2]

THE DIVISION AND COORDINATION OF LABOUR

Labour must be divided because individuals have physical and intellectual limitations. *Everyone* cannot do *everything*; even if this were possible, tremendous confusion and inefficiency would result. There are two basic dimensions to the division of labour: a vertical dimension and a horizontal dimension. Once labour is divided, it must be coordinated to achieve organizational effectiveness.

Vertical Division of Labour

The vertical division of labour is concerned primarily with apportioning authority for planning and decision making—who gets to tell whom what to do? As we see in Exhibit 14.1, in a manufacturing firm, the vertical division of labour is usually signi-

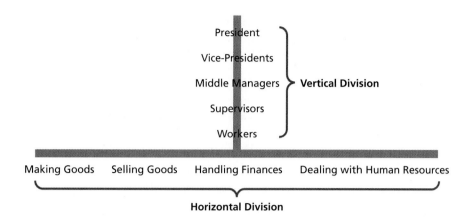

EXHIBIT 14.1
The dimensions of
division of labour in a
manufacturing firm.

fied by titles such as president, manager, and supervisor. In a university, it might be denoted by titles such as president, dean, and chairperson. Organizations differ greatly in the extent to which labour is divided vertically. For example, the Canadian Army has eighteen levels of command ranging from full generals to privates. Wal-Mart has five levels between its CEO and its store managers. On the other hand, an automobile dealership might have only two or three levels, and a university would usually fall between the extremes. Separate departments, units, or functions *within* an organization will also often vary in the extent to which they vertically divide labour. A production unit might have several levels of management, ranging from supervisor to general manager. A research unit in the same company might have only two levels of management. A couple of key themes or issues underlie the vertical division of labour.

Autonomy and Control. Holding other factors constant, the domain of decision making and authority is reduced as the number of levels in the hierarchy increases. Put another way, managers have less authority over fewer matters. On the other hand, a flatter hierarchy pushes authority lower and involves people further down the hierarchy in more decisions.

Communication. A second theme underlying the vertical division of labour is communication or coordination between levels. As labour is progressively divided vertically, timely communication and coordination can become harder to achieve. Recall our discussion in Chapter 10 on information filtering as a barrier to communication. As the number of levels in the hierarchy increases, filtering is more likely to occur.

These two themes illustrate that labour must be divided vertically enough to ensure proper control, but not so much as to make vertical communication and coordination impossible. The proper degree of such division will vary across organizations and across their functional units.

Horizontal Division of Labour

The horizontal division of labour groups the basic tasks that must be performed into jobs and then into departments so that the organization can achieve its goals. Required workflow is the main basis for this division. The firm schematized in Exhibit 14.1 must produce and sell goods, keep its finances straight, and keep its employees happy. A hospital must admit patients, subject them to lab tests, fix what ails them, and keep them comfortable, all the while staying within its budget. Just as organizations differ in the extent to which they divide labour vertically, they also differ in the extent of horizontal division of labour. In a small business, the owner might be a "jack-of-all-trades," making estimates, delivering the product or service, and keeping the books. As the organization grows, horizontal division of labour is likely, with different groups of employees assigned to perform each of these tasks. Thus, the horizontal division of labour suggests some specialization on the part of the workforce. Up to a point, this increased specialization can promote efficiency. A couple of key themes or issues underlie the horizontal division of labour.

Job Design. The horizontal division of labour is closely tied to our earlier consideration of job design (Chapter 6). An example will clarify this. Suppose that an organization offers a product or service that consists of A work, B work, and C work (e.g., fabrication, inspection, and packaging). There are at least three basic ways in which it might structure these tasks:

- Form an ABC Department in which all workers do ABC work.
- Form an ABC Department in which workers specialize in A work, B work, or C work.
- Form a separate A Department, B Department, and C Department.

There is nothing inherently superior about any of these three designs. Notice, however, that each has implications for the jobs involved and how these jobs are coordinated. The first design provides for enriched jobs in which each worker can coordinate his or her own A work, B work, and C work. It also reduces the need for supervision and allows for self-managed teams. However, this design might require highly trained workers, and it might be impossible if A work, B work, and C work are complex specialties that require (for example) engineering, accounting, and legal skills. The second design involves increased horizontal division of labour in which employees specialize in tasks and in which the coordination of A work, B work, and C work becomes more critical. However, much of this coordination could be handled by properly designing the head of the department's job. Finally, the third design offers the greatest horizontal division of labour in that A work, B work, and C work are actually performed in separate departments. This design provides for great control and accountability for the separate tasks, but it also suggests that someone above the department heads will have to get involved in coordination. There are several lessons here. First, the horizontal division of labour strongly affects job design. Second, it has profound implications for the degree of coordination necessary. Finally, it also has implications for the vertical division of labour and where control over work processes should logically reside.

Differentiation. A second theme occasioned by the horizontal division of labour is related to the first. As organizations engage in increased horizontal division of labour, they usually become more and more differentiated. **Differentiation** is the tendency for managers in separate units, functions, or departments to differ in terms of goals, time spans, and interpersonal styles.[3] In tending to their own domains and problems, managers often develop distinctly different psychological orientations toward the organization and its products or services. Under high differentiation, various organizational units tend to operate more autonomously.

A classic case of differentiation is that which often occurs between marketing managers and those in research and development. The goals of the marketing managers might be external to the organization and oriented toward servicing the marketplace. Those of R&D managers might be oriented more toward excellence in design and state-of-the-art use of materials. While marketing managers want products to sell *now*, R&D managers might feel that "good designs take time." Finally, marketing managers might believe that they can handle dispute resolution with R&D through interpersonal tactics learned when they were on the sales force ("Let's discuss this over lunch"). R&D managers might feel that "the design speaks for itself" when a conflict occurs. The essential problem here is that the marketing department and the R&D department *need* each other to do their jobs properly![4] Shortly, we will review some tactics to help achieve necessary coordination.

Differentiation. The tendency for managers in separate units, functions, or departments to differ in terms of goals, time spans, and interpersonal styles.

Differentiation is a natural and necessary consequence of the horizontal division of labour, but it again points to the need for coordination, a topic that we will consider in more detail below. For now, let's examine more closely how organizations can allocate work to departments.

Departmentation

As we suggested above, once basic tasks have been combined into jobs, a question still remains as to how to group these jobs so that they can be managed effectively. The assignment of jobs to departments is called departmentation, and it represents one of the core aspects of the horizontal division of labour. It should be recognized that "department" is a generic term; some organizations use an alternative term, such as unit, group, or section. There are several methods of departmentation, each of which has its strengths and weaknesses.

Functional Departmentation. This form of organization is basic and familiar. Under **functional departmentation**, employees with closely related skills and responsibilities (functions) are located in the same department (Exhibit 14.2). Thus, those with skills in sales and advertising are assigned to the marketing department, and those with skills in accounting and credit are assigned to the finance department. Under this kind of design, employees are grouped according to the kind of resources they contribute to achieving the overall goals of the organization.[5]

Functional departmentation. Employees with closely related skills and responsibilities are assigned to the same department.

What are the advantages of functional departmentation? The most cited advantage is that of efficiency. When all the engineers are located in an engineering department, rather than scattered throughout the organization, it is easier to be sure that they are neither overloaded nor underloaded with work. Also, support factors, such as reference books, specialized software, and laboratory space can be allocated more efficiently with less duplication. Some other advantages of functional departmentation include the following:

- Communication within departments should be enhanced, since everyone "speaks the same language."

- Career ladders and training opportunities within the function are enhanced because all parties will share the same view of career progression.

- It should be easier to measure and evaluate the performance of functional specialists when they are all located in the same department.

What are the disadvantages of functional departmentation? Most of them stem from the specialization within departments that occurs in the functional arrangement. As a result, a high degree of differentiation can occur between functional departments. At best, this can lead to poor coordination and slow response to organizational problems. At worst, it can lead to open conflict between departments, in which the needs of clients and customers are ignored. Departmental empires might be built at the expense of pursuing organizational goals.

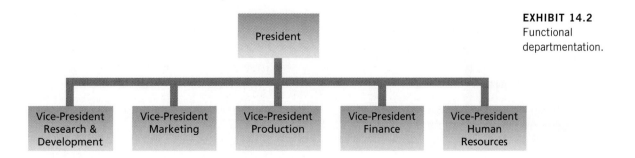

EXHIBIT 14.2
Functional departmentation.

There is consensus that functional departmentation works best in small to medium-sized firms that offer relatively few product lines or services. It can also be an effective means of organizing the smaller divisions of large corporations. When the scale gets bigger and the output of the organization gets more complex, most firms gravitate toward product departmentation or its variations.

Product Departmentation. Under **product departmentation**, departments are formed on the basis of a particular product, product line, or service. Each of these departments can operate fairly autonomously because it has its own set of functional specialists dedicated to the output of that department. For example, a personal care firm might have a shampoo division and a cosmetics division, each with its own staff of production people, marketers, and research and development personnel (Exhibit 14.3).

What are the advantages of product departmentation? One key advantage is better coordination among the functional specialists who work on a particular product line. Since their attentions are focused on one product and they have fewer functional peers, fewer barriers to communication should develop. Other advantages include flexibility, since product lines can be added or deleted without great implications for the rest of the organization. Also, product-focused departments can be evaluated as profit centres, since they have independent control over costs and revenues. This is not feasible for most functional departments (e.g., the research and development department does not have revenues). Finally, product departmentation often serves the customer or client better, since the client can see more easily who produced the product (the software group, not Ajax Consulting). All in all, product structures have more potential than functional structures for responding to customers in a timely way.

Are there any disadvantages to product departmentation? Professional development might suffer without a critical mass of professionals working in the same place at the same time. Also, economies of scale might be threatened and inefficiency might occur if relatively autonomous product-oriented departments are not coordinated. R&D personnel in an industrial products division and a consumer products division might work on a similar problem for months without being aware of each other's efforts. Worse, product-oriented departments might actually work at cross purposes.

Matrix Departmentation. The system of **matrix departmentation** is an attempt to capitalize simultaneously on the strengths of both functional and product departmentation.[6] In its most literal form, employees remain tied to a functional department such as marketing or production, but they also report to a product manager who draws on their services (Exhibit 14.4). For example, in a firm in the chemical industry, a marketing expert might matrix with the household cleaning products group.

 Product departmentation. Departments are formed on the basis of a particular product, product line, or service.

Matrix departmentation. Employees remain members of a functional department while also reporting to a product or project manager.

EXHIBIT 14.3
Product departmentation.

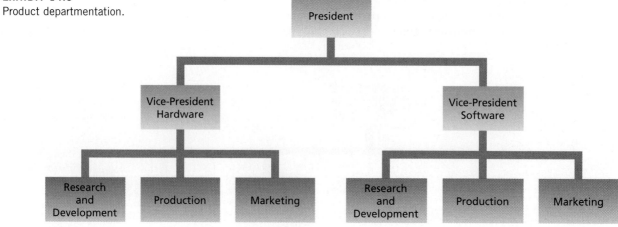

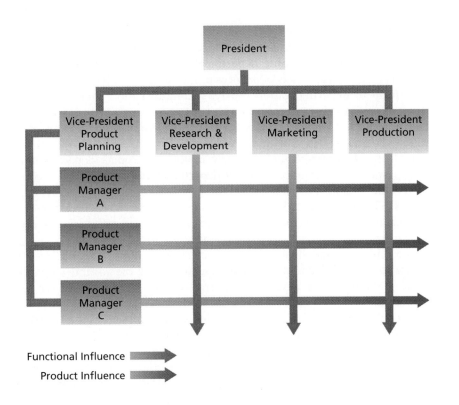

EXHIBIT 14.4
Matrix departmentation.

There are many variations on matrix design. Most of them boil down to what exactly gets crossed with functional areas to form the matrix and the degree of stability of the matrix relationships. For example, besides products, a matrix could be based on geographical regions or projects. For instance, a mechanical engineer in a global engineering company could report both to the mechanical engineering department at world headquarters and the regional manager for Middle East operations. This would probably be a fairly stable arrangement.

On the other hand, a matrix could be based on shorter-term projects. NASA uses this system, as do many consulting firms and research labs. The cross-functional teams that design cars (Chapter 7) draw members from various functions (e.g., styling, marketing, engineering). When the design is completed, members go on to other assignments.

NASA
www.nasa.gov

The matrix system is quite elegant when it works well. Ideally, it provides a degree of *balance* between the abstract demands of the product or project and the people who actually do the work, resulting in a better outcome. Also, it is very flexible. People can be moved around as project flow dictates, and projects, products, or new regions can be added without total restructuring. Being focused on a particular product or project can also lead to better communication among the representatives from the various functional areas (precisely why cross-functional teams are used to design cars).

Two interrelated problems threaten the matrix structure. First, there is no guarantee that product or project managers will see eye-to-eye with various functional managers. This can create conflict that reduces the advantages of the matrix. Also, employees assigned to a product or project team in essence report to two managers, their functional manager and their product or project manager. This violation of a classical management principle (every employee should have only one boss) can result in role conflict and stress, especially at performance review time. The upshot of this is that managers need to be well trained under matrix structures. In your authors' opinion, some of the bad press that matrix designs have received in the past stems from their early application in technical environments where neither functional managers nor project managers had well-developed people-management skills.

Geographic departmentation. Relatively self-contained units deliver an organization's products or services in a specific geographic territory.

Customer departmentation. Relatively self-contained units deliver an organization's products or services to specific customer groups.

Hybrid departmentation. A structure based on some mixture of functional, product, geographic, or customer departmentation.

Coordination. A process of facilitating timing, communication, and feedback among work tasks.

Other Forms of Departmentation. Several other forms of departmentation also exist.[7] Two of these are simply variations on product departmentation. One is geographic departmentation. Under **geographic departmentation**, relatively self-contained units deliver the organization's products or services in specific geographic territories (Exhibit 14.5). This form of departmentation shortens communication channels, allows the organization to cater to regional tastes, and gives some appearance of local control to clients and customers. National retailers, insurance companies, and oil companies generally exhibit geographic departmentation.

Another form of departmentation closely related to product departmentation is customer departmentation. Under **customer departmentation**, relatively self-contained units deliver the organization's products or services to specific customer groups (Exhibit 14.6). The obvious goal is to provide better service to each customer group through specialization. For example, many banks have commercial lending divisions that are separate from the consumer loan operations. Universities might have separate graduate and undergraduate divisions. An engineering firm might have separate divisions to cater to civilian and military customers. In general, the advantages and disadvantages of geographic and customer departmentation parallel those for product departmentation.

Finally, we should recognize that few organizations represent "pure" examples of functional, product, geographic, or customer departmentation. It is not unusual to see **hybrid departmentation**, which involves some combination of these structures. For example, a manufacturing firm might retain human resources, finance, and legal services in a functional form at headquarters, but use product departmentation to organize separate production and sales staffs for each product. Similarly, McDonald's and Wal-Mart centralize many activities at their respective headquarters, but also have geographic divisions that cater to regional tastes and make for efficient distribution. The hybrids attempt to capitalize on the strengths of various structures, while avoiding the weaknesses of others.

Basic Methods of Coordinating Divided Labour

When the tasks that will help the organization achieve its goals have been divided among individuals and departments, they must be coordinated so that goal accomplishment is actually realized. We can identify five basic methods of **coordination**, which is a process of facilitating timing, communication, and feedback.[8]

EXHIBIT 14.5
Geographic departmentation.

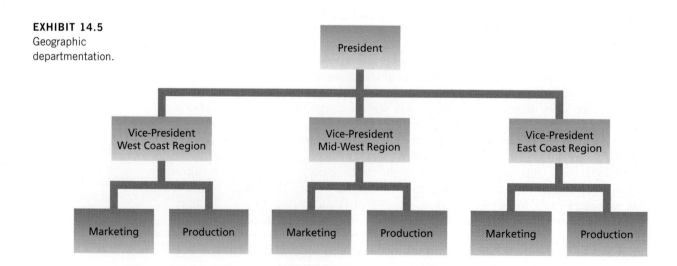

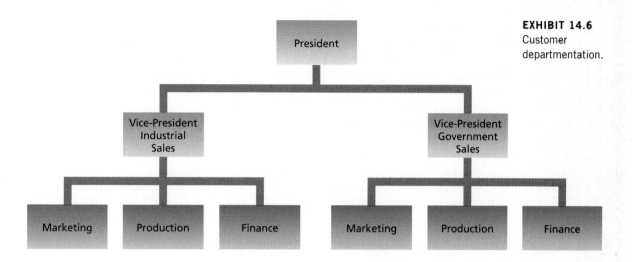

EXHIBIT 14.6
Customer
departmentation.

Direct Supervision. This is a very traditional form of coordination. Working through the chain of command, designated supervisors or managers coordinate the work of their subordinates. For instance, a production supervisor coordinates the work of his or her subordinates. In turn, the production superintendent coordinates the activities of all the supervisors. This method of coordination is closely associated with our discussion of leadership in Chapter 9.

Standardization of Work Processes. Some jobs are so routine that the technology itself provides a means of coordination. Little direct supervision is necessary for these jobs to be coordinated. The automobile assembly line provides a good example. When a car comes by, worker X bolts on the left A-frame assembly, and worker Y bolts on the right assembly. These workers do not have to interact, and they require minimal supervision. Work processes can also be standardized by rules and regulations. McDonald's stringent routine for constructing a burger is such an example.

McDonald's
www.mcdonalds.ca

Standardization of Outputs. Even when direct supervision is minimal and work processes are not standardized, coordination can be achieved through the standardization of work outputs. Concern shifts from how the work is done to ensuring that the work meets certain physical or economic standards. For instance, employees in a machine shop might be required to construct complex valves that require a mixture of drilling, lathe work, and finishing. The physical specifications of the valves will dictate how this work is to be coordinated. Standardization of outputs is often used to coordinate the work of separate product or geographic divisions. Frequently, top management assigns each division a profit target. These standards ensure that each division "pulls its weight" in contributing to the overall profit goals. Thus, budgets are a form of standardizing outputs.

Standardization of Skills. Even when work processes and output cannot be standardized, and direct supervision is unfeasible, coordination can be achieved through standardization of skills. This is seen very commonly in the case of technicians and professionals. For example, a large surgery team can often coordinate its work with minimal verbal communication because of its high degree of interlocked training—surgeons, anesthesiologists, and nurses all know what to expect from each other because of their standard training. MBA programs provide some standardized skills (e.g., the ability to read a balance sheet) to people with different functional specialties.

Mutual Adjustment. Mutual adjustment relies on informal communication to coordinate tasks. Paradoxically, it is useful for coordinating the most simple and the most complicated divisions of labour. For example, imagine a small florist shop that consists of the owner-operator, a shop assistant, and a delivery person. It is very likely that these individuals will coordinate their work through informal processes, mutually adjusting to each other's needs. At the other extreme, consider the top executive team of virtually any corporation. Such teams are generally composed of people with a variety of skills and backgrounds (e.g., finance, marketing) and tend to be preoccupied with very nonroutine problems. Again, mutual adjustment would be necessary to coordinate their efforts because standardization would be impossible.

Now that we have reviewed the five basic methods of coordinating divided labour, a few comments are in order. First, as we see in Exhibit 14.7, the methods can be crudely ordered in terms of the degree of *discretion* they permit in terms of task performance. Applied strictly, direct supervision permits little discretion. Standardization of processes and outputs permits successively more discretion. (However, clever employees can "beat" these forms of standardization.) Finally, standardization of skills and mutual adjustment put even more control into the hands of those who are actually doing the work. Obviously, W.L. Gore leans toward the right of the continuum.

Notice that just as division of labour affects the design of jobs, so does the method of coordination employed. As we move from the left side to the right side of the continuum of coordination, there is greater potential for jobs to be designed in an enriched manner. By the same token, an improper coordination strategy can destroy the intrinsic motivation of a job. Traditionally, much work performed by professionals (e.g., scientists and engineers) is coordinated by their own skill standardization. If the manager of a research lab decides to coordinate work with a high degree of direct supervision, the motivating potential of the scientists' jobs might be damaged. *The manager* is doing the work that *they* should be doing.

The use of the various methods of coordination tends to vary across different parts of the organization. These differences in coordination stem from the way labour has been divided. As we noted, upper management relies heavily on mutual adjustment for coordination. Where tasks are more routine, such as in the lower part of the production subunit, we tend to see coordination via direct supervision or standardization of work processes or outputs.[9] Advisory subunits staffed by professionals, such as a legal department or a marketing research group, often rely on a combination of skill standardization and mutual adjustment.

Finally, methods of coordination may change as task demands change. Under peacetime conditions or routine wartime conditions, the army relies heavily on direct supervision through a strict chain of command. However, this method of coordination can prove ineffective for fighting units under heavy fire. Here, we might see a sergeant with a radio instructing a captain where to direct artillery fire. This reversal of the chain of command is indicative of mutual adjustment. Similarly, the trend toward self-managed work teams (Chapter 7) downplays direct supervision and focuses on mutual adjustment among team members.

EXHIBIT 14.7
Methods of coordination as a continuum of worker discretion.

Source: From Mintzberg, H. (1979). *The structuring of organizations: A synthesis of research.* Englewood Cliffs, NJ: Prentice-Hall, p. 198. © 1979. Reprinted by permission of Prentice-Hall, Inc., Englewood Cliffs, NJ.

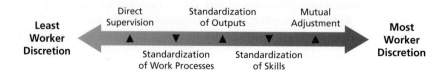

Other Methods of Coordination

The forms of coordination we discussed above are very basic, in that almost every organization uses them. After all, when do we see an organization that *does not* exhibit some supervision, some standardization, and some talking things out? Sometimes, however, coordination problems are such that more customized, elaborate mechanisms are necessary to achieve coordination. This is especially true when we are speaking of lateral coordination across highly differentiated departments. Recall that the managers of such departments might vary greatly in goals, time spans, and interpersonal orientation. Figuratively at least, they often "speak different languages." The process of attaining coordination across differentiated departments usually goes by the special name of **integration**.[10] Good integration achieves coordination without reducing the differences that enable each department to do its own job well.[11] For example, in a high-technology firm, we do not *want* production and engineering to be so cosy that innovative tension is lost.[12]

> **Integration.** The process of attaining coordination across differentiated departments.

In ascending order of elaboration, three methods of achieving integration include the use of liaison roles, task forces, and full-time integrators.[13]

Liaison Roles. A **liaison role** is occupied by a person in one department who is assigned, as part of his or her job, to achieve coordination with another department. In other words, one person serves as a part-time link between two departments. Sometimes the second department might reciprocate by nominating its own liaison person. For example, in a university library, reference librarians might be required to serve as liaison people for certain academic departments or schools. In turn, an academic department might assign a faculty member to "touch base" with its liaison in the library. Sometimes, liaison people might actually be located physically in the corresponding department.

> **Liaison role.** A person who is assigned to help achieve coordination between his or her department and another department.

Task Forces and Teams. When coordination problems arise that involve several departments simultaneously, liaison roles are not very effective. **Task forces** are temporary groups set up to solve coordination problems across several departments. Representatives from each department are included on a full-time or part-time basis, but when adequate integration is achieved, the task force is disbanded. Citicorp, Xerox, and Ford are firms that have made extensive use of task forces.

> **Task forces.** Temporary groups set up to solve coordination problems across several departments.

Self-managed and cross-functional teams (Chapter 7) are also an effective means of achieving coordination. Such teams require interaction among employees who might otherwise operate in an independent vacuum. Cross-functional teams are especially useful in achieving coordination for new product development and introduction.

Integrators. **Integrators** are organizational members who are permanently installed between two departments that are in clear need of coordination. In a sense, they are full-time problem solvers. Integrators are especially useful for dealing with conflict between (1) highly interdependent departments, (2) which have very diverse goals and orientations, (3) in a very ambiguous environment. Such a situation occurs in many high-tech companies.[14] For example, a bio-tech firm might introduce new products almost every month. This is a real strain on the production department, which might need the assistance of the lab to implement a production run. The lab scientists, on the other hand, rely on production to implement last-minute changes because of the rapidly changing technology. This situation badly requires coordination.

> **Integrators.** Organizational members permanently assigned to facilitate coordination between departments.

Integrators usually report directly to the executive to whom the heads of the two departments report. Ideally, they are rewarded according to the success of both units. A special kind of person is required for this job, since he or she has great responsibility but no direct authority in either department. The integrator must be unbiased, "speak the language" of both departments, and rely heavily on expert power.[15] An engineer with excellent interpersonal skills might be an effective integrator for the electronics firm. A typical job title might be project coordinator.

TRADITIONAL STRUCTURAL CHARACTERISTICS

Every organization is unique in the exact way that it divides and coordinates labour. Few business firms, hospitals, or schools have perfectly identical structures. What is needed, then, is some efficient way to summarize the effects of the vertical and horizontal division of labour and its coordination on the structure of the organization. Over the years, management scholars and practising managers have agreed on a number of characteristics that summarize the structure of organizations.[16]

Span of Control

Span of control. The number of subordinates supervised by a manager.

The **span of control** is the number of subordinates supervised by a manager. There is one essential fact about span of control: The larger the span, the less *potential* there is for coordination by direct supervision. As the span increases, the attention that a supervisor can devote to each subordinate decreases. When work tasks are routine, coordination of labour through standardization of work processes or output often substitutes for direct supervision. Thus, at lower levels in production units, it is not unusual to see spans of control ranging to over 20. In the managerial ranks, tasks are less routine and adequate time is necessary for informal mutual adjustment. As a result, spans at the upper levels tend to be smaller. Also, at lower organizational levels, workers with only one or a few specialties report to a supervisor. For instance, an office supervisor might supervise only clerks. As we climb the hierarchy, workers with radically different specialties might report to the boss. For example, the president might have to deal with vice-presidents of human resources, finance, production, and marketing. Again, the complexity of this task might dictate smaller spans.[17]

Flat versus Tall

Flat organization. An organization with relatively few levels in its hierarchy of authority.

Tall organization. An organization with relatively many levels in its hierarchy of authority.

Holding size constant, a **flat organization** has relatively few levels in its hierarchy of authority, while a **tall organization** has many levels. Thus, flatness versus tallness is an index of the vertical division of labour. Again, holding size constant, it should be obvious that flatness and tallness are associated with the average span of control. This is shown in Exhibit 14.8. Both schematized organizations have 31 members. However, the taller one has five hierarchical levels and an average span of two, while the flatter one has three levels and an average span of five. Flatter structures tend to push decision-making powers downward in the organization because a given number of decisions are apportioned among fewer levels. Also, flatter structures generally enhance vertical communication and coordination.

Differences in organizational height can exist even within industries. Some analysts have argued that the flatter Japanese car manufacturers are able to make decisions more quickly and get new products to market faster than the taller US automakers.[18] In general, there has been a North American trend toward flatter organizations, especially with downsizing, a topic we will cover shortly.

Formalization

Formalization. The extent to which work roles are highly defined by an organization.

Formalization is the extent to which work roles are highly defined by the organization.[19] A very formalized organization tolerates little variability in the way members perform their tasks. Some formalization stems from the nature of the job itself; the work requirements of the assembly line provide a good example of this. More interesting, however, is formalization that stems from rules, regulations, and procedures that the firm or institution chooses to implement. Detailed, written job descriptions, thick procedure manuals, and the requirement to "put everything in writing" are evidence of such formalization. At McDonald's, strict standards dictate how customers are greeted, how burgers are cooked, and how employees are to be dressed and groomed.

Tall Organization: 31 Members; 5 Levels; Average Span of Control Is 2

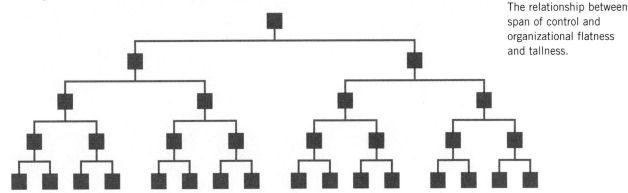

EXHIBIT 14.8
The relationship between span of control and organizational flatness and tallness.

Flat Organization: 31 Members; 3 Levels; Average Span of Control Is 5

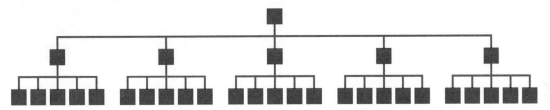

Very complex tasks dictate high formalization. In designing its 777 aircraft, Boeing used information technology to manage the development and modification of thousands of drawings and documents, thus coordinating the work of 5000 individuals at more than 20 locations.[20]

The Boeing Company
www.boeing.com

Sometimes, formalization seems excessive. Perhaps this is why so many fast-food employees ignore the hairnet rule. A US Department of Energy document detailing how to change a light bulb in a radioactive area is 317 pages long and specifies duties for 43 people.[21]

Centralization

Centralization is the extent to which decision-making power is localized in a particular part of the organization. In the most centralized organization, the power for all key decisions would rest in a single individual, such as the president. In a more decentralized organization, decision-making power would be dispersed down through the hierarchy and across departments. One observer suggests that limitations to individual brainpower often prompt decentralization:

> *How can the Baghdad salesperson explain the nature of his clients to the Birmingham manager? Sometimes the information can be transmitted to one centre, but a lack of cognitive capacity (brainpower) precludes it from being comprehended there. How can the president of the conglomerate corporation possibly learn about, say, 100 different product lines? Even if a report could be written on each, he would lack the time to study them all.*[22]

Of course, the information-processing capacity of executives is not the only factor that dictates the degree of centralization. Some organizations consciously pursue a more participative climate through decentralization. Bill Gore thought this way very explicitly. In others, top management might wish to maintain greater control and opt for stronger centralization. One of founder Ray Kroc's innovations was not to permit *regional* franchises that could grow powerful and challenge the basic business principles

Centralization. The extent to which decision-making power is localized in a particular part of an organization.

At Food Lion, buying is centralized, but local managers have autonomy to stay close to customers.

Food Lion
www.foodlion.com

of McDonald's.[23] The successful North Carolina-based supermarket chain Food Lion has generally decentralized with growth, giving local managers more autonomy to stay close to customers and cater to regional differences. However, the buying function and store design and construction have remained centralized to maintain efficiency and contain costs. Also, the lighting in all of its over 1200 stores spanning eleven states is centralized via a computer system.[24]

The proper degree of centralization should put decision-making power where the best *knowledge* is located. Often, this means decentralizing functions with direct customer contact, while centralizing functions that have a more internal orientation (e.g., information technology group). For an example of decentralization, see "Applied Focus: *Decentralizing Schools for Student Success*."

Complexity

Complexity. The extent to which an organization divides labour vertically, horizontally, and geographically.

Complexity is the extent to which organizations divide labour vertically, horizontally, and geographically.[25] A fairly simple organization will have few management levels (vertical division) and not many separate job titles (horizontal division). In addition, jobs will be grouped into a small number of departments, and work will be performed in only one physical location (geographic division). At the other extreme, a very complex organization will be tall, will have a large number of job titles and departments, and might be spread around the world. The essential characteristic of complexity is *variety*—as the organization becomes more complex, it has more kinds of people performing more kinds of tasks in more places, whether these places are departments or geographic territories.

Before continuing, consider the You Be the Manager feature on page 496.

SUMMARIZING STRUCTURE—ORGANIC VERSUS MECHANISTIC

Do the various structural characteristics that we have been reviewing have any natural relationship to one another? Is there any way to summarize how they tend to go together?

APPLIED FOCUS

Decentralizing Schools for Student Success

Most large urban North American school districts tend to be highly centralized. In practice, this means that various departments in the school district's headquarters are responsible for making decisions about curriculum, class schedules, teacher hiring and professional development, special education, and so on. In turn, principals of individual schools have little decision-making power and almost no budgetary control—what is taught, how it is taught, and the infrastructure for teaching are all centrally controlled. This high degree of centralization is often defended as providing economies of scale, ensuring equality among schools, and enabling decision input from specialized professionals. In recent years, some educators have begun to question such centralization, wondering whether it puts decision-making power and accountability close enough to where the knowledge is, in the local schools. Poor student performance and the recognition that schools have different student populations have led to questions about the "one size fits all" philosophy of centralization.

Professor William Ouchi of UCLA studied three school districts that have implemented decentralization over the years. These include Edmonton, Alberta (the pioneer, under visionary superintendent Mike Strembitsky), as well as Houston and Seattle. Speaking generally, decentralization permits principals to institute unique class schedules and hire teachers, librarians, and custodians as needed. Decentralized schools can determine their own teaching methods and purchase the instructional materials to match these methods. A feature of the structure is that students are free to choose a school that meets their needs rather than being assigned to a school by the district headquarters. This means that schools "compete" for students and thus have a strong incentive to improve. An absolutely key feature of decentralization is shifting potent budgetary control to the local schools. At one Seattle elementary school, the principal went from controlling $25 000 per year to $2 000 000 per year! The percentage of the school budgets controlled by principals ranged from 92 percent (Edmonton) to 59 percent (Houston). Comparisons were made with the centralized districts in Chicago, New York, and Los Angeles, where these percentages ranged from only 6 percent to 19 percent.

Does decentralization help student performance? Despite spotty data, Ouchi concludes that decentralization boosts Scholastic Aptitude Test (SAT) performance and reduces traditional achievement differences between racial groups. Local control helps tailor the educational experience to the unique needs of particular student bodies. It also makes principals and teachers accountable for the success of their schools.

Source: Ouchi, W.G. (2006). Power to the principals: Decentralization in three large school districts. *Organization Science, 17*, 298–307.

If you think back to the very first chapter of the book, you will recall how early prescriptions about management tended to stress employee specialization along with a very high degree of control and coordination. These themes were common to the classical management theorists, Taylor's Scientific Management, and Weber's bureaucracy. On the other hand, you will also recall how the human relations movement detected some of the problems that specialization and control can lead to—boredom, resentment, and low motivation. Consequently, these human relations advocates favoured more flexible management systems, open communication, employee participation, and so on.

In general, the classical theorists tended to favour **mechanistic structures.**[26] As Exhibit 14.9 demonstrates, these structures tend toward tallness, narrow spans of control, specialization, high centralization, and high formalization. The other structural and human resources aspects in the exhibit complement these basic structural prescriptions. By analogy, the organization is structured as a mechanical device, each part serving a separate function, each part closely coordinated with the others. Speaking generally, functional structures tend to be rather mechanistic.

Mechanistic structures. Organizational structures characterized by tallness, specialization, centralization, and formalization.

YOU BE THE Manager

IT Integration at Cardinal Health

In 2005, Cardinal Health was ranked 19th on *Fortune's* annual ranking of America's largest corporations, with over $75 billion in revenue, and was the second-largest distributor of pharmaceuticals and other medical supplies and equipment in the United States. The company has grown primarily through acquisitions—close to 100 over a 35-year period. While the acquisitions have made Cardinal Health one of the largest companies in the industry, it was mainly a holding company of individual businesses. Cardinal's leadership team decided that, in order to focus on quality and retain its position as a leading provider of health care products and services, the company would need to become a more integrated operation to better align the strengths of its various care businesses.

As an important first step, management began a redesign of its information technology (IT) operations, away from a business-unit focus and toward an integrated IT group servicing the entire organization. At the time, the infrastructure included 42 data centres, 15 help desks, 10-call tracking tools, multiple hardware vendors and cell phone service providers, and more than 1000 software applications. The business had grown rapidly, and like the rest of Cardinal Health, IT was very decentralized and under some strain. In the health care business, IT is critical. Every day Cardinal Health makes more than 50 000 deliveries of medicine and medical supplies to 40 000 customer sites, including hospitals, pharmacies, and other points of care. Efficient IT systems to support this level of mission-critical service are essential to customers.

Executive VP and CIO Jody Davids was involved in the original vision of Cardinal Health's technology integration and was responsible for executing the transition process. One of the first things she and her team learned was that in the current configuration, it could take weeks for the corporate group to collect routine information, such as the number of resources at each site, the technology blueprint at each site, the manner in which services were delivered at each site, and total IT costs. Prior to the transformation, the sheer volume of equipment and programming was as varied as it could possibly be, with asset tracking maintained at each

> **IT integration at Cardinal Health proved to be more difficult than it at first appeared.**

business unit. Computers, PDAs, and cell phones were all managed by the individual business. Employees could order the brand of their choice for electronic devices, and their computers were often customized with special software. Each unit might have assets tracked in a database, but that information wasn't shared with corporate IT in most instances.

Davids and her team quickly realized that major structural changes would be needed to achieve Cardinal's integration goals. But how to go about it? You be the manager.

QUESTIONS

1. Describe Cardinal's current IT set up in terms of departmentation. What form of departmentation would be consistent with the new vision at Cardinal?

2. In the new IT structure, what methods of coordination can be put in place to make things run smoothly?

To learn about what Cardinal Health did, see The Manager's Notebook at the end of the chapter.

Source: Adapted from Davids, J. (2006, May). Bringing unity to Cardinal Health. *Optimize*, 28–32.

Organizational Characteristics	Types of Organization Structure	
Index	**Organic**	**Mechanistic**
Span of control	Wide	Narrow
Number of levels of authority	Few	Many
Ratio of administrative to production personnel	High	Low
Range of time span over which an employee can commit resources	Long	Short
Degree of centralization in decision making	Low	High
Proportion of persons in one unit having opportunity to interact with persons in other units	High	Low
Quantity of formal rules	Low	High
Specificity of job goals	Low	High
Specificity of required activities	Low	High
Content of communications	Advice and information	Instructions and decisions
Range of compensation	Narrow	Wide
Range of skill levels	Narrow	Wide
Knowledge-based authority	High	Low
Position-based authority	Low	High

EXHIBIT 14.9
Mechanistic and organic structures.

Source: From Seiler, J.A. (1967). *Systems analysis in organizational behavior*. Homewood, IL: Irwin, p. 168. © Richard D. Irwin, Inc. 1967. This exhibit is an adaptation of one prepared by Paul R. Lawrence and Jay W. Lorsch in an unpublished "Working Paper on Scientific Transfer and Organizational Structure," 1963. The latter, in turn, draws heavily on criteria suggested by W. Evans (1963) "Indices of the Hierarchical Structure of Industrial Organizations," *Management Science, 9,* 468–477, Burns and Stalker, *op. cit.*, and Woodward, *op. cit.*, as well as those suggested by R.H. Hall, "Intraorganizational Structure Variables," *Administrative Science Quarterly, 9,* 295–308.

We can contrast mechanistic structures with organic structures. As shown in Exhibit 14.9, **organic structures** tend to favour wider spans of control, fewer authority levels, less specialization, less formalization, and decentralization. Flexibility and informal communication are favoured over rigidity and the strict chain of command. Thus, organic structures are more in line with the dictates of the human relations movement. Speaking generally, the matrix form is organic.

The labels *mechanistic* and *organic* represent theoretical extremes, and structures can and do fall between these extremes. But is one of these structures superior to the other? To answer this, pause for a moment and consider the structures of a fast-food restaurant chain like McDonald's and the structure of W.L. Gore & Associates, Inc. discussed in the chapter-opening vignette. At the restaurant level, McDonald's is structured very mechanistically. This structure makes perfect sense for the rather routine task of delivering basic convenience food to thousands of people every day and doing it with uniform quality and speed. Of course, McDonald's headquarters, which deals with less routine tasks (e.g., product development, strategic planning), would be more organically structured. W.L. Gore & Associates, Inc. develops and manufactures products that are highly dependent on fast-changing high technology. Its founder also despised bureaucracy. An organic structure suits Gore perfectly.

There is no "one best way" to organize. In general, more mechanistic structures are called for when an organization's external environment is more stable and its technology is more routine. Organic structures work better when the environment is uncertain, the technology is less routine, and innovation is important. We will examine these matters in more detail in the next chapter.

It has to be emphasized that many organizations do not have only a single structure and that structure can and should change over time. Innovation (which we will study in detail in Chapter 16) is one factor that often dictates multiple structures. When a large and established firm gets into a new line of business either on its own or by acquiring a smaller and newer innovative firm, the innovative unit often requires some autonomy (i.e., differentiation) and a more organic structure than the established parent. This is illustrated in "Applied Focus: *E-Commerce Structural Choices at Walgreens, CVS, Charles Schwab, and Merrill Lynch*." As innovative units mature, they often tend to become more mechanistic and more integrated into the larger organization.[27]

Organic structures.
Organizational structures characterized by flatness, low specialization, low formalization, and decentralization.

E-Commerce Structural Choices at Walgreens, CVS, Charles Schwab, and Merrill Lynch

Innovations in organizations often require difficult decisions about existing organizational structures and how to incorporate the innovation. A particular dilemma is the following: Innovations entail a good deal of uncertainty, and more organic structures are best for dealing with uncertainty because of their capacity for adjustment. However, existing organizations are often structured more mechanistically to capitalize on the efficiencies of such a structure. George Westerman, F. Warren McFarlan, and Marco Iansiti studied how existing firms in the pharmacy and brokerage industries responded to an important innovation—the advent of electronic commerce. Their research illustrates that firms have choices about how to structure and that these choices matter.

The drug chain CVS opted for a highly differentiated structure in that its e-commerce unit was largely autonomous and located at the opposite end of the country from the CVS headquarters. This more organic structure enabled CVS to get an early jump on its competitors. On the other hand, Walgreens pursued a much more integrated structure, fitting the e-commerce operation into its existing offline business, using senior executives as integrators to ensure that the offliners helped the online personnel. There were teething problems, but the integrated approach gradually paid off in efficiency as e-commerce became a more routine business model. Indeed, competitor CVS restructured to a more integrated, less autonomous design as the merits of that approach became apparent. The same trend was observed in the brokerage industry. Discount broker Charles Schwab was an early adopter and chose the more autonomous approach, with the e-commerce unit reporting directly to a co-CEO. Traditional broker Merrill Lynch was a later adopter and opted to integrate online services with its existing business. Schwab eventually followed suit, integrating online and offline operations.

The lesson to be learned here, according to Westerman and colleagues, is that innovations have life cycles and that organizational structures have to correspond to these cycles. Autonomy and differentiation are helpful for introducing innovations, but more integration leads to efficiency as the innovation becomes commonplace.

Source: Westerman, G., McFarlan, F.W., & Iansiti, M. (2006). Organization design and effectiveness over the innovation life cycle. *Organization Science, 17*, 230–238.

CONTEMPORARY ORGANIC STRUCTURES

Recent years have seen the advent of new, more organic organizational structures. Global competition and deregulation, as well as advances in technology and communications, have motivated these structures. Typically, the removal of unnecessary bureaucracy and the decentralization of decision making result in a more adaptable organization. Let's examine some contemporary organic organizational structures.

Network and Virtual Organizations

Network organization.
Liaisons between specialist organizations that rely strongly on market mechanisms for coordination.

In a **network organization**, various functions are coordinated as much by market mechanisms as by managers and formal lines of authority.[28] That is, emphasis is placed on who can do what most effectively and economically rather than on fixed ties dictated by an organizational chart. All the assets necessary to produce a finished product or service are present in the network as a whole, not held in-house by one firm. Ideally, the network members cooperate, share information, and customize their services to meet the needs of the network. Indeed, the diffusion of information and innovation are two important outcomes of network forms.[29]

In stable networks, core firms that are departmentalized by function, product, or some other factor contract out some functions to favoured partners so that they can concentrate on the things that they do best (see the left side of Exhibit 14.10).

Stable Network

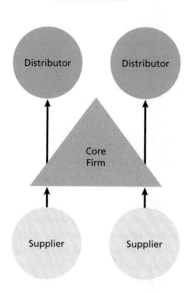

Virtual Organization (Dynamic Network)

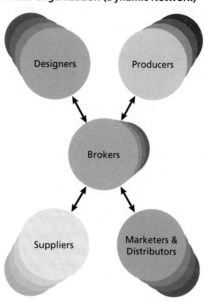

EXHIBIT 14.10
Types of network organizations.

Source: From R.E. Miles and C.C. Snow. "Causes of failure in network organizations." Copyright © 1985 by The Regents of the University of California. Reprinted from the *California Management Review,* Vol. 34, No. 4., by permission of The Regents.

DaimlerChrysler, for instance, has its car seats supplied by an upstream firm that also does all the research associated with seating.

Particularly interesting networks are dynamic or virtual organizations, such as that illustrated on the right side of Exhibit 14.10. In a **virtual organization,** an alliance of independent companies share skills, costs, and access to one another's markets. Thus, they consist of a network of continually evolving independent companies.[30] A "broker" firm with a good idea invents a network in which a large amount of the work is done by other network partners who might change over time or projects. Each partner in a virtual organization contributes only in its area of core competencies. Contemporary book publishers are good examples. These firms do not employ authors, print books, or distribute books. Rather, they specialize in contracting authors for a particular project, providing developmental assistance, and marketing the final product. Printing, distribution, and some editorial and design work are handled by others in the network. Such networks are not new, as they have been used for years in the fashion and film industries. However, more firms in other industries, such as computers and biotechnology, now adopt network forms. A familiar organization that is essentially virtual is Visa, which is at the centre of a network of thousands of financial institutions and many more retailers.

As indicated, a key advantage of the network form is its flexibility and adaptability. A virtual organization is even more flexible than a matrix. Networks also allow organizations to specialize in what they do best. In its network, DaimlerChrysler has intentionally positioned itself as a car manufacturer, not a car seat manufacturer. In turn, its supplier has a strong incentive to specialize in its product because DaimlerChrysler is a good, stable customer.

The joint operation of specialization and flexibility can be seen in the video game industry.[31] Although there are some exceptions, the development of video games (e.g., *Madden NFL 07*) and the design and sale of video game consoles (e.g., Xbox, PlayStation, GameCube) are done by separate, specialist organizations. In fact, there are hundreds of game developers and just a few console producers. Game developers can and do make choices about which consoles their games can run on, thus establishing a network tie. Factors such as the age and market dominance of the console

Virtual organization. A network of continually evolving independent organizations that share skills, costs, and access to one another's markets.

DaimlerChrysler
www.daimlerchrysler.ca

The video game industry uses networks extensively to develop and design games and gaming consoles.

affect this choice. On their part, console designers such as Sony and Nintendo have to think about the nature and timing of new products so as to cater to the needs of game designers and thus maintain and enlarge their networks. In a first for Sony, it subcontracted the actual production of its PlayStation 3 to Taiwan's Asustek Computer.[32] Thus, its network includes various game producers as well as supplier Asustek.

Network and virtual organizations face some special problems.[33] Stable networks can deteriorate when the companies dealing with the core firm devote so much of their effort to this firm that they are isolated from normal market demands. This can make them "lazy," resulting in a loss of their technological edge. Virtual organizations lose their organic advantage when they become legalistic, secretive, and too binding of the other partners. On the other side of the coin, virtual partners sometimes exploit their loose structure to profit at the expense of the core firm. The computer industry has experienced both problems with its network arrangements. For instance, the main beneficiaries of the advent of the PC were Microsoft (the operating system supplier) and Intel (the microprocessor supplier), not IBM.[34] Finally, and ironically, despite their capacity for flexibility, network firms sometimes suffer from "structural inertia." That is, network ties are maintained even when they are not economical. This may occur especially among older, larger organizations with large networks.[35]

The Modular Organization

In today's highly uncertain and fast-changing environment, many organizations are realizing that there are advantages to not becoming a large and vertically integrated bureaucracy. Instead, they focus on a few core activities that they do best, such as designing and marketing computers, and let other companies perform all the other activities. A **modular organization** is an organization that performs a few core functions and outsources noncore activities to specialists and suppliers. Services that are often outsourced include the manufacturing of parts, trucking, catering, data processing, and accounting. Thus, modular organizations are like hubs that are surrounded by networks of suppliers that can be added or removed as needed. And unlike a virtual organization, in which the participating firms give up part of their control and are interdependent, the modular organization maintains complete strategic control.[36]

By outsourcing noncore activities, modular organizations are able to keep unit costs low and develop new products more rapidly. It also allows them to use their capital in areas where they have a competitive advantage, such as design and marketing. This has enabled companies such as Dell Computer and Nike to experience large and rapid growth in a relatively short period of time, as they have not had to invest heavily in fixed assets. Nike and Reebok concentrate on designing and marketing high-tech fashionable sports and fitness footwear. Both organizations contract out production to suppliers in countries with low-cost labour.[37]

Modular organizations in the electronics industry buy their products already built, or they buy the parts from suppliers and then assemble them. Dell Computer, for example, assembles computers from outsourced parts, and this allows it to focus on marketing and service. Given this leanness, Dell can afford to invest in areas such as training salespeople and service technicians, although even most of its technicians are outsourced.[38] The automotive industry in North America has also begun to be heavily involved in outsourcing and to become increasingly modular. A major player in the outsourcing of auto parts is Canada's Magna International, a leading auto parts supplier. Consider DaimlerChrysler's minivan. Magna designs, engineers, and manufactures a great deal of the vehicle, including the seats, mirrors, door panels, locks, and more. An increasing number of auto makers are now outsourcing major parts of their vehicles to parts suppliers like Magna in an effort to improve efficiency and quality. The trend is also catching on in Europe and Japan.[39] For example, Toyota has achieved great success by relying on a network of suppliers.[40] Outsourcing is also taking place

Modular organization. An organization that performs a few core functions and outsources noncore activities to specialists and suppliers.

among auto parts suppliers, as manufacturers of smaller parts are providing the supplies for those who make the larger parts.[41]

Although there are many advantages to the modular organization, there are also some disadvantages. Modular organizations work best when they focus on the right speciality and have good suppliers. Because they are dependent on so many outsiders, it is critical that they find suppliers who are reliable and loyal and can be trusted with trade secrets. Modular organizations also must be careful not to outsource critical technologies, which could diminish future competitive advantages. Another disadvantage of the modular organization is that it decreases operational control due to its dependence on outsiders.[42]

In summary, the modular organization is a lean and streamlined organizational structure with great flexibility, making it particularly well-suited to organizations in rapidly changing environments. Many modular organizations have become extremely profitable and competitive. And although modular organizational structures have been most popular in the trendy, fast-paced apparel and electronics industries, other industries, such as automotive, steel, chemicals, and photographic equipment, are also becoming more modular.[43]

The Boundaryless Organization

An important outcome of the division and coordination of labour is that the structure of most organizations consists of a rigid vertical hierarchy and many departments. As a result, traditional organizational structures consist of boundaries or barriers that divide people at different hierarchical levels and separate those in different departments. This can be problematic to the extent that the different levels and departments are interdependent, as is usually the case in most organizations. In other words, the work in one department is dependent on and affects the performance of other departments. Such interdependence often results in open conflict. For example, in organizations with a tall vertical hierarchy, there can be conflict between employees at the lower levels and management in the upper ranks. In organizations with a functional structure, the various departments often do not communicate or coordinate their efforts, even though their tasks are interdependent. Thus, the barriers that exist in traditional organizational structures can stifle productivity and innovation.[44]

Former General Electric CEO Jack Welch says boundaries are dysfunctional because they separate employees from management, and the organization from its customers and suppliers. To remove the vertical and horizontal boundaries in organizations, Welch developed the idea of the boundaryless organization. In a **boundaryless organization**, the boundaries that divide employees, such as hierarchy, job function, and geography, as well as those that distance companies from suppliers and customers are broken down.[45] Thus, a boundaryless organization removes vertical, horizontal, and external barriers so that employees, managers, customers, and suppliers can work together, share ideas, and identify the best ideas for the organization.

What does the structure of a boundaryless organization look like? Instead of being organized around functions with many hierarchical levels, the boundaryless organization is made up of self-managing and cross-functional teams that are organized around core business processes that are critical for satisfying customers, such as new-product development or materials handling. The teams comprise individuals from different functional areas within the organization, as well as customers and suppliers. Each business process has an owner who is in charge of the process and process performance. Thus, the traditional vertical hierarchy is flattened and replaced by layers of teams making the organization look more horizontal than vertical.[46] Information and knowledge can be quickly distributed throughout the organization and directly to where it is needed without first being filtered by a tall vertical hierarchy.[47] Boundaryless organizations are able to achieve greater integration and coordination within the organization and with external stakeholders.

Boundaryless organization. An organization that removes vertical, horizontal, and external barriers so that employees, managers, customers, and suppliers can work together, share ideas, and identify the best ideas for the organization.

A good example is Chrysler's development of the Neon before the merger with Daimler-Benz. Chrysler wanted to develop a profitable subcompact vehicle, something that it had previously been unable to do. Rather than find a partner as some other automobile makers had done, the company decided to try something new. They involved many internal and external stakeholders, including personnel from different functional areas such as engineering, marketing, purchasing, finance, and labour, as well as suppliers and consumers. By removing the boundaries between these groups and having them work together, the company was able to avoid delays that are often the result of disagreements and misunderstandings. As a result, Chrysler developed the Neon in a record 42 months at a price tag of $1.3 billion. By comparison, Ford spent $2 billion and took five years to develop the money-losing Ford Escort, and GM spent $5 billion and took seven years to develop the Saturn.[48]

While boundaryless organizations have a number of advantages, including the ability to adapt to environmental changes, they have a number of disadvantages. For example, it can be difficult to overcome political and authority boundaries, and it can be time consuming to manage the democratic processes required to coordinate the efforts of many stakeholders.[49] Even General Electric realizes that it will take years before being boundaryless becomes natural.[50] Nonetheless, some believe that the boundaryless organization is the perfect organizational structure for the twenty-first century.[51]

In summary, many of the traditional organizational structures are being replaced by more flexible structures that break down external and internal boundaries. Network or virtual organizations and modular organizations represent structures that break down or modify external organizational boundaries, and the boundaryless organization is an attempt to remove both external and internal boundaries. For many organizations, traditional organizational structures are no longer effective, and so they must find new ways to structure and coordinate their efforts to adapt to environmental changes and to remain competitive.

THE IMPACT OF SIZE

It is perhaps trivial to note that the giant General Motors Corporation is structured differently from a small DVD rental shop. But exactly how does organizational size (measured by number of employees) affect the structure of organizations?[52]

Size and Structure

In general, large organizations are more complex than small organizations.[53] For example, a small organization is unlikely to have its own legal department or market research group, and these tasks will probably be contracted out. Economies of scale enable large organizations to perform these functions themselves, but with a consequent increase in the number of departments and job titles. In turn, this horizontal specialization often stimulates the need for additional complexity in the form of appointing integrators or creating planning departments. As horizontal specialization increases, management levels must be added (making the organization taller) so that spans of control do not get out of hand.[54] To repeat, size is associated with increased complexity.

Complexity means coordination problems, in spite of integrators, planning departments, and the like. This is where other structural characteristics come into play. In general, bigger organizations are less centralized than smaller organizations.[55] In a small company, the president might be involved in all but the least critical decisions. In a large company, the president would be overloaded with such decisions, and they could not be made in a timely manner. In addition, since the large organization will also be taller, top management is often too far removed from the action to make many operating decisions. How is control retained with decentralization? The answer is for-malization—large organizations tend to be more formal than small organizations. Rules, regulations, and standard procedures help to ensure that decentralized decisions fall within accepted boundaries.

One exception to the general rule that growth leads to decentralization occurs when the growth comes from acquisitions of other firms. The forest product company Weyerhaeuser found that such growth led to too much decentralization, in that a home builder often had to place orders with multiple divisions. The structure was revised via centralization so that a single salesperson could handle all requests from a builder.[56]

Weyerhaeuser
www.weyerhaeuser.com

Two further points about the relationship between size and structure should be emphasized. First, you will recall that product departmentation is often preferable to functional departmentation as the organization increases in size. Logically, then, orga-nizations with product departmentation should exhibit more complexity and more decentralization than those with functional departmentation. A careful comparison of Exhibits 14.2 and 14.3 will confirm this logic. In the firm with the product structure, research, production, and marketing are duplicated, increasing complexity. In addition, since each product line is essentially self-contained, decisions can be made at a lower organizational level.

Finally, we should recognize that size is only one determinant of organizational structure. Even at a given size, organizations might require different structures to be maximally effective. In the next chapter, we will examine other determinants of struc-ture, principally environmental pressures and technology.

Exhibit 14.11 summarizes the relationship between size and structural variables.

Downsizing

A reduction in workforce size, popularly called *downsizing*, has been an organizational trend in recent years. Millions of jobs have disappeared as organizations seek to bol-ster efficiency and cut costs in an era of global competition, government deregulation, mergers, changing consumer preferences, and advancing technologies.[57] Downsizing has a number of implications for organizational structure.

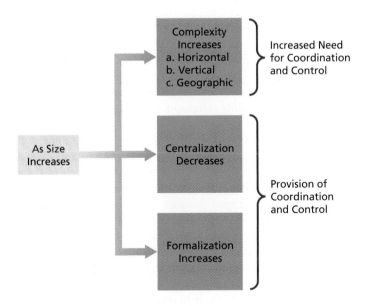

EXHIBIT 14.11
The relationship between size and structure.

Downsizing. The intentional reduction in workforce size with the goal of improving organizational efficiency or effectiveness.

Downsizing and Structure. Downsizing might be formally defined as the intentional reduction in workforce size with the goal of improving organizational efficiency or effectiveness.[58] Notice that this definition does not imply that the organization's fortunes are necessarily in decline, although a shrinking market could motivate downsizing. In fact, Compaq Computer announced substantial downsizing during a year of record revenues and shipments in anticipation of the need to be more competitive in the future.[59]

How should downsizing affect organizational structure? It is tempting to "work backwards" through Exhibit 14.11 and simply say that as size *decreases* the firm should reduce its complexity, centralize, and become less formalized. In the case of a very simple downsizing, this logic might work. However, notice its limitations. First, some of the conditions listed above that often prompt downsizing are *new* conditions, not simply the opposite of the factors that led to organizational growth in the past. For example, deregulation has led to a completely new cast of competitors in the banking and telecommunications industries. Second, the logic of simply working backwards through Exhibit 14.11 would assume that downsizing occurs proportionally in all parts of an organization. As you may know, this is not the case. White-collar managerial and staff jobs have been disproportionately reduced in the most recent downsizings, for reasons varying from high salaries to improvements in information technology. The upshot of all this is that a new downsized structure should not necessarily look like a mini-version of the old structure.

Downsizing can be accomplished in a variety of ways. Although layoffs have been common, some organizations have relied on hiring freezes and natural attrition. In practice, downsizing is often accompanied by reducing horizontal or vertical complexity. Vertically, management levels have been removed to make organizations flatter. This has sometimes made sense when information technology enables the remaining managers to more effectively monitor the performance of their subordinates. Also, self-managed teams (Chapter 7) can act as substitutes for a level of management. Horizontally, functions can be combined (e.g., inspection and quality) or removed altogether by contracting them out.

Problems with Downsizing. Many organizations have not done a good job of anticipating and managing the structural and human consequences of downsizing. For instance, when faced with serious decline, organizations have a decided tendency to become more mechanistic, particularly more formalized and centralized.[60] Rules are closely enforced, and higher levels of management take part in more day-to-day decisions. This can be useful to get the organization back on track, but it can also reduce flexibility just when it is needed. A good rule to follow is to avoid unnecessary formalization or centralization of matters that might have a negative impact on customers or clients. In other words, do not allow internal tightening up to damage external relationships.

One downsizing tactic has been to greatly reduce or even to eliminate whole departments of headquarters advisory staff. For instance, a human resources department might be downsized or the legal department eliminated. Many such staff units become bloated over the years, and they have been known to isolate top management from divisional concerns and to bureaucratize decision making. Thus, downsizing can provoke decentralization, giving line managers more power and speeding up decisions. On the other hand, some firms have eliminated such positions and then turned around and hired consultants to do the same work. Contracting work out can be a viable strategy, but it is clear that some consulting arrangements have proven more expensive than the original in-house unit.[61] A good rule to follow is to think very carefully about the *work* that needs to be done and *who* should do it before downsizing.

A common structural downsizing error has been to flatten organizations by removing management levels without considering the implications for job design and workload. A glance at Exhibit 14.8 illustrates the crux of the problem: If only the management ranks are thinned, managers have larger spans below them and less support above them. This works well if decentralization is called for and if the people in the lower ranks are ready to assume greater decision-making responsibility. It does not work well if managers are overloaded with work or are incapable of delegating to subordinates. Advanced information technology and training can sometimes assist managers in coping with increased spans of control.

The increased spans that accompany flatter structures have also been implicated in some cases of ethical violation and corporate fraud. Less direct supervision coupled with unclear responsibilities mean that traditional guards against unethical activities may be lacking.

Thinking in advance about the structural aspects of downsizing is not a substitute for involving employees in downsizing plans. Surprising people with workforce cuts is very likely to result in low morale, reduced personal productivity, and continuing distrust of management. Some survivors of downsizing have even reported feeling guilty because they retained their jobs.[62]

In summary, downsizing has the potential to improve organizational effectiveness in certain circumstances, but its impact on structure and morale must be anticipated and managed. A fair amount of evidence shows that downsizing often leads to reduced satisfaction and commitment, increased absenteeism, and damaged health.[63] Perhaps as a result, research has shown that contrary to expectations, downsizing does not result in cost reductions in the long run or improvements in productivity. The negative outcomes of downsizing, however, are primarily due to poor implementation, such as a lack of supporting activities. When carefully and properly implemented, downsizing can have positive consequences. For example, when discount broker Charles Schwab experienced business losses, it first cut back on management perks and cut executive pay. When the layoffs occurred, employees were given stock options, outplacement services, and $20 000 tuition vouchers.[64]

Charles Schwab
www.schwab.com

A FOOTNOTE: SYMPTOMS OF STRUCTURAL PROBLEMS

Let's conclude the chapter by considering some symptoms of structural problems in organizations.

- *Bad job design.* As we noted at several points, there is a reciprocal relationship between job design and organizational structure. Frequently, improper structural arrangements turn good jobs on paper into poor jobs in practice. A tall structure and narrow span of control in a research and development unit can reduce autonomy and turn exciting jobs into drudgery. An extremely large span of control can overload the most dedicated manager.

- *The right hand does not know what the left is doing.* If repeated examples of duplication of effort occur, or if parts of the organization work at cross-purposes, structure is suspect. One author gives the example of one division of a large organization laying off workers while another division was busy recruiting from the same labour pool![65] The general problem here is one of coordination and integration.

- *Persistent conflict between departments.* Managers are often inclined to attribute such conflicts to personality clashes between key personnel in the warring departments. Just as often, a failure of integration is the problem. One clue here is whether the conflict persists even when personnel changes occur.

- *Slow response times.* Ideally, labour is divided and coordinated to do business quickly. Delayed responses might be due to improper structure. Centralization might speed responses when a few decisions about a few products are required (dictating functional departmentation). Decentralization might speed responses when many decisions about many products are required (dictating product departmentation).

- *Decisions made with incomplete information.* In Chapter 11, we noted that managers generally acquire more than enough information to make decisions. After the fact, if we find that decisions have been made with incomplete information, and the information existed somewhere in the organization, structure could be at fault. It is clear that structural deficiencies were, in part, responsible for keeping top NASA administrators unaware of the mechanical problems that contributed to the explosion of the space shuttle *Challenger*.[66] This information was known to NASA personnel, but it did not move up the hierarchy properly.

- *A proliferation of committees.* Committees exist in all organizations, and they often serve as one of the more routine kinds of integrating mechanisms. However, when committee is piled on committee, or when task forces are being formed with great regularity, it is often a sign that the basic structure of the organization is being "patched up" because it does not work well.[67] A structural review might be in order if too many people are spending too much time in committee meetings.

 THE MANAGER'S

Notebook

IT Integration at Cardinal Health

1. The previous structure at Cardinal was a variation on product departmentation in which each business unit was relatively self-contained. This structure allows for the business units to be very responsive to their customers and for each business unit to be focused and cohesive. At Cardinal, one of the barriers to changing the structure of the IT function was that business units previously had a live support team to "tap on the shoulder" when problems arose. At the same time, this structure also had many disadvantages. First, the duplication was expensive. Second, the duplication was both inefficient and did not allow for tracking to determine and fix root causes of problems. As an example of inefficiency, it previously took IT staffers two weeks to literally put their hands on every computer to scan for viruses and clean hard drives. By company estimates, there were hundreds of thousands of different entry points for viruses. With the new structure and centralization, every computer can be accessed and scanned for viruses remotely. Overall, Cardinal greatly centralized and streamlined the IT function. The number of data centres was reduced from 42 to 7, with a goal of eventually having only 2. Fifteen disparate help desks and technical customer support groups have been consolidated into one central location, and call tracking tools were reduced from more than 10 down to a single package. The new structure is an example of hybrid departmentation in which the IT function is centralized while product and service delivery is otherwise decentralized.

2. The new IT structure at Cardinal depends primarily on the standardization of work processes. The first integration goal was to streamline and centralize the structure *and* processes by consolidating six major IT groups aligned with many business units into a single enterprise IT team, known as Enterprise IT (EIT). To get started, a catalogue detailing the services EIT would offer and the levels of support provided for each was established. Internal users' expectations for each of these were managed by setting a delivery standard. Service-level agreements were also established for resolution of issues and for availability of critical IT systems. This common Service Delivery Model (SDM) helped Cardinal benchmark protocols and work, including equipment orders, managing the help desk, tracking system availability, and even clearing viruses. They now track the work of all 1600 IT team members to achieve consistency and deliver results, and they have established metric guidelines for them to meet. Also, Cardinal no longer has dozens of desktop hardware vendors and cellular service providers; just a few industry leaders now meet their global service, quality, and price standards. To date, the results of the standardization and streamlining have been impressive. Service-delivery performance improved by 25 percent during the first four months, driving client satisfaction up to 93 percent. The centralized help desk and customer support centre supports nearly 500 000 annual calls and cases for more than 125 000 Cardinal Health customers. These calls now average just 45 seconds and are resolved within the service centre 79 percent of the time.

LEARNING OBJECTIVES CHECKLIST

1. *Organizational structure* is the manner in which an organization divides its labour into specific tasks and achieves coordination among these tasks. Labour is divided vertically and horizontally. *Vertical division of labour* concerns the apportioning of authority. *Horizontal division of labour* involves designing jobs and grouping them into departments.

2. While *functional departmentation* locates employees with similar skills in the same department, other forms of departmentation locate employees in accordance with *product, geography,* or *customer requirements.*

3. Basic methods of *coordinating* divided labour include direct supervision, standardization of work processes, standardization of outputs, standardization of skills, and mutual adjustment. Workers are permitted more discretion as coordination moves from direct supervision through mutual adjustment. More elaborate methods of coordination are aimed specifically at achieving integration across departments. These include liaison roles, task forces, teams, and integrators.

4. *Traditional structural characteristics* include span of control, flatness versus tallness, formalization, centralization, and complexity. Larger organizations tend to be more complex, more formal, and less centralized than smaller organizations.

5. The classical organizational theorists tended to favour *mechanistic organizational structures* (small spans, tall, formalized, and fairly centralized). The human relations theorists, having noted the flaws of bureaucracy, tended to favour *organic structures* (larger spans, flat, less formalized, and less centralized). However, there is no one best way to organize, and both mechanistic and organic structures have their places.

6. Many of the traditional organizational structures are being replaced by more flexible structures that break down external and internal boundaries. *Network* or *virtual organizations* and *modular organizations* are structures that break down or modify external barriers, and the *boundaryless organization* removes both internal and external barriers. As organizations grow in size they tend to become more complex (vertically, horizontally, geographically), more formalized, and less centralized.

7. *Downsizing* is the intentional reduction in workforce size with the goal of improving organizational efficiency or effectiveness. Sensible downsizing avoids mechanistic tendencies, retains necessary personnel, and respects good job design principles.

8. Symptoms of structural problems include poor job design, extreme duplication of effort, conflict between departments, slow responses, too many committees, and decisions made with incomplete information.

DISCUSSION QUESTIONS

1. Discuss the division of labour in a restaurant. What methods are used to coordinate this divided labour? Do differences exist between fast-food versus more formal restaurants?

2. Is the departmentation in a small college essentially functional or product oriented? Defend your answer. (*Hint:* In what department will the historians find themselves? In what department will the groundskeepers find themselves?)

3. Which basic method(s) of coordination is (are) most likely to be found in a pure research laboratory? On a football team? In a supermarket?

4. What are the relative merits of mechanistic versus organic structures?

5. Discuss the logic behind the following statement: "We don't want to remove the differentiation that exists between sales and production. What we want to do is achieve integration."

6. As Spinelli Construction Company grew in size, its founder and president, Joe Spinelli, found that he was overloaded with decisions. What two basic structural changes should Spinelli make to rectify this situation without losing control of the company?

7. Describe a situation in which a narrow span of control might be appropriate and contrast it with a situation in which a broad span might be appropriate.

8. Make up a list of criteria that would define a good downsizing effort.

INTEGRATIVE DISCUSSION QUESTIONS

1. How do the structural characteristics of organizations influence leadership, communication, decision making, and power in organizations? Discuss the implications of each of the structural characteristics (i.e., span of control, organization levels, formalization, centralization, and complexity) for leadership behaviour, communication and decision-making processes, and the distribution and use of power in organizations.

2. How do the new forms of organizational structure, such as virtual, modular, and boundaryless organizations, influence the culture of an organization? In other words, what is the relationship between these types of structures and an organization's culture? What is the relationship between these structures and the use and effectiveness of teams?

ON-THE-JOB CHALLENGE QUESTION

Google, the Internet innovator par excellence, relies less on top-down strategies and more on grassroots ideas for new products and services. These ideas are often developed in small project teams that have little supervision. In a typical organization, the span of control of a manager might range between 5 and 30 subordinates. However, according to consultant Gary Hamel, a single manager at Google professed to have 160 employees reporting to him!

What does this structural feature tell you about how work is organized at Google? How does a large span of control promote grassroots innovation?

Source: Hamel, G. (2006, February). The why, what, and how of management innovation. *Harvard Business Review*, 72–84.

EXPERIENTIAL EXERCISE

Organizational Structure Preference Scale

In most organizations, there are differences of opinion and preferences as to how the organization should be structured and how people should conduct themselves. Following are a number of statements concerning these matters. The purpose of this survey is for you to learn about your own preferences regarding the structure of organizations. Please use the response scale below to indicate the extent to which you agree with each statement.

1 — Disagree strongly
2 — Disagree
3 — Neither agree nor disagree
4 — Agree
5 — Agree strongly

_____ 1. I get most of my motivation to work from the job itself rather than from the rewards the company gives me for doing it.

_____ 2. I respect my supervisors for what they know rather than for the fact that the company has put them in charge.

_____ 3. I work best when things are exciting and filled with energy. I can feel the adrenalin rushing through me and I like it.

_____ 4. I like it best if we can play things by ear. Going by the book means you do not have any imagination.

_____ 5. People who seek security at work are boring. I don't go to work to plan my retirement.

_____ 6. I believe that planning should focus on the short term. Long-term planning is unrealistic. I want to see the results of my plan.

_____ 7. Don't give me a detailed job description. Just point me in the general direction and I will figure out what needs to be done.

____ 8. I don't expect to be introduced to new people. If I like their looks, I'll introduce myself.

____ 9. Goals should be set by everyone in the organization. I prefer to achieve my own goals rather than those of someone else.

____ 10. One of the things I prefer most about a job is that it be full of surprises.

____ 11. I like a job that is full of challenges.

____ 12. Organization charts are only needed by people who are already lost.

____ 13. Technology is constantly changing.

____ 14. Supervision and control should be face to face.

____ 15. If organizations focus on problem solving, the bottom line will take care of itself.

____ 16. I would never take a job that involved repetitive activities.

____ 17. Organizations are constantly in a state of change. I don't worry about how the players line up.

____ 18. Every decision I make is a new one. I don't look for precedents.

____ 19. When people talk about efficiency, I think they really don't want to do a good job.

____ 20. The people who know the most about the work should be put in charge.

Scoring and Interpretation

To calculate your organizational structure preference score, simply add up your responses to each of the 20 questions. Scores can range from 20 to 100. Your score on this survey indicates your preference for a mechanistic or organic organizational structure. A score of less than 50 indicates a preference for a mechanistic or formal organizational structure. Mechanistic structures tend to favour tallness, narrow spans of control, specialization, centralization, and formalization. Scores above 50 indicate a preference for a more organic or informal organizational structure. Organic structures tend to favour wider spans of control, fewer authority levels, less specialization, less formalization, and decentralization. Flexibility and informal communication are favoured over rigidity and the strict chain of command.

Source: Hoffman, R. & Ruemper, F. (1997). Exercise 20: Mechanistic or organic organizational design. In *Organizational behaviour: Canadian cases and exercises*, 3rd ed. Toronto: Captus Press, 298–299. Reprinted by permission of Captus Press Inc.

CASE INCIDENT

Conway Manufacturing

Conway Manufacturing is a large organization that manufactures machine tools that are used by workers in various industries. In recent years, sales of the company's products have begun to fall as a result of increasing competition. Customers have also begun to complain about the quality of Conway's products. In response, Conway decided to design some new high-quality products.

The research and development department was asked to develop some new designs for several of Conway's best-selling products. When the engineering department looked at the designs, they rejected them outright saying that they were not very good. Engineering then revised the designs and sent them to the production department. However, the production department responded by sending them back to the engineering department, insisting that they would be impossible to produce. In the meantime, the marketing department had begun a campaign based on the material they had received from the research and development department. One year later, Conway was still no closer to producing new products. In the meantime, more customers were complaining and threatening to find new suppliers, and the competition continued to take more and more of Conway's business.

1. Describe the structure of Conway Manufacturing. What are some of the problems that Conway is having, and is organizational structure a factor?

2. What would be the most effective structure to design new high-quality products in a short period of time? What are some methods for improving coordination?

CASE STUDY

IVE

Richard Ivey School of
The University of Wester

Trojan Technologies

In March 1998, a group of Trojan Technologies Inc. (Trojan) employees grappled with the issue of how to structure the business to effectively interact with their customers and to manage the company's dramatic growth. The London, Ontario, manufacturer of ultra-violet (UV) water disinfection systems believed that strong customer service was key to its recent and projected growth and had come to the realization that changes would have to be made to continue to achieve both simultaneously. The group hoped to develop a structure to address these issues. Marvin DeVries, executive vice-president, was to lead the development and implementation of the new structure. The transition to the new structure was to begin as of September 1998 to coincide with the new fiscal year.

The Business

Technology

Since 1977, the company had specialized in UV light applications for disinfecting water and wastewater. In essence, Trojan's products killed micro-organisms using high-intensity UV lamps. Water was channelled past the lamps at various speeds, based on the clarity of the water and the strength of the lamps, to achieve the required "kill" rate.

Trojan's UV technology had proved to be an environmentally safe and cost effective alternative to chlorination and was gaining wider recognition and acceptance. Even so, a significant market remained to be tapped, as the company estimated " . . . that only 5 percent to 10 percent of municipal wastewater sites in North America use UV-based technology . . . [and] of the approximate 62 000 wastewater treatment facilities operating worldwide, only 2500 currently utilize UV disinfection systems."[1]

Trojan Technologies Inc.[2]

Trojan was established in 1977 with a staff of three with the goal of developing a viable UV wastewater disinfection technology. Following several years of work, the first UV disinfection system (System UV2000™) was installed in Tillsonburg, Ontario, in 1981. It took another two years, however, before the regulatory approvals were in place to market the technology for municipal wastewater treatment in Canada and the United States. During this time, the company generated revenues through the sale of small residential and industrial cleanwater UV systems.

By 1991, the company had sales in excess of $10 million and had introduced its second-generation technology in the System UV3000™ wastewater disinfection system. As the company's growth continued, a staff of 50 was in place by 1992. The following year, due to capital requirements created by the company's strong growth, an initial public offering on the Toronto Stock Exchange was completed. Also in 1993, a branch office was established in The Hague, Netherlands, expanding Trojan's reach across the Atlantic.

The following year, 1994, saw the launch of the System UV4000™, the construction of a new head office, and sales exceeding $20 million. In 1995, a branch office was opened in California to service the enormous market for wastewater treatment in that state. Two years later, an expansion doubled head office capacity to house 190 staff and meet the demand for sales of more than $50 million.

Well into 1998, the expectation was that sales would reach $70 million by year end and continue to grow by more than 30 percent each year over the next five years, reaching $300 million by 2003. The company was in the process of planning additional capacity expansion in the form of building and property purchases adjacent to head office and expected to quadruple its headcount by 2003 to more than 1000 employees.

Products

In 1997, 93 percent of Trojan's sales were of wastewater products (System UV4000™ and System UV3000™). These systems were designed for use at small to very large wastewater treatment plants and more complex wastewater treatment applications with varying degrees of effluent treatment. The remaining 7 percent of sales were cleanwater products (primarily the System UV8000™ and Aqua UV™) for municipal and residential drinking water and industrial process applications. Growth in the coming year would be driven by increased sales of the wastewater disinfection products in both current and new geographic markets. In the longer term, new products such as the A•I•R•2000™, which was to use UV light with an advanced photocatalytic technology to destroy volatile organic compounds in the air, were expected to further Trojan's sales growth.

Products were typically assembled from component parts at Trojan's head office. The complexity of the product design, manufacture, and service arose from the integration of skills in electronics, biology, controls programming, and mechanical engineering. The company owned patents on its products and was prepared to defend them to preserve its intellectual capital.

Customers

Trojan sold its wastewater treatment products to contractors working on projects for municipalities or directly to municipalities. Typically, the process involved bidding on a project based on the Trojan products required to meet the municipality's specifications, and, therefore, engineering expertise was required as part of the selling process. Project sales typically fell in a $100 000 to $500 000 range, and given the large value of each sale, the sales and marketing function was critical to the company's success. However, for marketing to be effective, this new technology had to be well supported. Municipalities purchasing the wastewater disinfection systems required rapid response to any problems, and expected superior service given the consequences of breakdowns for the quality of water being discharged from their facility. Municipalities also had the ability to discuss Trojan and their UV products with other municipalities before deciding to make their purchase, further underlining the importance of warranty and aftermarket service to customers to ensure positive word-of-mouth advertising.

Trojan's smaller product line, the cleanwater segment, focused on a different customer base from wastewater, and it was difficult to generalize about the nature of this segment's customers. These customers ranged from municipalities to industrial companies to individuals.

Interaction with Customers

The Process

The main points of customer interaction in the wastewater product line included:

1. Quote/bid process
2. Configuration of the project structure
3. Project shipment and system installation
4. Technical support and warranty claims
5. Parts order processing

Each of these is described briefly below.

The quote/bid process was a major function of the marketing department with support from the project engineering department. Although the marketing department took the lead role in assembling the appropriate bid and pricing, the customer would on occasion wish to speak directly to the project engineering department on specific technical questions related to the function of the UV unit within the particular wastewater setting.

After winning a bid, the configuration of project structure involved working with the customer on the detailed specifications for the project and applying the appropriate Trojan systems in a configuration that would meet the customer's needs. The project engineering department took the lead role in this work and either worked through the marketing representative in transmitting technical information to and from the customer or communicated directly with the customer's technical personnel.

Once the project had been configured, it was scheduled for manufacture by the operations department. On completion, and when the customer was ready to integrate the UV system into their wastewater facility, the service department completed the installation and start-up of the unit. The service department would also be involved in demonstrating the proper use of the system to the customer.

After the system was in use by the customer, further interaction came in the form of technical support. The service department would deal with phone calls, site visits, and warranty claims and was the primary contact point for the customer. By its nature, most service work at this stage of the process was completed on an "as-needed" basis by the first available service representative. As a result, it was difficult or impossible to have the same service representative available to respond to a particular customer on every occasion. The service department, therefore, kept a detailed file on each UV installation and all customer contact to ensure the most informed response on each service call.

The final stage of customer interaction was the ordering of replacement parts by the customer after the warranty period was complete. This was handled by a call centre at the Trojan head office in London that was separate from the other departments that had dealt with the customer. The call centre was staffed to receive orders for Trojan replacement parts, but not to provide technical support as with the service department, and would generally not access customer service files in taking the order.

In summary, customers would deal with as many as four different departments during their interaction with Trojan. During the early days of Trojan's growth, the "close-knit" nature of Trojan's workforce allowed a seamless transition between "departments." However, as described below, the company's continued growth began to complicate the transition between departments.

Customer Support in the Early Days

In the 1980s and early 1990s, when Trojan had less than 50 employees and worked on a limited number of wastewater bids and projects during the course of the year, customer support was a collective effort across the entire company. In fact, it was not unusual that virtually everyone in Trojan knew the details of all the major projects in process at any given time. There was a common knowledge base of customer names and issues, which resulted, in DeVries' words, in an "immediate connectivity" to the job at hand. At times during those early days, there were as few as two employees in a "department." Under these conditions, every project received immediate and constant attention from start to finish, ensuring the customer was satisfied and potential issues were addressed in a proactive manner.

Challenges Created by Growth

As the company grew, departments grew. Very quickly, the number of projects multiplied and it became impossible for everyone to know all the customers and active projects, or even all the people in the organization. As departments grew from two to five to ten people, communications became focused internally within the departments. This made it progressively more difficult to ensure timely and effective communication on project status between departments, and the "immediate connectivity" described by DeVries began to break down. The situation was described by many as one where "things began to slip between the cracks" in terms of customer service excellence, because it was no longer possible for employees to shepherd a project though the company from start to finish as had been done in the early days. Once a particular department had finished their component of a project, they immediately had to turn their attention to the other projects they had ongoing, creating the potential for a lag before the next department picked up the customer file.

Project Engineering

Project engineering was one example of a department that had begun to experience problems maintaining service levels to the end-customer as a result of growth. By 1997, there were seven engineers in the department handling the regular support to the marketing department and acting as "specialists" for the various technical components of the products. When engineers were hired into this group, there was no formal training or apprenticeship program in place. The new hire would simply follow along as best he or she could and attempt to learn the complex product line though observation and assistance from others in the department. This type of training was strained by the demand for project engineering services brought on by Trojan's growth.

A "specialist" role, in addition to their support of the marketing department's project bids, had evolved within the project engineering group. To handle specific technical requests, this informal addition to the project engineer's role had occurred somewhat spontaneously within the department. For example, if one of the project engineers had developed a detailed understanding of the electronics included in the System UV4000™ products, that employee acted as the reference point for most detailed queries on this subject and was considered the "electronics specialist." There was no specific training or support to develop these specialists for their roles in place in 1997, nor was hiring particularly targeted at filling the specialist roles described above, as it was a secondary role for the department. As a result of the dual roles and the company's rapid growth, project engineers could not take responsibility to guide a project from bid through customer queries to production and commissioning of the project. The demand for assistance on many bids, coupled with the need to respond to queries in their "specialist" area on active projects, prevented project engineers from acting as a steward on specific projects as they passed through the company. Instead, the department operated more as a pooled resource that was accessed as needed by the marketing department to support bids and by the service group to assist with product support.

Service

The growth of the company and the establishment of new product lines had caused an amplified growth in the service group, because for each new project installed there was a long-term source of potential queries and service needs. The service group covered a broad spectrum of needs, from the initial set up of UV systems to emergency responses to equipment problems or queries (which frequently required site visits). A formal training program had been instituted during early 1998 when the new service manager recognized the need to quickly develop new employees to ensure they could contribute a strong technical background and familiarity with the product. An existing service group member typically instructed new employees for approximately one week, and new employees learned the balance "on the job" through observation and discussion of issues with other service employees. Again, company growth had caused some difficulty in ensuring that new employees received adequate training before they were needed to actively service customer inquiries.

There was a fundamental structuring conflict within the service area on how to best serve the customer. On one hand, customers appreciated the ability to contact one person whenever they had a concern or question. Also, customers frequently needed quick response times to their site for in-person assessments and action by the service employees. This appeared to suggest a need to place service employees physically as close to the end-customer as possible, especially given the company's expanded geographic marketing area. However, the timing of service work was very uncertain. Whereas the project engineering department had some ability to prioritize and schedule their workload, the service department typically had to respond to customer calls immediately, and the geographic distribution of calls was not predictable. Therefore, if Trojan received significant service requests in California, the company could be forced to respond by sending all available service employees there. The uncertainty of the timing and geographic distribution of service calls lent itself more to the centralized pooling of resources that Trojan currently used.

As Trojan had a significant geographic distribution of sales, service work involved substantial travel. In fact, the constant travel presented an additional risk of "burnout" that was unique to the department. To address this, and to ensure a reliable response to calls for assistance from customers, a head office call centre was created in 1998. The call centre was staffed by service technicians who could respond to many customer situations over the phone and by using sophisticated remote monitoring of the UV instalments in some cases. The call centre also provided a place where experienced service personnel who were at risk of "burnout" from constant travel could use their expertise. Also, the call centre provided another opportunity to train new employees before dispatching them directly to customer locations.

Related Issues

Career Ladders

In a small company, career progression and satisfaction typically comes with successes achieved that significantly affect the organization. There was generally not the expectation or the possibility of significant promotion or role development, but this was offset by the potential for involvement of everyone in several major components of company activity. This was certainly the case at Trojan in the early days. As the company grew, however, a need to distinguish between and recognize the various levels of experience developed. The current department structure did not provide for much differentiation of job requirements within the departments, and, therefore, did not recognize the significant difference in experience levels between new and veteran employees.

Training Issues

As Trojan's sales continued to grow, the need to increase staffing was accelerating. In the early days, the addition of a person to the company was informal and supportive. The new employee would be introduced to everyone and would easily be able to approach the appropriate person to ask questions and learn their role within the company. Given the rapid expansion of the company, this informal introduction to the company and its processes was rapidly becoming insufficient to allow new employees to become effective in their new position. Training, therefore, needed to be addressed in many areas.

Decisions

Given the issues developing as Trojan grew, the structuring issue was becoming steadily more important. The structuring team under DeVries envisioned a regional, team-based approach to customer interaction that would replicate the structure used by the company in the early days. One of the difficulties in implementing such a structure, however, would be ensuring that the groups still operated as though they were one company, sharing knowledge and resources as appro-

priate. Another would be determining what level of centralized support would be appropriate, bearing in mind the need to avoid duplicating activities at head office that should be handled by the regional teams. Employees were now aware that there would be a change in the company structure, and there was a need to come to some conclusions on the new structure quickly to reduce anxiety about the change within the organization.

Notes

1. From the Trojan 1998 annual report.

2. The information in this section was primarily gathered from the Trojan 1997 annual report.

Source: Case prepared by Greg Upton under the supervision of professor John Eggers. Copyright © 1999, Ivey Management Services. Version: (A) 1999-08-19.

1. Discuss how Trojan Technologies coordinated labour in its early days.

2. Discuss the kind of departmentation and the related structure used by Trojan at the time the change is being contemplated. Critique it from the standpoint of differentiation and integration.

3. Discuss the tensions between centralization and decentralization that Trojan faces. What are the merits and demerits of more or less centralization as they apply to Trojan?

4. The Trojan call centre actually uses technology to supplement organizational structure. Explain this.

5. Given the material in the chapter, reflect on how the change in size due to business growth has affected Trojan.

6. What kind of departmentation and structure is being contemplated at the end of the case?

7. Compare the current and contemplated structures in terms of responsiveness to customers.

CHAPTER 15

Environment, Strategy, and Technology

FORD MOTOR COMPANY

On October 29, 2004, Ford Motor Company announced plans to invest $1 billion (CDN) in its operation in Oakville to make it Ford's first flexible assembly plant in Canada and one of the most advanced automotive manufacturing facilities in North America. The new Oakville Assembly Complex (OAC) will also be home to a ground-breaking research and development centre, the first of its kind in Canada, focusing on fuel cell technology.

OAC will implement Ford's most advanced technology through a next-generation flexible manufacturing system. By the end of the decade, Ford expects that 75 percent of its 19 assembly plants in North America will be flexible. The company is on track to meet this target with OAC becoming its seventh flexible facility. The other six plants are in Flat Rock, Chicago, Norfolk, Kansas City, Dearborn, and Hermosillo, Mexico.

The $1 billion redevelopment that will lead to the production of the Ford Edge and Lincoln MKX crossover utility vehicles is happening entirely indoors. Crews are installing robots and erecting an assembly line in parts of the shuttered Ontario Truck Plant, which are being transformed into body shops for the new complex.

Why is Ford investing so much in flexible manufacturing? Flex, or flexible, manufacturing is critical to Ford's attempt to restore profit to its North American automotive operations and represents the future for the company's 60-year-old assembly complex a half-hour drive west of Toronto.

A key factor that is driving the adoption of flexible manufacturing by Ford and its competitors is market demand. The vehicle market has become so fragmented that companies must react quickly to changes in consumer demand. Instead of one or two plants cranking out 250 000 to 500 000 cars or trucks a year of the same variety, one plant will have to turn out several models off one or more platforms or basic underbodies.

Flexible manufacturing enables a plant to change the mix, volume, and options of products in response to consumer demand. It is a vital link to

LEARNING OBJECTIVES

After reading Chapter 15, you should be able to:

1. Discuss the *open systems* concept of an organization and the components of an organization's *external environment*.

2. Explain how *environmental uncertainty* and *resource dependence* affect what happens in organizations.

3. Define *strategy* and describe how organizational structure can serve as a strategic response to environmental demands.

4. Explain how *vertical integration, mergers, acquisitions, strategic alliances, interlocking directorates*, and the establishment of *legitimacy* reflect strategic responses.

5. Describe the basic dimensions of organizational *technology*.

6. Explain how organizations must match organizational structure to technology.

7. Discuss the impact of *advanced information technology* on job design and organizational structure.

Ford Motor Company's new Oakville Assembly Complex (OAC) is the company's first flexible assembly plant in Canada and one of the most advanced automotive manufacturing facilities in North America.

Ford's commitment to deliver new products—65 new Ford, Mercury, and Lincoln products in five years—by enabling the company to build the vehicles that customers want, when they want them. Through the use of reprogrammable tooling, Ford can respond quickly to market demand changes without the lengthy and expensive retooling process required for traditional vehicle model changeovers.

Ford Motor Company of Canada
www.ford.ca

Undergoing major model changes in traditional plants means weeks of downtime and millions spent on new tooling and equipment. Once a flexible body shop is installed, downtime is reduced dramatically and the equipment changes consist mainly of reprogramming robots. The point is to be able to cease assembly of one model on a Friday and start a new one on a Monday, instead of six, eight, or ten weeks later. It can cut changeover time from 26 weeks to 1.

The new assembly means more robots—about 580 in the new plant compared with a little more than 400 in the existing Oakville Assembly Plant, which turns out the Ford Freestar and Mercury Monterey minivans. But the increased number isn't as important as what the robots can do. At one station, a turntable eliminates downtime. Under the old system, a worker would push pieces of metal into a "tooling monument," then wait for clamps, arms, and welding guns to weld pieces together. The worker would have to wait before he could feed in new pieces of metal. Now, the worker feeds in the metal, then the turntable rotates. While the robot does its job, the worker puts on new parts.

On the existing assembly line, it takes 23 bays of equipment stretching the length of the plant to weld together a side body panel for a minivan. In the flexible system, seven or eight cells of robots do the work in about one-third the space.

There are also changes in store for employees. Plant manager, Frank Gourneau, now calls employees "our business partners," a far cry from a generation ago when the us-versus-them mentality dominated labour relations. "We want them to take ownership and be accountable for the things we expect them to deliver on cost, safety, delivery and quality . . . We want them to be owners." There will be more standards that workers will need to apply, but at the same time, the company wants employees to think and find ways of improving quality and efficiency. This involves a dramatic change in culture. For many years, senior staff managed with little input from workers. But now instead of simply taking direction, employees will have more power to make decisions because of technology and flexibility in operations. In addition, jobs and some processes have been organized better to reduce downtime for both workers and robots.

The OAC will be capable of producing more new vehicles more quickly and more efficiently. With its new flexible manufacturing system, OAC will be capable of producing four different vehicles based on two unique product platforms. To improve efficiency, different models will use scores of common parts. Ford also has plans to raise annual output from 335 000 to 364 000, and workers have voted in favour of shift schedule changes if demand surges. Gourneau estimates productivity will improve at least 20 percent in the new plant. Ford said it expects to achieve $2 billion in production cost savings alone during the next decade.[1]

The story of the new Oakville Assembly Complex illustrates some of the major questions that we will consider in this chapter. How does the external environment influence organizations? How can an organization develop a strategy to cope with this environment? And how can technology and other factors be used to implement strategy? In the previous chapter, we concluded that there is no one best way to design an organization. In this chapter, we will see that the proper organizational structure is contingent on environmental, strategic, and technological factors.

THE EXTERNAL ENVIRONMENT OF ORGANIZATIONS

In previous chapters, we have been concerned primarily with the internal environments of organizations—those events and conditions inside the organization—that affect the attitudes and behaviours of members. In this section, we turn our interest to the impact of the **external environment**—those events and conditions surrounding the organization that influence its activities.

External environment.
Events and conditions surrounding an organization that influence its activities.

There is ample evidence in everyday life that the external environment has tremendous influence on organizations. The OPEC oil embargo of 1973 and subsequent oil price increases shook North American automobile manufacturers to their foundations. Faced with gasoline shortages, increasing gasoline prices, and rising interest rates, consumers postponed automobile purchases or shifted to more economical foreign vehicles. As a consequence, workers were laid off, plants were closed, and dealerships failed, while the manufacturers scrambled to develop more fuel-efficient, smaller cars. The emphasis of advertising strategies changed from styling and comfort to economy and value. Significant portions of the manufacturers' environment (Middle East oil suppliers, American consumers, and Japanese competitors) prompted this radical regrouping.

Environmental conditions changed, and by the mid-1980s an international oil surplus pushed gasoline prices down. Consumers responded with increased interest in size, styling, and performance. Auto industry analysts noted that some manufacturers responded to this shift faster than others. Chrysler, trimmed of bureaucracy by its near demise several years earlier, responded quickly and scored a number of marketing coups.

In the new millennium, the auto industry faces an increasingly fragmented market as well as accelerated global competition, especially to supply the burgeoning middle class in developing countries. The implementation of flexible manufacturing systems as well as joint ventures and mergers between companies, such as the $48 billion global merger between Chrysler and Daimler-Benz, have become common.

A more recent example of the influence of the external environment on organizations is the terrorist attacks in the United States on September 11, 2001. This had a major effect on many companies, such as World Markets, the investment banking arm of CIBC and the Canadian company hit hardest by the terrorist attacks. The company was forced to evacuate nearly 2000 employees from its offices across the street from where the World Trade Center once stood. All of the company's employees survived the attacks, but the firm lost its equities trading floor, which was the centrepiece of its US business. Teamwork and esprit de corps helped World Markets build a new trading floor from scratch in six weeks, instead of the six to nine months that it would normally take.[2] Other companies had to lay off workers and some had to change the way they conduct their business. For example, because many employees were unwilling to travel following the terrorist attacks, the use of technology like videoconferencing became much more popular for communication and training. Organizations have also become much more sensitive to work–life balance issues and workplace diversity.

CIBC World Markets
www.cibcwm.com

CIBC World Markets had to evacuate nearly 2000 employees from its offices across the street from where the World Trade Center once stood and build a new trading floor from scratch.

The SARS outbreak is also a good example of the influence of the external environment. When SARS hit Toronto, bus, hotel, restaurant, theatre, and travel companies were deluged with cancellations and experienced a sharp decline in business. SARS forced Toronto-based Cullingford Coaches to idle many of its 17 coaches and face the prospect of having part of its fleet repossessed.[3] It has been estimated that the overall effect of SARS on the economy from lost tourism and airport revenues is about $570 million in Toronto and another $380 million in the rest of Canada. The losses are even greater in the Asian countries that experienced SARS outbreaks that were much worse than what Canada experienced.[4] In addition, many companies noticed that they could operate just as well with less business travel than they did before SARS. Some realized large savings in time and money by using technology like videoconferencing.[5] Both the terrorist attacks and SARS have resulted in lasting changes in the way many companies now do business, especially in terms of the use of technology. As always, the external environment profoundly shapes organizational behaviour.

Organizations as Open Systems

Open systems. Systems that take inputs from the external environment, transform some of them, and send them back into the environment as outputs.

Organizations can be described as open systems. **Open systems** are systems that take inputs from the external environment, transform some of these inputs, and send them back into the external environment as outputs (Exhibit 15.1).[6] Inputs include capital, energy, materials, information, technology, and people; outputs include various products and services. Some inputs are transformed (e.g., raw materials), while other inputs (e.g., skilled craftspeople) assist in the transformation process. Transformation processes may be physical (e.g., manufacturing or surgery), intellectual (e.g., teaching or programming), or even emotional (e.g., psychotherapy). For example, an insurance company imports actuarial experts, information about accidents and mortality, and capital in the form of insurance premiums. Through the application of financial knowledge, it transforms the capital into insurance coverage and investments in areas like real estate. Universities and colleges import seasoned scholars and aspiring students from the environment. Through the teaching process, educated individuals are returned to the community as outputs.

The value of the open systems concept is that it sensitizes us to the need for organizations to cope with the demands of the environment on both the input side and the output side. As we will see, some of this coping involves adaptation to environmental demands. On the other hand, some coping may be oriented toward changing the environment.

First, let's examine the external environment in greater detail.

EXHIBIT 15.1
The organization as an open system.

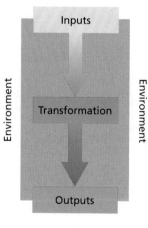

Components of the External Environment

The external environment of any given organization is obviously a "big" concept. Technically, it involves any person, group, event, or condition outside the direct domain of the organization. For this reason, it is useful to divide the environment into a manageable number of components.[7]

The General Economy. Organizations that survive through selling products or services often suffer from an economic downturn and profit by an upturn. When a downturn occurs, competition for remaining customers increases, and organizations might postpone needed capital improvements. Of course, some organizations thrive under a poor economy, including welfare offices and law firms that deal heavily in bankruptcies. In addition, if a poor economy is accompanied by high unemployment, some organizations might find it opportune to upgrade the quality of their staffs, since they will have an ample selection of candidates.

We see a clear example of the impact of the general economy in the most recent recession. Faced with falling orders (reduced inputs), thousands of organizations engaged in radical downsizing as a means of cutting costs.

Customers. All organizations have potential customers for their products and services. Piano makers have musicians, and consumer activist associations have disgruntled consumers. The customers of universities include not only students, but also the firms that employ their graduates and seek their research assistance. Organizations must be sensitive to changes in customer demands. For example, the small liberal arts college that resists developing a business school might be faced with declining enrolment.

Successful firms are generally highly sensitive to customer reactions. L'Oréal, the world's largest producer of cosmetics, announced that it would no longer test its products on animals in response to customer demand. More recently, companies like Kraft Foods have begun to remove trans fat from their products, and restaurants like KFC have promised to begin using trans-fat-free cooking oil and to eliminate trans fat from items on their menus. Ford's investment in flexible manufacturing is an attempt to respond quickly to changes in consumer demands.

L'Oréal
www.loreal.com

Suppliers. Organizations are dependent on the environment for supplies that include labour, raw materials, equipment, and component parts. Shortages can cause severe difficulties. For instance, the lack of a local technical school might prove troublesome for an electronics firm that requires skilled labour. Similarly, a strike by a company that supplies component parts might cause the purchaser to shut down its assembly line.

As alluded to earlier in the text, many contemporary firms have changed their strategy for dealing with suppliers. It used to be standard practice to have many of them and to keep them in stiff competition for one's business, mainly by extracting the lowest price. For example, auto manufacturers tend to pressure their suppliers to lower costs, and perhaps not surprisingly, suppliers report poor working relationships with most auto manufacturers.[8] However, more exclusive relationships with suppliers, on the basis of quality and reliable delivery, are becoming more common. Dell Computer reduced its suppliers from 140 to 80 and its freight carriers from 21 to 3.

Competitors. Environmental competitors vie for resources that include both customers and suppliers.[9] Thus, hospitals compete for patients, and consulting firms compete for clients. Similarly, utility companies compete for coal, and professional baseball teams compete for free-agent ballplayers. Successful organizations devote considerable energy to monitoring the activities of competitors.

The computer software industry provides an instructive lesson in how competition can change over time. In the early days of software development (not very long ago!), there were a large number of players in the field, and small companies could find a profitable niche. There was plenty of room for many competitors in what was an essentially technology-driven business. However, the growing domination of Microsoft, which slashed prices and consolidated multiple functions in its programs, has prompted a great number of mergers, acquisitions, and failures among firms dealing in basic consumer software, such as word processing and spreadsheets.[10]

Microsoft
www.microsoft.com

For many organizations today the competition has become so aggressive that their environments have been described as hypercompetitive. Organizations that find themselves in hypercompetitive environments must become extremely flexible to respond quickly to changes and cope with hypercompetition. Flexible manufacturing is a necessary response on the part of Ford and other automobile manufacturers to the increasingly competitive automotive industry.[11]

Social/Political Factors. Organizations cannot ignore the social and political events that occur around them. Changes in public attitudes toward ethnic diversity, the proper age for retirement, or the proper role of big business will soon affect them. Frequently, these attitudes find expression in law through the political process. Thus, organizations must cope with a series of legal regulations that prescribe fair employment practices, proper competitive activities, product safety, and clients' rights.

One example of the impact of social trends on organizations is Wal-Mart's move to ban handgun sales in its stores. Another is the increasing public interest in environmentalism. Many firms have been fairly proactive in their responses. For example, Pacific Gas and Electric works closely with environmental groups and has a dedicated environmentalist on its board. McDonald's has become a visible proponent of recycling and an active educator of the public on environmental issues.[12]

Technology. The environment contains a variety of technologies that are useful for achieving organizational goals. As we shall see, technology refers to ways of doing things, not simply to some form of machinery. The ability to adopt the proper technology should enhance an organization's effectiveness. For a business firm, this might involve the choice of a proper computer system or production technique. For a mental health clinic, it might involve implementing a particular form of psychotherapy that is effective for the kinds of clients serviced. For an automotive firm like Ford, it involves flexible manufacturing and smart robots.

An example of the impact of technology on organizational life is the advent of computer-aided design (CAD). With CAD, designers, engineers, and draftspeople can produce quick, accurate drawings via computer. They can store databases and run simulations that produce visual records of the reaction of objects to stress, vibration, and design changes. Some firms have found that CAD reduces design lead times and increases productivity. Others have had a difficult time reorganizing to exploit this technology. In general, CAD has broken down the traditional role differences between designers, engineers, and drawing technicians.

Interest groups. Parties or organizations other than direct competitors that have some vested interest in how an organization is managed.

Now that we have outlined the basic components of organizational environments, a few more detailed comments are in order. First, this brief list does not provide a perfect picture of the large number of actual interest groups that can exist in an organization's environment. **Interest groups** are parties or organizations other than direct competitors that have some vested interest in how an organization is managed. For example, Exhibit 15.2 shows the interest groups that surround a small private college. As you can see, our list of six environmental components actually involves quite an array of individuals and agencies with which the college must contend. To complicate

EXHIBIT 15.2

Interest groups in the external environment of a small private college.

Source: From Brown, W.B., & Moberg, D.J. (1980). *Organization theory and management*, p. 45. Copyright © 1980 by John Wiley & Sons, Inc. Reprinted by permission of John Wiley & Sons, Inc.

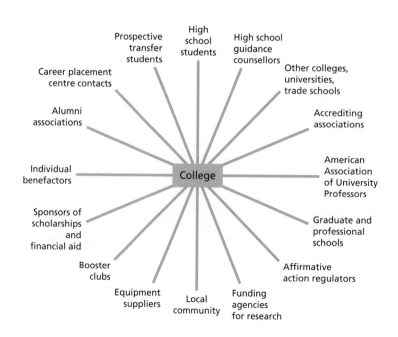

matters, some of these individuals and agencies might make competing or conflicting demands on the college. For instance, booster clubs might press the college to allocate more funds to field a winning football team, while scholarship sponsors might insist that the college match their donations for academic purposes.

Such competition for attention from different segments of the environment is not unusual. While anti-drug organizations have sometimes supported the screening of employees for drug use, the American Civil Liberties Union has taken a keen interest in the violation of privacy that such tests can involve. Obviously, different interest groups evaluate organizational effectiveness according to different criteria.[13]

American Civil Liberties Union
www.aclu.org

Different parts of the organization will often be concerned with different environmental components. For instance, we can expect a marketing department to be tuned in to customer demands and a legal department to be interested in regulations stemming from the social/political component. As we indicated in the previous chapter, coordination of this natural division of interests is a crucial concern for all organizations. Also, as environmental demands change, it is important that power shifts occur to allow the appropriate functional units to cope with these demands.

Finally, events in various components of the environment provide both constraints and opportunities for organizations. Although environments with many constraints (e.g., high interest rates, strong competition, and so on) appear pretty hostile, an opportunity in one environmental sector might offset a constraint in another. For example, the firm that is faced with a dwindling customer base might find its salvation by exploiting new technologies that give it an edge in costs or new product development.

Environmental Uncertainty

In our earlier discussion of environmental components, we implied that environments have considerable potential for causing confusion among managers. Customers may come and go, suppliers may turn from good to bad, and competitors may make surprising decisions. The resulting uncertainty can be both challenging and frustrating. **Environmental uncertainty** exists when an environment is vague, difficult to diagnose, and unpredictable. We all know that some environments are less certain than others. Your hometown provides you with a fairly certain environment. There, you are familiar with the transportation system, the language, and necessary social conventions. Thrust into the midst of a foreign culture, you encounter a much less certain environment. How to greet a stranger, order a meal, and get around town become significant issues. There is nothing intrinsically bad about this uncertainty. It simply requires you to marshal a particular set of skills to be an effective visitor.

Environmental uncertainty. A condition that exists when the external environment is vague, difficult to diagnose, and unpredictable.

Like individuals, organizations can find themselves in more or less certain environments. But just exactly what makes an organizational environment uncertain? Put simply, uncertainty depends on the environment's *complexity* (simple versus complex) and its *rate of change* (static versus dynamic).[14]

- *Simple environment.* A simple environment involves relatively few factors, and these factors are fairly similar to each other. For example, consider the pottery manufacturer that obtains its raw materials from two small firms and sells its entire output to three small pottery outlets.

- *Complex environment.* A complex environment contains a large number of dissimilar factors that affect the organization. For example, the college in Exhibit 15.2 has a more complex environment than the pottery manufacturer. In turn, Ford has a more complex environment than the college.

- *Static environment.* The components of this environment remain fairly stable over time. The small-town radio station that plays the same music format, relies on the same advertisers, and works under the same CRTC regulations year after year has a stable environment. (Of course, no environment is *completely* static; we are speaking in relative terms here.)

● *Dynamic environment.* The components of a highly dynamic environment are in a constant state of change, which is unpredictable and irregular, not cyclical. For example, consider the firm that designs and manufactures microchips for electronics applications. New scientific and technological advances occur rapidly and unpredictably in this field. In addition, customer demands are highly dynamic as firms devise new uses for microchips. A similar dynamic environment faces Ford, in part owing to the vagaries of the energy situation and cost of fuel, and in part owing to the fact that marketing automobiles has become an international rather than a national business. For example, fluctuations in the relative value of international currencies can radically alter the cost of competing imported cars quite independently of anything Ford management does.

As we see in Exhibit 15.3, it is possible to arrange rate of change and complexity in a matrix. A simple/static environment (cell 1) should provoke the least uncertainty, while a dynamic/complex environment (cell 4) should provoke the most. Some research suggests that change has more influence than complexity on uncertainty.[15] Thus, we might expect a static/complex environment (cell 2) to be somewhat more certain than a dynamic/simple environment (cell 3).

Earlier, we stated that different parts of the organization are often interested in different components of the environment. To go a step further, it stands to reason that some aspects of the environment are less certain than others. Thus, some subunits might be faced with more uncertainty than others. For example, the research and development department of a microchip company would seem to face a more uncertain environment than the human resources department.

Increasing uncertainty has several predictable effects on organizations and their decision makers.[16] For one thing, as uncertainty increases, cause-and-effect relationships become less clear. If we are certain that a key competitor will not match our increased advertising budget, we may be confident that our escalated ad campaign will

EXHIBIT 15.3
Environmental uncertainty as a function of complexity and rate of change.

"Characteristics of Organizational Environments and Perceived Environment Uncertainty," by Robert B. Duncan, *Administrative Science Quarterly*, Vol. 17, No. 3, 313–327, p. 320, September 1972.

	Complexity	
	Simple	**Complex**
Static	**CELL 1** *Low Perceived Uncertainty* 1. Small number of factors and components in the environment 2. Factors and components are somewhat similar to one another 3. Factors and components remain basically the same and are not changing	**CELL 2** *Moderately Low Perceived Uncertainty* 1. Large number of factors and components in the environment 2. Factors and components are not similar to one another 3. Factors and components remain basically the same
Dynamic	**CELL 3** *Moderately High Perceived Uncertainty* 1. Small number of factors and components in the environment 2. Factors and components are somewhat similar to one another 3. Factors and components of the environment are in continual process of change	**CELL 4** *High Perceived Uncertainty* 1. Large number of factors and components in the environment 2. Factors and components are not similar to one another 3. Factors and components of environment are in a continual process of change

Rate of Change

increase our market share. Uncertainty about the competitor's response reduces confidence in this causal inference. Second, environmental uncertainty tends to make priorities harder to agree on, and it often stimulates a fair degree of political jockeying within the organization. To continue the example, if the consequences of increased advertising are unclear, other functional units might see the increased budget allocation as being "up for grabs." Finally, as environmental uncertainty increases, more information must be processed by the organization to make adequate decisions. Environmental scanning, boundary spanning, planning, and formal management information systems will become more prominent.[17] This illustrates that organizations will act to cope with or reduce uncertainty because uncertainty increases the difficulty of decision making and thus threatens organizational effectiveness. Shortly, we will examine in greater detail the means of managing uncertainty. First, we explore another aspect of the impact of the environment on organizations.

Resource Dependence

Earlier, we noted that organizations are open systems that receive inputs from the external environment and transfer outputs into this environment. Many inputs from various components of the environment are valuable resources that are necessary for organizational survival. These include things such as capital, raw materials, and human resources. By the same token, other components of the environment (such as customers) represent valuable resources on the output end of the equation. All this suggests that organizations are in a state of **resource dependence** with regard to their environments.[18] Carefully managing and coping with this resource dependence is a key to survival and success.

Although all organizations are dependent on their environments for resources, some organizations are more dependent than others. This is because some environments have a larger amount of readily accessible resources.[19] A classic case of a highly resource-dependent organization is a newly formed small business. Cautious bank managers, credit-wary suppliers, and a dearth of customers all teach the aspiring owner the meaning of dependence. Also, many organizations in traditional manufacturing industries encounter a much less munificent environment. Investors are wary, customers are disappearing, and skilled human resources are attracted to situations with better career prospects. Historically, the computer and software industries were located in munificent environments. Capital was readily available, human resources were trained in relevant fields, and new uses for computers were continually being developed. Although this is still to some extent the case, we have already alluded to the shakeout in the market for basic software. The days are gone when business amateurs can develop a new word-processing package and become multimillionaires, like the founders of WordPerfect. The big firms have consolidated the market.

Resource dependence can be fairly independent of environmental uncertainty, and dealing with one issue will not necessarily have an effect on the other. For example, although the computer industry generally faces a fairly munificent environment, this environment is uncertain, especially with regard to rate of change. On the other hand, many mature small businesses exist in a fairly certain environment, but remain highly resource dependent.

Competitors, regulatory agencies, and various interest groups can have a considerable stake in how an organization obtains and transforms its resources.[20] In effect, the organization might be indirectly resource dependent on these bodies and thus susceptible to a fair degree of social control.

The concept of resource dependence does not mean that organizations are totally at the mercy of their environments. Rather, it means that they must develop strategies for managing both resource dependence and environmental uncertainty.

Resource dependence.
The dependency of organizations on environmental inputs, such as capital, raw materials, and human resources.

STRATEGIC RESPONSES TO UNCERTAINTY AND RESOURCE DEPENDENCE

Organizations devote considerable effort to developing and implementing strategies to cope with environmental uncertainty and resource dependence. **Strategy** can be defined as the process by which top executives seek to cope with the constraints and opportunities posed by an organization's environment. Before continuing, consider how Abitibi-Consolidated Inc. responded to environmental uncertainty in the You Be the Manger feature.

Exhibit 15.4 outlines the nature of the relationship between environment and strategy. At the top, the objective organizational environment is portrayed in terms of uncertainty and available resources, as we discussed above. However, much of the impact that the environment has on organizations is indirect rather than direct, filtered through the perceptual system of managers and other organizational members.[21] By means of the perceptual process we discussed in Chapter 3, personality characteristics and experience may colour managers' perceptions of the environment. For example, the environment might seem much more complex and unstable for a manager who is new to his job than for one who has years of experience. Similarly, the optimistic manager might perceive more resources than the pessimistic manager.[22] It is the perceived environment that comprises the basis for strategy formulation.

Strategy formulation itself involves determining the mission, goals, and objectives of the organization. At the most basic level, for a business firm, this would even involve consideration of just what business the organization should pursue. Then, the organi-

Strategy. The process by which top executives seek to cope with the constraints and opportunities that an organization's environment poses.

Abitibi-Consolidated Inc.
www.abitibiconsolidated.com

EXHIBIT 15.4
Environment, strategy, and organizational effectiveness.

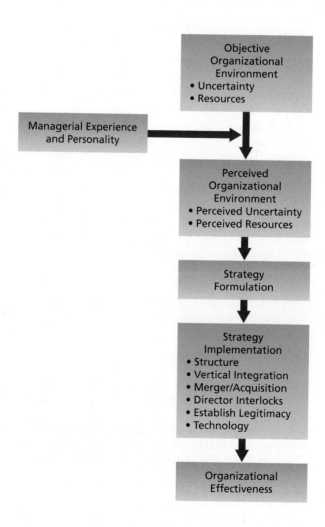

🖝 YOU BE THE
Manager

Abitibi-Consolidated Inc.'s Makeover

Abitibi-Consolidated Inc. is the world's largest newsprint producer. Like most of its counterparts, it has been grappling with a host of industry-wide challenges, including a high Canadian dollar that blows a hole in exports to the United States, soaring wood fibre prices in Eastern Canada, and a shrinking newsprint market.

Not long ago, Abitibi's president and CEO, John Weaver, found himself taking a close look at the can industry. Weaver and his management team were evaluating every aspect of what Abitibi does as part of a sweeping review aimed at repositioning the company. Studying successful companies in the can business was part of a one-year exercise aimed at learning how to thrive even though the industry you are in is a mature one, such as cans or newsprint or paper.

The management rethink—with lots of input from the board—began in earnest at the end of 2003, when Montreal-based Abitibi decided that a significant decline in the newsprint market wasn't the usual cyclical downturn. "Everyone expected there would be a cyclical recovery over time, but as we watched the data we realized the industry was undergoing a structural shift and we had to begin to plan for a mature industry in which there is little growth," said Weaver in an interview. "Many industries are successful and profitable in mature industries. We stepped back and examined what strategic initiatives were necessary for that to happen."

What Weaver and his team, including chief financial officer Pierre Rougeau, did was take a hard look at each and every asset and determine which ones simply could not be profitable over the longer term. They had prolonged discussions with the top 10 senior executives and hired consultants in addition to the board to test their strategies. One of the questions they put to the board was: "What's the answer if newsprint demand never recovers?"

"We got their feedback on the conclusions we were reaching and we used that to refine the strategy," said Weaver.

External events forced Abitibi-Consolidated to reposition itself.

What strategic initiatives do you think the company should consider? You be the manager.

QUESTIONS

1. **What are the environmental constraints and opportunities facing Abitibi?**

2. **What strategic initiatives do you think Abitibi should pursue? Should they change their focus on the newsprint market and consider other markets?**

To find out what Abitibi did, consult The Manager's Notebook at the end of the chapter.

Source: Excerpt from Marotte, B. 2005, July 30). Executive decision: In revamp, no Abitibi asset was untouchable. *Globe and Mail*, B3. Reprinted with permission from the *Globe and Mail*.

---

zation's orientation toward the perceived environment must be determined. This might range from being defensive and protective of current interests (such as holding market share) to prospecting vigorously for new interests to exploit (such as developing totally new products).[23] There is no single correct strategy along this continuum. Rather, the chosen strategy must correspond to the constraints and opportunities of the environment. Finally, the strategy must be implemented by selecting appropriate managers for the task and employing appropriate techniques, as shown in Exhibit 15.4.

Organizational Structure as a Strategic Response

How should organizations be structured to cope with environmental uncertainty? Paul Lawrence and Jay Lorsch of Harvard University have studied this problem.[24]

Lawrence and Lorsch chose for their research more and less successful organizations in three industries—plastics, packaged food products, and paper containers. These industries were chosen intentionally because it was assumed that they faced environments that differed in perceived uncertainty. This was subsequently confirmed by questionnaires and interviews. The environment of the plastics firms was perceived as very uncertain because of rapidly changing scientific knowledge, technology, and customer demands. Decisions had to be made even though feedback about their accuracy often involved considerable delay. At the opposite extreme, the container firms faced an environment that was perceived as much more certain. No major changes in technology had occurred in 20 years, and the name of the game was simply to produce high-quality standardized containers and get them to the customer quickly. The consequences of decisions could be learned in a short period of time. The perceived uncertainty faced by the producers of packaged foods fell between that experienced by the plastics producers and that faced by container firms.

Going a step further, Lawrence and Lorsch also examined the sectors of the environment that were faced by three departments in each company: sales (market environment), production (technical environment), and research (scientific environment). Their findings are shown in Exhibit 15.5. The crucial factor here is the *range* of uncertainty across the subenvironments faced by the various departments. In the container companies, producing, selling, and research (mostly quality control) were all fairly certain activities. In contrast, the range of uncertainty encountered by the plastics firms was quite broad. Research worked in a scientific environment that was extremely uncertain. On the other hand, production faced a technical environment that was a good bit more routine.

When Lawrence and Lorsch examined the attitudes of organizational managers, the impact of perceived environmental uncertainty became apparent. First of all, because the departments of the plastics firms had to cope with sectors of the environment that differed in certainty, the plastics firms tended to be highly differentiated (Chapter 14). Thus, their managers tended to differ rather greatly in terms of goals, interpersonal relationships, and time spans. For example, production managers were interested in immediate, short-term problems, while managers in the research department were concerned with longer-range scientific development. Conversely, the container firms were not highly differentiated because the environmental sectors with which they dealt were more similar in perceived certainty. The food packaging firms were more differentiated than the container firms but less differentiated than the plastic companies.

EXHIBIT 15.5
Relative perceived uncertainty of environmental sectors in the Lawrence and Lorsch study.

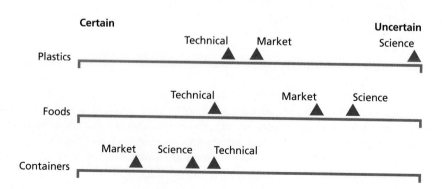

Because they faced a relatively certain environment and since they were fairly undifferentiated, the container firms had adopted mechanistic structures. The most successful was organized along strict functional lines and was highly centralized. Coordination was achieved through direct supervision and formalized written schedules. All in all, this container firm conformed closely to the classical prescriptions for structure. At the other extreme, the most successful plastics company had adopted an organic structure. This was the most sensible way to deal with an uncertain environment and high differentiation. Decision-making power was decentralized to locate it where the appropriate knowledge existed. Coordination was achieved through informal mutual adjustment, ad hoc teams that cut across departments, and special integrators who coordinated between departments (Chapter 14). In addition, the departments themselves were structured somewhat differently, research being the most organic and production the least organic.

The Lawrence and Lorsch study is important because it demonstrates a close connection among environment, structure, and effectiveness. However, follow-up research has not been entirely supportive of their findings, and several contradictory studies exist.[25] For example, a recent study of new ventures in the emergent Internet sector where the environment is dynamic, turbulent, and uncertain, found that new ventures with a more mechanistic structure (i.e., greater founding team formalization, functional specialization, and administrative intensity) outperformed those with more organic structures. Further, the effect of formalization, specialization, and administrative intensity was greater for larger new ventures. Thus, while mature organizations typically need to become more organic and flexible to adapt to dynamic environments, the opposite seems to be true for new ventures, which tend to be flexible and attuned to their environment but lack the benefits of structure.[26]

The argument presented so far suggests that strategy always determines structure, rather than the other way around. This is a reasonable conclusion when considering an organization undergoing great change or the formation of a new organization. However, for ongoing organizations, structure sometimes dictates strategy formulation. For instance, highly complex, decentralized structures might dictate strategies that are the product of political bargaining between functional units. More centralized, simple structures might produce strategies that appear more rational and less political (although not necessarily superior in effectiveness).[27]

Other Forms of Strategic Response

Variations on organizational structure are not the only strategic response that organizations can make. Structural variations often accompany other responses that are oriented toward coping with environmental uncertainty or resource dependence. Some forms of strategy implementation appear extremely routine, yet they might have a strong effect on the performance of the organization. For example, economic forecasting might be used to predict the demand for goods and services. In turn, formal planning might be employed to synchronize the organization's actions with the forecasts. All this is done to reduce uncertainty and to predict trends in resource availability. Lobbying and public relations are also common strategic responses. Simple negotiating and contracting are other forms of implementing strategy.

Some more elaborate forms of strategic response are worth a more detailed look. Notice how many of these concern relationships *between* organizations.

Vertical Integration. Many managers live in fear of disruption on the input or output end of their organizations. A lack of raw materials to process or a snag in marketing products or services can threaten the very existence of the organization. One basic way to buffer the organization against such uncertainty over resource control is to use an inventory policy of stockpiling both inputs and outputs. For example, an automaker might stockpile needed parts in advance of an anticipated strike at a supplier. At the same time, it might have a 30 days supply of new cars in its distribution system at all times. Both inventories serve as environmental "shock absorbers." A natural extension of this logic is **vertical integration**, the strategy of formally taking control of sources of supply and distribution.[28] Major oil companies, for instance, are highly vertically integrated, handling their own exploration, drilling, transport, refining, retail sales, and credit. Starbucks, the Seattle-based chain of espresso bars, imports, roasts, and packages its own coffee and refuses to franchise its bars in order to maintain high quality.

Vertical integration can reduce risk for an organization in many cases. However, when the environment becomes very turbulent, it can reduce flexibility and actually increase risk.[29] Managerial inefficiencies can also develop as a result of control and coordination difficulties, and various bureaucratic costs can also result. However, the results of a recent study indicate that the benefits of vertical integration outweigh the costs.[30]

Mergers and Acquisitions. In the last few years, there have been a number of very high-profile mergers and acquisitions. Topping the list was the very bitter and highly contested merger between Hewlett-Packard and Compaq Computer in which Hewlett-Packard's former CEO Carly Fiorina had to contend with a shareholder revolt against her plan for the merger. Shareholders eventually approved the $19 billion merger, making it the largest technology merger ever. As well, a number of very big Canadian mergers and acquisitions have recently taken place. For example, Kingdom Hotels International and Colony Capital, LLC purchased Toronto-based Fairmont Hotels & Resorts Inc. as part of a US$3.3 billion deal that would create a new global luxury chain. In one of the most heated takeover battles in Canadian history, Swiss-based mining giant Xstrata PLC acquired Falconbridge Ltd. after Inco Ltd. was unsuccessful in its bid to merge with Falconbridge. And in what is being called a historic agreement, Domtar Inc. is merging with Weyerhaeuser Company to become the largest manufacturer of uncoated free-sheet paper in North America and the second largest in the World.[31]

Such **mergers** or joining of two firms and the **acquisition** of one firm by another are increasingly common strategic responses. Some mergers and acquisitions are stimulated by simple economies of scale. For example, a motel chain with 100 motels might have the same advertising costs as one with 50 motels. Other mergers and acquisitions are pursued for purposes of vertical integration. For instance, a paper manufacturer

Vertical integration. The strategy of formally taking control of sources of organizational supply and distribution.

Mergers and acquisitions. The joining together of two organizations and the acquiring of one organization by another.

Mergers of two firms or the acquisition of one firm by another, such as the attempted merger between INCO and Falconbridge, have become increasingly common strategic responses in recent years.

Scott M. Hand
Chairman & Chief Executive Officer,
Inco Limited

Derek Pannell
Chief Executive Officer,
Falconbridge Limited

might purchase a timber company. When mergers and acquisitions occur within the *same* industry, they are being effected partly to reduce the uncertainty prompted by competition. When they occur across *different* industries (a diversification strategy), the goal is often to reduce resource dependence on a particular segment of the environment. A portfolio is created so that if resources become threatened in one part of the environment, the organization can still prosper.[32] This was one motive for Philip Morris to take over food companies such as Kraft; anti-smoking sentiments and legislation have provided much uncertainty for the firm's core cigarette business. However, the benefits and success of mergers and acquisitions are often disappointing. For a good example, see "Global Focus: *The DaimlerChrysler Merger of Equals.*"

DaimlerChrysler
www.daimlerchrysler.com

Strategic Alliances. We have all heard about bad blood following a merger or acquisition, especially after a hostile takeover. This failure of cultures to integrate smoothly (Chapter 8) is only one reason that mergers that look good from a financial point of

GLOBAL FOCUS

The DaimlerChrysler Merger of Equals

The $48-billion merger between Chrysler and Daimler-Benz in 1998 was unprecedented, as global mergers go—in fact, it was the largest-ever industrial merger. After the deal was struck by Chrysler Chairman Robert Eaton and Daimler-Benz Chairman Jürgen Schrempp, it was described as a "brilliant marriage of opportunity," even though nobody saw it coming.

According to the chairmen of both companies, mergers within the automobile industry were inevitable, given the excess capacity in the world. Both realized that a partnership could bring endless possibilities and opportunities. The merger was said to be a "merger of equals," and the newly formed DaimlerChrysler vowed to become the world's most profitable automobile company.

Unfortunately, this doesn't appear to have happened. The merger has been more difficult to implement than most thought it would. The company has become stagnant under the effects of infighting and profit breakdowns at its Chrysler and Mercedes divisions. The engineer of the deal, Daimler-Benz Chairman Schrempp, stepped down after angry shareholders made it clear he was no longer wanted.

What went wrong? DaimlerChrysler's first years after the merger were characterized by a lack of trust between the old Chrysler and Daimler-Benz divisions. Efforts to share parts and cooperate moved slowly. Mercedes engineers saw little point in sharing their technology with Chrysler and guarded it carefully,

resulting in massive losses to both divisions. Eventually, Dieter Zetsche, a veteran Mercedes manager and Schrempp's successor, was able to bring the two sides together to work on Chrysler's 300 sedan, which uses Mercedes real-wheel drive expertise and has become one of Chrysler's most popular models.

Even the "merger of equals" has been questioned. Kirk Kerkorian, Chrysler's largest shareholder at the time of the merger, has called the merger a fraud, saying that it was portrayed as a "merger of equals" to mislead Chrysler executives and shareholders, the United States Securities and Exchange Commission, and the public. He contends that Schrempp only called the deal a "merger" rather than a takeover to lower the transaction price and avoid paying investors a "control premium."

Zetsche has said, "It's pretty tough getting an organization to go in a direction it doesn't want to go in voluntarily." Several years have passed since the merger and the company is still trying to realize "some of the major benefits" of the deal, he said. And the numbers tell us that this appears to be true. In 2006, DaimlerChrysler's market value was about US$34 billion less than in the days directly after the merger was first announced.

Source: Boudette, N.E., Shirouzu, N., & Powe, S. (2006, July 3). Daimler to GM: Watch out for the potholes. *Globe and Mail*, B1, B4; Brown, T. (2004, April 23). Daimler "merger of equals" claim a fraud—Kerkorian. *Reuters News*.

Strategic alliances.
Actively cooperative relationships between legally separate organizations.

view often end up as operational disasters. Is there any way to have the benefits of matrimony without the attendant risks? Increasingly, the answer seems to be **strategic alliances**—that is, actively cooperative relationships between legally separate organizations. The organizations in question retain their own cultures, but true cooperation replaces distrust, competition, or conflict for the project at hand. Properly designed, such alliances reduce risk and uncertainty for all parties, and resource *interdependence* is recognized. The network organization we discussed in the previous chapter is one form of strategic alliance.

Organizations can engage in strategic alliances with competitors, suppliers, customers, and unions.[33] Among competitors, one common alliance is a research and development consortium in which companies band together to support basic research that is relevant for their products. For example, several Canadian producers of audio speakers formed a consortium under the National Research Council to perfect the technology for "smart speakers" that adjust automatically to room configuration. Another common alliance between competitors is the joint venture, in which organizations combine complementary advantages for economic gain or new experience. The Toyota–General Motors joint venture in a California auto plant gave Toyota manufacturing access to the United States and gave GM experience with Japanese management techniques. In some cases, competitors might form alliances to tackle economic and social concerns. For example, several years ago America Online, Microsoft, and Yahoo! formed an alliance to address the e-mail spam problem. Spam accounts for an estimated 40 percent of all e-mail traffic and costs businesses $8 to $10 billion a year. The companies said that they intend to share complaint data and build evidence files that can be used by state and federal prosecutors.[34]

Strategic alliances with suppliers and customers have a similar theme of reducing friction and building trust and cooperation. At Union Pacific, for example, customers can place orders and track the progress of their own shipments by accessing UP's own mainframe. Finally, strategic alliances can occur between companies and unions. For example, the Canadian Auto Workers union has offered to make wage concessions and more shop floor flexibility if Ford agrees to build a US$750 million assembly plant in St. Thomas, Ontario.[35]

Union Pacific
www.up.com

There are many risks associated with strategic alliances and almost half of them fail. According to one study, strategic alliances are most successful when there is a vice-president or director of strategic alliances with his or her own staff and resources. Organizations with such a dedicated alliance function achieved a 25 percent higher long-term success rate with their alliances than those without such a function and generated almost four times the market wealth whenever they announced the formation of a new alliance. Strategic alliances are also more likely to be successful and stable when the senior managers of the firms meet frequently and when the firms behave "transparently" toward one another, exchanging information quickly and accurately. A prior history of cooperation and a feeling that the partner is not taking unfair advantage of the alliance are also important.[36]

Strategic alliances between global partners are increasingly common. Examples include the Ford–Mazda connection, the European Airbus consortium, and a Canon–Olivetti joint venture in copiers. These global alliances can be especially difficult to manage due to cross-cultural differences in expectations. For example, North Americans favour shorter time horizons and a rather direct approach to conflicts. East Asian cultures favour longer time horizons and "talking around" overt conflict.[37]

Interlocking directorates.
A condition existing when one person serves on two or more boards of directors.

Interlocking Directorates. If we added up all the positions on boards of directors in the country and then added up all the people who serve as directors, the second number would be considerably smaller than the first. This is because of **interlocking directorates**, the condition that is said to exist when one person serves as a director on two or more boards. Such interlocking is legally prohibited when the firms are direct competitors; but as you can imagine, a fine line may exist as to the definition of a direct competitor. Many have recognized that interlocking directorates provide a subtle but effective means of coping with environmental uncertainty and resource dependence. The director's expertise and experience with one organization can provide valuable information for another. Sometimes the value of the interlock is more direct. This is especially true when it is a "vertical interlock" in which one firm provides inputs to or receives outputs from the other (for instance, a director might serve on the board of a steel company and that of an auto producer):

> *In addition to reducing uncertainty concerning inputs or outputs, a vertical interlock may also create a more efficient method of dealing with the environment. The outside director might be able not only to obtain the critical input but also to procure favourable treatment, such as a better price, better payment terms, or better delivery schedules. In addition, the search costs or the complexity involved in dealing with the environment may be reduced.*[38]

Interlocks can also serve as a means of influencing public opinion about the wealth, status, or social conscience of a particular organization. Highly placed university officials, clergy, and union leaders are effectively board members in their own organizations, and they may be sought as board members by business firms to convey an impression of social responsibility to the wider public.[39] Resources are easier to obtain from a friendly environment than from a hostile environment!

Establishing Legitimacy. It is something of a paradox that environmental uncertainty seems to increase the need to make correct organizational responses, but at the same time makes it harder to know which response is correct! One strategic response to this dilemma is to do things that make the organization appear *legitimate* to various constituents.[40] **Establishing legitimacy** involves taking actions that conform to prevailing norms and expectations. This will often be strategically correct, but equally important, it will have the *appearance* of being strategically correct. In turn, management will appear to be rational, and providers of resources will feel comfortable with the organization's actions.

Establishing legitimacy. Taking actions that conform to prevailing norms and expectations.

How can legitimacy be achieved? One way is by association with higher status individuals or organizations. For example, an organization without much established status might put a high-status outsider on its board or form a strategic alliance with a more prestigious partner. For example, consider how WestJet first established its legitimacy:

WestJet Airlines
www.westjet.com

> *In its formative year, the Calgary-based company had no direct experience in running an airline and it expected to be treated with skepticism by potential investors. To pre-empt this, it approached David Neeleman, former president of Morris Air, which had just been acquired by Dallas-based Southwest Airlines. Mr. Neeleman became one of WestJet's initial investors and joined its board of directors. In this way, WestJet was able to demonstrate that it had not just a business plan that copied Southwest's successful style, but also an experienced entrepreneur on side, committed to the idea. WestJet took off. WestJet continues to pay attention to public legitimacy, or what its CEO, Clive Beddoe, describes as "winning the hearts and minds of customers and employees."*[41]

Another way to achieve legitimacy is to be seen as doing good deeds in the community. Thus, many companies engage in corporate philanthropy and various charity activities. A third way is to make very visible responses to social trends and legal legislation. For example, many firms have appointed task forces and directors of workforce diversity or established official units to deal with employment equity guidelines. You might recall from Chapter 3 that the Bank of Montreal has an executive committee that oversees equity and diversity issues. Although such highly visible responses are not the only way to proceed with these matters, they do send obvious signals to external constituents that the organization is meeting social expectations. Probably the most common way of achieving legitimacy is to imitate management practices that other firms have institutionalized.

Attempts to achieve legitimacy can backfire. This is especially evident when management practices from other firms are copied without careful thought. Firms that "got on the bandwagon" of total quality management (a program aimed at improving the quality of an organization's goods or services, discussed in Chapter 16) or downsizing without clear rationale have often had unsuccessful experiences, despite the appearance of following recognized business trends.

The preceding are just a few examples of the kinds of strategic responses that organizations can implement to cope with the environment. Now, let's examine in greater detail another such response—technological choice.

THE TECHNOLOGIES OF ORGANIZATIONS

Technology. The activities, equipment, and knowledge necessary to turn organizational inputs into desired outputs.

The term *technology* brings to mind physical devices, such as turret lathes, handsaws, computers, and electron microscopes. However, as we pointed out earlier, this is an overly narrow view of the concept. To broaden this view, we might define **technology** as the activities, equipment, and knowledge necessary to turn organizational inputs into desired outputs. In a hospital, relevant inputs might include sick patients and naïve interns, while desired outputs include well people and experienced doctors. In a steel mill, crucial inputs include scrap metal and energy, while desired outputs consist of finished steel. What technologies should the hospital and the steel mill use to facilitate this transformation? More important for our purposes, do different technologies require different organizational structures to be effective?

The concepts of *technology* and *environment* are closely related.[42] The inputs that are transformed by the technology come from various segments of the organization's environment. In turn, the outputs that the technology creates are returned to the environment. In addition, the activities, equipment, and knowledge that constitute the technology itself seldom spring to life within the organization. Rather, they are imported from the technological segment of the environment to meet the organization's needs.

Organizations choose their technologies.[43] In general, this choice will be predicated on a desired strategy. For example, the directors of a university mental health centre might decide that they wish to deal only with students suffering from transitory anxiety or mild neuroses. Given these inputs, certain short-term psychotherapies would constitute a sensible technology. More disturbed students would be referred to clinics that have different strategies and different technologies. As described earlier, Ford wants to implement its most advanced technology through its flexible manufacturing system in most of its plants in North America by the end of the decade.

Different parts of the organization rely on different technologies, just as they respond to different aspects of the environment as a whole. For example, the human resources department uses a different technology from the finance department. However, research has often skirted this problem, concentrating on the "core" technology used by the key operating function (e.g., the production department in manufacturing firms).

Basic Dimensions of Technology

Organizational technology has been defined, conceptualized, and measured in literally dozens of different ways.[44] Some analysts have concentrated on the degree of automation; others have focused on the degree of discretion granted to workers. Here we will consider other classifications of technologies, specifically those of Charles Perrow, James D. Thompson, and Joan Woodward. These classification schemes are advantageous because we can apply them both to manufacturing firms and to service organizations, such as banks and schools.

Perrow's Routineness. According to Perrow, the key factor that differentiates various technologies is the routineness of the transformation task that confronts the department or organization.[45] **Technological routineness** is a function of two factors:

- *Exceptions*. Is the organization taking in standardized inputs and turning out standardized outputs (few exceptions)? Or is the organization encountering varied inputs or turning out varied outputs (many exceptions)? The technology becomes less routine as exceptions increase.

- *Problems*. When exceptions occur, are the problems easy to analyze or difficult to analyze? That is, can programmed decision making occur, or must workers resort to nonprogrammed decision making? The technology becomes less routine as problems become more difficult to analyze.

As Exhibit 15.6 demonstrates, the exceptions and problems dimensions can be arranged to produce a matrix of technologies. This matrix includes the following technologies:

- *Craft technologies* typically deal with fairly standard inputs and outputs. Cabinet makers use wood to make cabinets, and public schools attempt to educate "typical" students. However, when exceptions are encountered (a special order or a slow learner), analysis of the correct action might be difficult.

- *Routine technologies*, such as assembly line operations and technical schools, also deal with standardized inputs and outputs. However, when exceptions do occur (a new product line or a new subject to teach), the correct response is fairly obvious.

- *Nonroutine technologies* must deal frequently with exceptional inputs or outputs, and the analysis of these exceptions is often difficult. By definition, research units are set up to deal with difficult, exceptional problems. Similarly, psychiatric hospitals encounter patients with a wide variety of disturbances. Deciding on a proper course of therapy can be problematic.

- *Engineering technologies* encounter many exceptions of input or required output, but these exceptions can be dealt with by using standardized responses. For example, individuals with a wide variety of physical conditions visit health spas, and each has a particular goal (e.g., weight loss, muscle development). Despite this variety, the recommendation of a training regimen for each individual is a fairly easy decision.

From most routine to least routine, we can order Perrow's four technological classifications in the following manner: routine, engineering, craft, nonroutine. Shortly, we will consider which structures are appropriate for these technologies. First, though, let's examine Thompson's technological classification.

Technological routineness. The extent to which exceptions and problems affect the task of converting inputs into outputs.

Exceptions

	Few	Many
Difficult Analysis	**Craft Technology** Cabinet Making Public School	**Nonroutine Technology** Research Unit Psychiatric Hospital
Easy Analysis	**Routine Technology** Assembly Line Vocational Training	**Engineering Technology** Heavy Machinery Construction Health Spa

Problems

EXHIBIT 15.6
Perrow's matrix of technologies.

Source: From Perrow, C. (1967, April). Framework for the comparative analysis of organizations, *ASR, 32(2)*, Figures 1 and 2, pp. 196, 198. Copyright © 1967 by the American Sociological Association. Reprinted by permission.

Technological interdependence. The extent to which organizational subunits depend on each other for resources, raw materials or information.

Pooled interdependence. A condition in which organizational subunits are dependent on the pooled resources generated by other subunits but are otherwise fairly independent.

Sequential interdependence. A condition in which organizational subunits are dependent on the resources generated by units that precede them in a sequence of work.

Reciprocal interdependence. A condition in which organizational subunits must engage in considerable interplay and mutual feedback to accomplish a task.

Thompson's Interdependence. In contrast to Perrow, James D. Thompson was interested in the way in which work activities are sequenced or "put together" during the transformation process.[46] A key factor here is **technological interdependence**, the extent to which organizational subunits depend on each other for resources, such as raw materials or information. In order of increasing interdependence, Thompson proposed three classifications of technology (Exhibit 15.7). These classifications are as follows:

- *Mediating technologies* operate under **pooled interdependence**. This means that each unit is to some extent dependent on the pooled resources generated by the other units but is otherwise fairly independent of those units. Thompson gives rather abstract examples, such as banks, which mediate between depositors and borrowers, and post offices, which mediate between the senders and receivers of letters. However, the same argument can be applied more clearly to the branches of banks or post offices. The health of a bank as a whole might depend on the existence of several branches, but these branches operate almost independently of each other. Each has its own borrowers and depositors. Similarly, post office branches are dependent on other branches to forward and receive mail, but this is the limit of their required interaction. A taxi company is another good example of pooled interdependence.

- *Long-linked technologies* operate under **sequential interdependence**. This means that each unit in the technology is dependent on the activity of the unit that preceded it in a sequence. The transformed product of each unit becomes a resource or raw material for the next unit. Mass production assembly lines are the classic example of long-linked technology. However, many "paper-processing" technologies, such as the claims department of an insurance company, are also sequentially interdependent (claims must be verified before they are adjusted and must be adjusted before they are settled).

- *Intensive technologies* operate under **reciprocal interdependence**. This means that considerable interplay and mutual feedback must occur between the units performing the task to accomplish it properly. This is necessary because each task is unique, and the intensive technology is thus a customized technology. One example might be the technology employed by a multidisciplinary research team. Thompson cites a general hospital as a prime example of intensive technology:

EXHIBIT 15.7
Thompson's technology classification.

Mediating Technology (Pooled Interdependence):

Long-Linked Technology (Sequential Interdependence):

Intensive Technology (Reciprocal Interdependence):

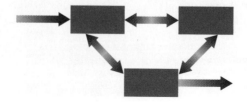

At any moment, an emergency admission may require some combination of dietary, x-ray, laboratory, and housekeeping or hotel services, together with the various medical specialities, pharmaceutical services, occupational therapies, social work services, and spiritual or religious services. Which of these is needed, and when, can be determined only from evidence about the state of the patient.[47]

As technologies become increasingly interdependent, problems of coordination, communication, and decision making increase. To perform effectively, each technology requires a tailored structure to facilitate these tasks.

Woodward's Production Processes. The most famous study of the relationship between technology and structure is that of Joan Woodward. Woodward examined the technology, structure, and organizational effectiveness of 100 firms in South Essex, England.[48] This study is especially interesting because it began as an attempt to test the argument that mechanistic structures will prove most effective in all cases. In brief, this test failed—there was no simple, consistent relationship between organizational structure and effectiveness—and many of the successful firms exhibited organic structures. Woodward then analyzed and classified the technologies of the 80 firms in her sample that had clear-cut, stable production processes. She used the classifications unit, mass, and process production. Some examples of these classifications include the following:

- *Unit* (production of single units or small batches)

  Custom-tailored units

  Prototype production

  Fabrication of large equipment in stages (e.g., locomotives)

  Small batches to order

- *Mass* (production of large batches or mass production)

  Large batches on assembly lines

  Mass production (e.g., bakeries)

- *Process* (input transformed as an ongoing process)

  Chemicals processed in batches

  Continuous-flow production (e.g., gasoline, propane)

From top to bottom, this scale of technology reflects both increasing smoothness of production and increasing impersonalization of task requirements.[49] Less and less personal intervention is necessary as machines control more and more of the work. Woodward's mass technology incorporates aspects of Perrow's routine technology and Thompson's long-linked technology. Her unit technology seems to cover Perrow's craft and engineering technologies and some aspects of Thompson's intensive technology. It is difficult to isolate Woodward's process technology in the Perrow or Thompson classifications.

Structuring to Cope with Technology

Now for the key question: How does technology affect organizational structure?

Perrow. According to Perrow, routine technologies should function best under mechanistic structures, while nonroutine technologies call for more organic structures. In the former case, few exceptions to the normal course of events and easily analyzable problems suggest high formalization and centralization. In the latter case, many exceptions and difficult problems suggest that decision-making power should be located "where the action is." The craft and engineering technologies fall between these prescriptions.

Research has generally supported his notion that more routine technologies adopt more mechanistic structures.[50]

Thompson. According to Thompson, increasing technological interdependence must be accompanied by increased coordination or integration mechanisms. There is research evidence to support this proposition.[51] Furthermore, the *methods* used to achieve coordination should be reflected in structural differences across the technologies. Mediating technologies, operating only under pooled interdependence, should be able to achieve coordination via standardization of rules, regulations, and procedures. This formalization is indicative of a mechanistic structure (consider banks and the post office). Long-linked technologies must also be structured mechanistically, but the increased demands for coordination prompted by sequential interdependence must be met by planning, scheduling, and meetings. Finally, intensive technologies require intensive coordination, and this is best achieved by mutual adjustment and an organic structure that permits the free and ready flow of information among units.[52]

Woodward. According to Woodward, structures should vary with technology and this variance should be related to organizational effectiveness. The research evidence supports this. Each of the three technologies tended to have distinctive structures, and the most successful firms had structures that closely approximated the average of their technological groups. For instance, Woodward found that as the production process became smoother, more continuous, and more impersonal, the management of the system took on increasing importance. That is, moving from unit to mass to process, there were more managers relative to workers, more hierarchical levels, and lower labour costs. This is not difficult to understand. Unit production involves custom-tailored craftswork in which the workers can essentially manage their own work activity. However, it is very labour intensive. On the other hand, sophisticated continuous-process systems (such as those used to refine gasoline) take a great amount of management skill and technical attention to start up. Once rolling, a handful of workers can monitor and maintain the system.

Successful firms with unit and process technologies relied on organic structures, while successful firms that engaged in mass production relied on mechanistic structures. For example, the latter firms had more specialization of labour, more controls, and greater formalization (a reliance on written rather than verbal communication). At first glance, it might strike you as unusual that the firms at the extremes of the technology scale (unit and process) both tended to rely on organic structures. However, close consideration of the actual tasks performed under each technology resolves this apparent contradiction. Unit production generally involves custom-building complete units to customer specifications. As such, it relies on skilled labour, teamwork, and coordination by mutual adjustment and standardized skills. The work itself is not machine paced and is far from mechanistic. At the other extreme, process production is almost totally automated. The workers are essentially skilled technicians who monitor and maintain the system, and they again tend to work in teams. While the machinery itself operates according to a rigid schedule, workers can monitor and maintain it at their own pace. Informal relationships with supervisors replace close control.

Woodward's research is a landmark in demonstrating the general proposition that structure must be tailored to the technology the organization adopts to achieve its strategic goals. Her findings have been replicated and extended by others.[53] However, there have been disconfirming studies, and a constant debate has gone on about the relative importance of organizational size versus technology in determining structure.[54]

IMPLICATIONS OF ADVANCED INFORMATION TECHNOLOGY

In concluding the chapter, let's consider some of the implications that ongoing advances in information technology are having for organizational behaviour. Speaking broadly, **advanced information technology** refers to the generation, aggregation, storage, modification, and speedy transmission of information made possible by the advent of computers and related devices. Information technology is equally applicable in the factory or the office. In the factory, examples include robots, computer-controlled machine tools, and automated inventory management. In the office, it covers everything from word processing to e-mail to automated filing to expert systems. Between the office and the factory, it includes computer-aided design and engineering.

Advanced information technology. The generation, aggregation, storage, modification, and speedy transmission of information made possible by the advent of computers and related devices.

The Two Faces of Advanced Technology

It is important to recognize that there has been much inaccurate hoopla about advanced information technology. This began even before the first mainframe computers were perfected, and it continues today. To exaggerate only slightly, doomsayers have painted a dark picture of job loss and de-skilling, with technology running wild and stifling the human spirit. Opponents of this view (often vendors of hardware and software) have painted a rosy picture of improved productivity, superior decision making, and upgraded, happy employees. It probably does not surprise you that research fails to support either of these extremes as a general state of affairs. In the early days of mainframe batch data processing, de-skilling, job pacing, and loss of routine clerical jobs did occur. However, as we shall see, the consequences of current advanced information technology are much less deterministic.

This discussion of extremes alerts us to a more realistic issue that we might call the "two faces" of technology.[55] This means that a given form of advanced information technology can have exactly *opposite* effects, depending on how it is employed. For example, the same system that is designed to monitor and control employees (say, by counting keystrokes) can also provide feedback and reduce supervision. Additionally, the same technology that can de-skill jobs can build skills *into* jobs. How can these opposite effects occur? They are possible because information technology is so *flexible*. In fact, we are discussing information technology separately from the core technologies discussed earlier because it is so flexible that it can be applied in conjunction with any of them.

The flexibility of information technology means that it is not deterministic of a particular organization structure or job design. Rather, it gives organizations *choices* about how to organize work. The company that wishes to decentralize can use information technology to provide lower-level employees with data to make decisions. The company that wishes to centralize can use the other face of the same technology to gather information from below to retain control. Such choices are a function of organizational culture and management values rather than inherent in the hardware. They should match the strategy the organization is pursuing, as our discussion of advanced manufacturing will show.

For purposes of discussion, we will distinguish between advanced manufacturing technology and advanced office technology. However, as we shall see, this distinction is artificial, since advanced technology has the capability to link the office more closely to the factory or to clients, customers, and suppliers in the outside environment.

Advanced Manufacturing Technology

Three major trends underlie advanced manufacturing technology.[56] The first is an obvious capitalization on computer intelligence and memory. The second is flexibility, in that the technology can accomplish a changing variety of tasks. This is usually the product of an organizational strategy that favours adaptiveness, small batch production, and fast response. In turn, this strategy follows from attempting to find and exploit short-term "niches" in the marketplace rather than hoping to produce large volumes of the same product year after year—precisely why Ford has implemented flexible manufacturing. Consider this textile firm:

> Milliken has reduced its average production run from 20 000 to 4000 yards and can dye lots as small as 1000 yards. Apparel makers, textile and fibre firms, and retailers have recently joined to launch the so-called Quick Response program, designed to improve the flow of information among the various groups and speed order times. The program's goal is to cut the 66-week cycle from fibre to retail in the United States to 21 weeks.[57]

As indicated, the same thing is happening in the auto industry where there is a trend toward more efficient, flexible manufacturing systems. With flexible manufacturing, a plant can manufacture a number of different vehicles in the same plant rather than just one vehicle and it can also quickly and more easily switch model production. Another good example of this is Honda of Canada Manufacturing Inc. in Alliston, Ontario. The plant produces the Odyssey minivan and the Pilot SUV for Honda and the MDX for the automaker's luxury Acura line. On another assembly line, Civic sedans and Acura 1.7EL models are made. General Motors is spending half a billion dollars to transform its plant in Oshawa, Ontario, into a flexible manufacturing facility where it plans to begin production of the new Chevrolet Camaro in 2008. With flexible manufacturing, the plant can switch production between different types of cars depending on customer demand simply by reprogramming the robots in the body shop. Flexible manufacturing also makes it possible to serve smaller niches, something that would not be profitable in a traditional plant that is designed to manufacture large numbers of a single vehicle.[58]

As a third trend, advanced manufacturing technologies are increasingly being designed to be integrated with *other* advanced technologies that organizations use. For example, the computer-aided design system that is used to design and modify a product can also be used to design, operate, and modify its production process via computer-aided manufacturing programs (the result being a so-called CAD/CAM system). Ultimately, using most of the technologies mentioned here, computer-integrated manufacturing systems (CIM) that integrate and automate all aspects of design, manufacturing, assembly, and inspection can be put in place. In turn, computerized information systems can link these tasks to supply and sales networks. Exhibit 15.8 compares highly flexible manufacturing systems with traditional mass production.[59]

Honda Canada
www.honda.ca

EXHIBIT 15.8
Flexible manufacturing compared with traditional mass production.

Organizational Characteristic	Flexible Manufacturing	Mass Production
Strategy	• Adapt to environment • Produce small batches • Small inventory, fast turnover • Respond fast	• Buffer against environment • Produce large batches • Large inventory, slow turnover • Respond predictably
Product	• Many variations, variable life cycles	• Few variations, long life cycles
Marketing	• Exploit niche markets	• Cater to mass market
Structure	• Organic, integrated	• Mechanistic, differentiated
Suppliers	• Few, chosen for reliability and responsiveness	• Many, chosen on basis of cost
Jobs	• Flexible jobs; teamwork	• Rigid, specialized jobs; little teamwork

What are the general implications of advanced manufacturing technology for organizational behaviour? Such technology tends to automate the more routine information-processing and decision-making tasks. Depending on job design, what might remain for operators are the more complex, nonroutine tasks—those dealing with system problems and exceptions. In addition, task interdependence tends to increase under advanced technologies. For example, design, manufacturing, and marketing become more reciprocally than sequentially interdependent in a flexible manufacturing system. Finally, let's remember that such advanced technologies are adopted, in part, to cope with a less certain environment. Thus, many advanced technological systems result in nonroutine, highly interdependent tasks that are embedded in an uncertain environment.[60]

Organizational Structure. What are the implications of this shift in technology? As Exhibit 15.8 shows, one effect is a movement toward flatter, more organic structures to capitalize on the technology's flexibility.[61] This corresponds to Woodward's finding that unit technologies require more organic designs than mass technologies, and the adoption of more flexible, short-term production batches is an example of unit technology. The expectation of flatter structures stems from the fact that more highly automated systems will handle information processing and diagnoses that were formerly performed by middle managers.

Implications of advanced technology for centralization are interesting. On the one hand, matters such as ordering raw materials and scheduling production should become more highly centralized. This is both required by the flexibility of the system and permitted by its enhanced information-processing capability. On the other hand, when problems or exceptions occur or when new designs are conceived, decentralization might be called for to locate decision making in the hands of lower-level specialists. However, the whole thrust of advanced technology dictates greater integration among specialities, such as design, engineering, production, and marketing. This might require a retreat from the rigid functional structures (Chapter 14) that are common in manufacturing firms. Minimally, it suggests the increased use of integrators, task forces, planning committees, and other mechanisms that stimulate coordination. One study of 185 firms that adopted advanced manufacturing technology found a general trend toward decentralization with more formalized rules and procedures to ensure coordination and effective exploitation of the technology.[62] However, another recent study on the effects of computer-based technology in manufacturing organizations found that it reduced the number of levels in the hierarchy and centralized operational authority and influence.[63]

Job Design. Advanced manufacturing technology can be expected to affect the design of jobs, and this is where the issue of choice we alluded to earlier clearly comes into play. There is evidence that such technology can reduce worker control over shop floor jobs and water down existing skills.[64] An example is having skilled machinists operate lathes that have been programmed by a remote technician. However, other choices are possible, including teaching the machinists to program the lathe or at least to edit existing programs for local conditions. The latter approaches have been shown to gain cooperation and commitment to the new technology and to enhance performance.[65] Following this logic, since advanced technology tends to automate routine tasks, operative workers must usually acquire advanced skills (e.g., computer skills). Also, since advanced technology tends to be flexible as well as expensive to operate, workers themselves must be flexible and fast to respond to problems. Extreme division of labour can be counterproductive in advanced technology. For example, operators simply might not be able to wait for someone else to perform routine maintenance and thus might have to have the flexibility to do this themselves. Similarly, traditional distinctions between roles (electrical maintenance versus mechanical maintenance or drafting versus design) begin to blur when the needs for coordination that advanced technology imposes are recognized.

All this points to the design of jobs for advanced manufacturing technology according to the principles of job enrichment we discussed in Chapter 6. Just consider the effect of flexible manufacturing on employees at Ford. Management now refers to employees as business partners and the company wants employees to think and find ways of improving quality and efficiency. The results of a recent study of 80 manufacturing companies found that integrated manufacturing was positively associated with job enrichment and employee skills development rather than impoverished, low-skill work.[66]

As described in Chapter 6, when jobs are enriched, proper training is critical and pay levels should be revised to fit the additional skills and responsibilities prompted by the technology. Many observers have recommended that self-managed teams (Chapter 7) be made responsible for setting up, running, and maintaining the system.[67] Such teams permit cross-transfer of skills and provide the cross-task integration that is necessary to keep things working smoothly. The team concept is also applicable to other forms of advanced technology. For example, one company organized its CAD/CAM users into teams composed of two designers, a draftsperson, and a toolmaker.[68]

Advanced Office Technology

As we noted above, the label *advanced office technology* can be applied sensibly to everything from word processing to exotic expert decision systems. Advanced office technology illustrates the coming together of some combination of three previously separate technologies—computers, office machines, and telecommunications (for example, a word processor combines a computer and a typewriter). The most common basic functions of the technology are the following:[69]

- Text processing
- Communication (e.g., e-mail, fax)
- Information storage and retrieval
- Analysis and manipulation of information
- Administrative support (e.g., electronic calendars)

As with advanced manufacturing technology, we can point to some environmental and strategic concerns that have stimulated the adoption of advanced office technology, although these concerns are more general. One is obviously the potential for *labour saving*. Consider, for example, word processing (revisions are easy), videoconferencing (a trip to the coast is unnecessary), or spreadsheet analysis (many "What if?" scenarios can be probed by one manager). Another major concern stimulating the adoption of advanced technology is *responsiveness*, both within the organization and also to customers and suppliers. Speed and personalization of response are common goals. Finally, *improved decision making* is a goal of various decision support systems, expert systems, and the like.

The implications of advanced office technology are far reaching. What follows is an illustrative sample, again focusing on organizational structure and job design.

Organizational Structure. At least as it pertains to management jobs, the link between office technology and organizational structure has been dominated by two related issues—the impact of information technology on tallness/flatness and centralization. Regarding tallness and flatness, advanced technology has enabled a reduction in the number of supervisory and middle-management personnel.[70] Fewer supervisors are needed because electronic monitoring and feedback often replace routine supervision, and existing supervisors can handle larger spans of control. With fewer supervisors, fewer middle managers are required. Also, some advanced technology, such as decision support and expert systems, can make up for analyses performed by middle managers. For its size (over 200 000 employees), FedEx is a flat organization, having only five levels. This is due, in part, to advanced electronic communication systems.

FedEx
www.fedex.com

Actual research evidence on all this is rather scanty and mainly targeted at the middle-management issue. Although there are reports of staff reductions, it is difficult to know how much of this is a direct result of office technology as opposed to the imposition of flatness to make organizations more responsive to the external environment. Some research points to increased demands on middle-management jobs as larger spans require them to be in charge of more diverse areas and as their performance is more monitorable by top management due to the technology.[71]

The impact of advanced office technology on centralization of decision making is variable, precisely as it should be.[72] Again, the key is the extreme flexibility of information technology. The same systems that allow senior managers to meddle in lower-level operations might enable junior staffers to assemble data and make decisions. Notice, though, that advanced technology does imply a freer, more democratic flow of information and general communication. This suggests that advanced technology enables a wider range of people at more levels to be involved in organizational decision making.[73] Exactly how this capacity gets played out in decision-making practice is most likely a function of strategy and prevailing culture.

Job Design. The impact of advanced office technology on job design and related quality of working life differs considerably with job status. Among clerical and secretarial employees, when jobs have not been lost altogether, there is the potential for deskilling and reduced motivating potential.[74] A good case in point occurred in many organizations when word processing was introduced. Because the equipment was then expensive, secretarial support was often shifted into word processing pools to make efficient use of the hardware.[75] This frequently resulted in task specialization and a reduction in task identity. However, most observers agree that such technology can actually upgrade skills if it is used to optimal capacity and the work is not highly fragmented.[76] In fact, one study found that the extent to which computers have a positive or negative effect on job characteristics depends on several factors, such as the amount of time spent on computing and noncomputing components of a job, the nature of the work done on the computer, and the nature of the work that is done apart from the computer.[77]

Turning to quality of working life, word processing and related video display work have been known to provoke eyestrain, muscular strain, and stress symptoms. However, proper work station design and work pacing can help employees cope with these problems. Computer monitoring (such as counting keystrokes or timing the length of phone calls by service workers) has also been linked to stress reactions. However, there are studies that show that such monitoring may be viewed favourably by employees when it is used for job feedback rather than as a basis for punishment.[78] However, some forms of monitoring that are meant to improve communication between workers in different locations might have a number of negative consequences. To learn more, see "Research Focus: *The Psychological Effects of Awareness Monitoring Technology.*"

There are many examples of organizations that have had poor success in introducing advanced technology because they ignored the human dimension. This raises the issue of implementing change in organizations, a concern of the next chapter.

RESEARCH FOCUS

The Psychological Effects of Awareness Monitoring Technology

Imagine having a camera mounted on your computer monitor that captures your actions (and whatever you happen to be doing at the time) and transmits these images to your colleagues around the world. Sound far-fetched? Well, new technologies, called *awareness monitoring systems* or *benign surveillance systems* are being designed to enhance communication between geographically distributed colleagues (e.g., tele-workers, multinational team members). The idea behind awareness monitoring is that if I know where my colleague is, we can communicate more effectively. Awareness monitoring systems have been implemented in organizations such as Nynex and Xerox in the United States.

With over 78 percent of firms in the United States already engaging in some form of electronic moni-toring, these new awareness technologies raise a number of important questions about employee sur-veillance. For example, do people really want to be monitored so closely at work? Will these new technolo-gies really enhance communication and collaboration? To answer these questions, David Zweig and Jane Webster asked over 600 people to share their percep-tions of awareness monitoring systems.

It was no surprise that, overall, people found these systems to be highly invasive and unfair. People ques-tioned the usefulness of the technology and even sug-gested that they would not work for an organization that implements awareness monitoring technologies. However, even when safeguards were put in place to protect privacy and respect fairness, people responded negatively to awareness monitoring technologies.

Specifically, offering people control over how their awareness information is shared, giving them knowl-edge of who is using the system to determine their availability, limiting the frequency of image capture, and blurring their image still resulted in negative atti-tudes and low levels of acceptance as compared to when these privacy and fairness enhancing modifica-tions were not available.

In a follow-up study, a potential reason for these findings emerged. People felt that the awareness mon-itoring system violated their personal boundaries for how much information they were willing to share with their colleagues—regardless of the privacy and fairness safeguards in place. Furthermore, all of the partici-pants were concerned about having their performance evaluated by presence. In other words, having pres-ence monitored by a technology that captures and transmits a person's image at a workstation to others at any point in time during the workday could serve as an inaccurate measure of performance.

What's the bottom line? As technology advances and organizations continue to disperse geographically, there is little doubt that efforts to design and imple-ment monitoring technologies to enhance communica-tion will continue. However, any new technology that violates employee expectations of privacy and fairness might have a significant impact on employee satisfac-tion, stress, retention, and performance.

Source: Written by David Zweig. Based on Zweig, D. and Webster, J. (2002). Where is the line between benign and invasive? An examination of psychological barriers to the acceptance of awareness monitoring systems. *Journal of Organizational Behavior, 23,* 605–633. © 2002 John Wiley & Sons Ltd. Reproduced with permission.

Notebook

Abitibi-Consolidated Inc.'s Makeover

1. The constraints facing Abitibi and the paper industry are a declining market for newsprint along with the high Canadian dollar and the cost of wood fibre. This suggests curtailing existing newsprint operations and perhaps a change in strategy toward other types of paper. There may be opportunities for other more lucrative areas of paper production. According to John Weaver, "Our in-depth review can be summarized as a concerted effort to make existing operations more profitable, pay down debt, and identify future growth options such as the commercial printing business in both the super high brights and the high-end glossy."

2. With the decline in the newsprint market, the decision was made to close all or part of the operations at three facilities and to sell one mill along with the 500 000 acres of nearby timberland. The remaining 20 or so paper mills in Canada and the United States, Asia and Britain have been subject to a rigorous overhaul to ensure they are all efficient, low-cost producers. At the same time, Abitibi is positioning itself in more lucrative, higher-growth markets, such as commercial printing paper. One mill is being considered for possible conversion to production of coated groundwood paper, which is a higher grade than newsprint.

LEARNING OBJECTIVES CHECKLIST

1. Organizations are *open systems* that take inputs from the external environment, transform some of these inputs, and send them back into the environment as outputs. The *external environment* includes all the events and conditions surrounding the organization that influence this process. Major components of the environment include the economy, customers, suppliers, competitors, social/political factors, and existing technologies.

2. One key aspect of the external environment is its uncertainty. More uncertain environments are vague, difficult to diagnose, and unpredictable. Uncertainty is a function of complexity and rate of change. The most uncertain environments are complex and dynamic—they involve a large number of dissimilar components that are changing unpredictably. More certain environments are simple and stable—they involve a few similar components that exhibit little change. As *environmental uncertainty* increases, cause-and-effect relationships get harder to diagnose, and agreeing on priorities becomes more difficult because more information must be processed. Another key aspect of the external environment is the amount of resources it contains. Some environments are richer or more munificent than others, and all organizations are dependent on their environments for resources. Organizations must develop strategies for managing environmental uncertainty and *resource dependence* for their survival and success.

3. *Strategy* is the process that executives use to cope with the constraints and opportunities posed by the organization's environment, including uncertainty and scarce resources. One critical strategic response involves tailoring the organization's structure to suit the environment. In general, as the Lawrence and Lorsch study demonstrates, mechanistic structures are most suitable for more certain environments, and organic structures are better suited to uncertain environments.

4. Some of the more elaborate strategic responses include *vertical integration, mergers* and *acquisitions, strategic alliances, interlocking directorates,* and *establishing legitimacy.* Many of these involve relationships between organizations. Vertical integration involves taking control of sources of organizational supply and distribution; mergers and acquisitions involve two firms joining together or one taking over another; strategic alliances involve cooperative relationships

between legally separate organizations; interlocking directorates exist when one person serves on two or more boards of directors; and establishing legitimacy involves taking actions that conform to prevailing norms and expectations.

5. *Technology* includes the activities, equipment, and knowledge necessary to turn organizational inputs into desired outputs. One key aspect of technology is the extent of its routineness. A routine technology involves few exceptions to usual inputs or outputs and readily analyzable problems. A nonroutine technology involves many exceptions that are difficult to analyze. Another key aspect of technology is the degree of interdependence that exists between organizational units. This may range from simple pooling of resources, to sequential activities, to complex reciprocal interdependence. Woodward classified technologies as unit, mass, or process production and reflects both increasing smoothness of production and increasing impersonalization of task requirements.

6. According to Perrow, routine technologies should function best under mechanistic struc-tures, while nonroutine technologies call for more organic structures. According to Thompson, mediating technologies require formalization that calls for a mechanistic structure; long-linked technologies must also be structured mechanistically; and intensive technologies require intensive coordination, which is best achieved with an organic structure. The most famous study of the relationship between technology and structure was Joan Woodward's. She determined that unit and process technologies performed best under organic structures, while mass production functioned best under a mechanistic structure. In general, less routine technologies and more interdependent technologies call for more organic structures.

7. *Advanced information technology* generates, aggregates, stores, modifies, and speedily transmits information. In the factory, it permits flexible manufacturing that calls for organic structures, enriched jobs, and increased teamwork. In the office and the organization as a whole, the flexibility of advanced information technology means that its effects are highly dependent on management values and culture.

DISCUSSION QUESTIONS

1. Construct a diagram of the various interest groups in the external environment of CBC Television. Discuss how some of these interest groups might make competing or contradictory demands on the CBC.

2. Give an example of vertical integration. Use the concept of resource dependence to explain why an organization might choose a strategic response of vertical integration.

3. Discuss how interlocking directorates can reduce environmental uncertainty and help manage resource dependence.

4. Explain why organizations operating in more uncertain environments require more organic structures.

5. Distinguish among pooled interdependence, sequential interdependence, and reciprocal interdependence in terms of the key problem each poses for organizational effectiveness.

6. Give an example of unit technology, mass technology, and process technology. For which type of technology are the prescriptions of the classical organizational theorists best suited?

7. Imagine that a company is converting from conventional mass technology to a highly flexible, computerized, integrated production system. List structural and behavioural problems that the company might have to anticipate in making this conversion.

8. Discuss this statement: The effects of advanced information technology on job design and organizational structure are highly predictable.

New Production Processes Require Job Enrichment

Recently, major changes have been taking place in manufacturing. The traditional practices centred on mass production are giving way to new ways of thinking about production. Practices such as "lean production," "world class manufacturing," "integrated manufacturing," "time-based flexible manufacturing," and "new wave manufacturing" represent new approaches that are aimed at making organizations more efficient and competitive.

These new approaches focus on being more responsiveness to customer demands by controlling costs while also improving quality and tailoring output to customer requirements. To accomplish this, enabling technologies and techniques such as just-in-time (JIT) and total quality management (TQM) are being employed now more than ever. Total quality management is a systematic attempt to achieve continuous improvement in the quality of an organization's products or services.

An important question raised when implementing these approaches is whether they are sufficient in themselves to realize new competitive goals, or whether wider individual and organizational change is also necessary. In particular, what is the role of employees and should their work be enriched, as discussed in Chapter 6?

To answer this question, Sharon Parker, Toby Wall, and Paul Jackson conducted two studies to examine the implementation of new production techniques. They argued that the successful implementation of new manufacturing practices hinges on the production employees themselves. These workers need to develop a broader role orientation that includes a concern for high product quality, customer satisfaction, working as part of a team, and understanding the importance of gaining and using a wide range of skills and knowledge. Furthermore, the development of a broader role orientation requires an increase in job autonomy.

The first study involved the implementation of a JIT-TQM initiative that did not involve any change in employees' autonomy. The assembly section of a company that designs and manufactures vehicle seats and seat mechanisms for car manufacturers in the United Kingdom and Europe was used for this study. The second study involved the introduction of a JIT-TQM initiative that was accompanied by enhanced autonomy. This study took place in the production department of an American-owned electronics company in the United Kingdom that designs and produces control equipment for use in process industries. At this site, autonomous work teams (Chapter 7) were formed and multiskilled employees were given the authority to manage day-to-day activities geared toward meeting production targets as well as the responsibility for testing and quality inspection.

The results indicated that employees in the first study, who did not experience a change in autonomy, did not develop a broader role orientation. In fact, they attached less importance to various skills and types of knowledge that would enable high performance. Employees in the second study, whose job autonomy was enhanced, developed a broader and more flexible role orientation. Overall, the adoption of the JIT-TQM initiative in this company was very successful. Lead times were reduced from 14 weeks to two days; inventory costs were reduced to 20 percent of the initial costs; delivery integrity (meeting customer delivery dates) was improved from 50 percent to 97 percent; and quality (monitored in terms of zero-defect boards and quality yield) was substantially improved.

The results of this research demonstrate that employees' jobs must be enriched so that they develop a broader and more flexible role orientation, which is required for the successful implementation of new manufacturing practices.

Source: Parker, S.K., Wall, T.D., & Jackson, P.R. (1997). "That's not my job": Developing flexible employee work orientations. *Academy of Management Journal, 40,* 899–929.

INTEGRATIVE DISCUSSION QUESTIONS

1. Consider the effect of environmental uncertainty and resource dependence on power and politics in organizations. To what extent is subunit power and organizational politics a function of environmental uncertainty and resource dependence? Does environmental uncertainty and resource dependence predict and explain the distribution and use of power and politics in organizations?

2. How does technology influence job design? Discuss the effect of technology according to Perrow, Thompson, and Woodward on the following approaches to job design described in Chapter 6: traditional views of job design, the Job Characteristics Model, and job enrichment.

3. Discuss the implications of mergers and acquisitions for organizational culture. In particular, consider mergers and acquisitions in light of the assets and liabilities of strong cultures. How will culture influence the success or failure of mergers and acquisitions, and what can organizations do to increase the chances of success?

ON-THE-JOB CHALLENGE QUESTION

General Motors, Renault SA, and Nissan have begun to consider a proposal for a three-way alliance. Renault and Nissan would pay US$3 billion for a 20 percent stake in GM. In letters sent to Renault and Nissan, it was stated that the alliance would be in the best interests of all three companies as each faces market and financial challenges. The alliance would rank among the most important deals in recent automotive history, like the one between Renault and Nissan in 1999 and the merger of Daimler-Benz and Chrysler in 1998.

What do you think about the proposal for a three-way alliance? What factors might be driving the proposal? What are the potential advantages and disadvantages of such an alliance? What are some other strategic responses the organizations might consider?

Source: Maynard, M. (2006, July 1). Nissan, Renault consider three-way deal with GM. *Toronto Star*, D1, D14.

EXPERIENTIAL EXERCISE

Diagnosing an Organization

The purpose of this exercise is to choose an organization and to diagnose it in terms of the concepts we covered in the chapter. Doing such a diagnosis should enable you to see better how the degree of "fit" among organizational structure, environment, strategy, and technology influences the effectiveness of the organization.

This exercise is suitable for an individual, a group project completed outside the class, or a class discussion guided by the instructor. In the case of the group project, each group might choose and contact a local organization for information. Alternatively, library resources might be consulted to diagnose a prominent national or international organization. Your instructor might suggest one or more organizations for diagnosis.

1. Discuss in detail the external environment of the chosen organization.
   a) How has the general economy affected this organization recently? Is the organization especially sensitive to swings in the economy?
   b) Who are the organization's key customers? What demands do they make on the organization?
   c) Who are the organization's key suppliers? What impact do they have on the organization?
   d) Who are the organization's important competitors? What threats or opportunities do they pose for the organization?
   e) What general social and political factors (e.g., the law, social trends, environmental concerns) affect the organization in critical ways?

2. Drawing on your answers to question 1, discuss both the degree of environmental uncertainty and the nature of resource dependence the organization faces. Be sure to locate the firm or institution in the appropriate cell of Exhibit 15.3, and defend your answer.

3. What broad strategies (excluding structure) has the organization chosen to cope with its environment?

4. Describe in as much detail as possible the structure of the organization, and explain how this structure represents a strategic response to the demands of the environment. Is this the proper structure for the environment and broad strategies that you described in response to the earlier questions?
   a) How big is the organization?
   b) What form of departmentation is used?
   c) How big are the spans of control?
   d) How tall is the organization?
   e) How much formalization is apparent?
   f) To what extent is the organization centralized?
   g) How complex is the organization?
   h) Where does the organization fall on a continuum from mechanistic to organic?

5. Describe the organization's core technology in terms of routineness (Exhibit 15.6) and interdependence (Exhibit 15.7). Is its structure appropriate for its technology?

6. What impact has advanced information technology had on the organization?

CASE INCIDENT

GTE

Telephone operations account for four-fifths of GTE's $20 billion in annual revenues. With deregulation, the telephone business has become intensely competitive, and GTE is looking for ways to both cut costs and improve customer service. Improved service can reduce service costs in the field, improve existing customers' relationships, and attract new customers. The traditional approach to such improvements has been to try to "fine-tune" existing procedures in the repair, billing, and marketing departments. However, GTE sees merit in trying to totally reengineer the way customers interact with the company to make the process more efficient and satisfying, perhaps using some of its own technology.

GTE is currently using a traditional system in which a customer needing repair service calls an operator who takes down basic information and then bounces the customer around various departments until someone can solve his or her problem. This system of passing on customers is both expensive and inefficient. What if a single customer wants to question a bill, obtain a calling card, and report a dial tone problem?

1. Describe the external environment of GTE and the relevant components of it. What influence does the external environment have on GTE?

2. What would you do to improve customer service at GTE and how does advanced information technology provide opportunities for improved customer service?

Sources: Greengard, S. (1993, December). Reengineering: Out of the rubble. *Personnel Journal*, 48A–48O; Brian Blevins, GTE; Sager, I. (1994). The great equalizer. *Business Week* (Special issue: The Information Revolution). 100–107; Stewart, T.A. (1993, August 23). Reengineering: The hot new management tool. *Fortune*, 41–48.

CASE STUDY

The Saturn Experiment

In February of 1984, a radical new experiment began with the establishment of the Group of 99, which consisted of 99 individuals representing a broad cross-section of members of the United Auto Workers (UAW), General Motors (GM) managers and staff from 55 plants and 14 UAW regions. The group's mission was to study GM divisions as well as other organizations and to create a new approach to building automobiles. The group travelled some two million miles and concluded that employees perform best when they feel part of the decision-making process and that if Saturn was to overcome the traditional difficulties of automobile manufacturing, they would have to operate under a different philosophy.

Saturn was conceived as a totally new corporation, a wholly owned General Motors subsidiary that delivered its first cars in the fall of 1990. The formerly autonomous division, headquartered in Spring Hill, Tennessee, has its own sales and service operations. At the time, why did GM decide to separate Saturn so decisively from the existing corporate structure, rather than just add yet another product line to its Chevrolet, Oldsmobile, Pontiac, Buick, and Cadillac lines?

General Motors insiders and auto industry analysts cited two primary reasons. First, GM badly needed to find ways to cut costs to compete in the small car market, in which estimates suggested that Japanese manufacturers enjoyed a great cost advantage. Second, top GM executives hoped to use the Saturn venture as a testing ground for innovations that could be applied throughout the rest of the organization, especially ones that could get new models to the market more quickly. According to then GM chairman Roger Smith, the techniques GM learns from Saturn will spread throughout the company, "improving the efficiency and competitiveness of every plant we operate . . . Saturn is the key to GM's long-term competitiveness, survival and success as a domestic producer." To accomplish both these goals, the freedom of a completely "fresh start" and the protection autonomy offered seemed to be essential.

With the exception of the use of plastic for vertical body parts, Saturn cars did not represent a radical technical departure for GM. Rather, it is the way in which the cars are built and marketed that is innovative. A primary goal was to create a culture in which employees have a sense of ownership over the functions they perform and a better understanding and bigger picture of the business. Tasks traditionally performed by management are performed by assembly workers. Extensively trained self-managed work teams assemble the cars, maintain their own equipment, order supplies, set work schedules, and even select new team members. In addition, a consensus-based decision-making process involves employees in decisions that affect them. Each team must feel 70 percent comfortable with a decision.

To control quality and reduce transport costs, much subassembly is done by suppliers that are located close to the plant or even within the plant itself, thus fostering a close cooperative arrangement. Parts that do come in from the outside are delivered precisely when they are needed and directly to the location where they are used in assembly. In the marketing domain, dealers are given more exclusive territories than is typical of North American auto manufacturers. As long as they meet stiff requirements in several key areas, they are given substantial autonomy to tailor their operations to local needs.

These changes in manufacturing and marketing are supported by a number of departures from conventional structure, management style, and labour relations practices. Saturn has a flatter management structure than the traditional GM divisions. A computerized "paperless" operation of e-mail and a single, highly integrated database speed decisions and counter bureaucracy. Finally, GM agreed to a truly groundbreaking labour contract with the United Auto Workers. There are no time clocks, and workers are on salaries, although these salaries average less than industry hourly wages. In addition, restrictive work rules were eliminated to support the team assembly concept. In exchange for these concessions, GM devotes a percentage of the industry hourly wage to performance incentives and a profit sharing plan for Saturn workers. Also, 80 percent of the workforce is granted what amounts to lifetime employment security. Union representatives sit on planning and organizing committees.

Has Saturn fulfilled the promise of its multibillion-dollar investment? Early cars suffered from quality glitches that the company attended to quickly, even replacing some faulty cars for free. As a result of such tactics and extremely cooperative dealers (many of whom organize customer picnics and car clinics), intense customer loyalty resulted in Saturn turning a profit three years after the first car rolled off the assembly line. However, the company has been in the red most years and has not recouped the initial investment. Many observers have noted the failure of other parts of GM to embrace the Saturn innovations. The United Auto Workers have consistently resisted Saturn-type labour agreements at any other manufacturing sites. Saturn has been slow to develop new models, and competitors are outpacing the company in terms of technical refinement and safety, even copying some of its "buyer-friendly" sales techniques. Although Saturn buyers have good demographics in terms of income and education, the company has been slow to develop larger sedans, minivans, and sport utility vehicles to offer them. Gaining investment funds for such projects from GM has been difficult because the parent firm has been busy recentralizing much vehicle development and engineering.

Four years after its start-up, Saturn became part of the GM Small Car Group. This required Saturn leadership to work even harder to ensure the spirit of the Saturn partnership remained strong. Even though organizational and market changes challenged Saturn's unique culture, the original memorandum of agreement between Saturn and its workers was renewed in late 1999.

In recent years, Saturn has been rebuilding its aging product line. In a long-awaited move, it finally introduced a sport utility vehicle, marking the first expansion in the division's history beyond its coupes, sedans, and station wagons, sending a signal that Saturn is now in the truck business. In December of 2001, the new Vue sport utility vehicle was unveiled followed by a complete restyling of its mid-sized L-Series. In 2002, Saturn unveiled the Ion to replace the S-Series, the car that first launched Saturn more than thirteen years ago, and in 2003 unveiled the Relay minivan. In addition, GM recently opened its first new assembly plant in 15 years. The new Lansing Grand River plant has been designed to improve efficiency and to create a worker-friendly environment and features a new manufacturing system. However, in 2004, GM absorbed Saturn into its companywide Global Manufacturing System. Saturn workers now have the same contract as the rest of GM's workforce.

In November of 2005, General Motors announced that it would be eliminating 5000 more jobs in addition to 25 000 previously announced cuts and would be closing all or part of a dozen plants. This time, however, even Saturn was not to be spared. What had once been the company's centrepiece of workplace innovation was now slated to lose one of its two production lines and as many as 1500 jobs. Production of the Ion compact will be shifted to another GM plant and the Saturn plant will make some non-Saturn vehicles. Why Saturn? According to a GM spokesman, "We really consider it to be another GM facility, just like any other."

Although it is not likely there will be any direct effort to transfer knowledge from the Saturn plant or any of the other facilities being closed, insiders say that Saturn's collaborative practices have already influenced the rest of GM.

Sources: Austen, I. (1999, March 26). Problem child. *Canadian Business*, 22–31; Bennet, J. (1994, March 29). Saturn, GM's big hope, is taking its first lumps. *New York Times*, A1, A12; Fisher, A.B. (1985, November 11). Behind the hype at GM's Saturn. *Fortune*, 34–49; Garsten, E. (2002, March 28). Saturn jazzes up small-car offerings. *Toronto Star*, C6; Keenan, G. (2002, February 6). GM driven to improve. *Globe and Mail*, C1; Staff. (1994, October 17). Will it work this time? *Autoweek*, 4–5; Taylor, A., III. (1988, August 1). Back to the future at Saturn. *Fortune*, 63–69; Treece, J.B. (1990, April 9). Here comes GM's Saturn. *Business Week*, 56–62; Vaughn, M. (1999, July 5). Smiling happy people. *Autoweek*, 20–21; Woodruff, J. (1992, August 17). Saturn. *Business Week*, 86–91; Kiger, P.J. (2005, December 12). Saturn plant's innovations live on at GM despite cutbacks. *Workforce Management, 84(14)*, 3–4; Solomon, C.M. (1991, June). Behind the wheel at Saturn. *Personnel Journal, 70(6)*, 72–74.

1. Discuss the role that environmental constraints and opportunities might have played in the creation of Saturn.

2. Apply the concepts of environmental uncertainty, resource dependence, and strategy to the Saturn case. To what extent does the strategy correspond to the constraints and opportunities of the environment?

3. Consider the relationship between the strategy and structure of the Saturn plant. What came first and how and why is the structure different from the rest of GM?

4. What strategic responses were used by Saturn to try to cope with environmental uncertainty? What other strategic responses might have been considered?

5. Describe the technology of Saturn in terms of Perrow's routineness, Thompson's interdependence, and Woodward's production processes.

6. Describe the relationship between structure and technology at Saturn. To what extent is there a match between structure and technology? What effect did technology have on structure and job design?

CHAPTER 16

Organizational Change, Development, and Innovation

SAMSUNG ELECTRONICS

Samsung Electronics is the world's most profitable high-tech company with over $55 billion in annual sales, and leads the global market for LCD panels, colour televisions, flash memory, and CDMA cell phones. Beyond Samsung brand products, chances are high that there are Samsung components in your favourite high-tech device, such as Apple's iPod, Microsoft's Xbox, Nokia's phone, or Sony's PlayStation portables.

What makes Samsung's success particularly remarkable is that less than fifteen years ago, the South Korean company's products were regarded as low-quality knockoffs, and the idea that the company could rival powerhouse Sony was almost laughable. This point was painfully understood by Samsung's chairman Kun-Hee Lee, who experienced two eye-opening episodes in the mid-1990s. In 1993, Lee visited a small electronics retailer in Los Angeles and found that his company's products were ignored by salespeople and gathering dust on the back shelves or in the discount bins. In 1995, to celebrate a profitable year, Lee gave Samsung mobile phones to friends and key workers. Unfortunately, the phones were defective and Lee received complaints. Embarrassed, he ordered the entire inventory of the company's leading factory, amounting to 150 000 wireless handsets, cordless phones, and fax machines, to be destroyed with hammers and thrown into a giant bonfire. Lee knew that radical change was needed if Samsung was ever to become a world leader.

Lee's vision was to transform Samsung from a company focused on quantity and out-selling competitors through low prices into a company in which quality and innovation would be the top priorities. Following his disappointing visit to the electronics store in LA, Lee had his design adviser assess Samsung's positions. The conclusion, which was also reached by outside consultants, was that Samsung lacked a design identity, had primitive product development, and tended to focus on imitating leaders such as Sony and IBM—middle and top managers cared nothing for design. In fact, managers were so internally competitive and focused

SAMSUNG in the World

Tokyo

London

SAMSUNG HongKong

SAMSUNG

Budweiser

BURGER KI

on sales volume that they kept ideas to themselves, rarely took risks, and created an environment where collaboration was almost nonexistent. Samsung had an R&D unit since 1987, but the unit was stymied by its uncomfortable relationship with the business units and the company's lack of emphasis on innovation.

Samsung Electronics
www.samsung.com

How did Samsung transform itself from a maker of cheap, low-quality products to arguably the most innovative high-tech manufacturer in the world? Through a combination of strong leadership, organizational restructuring, a focus on learning, and cultural transformation. Chairman Lee began by issuing a manifesto to Samsung's top executives in 1996 stating that quality must become the top priority and that the company must radically change. In a decree that is still talked about at Samsung today, Lee implored workers to "change everything except your wife and family." He also ordered every Samsung employee to henceforth report to work two hours early in a move to break old work habits. Samsung's corporate R&D centre—Samsung Advanced Institute of Technology (SAIT)—altered its organizational structure from a business-unit focus to research laboratories around major research fields, focusing on long-term projects as opposed to short-term development-oriented efforts. SAIT also invested in continuous improvement and implemented total quality processes. As a result, SAIT is now a central part of Samsung compared to its peripheral status in the late 1980s.

Lee also created new facilities aimed not only at fostering innovation, but altering the corporate mindset characterized by imitation, hypercompetitiveness, and resistance to change. Samsung built a $10 million state-of-the-art facility in downtown Seoul to house the Innovation Design Lab of Samsung (IDS) and brought in consultants from California's Art Center College of Design to make IDS a top-notch in-house design school. The curriculum was aimed as much at fostering a collaborative work environ-ment among Samsung designers as creating technical excellence. In addition to the requirement that designers take a year-long course in mechanical engineering, up-and-coming engineers and managers from other disciplines were brought into IDS to forge collaborative working relationships. Breaking the Korean practice of education through memorization, students at IDS learn by doing. IDS also launched the Global Design Workshop in which a few dozen students visit the world's great design cen-tres—Athens, Delhi, Florence, Paris, London, Berlin, New York—in a sort of travelling tutorial. Samsung also began sending its most promising designers to study at the world's top universities and institutions.

Samsung also created the VIP Center, which stands for Value Innovation Program, where Samsung's top researchers, engineers, and designers come together to solve the company's toughest problems. The setup consists of locating everyone who is working on a project in the same room in order to foster communication and facilitate fast decision making. At the new Samsung, recruiting top individuals has also become key. Task forces have been used to define and create Samsung's new corporate culture, focusing on quality, collaboration, and innovation, while integrating the traditional Korean cultural character of balancing reason with feeling.

The results of the corporate change initiative started by Chairman Lee speak for them-selves. In addition to the billions in sales and profits, Samsung has won more awards from the Industrial Designers Society of America over the last five years than any other corporation on the planet. Even Sony, the company that Samsung used to strive to imitate, turned to Samsung to help develop its flat-panel TV. Not bad for a company whose wares were regarded as cheap, toy-like knockoffs in the not too distant past.[1]

This story reflects some key themes of our chapter. Samsung implemented radical change in business strategy and organizational culture to foster innovation. In this chapter, we will discuss the concept of organizational change, including the whys and whats of change. Then, we will consider the process by which change occurs and examine problems involved in managing change. Following this, we will define orga-nizational development and explore several development strategies as well as innova-tion, a special class of organizational change.

THE CONCEPT OF ORGANIZATIONAL CHANGE

Common experience indicates that organizations are far from static. Our favourite small restaurant experiences success and expands. We return for a visit to our alma mater and observe a variety of new programs and new buildings. The local Chevy dealer begins to sell Korean-built Aveos. As consumers, we are aware that such changes may have a profound impact on our satisfaction with the product or service offered. By extension, we can also imagine that these changes have a strong impact on the people who work at the restaurant, university, or car dealership. In and of themselves, such changes are neither good nor bad. Rather, it is the way in which the changes are *implemented* and *managed* that is crucial to both customers and members. This is the focus of the present chapter.

Why Organizations Must Change

All organizations face two basic sources of pressure to change—external sources and internal sources.

In Chapter 15, we pointed out that organizations are open systems that take inputs from the environment, transform some of these inputs, and send them back into the environment as outputs. Organizations work hard to stabilize their inputs and outputs. For example, a manufacturing firm might use a variety of suppliers to avoid a shortage of raw materials and attempt to turn out quality products to ensure demand. However, there are limits on the extent to which such control over the environment can occur. In this case, environmental changes must be matched by organizational changes, if the organization is to remain effective. For example, consider the successful producer of record turntables in 1970. In only a few years, the turntable market virtually disappeared with the advent of reasonably priced cassette and CD players. Now, downloaded music is commonplace. Firms unable to anticipate or cope with such trends will cease to exist, a point recognized by Samsung's Kun-Hee Lee.

Probably the best recent example of the impact of the external environment in stimulating organizational change is the increased competitiveness of business. Brought on, in part, by a more global economy, deregulation, and advanced technology, businesses have had to become, as the cliché goes, leaner and meaner. Companies such as IBM and GM have laid off thousands of employees. Many firms did away with layers of middle managers, developing flatter structures that are more responsive to competitive demands. Mergers, acquisitions, and joint ventures with foreign firms have become commonplace, as have less adversarial relationships with unions and suppliers. For another example of how the external environment has prompted change, see "Applied Focus: *Business School Rankings Prompt Big Changes.*"

Change can also be provoked by forces in the internal environment of the organization. Low productivity, conflict, strikes, sabotage, and high absenteeism and turnover are some of the factors that signal that change is necessary. Employee opinion can also be a force for change. For example, about 2000 Microsoft employees publish online blogs, a number of which are critical of the firm's business strategy and share price.[2] Very often, internal forces for change occur in response to organizational changes that are designed to deal with the external environment. Thus, many mergers and acquisitions that were to bolster the competitiveness of an organization have been followed by cultural conflict between the merged parties. This conflict often stimulates further changes that were not anticipated at the time of the merger.

Microsoft
www.microsoft.com

A word should be said about the perception of threat and change. Sometimes, when threat is perceived, organizations "unfreeze" (see below), scan the environment for solutions, and use the threat as a motivator for change. Other times, though, organizations seem paralyzed by threat, behave rigidly, and exhibit extreme inertia. Change almost always entails some investment of resources, be it money or management time. Also, it almost always requires some modification of routines and processes.[3] If either of these prerequisites is missing, inertia will occur. For example, one of your authors observed a university program threatened by low enrolment. The involved faculty spent many hours ostensibly revising the curriculum. However, the revised curriculum looked much like the old curriculum. Here, resources were invested, but the routines of teaching were not modified to counter the threat.

In spite of trends toward change, the internal and external environments of various organizations will be more or less dynamic. In responding to this, organizations should differ in the amount of change they display. Exhibit 16.1 shows that organizations in a dynamic environment must generally show more change to be effective than those operating in a more stable environment. Also, change in and of itself is not a good

APPLIED FOCUS

Business School Rankings Prompt Big Changes

In 1988, *Business Week* published the first ranking of university business schools. In short order, this ranking, which was to become a yearly fixture, spawned other such rankings, using various criteria, and expanded the purview to include Canada, Europe, and Asia. These include rankings found in *U.S. News & World Report* and the *Financial Times*, among others. Although methodologies vary, most centre on evaluations of the business schools by graduates and corporate recruiters and concentrate on MBA programs.

The rankings, despite being viewed by many as rather arbitrary, have had a profound effect on the strategy and management of business schools, representing one of the most salient forces for change in higher education. This is because the rankings signal an incredibly valuable resource—reputation. This reputation attracts the best faculty and students, who attract the most ardent recruiters, who in turn supply the best jobs. In short, the rankings have created incredible competition among business schools for students and faculty, and not just between Harvard and Stanford, perennially high on the list. Even schools with more modest resources can claim to be in the top 50 or the best in their region.

Dennis Gioia and Kevin Corley summarize the changes that the business school rankings have occasioned, many of which they are less than enthusiastic about. In their words, the pursuit of resources has replaced the pursuit of knowledge, and short-term image and brand management have often replaced long-term substance. For instance, some rankings take into account the average Graduate Management Admission Test (GMAT) score of incoming classes. By increasing the weight of this admission criterion to keep the average up, the diversity of the student body is reduced. Because it is MBA programs that feature in the rankings, Gioia and Corley contend that various resources, including the best teachers, are often diverted from the much larger undergraduate programs. Many programs engage in curriculum changes just to convey the image that their product is new and improved. Because surveys of graduates are a critical component of the rankings, some schools are excessively customer focused, designing the curriculum by student popularity rather than needed knowledge.

Gioia and Corley do note a couple of positive changes occasioned by the rankings game. For one thing, it has forced business schools to pay more attention to emergent business practices, such as the use of teams. Also, it has put more emphasis on hiring professors who are good teachers in addition to being promising researchers.

Luis Martins examined why business schools changed or did not change in light of the rankings. He found that when a school's ranking was discrepant with the perception of the school's identity held by the school's administrators, change was most likely to occur. Views about the validity of the rankings did not affect the tendency to make changes. However, views about the strategic impact of the rankings (i.e., their image factor) did. Schools with strong identities saw themselves as unique and were less likely to be swayed by the rankings, thus pursuing a niche strategy.

Sources: Gioia, D.A., & Corley, K.G. (2002, September). Being good versus looking good: Business school rankings and the Circean transformation from substance to image. *Academy of Management Learning and Education*, 107–120; Martins, L.L. (2005). A model of the effects of reputational rankings on organizational change. *Organization Science, 16*, 701–720.

thing, and organizations can exhibit too much change as well as too little. The company that is in constant flux fails to establish the regular patterns of organizational behaviour that are necessary for effectiveness, and employees become cynical about the competence of management.

What Organizations Can Change

In theory, organizations can change just about any aspect of their operations. Since *change* is a broad concept, it is useful to identify several specific domains in which modifications can occur. Of course, the choice of *what* to change depends on a well-informed analysis of the internal and external forces signalling that change is necessary.[4] Factors that can be changed include:

EXHIBIT 16.1
Relationships among environmental change, organizational change, and organizational effectiveness.

- *Goals and strategies.* Organizations frequently change their goals and the strategies they use to reach these goals. Expansion, the introduction of new products, and the pursuit of new markets represent such changes. Samsung changed its strategy from producing low cost, imitative products to pursuing quality, collaboration, and innovation.

- *Technology.* Technological changes can vary from minor to major. The introduction of online portal access for employees is a fairly minor change. Moving from a rigid assembly line to flexible manufacturing is a major change.

- *Job design.* Companies can redesign individual groups of jobs to offer more or less variety, autonomy, identity, significance, and feedback, as we discussed in Chapter 6.

- *Structure.* Organizations can be modified from a functional to a product form or vice versa. Formalization and centralization can be manipulated, as can tallness, spans of control, and networking with other firms. Structural changes also include modifications in rules, policies, and procedures.

- *Processes.* The basic processes by which work is accomplished can be changed. For instance, some stages of a project might be done concurrently rather than sequentially.

- *Culture.* As we discussed in Chapter 8, organizational culture refers to the shared beliefs, values, and assumptions that exist in an organization. An organization's culture has a strong influence on the attitudes and behaviours of organizational members. As a result, one of the most important changes that an organization can make is to change its culture. In fact, culture change is so critical that the main reason reported for the failure of organizational change programs is the failure to change an organization's culture. In addition, because organizational culture is known to be a major factor in providing an organization with a competitive advantage and long-term effectiveness, changing an organization's culture is considered to be a fundamental aspect of organizational change.[5] At Samsung, an inward-focused culture was replaced by one that stressed the firm's identity as a design leader in the external marketplace.

- *People.* The membership of an organization can be changed in two senses. First, the actual *content* of the membership can be changed through a revised hiring process. This is often done to introduce "new blood" or to take advantage of the opportunities that a more diverse labour pool offers. Second, the existing membership can be changed in terms of skills and attitudes by various training and development methods. Thus, Samsung recruits bright personnel from a broad array of disciplines but also sends existing employees to the world's best universities.

Three important points should be made about the various areas in which organizations can introduce change. First, a change in one area very often calls for changes in others. Failure to recognize this systemic nature of change can lead to severe problems. For example, consider the functionally organized East Coast chemical firm that decides to expand its operations to the West Coast. To be effective, this goal and strategy change might require some major structural changes, including a more geographic form and decentralization of decision-making power.

Second, changes in goals, strategies, technology, structure, process, job design, and culture almost always require that organizations give serious attention to people changes. As much as possible, necessary skills and favourable attitudes should be fostered *before* these changes are introduced. For example, although providing bank employees with a revised IT system is a fairly minor technological change, it might provoke anxiety on the part of those whose jobs are affected. Adequate technical training and clear, open communication about the change can do much to alleviate this anxiety.

Third, as indicated above, change requires employees to learn new skills and change their attitudes. However, for people to learn, organizations must also learn. After all, how can an organization change and improve itself without first learning something new? Without learning, neither individuals nor organizations can change, and both will simply repeat old practices and ways of doing things. In fact, many change programs fail because of the absence of learning.[6] But just what is organizational learning?

The Learning Organization

Organizational learning refers to the process through which organizations acquire, develop, and transfer knowledge throughout the organization. There are two primary methods of organizational learning. First, organizations learn through *knowledge acquisition*. This involves the acquisition, distribution, and interpretation of knowledge that already exists but which is external to the organization. Second, organizations also learn through *knowledge development*. This involves the development of new knowledge that occurs in an organization primarily through dialogue and experience. Organizational learning occurs when organizational members interact and share experiences and knowledge, and through the distribution of new knowledge and information throughout the organization.[7]

Some organizations are better at learning than others because they have processes and systems in place to facilitate learning and the transfer of knowledge throughout the organization. These kinds of organizations are known as learning organizations. A **learning organization** is an organization that has systems and processes for creating, acquiring, and transferring knowledge to modify and change its behaviour to reflect new knowledge and insights.[8] As a result, organizational change is much more likely to occur in a learning organization. In fact, it has even been suggested that a learning organization is "an organization that is adaptive in its capacity for change."[9]

There are four key dimensions that are critical for a learning organization:[10]

- *Vision/support.* Leaders must communicate a clear vision of the organization's strategy and goals in which learning is a critical part and key to organizational success.

- *Culture.* A learning organization has a culture that supports learning. Knowledge and information sharing, risk taking, and experimentation are supported, and continuous learning is considered to be a regular part of organizational life and the responsibility of everybody in the organization.

- *Learning systems/dynamics.* Employees are challenged to think, solve problems, make decisions, and act according to a systems approach by considering patterns of interdependencies and by "learning by doing," just like at the Samsung Innovation Design Lab. Managers must be active in coaching, mentoring, and facilitating learning.

Organizational learning. The process through which an organization acquires, develops, and transfers knowledge throughout the organization.

Learning organization. An organization that has systems and processes for creating, acquiring, and transferring knowledge to modify and change its behaviour to reflect new knowledge and insights.

- *Knowledge management/infrastructure.* Learning organizations have established systems and structures to acquire, code, store, and distribute important information and knowledge so that it is available to those who need it, when they need it. This requires the integration of people, processes, and technology.

Research by the Conference Board of Canada indicates that not very many Canadian organizations consider themselves to be learning organizations. In fact, the average organization-respondent rated itself as "somewhat" of a learning organization, and only 15 percent rated themselves "highly" as learning organizations. Approximately 30 percent of the respondents rated their organizations as very low. The research also showed that learning organizations are almost 50 percent more likely to have higher overall levels of profitability than those organizations not rated as learning organizations, and they are also better able to retain essential employees.[11] Another study also found a positive relationship between learning organization practices and a firm's financial performance.[12]

Some companies, like BMO Financial Group (formerly Bank of Montreal), have realized the strategic importance of learning and the link between learning and achieving business objectives; as such, they have created systems and processes to facilitate both. In 1994, the bank invested in the construction of the Institute for Learning, which continues to serve as the organization's strategic learning base and a tangible symbol of BMO's commitment to life-long learning. The Institute serves as an agent of strategic and cultural alignment by providing individuals and teams with opportunities to acquire corporate knowledge and perspective through the learning process, both in a centralized classroom and through distributed learning at or near the employee's work site, thereby increasing access to relevant learning.[13]

Learning organizations are better able to change and transform themselves because of their greater capacity for acquiring and transferring knowledge. Thus, learning is an important prerequisite for organizational change and transformation. Let's now consider the change process.

BMO Financial Group's Institute for Learning serves as the organization's strategic learning base and is a tangible symbol of the company's commitment to life-long learning.

Bank of Montreal
www.bmo.com

The Change Process

By definition, change involves a sequence of organizational events or a psychological process that occurs over time. The distinguished psychologist Kurt Lewin has suggested that this sequence or process involves three basic stages—unfreezing, changing, and refreezing.[14]

Unfreezing. Unfreezing occurs when recognition exists that some current state of affairs is unsatisfactory. This might involve the realization that the present structure, task design, or technology is ineffective, or that member skills or attitudes are inappropriate. *Crises* are especially likely to stimulate unfreezing. A dramatic drop in sales, a big lawsuit, or an unexpected strike are examples of such crises. Unfreezing at Ontario Power Generation occurred when Ontario's new government fired the company's top three executives who were responsible for massive cost overruns in the rebuilding of the Pickering nuclear generating station. Talk about getting people's attention! A visit to Honda's American motorcycle plant by Harley-Davidson executives shocked them. The plant's great efficiency was obtained without extensive information technology and with very few support staff. Of course, unfreezing can also occur without crisis. Employee attitude surveys, customer surveys, and accounting data are often used to anticipate problems and to initiate change before crises are reached. At Samsung, Mr. Lee's telephone bonfire was a dramatic unfreezing ploy meant to signal crisis.

Unfreezing. The recognition that some current state of affairs is unsatisfactory.

Change. Change occurs when some program or plan is implemented to move the organization or its members to a more satisfactory state. The terms *program* and *plan* are used rather loosely here, since some change efforts reveal inadequate planning. Change

Change. The implementation of a program or plan to move the organization or its members to a more satisfactory state.

efforts can range from minor to major. A simple skills training program and a revised hiring procedure constitute fairly minor changes in which few organizational members are involved. Conversely, major changes that involve many members might include extensive job enrichment, radical restructuring, or serious attempts at empowering the workforce.

Refreezing. When changes occur, the newly developed behaviours, attitudes, or structures must be subjected to **refreezing**—that is, they must become an enduring part of the organization. At this point, the effectiveness of the change can be examined, and the desirability of extending the change further can be considered. It should be emphasized that refreezing is a relative and temporary state of affairs.

Refreezing. The condition that exists when newly developed behaviours, attitudes, or structures become an enduring part of the organization.

ISSUES IN THE CHANGE PROCESS

The simple sketch of the change process presented in the preceding section ignores several important issues that organizations must confront during the process. These issues represent problems that must be overcome if the process is to be effective. Exhibit 16.2 illustrates the relationship between the stages of change and these problems, which include diagnosis, resistance, evaluation, and institutionalization.

EXHIBIT 16.2
The change process and change problems.

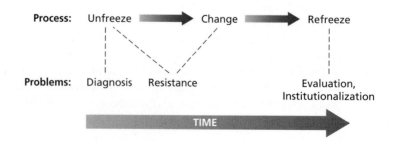

Diagnosis

Diagnosis is the systematic collection of information relevant to impending organizational change. Initial diagnosis can provide information that contributes to unfreezing by showing that a problem exists. Once unfreezing occurs, further diagnosis can clarify the problem and suggest just what changes should be implemented. It is one thing to feel that "hospital morale has fallen drastically," but quite another to be sure that this is true and to decide what to do about it.

Relatively routine diagnosis might be handled through existing channels. For example, suppose the director of a hospital laboratory believes that many of his lab technicians do not possess adequate technical skills. In conjunction with the hospital human resources manager, the director might arrange for a formal test of these skills. The hospital could devise a training program to correct inadequacies and establish a more stringent selection program to hire better personnel.

For more complex, nonroutine problems, there is considerable merit in seeking out the diagnostic skills of a change agent. **Change agents** are experts in the application of behavioural science knowledge to organizational diagnosis and change. Some large firms have in-house change agents who are available for consultation. In other cases, outside consultants might be brought in. In any event, the change agent brings an independent, objective perspective to the diagnosis while working with the people who are about to undergo change.

It is possible to obtain diagnostic information through a combination of observations, interviews, questionnaires, and the scrutiny of records. Attention to the views of customers or clients is critical. As the next section will show, there is usually considerable merit in using questionnaires and interviews to involve the intended targets of change in the diagnostic process. The next section will also show why the change agent must be perceived as *trustworthy* by his or her clients.

The importance of careful diagnosis cannot be overemphasized. Proper diagnosis clarifies the problem and suggests *what* should be changed and the proper *strategy* for implementing change without resistance.[15] Unfortunately, many firms imitate the change programs of their competitors or other visible firms without doing a careful diagnosis of their own specific needs. A symptom of this is buying some pre-packaged intervention from a consulting firm. Similarly, managers sometimes confuse symptoms with underlying problems. This usually leads to trouble.

Diagnosis. The systematic collection of information relevant to impending organizational change.

Change agents. Experts in the application of behavioural science knowledge to organizational diagnosis and change.

Resistance

As the saying goes, people are creatures of habit, and change is frequently resisted by those at whom it is targeted. More precisely, people may resist both unfreezing and change. At the unfreezing stage, defence mechanisms (Chapter 13) might be activated to deny or rationalize the signals that change is needed. Even if there is agreement that change is necessary, any specific plan for change might be resisted.

When Carly Fiorina became CEO of Hewlett-Packard, there was a great deal of resistance to her plans for change. Although managers and employees did not openly attack her ideas, if they did not like what they heard they would simply ignore it. The resistance was subtle and pervasive.[16] However, when she announced plans to merge with Compaq Computer, she was met with fierce resistance from the founder's families, shareholders, and employees. Many employees were concerned that the changes she was making would destroy the company's cherished culture.

Hewlett-Packard
www.hp.com

Causes of Resistance. **Resistance** to change occurs when people either overtly or covertly fail to support the change effort. Why does such failure of support occur? Several common reasons include the following:[17]

- *Politics and self-interest.* People might feel that they personally will lose status, power, or even their jobs with the advent of the change. For example, individual

Resistance. Overt or covert failure by organizational members to support a change effort.

departments will lose power and autonomy when a flat and decentralized structure is centralized and made more hierarchical.

- *Low individual tolerance for change.* Predispositions in personality might make some people uncomfortable with changes in established routines.

- *Misunderstanding.* The reason for the change or the exact course that the change will take might be misunderstood.

- *Lack of trust.* People might clearly understand the arguments being made for change, but not trust the motives of those proposing the change.

- *Different assessments of the situation.* The targets of change might sincerely feel that the situation does not warrant the proposed change and that the advocates of change have misread the situation. At UPS, managers saw the introduction of scanning bar-coded packages as a way to help customers trace goods. Employees saw it as a way to track them and spy on them.[18]

- *A resistant organizational culture.* Some organizational cultures have especially stressed and rewarded stability and tradition. Advocates of change in such cultures are viewed as misguided deviants or aberrant outsiders. When deregulation forced massive changes at AT&T, the resistant traditionalists were labelled "bellheads" by the new guard![19]

UPS
www.ups.com

Underlying these various reasons for resistance are two major themes: (1) change is unnecessary because there is only a small gap between the organization's current identity and its ideal identity; and (2) change is unobtainable (and threatening) because the gap between the current and ideal identities is too large. Exhibit 16.3 shows that a moderate identity gap is probably most conducive to increased acceptance of change because it unfreezes people while not provoking maximum resistance.[20]

Dealing with Resistance. Low tolerance for change is mainly an individual matter, and it can often be overcome with supportive, patient supervision.

If politics and self-interest are at the root of resistance, it might be possible to co-opt the reluctant by giving them a special, desirable role in the change process or by negotiating special incentives for change. For example, consider office computing. Many IT directors resisted the proliferation of personal computers, feeling that this change would reduce their power as departments moved away from dependence on the mainframe. Some organizations countered this resistance by giving IT control over the purchase, maintenance, and networking of personal computers, providing an incentive for change.

EXHIBIT 16.3
Probability of acceptance of change.

Source: Reger, R.K., Gustafson, L.T., DeMarie, S.M., & Mullane, J.V. (1994). Reframing the organization: Why implementing total quality is easier said than done. *Academy of Management Review, 19,* 565–584.

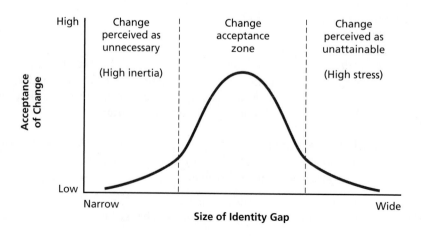

If misunderstanding, lack of trust, or different assessments are provoking resistance, good communication can pay off. Contemporary organizations are learning that obsessive secrecy about strategy and competition can have more internal costs than external benefits. It is particularly critical that lower-level managers understand the diagnosis underlying intended change and the details of the change so that they can convey this information to employees accurately. Springing "secret" changes on employees, especially when these changes involve matters such as workforce reduction, is sure to provoke resistance.

Involving the people who are the targets of change in the change process often reduces their resistance.[21] This is especially appropriate when there is adequate time for participation, when true commitment ("ownership") to the change is critical, and when the people who will be affected by the change have unique knowledge to offer.

Finally, transformational leaders (Chapter 9) are particularly adept at overcoming resistance to change. One way they accomplish this is by "striking while the iron is hot"—that is, by being especially sensitive to when followers are *ready* for change. The other way is to unfreeze current thinking by installing practices that constantly examine and question the status quo. One research study of CEOs who were transformational leaders noted the following unfreezing practices:[22]

- An atmosphere is established in which dissent is not only tolerated but encouraged. Proposals and ideas are given tough objective reviews, and disagreement is not viewed as disloyalty.

- The environment is scanned for objective information about the organization's true performance. This might involve putting lots of outsiders on the board of directors or sending technical types out to meet customers.

- Organizational members are sent to other organizations and even other countries to see how things are done elsewhere.

- The organization compares itself along a wide range of criteria *against the competition,* rather than simply comparing its performance against last year's. This avoids complacency.

Transformational leaders are skilled at using the new ideas that stem from these practices to create a revised vision for followers about what the organization can do or be. Often, a radically reshaped culture is the result. In the process, as we suggested in Chapter 9, transformational leaders are good at inspiring trust and encouraging followers to subordinate their individual self-interests for the good of the organization. They are also adept at countering employee cynicism so that the proposed change is not seen as the new "flavour of the month."[23] This combination of tactics keeps followers within the zone of acceptance shown in Exhibit 16.3.

Evaluation and Institutionalization

It seems only reasonable to evaluate changes to determine whether they accomplished what they were supposed to and whether that accomplishment is now considered adequate. Obviously, objective goals, such as return on investment or market share, might be easiest and most likely to be evaluated. Of course, organizational politics can intrude to cloud even the most objective evaluation.

Organizations are notorious for doing a weak job of evaluating "soft" change programs that involve skills, attitudes, and values. However, it is possible to do a thorough evaluation by considering a range of variables:

- Reactions—did participants like the change program?
- Learning—what knowledge was acquired in the program?
- Behaviour—what changes in job behaviour occurred?
- Outcomes—what changes in productivity, absence, etc. occurred?[24]

To some extent, reactions measure resistance, learning reflects change, and behaviour reflects successful refreezing. Outcomes indicate whether refreezing is useful for the organization. Unfortunately, many evaluations of change efforts never go beyond the measurement of reactions. Again, part of the reason for this may be political. The people who propose the change effort fear reprisal if failure occurs.

If the outcome of change is evaluated favourably, the organization will wish to institutionalize that change. This means that the change becomes a permanent part of the organizational system, a social fact that persists over time, despite possible turnover by the members who originally experienced the change.[25]

Logic suggests that it should be fairly easy to institutionalize a change that has been deemed successful. However, we noted that many change efforts go unevaluated or are only weakly evaluated, and without hard proof of success it is very easy for institutionalization to be rejected by disaffected parties. This is a special problem for extensive, broad-based change programs that call for a large amount of commitment from a variety of parties (e.g., extensive participation, job enrichment, or work restructuring). It is one thing to institutionalize a simple training program, but quite another to do the same for complex interventions that can be judged from a variety of perspectives.

Studies of more complex change efforts indicate that a number of factors can inhibit institutionalization. For example, promised extrinsic rewards (such as pay bonuses) might not be developed to accompany changes. Similarly, initial changes might provide intrinsic rewards that create higher expectations that cannot be fulfilled. Institutionalization might also be damaged if new hires are not carefully socialized to understand the unique environment of the changed organization. As turnover occurs naturally, the change effort might backslide. In a similar vein, key management supporters of the change effort might resign or be transferred. Finally, environmental pressures, such as decreased sales or profits, can cause management to regress to more familiar behaviours and abandon change efforts.[26]

It stands to reason that many of the problems of evaluation and institutionalization can be overcome by careful planning and goal setting during the diagnostic stage. In fact, *planning* is a key issue in any change effort. Let's now examine organizational development, a means of effecting planned change. But first, please consult the You Be the Manager feature, *Knowledge Sharing at Siemens AG* on pages 564–565, which is concerned with fostering change to build a learning organization.

Siemens AG
www.siemens.com

ORGANIZATIONAL DEVELOPMENT: PLANNED ORGANIZATIONAL CHANGE

Organizational development (OD). A planned, ongoing effort to change organizations to be more effective and more human.

Organizational development (OD) is a planned, ongoing effort to change organizations to be more effective and more human. It uses the knowledge of behavioural science to foster a culture of organizational self-examination and readiness for change. A strong emphasis is placed on interpersonal and group processes.[27]

The fact that OD is *planned* distinguishes it from the haphazard, accidental, or routine changes that occur in all organizations. OD efforts tend to be *ongoing* in at least two senses. First, many OD programs extend over a long period of time, involving several distinct phases of activities. Second, if OD becomes institutionalized, continual re-examination and readiness for further change become permanent parts of the culture. In trying to make organizations more *effective* and more *human*, OD gives recognition to the critical link between personal processes, such as leadership, decision making, and communication, and organizational outcomes, such as productivity and efficiency. The fact that OD uses *behavioural science knowledge* distinguishes it from other change strategies that rely solely on principles of accounting, finance, or engineering. However, an OD intervention may also incorporate these principles. OD seeks to modify *cultural norms and roles* so that the organization remains self-conscious and prepared for adaptation. Finally, a focus on *interpersonal* and *group* processes recognizes that all organizational change affects members, and their cooperation is necessary to implement change.

To summarize the above, we can say that OD recognizes that systematic attitude change must accompany changes in behaviour, whether these behaviour changes are required by revisions in tasks, work processes, organizational structure, or business strategies.

Traditionally, the values and assumptions of OD change agents were decidedly humanistic and democratic. Thus, self-actualization, trust, cooperation, and the open expression of feelings among all organizational members have been viewed as desirable.[28] In recent years, OD practitioners have shown a more active concern with organizational effectiveness and with using development practices to further the strategy of the organization. This joint concern with both people and performance has thus become the credo of many contemporary OD change agents. The focus has shifted from simple humanistic advocacy to generating data or alternatives that allow organizational members to make informed choices.[29]

SOME SPECIFIC ORGANIZATIONAL DEVELOPMENT STRATEGIES

The organization that seeks to "develop itself" has recourse to a wide variety of specific techniques, and many have been used in combination. We discussed some of these techniques earlier in the book. For example, job enrichment and management by objectives (Chapter 6) are usually classed as OD efforts, as are diversity training (Chapter 3), self-managed and cross-functional teams (Chapter 7), and empowerment (Chapter 12). In this section, we will discuss four additional OD strategies that illustrate the diversity of the practice. Team building illustrates how work teams can be fine-tuned to work well together. Survey feedback shows how OD can be conceived of as an ongoing applied research effort. Total quality management shows how organizations can foster continuous improvement. Finally, reengineering illustrates the radical redesign of organizational processes. The first two methods are limited in scope and are often a part of other change efforts. The second two methods are broader in scope and lead to more sweeping organizational change.

Team Building

Team building attempts to increase the effectiveness of work teams by improving interpersonal processes, goal clarification, and role clarification.[30] (What is our team trying to accomplish, and who is responsible for what?) As such, it can facilitate communication and coordination. The term *team* can refer to intact work groups, special task forces, new work units, or people from various parts of an organization who must work together to achieve a common goal.

Team building usually begins with a diagnostic session, often held away from the workplace, in which the team explores its current level of functioning. The team might use several sources of data to accomplish its diagnosis. Some data might be generated through sensitivity training, outdoor "survival" exercises, or open-ended discussion sessions. In addition, "hard" data, such as attitude survey results and production figures, might be used. The goal at this stage is to paint a picture of the current strengths and weaknesses of the team. The ideal outcome of the diagnostic session is a list of needed changes to improve team functioning. Subsequent team-building sessions usually have a decidedly task-oriented slant—how can we actually implement the changes indicated by the diagnosis? Problem solving by subgroups might be used at this stage. Between the diagnostic and follow-up sessions, the change agent might hold confidential interviews with team members to anticipate implementation problems. Throughout, the change agent acts as a catalyst and resource person.

Team building. An effort to increase the effectiveness of work teams by improving interpersonal processes, goal clarification, and role clarification.

☞ YOU BE THE
Manager

Knowledge Sharing at Siemens AG

Siemens AG is a huge multinational electronics company based in Munich, employing over 460 000 people in 190 countries. The Siemens corporate structure is highly decentralized: Every unit is run by its own executive and has its own supervisory groups, regional and corporate units, and services.

Siemens' largest unit is Information and Communication Networks (ICN). In 1998, the telecommunications industry in Germany, its largest market, was deregulated, and ICN started a process to transform itself from simply a seller of telecommunications products to a global provider of custom solutions and services. Knowledge management had been an important part of Siemens' strategy for several years, but this deregulation forced the company to restructure so it could benefit from and improve the expertise of its employees.

ICN's president of group strategy, Joachim Döring, set out to design a system that would not only draw upon Siemens employees' explicit knowledge but effectively tap into their tacit knowledge as well. The system Döring ultimately came up with combines a knowledge library, a forum for urgent requests, community news bulletin boards, discussion groups for certain topics, and live chat rooms—all designed to put the collective knowledge and expertise of Siemens employees worldwide to work more efficiently. The new system was named ShareNet.

In July 1999, Döring ran an intensive training session involving 60 managers—from every country ICN operated in—to explain the new ShareNet system. He created a committee to take care of ShareNet's strategic direction. Its 11 members include a representative from ICN's board and two from ICN's Group Strategy board. He also appointed people excited by the knowledge-sharing concept to be ShareNet managers and represent their local region, promote the ShareNet system, supervise local use, and deal with urgent requests during the start-up.

Managers put a lot of energy and resources into convincing employees to contribute to and use ShareNet, but often to little effect. One of the people first chosen to manage ShareNet, Gerhard Hirschler, recalled that "there were always excuses. People said, 'I don't have the time to spend on this.' Others were reluctant to share. The network consultants, for example, said,

> **Electronic knowledge sharing proves to be difficult to implement at Siemens AG.**

'Sure, we have knowledge, but it's for sale, it's not for free.' Still others said 'Everyone has a certain clarity regarding their own projects in their heads, but it won't translate well for others.'"

To motivate people to make better use of ShareNet, Siemens created incentives such as cash bonuses and ShareNet "shares," which could be redeemed for various prizes. The ShareNet team realized, however, that for the system to really work, Siemens would need to fundamentally change its organizational culture from one with single business units working in a vertical hierarchy to one with a network of units capable of horizontal collaboration.

Such profound changes do not happen easily. As the cost of the ShareNet system rose to over 16 million euros, global knowledge sharing through the system did, indeed, begin to flow, but it was still not possible to tell whether all this would be money and effort well spent.

QUESTIONS

1. **How did Siemens' management diagnose the need for change and how can its transformation into a learning organization create value to the company?**

2. Identify some sources of resistance to change at Siemens and explain how the ShareNet team attempted to overcome them.

To see what Siemens did, check The Manager's Notebook at the end of the chapter.

Source: Voelpel, S.C., Dous, M., & Davenport, T.H. (2005, May). Five steps to creating a global knowledge-sharing system: Siemens' ShareNet. *Academy of Management Executive*, 9–23.

When team building is used to develop *new* work teams, the preliminary diagnostic session might involve attempts to clarify expected role relationships and additional training to build trust among team members. In subsequent sessions, the expected task environment might be simulated with role-playing exercises.

One company used this integrated approach to develop the management team of a new plant.[31] In the simulation portion of the development, typical problems encountered in opening a new plant were presented to team members via hypothetical in-basket memos and telephone calls. In role-playing the solutions to these problems, they reached agreement about how they would have to work together on the job and gained a clear understanding of each other's competencies. Plant start-ups were always problem laden, but this was the smoothest in the history of the company. Team building can also work to facilitate change. Harley-Davidson used it to introduce resistant middle managers to employee-involvement concepts.

Harley-Davidson
www.harley-davidson.com

Ideally, team building is a continuing process that involves regular diagnostic sessions and further development exercises as needed. This permits the team to anticipate new problems and to avoid the tendency to regress to less effective predevelopment habits.

Outdoor training programs are a popular method of team building in which team members participate in structured outdoor activities to improve their communication and coordination skills and learn how to work together as a team.

Survey Feedback

Survey feedback. The collection of data from organizational members and the provision of feedback about the results.

In bare-bones form, **survey feedback** involves collecting data from organizational members and feeding these data back to them in a series of meetings in which members explore and discuss the data.[32] The purpose of the meetings is to suggest or formulate changes that emerge from the data. In some respects, survey feedback is similar to team building. However, survey feedback places more emphasis on the collection of valid data and less emphasis on the interpersonal processes of specific work teams. Rather, it tends to focus on the relationship between organizational members and the larger organization.

As its name implies, survey feedback's basic data generally consist of either interviews or questionnaires completed by organizational members. Before data are collected, a number of critical decisions must be made by the change agent and organizational management. First, who should participate in the survey? Sometimes, especially in large organizations, the survey could be restricted to particular departments, jobs, or organizational levels where problems exist. However, most survey feedback efforts attempt to cover the entire organization. This approach recognizes the systemic nature of organizations and permits a comparison of survey results across various subunits.

Second, should questionnaires or interviews be used to gather data? The key issues here are coverage and cost. It is generally conceded that *all* members of a target group should be surveyed. This procedure builds trust and confidence in survey results. If the number of members is small, the change agent could conduct structured interviews with each person. Otherwise, cost considerations dictate the use of a questionnaire. In practice, this is the most typical data-gathering approach.

Finally, what questions should the survey ask? Two approaches are available. Some change agents use pre-packaged, standardized surveys, such as the University of Michigan Survey of Organizations.[33] This questionnaire covers areas such as communication and decision-making practices and employee satisfaction. Such questionnaires are usually carefully constructed and permit comparisons with other organizations in which the survey has been conducted. However, there is some danger that pre-packaged surveys might neglect critical areas for specific consideration and so many change agents choose to devise their own custom-tailored surveys.

Feedback seems to be most effective when it is presented to natural working units in face-to-face meetings. This method rules out presenting only written feedback or feedback that covers only the organization as a whole. In a manufacturing firm, a natural working unit might consist of a department, such as production or marketing. In a school district, such units might consist of individual schools. Many change agents prefer that the manager of the working unit conduct the feedback meeting. This demonstrates management commitment and acceptance of the data. The change agent attends such meetings and helps facilitate discussion of the data and plans for change.

IBM
www.ibm.com

IBM was one of the pioneers in employee surveys, beginning back in 1957. Given its business sector, it was also one of the first firms to use computerized surveying with integrated data collection and data processing, allowing for fast feedback. The company currently uses quarterly surveys of random samples of employees in 70 countries using 13 languages.[34] There are 25 core questions and 5 more tailored to local concerns. IBM benchmarks responses against those shared by a consortium of other world-class organizations as well as a similar IT industry consortium. The company has validated the links from employee job satisfaction to client satisfaction to business performance.

Ford Motor Company also has a comprehensive, yearly, worldwide employee attitude survey called Ford Pulse.[35] Fifty-five core questions that are linked to strategic issues are always completed by salaried employees. Supplemental questions are custom-developed to cover local issues. On average, around 65 000 employees in 50 countries respond online in 23 languages. Ford validated the importance of the Pulse results at 147 Ford Credit branches in Canada and the United States.[36] The results showed that branches with higher Pulse scores had higher customer satisfaction, market share, and business volume and lower loan delinquency and employee turnover. The top part of Exhibit 16.4 shows the association between several Pulse dimensions and customer satisfaction with the branch. The lower part shows the association between Pulse scores and market share. These kinds of bottom-line results go a long way toward enhancing the credibility of the survey to managers and underlining the importance of accountability for "people issues."

Ford Credit
www.fordcredit.com

Total Quality Management

Total quality management (TQM) is a systematic attempt to achieve continuous improvement in the quality of an organization's products or services. Typical characteristics of TQM programs include an obsession with customer satisfaction; a concern for good relations with suppliers; continuous improvement of work processes; the prevention of quality errors; frequent measurement and assessment; extensive training; and high employee involvement and teamwork.[37] TQM was one of the tactics Samsung used to improve its corporate performance.

Prominent names associated with the quality movement include W. Edwards Deming, Joseph Juran, and Philip Crosby.[38] Although each of these "quality gurus" advocates somewhat different paths to quality, all three are concerned with using teamwork to achieve continuous improvement to please customers. Exhibit 16.5 highlights the key principles underlying customer focus, continuous improvement, and teamwork. In turn, each of these principles is associated with certain practices and specific techniques that typify TQM.

Total quality management (TQM). A systematic attempt to achieve continuous improvement in the quality of an organization's products or services.

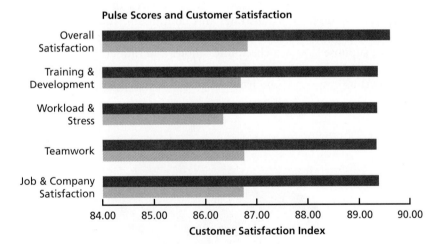

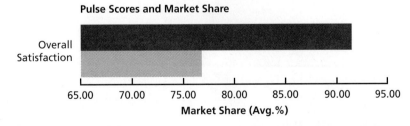

Top 25% Branches on Pulse

Bottom 25% Branches on Pulse

EXHIBIT 16.4
Relationship between Ford Pulse survey scores and customer satisfaction and market share at Ford Credit branches.

Source: Johnson, R.H., Ryan, A.M., & Schmit, M. (1994). *Employee attitudes and branch performance at Ford Motor Credit.* Presentation at the annual conference of the Society for Industrial and Organizational Psychology, Nashville, Tennessee.

	Customer Focus	Continuous Improvement	Teamwork
Principles	Paramount importance of providing products and services that fulfill customer needs; requires organizationwide focus on customers	Consistent customer satisfaction can be attained only through relentless improvement of processes that create products and services	Customer focus and continuous improvement are best achieved by collaboration throughout an organization as well as with customers and suppliers
Practices	Direct customer contact Collecting information about customer needs Using information to design and deliver products and services	Process analysis Reengineering Problem solving Plan/do/check/act	Search for arrangements that benefit all units involved in a process Formation of various types of teams Group skills training
Techniques	Customer surveys and focus groups Quality function deployment (translates customer information into product specifications)	Flowcharts Pareto analysis Statistical process control Fishbone diagrams	Organizational development methods such as the nominal group technique Team-building methods (e.g., role clarification and group feedback)

EXHIBIT 16.5

Principles, practices, and techniques of total quality management.

Source: Dean, J.W., Jr., & Bowen, D.E. (1994). Management theory and total quality: Improving research and practice through theory development. *Academy of Management Review, 19,* 392–418.

The concept of continuous improvement sometimes confuses students of TQM—how can something be more than 100 percent good? To clarify this, it is helpful to view improvement as a continuum ranging from responding to product or service problems (a reactive strategy) to creating new products or services that please customers (a proactive strategy). Exhibit 16.6 illustrates this continuum. Improvement can occur within each stage as well as between stages.[39]

For example, suppose that you check into a hotel and find no towels in your room. Obviously, a fast and friendly correction of this error is better than a slow and surly response, and cutting response time from 15 minutes to 5 minutes would be a great

EXHIBIT 16.6
A continuum of continuous improvement.

Source: Adapted from Kinlaw, D.C. (1992). *Continuous improvement and measurement for total quality: A team-based approach.* San Diego: Pfeiffer.

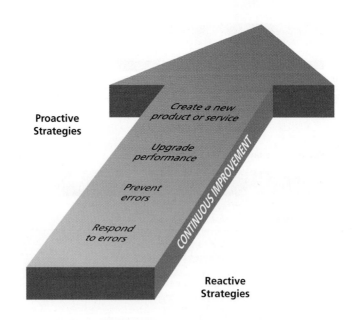

Proactive Strategies

Create a new product or service

Upgrade performance

Prevent errors

Respond to errors

CONTINUOUS IMPROVEMENT

Reactive Strategies

improvement. Better yet, management will try to prevent missing-towel episodes altogether, perhaps using training to move from 96 percent toward 100 percent error-free towel stocking. Although such error *prevention* is a hallmark of TQM, it is also possible to upgrade the service episode. For example, the hotel might work closely with suppliers to provide fluffier towels at the same price or encourage guests to not use too many towels, thus reducing laundry and room costs. Finally, a new service opportunity might be identified and acted on. For example, the Chicago Marriott hotel discovered (after 15 years of operation) that 66 percent of all guests' calls to the housekeeping department were requests for irons or ironing boards. The manager took funds earmarked to replace black-and-white bathroom TVs with colour sets and instead equipped each room with an iron and ironing board. No one had ever complained about black-and-white TVs in the bathroom.[40]

This series of hotel examples illustrates several features of the continuous improvement concept and TQM in general.[41] First, continuous improvement can come from small gains over time (e.g., gradually approaching 100 percent error-free room servicing) or from more radical innovation (e.g., offering a new service). In both cases, the goal is long-term improvement, not a short-term "fix." Next, improvement requires knowing where we are in the first place. Thus, TQM is very concerned with measurement and data collection—in our examples, we alluded to speed of service, percent of error-free performance, and frequency of customer requests as examples. Next, TQM stresses teamwork among employees and (in the examples given here) with suppliers and customers. Finally, TQM relies heavily on training to achieve continuous improvement.

Although simple job training can contribute to continuous improvement (as in the towel-stocking example), TQM is particularly known for using specialized training in tools that empower employees to diagnose and solve quality problems on an ongoing basis. Some tools, noted in the bottom row of Exhibit 16.5, include:

- *Flowcharts of work processes.* Flowcharts illustrate graphically the operations and steps in accomplishing some task, noting who does what, and when. For instance, what happens when hotel housekeeping receives a guest request for towels?

- *Pareto analysis.* Pareto analysis collects frequency data on the causes of errors and problems, showing where attention should be directed for maximum improvement. For instance, the Marriott data on reasons for calls to housekeeping corresponds to Pareto data.

- *Fishbone diagrams.* Fishbone (cause-and-effect) diagrams illustrate graphically the factors that could contribute to a particular quality problem. Very specific causes ("small bones") are divided into logical classes or groups ("large bones"). In the hotel example, classes of causes might include people, equipment, methods, and materials.

- *Statistical process control.* Statistical process control gives employees hard data about the quality of their own output that enables them to correct any deviations from standard. TQM places particular emphasis on reducing *variation* in performance over time.

These tools to improve the diagnosis and correction of quality problems will not have the desired impact if they fail to improve quality in the eyes of the customer. An essential problem here is that *quality* has many different and potentially incompatible definitions. For example, *ultimate excellence, value for the money, conformance to specifications,* or *meeting or exceeding customer expectations* are all potential definitions of quality.[42] Although this last definition would seem to be closest to the TQM principle of customer focus, it is not without its weaknesses. For example, customers might have contradictory expectations. Also, they are more likely to have clear expectations about familiar products and services than new or creative products or services. Nevertheless, organizations with a real commitment to TQM make heavy use of customer surveys, focus groups, mystery shoppers, and customer clinics to stay close to their customers. Harley-Davidson holds customer clinics and sponsors bike rallies to learn from its customers. Also, survey feedback programs allow organizations to obtain information about internal customers (such as how the adjacent department views your department's performance).

L.L.Bean
www.llbean.com

TQM programs reveal a large number of successes in firms such as L.L.Bean, Motorola, and Ritz-Carlton Hotels. However, they have also had their share of problems, all of which ultimately get expressed as resistance. Despite allowing for radical innovation, TQM is mainly about achieving small gains over a long period of time. This long-term focus can be hard to maintain, especially if managers or employees expect extreme improvements in the short term.

Finally, a number of organizations have implemented TQM programs at the same time that they were engaged in radical restructuring or downsizing (e.g., IBM, GM). Speaking generally, this is not a good recipe for the success of the TQM effort. Employees are likely to be insecure during such periods and unreceptive to calls for initiative and innovation.[43] Cynics may say, "The company cares about the customer more than it cares about me."

Despite these problems, the quality movement continues to be one of the most popular of the more elaborate OD efforts.

Reengineering

Reengineering. The radical redesign of organizational processes to achieve major improvements in factors such as time, cost, quality, or service.

Of all the forms of change that we are discussing in this chapter, reengineering is the most fundamental and radical. **Reengineering** is the radical redesign of organizational processes to achieve major improvements in factors such as time, cost, quality, or service.[44]

Reengineering does not fine-tune existing jobs, structures, technology, or human resources policies. Rather, it uses a "clean slate" approach that asks basic questions, such as "What business are we really in?" and "If we were creating this organization today, what would it look like?" Then, jobs, structure, technology, and policy are redesigned around the answers to these questions. Reengineering can be applied to an entire organization, but it can also be applied to a major function, such as research and development.

Organizational processes. Activities or work that have to be accomplished to create outputs that internal or external customers value.

A key word in our definition of reengineering is *processes*. Processes do not refer to job titles or organizational departments. Rather, **organizational processes** are *activities* or *work* that the organization must accomplish to create outputs that customers (internal or external) value.[45] For example, designing a new product is a process that might involve people holding a variety of jobs in several different departments (R&D, marketing, production, and finance). In theory, the gains from reengineering will be greatest when the process is complex and cuts across a number of jobs and departments.

We can contrast reengineering with TQM, in that TQM usually seeks incremental improvements in existing processes rather than radical revisions of processes. However, a TQM effort could certainly be part of a reengineering project.

What factors have prompted interest in reengineering? One factor is "creeping bureaucracy," which is especially common in large, established firms. With growth, rather than rethinking basic work processes, many firms have simply tacked on more bureaucratic controls to maintain order. This leads to overcomplicated processes and an internal focus on satisfying bureaucratic procedures rather than tending to the customer. Many corporate downsizings have been unsuccessful because they failed to confront bureaucratic controls and basic work processes.

New information technology has also stimulated reengineering. Many firms were disappointed that initial investments in information technology did not result in anticipated reductions in costs or improved productivity. This is because existing processes were simply automated rather than reengineered to correspond to the capabilities of the new technology. Now, it is commonly recognized that advanced technology allows organizations to radically modify (and usually radically simplify) important organizational processes. In other words, work is modified to fit technological capabilities rather than simply fitting the technology to existing jobs. At Ford Motor Company, for example, a look at the entire process for procuring supplies revealed great inefficiencies.[46] Ford employed a large accounts payable staff to issue payments to suppliers when it received invoices. Now, employees at the receiving dock can approve payment when the *goods* are received. Information technology enables them to tap a database to verify that the goods were ordered and issue a payment to the supplier. Needless to say, Ford has radically streamlined the payment process, and the accounts payable department now has fewer employees.

Ford Motor Company
www.ford.com

How does reengineering actually proceed? In essence, much reengineering is oriented toward one or both of the following goals:[47]

- The number of mediating steps in a process is reduced, making the process more efficient.
- Collaboration among the people involved in the process is enhanced.

Removing the number of mediating steps in a process, if done properly, reduces labour requirements, removes redundancies, decreases chances for errors, and speeds up the production of the final output. All of this happened with Ford's revision of its procurement process. Enhanced collaboration often permits simultaneous, rather than sequential, work on a process and reduces the chances for misunderstanding and conflict.

Some of the nitty-gritty aspects of reengineering include the following practices. You will notice that we have covered many of them in other contexts earlier in the book.[48]

- *Jobs are redesigned, and usually enriched.* Frequently, several jobs are combined into one to reduce mediating steps and provide greater employee control.
- *A strong emphasis is placed on teamwork.* Teamwork (especially cross-functional) is a potent method of enhancing collaboration.
- *Work is performed by the most logical people.* Some firms train customers to do minor maintenance and repairs themselves or turn over the management of some inventory to their suppliers.
- *Unnecessary checks and balances are removed.* When processes are simplified and employees are more collaborative, expensive and redundant controls can sometimes be removed.
- *Advanced technology is exploited.* Computerized technology not only permits combining of jobs, it also enhances collaboration via e-mail, groupware, and so on.

It is easiest to get a feel for the success of reengineering by considering some of the reductions in mediating steps and improvements in speed that have resulted. CTB Macmillan/McGraw-Hill, a publisher of standardized achievement tests, reduced the steps in its test scoring process from 154 to 68 and its turnaround time for scoring from 21 days to 5. Using software that allows clients to file electronic claims, Blue Cross of Washington and Alaska handled 17 percent more volume with a 12 percent smaller workforce and halved the time to handle a claim. Using cross-functional teams and advanced technology before its merger with Daimler-Benz, Chrysler cut the design time of its successful Jeep Cherokee from 5 years to 39 months.[49] Such "concurrent engineering" is now the norm. At popular clothing stores, fashions move from design to store in two months rather than the former two *seasons*. Thus, the firm is much more responsive to fickle swings in trends and taste. Computer technology, flatter structures, fewer "signoffs" on new ideas, and a sense of urgency on the part of management often play a role in such transformations.[50]

Reengineering is most extensive in industries where (1) much creeping bureaucracy has set in, (2) large gains were available with advanced technology, and (3) deregulation increased the heat of competition. These include the insurance, banking, brokerage, and telecommunications industries.

Because reengineering has the goal of radical change, it requires strong CEO support and transformational leadership qualities. Also, before reengineering begins, it is essential that the organization clarify its overall strategy. What business should we really be in? (Do we want to produce hardware, software, or both?) Given this, who are our customers, and what core processes create value for them? If such strategic clarification is lacking, processes that do not matter to the customer will be reengineered. Strong CEO support and a clear strategy are important for overcoming resistance that simply dismisses people who advocate reengineering as "more efficiency experts." Resistance due to self-interest and organizational politics is likely when radical change may lead to layoffs or major changes in work responsibilities.

Reengineering must be both broad and deep to have long-lasting, bottom-line results—that is, it should span a large number of activities that cut costs or add customer value, and it should affect a number of elements including skills, values, roles, incentives, structure, and technology.[51] Half-hearted attempts do not pay off.

DOES ORGANIZATIONAL DEVELOPMENT WORK?

Does it work? That is, do the benefits of OD outweigh the heavy investment of time, effort, and money? At the outset, we should reemphasize that most OD efforts are *not* carefully evaluated. Political factors and budget limitations might be prime culprits, but the situation is not helped by some OD practitioners who argue that certain OD goals (e.g., making the organization more human) are incompatible with impersonal, scientifically rigorous evaluation.

At the very broadest level, two large-scale reviews of a wide variety of OD techniques (including some we discussed in this chapter as well as job redesign, MBO, and goal setting from Chapters 5 and 6) reached the following conclusions:[52]

- Most OD techniques have a positive impact on productivity, job satisfaction, or other work attitudes.
- OD seems to work better for supervisors or managers than for blue-collar workers.
- Changes that use more than one technique seem to have more impact.
- There are great differences across sites in the success of OD interventions.

The last finding is probably due to differences in the skill and seriousness with which various organizations have undertaken OD projects. In addition, TQM and reengineering programs are most likely to be successful when they are accompanied by a change in organizational culture.[53]

Exhibit 16.7 summarizes the results of a large number of research studies on the impact of OD change efforts on changes in a variety of outcomes. Organizational arrangements included changes in formal structure and some quality interventions. Social factors included the use of team building and survey feedback. Technology changes mainly involved job redesign. Finally, physical-setting interventions (which were rare) included things such as changes to open-plan offices.

As you can see, a healthy percentage of studies reported positive changes following an OD effort. However, many studies also reported no change. This underlines the difficulty of introducing change, and it also suggests that variations in how organizations actually implement change may greatly determine its success. The relative lack of negative change is encouraging, but it is also possible that there is a bias against reporting bad outcomes.[54]

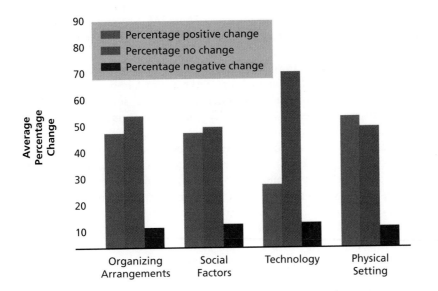

EXHIBIT 16.7
Organizational change
due to organizational
development efforts.

Source: Modified and reproduced by
special permission of the Publisher,
Davies-Black Publishing, an imprint of
CCP Inc., Palo Alto, CA 94303 from
*Handbook of Industrial and
Organizational Psychology,* Second
Edition, Volume 3, by Marvin D.
Dunnette and Leaetta M. Hough,
Editors. Copyright 1992 by Davies-
Black Publishing, an imprint of CPP,
Inc. All rights reserved. Further repro-
duction is prohibited without the
Publisher's written consent.

Weak methodology has sometimes plagued research evaluations on the success of OD interventions, although the quality of research seems to be improving over time.[55] Some specific problems include the following:[56]

- OD efforts involve a complex series of changes. There is little evidence of exactly which of these changes produce changes in processes or outcomes.

- Novelty effects or the fact that participants receive special treatment might produce short-term gains that really do not persist over time.

- Self-reports of changes after OD might involve unconscious attempts to please the change agent.

- Organizations may be reluctant to publicize failures.

For these reasons and others, OD continues to be characterized by both problems and promise. Let's hope that promise will overcome problems as organizations try to respond effectively to their increasingly complex and dynamic environments. Speaking of such response, let's turn now to innovation.

THE INNOVATION PROCESS

Do you recognize the name Arthur Fry? Probably not. But Arthur Fry is famous in his own way as the inventor of the ubiquitous, sticky-backed Post-it notes, a top seller among paper office supplies. Fry, a researcher at the innovative 3M Company, developed the product that became Post-its in response to a personal problem—how to keep his place marker from falling out of his church choir hymnal.

3M
www.3m.com

What accounts for the ability of individuals like Arthur Fry and organizations like 3M to think up and exploit such innovative ideas? This is the focus of this section of the chapter.[57]

What Is Innovation?

Innovation is the process of developing and implementing new ideas in an organization. The term *developing* is intentionally broad. It covers everything from the genuine invention of a new idea to recognizing an idea in the environment, importing it to the organization, and giving it a unique application.[58] The essential point is a degree of creativity. Arthur Fry did not invent glue, and he did not invent paper, but he did

Innovation. The process of developing and implementing new ideas in an organization.

develop a creative way to use them together. Then 3M was creative enough to figure out how to market what might have appeared to less probing minds to be a pretty mundane product.

We can roughly classify innovations as product (including service) innovations or process innovations.[59] *Product innovations* have a direct impact on the cost, quality, style, or availability of a product or service. Thus, they should be very obvious to clients or customers. It is easiest to identify with innovations that result in tangible products, especially everyday consumer products. Thus, we can surely recognize that digital cameras, the iPod, and Post-it notes have been innovative products. As seen in the chapter opening vignette, Samsung has become a master product innovator in the field of electronics. Perhaps coming less readily to mind are service innovations, such as purchasing via eBay, researching via Google, and downloading music via Kazaa.

Process innovations are new ways of designing products, making products, or delivering services. In many cases, process changes are invisible to customers or clients, although they help the organization to perform more effectively or efficiently. Thus, new technology is a process innovation, whether it be new manufacturing technology or a new management information system. New forms of management and work organization, including job enrichment, participation, reengineering, and quality programs, are also process innovations. Visa, GE, DuPont, and Procter & Gamble are particularly noted for management innovations.[60]

Innovation is often conceived of as a stage-like process that begins with idea generation and proceeds to idea implementation. For some kinds of innovations, it is also hoped that the implemented innovation will diffuse to other sites or locations. This applies especially to process innovations that have begun as pilot or demonstration projects:

IDEA GENERATION → IDEA IMPLEMENTATION → IDEA DIFFUSION

In advance of discussing these stages, let us note several interesting themes that underlie the process of innovation. First, the beginning of innovation can be pretty haphazard and chaotic, and the conditions necessary to create new ideas might be very different from the conditions necessary to get these ideas implemented. In a related vein, although organizations have to innovate to survive, such innovation might be resisted just like any other organizational change. The result of these tensions is that innovation is frequently a highly political process (Chapter 12).[61] This important point is sometimes overlooked because innovation often involves science and technology, domains that have a connotation of rationality about them. However, both the champions of innovation and the resisters might behave politically to secure or hold onto critical organizational resources.

Generating and Implementing Innovative Ideas

Innovation requires creative ideas, someone to fight for these ideas, good communication, and the proper application of resources and rewards. Let's examine these factors in detail.

Individual Creativity. Creative thinking by individuals or small groups is at the core of the innovation process. **Creativity** is usually defined as the production of novel but potentially useful ideas. Thus, creativity is a key aspect of the "developing new ideas" part of our earlier definition of innovation. However, innovation is a broader concept, in that it also involves an attempt to implement new ideas. Not every creative idea gets implemented.

When we see a company like Corning that is known for its innovations, or we see an innovative project completed successfully, we sometimes forget about the role that individual creativity plays in such innovations. However, organizations that have a consistent reputation for innovation have a talent for selecting, cultivating, and moti-

Creativity. The production of novel but potentially useful ideas.

vating creative individuals. Such creativity can come into play at many "locations" during the process of innovation. Thus, the salesperson who discovers a new market for a product might be just as creative as the scientist who developed the product.

What makes a person creative?[62] For one thing, you can pretty much discount the romantic notion of the naïve creative genius. Research shows that creative people tend to have an excellent technical understanding of their domain—that is, they understand its basic practices, procedures, and techniques. Thus, creative chemists will emerge from those who are well trained and up-to-date in their field. Similarly, creative money managers will be among those who have a truly excellent grasp of finance and economics. Notice, however, that the fact that creative people have good skills in their area of specialty does not mean that they are extraordinarily intelligent. Once we get beyond subnormal intelligence, there is no correlation between level of intelligence and creativity.

Most people with good basic skills in their area are still not creative. What sets the creative people apart are additional *creativity-relevant* skills. These include the ability to tolerate ambiguity, withhold early judgment, see things in new ways, and be open to new and diverse experiences. Some of these skills reflect certain personality characteristics, such as curiosity and persistence. Interestingly, creative people tend to be socially skilled but lower than average in need for social approval. They can often interact well with others to learn and discuss new ideas, but they do not see the need to conform just to get others to like them.

Many creativity-related skills can actually be improved by training people to think in divergent ways and to withhold early evaluation of ideas.[63] Some of the methods we discussed in Chapter 11 (electronic brainstorming, nominal groups, and Delphi techniques) can be used to hone creative skills. Frito-Lay and DuPont are two companies that engage in extensive creativity training.

Frito-Lay
www.fritolay.com

DuPont
www.dupont.com

Finally, people can be experts in their field and have creativity skills, but still not be creative if they lack intrinsic motivation for generating new ideas. Such motivation is most likely to occur when there is genuine interest in and fascination with the task at hand. This is not to say that extrinsic motivation is not important in innovation, as we shall see shortly. Rather, it means that creativity itself is not very susceptible to extrinsic rewards.

Having a lot of potentially creative individuals is no guarantee in itself that an organization will innovate. Let's now turn to some other factors that influence innovation. But first, consider "Applied Focus: *Innovation at Whirlpool*."

Whirlpool
www.whirlpool.com

Idea Champions. Again and again, case studies of successful innovations reveal the presence of one or more **idea champions**, people who see the kernel of an innovative idea and help guide it through to implementation.[64] This role of idea champion is often an informal emergent role, and "guiding" the idea might involve talking it up to peers, selling it to management, garnering resources for its development, or protecting it from political attack by guardians of the status quo. Champions often have a real sense of mission about the innovation. Idea champions have frequently been given other labels, some of which depend on the exact context or content of the innovation. For example, in larger organizations, such champions might be labelled *intrapreneurs* or *corporate entrepreneurs*. In R&D settings, one often hears the term *project champion*; *product champion* is another familiar moniker. The exact label is less important than the function, which is one of sponsorship and support, often outside of routine job duties.

Idea champions. People who recognize an innovative idea and guide it through to implementation.

For a modest innovation whose merits are extremely clear, it is possible for the creative person who thinks up the idea to serve as its sole champion and to push the idea into practice. In the case of more complex and radical innovations, especially those that demand heavy resource commitment, it is common to see more than one idea champion emerge during the innovation process. For example, a laser scientist might invent a new twist to laser technology and champion the technical idea within her

APPLIED FOCUS

Innovation at Whirlpool

In 1999, Dave Whitwam, Whirlpool's then chairman and CEO, was frustrated by the lack of brand loyalty demonstrated by appliance buyers. To remedy this situation, he issued a challenge to his leadership team: Turn Whirlpool into a rule-breaking, customer-pleasing, innovative company. This was no easy task for the world's largest manufacturer of household appliances, and right from the start it was clear that "innovation from everyone, everywhere," Whitwam's ultimate goal, would require major organizational changes.

Up to this point, the company's management processes had been designed to drive operational efficiency. However, Nancy Snyder, a corporate vice-president who was given the task of reorganizing the company to meet Whitwam's goals, pulled her colleagues into what would become a five-year process to reinvent the company. Whirlpool changed their training and development programs to focus more on innovation, allocated money specifically to go toward innovation, used technology to facilitate collaboration, and implemented an overall organizational shift to recognize the importance of innovation.

For example, Whirlpool trained more than 600 innovation mentors to encourage innovative thinking throughout the company and enrolled every salaried employee in an online course on business innovation. Fiscally, they set aside considerable sums of money every year to go exclusively toward developing projects that showed an extremely high level of innovation. Whirlpool also made a large portion of top management's bonuses contingent on how innovative their division had been.

Realizing that innovation is best achieved through collaboration, Whirlpool built an online portal that gave employees access to tools and data and allowed them to share ideas globally. And to really diffuse innovation throughout the company, Whirlpool required that all new product development plans have some element of new-to-market innovation and set aside time in business meetings to discuss new initiatives and progress.

Whirlpool didn't make all these changes at once, and there were plenty of problems along the way. Obviously, translating a new and abstract management idea into practice requires a long-term effort, but the payoff can be substantial. Jeff Fettig, Whirlpool's current chairman, estimates that by 2007 the innovation program will add more than $500 million a year to the company's top line.

Source: Hamel, G. (2006, February). The why, what, and how of management innovation. *Harvard Business Review*, 72–84, p. 76.

R&D lab. In turn, a product division line manager might hear of the technical innovation and offer to provide sponsorship to develop it into an actual commercial product. This joint emergence of a technical champion and a management champion is typical. Additional idea champions might also emerge. For example, a sales manager in the medical division might lobby to import the innovation from the optics division.

What kind of people are idea champions, and what are their tactics? An interesting program of research headed by Jane Howell examined champions who spearheaded the introduction of technology or product innovations in their firms (e.g., new management information systems).[65] This research compared "project champions" with nonchampions who had also worked on the same project. The champions had very broad interests and saw their roles as being broad. They were very active in scouting for new ideas, using a wide variety of media for stimulation. They were also skilled at presenting the innovation in question as an opportunity rather than framing it as countering a threat (e.g., "this will give us a whole new line of business" versus "this will keep us from getting sued"). Also, they exhibited clear signs of transformational leadership (Chapter 9), using charisma, inspiration, and intellectual stimulation to get people to see the potential of the innovation. They used a wide variety of influence tactics to gain support for the new system. In short, the champions made people truly *want* the innovation despite its disruption of the status quo.

Communication. Effective communication with the external environment and effective communication within the organization are vital for successful innovation. In fact, at Samsung, both the Innovation Design Lab and the VIP Center are oriented toward enhancing communication.

The most innovative firms seem to be those that are best at recognizing the relevance of new, external information, importing and assimilating this information, and then applying it.[66] You might recall from earlier in the chapter that such processes are consistent with organizational learning. Experience shows that the recognition and assimilation are a lot more chaotic and informal than one might imagine. Rather than relying on a formal network of journal articles, technical reports, and internal memoranda, technical personnel are more likely to be exposed to new ideas via informal oral communication networks. In these networks, key personnel function as **gatekeepers** who span the boundary between the organization and the environment, importing new information, translating it for local use, and disseminating it to project members. These people tend to have well-developed communication networks with other professionals outside the organization and with the professionals on their own team or project. Thus, they are in key positions to both receive and transmit new technical information.[67] Also, they are perceived as highly competent and as a good source of new ideas. Furthermore, they have an innovative orientation, they read extensively, and they can tolerate ambiguity.[68] It is important to note that gatekeeping is essentially an informal, emergent role, since many gatekeepers are not in supervisory positions. However, organizations can do several things to enhance the external contact of actual or potential gatekeepers. Generous allowances for subscriptions, telephone use, and database access might be helpful. The same applies to travel allowances for seminars, short courses, and professional meetings.

Technical gatekeepers are not the only means of extracting information from the environment. Many successful innovative firms excel at going directly to users, clients, or customers to obtain ideas for product or service innovation. This works against the development of technically sound ideas that nobody wants, and it also provides some real focus for getting ideas implemented quickly. For example, Sony requires new employees in technical areas to do a stint in retail sales, and Raytheon's New Products Center organizes expeditions by technical types to trade shows, manufacturing facilities, and retail outlets.[69] Willie G. Davidson, chief designer and grandson of one of the founders of Harley-Davidson, gets ideas from customers at Harley-Davidson bike rallies where he is often seen walking around with a notebook in hand and having one-on-one sessions with customers.[70] Notice that we are speaking here about truly getting "close to the customer," not simply doing abstract market research on large samples of people. Such research does not have a great track record in prompting innovation; talking directly to users does.

Now that we have covered the importation of information into the organization, what are the requirements of *internal* communication for innovation? At least during the idea generation and early design phase, the more the better. Thus, it is generally true that organic structures (Chapter 14) facilitate innovation more easily than mechanistic structures.[71] Decentralization, informality, and a lack of bureaucracy all foster the exchange of information that innovation requires. To this mixture, add small project teams or business units and a diversity of member backgrounds to stimulate cross-fertilization of ideas.

In general, internal communication can be stimulated with in-house training, cross-functional transfers, and varied job assignments.[72] One study even found that the actual physical location of gatekeepers was important to their ability to convey new

Gatekeepers. People who span organizational boundaries to import new information, translate it for local use, and disseminate it.

Raytheon
www.raytheon.com

information to co-workers.[73] This suggests the clustering of offices and the use of common lounge areas as a means of facilitating communication. Organizations could also give equal thought to the design of electronic communication media.

One especially interesting line of research suggests just how important communication is to the performance of research and development project groups.[74] This research found that groups with members who had worked together a short time or a long time engaged in less communication (within the group, within the organization, and externally) than groups that had medium longevity. In turn, performance mirrored communication, the high-communicating, medium-longevity groups being the best performers (Exhibit 16.8). Evidently, when groups are new, it takes time for members to decide what information they require and to forge the appropriate communication networks. When groups get "old," they sometimes get comfortable and isolate themselves from critical sources of feedback. It is important to emphasize that the age of the group is at issue here, not the age of the employees or their tenure in the organization.

Although organic structures seem best in the idea generation and design phases of innovation, more mechanistic structures are often better for actually implementing innovations.[75] Thinking up new computer programs is an organic task. Reproducing these programs in the thousands and marketing them require more bureaucratic procedures. This transition is important. Although audio and video recording innovations were pioneered in the United States, it was the Japanese who successfully implemented recording products in the marketplace. In part, this stemmed from a recognition of the different organizational requirements for idea generation versus the implementation of ideas.

Resources and Rewards. Despite the romance surrounding the development of innovations on a shoestring using unauthorized "bootlegged" funds, abundant resources greatly enhance the chances of successful innovation. Not only do these resources provide funds in the obvious sense, they also serve as a strong cultural symbol that the organization truly supports innovation.[76]

EXHIBIT 16.8
Group longevity, communication, and performance of research and development groups.

"The Effects of Group Longevity of Project Communication and Performance," by Ralph Katz, *Administrative Science Quarterly*, Vol. 27, No. 1, 81–104, p. 96, March 1982.

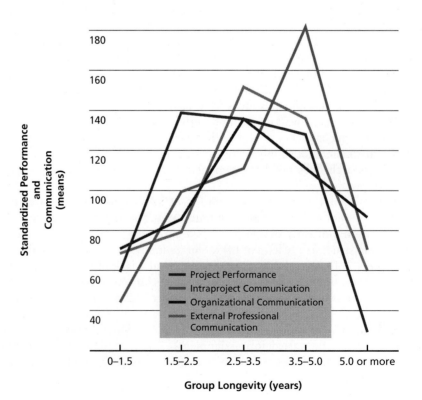

Funds for innovation are seen as an *investment,* not a *cost.* Several observers have noted that such a culture is most likely when the availability of funding is anarchic and multisourced—that is, because innovative ideas often encounter resistance from the status quo under the best of circumstances, innovators should have the opportunity to seek support from more than one source. At 3M, for instance, intrapreneurs can seek support from their own division, from another division, from corporate R&D, or from a new ventures group.[77] (Notice how other idea champions might be cultivated during this process.)

Money is not the only resource that spurs innovation. *Time* can be an even more crucial factor for some innovations. At Google, employees can devote up to 20 percent of work time to any personal project that will help advertisers or users.[78]

Reward systems must match the culture that is seeded by the resource system. Coming up with new ideas is no easy job, so organizations should avoid punishing failure. Many false starts with dead ends will be encountered, and innovators need support and constructive criticism, not punishment. In fact, Hallmark puts its executives through a simulation in which they must design a line of greeting cards so that they can better appreciate the frustrations felt by the creative staff.

Hallmark
www.hallmark.com

A survey of research scientists found that freedom and autonomy were the *most* cited organizational factors leading to creativity.[79] Since intrinsic motivation is necessary for creativity, these results support rewarding good past performance with enhanced freedom to pursue personal ideas. In a related vein, many organizations have wised up about extrinsic rewards and innovation. In the past, it was common for creative scientists and engineers to have to move into management ranks to obtain raises and promotions. Many firms now offer dual career ladders that enable these people to be extrinsically rewarded while still doing actual science or engineering. When Hewlett-Packard implemented an incentive program to pay researchers for each patent they filed, the number of filings doubled.[80]

We have been concerned here mainly with rewarding the people who actually generate innovative ideas. But how about those other champions who sponsor such ideas and push them into the implementation stage? At 3M, bonuses for division managers are contingent on 25 percent of their revenues coming from products that are less than five years old.[81] This stimulates the managers to pay attention when someone drops by with a new idea, and it also stimulates them to turn that new idea into a real product quickly!

To summarize this section, we can conclude that innovation depends on individual factors (creativity), social factors (a dedicated champion and good communication), and organizational factors (resources and rewards).

Diffusing Innovative Ideas

Many innovations, especially process innovations, begin as limited experiments in one section or division of an organization. This is a cautious and reasonable approach. For example, a company might introduce new automated technology for evaluation in one plant of its multiplant organization. Similarly, an insurance company might begin a limited exploration of job enrichment by concentrating only on clerical jobs at the head office. If such efforts are judged successful, it seems logical to extend them to other parts of the organization. **Diffusion** is the process by which innovations move through an organization. However, this is not always as easy as it might seem!

Diffusion. The process by which innovations move through an organization.

Richard Walton of Harvard University studied the diffusion of eight major process innovations in firms such as Volvo, Alcan, General Foods, Corning Inc., and Shell UK. Each effort was rigorous and broad based, generally including changes in job design, compensation, and supervision.[82]

Volvo
www.volvo.com

All the pilot projects that Walton studied were initially judged successful, and each received substantial publicity, a factor that often contributes to increased commitment to further change. Despite this, substantial diffusion occurred in only one of the observed firms—Volvo. What accounts for this poor record of diffusion? Walton identified these factors:

- Lack of support and commitment from top management.

- Significant differences between the technology or setting of the pilot project and those of other units in the organization, raising arguments that "it won't work here."

- Attempts to diffuse particular *techniques* rather than *goals* that could be tailored to other situations.

- Management reward systems that concentrate on traditional performance measures while ignoring success at implementing innovation.

- Union resistance to extending the negotiated "exceptions" in the pilot project.

- Fears that pilot projects begun in nonunionized locations could not be implemented in unionized portions of the firm.

- Conflict between the pilot project and the bureaucratic structures in the rest of the firm (e.g., pay policies and staffing requirements).

Because of these problems, Walton raises the depressing spectre of a "diffuse or die" principle. That is, if diffusion does not occur, the pilot project and its leaders become more and more isolated from the mainstream of the organization and less and less able to proceed alone. As we noted earlier, innovation can be a highly politicized process. Several of the barriers to diffusion that Walton cites have been implicated in limiting the influence that the Saturn project has had on General Motors, including top management changes, union resistance, and competition for resources from old-line GM divisions.

General Motors
www.gm.com

Some research suggests that innovations are especially difficult to diffuse in organizations dominated by professionals, who tend to focus on their own "silos." Thus, in hospitals, doctors, nurses, and physiotherapists can have trouble working as multidisciplinary teams to introduce new practices.[83]

One classic review suggests that the following factors are critical determinants of the rate of diffusion of a wide variety of innovations:[84]

- *Relative advantage.* Diffusion is more likely when the new idea is perceived as truly better than the one it replaces.

- *Compatibility.* Diffusion is easier when the innovation is compatible with the values, beliefs, needs, and current practices of potential new adopters.

- *Complexity.* Complex innovations that are fairly difficult to comprehend and use are less likely to diffuse.

- *Trialability.* If an innovation can be given a limited trial run, its chances of diffusion will be improved.

- *Observability.* When the consequences of an innovation are more visible, diffusion will be more likely to occur.

In combination, these determinants suggest that there is considerable advantage to thinking about how innovations are "packaged" and "sold" so as to increase their chances of more widespread adoption. Also, they suggest the value of finding strong champions to sponsor the innovation at the new site.

A FOOTNOTE: THE KNOWING-DOING GAP

Despite the need for organizations to change, develop, and innovate, they often exhibit considerable inertia. This is particularly ironic in that managers are better educated than ever, and there are well developed bodies of research (many documented in your text) that show that some management practices are better than others. In addition, short courses, consulting firms, and popular books by management gurus frequently describe in detail the "best practices" of successful firms in various industries. Thus, it seems that many managers *know* what to do, but have considerable trouble *implementing* this knowledge in the form of action. In a very insightful book, Jeffrey Pfeffer and Robert Sutton describe this situation as the *knowing-doing gap*.[85] To take just one of their examples, the much admired and highly efficient Toyota Production System (TPS) has been featured in many books and articles. Toyota readily gives plant tours to illustrate its features. Despite this, firms have had considerable trouble in trying to imitate Toyota.

Toyota Canada
www.toyota.ca

Why does the knowing-doing gap happen? Pfeffer and Sutton cite a number of reasons. One is the tendency for some organizational cultures to reward short-term talk rather than longer-term action. Meetings, presentations, documentation, and mission statements thus take precedence over action and experimentation. This is only reinforced when mistrust permeates a firm and employees fear reprisals for mistakes. Also,

 THE MANAGER'S

Notebook

1. The unfreezing process at Siemens was precipitated by deregulation in Germany and the recognition that customers' demands for total solutions were somewhat at odds with Siemens' highly diversified organization structure and culture. With activities in information and communication systems, products and services, semiconductors, passive and electromechanical components, transportation, energy, health care, household appliances, lighting, and other businesses, Siemens had a wealth of knowledge but it was incredibly dispersed. Joachim Döring emerged as a primary change agent, although he smartly created a team of dedicated partners at different levels to garner support for the ShareNet project. Döring's efforts can easily be conceptualized as an effort to transform Siemens into a learning organization. ShareNet is both a knowledge acquisition and a knowledge development system. ShareNet's "urgent request" component created a platform where users would regularly scan through this forum to check if they could answer questions. In practice this component revealed its value when, for example, an ICN project manager in South America tried to discover how dangerous it was to lay cables in the Amazon rainforest. He posted an urgent request asking for help from anyone with a similar project in a similar environment. A project manager in Senegal responded within several hours. Obtaining the right information before the cables went underground saved Siemens approximately US$1 million.

2. Creating a true learning organization involves creating a knowledge management infrastructure, management coaching and mentoring, leadership vision and support, and a supportive organizational culture. While the first three elements were in place through the ShareNet implementation process, the organizational culture aspect represented the biggest challenge to Döring and his team. Another source of resistance was ShareNet's use of English. Although the English literacy at Siemens Germany was sufficiently high, many employees still did not dare to post a question in a forum where several thousand people could see their grammar or spelling mistakes. Others were of the opinion that in a German-based company, the first language should still be German. Siemens' management used different tactics to counter resistance. The use of individual rewards was aimed at reducing politics and self-interest surrounding the system. Misunderstandings and trust issues were dealt with by enlisting managers in each location to champion the system and through extensive training. Finally, the ShareNet project involved extensive planning at the highest levels of the organization. In all, this broad range of tactics facilitated unfreezing and allowed change to occur. By July 2002, ShareNet was utilized by more than 19 000 registered users in more than 80 countries. They were supported by 53 ShareNet managers from different nations all over the world. More than 20 000 knowledge bids populated the system, half of which had been published within the previous year. Over 2.5 million ShareNet shares had been distributed with almost 300 users within reach of an award.

many changes require cooperation between organizational units, but many organizations foster internal competition that is not conducive to such cooperation. Finally, Pfeffer and Sutton note that when managers do manage to make changes, these changes sometimes fail because techniques are adopted without understanding their underlying philosophy. For instance, the TPS is based in part on TQM principles described earlier in this chapter, but some observers just see visible manifestations such as the cords that workers can pull to stop the assembly line. Similarly, one of your authors once heard a consultant say that one of his clients was all in favour of teamwork but didn't want to actually implement any teams!

We hope that our book has provided you with the knowing. Now it's your turn to do the doing!

LEARNING OBJECTIVES CHECKLIST

1. All organizations must change because of forces in the external and internal environments. Although more environmental change usually requires more organizational change, organizations can exhibit too much change as well as too little. Organizations can change goals and strategies, technology, job design, structure, processes, culture, and people. People changes should almost always accompany changes in other factors.

2. Organizations learn through the acquisition, distribution, and interpretation of knowledge that already exists but is external to the organization, and through the development of new knowledge that occurs in an organization primarily through dialogue and experience. *Learning organizations* have systems and processes for creating, acquiring, and transferring knowledge throughout the organization to modify and change behaviour.

3. The general *change process* involves unfreezing current attitudes and behaviours, changing them, and then refreezing the newly acquired attitudes and behaviours. Several key issues or problems must be dealt with during the general change process. One is accurate diagnosis of the current situation. Another is the resistance that might be provoked by unfreezing and change. A third issue is performing an adequate evaluation of the success of the change effort. Many such evaluations are weak or nonexistent.

4. Organizations can deal with *resistance to change* by being supportive, providing clear and upfront communication about the details of the intended change, involving those who

are targets of the change in the change process, and by co-opting reluctant individuals by giving them a special or desirable role in the change process or by negotiating special incentives for change. Transformational leaders are particularly adept at overcoming resistance to change.

5. *Organizational development (OD)* is a planned, ongoing effort to change organizations to be more effective and more human. It uses the knowledge of behavioural science to foster a culture of organizational self-examination and readiness for change. A strong emphasis is placed on interpersonal and group processes.

6. Four popular OD techniques are team building, survey feedback, total quality management, and reengineering. *Team building* attempts to increase the effectiveness of work teams by concentrating on interpersonal processes, goal clarification, and role clarification. *Survey feedback* requires organizational members to generate data that are fed back to them as a basis for inducing change. *Total quality management* (TQM) is an attempt to achieve continuous improvement in the quality of products or services. *Reengineering* is the radical redesign of organizational processes to achieve major improvements in time, cost, quality, or service.

7. The careful evaluation of OD programs poses special challenges to researchers. OD efforts involve a complex series of changes, so it is difficult to know exactly what changes produce changes in processes or outcomes.

Novelty effects or the fact that participants receive special treatment might produce short-term gains that really do not persist over time. Self-reports of changes after OD might involve unconscious attempts to please the change agent, and organizations might be reluctant to publicize failures.

8. *Innovation* is the process of developing and implementing new ideas in an organization. It can include both new products and new processes. Innovation requires individual creativity and adequate resources and rewards to stimulate and channel that creativity. Also, *idea champions* who recognize and sponsor creative ideas are critical. Finally, internal and external communication is important for innovation. The role of *gatekeepers* who import and disseminate technical information is especially noteworthy.

9. Innovations will diffuse most easily when they are not too complex, can be given a trial run, are compatible with existing practices, and offer a visible advantage over current practices. Factors that can hurt diffusion include a lack of support and commitment from top management, reward systems that focus on traditional performance and ignore success at implementing innovation, union resistance, and conflict between pilot projects and the bureaucratic structures in the rest of the organization.

OB FLASHBACK

Emotions and Organizational Change

As you know from reading this chapter, organizational change programs are often met with a great deal of resistance. Thus, managers must create positive attitudes toward change among members of an organization. But how successful are managers at creating positive attitudes toward organizational change programs, and how should they persuade employees to change?

As it turns out, managers are not very effective when it comes to managing change. Perhaps not surprisingly, many organizational change programs fail. This is largely due to a failure to obtain the acceptance, support, and commitment of organizational members and to overcome resistance to change.

In Chapter 4, we described attitudes as "a fairly stable evaluative tendency to respond consistently to some specific object, situation, person, or category of people." We also noted that attitudes are a function of what we think and what we feel, or a product of a related belief and value. Attempts to change attitudes usually involve some form of persuasion to modify the beliefs or values of an audience.

When it comes to change programs, however, managers tend to focus on the belief component of attitude change rather than the feeling or emotional component. In other words, they emphasize the cognitive or thinking components of attitude change by using rationale arguments (e.g., why the change is needed, facts and information regarding the problems of the present situation, opportunities and benefits of the change program, etc.). However, persuading employees to accept change and overcoming resistance to change requires employees' emotional involvement. A focus on only the rational elements of change means that employees might remain *emotionally* resistant to change. Furthermore, the emotional aspects of a change effort are often more important and relevant than the cognitive aspects.

How can managers appeal to employees' emotions when promoting organizational change programs? Shaul Fox and Yair Amichai-Hamburger describe a number of methods for using emotions during the organizational change process. First, they suggest including emotions in the content of change messages. For example, managers should use words with strong negative emotional connotations, such as *danger*, *loss*, *unpleasantness*, and *risk* to describe the consequences of not implementing a change program, and positive words such as *comfortable*, *convenient*, *success*, *progress*, *pleasure*, and *relief* to describe the future after a change program has been implemented. Managers can also use metaphors that evoke positive feelings and emotions for a change program. Positive organizational metaphors (e.g., family) can be used to create a strong sense of caring and support during the change process.

Second, managers should use different modes of communication to evoke emotions toward a change program, such as pictures, slogans, music, and colours. The use of humour is also recommended because it can create a pleasant atmosphere, generate good feelings, gain people's attention, and show that the change agents are human, thus bridging the distance between managers and employees. Managers should also display their own emotions when communicating with employees about a change program—by smiling and by exhibiting enthusiasm, warmth, pride, and confidence in the change program.

Third, managers should allow employees to express their views and should be fair, honest, and sympathetic in their treatment of employees during the change process. This helps in the development of positive emotions toward change and can lower employees' resistance. By allowing employees to voice their objections, negative emotions can be changed to positive feelings toward a change program.

A final method of appealing to employees' emotions is by creating pleasant settings that arouse positive emotions for change. One way to do this is through the use of ceremonies that celebrate the introduction of a change program and significant changes. Ceremonies should be held in dignified and pleasant surroundings and should include decorations and adornments to enhance the sense of importance and positive aspects of a change program. In addition, information about change programs should be provided in pleasant, intimate, convenient, and aesthetic surroundings. This helps to create linkages between the pleasant environment, positive emotions, and the change program.

Finally, recall from Chapter 4 the discussion of affective events theory, which states that events and happenings in the workplace have the potential to provoke emotions and moods, depending on how the events and happenings are appraised. Change programs are one type of organizational event that is sure to evoke very strong emotions. Therefore, managers should incorporate emotional elements of persuasion into their messages about change programs to create positive emotions toward change, to obtain employee acceptance and support for change initiatives, to minimize resistance to change, and to improve the chances of success.

Source: Fox, S., & Amichai-Hamburger, Y. (2001). The power of emotional appeals in promoting organizational change programs. *Academy of Management Executive, 15*, 84–95.

DISCUSSION QUESTIONS

1. Describe an example of resistance to change that you have observed. Why did it occur?

2. You have been charged with staffing and organizing an R&D group in a new high-tech firm. What will you do to ensure that the group is innovative?

3. What qualities would the ideal gatekeeper possess to facilitate the communication of technical information in his or her firm?

4. Suppose a job enrichment effort in one plant of a manufacturing firm is judged to be very successful. You are the corporate change agent responsible for the project, and you wish to diffuse it to other plants that have a similar technology. How would you sell the project to other plant managers? What kinds of resistance might you encounter?

5. What personal qualities and skills would be useful for an OD change agent to possess? Describe the relative merits of using an internal staff change agent versus an external consultant.

6. Discuss: The best organizational structure to generate innovative ideas might not be the best structure to implement those ideas.

7. Discuss some of the things that an organization can do to improve organizational learning and to become a learning organization. What should organizations know about the linkages between organizational learning and change and innovation?

8. Debate this statement: Survey feedback can be a problematic OD technique because it permits people who are affected by organizational policies to generate data that speak against those policies.

INTEGRATIVE DISCUSSION QUESTIONS

1. Do leadership, organizational culture, and communication influence the effectiveness of organizational change programs? Discuss the effect that leadership behaviour, strong cultures, and personal and organizational approaches to communication have on the change process and change problems. What should organizations do in terms of leadership, culture, and communication to overcome problems and ensure that the change process is effective?

2. How can organizational learning practices, pay, and socialization influence organizational learning and innovation in organizations? Design a program to improve an organization's ability to learn or generate and implement innovative ideas that combines organizational learning practices (Chapter 2), pay systems (Chapter 6), and socialization methods (Chapter 8). What effect does organizational culture have on an organization's ability to learn and innovate?

3. Review the chapter opening vignette on Samsung and identify some of the most relevant issues that have been covered in previous chapters. In particular, consider the vignette in terms of some of the following topics: (1) Learning (Chapter 2), (2) Perceptions (Chapter 3), (3) Groups and teamwork (Chapter 7), (4) Culture (Chapter 8), (5) Leadership (Chapter 9), (6) Communication (Chapter 10), (7) Organizational structure (Chapter 14), and (8) Strategy (Chapter 15).

ON-THE-JOB CHALLENGE QUESTION

For over 100 years, Eastman Kodak dominated the photography industry in terms of cameras and film. By the end of the 1990s and into the 2000s, however, the company was in dire financial straits, having been slow to jump on the digital photography bandwagon. Tens of thousands of employees have been laid off over the last five years, and Kodak's stock has dropped almost 75 percent over the same period. Since 2004, Kodak has made digital photography a top priority and is striving to once again become a leader through its heavy investments in R&D. But in a digital camera market that has been growing at a rate of 600 to 700 percent over the last five years and that already has established brands, doubts exist that Kodak will be able to overcome the decline of its core business and get back to the top of the photography industry.

Why do you think Kodak had difficulty unfreezing until hit with financial meltdown, while companies like Canon took advantage of new technologies quickly? What would the main sources of resistance be in Kodak's move toward digital technology? Since innovation is being positioned as Kodak's strategy to regain its leadership in the photography industry, what will the company need to do to ensure that this change strategy is a success?

Source: Stone, B. (2006, January 16). What's Kodak's strategy? *Newsweek*, 46–47.

EXPERIENTIAL EXERCISE

Measuring Tolerance for Ambiguity

Please read each of the following statements carefully. Then use the following scale to rate each of them in terms of the extent to which you either agree or disagree with the statement.

Completely disagree		Neither agree nor disagree				Completely agree
1	2	3	4	5	6	7

Place the number that best describes your degree of agreement or disagreement in the blank to the left of each statement.

_____ 1. An expert who does not come up with a definite answer probably does not know too much.

_____ 2. I would like to live in a foreign country for a while.

_____ 3. The sooner we all acquire similar values and ideals, the better.

_____ 4. A good teacher is one who makes you wonder about your way of looking at things.

_____ 5. I like parties where I know most of the people more than ones where all or most of the people are complete strangers.

_____ 6. Teachers or supervisors who hand out vague assignments give a chance for one to show initiative and originality.

_____ 7. A person who leads an even, regular life in which few surprises or unexpected happenings arise really has a lot to be grateful for.

_____ 8. Many of our most important decisions are based on insufficient information.

_____ 9. There is really no such thing as a problem that cannot be solved.

_____ 10. People who fit their lives to a schedule probably miss most of the joy of living.

_____ 11. A good job is one in which what is to be done and how it is to be done are always clear.

_____ 12. It is more fun to tackle a complicated problem than to solve a simple one.

_____ 13. In the long run, it is possible to get more done by tackling small, simple problems than large and complicated ones.

_____ 14. Often the most interesting and stimulating people are those who do not mind being different and original.

_____ 15. What we are used to is always preferable to what is unfamiliar.

_____ 16. People who insist on a yes or no answer just do not know how complicated things really are.

Scoring and Interpretation

You have just completed the Tolerance for Ambiguity Scale. It was adapted by Paul Nutt from original work by S. Budner. The survey asks about personal and work-oriented situations that involve various degrees of ambiguity. To score your own survey, add 8 to each of your responses to the *odd* numbered items. Then, add up the renumbered odd items. From this total, subtract your score from the sum of the *even* numbered items. Your score should fall between 16 and 112. People with lower scores are tolerant of and even enjoy ambiguous situations. People with high scores are intolerant of ambiguity and prefer more structured situations. In Paul Nutt's research, people typically scored between 20 and 80 with a mean around 45. People with a high tolerance for ambiguity respond better to change. They also tend to be more creative and innovative than those with low tolerance for ambiguity.

Source: From Paul Nutt, *Making Tough Decisions.* © 1989 John Wiley & Sons. Reprinted with permission of John Wiley & Sons, Inc.

CASE INCIDENT

Dandy Toys

Company president George Reed had built a successful toy company called Dandy Toys, which specialized in manufacturing inexpensive imitations of more expensive products. However, with increasing domestic and global competition, he became concerned that his cheap imitations would not be enough to maintain the company's current success. George decided to call a meeting with all the company's managers to express his concerns. He told them that Dandy Toys must change and become more innovative in its products. Rather than just knock off other companies' toys, he told the managers that they must come up with creative and innovative ideas for new and more upscale toys. "By the end of this year," George told the managers, "Dandy Toys must begin making its own in-house designed quality toys." When the managers left the meeting, they were surprised, and some were even shocked, about this new direction for Dandy Toys.

Although a few of the managers suggested some ideas for new toys during the next couple of months,

nobody really seemed interested. In fact, business pretty much continued as always at Dandy Toys, and by the end of the year not a single new in-house toy had been made.

1. Comment on the change process at Dandy Toys. What advice would you give the president about how to improve the change process? What are some of the things that might be changed at Dandy Toys as part of the change process?

2. Why wasn't the innovation process more successful at Dandy Toys, and what can be done to improve it?

3. Consider the relevance of organizational learning for change and innovation at Dandy Toys. What should the company do to improve learning and will this help to create change and improve innovation?

CASE STUDY

Erehwon Management Consultants, Inc.

Erehwon Management Consultants, Inc. (EMC) is a general consulting firm with offices in six cities, employing about 100 full-time consultants. Until recently, it had exhibited an enviable growth record based on just two "products." The firm's president began to see a slowdown because both of these products were rapidly entering the mature phases of their respective life cycles. In addition, he felt that the pace of work had become too intense and that by gradually bringing down the consultant's workload, it would be advantageous to the firm in retaining less stressed employees.

Cultural Norms before the Change Program

EMC, like many other firms in the industry, saw its success equated to billable hours and high consultant utilization rates. In other words, the success and even continued existence of EMC depended on, at a minimum, covering the fixed expenses (salary plus overhead and fringes) for its consulting staff. As a result, everyone at EMC watched the weekly "hours billed to clients."

Consultants at all levels were encouraged, usually in indirect ways, to "keep busy" on client efforts and to sell follow-up engagements. At performance review time and at promotion time, it was made explicit that sales and hard work for clients were the keys to personnel career growth at EMC. Partners seemed to be always on the road, calling on potential and current clients, seeking to reach the sales quotas. No organized marketing was done as it implied (to the partners) an unprofessional image.

A New Strategy for EMC

The president and the six partners that headed up the offices of EMC met for two days to address his concerns of an impending slowdown and the "quality of life" issue. Since EMC had emphasized sales during its entire existence as a firm and had seen sales success equated with capitalizing on its two existing products, no R&D or new product development efforts had been attempted to date.

To address the slowdown and, at the same time, to enhance the consultant quality of worklife, the following strategy was formulated by the group:

- Deemphasize sales and billable hours as measures of consultant performance.

- Set aside approximately 5 percent of each consultant's time (i.e., three hours per week) for "R&D" time. Each consultant could use such time for self-improvement of consulting skills, new product idea generation, or researching new industries to which to market existing products.

- Try to schedule consultants so that those who spent extensive time on the road (i.e., on client work) were occasionally "rewarded" with local assignments or officially recognized with new product development projects (also not requiring travel).

The Change Program

The president's committee realized that this new strategy represented a substantial departure from the previous approach. However, a sense of urgency seemed to dictate that the new strategy must be put in place without delay.

The head of EMC's largest office, a partner with the firm's best sales record, was given responsibility for designing the implementation of the plan. His program centred on the following steps:

- Firm-wide, each consultant would receive a memo from the president stating the new strategy and the need to change.

- In each office, the partner in charge would convene the consultants to explain the new situation and encourage each consultant to develop new product ideas.

- Each office would decide on the travel and "time off" procedures so as to cause minimal disruption to clients.

The president's one-page memo was distributed about two weeks later. It took nearly three months to schedule each of the six offices to have their staff meetings, since clients seemed to continually uncover "major" crises that required consultants on-site.

Consultants' Response

The president's memo surprised and perplexed most of EMC's consultants. In essence, it stated that EMC was evolving into an organization that was willing to invest in its future through its employees. The arguments were vague and the memo seemed to lack the feeling of urgency that had originally motivated the President to act on his concerns. Few if any of the consultants seemed to seriously accept the memo as representing a real change affecting them, at least not in the near future.

The office meetings also seemed to be missing a clear sense of urgency or rationale. In several of these sessions, the partner in charge seemed less than enthusiastic and was even heard to convey that "this is temporary—don't let it affect your *real* work!"

After the meetings were over, life at EMC seemed unchanged. Partners still hustled about, responding to any and all sales leads, and consultants were promoted or let go on the basis of their "partnership potential," that is, the ability to generate business.

Moreover, as the expected sales slump began to be felt earlier than anticipated, cold calling and visiting previous clients seemed to become everyone's primary activities. Even some client work in progress was slowed to free up more staff to make sales calls.

Sales did ultimately resume, albeit spread across a variety of products and markets that lacked any cohesive theme. Partners and consultants never really changed their focus on sales. The "new program" quickly disappeared from the scene.

Source: Buchowicz, B. (1990, Summer). Culture transition and attitude change. *Journal of General Management*, 45–55.

1. Describe the culture of Erehwon Management Consultants before and after the change effort.

2. Discuss in detail the reasons for the failure of the change effort.

3. Account for the resistance the change effort encountered. After all, the changes seemed beneficial to the consultants.

4. Discuss how the techniques of team building and TQM might have been applied at EMC.

5. Explain the factors that appear to work against product innovation at EMC.

6. It is particularly important that consulting firms exhibit the qualities of learning organizations. Why is this so? What would this mean in the context of consulting?

7. With hindsight, how might the president have acted differently to achieve his goals?

INTEGRATIVE CASE

Ace Technology

At the end of Part Three of the text, on Social Behaviour and Organizational Processes, you answered a number of questions about the Ace Technology Integrative Case that dealt with issues related to culture, leadership, communication, and decision making. Now that you have completed Part Four of the text and the chapters on The Total Organization, you can return to the Ace Technology Integrative Case and enhance your understanding of some of the main issues associated with the total organization by answering the following questions.

QUESTIONS

1. Describe the external environment and its influence on Ace Technology.

2. Describe Ace Technology's response to uncertainty and resource dependence. How effective do you think its response will be, and what are some other strategic responses that it might consider?

3. Consider the concept of organizational change. Does Ace Technology need to change? Why or why not?

4. Discuss the change process and issues in relation to the new programs at Ace Technology. How effectively have the three basic stages been conducted and the main issues managed?

5. Consider the issue of resistance to change at Ace Technology. What factors explain the degree of resistance toward the new strategy and compensation program at Ace Technology?

6. How effective do you think the new compensation program will be for generating and implementing innovative ideas? What else can Ace Technology do to improve innovation?

Research in Organizational Behaviour

Research is a way of finding out about the world through objective and systematic information gathering. The key words here are *objective* and *systematic*, and it is these characteristics that separate the outcomes of the careful study of organizational behaviour from opinion and common sense.

Understanding how researchers conduct their research is important to the study of organizational behaviour for several reasons. First of all, you should be aware of how the information presented in this book was collected. This should increase your confidence in the advantages of systematic study over common sense. Second, you will likely encounter reports, in management periodicals and the popular press, of interventions to improve organizational behaviour, such as job redesign or employee development programs. A critical perspective is necessary to differentiate those interventions that are carefully designed and evaluated from useless or even damaging ones. Those backed by good research deserve the greatest confidence. Occasionally, a manager may have to evaluate a research proposal or consultant's intervention to be carried out in his or her own organization. A brief introduction to research methodology should enable you to ask some intelligent questions about such plans.

Trained behavioural scientists who have backgrounds in management, applied psychology, or applied sociology carry out research in organizational behaviour. While this introduction will not make you a trained behavioural scientist, it should provide an appreciation of the work that goes into generating accurate knowledge about organizational behaviour.

THE BASICS OF ORGANIZATIONAL BEHAVIOUR RESEARCH

All research in organizational behaviour begins with a question about work or organizations. Sometimes this question might stem from a formal theory in the field. For example, a motivation theory called equity theory (see Chapter 5) is concerned with peoples' reactions to fairness or lack of it. Equity theory suggests the following research question: What do people do when they perceive their pay to be too low in comparison to other people? Other times, a research question might stem from an immediate organizational problem. For example, a human resources manager might ask herself: How can we reduce absenteeism among our customer service personnel?

LEARNING OBJECTIVES

After reading the Appendix, you should be able to:

1 Explain what a *hypothesis* is and define the meaning of a *variable*.

2 Distinguish between *independent* and *dependent variables* and *moderating* and *mediating variables*.

3 Differentiate *reliability* from *validity* and *convergent validity* from *discriminant validity*.

4 Understand *observational research* and distinguish between *participant* and *direct observation*.

5 Describe *correlational research* and explain why causation cannot be inferred from correlation.

6 Explain *experimental research* and the meaning of *internal validity* and discuss threats to internal validity.

7 Discuss the relative advantages and disadvantages of various research techniques.

8 Describe *random sampling* and *external validity* and the role they play in the research process.

9 Explain the *Hawthorne effect* and how it can occur.

10 Discuss the basic ethical concerns to which researchers must attend.

Hypothesis. A formal statement of the expected relationship between two variables.

Variables. Measures that can take on two or more values.

Often, research questions are expressed as hypotheses. A **hypothesis** is a formal statement of the expected relationship between two variables. **Variables** are simply measures that can take on two or more values. Temperature is a variable, but so are pay, fairness, and absenteeism. A formal hypothesis stemming from equity theory might be: The less fair people perceive their pay to be, the more likely they will be to resign their jobs. Here, a variable that can take on many values, perceived fairness, is linked to a variable made up of two values, staying or leaving. The human resources manager might develop this hypothesis: The introduction of a small attendance bonus will reduce absenteeism. Here, a variable with two values, bonus versus no bonus, is related to one that can take on many values, days of absenteeism.

Types of Variables

Independent variable. The variable that predicts or is the cause of variation in a dependent variable.

Dependent variable. The variable that is expected to vary as a result of changes to the independent variable.

Moderating variable. A variable that affects the nature of the relationship between an independent and a dependent variable such that the relationship depends on the level of the moderating variable.

Mediating variable. A variable that intervenes or explains the relationship between an independent and a dependent variable.

In most research, we are concerned with two kinds of variables: the independent variable and the dependent variable. The **independent variable** is a predictor or cause of variation in a dependent variable. The **dependent variable** is a variable that will vary as a result of changes in the independent variable. So in the first example, pay fairness perceptions is the independent variable and resigning is the dependent variable. In the second example, the attendance bonus is the independent variable and absenteeism is the dependent variable. In both cases, scores on the dependent variable are expected to vary as a function of scores on the independent variable.

Two other kinds of variables that we are sometimes interested in are mediating variables and moderating variables. A **moderating variable** is a variable that affects the nature of the relationship between an independent and a dependent variable such that the relationship depends on the level of the moderating variable. Moderating variables are like contingency variables in that they indicate when an independent variable is most likely to be related to a dependent variable. In the example above about the attendance bonus, a moderating variable might be pay satisfaction. If the bonus only reduces the absenteeism of employees who are *not* satisfied with their pay and has no effect on the absenteeism of employees who are satisfied with their pay, then we would conclude that pay satisfaction moderates the effect of the bonus on absenteeism.

Sometimes we want to know why an independent variable predicts or causes a dependent variable. In such cases, we are interested in a mediating variable. A **mediating variable** is a variable that intervenes or explains the relationship between an independent and a dependent variable. To return to the attendance bonus example, we might want to know why the bonus reduces absenteeism. One possibility might be that the bonus increases people's motivation. Thus, motivation intervenes or mediates the relationship between the attendance bonus and absenteeism.

Measurement of Variables

Reliability. An index of the consistency of a research subject's responses.

Validity. An index of the extent to which a measure truly reflects what it is supposed to measure.

Good researchers carefully measure the variables they choose. For one thing, a measure should exhibit high reliability. **Reliability** is an index of the consistency of a research subject's responses. For example, if we ask someone several questions about how fair his or her pay is, the person should respond roughly the same way to each question. Similarly, the person should respond roughly the same way to the same questions next week or next month if there has been no change in pay.

Measures should also exhibit high validity. **Validity** is an index of the extent to which a measure truly reflects what it is supposed to measure. For instance, a good measure of perceived pay fairness should not be influenced by employees' feelings of fairness about other workplace factors like supervision. Also, a researcher would expect people who are objectively underpaid to report high pay unfairness and for them to report increased fairness if their pay were increased. Researchers are often able to choose measures with a known history of reliability and validity.

Good measures should also be strongly related to other measures of the same variable and should not be related to measures of different variables. For example, a measure of job satisfaction should be highly correlated to other measures of job satisfaction. This is known as **convergent validity**, and it exists when there is a strong relationship between different measures of the same variable. In addition, good measures should not be related to measures of different variables. For example, a measure of job satisfaction should not be strongly related to measures of job performance. This is known as **discriminant validity**, and it exists when there is a weak relationship between measures of different variables. Good measures should have both convergent and discriminant validity. Thus, a measure of job satisfaction should be more strongly related to other measures of job satisfaction than to measures of job performance.

There are three basic kinds of research techniques: observation, correlation, and experimentation. As you will see, each begins with a research question or questions. Correlation and experimentation are most likely to test specific hypotheses and devote explicit attention to measurement quality.

Convergent validity. When there is a strong relationship between different measures of the same variable.

Discriminant validity. When there is a weak relationship between measures of different variables.

OBSERVATIONAL TECHNIQUES

Observational research techniques are the most straightforward ways of finding out about behaviour in organizations and thus come closest to the ways in which we develop common-sense views about such behaviour. In this case, *observation* means just what it implies—the researcher proceeds to examine the natural activities of people in an organizational setting by listening to what they say and watching what they do. The difference between our everyday observations and the formal observations of the trained behavioural scientist is expressed by those key words *systematic* and *objective*.

First, the researcher approaches the organizational setting with extensive training concerning the nature of human behaviour and a particular set of questions that the observation is designed to answer. These factors provide a systematic framework for the business of observing. Second, the behavioural scientist attempts to keep a careful ongoing record of the events that he or she observes, either as they occur or as soon as possible afterwards. Thus, excessive reliance on memory, which may lead to inaccuracies, is unnecessary. Finally, the behavioural scientist is well informed of the dangers of influencing the behaviour of those whom he or she is observing and is trained to draw reasonable conclusions from his or her observations. These factors help ensure objectivity.

The outcomes of observational research are summarized in a narrative form, sometimes called a *case study*. This narrative specifies the nature of the organization, people, and events studied, the particular role of and techniques used by the observer, the research questions, and the events observed.

Observational research. Research that examines the natural activities of people in an organizational setting by listening to what they say and watching what they do.

Participant Observation

One obvious way for a researcher to find out about organizational behaviour is to actively participate in this behaviour. In **participant observation** the researcher becomes a functioning member of the organizational unit he or she is studying to conduct the research. At this point you may wonder, "Wait a minute. What about objectivity? What about influencing the behaviour of those being studied?" These are clearly legitimate questions, and they might be answered in the following way: In adopting participant observation, the researcher is making a conscious bet that the advantages of participation outweigh these problems. It is doubtless true in some cases that "there is no substitute for experience." For example, researcher Robert Sutton wanted to find out how employees cope with jobs that require them to express negative emotions.[1] To do this, he trained and then worked as a bill collector. This is obviously a more personal experience than simply interviewing bill collectors.

Participant observation. Observational research in which the researcher becomes a functioning member of the organizational unit being studied.

Another advantage to participant observation is its potential for secrecy—the subjects need not know that they are being observed. This potential for secrecy does raise some ethical issues, however. Sociologist Tom Lupton served as an industrial worker in two plants in England to study the factors that influenced productivity.[2] Although he could have acted in secrecy, he was required to inform management and union officials of his presence to secure records and documents, and he thus felt it unfair not to inform his workmates of his purpose. It should be stressed that his goals were academic, and he was *not* working for the managements of the companies involved. Sometimes, however, secrecy seems necessary to accomplish a research goal, as the following study of "illegal" industrial behaviour shows.

Joseph Bensman and Israel Gerver investigated an important organizational problem: What happens when the activities that appear to be required to get a job done conflict with official organizational policy?[3] Examples of such conflicts include the punch press operator who must remove the safety guard from his machine to meet productivity standards, the executive who must deliver corporate money to a political slush fund, or the police officer who cannot find time to complete an eight-page report to justify having drawn her revolver on a night patrol.

The behaviour of interest to Bensman and Gerver was the unauthorized use of taps by aircraft plant workers. A tap is a hard steel hand tool used to cut threads into metal. The possession of this device by aircraft assemblers was strictly forbidden because the workers could use it to correct sloppy or difficult work like the misalignment of bolt holes in two pieces of aircraft skin or stripped lock nuts; both of these problems could lead to potential structural weaknesses or maintenance problems.

Possession of a tap was a strict violation of company policy, and a worker could be fired on the spot for it. On the other hand, since supervisors were under extreme pressure to maintain a high quota of completed work, the occasional use of a tap to correct a problem could save hours of disassembly and realignment time. How was this conflict resolved? The answer was provided by one of the authors, who served as a participant observer while functioning as an assembler. Put simply, the supervisors and inspectors worked together to encourage the cautious and appropriate use of taps. New workers were gradually introduced to the mysteries of tapping by experienced workers, and the supervisors provided refinement of skills and signals as to when a tap might be used. Taps were not to be used in front of inspectors or to correct chronic sloppy work. If "caught," tappers were expected to act truly penitent in response to a chewing out by the supervisors, even if the supervisors themselves had suggested the use of the tap. In short, a *social ritual* was developed to teach and control the use of the tap to facilitate getting the work out without endangering the continued presence of the crucial tool. Clearly, this is the kind of information about organizational behaviour that would be extremely difficult to obtain except by participant observation.

Direct Observation

Direct observation.
Observational research in which the researcher observes organizational behaviour without taking part in the studied activity.

In **direct observation** the researcher observes organizational behaviour without participation in the activity being observed. There are a number of reasons why one might choose direct observation over participant observation. First, there are many situations in which the introduction of a new person into an existing work setting would severely disrupt and change the nature of the activities in that setting. These are cases in which the "influence" criticism of participant observation is especially true. Second, there are many job tasks that a trained behavioural scientist could not be expected to learn for research purposes. For example, it seems unreasonable to expect a researcher to spend years acquiring the skills of a pilot or banker to be able to investigate what happens in the cockpit of an airliner or in a boardroom. Finally, participant observation places rather severe limitations on the observers' opportunity to record information. Existence of these conditions suggests the use of direct observation. In theory, the researcher could carry out such observation covertly, but there are few studies of organizational behaviour in which the presence of the direct observer was not known and explained to those being observed.

Henry Mintzberg's study of the work performed by chief executives of two manufacturing companies, a hospital, a school system, and a consulting firm provides an excellent example of the use of direct observation.[4] At first glance, this might appear to be an inane thing to investigate. After all, everybody knows that managers plan, organize, lead, and control, or some similar combination of words. In fact, Mintzberg argues that we actually know very little about the routine, everyday behaviour managers use to achieve these vague goals. Furthermore, if we ask managers what they do (in an interview or questionnaire), they usually respond with a variation of the plan-organize-lead-control theme.

Mintzberg spent a week with each of his five executives, watching them at their desks, attending meetings with them, listening to their phone calls, and inspecting their mail. He kept detailed records of these activities and gradually developed a classification scheme to make sense of them. What Mintzberg found counters the common-sense view that some hold of managers—sitting behind a large desk, reflecting on their organization's performance, and affixing their signatures to impressive documents all day. In fact, Mintzberg found that his managers actually performed a terrific amount of work and had little time for reflection. On an average day, they examined 36 pieces of mail, engaged in five telephone conversations, attended eight meetings, and made one tour of their facilities. Work-related reading encroached on home lives. These activities were varied, unpatterned, and of short duration. Half the activities lasted less than nine minutes, and 90 percent less than one hour. Furthermore, these activities tended to be directed toward current, specific issues rather than past, general issues. Finally, the managers revealed a clear preference for verbal communications, by either telephone or unscheduled face-to-face meetings; in fact, two-thirds of their contacts were of this nature. In contrast, they generated an average of only one piece of mail a day.

In summary, both participant and direct observation capture the depth, breadth, richness, spontaneity, and realism of organizational behaviour. However, they also share some weaknesses. One of these weaknesses is a lack of control over the environment in which the study is being conducted. Thus, Mintzberg could not ensure that unusual events would not affect the executives' behaviour. Also, the small number of observers and situations in the typical observational study is problematic. With only one observer, there is a strong potential for selective perceptions and interpretations of observed events. Since only a few situations are analyzed, the extent to which the observed behaviours can be generalized to other settings is limited. (Do most executives behave like the five that Mintzberg studied?) It is probably safe to say that observational techniques are best used to make an initial examination of some organizational event on which little information is available and to generate ideas for further investigation with more refined techniques.

CORRELATIONAL TECHNIQUES

Correlational research attempts to measure variables precisely and examine relationships among these variables without introducing change into the research setting. Correlational research sacrifices some of the breadth and richness of the observational techniques for more precision of measurement and greater control. It necessarily involves some abstraction of the real event that is the focus of observation to accomplish this precision and control. More specifically, correlational approaches differ from observational approaches in terms of the nature of the data researchers collect and the issues they investigate.

The data of observational studies are most frequently observer notes. We hope that these data exhibit reliability and validity. Unfortunately, because observations are gen-

Correlational research. Research that attempts to measure variables precisely and examine relationships among these variables without introducing change into the research setting.

erally the products of a single individual viewing a unique event, we have very little basis on which to judge their reliability and validity.

The data of correlational studies involve surveys and interviews as well as existing data. **Surveys** involve the use of questionnaires to gather data from participants who answer questions on the relevant variables. The **interview** is a technique in which the researcher asks respondents a series of questions to gather data on the variables of interest. Interview data can be quantitative and similar to that obtained from a survey or it can be more qualitative and descriptive. The type of data obtained will depend on the purpose of the interview and the nature of the questions asked. **Existing data** come from organizational records and include productivity, absence, and demographic information (e.g., age, gender). Variables often measured by surveys and interviews include:

- employees' perceptions of how their managers behave on the job,
- the extent to which employees are satisfied with their jobs, and
- employees' reports about how much autonomy they have on their jobs.

It is possible to determine in advance of doing research the extent to which such measures are reliable and valid. Thus, when constructing a questionnaire to measure job satisfaction, the researcher can check its reliability by repeatedly administering it to a group of workers over a period of time. If individual responses remain fairly stable, there is evidence of reliability. Evidence of the validity of a questionnaire might come from its ability to predict which employees would quit the organization for work elsewhere. It seems reasonable that dissatisfied employees would be more likely to quit, and such an effect is partial evidence of the validity of a satisfaction measure.

In addition to the nature of the data collected, correlational studies differ from observational studies in terms of the kinds of events they investigate. Although the questions investigated by observational research appear fairly specific (What maintains an "illegal" behaviour such as tapping? What do executives do?), virtually any event relevant to the question is fair game for observation. Thus, such studies are extremely broad based. Correlational research sacrifices this broadness to investigate the relationship (correlation) between specific, well-defined variables. The relationship between the variables of interest is usually stated as a hypothesis of the relationship between an independent and a dependent variable. Using the variables mentioned above, we can construct three sample hypotheses and describe how they would be tested:

- Employees who are satisfied with their jobs will tend to be more productive than those who are less satisfied. To test this, a researcher might administer a reliable, valid questionnaire concerning satisfaction and obtain production data from company records.
- Employees who perceive their supervisor as friendly and considerate will be more satisfied with their jobs than those who do not. To test this, a researcher might use reliable, valid questionnaires or interview measures of both variables.
- Older employees will be absent less than younger employees. To test this, a researcher might obtain data concerning the age of employees and their absenteeism from organizational records.

In each case, the researcher is interested in a very specific set of variables, and he or she devotes effort to measuring them precisely.

A good example of a correlational study is that of Belle Rose Ragins and John Cotton, who studied employees' willingness to serve as mentors to newer organizational members.[5] Mentorship was defined as helping a junior person with career support and upward mobility. The major focus of the study was the relationship between gender (the independent variable) and willingness to mentor (the dependent variable). The authors reviewed literature that hypothesizes that women may face more barriers to becoming mentors than men because they are in a minority in many employment settings. The authors were also interested in the relationships between age, organizational rank, length of employment, and prior mentorship experience and willingness to mentor.

Surveys. The use of questionnaires to gather data from participants who answer questions on the relevant variables.

Interview. A technique in which the researcher asks respondents a series of questions to gather data on the variables of interest.

Existing data. Data that is obtained from organizational records, such as productivity, absence, and demographic information.

These variables were measured with questionnaires completed by over 500 employees in three research and development organizations. The researchers found that men and women were equally willing to serve as mentors, although the women perceived more barriers (e.g., lack of qualifications and time) to being a mentor. They also found that higher rank and prior experience as a mentor or a protégé were associated with greater willingness to mentor. Notice that a study such as this could also incorporate existing data from records. For example, we might hypothesize that those with better performance evaluations would be more confident about serving as mentors.

Correlation and Causation

A final important point should be made about correlational studies. Consider a hypothesis that friendly, considerate supervisors will have more productive employees than unfriendly, inconsiderate supervisors. In this case, a researcher might have some employees describe the friendliness of their supervisors on a reliable, valid questionnaire designed to measure this variable and obtain employees' productivity levels from company records. The results of this hypothetical study are plotted in Exhibit A.1, where each dot represents an employee's response to the questionnaire in conjunction with his or her productivity. In general, it would appear that the hypothesis is confirmed—that is, employees who describe their supervisor as friendly tend to be more productive than those who describe him or her as unfriendly. As a result of this study, should an organization attempt to select friendly supervisors or even train existing supervisors to be more friendly to obtain higher productivity? The answer is no. The training and selection proposal assumes that friendly supervisors *cause* their employees to be productive, and this might not be the case. Put simply, supervisors might be friendly *if* their employees are productive. This is a possible interpretation of the data, and it does not suggest that selection or training to make supervisors friendly will achieve higher productivity. This line of argument should not be unfamiliar to you. Heavy smokers and cigarette company lobbyists like to claim that smoking is related to the incidence of lung cancer because cancer proneness prompts smoking, rather than vice versa. The point here is that *correlation does not imply causation*. How can we find out which factors cause certain organizational behaviours? The answer is to perform an experiment.

EXPERIMENTAL TECHNIQUES

If observational research involves observing nature, and correlational research involves measuring nature, **experimental research** manipulates nature. In an experiment, a variable is manipulated or changed under controlled conditions, and the consequence of this manipulation for some other variable is measured. If all other conditions are truly

Experimental research. Research that changes or manipulates a variable under controlled conditions and examines the consequences of this manipulation for some other variable.

EXHIBIT A.1
Hypothetical data from a correlational study of the relationship between supervisory friendliness and employee productivity.

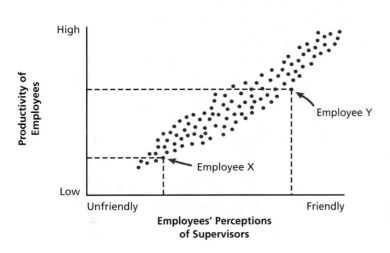

controlled, and a change in the second variable follows the change that was introduced in the first variable, we can infer that the first change has caused the second change.

In experimental language, the variable that the researcher manipulates or changes is the independent variable. The variable that the independent variable is expected to affect is the dependent variable. Consider the following hypothesis: The introduction of recorded music into the work setting will lead to increased productivity. In this hypothesis, the independent variable is music, which is expected to affect productivity, the dependent variable. Consider another hypothesis: Stimulating, challenging jobs will increase the satisfaction of the workforce. Here, the design of the job is the independent variable and satisfaction is the dependent variable.

Let's return to our hypothesis that friendly, considerate supervisors will tend to have more productive employees. If we wish to determine whether friendly supervision contributes to employee productivity, the style of supervision becomes the independent variable, and productivity becomes the dependent variable. This means that the researcher must manipulate or change the friendliness of some supervisors and observe what happens to the productivity of their employees. In practice, this would probably be accomplished by exposing the bosses to some form of human relations training designed to teach them to be more considerate and personable toward their workers.

Exhibit A.2 shows the results of this hypothetical experiment. The line on the graph represents the average productivity of a number of employees whose supervisors have received our training. We see that this productivity increased and remained higher following the introduction of the training. Does this mean that friendliness indeed increases productivity and that we should proceed to train all of our supervisors in this manner? The answer is again *no*. We cannot be sure that *something else* did not occur at the time of the training to influence productivity, such as a change in equipment or job insecurity prompted by rumoured layoffs. To control this possibility, we need a control group of supervisors who are not exposed to the training, and we need productivity data for their employees. A **control group** is a group of research subjects who have not been exposed to the experimental treatment, in this case not exposed to the training. Ideally, these supervisors should be as similar as possible in experience and background to those who receive the training, and their employees should be performing at the same level. The results of our improved experiment are shown in Exhibit A.3. Here, we see that the productivity of the employees whose supervisors were trained increases following training, while that of the control supervisors remains constant. We can, thus, infer that the human relations training affected employee productivity.

The extent to which a researcher can be confident that changes in a dependent variable are due to the independent variable is known as **internal validity**. Note that this is different from the validity of a measure, which was discussed earlier. Internal validity

Control group. A group of research subjects who have not been exposed to the experimental treatment.

Internal validity. The extent to which a researcher has confidence that changes in a dependent variable are due to the independent variable.

EXHIBIT A.2
Hypothetical data from an experiment concerning human relations training.

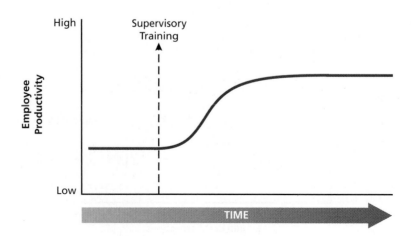

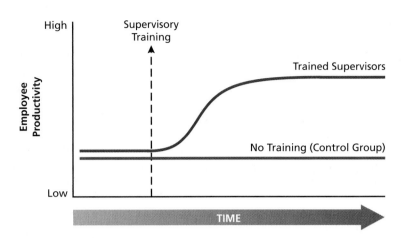

EXHIBIT A.3
Hypothetical data from an improved experiment concerning human relations training.

has to do with the validity of an experimental design. To return to the example above, if a control group was not included in the design, then the internal validity would be low because other factors might explain the improvement in productivity. What are some of these other factors? Perhaps something happened at the same time that the supervisors were trained, such as a pay increase or bonus, or perhaps new equipment or technology was implemented. Factors that are alternative explanations for the results of an experiment are called *threats to internal validity* (see Exhibit A.4). Without a control group, there are many threats to internal validity that might be responsible for a change in productivity. However, with a control group, one can have much more confidence that the improvement was due to the training program. Thus, internal validity increases the confidence that one has in concluding that the training program was the cause of the improvement in productivity and not something else.

John Ivancevich and Herbert Lyon conducted an interesting experiment that examined the effects of a shortened workweek on the employees of a company that manufactures food-packaging equipment.[6] The independent variable was the length of the workweek (4 days, 40 hours versus 5 days, 40 hours). Two of the company's divisions

EXHIBIT A.4
Threats to Internal Validity

Selection of participants. When participants selected for the experimental group differ from those in the control group in some way that influences the results of an experiment.

Testing. The process of completing a survey and answering questions at the start of an experiment might sensitize participants to the study and influence how they respond to the same questions after the experiment.

Instrumentation. If different measures are used at different times during the course of an experiment, then any changes in participants' scores might be due to differences in the measures used.

Statistical regression. This is the tendency of scores on a measure to shift over time toward the mean score. Participants who perform poorly on a test before an experiment might have higher scores after an experiment simply due to regression toward the mean.

History. Events or factors that occur during the course of an experiment and can explain changes in the dependent variable.

Maturation. Natural changes in participants that are due to the passage of time (e.g., job experience) and can result in changes in the dependent variable.

Mortality. When certain types of participants drop out of an experiment before it has ended and those who remain and complete the dependent measures differ in some way from those who dropped out.

were converted to a 4–40 week from a 5–40 week. A third division, remaining on the 5–40 schedule, served as a control group. Workers in the control division were similar to those in the other divisions in terms of age, seniority, education, and salary. The dependent variables (measured one month before the conversion and several times after) included the workers' responses to a questionnaire concerning job satisfaction and stress, absence data from company records, and performance appraisals conducted by supervisors. After 12 months, several aspects of satisfaction and performance showed a marked improvement for the 4–40 workers, when compared with the 5–40 workers. However, at 25 months this edge existed for only one aspect of satisfaction— satisfaction with personal worth. The authors concluded that benefits that had been proposed for the 4–40 workweek were of short-term duration.

A CONTINUUM OF RESEARCH TECHNIQUES

You might reasonably wonder which of the research techniques just discussed is most effective. As shown in Exhibit A.5, these methods can be placed on a continuum ranging from rich, broad based, and loosely controlled (observation) to specific, precise, and rigorous (experimentation). The method that researchers use to investigate organizational behaviour is dictated by the nature of the problem that interests them. In the writing of this section of the chapter, special pains were taken to choose examples of problems that were well suited to the research techniques employed to investigate them. Bensman and Gerver, as well as Mintzberg, were interested in variables that were not well defined. The variables were thus not easy to isolate and measure precisely, and observation was the appropriate technique. Furthermore, "tapping" was a controversial issue, and the researchers would have had to develop considerable trust to investigate it with questionnaires or formal interviews. Similarly, Mintzberg insists that questionnaires and interviews have failed to tell us what executives actually do. Ragins and Cotton, who studied mentoring, were interested in specific variables that were relatively easily measured. On the other hand, they were not in a position to manipulate the causes of intention to mentor. Ivancevich and Lyon were also interested in a specific set of variables, and they conducted their research on the short workweek in a situation where it was both possible and ethical to manipulate the workweek. In all these cases, the research technique the researchers chose was substantially better than dependence on common sense or opinion.

COMBINING RESEARCH TECHNIQUES

Robert Sutton and Anat Rafaeli tested what might seem to be an obvious hypothesis— that friendly, pleasant behaviour on the part of sales clerks would be positively associated with store sales.[7] As obvious as this might seem, it would be a good idea to confirm it before spending thousands of dollars on human relations training for clerks. The study combined correlational and observational methods. In the quantitative correlational part of the study, teams of researchers entered a large North American chain's 576 convenience stores and, posing as shoppers, evaluated the friendliness of the sales clerks on rating scales. They also recorded other factors, such as the length of the line at the register. Existing data from company records provided the total annual

EXHIBIT A.5
Continuum of research techniques.

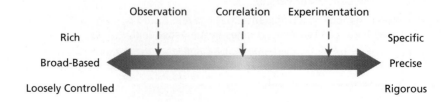

sales each store recorded. When the researchers analyzed the data, the results were surprising—the "unfriendly" stores tended to chalk up higher sales!

To understand this unexpected result, the authors resorted to qualitative, observational research techniques. Specifically, each author spent extensive time in many of the convenience stores directly observing transactions between customers and clerks. In addition, each spent time as a participant-observer, actually doing the sales clerk's job. This observation resolved the mystery. The researchers found that when the stores were busy, the sales clerks tended to stop the small talk, concentrate on their work, and process customers as quickly as possible. This behaviour corresponded to customers' expectations for fast service in a convenience store. When business was slow, clerks tended to be friendly and engage in small talk to relieve boredom. Since the busier stores generated higher sales, it is not surprising that their clerks were less friendly. In fact, further analysis of the correlational data showed that clerks were less friendly when the lines were longer.

This study illustrates how two research techniques can complement each other. It also shows that correlation does not imply causation. Although sales were negatively correlated with friendliness, volume of sales affected the expression of friendliness, not the other way around. Of course, these results would probably not generalize to sales settings in which customers expect more personal attention.

ISSUES AND CONCERNS IN ORGANIZATIONAL BEHAVIOUR RESEARCH

As in every field of study, particular issues confront researchers in organizational behaviour. Three of these issues include sampling, Hawthorne effects, and ethical concerns.

Sampling

Researchers are usually interested in generalizing the results of their research beyond their study. The extent to which the results of a study generalize to other samples and settings is known as **external validity**. External validity will be greater when the results of a study are based on large, random samples. Large samples ensure that the results they obtain are truly representative of the individuals, groups, or organizations being studied and not merely the product of an extreme case or two.

Random sampling means that the research participants have been randomly chosen from the population of interest. Random samples ensure that all relevant individuals, groups, or organizations have an equal probability of being studied and give confidence in the generalizability of the findings. As was noted earlier, observational studies usually involve small samples, and they are seldom randomized. Thus, generalizing from such studies is a problem. However, a well-designed observational study that answers important questions is surely superior to a large-sample, randomized correlational study that enables one to generalize about a trivial hypothesis.

In experimental research, randomization means randomly assigning subjects to experimental and control conditions. To illustrate the importance of this, we can reconsider the hypothetical study on human relations training. Suppose that instead of randomly assigning supervisors to the experimental and control groups, managers nominate supervisors for training. Suppose further that to "reward" them for their long service, more-experienced supervisors are nominated for the training. This results in an experimental group containing more-experienced supervisors and a control group containing less-experienced supervisors. If supervisory experience promotes employee productivity, we might erroneously conclude that it was the *human relations training* that led to any improved results and that our hypothesis is confirmed. Poor sampling due to a lack of randomization has biased the results in favour of our

External validity. The extent to which the results of a study generalize to other samples and settings.

Random sampling. The research participants are randomly chosen from the population of interest.

hypothesis. To achieve randomization, it would be a good idea to ascertain that the employees of the experimental and control supervisors were equally productive *before* the training began. Random sampling is another way to lower the threats to internal validity. In this example, the threat to internal validity was due to the fact that the supervisors in the experimental condition had more experience than those in the control group (as shown in Exhibit A.4, this threat to internal validity is called *selection of participants*), and this might explain the results of the experiment.

Hawthorne Effects

Hawthorne effect. A favourable response by subjects in an organizational experiment that is the result of a factor other than the independent variable that is formally being manipulated.

The Hawthorne effect was discovered as a result of a series of studies conducted at the Hawthorne plant of the Western Electric Company near Chicago many years ago. As explained in Chapter 1, these studies examined the effects of independent variables, such as rest pauses, lighting intensity, and pay incentives, on the productivity of assemblers of electrical components.[8] In a couple of these loosely controlled experiments, unusual results occurred. In the illumination study, both experimental and control workers improved their productivity. In another study, productivity increased and remained high despite the introduction and withdrawal of factors such as rest pauses, shortened workdays, and so on. These results gave rise to the **Hawthorne effect**, which might be defined as a favourable response of subjects in an organizational experiment to a factor other than the independent variable that is formally being manipulated. Researchers have concluded that this "other factor" is psychological in nature, although it is not well understood.[9] Likely candidates include subjects' reactions to special attention, including feelings of prestige, heightened morale, and so on. The point is that researchers might misinterpret the true reason for any observed change in behaviour because research subjects can have unmeasured feelings about their role in the research.

To return to the human relations training experiment, a Hawthorne effect might occur if the experimental subjects are grateful to management for selecting them for this special training and resolve to work harder back on the job. The supervisors might put in longer hours thinking up ways to improve productivity that have nothing to do with the training they received. However, the researcher could easily conclude that the human relations training improved productivity.

It is very difficult to prevent Hawthorne effects. However, it is possible, if expensive, to see whether they have occurred. To do so, investigators establish a second experimental group that receives special treatment and attention but is not exposed to the key independent variable. In the human relations experiment, this could involve training that is not expected to increase productivity. If the productivity of the supervisors' employees in both experimental groups increases equally, the Hawthorne effect is probably present. If productivity increases only in the human relations training condition, it is unlikely to be due to the Hawthorne effect.

Ethics

Researchers in organizational behaviour, no matter who employs them, have an ethical obligation to do rigorous research and to report that research accurately.[10] In all cases, the psychological and physical well-being of the research subjects is of prime importance. In general, ethical researchers avoid unnecessary deception, inform participants about the general purpose of their research, and protect the anonymity of research subjects. For example, in a correlational study involving the use of questionnaires, investigators should explain the general reason for the research and afford potential subjects the opportunity to decline participation. If names or company identification numbers are required to match responses with data in employee files (e.g., absenteeism or subsequent turnover), investigators must guarantee that they will not make individual responses public. In some observation studies and experiments, subjects may be unaware that their behaviour is under formal study. In these cases, researchers have special obligations to prevent negative consequences for subjects. Ethical research has a practical side as well as a moral side. Good cooperation from research subjects is necessary to do good research. Such cooperation is easier to obtain when people are confident that ethical procedures are the rule, not the exception.

LEARNING OBJECTIVES CHECKLIST

1. All research in organizational behaviour begins with a basic question about work or organizations. Frequently, researchers express the question as a *hypothesis*, a formal statement of the expected relationship between two variables. *Variables* are simply measures that can take on two or more values.

2. In most research, we are concerned with two kinds of variables. The *independent variable* is a predictor or cause of variation in a dependent variable. The *dependent variable* is a variable that will vary as a result of changes in the independent variable. Two other kinds of variables that we are sometimes interested in are mediating variables and moderating variables. A *moderating variable* is a variable that affects the nature of the relationship between an independent and dependent variable such that the relationship depends on the level of the moderating variable. A *mediating variable* is a variable that intervenes or explains the relationship between an independent and dependent variable.

3. Careful measurement of variables is important in research. *Reliability* is an index of the consistency of a research subject's responses. *Validity* is an index of the extent to which a measure truly reflects what it is supposed to measure. *Convergent validity* exists when there is a strong relationship between different measures of the same variable. *Discriminant validity* exists when there is a weak relationship between measures of different variables.

4. In *observational research,* one or a few observers assess one or a few instances of organizational behaviour in its natural setting. In *participant observation*, the observer actually takes part in the activity being observed. In *direct observation*, the assessment occurs without the active participation of the researcher.

5. Compared with observation, *correlational research* techniques attempt to measure the variables in question more precisely by using questionnaires, interviews, and existing data. No change is introduced into the research setting. One problem with correlational research is its inability to imply causation. Researchers use experiments to overcome this problem.

6. In *experimental research*, the investigator actually changes or manipulates some factor in the organizational setting and measures the effect that this manipulation has on behaviour. In experimental language, the variable that the researcher manipulates or changes is the independent variable and the variable that the independent variable is expected to affect is the dependent variable. Causation can be inferred from a carefully designed experiment that has high internal validity. *Internal validity* refers to the confidence that the researcher has in concluding that changes in the dependent variable are due to the independent variable. Threats to internal validity are alternative explanations for the results of an experiment. The use of a control group and random assignment to experimental and control conditions increases internal validity and lowers threats to internal validity.

7. The method that researchers use to investigate organizational behaviour is dictated by the nature of the problem under investigation. When variables are not well defined and not easy to isolate and measure precisely, *observation* is an appropriate technique. Some of the weaknesses of observational research include a lack of control over the environment in which the study is being conducted and the small number of observers and situations in the typical observational study. Observational techniques are best used to make an initial examination of some organizational event on which little information is available and to generate ideas for further investigation with

more refined techniques. When the researcher is interested in specific variables that are well defined and relatively easy to measure but cannot be manipulated, *correlational research* is an appropriate technique. Correlational research provides more precision and greater control than observational techniques; however, it cannot be used to study causation. When the researcher is interested in causation and the effect of an independent variable on a dependent variable and it is both possible and ethical to manipulate the independent variable, *experimental research* is an appropriate technique. Experimental research provides the greatest amount of rigour but sacrifices the breadth and richness of less rigorous techniques like observational research.

8. *External validity* refers to the extent to which the results of a study generalize to other samples and settings. External validity will be greater when the results of a study are based on large, random samples. A *random sample* means that the research participants have been randomly chosen from the population of interest. This ensures that all relevant individuals, groups, or organizations have an equal probability of being studied and give confidence in the generalizability of the findings.

9. The *Hawthorne effect* refers to a favourable response of subjects in an organizational experiment to a factor other than the independent variable that is formally being manipulated. Researchers have concluded that this "other factor" is psychological in nature, although it is not well understood. Likely candidates include subjects' reactions to special attention, including feelings of prestige, heightened morale, and so on. The point is that researchers might misinterpret the true reason for any observed change in behaviour because research subjects can have unmeasured feelings about their role in the research.

10. Researchers in organizational behaviour have an ethical obligation to do rigorous research and to report that research accurately. In all cases, the psychological and physical well-being of the research subjects is of prime importance. In general, ethical researchers avoid unnecessary deception, inform participants about the general purpose of their research, and protect the anonymity of research subjects.

REFERENCES

Chapter 1

1. Based on Wahl, A. (2006, April 23). On the money. *Canadian Business, 79(8)*, 68–69; Intini, J., & Snider, M. (2005, October 24). It's all in the perks. *Maclean's, 118(43)*, 34; Macklem, K. (2004, October, 11). Canada's top 100 employers: No.1 Vancity confidential. *Maclean's, 117(41/42)*, 22; Lee, J. (2005, October 29). Vancity employees feel the difference. *Vancouver Sun*, E1; www.vancity.com/MyBusiness/AboutUs/

2. Katz, D. (1964). The motivational basis of organizational behavior. *Behavioral Science, 9*, 131–146.

3. Peters, T. (1990, Fall). Get innovative or get dead. *California Management Review*, 9–26.

4. Pfeffer, J. (1994). *Competitive advantage through people: Unleashing the power of the work force*. Harvard Business School Press: Boston.

5. Chisholm, P. (2000, May 29). What the boss needs to know. *Maclean's, 113(22)*, 18–22.

6. Wren, D. (1987). *The evolution of management thought* (3rd ed.). New York: Wiley.

7. For a summary of their work and relevant references, see Wren, 1987.

8. Taylor, F.W. (1967). *The principles of scientific management*. New York: Norton.

9. Weber, M. (1974). *The theory of social and economic organization* (A. M. Henderson & T. Parsons, Trans.). New York: Free Press.

10. See Wren, 1987.

11. Roethlisberger, F.J., & Dickson, W.J. (1939). *Management and the worker*. Cambridge, MA: Harvard University Press; Wrege, C.D., & Greenwood, R.G. (1986). The Hawthorne studies. In D.A. Wren & J.A. Pearce II (Eds.), *Papers dedicated to the development of modern management*. Academy of Management.

12. Argyris, C. (1957). *Personality and organization*. New York: Harper.

13. Likert, R. (1961). *New patterns of management*. New York: McGraw-Hill.

14. Gouldner, A.W. (1954). *Patterns of industrial bureaucracy*. New York: Free Press.

15. Selznick, P. (1949). *TVA and the grass roots: A study in the sociology of formal organizations*. Berkeley: University of California Press.

16. Abrahamson, E. (1991). Managerial fads and fashions: The diffusion and rejection of innovations. *Academy of Management Review, 16*, 586–612; Johns, G. (1993). Constraints on the adoption of psychology-based personnel practices: Lessons from organizational innovation. *Personnel Psychology, 46*, 569–592.

17. Mintzberg, H. (1973). *The nature of managerial work*. New York: Harper & Row. See also Mintzberg, H. (1994, Fall). Rounding out the manager's job. *Sloan Management Review*, 11–26.

18. See Gibbs, B. (1994). The effects of environment and technology on managerial roles. *Journal of Management, 20, 581–604*; Kraut, A.I., Pedigo, P.R., McKenna, D.D., & Dunnette, M.D. (1989, November). The role of the manager: What's really important in different management jobs. *Academy of Management Executive*, 286–293.

19. Luthans, F., Hodgetts, R.M., & Rosenkrantz, S.A. (1988). *Real managers*. Cambridge, MA: Ballinger.

20. Kotter, J.P. (1982). *The general managers*. New York: Free Press.

21. Simon, H.A. (1987, February). Making management decisions: The role of intuition and emotion. *Academy of Management Executive*, 57–64; Isenberg, D.J. (1984, November–December). How senior managers think. *Harvard Business Review*, 80–90. See also Sims, H.P., Jr., & Gioia, D.A. (Eds.) (1986). *The thinking organization: Dynamics of organizational social cognition*. San Francisco: Jossey-Bass.

22. Hofstede, G. (1993, February). Cultural constraints in management theories. *Academy of Management Executive*, 81–94.

23. Crawford, M. (1993, May). The new office etiquette. *Canadian Business*, 22–31.

24. Kanungo, R.N. (1998). Leadership in organizations: Looking ahead to the 21st century. *Canadian Psychology, 39 (1–2)*, 71–82.

25. Mahoney, J. (2005, March 23). Visible majority by 2017. *Globe and Mail*, pp. A1, A7.

26. Mingail, H. (2004, September 29). Wise ways for retraining older workers. *Globe and Mail*, p. C8.

27. Galt, V. (2006, March 15). 65 means freedom to start a whole new career. *Globe and Mail*, pp. C1, C2.

28. Galt, V. (2005, September 20). Few firms adopt plans to retain aging staff. *Globe and Mail*, p. B7.

29. Javidan, M., Dorfman, P.W., de Luque, M.S., & House, R.J. (2006). In the eye of the beholder: Cross cultural lessons in leadership from Project GLOBE. *Academy of Management Perspectives, 20*, 67–90.

30. Armstrong-Stassen, M. (1998). Alternative work arrangements: Meeting the challenges. *Canadian Psychology, 39*, 108–123; Meyer, J.P., Allen, N.J., & Topolnytsky, L. (1998). Commitment in a changing world of work. *Canadian Psychology, 39*, 83–93.

31. Galt, V. (2003, January 28). One-third of employees loathe their jobs, consultants find. *Globe and Mail*, pp. B1, B6; Galt, V. (2005, November 15). Fewer workers willing to put in 110%. *Globe and Mail*, pp. B1, B6; Carniol, N. (2005, November 15). Fewer workers willing to give 100 per cent. *Toronto Star*, pp. D1, D11.

32. (2002, August 26). Workers' morale sliding. *Globe and Mail*, p. B11 (Reuters News Agency).

33. Attersley, J. (2005, November 7). Absence makes the bottom line wander. *Canadian HR Reporter*, p. R2; Chisholm, P. (2000, May 29); Galt, V. (2003, June 4). Workers rack up increased sick time. *Globe and Mail*, pp. C1, C3.

34. Duxbury, L., & Higgins, C. (2003). *Work–life conflict in Canada in the new millennium: A status report*. Ottawa: Health Canada.

35. Chisholm, P. (2001, March 5). Redesigning work. *Maclean's, 114 (10)*, 34–38.

36. See Bureau of Business Practice. (1992). *Profiles of Malcolm Baldrige Award winners*. Boston: Allyn & Bacon.

37. Shirouzu, N., & White, J.B. (2002, April 1). Car makers focus on quality. *Globe and Mail*, p. B8 (reprinted from the *Wall Street Journal*).

38. Shirouzu, N., & White, J. B. (2002, April 1).

39. Ansberry, C. (2002, March 27). Jobs morph to suit rapidly changing times. *Globe and Mail*, p. C2; Hitt, M.A., Keats, B.W., & DeMarie, S.M. (1998). Navigating in the new competitive landscape: Building strategic flexibility and competitive advantage in the 21st century. *Academy of Management Executive, 12*, 22–42.

40. McLaren, C. (2002, February 8). Ways to win top talent. *Globe and Mail*, p. C1.

41. McLaren, C. (2002, February 8).

42. (2000, January 17). How DuPont Canada keeps its employees. *Becoming the employer of choice. A special interest report published by the* Globe and Mail, p. E3.

43. Klie, S. (2005, September 26). 'Employees first' at CPX. *Canadian HR Reporter*, pp.1, 3; (2006, August 10). Breaking the rules: Hundreds of CPX o-o's see big raises from profit sharing program. *Today's Trucking Online*, www.todaystrucking.com/news.cfm?intDocID=16557&CFID=

44. McKay, S. (2001, February). The 35 best companies to work for in Canada. *Report on Business Magazine*, 53–62; Toda, B.H. (2000, February). The rewards: Being a good employer draws talent and unlocks success. *Report on Business Magazine*, 33.

Chapter 2

1. Based on Anonymous (2004, March 8). Telus awarded for development system. *Canadian HR Reporter, 17(5)*, p.16; Moralis, M. (2004, November 22). Trainers morph into new role. *Canadian HR Reporter, 17(20)*, p.G2, G10; Anonymous (2003, November). Canada calling. *T+D, 57(11)*, pp. 34, 46, 47; (2004, October 26). International award recognizes 'TELUS' training and development programs. http://about.telus.com/cgi-bin/news_viewer.cgi?news_id=510&mode=2&news_keywords=october%202004; (2003, November 14). American Society for Training & Development honours TELUS with 'Best Award.' http://about.telus.com/cgi-bin/news_viewer.cgi?news_id=406&mode=2&news_keywords=november%202003; (March 29, 2005). Executive honoured for making TELUS a learning organization. http://about.telus.com/cgi-bin/news_viewer.cgi?news_id=558&mode=2&news_year=2005; (2005, May 30). TELUS receives Program of the Year award at SkillSoft conference. http://about.telus.com/cgi-bin/news_viewer.cgi?news_id=581&mode=2&news_keywords=skillsoft.

2. George, J.M. (1992). The role of personality in organizational life: Issues and evidence. *Journal of Management, 18*, 185–213; Mount, M.K., & Barrick, M.R. (1995). The big five personality dimensions: Implications for research and practice in human resources management. In K.M. Rowland & G. Ferris (Eds.), *Research in personnel and human resources management* (Vol. 13, pp.153–200). Greenwich, CT: JAI Press.

3. George, 1992; Weiss, H.M., & Adler, S. (1984). Personality and organizational behavior. In B.M. Staw & L.L. Cummings (Eds.), *Research in organizational behavior* (Vol. 6, pp.1–50). Greenwich, CT: JAI Press.

4. Adler, S., & Weiss, H.M. (1988). Recent developments in the study of personality and organizational behavior. In C.L. Cooper & I. Robertson (Eds.), *International review of industrial and organizational psychology*. New York: Wiley.

5. Moses, S. (1991, November). Personality tests come back in I/O. *APA Monitor*, 9.

6. Mount & Barrick, 1995.

7. Digman, J.M. (1990). Personality structure: Emergence of the five-factor model. *Annual Review of Psychology, 41*, 417–440; Hogan, R.T. (1991). Personality and personality measurement. In M.D. Dunette & L.M. Hough (Eds.), *Handbook of industrial and organizational psychology* (2nd ed., Vol. 2). Palo Alto, CA: Consulting Psychologists Press; Barrick, M.R., & Mount, M.K. (1991). The big five personality dimensions and job performance: A meta-analysis. *Personnel Psychology, 44*, 1–26.

8. Judge, T.A., Higgins, C.A., Thorensen, C.J., & Barrick, M.R. (1999). The Big Five personality traits, general mental ability, and career success across the life span. *Personnel Psychology, 52*, 621–652.

9. Hough, L.M. et al. (1990). Criterion-related validities of personality constructs and the effect of response distortion on those validities. *Journal of Applied Psychology, 75*, 581–595; Tett, R.P., Jackson, D.N., & Rothstein, M. (1991). Personality measures as predictors of job performance: A meta-analytic review. *Personnel Psychology, 44,* 703–742.

10. Barrick & Mount, 1991.

11. Barrick, M.R., & Mount, M.K. (1993). Autonomy as a moderator of the relationship between the big five personality dimensions and job performance. *Journal of Applied Psychology, 78*, 111–118.

12. Ones, D.S., Viswesvaran, C., & Schmidt, F.L. (1993). Comprehensive meta-analysis of integrity test validities: Findings and implications for personnel selection and theories of job performance. *Journal of Applied Psychology, 78*, 679–703.

13. Judge, Higgins, Thorensen, & Barrick, 1999.

14. Judge, T. A., & Ilies, R. (2002). Relationship of personality to performance motivation: A meta-analytic review. *Journal of Applied Psychology, 87*, 797–807.

15. Judge, T.A., Heller, D., & Mount, M.K. (2002). Five-factor model of personality and job satisfaction: A meta-analysis. *Journal of Applied Psychology, 87*, 530–541; Morgeson, F.P., Reider, M.H., & Campion, M.A. (2005). Selecting individuals in team settings: The importance of social skills, personality characteristics, and team work knowledge. *Personnel Psychology, 58*, 583–611.

16. Kanfer, R., Wanberg, C.R., & Kantrowitz, T.M. (2001). Job search and employment: A personality-motivational analysis and meta-analytic review. *Journal of Applied Psychology, 86*, 837–855.

17. Judge, Higgins, Thorensen, & Barrick, 1999.

18. Barrick, M.R., Mount, M.K., & Gupta, R. (2003). Meta-analysis of the relationship between the five-factor model of personality and Holland's occupational types. *Personnel Psychology, 56*, 45–74.

19. Zhao, H. & Seibert, S.E. (2006). The big five personality dimensions and entrepreneurial status: A meta-analytic review. *Journal of Applied Psychology, 91*, 259–271.

20. Rotter, J.B. (1966). Generalized expectancies for internal versus external controls of reinforcement. *Psychological Monographs, 80* (Whole no. 609).

21. Szilagyi, A.D., & Sims, H.P., Jr. (1975). Locus of control and expectancies across multiple organizational levels. *Journal of Applied Psychology, 60*, 638–640.

22. Szilagyi, A.D., Sims, H.P., Jr., & Keller, R.T. (1976). Role dynamics, locus of control, and employee attitudes and behavior. *Academy of Management Journal, 19,* 259–276.

23. Andrisani, P.J., & Nestel, G. (1976). Internal-external control as contributor to and outcome of work experience. *Journal of Applied Psychology, 61,* 156–165.

24. For evidence on stress and locus of control, see Anderson, C.R. (1977). Locus of control, coping behaviors, and performance in a stress setting: A longitudinal study. *Journal of Applied Psychology, 62,* 446–451. For evidence on career planning, see Thornton, G.C., III. (1978). Differential effects of career planning on internals and externals. *Personnel Psychology, 31,* 471–476.

25. Snyder, M. (1987). *Public appearances/private realities: The psychology of self-monitoring.* New York: W.H. Freeman; Gangestad, S.W., & Snyder, M. (2000). Self-monitoring: Appraisal and reappraisal. *Psychological Bulletin, 126(4),* 530–555.

26. Snyder, 1987; Gangestad, S.W., & Snyder, M. (2000).

27. Day, D.V., Schleicher, D.J., Unckless, A.L., & Hiller, N.J. (2002). Self-monitoring personality at work: A meta-analytic investigation of construct validity. *Journal of Applied Psychology, 87,* 390–401.

28. Kilduff, M. & Day, D.V. (1994). Do chameleons get ahead? The effects of self-monitoring and managerial careers. *Academy of Management Journal, 37(4),* 1047–1060.

29. Brockner, J. (1988). *Self-esteem at work: Research, theory, and practice.* Lexington, MA: Lexington.

30. Brockner, 1988.

31. Brockner, 1988.

32. Pierce, J.L., Gardner, D.G., Cummings, L.L., & Dunham, R.B. (1989). Organization-based self-esteem: Construct definition, measurement, and validation. *Academy of Management Journal, 32,* 622–648; Tharanou, P. (1979). Employee self-esteem: A review of the literature. *Journal of Vocational Behavior, 15,* 1–29.

33. Pierce, J.L., Gardner, D.G., Dunham, R.B., & Cummings, L.L. (1993). Moderation by organization-based self-esteem of role condition–employee response relationships. *Academy of Management Journal, 36,* 271–288.

34. George, J.M. (1996). Trait and state affect. In K.R. Murphy (Ed.), *Individual differences and behavior in organizations.* San Francisco, CA: Jossey-Bass Publishers.

35. George, 1996; Thoresen, C.J., Kaplan, S.A., Barsky, A.P., Warren, C.R., & de Chermont, K. (2003). The affective underpinnings of job perceptions and attitudes: A meta-analytic review and integration. *Psychological Bulletin, 129,* 914–945; Lyubomirsky, S., King, L., & Diener, E. (2005). The benefits of frequent positive affect: Does happiness lead to success? *Psychological Bulletin, 131,* 803–855.

36. Crant, M.J. (2000). Proactive behaviour in organizations. *Journal of Management, 26,* 435–462; Seibert, S.E., Kraimer, M.L., & Crant, J.M. (2001). What do proactive people do? A longitudinal model linking proactive personality and career success. *Personnel Psychology, 54,* 845–874.

37. Bateman, T.S., & Crant, J.M. (1993). The proactive component of organizational behavior: A measure and correlates. *Journal of Organizational Behavior, 14,* 103–118.

38. Seibert, Kraimer, & Crant, 2001; Thompson, J.A. (2005). Proactive personality and job performance: A social capital perspective. *Journal of Applied Psychology, 90,* 1011–1017; Brown, D.J., Cober, R.T., Kane, K., Levy, P.E., & Shalhoop, J. (2006). Proactive personality and the successful job search: A field investigation with college graduates. *Journal of Applied Psychology, 91,* 717–726.

39. Chen, G., Gully, S.M., & Eden, D. (2001). Validation of a new general self-efficacy scale. *Organizational Research Methods, 4,* 62–83.

40. Chen, Gully, & Eden, 2001.

41. Judge, T.A., Erez, A., Bono, J.E., & Thoresen, C.J. (2003). The core self-evaluation scale: Development of a measure. *Personnel Psychology, 56,* 303–331.

42. Judge, T.A., & Bono, J.E. (2001). Relationship of core self-evaluations traits—self-esteem, generalized self-efficacy, locus of control, and emotional stability—with job satisfaction and job performance: A meta-analysis. *Journal of Applied Psychology, 86,* 80–92; Judge, T.A., Bono, J.E., & Locke, E.A. (2000). Personality and job satisfaction: The mediating role of job characteristics. *Journal of Applied Psychology, 85,* 237–249; Judge, Erez, Bono, & Thoresen, 2003; Judge, T.A., Locke, E.A., & Durham, C.C. (1997). The dispositional causes of job satisfaction: A core evaluations approach. In B.M. Staw & L.L. Cummings (Eds.), *Research in organizational behavior* (Vol. 19, 151–188). Greenwich, CT: JAI Press; Judge, T.A., Bono, J.E., Erez, A., & Locke, E.A. (2005). Core self-evaluations and job and life satisfaction: The role of self-concordance and goal attainment. *Journal of Applied Psychology, 90,* 257–268.

43. Day, N. (1998, June). Informal learning gets results. *Workforce,* 31–35.

44. Pfeffer, J. (1994). *Competitive advantage through people: Unleashing the power of the work force.* Boston, MA: Harvard Business School Press.

45. Peterson, S.J., & Luthans, F. (2006). The impact of financial and nonfinancial incentives on business-unit outcomes over time. *Journal of Applied Psychology, 91,* 156–165.

46. Peterson & Luthans, 2006.

47. Luthans, F., & Kreitner, R. (1975). *Organizational behavior modification.* Glenview, IL: Scott, Foresman.

48. However, more research is necessary to establish the extent of this in organizations. See Arvey, R.D., & Ivancevich, J M. (1980). Punishment in organizations: A review, propositions, and research suggestions. *Academy of Management Review, 5,* 123–132.

49. Punishment in front of others can be effective under restricted conditions. See Trevino, L.K. (1992). The social effects of punishment in organizations: A justice perspective. *Academy of Management Review, 17,* 647–676.

50. Orsgan, D.W., & Hamner, W.C. (1982). *Organizational behavior: An applied psychological approach* (Revised ed.). Plano, TX: Business Publications.

51. See Parmerlee, M.A., Near, J.P., & Jensen, T.C. (1982). Correlates of whistle-blowers' perceptions of organizational retaliation. *Administrative Science Quarterly, 27,* 17–34.

52. Bandura, A. (1991). Social cognitive theory of self-regulation. *Organizational Behavior and Human Decision Processes, 50,* 248–287.

53. Bandura, A. (1989). Human agency in social cognitive theory. *American Psychologists, 44,* 1175–1184. For a presentation of operant learning theory, see Honig, W.K., & Staddon, J.E.R. (Eds.). (1977). *Handbook of operant behavior.* Englewood Cliffs, NJ: Prentice-Hall. For a presentation of social learning theory, see Bandura, A. (1986). *Social foundations of thought and action.* Englewood Cliffs, NJ: Prentice-Hall.

54. Bandura, 1986.

55. Luthans, F., & Kreitner, R. (1985). *Organizational behavior modification and beyond: An operant and social learning approach.* Glenview, IL: Scott, Foresman; Manz, C.C., & Sims,

H.P., Jr. (1981). Vicarious learning: The influence of modeling on organizational behavior. *Academy of Management Review, 6*, 105–113.

56. Bandura, 1986; Goldstein, A.P., & Sorcher, M. (1974). *Changing supervisor behavior.* New York: Pergamon.

57. Robinson, S.L., & O'Leary-Kelly, A.M. (1998). Monkey see, monkey do: The influence of work groups on the antisocial behavior of employees. *Academy of Management Journal, 41*, 658–672; Goulet, L.R. (1997). Modelling aggression in the workplace: The role of role models. *Academy of Management Executive, 11*, 84–85.

58. Bandura, A. (1997). *Self-efficacy: The exercise of control.* New York, NY: W.H. Freeman.

59. Bandura, 1997; Stajkovic, A.D., & Luthans, F. (1998). Self-efficacy and work-related performance: A meta-analysis. *Psychological Bulletin, 124*, 240–261.

60. Bandura, 1991; Manz, C.C., & Sims, H.P., Jr. (1980). Self-management as a substitute for leadership: A social learning theory perspective. *Academy of Management Review, 5*, 361–367; Hackman, J.R. (1986). The psychology of self-management in organizations. In M.S. Pollack & R. Perloff (Eds.), *Psychology and work.* Washington, DC: American Psychological Association.

61. Bandura, 1986, 1989, 1991; Kanfer, F.H. (1980). Self-management methods. In F.H. Kanfer & A.P. Goldstein (Eds.), *Helping people change: A textbook of methods* (2nd ed.). New York: Pergamon.

62. Luthans & Kreitner, 1985; Manz & Sims, 1980.

63. Frayne, C., & Latham, G. (1987). Application of social learning theory to employee self-management of attendance. *Journal of Applied Psychology, 72*, 387–392.

64. Frayne, C.A., & Geringer, J.M. (2000). Self-management training for improving job performance: A field experiment involving salespeople. *Journal of Applied Psychology, 85*, 361–372.

65. Gist, M.E., Stevens, C.K., & Bavetta, A.G. (1991). Effects of self-efficacy and post-training intervention on the acquisition and maintenance of complex interpersonal skills. *Personnel Psychology, 44*, 837–861; Stevens, C.K., Bavetta, A.G., & Gist, M.E. (1993). Gender differences in the acquisition of salary negotiation skills: The role of goals, self-efficacy, and

perceived control. *Journal of Applied Psychology, 78*, 723–735.

66. Komaki, J., Barwick, K.D., & Scott, L.R. (1978). A behavioral approach to occupational safety: Pinpointing and reinforcing safe performance in a food manufacturing plant. *Journal of Applied Psychology, 63*, 434–445. For a similar study, see Haynes, R.S., Pine, R.C., & Fitch, H.G. (1982). Reducing accident rates with organizational behavior modification. *Academy of Management Journal, 25*, 407–416.

67. Stajkovic, A.D., & Lutans, F. (1997). A meta-analysis of the effects of organizational behavior modification on task performance, 1975–95. *Academy of Management Journal, 40*, 1122–1149; Stajkovic, A.D., & Luthans, F. (2003). Behavioral management and task performance in organizations: Conceptual background, meta-analysis, and test of alternative models. *Personnel Psychology, 56*, 155–194; Stajkovic, A.D., & Luthans, F. (2001). Differential effects of incentive motivators on work performance. *Academy of Management Journal, 44*, 580–590.

68. Markham, S.E., Scott, K.D., & McKee, G.H. (2002). Recognizing good attendance: A longitudinal, quasi-experimental field study. *Personnel Psychology, 55*, 639–660.

69. Markham, Scott, & McKee, 2002; Well-structured employee reward/recognition programs yield positive results. (1999, November). *HRFocus, 1*, 14, 15.

70. Markham, Scott, & McKee, 2002.

71. Brearton, S., & Daly, J. (2003, January). The fifty best companies to work for in Canada. *Report on Business, 19(7)*, 53–65; Gordon, A. (2000, February). 35 best companies to work for. *Report on Business Magazine, 16(8)*, 24–32.

72. Klie, S. (2006, August 14). Recognition equals profits. *Canadian HR Reporter, 19(14)*, 18.

73. Saks, A.M., & Haccoun, R.R. (2007). *Managing performance through training and development* (4th edition). Toronto, Canada: Nelson.

74. Taylor, P.J., Russ-Eft, D.F., & Chan, D.W.L. (2005). A meta-analytic review of behavior modeling training. *Journal of Applied Psychology, 90*, 692–709.

75. Taylor, Russ-Eft, & Chan, 2005.

76. Saks, A.M. (1997). Transfer of training and self-efficacy: What is the dilemma? *Applied Psychology: An International Review, 46*, 365–370.

77. DeSimone, R.L., Werner, J.M., & Harris, D.M. (2002). *Human resource development.* Orlando, FL: Harcourt College Publishers.

78. Harding, K. (2003, February 5). Firms offer a hand up the ladder. *Globe and Mail*, C3.

79. Brown, D. (2005, June 20). TD gives employees tool to chart career paths. *Canadian HR Reporter, 18(12)*, 11, 13.

Chapter 3

1. Sources include Dreyfus, J., Lee, M.J., & Totta, J.M. (1995, December). Mentoring at the Bank of Montreal: A case study of an intervention that exceeded expectations. *Human Resource Planning, 18(4)*, 45–49; Flynn, G. (1997, December). Bank of Montreal invests in its workers. *Workforce, 76(12)*, 30–38; Greengard, S. (2003, March). Optimas update: The best get better. *Workforce, 82(3)*, S5; Greffe, P. (1993, September). Workplace equality—pursuing a goal that makes the best of business sense. *CMA—The Management Accountant Magazine, 67(7)*, 11; Crawford, T. (2006, April 1). A better mix. *Toronto Star*, L1, L2; Stewart, S. (2006, July 20). Costello makes history as new Harris Bankcorp boss. *Globe and Mail*, B5; www.bmo.com.

2. Cox, T., Jr. (1993). *Cultural diversity in organizations: Theory, research, & practice.* San Francisco: Berrett-Koehler.

3. Ashforth, B.E. (2001). *Role transitions in organizational life: An identity-based persepctive.* Mahwah, NJ: Lawrence Erlbaum Associates, Inc.; Ashforth, B.E., & Mael, F. (1989). Social identity theory and the organization. *Academy of Management Review, 14*, 20–39.

4. Ashforth, 2001; Ashforth & Mael, 1989.

5. Bruner, J.S. (1957). On perceptual readiness. *Psychological Review, 64*, 123–152.

6. Eagly, A.H., Ashmore, R.D., Makhijani, M.G., & Longo, L.C. (1991). What is beautiful is good, but...: A meta-analytic review of research on the physical attractiveness stereotype. *Psychological Bulletin, 110*, 109–128; Hosoda, M., Stone-Romero, E.F., & Coats, G. (2003). The effects of physical attractiveness on job-related outcomes: A meta-analysis of experimental studies. *Personnel Psychology, 56*, 431–462.

7. Stone, E.F., Stone, D.L., & Dipboye, R.L. (1992). Stigmas in organizations: Race, handicaps, and physical unattractiveness. In K. Kelley (Ed.), *Issues, theory and research in industrial/organizational psychology*. New York: Elsevier; Hosoda, Stone-Romero, & Coats, 2003.

8. Judge, T.A., & Cable, D.M. (2004). The effect of physical height on workplace success and income: Preliminary test of a theoretical model. *Journal of Applied Psychology, 89,* 428–441.

9. See Krzystofiak, F., Cardy, R., & Newman, J.E. (1988). Implicit personality and performance appraisal: The influence of trait inferences on evaluations of behavior. *Journal of Applied Psychology, 73,* 515–521.

10. Fiske, S.T. (1993). Social cognition and social perception. *Annual Review of Psychology, 44,* 155–194.

11. Secord, P.F., Backman, C.W., & Slavitt, D.R. (1976). *Understanding social life: An introduction to social psychology*. New York: McGraw-Hill. For elaboration, see Wilder, D.A. (1986). Social categorization: Implications for creation and reduction of intergroup bias. *Advances in Experimental Social Psychology, 19,* 291–349.

12. Dion, K.L., & Schuller, R.A. (1991). The Ms. stereotype: Its generality and its relation to managerial and marital status stereotypes. *Canadian Journal of Behavioural Science, 23,* 25–40.

13. For a more complete treatment see Falkenberg, L. (1990). Improving the accuracy of stereotypes within the workplace. *Journal of Management, 16,* 107–118.

14. Kelley, H.H. (1972). Attribution in social interaction. In E.E. Jones et al. (Eds.), *Attribution: Perceiving the causes of behavior*. Morristown, NJ: General Learning Press. For an integrative attribution model, see Medcof, J.W. (1990). PEAT: An integrative model of attribution processes. *Advances in Experimental Social Psychology, 23,* 111–209.

15. Baron, R.A., Byrne, D., & Griffitt, W. (1974). *Social psychology: Understanding human interaction*. Boston: Allyn and Bacon.

16. This discussion of attribution biases draws upon Fiske, S.T., & Taylor, S.E. (1984). *Social cognition*. Reading, MA: Addison-Wesley.

17. Jones, E.E. (1979). The rocky road from acts to dispositions. *American Psychologist, 34,* 107–117; Ross, L. (1977). The intuitive psychologist and his shortcomings: Distortions in the attribution process. *Advances in Experimental Social Psychology, 10,* 173–220.

18. Mitchell, T.R., & Kalb, L.S. (1982). Effects of job experience on supervisor attributions for a subordinate's poor performance. *Journal of Applied Psychology, 67,* 181–188.

19. Watson, D. (1982). The actor and the observer: How are their perceptions of causality divergent? *Psychological Bulletin, 92,* 682–700.

20. Sonnenfeld, J. (1981). Executive apologies for price fixing: Role biased perceptions of causality. *Academy of Management Journal, 24,* 192–198; Waters, J.A. (1978, Spring). Catch 20.5. Corporate morality as an organizational phenomenon. *Organizational Dynamics,* 2–19.

21. Greenwald, A.G. (1980). The totalitarian ego: Fabrication and revision of personal history. *American Psychologist, 35,* 603–618; Tetlock, P.E. (1985). Accountability: The neglected social context of judgment and choice. *Research in Organizational Behavior, 7,* 297–332.

22. Pyszczynski, T., & Greenberg, J. (1987). Toward an integration of cognitive and motivational perspectives on social inference: A biased hypothesis-testing model. *Advances in Experimental Social Psychology, 20,* 197–340.

23. This section relies on Jackson, S.E., & Alvarez, E.B. (1992). Working through diversity as a strategic imperative. In S.E. Jackson (Ed.), *Diversity in the workplace: Human resources initiatives*. New York: Guilford Press; Mahoney, J. (2005, March 23). Visible majority by 2017. *Globe and Mail,* A1, A7.

24. Mahoney, 2005, March 23.

25. Mingail, H. (2004, September 29). Wise ways for retraining older workers. *Globe and Mail,* C8.

26. Crawford, 2006, April 1; Galt, V. (2005, March 2). Diversity efforts paying off: Shell CFO. *Globe and Mail,* B1, B20; Vu, U. (2004, November 8). FedEx holds managers accountable for diversity. *Canadian HR Reporter, 17(19),* 3; Shaw, A. (2006, May 22). Hiring immigrants makes good business sense. *Canadian HR Reporter, 19(10),* 21; Keung, N. (2006, March 18). Wanted: Minorities. *Toronto Star,* B1, B3.

27. Cox, 1993; Cox, T., Jr. (1991, May). The multicultural organization. *Academy of Management Executive, 5,* 34–47.

28. Crone, G. (1999, February 18). Companies embracing workplace diversity. *Financial Post,* C11; Galt, V. (2004, January 27). Firms excel with women in senior ranks: Study. *Globe and Mail,* B5.

29. Koonce, R. (2001, December). Redefining diversity. *T+D, 55(12),* 22–32; Galt, V. (2002, September 25). Top women still finding barriers. *Globe and Mail,* B7.

30. Hartley, E.L. (1946). *Problems in prejudice*. New York: King's Crown Press.

31. Alderfer, C.P., & Thomas, D.A. (1988). The significance of race and ethnicity for organizational behavior. In C.L. Cooper & I. Robertson (Eds.), *International review of industrial and organizational psychology*. New York: Wiley; Cox, T., Jr., & Nkomo, S.M. (1990). Invisible men and women: A status report on race as a variable in organization behavior research. *Journal of Organizational Behavior, 11,* 419–431.

32. Sharpe, R. (1993, September 14). Losing ground. *Wall Street Journal,* A1, 12, 13.

33. Brenner, O.C., Tomkiewicz, J., & Stevens, G.E. (1991). The relationship between attitudes toward women and attitudes toward blacks in management positions. *Canadian Journal of Administrative Sciences, 8(2),* 80–89.

34. Cox, 1993.

35. Greenhaus, J.H., & Parasuraman, S. (1993). Job performance attributions and career advancement prospects: An examination of gender and race effects. *Organizational Behavior and Human Decision Processes, 55,* 273–297.

36. Powell, G.N. (1992). The good manager: Business students' stereotypes of Japanese managers versus stereotypes of American managers. *Group & Organizational Management, 17,* 44–56.

37. Brief, A.P., Umphress, E.E., Dietz, J., Burrows, J.W., Butz, R.M., Scholten, L. (2005). Community matters: Realistic group conflict theory and the impact of diversity. *Academy of Management Journal, 48,* 830–844.

38. Galt, V. (2005, May 4). Glass ceiling still tough to crack. *Globe and Mail,* C1, C2; Flavelle, D. (2005, April 28). Women advance up ranks slowly. *Toronto Star,* D1, D12.

39. Brenner, O.C., Tomkiewicz, J., & Schein, V.E. (1989). The relationship between sex role stereotypes and requisite management characteristics revisited. *Academy of Management Journal, 32,* 662–669; Heilman, M.E.,

Block, C.J., Martell, R.F., & Simon, M.C. (1989). Has anything changed? Current characterizations of men, women, and managers. *Journal of Applied Psychology, 74*, 935–942; Schein, V.E. (1975). Relationships between sex role stereotypes and requisite management characteristics among female managers. *Journal of Applied Psychology, 60*, 340–344.

40. Brenner et al., 1989; Powell, G.N., Butterfield, D.A., & Parent, J.D. (2002). Gender and managerial stereotypes: Have the times changed? *Journal of Management, 28(2)*, 177–193.

41. Rosen, B., & Jerdee, T.H. (1974). Influence of sex role stereotypes on personnel decisions. *Journal of Applied Psychology, 59*, 9–14.

42. Cohen, S.L., & Bunker, K.A. (1975). Subtle effects of sex role stereotypes on recruiters' hiring decisions. *Journal of Applied Psychology, 60*, 566–572. See also Rose, G.L., & Andiappan, P. (1978). Sex effects on managerial hiring decisions. *Academy of Management Journal, 21*, 104–112.

43. Heilman, M.E., Wallen, A.S., Fuchs, D., & Tamkins, M.M. (2004). Penalties for success: Reactions to women who succeed at male gender-typed tasks. *Journal of Applied Psychology, 89*, 416–427.

44. Parasuraman, S., & Greenhaus, J.H. (1993). Personal portrait: The lifestyle of the woman manager. In E.A. Fagenson (Ed.), *Women in management: Trends, issues, and challenges in managerial diversity*. Newbury Park, CA: Sage; Cleveland, J. N., Vescio, T. K., & Barnes-Farrell, J. L. (2005). Gender discrimination in organizations. In R. L. Dipboye & A. Colella (Eds.), *Discrimination at work: The psychological and organizational bases*. Mahwah, NJ: Lawrence Erlbaum Associates.

45. Tosi, H.L., & Einbender, S.W. (1985). The effects of the type and amount of information in sex discrimination research: A meta-analysis. *Academy of Management Journal, 28*, 712–723.

46. For a review, see Latham, G.P., Skarlicki, D., Irvine, D., & Siegel, J.P. (1993). The increasing importance of performance appraisals to employee effectiveness in organizational settings in North America. In C.L. Cooper & I. Robertson (Eds.), *International review of industrial and organizational psychology*. New York: Wiley. For a representative study, see Pulakos, E.D., White, L.A., Oppler, S.A., & Borman, W.C. (1989).

Examination of race and sex effects on performance ratings. *Journal of Applied Psychology, 74*, 770–780; Cleveland, J. N., Vescio, T. K., & Barnes-Farrell, J. L. (2005).

47. Heilman, M.E., & Haynes, M.C. (2005). No credit where credit is due: Attributional rationalization of women's success in male-female teams. *Journal of Applied Psychology, 90*, 905–916.

48. Heilman, Wallen, Fuchs, & Tamkins, 2004.

49. Fiske, S.T., Beroff, D.N., Borgida, E., Deaux, K., & Heilman, M.E. (1991). Use of sex stereotyping research in Price Waterhouse v. Hopkins. *American Psychologist, 46*, 1049–1060.

50. Sackett, P.R., DuBois, C.L.Z., & Noe, A.W. (1991). Tokenism in performance evaluation: The effects of work group representation on male-female and white-black differences in performance ratings. *Journal of Applied Psychology, 76*, 263–267.

51. Galt, 2005, May 4.

52. Galt, 2005, March 2.

53. Galt, 2005, May 4.

54. Won, S. (2004, November 8). Women climbing the ranks at banks. *Globe and Mail*, C1, C2.

55. Rosen, B., & Jerdee, T.H. (1976). The nature of job-related age stereotypes. *Journal of Applied Psychology, 61*, 180–183. See also Gibson, K.J., Zerbe, W.J., & Franken, R.E. (1992). Job search strategies for older job hunters: Addressing employers' perceptions. *Canadian Journal of Counselling, 26*, 166–176.

56. Gibson et al., 1992.

57. Cole, T. (2000, June). Revenge of the fortysomethings. *Report on Business Magazine*, 34–40; McEvoy, G.M., & Cascio, W.F. (1989). Cumulative evidence of the relationship between employee age and job performance. *Journal of Applied Psychology, 74*, 11–17. For a broader review on age, see Rhodes, S.R. (1983). Age related differences in work attitudes and behavior. *Psychological Bulletin, 93*, 328–367.

58. Rosen, B., & Jerdee, T.H. (1976). The influence of age stereotypes on managerial decisions. *Journal of Applied Psychology, 61*, 428–432. Also see Dietrick, E.J., & Dobbins, G.J. (1991). The influence of subordinate age on managerial actions: An attributional analysis. *Journal of Organizational Behavior, 12*, 367–377.

59. Galt, V. (2002, October 16). What am i, chopped liver? *Globe and Mail*, C1, C6.

60. Galt, 2002, October 16.

61. Anonymous. (2004, September 27). Top employers for older workers. *Canadian HR Reporter, 17(16)*, 2.

62. Falkenberg, 1990; Fiske et al., 1991.

63. Business case study: Valuing and celebrating diversity makes good business sense. *Ford Motor Company of Australia*. Commonwealth Department of Immigration and Multicultural and Indigenous Affairs. http://www.diversityaustralia.gov.au/_inc/doc_pdf/da_ford_bc.pdf

64. Childs, J.T. Jr. (2005). Managing workforce diversity at IBM: A global HR topic that has arrived. *Human Resource Management, 44*, 73–77.

65. Vu, U. (2004, November 8). FedEx holds managers accountable for diversity. *Canadian HR Reporter, 17(19)*, 3.

66. Allerton, H.E. (2001, May). Building bridges in Vancouver. *T+D, 55(5)*, 84–97.

67. Caudron, S. (1993, April). Training can damage diversity efforts. *Personnel Journal*, 51–62.

68. Jayne, M.E.A., & Dipboye, R.L. (2004). Leveraging diversity to improve business performance: Research findings and recommendations for organizations. *Human Resource Management, 43*, 409–424.

69. Mayer, R.C., & Davis, J.H. (1999). The effect of the performance appraisal system on trust for management: A field quasi-experiment. *Journal of Applied Psychology, 84*, 123–136.

70. Lee, C. (1997, January). Trust. *Training, 34(1)*, 28–37.

71. Mayer & Davis, 1999; Davis, J.H., Mayer, R.C., & Schoorman, F.D. (1995, October). The trusted general manager and firm performance: Empirical evidence of a strategic advantage. Paper presented at the 15th annual meeting of the Strategic Management Society, Mexico City, Mexico. Cited in Mayer & Davis, 1999.

72. Davis, Mayer, & Schoorman, 1995; Mayer, R.C., Davis, J.H., & Schoorman, F.D. (1995). An integrative model of organizational trust. *Academy of Management Review, 20*, 709–734; Rousseau, D.M., Sitkin, S.B., Burt, R.S., & Camerer, C. (1998). Not so different after all: A cross-discipline view of trust. *Academy of Management Review, 23*, 393–404.

73. Mayer, Davis, & Schoorman, 1995.
74. Mayer & Davis, 1999; Mayer, Davis, & Schoorman, 1995.
75. Dirks, K.T., & Ferrin, D.L. (2002). Trust in leadership: Meta-analytic findings and implications for research and practice. *Journal of Applied Psychology, 87,* 611–628.
76. Mayer, R.C., & Gavin, M.B. (2005). Trust in management and performance: Who minds the shop while the employees watch the boss? *Academy of Management Journal, 48,* 874–888.
77. Rhoades, L., & Eisenberger, R. (2002). Perceived organizational support: A review of the literature. *Journal of Applied Psychology, 87,* 698–714.
78. Rhoades & Eisenberger, 2002.
79. Shanock, L.R., & Eisenberger, R. (2006). When supervisors feel supported: Relationships with subordinates' perceived supervisor support, perceived organizational support, and performance. *Journal of Applied Psychology, 91,* 689–695.
80. Allen, D.G., Shore, L.M., & Griffeth, R.W. (2003). The role of perceived organizational support and supportive human resource practices in the turnover process. *Journal of Management, 29(1),* 99–118.
81. Campion, M.A., Palmer, D.K., and Campion, J.E. (1997). A review of structure in the selection interview. *Personnel Psychology, 50,* 655–702; McDaniel, M.A., Whetzel, D.L., Schmidt, F.L., & Maurer, S.D. (1994). The validity of employment interviews: A comprehensive review and meta-analysis. *Journal of Applied Psychology, 79,* 599–616; Wiesner, W.H., & Cronshaw, S.F. (1988). A meta-analytic investigation of the impact of interview format and degree of structure on the validity of the employment interview. *Journal of Occupational Psychology, 61,* 275–290.
82. Hakel, M.D. (1982). Employment interviewing. In K.M. Rowland & G.R. Ferris (Eds.), *Personnel management.* Boston: Allyn and Bacon.
83. Hakel, 1982; Dipboye, R.L. (1989). Threats to the incremental validity of interviewer judgments. In R.W. Eder & G.R. Ferris (Eds.), *The employment interview: Theory, research, and practice.* Newbury Park, CA: Sage.
84. Hollmann, T.D. (1972). Employment interviewers' errors in processing positive and negative information. *Journal of Applied Psychology, 56,* 130–134.
85. Rowe, P.M. (1989). Unfavorable information in interview decisions. In R.W. Eder & G.R. Ferris (Eds.), *The employment interview: Theory, research, and practice.* Newbury Park, CA: Sage.
86. Maurer, T.J., & Alexander, R.A. (1991). Contrast effects in behavioral measurement: An investigation of alternative process explanations. *Journal of Applied Psychology, 76,* 3–10; Maurer, T.J., Palmer, J.K., & Ashe, D.K. (1993). Diaries, checklists, evaluations, and contrast effects in measurement of behavior. *Journal of Applied Psychology, 78,* 226–231; Schmitt, N. (1976). Social and situational determinants of interview decisions: Implications for the employment interview. *Personnel Psychology, 29,* 70–101.
87. Chapman, D.S., & Zweig, D.I. (2005). Developing a nomological network for interview structure: Antecedents and consequences of the structured selection interview. *Personnel Psychology, 58,* 673–702.
88. For other reasons and a review of the interview literature, see Harris, M.M. (1989). Reconsidering the employment interview: A review of recent literature and suggestions for future research. *Personnel Psychology, 42,* 691–726.
89. Rynes, S.L., Bretz, R., & Gerhart, B. (1991). The importance of recruitment in job choice: A different way of looking. *Personnel Psychology, 44,* 487–521.
90. Hausknecht, J.P., Day, D.V., & Thomas, S.C. (2004). Applicant reactions to selection procedures: An updated model and meta-analysis. *Personnel Psychology, 57,* 639–683.
91. Balzer, W.K., & Sulsky, L.M. (1992). Halo and performance appraisal research: A critical examination. *Journal of Applied Psychology, 77,* 975–985; Cooper, W.H. (1981). Ubiquitous halo. *Psychological Bulletin, 90,* 218–244; Murphy, K.R., Jako, R.A., & Anhalt, R.L. (1993). Nature and consequences of halo error: A critical analysis. *Journal of Applied Psychology, 78,* 218–225.
92. Kingstrom, P.D., & Bass, A.R. (1981). A critical analysis of studies comparing behaviorally anchored rating scales (BARS) and other rating formats. *Personnel Psychology, 34,* 263–289; Landy, F J., & Farr, J.L. (1983). *The measurement of work performance.* New York: Academic Press.
93. Mayer & Davis, 1999.

Chapter 4

1. Excerpt (with updates) from Livesey, B. (1997, March). Provide and con- quer. *Report on Business Magazine,* 34–43; also based on Lush, T. (1998, October 3). Company with a conscience. *The Gazette,* C3; Van Alphen, T. (2000, January 22). Good deeds earn equity at Husky. *Toronto Star,* B1, B8; Grant, T. (2001, August 20). Husky woos workers with unique perks. *Globe and Mail,* M1; Jaimet, K. (2002, April 8). Top CEO breaks ranks on Kyoto: Multi-millionaire "disappointed" by colleagues' stance, *Edmonton Journal,* A6; Starr, R. (2003, March 17). Breaking the mold. *Canadian Business, 76,* 17–18; Anonymous. (2003, November). Core values make good business sense. *Canadian Plastics, 61,* 22–23; Francis, D. (2004, August 14). Husky boss breaks mould. *National Post,* FP6; Anonymous. (2004, November 17). Husky's new Shanghai facility a model of sustainability. *Canada Newswire,* 1; Pitts, G. (2005, April). Green Piece. *Report on Business Magazine, 21,* 76; Anonymous (2005, September 22). Husky Injection Molding Systems Ltd. appoints John Galt as President and CEO. *Canada Newswire,* 1.
2. Hofstede, G. (1980). *Culture's Consequences: International differences in work-related values.* Beverly Hills, CA: Sage, 19.
3. Spranger, E. (1928). *Types of men.* New York: Stechat.
4. Rokeach, M. (1973). *The nature of human values.* New York: Free Press.
5. Meglino, B.M., Ravlin, E.C., & Adkins, C.L. (1989). A work values approach to corporate culture: A field test of the value congruence process and its relationship to individual outcomes. *Journal of Applied Psychology, 74,* 424–432.
6. Kristof, A.L. (1996). Person–organization fit: An integrative review of its conceptualizations, measurement, and implications. *Personnel Psychology, 49,* 1–49.
7. Judge, T.A., & Bretz, R.D., Jr. (1992). Effects of work values on job choice decisions. *Journal of Applied Psychology, 77,* 261–271.
8. Black, J.S., & Mendenhall, M. (1990). Cross-cultural training effectiveness: A review and theoretical framework for future research. *Academy of Management Review, 15,* 113–136.
9. MOW International Research Team. (1987). *The meaning of working.* London: Academic Press.
10. Hofstede, 1980. For a critique of this work, see Dorfman, P.W., & Howell, J.P. (1989). Dimensions of national culture and effective leadership patterns: Hofstede revisited. *Advances in*

International Comparative Management, 3, 127–150.

11. Hofstede, G. (1991). *Cultures and organizations: Software of the mind.* London: McGraw-Hill; Hofstede, G., & Bond, M.H. (1988). The Confucius connection: From cultural roots to economic growth. *Organizational Dynamics, 16(4),* 4–21.

12. House, R.J., Hanges, P.J., Javidan, M., Dorfman, P.W., & Gupta, V. (Eds.) (2004). *Culture, leadership, and organizations: The GLOBE study of 62 societies.* Thousand Oaks, CA: Sage.

13. Hofstede, G. (1984). The cultural relativity of the quality of life concept. *Academy of Management Review, 9,* 389–398; Hofstede, G. (1993, February). Cultural constraints in management theories. *Academy of Management Executive,* 81–94.

14. Young, S.M. (1992). A framework for successful adoption and performance of Japanese manufacturing practices in the United States. *Academy of Management Review, 17,* 677–700; Basadur, M. (1992, May). Managing creativity: A Japanese model. *Academy of Management Executive,* 29–42.

15. Staff reporter. (1992, December 30). Korea's biggest firm teaches junior execs strange foreign ways. *Wall Street Journal,* 1, 4.

16. Jones, E.E., & Gerard, H.B. (1967). *Foundations of social psychology.* New York: Wiley.

17. Wood, W. (2000). Attitude change: Persuasion and social influence. *Annual Review of Psychology, 51,* 539–570.

18. Harrison, D.A., Newman, D.A., & Roth, P.L. (2006). How important are job attitudes? Meta-analytic comparisons of integrative behavioral outcomes and time sequences. *Academy of Management Journal, 49,* 305–325.

19. Locke, E.A. (1976). The nature and causes of job satisfaction. In M.D. Dunnette (Ed.), *Handbook of industrial and organizational psychology.* Chicago: Rand McNally. See also Rice, R.W., Gentile, D.A., & McFarlin, D.B. (1991). Facet importance and job satisfaction. *Journal of Applied Psychology, 76,* 31–39.

20. Smith, P.C. (1992). In pursuit of happiness: Why study general job satisfaction? In C.J. Cranny, P.C. Smith, & E.F. Stone (Eds.), *Job satisfaction.* New York: Lexington.

21. Smith, P.C., Kendall, L.M., & Hulin, C.L. (1969). *The measurement of satisfaction in work and retirement.* Chicago: Rand McNally; Smith, P.C., Kendall, L.M., & Hulin, C.L. (1985).

The job descriptive index (Rev. ed.). Bowling Green, OH: Department of Psychology, Bowling Green State University.

22. Weiss, D.J., Dawis, R.V., England, G.W., & Lofquist, L.H. (1967). *Manual for the Minnesota satisfaction questionnaire: Minnesota studies in vocational rehabilitation.* Minneapolis: Vocational Psychology Research, University of Minnesota.

23. Locke, E.A. (1969). What is job satisfaction? *Organizational Behavior and Human Performance, 4,* 309–336; Rice, R.W., McFarlin, D.B., & Bennett, D.E. (1989). Standards of comparison and job satisfaction. *Journal of Applied Psychology, 74,* 591–598.

24. Williams, M.L., McDaniel, M.A., & Nguyen, N.T. (2006). A meta-analysis of the antecedents and consequences of pay level satisfaction. *Journal of Applied Psychology, 91,* 392–413.

25. For a good overview of fairness research, see Greenberg, J., & Colquitt, J.A. (2005). *Handbook of organizational justice.* Mahwah, NJ: Lawrence Erlbaum. For empirical reviews of the literature, see Colquitt, J.A., Conlon, D.E., Wesson, M.J., Porter, C.O.L.H., & Ng, K.Y. (2001). Justice at the millennium: A meta-analytic review of 25 years of organizational justice research. *Journal of Applied Psychology, 86,* 425–445; Cohen-Charash, Y., & Spector, P.E. (2001). The role of justice in organizations: A meta-analysis. *Organizational Behavior and Human Decision Processes, 86,* 278–321.

26. Adams, J.S. (1963). Toward an understanding of inequity. *Journal of Abnormal and Social Psychology, 67,* 422–436.

27. See Kulik, C.T., & Ambrose, M.L. (1992). Personal and situational determinants of referent choice. *Academy of Management Review, 17,* 212–237.

28. Freeze, C. (2006, May 16). Bell settles pay equity dispute. *Globe and Mail,* A7.

29. Greenberg, J. (1987). A taxonomy of organizational justice theories. *Academy of Management Review, 12,* 9–22.

30. Brockner, J., & Wisenfeld, B.M. (1996). An integrative framework for explaining reactions to decisions: Interactive effects of outcomes and procedures. *Psychological Bulletin, 120,* 189–208; Brockner, J., & Wiesenfeld, B. (2005). How, when, and why does outcome favorability interact with procedural fairness? In Greenberg & Colquitt, 2005.

31. Cropanzano, R., & Folger, R. (1989). Referent cognitions and task decision autonomy: Beyond equity theory. *Journal of Applied Psychology, 74,* 293. See also Folger, R. (1987). Reformulating the preconditions of resentment: A referent cognitions model. In J.C. Masters & W.P. Smith (Eds.), *Social comparison, justice, and relative deprivation: Theoretical, empirical, and policy perspectives.* Hillsdale, NJ: Erlbaum.

32. Colquitt, J.A., Greenberg, J., & Zapata-Phelan, C.P. (2005). What is organizational justice? A historical overview. In Greenberg & Colquitt, 2005; Bies, R.J. (2005). Are procedural justice and interactional justice conceptually distinct? In Greenberg & Colquitt, 2005.

33. Greenberg, J. (2006). Losing sleep over organizational injustice: Attenuating insomniac reactions to underpayment inequity with supervisory training in interactional justice. *Journal of Applied Psychology, 91,* 58–69.

34. Judge, T.A. (1992). The dispositional perspective in human resources research. *Research in Personnel and Human Resources Management, 10,* 31–72. See also Staw, B.M., & Cohen-Charash, Y. (2005). The dispositional approach to job satisfaction: More than a mirage, but not yet an oasis. *Journal of Organizational Behavior, 26,* 59–78.

35. Judge, T.A., Heller, D., & Mount, M.K. (2002). Five-factor model of personality and job satisfaction: A meta-analysis. *Journal of Applied Psychology, 87,* 530–541.

36. Judge, T.A., Bono, J.E., & Locke, E.A. (2000). Personality and job satisfaction: The mediating role of job characteristics. *Journal of Applied Psychology, 85,* 237–249.

37. Weiss, H.M., & Cropanzano, R. (1996). Affective events theory: A theoretical discussion of the structure, causes and consequences of affective experiences at work. *Research in Organizational Behavior, 18,* 1–74.

38. Barsade, S.G. (2002). The ripple effect: Emotional contagion and its influence on group behavior. *Administrative Science Quarterly, 47,* 644–675.

39. Grandey, A.A., Dickter, D.N., & Sin, H.P. (2004). The customer is *not* always right: Customer aggression and emotion regulation of service employees. *Journal of Organizational Behavior, 25,* 397–418.

40. Côté, S., & Morgan, L.M. (2002). A longitudinal analysis of the association

between emotion regulation, job satisfaction, and intentions to quit. *Journal of Organizational Behavior, 23,* 947–962; Diefendorff, J.M., & Richard, E.M. (2003). Antecedents and consequences of emotional display rule perceptions. *Journal of Applied Psychology, 88,* 284–294; Schaubroeck, J., & Jones, J.R. (2000). Antecedents of workplace emotional labor dimensions and moderators of their effects on physical symptoms. *Journal of Organizational Behavior, 21,* 163–183.

41. Côté & Morgan, 2002.

42. Glomb, T.M., Kammeyer-Mueller, J.D., & Rotundo, M. (2004). Emotional labor demands and compensating wage differentials. *Journal of Applied Psychology, 89,* 700–714.

43. This material draws upon Locke, 1976.

44. Lu, V. (1999, August 15). Rising sick days cost billions. *Toronto Star,* A1, A10.

45. Hackett, R.D. (1989). Work attitudes and employee absenteeism: A synthesis of the literature. *Journal of Occupational Psychology, 62,* 235–248; Hackett, R.D., & Guion, R.M. (1985). A reevaluation of the absenteeism-job satisfaction relationship. *Organizational Behavior and Human Decision Processes, 35,* 340–381.

46. Johns, G. (2002). Absenteeism and mental health. In J.C. Thomas & M. Hersen (Eds.), *Handbook of mental health in the workplace.* Thousand Oaks, CA: Sage; Nicholson, N., & Johns, G. (1985). The absence culture and the psychological contract—Who's in control of absence? *Academy of Management Review, 10,* 397–407.

47. Warr, P.B. (1987). *Work, unemployment, and mental health.* Oxford: Oxford University Press; Jamal, M., & Mitchell, V.F. (1980). Work, nonwork, and mental health: A model and a test. *Industrial Relations, 19,* 88–93; Judge, T.A., & Watanabe, S. (1993). Another look at the job satisfaction-life satisfaction relationship. *Journal of Applied Psychology, 78,* 939–948.

48. Farris, G.F. (1971). A predictive study of turnover. *Personnel Psychology, 24,* 311–328. However, the more general relationship between performance and voluntary turnover is negative, as shown by Bycio, P., Hackett, R.D., & Alvares, K.M. (1990). Job performance and turnover: A review and meta-analysis. *Applied Psychology: An International Review, 39,* 47–76; Williams, C.R., & Livingstone, L.P.

(1994). Another look at the relationship between performance and voluntary turnover. *Academy of Management Journal, 37,* 269–298.

49. Hom, P.W., & Griffeth, R.W. (1995). *Employee turnover.* Cincinnati, OH: South-Western.

50. This model is based on Hom & Griffeth, 1995; Lee, T.W., & Mitchell, T.R. (1994). An alternative approach: The unfolding model of voluntary employee turnover. *Academy of Management Review, 19,* 51–89; Mitchell, T.R., Holtom, B.C., Lee, T.W., Sablynski, C.J., & Erez, M. (2001). Why people stay: Using job embeddedness to predict voluntary turnover. *Academy of Management Journal, 44,* 1102–1121.

51. Hom & Griffeth, 1995.

52. Carsten, J.M., & Spector, P.E. (1987). Unemployment, job satisfaction, and employee turnover: A meta-analytic test of the Muchinsky model. *Journal of Applied Psychology, 72,* 374–381.

53. Boswell, W.R., Boudreau, J.W., & Tichy, J. (2005). The relationship between employee job change and job satisfaction: The honeymoon-hangover effect. *Journal of Applied Psychology, 90,* 882–892.

54. Judge, T.A., Thoresen, C.J., Bono, J.E., & Patton, G.K. (2001). The job satisfaction-job performance relationship: A qualitative and quantitative review. *Psychological Bulletin, 127,* 376–407.

55. Iaffaldano, M.T., & Muchinsky, P.M. (1985). Job satisfaction and job performance: A meta-analysis. *Psychological Bulletin, 97,* 251–273.

56. Lawler, E.E., III (1973). *Motivation in organizations.* Monterey, CA: Brooks/Cole.

57. Organ, D.W. (1988). *Organizational citizenship behavior: The good soldier syndrome.* Lexington, MA: Lexington; Podsakoff, P.M., MacKenzie, S.B., Paine, J.B., & Bachrach, D.G. (2000). Organizational citizenship behaviors: A critical review of the theoretical and empirical literature and suggestions for future research. *Journal of Management, 26,* 513–563.

58. Lepine, J.A., Erez, A., & Johnson, D.E. (2002). The nature and dimensionality of organizational citizenship behavior: A critical review and meta-analysis. *Journal of Applied Psychology, 87,* 52–65; Organ, D.W., & Ryan, K. (1995). A meta-analytic review of attitudinal and dispositional predictors of organizational citizenship behavior. *Personnel Psychology, 48,* 775–802.

59. Organ, 1988.

60. Organ, 1988; Organ, D.W., & Konovsky, M. (1989). Cognitive versus affective determinants of organizational citizenship behavior. *Journal of Applied Psychology, 74,* 157–164.

61. Lepine et al., 2002.

62. George, J.M. (1991). State or trait: Effects of positive mood on prosocial behaviors at work. *Journal of Applied Psychology, 76,* 299–307.

63. Harter, J.k, Schmidt, F.L., & Hayes, T.L. (2002). Business-unit level relationship between employee satisfaction, employee engagement, and business outcomes: A meta-analysis. *Journal of Applied Psychology, 87,* 268–279.

64. Laabs, J. (1999, March). The HR side of Sears' comeback. *Workforce,* 24–29.

65. Meyer, J.P., & Allen, N.J. (1997). *Commitment in the workplace.* Thousand Oaks, CA: Sage.

66. Meyer, J.P., Allen, N.J., & Topolnytsky, L. (1998). Commitment in a changing world of work. *Canadian Psychology, 39(1–2),* 83–93.

67. Meyer, J.p, Stanley, D.J., Herscovitch, L., & Topolnytsky, L. (2002). Affective, continuance, and normative commitment to the organization: A meta-analysis of antecedents, correlates, and consequences. *Journal of Vocational Behavior, 61,* 20–52.

68. Meyer et al., 2002.

69. Meyer et al., 2002; For a careful study, see Jaros, S.J., Jermier, J.M., Koehler, J.W., & Sincich, T. (1993). Effects of continuance, affective, and moral commitment on the withdrawal process: An evaluation of eight structural equation models. *Academy of Management Journal, 36,* 951–995.

70. Meyer, J.P., Becker, T.E., & Vandenberghe, C. (2004). Employee commitment and motivation: A conceptual analysis and integrative model. *Journal of Applied Psychology, 89,* 991–1007.

71. Meyer, J.P., Paunonen, S.V., Gellatly, I.R., Goffin, R.D., & Jackson, D.N. (1989). Organizational commitment and job performance: It's the nature of the commitment that counts. *Journal of Applied Psychology, 74,* 152–156.

72. Randall, D.M. (1987). Commitment and the organization: The organization man revisited. *Academy of Management Review, 12,* 460–471.

73. Meyer, Allen, & Topolnytsky, 1998.

74. Cascio, W.F. (1993, February). Downsizing: What do we know?

What have we learned? *Academy of Management Executive*, 95–104.

75. Meyer, Allen, & Topolnytsky, 1998.

Chapter 5

1. Alphonso, C. (2002, March 15). Street expects soaring WestJet to fly higher. *Globe and Mail*, B9; Heath-Rawlings, J. (2003, June 6). WestJet seen gliding through turbulence. *Globe and Mail*, B12; Menzies, P. (1999, July 2). Upstart WestJet proves free market can fly. *National Post*, C7; Verburg, P. (2000, December 25). Prepare for takeoff. *Canadian Business, 73(24)*, 94–99; Davis, A.A. (2006). Missing the turbulence. *WestJet's 10th Anniversary Magazine*. Calgary, Alberta: Red Point Media Group Inc.; Davis, A.A. (2006). Looking back to the future. *WestJet's 10th Anniversary Magazine*. Calgary, Alberta: Red Point Media Group Inc.; Magnan, M. (2005, October 10–23). People power. *Canadian Business, 78(20)*, 125; Wahl, A. (2005, October 10–23). Culture shock. *Canadian Business, 78(20)*, 115; Jang, B. (2006, April 28). WestJet soars to record profit. *Globe and Mail*, B5; Anonymous (2006, August 3). WestJet earnings soar to record. *Toronto Star*, C3.

2. Campbell, J.P., Dunnette, M.D., Lawler, E.E., Iii, & Weick, K.E., Jr. (1970). *Managerial behavior, performance, and effectiveness*. New York: McGraw-Hill. Also see Blau, G. (1993). Operationalizing direction and level of effort and testing their relationship to job performance. *Organizational Behavior and Human Decision Processes, 55*, 152–170.

3. Dyer, L., & Parker, D.F. (1975). Classifying outcomes in work motivation research: An examination of the intrinsic-extrinsic dichotomy. *Journal of Applied Psychology, 60*, 455–458; Kanungo, R.N., & Hartwick, J. (1987). An alternative to the intrinsic-extrinsic dichotomy of work rewards. *Journal of Management, 13*, 751–766. Also see Brief, A.P., & Aldag, R.J. (1977). The intrinsic-extrinsic dichotomy: Toward conceptual clarity. *Academy of Management Review, 2*, 496–500.

4. Vallerand, R.J. (1997). Toward a hierarchical model of intrinsic and extrinsic motivation. *Advances in Experimental Social Psychology, 29*, 271–360.

5. Deci, E.L., & Ryan, R.M. (1985). *Intrinsic motivation and self-determination in human behavior*. New York: Plenum.

6. Deci & Ryan, 1985.

7. Eisenberger, R., & Cameron, J. (1996). Detrimental effects of reward: Reality or myth? *American Psychologist, 51*, 1153–1166.

8. Guzzo, R.A. (1979). Types of rewards, cognitions, and work motivation. *Academy of Management Review, 4*, 75–86; Wiersma, U.J. (1992). The effects of extrinsic rewards in intrinsic motivation: A meta-analysis. *Journal of Occupational and Organizational Psychology, 65*, 101–114.

9. Based on Campbell, J.P., & Pritchard, R.D. (1976). Motivation theory in industrial and organizational psychology. In M.D. Dunnette (Ed.), *Handbook of industrial and organizational psychology*. Chicago: Rand McNally.

10. O'Reilly, C.A. Iii, & Chatman, J.A. (1994). Working smarter and harder: A longitudinal study of managerial success. *Administrative Science Quarterly, 39*, 603–627.

11. Hunter, J.E. (1986). Cognitive ability, cognitive aptitudes, job knowledge, and job performance. *Journal of Vocational Behavior, 29*, 340–362; Schmidt, F.L., & Hunter, J.E. (1998). The validity and utility of selection methods in personnel psychology: Practical and theoretical implications of 85 years of research findings. *Psychological Bulletin, 124*, 262–274.

12. O'Reilly & Chatman, 1994.

13. Mayer, J.D., Caruso, D.R., & Salovey, P. (2000). Emotional intelligence meets traditional standards for an intelligence. *Intelligence, 27*, 267–298; Salovey, P., & Mayer, J.D. (1990). Emotional intelligence. *Imagination, Cognition and Personality, 9*, 185–211.

14. Mayer, Caruso, & Salovey, 2000.

15. George, J.M. (2000). Emotions and leadership: The role of emotional intelligence. *Human Relations, 53*, 1027–1055.

16. George, 2000.

17. George, 2000.

18. Van Rooy, D.L., & Viswesvaran, C. (2004). Emotional intelligence: A meta-analytic investigation of predictive validity and nomological net. *Journal of Vocational Behavior, 65*, 71–95.

19. Schutte, N.S., Malouff, J.M., Hall, L.E., Haggerty, D.J., Cooper, J.T., Golden, C.J., & Dornheim, L. (1998). Development and validation of a measure of emotional intelligence. *Personality and Individual Differences, 25*, 167–177; Wong, C., & Law, K.S. (2002). The effects of leader and follower emotional intelli-

gence on performance and attitude: An exploratory study. *The Leadership Quarterly, 13*, 243–274; Daus, C.S., & Ashkanasy, N.M. (2005). The case for the ability-based model of emotional intelligence in organizational behaviour. *Journal of Organizational Behavior, 26*, 453–466.

20. See Henkoff, R. (1993, March 22). Companies that train best. *Fortune*, 62–75.

21. Galt, V. (2005, November 15). Fewer workers willing to put in 110%. *Globe and Mail*, B8; Carniol, N. (2005, November 15). Fewer workers willing to give 100 percent. *Toronto Star*, D1, D11; Galt, V. (2005, January 26). This just in: half your employees ready to jump ship. *Globe and Mail*, B1, B9.

22. Kahn, W.A. (1990). Psychological conditions of personal engagement and disengagement at work. *Academy of Management Journal, 33*, 692–724; Kahn, W.A. (1992). To be full there: Psychological presence at work. *Human Relations, 45*, 321–349.

23. Rothbard, N.P. (2001). Enriching or depleting? The dynamics of engagement in work and family roles. *Administrative Science Quarterly, 46*, 655–684; Kahn, 1992.

24. Kahn, 1990.

25. May, D.R., Gilson, R.L., & Harter, L.M. (2004). The psychological conditions of meaningfulness, safety and availability and the engagement of the human spirit at work. *Journal of Occupational and Organizational Psychology, 77*, 11–37; Saks, A.M. (in press). Antecedents and consequences of employee engagement. *Journal of Managerial Psychology*.

26. Harter, J.K., Schmidt, F.L., & Hayes, T.L. (2002). Business-unit level relationship between employee satisfaction, employee engagement, and business outcomes: A meta-analysis. *Journal of Applied Psychology, 87*, 268–279.

27. The distinction between need (content) and process theories was first made by Campbell et al., 1970.

28. Maslow, A.H. (1970). *Motivation and personality* (2nd ed.). New York: Harper & Row.

29. Alderfer, C.P. (1969). An empirical test of a new theory of human needs. *Organizational Behavior and Human Performance, 4*, 142–175. Also see Alderfer, C.P. (1972). *Existence, relatedness, and growth: Human needs in organizational settings*. New York: The Free Press.

30. McClelland, D.C. (1985). *Human motivation*. Glenview, IL: Scott, Foresman.

31. McClelland, D.C., & Winter, D.G. (1969). *Motivating economic achievement*. New York: The Free Press, 50–52.

32. McClelland, D.C., & Boyatzis, R.E. (1982). Leadership motive pattern and long-term success in management. *Journal of Applied Psychology, 67*, 737–743; McClelland, D.C., & Burnham, D. (1976, March–April). Power is the great motivator. *Harvard Business Review*, 159–166. However, need for power might not be the best motive pattern for managers of technical and professional people. See Cornelius, E.T., Iii, & Lane, F.B. (1984). The power motive and managerial success in a professionally oriented service industry organization. *Journal of Applied Psychology, 69*, 32–39.

33. Wahba, M.A., & Bridwell, L.G. (1976). Maslow reconsidered: A review of research on the need hierarchy theory. *Organizational Behavior and Human Performance, 15*, 212–240.

34. Schneider, B., & Alderfer, C.P. (1973). Three studies of measures of need satisfaction in organizations. *Administrative Science Quarterly, 18*, 498–505. Also see Alderfer, C.P., Kaplan, R.E., & Smith, K.K. (1974). The effect of relatedness need satisfaction on relatedness desires. *Administrative Science Quarterly, 19*, 507–532. For a disconfirming test, see Rauschenberger, J., Schmitt, N., & Hunter, J.E. (1980). A test of the need hierarchy concept by a Markov model of change in need strength. *Administrative Science Quarterly, 25*, 654–670.

35. McClelland, 1985; Spangler, W.D. (1992). Validity of questionnaire and TAT measures of need for achievement: Two meta-analyses. *Psychological Bulletin, 112*, 140–154.

36. Herzberg, F. (1966). *Work and the nature of man*. Cleveland: World Publishing.

37. Lawler, E.E., III. (1973). *Motivation in work organizations*. Monterey, CA: Brooks/Cole.

38. Vroom, V.H. (1964). *Work and motivation*. New York: Wiley.

39. Mitchell, T.R. (1974). Expectancy models of job satisfaction, occupational preference, and effort: A theoretical, methodological, and empirical appraisal. *Psychological Bulletin, 81*, 1053–1077. Also see Pinder, C.C.

(1984). *Work motivation: Theory, issues, and applications*. Glenview, IL: Scott, Foresman; Kanfer, R. (1990). Motivation theory in industrial and organizational psychology. In M.D. Dunnette & L.M. Hough (Eds.), *Handbook of industrial and organizational psychology* (2nd ed., Vol. 1). Palo Alto, CA: Consulting Psychologists Press.

40. A good discussion of how managers can strengthen expectancy and instrumentality relationships is presented by Strauss, G. (1977). Managerial practices. In J.R. Hackman & J.L. Suttle (Eds.), *Improving life at work: Behavioral science approaches to organizational change*. Glenview, IL: Scott, Foresman.

41. Adams, J.S. (1965). Injustice in social exchange. *Advances in Experimental Social Psychology, 2*, 267–299.

42. Kulik, C.T., & Ambrose, M.L. (1992). Personal and situational determinants of referent choice. *Academy of Management Review, 17*, 212–237.

43. Carrell, M.R., & Dittrich, J.E. (1978). Equity theory: The recent literature, methodological considerations, and new directions. *Academy of Management Review, 3*, 202–210; Mowday, R.T. (1991). Equity theory predictions of behavior in organizations. In R.M. Steers & L.W. Porter (Eds.), *Motivation and work behavior*, 111–131. New York: McGraw-Hill.

44. Mowday, 1991; Carrell & Dittrich, 1978.

45. See Kulik & Ambrose, 1992.

46. Locke, E.A., & Latham, G.P. (2002). Building a practically useful theory of goal setting and task motivation. *American Psychologist, 57*, 705–717.

47. The best-developed theoretical position is that of Locke, E.A., & Latham, G.P. (1990). *A theory of goal setting and task performance*. Englewood Cliffs, NJ: Prentice-Hall.

48. Locke & Latham, 2002.

49. Locke & Latham, 2002.

50. Locke, E.A., Latham, G.P., & Erez, M. (1988). The determinants of goal commitment. *Academy of Management Review, 13*, 23–39.

51. See Erez, M., Earley, P.C., & Hulin, C.L. (1985). The impact of participation on goal acceptance and performance: A two-step model. *Academy of Management Journal, 28*, 50–66.

52. Latham, G.P., Erez, M., & Locke, E.A. (1988). Resolving scientific disputes by the joint design of crucial experiments by the antagonists: Application to the Erez-Latham dispute regarding participation in goal

setting. *Journal of Applied Psychology, 73*, 753–772.

53. Latham, G.P., Mitchell, T.R., & Dosset, D.L. (1978). The importance of participative goal setting and anticipated rewards on goal difficulty and job performance. *Journal of Applied Psychology, 63*, 163–171; Saari, L.M., & Latham, G.P. (1979). The effects of holding goal difficulty constant on assigned and participatively set goals. *Academy of Management Journal, 22*, 163–168.

54. For a discussion of this issue, see Saari & Latham, 1979.

55. Button, S.B., Mathieu, J.E., & Zajac, D.M. (1996). Goal orientation in organizational research: A conceptual and empirical foundation. *Organizational Behavior and Human Decision Processes, 67*, 26–48; VandeWalle, D., Brown, S.P., Cron, W.L., & Slocum, J.W., Jr. (1999). The influence of goal orientation and self-regulation tactics on sales performance: A longitudinal field test. *Journal of Applied Psychology, 84*, 249–259; VandeWalle, D., Cron, W.L., & Slocum, J.W., Jr. (2001). The role of goal orientation following performance feedback. *Journal of Applied Psychology, 86*, 629–640.

56. VandeWalle, Brown, Cron, & Slocum, 1999; Seijts, G.H., Latham, G.P., Tasa, K., & Latham, B.W. (2004). Goal setting and goal orientation: An integration of two different yet related literatures. *Academy of Management Journal, 47*, 227–239.

57. Kozlowski, S.W.J., Gully, S.M., Brown, K.G., Salas, E., Smith, E.M., & Nason, E.R. (2001). Effects of training goals and goal orientation traits on multidimensional training outcomes and performance adaptability. *Organizational Behavior and Human Decision Processes, 85*, 1–31; VandeWalle, Brown, Cron, & Slocum, 1999.

58. Locke, E.A., & Latham, G.P. (1984). *Goal setting—A motivational technique that works*. Englewood Cliffs, NJ: Prentice-Hall.

59. Latham, G.P., & Baldes, J.J. (1975). The "practical significance" of Locke's theory of goal setting. *Journal of Applied Psychology, 60*, 122–124; Latham, G.P., & Locke, E. (1979, Autumn). Goal setting—a motivational technique that works. *Organizational Dynamics, 8(2)*, 68–80.

60. Seijts, Latham, Tasa, & Latham, 2004; Seijts, G., & Latham, G.P. (2005). Learning versus performance

goals: When should each be used? *Academy of Management Executive, 19,* 124–131.

61. O'Leary-Kelly, A.M., Martocchio, J.J., & Frink, D.D. (1994). A review of the influence of group goals on group performance. *Academy of Management Journal, 37,* 1285–1301.

62. Seijts, Latham, Tasa, & Latham, 2004; Seijts, & Latham, 2005.

63. Shaw, K.N. (2004). Changing the goal-setting process at Microsoft. *Academy of Management Executive, 18,* 139–142; Kerr, S., & Landauer, S. (2004). Using stretch goals to promote organizational effectiveness and personal growth: General Electric and Goldman Sachs. *Academy of Management Executive, 18,* 134–138.

64. Kagitcibasi, C., & Berry, J.W. (1989). Cross-cultural psychology: Current research and trends. *Annual Review of Psychology, 40,* 493–531.

65. Hofstede, G. (1980). *Culture's consequences: International differences in work-related values.* Beverly Hills, CA: Sage.

66. For a review, see Kagitcibasi & Berry, 1989.

67. Adler, N.J. (1992). *International dimensions of organizational behavior* (2nd ed.). Belmont, CA: Wadsworth.

68. Locke & Latham, 2002.

69. Kirkman, B.L., & Shapiro, D.L. (1997). The impact of cultural values on employee resistance to teams: Toward a model of globalized self-managing work team effectiveness. *Academy of Management Review, 22,* 730–757.

70. Adler, 1992, p. 159.

Chapter 6

1. www.bcbio.com. Brearton, S. & Daly, J. (2003, January). The 50 Best Companies to Work for in Canada. *Report on Business Magazine, 58;* Kupchuk, R. (2002, January 9). A great place to work. *Surrey/North Delta Leader.* Retrieved November 19, 2003, from www.bcbio.com; Penner, D. (2002, December 28). How to win top spot as the place to work: Flex-time, flat structure and parties a winning formula for B.C. company. *Vancouver Sun.* Retrieved November 19, 2003, from www.bcbio.com; Sutherland, J. (2005, January). Fifty best employers in Canada. *Report on Business, 21(6),* 45-50; Brearton, S. (2004). All for one. *Report on Business, 20(7),* 40.

2. Rynes, S.L., Gerhart, B., & Minette, K.A. (2004). The importance of pay in employee motivation: Discrepancies between what people say and what they do. *Human Resource Management, 43,* 381–394.

3. Jenkins, G.D., Jr., Mitra, A., Gupta, N., & Shaw, J.D. (1998). Are financial incentives related to performance? A meta-analytic review of empirical research. *Journal of Applied Psychology, 83,* 777–787; Sturman, M.C., Trevor, C.O., Boudreau, J.W., & Gerhart, B. (2003). Is it worth it to win the talent war? Evaluating the utility of performance-based pay. *Personnel Psychology, 56,* 997–1035; Rynes, Gerhart, & Minette, 2004.

4. For reviews, see Chung, K.H. (1977). *Motivational theories and practices.* Columbus, OH: Grid; Lawler, E.E., III. (1971). *Pay and organizational effectiveness: A psychological view.* New York: McGraw-Hill. For a careful study, see Wagner, J.A., Iii, Rubin, P.A., & Callahan, T.J. (1988). Incentive payment and nonmanagerial productivity: An interrupted time series analysis of magnitude and trend. *Organizational Behavior and Human Decision Processes, 42,* 47–74.

5. Locke, E.A., Feren, D.B., McCaleb, V.M., Shaw, K.N., & Denny, A.T. (1980). The relative effectiveness of four methods of motivating employee performance. In K.D. Duncan, M.M. Gruneberg, & D. Wallis (Eds.), *Changes in working life.* London: Wiley.

6. Fein, M. (1973, September). Work measurement and wage incentives. *Industrial Engineering,* 49–51.

7. Inspire your team. *Success,* 12; Perry, N.J. (1988, December 19). Here come richer, riskier pay plans. *Fortune,* 50–58; Sharplin, A.D. (1990). Lincoln Electric Company, 1989. In A.A. Thompson, Jr., & A.J. Strickland, III. *Strategic management: Concepts and cases.* Homewood, IL: BPI/Irwin.

8. For a general treatment of why firms fail to adopt state-of-the-art personnel practices, see Johns, G. (1993). Constraints on the adoption of psychology-based personnel practices: Lessons from organizational innovation. *Personnel Psychology, 46,* 569–592.

9. Posner, B.G. (1989, May). If at first you don't succeed. *Inc.,* 132–134, 132.

10. Lawler, 1971.

11. Lawler, 1971; Nash, A., & Carrol, S. (1975). *The management of compensation.* Monterey, CA: Brooks/Cole.

12. Bertin, O. (2003, January 31). Is there any merit in giving merit pay? *Globe and Mail,* C1, C7.

13. Sethi, C. (2006, September 5). Calgary wages rising at record pace. *Globe and Mail,* B1, B2.

14. Chu, K. (2004, June 15). Firms report lacklustre results from pay-for-performance plans. *Wall Street Journal,* D2.

15. Heneman, R.L. (1990). Merit pay research. *Research in Personnel and Human Resources Management, 8,* 203–263; Tosi, H.L., & Gomez-Mejia, L.R. (1989). The decoupling of CEO pay and performance: An agency theory perspective. *Administrative Science Quarterly, 34,* 169–189; Ungson, G.R., & Steers, R.M. (1984). Motivation and politics in executive compensation. *Academy of Management Review, 9,* 313–323.

16. Haire, M., Ghiselli, E.E., & Gordon, M.E. (1967). A psychological study of pay. *Journal of Applied Psychology Monograph, 51,* (Whole No. 636).

17. Lublin, J.S. (1997, January 8). Why more people are battling over bonuses. *Wall Street Journal,* B1, B7.

18. Meyer, H.H. (1991, February). A solution to the performance appraisal feedback enigma. *Academy of Management Executive,* 68–76.

19. See Zenga, T.R. (1992). Why do employers only reward extreme performance? Examining the relationships among pay, performance, and turnover. *Administrative Science Quarterly, 37,* 198–219.

20. Koenig, B. (2005, February 14). Ford to reinstate employee bonuses. *Globe and Mail,* B13.

21. Lawler, E.E., Iii, (1972). Secrecy and the need to know. In H.L. Tosi, R.J. House, & M.D. Dunnette (Eds.), *Managerial motivation and compensation.* East Lansing, MI: Michigan State University Press.

22. Futrell, C.M., & Jenkins, O.C. (1978). Pay secrecy versus pay disclosure for salesmen: A longitudinal study. *Journal of Marketing Research, 15,* 214–219, p. 215.

23. For a study of the prevalence of these plans, see Lawler, E.E. Iii, Mohrman, S.A., & Ledford, G.E. (1992). *Employee involvement and total quality management: Practices and results in Fortune 1000 companies.* San Francisco: Jossey-Bass.

24. Anonymous (2006, March 22). Ace offers profit sharing and all that jazz talks begin. *National Post,* FP6.

25. (2003, October). The goals of stock option programs. www.workforce.com.

26. Gordon, A. (February 2000). 35 best companies to work for. *Report on Business Magazine,* 24–32.

27. Brearton, S., & Daly, J. (2003, January). The 50 Best Companies to Work for in Canada. *Report on Business,* 53–65.

28. Hays, S. (February 1990). "Ownership cultures" create unity. *Workforce, 78(2),* 60–64.

29. Graham-Moore, B., & Ross, T.L. (1990). *Gainsharing: Plans for improving performance.* Washington, DC: Bureau of National Affairs; Markham, S.E., Scott, K.D., & Little, B.L. (1992, January–February). National gainsharing study: The importance of industry differences. *Compensation & Benefits Review,* 34–45; Miller, C.S., & Shuster, M.H. (1987, Summer). Gainsharing plans: A comparative analysis. *Organizational Dynamics,* 44–67.

30. Davis, V. (1989, April). Eyes on the prize. *Canadian Business,* 93–106.

31. Graham-Moore & Ross, 1990; Moore, B.e, & Ross, T.L. (1978). *The Scanlon way to improved productivity: A practical guide.* New York: Wiley.

32. Perry, N.J. (1988, December 19). Here come richer, riskier pay plans. *Fortune,* 50–58; Lawler, E.E. (1984). Whatever happened to incentive pay? *New Management, 1(4),* 37–41.

33. Arthur, J.B., & Huntley, C.L. (2005). Ramping up the organizational learning curve: Assessing the impact of deliberate learning on organizational performance under gainsharing. *Academy of Management Journal, 48,* 1159–1170.

34. Hammer, T.H. (1988). New developments in profit sharing, gainsharing, and employee ownership. In J.P. Campbell & R.J. Campbell (Eds.), *Productivity in organizations.* San Francisco: Jossey-Bass.

35. Cooper, C.L., Dyck, B., & Frohlich, N. (1992). Improving the effectiveness of gainsharing: The role of fairness and participation. *Administrative Science Quarterly, 37,* 471–490.

36. Lawler, E.E., Ili, & Jenkins, G.D., Jr. (1992). Strategic reward systems. In M.D. Dunette & L.M. Hough (Eds.), *Handbook of industrial and organizational psychology* (2nd ed., Vol. 3). Palo Alto, CA: Consulting Psychologists Press.

37. Murray, B., & Gerhart, B. (1998). An empirical analysis of a skill–based pay program and plant performance outcomes. *Academy of Management Journal, 41,* 68–78.

38. Taylor, F.W. (1967). *The principles of scientific management.* New York: Norton.

39. This discussion draws upon Gibson, J.L., Ivancevich, J.M., & Donnelly, J.H., Jr. (1991). *Organizations,* 7th edition. Homewood, IL: Irwin.

40. Ray, R. (2006, April 19). New assignments a stretch but not a yawn. *Globe and Mail,* C1, C6.

41. Hackman, J.R., & Oldham, G.R. (1980). *Work redesign.* Reading, MA: Addison-Wesley.

42. Oldham, G.R., Hackman, J.R., & Stepina, L.P. (1979). Norms for the job diagnostic survey. *JSAS Catalog of Selected Documents in Psychology, 9,* 14. (Ms. No. 1819).

43. See, for example, Johns, G., Xie, J.L., & Fang, Y. (1992). Mediating and moderating effects in job design. *Journal of Management, 18,* 657–676.

44. Rentsch, J.R., & Steel, R.P. (1998). Testing the durability of job characteristics as predictors of absenteeism over a six–year period. *Personnel Psychology, 51,* 165–190.

45. Johns et al., 1992; Tiegs, R.B., Tetrick, L.E., & Fried, Y. (1992). Growth need strength and context satisfactions as moderators of the relations of the Job Characteristics Model. *Journal of Management, 18,* 575–593.

46. Brown, S.P. (1996). A meta-analysis and review of organizational research on job involvement. *Psychological Bulletin, 120,* 235–255.

47. This section draws in part on Hackman & Oldham, 1980.

48. Dumaine, B. (1989, November 6). P&G rewrites the marketing rules. *Fortune,* 34–48, p. 46.

49. Campion, M.A., Mumford, T.V., Morgeson, F.P., & Nahrgang, J.D. (2005). Work redesign: Eight obstacles and opportunities. *Human Resource Management, 44,* 367–390.

50. Dowling, W.F. (1973). Job redesign on the assembly line: Farewell to the blue collar blues? *Organizational Dynamics,* 51–67.

51. Locke, E.A., Sirota, D., & Wolfson, A.D. (1976). An experimental case study of the successes and failure of job enrichment in a government agency. *Journal of Applied Psychology, 61,* 701–711.

52. Stonewalling plant democracy (1977, March 28). *Business Week.*

53. Good descriptions of MBO programs can be found in Mali, P. (1986). *MBO updated: A handbook of practices and techniques for managing by objectives.* New York: Wiley; Odiorne, G.S. (1965). *Management by objectives.* New York: Pitman; Raia, A.P. (1974). *Managing by objectives.* Glenview, IL: Scott, Foresman.

54. Beer, M., & Cannon, D. (2004). Promise and peril in implementing pay-for-performance. *Human Resource Management, 43,* 3–48.

55. Brearton, S., & Daly, J. (2003, January). The 50 best companies to work for in Canada. *Report on Business,* 53–66.

56. Brearton & Daly, 2003; Rodgers, R., & Hunter, J.E. (1991). Impact of management by objectives on organization productivity. *Journal of Applied Psychology, 76,* 322–336.

57. Rodgers & Hunter, 1991.

58. See Rodgers, R., Hunter, J.E., & Rogers, D.L. (1993). Influence of top management commitment on management program success. *Journal of Applied Psychology, 78,* 151–155.

59. For discussions of these and other problems with MBo, see Levinson, H. (1979, July–August). Management by whose objectives. *Harvard Business Review,* 125–134; McConkey, D.D. (1972, October). 20 ways to kill management by objectives. *Management Review,* 4–13; Pringle, C.D., & Longenecker, J.G. (1982). The ethics of MBO. *Academy of Management Review, 7,* 305–312.

60. Chisholm, P. (2000, May 29). What the boss needs to know. *Maclean's, 113(22),* 18–22; Chisholm, P. (2001, March 5). Redesigning work. *Maclean's, 114(10),* 34–38.

61. See Nollen, S.D. (1982). *New work schedules in practice: Managing time in a changing society.* New York: Van Nostrand Reinhold; Ronen, S. (1981). *Flexible working hours: An innovation in the quality of work life.* New York: McGraw-Hill; Ronen, S. (1984). *Alternative work schedules: Selecting, implementing, and evaluating.* Homewood, IL: Dow Jones-Irwin.

62. For a good study showing absence reduction, see Dalton, D.R., & Mesch, D.J. (1990). The impact of flexible scheduling on employee attendance and turnover. *Administrative Science Quarterly, 35,* 370–387.

63. Baltes, B., Briggs, T.E., Huff, J.W., Wright, J.A., & Neuman, G.A. (1999). Flexible and compressed workweek schedules: A meta-analysis of their effects on work-related criteria. *Journal of Applied Psychology, 84,* 496–513.

64. Golembiewski, R.T., & Proehl, C.W. (1978). A survey of the empirical literature on flexible workhours: Character and consequences of a major innovation. *Academy of Management Review, 3,* 837–853; Pierce, J.L., Newstrom, J.W., Dunham,

R.B., & Barber, A.E. (1989). *Alternative work schedules*. Boston: Allyn and Bacon; Ronen, 1981 and 1984.

65. Baltes et al, 1999.

66. Ronen, 1984; Nollen, 1982.

67. Pierce et al., 1989; Ronen, 1984; Ronen, S., & Primps, S.B. (1981). The compressed workweek as organizational change: Behavioral and attitudinal outcomes. *Academy of Management Review, 6*, 61–74.

68. Pierce et al., 1989; Ivancevich, J.M., & Lyon, H.L. (1977). The shortened workweek: A field experiment. *Journal of Applied Psychology, 62*, 34–37.

69. Johns, G. (1987). Understanding and managing absence from work. In S.L. Dolan & R.S. Schuler (Eds.), *Canadian readings in personnel and human resource management*. St. Paul, MN: West.

70. Ivancevich & Lyon, 1977; Calvasina, E.J., & Boxx, W.R. (1975). Efficiency of workers on the four-day workweek. *Academy of Management Journal, 18*, 604–610; Goodale, J.G., & Aagaard, A.K. (1975). Factors relating to varying reactions to the 4-day workweek. *Journal of Applied Psychology, 60*, 33–38.

71. Baltes et al, 1999.

72. This section relies on Pierce et al, 1989.

73. MacGregor, A. (2001, December 29). Sharing jobs gets trendy. *The Gazette, Montreal*, C1.

74. DeFrank, R.S., & Ivancevich, J.M. (1998). Stress on the job: An executive update. *Academy of Management Executive, 12*, 55–66.

75. Grensing-Pophal, L. (1997, March). Employing the best people—from afar. *Workforce, 76(3)*, 30–38; Piskurich, G.M. (1998). *An organizational guide to telecommuting: Setting up and running a successful telecommuter program*. Alexandria, VA: American Society for Training and Development.

76. Grensing-Pophal, 1997.

77. DeFrank & Ivancevich, 1998; Goldsborough, R. (1999, May 14). Make telecommuting work for you. *Computer Dealer News*, 19–20; Fortier, B. (2005, June 6). Ergonomics for teleworkers often overlooked. *Canadian HR Reporter, 18(11)*, 18, 21.

78. Galt, V. (2003, September 24). Drive is on for telework. *Globe and Mail*, C7; Vu, U. (2006, August 14). A variety of options gives boost to remote work. *Canadian HR Reporter, 19(14)*, 15, 21.

79. DeFrank & Ivancevich, 1998; Grensing-Pophal, 1997.

80. Hill, E.J., Miller, B.C., Weiner, S.P., & Colihan, J. (1998). Influences of the virtual office on aspects of work and work/life balance. *Personnel Psychology, 51*, 667–683.

81. Galt, 2003.

82. Bailey, D.S., & Foley, J. (1990, August). Pacific Bell works long distance. *HRMagazine*, 50–52.

83. Grensing-Pophal, 1997.

84. Rynes, Gerhart, & Minette, 2004.

85. Rynes, Gerhart, & Minette, 2004.

Chapter 7

1. Excerpted with minor edits from Kibbe, D.R., & Casner-Lotto, J. (2002, Summer). Ralston Foods: From greenfield to maturity in a team-based plant. *Journal of Organizational Excellence*, 57–67. Reprinted with permission of John Wiley & Sons, Inc.

2. Tuckman, B.W. (1965). Developmental sequence in small groups. *Psychological Bulletin, 63*, 384–399; Tuckman, B.W., & Jensen, M.A.C. (1977). Stages of small-group development revisited. *Group & Organization Studies, 2*, 419–427.

3. Harris, S.G., & Sutton, R.I. (1986). Functions of parting ceremonies in dying organizations. *Academy of Management Journal, 29*, 5–30.

4. Seger, J.A. (1983). No innate phases in group problem solving. *Academy of Management Review, 8*, 683–689. For a study comparing phases with punctuated equilibrium, see Chang, A., Bordia, P., & Duck, J. (2003). Punctuated equilibrium and linear progression: Toward a new understanding of group development. *Academy of Management Journal, 46*, 106–117.

5. Ginnett, R.C. (1990). Airline cockpit crew. In J.R. Hackman (Ed.), *Groups that work (and those that don't)*. San Francisco: Jossey-Bass.

6. Gersick, C.J.G. (1989). Marking time: Predictable transitions in task groups. *Academy of Management Journal, 32*, 274–309; Gersick, C.J.G. (1988). Time and transition in work teams: Toward a new model of group development. *Academy of Management Journal, 31*, 9–41.

7. Gersick, 1989, 1988; Hackman, J.R., & Wageman, R. (2005). A theory of team coaching. *Academy of Management Review, 30*, 269–287.

8. Hare, A.P. (1976). *A handbook of small group research*. New York: The Free Press; Shaw, M.E. (1981). *Group dynamics: The psychology of small group behavior* (3rd ed.). New York: McGraw-Hill; Jones, E.E., & Gerard, H.B. (1967). *Foundations of social psychology*. New York: Wiley.

9. Hare, 1976; Shaw, 1981.

10. The following discussion relies upon Steiner, I.D. (1972). *Group process and productivity*. New York: Academic Press.

11. Steiner, 1972; Hill, G.W. (1982). Group versus individual performance: Are n+1 heads better than one? *Psychological Bulletin, 91*, 517–539.

12. Williams, K.Y., & O'Reilly, C.A. III. (1998). Demography and diversity in organizations: A review of 40 years of research. *Research in Organizational Behavior, 20*, 77–140; Jackson, S.E., Stone, V.K., & Alvarez, E.B. (1993). Socialization amidst diversity: The impact of demographics on work team oldtimers and newcomers. *Research in Organizational Behavior, 15*, 45–109.

13. Watson, W.E., Kumar, K., & Michaelson, L.K. (1993). Cultural diversity's impact on interaction process and performance: Comparing homogeneous and diverse task groups. *Academy of Management Journal, 36*, 590–602.

14. Webber, S.S., & Donahue, L.M. (2001). Impact of highly and less job-related diversity on work group cohesion and performance: A meta-analysis. *Journal of Management, 27*, 141–162.

15. Guzzo, R.A., & Dickson, M.W. (1996). Teams in organizations: Recent research on performance and effectiveness. *Annual Review of Psychology, 47*, 307–338.

16. Harrison, D.A., Price, K.H., & Bell, M.P. (1998). Beyond relational demography: Time and effects of surface- and deep-level diversity on work group cohesion. *Academy of Management Journal, 41*, 96–107.

17. For an example of the social process by which this sharing may be negotiated in a new group, see Bettenhausen, K., & Murnighan, J.K. (1991). The development of an intragroup norm and the effects of interpersonal and structural challenges. *Administrative Science Quarterly, 36*, 20–35.

18. Kanter, R.M. (1977). *Men and women of the corporation*. New York: Basic Books, p. 37.

19. Leventhal, G.S. (1976). The distribution of rewards and resources in groups and organizations. In L. Berkowitz & E. Walster (Eds.), *Advances in experimental social psy-*

chology (Vol. 9). New York: Academic Press.

20. See Mitchell, T.R., Rothman, M., & Liden, R.C. (1985). Effects of normative information on task performance. *Journal of Applied Psychology, 70,* 48–55.

21. Jackson, S.E., & Schuler, R.S. (1985). A meta-analysis and conceptual critique of research on role ambiguity and role conflict in work settings. *Organizational Behavior and Human Decision Processes, 36,* 16–78. For a methodological critique of this domain, see King, L.A., & King, D.W. (1990). Role conflict and role ambiguity: A critical assessment of construct validity. *Psychological Bulletin, 107,* 48–64.

22. Jackson & Schuler, 1985; Tubre, T.C., & Collins, J.M. (2000). Jackson and Shuler (1985) revisited: A meta-analysis of the relationship between role ambiguity, role conflict, and job performance. *Journal of Management, 26,* 155–169.

23. O'Driscoll, M.P., Ilgen, D.R., & Hildreth, K. (1992). Time devoted to job and off-job activities, interrole conflict, and affective experiences. *Journal of Applied Psychology, 77,* 272–279.

24. See Latack, J.C. (1981). Person/role conflict: Holland's model extended to role-stress research, stress management, and career development. *Academy of Management Review, 6,* 89–103.

25. Jackson & Schuler, 1985.

26. Shaw, 1981.

27. Kiesler, S., & Sproull, L. (1992). Group decision making and communication technology. *Organizational Behavior and Human Decision Processes, 52,* 96–123.

28. Strodbeck, F.L., James, R.M., & Hawkins, C. (1957). Social status in jury deliberations. *American Sociological Review, 22,* 713–719.

29. Gordon A. (2000, February). 35 best companies to work for. *Report on Business Magazine,* 24–32.

30. Kiesler & Sproull, 1992.

31. For other definitions and a discussion of their differences, see Mudrack, P.E. (1989). Defining group cohesiveness: A legacy of confusion? *Small Group Behavior, 20,* 37–49.

32. Stein, A. (1976). Conflict and cohesion: A review of the literature. *Journal of Conflict Resolution, 20,* 143–172.

33. Cartwright, D. (1968). The nature of group cohesiveness. In D. Cartwright & A. Zander (Eds.), *Group dynamics* (3rd ed.). New York: Harper & Row.

34. Lott, A., & Lott, B. (1965). Group cohesiveness as interpersonal attraction: A review of relationships with antecedent and consequent variables. *Psychological Bulletin, 64,* 259–309.

35. Anderson, A.B. (1975). Combined effects of interpersonal attraction and goal-path clarity on the cohesiveness of task-oriented groups. *Journal of Personality and Social Psychology, 31,* 68–75. Also see Cartwright, 1968.

36. Seashore, S. (1954). *Group cohesiveness in the industrial workgroup.* Ann Arbor, MI: Institute for Social Research.

37. Blanchard, F.A., Adelman, L., & Cook, S.W. (1975). Effect of group success and failure upon interpersonal attraction in cooperating interracial groups. *Journal of Personality and Social Psychology, 31,* 1020–1030.

38. Aronson, E., & Mills, J. (1959). The effects of severity of initiation on liking for a group. *Journal of Abnormal and Social Psychology, 59,* 177–181.

39. Cartwright, 1968; Shaw, 1981.

40. Schacter, S. (1951). Deviation, rejection, and communication. *Journal of Abnormal and Social Psychology, 46,* 190–207. See also Barker, J.R. (1993). Tightening the iron cage: Concertive control in self-managing teams. *Administrative Science Quarterly, 38,* 408–437.

41. Beal, D.J., Cohen, R.R., Burke, M.J., & McLendon, C.L. (2003). Cohesion and performance in groups: A meta-analytic clarification of construct relations. *Journal of Applied Psychology, 88,* 989–1004; Mullen, B., & Copper, C. (1994). The relation between group cohesiveness and performance: An integration. *Psychological Bulletin, 115,* 210–227.

42. Podsakoff, P.M., MacKenzie, S.B., & Ahearne, M. (1997). Moderating effects of goal acceptance on the relationship between group cohesiveness and productivity. *Journal of Applied Psychology, 82,* 974–983.

43. Seashore, 1954. Also see Stogdill, R.M. (1972). Group productivity, drive, and cohesiveness. *Organizational Behavior and Human Performance, 8,* 26–43. For a critique, see Mudrack, P.E. (1989). Group cohesiveness and productivity: A closer look. *Human Relations, 42,* 771–785.

44. Gulley, S.M., Devine, D.J., & Whitney, D.J. (1995). A meta-analysis of cohesion and performance: Effects of level of analysis and task interdependence. *Small Group Research, 26,* 497–520.

45. Shepperd, J.A. (1993). Productivity loss in small groups: A motivation analysis. *Psychological Bulletin, 113,* 67–81; Kidwell, R.E., Ili, & Bennett, N. (1993). Employee propensity to withhold effort: A conceptual model to intersect three avenues of research. *Academy of Management Review, 18,* 429–456.

46. Shepperd, 1993; Kidwell & Bennett, 1993; George, J.M. (1992). Extrinsic and intrinsic origins of perceived social loafing in organizations. *Academy of Management Journal, 35,* 191–202.

47. Guzzo & Dickinson, 1996.

48. Kirkman, B.L., & Shapiro, D.L. (1997). The impact of cultural values on employee resistance to teams: Toward a model of globalized self-managing work team effectiveness. *Academy of Management Review, 22,* 730–757.

49. Guzzo & Dickinson, 1996; Kirkman & Shapiro, 1997; Banker, R.D., Field, J.M., Schroeder, R.G., & Sinha, K.K. (1996). Impact of work teams on manufacturing performance: A longitudinal field study. *Academy of Management Journal, 39,* 867–890.

50. Hackman, J.R. (1987). The design of work teams. In J.W. Lorsch (Ed.), *Handbook of organizational behavior.* Englewood Cliffs, NJ: Prentice-Hall. See also Hackman, J.R. (2002). *Leading teams: Setting the stage for great performances.* Boston: Harvard Business School Press.

51. Campion, M.A., Medsker, G.J., & Higgs, A.C. (1993). Relations between work group characteristics and effectiveness: Implications for designing effective work groups. *Personnel Psychology, 46,* 823–850.

52. Dumaine, B. (1990, May 7). Who needs a boss? *Fortune,* 52–60.

53. Wall, T.D., Kemp, N.J., Jackson, P.R., & Clegg, C.W. (1986). Outcomes of autonomous workgroups: A field experiment. *Academy of Management Journal, 29,* 280–304, p. 283.

54. Parts of this section rely on Hackman, 1987.

55. See Ashforth, B.E., & Mael, F. (1989). Social identity theory and the organization. *Academy of Management Review, 14,* 20–39.

56. Treece, J. (1990, April 9). Here comes GM's Saturn. *Business Week,* 56–62.

57. Wall et al., 1986; Cordery, J.L., Mueller, W.S., & Smith, L.M. (1991). Attitudinal and behavioral effects of

autonomous group working: A longitudinal field study. *Academy of Management Journal, 34,* 264–276.

58. Hayward, D. (2003, May 20). Management through measurement. *Financial Post,* BE5.

59. Manz, C.C., & Sims, H.P., Jr. (1987). Leading workers to lead themselves: The external leadership of self-managing work teams. *Administrative Science Quarterly, 32,* 106–128.

60. For reviews of research on self-managed teams, see Chapter 3 of Cummings, T.G., & Molloy, E.S. (1977). *Improving productivity and the quality of working life.* New York: Praeger; Goodman, P.S., Devadas, R., & Hughes, T.L.G. (1988). Groups and productivity: Analyzing the effectiveness of self-managing teams. In J.P. Campbell & R.J. Campbell (Eds.), *Productivity in organizations.* San Francisco: Jossey-Bass; Pearce, J.A., Iii, & Ravlin, E.C. (1987). The design and activation of self-regulating work groups. *Human Relations, 40,* 751–782.

61. Campion, M.A., Papper, E.M., & Medsker, G.J. (1996). Relations between work team characteristics and effectiveness: A replication and extension. *Personnel Psychology, 49,* 429–452; Campion, Medsker, & Higgs, 1993.

62. Hyatt, D.E., & Ruddy, T.M. (1997). An examination of the relationship between work group characteristics and performance: Once more into the breech. *Personnel Psychology, 50,* 553–585.

63. Kirkman & Shapiro, 1997; Banker et al., 1996.

64. Farnham, A. (1994, February 7). America's most admired company. *Fortune,* 50–54; Dumaine, B. (1993, December 13). Payoff from the new management. *Fortune,* 103–110.

65. Waterman, R.H., Jr. (1987). *The renewal factor.* New York: Bantam Books; McElroy, J. (1985, April). Ford's new way to build cars. *Road & Track,* 156–158.

66. Pinto, M.B., Pinto, J.k, & Prescott, J.E. (1993). Antecedents and consequences of project team cross-functional cooperation. *Management Science, 39,* 1281–1297; Henke, J.W., Krachenberg, A.R., & Lyons, T.F. (1993). Cross-functional teams: Good concept, poor implementation! *Journal of Product Innovation Management, 10,* 216–229. Mustang examples from White, J.B., & Suris, O. (1993, September 21). How a 'skunk works' kept the Mustang

alive—on a tight budget. *Wall Street Journal,* A1, A12.

67. Lipnack, J., & Stamps, J. (2000). Virtual teams: People working across boundaries with technology. (2nd ed.). New York: Wiley; Axtell, C.M., Fleck, S.J., & Turner, N. (2004). Virtual Teams: Collaborating across distance. *International Review of Industrial and Organizational Psychology, 19,* 205–248.

68. Willmore, J. (2000, February). Managing virtual teams. *Training Journal,* 18–21.

69. Joinson, C. (2002, June). Managing virtual teams. *HR Magazine,* 68–73.

70. Cascio, W.F. (2000, August). Managing a virtual workplace. *Academy of Management Executive,* 81–90.

71. Willmore, 2000.

72. Kirkman, B.L., Rosen, B., Gibson, C.B., Telusk, P.E., & McPherson, S.O. (2002, August). Five challenges to virtual team success: Lessons from Sabre, Inc. *Academy of Management Executive,* 67–79.

73. Cascio, 2000; Joinson, 2002; Kirkman et al. 2002.

74. Allen, N.J., & Hecht, T.D. (2004). The 'romance of teams': Toward an understanding of its psychological underpinnings and implications. *Journal of Occupational and Organizational Psychology, 77,* 439–461.

75. Vallas, S.P. (2003). Why teamwork fails: Obstacles to workplace change in four manufacturing plants. *American Sociological Review, 68,* 223–250; Tudor, T.R., Trumble, R.R., & Diaz, J.J. (1996, Autumn). Workteams: Why do they often fail? *S.A.M. Advanced Management Journal,* 31–39.

Chapter 8

1. Schettler, J. (2002, August). Welcome to ACME Inc. *Training, 39(8),* 36–43; Durett, J. (2006, March). Plug in and perform: Technology opens the door to success at Ritz-Carlton. *Training, 43(3),* 30–34; www.ritzcarlton.com; www.fairmont.com.

2. See Morrison, E.W. (1993). Newcomer information seeking: Exploring types, modes, sources, and outcomes. *Academy of Management Journal, 36,* 557–589.

3. The terms information dependence and effect dependence are used by Jones, E.E., & Gerard, H.B. (1967). *Foundations of social psychology.* New York: Wiley.

4. Festinger, L. (1954). A theory of social comparison processes. *Human Relations, 7,* 117–140; Thomas, J., & Griffin, R. (1983). The social information processing model of task design: A review of the literature. *Academy of Management Review, 8,* 672–682.

5. Kelman, H.C. (1961). Processes of opinion change. *Public Opinion Quarterly, 25,* 57–78.

6. Saks, A.M., & Ashforth, B.E. (1997). A longitudinal investigation of the relationships between job information sources, applicant perceptions of fit, and work outcomes. *Personnel Psychology, 50,* 395–426.

7. Kristof-Brown, A.L., Zimmerman, R.D., & Johnson, E.C. (2005). Consequences of individuals' fit at work: A meta-analysis of person-job, person-organization, person-group, and person-supervisor fit. *Personnel Psychology, 58,* 281–342; Kristof, A.L. (1996). Person-organization fit: An integrative review of its conceptualizations, measurement, and implications. *Personnel Psychology, 49,* 1–49; Saks & Ashforth, 1997; Saks, A.M., & Ashforth, B.E. (2002). Is job search related to employment quality? It all depends on the fit. *Journal of Applied Psychology, 87,* 646–654.

8. Van Maanen, J., & Schein, E.H. (1979). Toward a theory of organizational socialization. *Research in Organizational Behavior, 1,* 209–264.

9. Feldman, D.C. (1976). A contingency theory of socialization. *Administrative Science Quarterly, 21,* 433–452.

10. Wanous, J.P. (1992). *Organizational entry: Recruitment, selection, orientation, and socialization of newcomers.* (2nd ed.). Reading, MA: Addison-Wesley.

11. Wanous, J.P. (1976). Organizational entry: From naive expectations to realistic beliefs. *Journal of Applied Psychology, 61,* 22–29.

12. See Breaugh, J.A. (1992). *Recruitment: Science and practice.* Boston: PWS-Kent.

13. Morrison, E.W., & Robinson, S.L. (1997). When employees feel betrayed: A model of how psychological contract violation develops. *Academy of Management Review, 22,* 226–256.

14. Robinson, S.L., & Rousseau, D.M. (1994). Violating the psychological contract: Not the exception but the norm. *Journal of Organizational Behavior, 15,* 245–259.

15. Morrison & Robinson, 1997; Robinson, S.L. (1996). Trust and breach of the psychological contract. *Administrative Science Quarterly, 41,*

574–599; Raja, U., Johns, G., & Ntalianis, F. (2004). The impact of personality on psychological contracts. *Academy of Management Journal, 47,* 350–367; Deery, S.J., Iverson, R.D., & Walsh, J.T. (2006). Toward a better understanding of psychological contract breach: A study of customer service employees. *Journal of Applied Psychology, 91,* 166–175.

16. Morrison & Robinson, 1997.
17. Morrison & Robinson, 1997.
18. Wanous, 1992; Breaugh, 1992.
19. Wanous, 1992; Breaugh, 1992.
20. Galt, V. (2005, March 9). Kid-glove approach woes new grads. *Globe and Mail,* C1, C3.
21. Harding, K. (2003, July 16). Police aim to hire officers. *Globe and Mail,* C1.
22. Phillips, J.M. (1998). Effects of realistic job previews on multiple organizational outcomes: A meta-analysis. *Academy of Management Journal, 41,* 673–690.
23. Premack, S.L., & Wanous, J.P. (1985). A meta-analysis of realistic job preview experiments. *Journal of Applied Psychology, 70,* 706–719. See also Wanous, J.P., Poland, T.D., Premack, S.L., & Davis, K.S. (1992). The effects of met expectations on newcomer attitudes and behaviors: A review and meta-analysis. *Journal of Applied Psychology, 77,* 288–297.
24. Premack & Wanous, 1985; McEvoy, G.M. & Cascio, W.F. (1985). Strategies for reducing employee turnover: A meta-analysis. *Journal of Applied Psychology, 70,* 342–353.
25. Morrison & Robinson, 1997.
26. Wanous, J.P., & Reichers, A.E. (2000). New employee orientation programs. *Human Resource Management Review, 10,* 435–451.
27. Gruner, S. (1998, July). Lasting impressions. *Inc., 20(10),* 126.
28. Klein, H.J. & Weaver, N.A. (2000). The effectiveness of an organizational-level orientation training program in the socialization of new hires. *Personnel Psychology, 53,* 47–66.
29. Schettler, J. (2002, August). Welcome to ACME Inc. *Training, 39(8),* 36–43.
30. Van Maanen, J., & Schein, E.H. (1979). Toward a theory of organizational socialization. In B.M. Staw (Ed.), *Research in organizational behavior,* Vol. 1. Greenwich, CT: JAI Press, 209–264.
31. Ashforth, B.E., & Saks, A.M. (1996). Socialization tactics: Longitudinal effects on newcomer adjustment. *Academy of Management Journal, 39,* 149–178; Jones, G.R. (1986). Socialization tactics, self-efficacy, and newcomers' adjustments to organizations. *Academy of Management Journal, 29,* 262–279.
32. Ashforth & Saks, 1996; Jones, 1986; Cable, D.M., & Parsons, C.K. (2001). Socialization tactics and person-organization fit. *Personnel Psychology, 54,* 1–23; Rollag, K., Parise, S., & Cross, R. (2005). Getting new hires up to speed quickly. *MIT Sloan Management Review,* 35–41.
33. Kram, K. (1985). *Mentoring.* Glenview, IL: Scott, Foresman.
34. Dalton, G.W., Thompson, P.H., & Price, R. (1977, Summer). The four stages of professional careers—A new look at performance by professionals. *Organizational Dynamics,* 19–42; Fagenson, E. (1988). The power of a mentor: Protégés and nonprotégés' perceptions of their own power in organizations. *Group and Organization Studies, 13,* 182–192; Fagenson, E. (1989). The mentor advantage: Perceived career/job experiences of protégés versus non-protégés. *Journal of Organizational Behavior, 10,* 309–320; Scandura, T. (1992). Mentorship and career mobility: An empirical investigation. *Journal of Organizational Behavior, 13,* 169–174; Dreher, G., & Ash, R. (1990). A comparative study of mentoring among men and women in managerial, professional and technical positions. *Journal of Applied Psychology, 75,* 539–546; Whitely, W., Dougherty, T., & Dreher, G. (1991). Relationship of career mentoring and socioeconomic origin to managers' and professionals' early career progress. *Academy of Management Journal, 34,* 331–351.
35. Allen, T.D., Eby, L.T., Poteet, M.L., Lentz, E., & Lima, L. (2004). Career benefits associated with mentoring for protégés: A meta-analysis. *Journal of Applied Psychology, 89,* 127–136.
36. Allen, T.D., McManus, S.E., & Russell, J.E.A. (1999). Newcomer socialization and stress: Formal peer relationships as a source of support. *Journal of Vocational Behavior, 54,* 453–470.
37. Allen, T.D., Eby, L.T., & Lentz, E. (2006). Mentorship behaviours and mentorship quality associated with formal mentoring programs: Closing the gap between research and practice. *Journal of Applied Psychology, 91,* 567–578; Murray, M. (1991). *Beyond the myths and magic of mentoring: How to facilitate an effective mentoring program.* San Francisco, CA: Jossey-Bass; Lawrie, J. (1987). How to establish a mentoring program.
38. Harding. K. (2003, March 12). Your new best friend. *Globe and Mail,* C1, C10.
39. Chao, G., Walz, P., & Gardner, P. (1992). Formal and informal mentorships: A comparison on mentoring functions and contrast with nonmentored counterparts. *Personnel Psychology, 45,* 619–636; Noe, R. (1988). An investigation of the determinants of successful assigned mentoring relationships. *Personnel Psychology, 41,* 457–479; Allen, Eby, & Lentz, 2006; Allen, T.D., Eby, L.T., & Lentz, E. (2006). The relationship between formal mentoring program characteristics and perceived program effectiveness. *Personnel Psychology, 59,* 125–153.
40. Kram, K.E., & Isabella, L.A. (1985). Mentoring alternatives: The role of peer relationships in career development. *Academy of Management Journal, 28,* 110–132.
41. Cox, T., Jr. (1993). *Cultural diversity in organizations: Theory, research, & practice.* San Francisco: Berrett-Koehler; Noe, R.A. (1988). Women and mentoring: A review and research agenda. *Academy of Management Review, 13,* 65–78; Ragins, B.R. (1989). Barriers to mentoring: The female manager's dilemma. *Human Relations, 42,* 1–22.
42. Dreyfus, J., Lee, M.J., & Totta, J.M. (1995, December). Mentoring at the Bank of Montreal: A case study of an intervention that exceeded expectations. *Human Resource Planning, 18(4),* 45–49.
43. Ragins, B., & McFarlin, D. (1990). Perceptions of mentor roles in cross-gender mentoring relationships. *Journal of Vocational Behavior, 37,* 321–339.
44. Burke, R., & McKeen, C. (1990). Mentoring in organizations: Implications for women. *Journal of Business Ethics, 9,* 317–322; Dennett, D. (1985, November). Risks, mentoring helps women to the top. *APA Monitor, 26;* Morrison, A., White, R., & Van Velsor, E. (1987). *Breaking the glass ceiling: Can women reach the top of America's largest corporations?* Reading, MA: Addison-Wesley;.
45. Purden, C. (2001, June). Rising to the challenge. *Report on Business Magazine, 17(12),* 31.
46. Purden, 2001.
47. Church, E. (2001, March 8). Mentors guide women through career roadblocks. *Globe and Mail,* B12.
48. Dreyfus, Lee, & Totta, 1995.

49. Cox, 1993; Ibarra, H. (1993). Personal networks of women and minorities in management. *Academy of Management Review, 18,* 56–87.

50. Nkomo, S., & Cox, T. (1989). Gender differences in the upward mobility of black managers: Double whammy or double advantage? *Sex Roles, 21,* 825–839.

51. Thomas, D. (1989). Mentoring and irrationality: The role of racial taboos. *Human Resource Management, 28,* 279–290; Thomas, D. (1990). The impact of race on managers' experiences of developmental relationships: An intraorganizational study. *Journal of Organizational Behavior, 11,* 479–492.

52. Papmehl, A. (2002, October 7). Diversity in workforce paying off, IBM finds. *Toronto Star.* Retrieved November 30, 2003, from www.thestar.com

53. Ostroff, C., & Kozlowski, S.W.J. (1992). Organizational socialization as a learning process: The role of information acquisition. *Personnel Psychology, 45,* 849–874; Saks, A.M., & Ashforth, B.E. (1996). Proactive socialization and behavioral self-management. *Journal of Vocational Behavior, 48,* 301–323.

54. Morrison, E.W. (1993). Newcomer information seeking: Exploring types, modes, sources, and outcomes. *Academy of Management Journal, 36,* 557–589; Morrison, E.W. (1993). Longitudinal study of the effects of information seeking on newcomer socialization. *Journal of Applied Psychology, 78,* 173–183.

55. Ostroff & Kozlowski, 1992.

56. Ashford, S.J., & Black, J.S. (1996). Proactivity during organizational entry: The role of desire for control. *Journal of Applied Psychology, 81,* 199–214; Griffin, A.E.C., Colella, A., & Goparaju, S. (2000). Newcomer and organizational socialization tactics: An interactionist perspective. *Human Resource Management Review, 10,* 453–474; Wanberg, C.R. & Kammeyer-Mueller, J.D. (2000). Predictors and outcomes of proactivity in the socialization process. *Journal of Applied Psychology, 85,* 373–385; Whitely, W.T., Peiró, J.M., Feij, J.A., & Taris, T.W. (1995). Conceptual, epistemological, methodological, and outcome issues in work-role development: A reply. *Journal of Vocational Behavior, 46,* 283–291.

57. Ashforth & Saks, 1996; Riketta, M. (2005). Organizational identification: A meta-analysis. *Journal of Vocational Behavior, 66,* 358–384.

58. For a more complete discussion of various definitions, theories, and concepts of culture, see Allaire, Y., & Firsirotu, M.E. (1984). Theories of organizational culture. *Organization Studies, 5,* 193–226; Hatch, M.J. (1993). The dynamics of organizational culture. *Academy of Management Review, 18,* 657–693; Schein, E.H. (1992). *Organizational culture and leadership,* 2nd edition. San Francisco: Jossey-Bass; Smircich, L. (1983). Concepts of culture and organizational analysis. *Administrative Science Quarterly, 28,* 339–358.

59. Sackmann, S.A. (1992). Culture and subculture: An analysis of organizational knowledge. *Administrative Science Quarterly, 37,* 140–161.

60. Gregory, K.L. (1983). Native-view paradigms: Multiple cultures and culture conflicts in organizations. *Administrative Science Quarterly, 28,* 359–376.

61. Deal, T.E., & Kennedy, A.A. (1982). *Corporate cultures: The rites and rituals of corporate life.* Reading, MA: Addison-Wesley; Kilmann, R., Saxton, M.J., & Serpa, R. (1986, Winter). Issues in understanding and changing culture. *California Management Review,* 87–94. For a critique, see Saffold, G.S., III. (1988). Culture traits, strength, and organizational performance: Moving beyond "strong" culture. *Academy of Management Review, 13,* 546–558.

62. Holloway, A. (2006, April 10–23). Hilti (Canada) Corp. *Canadian Business, 79(8),* 78.

63. Brearton, S., & Daly, J. (2003, January). The fifty best companies to work for in Canada. *Report on Business Magazine, 19(2),* 61; Hannon, G. (2002, January). Flight Centre. *Report on Business Magazine, 18(7),* 44–46.

64. Wahl, A. (2005, October 10–23). Culture shock. *Canadian Business, 78(20),* 115.

65. Verburg, P. (2000, December 25). Prepare for takeoff. *Canadian Business, 73(24),* 94–99; Wahl, A. (2005, October 10–23).

66. Raynal, W. (1993, December 20). Down, but not out. *Autoweek,* 15.

67. Gordon, G.G., & Di Tomaso, N. (1992). Predicting corporate performance from organizational culture. *Journal of Management Studies, 29,* 783–798. For a critique of such work, see Siehl, C., & Martin, J. (1990).

Organizational culture: A key to financial performance. In B. Schneider (Ed.), *Organizational climate and culture.* San Francisco: Jossey-Bass.

68. Sheridan, J.E. (1992). Organizational culture and employee retention. *Academy of Management Journal, 35,* 1036–1056.

69. Lorsch, J.W. (1986, Winter). Managing culture: The invisible barrier to strategic change. *California Management Review,* 95–109.

70. Verburg, P. (2000, December 25).

71. (2006). The corporate culture paradox. Toronto, Ontario: Waterstone Human Capital Ltd.

72. Mount, I. (2002, August). Out of control. *Business 2.0, 3(8),* 38–44.

73. Cartwright, S., & Cooper, C.L. (1993, May). The role of culture compatibility in successful organizational marriage. *Academy of Management Executive,* 57–70.

74. Fordahl, M. (2002, March 28). Hp, Compaq face ghosts of mega-mergers past. *Globe and Mail,* B17.

75. Kets de Vries, M.F.R., & Miller, D. (1984). *The neurotic organization: Diagnosing and changing counterproductive styles of management.* San Francisco: Jossey-Bass.

76. Lardner, J. (2002, March). Why should anyone believe you? *Business 2.0, 3(3),* 40–48; Waldie, P., & Howlett, K. (2003, June 11). Reports reveal tight grip of Ebbers on WorldCom. *Globe and Mail,* B1, B7.

77. McKenna, B. (2003, August 27). Shuttle probe blasts NASA's dysfunctional atmosphere. *Globe and Mail,* A9; Schwartz, J., & Wald, M.L. (2003, August 27). Shuttle probe faults NASA. *Toronto Star.* Retrieved November 30, 2003, from www.thestar.ca (orig. pub. *New York Times*).

78. See Schein, 1992.

79. Papmehl, 2002.

80. Uttal, B. (1985, August 5). Behind the fall of Steve Jobs. *Fortune,* 20–24.

81. Pascale, R. (1985, Winter). The paradox of "corporate culture": Reconciling ourselves to socialization. *California Management Review,* 26–41. For some research support, see Caldwell, D.F., Chatman, J.A., & O'Reilly, C.A. (1990). Building organizational commitment: A multifirm study. *Journal of Occupational Psychology, 63,* 245–261.

82. Gordon, A. (2000, February). 35 best companies to work for. *Report on Business Magazine,* 24–32.

83. Hatch, 1993; Ornstein, S. (1986). Organizational symbols: A study of

their meanings and influences on perceived organizational climate. *Organizational Behavior and Human Decision Processes, 38,* 207–229.

84. Nulty, P. (1989, February 27). America's toughest bosses. *Fortune,* 40–54.

85. Trice, H.M., and Beyer, J.M. (1984). Studying organizational cultures through rites and ceremonials. *Academy of Management Review, 9,* 653–669.

86. Martin, J., Feldman, M.S., Hatch, M.J., & Sitkin, S.B. (1983). The uniqueness paradox in organizational stories. *Administrative Science Quarterly, 28,* 438–453.

87. Peters, T., & Austin, N. (1985). *A passion for excellence: The leadership difference.* New York: Random House.

Chapter 9

1. Based on Yelaja, P. (2005, July 17). A CEO who delivers. *Toronto Star,* A19. Reprinted with permission from Torstar Syndication Services; Anonymous (2006, March 29). FedEx Canada president wins Excellence in Communication Leadership (EXCEL) Award. International Association of Business Communicators, www.news.iabc.com/index.php?s= press_release&item=92.

2. Daly, J. (2003, February). The toughest SOBs in business. *Report on Business Magazine, 19(8),* 34–42; Various contributors (2005, November). The power 25. *Report on Business Magazine, 22(4),* 49–82.

3. Bass, B.M. (1990). *Bass & Stogdill's handbook of leadership: A survey of research* (3rd ed.). New York: Free Press.

4. This list is derived from Bass, 1990; House, R.J., & Baetz, M.L. (1979). Leadership: Some empirical generalizations and new research directions. *Research in Organizational Behavior, 1,* 341–423; Locke, E.A., et al. (1992). *The essence of leadership: The four keys to leading effectively.* New York: Free Press; Lord, R.G., DeVader, C.L., & Alliger, G.M. (1986). A meta-analysis of the relationship between personality traits and leadership perceptions: An application of validity generalization procedures. *Journal of Applied Psychology, 71,* 402–410.

5. Judge, T.A., Colbert, A.E., & Ilies, R. (2004). Intelligence and leadership: A quantitative review and test of theoretical propositions. *Journal of Applied Psychology, 89,* 542–552.

6. Goleman, D. (1998, November–December). What makes a leader? *Harvard Business Review,* 93–102; Judge, T.A., & Bono, J.E. (2000). Five-factor model of personality and transformational leadership. *Journal of Applied Psychology, 85,* 751–765; Wong, C., & Law, K.S. (2002). The effects of leader and follower emotional intelligence on performance and attitude: An exploratory study. *The Leadership Quarterly, 13,* 243–274.

7. Kirkpatrick, S.A., & Locke, E.A. (1991). Leadership: Do traits matter? *Academy of Management Executive, 5,* 48–60.

8. Bottger, P.C. (1984). Expertise and air time as bases of actual and perceived influence in problem-solving groups. *Journal of Applied Psychology, 69,* 214–221.

9. Lewis, G.H. (1972). Role differentiation. *American Sociological Review, 37,* 424–434.

10. Bales, R.F., & Slater, P.E. (1955). Role differentiation in small decision-making groups. In T. Parsons, et al. (Eds.), *Family, socialization, and interaction process.* Glencoe, IL: Free Press; Slater, P.E. (1955). Role differentiation in small groups. *American Sociological Review, 20,* 300–310.

11. Hannon, G. (2004, January). The great transformation. *Report on Business Magazine, 20(7),* 43–46.

12. Judge, T.A., Piccolo, R.F., & Ilies, R. (2004). The forgotten ones? The validity of consideration and initiating structure in leadership research. *Journal of Applied Psychology, 89,* 36–51.

13. Kerr, S., Schriesheim, C.A., Murphy, C.J., & Stogdill, R.M. (1974). Toward a contingency theory of leadership based upon the consideration and initiating structure literature. *Organizational Behavior and Human Performance, 12,* 62–82.

14. Podsakoff, P.M., Bommer, W.H., Podsakoff, N.P., & MacKenzie, S.B. (2006). Relationships between leader reward and punishment behaviour and subordinate attitudes, perceptions, and behaviors: A meta-analytic review of existing and new research. *Organizational Behavior and Human Decision Processes, 99,* 113–142.

15. Verburg, P. (2000, December 25). Prepare for takeoff. *Canadian Business, 73(24),* 94–99.

16. Fiedler, F.E. (1967). *A theory of leadership effectiveness.* New York: McGraw-Hill; Fiedler, F.E. (1978). The contingency model and the dynamics of the leadership process. In

L. Berkowitz (Ed.), *Advances in experimental social psychology* (Vol. 11). New York: Academic Press; Fiedler, F.E., & Chemers, M.M. (1974). *Leadership and effective management.* Glenview, IL: Scott, Foresman.

17. For a summary, see Fiedler, 1978.

18. See Ashour, A.S. (1973). The contingency model of leader effectiveness: An evaluation. *Organizational Behavior and Human Performance, 9,* 339–355; Graen, G.B., Alvares, D., Orris, J.B., & Martella, J.A. (1970). The contingency model of leadership effectiveness: Antecedent and evidential results. *Psychological Bulletin, 74,* 285–296.

19. Peters, L.H., Hartke, D.D., & Pohlmann, J.T. (1985). Fiedler's contingency theory of leadership: An application of the meta-analysis procedures of Schmidt and Hunter. *Psychological Bulletin, 97,* 274–285; Schriesheim, C.A., Tepper, B.J., & Tetreault, L.A. (1994). Least preferred co-worker score, situational control, and leadership effectiveness: A meta-analysis of contingency and performance predictions. *Journal of Applied Psychology, 79,* 561–573; Strube, M.J. & Garcia, J.E. (1981). A meta-analytic investigation of Fiedler's contingency model of leadership effectiveness. *Psychological Bulletin, 90,* 307–321.

20. House, R.J., & Dessler, G. (1974). The path-goal theory of leadership: Some post hoc and a priori tests. In J.G. Hunt & L.L. Larson (Eds.), *Contingency approaches to leadership.* Carbondale, IL: Southern Illinois University Press; House, R.J., & Mitchell, T.R. (1974, Autumn). Path-goal theory of leadership. *Journal of Contemporary Business,* 81–97. See also Evans, M.G. (1970). The effects of supervisory behavior on the path-goal relationship. *Organizational Behavior and Human Performance, 5,* 277–298.

21. Filley, A. C., House, R. J., & Kerr, S. (1976). *Managerial process and organizational behavior* (2nd ed.). Glenview, IL: Scott, Foresman; House & Dessler, 1974; House & Mitchell, 1974; Wofford, J.C., & Liska, L.Z. (1993). Path-goal theories of leadership: A meta-analysis. *Journal of Management, 19,* 857–876.

22. See, for example, Greene, C.N. (1979). Questions of causation in the path-goal theory of leadership. *Academy of Management Journal, 22,* 22–41; Griffin, R.W. (1980). Relationships among individual, task

design, and leader behavior variables. *Academy of Management Journal, 23,* 665–683.

23. Mitchell, T.R. (1973). Motivation and participation: An integration. *Academy of Management Journal, 16,* 160–179.

24. Maier, N.R.F. (1970). *Problem solving and creativity in individuals and groups.* Belmont, CA: Brooks/Cole; Maier, N.R.F. (1973). *Psychology in industrial organizations* (4th ed.). Boston: Houghton Mifflin.

25. Maier, 1970, 1973.

26. Vroom, V.H. & Jago, A.G. (1988). *The new leadership: Managing participation in organizations.* Englewood Cliffs, NJ: Prentice-Hall; Vroom, V.H., & Yetton, P.W. (1973). *Leadership and decision-making.* Pittsburgh: University of Pittsburgh Press.

27. Vroom & Yetton, 1973, p. 13.

28. See Vroom & Jago, 1988, for a review. See also Field, R.H.G., Wedley, W.C., & Hayward, M.W.J. (1989). Criteria used in selecting Vroom-Yetton decision styles. *Canadian Journal of Administrative Sciences, 6(2),* 18–24.

29. Reviews on participation reveal a complicated pattern of results. See Miller, K.I. & Monge, P.R. (1986). Participation, satisfaction, and productivity: A meta-analytic review. *Academy of Management Journal, 29,* 727–753; Wagner, J.A., Iii, & Gooding, R.Z. (1987a). Shared influence and organizational behavior: A meta-analysis of situational variables expected to moderate participation–outcome relationships. *Academy of Management Journal, 30,* 524–541; Wagner, J.A., Iii, & Gooding, R.Z. (1987b). Effects of societal trends on participation research. *Administrative Science Quarterly, 32,* 241–262.

30. Graen, G.B., & Uhl-Bien, M. (1995). Relationship-based approach to leadership: Development of leader–member exchange (LMX) theory of leadership over 25 years: Applying a multi-level, multi-domain perspective. *Leadership Quarterly, 6(2),* 219–247.

31. Gerstner, C.R., & Day, D.V. (1997). Meta-analytic review of leader-member exchange theory: Correlates and construct issues. *Journal of Applied Psychology, 82,* 827–844; Graen, & Uhl-Bien, 1995; Schriesheim, C.A., Castro, S.L., & Cogliser, C.C. (1999). Leader–member exchange (LMX) research: A comprehensive review of theory, measurement, and data-analytic practices. *Leadership Quarterly, 10(1),* 63–113; House, R.J., & Aditya, R.N. (1997). The social scientific study of leadership: Quo vadis? *Journal of Management, 23,* 409–473; Tierney, P., Farmer, S.M., & Graen, G.B. (1999). An examination of leadership and employee creativity: The relevance of traits and relationships. *Personnel Psychology, 52,* 591–620.

32. Gerstner, & Day, 1997; Graen, & Uhl-Bien, 1995.

33. Judge, T.A. & Piccolo, R.F. (2004). Transformational and transactional leadership: A meta-analytic test of their relative validity. *Journal of Applied Psychology, 89,* 755–768.

34. The transformational/transactional distinction is credited to Burns, J.M. (1978). *Leadership.* New York: Harper & Row.

35. Bass, B.M. (1985). *Leadership and performance beyond expectations.* New York: Free Press; Bass, B.M. (1990, Winter). From transactional to transformational leadership: Learning to share the vision. *Organizational Dynamics,* 19–31.

36. Judge & Piccolo, 2004.

37. Judge & Piccolo, 2004; Bono, J.E., & Judge, T.A. (2004). Personality and transformational and transactional leadership: A meta-analysis. *Journal of Applied Psychology, 89,* 901–910.

38. House, R.J. (1977). A 1976 theory of charismatic leadership. In J.G. Hunt & L.L. Larson (Eds.), *Leadership: The cutting edge.* Carbondale, IL: Southern Illinois University Press.

39. House, R.J., Woycke, J., & Fodor, E.M. (1988). Charismatic and non-charismatic leaders: Differences in behavior and effectiveness. In J.A. Conger & R.N. Kanungo (Eds.), *Charismatic leadership: The elusive factor in organizational effectiveness.* San Francisco: Jossey-Bass.

40. DeGroot, T., Kilker, D.S., & Cross, T.C. (2000). A meta-analysis to review organizational outcomes related to charismatic leadership. *Canadian Journal of Administrative Sciences, 17,* 356–371; Fuller, J.B., Patterson, C.E.P., Hester, K., & Stringer, D.Y. (1996). A quantitative review of research on charismatic leadership. *Psychological Reports, 78,* 271–287.

41. Agle, B.R., Nagarajan, N J., Sonnenfeld, J.A., & Srinivasan, D. (2006). Does CEO charisma matter? An empirical analysis of the relationships among organizational performance, environmental uncertainty, and top management team perceptions of CEO charisma. *Academy of Management Journal, 49,* 161–174; Waldman, D.A., Ramirez, G.G., House, R.J., & Puranam, P. (2001). Does leadership matter? CEO leadership attributes and profitability under conditions of perceived environmental uncertainty. *Academy of Management Journal, 44,* 134–143.

42. Howell, J.M. (1988). Two faces of charisma: Socialized and personalized leadership in organizations. In J.A. Conger & R.N. Kanungo (Eds.), *Charismatic leadership: The elusive factor in organizational effectiveness.* San Francisco: Jossey-Bass; Howell, J.M., & Avolio, B.J. (1992, May). The ethics of charismatic leadership. Submission or liberation? *Academy of Management Executive,* 43–54.

43. Judge & Piccolo, 2004.

44. Wang, H., Law, K.S., Hackett, R.D., Wang, D., & Chen, Z.X. (2005). Leader-member exchange as a mediator of the relationship between transformational leadership and followers' performance and organizational citizenship behaviour. *Academy of Management Journal, 48,* 420–432; Piccolo, R.F. & Colquitt, J.A. (2006). Transformational leadership and job behaviours: The mediating role of core job characteristics. *Academy of Management Journal, 49,* 327–340.

45. Ireland, R.D., & Hitt, M.A. (1999). Achieving and maintaining strategic competitiveness in the 21st century: The role of strategic leadership. *Academy of Management Executive, 13,* 43–57.

46. Ireland & Hitt, 1999.

47. Ireland & Hitt, 1999.

48. Ireland & Hitt, 1999.

49. Javidan, M., Dorfman, P.W., de Luque, M.S., & House, R.J. (2006). In the eye of the beholder: Cross-cultural lessons in leadership from Project GLOBE. *Academy of Management Perspectives, 20,* 67–90.

50. Javidan, Dorfman, de Luque, & House, 2006.

51. Javidan, Dorfman, de Luque, & House, 2006.

52. Gregersen, H.B., Morrison, A.J., & Black, J.S. (1998, Fall). Developing leaders for the global frontier. *Sloan Management Review,* 21–32.

53. Javidan, Dorfman, de Luque, & House, 2006.

54. Yakabuski, K. (2006, August 26). Building the world, Canadian style. *Globe and Mail,* B4.

55. Gregersen, Morrison, & Black, 1998.

56. Gregersen, Morrison, & Black, 1998; Javidan, Dorfman, de Luque, & House, 2006.

57. Javidan, Dorfman, de Luque, & House, 2006.

58. Gregersen, Morrison, & Black, 1998; Church, E. (1999, January 7). Born to be a global business leader. *Globe and Mail*, B8.

59. Moore, K. (2002, August 21). Multicultural Canada breeds managers with global outlook. *Globe and Mail*, B9.

60. Thomas, T., Schermerhorn, J.R., Jr., & Dienhart, J.W. (2004). Strategic leadership of ethical behavior in business. *Academy of Management Executive*, *18*, 56–66; Seidman, D. (2004). The case for ethical leadership. *Academy of Management Executive*, *18*, 134–138; Schminke, M., Ambrose, M.L., & Neubaum, D.O. (2005). The effect of leader moral development on ethical climate and employee attitudes. *Organizational Behavior and Human Decision Processes*, *97*, 135–151.

61. Olive, D. (2006, June 25). Nothing like a crisis to test corporate mettle. *Globe and Mail*, A19; Various contributors (2005, November). The power 25: Rick George. *Report on Business Magazine*, *22(4)*, 49–82.

62. Brown, M.E., Trevino, L.K., & Harrison, D.A. (2005). Ethical leadership: A social learning perspective for construct development and testing. *Organizational Behavior and Human Decision Processes*, *97*, 117–134.

63. Thomas, Schermerhorn, & Dienhart, 2004.

64. Thomas, Schermerhorn, & Dienhart, 2004.

65. Carpenter, D. (2006, July 3). Boeing CEO sitting pretty one year in. *Globe and Mail*, B5.

66. Brown, Trevino, & Harrison, 2005; Schminke, Ambrose, & Neubaum, 2005.

67. Eagley, A.H., & Johnson, B.T. (1990). Gender and leadership style: A meta-analysis. *Psychological Bulletin*, *108*, 233–256.

68. Kass, S. (September 1999). Employees perceive women as better managers than men, finds five-year study. *ADA Monitor*, *30(8)*, 6.

69. Eagly, A.H., Johannesen-Schmidt, M.C., & van Engen, M.L. (2003). Transformational, transactional, and laissez-faire leadership styles: A meta-analysis comparing women and men. *Psychological Bulletin*, *120*, 569–591.

Chapter 10

1. Adapted from Soupata, L. (2005). Engaging employees in company success: The UPS approach to a winning team. *Human Resource Management*, *44*, 95–98. Reprinted with permission of John Wiley & Sons, Inc.

2. Very few organizations formally institute such policies. See Saunders, D.M., & Leck, J.D. (1993). Formal upward communication procedures: Organizational and employee perspectives. *Canadian Journal of Administrative Sciences*, *10*, 255–268.

3. Snyder, R.A., & Morris, J.H. (1984). Organizational communication and performance. *Journal of Applied Psychology*, *69*, 461–465.

4. From an unpublished review by Gary Johns. Some studies are cited in Jablin, F.M. (1979). Superior–subordinate communication: The state of the art. *Psychological Bulletin*, *86*, 1201–1222. See also Dansereau, F., & Markham, S.E. (1987). Superior–subordinate communication: Multiple levels of analysis. In F. Jablin, L. Putnam, K.H. Roberts, & L.W. Porter (Eds.), *Handbook of organizational communication*. Newbury Park, CA: Sage; Harris, M.M., & Schaubroeck, J. (1988). A meta-analysis of self-supervisor, self-peer, and peer–supervisor ratings. *Personnel Psychology*, *41*, 43–62.

5. Jablin, 1979.

6. Tesser, A., & Rosen, S. (1975). The reluctance to transmit bad news. In L. Berkowitz (Ed.), *Advances in experimental social psychology* (Vol. 8). New York: Academic Press.

7. Read, W. (1962). Upward communication in industrial hierarchies. *Human Relations*, *15*, 3–16; for related studies, see Jablin, 1979.

8. Evidence that subordinates suppress communicating negative news to the boss can be found in O'Reilly, C.A., & Roberts, K.H. (1974). Information filtration in organizations: Three experiments. *Organizational Behavior and Human Performance*, *11*, 253–265. For evidence that this is probably self-presentational, see Bond, C.F., Jr., & Anderson, E.L. (1987). The reluctance to transmit bad news: Private discomfort or public display? *Journal of Experimental Social Psychology*, *23*, 176–187.

9. Ashford, S.J. (1989). Self-assessments in organizations: A literature review and integrated model. *Research in Organizational Behavior*, *11*, 133–174; Harris & Shaubroeck, 1988.

10. Noon, M., & Delbridge, R. (1993). News from behind my hand: Gossip in organizations. *Organization Studies*, *14*, 23–36.

11. Davis, K. (1977). *Human behavior at work* (5th ed.). New York: McGraw-Hill.

12. Davis, K. (1953). Management communication and the grapevine. *Harvard Business Review*, *31(5)*, 43–49; Sutton, H., & Porter, L.W. (1968). A study of the grapevine in a governmental organization. *Personnel Psychology*, *21*, 223–230.

13. Bartlett, C.A., & Ghosal, S. (1995, May–June). Changing the role of top management: Beyond systems to people. *Harvard Business Review*, 132–142; for more on gossip, see the June 2004 special issue of the *Review of General Psychology*.

14. Rosnow, R.L. (1980). Psychology of rumor reconsidered. *Psychological Bulletin*, *87*, 578–591.

15. Rosnow, R.L. (1991) Inside rumor: A personal journey. *American Psychologist*, *46*, 484–496.

16. Kanter, R.M. (1977). *Men and women of the corporation*. New York: Basic Books.

17. For reviews, see Heslin, R., & Patterson, M.L. (1982). *Nonverbal behavior and social psychology*. New York: Plenum; Harper, R.G., Wiens, A.N., & Matarazzo, J.D. (1978). *Nonverbal communication: The state of the art*. New York: Wiley.

18. Mehrabian, A. (1972). *Nonverbal communication*. Chicago: Aldine-Atherton.

19. Mehrabian, 1972; see also Hall, J.A., Coats, E.J., & Smith LeBeau, L. (2005). Nonverbal behavior and the vertical dimension of social relations: A meta-analysis. *Psychological Bulletin*, *131*, 898–924.

20. DePaulo, B.M. (1992). Nonverbal behavior and self-presentation. *Psychological Bulletin*, *111*, 203–243.

21. Edinger, J.A., & Patterson, M.L. (1983). Nonverbal involvement and social control. *Psychological Bulletin*, *93*, 30–56.

22. Rasmussen, K.G., Jr. (1984). Nonverbal behavior, verbal behavior, resume credentials, and selection interview outcomes. *Journal of Applied Psychology*, *69*, 551–556.

23. Campbell, D.E. (1979). Interior office design and visitor response. *Journal of Applied Psychology*, *64*, 648–653. For a replication, see Morrow, P.C., & McElroy, J.C. (1981). Interior office design and visitor response: A constructive replication. *Journal of Applied Psychology*, *66*, 646–650.

24. Gosling, S.D., Ko, S.J., Mannarelli, T., & Morris, M.E. (2002). A room with a cue: Personality judgments based on

offices and bedrooms. *Journal of Personality and Social Psychology, 82*, 379–398.

25. Elsbach, K.D. (2004). Interpreting workplace identities: The role of office decor. *Journal of Organizational Behavior, 25*, 99–128.

26 Molloy, J.T. (1993). *John T. Molloy's new dress for success*. New York: Warner; Molloy, J.T. (1987). *The woman's dress for success book*. New York: Warner.

27. Rafaeli, A., & Pratt, M.G. (1993). Tailored meanings: On the meaning and impact of organizational dress. *Academy of Management Review, 18*, 32–55; Solomon, M.R. (Ed.). (1985). *The psychology of fashion*. New York: Lexington; Solomon, M.R. (1986, April). Dress for effect. *Psychology Today*, 20–28.

28. Forsythe, S., Drake, M.F., & Cox, C.E. (1985). Influence of applicant's dress on interviewer's selection decisions. *Journal of Applied Psychology, 70*, 374–378.

29. Solomon, 1986.

30. Tannen, D. (1994). *Talking from 9 to 5*. New York: William Morrow.

31. Koonce, R. (1997, September). Language, sex, and power: Women and men in the workplace. *Training & Development*, 34–39.

32. Tannen, D. (1995, September–October). The power of talk: Who gets heard and why. *Harvard Business Review*, 138–148.

33. Koonce, 1997.

34. Tannen, 1994.

35. Koonce, 1997; Tannen, 1995.

36. Adler, N.J. (1992). *International dimensions of organizational behavior* (2nd ed.). Belmont, CA: Wadsworth, p. 66.

37. Ramsey, S., & Birk, J. (1983). Preparation of North Americans for interaction with Japanese: Considerations of language and communication style. In D. Landis & R.W. Brislin (Eds.), *Handbook of intercultural training* (Vol. III). New York: Pergamon.

38. Ekman, P., & Rosenberg, E. (1997). *What the face reveals*. New York: Oxford University Press.

39. Furnham, A., & Bochner, S. (1986). *Culture shock: Psychological reactions to unfamiliar environments*. London: Methuen, pp. 207–208.

40. Examples on gaze and touch draw on Argyle, M. (1982). Inter-cultural communication. In S. Bochner (Ed.), *Cultures in contact: Studies in cross-cultural interaction*. Oxford:

Pergamon; Furnham & Bochner, 1986.

41. Collett, P. (1971). Training Englishmen in the non-verbal behaviour of Arabs: An experiment on intercultural communication. *International Journal of Psychology, 6*, 209–215.

42. Furnham & Bochner, 1986; Argyle, 1982.

43. Ramsey & Birk, 1983.

44. Furnham & Bochner, 1986; Argyle, 1982.

45. Tannen, 1995.

46. Levine, R., West, L.J., & Reis, H.T. (1980). Perceptions of time and punctuality in the United States and Brazil. *Journal of Personality and Social Psychology, 38*, 541–550.

47. Hall, E.T., & Hall, M.R. (1990). *Understanding cultural differences*. Yarmouth, ME: Intercultural Press.

48. Dulek, R.E., Fielden, J.S., & Hill, J.S. (1991, January–February). International communication: An executive primer. *Business Horizons*, 20–25.

49. Daft, R.L., & Lengel, R.H. (1984). Information richness: A new approach to managerial behavior and organizational design. *Research in Organizational Behavior, 6*, 191–233.

50. Dennis, A.R., & Wixom, B.H. (2001). Investigating the moderators of the group support systems use with meta-analysis. *Journal of Management Information Systems, 18*, 235–257.

51. McGuire, T., Kiesler, S., & Siegel, J. (1987). Group and computer-mediated discussion effects in risk decision making. *Journal of Personality and Social Psychology, 52*, 917–930.

52. Baltes, B., Dickson, M.W., Sherman, M.P., Bauer, C.C., & LaGanke, J.S. (2002). Computer-mediated communication and group decision making: A meta-analysis. *Organizational Behavior and Human Decision Processes, 87*, 156–179, p. 175.

53. Wilson, J.M., Straus, S.G., & McEvily, B. (2006). All in due time: The development of trust in computer-mediated and face-to-face teams. *Organizational Behavior and Human Decision Processes, 99*, 16–33.

54. Kasper-Fuehrer, E.C., & Askanasy, N.M. (2001). Communicating trustworthiness and building trust in interorganizational virtual organizations. *Journal of Management, 27*, 235–254.

55. O'Mahony, S., & Barley, S.R. (1999). Do digital telecommunications affect work organization? The state of our knowledge. *Research in*

Organizational Behavior, 21, 125–161; Thomson, R., & Murachver, T. (2001). Predicting gender from electronic discourse. *British Journal of Social Psychology, 40*, 193–208.

56. Kruger, J., Epley, N., Parker, J., & Ng, Z.W. (2005), Egocentrism over e-mail: Can we communicate as well as we think? *Journal of Personality and Social Psychology, 89*, 925–936.

57. Lengel, R.H., & Daft, R.L. (1988, August). The selection of communication media as an executive skill. *Academy of Management Executive*, 225–232.

58. The following relies in part on Athos, A.G., & Gabarro, J.J. (1978). *Interpersonal behavior*. Englewood Cliffs, NJ: Prentice-Hall; DeVito, J.A. (1992). *The interpersonal communication book* (6th ed.). New York: HarperCollins; Whetten, D.A., & Cameron, K.S. (1991). *Developing management skills* (2nd ed.). New York: HarperCollins.

59. Chamberlin, J. (2000, January). Cops trust cops, even one with a PhD. *Monitor on Psychology*, 74–76.

60. Dulek et al., 1991.

61. Cardy, B., & Dobbins, G. (1993, Spring). The changing face of performance appraisal: Customer evaluations and 360 appraisals. *Human Resources Division News*, 17–18; Newman, R.J. (1993, November 1). Job reviews go full circle. *U.S. News & World Report*; Prince, J.B. (1994, January). Performance appraisal and reward practices for total quality organizations. *Quality Management Journal*, 36–46.

62. Walker, A.G., & Smither, J.W. (1999). A five-year study of upward feedback: What managers do with their results matters. *Personal Psychology, 52*, 393–423.

63. For a good description of how to develop and use organizational surveys, see Kraut, A.I. (Ed.). (1996) *Organizational surveys*. San Francisco: Jossey-Bass; Edwards, J.E., Thomas, M.D., Rosenfeld, P., & Booth-Kewley, S. (1996). *How to conduct organizational surveys: A step-by-step guide*. Thousand Oaks, CA: Sage.

64. Wintrob, S. (2003, May 20). Awards can bring rewards. *Financial Post*, BE1, BE6.

65. Taft, W.F. (1985). Bulletin boards, exhibits, hotlines. In C. Reuss & D. Silvis (Eds.), *Inside organizational communication* (2nd ed.). New York: Longman.

66. Chamine, S. (1998, December). Making your intranet an effective HR tool. *HR Focus,* 11–12.

67. Burnaska, R. (1976). The effects of behavior modeling training upon managers' behaviors and employees' perceptions. *Personnel Psychology, 29,* 329–335.

68. Capella, J.N. (1981). Mutual influence in expressive behavior: Adult–adult and infant–adult dyadic interaction. *Psychological Bulletin, 89,* 101–132.

Chapter 11

1. Sources include Alberts, S. (2005, August 8). Two wings and many prayers. *The Gazette (Montreal),* A1; Alberts, S. (2005, August 10). Nail-biter ends with textbook landing. *The Gazette (Montreal),* A1; Capers, R.S., & Lipton, E. (1993, November). Hubble error: Time, money, and millionths of an inch. *Academy of Management Executive,* 41–57 (originally published in *Hartford Courant*); Columbia tragedy forces nation, NASA to reassess. (2003, February 3). *USA Today,* 22A; Covault, C. (2003, March 5). Columbia revelations. Alarming e-mails speak for themselves. But administrator O'Keefe is more concerned about board findings on NASA's decision-making. *Aviation Week & Space Technology,* 26–28; Covault, C. (2003, April 28). Echoes of Challenger. Evidence is growing that NASA's failure to fully implement lessons from the earlier accident played a key role in the loss of Columbia. (Vaughan quote). *Aviation Week & Space Technology,* 29–31; Dunn, M. (2005, August 3). Pass the duct tape: Shuttle's Mr. Fix-it tries risky repair. *The Gazette (Montreal),* A1; Guterl, F. (2003, February 17). The human factor; as NASA searches for the cause of the Columbia disaster, the manned space program is on trial. It's time to ask: what is the point of putting people into space? *Newsweek,* 46; Kluger, J. (2005, August 8). Why NASA can't get it right. *Time,* 22–25; Levin, A. (2003, April 24). NASA took too great a risk, witnesses say. *USA Today,* 3A; Levin, A., & Watson, T. (2003, May 7). Shuttle problems seen as surmountable. *USA Today,* 4A; Petit, C.W. (2005, July 18). Ready for liftoff; NASA prepares to launch new shuttle, putting it all on the line in an attempt to stay in space. *U.S. News & World Report,* 48–55; Schwartz, J., & Wald, M.L. (2003, March 29). Space agency culture comes under scrutiny. *New York Times,* A7.

2. Mintzberg, H. (1979). *The structuring of organizations.* Englewood Cliffs, NJ: Prentice-Hall.

3. MacCrimmon, K.R., & Taylor, R.N. (1976). Decision making and problem solving. In M.D. Dunnette (Ed.), *Handbook of industrial and organizational psychology.* Chicago: Rand McNally.

4. Simon, H.A. (1957). *Administrative behavior* (2nd ed.). New York: Free Press. See also: Kahneman, D. (2003). A perspective in judgment and choice: Mapping bounded rationality. *American Psychologist, 56,* 697–720.

5. Bazerman, M. (2006). *Judgment in managerial decision making* (6th ed.). Hoboken, NJ: Wiley; Kahneman, 2003.

6. Russo, J.E., & Schoemaker, P.J.H. (1989). *Decision traps.* New York: Doubleday; Whyte, G. (1991, August). Decision failures: Why they occur and how to prevent them. *Academy of Management Executive,* 23–31.

7. The latter two difficulties are discussed by Huber, G.P. (1980). *Managerial decision making.* Glenview, IL: Scott, Foresman. For further discussion of problem identification, see Cowan, D.A. (1986). Developing a process model of problem recognition. *Academy of Management Review, 11,* 763–776; Kiesler, S., & Sproull, L. (1982). Managerial response to changing environments: Perspectives on problem sensing from social cognition. *Administrative Science Quarterly, 27,* 548–570.

8. Whyte, 1991; Russo & Schoemaker, 1989.

9. Tversky, A., & Kahneman, D. (1973). Availability: A heuristic for judging frequency and probability. *Cognitive Psychology, 5,* 207–232. Also see Taylor, S.E., & Fiske, S.T. (1978). Salience, attention, and attribution: Top of the head phenomena. In L. Berkowitz (Ed.), *Advances in experimental social psychology* (Vol. 11). New York: Academic Press.

10. Lichtenstein, S., Fischhoff, B., & Phillips, L.D. (1982). Calibration of probabilities: The state of the art in 1980. In D. Kahneman, P. Slovic, & A. Tversky (Eds.), *Judgment under uncertainty: Heuristics and biases.* Cambridge: Cambridge University Press.

11. Miller, J.G. (1960). Information input, overload, and psychopathology. *American Journal of Psychiatry, 116,* 695–704.

12. Manis, M., Fichman, M., & Platt, M. (1978). Cognitive integration and referential communication: Effects of information quality and quantity in message decoding. *Organizational Behavior and Human Performance, 22,* 417–430; Troutman, C.M., & Shanteau, J. (1977). Inferences based on nondiagnostic information. *Organizational Behavior and Human Performance, 19,* 43–55.

13. O'Reilly, C.A., III. (1980). Individuals and information overload in organizations: Is more necessarily better? *Academy of Management Journal, 23,* 684–696.

14. Feldman, M.S., & March, J.G. (1981). Information in organizations as signal and symbol. *Administrative Science Quarterly, 26,* 171–186.

15. Kahneman et al, 1982; Tversky, A., & Kahneman, D. (1976). Judgment under uncertainty: Heuristics and biases. *Science, 185,* 1124–1131.

16. Northcraft, G.B., & Neale, M.A. (1987). Experts, amateurs, and real estate: An anchoring-and-adjustment perspective on property pricing decisions. *Organizational Behavior and Human Decision Processes, 39,* 84–97.

17. Johns, G. (1999). A multi-level theory of self-serving behavior in and by organizations. *Research in Organizational Behavior, 21,* 1–38; Tetlock, P.E. (1999). Accountability theory: Mixing properties of human agents with properties of social systems. In L.L. Thompson, J.M. Levine, & D.M. Messick (Eds.), *Shared cognition in organizations: The management of knowledge.* Mahwah, N.J.: Lawrence Erlbaum.

18. Nutt, P.C. (2004, November). Expanding the search for alternatives during strategic decision-making. *Academy of Management Executive,* 13–28.

19. Simon, H.A. (1957). *Models of man.* New York: Wiley; Cyert, R.M., & March, J.G. (1963). *A behavioral theory of the firm.* Englewood Cliffs, NJ: Prentice-Hall. For an example, see Bower, J., & Zi-Lei, Q. (1992). Satisficing when buying information. *Organizational Behavior and Human Decision Processes, 51,* 471–481.

20. Bazerman, M. (1990). *Judgment in managerial decision making* (2nd ed.). New York: Wiley.

21. Kahneman, D., & Tversky, A. (1979). Prospect theory: An analysis of decision under risk. *Econometrica, 47,* 263–291.

22. Sitkin, S.B., & Pablo, A.L. (1992). Conceptualizing the determinants of risk behavior. *Academy of Management Review, 17*, 9–38.

23. For a detailed treatment and other perspectives, see Northcraft, G.B., & Wolf, G. (1984). Dollars, sense, and sunk costs: A life cycle model of resource allocation decisions. *Academy of Management Review, 9*, 225–234.

24. Brockner, J. (1992). The escalation of commitment to a failing course of action: Toward theoretical progress. *Academy of Management Review, 17*, 39–61; Staw, B.M. (1997). Escalation of commitment: An update and appraisal. In Z. Shapira (Ed.), *Organizational decision making*. Cambridge: Cambridge University Press.

25. Staw, B.M. (1981). The escalation of commitment to a course of action. *Academy of Management Review, 6*, 577–587. For the limitations on this view, see Knight, P.A. (1984). Heroism versus competence: Competing explanations for the effects of experimenting and consistent management. *Organizational Behavior and Human Performance, 33*, 307–322.

26. Arkes, H.R., & Blumer, C. (1985). The psychology of sunk cost. *Organizational Behavior and Human Decision Processes, 35*, 124–140.

27. Whyte, G. (1986). Escalating commitment to a course of action: A reinterpretation. *Academy of Management Review, 11*, 311–321.

28. Wong, K.F.E., Yik, M., & Kwong, J.Y.Y. (2006). Understanding the emotional aspects of escalation of commitment: The role of negative affect. *Journal of Applied Psychology, 91*, 282–297.

29. Ku, G., Malhorta, D., & Murnighan, J.K. (2005). Towards a competitive arousal model of decision-making: A study of auction fever in live and internet auctions. *Organizational Behavior and Human Decision Processes, 96*, 89–103.

30. Simonson, I., & Nye, P. (1992). The effect of accountability on susceptibility to decision errors. *Organizational Behavior and Human Decision Processes, 51*, 416–446; Simonson, I., & Staw, B.M. (1992). Deescalation strategies: A comparison of techniques for reducing commitment to losing courses of action. *Journal of Applied Psychology, 77*, 419–426; Whyte, 1991.

31. Whyte, G. (1993). Escalating commitment in individual and group decision making: A prospect theory approach. *Organizational Behavior and Human Decision Processes, 54*, 430–455.

32. Hawkins, S.A., & Hastie, R. (1990). Hindsight: Biased judgments of past events after outcomes are known. *Psychological Bulletin, 107*, 311–327.

33. Greenwald, A.G. (1980). The totalitarian ego: Fabrication and revision of personal history. *American Psychologist, 35*, 603–618.

34. Forgas, J.P., & George, J.M. (2001). Affective influences on judgments and behavior in organizations: An information processing perspective. *Organizational Behavior and Human Decision Processes, 86*, 3–34.

35. Hayward, M.L.A., & Hambrick, D.C. (1997). Explaining the premiums paid for large acquisitions: Evidence of CEO hubris. *Administrative Science Quarterly, 42*, 103–127.

36. Forgas & George, 2001; Weiss, H.M. (2002). Conceptual and empirical foundations for the study of affect at work. In R.G. Lord, R.J. Klimoski, & R. Kanfer (Eds), *Emotions in the workplace: Understanding the structure and role of emotions in organizational behavior*. San Francisco: Jossey-Bass; Amabile, T.M., Barsade, S.G., Mueller, J.S., & Staw, B.M. (2005). Affect and creativity at work. *Administrative Science Quarterly, 50*, 367–403.

37. Au, K., Chan, F., Wang, D., & Vertinsky, I. (2003). Mood in foreign exchange trading: Cognitive processes and performance. *Organizational Behavior and Human Decision Processes, 91*, 322–338.

38. Mitchell, T.R., & Beach, L.R. (1977). Expectancy theory, decision theory, and occupational preference and choice. In M.F. Kaplan & S. Schwartz (Eds.), *Human judgment and decision processes in applied settings*. New York: Academic Press.

39. Pinfield, L.T. (1986). A field evaluation of perspectives on organizational decision making. *Administrative Science Quarterly, 31*, 365–388.

40. Nutt, P.C. (1989). *Making tough decisions*. San Francisco: Jossey-Bass.

41. Nutt, P.C. (1999, November). Surprising but true: Half the decisions in organizations fail. *Academy of Management Executive*, 75–90.

42. Lord, R.G., & Maher, K.J. (1990). Alternative information-processing models and their implications for theory, research, and practice. *Academy of Management Review, 15*, 9–28.

43. Shaw, M.E. (1981). *Group dynamics* (3rd ed.). New York: McGraw-Hill, p. 78.

44. Hill, G.W. (1982). Group versus individual performance: Are n+1 heads better than one? *Psychological Bulletin, 91*, 517–539.

45. Shaw, 1981; Davis, J.H. (1969). *Group performance*. Reading, MA: Addison-Wesley; Libby, R., Trotman, K.T., & Zimmer, I. (1987). Member variation, recognition of expertise, and group performance. *Journal of Applied Psychology, 72*, 81–87.

46. Janis, I.L. (1972). *Victims of groupthink*. Boston: Houghton Mifflin.

47. Esser, J.K. (1998). Alive and well after 25 years: A review of groupthink research. *Organizational Behavior and Human Decision Processes, 73*, 116–141.

48. Aldag, R.J., & Fuller, S.R. (1993) Beyond fiasco: A reappraisal of the groupthink phenomenon and a new model of group decision processes. *Psychological Bulletin, 113*, 533–552; McCauley, C. (1989). The nature of social influence in groupthink: Compliance and internalization. *Journal of Personality and Social Psychology, 57*, 250–260; Baron, R.S. (2005). So right it's wrong: Groupthink and the ubiquitous nature of polarized group decision making. *Advances in Experimental Social Psychology, 37*, 219–253.

49. Janis, 1972.

50. Moorhead, G., Ference, R., & Neck, C.P. (1991). Group decision fiascos continue: Space shuttle Challenger and a revised groupthink framework. *Human Relations*, 539–550. Esser, 1998.

51. This is our analysis. The data cited is from Capers & Lipton, 1993.

52. Hart, P. (1998). Preventing groupthink revisited: Evaluating and reforming groups in government. *Organizational Behavior and Human Decision Processes, 73*, 306–326.

53. Stoner, J.A.F. (1961). *A comparison of individual and group decisions involving risk*. Unpublished Master's thesis. School of Industrial Management, Massachusetts Institute of Technology.

54. Lamm, H., & Myers, D.G. (1978). Group-induced polarization of attitudes and behavior. In L. Berkowitz (Ed.), *Advances in experimental social psychology* (Vol. 11). New York: Academic Press.

55. Isenberg, D.J. (1986). Group polarization: A critical review and meta-analysis. *Journal of Personality and Social Psychology, 50*, 1141–1151.

56. Kiesler, S., & Sproull, L. (1992). Group decision making and communication technology. *Organizational*

Behavior and Human Decision Processes, 52, 96–123; Sia, C.L., Tan, B.C.Y., & Wei, K.K. (1999). Can a GSS stimulate group polarization? An empirical study. *IEEE Transactions on Systems, Man, and Cybernetics Part C—Applications and Reviews, 29,* 227–237.

57. Nutt, 1999.

58. Maier, N.R.F. (1973). *Psychology in industrial organizations* (4th ed.). Boston: Houghton Mifflin; Maier, N.R.F. (1970). *Problem solving and creativity in individuals and groups.* Belmont, CA: Brooks/Cole.

59. Tjosvold, D. (1985). Implications of controversy research for management. *Journal of Management, 11(3),* 21–37.

60. Schwenk, C.R. (1984). Devil's advocacy in managerial decision-making. *Journal of Management Studies, 21,* 153–168. For a study, see Schwenk, C., & Valacich, J.S. (1994). Effects of devil's advocacy and dialectical inquiry on individuals versus groups. *Organizational Behavior and Human Decision Processes, 59,* 210–222.

61. Osborn, A.F. (1957). *Applied imagination.* New York: Scribners.

62. See for example Madsen, D.B., & Finger, J.R., Jr. (1978). Comparison of a written feedback procedure, group brainstorming, and individual brainstorming. *Journal of Applied Psychology, 63,* 120–123.

63. Gallupe, R.B., Dennis, A.R., Cooper, W.H., Valacich, J.S., Bastianutti, L.M., & Nunamaker, J.F., Jr. (1992). Electronic brainstorming and group size. *Academy of Management Journal, 35,* 350–369. See also Dennis, A.R., & Valacich, J.S. (1993). Computer brainstorms: More heads are better than one. *Journal of Applied Psychology, 78,* 531–537.

64. Delbecq, A.L., Van de Ven, A.H., & Gustafson, D.H. (1975). *Group techniques for program planning.* Glenview, IL: Scott, Foresman, p. 8.

65. Delbecq et al., 1975.

Chapter 12

1. Sources include Backover, A. (2002, July 22). WorldCom files for Chapter 11 protection. *USA Today,* A1; Broughton, P.D. (2002, January 29). Enron lived "on edge—sex, money, all of it." *National Post,* A1; Dube, R. (2006, July 6). Will Lay's legacy be greed or innovation? *Globe and Mail,* B1; Farrell, G. (2003, March 3). Former Andersen exec tells of stressful internal culture. *USA Today,* 3B; Farrell, G., & Jones, D. (2002, January 14). How did Enron come

unplugged? *USA Today,* 1B; Feder, B. J. (2003, June 10). Management practices enabled huge fraud, 2 investigations find. *New York Times,* C1; Fonda, D. (2005, March 28). After Bernie, who's next? *Time,* 44–46; Haddad, C., Foust, D., Rosenbush, S. (2002, July 8). WorldCom's sorry legacy. *Business Week,* 38–40; Morton, P. (2005, July 14). Ebbers will 'die in jail': 25 years for WorldCom founder from Edmonton. *National Post,* A1; Roberts, J.L., & Thomas, E. (2002, March 11). Enron's dirty laundry. *Newsweek,* 22–28; Sloan, A., & Isikoff, M. (2002, January 28). The Enron effect. *Newsweek,* 34–36; Sloan, A. (2006, June 5). Laying Enron to rest; convicted felons Ken Lay and Jeff Skilling may be trading pinstripes for prison stripes. These were 'the smartest guys in the room'? *Newsweek,* 24–30; Zellner, W. et al. (2001, December 17). The fall of Enron. *Business Week,* 30–36; Zellner, W., Palmeri, C., France, M., Weber, J., & Carney, D. (2002, February 11). Jeff Skilling: Enron's missing man. *Business Week,* 38–40.

2. Brass, D.J., & Burkhardt, M.E. (1993). Potential power and power use: An investigation of structure and behavior. *Academy of Management Journal, 36,* 441–470; see also Kim, P.H., Pinkley, R.L., & Fragale, A.R. (2005). Power dynamics in negotiation. *Academy of Management Review, 30,* 799–822.

3. These descriptions of bases of power were developed by French, J.R.P., Jr., & Raven, B. (1959). In D. Cartwright (Ed.), *Studies in social power.* Ann Arbor, MI: Institute for Social Research.

4. Rahim, M.A. (1989). Relationships of leader power to compliance and satisfaction with supervision: Evidence from a national sample of managers. *Journal of Management, 15,* 545–556; Tannenbaum, A.S. (1974). *Hierarchy in organizations.* San Francisco: Jossey-Bass.

5. Podsakoff, P.M., & Schriesheim, C.A. (1985). Field studies of French and Raven's bases of power: Critique, reanalysis, and suggestions for future research. *Psychological Bulletin, 97,* 387–411.

6. Heider, F. (1958). *The psychology of interpersonal relations.* New York: Wiley.

7. Podsakoff & Schriesheim, 1985.

8. Ragins, B.R., & Sundstrom, E. (1990). Gender and perceived power in manager-subordinate dyads. *Journal of*

Occupational Psychology, 63, 273–287.

9. The following is based upon Kanter, R.M. (1977). *Men and women of the corporation.* New York: Basic Books. For additional treatment see Pfeffer, J. (1992). *Managing with power: Politics and influence in organizations.* Boston: Harvard Business School Press.

10. See Thomas, K.W., & Velthouse, B.A. (1990). Cognitive elements of empowerment: An "interpretative" model of intrinsic task motivation. *Academy of Management Review, 15,* 668–681; Conger, J.A., & Kanungo, R.N. (1988). The empowerment process: Integrating theory and practice. *Academy of Management Review, 13,* 471–482.

11. Tichy, N.M., & Sherman, S. (1993, June). Walking the talk at GE. *Training and Development,* 26–35.

12. Seibert, S.E., Silver, S.R., & Randolph, W.A. (2004). Taking empowerment to the next level: A multiple-level model of empowerment, performance, and satisfaction. *Academy of Management Journal, 47,* 332–349; Laschinger, H.K.S., Finegan, J.E., Shamian, J., & Wilk, P. (2004). A longitudinal analysis of the impact of workplace empowerment on work satisfaction. *Journal of Organizational Behavior, 25,* 527–545; Patterson, M.G., West, M.A., & Wall, T.D. (2004). Integrated manufacturing, empowerment, and company performance. *Journal of Organizational Behavior, 25,* 641–665; Wall, T.D., Wood, S.J., & Leach, D.J. (2004). Empowerment and performance. *International Review of Industrial and Organizational Psychology, 19,* 1–46.

13. Bowen, D.E., & Lawler, E.E., III. (1992, Spring). The empowerment of service workers: What, why, how, and when. *Sloan Management Review,* 31–39.

14. Kipnis, D., Schmidt, S.M., & Wilkinson, I. (1980). Intra-organizational influence tactics: Explorations in getting one's way. *Journal of Applied Psychology, 65,* 440–452; Kipnis, D., & Schmidt, S.M. (1988). Upward-influence styles: Relationship with performance evaluation, salary, and stress. *Administrative Science Quarterly, 33,* 528–542.

15. See Brass & Burkhardt, 1993.

16. Kipnis et al., 1980. See also Keys, B., & Case, T. (1990, November). How to become an influential manager. *Academy of Management Executive,* 38–51.

17. Kipnis & Schmidt, 1988.

18. Kipnis, D. (1976). *The powerholders.* Chicago: University of Chicago Press.

19. McClelland, D.C. (1975). *Power: The inner experience.* New York: Irvington.

20. Winter, D.G. (1988). The power motive in women—and men. *Journal of Personality and Social Psychology, 54,* 510–519.

21. McClelland, D.C., & Burnham, D.H. (1976, March–April). Power is the great motivator. *Harvard Business Review,* 100–110.

22. Ashforth, B.E. (1989). The experience of powerlessness in organizations. *Organizational Behavior and Human Decision Processes, 43,* 207–242.

23. Salancik, G.R., & Pfeffer, J. (1977, Winter). Who gets power—and how they hold on to it: A strategic contingency model of power. *Organizational Dynamics,* 3–21.

24. Salancik, G.R., & Pfeffer, J. (1974). The bases and use of power in organizational decision making: The case of a university. *Administrative Science Quarterly, 19,* 453–473. Also see Pfeffer, J., & Moore, W.L. (1980). Power in university budgeting: A replication and extension. *Administrative Science Quarterly, 25,* 637–653. For conditions under which the power thesis breaks down, see Schick, A.G., Birch, J.B., & Tripp, R.E. (1986). Authority and power in university decision making: The case of a university personnel budget. *Canadian Journal of Administrative Sciences, 3,* 41–64.

25. Hickson, D.J., Hinings, C.R., Lee, C.A., Schneck, R.E., & Pennings, J.M. (1971). A strategic contingency theory of intraorganizational power. *Administrative Science Quarterly, 16,* 216–229; for support of this theory, see Hinings, C.R., Hickson, D.J., Pennings, J.M., & Schneck, R.E. (1974). Structural conditions of intraorganizational power. *Administrative Science Quarterly, 19,* 22–44; Saunders, C.S., & Scamell, R. (1982). Intraorganizational distributions of power: Replication research. *Academy of Management Journal, 25,* 192–200; Hambrick, D.C. (1981). Environment, strategy, and power within top management teams. *Administrative Science Quarterly, 26,* 253–276.

26. Kanter, 1977, pp. 170–171.

27. Hickson et al., 1971; Hinings et al., 1974.

28. Hickson et al., 1971; Hinings et al., 1974; Saunders & Scamell, 1982.

29. Nulty, P. (1989, July 31). The hot demand for new scientists. *Fortune,* 155–163.

30. Nord, W.R., & Tucker, S. (1987). *Implementing routine and radical innovations.* Lexington, MA: Lexington Books.

31. Mayes, B.T., & Allen, R.W. (1977). Toward a definition of organizational politics. *Academy of Management Review, 2,* 672–678.

32. Porter, L.W., Allen, R.W., & Angle, H.L. (1981). The politics of upward influence in organizations. *Research in Organizational Behavior, 3,* 109–149.

33. Porter et al., 1981; Madison, D.L., Allen, R.W., Porter, L.W., Renwick, P.A., & Mayes, B.T. (1980). Organizational politics: An exploration of managers' perceptions. *Human Relations, 33,* 79–100.

34. Kacmar, K.m, & Baron, R.A. (1999). Organizational politics: The state of the field, links to related processes, and an agenda for future research. *Research in Personnel and Human Resources Management, 17,* 1–39.

35. Treadway, D.C., Ferris, G.R., Hochwarter, W., Perrewé, P., Witt. L.A., & Goodman, J.M. (2005). The role of age in the perceptions of politics-job performance relationship: A three-study constructive replication. *Journal of Applied Psychology, 90,* 872–881.

36. Ferris, G.D., Davidson, S.L., & Perrewé, P.L. (2005). *Political skill at work: Impact on effectiveness.* Mountain View, CA: Davies-Black, 7; see also Ferris, G.R., Treadway, D.C., Kolodinsky, R.W., Hochwarter, W.A., Kacmar, C.J., Douglas, C., & Frink, D.D. (2005). Development and validation of the Political Skill Inventory. *Journal of Management, 31,* 126–152.

37. Perrewé, P.L., Zellars, K.L., Ferris, G.R., Rossi, A.M., Kacmar, C.J., & Ralston, D.A. (2004). Neutralizing job stressors: Political skill as an antidote to the dysfunctional consequences of role conflict. *Academy of Management Journal, 47,* 141–152.

38. Kotter, J.P. (1982). *The general managers.* New York: Free Press.

39. Forret, M.L., & Dougherty, T.W. (2004). Networking behaviors and career outcomes: Differences for men and women. *Journal of Organizational Behavior, 25,* 419–437; Forret, M.L., & Dougherty, T.W. (2001). Correlates of networking behavior for managerial and professional employees. *Group & Organization Management, 26,* 283–311.

40. Brass, D.J., Galaskiewicz, J., Greve, H.R., & Tsai, W. (2004). Taking stock of networks and organizations: A mul-

tilevel perspective. *Academy of Management Journal, 47,* 795–817.

41. Shellenbarger, S. (1993, December 16). I'm still here! Home workers worry they're invisible. *Wall Street Journal,* B1, B4.

42. Geis, F., & Christie, R. (1970). Overview of experimental research. In R. Christie & F. Geis (Eds.), *Studies in Machiavellianism.* New York: Academic Press; Wilson, D.S., Near, D., & Miller, R.W. (1996). Machiavellianism: A synthesis of the evolutionary and psychological literatures. *Psychological Bulletin, 119,* 285–299.

43. Geis & Christie, 1970; Wilson et al., 1996.

44. What follows relies on Ashforth, B.E., & Lee, R.T. (1990). Defensive behavior in organizations: A preliminary model. *Human Relations, 43,* 621–648.

45. Boeker, W. (1992). Power and managerial dismissal: Scapegoating at the top. *Administrative Science Quarterly, 37,* 400–421.

46. Maich, S. (2002, September 24). Grubman's rise and fall. *Financial Post,* FP1, FP6.

47. This draws loosely on Glenn, J.R., Jr. (1986). *Ethics in decision making.* New York: Wiley.

48. For reviews, see Trevino, L.K. (1986). Ethical decision making in organizations: A person-situation interactionist model. *Academy of Management Review, 11,* 601–617; Tsalikis, J., & Fritzsche, D.J. (1989). Business ethics: A literature review with a focus on marketing ethics. *Journal of Business Ethics, 8,* 695–743.

49. Tyson, T. (1992). Does believing that everyone else is less ethical have an impact on work behavior? *Journal of Business Ethics, 11,* 707–717.

50. Tsalikis & Fritzsche, 1989.

51. Kaynama, S.A., King, A., & Smith, L.W. (1996). The impact of a shift in organizational role on ethical perceptions: A comparative study. *Journal of Business Ethics, 15,* 581–590.

52. Franke, G.R., Crown, D.F., and Spake, D.F. (1997). Gender differences in ethical perceptions of business practices: A social role theory perspective. *Journal of Applied Psychology, 82,* 920–934.

53. Tsalikis & Fritzsche, 1989.

54. Bird, F., & Waters, J.A. (1987). The nature of managerial moral standards. *Journal of Business Ethics, 6,* 1–13.

55. Hegarty, W.H., & Sims, H.P., Jr. (1978). Some determinants of unethical behavior: An experiment. *Journal of Applied Psychology, 63,* 451–457;

Trevino, L.K., Sutton, C.D., & Woodman, R.W. (1985). *Effects of reinforcement contingencies and cognitive moral development on ethical decision-making behavior: An experiment.* Paper presented at the annual meeting of the Academy of Management, San Diego.

56. Levine, D.B. (1990, May 21). The inside story of an inside trader. *Fortune*, 80–89, p. 82.

57. Grover, S.L. (1993). Why professionals lie: The impact of professional role conflict on reporting accuracy. *Organizational Behavior and Human Decision Processes, 55*, 251–272.

58. Staw, B.M., & Szwajkowski, E.W. (1975). The scarcity-munificence component of organizational environments and the commission of illegal acts. *Administrative Science Quarterly, 20*, 345–354.

59. Sonnenfeld, J., & Lawrence, P.R. (1989). Why do companies succumb to price fixing? In K.R. Andrew (Ed.), *Ethics in practice: Managing the moral corporation.* Boston: Harvard Business School Press.

60. Hegarty & Sims, 1978; Hegarty, W.H., & Sims, H.P., Jr. (1979). Organizational philosophy, policies, and objectives related to unethical decision behavior: A laboratory experiment. *Journal of Applied Psychology, 64*, 331–338.

61. Colby, A., & Kohlberg, L. (1987). *The measurement of moral judgment. Volume 1: Theoretical foundations and research validation.* Cambridge: Cambridge University Press; also see Trevino, 1986; Grover, 1993.

62. Victor, B., & Cullen, J.B. (1988). The organizational bases of ethical work climates. *Administrative Science Quarterly, 33*, 101–125.

63. Baucus, M.S., & Near, J.P. (1991). Can illegal corporate behavior be predicted? An event history analysis. *Academy of Management Journal, 34*, 9–16.

64. Anand, V., Ashforth, B.E., & Joshi, M. (2004, May). Business as usual: The acceptance and perpetuation of corruption in organizations. *Academy of Management Executive*, 39–53.

65. Sonnenfeld & Lawrence, 1989. See also Hosmer, L.T. (1987). The institutionalization of unethical behavior. *Journal of Business Ethics, 6*, 439–447.

66. Morgan, R.B. (1993). Self- and coworker perceptions of ethics and their relationships to leadership and salary. *Academy of Management Journal, 36*, 200–214.

67. This definition and other material from this paragraph are from Miceli, M.P., & Near, J.P. (2005). Standing up or standing by: What predicts blowing the whistle on organizational wrongdoing? *Research in Personnel and Human Resources Management, 24*, 95–136.

68. Moore, D.a, Tetlock, P.H., Tanlu, L., & Bazerman, M.H. (2006). Conflicts of interest and the case of auditor independence: Moral seduction and strategic issue cycling. *Academy of Management Review, 31*, 10–29.

69. Ripley, A. (2002, December 30/2003, January 6). The night detective. *Time*, 45; Morse, J., & Bower, A. (2002, December 30/2003, January 6). The party crasher. *Time*, 53.

70. O'Hara, J. (1998, May 25). Rape in the military. *Maclean's*, 14.

71. Peirce, E., Smolinski, C.A., & Rosen, B. (1998, August). Why sexual harassment complaints fall on deaf ears. *Academy of Management Executive*, 41–54.

72. Seppa, N. (1997, May). Sexual harassment in the military lingers on. *APA Monitor*, 40–41.

73. Schneider, K.T., Swan, S., & Fitzgerald, L.F. (1997). Job-related and psychological effects of sexual harassment in the workplace: Empirical evidence from two organizations. *Journal of Applied Psychology, 82*, 401–415.

74. Schneider, Swan, & Fitzgerald, 1997.

75. Cleveland, J.N., & Kerst, M.E. (1993). Sexual harassment and perceptions of power: An underarticulated relationship. *Journal of Vocational Behavior, 42*, 49–67.

76. Seppa, 1997.

77. Seppa, 1997.

78. Peirce, Smolinski, & Rosen, 1998; Seppa, 1997.

79. O'Hara, 1998.

80. Peirce, Smolinski, & Rosen, 1998.

81. Peirce, Smolinski, & Rosen, 1998.

82. Peirce, Smolinski, & Rosen, 1998.

83. Flynn, G. (1997, February). Respect is key to stopping harassment. *Workforce*, 56.

84. Peirce, Smolinski, & Rosen, 1998.

85. This draws on Waters, J.A., & Bird, F. (1988). *A note on what a well-educated manager should be able to do with respect to moral issues in management.* Unpublished manuscript.

86. See Jones, T.M. (1991). Ethical decision making by individuals in organizations: An issue-contingent model. *Academy of Management Journal, 16*, 366–395.

87. Weber, J. (1990). Measuring the impact of teaching ethics to future managers: A review, assessment, and recommendations. *Journal of Business Ethics, 9*, 183–190.

Chapter 13

1. Sources include Fonda, D. (2003, December 15). Eisner's wild ride. *Time*, 38–39; Fonda, D. (2003, February 23). M-I-C..see ya real soon? *Time*, 36–39; Gunther, M. (2004, March 8). Eisner's last act. *Fortune*, 123–128; Jefferson, D.J., & Roberts, J.L. (2004, March 15). The magic is gone. *Newsweek*, 52–54; Gunther, M. (2004, March 22). Disney's board game. *Fortune*, 35–38; Sellers, P. (2004, October 4). The mouse hunt begins. *Fortune*, 33–38 (quote); Smith, S. (2004, October 11). Life isn't beautiful. *Newsweek*, 54–55; Anonymous (2005, February 19). Business: A new king for the Magic Kingdom. *The Economist*, 72; Grover, R. (2005, February 28). Emperor Eisner. *Business Week*, 24–25; Anonymous (2005, July 16). Business: Restoring magic. *The Economist*, 59; Serwer, A. (2005, July 25). What if Eisner had listened to Ovitz? *Fortune*, 55–56; Pulley, B. (2005, October 17). Last days of the Lion King. *Forbes*, 47; Schlender, B. (2006, May 29). Pixar's magic man. *Fortune*, 139–149.

2. Kolb, D.M., & Bartunek, J.M. (Eds.) (1992). *Hidden conflict in organizations: Uncovering behind-the-scenes disputes.* Newbury Park, CA: Sage.

3. This section relies partly on Walton, R.E., & Dutton, J.M. (1969). The management of interdepartmental conflict: A model and review. *Administrative Science Quarterly, 14*, 73–84.

4. Ashforth, B.E., & Mael, F. (1989). Social identity theory and the organization. *Academy of Management Review, 14*, 20–39; Kramer, R.M. (1991). Intergroup relations and organizational dilemmas: The role of categorization processes. *Research in Organizational Behavior, 13*, 191–228; Messick, D.M., & Mackie, D.M. (1989). Intergroup relations. *Annual Review of Psychology, 40*, 45–81.

5. Johns, G. (1994). Absenteeism estimates by employees and managers: Divergent perspectives and self-serving perceptions. *Journal of Applied Psychology, 79*, 229–239.

6. See Whyte, W.F. (1948). *Human relations in the restaurant industry.* New York: McGraw-Hill.

7. Moritz, M. (1984). *The little kingdom: The private story of Apple*

Computer. New York: Morrow, 246–247.

8. Jehn, K.A., & Mannix, E.A. (2001). The dynamic nature of conflict: A longitudinal study of intragroup conflict and group performance. *Academy of Management Journal, 44,* 238–251.

9. For evidence of the pervasively negative impact of conflict, see De Dreu, C.K.W., & Weingart, L.R. (2003). Task versus relationship conflict, team performance, and team member satisfaction: A meta-analysis. *Journal of Applied Psychology, 88,* 741–749. For exceptions for task conflict, see Jehn & Mannix, 2001; Jehn, K.A. (1997). A qualitative analysis of conflict types and dimensions in organizational groups. *Administrative Science Quarterly, 42,* 530–557.

10. See Blake, R.R., Shepard, M.A., & Mouton, J.S. (1964). *Managing intergroup conflict in industry.* Houston: Gulf; Sherif, M. (1966). *In common predicament: Social psychology of intergroup conflict and cooperation.* Boston: Houghton Mifflin; Wilder, D.A. (1986). Social categorization: Implications for creation and reduction of intergroup bias. *Advances in Experimental Social Psychology, 19,* 291–349.

11. Thomas, K.W. (1992). Conflict and negotiation in organizations. In M.D. Dunnette & L.M. Hough (Eds.), *Handbook of industrial and organizational psychology* (2nd ed., Vol. 3). Palo Alto, CA: Consulting Psychologists Press.

12. Seabrook, J. (1994, January 10). E-mail from Bill. *The New Yorker,* 48–61, p. 52.

13. Kramer, R.M. (2006, February). The great intimidators. *Harvard Business Review,* 88–96.

14. Johnson, D.W., Maruyama, G., Johnson, R., Nelson, D., & Skon, L. (1981). Effects of cooperative and individualistic goal structures on achievement: A meta-analysis. *Psychological Bulletin, 89,* 47–62. See also Tjosvold, D. (1991). *The conflict-positive organization.* Reading, MA: Addison-Wesley.

15. Tjosvold, D., Dann, V., & Wong, C. (1992). Managing conflict between departments to serve customers. *Human Relations, 45,* 1035–1054.

16. Neale, M.A., & Bazerman, M.H. (1992, August). Negotiating rationally: The power and impact of the negotiator's frame. *Academy of Management Executive,* 42–51, p. 42.

17. Wall, J.A., Jr. (1985). *Negotiation: Theory and practice.* Glenview, IL: Scott, Foresman.

18. Walton, R.E., & McKerzie, R.B. (1991). *A behavioral theory of labor negotiations* (2nd ed.). Ithaca, NY: ILR Press.

19. What follows draws on Pruitt, D.G. (1981). *Negotiation behavior.* New York: Academic Press.

20. Wall, J.A., Jr., & Blum, M. (1991). Negotiations. *Journal of Management, 17,* 273–303.

21. Wall & Blum, 1991.

22. Stuhlmacher, A.F., and Walters, A.E. (1999). Gender differences in negotiation outcome: A meta-analysis. *Personnel Psychology, 52,* 653–677.

23. Bazerman, M.H. (1990). *Judgment in managerial decision making* (2nd ed.). New York: Wiley.

24. The following draws on Bazerman, M.H., & Neale, M.A. (1992). *Negotiating rationally.* New York: The Free Press; see also Bazerman, M.H. (2006). *Judgment in managerial decision making* (6th ed.) Hoboken, NJ: Wiley.

25. Sherif, 1966; Hunger, J.D., & Stern, L.W. (1976). An assessment of the functionality of the superordinate goal in reducing conflict. *Academy of Management Journal, 19,* 591–605.

26. Pruitt, 1981; Kressel, K., & Pruitt, D.G. (1989). *Mediation research.* San Francisco: Jossey-Bass.

27. Kressel & Pruitt, 1989.

28. Pruitt, 1981; Wall & Blum, 1991.

29. Moore, M.L., Nichol, V.W., & McHugh, P.P. (1992). Review of no-fault absenteeism cases taken to arbitration, 1980–1989: A rights and responsibilities analysis. *Employee Rights and Responsibilities Journal, 5,* 29–48; Scott, K.D., & Taylor, G.S. (1983, September). An analysis of absenteeism cases taken to arbitration: 1975–1981. *The Arbitration Journal,* 61–70.

30. Robbins, S.P. (1974). *Managing organizational conflict: A nontraditional approach.* Englewood, Cliffs, NJ: Prentice-Hall, p. 20.

31. Brown, L.D. (1983). *Managing conflict at organizational interfaces.* Reading, MA: Addison-Wesley.

32. Robbins, 1974; also see Brown, 1983.

33. Raynal, W. & Wilson, K.A. (2001, October 15). What about Bob? *Autoweek,* 5.

34. Ramsay, L. (1999, March 15). Stress, the plague of the 1990s. *National Post,* D10. Best, P. (1999, February). All work (Stressed to the max? Join the club). *Report on Business Magazine,* 3.

35. Keita, G.P. (2006, June). The national push for workplace health. *Monitor on Psychology, 32.*

36. Xie, J.L., & Johns, G. (1995). Job scope and stress: Can job scope be too high? *Academy of Management Journal, 38,* 1288–1309.

37. Cole, T. (1999, February). All the rage. *Report on Business Magazine,* 50–57.

38. This model has much in common with many contemporary models of work stress. For a comprehensive summary, see Kahn, R.L., & Byosiere, P. (1992). Stress in organizations. In M.D. Dunnette & L.M. Hough (Eds.), *Handbook of industrial and organizational psychology* (2nd ed., Vol. 3). Palo Alto, CA: Consulting Psychologists Press.

39. McGrath, J.E. (1970). A conceptual formulation for research on stress. In J.E. McGrath (Ed.), *Social and psychological factors in stress.* New York: Holt, Rinehart, Winston.

40. Roth, S., & Cohen, L.J. (1986). Approach, avoidance, and coping with stress. *American Psychologist, 41,* 813–819.

41. Glazer, S., & Beehr, T.A. (2005). Consistency of implications of three role stressors across four countries. *Journal of Organizational Behavior, 26,* 467–487.

42. Kahn & Byosiere, 1992. For a typical study, see Spector, P.E., & O'Connell, B.J. (1994). The contribution of personality traits, negative affectivity, locus of control, and Type A to the subsequent reports of job stressors and job strains. *Journal of Occupational and Organizational Psychology, 67,* 1–11.

43. Friedman, M., & Rosenman, R. (1974). *Type A Behavior and your heart.* New York: Knopf.

44. Chesney, M.A., & Rosenman, R. (1980). Type A behavior in the work setting. In C.L. Cooper and R. Payne (Eds.), *Current concerns in occupational stress.* Chichester, England: Wiley. For a typical study, see Jamal, M., & Baba, V.V. (1991). Type A behavior, its prevalence and consequences among women nurses: An empirical examination. *Human Relations, 44,* 1213–1228.

45. Fine, S. & Stinson, M. (2000, February 3). Stress is overwhelming people, study shows. *Globe and Mail,* A1, A7; Matthews, K.A. (1982). Psychological perspectives on the Type A behavior pattern. *Psychological Bulletin, 91,* 293–323.

46. Booth-Kewley, S., & Friedman, H.S. (1987). Psychological predictors of heart disease: A quantitative review. *Psychological Bulletin, 101,* 343–362; Smith, D. (2003, March). Angry

thoughts, at-risk hearts. *Monitor on Psychology*, 46–48; Ganster, D.C., Schaubroeck, J., Sime, W.E., & Mayes, B.T. (1991). The nomological validity of the Type A personality among employed adults. *Journal of Applied Psychology, 76,* 143–168.

47. See for example Houkes, I., Janssen, P.P.M., de Jonge, J., & Bakker, A.B. (2003). Personality, work characteristics, and employee well-being: A longitudinal analysis of additive and moderating effects. *Journal of Occupational Health Psychology, 8,* 20–38.

48. Spector, P.E., Zapf, D., Chen, P.Y., & Frese, M. (2000). Why negative affectivity should not be controlled in stress research: Don't throw out the baby with the bath water. *Journal of Organizational Behavior, 21,* 79–95; for a relevant study, see Barsky, A., Thoresen, C.J., Warren, C.R., & Kaplan, S.A. (2004). Modeling negative affectivity and job stress: A contingency-based approach. *Journal of Organizational Behavior, 25,* 915–936.

49. Fine, S. & Stinson, M. (2000, February 3). Stress is overwhelming people, study shows. *Globe and Mail,* A1, A7.

50. Parasuraman, S., & Alutto, J.A. (1981). An examination of the organizational antecedents of stressors at work. *Academy of Management Journal, 24,* 48–67.

51. Mintzberg, H. (1973). *The nature of managerial work.* New York: Harper & Row.

52. An excellent review of managerial stressors can be found in Marshall, J., & Cooper, C.L. (1979). *Executives under pressure.* New York: Praeger.

53. Xie & Johns, 1995.

54. Karasek, R.A., Jr. (1979). Job demands, job decision latitude, and mental strain: Implications for job redesign. *Administrative Science Quarterly, 24,* 285–308.

55. For reviews, see Xie, J.L., & Shaubroeck, J. (2001). Bridging approaches and findings across disciplines to improve job stress research. In P.L. Perrewé & D.C. Ganster (Eds.) *Research in occupational stress and well being.* Oxford: JAI; Van Der Doef, M., & Maes, S. (1999). The Job Demand-Control (-Support) model and psychological well-being: A review of 20 years of empirical research. *Work & Stress, 13,* 87–114; for a recent study see Totterdell, P., Wood, S., & Wall, T. (2006). An intra-individual test of the demands-control model: A weekly diary study

of psychological strain in portfolio workers. *Journal of Occupational and Organizational Psychology, 79,* 63–84.

56. Maslach, C., & Jackson, S.E. (1984). Burnout in organizational settings. In S. Oskamp (Ed.), *Applied social psychology annual* (Vol. 5). Beverly Hills, CA: Sage, p. 134.

57. Maslach, C., Schaufeli, W.B., & Leiter, M.P. (2001). Job burnout. *Annual Review of Psychology, 52,* 397–422; Cordes, C.L., & Dougherty, T.W. (1993). A review and integration of research on job burnout. *Academy of Management Review, 18,* 621–656; for a comprehensive study, see Lee, R.T., & Ashforth, B.E. (1993). A longitudinal study of burnout among supervisors and managers: Comparisons of the Leiter and Maslach (1988) and Golembiewski et al. (1986) models. *Organizational Behavior and Human Decision Processes, 54,* 369–398.

58. For a study of burnout among police personnel, see Burke, R.J., & Deszca, E. (1986). Correlates of psychological burnout phases among police officers. *Human Relations, 39,* 487–501.

59. See Pines, A.M., & Aronson, E. (1981). *Burnout: From tedium to personal growth.* New York: The Free Press.

60. Salin, D. (2003). Ways of explaining workplace bullying: A review of enabling, motivating and precipitating structures in the work environment. *Human Relations, 56,* 1213–1232.

61. Salin, 2003; Rayner, C., & Keashly, L. (2005). Bullying at work; A perspective from Britain and North America. In S. Fox & P.E. Spector (Eds.), *Counterproductive work behavior: Investigations of actors and targets.* Washington, DC: American Psychological Association.

62. This is one interpretation of the distinction between bullying and mobbing. See Zapf, D., & Einarsen, S. Mobbing at work: Escalated conflicts in organizations. In Fox & Spector, 2005.

63. Meyers, L. (2006, July/August). Still wearing the 'kick me' sign. *Monitor on Psychology,* 68–70.

64. Dingfelder, S.F. (2006, July/August). Banishing bullying. *Monitor on Psychology,* 76–78.

65. Gibb-Clark, M. (1999, June 4). Work v. family: The $2.7-billion crisis. *Globe and Mail,* M1; Duxbury, L., & Higgins, C. (2003). *Work–life conflict in Canada in the new millennium: A status report.* Ottawa: Health Canada.

66. Gibb-Clark, 1999.

67. For job loss in particular, see McKee-Ryan, F.M., Song, Z., Wanberg, C.R., & Kinicki, A.J. (2005). Psychological and physical well-being during unemployment: A meta-analytic study. *Journal of Applied Psychology, 90,* 53–76; for mergers and acquisitions, see Cartwright, S. (2005). Mergers and acquisitions: An update and appraisal. *International Review of Industrial and Organizational Psychology, 20,* 1–38.

68. Bellavia, G.M., & Frone, M.R. (2005). Work-family conflict. In J. Barling, E.K. Kelloway, & M.R. Frone (Eds.), *Handbook of work stress.* Thousand Oaks, CA: Sage.

69. DeFrank, R.S., & Ivancevich, J.M. (1998, August). Stress on the job: An executive update. *Academy of Management Executive,* 55–66.

70. Jackson, S.E., & Schuler, R.S. (1985). Meta-analysis and conceptual critique of research on role ambiguity and conflict in work settings. *Organizational Behavior and Human Decision Processes, 36,* 16–78. For a critique of some of this research, see Fineman, S., & Payne, R. (1981). Role stress—A methodological trap? *Journal of Occupational Behaviour, 2,* 51–64.

71. Fitzgerald, L.F., Drasgow, F., Hulin, C.L., Gelfand, M.J., & Magley, V.J. (1997). Antecedents and consequences of sexual harassment in organizations: A test of an integrated model. *Journal of Applied Psychology, 82,* 578–589; Schneider, K.T., Swan, S., & Fitzgerald, L.F. (1997). Job-related and psychological effects of sexual harassment in the workplace: Empirical evidence from two organizations. *Journal of Applied Psychology, 82,* 401–415.

72. Fitzgerald et al., 1997; Schneider et al., 1997.

73. Schneider et al., 1997.

74. Peirce, E., Smolinski, C.A., & Rosen, B. (1998, August). Why sexual harassment complaints fall on deaf ears. *Academy of Management Executive,* 41–54; Schneider et al., 1997.

75. Fitzgerald et al., 1997; Glomb, T.M., Munson, L.J., Hulin, C.L., Bergman, M.E., & Drasgow, F. (1999). Structural equation models of sexual harassment: Longitudinal explorations and cross-sectional generalizations. *Journal of Applied Psychology, 84,* 14–28.

76. Jamal, M. (1984). Job stress and job performance controversy: An empirical assessment. *Organizational Behavior and Human Performance, 33,* 1–21; Motowidlo, S.J., Packard,

J.S., & Manning, M.R. (1986). Occupational stress: Its causes and consequences for job performance. *Journal of Applied Psychology, 71,* 618–629.

77. Lepine, J.A., Podsakoff, N.P., & Lepine, M.A. (2005). A meta-analytic test of the challenge stressor-hindrance stressor framework: An explanation for inconsistent relationships among stressors and performance. *Academy of Management Journal, 48,* 764–775.

78. Johns, G. (1997). Contemporary research on absence from work: Correlates, causes and consequences. *International Review of Industrial and Organizational Psychology, 12,* 115–173; Darr, W., & Johns, G. (2006). *Stress, health, and absenteeism from work: A meta-analysis.* Manuscript under review.

79. Beehr, T.A., & Newman, J.E. (1978). Job stress, employee health, and organizational effectiveness: A facet analysis, model, and literature review. *Personnel Psychology, 32,* 665–699; Kahn & Byosiere, 1992; Cooper, M.L., Russell, M., & Frone, M.R. (1990). Work stress and alcohol effects: A test of stress-induced drinking. *Journal of Health and Social Behavior, 31,* 260–276; Frone, M.R. (1999). Work stress and alcohol use. *Alcohol Research and Health, 23,* 284–291.

80. For reviews see Cramer, P. (2000). Defense mechanisms in psychology today: Further processes for adaptation. *American Psychologist, 55,* 637–646; Baumeister, R.F., Dale, K., & Sommer, K.L. (1998). Freudian defense mechanisms and empirical findings in modern social psychology: Reaction formation, projection, displacement, undoing, isolation, sublimation, and denial. *Journal of Personality, 66,* 1081–1124.

81. Beehr & Newman, 1978. For a later review and a strong critique of this work, see Fried, Y., Rowland, K.M., & Ferris, G.R. (1984). The physiological measurement of work stress: A critique. *Personnel Psychology, 37,* 583–615. See also Fried, Y. (1989). The future of physiological assessments in work situations. In C.L. Cooper & R. Payne (Eds.), *Causes, coping, and consequences of stress at work.* Chichester, England: Wiley & Sons

82. Cooper, C.L., Mallinger, M., & Kahn, R. (1978). Identifying sources of occupational stress among dentists. *Journal of Occupational Psychology, 61,* 163–174. See also DiMatteo, M.r,

Shugars, D.A., & Hays, R.D. (1993). Occupational stress, life stress and mental health among dentists. *Journal of Occupational and Organizational Psychology, 66,* 153–162.

83. Cohen, S. & Herbert, T.B. (1996). Health psychology: Psychological and physical disease from the perspective of human psychoneuroimmunology. *Annual Review of Psychology, 47,* 113–142; Cohen, S., & Williamson, G.M. (1991). Stress and infectious disease in humans. *Psychological Bulletin, 109,* 5–24.

84. Melamed, S., Shirom, A., Toker, S., Berliner, S., & Shapira, I. (2006). Burnout and risk of cardiovascular disease: Evidence, possible causal paths, and promising research directions. *Psychological Bulletin, 132,* 327–353.

85. Grandey, A.A., Fisk, G.M., & Steiner, D.D. (2005). Must "service with a smile" be stressful? The moderating role of personal control for American and French employees. *Journal of Applied Psychology, 90,* 893–904; Grandey, A.A., Dicter, D.N., & Sin, H.P. (2004). The customer is *not* always right: Customer aggression and emotion regulation of service employees. *Journal of Organizational Behavior, 25,* 397–418.

86. Cohen, S., & Wills, T.A. (1985). Stress, social support, and the buffering hypothesis. *Psychological Bulletin, 98,* 310–357; Kahn & Byosiere, 1992.

87. Chamberlin, J. (2000, January). Cops trust cops, even with a PhD. *Monitor on Psychology,* 74–76.

88. This section relies on a *Wall Street Journal* special section on Work & Family (1993, June 21) and Shellenbarger, S. (1993, June 29). Work & family. *Wall Street Journal,* B1.

89. Ivancevich, J.M., Matteson, M.T., Freedman, S.M., & Phillips, J.S. (1990). Worksite stress management interventions. *American Psychologist, 45,* 252–261; Murphy, L.R. (1984). Occupational stress management: A review and appraisal. *Journal of Occupational Psychology, 57,* 1–15; Cartwright, S. & Cooper, C. (2005). Individually targeted interventions. In Barling et al., 2005.

90. Ivancevich et al., 1990; Murphy, 1984.

91. Faught, L. (1997, April). At Eddie Bauer you can work and have a life. *Workforce,* 83–90.

92. Lush, T. (1998, October 3). Company with a conscience. *The Gazette,* C3.

93. Weiss, N. (1998, August). How Starbucks impassions workers to drive growth. *Workforce,* 61–64.

94. DeGroot, T., & Kiker, D.S. (2003). A meta-analysis of the non-monetary effects of employee health management programs. *Human Resource Management, 42,* 53–69; Falkenberg, L.E. (1987). Employee fitness programs: Their impact on the employee and the organization. *Academy of Management Review, 12,* 511–522; Jex, S.M. (1991). The psychological benefits of exercise in work settings: A review, critique, and dispositional model. *Work & Stress, 5,* 133–147.

Chapter 14

1. Anfuso, D. (1999, March). Core values shape W. L. Gore's innovative culture. *Workforce,* 48–53 (quote); Deutschman, A. (2004, December). The fabric of creativity. *Fast Company,* 54–62; Weinreb, M. (2003, April). Power to the people. *Sales and Marketing Management,* 30–35.

2. Mintzberg, H. (1979). *The structuring of organizations.* Englewood Cliffs, NJ: Prentice-Hall. For a recent review of some of the issues involved in structuring organizations, see Dunbar, R.L., & Starbuck, W.H. (2006). Learning to design organizations and learning from designing them. *Organization Science, 17,* 171–178.

3. Lawrence, P.R., & Lorsch, J.W. (1969). *Organization and environment: Managing differentiation and integration.* Homewood, IL: Irwin.

4. For an extended treatment of the role of interdependence between departments, see McCann, J., & Galbraith, J.R. (1981). Interdepartmental relations. In P.C. Nystrom & W.H. Starbuck (Eds.), *Handbook of organizational design* (Vol. 2). Oxford: Oxford University Press.

5. For a comparison of functional and product departmentation, see McCann & Galbraith, 1981; Walker, A.H., & Lorsch, J.W. (1968, November–December). Organizational choice: Product vs. function. *Harvard Business Review,* 129–138.

6. See Davis, S.M., & Lawrence, P.M. (1977). *Matrix.* Reading, MA: Addison-Wesley.

7. Treatment of these forms of departmentation can be found in Daft, R.L. (2007). *Organization theory and design* (9th ed.). Cincinnati, OH: Thompson South-Western; Robey, D. (1991). *Designing organizations* (3rd ed.). Homewood, IL: Irwin.

8. Mintzberg, 1979.
9. See Hall, R.H. (1962). Intraorganizational structural variation: Application of the bureaucratic model. *Administrative Science Quarterly, 7,* 295–308.
10. Lawrence & Lorsch, 1969.
11. Galbraith, J.R. (1977). *Organization design.* Reading, MA: Addison-Wesley.
12. See Birnbaum, P.H. (1981). Integration and specialization in academic research. *Academy of Management Journal, 24,* 487–503.
13. This discussion relies on Galbraith, 1977.
14. Lawrence & Lorsch, 1969.
15. Galbraith, 1977.
16. These definitions of structural variables are common. However, there is considerable disagreement about how some should be measured. See Walton, E.J. (1981). The comparison of measures of organizational structure. *Academy of Management Review, 6,* 155–160.
17. Research on these hypotheses is sparse and not always in agreement. See Dewar, R.D., & Simet, D.P. (1981). A level specific prediction of spans of control examining effects of size, technology, and specialization. *Academy of Management Journal, 24,* 5–24; Van Fleet, D.D. (1983). Span of management research and issues. *Academy of Management Journal, 26,* 546–552.
18. Treece, J.B. (1990, April 9). Here comes GM's Saturn. *Business Week,* 56–62.
19. For a study, see Hetherington, R.W. (1991). The effects of formalization on departments of a multi-hospital system. *Journal of Management Studies, 28,* 103–141.
20. Groth, L. (1999). *Future organizational design: The scope for the IT-based enterprise.* Chichester, England: Wiley.
21. *60 Minutes,* October 17, 1993.
22. Mintzberg, 1979, p. 182.
23. Ritzer, G., (1993). *The McDonaldization of society.* Thousand Oaks, CA: Pine Forge Press.
24. Personal communication from Food Lion's Jeff Lowrance, August 7, 2006.
25. Daft, 2007.
26. The terms *mechanistic* and *organic* (to follow) were first used by Burns, T., & Stalker, G.M. (1961). *The management of innovation.* London: Tavistock Publications. For a relevant study, see Courtright, J.A., Fairhurst, G.T., & Rogers, L.E. (1989). Interaction patterns in organic and mechanistic systems. *Academy of Management Journal, 32,* 773–802.
27. Westerman, G., McFarlan, F.W., & Iansiti, M. (2006). Organization design and effectiveness over the innovation life cycle. *Organization Science, 17,* 230–238; Puranam, P., Singh, H., & Zollo, M. (2006). Organizing for innovation: Managing the coordination-autonomy dilemma in technology acquisitions. *Academy of Management Journal, 49,* 263–280.
28. Miles, R.E., & Snow, C.C. (1992, Summer). Causes of failure in network organizations. *California Management Review,* 53–72; Snow, C.C., Miles, R.F., & Coleman, H.J., Jr. (1992, Winter). Managing 21st century network organizations. *Organizational Dynamics,* 5–19.
29. Brass, D.J., Galaskiewicz, J., Greve, H.R., & Tsai, W. (2004). Taking stock of networks and organizations: A multilevel perspective. *Academy of Management Journal, 47,* 795–817.
30. Dess, G.G., Rasheed, A.M.A., McLaughlin, K.J., and Priem, R.L. (1995, August). The new corporate architecture. *Academy of Management Executive,* 7–20.
31. This example is from Venkatraman, N., & Lee, C.H. (2004). Preferential linkage and network evolution: A conceptual model and empirical test in the U.S. video game sector. *Academy of Management Journal, 47,* 876–892.
32. Anonymous. (2006, July 20). Sony to receive first shipments of PlayStation 3 consoles early. *National Post.*
33. Miles & Snow, 1992.
34. Chesbrough, H.W., & Teece, D.J. (2002, August). Organizing for innovation: When is virtual virtuous? *The Innovative Enterprise,* 127–134.
35. Kim, T.Y., Oh, H., & Swaminathan, A. (2006). Framing interorganizational network change: A network inertia perspective. *Academy of Management Review, 31,* 704–720.
36. Dess, et al., 1995; Tully, S. (1993, February 8). The modular corporation. *Fortune,* 106–114.
37. Tully, 1993; Dess, et al., 1995.
38. Magretta, J. (1998, March–April). The power of virtual integration: An interview with Dell Computer's Michael Dell. *Harvard Business Review,* 72–84; Tully, 1993.
39. Berman, D. (1996, September). Car and striver. *Canadian Business,* 92–99.
40. Dess, et al., 1995.
41. Berman, 1996.
42. Dess, et al., 1995; Tully, 1993.
43. Tully, 1993.
44. Dess, et al., 1995.
45. Tichy, N.M., & Sherman, S. (1993, January 25). Jack Welch's lessons for success. *Fortune,* 86–93. Excerpt from *Control your destiny or someone else will* (1993), Toronto: Doubleday.
46. Jacob, R. (1992, May 18). The search for the organization of tomorrow. *Fortune,* 92–98; Rao, R.M. (1995, April 3). The struggle to create an organization for the 21st century. *Fortune,* 90–99.
47. Jacob, 1992.
48. Dess, et al., 1995.
49. Dess, et al., 1995.
50. Tichy & Sherman, 1993. Excerpt from *Control your destiny or someone else will* (1993), Toronto: Doubleday.
51. Rao, 1995; Jacob, 1992.
52. For a good general review of size research, see Bluedorn, A.C. (1993). Pilgrim's progress: Trends and convergence in research on organizational size and environments. *Journal of Management, 19,* 163–191.
53. Much of this research was stimulated by Blau, P.M. (1970). A theory of differentiation in organizations. *American Sociological Review, 35,* 201–218. For a review and test, see Cullen, J.B., Anderson, K.S., & Baker, D.D. (1986). Blau's theory of structural differentiation revisited: A theory of structural change or scale? *Academy of Management Journal, 29,* 203–229.
54. Dewar, R., & Hage, J. (1978). Size, technology, complexity, and structural differentiation: Toward a theoretical synthesis. *Administrative Science Quarterly, 23,* 111–136; Marsh, R.M., & Mannari, H. (1981). Technology and size as determinants of the organizational structure of Japanese factories. *Administrative Science Quarterly, 26,* 33–57.
55. Hage, J., & Aiken, M. (1967). Relationship of centralization to other structural properties. *Administrative Science Quarterly, 12,* 79–91; Mansfield, R. (1973). Bureaucracy and centralization: An examination of organizational structure. *Administrative Science Quarterly, 18,* 77–88.
56. Carleton, J. (2006, April 20). Forestry company Weyerhaeuser tries to become more nimble. *Globe and Mail,* B16.
57. DeWitt, R.L. (1993). The structural consequences of downsizing. *Organization Science, 4,* 30–40.
58. Freeman, S.J., & Cameron, K.S. (1993). Organizational downsizing: A convergence and reorientation framework. *Organization Science, 4,* 10–29.
59. Cascio, W.F. (1993, February). Downsizing: what do we know? What

have we learned? *Academy of Management Executive*, 95–104.

60. DeWitt, 1993; Sutton, R.L., & D'Aunno, T. (1989). Decreasing organizational size: Untangling the effects of money and people. *Academy of Management Review, 14*, 194–212.

61. Cascio, 1993.

62. Brockner, J. (1988). The effects of work layoffs on survivors: Research, theory, and practice. *Research in Organizational Behavior, 10*, 213–255.

63. Kammeyer-Mueller, J., Liao, H., & Arvey, R.D. (2001). Downsizing and organizational performance: A review of the literature from a stakeholder perspective. *Research in Personnel and Human Resources Management, 20*, 269–329; Johns, G. (2006, June). Presenteeism at work: An introduction for psychologists. Theory review session, Annual convention of the Canadian Psychological Association, Calgary, Alberta. (Abstracted in *Canadian Psychology, 47*; 2a, 2006).

64. Cascio, W.F. (2002, August). Strategies for responsible restructuring. *Academy of Management Executive*, 80–91; see also Burke, W.W. (1997, Summer). The new agenda for organization development. *Organizational Dynamics*, 7–18.

65. Child, J. (1984). *Organization: A guide to problems and practice*. London: Harper & Row.

66. Presidential Commission. (1986). *The report on the space shuttle Challenger accident*. Washington, DC: U.S. Government Printing Office.

67. Pugh, D. (1979, Winter). Effective coordination in organizations. *Advanced Management Journal*, 28–35.

Chapter 15

1. Sources include: Van Alphen, T. (2006, May 10). Oakville plant breaks mould. *Toronto Star*, F1, F8; Keenan, G. (2006, May 10). Ford's new maxim: Flex manufacturing. *Globe and Mail*, B3; Van Alphen, T. (2006, March 23). Ford changes in shifts okayed. *Toronto Star*, D3; (2004, October 29). Ford invests $1 billion in Oakville assembly complex. www.media.ford.com/newsroom/release_display.cfm?relese=19503.

2. Howlett, K. (2001, December 21). CIBC regroups after Sept. 11 devastation. *Globe and Mail*, B1, B5.

3. McNish, J. (2003, June 11). Skittish travelers shifting bus tour firm into reverse. *Globe and Mail*, B1, B4.

4. Little, B. (2003, June 11). Second SARS outbreak barely noticed. *Globe and Mail*, B4.

5. Neuman, S. (2003, June 4). SARS travel slump could last. *Globe and Mail*, B6.

6. Katz, D., & Kahn, R.L. (1978). *The social psychology of organizations* (2nd ed.). New York: Wiley.

7. This list relies on Duncan, R. (1972). Characteristics of organization environments and perceived environmental uncertainty. *Administrative Science Quarterly, 17*, 313–327.

8. Durbin, D. (2005, May 31). Parts firms' trust in big three drops. *Globe and Mail*, B12.

9. See Khandwalla, P. (1981). Properties of competing organizations. In P.C. Nystrom & W.H. Starbuck (Eds.), *Handbook of organization design* (Vol. 1). Oxford: Oxford University Press.

10. Zachary, G.P. (1994). Consolidation sweeps the software industry; small firms imperiled. *Wall Street Journal*, A1, A6.

11. Volberda, H.W. (1996). Toward the flexible form: How to remain vital in hypercompetitive environments. *Organization Scene, 7*, 359–374.

12. Kirkpatrick, D. (1990, February 12). Environmentalism: The new crusade. *Fortune*, 44–55.

13. Connolly, T., Conlon, E.J., & Deutsch, S.J. (1980). Organizational effectiveness: A multiple-constituency approach. *Academy of Management Review, 5*, 211–217.

14. Duncan, 1972. Just how to measure uncertainty has provoked controversy; see Downey, H.K., & Ireland, R.D. (1979). Quantitative versus qualitative: Environmental assessment in organizational studies. *Administrative Science Quarterly, 24*, 630–637; Milliken, F.J. (1987). Three types of perceived uncertainty about the environment: State, effect, and response uncertainty. *Academy of Management Review, 12*, 133–143.

15. Duncan, 1972; Tung, R.L. (1979). Dimensions of organizational environments: An exploratory study of their impact on organization structure. *Academy of Management Journal, 22*, 672–693. For contrary evidence, see Downey, H., Hellriegel, D., & Slocum, J. (1975). Environmental uncertainty: The construct and its application. *Administrative Science Quarterly, 20*, 613–629.

16. See Leblebici, H., & Salancik, G.R. (1981). Effects of environmental uncertainty on information and deci-sion processes in banks. *Administrative Science Quarterly, 26*, 578–596.

17. See At-Twaijri, M.I.A., & Montanari, J.R. (1987). The impact of context and choice on the boundary-spanning process: An empirical extension. *Human Relations, 40*, 783–798.

18. Pfeffer, J., & Salancik, G.R. (1978). *The external control of organizations: A resource dependence perspective*. New York: Harper & Row; Yasai-Ardekani, M. (1989). Effects of environmental scarcity and munificence on the relationship of context to organizational structure. *Academy of Management Journal, 32*, 131–156.

19. Castrogiovanni, G.J., (1991). Environmental munificence: A theoretical assessment. *Academy of Management Review, 16*, 542–565.

20. Pfeffer & Salancik, 1978.

21. Boyd, B.K., Dess, G.G., & Rasheed, A.M.A. (1993). Divergence between archival and perceptual measures of the environment: Causes and consequences. *Academy of Management Review, 18*, 204–226.

22. For an analogue, see Miller, D., Dröge, C., & Toulouse, J.M. (1988). Strategic process and content as mediators between organizational context and structure. *Academy of Management Journal, 31*, 544–569.

23. Miles, R.C., & Snow, C.C. (1978). *Organizational strategy, structure, and process*. New York: McGraw-Hill.

24. Lawrence, P.R., & Lorsch, J.W. (1967). *Organization and environment: Managing differentiation and integration*. Homewood, IL: Irwin. For a follow-up study, see Lorsch, J.W., & Morse, J.J. (1974). *Organizations and their members: A contingency approach*. New York: Harper & Row.

25. For a review, see Miner, J.B. (1982). *Theories of organizational structure and process*. Chicago: Dryden.

26. Sine, W.D., Mitsuhashi, H., & Kirsch, D.A. (2006). Revisiting Burns and Stalker: Formal structure and new venture performance in emerging economic sectors. *Academy of Management Journal, 49*, 121–132.

27. Frederickson, J.W. (1986). The strategic decision process and organizational structure. *Academy of Management Review, 11*, 280–297.

28. Romme, A.G.L. (1990). Vertical integration as organizational strategy formation. *Organization Studies, 11*, 239–260.

29. Chatterjee, S., Lubatkin, M., & Schoenecker, T. (1992). Vertical strate-

gies and market structure: A systematic risk analysis. *Organization Science, 3*, 138–156; D'Aveni, R.A., & Ilinitch, A.Y. (1992). Complex patterns of vertical integration in the forest products industry: Systematic and bankruptcy risks. *Academy of Management Journal, 35*, 596–625.

30. D'Aveni, R.A., & Ravenscraft, D.J. (1994). Economies of integration versus bureaucracy costs: Does vertical integration improve performance? *Academy of Management Journal, 37(5)*, 1167–1206.

31. Anders, G. (2003, February). The Carly Chronicles. *Fast Company*, 66–73; Wong, T. (2006, January 31). Fairmont fetches $3.9 billion U.S.; Saudi prince, allies purchase chain Royal York among hotels, resorts sold. *Toronto Star*, D1; Perkins, T. (2006, August 18). Executive suite vacated at mining firm's headquarters. *Toronto Star*, F1, F8; Perkins, T. (2006, August 24). Domtar creates fine-paper giant in deal with U.S. firm. *Toronto Star*, C1, C8.

32. Lubatkin, M., & O'Neill, H.M. (1987). Merger strategies and capital market risk. *Academy of Management Journal, 30*, 665–684; Pfeffer & Salancik, 1978; Hill, C.W.L., & Hoskisson, R.E. (1987). Strategy and structure in the multiproduct firm. *Academy of Management Review, 12*, 331–341.

33. Kanter, R.M. (1989, August). Becoming PALS: Pooling, allying, and linking across companies. *Academy of Management Executive*, 183–193.

34. Krim, J. (2003, April 28). 3 E-mail providers join spam fight: AOl, Microsoft, Yahoo seek ways to curtail unwanted solicitations. *The Washington Post*, A2.

35. Van Alphen, T. (2006, August 30). CAW makes unusual pitch to Ford. *Toronto Star*, F1, F7.

36. Dyer, J.H., Kale, P., & Singh, H. (2001). How to make strategic alliances work. *MIT Sloan Management Review, 42(4)*, 37–43; Parkhe, A. (1993). Strategic alliance structuring: A game theoretic and transaction cost examination of interfirm cooperation. *Academy of Management Journal, 36*, 794–829. See also Ring, P.S., & Van de Ven, A.H. (1994). Developmental processes of cooperative interorganizational relationships. *Academy of Management Review, 19*, 90–118.

37. Parkhe, A. (1993). Partner nationality and the structure-performance relationship in strategic alliances. *Organizational Science, 4*, 301–324.

38. Schoorman, F.D., Bazerman, M.H., & Atkin, R.S. (1981). Interlocking directorates: A strategy for reducing environmental uncertainty. *Academy of Management Review, 6*, 243–251, p. 244. For a recent study, see Haunschild, P.R., (1993). Interorganizational imitation: The impact of interlocks on corporate acquisition activity. *Administrative Science Quarterly, 38*, 564–592.

39. Schoorman et al., 1981.

40. See Davis, G.F., & Powell, W.W. (1992). Organization-environment relations. In M.D. Dunnette & L.M. Hough (Eds.), *Handbook of industrial and organizational psychology* (2nd ed., Vol. 3). Palo Alto, CA: Consulting Psychologists Press; Oliver, C. (1991). Strategic responses to institutional processes. *Academy of Management Review, 16*, 145–179.

41. Greenwood, R., & Deephouse, D. (2001, December 26). Legitimacy seen as key. *Globe and Mail*, B7.

42. Rousseau, D.M. (1979). Assessment of technology in organizations: Closed versus open systems approaches. *Academy of Management Review, 4*, 531–542.

43. Child, J. (1972). Organizational structure, environment and performance: The role of strategic choice. *Sociology, 6*, 2–22.

44. Gillespie, D.F., & Mileti, D.S. (1977). Technology and the study of organizations: An overview and appraisal. *Academy of Management Review, 2*, 7–16; Rousseau, 1979.

45. Perrow, C.A. (1967). A framework for the comparative analysis of organizations. *American Sociological Review, 32*, 194–208.

46. Thompson, J.D. (1967). *Organizations in action*. New York: McGraw-Hill.

47. Thompson, 1967, p. 17.

48. Woodward, J. (1965). *Industrial organization: Theory and practice*. London: Oxford University Press.

49. Mintzberg, H. (1979). *The structuring of organizations*. Englewood Cliffs, NJ: Prentice-Hall.

50. Miller, C.C., Glick, W.H., Wang, Y.D., & Huber, G.P. (1991). Understanding technology-structure relationships: Theory development and meta-analytic theory testing. *Academy of Management Journal, 34*, 370–399. For information on measurement, see Withey, M., Daft, R.L., & Cooper, W.H. (1983). Measures of Perrow's work unit technology: An empirical assessment and a new scale. *Academy of Management Journal, 26*, 45–63.

51. Cheng, J.L.C. (1983). Interdependence and coordination in organizations: A role-system analysis. *Academy of Management Journal, 26*, 156–162.

52. Van de Ven, A.H., Delbecq, A.L., & Koenig, R., Jr. (1976). Determinants of coordination modes within organizations. *American Sociological Review, 41*, 322–338.

53. Keller, R.T., Slocum, J.W., Jr., & Susman, G.J. (1974). Uncertainty and type of management in continuous process organizations. *Academy of Management Journal, 17*, 56–68; Marsh, R.M., & Mannari, H. (1981). Technology and size as determinants of the organizational structure of Japanese factories. *Administrative Science Quarterly, 26*, 33–57; Zwerman, W.L. (1970). *New perspectives on organizational theory*. Westport, CT: Greenwood.

54. Singh, J.V. (1986). Technology, size, and organizational structure: A reexamination of the Okayma study data. *Academy of Management Journal, 29*, 800–812.

55. Walton, R.E. (1989). *Up and running: Integrating information technology and the organization*. Boston: Harvard Business School Press.

56. Child, J. (1987). Organizational design for advanced manufacturing technology. In T.D. Wall, C.W. Clegg, & N.J. Kemp (Eds.), *The human side of advanced manufacturing technology*. Sussex, England: Wiley.

57. From the Massachusetts Institute of Technology report *Made in America*, as excerpted in *Fortune*, May 22, 1989, p. 94.

58. Keenan, G. (2003, May 24). Chrysler future lies in flexibility. *Globe and Mail*, B3.

59. This table draws in part on Jelinek, M., & Goldhar, J.D. (1986). Maximizing strategic opportunities in implementing advanced manufacturing systems. In D.D. Davis (Ed.), *Managing technological innovation*. San Francisco: Jossey-Bass; Main, J. (1990, May 21). Manufacturing the right way. *Fortune*, 54–64; Nemetz, P.L., & Fry, L.W. (1988). Flexible manufacturing organizations: Implications for strategy formulation and organization design. *Academy of Management Review, 13*, 627–638.

60. Cummings, T.G., & Blumberg, M. (1987). Advanced manufacturing technology and work design. In T.D. Wall, C.W. Clegg, & N.J. Kemp (Eds.), *The human side of advanced manufacturing technology*. Sussex, England: Wiley.

61. The following draws upon Child, 1987; Nemetz & Fry, 1988; Zammuto, R.F., & O'Connor, E.J. (1992). Gaining advanced manufacturing technologies' benefits: The roles of organizational design and culture. *Academy of Management Review, 17,* 701–728.

62. Dean, J.W., Jr., Yook, S.J., & Susman, G.I. (1992). Advanced manufacturing technology and organizational structure: Empowerment or subordination? *Organization Science, 3,* 203–229.

63. Collins, P.D., Ryan, L.V., & Matusik, S.F. (1999). Programmable automation and the locus of decision-making power. *Journal of Management, 25,* 29–53.

64. Wall, T.D., & Davids, K. (1992). Shopfloor work organization and advanced manufacturing technology. *International Review of Industrial and Organizational Psychology, 7,* 363–398.

65. Wall, T.D., Corbett, J.M., Martin, R., Clegg, C.W., & Jackson, P.R. (1990). Advanced manufacturing technology, work design, and performance: A change study. *Journal of Applied Psychology, 75,* 691–697; Wall, T.D., Jackson, P.R., & Davids, K. (1992). Operator work design and robotics systems performance: A serendipitous field study. *Journal of Applied Psychology, 77,* 353–362.

66. Patterson, M.G., West, M.A., & Wall, T.D. (2004). Integrated manufacturing, empowerment, and company performance. *Journal of Organizational Behavior, 25,* 641–665.

67. Cummings & Blumberg, 1987; Blumberg, M., & Gerwin, D. (1984). Coping with advanced manufacturing technology. *Journal of Occupational Behaviour, 5,* 113–130.

68. From an unpublished paper by C.A. Voss, cited in Child, 1987.

69. Long, R.J. (1987). *New office information technology: Human and managerial implications.* London: Croom Helm.

70. Long, 1987.

71. Dopson, S., & Stewart, R. (1990). What is happening to middle management? *British Journal of Management, 1,* 3–16.

72. See Bloomfield, B.P., & Coombs, R. (1992). Information technology, control and power: The centralization and decentralization debate revisited. *Journal of Management Studies, 29,* 459–484; Dewett, T., & Jones, G.R. (2001). The role of information technology in the organization: A review,

model and assessment. *Journal of Management, 27,* 313–346.

73. Huber, G.P. (1990). A theory of the effects of advanced information technologies on organizational design, intelligence, and decision making. *Academy of Management Review, 15,* 47–71.

74. Long, 1987; Hughes, K.D. (1989). Office automation: A review of the literature. *Relations Industrielles, 44,* 654–679.

75. Long, 1987.

76. Medcof, J.W. (1989). The effect and extent of use of information technology and job of the user upon task characteristics. *Human Relations, 42,* 23–41.

77. Medcof, J.W. (1996). The job characteristics of computing and non-computing work activities. *Journal of Occupational and Organizational Psychology, 69,* 199–212.

78. Long, 1987.

Chapter 16

1. Breen, B. (2005, December). The Seoul of design. *Fast Company,* 90–97; Lewis, P. (2005, September 19). A perpetual crisis machine. *Fortune,* 58–76; Park, S., & Gil, Y. (2006, July/August). How Samsung transformed its corporate R&D center. *Research Technology Management,* 24–29.

2. Kirby, J. (2006, June 19). Awakening Microsoft. *National Post,* FP1, FP4.

3. Gilbert, C.G. (2005). Unbundling the structure of inertia: Resource versus routine rigidity. *Academy of Management Journal, 48,* 741–763; see also Vincente-Lorente, J.D., & Zúñiga-Vincente, J.A. (2006). Testing the time-variancy of explanatory factors of strategic change. *British Journal of Management, 17,* 93–114.

4. This list relies mostly on Leavitt, H. (1965). Applied organizational changes in industry: Structural, technological, and humanistic approaches. In J.G. March (Ed.), *Handbook of organizations.* Chicago: Rand McNally.

5. Cameron, K.S., & Quinn, R.E. (1999). *Diagnosing and changing organizational culture.* Reading: MA. Addison-Wesley.

6. Garvin, D.A. (1993, July–August). Building a learning organization. *Harvard Business Review,* 78–91.

7. Tetrick, L.E., & Da Silva, N. (2003). Assessing the culture and climate for organizational learning. In S.E. Jackson, M.A. Hitt, and A.S. Denisi

(Eds.), *Managing knowledge for sustained competitive advantage.* San Francisco, CA: Jossey-Bass.

8. Garvin, 1993.

9. Corley, K.G., & Gioia, D.A. (2003). Semantic learning as change enabler: Relating organizational identity and organizational learning. In M. Easterby-Smith and M.A. Lyles (Eds.), *Handbook of organizational learning and knowledge management.* Oxford: Blackwell.

10. Harris-Lalonde, S. (2001). *Training and development outlook 2001.* Ottawa: The Conference Board of Canada.

11. Harris-Lalonde, 2001.

12. Ellinger, A.D., Ellinger, A.E., Baiyin, Y., & Howton, S.W. (2002). The relationship between the learning organization concept and firms' financial performance: An empirical assessment. *Human Resource Development Quarterly, 13,* 5–21.

13. Flynn, G. (1997, December). Bank of Montreal invests in its workers. *Workforce,* 30–38.

14. Lewin, K. (1951). *Field theory in social science.* New York: Harper & Row.

15. See Levinson, H. (2002). *Organizational assessment: A step-by-step guide to effective consulting.* Washington, DC: American Psychological Association; Howard, A. (Ed.) (1994). *Diagnosis for organizational change: Methods and models.* New York: Guilford.

16. Anders, G. (2003, February). The Carly chronicles. *Fast Company,* 66–73.

17. The first five reasons are from Kotter, J.P., & Schlesinger, L.A. (1979, March–April). Choosing strategies for change. *Harvard Business Review,* 106–114.

18. Frank, R. (1994, May 23). As UPS tries to deliver more to its customers, labor problems grow. *Wall Street Journal,* A1, A8.

19. Tichy, N.M., & Devanna, M.A. (1986). *The transformational leader.* New York: Wiley.

20. The following relies partly on Kotter & Schlesinger, 1979.

21. For reviews, see Macy, B.A., Peterson, M.F., & Norton, L.W. (1989). A test of participation theory in a work redesign field setting: Degree of participation and comparison site contrasts. *Human Relations, 42,* 1095–1165; Filley, A.C., House, R.J., & Kerr, S. (1976). *Managerial process and organizational behavior* (2nd ed.). Glenview, IL: Scott, Foresman.

22. Tichy & Devanna, 1986.

23. Bommer, W.H., Rich, G.A., & Rubin, R.S. (2005). Changing attitudes about change: Longitudinal effects of transformational leader behavior on employee cynicism about organizational change. *Journal of Organizational Behavior, 26,* 733–753.

24. Catalanello, R.F., & Kirkpatrick, D.L. (1968). Evaluating training programs—The state of the art. *Training and Development Journal, 22,* 2–9.

25. Goodman, P.S., Bazerman, M., & Conlon, E. (1980). Institutionalization of planned organizational change. *Research in Organizational Behavior, 2,* 215–246.

26. Goodman et al., 1980.

27. For a review of various definitions, see Porras, J.I., & Robertson, P.J. (1992). Organizational development: Theory, practice, and research. In M.D. Dunnette & L.M. Hough (Eds.), *Handbook of industrial and organizational psychology,* (2nd ed., Vol. 3). Palo Alto, CA: Consulting Psychologists Press.

28. French, W.L., & Bell, C.H., Jr. (1973). *Organization development.* Englewood Cliffs, NJ: Prentice-Hall.

29. Beer, M. (1980). *Organization change and development: A systems view.* Glenview, IL: Scott, Foresman; Beer, M., & Walton, E. (1990). Developing the competitive organization: Interventions and strategies. *American Psychologist, 45,* 154–161.

30. Beer, M. (1976). The technology of organizational development. In M.D. Dunnette (Ed.) *Handbook of industrial and organizational psychology.* Chicago: Rand McNally. See also Dyer, W. (1987). *Team building: Issues and alternatives* (2nd ed.). Reading, MA: Addison-Wesley.

31. Wakeley, J.H., & Shaw, M.E. (1965). Management training: An integrated approach. *Training Directors Journal, 19,* 2–13.

32. This description relies upon Beer, 1980; Huse, E.F., & Cummings, T.G. (1985). *Organization development and change* (3rd ed.). St. Paul, MN: West; Nadler, D.A. (1977). *Feedback and organization development: Using data-based methods.* Reading, MA: Addison-Wesley.

33. Taylor, J., & Bowers, D. (1972). *Survey of organizations: A machine-scored standardized questionnaire instrument.* Ann Arbor, MI: Center for Research on Utilization of Scientific Knowledge, Institute for Social Research, University of Michigan.

34. Weiner, S.P. (2006). *Driving change with IBM's bimonthly global pulse survey.* Presented at the annual conference of the Society for Industrial and Organizational Psychology, Dallas, Texas.

35. Smith, R.L., Rauschenberger, J.M., Bastos, M.W., Jayne, M.A.E., Mills, N.E., & Tripp, R.E. (2006). *Ford Motor Company Pulse trend analysis—Making and breaking trends.* Presented at the annual conference of the Society for Industrial and Organizational Psychology, Dallas, Texas.

36. Johnson, R.H., Ryan, A.M., & Schmit, M. (1994). *Employee attitudes and branch performance at Ford Motor Credit.* Presentation at the annual conference of the Society for Industrial and Organizational Psychology, Nashville, Tennessee.

37. For an eclectic view of TQM concerns, see the Total Quality Special Issue of the July 1994 *Academy of Management Review.*

38. Crosby, P.B. (1979). *Quality is free.* New York: McGraw-Hill; Deming, W.E. (1986). *Out of the crisis.* Cambridge, MA: Massachusetts Institute of Technology Center for Advanced Engineering Study; Juran J.M. (1992). *Juran on quality by design.* New York: Free Press.

39. Kinlaw, D.C. (1992). *Continuous improvement and measurement for total quality: A team-based approach.* San Diego: Pfeiffer.

40. Berry, L.L., Parasuraman, A., & Zeithaml, V.A. (1994, May). Improving service quality in America: Lessons learned. *Academy of Management Executive,* 32–45.

41. Kinlaw, 1992; Bounds, G., Yorks, L., Adams, M., & Ranney, G. (1994). *Beyond total quality management: Toward the emerging paradigm.* New York: McGraw-Hill.

42. Reeves, C.A., & Bednar, D.A. (1994). Defining quality: Alternatives and implications. *Academy of Management Review, 19,* 419–445.

43. Krishnan, R., Shani, A.B., Grant, R.M., & Baer, R. (1993, November). In search of quality improvement: Problems of design and implementation. *Academy of Management Executive,* 7–20.

44. Greengard, S. (1993, December). Reengineering: Out of the rubble. *Personnel Journal,* 48B–48O; Hammer, M., & Champy, J. (1993). *Reengineering the corporation: A manifesto for business revolution.* New York: HarperBusiness; Stewart, T.A. (1993, August 23). Reengineering: The hot new management tool. *Fortune,* 41–48.

45. Hammer & Champy, 1993.

46. Hammer & Champy, 1993.

47. Teng, J.T.C., Grover, V., & Fiedler, K.D. (1994, Spring). Business process reengineering: Charting a strategic path for the information age. *California Management Review,* 9–31.

48. Hammer & Champy, 1993; Teng et al., 1994.

49. Examples from Greengard, 1993; Teng et al., 1994.

50. See Dumaine, B. (1989, February 14). How managers can succeed through speed. *Fortune,* 54–59.

51. Hall, G., Rosenthal, J., & Wade, J. (1993, November–December). How to make reengineering really work. *Harvard Business Review,* 119–131.

52. Guzzo, R.A., Jette, R.D., & Katzell, R.A. (1985). The effects of psychologically based intervention programs on worker productivity: A meta-analysis. *Personnel Psychology, 38,* 275–291; Neuman, G.A., Edwards, J.E., & Raju, N.S. (1989). Organizational development interventions: A meta-analysis of their effects on satisfaction and other attitudes. *Personnel Psychology, 42,* 461–489.

53. Cameron, & Quinn, 1999.

54. For a meta-analytic summary, see Robertson, P.J., Roberts, D.R., & Porras, J.I. (1993). Dynamics of planned organizational change: Assessing support for a theoretical model. *Academy of Management Journal, 36,* 619–634. See also Macy, B.A., & Izumi, H. (1993). Organizational change, design, and work innovation: A meta-analysis of 131 North American field studies—1961–1991. *Research in Organizational Change and Development, 7,* 235–313.

55. Porras, & Robertson, 1992; Nicholas, J.M., & Katz, M. (1985). Research methods and reporting practices in organization development: A review and some guidelines. *Academy of Management Review, 10,* 737–749.

56. White, S.E., & Mitchell, T.R. (1976). Organization development: A review of research content and research design. *Academy of Management Review, 1,* 57–73.

57. For recent reviews of creativity and innovation research, see Shalley, C.E., & Gibson, L.L. (2004). What leaders need to know: A review of social and contextual factors that can foster or hinder creativity. *The Leadership Quarterly, 15,* 33–53; Anderson, N.,

De Dreu, C.K.W., & Nijstad, B.A. (2004). The routinization of innovation research: A constructively critical review of the state-of-the-science. *Journal of Organizational Behavior, 25*, 147–173.

58. For an attempt to provide some order to this subject, see Wolfe, R.A. (1994). Organizational innovation: Review, critique and suggested research directions. *Journal of Management Studies, 31*, 405–431.

59. Tushman, M., & Nadler, D. (1986, Spring). Organizing for innovation. *California Management Review,* 74–92.

60. Hamel, G. (2006, February). The why, what, and how of management innovation. *Harvard Business Review,* 72–84.

61. Frost, P.J., & Egri, C.P. (1991). The political process of innovation. *Research in Organizational Behavior, 13*, 229–295.

62. This three-part view of creativity is from Amabile, T.M. (1988). A model of creativity and innovation in organizations. *Research in Organizational Behavior, 10*, 123–167. See also Woodman, R.W., Sawyer, J.E., & Griffin, R.W. (1993). Toward a theory of organizational creativity. *Academy of Management Review, 18*, 293–321.

63. Basadur, M. (1994). Managing the creative process in organizations. In M.A. Runco (Ed.), *Problem finding, problem solving, and creativity.* Norwood, NJ: Ablex; Kabanoff, B., & Rossiter, J.R. (1994). Recent developments in applied creativity. *International Review of Industrial and Organizational Psychology, 9,* 283–324.

64. Galbraith, J.R. (1982, Winter). Designing the innovating organization. *Organizational Dynamics,* 4–25.

65. Howell, J.M. (2005, May). The right stuff: Identifying and developing effective champions of innovation. *Academy of Management Executive,* 108–119; Howell, J.M., & Higgins, C.A. (1990). Champions of technological innovation. *Administrative Science Quarterly, 35,* 317–341.

66. Cohen, W.M., & Levinthal, D.A. (1990). Absorptive capacity: A new perspective on learning and innovation. *Administrative Science Quarterly, 35,* 128–152.

67. Tushman, M.L., & Scanlan, T.J. (1981a). Characteristics and external orientations of boundary spanning individuals. *Academy of Management Journal, 24,* 83–98; Tushman, M.L.,

& Scanlan, T.J. (1981b). Boundary spanning individuals: Their role in information transfer and their antecedents. *Academy of Management Journal, 24,* 289–305.

68. Keller, R.T., & Holland, W.E. (1983). Communicators and innovators in research and development organizations. *Academy of Management Journal, 26,* 742–749.

69. Kanter, R.M. (1988). When a thousand flowers bloom: Structural, collective, and social conditions for innovation in organization. *Research in Organizational Behavior, 10,* 169–211.

70. Bertin, O. (2003, July 14). Harley-Davidson's great ride to the top. *Globe and Mail,* B1, B4.

71. Kanter, 1988; Nord, W.R., & Tucker, S. (1987). *Implementing routine and radical innovations.* Lexington, MA: Lexington Books; Damanpour, F. (1991). Organizational innovation: A meta-analysis of effects of determinants and moderators. *Academy of Management Journal, 34,* 555–590.

72. Tushman & Scanlan, 1981b.

73. Keller & Holland, 1983.

74. Katz, R. (1982). The effects of group longevity on project communication and performance. *Administrative Science Quarterly, 27,* 81–104.

75. For a review, see Nord & Tucker, 1987. However, this prescription is controversial. For other views, see Kanter, 1988; Marcus A.A. (1988). Implementing externally induced innovations: A comparison of rule-bound and autonomous approaches. *Academy of Management Journal, 31,* 235–256.

76. Damanpour, 1991; Kanter, 1988.

77. Galbraith, 1982.

78. Hamel, 2006.

79. Amabile, 1988.

80. Damsell, K. (2003, October 29). CEO Fiorina touts HP's ability to adapt. *Globe and Mail,* B3.

81. Galbraith, 1982.

82. Walton, R.E. (1975, Winter). The diffusion of new work structures: Explaining why success didn't take. *Organizational Dynamics,* 3–22.

83. Ferlie, E., Fitzgerald, L., Wood, M., & Hawkins, C. (2005). The nonspread of innovations: The mediating role of professionals. *Academy of Management Journal, 48,* 117–134.

84. Rogers, E.M. (1995). *Diffusion of innovations* (4th ed.). New York: Free Press.

85. Pfeffer, J., & Sutton, R.I. (2000). *The knowing-doing gap: How smart companies turn knowledge into action.* Boston: Harvard Business School Press; see also Johns, G. (1993). Constraints on the adoption of psychology-based personnel practices: Lessons from organization innovation. *Personnel Psychology, 46,* 569–592.

Appendix

1. Sutton, R.I. (1991). Maintaining norms about expressed emotions: The case of bill collectors. *Administrative Science Quarterly, 36,* 245–268.

2. Lupton, T. (1963). *On the shop floor.* Oxford: Pergamon.

3. Bensman, J., & Gerver, I. (1963). Crime and punishment in the factory: The function of deviancy in maintaining the social system. *American Sociological Review, 28,* 588–598.

4. Mintzberg, H. (1973). *The nature of managerial work.* New York: Harper & Row.

5. Ragins, B.R., & Cotton, J.L. (1993). Gender and willingness to mentor in organizations. *Journal of Management, 19,* 97–111.

6. Ivancevich, J.M., & Lyon, H.L. (1977). The shortened workweek: A field experiment. *Journal of Applied Psychology, 62,* 34–37.

7. Sutton, R.I., & Rafaeli, A. (1988). Untangling the relationship between displayed emotions and organizational sales: The case of convenience stores. *Academy of Management Journal, 31,* 461–487.

8. Greenwood, R.G., & Wrege, C.D. (1986). The Hawthorne studies. In D.A. Wren & J.A. Pearce II (Eds.), *Papers dedicated to the development of modern management.* The Academy of Management; Roethlisberger, F.J., & Dickson, W.J. (1939). *Management and the worker.* Cambridge, MA: Harvard University Press.

9. Adair, J.G. (1984). The Hawthorne effect: A reconsideration of the methodological artifact. *Journal of Applied Psychology, 69,* 334–345.

10. See Academy of Management. (2002). Academy of Management code of ethical conduct. *Academy of Management Journal, 45,* 291–294; Lowman, R.L. (Ed.). (1985) *Casebook on ethics and standards for the practice of psychology in organizations.* College Park, MD: Society for Industrial and Organizational Psychology.

INDEX

● PHOTO CREDITS